THE WINES OF BURGUNDY

THE WINES OF BURGUNDY

by

Clive Coates MW

UNIVERSITY OF CALIFORNIA PRESS
Berkeley Los Angeles London

University of California Press, one of the most distinguished university presses in the United States, enriches lives around the world by advancing scholarship in the humanities, social sciences, and natural sciences. Its activities are supported by the UC Press Foundation and by philanthropic contributions from individuals and institutions. For more information, visit www.ucpress.edu.

The publisher acknowledges the *Nouvel Atlas des Grands Vignobles de Bourgogne* by Sylvain Pitiot and Pierre Poupon as a source of site information for a portion of the map program.

University of California Press
Berkeley and Los Angeles, California

University of California Press, Ltd.
London, England

Library of Congress Cataloging-in-Publication Data

Coates, Clive.
   The wines of Burgundy / by Clive Coates.—Rev. ed.
      p.   cm.
   Rev. ed. of: Côte d'Or. 1997.
   Includes bibliographical references and index.
   ISBN 978-0-520-25050-5 (cloth : alk. paper)
   1. Wine and wine making—France—Burgundy.   I. Title.

TP553.C567 2008
641.2'2094441—dc22   2007043526

Manufactured in the United States of America
10   09   08
10   9   8   7   6   5   4   3   2

The paper used in this publication meets the minimum requirements of ANSI/NISO Z39.48-1992 (R 1997) *(Permanence of Paper)*.

Cover illustration: Château du Clos de Vougeot, Côte d'Or (Photograph by Nigel Blythe/Cephas Picture Library Ltd.).

ONCE AGAIN, TO BECKY AND RUSSELL
AND ALL MY FRIENDS, THE TOP
WINE-GROWERS IN BURGUNDY

CONTENTS

PREFACE

Ten years ago I published a book called *Côte d'Or: A Celebration of the Great Wines of Burgundy*. Burgundy moves fast. So great have been the changes since then and so large the number of new domaines worth considering that an update is long overdue. Here it is.

Côte d'Or consisted of three parts: a discussion of the land, the history of each commune, the vineyards and the properties formed the first section; an in-depth profile of 60 top estates with notes of a vertical tasting then followed; and an assessment of the last 40 vintages was the final element.

I have retained the first and the last segments. They have been completely revised and rewritten: all the tasting notes date from post–2000. Much of what was in the domaine profiles would not need to have been greatly changed. Not wishing to repeat myself, I have therefore put these aside. This has given me space to add chapters on Chablis and the Côte Chalonnaise.

I have loved red Burgundy for decades, ever since the first really great Pinot Noir passed my lips. Who could fail to be entranced? Here is a wine which can sing like a nightingale, shine forth like a sapphire, intrigue like the most complex of chess problems and seduce like the first kiss of someone you are just about to fall in love with. Moreover, great Burgundy can inspire like a great orator, satisfy like the most subtle of three-star meals, and leave you at peace at the end like the slow movement of a Mozart piano concerto. At its best the wine is complex but not puzzling, profound but not didactic, perfect but not intimidating, and magnificent but never anything less than friendly.

Chardonnay too is a majestic grape variety. There is more competition here from outside Burgundy. There are also more disappointing Chardonnay cellars and wines within Burgundy than is the case with Pinot Noir. Nevertheless, the great Pulignys, Meursaults and Chassagnes make the most complete statement white wine is capable of uttering; they are as "serious" as their counterparts in red. Great white Burgundy is ripe but dry, austere in the best sense, rich without a suggestion of residual sugar, nutty, honeyed, gently oaky, subtle, profoundly elegant and persistent on the finish. It can age almost as well as a red wine.

Burgundy is the most fascinating, the most complex and the most intractable fine wine region in the world. It is also the most personal and the most individual. Nowhere is fine wine—occasionally great wine, but also, sadly, frequently disappointing wine—made in such small quantities, in so many different ways, and by so many characters, each convinced that only he or she has the magic recipe for success. Nowhere else is wine made which demonstrates quite such an expression of the soil the vines lie in and the particular way they are tended and the wines made and reared. Nowhere else is the personality and the expertise, the passion and the sweat of the winemaker so closely paralleled by the wine in the glass. This is winemaking at its most committed, yet most humble and most artisanal. But this is where—just from time to time, frequently enough to fill your heart with joy, but sufficiently rarely to be a continued source of exasperation—something so sublimely correct and so breathtakingly individual is created that to experience it is to experience life itself.

Burgundy, says Hugh Johnson, is easier to judge, taste and understand than Bordeaux. Here I must take issue. Appreciate and enjoy: yes. Understand: no. Burgundy is an enigma. I have spent more than forty years as a wine professional, first as a merchant, now as a writer. I feel I understand Bordeaux. I doubt I will ever fully comprehend Burgundy. Yet I visit perhaps 250 growers in the Côte d'Or every year, as well as a few dozen or more in both Chablis and the Côte Chalonnaise, and I now live there. Visit Bordeaux, and you can sample with relative ease the wares (usually one single *grand vin*) of the top 150 *châteaux*. You will have tasted all the best, all made more or less in the same way, and you can form your judgment over the vintage and the wines which stand out or fail to sing. To do justice to Burgundy in the same way would entail not only visiting twice as many addresses and sampling perhaps six or ten wines at each, but also investing the time and curiosity to learn the different approach of each winemaker. Moreover, while the main wines of Bordeaux can be amassed together to be reviewed subsequently in bottle, to locate all the Burgundies even once several years later is a daunting task. One can only be familiar with the tip of the iceberg.

Anyone who is honest will therefore commence writing a book on Burgundy with not only due humility, but also with a faint sense of futility. Can anyone do justice to such an impossible task? On the other hand, such has been the improvement in quality in the region over the last decade, the reasonableness of price—in French Franc terms the wines cost hardly more in 2006 than they did in 1996—and the rate of emergence of dozens and dozens of unsung Burgundian heroines and heroes producing such very good wine that it is unfair not to give them their due recognition and exposure, and thus aid their commercial success. If my first justification for writing this book is that I have probably covered more ground more regularly in Burgundy than any other writer in the last 35 years, then the second must be the quality and the value of the wines today.

Wine people are generous people. In England, the United States and mainland Europe, there are groups of Burgundy-lovers, amateurs and professionals, who have helped me set up tastings, invited me to share bottles and generally given me immeasurable opportunities to increase my experience of Burgundy. In Burgundy itself I have sampled at most of the top domaines every year and most of the rest one year in two or three, and occasionally isolated a commune on most visits to pay a call on absolutely everybody in the appellation. In addition, I invited those I know best to an annual party to examine the vintage that is ten years old. This is held at the Bouilland farmhouse of Becky Wasserman and her husband Russell Hone. I arrive with a few cases of champagne, some sides of smoked salmon and large quantities of fine mature unpasteurized English cheese (so much better for wine than the French counterparts!). The growers come with their bottles. It is fun, as well as instructive.

Additionally, each July, with a group of professional friends, usually in England, I hold a tasting of the vintage which is approaching its fourth birthday. To this group—regular members of which include John Avery MW of Avery's of Bristol; Bill Baker of Reid Wines; Hew Blair of Justerini and Brooks; Stephen Browett and Lindsay Hamilton of Farr Vintners; Andrew Bruce; Simon Cock of Heyman, Barwell, Jones; Chris Davey of O.W. Loeb; Toby Morrhal of The Wine Society; Jasper Morris MW of Berry Bros and Rudd; Barry Philipps of the Four Walls Wine Co.; Roy Richards of Richards Walford; David Roberts MW; Robert Rolls; and Mark Savage MW—I must extend my special thanks. I am particularly grateful to Simon Cock for providing me with the material for the movement of opening prices, which you will find in Appendix Six.

In the United States, there is the annual meeting of what I call the Connecticut Group, which takes place in Guildford, CT, at the end of March. Regular members, generously providing old bottles from their cellars, include Jim and Debbie Cianciolo, Gregg Cook, Tony and Judy Dietrich, Bob Feinn of Mount Carmel Wines, Roger Forbes, Jack and Thelma Hewitt, George Sape, Bruce and Pam Simonds and Alvin Wakamia.

I would also like to thank the team at the University of California Press and their associates: Blake Edgar and Scott Norton, Bart Wright of Wright Lohnes GIS and Mapping, and Megan Washburn of Publication Services, Inc.

Last, but by no means least, I owe a huge debt to Sonia Portalès who has been deciphering my scrawl, typing up my tasting notes, and proofreading and translating some of my writings for more than fifteen years. I'd be lost without you. *Merci*!

Introduction

TODAY'S CÔTE D'OR is the most exciting wine region in the world. There has been an explosion in quality over the last 25 years. The villages are vibrant with a new generation of qualified, talented, committed men and women, infinitely curious about all the wines of the world, willing and able to share their experience and expertise with their neighbours and to taste their wines one with another, and continually seeking to fine-tune their techniques of viticulture, vinification and *élevage* in order to further increase the quality of the bottles they are producing. There is one goal: perfection.

Moreover, while no one would call Burgundy cheap—the wine cannot be inexpensive for all sorts of reasons, not least of which are the price of land, the pitifully small scale of the operations and the impossibility of making top quality wine without reducing yields to a minimum—prices have remained remarkably stable, despite increasing demand for the starry wines. I refer readers to Appendix Five.

And there has been a further cause for celebration. Since 1985 Burgundy has enjoyed a 21-year (as I write this introduction), and perhaps continuing, run of good to very fine vintages. Though one could argue that the average vintage standard for white wines has been not as high as that for the reds, the reds have not produced a less than "good" vintage year since 1984—and the best 1984s, though aging now, are by no means to be decried. God seems to be smiling on the resurgence of modern Burgundy. In 1985, again in 1988 and 1989, triumphantly so in 1990, again in 1991, 1993, 1995, 1996, 1998, brilliantly in 1999, partially in 2001, in 2002, 2004 and spectacularly in 2005, we have seen red wine vintages which are very good if not very fine. Even in the softer and less consistent vintages, such as 1997 and 2000, and in the vintages of the heat-wave conditions of 2003, there is much to enjoy, and these wines can be enjoyed soon, thus preventing the infanticide that occurs in the greater years.

Burgundy has evolved considerably since the early 1980s. Growers now act like *négociants*, bottling and commercialising their wares, as well as tending the vines and making the wine. Increasingly, perhaps to make up for land they have lost as estates are split up in the natural process of being passed down from one generation to another or as leases and share-cropping arrangements come to an end, some growers have set up in a small way as merchants who buy others' fruit, must or finished wine.

Merchants, for their part, are increasingly acting as growers. Most now prefer not to buy finished wine but to contract for the fruit and vinify it themselves, alongside the produce of their own estates, these estates having themselves been enlarged by acquisition over the years. In their dealings with their suppliers, *négociants* are more and more frequently taking an active role in the vineyards, a partnership which hitherto did not exist.

Unlike their fathers and grandfathers—and unlike today, in previous generations, it would have been unheard of for women to take an active role in winemaking—today's Burgundian winemaker has been to wine school. While not all one is taught at the *Viti* in Beaune or at the University of Dijon is entirely compatible with the demands associated with the role of a producer of serious *premier* or *grand cru*, growers today do have the technical background to help them comprehend why it is that they do what they do and what the result would be if they modified their approach. Today they have the knowledge and the confidence to help them experiment in their search for improvement, and what could be a greater impetus toward higher standards than the fact that one's name is eventually going to be on the bottle?

A generation or more ago, Burgundy was on its knees. Over-fertilisation in the 1960s and 1970s, the introduction of high-yield, low-quality clones and the clampdown on bolster wines from

the south of France and Algeria all led to wine which was thin, pallid, fruitless and short-lived. The vineyard is still weak in this respect, for it takes time and money to replant, and Burgundy's reputation has taken a long time to recover. But at least the problems are being faced. Good husbandry, *biologique* if not *biodynamique*, is the order of the day. Growers understand the crucial importance of low yields. Today's clones are judged by quality rather than quantity. Action can be taken to reduce erosion, sterilise the vineyard against viral diseases, improve drainage, counteract the effects of past fertilisation mistakes, space out the fruit to reduce depredation, protect it against rot, increase the efficiency of the ripening process, mitigate against the effects of last minute rain, eliminate all but the very best fruit before vinification begins, concentrate the must by equalising the solid-liquid ratio, control the fermentations, improve the wine's ability to settle out its impurities naturally, and prevent it from contamination and deterioration during the process of *élevage*: in short, to translate as purely as possible the very best fruit into the very best wine.

Combined with a new understanding, a new mind-set and new techniques is new equipment. Cellars are temperature-controlled where necessary, and so are the fermentation vats. There are all sorts of new machines to help the winemaker in his task, to reduce his physical labour in the vineyard and in the cellar and to enable him to control the winemaking process in exactly the way he wishes. Moreover, today's winery is increasingly spotlessly clean. The old, bug-infested barrels have been taken out and burnt, and if there is sometimes a little too much new oak, this problem is not as bad as it was a few years ago.

Winemaking, at least for great Burgundy, does not, however, involve as much creativity of approach as most outsiders think. Winemakers can destroy, you will be told, through incompetence or ignorance, but they cannot make any better wine than the potential quality of the fruit, the *matière première*, will allow in the first place. The winemaker's role is one of preventive medicator. And increasingly, the move is toward a hands-off approach. The more you manipulate the wine, the more you risk reducing what is good and individual about it. The greater the quality of the fruit at the time of the harvest, the better the possibility of the wine. The last 30 years have seen a revolution in the cellar and in the understanding of winemaking. We are now in the middle of just as important a revolution out there in the vineyard.

A MARKED INCREASE IN QUALITY

Ten years ago, in Côte d'Or, I awarded stars (one, two or three: in the Michelin Red Guide style) to the top domaines. In the Côte d'Or, 17 domaines earned three stars, 29 two stars and 97 one star. I have repeated this exercise in *The Wines of Burgundy*. Within the Côte d'Or again, we now have 11 three-star estates, 29 two-stars and 99 one-stars. Overall, there are now more than 50 percent more domaines worthy of a star rating than there were 10 years ago. This is good for Burgundy and good for the customer, and it shows the progress that has been made in the last decade. See Appendix Three for a list of the Côte d'Or starred domaines, and for my star ratings of Chablis and of the Côte Chalonnaise.

BURGUNDY: THE ARCANE AND THE FRAGMENTED

Burgundy is considered complicated, difficult and confusing. It is certainly complex, with an extraordinary variety of individual vineyards, estates and winemaking styles and techniques crammed into a very small region.

In the Côte d'Or there are some 5,550 hectares producing some 250,000 hectolitres (2.75 million cases) of wine a year (all figures exclude generics), of which 75 percent is red wine from the Pinot Noir grape and 25 percent is white wine from the Chardonnay grape. There are two village-overlapping appellations (Côte-de-Beaune-Villages and Côte-de-Nuits-Villages), and twenty-five village appellations, most of which can produce both red and white wine

(plus Côte-de-Beaune, not to be confused with the above and described on page 204). Within the villages there are a total of 539 *premiers crus*, probably an equal number of *lieux-dits* which are not *premiers crus* and thirty-two *grands crus*. Moreover, there are quite a number of special wine place-names individual to particular growers—such as Bouchard Père et Fils' Vigne de l'Enfant Jésus, from Beaune's *premier cru* Les Grèves, or Louis Latour's Château Corton-Grancey.

While there are a couple of dozen important monopolies—whole appellations or vineyards within the fief of a single owner—most vineyards (or *climats*, to use the Burgundian expression) are divided up among a number of individual owners. The most commonly cited example of this is the 50-hectare Clos-de-Vougeot, which has 100 plots and eighty owners, with an average of 62 acres each.

It is this fragmentation which causes the confusion. Unlike Bordeaux, an area of large estates producing (usually) a single *grand vin*, Burgundy is a region of small domaines spread over a number of different *climats*, producing everything from various generics to, if they are lucky, *grands crus*. And of course the quantities of each wine produced will be miniscule, in Bordeaux terms. Château Lafite produces 21,000 cases a year of *grand vin* and 15,000 cases of Carruades. Romanée-Conti the vineyard yields 540 cases and Romanée-Conti the domaine 8,310. A typical top Burgundian domaine, today marketing most of its produce in bottle—although a little may be sold off in bulk at the outset to help with the cash flow—would probably be one like that of Michel Lafarge in Volnay, which comprises only 11.5 hectares, but commercialises fifteen different wines.

Burgundy seems perplexing because of its nomenclature. During the 80 or so years after 1848—Gevrey was the first, Morey the last—the Côte d'Or villages complicated matters by tagging the name of their best vineyard onto that of the village, in order to raise the prestige of these lesser wines. Thus Gevrey became Gevrey-Chambertin, and Aloxe, Aloxe-Corton, while both Puligny and Chassagne chose Montrachet, whose *climat* straddles their borders, as a suffix. Meanwhile in Gevrey, but thankfully only in that commune, certain *climats*, later to be confirmed as *grands crus*, claimed Chambertin, to which they were contiguous, also as a suffix. Thus Gevrey-Chambertin is a village, Charmes-Chambertin a *grand cru*. The only solution to these complications is knowledge.

There is another tradition, now a legal rule, which needs appreciation. The thirty-two *grands crus* exist in their own right. No further geographical clarification is necessary. A name such as Le Musigny says it all. The *premier cru* and *lieu-dit* designations, on the other hand, need to be preceded and qualified by the name of the village. Thus, a wine from Les Amoureuses is described as Chambolle-Musigny, Les Amoureuses, with or without (this is optional) the mention that the *climat* is a *premier cru*. Each *premier* and *grand cru* is an appellation in its own right.

So if Burgundy seems difficult to comprehend at first, a little perseverance will soon clarify matters. And the solution to the fact that, on the face of it, a number of people seem to be offering the same wine is to understand that, even more than the geographical origin, it is the name of the domaine which made the wine that is important. Bordeaux *châteaux* names are brand names, and the top ones have a classification, which is a help to the consumer, even if that of 1855 is somewhat out of date. It is the land in Burgundy, not the winemaker or his estate, which is classified. The classification is based on geographical possibility, not on the quality in the bottle. And there are good winemakers and bad. One grower's Chambertin can be sublime, another's beneath contempt. In the pages that follow, you will see a personal classification of these winemakers, something which will never be attempted officially. I hope it helps clarify the level of individual estate quality today.

HOW BURGUNDY WORKS

Once upon a time, back before the French Revolution, the vineyards of the Côte d'Or were owned by the church and the aristocracy. Even then, they were fragmented and leased out, often at second-, third- or even fourth-hand, with the ultimate owners letting to the local *bourgeoisie*, who then sublet to tenant farmers who actually did the work.

Essentially, there were, and still are, two forms of leasing arrangement. The first (*fermage*) was a simple rental arrangement, in which the tenant paid in cash, after which he was a free man, but responsible for all expenses. The second (*métayage*) was a share-cropping agreement, in which the landlord usually continued to pay the capital costs (replanting and so on) and was recompensed with a portion, normally half, of the fruit. The tenant could render his share in grapes or go as far as to make the wine and sell it (in bulk or in bottle) on his landlord's behalf, but the principle was a share of the crop to each side.

Employees, too, were recompensed in different ways. One way was through payment of the usual so-much-per-hour or month, under the direct supervision of the *patron*. The second was a looser arrangement: *à la tâche*. Here the worker was paid by the job, for example for looking after a plot of land for the whole year. When and how the job was done—and how time-consuming the task—then lay in the worker's hands.

These arrangements still continue. It is impossible to assess what proportion of the Côte d'Or vineyard is leased rather than exploited by the owner, for very many leasing arrangements are between close members of the same family and are, in practice, owner-occupier operated, so to speak. My guess is that a good third of the Côte d'Or is leased.

These leases normally run on an ongoing 9-year basis until the *vigneron* reaches retirement age. Landlords are not allowed, even at the end of the 9 years, to rescind the lease unless they are prepared to work the land themselves. A fortunate incompetent can, therefore, be in for life. In the 1980s two great domaines, Lafon and Méo-Camuzet, have taken back their *métayer's*—highly competent, it has to be underlined—vines as the leases came to their end. Other owners, however, have not; even when their leaseholders have reached sixty, such owners have been prepared to sign a new lease with their sons or daughters.

Ownership of the Côte d'Or vineyard, operationally already largely split up into family exploitable-portions, was totally transformed by the French Revolution. The lands of the church were very quickly seized and sold off in 1791. Those of the nobility followed a couple of years later. It was not, however, the peasant farmer who benefited. He did not have the means. Instead, it was the *bourgeoisie*, in many cases those who had been around before 1789. The *Code Napoléon* abolished primogeniture, however, and thus began the fragmentation of ownership which has led inexorably to the morcellation of Burgundy today.

The grower, then, can be an owner in his own right, an exploiter on behalf of his parents or the rest of his family, a *fermier* or *métayer*, or indeed a combination of the lot! While today almost everybody keeps a little back for bottling, to sell at the garden gate or consume at home, the next great divide is between those who sell the bulk of their domaine off as fruit, must or young wine, and those who keep the majority back for eventual sale in bottle. The last 25 years have seen amazing changes here. In the early 1970s hardly 15 percent of Côte d'Or wine was domaine bottled. Today the proportion is well over 60 percent, and the more prestigious the origin, the more likely it will be to leave Burgundy with the owner's, not a *négociant*'s, name on it. What this means, of course, is that today fine Burgundy can really only come direct from the domaines.

For both merchants and growers, the next step after the wine is made is to sell it. The bigger firms will have their own teams of salesmen and agents within metropolitan France. The smaller growers will tend to go direct, hoping to place their wines in the top Michelin-starred restaurants, a sure way to fame and fortune. Both will do extensive mail-order business within France.

Exporting can be a nightmare, certainly outside of the European Community, where different rules and regulations apply. For instance capacity within the Community is expressed in centilitres (e.g., 75 cl). Officially this won't do for the United States, whose authorities insist on seeing 750 millilitres printed on the label, though it means exactly the same thing. For the larger *négociant* this is a small problem. The small grower can be forgiven if he decides it is not worth the bother.

The established merchants will tend to export directly to agents, whereas the smaller will deal through brokers, who can be established either in Burgundy or in the exporting country. Sales, naturally, are almost by allocation, especially for the limited stock of the better wines. Only a small number of retail outlets will eventually get hold of some stock, for no single domaine can deal with everybody. Moreover, in order to keep its place in the queue, an outlet must buy the bad with the good, the Bourgogne *rouge* together with the Richebourg, the badly quoted vintage together with the triumphant success. The implications of this for the consumer who wishes to buy top Burgundy are discussed on page 33.

THE ROLE OF THE *NÉGOCIANT*

As mentioned above, until very recently the vast majority of Burgundy was sold under a *négociant* or merchant label. Individual landholdings were (and continue to be) tiny, prices were low, and growers simply did not have the wherewithal, space, or experience to enable them to look after the wine, bottle it, and subsequently market it. It was simpler and more economical to divide the process: the grower tended the vines and made the wine, and the merchant—or brokers on his behalf—would tour the area soon after, buy up the stock, blend parcels of the same wine together into more economical units, and see to the product's sale. The advantages to the grower were that he could receive payment sooner, rather than later, and that he could avoid the need for any investment in a maturation cellar or bottling plant. Indeed his responsibilities ceased after the *malos* had finished and the wine was collected. For the merchant the attractions were the availability of the pick of the crop, without the capital expense of land ownership, and the benefits of scale, such as the creation of a brand image.

As I have said, the position has radically changed since the early 1980s. Yet the role of the *négociant*, particularly at the bottom end of the hierarchical scale—and, it must be said, at the lower end of the quality scale too—is still important. Wines that continue to be sold through this process are now rarely seen on the export market in Britain or the United States, but a walk through a French supermarket is instructive.

THE RISE OF THE *PETIT NÉGOCIANT*

More and more growers, however, are becoming *négociants* in their own right, if on a small scale. Growers lose vineyards they have farmed, domaines are split or have more customers than they can serve, or producers are simply ambitious: it is easy for a grower to acquire a merchant's licence. This is an element of Burgundy which is growing. By and large the product is bought in as fruit, and then vinified and reared in just the same way as the domaine wine. You can't tell the difference.

THE ROLE OF THE MEDIA

Of increasing importance over the last 25 years—and an influence which is both beneficial and malign—is the wine writer. Wine writers can range from journalists who know nothing whatsoever about wine to those who wear another hat, that of wine professional, most of the time. Here I must declare an interest. Today I am a writer; yesterday (that is, up to 1984) I was a wine merchant. I still consider myself a "professional," whatever that may precisely mean, and I have a certificate, having passed the Master of Wine examination, to prove at least some competence in this respect.

Prior to the mediatisation of the world of wine, reputations took time to expand, particularly in a region of reduced quantity, such as the Côte d'Or. About the only way for a producer to bypass this slow progression was to get his wine into a three-star restaurant. Equally, it was years before a decline in quality was recognised. Today, a newcomer like the Domaine d'Ardhuy, which produced its first vintage in 2003, can achieve fame almost overnight. And the underachievers, either permanent or temporary, can be fingered from the outset. The consumer is advised before he or she even receives his or her opening offer. On the face of it, this, surely, is to be welcomed: a good, honest, up-to-date opinion, informed and unprejudiced, is available to guide the private customer to spend his money in the best way possible.

Sadly, however, life is not perfect. Wine critics are often misinformed or just plain pig-ignorant. They *are* prejudiced. They set about doing the job of sampling Burgundy in the wrong way and at the wrong time. They try to imply that there is only one way to judge a wine (i.e., according to the personal taste of that critic), forgetting how subjective and temperamental taste can be, and also ignoring the fact that most wine is made to be consumed and judged mature with food and friends, and not immature alongside numerous other bottles. The bad critics look at Pinot through Cabernet-tinted spectacles and so criticise it for being what it never set out to be. Generally, they cause anger in the Côte d'Or and confusion at home. Moreover—and this is a situation which is almost universal in the United States, though thankfully largely absent in Britain—the trade has allowed itself to be emasculated. Instead of continuing to buy and sell based on their own professional judgement, they have consigned themselves to the role of mere purveyors. They buy what the *Wine Spectator* and the *Wine Advocate* score highly and then sell their wares by proclaiming the magazines' marks. It is totally crazy.

The only way to become a competent judge of young Burgundy is to spend many years at the coal-face: to go down there as often as possible, to listen a lot, to say little, and to learn much.

This is what I do. Sadly, I seem to be largely alone. There are many growers I visit who have never seen another writer; many cellars who would dearly love to welcome others to explain what they are trying to do. Let us not forget the hundreds of different ways Burgundy can be made. All one has to do is permute between zero and 100 percent stems, use zero to 100 percent new wood, ferment at temperatures from 25°C all the way up to 35°C and above, and employ cold soaking or not. All of these conditions *can* result in great Burgundy. But you need to understand what the grower is doing, and his/her personality and philosophy, in order to understand and be able to judge the wine.

Burgundy is a wine which suffers more than more tannic wines from manipulations such as racking, fining and bottling. It is therefore advisable to descend when the majority of the wines are in good form. June is a good time for whites, provided the *malos* are not late to complete. November is a good time for last year's reds. It is necessary not only to understand where the wine is in its development, but also, for instance, to know whether the *cuvée* is from young vines, and whether what you are being given to sample is the finished blend: in short, how close is what you are tasting to the finished article? If what you are given to taste is a sample from the single new oak cask (out of six) of a wine which was racked the previous week and to which is to be added half as much again of a separate *cuvée* of young vine wine, then you are wasting your time (and that of your reader). If, further, you are doing your sampling in a hotel or another cellar among a hundred other samples in a great rush, you risk missing the fragrance, delicacy and complexity—which is what Pinot Noir and Chardonnay in Burgundy are all about—in favour of extreme colour and quantities of tannin, alcohol and new oak. And you are falling into the trap of judging Burgundy by its immediacy, rather than by its true potential.

Burgundy has been much maligned—more so than any other region—by certain elements of the media. Robert Parker proclaimed that the region was a dinosaur of poor quality and high prices: the exact opposite of the truth. The *Wine Spectator* has criticised the increasing bunch of estates that refuse to play ball with its *modus operandi* and submit samples for mammoth tastings. The magazine's representatives arrive in the region only a few months after the wines have been bottled, before they have had a chance to recover, and attempt to rate every wine in percentage points out of 100. The time for accurate ratings such as this is much later, a year or two after bottling and shipment, dispassionately, in groups of twenty-five or so. At the outset, it is sufficient merely to note how successful the estate has been, given its reputation and the standing in the hierarchy of each of its wines.

Moreover, the British media has been accused, if not of being corrupt, of having vested interests. It so happens that most of us who write seriously about Burgundy are, or were, professionals. The majority are Masters of Wine. In my view, this is nothing but a good thing: we have years of experience behind us to back up our judgments and qualifications to prove our competence. The three best recent books on Burgundy have been written by Anthony Hanson, a merchant who has been scrupulously meticulous about pointing out cases in which he has a personal and commercial involvement; by Remington Norman, who used to be a full-time merchant but is no longer; and by Serena Sutcliffe, who used to represent a couple of houses in Burgundy together with her husband David Peppercorn, but is now the director of the wine department of Sotheby's. All three are Masters of Wine (Norman has since resigned from the Institute of Masters of Wine). To those who accuse these professionals or ex-professionals of pulling punches, overpraising or whatever, I say where is your proof? What is perhaps also noteworthy is that while there are many MWs who have crossed over to become writers, there have so far—and not for want of trying—been only a couple of journalists who have successfully sat the Master of Wine exam. Give me a professional approach every time!

HOW TOP BURGUNDY IS MADE

Geology and the Concept of Terroir

Of all the various factors which influence a wine's character and flavour—the variety; the viticultural, vinification and maturation methods; and, of course, the climate—the most fundamental, the one least open to radical alteration or change, is the land in which the grower has planted his/her vines. The land is *there*. It faces in a particular direction; it drains so; it is protected so; its physical, chemical and biological make-up is such and such. One can tinker at the edges, but one cannot really modify the basic structure.

It is here, literally on the bedrock, that the difference between great wine and merely good wine lies. Some vineyards can produce great wine; others never will. The Côte d'Or consists of a 40-kilometre southeast-facing slope where, in the middle of the incline, lie all the physical characteristics of the "right place" on a soil and sub-soil of the "right type," and great wine can be produced.

Moreover, such is the complexity, within a basic geological formula, and such is the multiplicity of important aspects—microclimates and other elements that fall within the concept of *terroir*—that if you move a matter of a few dozen metres up, down or sideways, you will find that while the wine is fundamentally the same, it will be, yes, just that little bit different—sufficiently separate to merit its being called by another name and bottled apart. It is for this reason that we can accept that the existence of as many as 539 *premiers crus* and thirty-two *grands crus*, some of them very small, others impossibly tiny, *is* justified. Find a grower who can offer you wines from several adjoining *climats*, all of them the same age and clone, all made in exactly the same way, and you will notice the differences. They are real, and they will be the same, whatever the vintage, whatever the climate.

There are limited places in the world—more than we realise today, for some are still to be discovered, but few and far between nonetheless—where the right choice of grape complements great *terroir* and can produce great wine. The Côte d'Or is manifestly one of them. Within the obvious climatic limits, modern technology allows for good wine to be produced almost anywhere, even on the quasi-hydroponic sands of the Salins du Midi in the south of France. Great wine is rare because the great *terroirs* are rare.

This conveys by implication an important duty on the Burgundian winemaker. If he possesses great land and is unable or unwilling to do his utmost to produce as great a wine from it as he can, then, quite simply, he should be taken out and shot and his vines given to one of the other small domaines whose proprietor *does* take his or her responsibilities seriously. Otherwise, humanity is being deprived of its just deserts, and that is too important a matter to be left unattended.

The geology of the Côte d'Or is complex but not inexplicable. During the time of the dinosaurs, the Jurassic Period of some 195 to 135 million years ago, what is now Burgundy was underwater. In this sea, countless small animals, such as oysters, molluscs of various types, sea urchins, chrinoids and brachiopods, lived, died and were deposited on the bottom. The soil that has resulted is rich in these fossils. Clay, sand and gravel, formed out of the decomposition and erosion of other soils, combined with the calcium carbonate in the water to deposit marl and other variations of mudstone. Elsewhere, a third type of rock was formed by the precipitation of carbonate of lime from seawater and its subsequent settling out to form oolitic limestone.

Somewhat later, beginning about 35 million years ago in the Oligocene Period and continuing into the Miocene (from 26 million years ago onwards), as the Alps and other European mountain ranges were being formed, a rift began to form the flatland and lagoons of the Bresse, the Saône and the Doubs. Where, abruptly, the Morvan came to its easterly end and fell into the plain, there was, exposed for all to see and facing precisely in the direction where it would be bathed in sun from the first rays of the morning, a golden slope. Later it would be found to be an ideal site for the grape.

The Côte d'Or, then, is largely limestone, but limestone of a number of different types, thicknesses, permeabilities, hardnesses and colours and with a variety of percentages of clay therein. There are faults. There are valleys formed by rivers tumbling out of the higher ground from the west. There are places where a number of different surface soils lie within the space of 50 metres. On most slopes the age and character of the rock changes abruptly as you descend from the trees above to the road below.

In essence the oldest of the limestones, the fossil-rich Bajocian—on top of which can be found Bathonian, and between which is located a softer marly limestone—will be found in the northern Côte de Nuits. Sub-varieties of the Bathonian limestone are the pink marble of Prémeaux and the more creamy marble of Comblanchien, and these will be found in Nuits-Saint-Georges.

Once you move into the Côte de Beaune, these older limestones sink beneath the ground, to surface again in Chassagne, and the surface limestone rock becomes the later Callovian, Argovian or, most recent of all, Rauracian, and contains fossilised sea urchins. These limestones are, in general, more prone to erosion. There are parts where they have degenerated into what the Burgundians call *lave*, and can be easily broken up manually.

As important as the bedrock is the surface soil. Upslope, there is little of this, as erosion is a perennial problem in the Côte d'Or, particularly in the Côte de Nuits. The earth can consist of any blend of decomposed limestone debris, harder stones such as flints and even larger rocks, gravels of various sizes, sands and accumulations of clay. In general, there is more clay and more nitrogenous matter, and of course worse drainage, at the foot of the slope; hence, the least clay and the most "pure" limestone provide an auspicious home for the Chardonnay at the top.

The golden slope is divided into two halves. In the north, the Côte de Nuits, the aspect is,

in principle, to the east; the slope is generally steeper; and the width of the vineyard area is narrower, hardly a couple of hundred metres at Prémeaux. Beyond the hill of Corton, the orientation of the Côte de Beaune turns toward the southeast, there are more valleys into the hillsides, the slope is more gentle and the east–west extent of the vines is wider—almost 4 kilometres at Savigny and Chorey.

Climate

Less so than in Alsace, more so than in Bordeaux, Burgundy enjoys a continental climate. What this means is that the climate is more uneven than at the coast. Yet if you take all four climatic parameters together (rainfall, relative humidity, temperature and hours of sunshine), the climate in Bordeaux and Burgundy is really very similar.

The Côte d'Or is drier, particularly in July and August, than both the Côtes Chalonnaise and Mâconnais and the Hautes-Côtes. Overall precipitation corresponds very closely to that of Bordeaux, but is less even, with Burgundy experiencing more very heavy storms—often accompanied by hail—and more periods of drought. Early spring (February, March and April) is dry, as is July, but May and June can be wet, which does not help the flowering. Luckily, September and October tend to be dry as well, which helps prevent rot.

As a result of the proximity of the ocean, relative humidity is greater in Bordeaux than in Burgundy at the beginning of the day, but is lower by the end of it. Overall, the figures are very close. Burgundy, however, is both cooler and sunnier than Bordeaux, not so much because it is less hot in summer but because it is colder in winter, and the days are longer. It is warmer in Dijon than it is in the Côte Chalonnaise, but warmer still in Beaune, and being marginally further to the north, as well as inland, Burgundy's late summer days are longer and sunnier those of Bordeaux, helping maturity. Light, as Benjamin Leroux of the Clos des Epeneaux points out, is more important than heat in promoting maturity. The Côte de Beaune starts picking around the time the Merlots are collected in the Gironde. The Côte de Nuits begins a week later, on the same sort of day the Cabernets are attacked.

Burgundy, however, has a great advantage over Bordeaux. In the Gironde there are, in general, larger estates and more grape varieties. Hence, the harvest can extend over 3 weeks. In the Côte d'Or a week is usually the maximum, and a glance at the projected weather forecast can ensure that the growers' best sites are reserved for collection during the best periods, if the weather seems inclement.

GLOBAL WARMING

The effects of global warming are there in Burgundy for all to see. The area is much drier than it used to be, and summers are overall hotter—a trend that is fine if you are on holiday there, but is not of much comfort to the viticulturalist. Moreover, winters are tending to be longer and colder—and also drier—thus leading to a later bud-break. Together with an earlier harvest, which has as much to do with lower crops and better viticultural husbandry as it does with climate change, the gestation period from bud to harvest is shortening, which, in principle, leads to less complexity in the wine. A comparison of the dates of the harvest—and the trend is the same in Bordeaux—shows that the vintage is starting 4 days earlier, on average, every decade.

Grape Varieties

PINOT NOIR

There is a very large number of Pinots, both beyond the simple Pinot Noir and within the aegis of this single variety. A gypsy of a grape, it has been called. And if by gypsy, you think of the temperamental Carmen, then you have got it in one. The variety is sensitive to cold, both during the winter and during the flowering. It buds early, making spring frost a potential hazard, and it ripens early. The Pinot Noir produces a small cylindrical-conical cluster of densely-packed, slightly oval berries. As a result of their being close together, and the Pinot Noir skin being thin, grey rot can be a serious problem if the weather turns humid towards harvest time.

As important are two other traits: Wine made from Pinot Noir is much more susceptible than other varieties to overproduction. The concentration and character dissolve rapidly if the yield is excessive, and this point of diminishing returns starts at a much lower level than is the case with other varieties. A Cabernet or a Merlot can yield satisfactory wine at 55 or even 60 hectolitres per hectare. The limit for Pinot Noir is 45, and apart from exceptional years such as 1990 and 1999, anything over 35 for *grand cru* and 40 for *premier cru* is an admission that the grower has not set his sights as high as he should.

Moreover, Pinot Noir is very susceptible to temperature as it reaches the end of its ripening cycle. As with other varieties, the wine can be mean and unripe if the sun fails to shine, but if the weather is too hot and roasted, as in 2003, a Pinot Noir is also prone to being coarse and leaden-footed.

Pinot is said to be an old variety, close to wild *vitis vinifera*. There are a number of legends as to how it arrived in the region. One concerns the Celtic tribe, the Aedui, ancestors of today's Burgundians, who were seduced by the delicious wines of Lombardy, invaded Italy to enjoy them further and then stayed there until they were forced out by the emerging Roman empire a couple of hundred years later in about 200 BC. They brought the Pinot Noir back with them. It's a nice story, until you start looking for Pinots in northern Italy.

Other historians like to suggest that the Pinot is indigenous and only needed to be adapted from the wild—by the Aedui or anyone else. A third story, which follows on from the generally accepted origin of French viticulture as lying with the establishment of a Phoenician Greek colony in what is now Marseilles in around 600 BC and posits the gradual dissemination of the science of vine farming as proceeding up the Rhône and beyond, cites the origin of the Pinot Noir and other local grapes as lying in the Middle East.

What is not explained by any of these theories, but is clear from Roman records, is that wine was not definitely *made* in Burgundy (as opposed to being consumed) until about AD 200. The first recorded mention of the Pinot Noir dates from as late as 1375.

A Pinot Noir wine is rarely a blockbuster. Fragrance, finesse and delicacy are the keynotes, not size, muscle and overwhelming tannins. Because the thickness of the skins is less than, say, that of Cabernet-Sauvignon or Syrah, there is less colour, Pinot Noir has less tannin and less body. Nevertheless, there should be no lack of intensity, grip, depth and complexity.

The flavour of a young Pinot Noir is of slightly sweet, freshly crushed soft summer fruits: a fragrant, silky, multifaceted and delicately elegant combination of raspberries, strawberries, cherries, mulberries and currants of different types. Concentrated young Burgundy often offers up a hint of coffee. From the oak—and this element should not be excessive—there can come vanilla and fondant, mocha and cigar-box. The character of Pinot Noir is fragile and elusive, though, and it should not be swamped, either by too much oak or by excessive maceration.

As a Pinot Noir evolves it takes on a totally different character. As with all wines the spice elements of the flavours of maturity begin to emerge. The oak changes into cedar or sandalwood. An animal, gamey, almost vegetal character begins to emerge. The fruit flavours deepen, incorporating hints of damson and blackberry. The whole thing becomes more sensuous. The residual flavours are sweet, but naturally sweet—ethereal, multifaceted and totally magical.

Sadly, few of us get the chance to consume magical old Burgundy. Some wines are just not made for this sort of long-term keeping. Others come from less illustrious vintages, less auspicious *terroirs*. Most are consumed far in advance of their prime, for the simple reason that there is nothing else to buy within our budgets. Some authorities misleadingly believe Burgundy doesn't keep. Nonsense: all properly balanced wine will keep much longer than we think it will—hence the tasting notes of vigorous 1964s and earlier vintages located further on in these pages.

There is a fashion, encouraged if not insisted upon by certain American writers, for Burgundies to be reared, whatever their provenance, in 100 percent new oak; for the wine to have the deepest colour possible—or the reverse, to be marked down if the colour is light; to be big and tannic; and to generally be the sort of wine a Pinot Noir is impossible of being. I shall discuss these "misnomers" in the pages that follow. Suffice it to say here that these wines do not age and will not make the lovely fragrant old Burgundies that, every now and then, we are lucky enough to encounter: Burgundies which set our hearts afire.

CHARDONNAY

Though it was called Pinot-Chardonnay in the past, Chardonnay has, in fact, no close connection with the Pinot family. The variety is fairly vigorous. It starts and finishes its growing season just a little after the Pinot Noir but is nevertheless susceptible to spring frost. *Coulure* is also a problem. Chardonnay forms a small, relatively compact winged-cylindrical cluster of small berries, not as densely closed as that of the Pinot Noir, and so is less prone to grey rot. Overmaturity is much more of a problem. At this stage, somewhere between full ripeness and the onset of *pourriture noble*, the acidity of the grape is at its lowest, and the wines therefrom will attenuate quickly. In vineyards where the vines are over-cropped—and Chardonnay, too, has its low limits if the objective is truly *premier* and *grand cru* wine (say, 38 hl/ha for *grand cru*, 43 for *premier cru* and 48 for village wine)— the fruit can pass from only-just-ripe to overripe without ever becoming properly concentrated, and thus it will never have sufficient acidity to produce a balanced and stylish wine which will improve in bottle.

Chardonnay grows well on soils with more limestone and less clay. If the latter is too preponderant, the wine will be leaden-footed, heavy and four-square. Hence, in general, up at the top of the slope is where it will thrive best. Moreover, because it requires fewer sun-hours to ripen, and in any case because it is not vinified with its stems, Chardonnay can make good wine where the red results would be a bit weak and thin: hence the preference for Chardonnay up in the valleys at higher altitudes and on west-facing slopes.

The best Côte d'Or white Burgundies are, of course, vinified in wood, a percentage of which will be new. If the vineyard has not been over-cropped, then Chardonnay, with its blend of ripe, subtle, opulent, peachy or nutty-buttery fruit and oak, and with its round, rich mouth-feel, can be one of the great wine flavours of the world. And it can age exceptionally well in bottle.

Viticulture

BACK FROM THE BRAIN-DEAD: MOVEMENTS TOWARD A LIVING SOIL

It is alarming to see how much damage can be done so rapidly. Through a combination of ignorance, negligence, cynicism and a regard for solely short-term profit (and damn the consequences), the Burgundian vineyard was reduced to the status of almost desert, in terms of its natural nutrient and micro-flora and fauna content, in little more than 30 years. The misuse of fertilisers, chemical weed-killers and heavier and heavier tractors not only had the effect of neutralising and homogenising the soil, compacting it such that it was rendered less permeable (and more prone to erosion) and reducing its acidity by increasing the amounts of nitrogen and potassium therein; evading the need to plough also encouraged the vines to be lazy and to only extend their roots on the surface, where the artificial nutrients were found, rather than to dig deep into the bedrock, where they could find the elements that were special and unique about the particular *climat*.

It took a mere 30 years for things to go downhill. It may take more than that to climb back up. There are today some vineyards, not fertilised since the end of the 1970s, which *still* have too high a potassium content. There are others which cannot be ploughed because important root systems lie close to the surface, so ploughing would cause the vines to be decapitated. In these cases, we will have to wait until the vineyard is replanted. There are still vines belonging to that infamous strain, the Pinot Droit, planted in the 1960s for quantity and not quality. Vineyard husbandry is a long-term process.

Happily, almost at the brink, and aided by agricultural engineers such as Claude Bourguignon and other experts, the Burgundian *vigneron* began to realise he was not only ruining his soil, but also taking out the very individuality which lies at the heart of the word *terroir*. Today everybody is at least *biologique*—which I would argue is mere common sense—or *biodynamique*.

BIOLOGIQUE

This concept starts with the principle that what is unique about a particular *terroir* must at all costs be preserved. Not only is this *terroir* an expression of the chemical composition of the surface soil and the sub-soil beneath it, but it is also characterized by the micro-flora and -fauna within it. Those who are proponents of natural yeasts will point out that each individual site will or should have its own family of natural yeasts. The soil must be able to breathe. Hence, it must be ploughed. One of the beneficial side effects of traditional ploughing is that the earth can be banked up against the vine in the autumn, so protecting it against cold. To avoid compacting the soil too much, a new, lighter breed of tractors with balloon wheels is being evolved.

It has been discovered that a return to traditional methods has a number of beneficial side effects. Not only does the elimination of all fertilisation apart from a delicate composting one year in three encourage the vine to send its roots deep down into the sub-soil in search of nutrients, a process which gives these vines a more distinctive, better balanced wine, but it also leaves the plant itself healthier. It will suffer less from cryptogamic disease (mildew, oïdium); it will react better to cold, as well as to heat and drought; and it will be more efficient in turning sun hours into sugar in the grape.

La lutte biologique (organic viticulture) and *la lutte raisonnée* (reactive viticulture) follow naturally on from this logical approach to the *terroir*. Instead of spraying against insect depredation as a matter of rote, cultivate predators and release them just when the next generation of spider or grape-worm is due to appear. Instead of using synthetic or systematic sprays against mildew and oïdium, and in enormous quantities, use just the exact amount of sulphur and copper sulphate, perfectly natural chemicals. Moreover, in today's world where keeping the yield under control and not letting it get too high is as important as encouraging a harvest in the first place, is it so bad if your vines *do* naturally lose a little of their fruit during the summer?

BIODYNAMIQUE

Biodynamism is thus far practised by few—but an increasing number—in Burgundy. However those few include such big names as Lalou Bize at the Domaines Leroy and Auvenay and the Domaines Leflaive, Lafon, Lafarge, Trapet, De Montille, Pierre Morey and Comte Armand, as well as Jean-Claude Rateau in Beaune, Thierry Guyot in Saint-Romain and others. Moreover, there are many illustrious domaines outside the Côte d'Or who have "gone biodynamic" recently.

The principle behind biodynamism is cosmic: that not only the moon, but also the position of the planets in the Zodiac should govern when we should plant, when we should plough, when we should treat and when we should harvest—that the planets, not just the moon, exert an influence on agriculture on the earth.

There are four elements in any plant: the root, the leaf, the flower and the fruit. Indeed there are four types of plant: those cultivated for their root, such as carrots; their leaf, such as lettuce; their flower, such as sunflowers; and their fruit, such as the vine. These correspond to the four elements of Earth, Water, Air and Fire as follows:

Earth	Root	Taurus, Virgo, Capricorn
Water	Leaf	Cancer, Scorpio, Pisces
Air	Flower	Gemini, Libra, Aquarius
Fire	Fruit	Aries, Leo, Sagittarius

Every 9 days the moon passes in front of one of these constellations; its force will be greater or lesser depending on the wax and wane of the moon itself and on the position of the planets.

What all this boils down to is that there are certain dates when the efficiency of a treatment can be much greater than others, certain dates which are appropriate and others which are not. A friend in Burgundy, no mean gardener, planted three rows of new potatoes at 10-day intervals in 1995. The first and the third, she later found out, happened to coincide with a biodynamically recommended day. These thrived. The second, sown on a bad day, produced a meagre harvest.

Biodynamic treatments are homeopathic. Sulphur and copper sulphate, against oïdium and mildew, are allowed. Against other depredations, preparations based on silica and infused with plants as varied as nettle, dandelion, bracken, camomile, arsenic and valerian are used. Homemade compost, based on cattle dung, is recommended. In some cases the treatment is placed inside a cow horn, buried in the earth on one special date and dug up on another, before being diluted by 10 million parts and applied.

Sometimes the extremes of biodynamism sound like black magic. But the point is: it works. We should learn not to scoff.

PREPARATION OF THE SOIL

A virgin, or a least cleared, piece of land presents the farmer with what, in the case of a Côte d'Or vineyard, can be a once-in-a-lifetime opportunity. Now is the time, before replanting, to have the soil analysed and to remedy any defects, to inject it against viral and other diseases, to install an efficient drainage system, to break up the land in order to crush or eliminate really large rocks, to renew all the stakes and wires and to renew the surface soil at the top with the earth that has been washed down to the bottom.

What is a clone? A clone is a population of vines all deriving from the same mother plant. Each vine will be genetically the same as its neighbour.

The advantage of clonal selection is that clones, by and large, are more resistant to disease and crop more uniformly. Their disadvantages? Uniformity, a lack of variety. Conversely, *sélection massale*, propagation from a number of the vineyard's own most successful plants, will bring with it all the defects of these plants, but it will also give diversity.

Clonal selection is becoming more popular, but this pace is hindered by the very time-scale of producing and testing the clones in the first place. It *is* a slow process, and it is only relatively recently—since 1980 or so—that clones which will be useful to the *grand cru* owner in Vosne-Romanée, as opposed to the bulk grower in the Mâconnais, have been evolved. We are only now into the second generation of these clones. Currently, clone numbers 667, 777 and 828 are yielding good results. Another, 943, seems promising.

The ideal, of course, is a combination of the two: the availability of a dozen or more high-quality, relatively low-yielding, disease-resistant clones. A *sélection massale* of clones: this is the future.

SELECTION OF ROOT-STOCK

As important as the fruit-bearing end of the piece of wood to be propagated is the end that will produce the root system. As a result of a nasty little aphid called *phylloxera*, a *vitis vinifera* variety such as a Pinot Noir or a Chardonnay will not thrive in the soils of nearly all the vineyard areas of Europe, including Burgundy. As a consequence, a graft is required: Pinot Noir onto a non-*vinifera* root such as *rupestris* or *berlandieri*—these having a more aphid-resistant, harder bark. Once again progress here

is only just beginning: the task is to adapt precisely not only the root-stock to the clonal or *massale* selection of the grape variety, but also to the land on which it is to be planted. Here, the type of surface soil (how much clay, sand, gravel) on top of the basic limestone, the pH of the soil and its physical condition (exposure, drainage) need to be calculated, and the root-stock chosen accordingly. Moreover, some root-stocks are more vigorous than others. Some race toward overmaturity in September. The SO4 is notorious in both respects. Is this a good or a bad thing? It is up to the *vigneron* to decide.

In Burgundy domaines, favoured root-stocks—and they always seem to be branded with complicated numbers—include 161/49C, or Fercal, for Pinot Noir and for Chardonnay, Riparia, 3309C and 101-14MG. In Chablis you will find 41B, a *vinifera-berlandieri* hybrid.

SPACING

The Côte d'Or is a densely populated vineyard. Unlike in the New World, it is felt that the greater the population, the better the wine, for there will be more competition among the root systems, so they will have to dig deeper, and thus become more complex, and further, which will cause the vigour of each vine, and so its tendency to overproduce, to be reduced. Densities of up to 12,500 vines per hectare (less than 1 m between vines and rows) are commonplace; 10,000 (1 m by 1 m) is the norm.

RAY-GRASS AND OTHER METHODS OF COMBATING EROSION

Côte d'Or vineyards, generally inclining east to southeast, are usually planted up and down the slope. This does not maximise the vines' ability to take in the sun—that would be a north-south planting—but it aids the flow of water away from the vines when it rains.

Unfortunately, on the Côte d'Or's steep slopes, with its sometimes violent thunderstorms, erosion can be a problem. One solution to this is the planting of a special grass between the rows. This practice has been pioneered by the Gouges family in Nuits-Saint-Georges. The addition of the grass has a minor disadvantage: the rate of frost damage is increased. But as well as combating erosion, there are a number of other advantages caused by the competition between the grass and the root-system, which forces the latter to seek lower down for its nutrients. The result is an increase not only in the concentration and character of the wine, but also in its potential alcohol and acidity. Not surprisingly, other Burgundians, cautious at first, are following suit.

PRUNING AND TRAINING SYSTEMS

Having got this far, the Côte d'Or *vigneron* will be aware of two things. His, not the winemaker's (for all that they may be the same individual) is the creative role. This role is to produce, at the time of harvest, fruit which is in as ripe and healthy a condition as possible and at a yield per hectare which is compatible with the production of high quality, concentrated wine. As any Burgundian winemaker will tell you, 90 percent of the potential quality lies in the quality of the fruit in the first place. The winemaker's task is (merely?) to translate this into the finest possible wine. He will not be able to *add* quality. His role is (merely, again) not to screw it up. Viticultural tasks therefore have two objectives: to keep the plant and its fruit healthy and to keep the yield within acceptable limits.

The way the vine is pruned and trained is vital to both of these pursuits. Pruning must be severe, to six or so buds per vine. And there are essentially two systems of training the adult vine: *Guyot* and *Cordon du Royat*. The cane should point downslope, away from the trunk. This trains the sap efficiently right to the end, ensuring a more even ripeness.

The first system, *Guyot*—though recent in Burgundy, having only been introduced in the 1930s—is the most widespread. This is a single *Guyot*, one cane extending horizontally from the mother trunk, on which are the six buds, plus a short spur near the trunk, on which there is one bud which will usually produce next year's cane.

The *Cordon* system involves spur, not cane pruning. The lateral, horizontal branch will be old wood, not a cane from last year, and at intervals along it will be spurs of one or two buds.

For Chardonnay most growers prefer the single *Guyot* system. Increasingly, for Pinot Noir, because the bunches can be spaced out, reducing the risk of rot, and because the harvest can be more easily controlled, growers in the Côte d'Or are opting for the *Cordon* method.

HIGH-TRAINING AND THE IMPORTANCE OF THE LEAF CANOPY

There are always those who have quite other ideas. One such is Henri Latour in Auxey-Duresses. He has developed his own *Lyre* system, high-trained, with the canopy divided at the top to let in the sun. Others in Auxey-Duresses—the domaines Roy and Labry—also see the advantage of *Lyre*-trained vines. The Burgundians being fuddy-duddies, this is only "tolerated" by the authorities. Latour's wines, however, are very good. And that should be enough justification.

The leaf canopy, of course, is the engine room of the vine. It is here that the vital process of photosynthesis takes place. Train the vines a bit higher, maximise the leaf space and you will gain sugar, say people such as Christophe Roumier and Jacques Seysses: so a higher hedge in their vineyards. But you can exaggerate this, says Étienne Grivot: too much and, yes, the wine is richer and riper, but it has less acidity—lovely when young, but less finesse and capacity to age.

ROGNAGE

Rognage is the clipping away, by hand or by machine, of excess foliage. This is usually begun at about the time the vine flowers—it should not take place until *after* flowering has completed, say some, for to commence before leads to too much second generation fruit—and repeated periodically afterwards.

In the last few seasons, Lalou Bize of the Domaine Leroy has decided not to *rogner*. She believes it stresses the vine. Instead, one vine's excess foliage is bent over to join its neighbour, forming a hoop. It makes the Leroy vines easy to pick out. The Domaine Roblot-Monnot also follows this practice, pointing out that it increases the leaf canopy, thus maximising photosynthesis.

LEAF-STRIPPING

As the harvest approaches, it is usual to strip away the leaves surrounding the fruit. This will aid aeration, so reducing the risk of rot. In August this is done on the north or non-sunny side of the vine. Early in September, those on the sunny side are removed. It also helps fix the colour as the skin is thickened. Obviously, with hindsight, this was a great mistake in 2003.

PLOUGHING WITH HORSES

In order to plough without compacting the soil with a tractor, horses are once again being seen in the Burgundian vineyards. Again, Lalou Bize was one of the first to revert to the use of animals. Obviously, if you do not *rogner*, you can't use tractors.

KEEPING THE HARVEST DOWN: IS GREEN HARVESTING EFFECTIVE?

The earlier steps are taken to keep the harvest within limits, the better. Techniques such as green harvesting pale into inefficient insignificance when compared with the pruning itself and with the subsequent de-budding, even before the flowering takes place.

What is the objective? Six bunches per vine for Pinot Noir, eight for Chardonnay. So prune to six or eight in the first place. Some buds will be double-yolkers, so to speak, so one embryonic bunch must be rubbed out, one embryonic flower removed. Moreover, to eliminate the second generation, once the danger of frost has gone, nip out this bud, on the opposite side of the cane to the first, as well. Drastic action perhaps, and if the flowering is unsuccessful, perhaps unnecessary; but best done at this time than later. Obviously, you *can* reduce the harvest immediately after flowering, or just before the *véraison*, this latter practice being what is generally known as green harvesting, but what will probably happen, say opponents, is that

the remaining bunches will simply expand to compensate, and your juice-to-solid ratio will be worse than it would have been in the first place. In my view green harvesting should be a last resort and needs to be as drastic as one in two bunches being eliminated to have any material effect.

OLD VINES AND LOW YIELDS

Vines, like people, decline in vigour as they age. Like some people, what they produce gets better. As the root system gets more impressive, the fruit becomes more complex. When it gets concentrated by a lower production—and a yield which is naturally rather than artificially small—the resultant wine will be richer and creamier in mouth-feel: the taste of old vines. Naturally, growers will boast about the venerable age of certain of their plots. Let's hope they are not encouraged to exaggerate.

With old vines, of course, come low yields. But beware the sort of low yield which comes from a vineyard where half the vines are dead or long since ripped out. Beware irregularity. There are many vineyards where old vines, as they have given up the ghost, have been replaced with young ones (this process is known as *repiquage*). In this case you could have a row which goes young vine (thirteen bunches), old vine (one bunch), young vine (sixteen bunches), old vine (two bunches), and so on, for an average of eight bunches per vine: probably 35 to 40 hectolitres per hectare. But you will get no low-*rendement* feel in the resultant wine, nor, of course, any old-vine flavour. I should point out here that the phrase *vieilles vignes* is not controlled by law.

WHERE A LARGE(-ISH) HARVEST CAN BE AN ADVANTAGE

Have you ever wondered why 1973, 1979, 1982 and 1999 were all surprisingly good white wine Côte d'Or vintages? So did I, until suddenly a bit of lateral thinking gave me the explanation. As we all know, in Champagne, the first pressing gives the best wine. Subsequent pressings provide lesser quality, and it is beneath the dignity of the top *grande marque* houses to allow them house-room. What would be the effect on the wine, in what promised to be an abundant harvest, if a first gentle pressing of Côte d'Or Chardonnay produced sufficient wine to fill the allowed *rendement*, and the juice from any subsequent pressings was spirited away separately to provide *vin ordinaire* for the workers? Would this not produce a *grand vin* of above average quality, above expectation for the vintage? Was this the explanation for the white wine success of these vintages? Is there a lesson to be learned?

WHERE THE AC LAWS NEED TO BE REWRITTEN
Politicians rarely have the courage of their own convictions. Prior to 1974 there was the Cascade System. Effectively there was no limit to what the Burgundian *vigneron* could produce: only to what he was allowed to label. Thus, if the wine in question was a *grand cru* (where the maximum *rendement* was 30 hl/ha) and the production was in fact 60 hectolitres per hectare, the first 30 hectolitres would be labelled *grand cru*, the next 5 as village or *premier cru* (where the maximum was 35 hl/ha), the next 15 as *Bourgogne* (the limit being 50 hl/ha) and the remainder as *vin ordinaire*. Yet all the wine was the same.

This was obviously an unsatisfactory state of affairs, open to abuse; foreigners could ship the *vin ordinaire*—or another wine, perhaps—in bulk and label it *grand cru*, for example.

Instead of merely limiting the grower to a simple maximum, implying that if he/she overproduced, then the A.C would be withheld, the Institut National des Appellations d'Origine (INAO) not only increased the *rendement de base* (from 30 hl to 35 hl for *grand cru rouge*, and from 35 hl to 42 hl for *premier cru* and village wine), but also allowed—indeed encouraged—the grower to overproduce by advancing the possibility of an extra 20 percent above the maximum, subject to tasting. This is called *plafond limite de classement* (*PLC*).

There are three fundamental flaws here. Firstly, except in exceptional vintages such as 1990 and 1999, diminishing returns, as I have

already pointed out, set in at 35, 40 and 45 hectolitres per hectare for *grand cru, premier cru* and village red wines, respectively. You simply cannot produce *grand cru* worthy of the name at 42 hectolitres per hectare, or *premier cru* at 48. Secondly, the *rendement annuel* (as opposed to the *rendement de base*) and the percentage of *PLC* were supposed to be varied according to nature of the vintage (e.g., if there were frost or hail damage, it would be reduced). In fact, it rarely varies. Thirdly, the so-called tasting inspection takes place once, long before bottling (why not judge the finished article as well), and the judges are the local trade: growers, brokers and *négociants*. You can be faulted on typicity—rarely, if ever, on a lack of basic quality or concentration.

What needs to be done? Eliminate the concept of *PLC* for a start. Differentiate between *premier cru* and village wine, but raise the *rendement de base* for village *rouge* from 40 to 45 hectolitres. And set these as absolute limits. Anyone who continually (not just during a one-off unfortunate experience with rain) overproduces should be heavily fined, and the whole *cuvée* confiscated (this could make an interesting third auction sale, to add to the Hospices de Beaune and Hospices de Nuits). Moreover, bottled wine should be sampled, and the judging be somewhat less of a formality.

RECENT CHANGES TO THE LAW
With a cautiousness that seems almost excessive, the wine *syndicats* in the Côte d'Or (please note this does not cover Chablis, the Côte Chalonnaise, Mâconnais, or Beaujolais) have agreed on a new system, starting in 2004, which gives individual growers more responsibility for restricting yields. The new benchmark will be the *rendement moyen décennal* (RMD), or 10-year average. For instance, the permitted maximum yield for village and *premier cru* Gevrey-Chambertin is 47 hectolitres per hectare, or 470 over 10 years. Growers will be allowed to vary yields up and down, making it easier for them to adjust to climatic conditions, by a maximum of 3 hectolitres, provided the total does not exceed 470 hectolitres over 10 years.

As of the 2005 vintage, Burgundy has adopted these new regulations regarding yields. Out goes the controversial *PLC*, whereby, in most vintages, growers were permitted to produce 20 percent more than the *rendement de base* or basic permitted yield. In some cases, though, the *rendement de base* will be increased. In addition, inspectors will have the authority to warn growers during the summer that certain parcels look as if they will overproduce. Moreover, following frost or hail depredation, the authorities will be permitted to specify reduced maximum yields. This happened in 2005 in Santenay. This will deter growers from overproducing in one vineyard to compensate for reduced crops elsewhere. All this is much to be welcomed.

Moves are afoot to change the time when Burgundy wines are submitted for appellation approval. Currently this occurs in the spring after the vintage, when the malolactic fermentation has completed itself. In the future, domaine-bottled wines will be assessed just before bottling, at a time when the *élevage* is just about finished. This new move will help to eliminate those wines ruined in cask by bad handling.

As of the 2005 vintage, the wines of Volnay, Chassagne-Montrachet, Santenay and Viré-Clessé in the Mâconnais were assessed for AOC approval later rather than sooner. This system will cover all of Burgundy from the 2007 vintage onward.

COMBATTING CRYPTOGAMIC DISEASES, INSECT DEPREDATION AND GREY ROT

In Burgundy's marginal climate, and with at least one sensitive grape (though I believe the Chardonnay is not as hardy as some people think), keeping pests and diseases at bay is a continual problem. In fact the most effective way of reducing contamination happens to be precisely what any grower should be looking for: a healthy plant, in a living soil, with a deep and complex root-system, baring only a modicum of fruit.

From the word go, at the beginning of the season, you will see the curious, insect-like vineyard tractors travelling up and down the vine rows pumping out clouds of moist insect repellent combined with sulphur and/or copper sulphate against the diseases and pests which threaten the vine. In the main, these are now under control and have been for some time, though the incidence of grape-worm seems to be on the increase.

Grey rot is a more serious problem. It is the same fungus as that of noble rot, yet it is rarely noble in Burgundy, and always disastrous for Pinot Noir. Any seriously lengthy outbreak of rain will encourage rot, if the temperature remains high. The thinner the skin of the fruit, the quicker it will set in. And rotten grapes give rotten wine, wine without colour, which will tend to be high in volatile acidity and which will not clarify well.

Spacing out the bunches and removing of some or all of the covering leaves to aid aeration can help (see above). There are also anti-rot sprays, which harden the skin (as does the application of copper sulphate). The long-term solution, I believe, is clonal: the eventual production of a Pinot Noir with a thicker skin. In the meanwhile, it makes the necessity to *trier* (sort through the fruit to eliminate what is substandard at the time of the harvest) all the more acute.

As far as insects are concerned, there are two main pests: grape-worm and red spider. The latter has been suppressed by giving up the use of insecticides, thus releasing these arachnids' natural predators.

SEXUAL CONFUSION

Small plastic capsules that excrete female grape-moth pheromones are becoming more and more widespread. This confuses the male *cochylis* and *eudemis* moths, which are then unable to find a female mate, preventing a second generation of moths and, more immediately important, the adolescent form of grape-worm or *ver de la grappe* which wreaks havoc in vineyards by feeding on embryonic flowers, the flowers themselves and young berries. In Burgundy the *cochylis* and *eudemis* are considered to be second only to *phylloxera* in terms of potential damage, but this form of biotechnological control can only be effective if whole communes agree on its implementation. Today, the whole of the southern part of the Côte de Nuits, from Bonnes Mares to Nuits-Saint-Georges, Clos de la Maréchale, is protected, as are, in the Côte de Beaune, the white wine communes of Chassagne-Montrachet and Puligny-Montrachet, as well as Beaune itself. It was tried, but then abandoned, in Meursault, too. It proved impossible to get everyone to agree. Visitors to the vineyards will notice these little brown pheromone-excreting sachets, called *rates*, on every fifth vine in every fifth row.

MACHINE HARVESTING?

We arrive at the date of the harvest. The winery has had its annual spring clean. The fermentation vats have been scrubbed and sterilised. The pipes have been washed and sterilised. The crusher/de-stemmer is back from servicing. The new barrels have been broken in with a mixture of hot water, salt and something abrasive like gravel, to leach out their green tannins. Space has been cleared. Everyone is keeping a nervous eye on the weather forecast, but is otherwise raring to go. Finally, sugar readings in the vineyards indicate the fruit is ripe. A plan of campaign—the order in which the vineyards are to be attacked—is drawn up. Does the quality Côte d'Or *vigneron* climb up onto his harvesting machine and gallop off to battle? The answer is no. These are useful, indeed today essential, tools in the production of merely good wine. But not of fine wine. For a start, they prevent *triage* in the vineyard—and it is in the vineyard that *triage* should commence, for the contact between mouldy and clean fruits, and the intermingling of their juices, can make the effort pointless. Secondly, they separate the fruit from its stem too early, encouraging oxidation. Thirdly, they do not differentiate between the ripe fruit and the *verjus*, that of the second generation. And fourthly, there is a direct relation between slightly unripe fruit and a herbaceous taint in the wine if the fruit is machine harvested.

You will see plenty of machines in Chablis and in the Mâconnais. There are some in the Hautes Côtes. But they are out of place in the Côte d'Or. Sadly—and I think they should be outlawed in *premiers* and *grands crus climats*—there are some, even here, who employ them.

Viniculture

A few general axioms to start off with:

- The grander the *terroir* the more hands-off and anonymous must the thumb-print of the winemaker be. The public wants to taste the character of Chambertin, not the winemaking signature of M. Machin.

- Ninety percent of the quality of the wine derives from the fruit in the first place (I have said this before, but it cannot be emphasised enough).

- The art of winemaking is disaster-preventative, not creative. You cannot make a silk purse out of a sow's ear. (I have also said this before.) On the other hand, the winemaker is no mere cypher. He or she can exert a lot of influence over the character of the wine, which is why one Chambertin is different from another. A great winemaker needs flair, imagination and the inspiration of divine discontent.

- There are numerous different ways to produce high quality Burgundy—not one magic recipe. And Burgundy, for this reason, is the most individualistic wine growing area in the world.

- Every vintage poses its own problems and solutions. Above all, winemakers must be flexible.

TRIAGE

In order to maximise the quality of the fruit, the first thing to do once the harvest reaches the winery is to perform another *triage* (why doesn't Burgundian law, like that in Châteauneuf du Pape, make this compulsory?). The fruit is poured out onto a conveyor belt and picked over by a team who reject anything unripe, bruised or rotten. The belt can have a light underneath (which helps eliminate unripe berries or bunches), as *chez* Philippe Charlopin. It can have a device which riddles it from side to side (which helps shake off rain-drops), as at the Domaine de Courcel. There can even be a wind tunnel (to dry the fruit), as *chez* Faiveley.

Then comes the moment of segregation. Is the fruit Pinot Noir or Chardonnay? Are we producing Chambertin or Montrachet?

Red Wine

SAIGNÉE AND OTHER METHODS OF CONCENTRATING THE MUST

Saigner means to bleed. Some of the free run juice is allowed to seep away (it can make a very pleasant *rosé*), with the object of equalising the solid-liquid ratio in the must. Increasingly used since the early 1970s, this is a useful technique. Sadly, there are one or two disadvantages. Firstly this free run juice is very aromatic, and a wine without these aromas risks being a little hum-drum, lacking high tones. The eventual result can be a bit four-square. Secondly it is difficult to anticipate at the outset quite what is the optimum percentage of juice which needs to be tapped off. For obvious reasons, you cannot do a trial run. If too much is run off, the wine can be a little too dense and solid.

Today, various people in Burgundy are experimenting with machines which can concentrate the must by eliminating merely the water, not the esters which make up the flavour. Sadly, most of the top growers who have experimented have come to the conclusion that the elegance of the wine is compromised.

Once again, however, the moral of the story is not to overproduce in the first place. If your vines are old, and the pruning severe, the berries will be small and concentrated in all but the most depressingly rainy harvests.

CHAPTALISATION AND ACIDIFICATION

Chaptalisation is permitted up to a level which would increase the alcohol content of the wine by 2°. At long last, it is up to the winemaker how and when he adds his sugar. Officially, he used to have to do this all at once, and at the beginning of fermentation. Most winemakers would rather do this in stages, and at the end, for this keeps the temperature high, resulting in a better extract of flavour and structural elements from the fruit. Two degrees (i.e., increasing the alcohol level of an 11° wine by 18 percent) seems already quite enough, but many Burgundians are lobbying to have the level raised to 2.5°. I consider this would only be an excuse for greater overproduction and worse husbandry. I trust this lobby is resisted.

You are not allowed to both chaptalise and acidify. Does this seem churlish? If so, imagine a wine which needed both to make it palatable. Should it be allowed to be anything but *vin ordinaire*? Is it going to taste any better than that, even after it has been concocted?

Some winemakers will argue—and it affects whites more than reds—that acidified wines never integrate properly; the acidity always appears to be "separate" from the fruit. I have found this to be less of a problem with reds, and I can understand those who turn a blind eye in the direction of the law and acidify a little, at the same time as chaptalising a little. The answer, of course, is to keep the *rendement* down. This will reduce the need to do either.

While we are on the subject, what is the optimum alcoholic level for red Burgundy? I would suggest for *grand* and *premier cru* somewhere between 12.5° and 13.5°; the more concentrated and full-bodied the wine, the nearer it should approach this upper limit. Bearing in mind a loss of about half a degree during fermentation, this means chaptalising up to 14°. But a wine which was only at 12° naturally would not be "concentrated and full bodied," for it is only after reaching 11.5° that the wine begins to develop the higher alcohols and double sugars that give the rich, full mouth-feel we call concentrated, and if it were to be chaptalised to the limit, it would be unbalanced, giving a "hot" effect on the aftertaste. This is another argument for keeping the rules unchanged. Leave the job to photosynthesis, not to the sugar bags! Too much Burgundy is still today, sadly, over-chaptalised.

THE STEMS

In the past, top red Burgundy was rarely de-stemmed. Today, with the exception of some—but these some include illustrious names such as the Domaine de la Romanée-Conti and Leroy—most Côte d'Or reds come from de-stemmed fruit. What are the arguments for and against?

The arguments for the stems are as follows: that they add tannin and structure, and also acidity; that they help to produce a more even fermentation because they will absorb some of the heat (fermentation is an exothermic reaction); that at least some of the fermentation can begin within the unbroken grape, so producing more complex flavours; that they add to the solid matter of the fermenting environment; and that they physically aid the fermentation by furthering aeration, helping with the drainage of the juice and so on. Many growers retain 10 or 15 percent just for this purpose. But it would appear from my discussions with growers that the main reason for not eliminating the stems is that this is the way a particular domaine has always made its red Burgundy.

Critics will argue that, while the fruit may be ripe, the wood may not be, so the presence of the stems may impart a harsh, green, twiggy taste; that, even if ripe, the flavours will mask the finesse of the crushed soft red fruit of the Pinot Noir; that the colour of the wine will be reduced; and that (in opposition to the argument that the stems *add* acidity) they may bring potassium with them (if that is still in excess in the soil), and so *reduce* the acidity of the wine. Vinifying with no stems results in a slightly higher alcohol level—for the fermentation is more efficient, and produces a more mellow wine with a richer, fatter mouth-feel, especially in the poorer vintages. Again, as with all Burgundy, it boils down to personal taste. I, lover of La Tâche as I am, personally find that I usually prefer wine from de-stemmed or largely de-stemmed fruit, especially if it is a wine from one of the minor *communes*, and so does most of the new

generation of Burgundian winemakers. The wine seems smoother and richer; the fruit more intense. But then, the diversity of Burgundy is one of its compelling charms. It would be tragic if the winemaking became standardised.

COLD-SOAKING

The theory behind cold-soaking, which involves a few days of macerating the grape skins in their own juice (a watery solution) prior to fermentation (i.e., without alcohol)—is that a better colour is fixed, more sophisticated tannins result and more vibrant fruit flavours are extracted.

As Burgundy is usually quite cool at the time of the harvest, fermentations, unless artificially heated, can take 3 or 4 days to get going; thus, most wines will, in fact, undergo a brief period of cold-soaking. What I am referring to here, however, is when this period is deliberately prolonged—to a week or more.

There are two main criticisms of prolonged cold-soaking. The first is that, unless you are equipped with a cooling unit, the must has to be very heavily sulphured in order to inhibit the fermentation from commencing; this sulphur takes months, if not years, to dissipate and combines with and degrades the flavour elements of the wine. The second, and most important, bone of contention is that the wine which results will taste untypical regardless.

Proponents will answer firstly that, on the sulphur side, the amount at bottling is no higher than that at other domaines, and that anyway, more and more people are now equipped to keep the temperature down (to 16–18° or even less) by cooling, thus eliminating the need to over-sulphur in the first place. To the accusation of non-typicity, they will argue firstly that a young, long-cold-soaked wine in fact tastes like young Burgundy used to taste 40 or 50 years ago, and secondly that after a decade, when the wine is mature, it *will* be typical (and, moreover, that what it tastes like in the meanwhile is immaterial).

I have listened to both sides carefully. There are many winemakers who favour long cold-soaking whom I admire, whose intelligence I respect, who make great wine. Equally, there are many who don't cold-soak who make great wine too.

Cold-soaking, however, is a relative term. It should not be "cold." It should ideally be at 13–15°. If too cold, at 10° or less, it is a waste of time. Nothing will happen. There will be no extraction of flavour and little of colour.

YEASTS: CULTURED OR NOT

The arguments for or against cultured yeasts flow along similar lines to those of clones versus *sélection massale*: we can either employ that little bit of control mankind has already achieved over nature, or let Mother Nature go rampant, with all the danger, but also with all the possibility for excitement, that might be involved.

Up to very recently, fermentations have traditionally been enabled by the presence in the vineyards and wineries of native wild yeasts, and the big argument for continuing to use them is that they are specific and individual to each particular *climat* and winemaker. Alter the yeast, and you change the flavour of the wine. Use the same yeast for several wines, and you risk standardising their flavours. So keep to the natural yeasts, and preserve the diversity.

There are, unfortunately, a number of downsides. Firstly, there needs to be a certain quantity of yeasts in the first place, and the amount of available yeasts can be reduced if there is rain at the time of the harvest. Secondly, their efficiency is variable, particularly at the beginning and end of fermentation. At the beginning this is not too much of a problem, but at the end, when there is only the barest element of non-fermented sugar left, and when the level of alcohol will be such as to inhibit yeast activity, a prolonged finish to the process can leave the wine open to oxidation or volatile acidity contamination.

Moreover, there are good yeasts as well as bad yeasts. Some wild yeasts can give very barnyardy flavours. One, *brettanomyces*, is very often cited as a cause of some unusual and rustic flavours in many a red wine.

In fact, there is not just one yeast out there in the wild, but a whole family of them, some useful at the start of fermentation, others at the end; some which will produce one flavour, others which will produce another; some which will suit one grape variety, others which will adapt to a different *cépage*. There are even yeasts which promote colour extraction or longevity, or increase the richness and creaminess of the mouth-feel. And there is no reason, in theory, why producing artificial strains of them, to suit the particular sort of wine you want to make, should not be warmly welcomed. Some domaines start off using the natural yeasts and then add artificial strains later. As I have said, the danger with cultured yeasts, particularly with white wines, is that all the resulting wines will taste the same. As with clones, this is a part of winemaking which is still very much in its infancy.

TEMPERATURES OF FERMENTATION

Fermentation is exothermic: it produces heat. The amount, in degrees Celsius, is the potential alcohol of the fruit plus 2. It is therefore crucial that the fermentation starts at 18–20°C or so. In hot vintages, the must will need to be cooled. In cold vintages, or after cold-soaking (see above), the juice will need to be warmed. Here again, as with attitudes toward the amount of stems and the amount of new oak, Burgundy shows a greater diversity of opinion than almost any other winemaking region in the world. There are those who insist on fermenting at a maximum of 28°C, others who choose to maintain the temperature within a very narrow band of 30–32°C, and winemakers who have no qualms about letting the thermometer rise to 35°C and above. François Faiveley likes low temperatures, his argument being that the flavour elements are volatile and will be lost if the fermentation is too hot. Above 32°C, with a fragile variety such as the Pinot Noir, the nose of the wine disappears. Patrice Rion, of Domaine Michèle and Patrice Rion, likes to ferment at exactly 32°C. Too little heat, in his view, leads to wines which lack body and structure; too much heat, and the wine risks being coarse, with the freshness of the fruit compromised. Jacques Lardière, at Jadot, on the other hand, is unconcerned if temperatures rise to 35°C plus. The wine doesn't suffer, he says, and he extracts more of the individuality of the *terroir* this way.

The point is that different elements in the wine get extracted at different temperatures: the fruit at cooler temperatures, the best of the tannins at a higher degree. Once again, the winemaker must be prepared to adapt. He or she must pay regard to the quality of the fruit in the first place and adapt accordingly. Flexibility should be the keynote.

PIGEAGE

Pigeage is the treading down of the "cap" of solid matter (grape skins and pips) which tends to rise up to the surface of the fermenting must. The winemaking team can either do this personally, or install a mechanical plunger. The object is threefold: to break up the cap and keep it submerged in the juice, to speed up the extraction, and to equalise the temperature. Normally this was done twice a day, for half an hour or so, while the wine was fermenting, and for a few days after that. Today in Burgundy, there is a tendency to tread down less but, in consequence, to extract for a longer period before running off the new wine.

POST-FERMENTATION

During fermentation the top of the vat will be at least partly open to allow some of the carbon dioxide to escape. After the fermentation is over, the vat is closed. This has several effects: the temperature is maintained, keeping it high; the maceration continues under the carbonic acid gas; the yeasts autolyse (degrade); aroma is released. It is here, if one needs to, that one chaptalises. It is here, if one desires to (to complete the fermentation and release further aromas), that one adds extra yeasts.

ENZYMES

Enzymes are used both for extraction (Vinozeme-Vintage: added 3 or 4 days into the fermentation process), and for clarification (Vinoflow: added the days before the wine is run off the residue of skins and pips). The object is to produce cleaner juice with greater purity of aromas, thus requiring neither fining nor filtration before bottling. Enzymes arrived in the early 1980s, when their use was considered by some, such as Dominique Lafon, to "*banaliser*" the wine (to reduce its flair and *terroir* definition). They have been refined since, and continue to be used by domaines such as Grivot: "It's a complement to all the other things we do. We don't systematically resort to enzymes ever year. But when we do, it is in very small doses: 3.5 grams per hectolitre. Enzymes must be used sparingly." Others are healthily sceptical. As André Porcheret, of Domaine Monthelie-Douhairet, says, "The fact that I do a severe *tri* of the fruit and then use a bladder press gives me such pure juice that I have no use for enzymes."

LENGTH OF MACERATION

The duration of the *cuvaison*, after which the wine, having finished its fermentation, is drawn off its lees, is also of profound importance and is closely allied with the temperature at which that maceration took place.

From the start, even before the fermentation—which lasts only a few days—begins, the effect of the skins macerating with the juice is to extract colouring matter, flavour and structure from the fruit. The colour comes from the phenolic compounds: anthocyanins and tannins. The former are extracted quickly (and break down in the wine over the next 5 years). The tannins, which preserve the colour and give the possibility of long aging, leach out at an even rate. Too short a maceration, and the wine is consequently light and ephemeral. Too long, and it will be coarse and dense. There will be an optimum moment, which will also depend on the temperature, that will be a desirable compromise between structure and fruit: at this time, the balance of wine will be at its best. Once again, today's winemaker will adjust to the quality of the harvested fruit. If there is a danger of rot, or of hail taint, then *cuvaison* must be reduced—but perhaps the temperature will be raised higher to maximise extraction quicker.

A TENDENCY TOWARD OVER-EXTRACTION AND OVER-OAKING

In the mid-1990s—and one can't help feeling, as a result of demands made by certain American wine importers, who thought (correctly) that the resultant wines would be awarded higher marks in their press—there was a tendency in Burgundy among some growers to over-macerate and/or over-oak. Bernard Dugat-Py, Christophe Perrot-Minot, the late Denis Mortet and Frédéric Magnien were some of those who erred in this respect. I wrote at the time that this was an error: the wines would not age with dignity. I was therefore gratified to note—after all these growers were not fools—that from the 1998 vintage, the foot was taken off the accelerator—that they had lightened up their techniques. I was at the Mortet domaine, alongside Becky Wasserman, with a group of our Bouilland Symposium clients in the summer of 2001. Denis asked the two of us if we would privately sample three wines blind and indicate our preference. He was pleased we both preferred the same wine, the one he had extracted the least. "I want to make wine like Charles Rousseau," he commented.

White Wine

A number of the subjects discussed in the previous pages—*triage*, chaptalisation, acidification, cultured yeasts or not—apply as equally to the production of white wine as to red. I refer readers to those paragraphs above.

Where white wine making differs most fundamentally from red is that it takes place without the skins and stems, in (and we are speaking here about the Côte d'Or's better wines—I discuss the different process in Chablis in the appropriate chapter) small wood rather than in tank or *foudre* (large wooden vats) and at much lower temperatures.

SKIN CONTACT

The flavour elements within a ripe grape are not distributed evenly. They are congregated towards the outside, within or very near the skin, not in the middle. The idea behind skin contact before pressing and fermentation—usually for 6 to 24 hours in a cool place—is to take advantage of the fruit's breakdown after picking and to leach out flavours from the skin into the juice. Otherwise, they would largely be lost. Obviously, if the skin is bruised or in any other way contaminated, this exercise would be inappropriate. But, say the adherents, if not, why not allow your fruit to rest overnight after picking in order to extract a bit more flavour this way?

Experience has shown, however, that skin-contacted wines—if I can describe them as such—do not age well. They are very upfront and aromatic when young, but they thin out, becoming vegetal and attenuated quite rapidly thereafter. This is appropriate for regional wines such as Mâcon Blanc, but not for fine Meursault.

PRESSING

Most white Burgundy is therefore sorted through and pressed as soon as possible after its entry into the winery. Of the various types of press, the most preferred is today the pneumatic horizontal type, within which is located an inflatable cylindrical balloon, the expansion of which presses the fruit gently against the outside. Today's machines are very sensitive, producing much more elegant musts than hitherto, and the winemaker can, if he or she so desires, make a number of different pressings of the same load of fruit. The first, obviously, will produce the best wine.

Moreover, pneumatically pressed musts—or in the case of reds, wines—produce finer lees, enabling the wines to be kept longer in cask and to need fewer rackings (see Keeping the Wine on its Lees, page 28).

FERMENTATION IN WOOD

In most cases (Ramonet is an exception), the growers then allow the pressed juice to settle out its gross lees (this is called *débourbage*), after which it is decanted into oak barrels and allowed to ferment. In some cases, fermentation may be encouraged to begin in bulk, and, once it is under way, to then continue in wood. But always, the principle that it takes place in wood is paramount. Only this way will a proper oak and wine integration of flavour be achieved. A wine which has been fermented in bulk and then matured in oak will never balance these elements correctly.

TEMPERATURES OF FERMENTATION
As noted, fermentation is an exothermic chemical reaction: it produces heat. But usually, cellars are cool, or environments temperature controlled, and the heat can conveniently escape easily from the barrel. The result is that top white Burgundy ferments at about 20–24°C. Higher temperatures (than 16–18°C, for most white wines) are desirable. They produce wines with richness, concentration and fat.

Élevage

The third part of winemaking, élevage, does not, I feel, receive the importance it deserves. Even if we might today take Henri Jayer's 1985 pronouncement—that 80 percent of Burgundy was good at the outset, but only 20 percent was good by the time it got into the bottle—with a pinch of salt, those of us who are used to tasting new wine out of cask are only too well aware of the pitfalls that can lie ahead of it and the ease with which it can deteriorate through incompetence and neglect.

Once again, there is a cardinal rule which should underlie every aspect of élevage. Just as the object of viticulture is to produce as superb fruit as possible, and that of viniculture to translate that superb fruit to superb young wine, so the principle behind the élevage of this wine is to look after it until it is time for it to be bottled, to make sure that it doesn't spoil and to prepare it for bottling so that it will mature thereafter into a great wine. And that means manipulating it as little as possible. The more you muck about with it, the more you risk taking out of it just those elements—for they are more fragile—that make one wine different from, and better

than, another. What is required is a hands-off, preventative approach.

MALOLACTIC FERMENTATION
Subsequent to the sugar-alcohol fermentation is the malolactic fermentation—from malic acid into lactic acid. Similarly, carbon dioxide is formed, which, if not allowed to escape, can help to protect the wine from oxidation (see below). The effect is to round off the wine, to reduce its acidity.

This fermentation is caused, not by yeasts secreting enzymes, as in the case of alcoholic fermentation, but by bacterial action, and if it is slow to commence (for some reason, it occurs much more tardily in Burgundy than in Bordeaux), it can be encouraged, both by warming up the cellar to 18°C or so, and by using inoculation. Most Burgundians, though, prefer to let nature take its course. Warming up the cellar excessively—Michelot in Meursault used to be guilty of this, and the combination of the heat and the natural dampness of his cellar made you feel you were going into a Turkish bath—can result in rather four-square wines with a lack of zip.

For red wines, an efficient malo is essential. The wine is rendered more supple, and it needs fully to complete rather than to continue in bottle, which would upset the balance and cause off-flavours.

As far as white wines are concerned, some establishments such as Jadot or Sauzet prefer to stop the malos of certain wines at some stage in order to preserve their natural acidities. This is far preferable to acidification. Critics, however, aver that it produces rather hard, unyielding wines.

With white wines, of course, malos take place in cask. While there is now a movement in Bordeaux which sponsors the achievement of red wine malos also in cask, rather than, as hitherto, in bulk before the wine is racked into small wood, red Burgundies have always undergone malo in cask in the top estates. These red wines are deemed to be richer and better integrated as a result.

There is no subject in Burgundian winemaking today which is more controversial, which causes more heated argument, than the amount of new oak which is applicable to the Pinot Noir and Chardonnays of differing qualities and pretensions produced up and down the Côte d'Or. As with all the other bones of contention—stems, temperatures of fermentation, etc.—the response you will get at the growers' end is as diverse as can be.

The public sees the flavour of new oak as a plus point, as an indication of quality. And indeed, the judicious marriage of wine and oak produces something with a more enhanced complex flavour than wine has on its own. The moot point is, of course, what percentage of new oak is "judicious"? Where do you draw the line and say that a wine has too much? And, often forgotten, how do very oaky young wines develop?

There are entrenched positions on both sides. And sadly, in some cases—and I view this with sorrow—growers are preparing two *cuvées* of the same wine: one very oaky for the American market, one less so for Europe and the rest of the world. Surely should not the producer him or herself decide what is best for his or her wine, rather than letting the market (or more simply, one broker's (or critic's) assessment of what will get high marks) dictate?

Because the wood is more porous, wine in a new oak cask will evolve faster, because it is more exposed to oxygen. (For this reason, as Thierry Matrot points out, disaster occurs in white wine vintages where, like in 1998, there has been some *pourriture*. The extra oxygenation only makes the wines even more coarse and unbalanced as they evolve.) The newer the cask, the faster the malo will complete, the sooner it will need racking, and the earlier it will need to be bottled. (Of course, what usually happens is that the winemaker will equalise the wine at each racking, so that the new oak element is the same in each cask.)

Moreover, and this is crucial, the tannins imparted by an oak cask are different from those the wine acquires during its maceration. Wine tannins slowly break down as the wine ages. Wood tannins are more rigid. When young, the "puppy fat" and primary fruit of the wine may seem sufficient to balance up with the new wood. But this may not be the case at 5 or 10 years old. If the wine is noticeably oaky at the time of bottling, it will be even more so later on down the road.

The flavours of Pinot Noir and Chardonnay, I submit, are delicate. These are wines of fragrance and complexity: wines of elegance. Unless they are very powerful and concentrated, *grands crus* of a great vintage, they will be overwhelmed by any more than a hint of new wood. Charles Rousseau gets it right, I think: 100 percent for Chambertin and Clos de Bèze, going down to 50 to 33 percent for the rest of his top wines, and hardly any at all for the village Gevrey-Chambertin. And that is just until the first racking in September6 months at most. Others, such as Ponsot and Gouges, believe in very much less, barely one tenth or none at all. Most growers row a path somewhere in the middle of these approaches.

But there are some who believe in 100 percent new oak for all their wines, and some even in 200 percent (by which we mean racking from new into *new* wood after 12 months or so). Among these are the wines of Dominique Laurent, some of the American *cuvées* imported by Bobby Kacher, and those which used to be made by Henri Jayer. Jayer was regarded by many as a god. I have had many a spectacular bottle from his range. But I have also had mature wines (the 1985 Cros Parentoux, for example) which were spoiled by too much oak. And the effect gets worse and worse as the wine gets exposed to air in the glass.

You can argue, as does my friend Mel Knox, who imports French barrels into California, that there is no such thing as over-oaked wine, just under-wined oak. And we mustn't forget that there are differences in the origins of the wood and their toasting, as well as in the quality of craftsmanship of the barrels. Nor should we forget the potentially deleterious effect of mouldy, bug-infested, far too *old* barrels. Nevertheless, in my view, Burgundy risks offering us today more wines which are over-oaked than under-oaked. As Robert Drouhin said to me once: "we are winemakers, not carpenters." Personally, I want to taste the fruit.

KEEPING THE WINE ON ITS LEES

The lees of a wine, the deposit which settles out at the bottom of the cask, consist of dead yeast cells, tartrate crystals, colouring matter and a number of other things. If these are "clean," they do nothing but good. The wine can gain richness and nutrients from them and increase in complexity and character. They also help protect the wine from oxidation. For this reason, rackings are never so drastic that a little turbid juice is not left in the cask, and the wines, both red and white, are kept as long as possible on their lees between rackings.

After the malo, the first racking tends to be aerobic, in order to allow most of the carbon dioxide to escape (but not all, for its presence also helps preserve the wine), and in order to admit a little oxygen in to aid the wine's development. Further rackings—and in Burgundy, there should usually only be the need for one more before preparation for bottling, as too many would risk the wine drying up and losing its fruit—will be anaerobic, without the presence of air. Many wines today are not racked at all until their preparation for bottling.

BÂTONNAGE

Bâtonnage is the periodic stirring up of the lees of a very young wine. This is a technique which is applied to white wines, but only rarely to reds. The object is to release into the liquid flavours presently locked up and to enable a more efficient extraction of the feeding matter in these lees. It is appropriate in the case of wines to be drunk young, which sadly is the case for even the most illustrious white Burgundies. It should not, in my view, be considered for *grands crus*. These should be allowed to release their flavours more gently and over a longer time-scale. I don't mind *bâtonnage* in ephemeral village Meursault, delicious after 2 years in bottle—but not in Le Montrachet!

CARE OF THE WINE IN CASK

Wine is at its most vulnerable during the period of its *élevage* in barrel. At the beginning, the carbon dioxide produced by the fermentations will protect it, as will, to a certain extent, the fine lees. But after a while, the CO_2 will have more or less escaped, and the amount of lees after the mid-summer/September racking will be much less.

It is vital, therefore, that the barrels are kept topped up, that the ambient temperature and humidity are correct, and that the wine is protected from bacterial contamination as well as oxygenation. So a judicious, light sulphiting is required. Wines in cask, especially when they approach the time when they need a racking, often exhibit reductive flavours—H_2S, and so on. These can be cleaned up by aeration. A wine which has just been racked may appear temporarily a bit oxidised. This again will go. But once serious oxidation or other off-flavours set in, there is little one can do except pour the wine down the drain.

The winemaker should therefore not continually attack the same cask when offering tasting samples. After being regularly exposed to aeration and then refurbished, it will not be representative of the lot as a whole. This was so *chez* Gouges, with all the casks *bande à côté* (bung to the side) except one, the tasting barrel. Once, when I found the sample puzzling, I asked to taste another cask. This involved a certain amount of heaving and rolling barrels about. But the result was a totally different wine. Today, all the barrels *chez* Gouges are *bande dessus* (bung upright) and, as elsewhere, I can chose which cask I want to sample.

What does one use for topping up? A bit of *vin de presse*? Some of the generic wine? Bottles left over after a tasting session? Obviously, it *should* be exactly the same wine. In the Burgundian situation, it is very unlikely that every single cask is topped up with the identical wine. But let's hope that today's serious growers realise that there is a problem here, and that they do not abuse it.

CLARIFICATION: FINING AND FILTRATION

Wines are fined and filtered not just to annoy Robert Parker, who has made somewhat of a fetish about the subject, but because there are or may be elements within them which have not settled out naturally, and which need to be removed to avoid their contaminating the wine after it has been bottled. Today, as I have already stated, the addition of certain enzymes at the time of fermentation aids the natural clarification process, so making fining and filtration less necessary. Moreover, a wine can be filtered using kieselguhr—a diatomaceous earth which has an electrostatic cleaning effect, like most fining agents—earlier in its career in cask.

Excessive fining and filtration, as well as the pumping of the wine which goes with it, is of course just as disastrous as excessive anything else. The process *can* strip a wine of all its beauty, if not carried out properly. And here the strictures of Robert Parker, Kermit Lynch and others have done the wine world a great service. But, I believe—and I have taken part in a number of tastings to test this theory out—both that "filtration properly carried out does not strip or attenuate a wine," to quote the late Professor Émile Peynaud, and also that after 5 or 10 years, you cannot tell the difference.

The answer is simple. If a detailed analysis indicates that there is no need to fine or filter, then don't. Subjecting the wine to as few manipulations as possible is, after all, the cardinal rule. But if one or other or both of these processes *are* necessary, then do it. No consumer 10 years on, with a contaminated bottle in his hand, is going to thank you for your policy of No Filtration.

WHEN TO BOTTLE

I strongly believe that the length of time the wine is allowed to rest in cask before bottling has a profound effect on its quality. Bottling a little too early may not be too bad a thing. Too late, however, is a significant error. Here, once again, the *éleveur* has to exercise discretion, imagination and flexibility. The humidity and ambient temperature of the cellar play as crucial a role as does the wine itself.

Most white wine, for example village Meursault, is bottled after a year, early in September, just before the vintage. This has the decided advantage of releasing the cask for the next year's wine. *Grands crus* may be held until November. More and more growers—Lafon, Coche-Dury, Pierre Morey, Leflaive, Roulot, Javillier—bottle later. They may have deep, cold, humid cellars, like Lafon, and/or have produced more concentrated wine in the first place. They may, like Leflaive, leave the wine in cask until September, but then give it 6 months more in stainless steel tanks. It is easy to point out that the best growers seem to bottle later. But that is putting the cart before the horse. Being the best growers, they produce the best, most concentrated wine, and this is the reason that their wine can keep 18 months in cask.

Quite a lot of red wine, for reasons more to do with cellar space than with personal conviction, apart from releasing the barrels, is also bottled after a little under a year. Here, I am unconvinced this is a good thing. Red wine—serious red wine, anyway—needs a year and a half or so to gain depth in cask. Few of the 12-month red wine growers rank up with the stars of the Burgundian firmament.

On the other hand, keeping wine, unless excessively tannic and concentrated (and even 1999 did not produce many of these) up to 2 years in wood is, in my view, a grave error. The resulting wine will be dry and astringent. Even Lalou Bize-Leroy, with her 13 hectolitres per hectare concentrated 1993s, did not leave them more than 15 months in cask. Indeed, an exception to my rule, she is now regularly bottling after 10 to 11 months. Most top red Burgundy is bottled between February and May on its second year: earlier if the vintage is a bit weak, and also earlier if a lot of new wood has been used in its *élevage*.

BOTTLING, PARTICULARLY HAND BOTTLING AND CONTRACT BOTTLING

On the principle that great wines should be handled with personal care, a number of larger concerns, as well as the tiny domaines which have always done it, have reverted to hand bottling by gravity rather than by machine. It is the gentlest way to approach what is probably the greatest shock the wine has yet to experience in its brief career. François Faiveley is one who practices hand bottling. It is an approach to be commended.

On the other hand, most of the small bottling lines you see in Burgundian cellars, if sensitively used, will not do the wine any long-term harm. The main thing to remember is that the bottling process *is* upsetting, and together with the subsequent transport all the way into the cellar of those who have bought *en primeur*, it will render a fragile wine like Burgundy unfit for judgement for maybe as much as a year.

An unquantifiable statistic (I forgot to include the question in my grower's questionnaire) is the number of domaines that use contract bottlers. Contract bottling *can* be perfectly good. But the danger is both that, in order to protect himself, the bottler will do a belt and braces job (i.e., he will fine and filter to excess) and that the speed with which the wine is bottled will further strip out its flavours.

NOTES FOR THE CONSUMER

Has the Style of Burgundy Evolved Over the Years?

Burgundy of the 1940s and 1950s was a sturdier animal than it is today. There are a number of reasons for this. Firstly, the average age of the vineyards was high, as the plants were essentially still the first generation of grafted vines planted after *phylloxera*. Secondly, the yield was lower. And thirdly, lest we forget, the 1945–1959 period offered a regular series of very good vintages.

How genuine the wines were (i.e., whether—and I am talking about the serious *négociants* and the few domaine bottlers of the period—what was in the bottle was 100 percent Pinot Noir) is difficult now to tell. Old wines exhibit all sorts of spice and other elements in their flavour, some to such an extent that it becomes very difficult to guess their variety and, therefore, their origin. Judging by the wines which have come my way over the last 6 years, during which I have made a particular point of buying up all the small lots of old wine I could afford, I would say that the vast majority *of these* were totally pure and unadulterated. (But this, it should be noted, is the *crème de la crème*. I am not talking about second-division merchants' Burgundy.)

In the 1960s and 1970s, as a result of increased but unregulated production thanks to the new clones and new fertilisers, the wines in general became lighter and weaker (though we should not forget 1964 and 1966, and even 1962 and 1969, as very good vintages). Burgundy became wishy-washy and expensive. At the top domaine level, however, this deterioration was less apparent.

Which brings us to the 1980s and 1990s, and the emergence as sellers in bottle rather than in cask, of perhaps 80 percent of the domaines discussed in the subsequent pages in this book. Here we can definitely talk about an evolution, and an ongoing one. Wines have clearly improved in quality. The tannins are more sophisticated, the wines have a better acidity, the fruit flavours are purer and there is more site specificity. Moreover, and just as important, the quality in the lesser years has improved in tandem. So far, there has been more progress in red wine than in white. But the lover of red Burgundy is now in the happy position of having a large number of quality estates to choose from.

How Does Burgundy Age?

The abiding principle here is that, provided the balance is correct, any wine will last much better than you think. The most important factor is the acidity in the wine. Acidity preserves the freshness and the fruit, and hence the balance and the elegance. Good levels of tannin and alcohol are equally valuable preservatives. Too many wines today, sadly—and the yield has a lot to do with this—lack the grip, this combination of youthful vigour and acidity, which will ensure that they can last. On the other hand, I have had many a wine—usually, it has to be said, red rather than white—which has been quite delicious, despite its having been way beyond even the most ambitious originally suggested drink-by date.

When to Drink Your Wine

YEARS AFTER THE VINTAGE

Red Wines

Village Côte Chalonnaise	2 to 8
Côte-de-Beaune/Nuits Villages	2 to 8
Mainstream Village Côte de Beaune	4 to 10
Mainstream Village Côte de Nuits	6 to 12
Premier Cru Côte de Beaune	7 to 12
Premier Cru Côte de Nuits	8 to 14
Lighter *Grand Cru*	8 to 15
Grand Cru	10 to 25

White Wines

Lighter Village Wines	2 to 5
Better Village Wines	4 to 8
Premier Cru	6 to 8
Grand Cru	8 to 15+

When to Drink Your Wine

As a general rule, assuming a better-than-usual vintage of normal proportions, a well balanced wine will be at its peak as described in the table above. You must make allowances, obviously, for different types of vintages. A lighter red wine year such as 2000 or 2004 will obviously come on stream earlier than 2002 or 2005. The converse is true for very rich, tannic vintages.

Naturally, the wine will change, becoming mellow but less fresh, during its period of optimum drinking. Here your own personal taste comes into it. Make regular notes. You will soon figure out where your own optimum is.

Above all, please, I implore you, do not commit infanticide. One of the *raisons d'être* of magazines like *The Vine* is to review vintages periodically, on their way to maturity, so that you, the reader, do not have to waste your precious bottles.

The Unhappy Evolution of Recent White Wine Vintages

In 2004 rumours began to circulate. Many of the top 1996 white Burgundies seemed to have suddenly oxidised. A couple of professional friends of mine telephoned me to ask if I had encountered any bad bottles. I hadn't, but I opened a few from my cellar: no problems. I was lucky.

At first it seemed to be only the 1996 vintage which was causing concern. As time went on, it became increasingly obvious that there was a problem, and it was widespread. A professional colleague had to withdraw both a stock of quality 1996 Chablis and another bin of top Corton-Charlemagne. I later found I had difficulties with some first-division Puligny-Montrachet, Les Combettes. Others reported similar disappointments.

As the months progressed, a number of factors became apparent.

- It was not just the 1996 vintage, but others: 1997, 1998 and even 1999 were oxidising.

- It was not a grower problem, nor even a wine problem. There were good and bad bottles even within the same case of wine.

- It also did not seem to be a question of bad storage or of transportation at excessively high temperatures. There were as many bad bottles in the cellars of the growers in Burgundy as elsewhere.

The Mystery of Bad White Burgundy has now been much discussed, within the profession as well as outside it, on, for instance, Mark Squires Wine Forum on the US Internet. A large number of absurd and mistaken explanations have been put forward. Let us eliminate the most stupid of these:

"The dominating acidity of the 1996 white Burgundies is the cause of their premature oxidation." This is idiotic, as any oenologue will tell you.

"The wines were under-sulphured." It is suggested that because of the high acidities, the 1996s were considered to need less sulphur protection than other vintages. I have not found a single grower who will admit to having sulphured his/her 1996s less than usual.

"White Burgundy is lees-stirred (*bâtonnage*) excessively these days." An arguable point. But there is no obvious connection between this and premature oxidation.

"With the widespread move to pneumatic presses, wines are more fragile today." They are certainly cleaner, as are the lees, which means there can be longer lees contact in cask without the onset of mercaptan. All in all this would give more, not less, concentrated wines.

"The size of the crops today produces weaker wines which age faster." An arguable point. But why then do the wines of the first-division producers, who do not over-crop, vary as much as the rest? And while 1996 and 1999 were plentiful years, 1997 and 1998 were not.

A number of other possibilities can also be eliminated by a bit of diligent research: the date of the bottling (many Burgundians are now bottling at 18 months rather than 12); the use of much or little new oak; the fact that a few producers regularly block the malos to ensure high levels of freshness; the use of enzymes; etc., etc. There is no pattern. All these are blind alleys.

Having exhausted all the possible viticultural and vinicultural explanations, we are left with one final cause. Yes, the problem lies with the corks. Some have suggested that it has been the move from chlorine-treated corks to peroxide-treated corks—peroxide being oxidative—that is the reason. I suggest it is more fundamental than that. The quality of corks has declined over the last generation or two (why do we have three or four times more bottles that are corky than we used to have?) The trees are stripped more often. There is less assiduous selection of the bark. And the result, quite simply, is that there is too much oxygen permeation through much of today's cork material. This leads to a collapse of the free and total sulphur levels in the wine and, therefore, to their premature oxidation. This is a scandalous situation, and we have no guarantee that it will not be repeated in subsequent vintages. So far, the delicious 2002s seem to be unaffected. I am keeping my fingers crossed.

One of the very few growers/merchants whose wines no one cited as problematic during the period I have been investigating this subject is Raveneau in Chablis. Is it a mere coincidence that Raveneau waxes the top of his bottles?

How to Judge Young Wine

Judging young wine requires time and concentration, a lack of interruption and, ideally, a certain amount of physical comfort, such that one can be as relaxed as possible. Moreover, one should be hungry and not tired, and the taste buds should not already be saturated by dozens of other samples. Manifestly, there is a finite limit to the amount of wine which can be assessed in one session or one day, and while the professional, because he or she does it regularly, can absorb more before the perception decreases, even he or she, in my experience, should enforce self-limits. Arrogantly, we always think we can attempt more than we in fact can.

Plenty of time is essential, as one cannot do the job properly if rushed. It is on and by the finish that a young wine is properly judged. The nose is a good clue, but it can be funky. The palate may be overloaded with tannin. On the finish and the aftertaste, however, one can assess if all the elements—fruit, tannin, acidity, oak, fat, elegance and complexity—are there, and whether they are in balance. The length is a vital clue.

Do not forget, also, that if you are in a Burgundian cellar, you will have someone with you—your host—who not only knows a great deal more about it than you do, but who will probably be only too happy to explain; in Burgundy, this will be the person responsible for making the wine. Use the opportunity: Ask questions. Say what you think and, if corrected, re-taste. Compare and contrast. In short, listen and learn.

How to Judge a Grower

Imagine the following scenario: You are in, say, Gevrey-Chambertin, and the vintage is good, and you have enjoyed what you have been given to taste. Do you trust your judgement? Do you get out your credit card and start filling up your boot? Putting aside the fact that you can always refer to a book such as this for a second opinion, one final tip is to ask to taste a lesser wine of a lesser vintage. Anyone can or should produce fine wine from fine land in a fine vintage (otherwise he should change his *métier*: go and sell sausages, as one grower put it to me once). But only the good growers produce good wine from lesser *climats* in lesser vintages. So if you want to be sure, you can rely on M. Machin's Lavaux-Saint-Jacques 2005, ask to see his Marsannay 2000 as well.

How to Buy Good Burgundy

It is important to be fully informed, which is why I have written this book. And here I refer readers to Appendices One, Two and Three: Rating the Vintages, Rating the Vineyards, and Rating the Growers. You may assume that each of these is of equal importance. Not so. The name of the grower on the label is paramount. The *climat* is of marginally less precedence, and the vintage very much the least.

Burgundy is not a tannic wine, so the poorer vintages will not be dominated by rather unripe tannins, as they are in Bordeaux. Even if the wine may be rather lean at the outset, provided the fruit was not rotten, it will eventually mellow and, indeed if from a top grower and a good site, become remarkably pleasant.

For a number of years, until my stock ran out, I used to amuse myself by serving a perfectly respectable village Gevrey-Chambertin, 1985 vintage, alongside a Clos-Saint-Jacques 1984 from Charles Rousseau. They had cost me the same amount of money. Which did my guests prefer? Inevitably, the 1984: not a rich, concentrated wine, but a wine of individuality, complexity and elegance.

Should You Buy Burgundy En Primeur?

Buying futures, taking advantage of your retailer's opening offer is, as far as Burgundy is concerned, sometimes the only way to get hold of the top wines. In Bordeaux, normally, and with the exception of a handful of *recherché* Pomerols, the wines can be bought several years down the road at the equivalent price in real terms. In Burgundy, the majority—certainly the *crème de la crème*—disappear out of sight the moment they are offered and are rarely seen again. Thus, buying futures is the only way to get them.

However, unlike Bordeaux, the "campaign" is extended all the way through the second year and into the third. Some growers and *négociants* fix a price, based on their costs, in the spring or summer following the vintage. Others wait until the next year's wine is in the cellar, so that they can take its quality and quantity into account. Yet more do not commercialise the wine until it is in bottle the following summer. This complicates life for the *en primeur* buyer. How can he or she compare prices? It is a nuisance which just has to be endured.

Getting Hold of It

This is the difficult bit. You have earmarked what you want. Then you find you can't get hold of it.

In order to avoid future frustration, I think every wine consumer—every Burgundy-lover certainly—however rich, must accept a certain vinous statute of limitation: not one of time, but one of availability. Great Burgundy is made in tiny quantities. There is never enough to go round. Each grower can only deal with a limited number of retailers. Those retailers are obviously going to favour their best customers—people like them who are prepared to take the rough with the smooth, the lesser *cuvées* and vintages, as well as the fine and grand.

Naturally, you as buyer want to cherry pick. But don't be surprised if sometimes you can't.

Getting the Most Out of Your Bottles

The correct storage and the eventual service of the wine at the right temperature and in the right environment is as vital as the choice of the best wine in the first place. The role of the owner does not stop at the moment he writes out his cheque.

Bottles should be stored on their side, away from light, heat and movement. They should be allowed to rest undisturbed at an ideal temperature of 11°C (52°F). Temperatures up to 14°C (59°F) can be tolerated, provided there are no sudden jumps. The wine will only mature sooner. The temperature can also fall to 8°C (45°F) without any harm being caused to the wine. Moreover, the atmosphere must be humid, a minimum of 70 percent. This is good for wine, but bad for labels. If your home environment cannot provide all this, then it is a waste of money not to go to the expense of leasing suitable space outside. Why pay £500 a dozen and then skimp on an extra £10 or so a year for proper storage?

Most red wines are served too warm; most white wines, too cold. White Burgundy is a rich wine, and to serve it straight from the depth of the refrigerator is only to stun its flavours. Ten to 11°C (50–52°F) is optimum.

At least the too-cold glass of Montrachet can be left to gently warm up. If the Musigny is too warm, it is irreparably ruined. When we used to talk about room temperature, we were referring to the times before universal central heating. What was meant was 16°C (63°F) not 20°C plus (70°F plus). If a red wine is served at too high a temperature, its freshness and fragrance are lost. If stored at this level, as sadly happens in restaurants, it very quickly becomes stewed.

Decant both red and white Burgundy if you wish, but at the last minute. Most Burgundians object, preferring the wine to evolve totally in the glass. I find decanting improves the wine. It also makes the service of it easier.

What Are You Looking For?
In a Word: Elegance

Elegance or finesse in a wine is like beauty or sex-appeal in human beings: you've either got it or you haven't. A lot of people think of elegance as merely the soft furnishing of a wine—the wallpaper of a room or the design of the curtains. No, it is much more fundamental than that. It is the very shape of the wine, the very

essence. If it is not potentially there in the fruit in the first place, there is very little the wine-maker can do to compensate. And the wine will be all the bereft for it. But, I submit, you are more likely to find this characteristic in Burgundy than in any other wine.

The Art of Good Living

The art of good living, in the gastronomic sense, is the service of good mature wine alongside the appropriate food in the company of good friends. If you have a really great wine to offer, precede it with something similar but lower down the scale. It will set it off better. It will taste even grander.

And then, forget about pecking orders and 90- or 19-point scores. Forget also about what it is worth or what it would cost you to replace it. Just enjoy it!

SPELLING IDIOSYNCRASIES

Burgundy is notoriously haphazard about spelling. Vineyard names can be singular or plural (Griotte or Griottes), can be hyphenated or not (Beaux-Monts or Beaumonts), can incorporate the definite article or not and can even use prepositions such as *aux* or *en* rather than *le* or *les*. Moreover, no one is quite sure whether and when to hyphenate. It is Nuits-Saint-Georges, but should it be Clos de la Roche or Clos-de-la-Roche?

By and large, I have tried to follow what the growers themselves put on their labels, except where I know them to be in error (e.g., Clos Vougeot instead of Clos de Vougeot). You will notice, therefore, a number of alternative spellings in the pages that follow. But this is one of the charms of Burgundy.

A NOTE ON THE STAR RATING SYSTEM

In Part Three of this book, the reader will find a multitude of tasting notes on individual wines. It is also necessary to rate the domaines as a whole, and that I have done in Part One.

I have chosen a system which is analogous to that used in the Michelin guide. Anyone who has used *Michelin* will be familiar with this, and with its rigorous—even mean—approach. In vinous terms, this can be translated as follows:

★★★ THE BEST

A domaine which will not only have significant holdings in *grand cru* vineyards, but which will consistently make very high-quality wines from them. Naturally they will ask high prices. These domaines are rare.

★★ A FINE DOMAINE

Again, it will have fine vineyard holdings. High results can be expected and will be priced accordingly.

★ A VERY GOOD DOMAINE

The customer can safely buy wines with confidence here.

PART ONE

The Villages, the Vineyards, the Domaines

Chablis

Domaine du Vieux Chateau

Domaine Benoît Droin

Domaine Joseph Drouhin

Domaine Gérard Duplessis

Domaine Jean Durup Père et Fils

Chateau de Maligny

Domaine de l'Églantière

Domaine William Fèvre

Domaine Garnier et Fils

Domaine Raoul Gautherin et Fils

Domaine Alain Gautheron

Domaine Corinne and Jean-Pierre Grossot

Domaine Perchaud

Domaine Thierry Hamelin

Jean and Romuald Hugot

Domaine de Pisse-Loup

Maison Jadot

Domaine Chantal and Claude Laroche

Domaine/Maison Michel Laroche

Maison Olivier Leflaive Frères

Bernard Legland

Domaine des Marronniers

Domaine Long-Depaquit

Lyne and Jean-Bernard Marchive

Domaine des Malandes

Domaine Louis Michel et Fils

Domaine Alice and Olivier De Moor

Domaine Christian Moreau Père et Fils

Domaine Louis Moreau

Domaine de Biéville

Domaine du Cèdre Doré

Domaine Moreau-Naudet

Domaine Sylvain Mosnier

Thierry Mothe

Domaine du Colombier

Domaine Christianne and Jean-Claude Oudin

Domaine Gilbert Picq et Fils

Frédéric Prain

Domaine d'Élise

Domaine Pinson Frères

Domaine Denis Race

Domaine Raveneau

Maison Regnard

Domaine Guy Robin

Domaine Francine and Olivier Savary

Domaine Roger Séguinot-Bordet

Domaine Servin

Domaine/Maison Simmonet-Fèbvre

Domaine Philippe Testut

Gérard Tremblay

Domaine des Iles

Domaine Laurent Tribut

Domaine Tribut-Dauvissat

Maison/Domaine Olivier Tricon

Domaine de Vauroux

Maison Verget

Claude Vilain

Domaine de la Chaude Écuelle

Domaine du Chateau de Viviers

Domaine Yvon Vocoret

Domaine Vocoret et Fils

EQUIDISTANT BETWEEN Champagne, Sancerre at the eastern end of the Loire Valley and the Côte d'Or, the isolated region of Chablis lies on the banks of the small river Serein in the Yonne *département*. A dozen kilometres away, the Paris-Lyon *autoroute* cuts a great concrete swathe through the fields of wheat, maize and pasture. Across the *autoroute* you come to the busy city of Auxerre, dominated by its cathedral of Saint-Étienne.

But Chablis lies in a backwater, on the road to nowhere of any importance. The town of the same name is sleepy and rural—hardly more, indeed, than a large village. There are no buildings of any note and nothing, really, to distinguish it from a hundred other small towns in arable France—nothing except for what is produced from a single noble grape which has found here an ideal soil in which to thrive. This grape is the Chardonnay. The soil is a peculiar and highly individual mixture of chalky limestone and clay, and the resulting wine is one of the world's best-known dry white wines, but one quite different from other Chardonnays produced 150 kilometres further south in the Côte de Beaune.

A century or more ago, before the arrival of *phylloxera*, the Burgundian vineyard began at Sens and continued, uninterrupted, through the Auxerrois and down to Montbard and Dijon. There were then in the Yonne as many as 40,000 hectares under vine. Much of the resulting wine, no doubt, was thin and very ordinary, destined to be consumed directly from the cask in the *comptoirs* of Paris and the other conurbations of northern France. Chablis and the other local vineyards benefited greatly from this close proximity to the capital; however, with the arrival of the *phylloxera* louse—rather later than in the Côte d'Or, for it did not seriously begin to affect the Chablis vines until 1893—coupled with increasing competition from the Midi once the railway system connecting Paris with the south had been completed, most of the Yonne vineyards disappeared. This decline was further accentuated by World War I and the resulting economic stagnation and rural depopulation. By 1945, when a particularly savage frost totally destroyed the potential harvest—not a single bottle of Chablis was produced in this vintage—the total area under vine was down to less than 500 hectares. As late as the severe winter of 1956, the locals were skiing in February down what is now the *grand cru* of Les Clos.

Since then, however, there has been a gradual but accelerating increase in the total area of vineyards to 4,755 hectares in 2005. As more efficient methods of combating the ever-present threat of frost damage have been devised, as greater control of other potential depredations of the yield has been introduced and as more prolific strains of Chardonnay have been planted, production has risen disproportionately from an average of around 24,000 hectolitres per annum in the 1960s to more than ten times as much in the early 2000s.

The local *Bureau Interprofessionnel* announced in 2003 that the *surfaces délimitées* (i.e., authorised for production) are as much as 6,830 hectares. In case you might think that the extra, over what is planted today, is in marginal land, I can only tell you that their potential *grand cru* and *premier cru* figures are only 2 hectares higher than the 2001 levels. So you may well be right. Will these theoretical 2,500 extra hectares *really* produce good Chablis, or will they produce just a palatable non-oaky Chardonnay, hardly indistinguishable from a Mâcon?

SOIL

The heartland of the Chablis region is the southwest-facing slope north of the town. Here all the *grands crus* are situated in a continuous line, adjacent to some of the best of the *premier*

Chablis

	SURFACE AREA (ha)	PRODUCTION (hl)	MAXIMUM YIELD (hl/ha)	MINIMUM ALCOHOLIC DEGREE
Grand Cru	104	5,032	45	11.0°
Premier Cru	775	44,094	50	10.5°
Chablis	3,163	186,377	50	10.0°
Petit Chablis	713	41,883	50	9.5°
Total AC Chablis	4,755	277,386		

cru vineyards. These famous vineyards lie on a soil of crumbly limestone, grey or even white in colour, which is named after Kimmeridge, a small village in Dorset. Elsewhere, particularly at Beines to the east and in the communes of Maligny, Villy and Lignorettes to the north, the soil has a different appearance, being more sandy in colour and marginally different— Portlandian limestone as opposed to Kimmeridgian. There has been much argument over whether the wines from Portlandian soils are as good as those from Kimmeridgian. At times there has been heated opposition, even lawsuits, between those who favour a strict delimitation of Chablis and those who favour expanding the vineyards. The first camp stresses the overriding importance of Kimmeridgian soil; the second believes that an extension of the Chablis vineyards over further suitable slopes of Portlandian soil will relieve pressure on the existing vineyard and better enable the whole community to exploit and benefit from the worldwide renown of its wine. Each grower has his own opinion and will probably be a member of one or the other of the two rival *syndicats*, or producer groups. Le Syndicat de la Défense de l'Appellation Chablis, as its name implies, is in favour of the strict delimitation of Chablis and was led, until his recent retirement, by William Fèvre of Domaine de la Maladière. The second group, La Fédération des Viticulteurs Chablisiens, is led by Jean Durup of Domaine de l'Églantière in Maligny.

Following a decision by the INAO in 1978, which effectively diminished the importance of the soil in favour of microclimate and aspect when considering a further revision of the area, the expansionists have been ascendant. Since then, the total vineyard area has tripled. New *premiers crus* have appeared on the scene. No one who has tasted the new *premier cru* Vau de Vey alongside other *premiers crus,* such as Vaillons or Montmains from the same grower, can be in any doubt that it can be at least as good. Whether this extension of vineyard area will help avoid some of the extreme fluctuations in the price of Chablis which have occurred in the past remains to be seen. Greater stability, in

my view, is crucial to the continuing commercial success of the wine.

So, too, is a higher and more consistent level of quality. The run of recent vintages has been kind, but half the *vignoble*, especially in plain Chablis *tout court,* is young vines, and production figures tend to be much higher than in the Côte de Beaune (nearly 59 hl/ha in 2005), inevitably necessitating chaptalisation up to the limit, even in the very best of vintages.

THE DANGER OF FROST

The Chablis vineyards lie very close to the northernmost limit for rearing the vine successfully. The vine will not start to develop in the early spring until the average temperature reaches 10°C, and the fruit must ripen before the leaves begin to fall in the autumn. The incidence of frost, therefore, is an important concern. Chablis, particularly the lower slopes adjacent to the river Serein, lies in a frost pocket. The *grand cru* vineyards are the most susceptible, but even on the higher plateaux used for the generic wine or plain Chablis, the young shoots are vulnerable from the time they break out of the buds in late March through the middle of May. The exposure and angle of the slope is critical, and there are a number of techniques the grower can use in order to protect his or her vines from being harmed.

The most primitive method, but one now frowned upon by the ecologists, is simply to install a little fuel burner or a paraffin *chaufferette* in the vineyard. The grower must be in the vineyard, usually by three o'clock in the morning (the coldest part of the night is normally just before sunrise), to light his or her burners, and these must then be refilled in readiness for the following night. More recently, automatic fuel-heating systems, connected to a nearby tank, and infrared devices have been installed in some vineyards. These are expensive, both in fuel and in labour, but they are effective.

Another technique is the aspersion method. First, a system of water sprinklers must be set up in the vineyard and connected to a supply of water. (There is a large reservoir outside

Beines which serves over 80 hectares of vines, chiefly in the *premier cru* Fourchaume.) When the temperature descends to zero, the system is switched on, spraying the vines with a continuous fine stream of water, just as you might do if you were sprinkling your garden. Water freezes at 0°C, but the vine buds will not suffer until the temperature sinks below minus 5°C, by which time the bud is protected by a snug coating of ice. This aspersion method, however, is costly to set up and difficult to maintain. You will find it only in the *grands* and *premiers crus*.

There are some Chablis producers who argue that regularly imprisoning the embryonic leaf cluster in ice for 5 or 6 hours a day, perhaps for a month or more, will do it no good. Nevertheless, and despite the difficulties of keeping the nozzles unblocked, this is a technique which has spread rapidly since it was first introduced in the late 1970s. Installation costs are high and maintenance is crucial, but operating expenses are minimal.

EDF (the French nationalised electricity company) has been running trials with William Fèvre and Long-Depaquit with a new anti-frost concept. The idea is to run an electric wire along the rows at the level of the embryonic bunch. When the electricity is turned on, a cocoon of heat measuring roughly 10 centimetres in diameter is created which will protect the embryonic harvest. Although costly to install, it is, so *EDF* argues, both cheap to run and easy to maintain. Ecologists, however, are worried. The presence of electricity nearby causes mutated and abnormal growth, they argue. Might this be, even infinitesimally, a cancer risk?

Irrespective of the point above, there is another problem with this solution to the frost problem. Frost occurs when the barometer is high and the sky is clear. This frequently coincides with the full moon. Not only can frost be a threat in early April, but it can still occur 4 weeks later. By this time the shoots can be much larger, 10 centimetres in extent, and the fruiting buds will be outside the cylinder of protection.

An alternative method, started in 1995, necessitates covering the vines with plastic sheeting, with holes at intervals for the sun's rays to enter and to prevent undue humidity. This effectively creates an artificial greenhouse effect. It is costly but effective. Strangely, it seems to be allowed here. Using plastic sheeting on the ground of the vineyards elsewhere (avoiding the effects of excessive rain in September) has been declared illegal by the INAO as it is "contrary to nature" and destroys the "uniqueness of the local *terroir.*"

THE *GRANDS CRUS*

There are currently almost 4,800 hectares of vineyard in production in the Chablis area. Just over a hundred of these are the *grand cru* vineyards, a continuous slope of undulating vines facing southwest and directly overlooking the town itself.

If you look up at the slope from the town, these *grands crus* are, from left to right, Bougros; Preuses; Vaudésir, incorporating La Moutonne of Domaine Long-Depaquit; Grenouilles; Valmur; Les Clos; and Blanchots. It is generally agreed that Les Clos is the best *grand cru*, producing the most powerful and long-lasting wines, the ones with the most intensity and richest flavour. Valmur and Vaudésir are also highly regarded (Valmur, in particular, also needs time to age). Preuses and Grenouilles produce more floral and delicate wines. Bougros and Blanchots are the least fine.

Opinions on these *grands crus* vary, and quite naturally, it is difficult to find a grower who can

⇒ Chablis *Grands Crus* ⇐	
	SURFACE AREA (ha) 2005
Blanchots	12.88
Bougros	15.47
Les Clos	27.61
Grenouilles	9.38
Preuses	10.70
Valmur	11.04
Vaudésir	16.83
Total	103.91
Production (2005)	5,032 hl
Maximum Yield	45 hl/ha
Grape Variety	Chardonnay

be totally objective. Michel Remon, erstwhile owner of the *négociant* Regnard, who could afford to be more dispassionate than most at this firm, and who did not at any time own any vineyards at all, held the following views: he described wine from Blanchots as the most rustic, and he condemned Grenouilles for its lack of class; in his opinion, it was only a *grand cru* because it lay alongside the rest. In his view Les Clos was racy and the most *nerveux*; Vaudésir was the roundest and richest, but occasionally a bit heavy; Preuses was similar, but with less style; and Bougros produced wine somewhat like it on its upper slopes, but it was more like Grenouilles on the lower land. Monsieur Remon gave first prize to Valmur—a feminine wine, the most elegant and full of depth.

The now-retired but until recently important grower William Fèvre sees three different categories. Leading his list is Les Clos, which he describes as intense and long on the palate, with a toasted, gamey flavour. Bougros is *tendre* and *douceâtre* (soft and sweetish) with elements of chocolate. The wine is less steely and more obviously fruity than Preuses. Grenouilles and Vaudésir come somewhere between the two in style—less powerful than Les Clos, with more delicate and floral perfumes and a touch of violets. Christian Moreau simply says that Les Clos, Valmur and Vaudésir are the three finest *climats*, and the remainder do not merit *grand cru* prices. Les Clos, he adds, is a combination of the finesse of Vaudésir and the structure of Valmur. Jean-Pierre Simonnet, an important *négociant-éleveur*, finds the quality-price ratio for all the *grands crus* to have ceased to be useful. These wines are difficult to buy, finance or sell, he will tell you. He concentrates now on *premiers crus*.

BLANCHOTS

SURFACE AREA: 12.88 ha
SIGNIFICANT OWNERS: Laroche (4.50 ha), Vocoret (1.77 ha), Long-Depaquit (1.65 ha), La Chablisienne (1 ha), Servin (0.91 ha), Vauroux (0.69 ha), Raveneau (0.60 ha), Viviers (0.50 ha), P. Bouchard (0.25), D. Defaix (0.20 ha), Robin (0.20 ha), Billaud-Simon (0.18 ha), Droin (0.16 ha), C. Moreau (0.10 ha), J. Moreau (0.10 ha).

Blanchot, or Blanchots, is the most southeasterly *grand cru* and rises up above the road to Fyé, sandwiched between Montée de Tonnerre and Les Clos. The aspect is southeast, and the soil drains well. A typical Blanchots is a delicate wine, highly floral, maturing earlier than, say, a Les Clos or Valmur. Not having the backbone of these neighbours, Blanchots is more susceptible, I would suggest, to overproduction.

BOUGROS

SURFACE AREA: 15.47 ha
SIGNIFICANT OWNERS: Fèvre (6.20 ha), Colombier (1.20 ha), Long-Depaquit (0.52 ha), Robin (0.50 ha), Servin (0.46 ha), Drouhin (0.33 ha), Laroche (0.31 ha), La Chablisienne (0.25 ha).

There are two distinct wines produced in this, the most northwesterly of the *grands crus*. Most Bougros is fullish bodied, four-square, bordering on rustic. It lacks the minerally thrust of a typical *grand cru*. Within the *climat*, however, facing southwest rather than due south, is a very steep section which gives an altogether better wine, combining the power of Bougros with no lack of finesse. William Fèvre, whose estate was bought by Champagne Henriot in 1997, owns a large parcel in this part of Bougros which is labelled as Clos des Bouguerots.

LES CLOS

SURFACE AREA: 27.61 ha
SIGNIFICANT OWNERS: Fèvre (4.15 ha), J. Moreau (3.61 ha), C. Moreau (3.60 ha), Pinson (2.50 ha), V. Dauvissat (1.70 ha), Vocoret (1.62 ha), Long-Depaquit (1.54 ha), Laroche (1.12 ha), Drouhin (1.03 ha), Droin (0.99 ha), P. Bouchard (0.70 ha), Servin (0.63 ha), Raveneau (0.54 ha), Malandes (0.53 ha), La Chablisienne (0.50 ha), L. Michel (0.50 ha), Billaud-Simon (0.44 ha), Duplessis (0.36 ha), Robin (0.20 ha), Gautherin (0.18 ha).

Les Clos is the largest of the *grands crus* and lies between Blanchots and Valmur, facing south.

The soil is rocky and very well drained. Here we have Chablis at its very, very best: firm, austere, racy, mineral, full and long lasting, combining depth, intensity and great elegance. A bottle of Les Clos requires time, but it is worth it. The famous Clos des Hospices, a 0.8-hectare shared monopoly between Christian Moreau and his nephew Louis (see page 61) lies toward the bottom of the hill.

LES GRENOUILLES

SURFACE AREA: 9.38 ha
SIGNIFICANT OWNERS: La Chablisienne (7.50 ha), Testut (0.55 ha), L. Michel (0.54 ha), Regnard (0.50 ha), Droin (0.48 ha), R. Gautherin (0.22 ha).

Les Grenouilles forms a triangle at the bottom of the slope, bordered by Valmur to the east and Vaudésir to the north and west. It is the smallest of the *grands crus*. Much of Les Grenouilles is controlled by the cooperative, and most of this is labelled as Château de Grenouilles. This is one of La Chablisienne's flagship wines, vinified using new oak; it is an exotic and nutty wine, with size and even muscle. Louis Michel's example is also rich and full bodied, more ample but less mineral than his Vaudésir. In principle I prefer both Vaudésir and Valmur and place Grenouilles in the second division. *Chez* Droin, comparing the same wines, the Grenouilles is more powerful, but perhaps less elegant.

LES PREUSES

SURFACE AREA: 10.7 ha
SIGNIFICANT OWNERS: La Chablisienne (4 ha), Fèvre (2.55 ha), V. Dauvissat (1 ha), J. Dauvissat (0.74 ha), Servin (0.69 ha), Billaud-Simon (0.40 ha), Simmonet-Fèbvre (0.29 ha), Long-Depaquit (0.25 ha), Drouhin (0.23 ha).

Les Preuses I rate in fourth place, above Les Grenouilles and Blanchots, but lower than Vaudésir and Valmur, and, of course, Les Clos. The *climat* lies on the northwestern edge of the flank of *grands crus*, between Bougros and Vaudésir. This is an undulating vineyard, facing mainly due south and producing a Chablis which is typically ripe and succulent, balanced and elegant, but without the steeliness of Valmur and Les Clos.

VALMUR

SURFACE AREA: 11.04 ha
SIGNIFICANT OWNERS: Robin (2.60 ha), Bessin (2.08 ha), Fèvre (1.10 ha), Droin (1.02 ha), C. Moreau (1 ha), J. Moreau (0.99 ha), Raveneau (0.75 ha), Moreau-Naudin (0.60 ha), Collet (0.51 ha), Vocoret (0.25 ha), La Chablisienne (0.25 ha).

Valmur lies northwest of Les Clos, above Les Grenouilles. Only a small part reaches down to the main road. The aspect is southwest. Valmur is a firm, full-bodied wine; properly steely, it should be backward and austere in its youth, rivalling Les Clos in the time it needs to mature. A top Les Clos is classier and more complete, but Valmur ranks with Vaudésir as an equal in the second spot in my personal hierarchy.

VAUDÉSIR

SURFACE AREA: 16.83 ha
SIGNIFICANT OWNERS: Long-Depaquit (2.60 ha), Besson (1.43 ha), Drouhin (1.41 ha), Fèvre (1.20 ha), L. Michel (1.17 ha), Droin (1.03 ha), Malandes (0.90 ha), Gautherin (0.89 ha), Billaud-Simon (0.71 ha), P. Bouchard (0.60 ha), Tremblay (0.60 ha), La Chablisienne (0.50 ha), C. Moreau (0.50 ha), J. Moreau (0.45 ha), Robin (0.25 ha), Vocoret (0.11 ha), plus La Moutonne, Long-Depaquit (*monopole*) (2.35 ha).

Lying between Les Grenouilles and Les Preuses, and primarily high up on the slope in the form of a well-protected, south-facing amphitheatrical bowl, Vaudésir has long been regarded as one of the best of the *grands crus*. Many consider it as *the* best. The reason, as always, lies in the quality, individuality and finesse of the fruit. A good Vaudésir shows very subtle floral tones, a little more high-toned than Valmur and Les Clos, slightly more feminine, perhaps, but not a bit lacking the essential Chablis minerality. La Moutonne, a monopoly of Domaine Long-Depaquit (see page 60) lies in the Vaudésir *climat*.

THE *PREMIERS CRUS*

There are 775 hectares of *premier cru* vineyards today—70 percent more than in 1978. In 1967, to facilitate their commercialisation, what was then a total of twenty-six original *lieux-dits* (site names) was reduced to eleven *premiers crus*. The grower now had a choice: he or she could either use the main *premier cru* name on the label—and blend the wine from several subsidiary vineyards under this title—or continue to use the old *lieu-dit*.

In 1986 this list of *premiers crus* was extended to include seven other sites, some of which incorporated several *lieux-dits*. Today, there are forty *lieux-dits*, but generally only seventeen names in common usage.

Of these, the longest established—and still considered the best—are Fourchaume, Montée de Tonnerre and Mont de Milieu. It is no coincidence that these three *premiers crus* all lie on the right bank of the Serein, on either side of the *grands crus*, facing southwest just as the *grands crus* do. The largest and most important of the rest, Beauroy, Vau de Vey, Côte de Léchet, Vaillons and Montmains, are all in side-valleys on the left bank and face southeast. The wines from Vaillons and Côte de Léchet are better than the rest. These wines are shorter in flavour, less powerful and more floral than those from the right bank of the Serein. When made from ripe grapes, they have a peachy, Granny-Smith appley flavour, while Fourchaume wines are rich and plump, and Montée de Tonnerre and Mont de Milieu wines are firm, nutty and steely,

and are the closest in style to Les Clos, the best *grand cru*.

As I have observed elsewhere, spellings are personal and idiosyncratic in Burgundy. Thus Vaillon, Montmain and the village of Beines, for instance, can be singular or plural. The use of the definitive article (Les Clos, Les Preuses) is optional. It can be Sécher or Séchets, Vau de Ligneau or Vau Ligneau, and so on.

CHABLIS AND PETIT CHABLIS

Not surprisingly, the largest increase in surface area has been in those vineyards which are merely generic Chablis. Since 1978 there has been a 350-percent-plus rise to 3,163 hectares.

The area delimited as Petit Chablis, the lowest ranking of the Chablis appellations, has tended to fluctuate greatly. New vineyards have come into production, while others have been upgraded to Chablis or declassified entirely. There were 184 hectares in 1976, decreasing to only 113 in 1981, when we were led to believe that the authorities were going to eliminate this appellation entirely. However, as the result of new vineyards being authorised, the figure has risen to over 700 hectares today. Good intentions have found it hard to compete with local politics. Petit Chablis wine is dry and crisp, but not as intensely flavoured as Chablis, and should be drunk young.

MANUAL VERSUS MECHANICAL HARVESTING

Along with the suitability of Portlandian soil and new oak (see the next section), the third great argument raging in Chablis concerns the use of picking machines. Machine harvesters began to arrive in the Chablis vineyards in the early 1980s. The harvesters were somewhat rudimentary in those days, difficult to control and abusive

Chablis *Premiers Crus*

LIEU TO DIT/ORIGINAL *PREMIER CRU*	COMMUNE	MAIN *PREMIERS CRUS* (OPTIONAL)	SIZE (ha)
Right Bank of Serein			
Berdiot	Fyé	Berdiot	2.56
Chapelot	Fyé	Montée de Tonnerre	0.35
Côte de Bréchin	Fyé	Montée de Tonnerre	—
Côte de Fontenay	Fontenay	Fourchaume	0.25
Côte de Prés Girots	Fleys	Les Fourneaux	0.33
Côte de Vaubarousse	Fyé	Côte de Vaubarousse	0.99
Fourchaume	La Chapelle Vaupelteigne	Fourchaume	108.00
L'Homme Mort	Maligny	Fourchaume	7.02
Les Fourneaux	Fleys	Les Fourneaux	25.83
Mont de Milieu	Fleys	Mont de Milieu	41.42
Montée de Tonnerre	Fyé	Montée de Tonnerre	40.22
Morein	Fleys	Les Fourneaux	3.90
Pied d'Aloup	Fyé	Montée de Tonnerre	—
Vaucoupin	Chichée	Vaucoupin	40.96
Vaulaurent	Poinchy	Fourchaume	7.43
Vaupoulent	La Chapelle Vaupelteigne	Fourchaume	9.90
Left Bank of Serein			
Beauroy	Poinchy	Beauroy	56.15
Beugnons	Chablis	Vaillons	2.88
Butteaux	Chablis	Montmains	7.74
Chatains	Chablis	Vaillons	—
Chaume de Talvat	Courgis	Chaume de Talvat	—
Côte de Léchet	Milly	Côte de Léchet	50.34
Côte de Cuissy	Courgis	Les Beauregards	0.92
Côte de Jouan	Courgis	Côte de Jouan	11.90
Côte de Savant	Beines	Beauroy	2.21
Forêts	Chablis	Montmains	13.33
Les Beauregards	Courgis	Les Beauregards	18.26
Les Epinottes	Chablis	Les Beauregards	—
Les Lys	Chablis	Vaillons	9.45
Mélinots	Chablis	Vaillons	—
Montmains	Chablis	Montmains	89.29
Roncières	Chablis	Vaillons	0.88
Sécher or Séchets	Chablis	Vaillons	2.76
Troesmes	Beines	Beauroy	4.38
Vau de Vey	Beines	Vau de Vey	40.57
Vaillons	Chablis	Vaillons	109.57
Vaugiraut	Chichée	Vogros	6.24
Vogros	Chichée	Vogros	13.26
Vau Ligneau	Beines	Vau Ligneau	28.56
Vaux Ragons	Beines	Vau de Vey	—

Note: Size is according to the declaration of the 2004 harvest. In addition, 15.22 hectares were declared as *premier cru tout court*.

to the vine, whose life they cut short. Nevertheless they soon caught on. They were cheap and convenient. Working hours were more flexible. Vineyards could be cleared quickly if bad weather threatened. One was saved the expense of paying pickers for sitting around doing nothing when it rained. On Chablis's rolling hills the picking machine soon became dominant. By 1990 it was estimated that up to 95 percent of the vineyard was machine harvested. As the machines became more sophisticated, the damage to the vines lessened, and with more careful control, the vibrating rods could be adjusted to cause both unripe and rotten berries to fall to the ground and only the best fruit to be collected. For generic Petit Chablis and Chablis, this was the obvious route to adopt.

But what about the *premiers* and *grands crus*? The purists amongst the locals—and I agree—say no. Firstly, the harvesting machine, which picks berries and not bunches, inevitably splits the entry of the stem to the fruit, opening up the risk of oxidation. Secondly, how can you perform a really serious *triage* (sorting through of the fruit)? And how are you going to produce optimum quality if you can't isolate the bad from the good and ensure that you only vinify the former? It was noteworthy that in a vintage of uneven maturity and sanitation such as 2001, machine-harvested fruit produced musts which needed much more serious *débourbage* (setting out) or even clarification by centrifugation to cleanse them. Moreover, certain parts of the Chablis *vignoble*, the *grands crus* particularly, are too steep and are therefore unsuitable for the machine. A further downside to mechanical harvesting—I am not a scientist, but I repeat what I am told by those who have the expertise—is that it releases potassium, ultimately lowering the effective acidity in the wine.

Certain domaines, for instance Raveneau and Vincent Dauvissat, have always resisted the harvesting machine entirely, picking even their generic wines by hand. Others—and an increasing number of them, for the pendulum has reversed its direction—machine pick the basic wines and hand harvest their *premiers* and *grands crus*. The Union des Grands Crus de Chablis, a trade organisation of fifteen members, all of whom, as the title indicates, possess *grand cru* vineyards, stipulates, inter alia, that as a condition of membership, these *grand cru* vineyards be handpicked. This is a logical commitment to quality. It is no coincidence that Raveneau and Vincent Dauvissat are the top two names in the area. I would like to see legislation outlawing the machine from all *grands* and *premiers crus* in the Chablis vineyard.

OAK OR NOT

In addition to the feud in Chablis between the restrictionists and the expansionists and the arguments for and against picking machines, there has been a vehement debate about whether the wine should or should not be vinified and matured in whole or in part in new or newish wood. William Fèvre, late of Domaine de la Maladière, used to lead the oak faction as he did that of the restrictionists. As a grower and the largest proprietor of *grand cru* vineyards, he was able to control the vinification of his wine from the start, as well as the *élevage* (most of the *négociants* buy must, not grapes), and he fermented all his own *grands crus* in wood. All his wines were partly matured in oak as well.

The non-oak faction has many supporters, including large landholders such as Jean-Marie Brocard and Jean Durup, the top growers Daniel Dampt, the Domaine des Malandes and Louis Michel, plus *négociants* such as J. Moreau and Maison Regnard.

All the above do not use any new oak at all. Their wine spends all its life in *cuve*, a stainless steel or glass and tile-lined concrete vat. Others, such as the much-respected growers Jean-Marie Raveneau and Vincent Dauvissat, do use oak, but it is old oak rather than new, and it imparts no oaky taste to the wine.

Their general belief is that Chablis should not try to ape the Côte de Beaune. Chablis should be as natural a wine as possible; its flavours are subtle and delicate, and its essential gun-flinty, steely character should not be swamped by the supplementary aromas which result from vinifying or maturing the wine in oak.

There are arguments in favour of both sides. I have had many a well-matured, non-oak-aged Chablis which have proven that tank-matured wine need not be ephemeral. Ageing potential is as much a result of the correct balance between fruit and acidity (plenty of each and plenty of concentration) as of maturation and fermentation in wood per se. On the other hand, the extra weight and tannins added by the wood do help, especially in the weaker vintages. Fèvre's wines and those of Joseph Drouhin in Beaune—an important Chablis proprietor and also a believer in new wood—do keep extremely well. Moreover, their capacity for ageing is not so dependent on the vagaries of the vintage.

With greater numbers of growers today—and at the cooperative, La Chablisienne—the customer can have it both ways. There is no new oak for the lesser wines, but at least one special *cuvée* which has been "*élevé en fût de chêne.*" What should be born in mind is that wines age quicker in oak than in tank. Personally, I find many of these special oaky *cuvées* over-evolved, atypical and unbalanced. *Caveat emptor*!

THE WINE

Chablis, at its best, is a magnificent wine and is quite unique. The colour should be a full, in the sense of quite viscous, greeny-gold. The aromas should combine steeliness and richness, gun flint, grilled nuts and crisp toast. The flavour should be long, individual and complex. Above all, the wine should be totally dry, but without greenness. The aftertaste must be rich rather than mean, ample rather than hard, generous rather than soulless. Chablis is an understated wine, so it should be subtle rather than obvious, reserved rather than too obviously charming.

Far too often, however, Chablis is a disappointing wine. Very frequently when I first taste the wines in bottle, I find myself thinking that they were at their best after six months in cask: the evolution since then has been downhill. Now, many white wines, like reds, will enter an adolescent phase once they have been imprisoned in bottle. But far too many Chablis just

deteriorate further, becoming thin and attenuated. Why? There are several answers:

- Ninety-five percent of the Chablis vineyard is picked by machine. Elimination of substandard fruit is therefore impossible. The entire crop, unripe as well as ripe, rotten as well as healthy, is vinified together.

- The Chablisiens overproduce. Overall in 2002, yields were 56 hectolitres per hectare in Petit Chablis, 59 in Chablis, 58 in Chablis *premier cru* and even 52 in Chablis *grand cru*. Compare this with the Côte d'Or: 53 hectolitres per hectare for village white wine, 51 for *premier cru* and 44 for *grand cru*. Moreover, consider Chablis's situation: it is much closer to the northerly limit of successful wine production. If anything, yields should be lower, not 10 to 15 percent higher!

- The vineyard, having expanded so fast in the last 25 years, is underage. Vines less than 20 years old are infants, incapable of producing wines of depth and concentration.

- Chablis is overmanipulated. I was struck by the times that I read, in the replies to the questionnaires that I had sent out to the best-known names, how many rackings, as well as finings, usually with bentonite, and filterings, usually with kieselguhr, the wines were subjected to. Some, in years of marginal ripeness and health such as 2001, had been clarified using a centrifuge in the first place. Côte de Beaune whites, which moreover are normally bottled later, are not racked three times! I also fear that most Chablis is over-*bâtonné*-ed. Too much stirring up of the lees brings out too much of the character and flavour too early, leaving nothing for the long term.

- Finally, there is the soil itself. Kimmeridgian is a younger limestone than that found in the Côte de Beaune. So is Portlandian. Moreover, the clays are different. These are not soils which will produce profound wine at yields of 58 hectolitres per hectare.

Those responsible for the wine will argue that at current prices, a reduction in yields is quite simply uneconomical. They are quite right. It is a vicious circle. But the circle will have to be broken. The world market will not accept weak, attenuated wine. As has been demonstrated in the Côte d'Or, those with the determination to make top-quality wine will flourish. The rest will go to the wall. Perfectionism is the only way forward.

CHABLIS'S BEST SOURCES

Many wine writers have been too diffident or too polite to come into the open with a hierarchy of the top Chablis growers and *négociants*. The position is complicated for various reasons: first, the controversy over whether the wine should be matured in wood or not; second, the arm's-length presence of the *négociants* in Beaune and Nuits-Saint-Georges, all of whom sell Chablis but few of whom, except Drouhin, own any Chablis vineyards; and third, the presence of a very powerful local cooperative, La Chablisienne, which accounts for a third of the Chablis crop. Not unnaturally, this latter concern has a major influence on the annual price of the wine. La Chablisienne was my major Chablis supplier throughout most of my professional life, and I never found anything in the quality of its best wines—obviously with such a large business you have to pick and choose—which was not of the very highest standard. You may criticise the cooperative for its policy of allowing commercial buyers to choose the name of one of the cooperative's members to put on its label: for example, Fèvre Frères for Fourchaume which, together with *"mise en bouteille à la propriété,"* is certainly misleading, but you cannot deny that the wine inside the bottle can be as good as anything the appellation can produce.

→ Chablis Production 2005 (hl) ←

Grand Cru	5,032
Premier Cru	44,094
Chablis	186,377
Petit Chablis	41,883
TOTAL	277,386
Area Under Vine	4,755 ha
Average Yield	58.30 hl/ha

WHEN SHOULD YOU DRINK CHABLIS?

Top-quality Chablis—the *grands crus* and the best *premiers crus*, from a fine vintage and a star-rated grower or merchant—will last a long time, rather longer than one would expect. A *cuvée* of Fourchaume 1978 I chose at La Chablisienne was still alive and delicious in 1990. Sadly, these wines are the tip of the iceberg.

A general rule is as follows:

Petit Chablis	6 months to 2 1/2 years (after the vintage)
Chablis	1 to 4 years
Chablis *premier cru*	3 to 8 years
Chablis *grand cru*	5 to 12 years

RECENT VINTAGES

For 2007 and 2006, see page 315.

2005

In November 2005 I was in Chablis to taste the 2004s. "I can't tell you whether 2005 is the vintage of the century," said Christian Moreau. "I'll tell you in 6 months' time. But I am sure it's very fine." It was a small crop because of poor flowering. But after that the weather was very good. Despite a week of cloud and rain just before the harvest—which led to a fear of rot—the fruit was very healthy: rich and concentrated musts with good acidity. *Chez* Moreau, they started picking on September 19—very early for Chablis, and an indication of a good vintage. Jean-Loup Michel, of Domaine Louis Michel, began picking on September 21 and also boasted of a smaller than usual crop, with high alcoholic levels (up to 14° natural in the *grands crus*) and balancing acidities.

I visited Chablis again early in May 2006. It was abundantly clear that the enthusiastic anticipation I had found 6 months earlier was amply justified. The wines are both full and concentrated, and are splendidly refreshing. To have both concentration and freshness at the same time is rare. Yes, it is a very fine vintage, and the wines should last well.

2004

This was a huge crop to compensate for the deficiency in 2003. A good summer was succeeded by a miserable August, but September saw a return to fine weather. The harvest began on September 29 and continued until October 11, interrupted by rain only on October 4. The wines are aromatic and have high natural acidities. Where the crop is not too excessive—there were many reports of yields in the range of 80 hectolitres per hectare—quality is very good. Elsewhere there is a great deal of dilute, ephemeral rubbish which should have been sold as *vin de table* or sent away for distillation. The best wines should keep well. I found few disappointments in the top estates when I was there in November 2005.

2003

As a result of April frosts, yields ranged from 20 hectolitres per hectare to the full amount allowed by the authorities and, naturally, were lowest where growers do not have frost protection—in Petit Chablis and Chablis itself rather than in the *grand* and *premier cru* vineyards. After an unprecedentedly hot summer, the harvest was the earliest on record. The *ban des vendanges* was declared on August 25. Many growers, fearful of both low acidities and high alcohols, rushed out to pick. Many of the best growers, though, preferred to wait. Despite the heat of the summer, they considered their fruit to be not ripe enough. These brave souls benefited from the decline in the heat wave and some showers which, perversely, allowed both ripeness and acidity to concentrate. Many growers acidified. The wines are full, sturdy and atypical. I fear they will not age well. I sampled widely in February 2005, and a little less extensively when I returned to Chablis 9 months later in November to sample the 2004s. Many wines had declined in the meanwhile. Avoid this vintage.

2002

A cold winter was succeeded by a mild spring—so no frost damage for once. But May was cold, retarding development. The second half of June, when the Chablis vineyard flowered, was fine, however, and a large crop, a couple of percentage points more prolific than 2000 and 2001, set into grapes. July and August were dry and warm, rather than hot. The first two weeks of September were unsettled, but from then on, the weather was fine, with a strong north wind. The fruit was healthy, and acidity levels were good. The grapes were concentrated, and sugar levels were all that could be asked for. There was no excuse not to make good wine. In my view—leaving the very promising 2005s aside—2002 is the most satisfactory of recent vintages. The wines in bottle have shown well, despite the high yields. They should keep very well.

→ Chablis Production ← 2004 (hl)	
Grand Cru	5,726
Premier Cru	45,963
Chablis	191,677
Petit Chablis	40,951
TOTAL	284,317
Area Under Vine	4,469 ha
Average Yield	63.60 hl/ha

→ Chablis Production ← 2002 (hl)	
Grand Cru	5,325
Premier Cru	44,642
Chablis	179,798
Petit Chablis	36,198
TOTAL	265,963
Area Under Vine	4,460 ha
Average Yield	59.63 hl/ha

→ Chablis Production ← 2003 (hl)	
Grand Cru	4,376
Premier Cru	37,036
Chablis	140,438
Petit Chablis	24,867
TOTAL	206,717
Area Under Vine	4,584 ha
Average Yield	45.10 hl/ha

July was cold and wet, but August was sunny and warm. It was this month, when yields were not too abundant, which gave the eventual wine richness and ensured that the skins were thick enough to prevent an early slide into rot. September saw a reversion to the July weather conditions. Better things were announced for October, the harvest beginning on October 1, a Monday. But the Wednesday was cold and wet, and this was followed by a violent storm on Saturday, October 6. After that, thankfully, the weather did improve, but the resultant fruit was nevertheless uneven in ripeness and far from being in perfect health.

The original musts and wine were slow to show their real character. Acidities, until the malolactic had taken place, were high. The wines seemed lean and fruitless. But they became suppler and showed better and better fruit as 2002 progressed. They proved to have, surprisingly, a very good *tenue à l'air* (resistance to oxidation). When I came across them, after bottling, opinions were relatively bullish. I found much to enjoy. But this is not as good a vintage as 1999, 2000 or 2002, and it should be drunk soon.

⇥ Chablis Production 2001 (hl) ⇤	
Grand Cru	5,329
Premier Cru	44,416
Chablis	171,723
Petit Chablis	33,421
TOTAL	254,889
Area Under Vine	4,308 ha
Average Yield	59.20 hl/ha

⇥ Chablis Production 2000 (hl) ⇤	
Grand Cru	5,621
Premier Cru	46,049
Chablis	171,437
Petit Chablis	33,022
TOTAL	256,129
Area Under Vine	4,171 ha
Average Yield	61.40 hl/ha

⇥ Chablis Production 1999 (hl) ⇤	
Grand Cru	5,522
Premier Cru	48,955
Chablis	182,432
Petit Chablis	34,583
TOTAL	271,492
Area Under Vine	4,171 ha
Average Yield	65.10 hl/ha

Although the climatic conditions earlier in the summer had been by no means propitious, with July being particularly chilly, August was warm, and September was sunny, even hot. This led to a precociously early harvest, the *ban* being fixed for Saturday, September 23, with several growers obtaining permission to pick even earlier. The vintage took place in hot, dry conditions, with the exception of one storm on Tuesday, September 26, and another on Thursday, September 28. By that time, since Chablis is collected today almost entirely by machine, the harvest was more or less over.

The fruit was in almost perfect health, with natural alcoholic degrees between 11.5 and 12.5. From the beginning it appeared that the wines were concentrated and balanced, and that 2000 would be the sort of vintage that would earn it the accolades given to 1990, 1997 and 1999. Indeed, to have had three splendid years out of four, all of them abundant (although 2000 wasn't quite as plethoric as 1999), seemed to the Chablisien to be fortune indeed. Sadly, the wines in bottle showed less depth, less class and less consistency than they had promised earlier. The vintages of 1999 and 2002 are finer and will last better.

1999

This was a large crop, following a generous *sortie* and good weather during the flowering. Following that, the summer was cool, although not too wet, but after mid-August, a 6-week period of very fine weather settled in. The *ban des vendanges* was announced from September 22, but many of the top growers obtained permission to begin harvesting a couple of days earlier. The weather began to deteriorate after September 28, but by this time most of the fruit was safely fermenting in the cellars. This year is a full, rich, concentrated, fine vintage for Chablis. The wines are lasting well.

THE LEADING DOMAINES AND MERCHANTS

For simplicity I list all these by proprietor, in alphabetical order. The following sources may be better known under their domaine names:

Domaine de la Conciergerie, Christian Adine

Domaine de Chantemerle, François Boudin

Domaine du Vieux Château, Daniel-Étienne Defaix

Domaine de Vaudon, Joseph Drouhin

Domaine de l'Églantière, Jean Durup

Château de Maligny, Jean Durup

Domaine de la Paulière, Jean Durup

Domaine des Valéry, Jean Durup

Domaine Perchaud, Corinne and Jean-Pierre Grossot

Domaine de Pisse-Loup, Jean and Romual Hugot

Domaine de la Meulière, Chantal and Claude Laroche

Domaine des Marronniers, Bernard Legland

Domaine des Malandes, Lyne and Jean-Bernard Marchive

Domaine de la Tour Vaubourg, Louis Michel

Domaine de Biéville, Louis Moreau

Domaine du Cèdre Doré, Louis Moreau

Domaine du Colombier, Thierry Mothe

Domaine d'Élise, Frédéric Prain

Domaine des Isles, Gérard Tremblay

Domaine de Vauroux, Olivier Tricon

Domaine de la Chaude Écuelle, Gérard Vilain

★ *Christian Adine*
Domaine de la Conciergerie
Location: Courgis
Owners: Adine family
19.2 ha. *Premiers crus* in Butteaux, Côte de Cuissy, Montmains; Chablis Vieilles Vignes; Petit Chablis.

Across the road from the family house in Courgis, which is where one normally tastes, is a relatively new winery. The Adines, Christian and his daughter Marie-Gaëtane, supplement their white wine production with a red from near Béziers in the Languedoc, called Domaine de la Bergerie d'Amilhac. No wood is used here. These are stylish wines which normally develop quite soon.

★ *Domaine Barat*
Location: Milly
Owners: Barat family
16 ha. *Premiers crus* in Les Fourneaux, Côte de Léchet, Mont de Milieu, Vaillons; Chablis.

Michel Barat retired in 2003, and his son Ludovic is now in charge at this friendly family domaine. No wood is used. Enzymes are used to clarify the wine, and fining is by casein "in order to precipitate and isolate the oxidase elements: very useful in 2001." Very good 2000s and 2001s (for the vintage). Sadly, the 2002s seemed a little over-evolved in May 2004.

★ *Domaine Jean-Claude Bessin*
Location: Chablis; cellars in La Chapelle Vaupelteigne
Owner: Jean-Claude Bessin
6.15 ha (half of 12.3 ha he exploits *en métayage* from his father-in-law). *Grand cru* in Valmur (2.08 ha); *premiers crus* in Fourchaume, Fourchaume Vieilles Vignes, Montmains, La Pièce du Comte; Chablis.

Jean-Claude Bessin's cellar lies underneath the church in La Chapelle Vaupelteigne. Here he retains the yield of the old vines he sharecrops. His father-in-law's portion is sold off in bulk. In 2000 he started using older barrels for the maturation of his wines: "à la Raveneau," as he puts it. Low yields (45–50 hl/ha in 2000 and 2001) and first-class quality exist here.

★ Domaine Alain Besson

Location: Chablis
Owner: Alain Besson
19.4 ha. *Grand cru* in Vaudésir (1.43 ha); *premiers crus* in Mont de Milieu, Montmains, Vaillons.

On the southern outskirts of Chablis lies Alain Besson's new, and recently enlarged, modern, over-ground, temperature-controlled cellar. Although he is in his mid-forties, he only decided to bottle the produce of his estate in 2000. He vinifies using 5 to 10 percent of new oak for the top wines. Despite this (and it is barely perceptible once the wine is in bottle), his wines are splendidly pure and minerally. The quality is usually impressive, but I was a little underwhelmed by his 2004s.

★★ Domaine Billaud-Simon

Location: Chablis
Owners: Billaud family
20 ha. *Grands crus* in Blanchots (0.18 ha), Les Clos (0.44 ha), Les Preuses (0.40 ha), Vaudésir (0.71 ha); *premiers crus* in Fourchaume, Mont de Milieu, Montée de Tonnerre, Vaillons; Chablis *premier cru*; Chablis Tête d'Or; Chablis; Petit Chablis.

Founded in 1815 when Charles Louis Noël Billaud, on his return from the Napoleonic wars, planted his first vines in the Mont de Milieu and then expanded on the occasion of the marriage between Jean Billaud and Renée Simon in the 1930s, this up-to-date and excellent domaine is today run by Bernard, Jean's son, and his nephew Samuel. You will find it alongside the river Serein, just south of the village. Across a courtyard behind the family house is a large, modern winery, constructed in 1991 and updated since, a new reception hall and a pneumatic press having been installed in 2001. Most of the wines are vinified and matured in stainless steel. Two of the prestige *cuvées*, the Chablis Tête d'Or and the Mont de Milieu (*vieilles vignes*), are partly vinified in 3- to 5-year-old wood. The Blanchots is entirely vinified in oak. Recent changes for the better include the restriction of the harvest to 35 to 45 hectolitres per hectare for *grand* and *premier cru*, more ploughing and less use of herbicides and a return to manual harvesting in the *grands crus* and some *premiers crus*. High-class wines come from here. My favourite is the Clos.

Domaine/Maison Pascal Bouchard

Location: Chablis
Owner: Pascal Bouchard
33 ha. *Grands crus* in Blanchots (0.25 ha), Les Clos (0.70 ha), Vaudésir (0.60 ha); *premiers crus* in Beauroy, Fourchaume, Mont de Milieu, Montmains; Chablis; Petit Chablis.

Pascal Bouchard married into the Tremblay family and took over from his father-in-law André in 1979. New premises were installed in 1995 on the western side of the town of Chablis, at the same time Pascal Bouchard was expanding the merchant's side of his business. The *grands crus* and the old vine *cuvées* Fourchaume, Mont de Milieu and generic Chablis are vinified in oak, up to 15 percent of which is new. This is a little exaggerated, I feel. It makes the wines evolve too quickly. The 2000s already showed age in February 2003. A second label is Tremblay-Bouchard.

★ François Boudin
Domaine de Chantemerle

Location: La Chapelle Vaupelteigne
Owners: Boudin family
15.5 ha. *Premiers crus* in Fourchaume, L'Homme Mort; Chablis.

François Boudin now runs his estate on his own since his father Adhémar has retired. The estate is based in the sleepy village of La Chapelle Vaupelteigne, on the opposite bank of the river Serein from the domaine's first-growth wines. Boudin is one of the few who bottles and labels L'Homme Mort, from the location said to have been the burial place of local convicts denied sites in a church cemetery. The Boudin take on this is different: it was the site of a battle in the fifteenth century. The harvest is entirely manual, and there is no oak here. Boudin is a nice man who produces very good wines.

Domaine/Maison Jean-Marc Brocard

Location: Préhy
Owner: Jean-Marc Brocard
64 ha. *Premiers crus* in Beauregard, Côte de Jouan, Montmains, Vaucoupin; Chablis; Petit Chablis; Sauvignon de Saint-Bris and Irancy.

The village of Préhy lies, somewhat isolated, on the southwestern edge of the Chablis *vignoble*. It has little to offer the tourist except for a worth-a-visit fifteenth-century church and the modern (1989) premises of Jean-Marc Brocard. This is a recent success story. Brocard married Claudine, a young lady from Saint-Bris-Le-Vineux, further to the west on the other side of the motorway, in 1972 and inherited 1 hectare. He now exploits as much as 110, offering the *grands crus* of Bougros, Les Clos and Vaudésir, as well as the wines of his own domaine, one fifth of which is now run on biodynamic lines. There is no oak here. Brocard and his children, I find *sympas*. The wines are variable. This is a very good source for Sauvignon de Saint-Bris, however.

Cave Coopérative La Chablisienne

Location: Chablis
Number of Adherents: 300
1,200 ha. *Grands crus* in Blanchots (1 ha), Bougros (0.25 ha), Les Clos (0.50 ha), Grenouilles including Château de Grenouilles (7.50 ha), Les Preuses (4 ha), Valmur (0.25 ha), Vaudésir (0.50 ha); *premiers crus* in Beauroy, Côte de Léchet, Fourchaume, Les Lys, Mont de Milieu, Montée de Tonnerre, Vaillons, Vaulovent; Chablis; Petit Chablis.

Founded in 1923 and responsible for one third of the total appellation, La Chablisienne is up-to-date, well established and very powerful. Once you have signed up, you are effectively a shareholder, and it is difficult and expensive to extract yourself and set up independently. Hervé Tucki, who took over from his father Michel in the late 1980s, is a sensitive winemaker. Regrettably, in my view, the last decade has seen an increase in the amount of wood used here. They now have 600 casks, renewing 100 each year. The Château de Grenouilles is one *cuvée* which is regularly oak-abused. So are many of the rest

of the *grands crus*. You can find good wines here, but you have to pick and choose, especially if you are also looking for a wine which will last.

★ Domaine Christophe et Fils

Location: Fyé
Owners: Christophe family
5.5 ha. *Premiers crus* in Fourchaume, Montée de Tonnerre; Chablis Vieilles Vignes; Chablis; Petit Chablis.

In the middle of nowhere on the plateau above Fyé and the *grands crus* lies the Ferme des Carrières. In addition to cultivating sugar beets and maize, the youthful Sébastien Christophe runs a small vineyard. The Petit Chablis and the *premiers crus* are recent additions and young vines. The estate has only been bottling since 1999. I can only judge by the Chablis *tout court* and the *vieilles vignes* and by one vintage of the Fourchaume, for the first vintage of the Fourchaume was 2004, and the Montée de Tonnerre, 2005. There is no wood. These are lovely wines.

★ Domaine Jean Collet et Fils

Location: Chablis
Owners: Collet family
35 ha. *Grand cru* in Valmur (0.51 ha); *premiers crus* in Mont de Milieu, Montée de Tonnerre, Montmains, Vaillons; Chablis; Petit Chablis.

Gilles Collet and his wife Dominique have run this well-known domaine, well situated in Chablis, since 1979. It is a major owner in Vaillons, with no less than 9.6 hectares. The Valmur, Montée de Tonnerre and Mont de Milieu are vinified in old wood (1 to 6 years of age); the rest are vinified in stainless steel. The 2003 Montée de Tonnerre was fermented in oak, 10 percent of which was new. I found this to be a mistake. Generally speaking, though, the quality is very good here.

★ Domaine Daniel Dampt

Location: Milly
Owners: Dampt family
26 ha. *Premiers crus* in Beauroy, Côte de Léchet, Fourchaume, Les Lys, Vaillons.

Daniel Dampt's modern winery, temperature controlled throughout since 2002, lies out in the vineyards on the eastern side of Milly. This is one of the very best domaines in the village. The building is spotless, and Daniel Dampt is a perceptive, as well as a punctilious, winemaker. There is no wood here. The products are fine, pure mineral wines. Some wines are also sold under the Jean Defaix label.

Domaine Agnès and Didier Dauvissat

Location: Beines
Owners: Agnès and Didier Dauvissat
10 ha. *Premier cru* in Beauroy; Chablis; Petit Chablis.

No relation to the other Dauvissats, Agnès and Didier are a charming young couple who make three nicely nuanced wines. The junior two are for early drinking. The Beauroy, not released until it is two years old, will keep well.

Domaine Jean and Sébastien Dauvissat

Location: Chablis
Owners: Dauvissat family
9 ha. *Grand cru* in Les Preuses (0.74 ha); *premiers crus* in Montmains, Séchet, Vaillons; Chablis Cuvée Saint-Pierre; Chablis.

This is the lesser and less well known of the two Dauvissat domaines. The owners are cousins of Vincent and his father René and have their premises round the corner next to that of the Raveneaus. The Cuvée Saint-Pierre (only sold, I am told, on the European market) is usually a selection from the Vaillons. The wines are vinified in barrel, 30 percent of which, in the case of the Cuvée Saint-Pierre and the Preuses, is new. This latter exaggeration is a mistake. The rest of the range is to be preferred.

★★ Domaine Vincent Dauvissat

Location: Chablis
Owners: Dauvissat family
12 ha. *Grands crus* in Les Clos (1.70 ha), Les Preuses (1 ha); *premiers crus* in Forest (sic), Séchet Vaillons; Chablis; Petit Chablis.

This Dauvissat domaine (it used to be René and Vincent Dauvissat) lies with that of the Raveneau brothers at the top of the Chablis hierarchy. Production methods are superficially similar: ploughing of the vineyard, total hand harvesting and vinification and *élevage* in old barrels. The main difference is that Vincent Dauvissat does not stir up the lees in the barrel (*bâtonnage*), a technique almost universally employed elsewhere in the appellation. He is also against fining his wines. This is a great estate. The Clos is my favourite. This is a great Chablis. Some wines are sold under the Dauvissat-Camus label.

★ Domaine Bernard Defaix
Maison Sylvain and Didier Defaix

Location: Milly
Owners: Defaix family
25 ha. *Premiers crus* in the Côte de Léchet, Les Lys, Vaillons; Chablis Vieilles Vignes; Chablis; Petit Chablis.

Since Bernard Defaix retired in 1995, it has been his sons Sylvain (in the cellar) and Didier (in the vineyards) who have been in charge here, and since 1999 they have supplemented the produce of their family estate with purchases of must from Fourchaume and Bougros. This domaine is the largest owner in the Côte de Léchet, which rises behind the winery. They possess 7.5 hectares and produce two *cuvées*, the better labelled *réserve*. Half of this *cuvée* matures in old wood, and 100 percent oak is used for the Bougros. The rest of the wines spend all their life in stainless steel. I find their excellent domaine Côte de Léchet far superior to their merchant Bougros.

★ Domaine Daniel-Étienne Defaix
Domaine du Vieux Chateau

Location: Milly
Owner: Daniel-Étienne Defaix
25 ha. *Grand cru* in Blanchots (0.20 ha); *premiers crus* in Côte de Léchet, Les Lys, Vaillons; Chablis; Petit Chablis.

Almost everyone in Milly is related to each other. This Defaix is a cousin of those above, as well as of Daniel Dampt, Lyne Marchive (see the Domaine des Malandes below) and Gérard Tremblay. In addition to maintaining his cellar in Milly, Daniel Defaix is busy renovating some medieval buildings in the centre of Chablis, behind his shop. He doesn't offer, or sell, *en primeur*. You will sample and be able to buy the wines when Defaix considers them ready for drinking. There is no oak here. These are very pure wines, with good *terroir* definition. They keep well too.

★★ Domaine Benoît Droin

Location: Chablis

Owners: Droin family

25.5 ha. *Grands crus* in Blanchots (0.17 ha), Les Clos (0.99 ha), Grenouilles (0.48 ha), Valmur (1.02 ha), Vaudésir (1.03 ha); *premiers crus* in Côte de Léchet, Fourchaume, Mont de Milieu, Montée de Tonnerre, Montmains, Vaillons, Vaucoupin, Vosgros; Chablis; Petit Chablis.

Benoît Droin took over from his father in 1999. His name appears on the label from the 2002 vintage. There is quite widespread use of oak here, although increasingly less than in Jean-Paul Droin's time, and most of the wines in most vintages can take it. Benoît is determined to treat each *cuvée* in a different way. Too much wood, he says, undermines the elegance and minerality of the wine. But each *cuvée* and each vintage reacts with the oak in a different way. This is a first-class estate. The Mont de Milieu vines are very young at the time of writing. Their first vintage was the 2003.

★★ Domaine Joseph Drouhin

Location: Beaune

Owners: Drouhin family

37.8 ha. *Grands crus* in Bougros (0.33 ha), Les Clos (1.30 ha), Les Preuses (0.23 ha), Vaudésir (1.41 ha); *premiers crus* in Montmains, Séchers, Vaillons, plus Mont de Milieu, Montée de Tonnerre, Morein and Roncières blended together as *premier cru tout court*; Chablis Domaine de Vaudon; Chablis.

The respected Beaunois house of Drouhin started expanding into the Chablis vineyard in 1968. The fruit is pressed here in Chablis, but the musts are transferred to Beaune for vinification and *élevage*. The *grands crus* and some of the *premiers crus*, as well as the Domaine de Vaudon, whose origins lie on slopes between the Montée de Tonnerre and the Mont de Milieu,

are fermented and stored at least partly in wood, with 15 percent being new for the *grands crus*. The percentage varies from vintage to vintage. As far as I am concerned, the Drouhins get the oak absolutely right. If you are going to have oaky Chablis, this is the model to follow, for the wines do not suffer from a lack of *typicité*. The Clos is the best wine, but the Vaudésir comes close.

Domaine Gérard Duplessis

Location: Chablis

Owners: Duplessis family

7 ha. *Grand cru* in Les Clos (0.36 ha); *premiers crus* in Fourchaume, Montée de Tonnerre, Montmains, Vaillon; Chablis.

Next door to Billaud-Simon on the Quai de Reugny on the left bank of the river Serein, presided over by the genial and splendidly bearded Gérard, is the Duplessis domaine. Vinification is in stainless steel, and *élevage* is split between tank and old wood. Bottling is late, after as long as 20 months. I used to rate this domaine highly, but in two recent visits, coinciding with a major programme of renovation to the cellars, running late and occasioning a multitude of disorder, I was underimpressed.

Domaine Jean Durup Père et Fils
Chateau de Maligny
Domaine de l'Églantière

Location: Maligny

Owners: Durup family

180 ha. *Premiers crus* in Fourchaume, L'Homme Mort, Montée de Tonnerre, Montmains, Vau de Vey; Chablis *premier cru* Cuvée La Reine Mathilde; Chablis Vieilles Vignes; Chablis Le Carré de Cézar; Chablis La Vigne de la Reine; Chablis La Marche du Roi; Chablis.

The Durups dominate Maligny. Not only is their domaine the largest in Chablis after the cooperative La Chablisienne—and there are still 35 hectares to be planted once permission has been granted—but the family is also undertaking a major restoration of the twelfth-century Château de Maligny and its neighbouring thirteenth-century nunnery. Jean-Paul

Durup is the man in charge on the spot. The winery is spotless, without a stave of wood to be seen, and quality is impressive, especially given the size of the operation.

★★ Domaine William Fèvre

Location: Chablis
Owners: Henriot Champagne
Local Director: Didier Seguier
48 ha. *Grands crus* in Bougros (6.20 ha) (most sold as Clos des Bouguerots), Les Clos (4.15 ha), Grenouilles (0.57 ha); Les Preuses (2.55 ha), Valmur (1.10 ha); Vaudésir (1.20 ha); *premiers crus* in Beauroy, Les Lys, Montmains, Montée de Tonnerre, Vaillons, Vaulorent; Chablis.

In 1998, upon his retirement at the age of sixty-seven, William Fèvre sold his domaine (but only a twenty-five–year lease on his vineyard) to Henriot Champagne, already proprietors of Bouchard Père et Fils in Beaune. It was a first-class domaine then; it is even better now. This is an estate which believes in wood for both fermentation and *élevage*, but there is much less new wood than previously (barely 2 percent), and the resultant wines are all the better for it, being more relaxed and having excellent *terroir* definition. Harvesting is by hand. The wines are not subjected to *bâtonnage*, are lightly fined only when necessary and are not filtered. Bottling takes place after the wines have had 4 to 8 months in wood, followed by the equivalent time in tank. This is a classy setup, producing very classy wines.

There is also a Fèvre merchant operation, offering inter alia Mont de Milieu and Blanchots.

Domaine Garnier et Fils

Location: Ligny le Châtel
Owners: Garnier family
19 ha. Chablis "Grains Dorés"; Chablis; Petit Chablis.

Xavier and Jérôme Garnier, the two *fils*, started planting vines on their family land above Fourchaume in 1986 and began to domaine bottle in 1992. Two thirds of the wine is still sold off in bulk. There are two *cuvées*. The basic is cropped at 60 hectolitres per hectare. The slightly oaky Grains Dorés, introduced in 1999, is from the

best parcels, where the yield is reduced to 35 to 40 hectolitres per hectare. This is an address worth exploring.

Domaine Raoul Gautherin et Fils

Location: Chablis
Owners: Gautherin family
16.6 ha. *Grands crus* in Les Clos (0.18 ha), Grenouilles (0.22 ha), Vaudésir (0.84 ha); *premiers crus* in Mont de Milieu, Montmains, Vaillons; Chablis Vieilles Vignes; Chablis; Petit Chablis.

Alain Gautherin's winery and tasting room are located across a courtyard from his house in the centre of Chablis. Harvesting is by hand, lees settling is undertaken with the use of enzymes and, for the most part, maturation takes place in stainless steel. The *vieilles vignes* and the Grenouilles spend some of their time in old oak. Gautherin works with the lees but does not approve of *bâtonnage*. Quality is good but not outstanding. Recently I have preferred his Grenouilles to his Vaudésir.

Domaine Alain Gautheron

Location: Fleys
Owners: Gautheron family
18 ha. *Premiers crus* in Les Fourneaux including a *vieilles vignes* cuvée, Mont de Milieu, Vaucoupin; Chablis Vieilles Vignes; Chablis; Petit Chablis.

This family domaine—son Cyril has recently joined his father, Alain—is found on the eastern side of the village of Fleys under the Fourneaux *premier cru*. The *vieilles vignes* from this *climat* are hand harvested, and this and the Chablis Vieilles Vignes age in old wood. These are the two best wines; otherwise, quality is patchy.

★ Domaine Corinne and Jean-Pierre Grossot
Domaine Perchaud

Location: Fleys
Owner: Corinne Perchaud and Jean-Pierre Grossot
18 ha. *Premiers crus* in Fourchaume, Les Fourneaux, Mont de Milieu, Côte de Troesmes, Vaucoupin; Chablis "La Part des Anges"; Chablis.

The modern premises of the Grossot domaine are isolated beneath the Mont de Milieu on the western side of Fleys. Part of the harvest is manual, and from the Part des Anges *cuvée* upward, the wines undergo part of their *élevage* in wood. I find this domaine produces very stylish wines and rate it the best in the village. My favourite is their Mont de Milieu.

Domaine Thierry Hamelin
Location: Lignorelles
Owners: Hamelin family
37 ha. *Premier cru* in Beauroy, Vau Ligneau; Chablis; Petit Chablis.

The large, robust Thierry Hamelin and his brother Bruno operate from an ugly, if functional, warehouse out in the sugar beet fields in the northern part of the appellation. The Chablis and the Petit Chablis come from Portlandian soils. There is no wood here. The wines are of sound quality, but not special.

Jean and Romuald Hugot
Domaine de Pisse-Loup
Location: Beines
Owners: Hugot family
13 ha. Chablis; Petit Chablis.

This estate, situated on the main road in Beines, dates from 1985 and is now run by Romuald, son of Jean Hugot. The family also owns the Château Lagarde-Rouffiac in Cahors. Since 2002 there has been an oaky special *cuvée* from hand-harvested grapes. The quality is sound but not special.

★★ Maison Jadot
Location: Beaune
Owners: Kopf family
PDG: Pierre-Henri Gagey
Winemaker: Jacques Lardière

Although Jadot do not own any vineyards in the Chablis area, they are important players in Burgundy and sell some 100,000 bottles of Chablis a year. Vinification and *élevage* take place in their cellars in Beaune. The generic wines are fermented and matured in stainless steel; the *premiers* and *grands crus* are fermented and matured at least partly in old wooden casks. As with Jadot's other white wines, indigenous yeasts are used, malolactic fermentations are blocked and the wines are bottled later than most. I admire Jadot's Chablis very much. They are made for keeping.

Domaine Chantal and Claude Laroche
Location: Fleys
Owners: Claude Laroche family
25 ha. *Premiers crus* in Fourchaume, Les Fourneaux, Mont de Milieu, Vaucoupin; Chablis Vieilles Vignes; Chablis; Petit Chablis.

Harvesting is by hand at this family domaine, founded in 1972, and until recently, no wood was to be found in the cellar. Today, the Fourchaume is 100 percent vinified and *élevé* in wood, 18 percent of which is new. This is too much. So, surely, is the Laroche habit of racking each wine four times. The Fourneaux is currently young wines.

Domaine/Maison Michel Laroche
Location: Chablis
Owners: Laroche family
98.8 ha. *Grands crus* in Blanchots (4.50 ha), Bougros (0.31 ha), Les Clos (1.12 ha); *premiers crus* in Beauroy, Côte de Léchet, Fourchaume (*vieilles vignes*), Montmains, Montée de Tonnerre, Vaillons (*vieilles vignes*), Vau de Vey; Chablis Saint-Martin (*vieilles vignes*); Chablis; Petit Chablis.

Although dating from 1850, the Laroche empire really started to expand in 1967 when Michel Laroche, then twenty-one, and his father, Henri, began to buy up land. The business is based at the Obédiencerie, a monastery which dates from the ninth century and is still a fine building. The *cuverie*, dating from 1992, lies west of the town, on the road to Auxerre. It works by gravity. Harvesting is done partly by hand, selected yeasts are used, and all the *grands crus* and most of the *premiers crus* are fermented and matured in wood. Although no new wood is used, I find the expression of oak in the Laroche wines excessive. The wine from a special half hectare of Blanchots, where Laroche is by far the largest landholder, produces a Réserve de l'Obédiencerie. Laroche buys in fruit at the village level.

Maison Olivier Leflaive Frères

Location: Puligny-Montrachet
Owners: Olivier Leflaive and associates. Winemaker: Patrick Duize

Olivier Leflaive Frères own no vineyards in Chablis but jointly possess, with Jean-Marie Guffens's Maison Verget in Sologny in the Mâconnais, a winemaking facility at Chitry. Leflaive's local manager here, reporting to Franck Grux back in Puligny, is the Canadian Patrick Duize. His contracts with his suppliers enable him to send in his own pickers to hand harvest in the best vineyards. After pressing, the wines are vinified in Puligny. Apart from a tendency to over-oak, the wines are very good here. Like their Côte de Beaune counterparts, they are for early drinking.

Bernard Legland
Domaine des Marronniers

Location: Préhy
Owners: Legland family
20 ha. *Premiers crus* in Côte de Jouan, Montmains; Chablis; Petit Chablis.

Bernard Legland's domaine dates from 1976, when he planted his first vines. He is a conscientious winemaker, eschewing the use of oak and *bâtonnage* and producing neat, clean wines from the medium term. Recently he has been inclined to bottle later and later, provided the vintage allows it. The *tenue à l'air* (the ability of the wine to withstand oxygen) is greater, and consequently, he can reduce the sulphur content required to protect the wines.

Domaine Long-Depaquit

Location: Chablis
Owner: Albert Bichot
63 ha. *Grands crus* in Blanchots (1.65 ha), Bougros (0.52 ha), Les Clos (1.54 ha), La Moutonne (2.35 ha), Les Preuses (0.25 ha), Vaudésir (2.60 ha); *premiers crus* in Beugnons, La Forêt, Les Lys, Montée de Tonnerre, Vaillons, Vaucoupin; Chablis.

Long-Depaquit dates from 1791. Its elegant buildings occupy a spacious park, strangely calm in the middle of the town. In 1971 the company was sold to Albert Bichot, the large

Beaune *négociant*. The new owners retained Long-Depaquit's oenologue and resident manager Gérard Vullien and largely left him to his own devices. The era came to an end in 2001, however: Vullien retired, there was a change of management, and more importantly, there was a change in attitude at the Beaune end. Jean-Didier Basch succeeded Vullien as *régisseur*, yields were reduced and the viticultural approach became more *biologique*. Today all the *grands crus*, the Vaucoupin and the Montée de Tonnerre are harvested by hand. The wines are made here in Chablis but bottled in Beaune. Now all that remains is to reduce the wood so that the wine tastes like true Chablis.

A separate Bichot-owned estate is the Domaine du Château de Viviers (see page 66).

★★ Lyne and Jean-Bernard Marchive
Domaine des Malandes

Location: Chablis
Owners: Lyne and Jean-Bernard Marchive and the Tremblay family
26 ha. *Grands crus* in Les Clos (0.53 ha), Vaudésir (0.90 ha); *premiers crus* in Côte de Léchet, Fourchaume, Montmains, Vau de Vey; Chablis Vieilles Vignes "Tour du Roi"; Chablis; Petit Chablis.

Jean-Bernard and Lyne Marchive, a charming and welcoming couple, started this domaine in 1986, and they are now being joined by their eldest daughter, Marion, and her husband, Josh. Lyne Marchive was née Tremblay, and the entire domaine is *en fermage*, part of the Vaudésir owned by English wine merchant Mark Reynier. Vinification is in tank after a preliminary passage through the vines to cut out all the unripe or rotten fruit, but the *grands crus* are wholly or partly fermented in old wood. All the wines go through a cold stabilisation process the following summer. You will find fine quality here: very clean, pure wines. They keep well, too.

★★ Domaine Louis Michel et Fils

Location: Chablis
Owners: Michel family
23 ha. *Grands crus* in Les Clos (0.50 ha), Grenouilles (0.54 ha), Vaudésir (1.17 ha); *premiers crus* in

Fourchaume, Forêts, Montée de Tonnerre, Montmains, Vaillons; Chablis; Petit Chablis.

The Michel domaine was founded in 1850 and, following his father's death in 1999, is run currently by Jean-Loup Michel, making the domaine fifth-generation family owned. Attached to the house, on a street which runs down to the river Serein in the middle of Chablis, is the ivy-covered Domaine de la Tour Vaubourg, under whose label some of the wines are sold, and beneath which is the cellar where you will taste the wines. The *grands crus* and some of the *premiers crus* are hand harvested. Apart from a few empty casks which are strictly for decorative purposes, there is not a stick of wood in the Michel cellar. The wines are vinified at 18°C, a low temperature, and there is no *bâtonnage*. This technique produces splendidly elegant, pure and fragrantly expressive wines. They can be austere in their youth, but they keep remarkably well. This is one of the top domaines in the appellation.

Domaine Alice and Olivier de Moor
Location: Courgis
Owners: Alice and Olivier de Moor
6.5 ha (3 of Chablis). Chablis "Rosette"; Chablis "Belair"; Sauvignon de Saint-Bris; Bourgogne Chitry (*blanc*); Bourgogne Aligoté.

Neither Olivier nor his wife is from a viticultural background, although both are qualified oenologists. They set up in 1988, produced their first vintage in 1993 and were rapidly recognised as rising stars. Everything is done by hand here. Fermentations are in old barrels, and the wines are neither fined nor filtered. Sulphuring is kept to the barest minimum. The wines are forward but well made—very clean and stylish.

★★ Domaine Christian Moreau Père et Fils
Location: Chablis
Owners: Moreau family
12 ha. *Grands crus* in Blanchot (0.10 ha), Les Clos (3.60 ha, of which 0.40 ha is Clos des Hospices, Valmur (1 ha), Vaudésir (0.50 ha); *premier cru* in Vaillons, including a Cuvée Guy Moreau; Chablis; Petit Chablis.

The year 2002 was the first vintage for Christian Moreau and his son Fabien, following the end of the lease of the family vines to Ets. J. Moreau et Fils, now owned by Boisset. Louis Moreau, his nephew, took on the other half (see below). Harvesting is entirely by hand, with the lesser wines fermented in stainless steel tanks and the *premier* and *grand cru* vinified 30 to 50 percent in wood. Christian Moreau describes himself as a "100 percent Chablisien." The 2002s and 2003s were an impressive start; the 2004s and 2005s are even better. Currently, because the vines are older, I prefer the straight Les Clos to the Clos des Hospices.

Domaine Louis Moreau
Domaine de Biéville
Domaine du Cèdre Doré
Location: Beines
Owners: Louis and Anne Moreau
DOMAINE LOUIS MOREAU: 50 ha. *Grands crus* in Blanchots (0.10 ha), Les Clos (3.61 ha including 0.41 ha which is Clos des Hospices (*monopole*), Valmur (0.99 ha), Vaudésir (0.45 ha); *premiers crus* in Fourneaux, Vaillons, Vaulignot; Chablis; Petit Chablis.

DOMAINE DE BIÉVILLE: 65 ha. Chablis.

DOMAINE DU CÈDRE DORÉ: 5 ha. Chablis.

Louis Moreau is the son of Jean-Jacques (Christian's brother; see above), who created the Viviers-based Domaine de Biéville in 1965 (Viviers lies on the eastern edge of the appellation). The Cèdre Doré followed, and Louis has since built up his own domaine. It now includes half the family vineyards once leased to merchants J. Moreau, which is no longer in the family hands (see above). Prior to the *grands crus* returning *en famille*, this was a no-wood, no-*bâtonnage* establishment, producing neat, clean wines for the medium term. The *grands crus* now go through a brief (4 to 8 weeks) *élevage en fûts*, 16 percent of which are new. They are good, but they lack the flair of those produced by the cousins above.

★ Domaine Moreau-Naudet
Location: Chablis
Owners: Moreau-Naudet family
22 ha. *Grand cru* in Valmur (0.60 ha); *premiers crus* in Beauregard, Côte de Jouan, La Forêt, Montée de Tonnerre, Montmains, Vaillons; Chablis; Petit Chablis.

Stéphane Moreau, who is no close relation to the above, took over from his father at the family domaine in 1999 and very quickly established it among the leading estates in the area. He harvests at low yields (35 to 45 maximum), hand picks the majority of his top wines, and has been experimenting with biodynamism (as far as I know, this is the only serious domaine in Chablis to move in this direction). The better wines are lightly oaked. These are concentrated, classy wines.

Domaine Sylvain Mosnier

Location: Beines
Owner: Mosnier family
17.2 ha. *Premiers crus* in Beauroy, Côte de Léchet; Chablis Vieilles Vignes; Chablis; Petit Chablis.

Sylvain Mosnier retired in 2005 and handed the domaine over to his daughter Stéphanie. This is a domaine which believes in low yields and uses no oak except for a passage in cask after fermentation for the *vieilles vignes cuvée* and the Beauroy. I have enjoyed the wines of this estate in the past, but I had a disappointing visit in February 2004 when I called to sample the 2001s and 2002s. This, however, seems to have been a temporary blip. The 2004s were very good indeed.

Thierry Mothe
Domaine du Colombier

Location: Fontenay-Près-Chablis
Owners: Mothe family
35 ha. *Grand cru* in Bougros (1.20 ha); *premiers crus* in Fourchaume, Vaucoupin; Chablis Vieilles Vignes; Chablis; Petit Chablis.

Thierry Mothe took over this domaine—Fontenay's best—in 1998 upon the retirement of his father, Guy, and has, I feel, further refined the quality here. There is no wood. The domaine produces intense, pure, elegant wines. This is the best source, along with William Fèvre, for Bougros.

Domaine Christianne and Jean-Claude Oudin

Location: Chichée
Owners: Oudin family
7.5 ha. *Premiers crus* in Vaucoupin, Vaugiraut; Chablis "Les Serres"; Chablis.

After 10 years in Paris as an aeronautical engineer, Jean-Claude Oudin returned to Chichée, south of Chablis, to take over the holdings of his wife's family. This was in 1988. There were 2 hectares then; now there are 7.5. Picking is by machine, but the land is ploughed, and a lot of attention is paid to ensuring a low harvest. There is no wood. The domaine produces very good wines.

Domaine Gilbert Picq et Fils

Location: Chichée
Owners: Picq family
13 ha. *Premiers crus* in Vaucoupin, Vosgros; Chablis Vieilles Vignes; Chablis.

Didier and his brother Pascal are in charge here at Chichée's best-known estate, created by Picq *père* in 1976. Vinification and *élevage* are entirely in stainless steel tanks, following pressing in a pneumatic apparatus; as of 2005, the fruit is picked through on a sorting table. The wines are left on their fine lees for 10 to 15 months before bottling. Neat, crisp wines are produced here. It is a good address.

Frédéric Prain
Domaine d'Élise

Location: Milly
Owners: Prain family
13.5 ha. *Premier cru* in Côte de Léchet; Chablis Cuvée Galilée; Chablis; Petit Chablis.

Not without difficulty (I got lost the first time, for there are no signposts), you will find the Prain domaine on the plateau above the Côte de Léchet. In 1982 Frédéric Prain retired from his job as a public works engineer in Paris. The house is still not finished. Prain picks by hand, not machine, sells half his crop to the *négoce* and bottles after 9 months. It is only recently that he achieved *premier cru* status for his 0.26 hectare of Côte de Léchet, which lies at the top of the slope and adjoins the rest of his estate, which is all in one piece. There is no wood here. Only the Cuvée Galilée undergoes *bâtonnage*. The domaine produces good wines for drinking fairly early.

★ Domaine Pinson Frères

Location: Chablis
Owners: Pinson family
11.8 ha *Grand cru* in Les Clos (2.50 ha); *premiers crus*
in Les Forêts, Mont de Milieu, Montmains, Vaillons,
Vaugiraut; Chablis.

Laurent and Christophe Pinson, cheerful, strapping young men in their mid-thirties, now run this popular domaine, whose headquarters is situated in the Quai Voltaire overlooking the river Serein. Father Louis is now retired. Noteworthy is that this is one of the very few Chablis properties which harvests entirely by hand. The wine is vinified in tank, with the top wines being aged for 6 months or so in wood, 10 percent of which is new, in a new extension to the cellar constructed in 2004. The Vaugiraut and Vaillons are currently from young vines. The wines are of fine quality.

Domaine Denis Race

Location: Chablis
Owners: Race family
15 ha. *Grand cru* in Blanchots (0.30 ha); *premiers crus* in Côte de Cuissy, Mont de Milieu, Montmains, Vaillons; Chablis; Petit Chablis.

Father Laurence is now semi-retired, and so this classy estate is now in the hands of his son Denis. You will find the headquarters next to that of Raveneau on the road to Chichée. The Races are firmly against wood. Of late, Denis has been pruning to the Guyot *simple* rather than *double*, with the intent of being able to control the size of the harvest more easily. Elegant wines for the medium term are found here.

★★ Domaine Raveneau

Location: Chablis
Owners: Raveneau family
7.5 ha. *Grands crus* in Blanchots (0.60 ha),
Les Clos (0.54 ha), Valmur (0.75 ha); *premiers crus* in
Butteaux, Chapelot, Forest (*sic*), Montée de Tonnerre,
Montmains, Vaillons; Chablis.

Brothers Jean-Marie and Bernard Raveneau run Chablis's best domaine—a surprisingly small establishment. Older bottles will be found with the Christian name of father François on the label. Harvesting is entirely by hand here. Yields are never excessive: 45 hectolitres per hectare in 2000 and 2001, 50 in 2002 and 35 in 2003—but 70 in 2004. The wines are vinified with natural or selected yeasts, depending on the vintage, and matured for up to 18 months in old barrels or half-barrels (*feuillettes*). Raveneau's corks are sealed with wax.

What is impressive about the Raveneau Chablis is that they are invariably very expressive of both their *terroirs* and their vintages. No two wines are alike. They are very pure and are capable of long ageing. This is the way to produce top-quality Chablis.

Maison Regnard

Location: Chablis
Owner: Baron Patrick de Ladoucette
Régisseur: Philippe Rossignol
10 ha. *Grand cru* in Les Grenouilles (0.50 ha). The firm buys in the equivalent of 125 hectares of fruit or must from some fifty growers.

Maison Regnard was founded in 1860, absorbed Maison Albert Pic in 1957, and was sold by Michel Remon, whose wife was *née* Regnard, to Patrick de Ladoucette of Pouilly-Fumé in 1984. Winemaking is entirely in stainless steel here, and the top wines are aged on their lees for 8 to 12 months before bottling. The firm produces about half a million bottles a year. All the *grands crus* are offered, plus the following *premiers crus*: Fourchaume, Montée de Tonnerre, Mont de Milieu and Montmains. Maison Regnard is clearly the best of the locally based *négociants*. Quality is generally very high.

Domaine Guy Robin

Location: Chablis
Owners: Robin family
20 ha. *Grands crus* in Blanchot (0.20 ha), Bougros (0.50 ha), Les Clos (0.20 ha), Valmur (2.60 ha), Vaudésir (0.25 ha); *premiers crus* in Mont de Milieu, Montée de Tonnerre, Montmains, Vaillons; Chablis.

The Robin estate consists of fine old vines. They pick entirely by hand. There is no reason why quality should not be splendid. Sadly, for many years the winery has been a hopeless mess, both dirty and smelly, and the bottles it has produced have reflected this neglect. There are, however, some positive signs for the future: Guy's son Jean-Pierre is now increasingly in charge. He, at least, is aware that there is a problem.

Domaine Francine and Olivier Savary

Location: Maligny
Owners: Savary family
16.5 ha. *Premiers crus* in Fourchaume, Vaillons; Chablis Vieilles Vignes; Chablis; Petit Chablis.

Since 1984 the charming husband and wife team of Olivier and Francine Savary have built up their domaine from nothing. The expanding estate necessitated a new stainless steel winery, working by gravity, in 2000, at which time *lutte raisonnée* (reactive viticulture) and a more severe approach to yields was adopted. Only the Chablis Vieilles Vignes sees any wood here, but the wood is not a bit excessive. The wines produced are of impressive quality.

Domaine Roger Séguinot-Bordet

Location: Maligny
Owners: Séguinot-Bordet family
23 ha. *Premier cru* in Fourchaume; Chablis Vieilles Vignes; Chablis; Petit Chablis.

Jean-François Bordet, grandson of Roger, took over here at the beginning of 1998 and has since installed a brand new *cuverie chez lui* in Maligny, which was first used in 2002. In 2003 Jean-François started buying in fruit from Vaudésir, Côte de Léchet and Vaillons. He is picking later than was the practice when Roger Séguinot was in charge, but still by machine, and he is keeping the wine longer on its lees, with more *bâtonnage*. There is certainly an enthusiastic will to make good wines here, with the intention of producing *vins de garde*, but the results so far are merely so-so. There is no wood.

★ Domaine Servin

Location: Chablis
Owners: Servin family
33.6 ha. *Grands crus* in Blanchot (0.91 ha), Bougros (0.46 ha), Les Clos (0.63 ha), Les Preuses (0.69 ha); *premiers crus* in Forêts, Montée de Tonnerre, Vaillons; Chablis Cuvée Massale; Chablis; Petit Chablis.

François Servin and his Australian brother-in-law, Mark Cameron, are in charge at this well-reputed estate, whose headquarters lie just across the river Serein bridge from the heart of the town. All new plantations are now at 8,000 to 9,000 per hectare (as opposed to the normal 5,000 to 6,000), and pruning is to a single *Guyot* rather than the standard double: a net increase of riper grapes with less disease, the domaine reports. All the *grands crus*, the Forêts and old *massale* vines are hand harvested. The must is then cold-settled for 24 hours before fermentation using selected yeasts. The Bougros, Les Clos and Preuses, but not the Blanchots, are vinified in barrels, with the first two getting the newer wood. The Vaillons and the Chablis *sélection massale* are also gently oaky. All this takes place in a new gravity-fed cellar, installed in 2002. There are very good wines here, but the oaky wines are sometimes excessively so.

Domaine/Maison Simmonet-Fèbvre

Location: Chablis
Owner: Louis Latour
5 ha. *Grand cru* in Les Preuses (0.29 ha); *premier cru* in Mont de Milieu; Chablis village.

The domaine was founded by Jean Fèbvre in 1840, whose daughter married a Simmonet. In June 2003 the Simmonet family sold the business to Maison Louis Latour of Beaune. As well as Chablis, Simmonet-Fèbvre also offers Crémant de Bourgogne, and such Yonne appellations as Saint-Bris and Coulanges la Vineuse. Cultured yeasts are used, but not a stick of wood. Critics are divided as to whether the own-domaine wines are superior to the merchant offerings. I confess I have not been particularly inspired by either, but I have not yet tasted the wines produced subsequent to the change of ownership.

Domaine Philippe Testut

Location: Chablis
Owners: Testut family
11 ha. *Grand cru* in Grenouilles (0.55 ha); *premiers crus* in Beugnons, Les Forêts, Montmains, Montée de Tonnerre, Vaucoupin; Chablis; Petit Chablis.

Philippe Testut—currently assisted by his son Cyrille—started this domaine in 1966, having previously worked at Long-Depaquit. In 1970 he took over the lease of the Château Grenouilles, only to lose this to the cooperative La Chablisienne in 1974. Vinification is in tank, with their own Grenouilles raised partly in cask. I like the style here. Like Philippe Testut, the wines are gentle and relaxed, but they do not lack intensity.

★★ Gérard Tremblay
Domaine des Iles

Location: Poinchy
Owners: Tremblay family
34 ha. *Grand cru* in Vaudésir (0.60 ha); *premiers crus* in Beauroy, Côte de Léchet, Fourchaume, including a *vieilles vignes cuvée*, Montmains; Chablis Cuvée Hélène; Chablis; Petit Chablis.

Gérard Tremblay, his wife Hélène (for whom a special oaky village wine *cuvée* was created in 2001) and their son Vincent run this excellent domaine in Poinchy, which lies on the road to Auxerre. The Vaudésir is handpicked; the rest is harvested by machine. The Vaudésir and the *premiers crus*, and now the *Cuvée Hélène*, are matured partly in newish wood, but only the latter shows signs of this. Very classy, pure, elegant wines are found here.

★ Domaine Laurent Tribut
Domaine Tribut-Dauvissat

Location: Poinchy
Owners: Tribut family
5.2 ha. *Premiers crus* in Beauroy, Côte de Léchet, Montmains; Chablis.

Together with the Domaines des Iles, this is the best estate in Poinchy. Laurent Tribut and his wife, Marie-Clothilde (she is Vincent Dauvissat's sister), set up this domaine in 1987. Picking is by hand. The wines are fermented using natural yeasts and are kept in tank until the malolactic fermentations are complete. They are then racked into old wood. There is no *bâtonnage*, nor cold-stabilisation. Bottling takes place after 12 to 18 months. The domaine produces lovely mineral, clean, classy wines.

★ Maison/Domaine Olivier Tricon
Domaine de Vauroux

Location: Chablis
Owners: Tricon family
28.7 ha. *Grand cru* in Bougros (0.69 ha); *premiers crus* in Montée de Tonnerre, Montmains; Chablis.

Travelling a few kilometres south of Chablis on the route to Avallon will bring you to the isolated Domaine de Vauroux, acquired by the Tricon family in 1954. The grandson of the original owner Olivier, also named Olivier, runs the estate today. In addition to the merchant wines, Olivier Tricon has his own domaine of 6 hectares, which sells under the Domaine Olivier Tricon label. The Bougros and the Montée de Tonnerre are harvested by hand. The former is partly vinified and *élevé* in wood; otherwise, there is no oak here. These are stylish, racy wines for relatively early drinking.

Maison Verget

Location: Sologny (Mâconnais)
Owner: Jean-Marie Guffens

Jean-Marie Guffens is vociferous, rude and indiscreet, irritating rather than congenial. But he has shown with his own domaine Mâconnais wines that he not only loves his *métier* but knows how to do it. His Verget Mâconnais are very good, too. When it comes to Chablis, though, he has a vinification centre on the spot in Chitry, which he shares with Olivier Leflaive Frères. There can be some alarming inconsistencies, particularly in difficult vintages. Nearly all the wines are either *premier cru* or, a neat touch, individual village Chablis such as "Terroirs de Chablis," "Terroirs de Fleys" and "Terroirs de Poinchy." Some wines are over-oaked, though.

Claude Vilain
Domaine de la Chaude Écuelle

Location: Chemilly-sur-Serein
Owners: Vilain family
30 ha. *Premiers crus* in Montée de Tonnerre, Montmains; Chablis; Petit Chablis.

An *écuelle* is a bowl in which *vignerons* in the past reheated their midday meals. This estate of the "hot bowl" is located in a sleepy village south of Chablis, enclosed by sugar beets and maize rather than vines. No wood is used. The estate produces minerally, quite full wines, with no lack of depth.

Domaine du Chateau de Viviers

Location: Viviers
Owners: Albert Bichot et Cie
17 ha. *Grand cru* in Blanchot (0.50 ha); *premiers crus* in Vaillons, Vaucoupin; Chablis.

This is a separate concern from that of Long-Depaquit, but run by the same team. The wines are vinified in stainless steel, after which the wine is transferred to Beaune for its maturation. There is no oak. Just as with the Long-Depaquit wines, quality here is improving.

Domaine Yvon Vocoret

Location: Maligny
Owners: Vocoret family
10 ha. *Premier cru* in Fourchaume; Chablis Vieilles Vignes; Chablis.

The Maligny-based Vocorets (the *c* is hard), Yvon and his father Maurice, are only distantly related to the Vocorets of Chablis (see below). Traditional winemaking is practiced here, with deliberately reduced harvests. No oak is used. These are quite substantial wines, and of good quality.

★ Domaine Vocoret et Fils

Location: Chablis
Owners: Vocoret family
47 ha. *Grands crus* in Blanchot (1.77 ha), Les Clos (1.62 ha), Valmur (0.29 ha), Vaudésir (0.11 ha); *premiers crus* in Côte de Léchet, La Forêt, Mont de Milieu, Montée de Tonnerre, Montmains, Vaillons; Chablis Vieilles Vignes; Chablis; Petit Chablis.

This Vocoret domaine lies on the main road next to the Hotel Ibis on the Auxerre side of Chablis, brilliantly situated to attract the maximum number of tourists. One should not fall into the trap of thinking that the quality of the wines is no more than acceptable, however. This is indeed a classy estate. It was founded in 1870 and built up by Robert Vocoret in the 1930s, and it is now run by his grandson Patrice

(in the cellar) and great-grandson Jérôme (in the vineyards). The bulk of the *grands crus* are hand harvested. Vinification and malolactic fermentation take place in vat, but the wine is then matured in wooden *foudres* until the following summer. So far, so good. But today there is also, or alternatively, a *passage en fût*, newish *demi-muids*, for the top wines. They are oakier than they used to be. This I regret.

OTHER WINES OF THE YONNE

After Chablis, the other wines of the Yonne can be divided into three groups: two separate village appellations, Irancy and Saint-Bris (although the latter only for its Sauvignon), and the generic wines. Some of these can be labelled with the name of the village after the word *Bourgogne* (e.g., Bourgogne-Coulanges-La-Vineuse). Others, where appropriate, can be labelled with the phrase *Côtes d'Auxerre*. Most of the wine does indeed come from the land south of Auxerre, but there are isolated pockets at Vézelay, Joigny, Épineuil near Tonnerre, and even Chatillon-sur-Seine. None of these areas is very large. The grand total of all of this comprises some 1,600 hectares producing 100,000 hectolitres of wine, one third of it red and *rosé*, two thirds of it white. These figures are dwarfed by Chablis: 4,670 hectares producing 284,000 hectolitres.

Outside Chablis, then, the grape is scarce. The climate is not propitious. We are rapidly approaching the point at which the vine will not ripen sufficiently to produce palatable wine. There is competition from cereals and pasture, and it is only in the most favourable pockets that the vine can thrive. Nevertheless, this is an expanding and thriving part of viticultural France. Land prices are not excessive, and the market for well-made wine of character is constantly growing.

As well as the Pinot Noir, the Chardonnay and the Aligoté, a number of rustic grape varieties, long since dispensed with elsewhere, continue to survive. To add to the Pinot Noir there is the César, which will beef up the colour and the alcohol. Officially, there is also the Tressot, although this is hardly seen today. Two white grape varieties, the Sacy (the Tresallier in Saint-Pourçain) and the Melon (Muscadet), are permitted for the Crémant, as is the Gamay for the *rosé*. And then there is the Sauvignon (see Saint-Bris, below).

IRANCY

Irancy lies 10 kilometres southeast of Auxerre and is visually one of France's vineyard gems. Above the village, a natural amphitheatre faces due south and captures all the sun that is available. The slopes are full of vines and cherry trees, with a little road winding down from the forest above. In the spring, when the wildflowers are out, the place is enchanting. You can also eat very well on the side of the river Yonne in the village of Vincelottes, below that of Irancy, at the Auberge des Tilleuils.

⇥ Irancy ⇤	
Surface Area (2005)	160 ha
Production (2005)	8,552 hl
Colour	Red
Maximum Yield	55 hl/ha
Minimum Alcohol	10.0°
Grape Varieties	Pinot Noir, César
Optimum Drinking	2 to 5 Years after the Vintage

The wine is red and is clearly the best of those in the Auxerrois—it is the only one which is more than a sort of half *rosé*. Drink it when it is between 2 and 5 years old. The hot year of 2003 produced some splendid Irancys.

SAINT-BRIS

This is a curious appellation. Until 1995 it was Burgundy's sole Vin Délimité de Qualité Superieure (VDQS), relegated to the second rank because the grape variety used was considered not properly Burgundian—except that we are only 80 miles west of Pouilly-sur-Loire, and the Nièvre *département*, in which Pouilly lies, has historically always been part of greater Burgundy. Nevertheless, here we

⇥ Saint-Bris ⇤	
Surface Area (2005)	103 ha
Production (2005)	6,953 hl
Colour	White
Maximum Yield	60 hl/ha
Minimum Alcohol	9.5°
Grape Varieties	Sauvignon Blanc
Optimum Drinking	Within 1.5 Years after the Vintage

have a wine from a variety not permitted elsewhere. It has had some difficulty competing with the improved quality of the local Chardonnays in past years, and the fact that Sauvignon is not allowed in the local Crémant has tended to discourage growers from planting it. Promotion to *appellation contrôlée* has given it a shot in the arm, though, and the surface area is increasing.

Saint-Bris lies on the road from Auxerre to Irancy and is really quite substantial. It is also a pretty town. We are in the centre of the Côtes d'Auxerre here, and most of the local growers make Bourgogne, in its various colours, as well as the local Sauvignon. This can be an attractive wine, but it has more in common with a generic Touraine than with a Sancerre.

BOURGOGNE

Chitry lies on the Chablis side of Saint-Bris and Irancy, and Coulanges-la-Vineuse on the other, some 8 kilometres due south of Auxerre, together with Saint-Bris-le-Vineux (to give it its full name) and eight other communes not grand enough to be allowed to use their names on the label. This comprises the Côte d'Auxerre. This is the home of increasing stylish light Chardonnays and almost *vin de l'année* Pinots, best drunk cool and soon.

Coulanges-la-Vineuse has made a speciality of its reds, and it obviously has ambitions to join Irancy as an appellation in its own right. At Chitry we are on the borders of *appellation contrôlée* Chablis, and the bias is toward Chardonnay.

Épineuil is a suburb of Tonnerre and offers a small amount of Pinot Noir from the south-facing slopes above the river Armançon. This, too, is a light wine for early drinking. It, too, can have elegance.

Tonnerre was granted an appellation in its own right in 2006, for white wines only. Not surprisingly, these wines resemble a minor Chablis and are best for early drinking.

The vineyards at Côte Saint-Jacques, above Joigny to the north, and Vézelay to the south, are recent and minuscule, the product of a few brave souls—pioneering spirits who would have us remember what an important *vignoble* the Yonne was in pre-*phylloxera* days. Not surprisingly the two local multi-starred Michelin chefs, Marc Meneau of L'Espérance at Saint-Père near Vézelay and Michel Lorain of, appropriately, La Côte Saint-Jacques at Joigny, are at the forefront of this revival.

YONNE LEADING DOMAINES

S.I.C.A. du Vignoble Auxerrois
Caves Bailly-Lapierre
Location: Bailly
Members: 80
500 ha. Crémant de Bourgogne; Bourgogne Aligoté; Irancy; Saint-Bris.

Founded in 1971, the local produce having previously been sent to Germany as a base wine for *sekt*, this domaine is the producer of the best Crémant de Bourgogne. The up-to-date premises, with cellars cut out of an old limestone quarry into which you can drive your car at least part-way, are worth a visit. The flagship Crémant is labelled *Bailly-Lapierre*—hence the recent change of name from Cave de Bailly.

Domaine Anita and Jean-Pierre Colinot
Location: Irancy
Owners: Anita and Jean-Pierre Colinot
10 ha. Irancy, including "Côte du Moutier," "Les Mazelots," "Palotte."

This is the source of the best Irancy, produced from 95 percent Pinot Noir and 5 percent César, with the *cuvées* from the best parcels being vinified and bottled separately. The fullest Irancy is the Côte du Moutier. The *cuvée* labelled *Palette* is supple and aromatic. Beware of Les Mazelots. This is pure César—not to my taste. The Colinots are charming, irrepressible and passionate about their wine, which does not see wood. Their 2003s are superb. A visit here is a delight.

Domaine Ghislaine and Jean-Hugues Goisot
Location: Saint-Bris-le-Vineux
Owners: Ghislaine and Jean-Hugues Goisot
27 ha. Bourgogne Côtes d'Auxerre; Bourgogne Aligoté; Saint-Bris; Irancy.

This is a splendid source of neatly made, elegant generic wine. The Goisots live in the village of Saint-Bris, but this represents only a third of their production. The best is labelled *Gourmand Fyé Gris*. The top Côtes d'Auxerres, both red and white, are hand harvested, vinified in wood and bottled under the name *Corps de Garde*. On top of this, there is the white "Biaumont" and the red "Gondonne," a superb selection. After a couple of years in bottle, these are admirable wines.

The Côte d'Or

THE CÔTE DE NUITS

Les Porrets or Poirets or Porrets-Saint-Georges
Les Perrières
Les Poulettes
Les Chaboeufs
Les Vallerots
Chaînes Carteaux
Les Saint-Georges
Les Cailles
Les Vaucrains
Les Didiers
Les Forêts or Clos des Forêts-Saint-Georges
Aux Corvées or Clos des Corvées
Aux Corvées (Clos Saint-Marc)
Les Corvées-Pagets
Aux Perdrix
Les Argillières
Clos des Argillières
Les Grandes-Vignes or
   Clos-des-Grandes-Vignes
Clos de l'Arlot
Clos de la Maréchale
Les Terres Blanches

The Growers and the Négociants
Nuits-Saints-Georges

Jean Chauvenet
Hubert Chauvenet-Chopin
Chevillon-Chezeaux
Robert Chevillon
Georges Chicotot
Dufouleur Père et Fils
Joseph Faiveley
Philippe Gavignet
Henri Gouges
Hospices de Nuits-Saint-Georges
Dominique Laurent
Fernand Lecheneaut et Fils
François Legros
Thibault Liger-Belair
Bertrand Machard de Gramont
Alain Michelot
Jean-Marc Millot
Maison Nicolas Potel
Domaine Nicolas Potel
Prieuré-Roch
Gilles Remoriquet
Charles Thomas

Prémeaux

Bertrand Ambroise
Domaine de l'Arlot
Jérôme Chézeaux
Jean-Jacques Confuron
R. Dubois et Fils
Chantal Lescure
Machard de Gramont
Perdrix
Château de Prémeaux
Protot
Daniel Rion et Fils
Michèle and Patrice Rion
Jean-Pierre Tréchutet
La Vougeraie

COMBLANCHIEN AND CORGOLOIN / 165
The Southern Côte-de-Nuits-Villages
The Growers

D'Ardhuy, Clos des Langres, Corgoloin
Chopin et Fils, Comblanchien
Anne-Marie Gille, Comblanchien
Damien and Liselotte Gachot-Monot,
   Gorgoloin
Gilles Jourdan, Corgoloin
Jean Petitot et Fils, Corgoloin
La Poulette, Corgoloin
Pierre Thibert, Corgoloin

HAUTES-CÔTES-DE-NUITS AND
   HAUTES-CÔTES-DE-BEAUNE / 167
The Growers

Cave des Hautes-Côtes, Beaune
François Charles et Fils, Nantoux
David Duband, Chevannes
François Feuillet
Féry, Echevronne
Henri Gros, Chamboeuf
Lucien Jacob, Echevronne
Gilles Jayer, Magny-lès-Villers
Olivier Jouan, Arcenant
Mazilly Père et Fils, Meloisey
Jean-Pierre Mugneret, Concoeur
Henri Naudin-Ferrand, Magny-lès-Villers
Agnès and Sébastien Pacquet, Meloisey
Parigot Père et Fils, Meloisey
Thierry Vigot, Messanges

The term Côte Dijonnaise applies to such vineyards as exist north of Marsannay in what are now the Dijon suburbs. There have never been a great number of vines here, and of course there are now even fewer, as the city has expanded. But stubbornly, a few still exist.

Anthony Hanson (*Burgundy*, 1995) has uncovered a grower called Jean Dubuis, at the Domaine de la Cras in Plombières-lès-Dijon, which is north of the river Ouche. A couple of kilometres further on, in Daix, the Mortet family of Gevrey owns land, and both the late Denis's estate and his brother Thierry cultivate a couple of hectares.

Further south, in Larrey, there is a vineyard called Montre-Cul, exploited by Régis Bouvier of Marsannay, and nearby, at Fontaine d'Ouche, another called Les Marcs d'Or, which is *en métayage* to the Derey family of Couchey.

It is the area round Daix, Hauteville-lès-Dijon and Ahuy, according to the late Denis Mortet, which is the most interesting. The aspect is right, the geology promising, and there is no reason why one shouldn't produce neat, correct examples of Bourgogne, Pinot Noir or Chardonnay which would have more finesse than the generics from the plain on the east side of the Nuits-Dijon highway. But the locals are not interested, unfortunately. The late Denis Mortet's estate and his brother seem to be the only ones prepared to bother. It is a sad state of affairs, an opportunity being missed.

MARSANNAY

In 1987, the wines of Marsannay, hitherto simple Bourgogne, but able to be specially differentiated as Bourgogne de Marsannay or Bourgogne de Marsannay-La-Côte, were elevated to village *appellation contrôlée* (AC).

This is the closest appellation to the city of Dijon; indeed, Marsannay and its neighbours Chenôve and Couchey, over which the vineyard overflows, are more or less suburbs of the city itself. For some years, since "invented" in

Marsannay

	SURFACE AREA (ha)	PRODUCTION (hl)
Rouge	27	6,061
Rosé	34	1,914
Blanc	31	1,434
Total	192	9,409

the 1920s by the Domaine Clair-Daü, then one of the leading local estates, the area has been famous for its *rosé*, and good Pinot Noir *rosé* can be a delicious drink, perhaps the best *rosé* of all; but strangely, since the elevation to village level, the production of *rosé* has declined.

This, at least, is what the locals say. In fact, as *rosé* statistics are usually incorporated into the figure for *rouge*, any trend is difficult to substantiate. Today the Union Générale des Syndicats, though not the BIVB (Bureau Interprofessionnel des Vins de Bourgogne), *does* publish separate figures. Since 1993 the total area under vines has grown from 174 hectares to 192, but the amount yielding *rosé* (where the *rendement de base* is 56 hl/ha, as opposed to 45 for red wine and 50 for white) has declined from 58 hectares to 31.

The *blanc* figure represents 52 percent of the total Côte de Nuits production.

The Vineyard

While there are no first growths, let alone *grands crus*, in Marsannay, there are a number of officially recognised *lieux-dits*. The important ones are as follows: Le Boivin, Les Champs-Perdrix, Les Champs-Salomon, Le Clos de Jeu, Clos-du-Roy, Les Echézeaux, Les Etalles, Les Favières, Les Finottes, Les Genelières, Les Grandes Vignes, Les Grasses-Têtes, Les Longeroies, Dessus des Longeroies, En La Montagne, En Montchevenoy, Les Récilles, Saint-Jacques, Les Vaudenelles, Les Vignes-Maries.

These occupy the land above (i.e., westward of) the Route des Grands Crus, which runs along the middle of the village. Below this road the vines can produce Marsannay *rosé*, but if the wine is red or white, it can only be called Bourgogne.

According to Olivier Guyot, 80 percent of Marsannay is harvested by machine. He, of course, is one of the exceptions; so are Bruno Clair and Sylvain Pataille.

The geology of the Marsannay slopes is complex. Essentially, it is good Bathonian or Bajocian limestone, but there are parts where this is replaced by loess or an argilo-siliceous silt, parts which are very clayey indeed, parts with an abundance of stone and gravel, parts where the soil resembles a black grit. Some of these are more propitious for the vine than others.

Of equal importance is the shelter afforded by the Côte itself. Above Marsannay an important valley winds up into the hills. The soil is very clayey here, and the vines very exposed, leading to an abruptly cooler microclimate. This land will never make good wine, and it ought to be declassified. Yet on some of the lower, more sheltered land on the wrong side of the village, there are some gravel soils which could and do in fact make a very nice little wine.

The Wine

When the elevation to full village status occurred, leaving the northern part of Brochon as Côte-de-Nuits-Villages, an appellation which can also be applied to the wines of Fixin if the growers so wish, I remember wondering why it hadn't been decided merely to raise the status of Marsannay to this halfway house. Why full village status, which seems to be a higher level?

I cannot speak for the authority's reasoning, but now that I know the wines better, I can view this separate village status as quite logical. The wines are, in fact, different.

The Brochon-Fixin red wines are bigger, and quite sturdy, with that robustness the French call *sauvage*. Marsannay reds are, or should be, rather lighter, though they gain in strength as one travels from north to south. It is a mistake to give them too much backbone and muscle. There should only be medium body—there should not be an excess of oak either—and the fruit, with as much red fruit flavour as black, should be allowed to sing out. Marsannay is not serious Burgundy: it is the Côte de Nuits's version of a Chorey-lès-Beaune or a good Bouzeron. But that is no reason for it not to be a very agreeable, stylish, fruity wine for reasonably early drinking.

While there is this big difference between Marsannay and Fixin *rouge*, there is less of a difference between the white wines, and indeed the resemblance continues into the white wines of Morey-Saint-Denis. When they are well made, such as in the cellar of Bruno Clair, where you can taste them side by side, all three—though the Marsannay is the lightest—have a crisp, fruity leanness (but lean in the best sense, which recalls a combination of apple, melon, greengage and peach). This is a long way from the honeyed butteriness of Meursault. They are best quite young, while still fresh. Incidentally, vintage years follow the quality of the local reds, which is logical, rather than the relative success of the white wine communes of the Côte de Beaune.

And so to the *rosé*. The *rosé* sells for less than the red and the white, which is good from the consumer's point of view, for I'm sure in the best cellars the *rendement* is not excessively higher. It can be commercial, confected and a bit sweet, if you find the wrong source; but it can be poised, racy and delightfully fruity and elegant if you stick to the best, such as those from Huguenot Père et Fils, Régis Bouvier and the aforementioned Bruno Clair. *Rosé* suffers from not being considered serious. But why do we have to be "serious" all the time? And surely it is no more or less serious than the red and the white. It deserves to be more popular. I would suggest that there are all manner of occasions and dishes, especially during the summer, when a Marsannay *rosé* would be just as appropriate as anything else—and twice as delicious.

The Growers of Chenôve, Marsannay and Couchey

All growers are in Marsannay unless otherwise stated.

Bart

20 ha owned and *en fermage*. Bonnes-Mares
(1.03 ha); Chambertin, Clos de Bèze (0.41 ha);
Fixin *premier cru* Les Hervelets; village Chambolle-
Musigny; village Santenay *rouge et blanc*; village
Marsannay *rouge*, including the *lieux-dits* Les
Echézeaux, Les Grandes Vignes and Les Longeroies,
blanc et rosé; Côte-de-Nuits-Villages.

Martin Bart's grandfather was a Clair of Clair-
Daü, and it is from the dismemberment of this
domaine in the early 1980s that much of the
estate derives: the Clos de Bèze, for instance, and
the Bonnes-Mares, whose vines were planted in
1935. Bart works the estate with his sister. Since
1998 the must has been cold-macerated for up
to a week and a new set of vats introduced, proportional to the size of the vineyard parcels.

    The wines are made in a large ugly *cuvier*
constructed in 1987. There is total de-stemming
and an average of 25 percent new oak. The
results are full and rich, with good intensity.
More and more is now bottled under the growers' own label.

Régis Bouvier

18 ha owned and *en fermage*. Marsannay *rouge*, *blanc
et rosé*, including the *lieux-dits* Clos-du-Roy and Les
Longeroies (both additionally available in *vieilles
vignes cuvées*); village Morey-Saint-Denis, including
the *lieu-dit* En La Rue de Vergy; village Gevrey-
Chambertin; village Fixin; Côte de Nuits Villages;
Bourgogne Montre-Cul (from Dijon).

Régis Bouvier struck out on his own—there is
a separate Domaine René et Bernard Bouvier
run by his father and brother—in 1981. He had
3 hectares then, which he has since extended,
particularly in Marsannay. This is a neat, efficient setup, with epoxy-resin-lined cement vats
and automatic *pigeage* in a cellar constructed
in 1987. The wines are good. The Marsannay
vieilles vignes cuvées are recent. A third of the production is sold off in bulk.

Marc Brocot

8.5 ha owned and *en fermage*. Village Gevrey-
Chambertin; Marsannay *rouge* in the *lieux-dits*
Les Echézeaux and Les Etalles; Marsannay *blanc*.

Marc Brocot is a large, dark-haired man in his
late forties, whose cave can be found on a road
going up to the hills, and who, up to 1988, sold
nearly everything he produced in bulk. Since
then, however, he's been keeping back more and
more for selling in bottle. The grapes are totally
de-stemmed, matured using one third new oak
and bottled just before the subsequent vintage.
These are attractively plump fruity wines for the
medium term.

★★ Bruno Clair

21.25 ha owned and *en fermage*. Chambertin,
Clos de Bèze (0.98 ha); Bonnes-Mares (0.41 ha);
Corton-Charlemagne (0.34 ha); Gevrey-Chambertin
premier cru in Clos du Fonteny (*monopole*),
Clos Saint-Jacques, Les Cazetiers and
Petite Chapelle; Savigny-lès-Beaune *premier cru*
La Dominode; village Morey-Saint-Denis *rouge*
in the *lieu-dit* En La Rue de Vergy; village Morey-
Saint-Denis *blanc*; village Chambolle-Musigny
in the *lieu-dit* Les Véroilles; village Vosne-Romanée
in the *lieu-dit* Les Champs-Perdrix; village Aloxe-
Corton; Pernand-Vergelesses *blanc*; Marsannay,
including the *lieux-dits* Les Grasses-Têtes, Les
Longeroies and Les Vaudenelles (all *rouge*);
Marsannay *blanc et rosé*.

This is the most important property in the village. Its origins, like those of the Domaine Bart
(see previous entry), lie in the old Clair-Daü
estate, broken up in the early 1980s. Bruno Clair
has expanded since, notably by rescuing land
above Clos-de-Tart and Bonnes-Mares. Some of
the vines in Savigny-lès-Beaune, La Dominode,
date from 1902.

    Clair is a meticulous winemaker, anxious
above all for purity and elegance. These are
not for those who like their Burgundies sweet,
syrupy and fat. He works alongside his oenologist Philippe Brun out of a splendidly cavernous cellar behind his house. The quality here,
from perfectly respectable beginnings in 1986,
has improved enormously (though I have never
been impressed with his 1997s). Since 2005
Bruno Clair has exploited all his Clos de Bèze
and Clos Saint-Jacques. Hitherto, Maison Jadot
had a lease on 50 percent of the fruit of these

two parcels. This is now one of the top domaines in Burgundy.

De Coillot

11 ha owned and *en fermage*. Marsannay *rouge* (including the *lieux-dits* Le Boivin, Les Grasses-Têtes and Les Longeroies) *et blanc*; village Gevrey-Chambertin *vieilles vignes*.

Much progress has been made here since the lean Christophe Coillot, in his late thirties, took over from his father Bernard in 1996. The harvest has been reduced to 40 hectolitres per hectare and the amount of new oak increased to 70 percent.

From the Grasses Têtes, Coillot produces a red for early drinking. The Longeroies is for maturing in bottle for 2 years. This is very good, as is the Gevrey-Chambertin.

Collotte

11 ha owned and *en fermage*. Marsannay *rouge* (including the *lieux-dits* Le Boivin, Champ Salomon and Le Clos de Jeu) *et blanc*; village Fixin.

Philippe Collotte, lean and in his mid-thirties, has been in charge of this family domaine since 1990, when it was enlarged to its present size. The fruit is totally de-stemmed, and the wine matured in one quarter new oak. There are very good wines here.

Derey Frères
Domaine de la Croix-Saint-Germain, Couchey

20 ha owned and *en fermage/en métayage*. Marsannay, *rouge*, *blanc et rosé*, including the *lieux-dits* Les Vignes Marie and Les Champs-Perdrix; Fixin *premier cru* Les Hervelets; village Fixin; village Gevrey-Chambertin; Côte-de-Nuits-village.

The Derey domaine has been passed down from father to son since 1650 and is currently, despite the current title, run by Philippe on his own, who has taken over from his father Albert and his uncle Hervé. One third new wood here is used here, and bottling occurs after a year, to release the casks for the next vintage. A curiosity in the portfolio is the Clos des Marcs d'Or, half a hectare of Chardonnay in Fontaine d'Ouche belonging to the City of Dijon, which the Dereys farm on a *métayage* basis. Since Philippe took over in 1998, there has been more new oak, more extended cold soaking and the introduction of a green harvest. Quality has improved.

Fougeray de Beauclair

21.68 ha owned and *en fermage*. Bonnes-Mares (1.20 ha); village Savigny-les-Beaune *rouge et blanc* in the *lieu-dit* Les Gollardes; village Vosne-Romanée in the *lieu-dit* Les Damodes; village Chambolle-Musigny in the *lieu-dit* Les Véroilles; village Gevrey-Chambertin in the *lieu-dit* Les Sauvrées; village Fixin, including the "Clos Marion"; Marsannay, *rouge, rosé et blanc*, including the *lieux-dits* Dessus des Longeroies, Les Favières, Les Grasses-Têtes and Les Saint-Jacques; Côtes-de-Nuits-Villages.

There have been improvements here in the last few years: a new cellar, the arrival of son-in-law Patrice Ollivier 10 years ago, more diligent *triage* and the installation of a pneumatic press in 2000. The domaine came into existence in 1986 when the late Bernard Clair, father of Bruno, leased to Jean-Louis Fougeray his Bonnes-Mares. This parcel is the majority—Bruno Clair now looks after the rest—of that part of the *grand cru* which lies in Morey-Saint-Denis. One third of the produce is sold to Maison Jadot as fruit. Since 1994 they have taken on the lease of the Domaine Marion's Fixin.

Jean Fournier

16 ha owned and *en fermage*. Marsannay *rouge, blanc et rosé*, including the *lieux-dits* Clos-du-Roy, Les Echézeaux, Les Longeroies and a *vieilles vignes cuvée*; village Gevrey-Chambertin.

No immediate relation to other Fourniers (there are two Fournier domaines in neighbouring Couchey), Laurent Fournier, who took over from his father Jean in 2001, ages his wines for eight months in barrels and then a further twelve in *foudre* before bottling. The wines are clean, not rustic, but could do with an extra zip of personality. Since Laurent has been in charge, he has introduced green harvesting, is slowly changing over the vineyards to *Cordon du Royat*, is cold soaking the must and has increased the amount of new wood. I expect to see more interesting wines in the future.

Alain Guyard

9 ha owned. Village Vosne-Romanée in the *lieu-dit* Aux Réas; village Gevrey-Chambertin; village Fixin; Côte-de-Nuits-Villages; Marsannay *rouge* (including the *lieu-dit* Les Genelières), *rosé et blanc*.

Alain Guyard has now taken over from his father Lucien at this friendly domaine next to the one-star restaurant Les Gourmets. There are no startling *climats* here, but the wines are competently made. "I find I become more and more anti–new wood," says Guyard *père*. "If the wine is good, it needs no more than a touch." A touch here is one fifth. The Vosne-Romanée is matured in oak from the Tronçais, the Gevrey in Chatillon.

★ Olivier Guyot

14 ha owned and *en fermage*. Gevrey-Chambertin *premier cru* Les Champeaux; village Gevrey-Chambertin in the *lieu-dit* En Champs; Marsannay *rouge* (including the *lieu-dit* La Montagne), *blanc et rosé*.

Olivier Guyot is in his late thirties and has built up his domaine since he took over from his parents in 1989. His wines are much loved by the French media and are in all the top restaurants. The vineyards are ploughed by a sturdy horse called Indigo, the fruit 60 percent de-stemmed, the wine reared in 100 percent new oak. It is a very good address.

Huguenot Père et Fils

25 ha owned and *en fermage*. Charmes-Chambertin (0.28 ha); Gevrey-Chambertin *premier cru* Les Fontenys; village Gevrey-Chambertin; village Fixin, including the *lieu-dit* Les Petits-Crais; Marsannay *rouge, blanc et rosé*, including the *lieux-dits* La Montagne, Les Echézeaux, Les Champs-Perdrix, Clos-du-Roy, Champ Salomon; Côte-de-Nuits-Villages.

The big, bearded Jean-Louis Huguenot and his son Philippe run one of the best domaines in the village, vinifying in epoxy-resin-lined concrete vats and stainless steel in a modern cellar, retaining 10 percent of the stems and using 15 percent new oak. Good clean-cut Marsannays are produced here. The Champs-Perdrix, adjoining the vineyards of Fixin, is the best of the Marsannays, rich, full and plummy. The Echézeaux is less fat and rich, but is a stylish example for medium-term drinking.

Château de Marsannay

45 ha owned. Clos Vougeot (21.00 ha); Ruchottes-Chambertin (0.10 ha); Vosne-Romanée *premier cru* En Orveaux; Gevrey-Chambertin *premier cru*; village Fixin; Marsannay *rouge* in the *lieu-dit* Les Echézeaux; Marsannay *rouge, rosé et blanc*.

This pretentious tourist trap was bought by Patriarche in 1990 when they acquired Charles Quillardet in order to become a sort of red counterpoint to the Château de Meursault. I am sure it is very successful. Sadly, the wines, sold under such fancy names as Cuvée Anne de Sault, Cuvée Charles le Téméraire and Cuvée Pierre de Baufremont, are very commercial. The reds are soulless, the *rosés* flat and suspiciously sweet.

★ Sylvain Pataille

12 ha owned. Marsannay *rouge* (including the *lieux-dits* La Montagne and Clos du Roy and a *cuvée* L'Ancestrale), *blanc et rosé*.

Sylvain Pataille is one of Burgundy's young tigers, already a superstar. His Ancestrale *cuvée* is not cheap, but it is an amazingly good wine. Pataille, having been a consultant oenologist, started off with 1 hectare of vines in 1999. His viticultural philosophy is to keep things as natural as possible. As to vinification, his approach to matters such as new wood and the percentage of the stems is totally flexible. The wines are made in a new cellar in Chenôve, above which he will reside once the renovations are finished.

Domaine du Vieux Collège

17 ha owned and *en fermage*. Gevrey-Chambertin *premier cru* Les Champeaux; Fixin *premier cru* Les Hervelets; village Fixin *rouge et blanc*; Marsannay *rouge* (including the *lieux-dits* Les Favières and Les Longeroies), *blanc et rosé*.

Éric Guyard, bearded and in his late thirties, took over from his father Jean-Pierre in 2002.

They do not seem to be any close relation to the other Guyard family in Marsannay.

The fruit is entirely de-stemmed, the must cold-soaked and the wine reared in one third new wood. The wine is bottled by a visiting contract bottler. Both the Marsannays and the Fixins can be a little *sauvage*, but the Gevrey is good.

CÔTE-DE-NUITS-VILLAGES

This is a useful local appellation encompassing peripheral minor villages of the Côte. Though not as well known as its equivalent, Côte-de-Beaune-Villages, Côte-de-Nuits-Villages provides an inexpensive introduction to the great wines of the Côte and is often as good as a lesser grower's village wine at half the price.

The villages entitled to the appellation Côte-de-Nuits-Villages are Fixin (which can also sell off wine as Fixin) and Brochon, which are both to the north; at the southern end of the Côte are Prissey, Comblanchien and Corgoloin.

According to Sylvain Pitiot and Pierre Poupon (*Atlas des Grands Vignobles de Bourgogne*) there are 310 hectares of land entitled to this appellation (this includes all of Fixin's Village AC). In 2005 the declaration, from 158 hectares under Pinot Noir and 7 hectares under white grapes, was 7,230 hectolitres of red wine and 355 of white wine.

Depending on where it comes from—for in practice there is little blending of the wines of the northern sector with those of the south—the wine can be either a lesser sort of Nuits-Saint-Georges or a Fixin look-alike. In general it will have medium to full body (more than a Marsannay or a Hautes-Côtes) and be robust, fruity and a little four-square. I find the wines of Fixin and Brochon origin more interesting—more elegant—than those of the south.

There is a little white, as noted previously, production of which has doubled in the last decade. I have rarely tasted it. Jadot produces a neat example.

RECOMMENDED SOURCES
Bertrand Ambroise; Domaine de l'Arlot; Denis Bachelet; Vincent and Denis Berthaut;

Caveau Saint-Vincent (Michel Defrance); Hubert Chauvenet-Chopin; Jean-Jacques Confuron; David Duband; Sylvie Esmonin; Gachot-Monnot; Jérôme Galeyrand; Louis Jadot; Jayer-Gilles; Gilles Jourdan; Henri Naudin-Ferrand; Jean Petitot et Fils; Daniel Rion; Philippe Rossignol; Jean-Pierre Tréchutet.

FIXIN

Fixin, pronounced "Fissin," is the next commune south on the Côte d'Or. It is in fact an amalgamation of two communes: Fixey and Fixin. The two villages, now part of the same sprawl, were originally a few hundred metres apart, with Fixey lying further up the slope and to the north.

Fixin's best-known estate, the Clos de la Perrière, lies underneath the trees above the village on the southern side. As its name suggests, it was once the site of a quarry. The Dukes of Burgundy used the *manoir* as a hunting lodge, but donated it in 1142 to the monks of Cîteaux, who used it as a convalescent home.

Two of the main vineyards of the village—Le Chapitre and Les Arvelets—came under the jurisdiction of another ecclesiastical establishment, Saint-Mammès-de-Langres, associated with the Abbey of Bèze.

The village also had Napoleonic connections. Some 160 years ago, Claude Noisot, a local aristocrat who had fought alongside the emperor in many a battle and who had even accompanied him in exile to Elba, arrived back in the village. He proceeded to re-christen one of his vineyards Clos Napoléon (prior to that it had been called Aux Cleusots or Les Echézeaux), to install a small museum of memorabilia and to commission a statue from the Dijon sculptor Rudé for the local village square. All this did much to help the esteem of the local wine.

Location

The appellation is roughly square, with the *premiers crus* (there are no *grands crus*) huddled together upslope at the southern end. The decree for village *appellation contrôlée* extends halfway down between the Route des Grands Crus and the main road, while in Gevrey-Chambertin, a kilometre or so to the south, village land extends across the Dijon-Nuits highway and beyond.

The soil structure is based on a hard Bajocian limestone, capable of taking a fine marble polish, and is a mixture of marl and limestone debris. It is stonier as one mounts the slope, and steeper to the south (Clos de la Perrière; Clos du Chapitre) than to the north (in Les Hervelets and Les Arvelets). Only in the Clos du Chapitre itself is the brown-coloured limestone of Bathonian origin found; here the soil is the stoniest of all. Overall, there is rather more clay than further south, which accounts for the burliness of the wines.

The Vineyard

PREMIERS CRUS There are eight, in whole or in part: Les Arvelets; Clos de la Perrière (*monopole*); Clos du Chapitre (*monopole*); Clos Napoléon (*monopole*); Les Hervelets; Les Meix-Bas; Queue de Hareng (which lies adjacent to the Clos-de-la-Perrière but is in the neighbouring commune of Brochon); and En Suchot. In practice only five of these are ever seen (see below).

The appellation Fixin *premier cru* exists for both red and white wine. Philippe Joliet, of the Clos de la Perrière—who made 23 hectolitres from half a hectare of young vines in 2003 (but nothing in 2004)—is the only producer of *premier cru* white wine that I know of. Altogether, these *premiers crus* cover 18.5 hectares (1.62 of which are in Brochon) and produce around 700 hectolitres per annum.

VILLAGE WINE Village Fixin can be sold as such or under the name Côte-de-Nuits-Villages (see page 79). This makes the precise area delimited as village wine in the commune difficult to establish. The list of *lieux-dits* enumerated in Pitiot and Poupon's *Atlas des Grands Vignobles de Bourgogne* add up to 107.35 hectares. This must be compared against the actual declaration in 2005 of 94 hectolitres (of which 3.2 hl were white) and a production figure of 4,152 hectolitres of red wine plus 155 hectolitres of white wine.

The word perennially used to describe the wines of Fixin is *sauvage*, a connotation equally applied to the wines of Brochon and, to some extent, to those vineyards in the northern part of Gevrey which lie on the same line of slope.

Sauvage wines, at their worst, can be merely lumpy and artisanal: size without grace. At their best, a richness as well as a power is indicated, and they display a hardness in youth, but an ability to age to produce something which, while always a little austere, is nevertheless of interest and depth when the wine softens up. Clos du Chapitre and Clos Napoléon have this, and so do some of the village wines, though obviously to a lesser degree of distinction. The Fixin from Les Arvelets and Les Hervelets, however, are lighter and softer: feminine, if one is still permitted to use the term.

The Premiers Crus

LES ARVELETS   (3.36 ha)
LES HERVELETS   (4.32 ha)

As it is permitted to declare the produce from the Les Meix-Bas as Les Hervelets, that is what everyone does, and Les Meix-Bas is never seen. To complicate matters further, Les Arvelets can be declared as Les Hervelets, but not, for some reason, vice versa. These two *premiers crus* are the only ones in Fixin that are not monopolies. They lie north of the three others on a slope which is more gentle and less stony. The wine is not as strong and manly here as it is in the *premiers crus* below. The volume is that of a Morey rather than a Gevrey, but in good hands there can be plenty of elegance. Dr. Lavalle was even prepared to compare the wine with that of Clos-Saint-Jacques in Gevrey-Chambertin. But that, I fear, is going a little too far.

RECOMMENDED SOURCES
Pierre Gelin (Les Hervelets); Vincent and Denis Berthaut (Les Arvelets).

CLOS-DE-LA-PERRIÈRE   (6.70 ha)

This *premier cru* incorporates En Suchot and Queue de Hareng and is the monopoly of Philippe Joliet (see below).

CLOS-DU-CHAPITRE   (4.79 ha)
CLOS NAPOLÉON   (1.83 ha)

These two *premiers crus* lie alongside each other, underneath the Clos de La Perrière. Both are monopolies. The Domaine Gelin owns the latter and farmed the former up to the 1984 vintage, on behalf of the Domaine Marion. Marion has since sold this to Guy Dufouleur (see below).

The Growers

Vincent and Denis Berthaut

13 ha *en fermage/en métayage*. Fixin *premier cru* Les Arvelets; village Fixin, including the *lieux-dits* Les Clos, Les Crais; Gevrey-Chambertin *premier cru* in Les Cazetiers and Lavaux Saint-Jacques; village Gevrey-Chambertin "Clos du Château"; Côte-de-Nuits-villages.

Vincent, bald and in his mid-fifties, and his younger, taller, bespectacled and also balding brother Denis run this domaine, much of which is rented or share-cropped. One of the Gevrey owners is the Domaine Chezaux, most of the rest of whose land is *en métayage* to the Domaine Ponsot in Morey-Saint-Denis. The Gevrey-Chambertin *premier cru* comes from Les Cazetiers and Lavaux-Saint-Jacques, but there is not a lot of it, and in short vintages it is incorporated into the village *cuvées* or blended together. Well-made, rich wines are found here, bottled as much as 2 years after the vintage, with the Arvelets showing much more sophisticated tannins than the village Fixins. The domaine is cautious about new oak, preferring the barrels to be "run in" by the Gerbet domaine in Vosne-Romanée, as Denis Berthaut is married to one of the Gerbet sisters.

Domaine du Clos Saint-Louis

11 ha owned and *en fermage*. Fixin *premier cru* Les Hervelets; Marsannay *rouge et* blanc; village Fixin; village Gevrey-Chambertin; Côte-de-Nuits-Villages.

Philippe and Martine Bernard run this domaine based in Fixey. The vineyard is green harvested, picking is by hand, and the fruit is sorted. The basic wines largely come from young vines and

are quite good. The Hervelets, however, is a serious example.

Pierre Gelin

11.45 ha owned and *en fermage*. Chambertin Clos de Bèze (0.60 ha); Gevrey-Chambertin *premier cru* Clos Prieur; Fixin *premier cru* Clos Napoléon (*monopole*) and Les Hervelets; village Fixin.

Stéphane Gelin, now aided by his son Emmanuel, presides at Fixin's best domaine. Until 1995 Stephen worked alongside his brother-in-law André Molin, but that year they went their separate ways. The Clos Napoléon, the estate's monopoly, lies behind Stéphane Gelin's house, under which is the barrel cellar. Nearby, in a deconsecrated church, is the winery.

Gelin believes in a long *cuvaison* at 30–32°C, without stalks, and uses about 20 percent new oak for his top wines. These are rich, substantial wines, the Clos Napoléon a little fatter and more masculine than the Hervelets.

Manoir de la Perrière

6.8 ha owned. Fixin, Clos de la Perrière (*monopole*) *rouge et blanc*.

Dominating the village, as it has done for nearly nine centuries, the Manoir de la Perrière dates in part from before the donation of the vineyard by Duke Eudes of Burgundy to his brother Henri, of the Abbey of Cîteaux, in 1102 or 1142, depending on the source of your information. Essentially, however, its construction can be placed between the thirteenth and fifteenth centuries. The cavernous, vaulted, earth-floored cellar contains a large and impressive medieval press.

The building and its splendidly situated vineyard have belonged to the Joliet family since 1853. There is but one *cuvée* of wine, which is a pity, given the potential economies of scale, and more often than not, it is a bit rustic. It spends its first year in *cuve*, and this is followed by 2 years in cask, of which 30 percent is new wood. It has improved since Philippe Joliet's son Benigne took over in the late 1990s. On the basis of the wines since then, I would suggest that the vineyard *could* certainly live up to its past reputation as the best in the commune and would produce a more feminine, less *sauvage* wine than the Clos du Chapitre and Clos Napoléon further down the slope.

From the 1994 vintage, there has been a little young-vine white wine: the only *premier cru* white in Fixin. Philippe Charlopin of Gevrey-Chambertin has been a consultant since the 2005 vintage.

Michel Moniot-Defrance, Caveau Saint-Vincent

3 ha owned. Village Fixin *rouge* (including the *lieux-dits* La Mazière and Les Champs-Perdrix) *et blanc*; Côte de Nuits Villages "La Croix Violette."

Ten years ago this was a small, somewhat artisanal set-up, run by the vigorous, seventy-something Gilbert Moniot. Today Gilbert's son Michel is in charge. There is good Fixin, the white being from young vines, but the star is the Côte de Nuits Villages "La Croix Violette." This is delicious. It is reared partly in wood (30 percent), partly in tank. It is individual: both ripe and with good grip.

Philippe Naddef

5 ha owned and *en fermage/en métayage*. Mazis-Chambertin (0.42 ha); Gevrey-Chambertin *premier cru* in Les Cazetiers and Les Champeaux; village Gevrey-Chambertin, including a *vieilles vignes cuvée*; village Fixin; Marsannay *rouge*.

Philippe Naddef, lean, dark, intense and perfectionistic, moved from Couchey to Fixin in 2001. He has been on his own since 1983, working mainly with the vines from his maternal grandfather.

The recipe is 100 percent de-stalking, 15–18 days maceration at temperatures up to 32°C with lots of *pigeages* and 100 percent new oak for all except the Marsannay. The results are full, rich, vibrant and long-lasting. The one thing that worries me is the intense, almost hard oakiness in the Naddef wines. This often dominates the wines in bottle. I would prefer a lighter touch.

GEVREY-CHAMBERTIN

With Gevrey we arrive at the beginning of the finest sector of the Burgundian vineyard. Gevrey-Chambertin is the largest of the great communes of the Côte de Nuits and can boast nine of the twenty-four Côte de Nuits *grands crus*. It therefore vies with Vosne—which has six—for the title of most important commune of them all: the apogee of Burgundy, the pinnacle of the Pinot Noir.

The wines are indeed—or should be—sumptuous. At the summit are Chambertin and Chambertin, Clos de Bèze: immaculate and full, firm and rich, concentrated and masculine, similar but subtly different from one another. Ruchottes and Mazis are less structured, but pure and intense. Chapelle and Griotte show a hint of red fruit, cherries or raspberries, according to taste, and the velvet changes discreetly to silk. Charmes and Mazoyères are softer and more feminine, Latricières coarser and more spicy. But all can inspire. Meanwhile, the brilliance and poise of Clos Saint-Jacques, denied *grand cru* status, forever points a finger at the errors of the *appellation contrôlée* ratings.

Gevrey is not only a large commune but also a large village, with some eighty families making a living out of wine. A great many of these now bottle their own produce and have set up in competition with larger, earlier-established domaines. As two or three of these senior exploitations are, sadly, currently underachieving, these new enterprises are not without customers. The village is today a happy hunting ground for those seeking out good wine.

Gevrey-Chambertin is a full and sturdy wine, rich and masculine, but with a touch of the fleshy and the exotic. Sensual and vigorous, it is more flamboyant than Vosne and more substantial than Chambolle. Musigny can be said to be the queen, the epitome of delicacy and finesse, but Le Chambertin is king: simply the complete Burgundy: "Tout le Grand Bourgogne possible," to quote the poet Gaston Roupnel.

History

The name Gevrey comes from Gabriacus, a name dating from Gallo-Roman times and first recorded in AD 640. About this time, the Abbey of Bèze was given land by Duke Amalgaire of

Burgundy, land which the monks planted with vines. Shortly afterward, as legend has it, a peasant named Bertin decided that he, too, would plant vines on his neighbouring plot. From the *Campus* or *Champ* Bertin comes the title of Gevrey's greatest vineyard.

In 894, the Abbey of Sainte-Benigne received land donated by another Burgundian Duke, Richard Le Justicier. This abbey soon came under the jurisdiction of the great ecclesiastical establishment at Cluny. The castle, built at the behest of the abbot, still stands. In the Middle Ages, the Abbey of Bèze sold its vineyards to the Cathedral Chapter of Saint-Mammès at Langres, who remained the nominal proprietors until the French Revolution. During the seventeenth century, the chapter leased out Clos de Bèze and other vineyards in their possession, as did other ecclesiastical establishments, such as the closer abbey at Cîteaux. Clos Saint-Jacques passed to the Morizot family. Claude Jomard, a local parliamentarian, took a 20-year lease over Clos de Bèze and, it is said, had to make some significant reparations to the state of the vineyard: it must originally have been a walled enclosure, but little of this stands today.

Meanwhile, alongside, we find an act dated 1276, signed by Guillaume de Grancey and the Abbey at Cluny, referring to vines in the Champ Bertin. At the end of the fifteenth century, there is a similar deed between the sire de Thénissey and the *chapitre* at Langres.

Chambertin, perhaps because it was leased into secular hands earlier, seems always to have had the edge in terms of reputation over Clos de Bèze. Claude Arnoux, an *émigré* Beaunois priest, published one of the first accounts of the wines of Burgundy in London in 1728. Chambertin, in Arnoux's opinion, is "the most considerable wine in all Burgundy. . . . It has all the qualities and none of the defects of the other wines." It sold for twice as much as the wines of Volnay, Pommard and Beaune, at 40 to 42 pounds sterling the *queue*. One hundred years later, André Jullien placed Chambertin second only to the Romanée-Conti of all the red wines of Burgundy. Clos de Bèze is not mentioned

at all. Perhaps the explanation is that the wine from either *climat* was sold as Chambertin, *tout court*, as is permitted today.

Much of the renown of Chambertin is due to the forceful promotion of the *négociant* Claude Jobert. Jobert arrived in Gevrey in 1731, started dealing with the successors to Claude Jomard and, by 1750, was in control of over half of Chambertin and Clos de Bèze. In all, he built up a domaine of over 500 *ouvrées* (more than 20 ha) in Gevrey-Chambertin, Morey-Saint-Denis and Chambolle-Musigny. He even succeeded in changing his name to Claude Jobert de Chambertin! By the time of his death in 1761, Chambertin was fetching 400 *livres* the *queue*—ten times the price it had commanded in the previous century.

Clos de Bèze and Chambertin were auctioned off as *biens nationaux* on January 29 and October 26, 1791, the price of Chambertin achieving 777 *livres* an *ouvrée* (Clos de Vougeot had fetched 606 *livres*), a record price. A certain Claude Antoine Gelquin soon found himself with 2 hectares of Chambertin, one of Clos de Bèze, three of Clos Saint-Jacques, Cazetiers, Charmes, Chapelle, Ruchottes, and so on. Fairly soon, the inevitable further parcellation was to begin.

Napoléon's predilection for the wines of Chambertin is well known. He is reputed to have drunk little else. It would seem that the emperor drank his Chambertin—bottled 5 or 6 years after the vintage with an embossed "N"—much diluted with water. On the retreat from Moscow, though, his cellar was stolen by Cossacks, or so his stewards alleged. The French market was soon flooded with fake Chambertin "returned from Russia," enough to have been the production of a number of vintages!

The wine of Chambertin and Clos de Bèze, not least because of this Napoleonic patronage, has a great reputation. Understandably, the neighbouring wines have sought to share its glory. If Chambertin and Clos de Bèze were undisputed first growths, went the argument, then any contiguous vineyard should be a sort of lesser first growth as well, and thus be entitled to the name. Moreover, thanks to some astute lobbying by the local mayor, by decree of Louis-Philippe in 1847, the village of Gevrey (and hence the wines too) was allowed to suffix its name with that of Chambertin. This established a trend which was soon followed by most of the other villages on the Côte.

In 1855 Dr. Lavalle (*Histoire et Statistiques de la Vigne et des Grands Vins de la Côte d'Or*) decreed one single *tête de cuvée* in Gevrey: Chambertin, by which he meant Chambertin and Chambertin and Clos de Bèze. As *premières cuvées* he listed Clos Saint-Jacques in first place, followed by "Fouchère," Chapelle (*haute*), Mazis (*haute*), Ruchottes (*du dessus*), Charmes (*haute*), Griotte (*haute*), Varoilles (*vieilles*), Estournelles and Cazetiers (*haute*). Latricières and Mazoyères were included among the *deuxièmes cuvées*.

As the nineteenth century progressed, little by little, discreetly and stealthily, a number of the *climats* surrounding Chambertin and Clos de Bèze began to tag the magic word onto their names, just as the Napoleonic decree had permitted the village itself to do. Mazis became Mazis-Chambertin; Griotte, Griotte-Chambertin; and so on. This proved useful when it came to the official codification of the concept of *grand cru* in the 1930s. At the same time, many *climats* were absorbed into superior neighbours, notably Les Gémeaux into Chapelle, and Fouchère (see above) into Chambertin itself.

The AOC laws of 1936 confirmed a number of historical practices—first, that Clos de Bèze could be prefixed with the name Chambertin, but that the six or seven other *grands crus* could only hyphenate it on as a suffix, and second, that Clos de Bèze could be sold as Chambertin *tout court*, but not vice versa. An allowance was given to the producers of Mazoyères-Chambertin, such that they could continue to call their wine Charmes-Chambertin instead. Moreover, the village appellation overlaps into the next commune to the north. Fifty hectares of Brochon can make wine which can be labelled village Gevrey-Chambertin.

Unlike nearly all the other villages of the Côte d'Or, Gevrey-Chambertin possesses a substantial amount of village AC land on the "wrong"—that is, eastern—side of the road.

Morey has a little, and Nuits-Saint-Georges, a scrap (although it includes a *premier cru*). But the only other commune with a large amount east of the N.74 is Chorey-lès-Beaune. The explanation is similar: the action of rivers rushing out of the Hautes-Côtes has pushed alluvial limestone debris and gravel—good land for the vine—further into the flatlands of the Saône.

Location

The village of Gevrey-Chambertin, south of Brochon, north of Morey-Saint-Denis, lies on the same level as its *grands crus*, at the point where the Combe de Lavaux opens out into the valley. It sprawls all the way down to the main road, and then beyond, toward the railway line; this side, which contains several *zones industrielles*, is the newest part.

At the top of the village is its château, constructed in the late thirteenth century by Yves de Chazan, Abbot of Cluny. Only two of the four original towers still remain. The cellars are impressive, as are the fortifications. Once inside, you were well and truly protected! Nearby is the church of Saint-Aignan, a bit of an architectural muddle, but externally medieval. More impressive is the restored Cellier des Dîmes, once a chapter house, and later the place where tenants of the church would come to pay their rent in kind. The ground floor and the loft above were used for storing the cereals; the cellar for wine. One local *vigneron*, the excellent Claude Dugat, rents the cellars today.

For 100 years the cobbles in the main part of Gevrey were taken up, to be replaced with tarmac, but the cobbles were replaced a decade ago, as the local authorities attempted to make the village pedestrian-friendly. As a result the poor motorist has to drive around the houses to get from A to B. The Route des Grands Crus is interrupted, and those who live on the periphery now get the noise which plagued those who were in the centre. Gevrey is nevertheless a friendly, bustling place, with several good restaurants of varying degrees of pretension and expense. Every September it hosts Le Roi Chambertin, a combination of a blind-tasting competition, similar to the Clos Vougeot *tastevinage*, a general open house and grand dinners.

The Vineyard

GRANDS CRUS There are eight or nine *grands crus*: Chambertin; Chambertin, Clos de Bèze; Chapelle-Chambertin; Charmes-Chambertin (incorporating Mazoyères-Chambertin); Griotte-Chambertin; Latricières-Chambertin; Mazis-Chambertin; and Ruchottes-Chambertin. These comprise some 87 hectares and produce an average of 2,600 hectolitres per annum. Charmes and Mazoyères together contribute over a third of this. The *grands crus* lie in one contiguous mass on the south side of the village, either above the Route des Grands Crus (Mazis, Ruchottes, Clos de Bèze, Chambertin, Latricières), or below it (Chapelle, Griotte, Charmes, Mazoyères), on the way to Morey-Saint-Denis.

PREMIERS CRUS There are twenty-six *premiers crus* in Gevrey-Chambertin, in whole or in part. Altogether, they cover some 86 hectares and produce 3,500 hectolitres a year. In alphabetical order, they are as follows: Bel Air (part); La Bossière (part); Les Cazetiers; Les Champeaux; Les Champitonnois (more commonly known as La Petite Chapelle); Champonnet; Les Cherbaudes; Clos du Chapitre; Clos Prieur (part); Clos Saint-Jacques, Clos des Varoilles; Au Closeau; La Combe au Moine; Aux Combottes; Les Corbeaux (part); Craipillot; Les Ergots; Les Estournelles (-Saint-Jacques); Le Fonteny; Les Goulots; Les Issarts; Lavaux-Saint-Jacques; Les Petits Cazetiers; La Perrière; Poissenot; La Romanée (part).

VILLAGE WINE Including the 50 hectares in the commune of Brochon, but entitled to the Gevrey-Chambertin *appellation contrôlée*, there are 369 hectares of village vineyard. The average production is 135,000 hectolitres. The appellation Gevrey-Chambertin, like that of Vosne-Romanée, but not that of Morey-Saint-Denis, applies to red wine only.

The village wines come from three distinct sections: the north, Brochon side of the village; the south, underneath the *grands crus*; and across the main Nuits-Saint-Georges to Dijon highway. The wines from the northern sector are full, rich, muscular and sometimes a bit burly; those from the south are lighter, more fragrant, more feminine; and those from the "wrong" side of the road have less definition and elegance and also tend to be on the lighter side. A judicious blend, agree most of the locals, makes the best of all possible worlds, though many growers produce village wines from single vineyards.

The Grands Crus

CHAMBERTIN

SURFACE AREA: 12.9 ha
AVERAGE PRODUCTION: 390 hl
PRINCIPAL PROPRIETORS: ★ Armand Rousseau (2.15 ha); ★ Jean and Jean-Louis Trapet (1.90 ha); ★ Rossignol-Trapet (1.60 ha); Camus (1.69 ha); Jacques Prieur (0.83 ha); ★ Madame Michèle Rolland (Héritiers Latour) (0.61 ha); ★ Leroy (0.50 ha); ★ Pierre Damoy (0.48 ha); Rebourseau (0.46 ha); Jean-Claude Belland (0.41 ha): Gabriel Tortochot (0.31 ha); Louis Remy (0.32 ha); ★ Dujac (0.30 ha); ★ Philippe Charlopin (Madame Baron) (0.21 ha); ★ Bertagna (0.20 ha); ★ Joseph Drouhin (0.20 ha); ★ Ponsot/De Chézeaux (0.20 ha); ★ Clos Frantin (Bichot) (0.17 ha); ★ Bouchard Père et Fils (0.15 ha); ★ Denis Mortet (Mme Quillardet) (0.15 ha).
[N.B. some of these figures include land in Clos de Bèze.]

There are some fifty-five separate parcels of land in the Chambertin *cadastre*, some as little as 50 square metres in size, yet four domaines—and it was not so long ago that it was three, the Trapet estate having been divided as recently as 1990— own over half this *grand cru*. There were twelve proprietors in 1829 and fifteen in 1910, and there are around twenty-five today, if one groups together several members of the same family where the wine is made in common, but ownership is split for tax and inheritance reasons.

Chambertin lies above the Route des *Grands Crus*, between Latricières and Clos de Bèze, sheltered under the Montagne de la Combe-Grisard, at an altitude of between 275 and 300 metres. Upslope, where it and Clos de Bèze meet, there is what looks like a quarry. It is merely the rock formation.

The soil is a limestone of Bajocian origin, and the incline is gentle: a little more so than that of Latricières, which is almost flat except just under the trees, but less so than that of Clos de Bèze. In parts, particularly to the south and upslope, the vines are on white oolite (*marnes blanches*). Elsewhere, the earth is browner, and mixed with clay and pebbles. The proportion of fine earth to rock and pebbles (68 percent to 32 percent) is identical to that at Montrachet. Purely a coincidence?

What is the difference between Chambertin and Clos de Bèze? Charles Rousseau, who produces plenty of each at a high level of quality, says of Chambertin, "It is male, and sturdy. It lacks a bit of finesse in its youth, but then it rounds off. Clos de Bèze is more complex, *plus racé* (more racy), more delicate."

These are virile wines. The tannins are more obvious than in the top wines of Vosne-Romanée. Chambertins are full, firm and austere at the outset and structured and fleshy, with initial flavours of black fruit, liquorice and coffee beans, mellowing into something rich, concentrated, generous and warm-hearted when they mature. The Clos de Bèze is more perfumed in its youth; the Chambertin more severe, and perhaps the bigger of the two. Both are true *vins de garde*, needing a decade at least to soften up. Perhaps neither is ever as subtle as the top wines of Vosne-Romanée. But both can be magnificent.

CLOS DE BÈZE

SURFACE AREA: 15.4 ha
AVERAGE PRODUCTION: 464 hl
PRINCIPAL PROPRIETORS: ★ Pierre Damoy (5.36 ha); ★ Armand Rousseau (1.42 ha); ★ Drouhin-Laroze (1.39 ha); ★ Faiveley (1.29 ha); Henri Roch (1.01 ha); ★ Bruno Clair (0.95 ha); Gelin (0.60 ha); ★ Louis Jadot (0.42 ha); ★ Robert Groffier (0.42 ha); Bart (0.41 ha); Rebourseau (0.33 ha); ★ Dujac (0.29 ha); Duroché (0.25 ha); Jacques Prieur (0.15 ha); ★ Joseph Drouhin (0.12 ha).
[N.B. Clos de Bèze can be bottled as Chambertin, but not vice versa.]

In all, there are some forty separate parcels in Clos de Bèze, but despite it being larger, it has a smaller number of proprietors. As can be seen, one domaine, sadly an underachiever for a long time but now happily under new and determinedly perfectionist management, has no less than 34.8 percent of the *climat*. Like Chambertin itself, the majority of the proprietors are Gibriacois (as the adjective of Gevrey is rendered).

Clos de Bèze lies due north of Chambertin, between it and Mazis, on the same altitude of 275 to 300 metres. The incline is a little steeper, particularly at the top of the slope, and the soil, brown in colour, is a little less deep. In parts, the Bajocian bedrock shows through. As in Chambertin, in parts, there are plenty of small stones and pebbles. If there is one difference from Chambertin, it is the absence of *marnes blanches*, the white oolite which is apparent in some of the upper sections of the more southerly *climat*.

Gaston Roupnel said of Chambertin and Clos-de-Bèze, "The wine blends grace and vigour. It combines austerity and power with finesse and delicacy. Together there is all that is necessary for a synthesis that is generosity and perfection itself."

At their best these two wines are certainly not just among the top wines of Burgundy, but among the top red wines of the world. And, good as the wines of next rung may be, be they from Mazis or Ruchottes or Clos Saint-Jacques, there is a considerable margin between them and those of the Clos-de-Bèze.

CHAPELLE-CHAMBERTIN

SURFACE AREA: 5.49 ha
AVERAGE PRODUCTION: 165 hl
PRINCIPAL PROPRIETORS: ★ Pierre Damoy (2.22 ha); Ponsot (0.70 ha); ★ Jean and Jean-Louis Trapet (0.60 ha); ★ Drouhin-Laroze (0.51 ha); Rossignol-Trapet (0.50 ha); ★ Louis Jadot (0.39 ha); Cécile Tremblay (0.38 ha); ★ Claude Dugat (0.10 ha).

Chapelle-Chambertin lies immediately underneath Clos de Bèze, with Griotte to the south and the *premier cru* Les Cherbaudes to the north. It takes its name from the chapel of Notre-Dame de Bèze, originally built in 1155 and reconstructed by Philippe de Beaujeu in 1547 (and reconsecrated by the Bishop of Bethlehem), but subsequently deliberately burnt to the ground in order to increase the land by two *ouvrées* in 1830. Originally, Chapelle was just the southerly section, but this *grand cru* absorbed the *climat* of Les Gémeaux (1.75 ha) during the course of the nineteenth century.

The slope is modest here. The shallow pebbly soil, based on hard rock, which sticks out in places, is a little richer than in neighbouring Griotte. Of all the *grands crus* downslope from the Route des *Grands Crus*—which are lighter and more "feminine" than those above it—this is the sturdiest wine, though not as full (or as fine) as Chambertin itself. It is rich and plummy and can resemble Clos de Bèze, but in the final analysis, it doesn't have quite the volume, the concentration or the flair.

CHARMES-CHAMBERTIN AND MAZOYÈRES-CHAMBERTIN

SURFACE AREA: 30.83 ha
AVERAGE PRODUCTION: 980 hl
PRINCIPAL PROPRIETORS: Camus (Charmes: 5.90 ha; Mazoyères: 1.01 ha); ★ Perrot-Minot (1.56 ha); Taupenot-Merme (1.42 ha); ★ Armand Rousseau (1.37 ha); Rebourseau (1.31 ha); ★ Arlaud (1.14 ha); Henri Richard (1.11 ha); Gérard Raphet (1 ha); Dupont-Tisserandot (0.80 ha); Naigeon/Domaine des Varoilles (0.75 ha); ★ Vougeraie (0.75 ha); ★ Dujac (0.70 ha); ★ Bernard Dugat-Py (0.69 ha); Feuillet (0.65 ha); Pierre Bourée (0.65 ha); Charlopin-Parizot (0.60 ha); Gabriel Tortochot (0.57 ha); Seguin (0.57 ha); Beaumont (0.52 ha); ★ Geantet-Pansiot (0.50 ha); ★ Denis Bachelet (0.43 ha); Duroché (0.41 ha); Guy Castagnier (0.40 ha); ★ Confuron-Cotétidot (0.39 ha); Coquard-Loison (0.32 ha); ★ Claude Dugat (0.31 ha); ★ Christian Sérafin (0.31 ha); ★ Ponsot (0.30 ha); ★ Dominique Gallois (0.29 ha); Huguenot (0.28 ha); Michel Magnien (0.28 ha); ★ Christophe Roumier (0.27 ha); Pierre Amiot (0.20 ha); ★ Humbert Frères (0.20 ha); Bernard Maume (0.17 ha); Thierry Odoul-Coquard (0.17 ha); ★ Joseph Roty (0.16 ha); Marchand Frères (0.14 ha); ★ Hubert Lignier (0.11 ha).

For 150 years growers in Mazoyères have been able to sell their wine under the more user-friendly label of Charmes. There are today few Mazoyères to be seen, save *chez* Camus, Perrot-Minot and Taupenot-Merme. Mazoyères lies under Latricières and, in part, stretches down to the main road—the only other *grand cru* in Burgundy apart from Clos Vougeot to do this. Charmes adjoins it to the north, under Chambertin. The etymology of Mazoyères is obscure. Could it, like Mazis, have something to do with *maisons* (houses)? But Charmes, though the wine is indeed charming, comes from *chaume*, a piece of vineyard abandoned at one time (*en friche*) and then replanted.

Once again, the slope is gentle. The surface soil is meagre, made up of decayed limestone (*lave*) with an abundance of gravel and stones at the lower levels. In the Charmes the rock is less decomposed. In the old days lumps of iron ore would be dug up in the course of ploughing the vineyard, and these would be sent off to a foundry in Langres to be worked into metal.

The wines of the Mazoyères section are firmer, fuller and gamier but less fine, less pure and fragrant, than those of the Charmes—certainly the Charmes-du-Haut, which is round and less sturdy, but can have plenty of finesse. All in all, this is the least exciting of the Gevrey *grands crus*, and the most forward. Yet in good hands, like the wines of Denis Bachelet, for example, it can nevertheless be very enticing, with a violet and raspberry perfume, with a texture which can be velvety, even silky-smooth, and with no lack of intensity: if not quite the Musigny of Gevrey, then perhaps its Amoureuses. As always, it depends on the grower.

GRIOTTE-CHAMBERTIN

SURFACE AREA: 2.73 ha
AVERAGE PRODUCTION: 90 hl

PRINCIPAL PROPRIETORS: ★ Ponsot/Domaine des Chézeaux (0.89 ha); René Leclerc/Domaine des Chézeaux (0.75 ha); ★ Joseph Drouhin (0.53 ha); ★ Fourrier (0.26 ha); ★ Claude Dugat (0.15 ha); Marchand Frères (0.13 ha); ★ Joseph Roty (0.08 ha).

This is the smallest of the Gevrey *grands crus*, and it lies squeezed in between Charmes and Chapelle, just under the point where Chambertin meets Clos de Bèze. As every book on Burgundy will tell you, *griotte* is a type of cherry, used for jam making, and that is what the wine tastes like. Yes, it can have a flavour of cherries, if you are looking for them—I find more of a cornucopia of all sorts of red and black small fruits, plus liquorice and violets—but the name has more mundane origins. As is so often the case, it derives from the soil, *criotte* or *crai*: chalk—as in Criots-Bâtard-Montrachet.

There is little surface soil here. The roots delve straight into broken-up rock impacted with pebbles and fossils. When it rains, the vineyard can get very wet, for there are a number of underground streams and springs. But it drains well. The wine, however, can be sublime. Whether it is just that most of the people able to show you a Griotte are fine producers or it is coincidence, I find a major difference between Griotte and Chapelle, particularly in terms of intensity and finesse. Moreover, Griotte has a poise and individuality which raises it above all but the very best Charmes. Griotte is never a blockbuster: the tannins are always soft, the acidity is usually gentle, and the wine is perfumed, harmonious and seductive—oh, ever so seductive!

LATRICIÈRES-CHAMBERTIN

SURFACE AREA: 7.35 ha
AVERAGE PRODUCTION: 255 hl
PRINCIPAL PROPRIETORS: Camus (1.51 ha); ★ Joseph Faiveley (1.21 ha); Rossignol-Trapet (0.76 ha); ★ Jean and Jean-Louis Trapet (0.75 ha); ★ Drouhin-Laroze (0.67 ha); ★ Louis Rémy (0.57 ha); ★ Leroy (0.57 ha); Castagnier/Newman (0.53 ha); Bize (0.40 ha); Duroché (0.28 ha).

Latricières—the word means poor, in the sense of infertile—lies directly to the south of Chambertin. It shares much of the same soil and subsoil, a white oolitic marl on a solid rock base with very little surface earth, but the land is flatter. There is almost no slope except at the upper end just under the trees.

Dr. Morelot (1831) ignored it—probably the wine was passed off as Chambertin in those days—and Lavalle (1855) classed it as a *deuxième cuvée*. One hundred and fifty years ago, there were three proprietors (MM Gournot, Ouvrard and Marion). Today, there are ten.

Latricières is a sturdy wine, robust in its youth, and spicy and gamey in its maturity, and it lacks both the distinction of Chambertin and Clos de Bèze and the finesse of Mazis and Ruchottes. In good hands, though, (Leroy and Faiveley, for example) we can find a thoroughly satisfactory, warm-hearted bottle. But a Latricières is a second-division *grand cru*, nonetheless.

MAZIS-CHAMBERTIN

SURFACE AREA: 9.1 ha
AVERAGE PRODUCTION: 320 hl
PRINCIPAL PROPRIETORS: ★ Hospices de Beaune (1.75 ha); ★ Bernard Dugat-Py (0.22 ha); ★ Joseph Faiveley (1.20 ha); Rebourseau (0.96 ha); Harmand-Geoffroy (0.73 ha); Bernard Maume (0.67 ha); ★ Armand Rousseau (0.53 ha); Frédéric Esmonin (0.42 ha); Gabriel Tortochot (0.42 ha); Philippe Naddef (0.42 ha); Camus (0.37 ha); Dupont-Tisserandot (0.35 ha); ★ D'Auvenay/Mme Bize-Leroy (0.26 ha); ★ Bernard Dugat-Py (0.22 ha); Castagnier/Newman (0.19 ha); Jean-Michel Guillon (0.18 ha); ★ Joseph Roty (0.12 ha); Philippe Charlopin-Parizot (0.09 ha); Confuron-Cotétidot (0.08 ha).

Mazis, often spelled with a "y," and with or without the final "s," has the same etymological origin, it is suggested, as Mazoyères, and indeed, various Maizières: the word means hamlet. It lies under Ruchottes, between Clos de Bèze and the village of Gevrey, above the Route des Grands Crus, and it is divided into the Mazis *haut* and the Mazis *bas*, the former being the choicer parcel. Since 1855 it has absorbed part of Les Corbeaux, increasing its surface area by about 0.60 hectares.

The soil is similar to that of Clos de Bèze— shallow, especially in the *haut*, with the Bajocian bedrock poking out in places—and the wine, at its best, comes the closest in quality, both in volume and in distinction, to the two great *grands crus*. Mazis is well-coloured and rich in tannin and has good grip and a most attractive, even opulent fruit: blackberry and black cherry to add to the *petits fruit rouges*. Madame Lalou Bize of Maison Leroy has for long produced a Mazis to conjure with: indisputably *grand vin*. Now she owns a parcel in her own right—and it houses the same vines whose wine she bought in the first place.

RUCHOTTES-CHAMBERTIN

SURFACE AREA: 3.30 ha

AVERAGE PRODUCTION: 115 hl

PRINCIPAL PROPRIETORS: ★ Armand Rousseau (Clos des Ruchottes) (1.06 ha); ★ Dr. Georges Mugneret (0.64 ha); Frédéric Esmonin (0.58 ha); ★ Christophe Roumier (0.51 ha); Henri Magnien (0.16 ha); Château de Marsannay (0.10 ha); Marchand-Grillot (0.08 ha).

Ruchottes—the word comes from *rochers* (rocks)—is always plural, whereas Griotte and Mazis can be either. The *climat*—small, steep, and much-parcellated—lies above Mazis and beneath a little road which disappears into the mountains on its way to Curley. Across the road is the *premier cru* Le Fonteny.

As in the top part of Chambertin and Latricières, there is oolitic *marnes blanches* here, and once again there is very little surface soil. The result is a wine of the same size as Mazis, but with more of the structure showing: less fat, less lush, more mineral. It is a *vin de garde*, and a very satisfactory one, if somewhat austere in its youth. Give it time. There is plenty of depth and a mulberry-type fruit balanced by a cool acidity.

All three starred proprietors owe their land to the break-up of the Thomas-Bassot domaine. Thomas Bassot was founded in 1852 and soon became the proprietor of the lion's share of Ruchottes. In 1976, after a succession of family problems and personal tragedies, the firm was sold to Jean-Claude Boisset, and the domaine was put on the market. Christophe Roumier farms the Ruchottes of Michel Bonnefond, a wine lover who lives near Rouen.

The Premiers Crus

The twenty-six *premiers crus* of Gevrey-Chambertin can be conveniently grouped into four sections:

The first section is upslope from the village itself, on the southeast-facing slope of the extension of the Combe de Lavaux.

Here you will find La Boissière (part *premier cru: monopole* of Domaine Harmand-Geoffroy), La Romanée (part), Clos des Varoilles (*monopole* of the Domaine des Varoilles), Poissenot, Lavaux-Saint-Jacques (or Lavaut-Saint-Jacques), Estournelles (-Saint-Jacques), Clos Saint-Jacques, Clos du Chapitre (which lies downslope from Clos Saint-Jacques), Les Cazetiers, Les Petits Cazetiers, La Combe-au-Moine, Les Champeaux and Les Goulots. This is the best area for *premier cru* Gevrey-Chambertin.

CLOS SAINT-JACQUES   (6.70 ha)

PRINCIPAL PROPRIETORS: ★ Armand Rousseau (2.20 ha); ★ Sylvie Esmonin (formerly Michel Esmonin et Fille) (1.60 ha); ★ Bruno Clair (1.00 ha); ★ Louis Jadot (1.00 ha); ★ Domaine Fourrier (0.89 ha).

When it came to be decreed what was *grand cru* and what was not in the 1930s, it was decided that only *climats* contiguous with Chambertin and Clos de Bèze would be considered for top rank. Ruchottes and Mazoyères scraped in, for a finger of each touches the magic core. Clos Saint-Jacques, on its own, but perfectly poised on the Combe de Lavaux flank, was excluded. No one who owns a part of this vineyard (there are only five, and they all today produce excellent wine) would agree with this judgement. Neither would other, more dispassionate outsiders.

In the Armand Rousseau cellar you are given the Saint-Jacques to taste *after* the Clos de la Roche, Ruchottes and Mazis, and the Saint-Jacques is awarded a higher percentage of new oak. It is always the best of the wines.

In the nineteenth century the vineyard belonged exclusively to the Comte de Moucheron. In 1953, at which time the *métayer* was Henri Esmonin, grandfather of Sylvie, it was divided and sold to antecedents of the present producers. It lies on the same elevation as Chambertin, and the soil is a white marl similar in constitution, though the incline is marginally greater. The fruit ripens just a little later, owing to a fresh wind which can flow out of the Combe. But the wine can be exquisite: rich, ample, full-bodied and distinctive. This is a wine of real depth and dimension, slightly lusher and plumper than the two greatest Gevrey wines, but no less classy, no less inspiring. It is clearly head and shoulders above all the other Gevrey *premiers crus*.

LAVAUX-SAINT-JACQUES	*(9.53 ha)*
ESTOURNELLES-SAINT-JACQUES	*(2.09 ha)*

Lavaux-Saint-Jacques lies immediately south of Clos Saint-Jacques, with the smaller Estournelles above it. Here it is not so much soil structure or exposition which precludes the wines from pretension to *grand cru* status, but the sheltering and cooling effect of the valley into which the road at the bottom of the slope rapidly disappears. Walk from the Clos Saint-Jacques boundary on the north side across to where Lavaux meets Varoilles and Poissenot on the other side—a distance of less than 400 metres—and you will notice a drop in temperature. In the winter, when frost or snow hits the ground, you can also see the microclimatic difference, as the ground warms up each morning.

Nevertheless, the wines from these two *climats* can be excellent *premier cru* examples: fullish, rich, plump, ample and meaty, without hard edges or rusticity, and with plenty of fruit. Local wisdom will opine that a blend of the two would make a wine superior to what either could accomplish on its own—a wine as good as Clos Saint-Jacques. But then, it could only be called *premier cru*.

RECOMMENDED SOURCES
LAVAUX-SAINT-JACQUES
Bernard Dugat-Py, Claude Dugat, Dupont-Tisserandot, Humbert Frères, Denis Mortet (all Gevrey-Chambertin); Louis Jadot (Beaune).

ESTOURNELLES-SAINT-JACQUES
Frédéric Esmomin; Humbert Frères, Phillppe Rossignol (all Gevrey-Chambertin); Jadot (Beaune).

Further into the valley, you will find Le Poissenot (2.20 ha): note the wines of Geantet-Pansiot and Humbert Frères in Gevrey-Chambertin and Louis Jadot in Beaune; La Romanée (1.06 ha) (see the Domaine des Varoilles); the Clos des Varoilles (5.97 ha) (the monopoly of the Domaine de Varoilles); and La Bossière, part of which (0.45 ha) is *premier cru*, and the monopoly of Domaine Harmand-Geoffroy. The wines get progressively leaner as one retreats into the valley. Sometimes the tannins can be a little unsophisticated.

LES CAZETIERS	*(8.43 ha)*
LES PETITS-CAZETIERS	*(0.45 ha)*
LA COMBE AU MOINE	*(4.77 ha)*
LES GOULOTS	*(1.81 ha)*
LES CHAMPEAUX	*(6.68 ha)*

These *climats* lie on the other side of Clos Saint-Jacques and have an exposure which is more to the east and even, in the case of La Combe-au-Moine, marginally to the north.

Les Cazetiers is almost as well exposed as Clos Saint-Jacques and can closely approach it, though it never seems to really equal it. You can taste the two alongside each other *chez* Bruno Clair, Rousseau and Jadot. It is an equally sizeable wine—just a little more to the sturdy, robust side—but it can be splendidly rich and satisfying.

Beyond Les Cazetiers, which is a wide, extensive vineyard, are Les Petits Cazetiers, La Combe-au-Moine and Les Goulots, with Les Champeaux lying underneath. This is rocky, stony territory, with the vineyard broken up into terraces. With the exception of one or two Combe au Moine, this is second-division territory; the microclimate is cooler, and the wines, though they can be quite substantial, do not have the proper definition and finesse.

RECOMMENDED SOURCES
LES CAZETIERS
Bruno Clair (Marsannay); Philippe Naddef (Couchey); Dupont-Tisserandot, Armand Rousseau, Christian Sérafin (all Gevrey-Chambertin); Joseph Faiveley (Nuits-Saint-Georges); Louis Jadot (Beaune).

LA COMBE AU MOINE
Joseph Faiveley (Nuits-Saint-Georges); Fourrier, Dominique Gallois (both Gevrey-Chambertin); Louis Jadot (Beaune).

LES GOULOTS
Fourrier (Gevrey-Chambertin).

LES CHAMPEAUX
Philippe Naddef (Couchey); Fourrier, Denis Mortet (both Gevrey-Chambertin).

The second sector lies between the *grands crus* of Ruchottes and Mazis and the village itself. Lowest down, marching with Mazis *bas*, is Les Corbeaux, a section of which is plain village *appellation contrôlée*. Just above is Le Fonteny (singular or plural), and above that Champonnet, Craipillot and the tiny Issarts, whose main proprietor is Faiveley.

Only the first three are of importance, in the sense that you are likely to see them on a label. They produce wines of a medium weight, with good fruit and an often charming balance, but without the weight or concentration of a good Lavaux-Saint-Jacques or Cazetiers.

LES CORBEAUX	(3.21 ha)
LE FONTENY	(3.73 ha)
CHAMPONNET	(3.32 ha)
CRAIPILLOT	(2.76 ha)
ISSARTS	(0.62 ha)

RECOMMENDED SOURCES
LES CORBEAUX
Denis Bachelet (Gevrey-Chambertin); Bruno Clavelier (Vosne-Romanée).

LE FONTENY
Bruno Clair (Marsannay); Christian Sérafin, Joseph Roty (both Gevrey-Chambertin).

CHAMPONNET
Frédéric Esmonin (Gevrey-Chambertin).

CRAIPILLOT
Confuron-Cotéditot (Vosne-Romaneé) Drouhin-Laroze, Humbert Frères (both Gevrey-Chambertin)

Downslope from Mazis and Chapelle-Chambertin lies the third sector of Gevrey-Chambertin *premiers crus*. Running from north to south, these are Au Closeau (I have only ever encountered that of Drouhin-Laroze), La Perrière, Clos Prieur *haut* (not to be confused with Clos Prieur *bas*, merely village AC), Les Cherbaudes, Les Champitonnois (usually declared as La Petite-Chapelle) and En Ergot (which has failed to come my way).

AU CLOSEAU	(0.53 ha)
LA PERRIÈRE	(2.47 ha)
CLOS PRIEUR (HAUT)	(1.98 ha)
CHERBAUDES	(2.18 ha)
LA PETITE CHAPELLE (LES CHAMPITONNOIS)	(4.00 ha)
EN ERGOT	(1.16 ha)

These are the most "feminine" of the Gevrey-Chambertin *premiers crus*: medium in body, soft-centred, aromatically *petits fruits rouges* and, when good, extremely charming. When not good, or in poor vintages, they can be weedy and will attenuate rapidly.

RECOMMENDED SOURCES
CHERBAUDES
Louis Boillot (Chambolle-Musigny); Fourrier (Gevrey-Chambertin).

LA PETITE CHAPELLE
Bernard Dugat-Py, Dupont-Tisserandot, Humbert Frères (all Gevrey-Chambertin).

This leaves Bel Air, which lies above Clos de Bèze, part of which (2.65 ha) is *premier cru*, and Aux Combottes (4.57 ha). I have rarely seen the former, but I have often been seduced by wines from this latter *climat*.

If you look at the map, you may be puzzled by the standing of Aux Combottes, for it lies directly between Latricières and Clos-de-la-Roche, on the same line as Chambertin itself. Why is this not *grand cru*? The answer lies in the microclimate. Combottes is in the faintest of hollows, and so drains marginally less well. Above it, there is a break in the hill where the Combe Grisard disappears into the Hautes-Côtes, and this lets a breeze flow over the Combottes vines. It's a small thing, but the result is that the grapes do not ripen as well as they do either in Clos-de-la-Roche or in Latricières. The wine is never as full or as concentrated.

However, it can nevertheless be delicious: elegant, supple, intense and full of cherry, raspberry and red currant fruit. It is a sort of Gevrey-Chambolle cross, but in a unique way: I find no Morey parallel.

RECOMMENDED SOURCES
AUX COMBOTTES
Pierre Amiot, Dujac, Hubert Lignier (all Morey-Saint-Denis); Leroy (Vosne-Romanée).

The Growers

★★★ *Denis Bachelet*

3.83 ha owned. Charmes-Chambertin (0.43 ha); Gevrey-Chambertin *premier cru* Les Corbeaux; village Gevrey-Chambertin; Côte-de-Nuits Villages.

Denis Bachelet took over his small family domaine in 1983, when he was in his early twenties, and he has since augmented it a little, but this is still essentially a one-man band. Happily, it is a perfectionistic and excellent one. Low yields are critical, in Bachelet's view. The fruit is completely de-stemmed, macerated at 15°C for 6 to 8 days, and given a *cuvaison* of medium length (7–11 days); 25 percent new oak is used for all the wines. These are kept on their lees as long as possible and hand bottled without filtration.

The Denis Bachelet style produces wines of intensity, great elegance and subtlety: feminine in the best sense. They are concentrated, harmonious, pure and understated. Bachelet's Charmes is a ravishing example—a wine which really sings. Except for his 1991s, which are marginally unimpressive, this domaine has not put a foot wrong. Here is not the only cellar where

the 2002s are superior to the 1999s (and they are very fine indeed!).

Pierre Bourée et Fils

5 ha owned. Charmes-Chambertin (0.65 ha); Gevrey-Chambertin *premier cru* Les Champeaux; village Gevrey-Chambertin, including the *lieu-dit* Clos-de-la-Justice *(monopole)*; Beaune *premier cru* Les Epenottes.

Bourée is as much a *négociant* as a domaine, and a very traditional one at that. Owned by Louis Vallet, a slight and somewhat shy man in his late sixties, and his sons Jean-Christophe and Bernard—all of them direct descendants of the original Bourée who founded the firm in 1864—this is an affair which is almost defiant in its insistence on not moving with the times. There is no temperature control, no de-stemming, some new oak—30 percent now—but a great deal more oak which looks incredibly aged and no bottling before at least 2 years or more.

I have had good Bourée wines in the past, and I remember a couple of 1969s bought by the Wine Society in my time there. But of late, I find myself unimpressed. The wines lack succulence and grip. All too often, I find them attenuated. Vallet Frères is a subsidiary name for the *négociant* business.

René Bouvier

17 ha owned and *en fermage*. Marsannay *rouge* (including the *lieux-dits* Clos du Roy, Champs Salomon and Longeroies) *et blanc*; Côte de Nuits Villages; Fixin; Gevrey-Chambertin, including a *vieilles vignes cuvée*.

Bernard Bouvier, son of René, took over the premises and some of the vines of Laurent Goillot-Bernollin in the spring of 2001 and moved down from Marsannay. His is the last house in the village on the main road, going north. Things are improving here. Following the move, it was decided to green harvest, to dispense with the picking machine, and to install a sorting table. Bernard Bouvier is also a merchant in a small way. Charmes-Chambertin is regularly offered.

★ Alain Burguet

5.35 ha owned and *en fermage*. Gevrey-Chambertin *premier cru* Les Champeaux; village Gevrey-Chambertin, including a *vieilles vignes cuvée* called "Ma Favorite" and the *lieux-dits* Les Billards, La Justice and Les Reniards.

Alain Burguet is an example of how it is still possible to build up a domaine from scratch, without ample resources and without having to make a "sensible" marriage, even with today's high prices of land. The man is in his late forties and is short, solid, quietly determined, even grim. The wine is similar: full and masculine, uncompromising, sturdy, concentrated and long-lasting.

The grapes are almost entirely de-stemmed and vinified at a high temperature. *Cuvaisons* are long. There is no fining and minimal filtration. Burguet is not seeking wines which are *flatteur* in their youth. These are deliberate *vins de garde*.

A decade ago there were two changes in Burguet's vinification techniques. Somewhat reluctantly, at least at first, he started to augment the amount of new oak. He also took over a cellar at the top of the village, enabling him to keep the wine longer in cask. Hitherto, it had been bottled after 14 months.

Burguet's village *vieilles vignes* "Ma Favorite" is at least the equal of most growers' *premiers crus*. If I were to pick one village wine as a yardstick, this would be it. The Champeaux dates from vines which were planted in 1985. From 2003 Burguet commenced a *négociant* business. He now offers Chambertin Clos de Bèze and Clos Vougeot.

Camus Père et Fils

18 ha owned. Charmes-Chambertin (3.03 ha); Chambertin (1.69 ha); Latricières-Chambertin (1.51 ha); Mazoyères-Chambertin (1.01 ha); Mazis-Chambertin (0.37 ha); village Gevrey-Chambertin.

What a magnificent line-up! But what a disappointment when you taste the wines today.

Joseph Camus built up the domaine in the crisis years of the 1930s, and even then, he was selling no inconsiderable percentage directly to private customers. Joseph was succeeded by his son Léon, and Léon by Hubert, today a handsome man in his late sixties. The unselfish Hubert spends most of his time on the committees of a large number of organisations which govern and promote what goes on in Burgundy: at the expense, I fear, of the wines. There is 100 percent de-stemming, a 3-week *cuvaison* and 10 to 30 percent new oak. Sadly, the wines lack freshness and concentration and evolve fast. The 1999s were already pruney in January 2002.

This is one of the few domaines to bottle Mazoyères under its real name. I have had plenty of fine old Camus wines from the 1960s and 1950s.

Philippe Charlopin-Parizot

18.5 ha owned and *en fermage/en métayage*. Clos de Vougeot (0.41 ha); Echézeaux (0.33 ha); Mazoyères-Chambertin (0.30 ha); Charmes-Chambertin (0.30 ha); Chambertin (0.21 ha—owned by Mme Baron, but made and bottled by Charlopin); Clos Saint-Denis (0.17 ha); Bonnes-Mares (0.12 ha); Mazis-Chambertin (0.09 ha); Gevrey-Chambertin *premier* cru in Bel Air; village Gevrey-Chambertin, including the *lieux-dits* Les Evocelles and La Justice; village Morey-Saint-Denis; village Chambolle-Musigny; village Vosne-Romanée; village Fixin.

Philippe Charlopin, a short, chubby man in his late forties, with an abundant mane of curly hair, inherited 1.8 hectares from his father in 1976 and has been gradually building up his domaine ever since. Originally from Gevrey, he moved to Marsannay in 1987, but has since returned, and now occupies part of the old Charles Quillardet cellars on the main road to Dijon. Increasingly, his son Yann is in charge, for Philippe additionally manages the Château de Pommard.

The grapes are de-stemmed, given a deliberate pre-fermentation maceration (up to 8 days in 1988), and fermented at a maximum of 30°C, with the *cuvaison* varying from 12 days to 20, depending on the vintage. Unusually, there is no racking; the wine is kept on its lees, without being de-gassed, and so under a lot of carbon dioxide, until bottling a year later.

The wines are plump and plummy, well-coloured and fullish without being too sturdy. They are of good quality, but are sometimes lacking in true *terroir* definition; they taste a bit too alike.

Des Chézeaux

4 ha all leased on a *métayage* basis (see below): Griotte-Chambertin (1.57 ha); Chambertin (0.20 ha); Clos Saint-Denis (0.60 ha); Gevrey-Chambertin *premier cru* in Les Cazetiers and Lavaux-Saint-Jacques; Chambolle-Musigny *premier cru* Les Charmes; village Gevrey-Chambertin.

Chantal Nemes-Mercier, who inherited this domaine upon the death of her father in 2000, has three share-croppers: the brothers Berthaut in Fixin look after the village Gevrey-Chambertin and the *premiers crus*; Laurent Ponsot is responsible for the Chambertin, the Chambolle-Musigny Les Charmes and part of the Griotte-Chambertin; and René Leclerc operates another segment of the Griotte, which the domaine bought in 1994.

It is this latter wine which causes confusion. Both Ponsot and Leclerc bottle their portions under their own label, and each separately bottle what they owe to the Domaine des Chézeaux under its label. But up until 2002, when the winemaker began to be specified, the consumer had no way of knowing what was which: important, as Leclerc is a far inferior operator to Ponsot. His 1999 Griotte is a disgrace. So, *caveat emptor*: approach the Chézeaux wines with caution!

★ Pierre Damoy

10.47 ha owned. Chambertin Clos de Bèze (5.36 ha); Chapelle-Chambertin (2.22 ha); Chambertin (0.48 ha); village Gevrey-Chambertin, including the *lieu-dit* Clos Tamisot (*monopole*).

After many years in the wilderness, this important domaine was taken in hand in 1992, on the arrival of Pierre Damoy, grandson of the eponymous Pierre and nephew of Jacques, the current proprietor. Everything, including the label, has been changed since then. Herbicides and insecticides have been outlawed, a sorting table has been added, the must has begun to be cold-macerated and the wine has begun to be racked only once, at bottling, without fining or filtration. Quality is now what it should be: the fruit from the worst part of the Clos de Bèze—parcels badly planted during the time of Damoy's uncle—are sold off separately. Since 2001 there has been a separate *vieilles vignes cuvée* of this wine.

★ Drouhin-Laroze

12 ha owned. Bonnes-Mares (1.49 ha); Chambertin, Clos de Bèze (1.39 ha); Clos de Vougeot (1.03 ha); Latricières-Chambertin (0.67 ha); Chapelle-Chambertin (0.51 ha); Musigny (0.12 ha); Gevrey-Chambertin *premier cru* in Au Closeau, Craipillot (these first two often blended together), Lavaux-Saint-Jacques and Clos Prieur; Chambolle-Musigny *premier cru* Les Baudes; village Gevrey-Chambertin; village Morey-Saint-Denis; village Chambolle-Musigny.

Founded by Jean-Baptiste Laroze around 1850, the domaine is today run by his descendant Philippe Drouhin. The relationship with Robert Drouhin of the Beaune *négociants* is distant.

I used to find quality disappointing here: the wines seemed a bit too jammy, lacking *terroir* definition, and moreover, over-oaked. Since 2001 they have improved. There is now a vibrating sorting table and more precise temperature control. They seem fresher, more individual, more stylish. The domaine is rich, the premises, in the middle of Gevrey-Chambertin, extensive and up-to-date, with a splendid first-year barrel cellar. Usually there are very good wines today, but they are occasionally still a bit over-extracted.

★★ Bernard Dugat-Py

9.81 ha owned and *en fermage/en métayage*. Charmes-Chambertin (0.69 ha); Mazis-Chambertin (0.22 ha); Le Chambertin (0.05 ha); Gevrey-Chambertin *premier cru* in Champeaux, Lavaux-Saint-Jacques and Petite-Chapelle; Chassagne-Montrachet *premier cru* Les Morgeots; village Gevrey-Chambertin, including the *lieu-dit* Les Evocelles and a *vieilles vignes cuvée* "Coeur du Roi"; village Vosne-Romanée Vieilles

Vignes; village Pommard Vieilles Vignes; village Meursault; village Chassagne-Montrachet *blanc*.

Having doubled in size in the last decade, this is now a reasonably substantial domaine, whose marvellous vaulted cellar was once the crypt of the church of a leprosarium. There was a period in the mid-1990s when I, like some others, felt the extraction had been exaggerated, but the wines now have an old-vine, minimum-yield concentration and are abundantly fruity and very stylish and well-balanced. The 2002s are splendid, even better than his 1999s. This is a high-class establishment presided over by a charming couple. The Dugats are still seeking to expand: to 12 or 13 hectares. The white wines are new.

From 2004 the domaine has been cultivated on biodynamic lines. There is no cold-soaking. Between 20 and 100 percent of the stems are retained, and the wine is vinified at 30°C. Some 80 percent of the wood is renewed each year. The 2005s are truly fine.

★★ *Claude Dugat*

6.05 ha owned. Charmes-Chambertin (0.31 ha); Griotte-Chambertin (0.15 ha); Chapelle-Chambertin (0.10 ha); Gevrey-Chambertin *premier cru* in Lavaux-Saint-Jacques, Craipillot and La Perrière (these last two usually blended together); village Gevrey-Chambertin.

Claude Dugat, born in 1956, and the elder and balding cousin of Bernard, is in charge here, and he keeps his wine in the cellars of the beautifully restored Cellier des Dîmes, once a chapter house, next to Gevrey's church. Until the 1991 vintage, the Lavaux-Saint-Jacques bore the label of his father Maurice, a familiar figure as one of the Cadets de Bourgogne who sing, clap and interrupt at the dinners at the Clos-de-Vougeot. The Griotte is bottled under the name Françoise, Claude's sister.

This Dugat makes his wine slightly differently from his cousin, totally de-stemming and using a little less new oak. But the wines are arguably even better: very rich and concentrated,

with marvellous classy fruit and very good grip. This is another fine source.

★ *Dupont-Tisserandot*

23 ha owned and *en fermage/en métayage*. Charmes-Chambertin (0.80 ha); Mazis-Chambertin (0.35 ha); Corton Le Rognet (0.33 ha); Gevrey-Chambertin *premier cru* in Bel Air, Les Cazetiers, Lavaux-Saint-Jacques and Petite-Chapelle; village Gevrey-Chambertin; village Nuits-Saint-Georges; village Savigny-lès-Beaune; village Fixin; Marsannay.

This is a large exploitation, and it still sells off some of its produce in bulk to the *négoce*. Bernard Dupont, who started the whole thing off in 1954 when he married Gisèle Tisserandot—he was a grocer before and was somewhat thrown in the deep end—is now *en retraite*. Responsibility has been ceded to his daughter and son-in-law, Patricia and Didier Chevillon. Didier has been totally responsible for the wines since 1999.

There has been much progress here since the last decade, when the cellar was a shambles and the wines unimpressive. Since 2000 the size of the harvest has been restrained. There is now a green harvest, total de-stemming, cold-soaking for up to a week and rather more new oak—up to 100 percent for the *grands crus*. In 2004 a *table de tri* was installed in the cellar, and in 2005 a new crusher/de-stemmer was acquired. The wines are lovely now. This is an address worth noting.

Gilles Duroché

8.26 ha Owned and *en fermage*. Charmes-Chambertin (0.41 ha); Latricières-Chambertin (0.28 ha); Chambertin Clos de Bèze (0.25 ha); Gevrey-Chambertin *premier cru* in Les Champeaux, Les Estournelles and Lavaux-Saint-Jacques; village Gevrey-Chambertin.

Philippe Duroché started off with 3 hectares in 1954 on the death of his father and slowly built up this domaine to the present size before handing over the reins to his son Gilles at the end of the 1980s.

This is a very efficient set-up, with a spotlessly tidy cellar in the centre of the village. There is total de-stemming, a few days of pre-fermentation maceration, a 12–15 day *cuvaison* and no fining. The vines in the Champeaux are still quite young, dating from 1986, and those in the Latricières and the Estournelles are only 25 years old or so, though in the Clos de Bèze they are venerable. Over the last decade, the quantity of new oak has been increased, and yields lowered. Quality is now very good, and the wines are rich and succulent. This is another address worth investigating.

Frédéric Esmonin, Domaine des Estournelles

6 ha owned and *en métayage*. Ruchottes-Chambertin (0.58 ha); Mazis-Chambertin (0.42 ha); Chambertin Clos de Bèze (0.13 ha); Bonnes-Mares (0.07 ha); Chambertin (0.03 ha); Gevrey-Chambertin *premier cru* in Champonnet, Les Estournelles-Saint-Jacques and Lavaux-Saint-Jacques; village Gevrey-Chambertin including Clos Prieur.

Much has changed here in recent years. The Esmonins, father André and son Frédéric, have lost their Griotte-Chambertin, which they share-cropped up until 1999, but have acquired some Chambertin and Chambertin Clos de Bèze (despite the small quantity of the latter, it is nevertheless produced separately) and also some Bonnes-Mares. They are also merchants in a small way and offer Clos de Vougeot and Charmes-Chambertin.

The recipe is 100 percent de-stemming, fermentation at a high temperature after 4–6 days cold maceration, 33 percent new oak and relatively early bottling. The wines are rich in colour, virile, profound and concentrated. I normally like what I sample when I visit. But sometimes I find less finesse when I encounter the wines later in bottle.

★ Sylvie Esmonin

7.13 ha owned and *en fermage/en métayage*. Gevrey-Chambertin *premier cru* Clos-Saint-Jacques; Volnay *premier* cru Santenots; village Gevrey-Chambertin, including a *vieilles vignes cuvée*; Côte de Nuits Villages.

The attractive, capable Sylvie, qualified both as an *ingénieur agronome* and an oenologue,

is in charge at this domaine, whose headquarters lie underneath the Clos Saint-Jacques vineyards.

There is only partial de-stemming, 2–5 days cold-maceration, fermentation at a maximum of 29°C, with a long *cuvaison*, and 100 percent new wood for the Clos Saint-Jacques. The atmosphere is tidy, competent and quietly confident, the wines suitably more feminine and more elegant when they are young than those of the cousins down the road. They have become fatter and more succulent since Sylvie has become an "item" with Dominique Laurent, merchant in Nuits-Saint-Georges. Up to 2002 the wines were bottled as Michel Esmonin et Fille.

★★ Fourrier

9 ha owned. Griotte-Chambertin (0.26 ha); Gevrey-Chambertin *premier cru* in Les Champeaux, Les Cherbaudes, Clos-Saint-Jacques, La Combe au Moine and Les Goulots; Vougeot *premier cru* in Les Petits-Vougeots; Morey-Saint-Denis *premier cru* Clos Sorbès; Chambolle-Musigny *premier cru* Les Gruenchers; village Gevrey-Chambertin, including the *lieu-dit* Aux Echézeaux; village Morey-Saint-Denis; village Chambolle-Musigny.

Following fine bottles in the 1950s and 1960s, when it sold under Pernot-Fourrier, this domaine went into decline until resurrected by Jean-Marie Fourrier in the early 1990s. Jean-Marie had worked for Henri Jayer and Domaine Drouhin in Oregon. He took over from his father Jean-Claude in 1995.

Everything is now as it should be, with ploughing in the vineyards via a vibrating sorting table, total de-stemming, temperatures up to 33°C after a short period of cold-soaking, minimal use of sulphur during the *élevage* and 20 percent new oak. This young man is a thinker. "I find that my way of doing things—not forcing the extraction, not raising the temperature at the end of the fermentation, retaining the carbon dioxide, not over-oaking—results in nobler tannins and fresher and more sophisticated fruit." There are brilliant wines here.

Jérôme Galeyrand

5 ha owned and *en fermage*. Village Gevrey-Chambertin, including a *vieilles vignes cuvée*; village Fixin; Côte de Nuits Villages.

Jérôme Galeyrand came to Burgundy from the Mayenne at the age of twenty-three to work the vintage with Alain Burguet. That was in 1996. He was a cheese wholesaler at the time. He now lives in Saint-Philibert outside Gevrey-Chambertin, where he has his barrel cellar. But the wines are made in Brochon. The domaine is small, but he supplements this by buying in fruit. He tends the Bonnes-Mares vines of Pierre Naigeon and purchases enough of the harvest to make one barrel. The year 2002 was his first vintage. This domaine is a rising star.

Dominique Gallois

3.5 ha owned. Charmes-Chambertin (0.29 ha); Gevrey-Chambertin *premier cru* in La Combe au Moine, Les Goulots and Les Petits Cazetiers; village Gevrey-Chambertin.

The dark-haired Dominique Gallois, cousin of Philippe Nadeff of Fixin, took over from his father in 1989, and it is only since then that we have seen these wines on the market. The vines are encouragingly old, the grapes 80 percent de-stemmed and macerated for a fortnight or so. There is no system for heating or cooling the must in the large, empty, deep, dark cellar. These wines have depth and are a little rigid at first but are slow to develop. This is a cellar to watch and one of the few to offer Petits-Cazetiers: most call their wine Cazetiers.

★ Vincent Geantet-Pansiot

13 ha owned and *en fermage*. Charmes-Chambertin (0.50 ha); Gevrey-Chambertin *premier cru* Le Poissenot; village Gevrey-Chambertin, including the *lieux-dits* Les Jeunes Rois and En Champs, and a *vieilles vignes cuvée*; Chambolle-Musigny *premier cru* (from Les Baudes, Les Feusselottes and Les Plantes); village Chambolle-Musigny; Marsannay.

Vincent Geantet has been in charge here since 1982, when his father Edmond handed over control, and things have been gently improving

ever since. No stems are used. Following a deliberate cooling down of the fruit for 8–10 days, the temperature is then allowed to rise to as much as 35°C during a 12–15 day *cuvaison*. One third new wood is employed for the *élevage*. The wines are bottled early—after 12 months or so—without fining or filtration to capture the fruit while it is fresh.

These are intensely flavoured wines, but not blockbusters. There is succulent perfumed fruit and good balance: no solidity, no hard edges. Geantet is a likeable man, and his domaine a very good source.

Jean-Michel Guillon

10 ha owned and *en fermage*. Clos de Vougeot (0.19 ha); Mazis-Chambertin (0.18 ha); Gevrey-Chambertin *premier cru* in La Petite Chapelle, Clos Prieur and Les Champonnets, plus a *vieilles vignes cuvée* of Les Champonnets; Morey-Saint-Denis *premier cru* La Riotte; village Gevrey-Chambertin, including a *vieilles vignes cuvée*; village Chambolle-Musigny.

The *sympa* Jean-Michel Guillon was in aeronautics. He lived for a while in Tahiti. Then, for some reason—for he has no family connections with Burgundy—he got the wine bug. Twenty-five years ago he installed himself in Gevrey-Chambertin. And he has since built up this domaine from scratch. His son Alexis joined him in 2004.

The *grands crus* are not de-stemmed; the Petite Chapelle is half; the rest totally. After a *saignée* Guillon macerates *à froid* for 6–7 days, then lets the temperature rise up to 36°C, even 37°C. Up to 100 percent new oak is used, and after that, the wine is left until bottling, which takes place 14 to 16 months after the vintage.

The set-up is clean, and the equipment up-to-date. Jean-Michel is a tall, handsome, vigorous and youthful fifty-ish man, and his wines are well made. But do they all taste a little too like each other? Are they a bit over-extracted and over-oaked?

Gérard Harmand-Geoffroy

8.91 ha owned and *en fermage*. Mazis-Chambertin (0.73 ha); Gevrey-Chambertin *premier cru* in La

Bossière (*monopole*), Les Champeaux, Lavaux-Saint-Jacques and La Perrière; village Gevrey-Chambertin, including the *lieux-dits* Clos Prieur and En Jouise, and a *vieilles vignes cuvée*.

The viticultural approach here is seriously *biologique*, encouraging the vine to produce its own defences to any depredatory attack, and the pruning is very short. When the fruit arrives in the modern winery in Gevrey's Place de Lois, it is 100 percent de-stemmed and cold-soaked for 5 days; there is a *cuvaison* of 15–21 days, and 25 to 50 percent new oak is employed during the *élevage*. Bottling takes place early in order to preserve the fruit.

The wines are plump and quite stylish, but not stunning enough to earn a star. Currently the Clos Prieur, a mix of *premier cru* and village wine, is preferable to the Bossière whose vines are still youthful.

★ Heresztyn

11 ha owned. Clos-Saint-Denis (0.23 ha); Gevrey-Chambertin *premier cru* in Les Champonnets, Les Corbeaux, Les Goulots and La Perrière; Morey-Saint-Denis *premier cru* Les Milandes; village Gevrey-Chambertin, including the *lieu-dit* Clos Village and a *vieilles vignes cuvée*; village Chambolle-Musigny.

The original Heresztyn, Jean, arrived from Poland in 1932, worked in the Gelin domaine in Fixin and for Jean Trapet in Gevrey-Chambertin and, slowly but surely, built up a domaine for himself. Now it is the third generation—an extended family of five brothers and sisters, husbands and wives—who run things, guarded by a noisy Alsatian, from premises in the centre of the villages. Christian Sérafin (q.v.) is a cousin.

Today all the fruit is de-stemmed. There is a cold-soaking for a week, and then a long *cuvaison* at a maximum temperature of 33°C; the wines are bottled after 18 months. They do not fine or filter.

Things are improving here. There is a *table de tri* now, and there seems to be a bit more new wood (30 to 40 percent) for the lesser *cuvées*. Since 1998 Heresztyn has deserved a star. The Goulots can be a little rustic, and the Perrière is

sometimes a little feeble. But the Milandes is a consistent success: one of the best *premier cru* Moreys on the market.

★ Humbert Frères

5.5 ha owned. Charmes-Chambertin (0.20 ha); Gevrey-Chambertin *premier cru* in Le Craipillot, Les Estournelles-Saint-Jacques, Lavaux-Saint-Jacques, La Petite-Chapelle, Le Poissenot; village Gevrey-Chambertin.

The Humbert brothers, Frédéric and Emmanuel, are cousins of the Dugats and live next door to Bernard. I used to wonder whether they were twins. Both are large, dark and solid. Until recently, Frédéric, the elder, made the wine, and Emmanuel worked the vineyards. A decade ago they switched roles, and from that point the wines became worthy of note. Total de-stemming, 5 days cold-maceration, fermentation temperatures up to 35°C, as little handling as possible and 100 percent new oak for the top wines before bottling after 16 months compose the usual recipe here. The wines are succulent, graceful and elegant, and by no means over-oaked.

Philippe Leclerc

7.84 ha owned. Gevrey-Chambertin *premier cru* in Les Cazetiers, Les Champeaux and La Combe au Moine; village Gevrey-Chambertin in the *lieux-dits* La Platière and En Champs; village Chambolle-Musigny.

The Leclerc domaine was split between Philippe, born 1951, and his elder brother René (see below) in 1974, and they have since gone entirely separate ways. Philippe, with his neat beard and elegant clothes, gives one the impression that he has just got off the set of some swashbuckling movie. He believes in picking late, macerating slowly at a high temperature with 20 percent of the stems, and then giving the wines a good 2 years in new wood with a very high toast, some of it from the Limousin region, delaying the malo, and bottling without either fining or filtration.

This used to result in big, spicy, almost brutally tannic and oaky wines. They could certainly be rich, but I found a lack of grace. From the 1999 vintage Leclerc began to forgo the Limousin in favour of oak from the Allier, and this and other touches made the wines more refined, less oaky. But there is still a way to go. The wines' olde-worlde presentation is uncompromisingly rustic, but for some reason this does not put off the tourists, who flock to his boutique in the centre of the village.

René Leclerc

9.5 ha owned and *en métayage*. Griotte-Chambertin (0.75 ha—Domaine des Chézeaux); Gevrey-Chambertin *premier cru* in La Combe au Moine, Lavaux-Saint-Jacques and Les Champeaux; village Gevrey-Chambertin, including the *lieu-dit* Clos Prieur.

The curly-headed, greying René, a decade or so older than Philippe, makes his wine with the help of his son François in a modern cellar down by the main road. He too has a shop in the middle of the village itself.

Again, there is a long *cuvaison*, but the grapes are de-stemmed, and the *cuvaison* temperature maintained at less than 30°C. Bottling takes place after 18 months. Here, however, there is only a third new oak and too much old wood. As a result, because the wines are never very concentrated in the first place, they tend to dry out and lose their focus and elegance.

Marchand Frères

7.2 ha owned. Charmes-Chambertin (0.14 ha); Griotte-Chambertin (0.13 ha); Clos de la Roche (0.07 ha); Gevrey-Chambertin *premier cru* Les Combottes; Morey-Saint-Denis *premier cru* Clos-Des-Ormes, Les Faconnières, Les Genavrières and Les Milandes; Chambolle-Musigny *premier cru* Les Sentiers; village Gevrey-Chambertin; village Morey-Saint-Denis; village Chambolle-Musigny in the *lieu-dit* Les Athées.

The Marchand brothers, Denis and Jean-Philippe, inherited the domaine of their Morey-Saint-Denis–based father Charles in 1983. In 1999 Jean-Philippe went his own way and set up a business under his own name, so it is Denis who is in charge here.

Ten percent of the stems are retained, and after 5 days cold-soaking, the fermentation proceeds at a maximum temperature of 32°C.

Thirty percent of the casks are new. The style of this estate is one of femininity and elegance rather than undue weight and power. It is good to very good, but it could be better.

Part of the Genavrières *premier cru* is to be converted to Chardonnay.

Marchand-Grillot et Fils

9 ha owned and *en fermage/en métayage*. Ruchottes-Chambertin (0.08 ha); Gevrey-Chambertin *premier cru* in La Petite Chapelle and Les Perrières, including the *lieu-dit* En Songe and a *vieilles vignes cuvée*; village Gevrey-Chambertin; village Morey-Saint-Denis; village Chambolle-Musigny.

Jacques Marchand, cousin of Jean-Philippe, runs this domaine from two separate cellars underneath the rear of two adjoining houses in the quaintly named Rue Aquatique. He occasionally thinks about joining them up, which would save a lot of manhandling. The trouble is they are not exactly on the same level. The fruit is now de-stemmed. There are a few days cold-maceration before the fermentation unleashes itself, and there is a *cuvaison* of 10–12 days at temperatures up to 32°C. These Marchands used to be no great fans of new oak, but they now use 50 percent for the *premiers crus*. Lighter vintages are bottled quite early, before the Christmas of the following year.

The wines used to be good here: stylish, balanced and fruity, on the feminine side. But in recent years, the domaine seems to have lost its way.

Maume

4.33 ha owned. Mazis-Chambertin (0.67 ha); Charmes-Chambertin (0.17 ha); Gevrey-Chambertin *premier cru* in Les Champeaux, Les Cherbaudes, Lavaux-Saint-Jacques and La Perrière (these last two are blended together and sold as Gevrey-Chambertin Premier Cru); village Gevrey-Chambertin, including the *lieux-dits* En Pallud and Aux Etelois.

Bernard Maume used to lead a double life. Though retired now, he would spend his days lecturing at the University of Dijon, or undertaking research into yeasts and starches, and his spare time running his small estate, inherited from an uncle, with his son Bertrand. He is an amiable man, thoughtful enough to provide a few warmed-up *gougères* for the travelling wine-writer to munch through as he samples the wines.

Naturally, much thought has gone into the winemaking process. Maume de-stems entirely, macerates at cool temperatures for 4 or 5 days, believes in a long *cuvaison* (3 or 4 weeks), at a maximum of 30°C, and lodges his wine in a selection of oak barrels from different origins, depending on the *cuvée*, a quarter of which, overall, is new. Racking is kept to a minimum, and the wines are not filtered.

What I like about Maume's wines is their rampant individuality. The Mazis is sexy and exotic, wanton and dangerous. The Charmes is more refined. I described them once in my newsletter *The Vine* as Eliza Doolittle and Professor Higgins. They are full, rich and concentrated, but sometimes they can lack a little grace.

★★ *Denis Mortet*

11.5 ha owned and *en fermage*. Clos de Vougeot (0.31 ha); Chambertin (0.15 ha); Gevrey-Chambertin *premier cru* in Lavaux-Saint-Jacques and Les Champeaux, plus a *premier cru* from a blend of Bel Air, Champonnets, Cherbaudes and Petite Chapelle; village Gevrey-Chambertin, including the *lieux-dits* En Champs *vieilles vignes*, Combe du Dessus, En Derée, Au Vellé and En Motrot (*monopole*); Chambolle-Musigny *premier cru* Aux Beaux Bruns; Fixin; Marsannay, Les Longeroies.

What was formerly the domaine Charles Mortet et Fils was divided after the 1991 harvest, Denis Mortet, born 1956, and his younger brother Thierry having decided to go their separate ways. Denis was then lucky enough to be approached by a neighbour about to retire, and he took over this man's 4.5 hectare domaine *en fermage*. This included a large parcel of Lavaux-Saint-Jacques.

Following a severe *triage*, the fruit is totally de-stemmed. There follows 5 to 7 days of pre-fermentation cold-maceration, a 13–15 day *cuvaison*, at a maximum temperature of 32°C, and a percentage of new oak which varies from 80 to 100 percent, depending on the *cuvée*. Moreover, there is a change in the origin of the wood

as well: a mixture for the lesser wines, solely Vosges for the best. There is no filtration, and usually no fining either.

But of course great winemaking cannot be encapsulated in a single paragraph. It is about a meticulous attention to detail from the vineyard onward, a very low yield, a very severe selection of fruit and, above all, flair and imagination. Denis Mortet had this in spades. The wines are full-bodied, concentrated, harmonious, intensely flavoured and splendidly elegant. There was a period in the mid-1990s when I felt they were a little over-extracted, but Mortet then, as he put it, took his foot off the accelerator "to let the *terroir* express itself." "I want to make wine like Charles Rousseau," he declared. As a result of this, his 2002s were better than his 1999s. From 2004 the various village Gevreys were simplified into two *cuvées*, one of which is called *vieilles vignes*.

Sadly and suddenly, Denis Mortet took his own life in January 2006, at the age of 49. It was a great loss. His son Arnaud, at age twenty-six, is now in charge. Fine 2005s were found here.

Thierry Mortet

4.5 ha owned and *en fermage*. Chambolle-Musigny *premier cru* Aux Beaux Bruns; village Chambolle-Musigny; village Gevrey-Chambertin, including the *lieu-dit* Clos Prieur.

Thierry Mortet's first vintage was 1992 (see above). He makes the wine in much the same way as his late brother did. They do not quite have the same flair, but they are nevertheless clean and attractive, if a little on the oaky side.

François Perrot

13 ha owned and *en métayage*. Gevrey-Chambertin *premier cru* La Petite-Chapelle; Chambolle-Musigny *premier cru* in Les Charmes and Les Baudes; village Gevrey-Chambertin, including the *lieu-dit* Champerrier; village Chambolle-Musigny; village Savigny-lès-Beaune; Marsannay.

François Perrot runs two domaines: what used to be Domaine les Perrières, which exploits the

Gevrey vines, and Les Tassées, which exploits those in Chambolle. The headquarters are a modern, ugly, disorderly winery up against the slope above the Champonnet *climat*. The fruit is largely, but not totally, de-stemmed; there is one week's cold-soaking before fermentation, and the wines are matured using 15 percent new oak. I used to find the wines thin and rustic, but despite the surroundings, recent visits have been more than satisfactory. I'd like to have more experience of the wines in bottle.

Henri Rebourseau

13.62 ha owned. Clos-de-Vougeot (2.21 ha); Charmes-Chambertin (1.31 ha); Mazis-Chambertin (0.96 ha); Chambertin (0.46 ha); Chambertin, Clos de Bèze (0.33 ha) (the last two are blended together); Gevrey-Chambertin *premier cru* Le Fonteny; village Gevrey-Chambertin.

The imperative that if you possess great land, you have a duty to mankind to produce great wine applies with more force, the greater the cornucopia of richness, as is the case here. Sadly, I can report only disappointment, though there have been one or two occasions in the last decade when I thought that things might have turned the corner. One explanation is that, coinciding with the arrival of Jean de Surrel, the present manager, at the end of the 1980s, much of the domaine was replanted.

The grapes are de-stemmed, vinified at up to 30°C after a couple of days *macération à froid*, with *cuvaison* lasting a fortnight, and there is 100 percent new oak for the Chambertin. The top 1999s are good. But this was an easy vintage to make good wine in. The 2000s reverted to being one-dimensional. And surely, it should be against the law to pick Chambertin by machine.

Henri Richard

3.2 ha owned. Charmes-Chambertin and Mazoyères-Chambertin (1.11 ha); village Gevrey-Chambertin.

From headquarters on the main road—one of the last houses on the Beaune side—this small domaine is one of the few which offer you both Charmes-Chambertin and Mazoyères-Chambertin, their large parcel overlapping the boundary between these two appellations. The Charmes is preferred and given a little more new oak. As a result, perhaps, I find the Mazoyères a little more robust.

Today run by Madame Richard (Henri died in 1985), her daughter Margaret Bastien-Richard and a young *caviste*, this domaine produces neat, fresh, fruity wines which evolve in the medium term. Bottling is by gravity, without filtration.

Philippe Rossignol

6 ha owned and *en fermage/en métayage*. Gevrey-Chambertin *premier cru* Les Corbeaux and Estournelles-Saint-Jacques; village Gevrey-Chambertin, including a *vieilles vignes cuvée*; village Fixin; Côte-de-Nuits-Villages *rouge et blanc*.

Philippe Rossignol, born in 1956, in Burgundy but not *dans les vignes*, as he puts it, is the brother-in-law of Joseph Roty and has built up his domaine from scratch since the mid-1970s. It was only in 1993 that he was proudly able to offer some *premier cru* wine. He's one of the few *vignerons* with premises below the main road on the way to the railway station.

The grapes are entirely de-stemmed and vinified after 5 or 6 days cold-maceration at a maximum temperature of 34°C. There is quite a lot of new wood and neither fining nor filtration. The results are very good, though sometimes a little hard and austere at the outset.

★ Rossignol-Trapet

14 ha owned. Chambertin (1.60 ha); Latricières-Chambertin (0.75 ha); Chapelle-Chambertin (0.50 ha); Gevrey-Chambertin *premier cru* in Clos Prieur and La Petite Chapelle; Beaune *premier cru* Les Teurons; village Gevrey-Chambertin; village Beaune in the *lieu-dit* Les Mariages; village Savigny-Lès Beaune in the *lieu-dit* Les Bas-Liards.

The well-known Trapet domaine was divided in 1990, at which time both Jean Trapet and his brother-in-law Jacques Rossignol officially retired. Jacques's half is today administered by his sons David and Nicolas.

Following their cousins across the road, this domaine is biodynamic—all the *grands crus* are from 2001. The fruit is now entirely de-stemmed. Fermentation is controlled at a maximum of 32°C, the percentage of new oak varies from a quarter to one half, and bottling takes place about 13–16 months after the vintage.

The result, just like over the road at what is now Jean and Jean-Louis Trapet, is good: round, medium-full, plump and fruity wines. With a great attention to matters in the vineyard—higher training, ploughing and green harvesting, plus a vibrating sorting table in the winery, no pumping and no filtration—quality has improved, especially since 1999. The vines in the Petite Chapelle and the Clos Prieur are still relatively young, having been planted in 1986. This is now a very good source.

★ Joseph and Philippe Roty

9.2 ha owned and *en fermage*. Charmes-Chambertin (0.16 ha), Mazis-Chambertin (0.12 ha); Griotte-Chambertin (0.08 ha); Gevrey-Chambertin *premier cru* Le Fonteny; village Gevrey-Chambertin, including the *lieux-dits* Brunelle, Les Champs Chenys and Clos Prieur, plus a *très vieilles vignes cuvée*; Marsannay, including the *lieux-dits* Le Boivin, Champs Saint-Etienne, Le Clos de Jeu, Les Quartiers and Les Ouzeloy.

Joseph Roty, *enfant terrible* of the Côte d'Or, has sadly aged fast. His son Philippe has been in charge for some years and has expanded the domaine holdings in Marsannay.

Viticulture is *biologique*, old vines are preserved, and the yields are cut to a minimum. He vinifies with some of the stems, for a long time, at a very cold temperature, never more than 28°C (and preferably at 25°C). The wine then goes into well-charred new wood: 100 percent for the *grands crus*. There is minimal racking, no filtration and no fining.

Roty's wines are very distinctive. They are full, very intense, very perfumed and very harmonious. They are certainly immensely seductive. Sometimes, though, I find them just a touch sweet, just a shade over-oaky.

★★★ Armand Rousseau

13.7 ha owned. Chambertin (2.15 ha); Chambertin, Clos-de-Bèze (1.42 ha); Charmes-Chambertin (1.37 ha);Clos-de-la-Roche (1.48 ha); Ruchottes-Chambertin, Clos-Des-Ruchottes (1.06 ha); Mazy-Chambertin (0.53 ha); Gevrey-Chambertin *premier cru* in Clos-Saint-Jacques, Les Cazetiers and Lavaux-Saint-Jacques; village Gevrey-Chambertin.

A visit to taste in Charles Rousseau's cellar is one of the delights of every Burgundy visit. This is a domaine with a proven record of producing fine wine which dates back to the 1930s, when Charles's father Armand was one of the very first to start putting his own wine into bottle. Armand died in 1959 at the age of seventy-five, and the mantle passed to Charles, born 1923, a short man with a large head, a voluble, expansive presence and a lush, squeaky laugh. His son Éric is now in charge in the cellar.

Fifteen percent of the stems are retained, to aid the efficiency of the fermentation as much as anything else. The *cuvaison* lasts 15 days, at a maximum temperature of 31°C, and the top three wines, the third being the Clos-Saint-Jacques (not the Mazy or the Ruchottes), get 100 percent new wood. The wine is bottled late, after 18–20 months. But it all starts in the vineyard, says Charles, with a low yield which is established early in the season, by hard pruning and de-budding. He is contemptuous of the current fashion of green harvesting. Yet, despite an increasing tendency elsewhere to reduce the number of rackings, Rousseau's wines used to be racked in the spring (he likes an early malo) as well as in September. Since 2003 the spring racking has been given up, and the cellar is no longer warmed to speed up the malo.

Rousseau's wines are rich in colour, pure in texture, never over-oaked, always concentrated, balanced, vigorous and very classy. They get round and velvety sooner than some. Moreover, they are all quite distinctive, each an expression of its own *terroir*. This is superb winemaking, from one of the gentlemen of Burgundy.

Gérard Seguin

5.5 ha owned. Gevrey-Chambertin *premier cru* in Craipillot and Lavaux-Saint-Jacques; village Gevrey-

Chambertin, including the *lieux-dits* Les Crais and La Justice and a *vieilles vignes cuvée*; village Chambolle-Musigny, including the *lieu-dit* Derrière le Four.

Gérard Seguin, whose premises are found between those of Armand Rousseau and the Humbert brothers on the road up into the Hautes-Côtes, supplements his income from his domaine by teaching at the local viticultural college. He ploughs his land, green harvests, usually concentrates the must by means of a *saignée*, de-stems, matures his wine using 30 percent new wood, and does not rack until the juice is being prepared for bottling. These are gentle wines, and quite stylish, but they could do with being more concentrated.

★ Christian Sérafin

5.35 ha owned. Charmes-Chambertin (0.31 ha); Gevrey-Chambertin *premier cru* in Les Cazetiers and Le Fonteny; Morey-Saint-Denis *premier* cru Les Milandes; Chambolle-Musigny *premier cru* Les Baudes; village Gevrey-Chambertin, including the *lieu-dit* Les Corbeaux and a *vieilles vignes cuvée*.

Stanislaus Sérafin arrived from Poland before the war (the family are cousins of the Heresztyns), worked first as a *maçon* (builder), and in 1947 bought a piece of land and set himself up as a *vigneron*. He gradually built up an estate, which his son Christian inherited in 1988, though the latter had been responsible for the wine for a decade or more before that point.

One would have agreed then: a good domaine, but not an exciting one. The last 20 years, however, have seen a distinct improvement, as if Christian had been somewhat constrained in the past. This is today an excellent source.

The vineyard is organically cultivated, great attention being paid to restricting the yield and, when it comes to the harvest, to a *triage* of the fruit. The grapes are now totally de-stemmed, and after 4 to 8 days of cold maceration, the fermentation is allowed to progress up to a maximum temperature of 33°C. *Cuvaisons* are long. There is 80 to 100 percent new wood, much more than hitherto, and no longer any filtration. The wines are bottled after 16–20 months.

Sérafin's wines are full-bodied, meaty, and abundantly rich, with a good touch of spice, and are nicely oaky rather than excessively so. His *vieilles vignes* village Gevrey-Chambertin is usually better than his Fonteny. This is a splendid address, save for a blip in 1996 and 1995.

Thibaut Père et Fils

8 ha owned and *en fermage/en métayage*. Village Gevrey-Chambertin; village Morey-Saint-Denis; village Chambolle-Musigny; village Vosne-Romanée.

The lean, if not gaunt, Denis Thibaut, who took over from his father in 1995, deserves to be better recognised, but he is almost too self-effacing, if not a touch morose. So it is we who will have to make the effort. He makes only village wines, but only the old vine elements of such (the rest is sold off in bulk); the grapes are totally de-stemmed and cold-soaked for 6 days or so and then fermented up to 35°C, matured with 20 percent new wood and bottled in the early spring, 16 months or so after the vintage. These are very clean, pure wines: admirable Pinot Noir. But little is sold in bottle.

Tortochot

11 ha owned. Chambertin (0.31 ha); Charmes-Chambertin (0.57 ha); Mazis-Chambertin (0.42 ha); Clos de Vougeot (0.21 ha); Gevrey-Chambertin *premier cru* in Les Champeaux and Lavaux-Saint-Jacques; Morey-Saint-Denis *premier cru* Aux Charmes; village Gevrey-Chambertin, including the *lieux-dits* Champerrier, Les Corvées, Les Jeunes Rois and a *vieilles vignes cuvée*; village Morey-Saint-Denis.

Gabriel Tortochot passed away in 2001, and his daughter, Chantal Michel, is now in charge. The *cave* is a splendid rabbit warren of different locations in different cellars.

The grapes are completely de-stemmed, cold-soaked for a week and vinified at 32–34°C, and the top wines get 100 percent new oak. There is no racking until bottling, which is done without fining or filtration after 15 months. The wines have improved over the last decade: they are less rustic than hitherto, but they nevertheless still lack succulence and concentration.

★ Jean and Jean-Louis Trapet

12 ha owned. Chambertin (1.90 ha); Chapelle-
Chambertin (0.60 ha); Latricières-Chambertin
(0.75 ha); Gevrey-Chambertin *premier cru* in Clos
Prieur and La Petite Chapelle; village Gevrey-
Chambertin; Marsannay.

This is the other half of the Trapet domaine (q.v.
Rossignol-Trapet), divided in 1990, and today it
is Jean-Louis, son of the ebullient Jean, who is
in charge. The domaine has been totally biodynamic since 1998.

Thirty percent of the fruit is de-stemmed.
There is a 5- to 8-day cold-maceration, and
then a long *cuvaison* (3 to 4 weeks) at a maximum temperature of 32°C. Plenty of new oak
is employed: from 30 to 75 percent for the top
wines. Bottling takes place after 15 to 18 months,
without filtration and by gravity.

Quality had dropped from high levels in
the 1950s and 1960s an only average level in
the 1980s, but since the split and Jean-Louis's
promotion to the man in charge, this trend has
been dramatically reversed. When you sample a
Trapet Chambertin against a Rousseau, the gap
is evident. But it is getting smaller.

Varoilles

10.5 ha owned and *en métayage*. Charmes-Chambertin
(0.75 ha); Clos de Vougeot (0.60 ha); Gevrey-
Chambertin *premier cru* in Clos des Varoilles
(*monopole*), Les Champonnets and La Romanée
(*monopole*); village Gevrey-Chambertin, including
lieux-dits of Clos du Meix des Ouches (*monopole*),
Clos du Couvent (*monopole*) and Clos Saint-Pierre.

The Domaine des Varoilles now belongs to
the Swiss businessman Gilbert Hammel, having previously belonged to the late Jean-Pierre
Naigeon of the *négociants* Naigeon-Chauveau.
Patrice Naigeon, son of Jean-Pierre, has now
gone his own way, and the contract with him for
the Bonnes-Mares ran out in 2002.

Complete de-stemming is practised here,
but instead of the more traditional *pigeage*, an
automatic device to break up the cap and sub-
merge it in the must is used. The *cuvaison* lasts

10–12 days, the wines are given up to 60 percent
new oak, and bottling takes place after a little
over a year.

The results are good here, sometimes very
good, but I find the style of the Varoilles wines,
though elegant, a little lean. I'd like a bit of fat.
It would give the wines more generosity and
sex appeal.

Alain Voegeli

2.5 ha owned. Village Gevrey-Chambertin.

Alain Voegeli now owns the land he used to
exploit on behalf of his late grandmother,
Madame Suzanne Servoz, which was once part
of the Domaine Etienne Grey (of Grey-Poupon
Mustard). He makes one wine—the young-vine
wine is sold off in bulk—and it is plump, elegant
and generous. It comes forward in the medium
term. There is total de-stemming, a few days
cold-soaking and 20 percent new wood.

MOREY-SAINT-DENIS

Morey-Saint-Denis leads a schizophrenic existence and has never achieved the reputation
of either Gevrey-Chambertin to the north or
Chambolle-Musigny to the south, despite being
the possessor of four and a bit *grands crus*—the
bit being a small part of Bonnes-Mares, most of
which lies across the border in Chambolle.

The reason for this is simple: for generations, the local growers, abetted by the *négoce*,
passed off their wines as Gevrey-Chambertin.
And for generations, wine writers have tended
to dismiss Morey as a sort of inferior halfway
house, neither Gevrey nor Chambolle and not
as good as either.

This is unfair, for the village possesses
an impossibly large number of tiny *premiers
crus*—only three out of twenty are larger than
3 hectares, and one of these, Monts-Luisants,
is planted with white grapes as well as red;
consequently, these lack definition in the
minds of all but the most experienced locals,
and despite the area of village appellation having been extended across the main road to

the east—a deleterious step in my view—the wines of Morey *do* have character and a distinct personality, and they *can* be just as fine (and sadly sometimes just as miserable) as all but the very, very best of either Chambolle-Musigny or Gevrey-Chambertin. Today there are plenty of very good estates in the commune.

History

The origins of Morey-Saint-Denis, known as Mirriacum in 1120 according to Dangay et Aubertin, are closely connected with the Cistercian Abbey of Cîteaux and its benefactors, the *seigneurs* of Vergy (though there is much archaeological evidence of a Gallo-Roman settlement centuries before the arrival of the monks). This heritage is illustrated by the survival of the word "Clos" in a number of *climats*.

It was in that year, 1120, that Savaric de Vergy ceded to Cîteaux much of the land in the village. In 1300 responsibility passed to the Abbey of Saint-Germain-des-Près, when it bought the priory of Gilly, to which the lands at Morey were tied. A century later, when the local Cistercians acquired the château at Gilly—now a splendidly renovated but expensive hotel—the village came back into local hands, and until the Revolution, the land was owned either by the Abbaye de Cîteaux or by the descendants of the Vergys and the other grand families of Burgundy, such as the Saulx-Tavannes and the Croonembourgs, owners at one time of La Romanée-Conti itself.

The first important vineyard settlement seems to have been that of the Clos de Tart. It was originally Tart-le-Haut, to distinguish it from the village in the plain beyond Dijon, and was exploited by the nuns of the newly created Notre-Dame-de-Tart almost from the foundation of their establishment in 1125 until the Revolution. Notably, it has remained, since regaining its present size in 1251, both unaltered and a monopoly.

Clos Saint-Denis, which was originally a mere 2.14 hectares instead of today's 6.62 hectares, takes its name from a college of Canons installed in 1023 up in the hill beyond Vergy. The college owned a number of parcels of land, including part of Les Saint-Georges in Nuits. Like the Clos de Tart, the land passed after the Revolution to the Marey-Monge family.

Clos des Lambrays, elevated to *grand cru* in 1981, seems never to have enjoyed ecclesiastical ownership; indeed, its origins are somewhat enshrouded in mist, though references to it date back to the fourteenth century. After the Revolution it was split among as many as seventy-four proprietors. Subsequently, under the Joly, Rodier and Cosson families, it was reassembled, and it is now for all intents and purposes a monopoly.

Clos de la Roche, as Henri Cannard says, is an enigma. The vineyard dates from much later and has never been enclosed. Some writers have suggested—for why La Roche rather than Les Roches?—that it was originally the site of some Druidic religious ritual. Originally, it covered a mere 4.57 hectares. Now, having absorbed several *premiers crus*, the last in 1971, it occupies 16.9 hectares.

A number of other *climats* have clear religious origins: the Clos-de-la-Bussière, for example, which belonged to the Cistercian abbey of Bussières-Sur-Ouche. There are also the Clos des Ormes, today sadly without a single elm tree (*orme*) in sight, the Clos Baulet and the Clos Sorbè.

Probably more so here than in the rest of the Côte de Nuits, a consequence of its lack of reputation perhaps, the village continued to plant a large quantity of Gamay until well into the last half of the nineteenth century. Only in the plum vineyards, suggests Dr. Lavalle, will you find solely the Pinot. In 1855 a mere 70 hectares out of 160 were planted with the noble grape.

In Lavalle's opinion, the wine of Clos de Tart was supreme: a *tête de cuvée*. Bonnes-Mares, that small part within the confines of the commune, Les Lambrays (not a Clos in those days!) and Clos-de-Laroche [*sic*] were regarded as *premières cuvées*, while Clos Saint-Denis was among half a dozen *deuxièmes*.

Morey was late to adopt the usual practice of tagging on the name of the most important cru to the village name. This did not happen until 1927, for the locals had found themselves in a dilemma. Which name? Morey-Tart did not sing, and neither did Morey-La-Roche. The anti-clerical lobby would disapprove of Morey-Saint-Denis. Some suggested Morey-Chambertin, but the neighbours would not hear of it. Morey-Les-Ormes was even put forward. But it wasn't vinous enough. The discussion went on for years. In the end, despite a certain opposition, Morey-Saint-Denis it became, for who would dare to criticise a saint with his head under his arm?

But as everyone has hitherto pointed out, Clos Saint-Denis is not Morey's best wine: it's Clos de la Roche, or Clos de Tart.

By the way, the Morey-Saint-Denis symbol is a wolf: the natives are called Les Loups de Morey.

Location

Only the excellent Gevrey-Chambertin *premier cru* Les Combottes separates the Latricières-Chambertin from Clos de la Roche, after which the rest of Morey's *grands crus* follow in a line above the Route des Grands Crus, which runs through the village until the *climat* of Bonnes-Mares overlaps into Chambolle-Musigny. With the exception of the Monts-Luisants, Les Chal-lots and Les Genavrières (spelled with an a), which lie upslope from Clos de la Roche and Clos Saint-Denis, Morey-Saint-Denis's *premiers crus* lie beneath the Route des Grands Crus on either side of the Grand Rue, which runs from the church opposite the entrance to the Clos de Tart down to the main road.

Morey is a compact village, with the Grand Rue as its main road, off which is many an imposing mansion fronted by a large courtyard, these being the headquarters of many of its leading growers. Above the village, and its Place du Monument, a road disappears into the hills behind the Domaine Ponsot, but only goes as far as a farm and an old marble quarry. Across the main road, where you will find Morey's winemaking cooperative, a rare foundation in the Côte d'Or, vines on the Gevrey side were

elevated to *appellation contrôlée* status in the early 1980s.

The appellation is only about a kilometre wide, from north to south, and forms a square, rising to 350 metres in the Monts Luisants, from which you can see the snows of Mont Blanc (but if you can, it means it's going to rain tomorrow!). Up at the top of the slope above the *grands crus*, white grape varieties, entitled to village AC (and indeed *premier cru* in Monts Luisants), are planted on light Bathonian limestone. Further down the slope, the soil is more of Bajocian origin, brown and calcareous. The Clos de Tart and the Bonnes-Mares are marked by their stones. There is more sand in the Clos des Lambrays. In the Clos Saint-Denis and the Clos de la Roche, there is marl, and it is less stony.

The Vineyard

GRANDS CRUS Morey has four *grands crus* in its own right. From north to south, they are Clos de la Roche, Clos Saint-Denis, Clos des Lambrays and Clos de Tart. Part of Bonnes-Mares lies in the commune. Ignoring this, the *grands crus* cover fractionally under 40 hectares and produce an average of 1,325 hectolitres per year.

PREMIERS CRUS Today there are twenty *premiers crus* in Morey-Saint-Denis, a number having been absorbed into Clos Saint-Denis and Clos de la Roche over the years. Altogether, they comprise some 33 hectares and produce 1,760 hectolitres per annum. In alphabetical order, they are as follows: Les Blanchards; La Bussière; Les Chaffots; Aux Charmes; Les Charrières; Les Chenevery; Aux Cheseaux; Clos Baulet; Clos des Ormes; Clos Sorbè; Côte Rôtie; Les Faconnières; Les Genavrières; Les Gruenchers; Les Milandes; Les Monts Luisants; La Riotte; Les Ruchots; Les Sorbès; Le Village.

In 1995 the local growers syndicate lodged an application with the Institut National des Appellations d'Origine (INAO) for the reclassification as *premier cru* of part (2.5 ha) of En la Rue de Vergy. The *climat* lies upslope from Clos de Tart. Nothing has been heard since.

VILLAGE WINE   There are some 64 hectares of village wine. These produce an average of 2,800 hectolitres a year.

The Morey-Saint-Denis appellation, unlike that of Gevrey-Chambertin or Chambolle-Musigny, applies to white wines as well as red. But the production is tiny, less than 4.2 hectares producing 196 hectolitres in 2005.

The red wine of Morey is said to be a cross between Gevrey and Chambolle, more structured but with less fragrance than the latter, and suppler and less sturdy than the former. This is simple, and it is true. There is a frank, lush fruitiness about a good Morey which makes it very appealing. Logic would also suggest that the wines to the north would be more Gevrey-like, those to the south more Chambolle-like. This is less easy to agree with. Remember that the vines to the south lie under Bonnes-Mares, itself a fuller, more tight-knit wine than Clos Saint-Denis and Clos de la Roche. Moreover, on this side we have the Roumier domaine's monopoly of the Clos de la Bussière: no Chambolle touches here! Happily—for glib simplification is boring—the commune does not generalise easily.

The Grands Crus

CLOS DE LA ROCHE

SURFACE AREA: 16.9 ha
AVERAGE PRODUCTION: 565 hl
PRINCIPAL PROPRIETORS: ★ Ponsot (3.34 ha); ★ Dujac (1.95 ha); ★ Armand Rousseau (1.48 ha); Pierre Amiot (1.20 ha); Coquard-Loison-Fleurot (1.17 ha); Georges Lignier (1.05 ha); ★ Hubert Lignier (1.01 ha); Peirazeau (0.80 ha); Morey Cooperative (0.79 ha); ★ Leroy (0.67 ha); ★ Louis Rémy (0.66 ha); Guy Castagnier (0.58 ha); ★ Hospices de Beaune (0.44 ha); ★ Arlaud (0.43 ha); Feuillet (0.41 ha); Gérard Raphet (0.38 ha); Michel Magnien (0.37 ha); ★ Lignier-Michelot (0.31 ha).

Clos de la Roche has grown from 4.57 hectares in 1861 to 16.9 hectares today, absorbing the *lieux-dits* of Chabiots, Fremières, Froichots, Mauchamps and the bottom of Monts Luisants in the process. (Who's to say it wouldn't have

gobbled up Gevrey-Chambertin, Les Combottes, if it hadn't been over the boundary?) If that sounds greedy, a glance at the map or a wander along between the vines will show that there is nothing unnatural here. The extra territory is at the same altitude (270–300 m) and of the same geological mixture—on a Bajocian limestone base, brown in colour, mixed gently with clay and limestone rock scree, and in places barely 30 centimetres deep. At least this *grand cru* has not extended itself below the Route des Grand Vins.

There is a gentle incline, more so than across the border in Latricières and in Chambertin itself, which aids the drainage, and the aspect is firmly to the east, while in the Clos Saint-Denis next door, there is a faint suggestion of a few degrees further to the north.

It is the biggest and the classiest of the Morey *grands crus*. But the structure has an inherent lushness to it. There is none of the austerity of Chambertin or the muscular density of Bonnes-Mares. The fruit has an element of the exotic, with a splendidly seductive perfume of *myrtille* (bilberry, huckleberry), sometimes black cherry, violets or truffles. Ample and classy it certainly is. But dignified? I think not. It definitely doesn't stand on its dignity.

CLOS SAINT-DENIS

SURFACE AREA: 6.62 ha
AVERAGE PRODUCTION: 230 hl
PRINCIPAL PROPRIETORS: Georges Lignier (1.49 ha); ★ Dujac (1.47 ha); ★ Drouhin (0.68 ha); ★ Bertagna (0.51 ha); De Chézeaux/★ Ponsot (0.60 ha); Henri Jouan (0.36 ha); Guy Castagnier (0.35 ha); Jean-Paul Magnien (0.32 ha); Heresztyn (0.23 ha); Peirazeau (0.20 ha); Pierre Amiot (0.17 ha); Coquard-Loison-Fleurot (0.17 ha); Charlopin-Parizot (0.17 ha); ★ Arlaud (0.17 ha); ★ Jadot (0.17 ha); Michel Magnien (0.12 ha).

If the extent of this Clos, prior to the Revolution, was a mere 2.12 hectares, there are, to quote Danguy et Aubertin, "no natural limits in Morey," and the *climat* has expanded to fill all the space between Clos de la Roche and the road up into the hills, absorbing part of Les Chaffots and La Calouère and all of Maison Brûlée in the meanwhile.

Clos Saint-Denis does not reach all the way down to the Route des Grand Vins, for what was Les Chabiots is now Clos de la Roche. But otherwise it is on the same level and has much the same soil structure—a brown Bajocian marl—mixed more with rock than pebbles, that is high in phosphorus, with perhaps just a little more clay than in the Clos de la Roche.

This is the most Chambolle-like of the Morey *grands crus* despite its position. The words *supple* and *delicate* spring to mind, as do *fragrant* and *"feminine."* There is a purity and class here when the wine is at its best, which is quite different from the Clos de la Roche, and though it is less structured, it is no less intense. The fruit flavours are of raspberries and red currants, and the structure gentle and quietly dignified. In Jacques Seysses's cellar at the Domaine Dujac, you can see the two side by side. On their own you might find each hard to place, but put together, the different origins are inescapable.

CLOS DES LAMBRAYS

SURFACE AREA: 8.84 ha
AVERAGE PRODUCTION: 295 hl
PRINCIPAL PROPRIETORS: Domaine des Lambrays (8.66 ha); Jean Taupenot-Merme owns 420 square metres.

It was not until 1981 that this *climat* was finally promoted to *grand cru*. Judging by the bottles it produced in the late 1940s, this was indisputably fully merited. But by then, the Domaine des Lambrays, in the hands of the Cosson family, had fallen on hard times. Having failed to take up the cudgels to get the land classed as *grand cru* in 1936, the widow Renée Cosson allowed the vineyard to decline, failing to replace dead vines. By the 1970s the winemaking had deteriorated too, and when it finally changed hands after her death in 1977—being bought in 1979—a major project of replantation and rehabilitation was necessary, and inevitably, with a low average age of vineyard, the wines that followed

under the new regime were somewhat thin and uninspiring.

The new owner was a consortium, whose shareholders were the Saier family, owners of an existing domaine in Mercurey and Aloxe-Corton, together with Roland Pelletier de Chambure. The latter died prematurely in 1988, and the Saier brothers bought up his share, at the top of the market. The Domaine des Lambrays was acquired by M. and Mme Günther Freund in 1997.

The Clos des Lambrays reaches furthest up the hill of all the Morey *grands crus* and inclines gently to the north as well as east. The soil is less marly and has more pure limestone than that of the other *climats*, and there is also sand. Because of the undulating nature of the terrain, much of the vineyard is planted north–south rather than the more usual east–west.

Charles Quittanson, who has written a monograph on the Clos, speaks of iron hands in velvet gloves, and others remark on the substance that this *climat* can produce. (*"Très corsé,"* says Henri Cannard, while Clos de Tart and Clos de la Roche are merely *"corsé."*)

I wrote in 1993, when I sampled it in cask, that it was "definitely Morey (rather than Gevrey or Bonnes-Mares) in its structure and texture"—rich and plummy, balanced and classy: not a blockbuster. But not (yet?) unmistakably of *proper grand cru* quality.

Nevertheless, the Freunds and their resident manager, Thierry Brouhin, have been unstinting in attention to detail to promote the quality of this wine, and the château, park and its outbuildings have been largely restored. Success, in the sense of the fabulous Clos des Lambrays of the past, has come in the last decade. I shall never forget a 1949 that Alexis Lichine was once kind enough to open for me at the Prieuré; nor the 1947; nor the 1945.

CLOS DE TART

SURFACE AREA: 7.53 ha
AVERAGE PRODUCTION: 230 hl
PROPRIETOR: Monopoly of Mommessin S.A.

Directly upslope from the village itself is the Clos de Tart. The large, impressive, two-level, deep cellar is nineteenth century, but the buildings opposite, comprising the offices and lodging for some of the vineyard workers, are medieval, once a monastic *dortoir*.

Sequestered by the revolutionary state, the Clos was sold at auction early in 1791, between the disposal of Romanée-Saint-Vivant and that of Chambertin, and acquired by Charles Dumand of Nuits-Saint-Georges for 68,200 francs. Dumand and Nicolas-Joseph Marey often acted in tandem, and perhaps on this occasion Dumand was acting on behalf of the Marey (later Marey-Monge) family, for it was into their hands that the Clos de Tart was to pass. In the crisis of the 1930s, having been first exploited by the *négociants* Champy of Beaune and then by Chauvenet of Nuits-Saint-Georges, descendants of the Marey-Monge dynasty sold the Clos de Tart to Mommessin of Mâcon. Other holdings in the Morey-Saint-Denis area passed to the Groffier family. Since 1932 the Clos de Tart has remained with Mommessin. The resident manager is currently Sylvain Pithiot.

The vines, unlike most of the Côte, are planted north–south rather than up and down the slope, a neat compromise between the need to protect against erosion and the requisite of efficient drainage. The vineyard here is very stony, resting on a Bathonian calcareous base at the top of the slope, evolving into Bajocian, with a little more clay and a little more depth of surface soil at the foot. Renewal of the vineyard is by *sélection massale* on a regular basis to ensure a 55-year average age.

Full-bodied but "feminine" is how Clos-de-Tart is described. "*Une grande dame*," says Bazin. I must demur. The wine is robust and tannic, with rich cherry fruit and a certain spice. Leaving Bonnes-Mares to the side, it is surely the most masculine of the Morey-Saint-Denis *grands crus*. Since 1999 quality has been indisputably first division.

The Premiers Crus

There are currently twenty *premiers crus* in Morey-Saint-Denis, and few are of a size significant enough to give them a distinct personality of their own. It is convenient to discuss them under four separate headings.

1.   There are those which lie upslope from Clos Saint-Denis and Clos de la Roche:

LES CHAFFOTS	*(2.62 ha)*
CÔTE RÔTIE	*(1.23 ha)*
LES GENAVRIÈRES—with	
an *a*, please note	*(1.19 ha)*
LES MONTS LUISANTS	*(5.39 ha)*

Hitherto a terrain given over to white wine, this sector has been gradually taken over by the Pinot Noir since 1960. Ponsot (see below) is one of the few who have not replanted all their land in black grapes. The land is poor and rocky, with very little surface soil, and up here at above 300 metres, it is marginally cooler. The result is wine with a good acidity, so it keeps well, but with a certain leanness. The fruit flavours combine red currants and cherries, with a hint of damsons in some years.

RECOMMENDED SOURCES
LES MONTS LUISANTS *BLANC*
Ponsot (Morey-Saint-Denis).

LES CHAFFOTS
Hubert Lignier (Morey-Saint-Denis).

2.   Underneath Clos-de-la-Roche, at the Gevrey-Chambertin end, you will find in a line from north to south the following:

AUX CHARMES	*(1.17 ha)*
AUX CHESEAUX (part)	*(1.49 ha)*
CLOS DES ORMES	*(3.15 ha)*
LES CHARRIÈRES	*(2.27 ha)*
LES FACONNIÈRES	*(1.67 ha)*
LES MILANDES (one of the larger climats)	*(4.20 ha)*

Underneath the last, part of Les Chenevery (1.90 ha) is also graded *premier cru*.

Premier cru land reaches down to within a couple hundred metres of the main road, roughly on a line with the last houses of the village and the hotel-restaurant Les Tres Girard.

This is where you will find the best of Morey's *premiers crus*. A good Clos des Ormes or Milandes, the two most commonly seen, is a rich, ample wine with good backbone and plenty of ripe black cherry and blackberry fruit: very much a lesser—but by no means ignoble—Clos de la Roche.

RECOMMENDED SOURCES
LES CHENEVERY
Lignier-Michelot (Morey-Saint-Denis).

AUX CHESEAUX
Arlaud (Morey-Saint-Denis).

CLOS DES ORMES
Georges Lignier (Morey-Saint-Denis).

LES FACONNIÈRES
Hubert Lignier, Lignier-Michelot (both Morey-Saint-Denis).

LES MILANDES
Pierre Amiot, Arlaud, Jean Raphet (all Morey-Saint-Denis); Heresztyn, Christian Sérafin (both Gevrey-Chambertin).

3.   Moving south toward the village of Morey, we find these:

LES GRUENCHERS	(0.51 ha)
LA RIOTTE	(2.45 ha)
LES BLANCHARDS	(1.97 ha)
LE VILLAGE (part)	(0.90 ha)
CLOS BAULET	(0.87 ha)
CLOS SORBÈ	(3.55 ha)
LES SORBÈS	(2.68 ha)

Here the wines are similar to those in the last category, but they have less definition and less finesse: good worthy Moreys, but rarely exciting.

RECOMMENDED SOURCES
CLOS SORBÈ
Fourrier (Gevrey-Chambertin)

LA RIOTTE
Hubert Lignier, Perrot-Minot (both Morey-Saint-Denis)

LES SORBÈS
Bernard Serveau (Morey-Saint-Denis)

4.   On the southern side of the village, under-neath Clos de Tart and Bonnes-Mares, lie the last two *premiers crus*:

LES RUCHOTS	(2.58 ha)
CLOS DE LA BUSSIÈRE (monopoly of the Domaine Georges Roumier of Chambolle-Musigny)	(2.59 ha)

If you stand on the Route des Grands Vins with your back to the Clos de Tart and look downslope, you will see the land sink into a little hollow in the Ruchots and then rise again. This keeps the Bussière—which is the land on the rise—very well drained, and in the hands of Christophe Roumier, it makes a very good wine, not a bit like the rest of his range: fullish, meaty, robust and animal, but rich and succulent after a goodly period of maturity.

RECOMMENDED SOURCES
LES RUCHOTS
Pierre Amiot, Arlaud (both Morey-Saint-Denis).

CLOS DE LA BUSSIÈRE
Georges Roumier (Chambolle-Musigny).

The Growers

Pierre Amiot et Fils

8.5 ha owned and *en métayage*. Clos de la Roche (1.20 ha); Clos-Saint-Denis (0.17 ha); Charmes-Chambertin (0.20 ha); Gevrey-Chambertin *premier cru* Les Combottes; Morey-Saint-Denis *premier cru* in Aux Charmes, Les Chevenery, Les Milandes and Les Ruchots; village Morey-Saint-Denis *rouge et blanc*; village Gevrey-Chambertin.

Pierre Amiot has now retired, and his place has been taken by two of his sons, Jean-Louis and Didier (another, Christian, looks after the Domaine Amiot-Servelle in Chambolle-Musigny).

Yields have been cut following more severe pruning and green harvesting, and quality has improved and become more consistent. Total de-stemming, a week of cold-soaking and one third or more new oak is the order of the day here.

The Ruchots is the best of the Moreys, but the Combottes is better still.

★ Arlaud Père et Fils

15 ha owned and *en fermage*. Charmes-Chambertin (1.14 ha); Clos de la Roche (0.43 ha); Clos Saint-Denis (0.17 ha); Bonnes-Mares (0.20 ha); Morey-Saint-Denis *premier cru* in Les Blanchards,

Aux Cheseaux, Les Milandes and Les Ruchots; Gevrey-Chambertin *premier cru* Aux Combottes; Chambolle-Musigny *premier cru* in Les Chatelots, Les Noirots and Les Sentiers; village Morey-Saint-Denis; village Gevrey-Chambertin; village Chambolle-Musigny.

Father Hervé having retired, Cyprien Arlaud has brought the winemaking back from somewhat cramped quarters in Nuits-Saint-Georges to a new, custom-built winery out on the flat land near the railway line. Quality is high here: the recipe is 100 percent de-stemming, 4–6 days of cold-maceration, fermentation temperatures up to 32°C, from 30 to 100 percent new oak, and bottling after 12–16 months, following only a single racking and neither fining nor filtration. I find the Arlaud wines very pure and fragrant. This is a very good address. In 2005 the Arlauds took over 2.5 ha from Guy Coguard on his retirement.

Domaine des Beaumont

4 ha owned. Charmes-Chambertin (0.52 ha); Gevrey-Chambertin *premier cru* Cherbaudes and Aux Combottes; Morey-Saint-Denis Les Sorbès and a *premier cru* (a blend of Milandes and Les Ruchots); Chambolle-Musigny *premier cru*; village Gevrey-Chambertin, including a *vieilles vignes cuvée*; village Morey-Saint-Denis; village Chambolle-Musigny.

Thierry Beaumont and his brother inherited this estate in 1991, but until 1998, they sold the produce off in bulk. They operate from a modern cellar on the "wrong" (i.e., downslope) side of the main road. The wines are racked into tank in September to liberate the casks for the next vintage, and bottled soon thereafter. It is a neat set-up, which now acts as a merchant as well as a domaine. But the wines could have more depth and personality, despite a relatively long *cuvaison* of up to 3 weeks.

Guy Castagnier
Christopher Newman

CASTAGNIER: 3.8 ha *en fermage/en métayage*. Clos de Vougeot (0.50 ha); Clos de la Roche (0.58 ha); Clos Saint-Denis (0.35 ha); Charmes-Chambertin (0.40 ha); village Morey-Saint-Denis; village Gevrey-Chambertin; village Chambolle-Musigny.

NEWMAN: 1.10 ha owned. Latricières-Chambertin (0.53 ha); Mazis-Chambertin (0.19 ha); Bonnes-Mares (0.33 ha).

One domaine, two labels. Firstly, we have the estate which has come down the female line from Odette Rameau, wife of Gilbert Vadey, which is now administered by their son-in-law Guy Castagnier, who will shortly be handing over the reins to his son Jérôme, once a professional trumpeter. Secondly, we have the small domaine Christopher Newman inherited from his father Robert. Robert Newman's original intention had been to set up a joint venture with Alexis Lichine, in which Lichine was to be responsible for making and selling the wine and would be allowed to buy a half share in due course. It never worked out, as Lichine neglected his side of the bargain, and so Newman kept everything for himself but entrusted the care of the land, on a *métayage* basis, to one of Lichine's favourite growers, Gilbert Vadey. This, Castagnier has inherited.

The wine is made at the top of the village, off the Place du Monument, but is now matured in Castagnier's new cellars below his house down in the plain. After a severe sort-through, the grapes are totally de-stemmed, vinified classically after 4 or 5 days cold-maceration, fermented at temperatures up to 34°C and given 50 percent new wood.

The Vadey wines had a high reputation in the 1970s, but when I first came to call on Guy Castagnier, I was not impressed. The 1993s, however, were an improvement, and progress has continued since. Quality could be more consistent though. Even some of the 1999s and 2002s were still a little rustic.

Étienne Cosson

3.5 ha owned. Morey-Saint-Denis *premier cru* in Les Blanchards, Clos Baulet and Clos Sorbè; village Morey-Saint-Denis; village Gevrey-Chambertin.

The thirty-something Étienne Cosson took over this family domaine, once owner of the Clos des Lambrays, in 1989. How does he make his wine? One hundred percent de-stemming, long macerations, 30 percent new wood. But "I'm still changing things to find out what is best," he says. I like his wines, particularly the Clos Sorbè.

★★ Dujac

14.69 ha owned. Clos de la Roche (1.95 ha); Clos Saint-Denis (1.47 ha); Charmes-Chambertin (0.70 ha); Bonnes-Mares (0.58 ha); Echézeaux (0.69 ha); Chambertin (0.30 ha); Romanée-Saint-Vivant (0.17 ha); Gevrey-Chambertin *premier cru* Aux Combottes; Morey-Saint-Denis *premier cru blanc* in Monts Luisants and a *premier cru rouge* (from Clos Sorbè, Les Charrières, Les Milandes and Les Ruchots); Chambolle-Musigny *premier cru* Les Gruenchers; Vosne-Romanée *premier cru* in Les Beaumonts and Les Malconsorts; village Morey-Saint-Denis *rouge et blanc*; village Chambolle-Musigny.

This is a splendid and perfectionistic domaine which has been in existence for only little over 35 years, when Jacques Seysses's father bought the Domaine Marcel Graillet for his son. Traditional in some ways (until recently, 100 percent of stems were retained—now it varies according to the vintage), ultra-modern in others, and with a healthily biological if not biodynamic approach to viticulture under vineyard manager Lilian Robin, the Dujac wines, almost entirely matured in new oak, are strikingly individual. They are never very deep in colour at first (because of the stems—the wines get deeper in colour as they age), yet they are intense, perfumed, silky-smooth and impeccably balanced.

In recent years Jacques Seysses and his charming American wife Rosalind have begun to take a back seat in favour of their elder son Jeremy and his oenologue-trained wife Diana Snowden-Seysses. Diana is now firmly in charge in the cellar. Malos are now done later, the new wine being cooled before it is descended into cask. As a result, the colour of the red wine is deeper, and the stems are less evident on the palate. In 2005, together with Étienne de Montille, the Charles Thomas domaine was acquired: Dujac has taken over the more northerly vineyards, Chambertin to Vosne.

There is a small associate *négociant* company, Dujac Fils et Père.

★ Robert Groffier Père et Fils

8 ha owned. Bonnes-Mares (0.97 ha); Chambertin, Clos de Bèze (0.41 ha); Chambolle-Musigny *premier cru* in Les Amoureuses, Les Hauts Doix and Les Sentiers; village Gevrey-Chambertin.

This Morey-based domaine is singular in that it owns not one vine in the commune. What it does possess is good-sized plots in all the *climats* it is present in, including the largest single slice of Chambolle-Musigny, Les Amoureuses (1.09 ha). As you drive up the hill from Vougeot to Chambolle, you will see Robert Groffier's large hoarding.

In all other ways, Robert Groffier, who works alongside his son Serge, is a self-effacing, somewhat shy and gentle man, and the wines are like the man himself: not rugged blockbusters, but pure, intense, understated and elegant.

He leaves about a third of the fruit stemmed and vinifies at 30–32°C after 5 days cold-maceration; the amount of new oak varies from 30 to 70 percent. The results are fine: very pure, silky and intense, with the oak noticeable but not exaggerated.

Alain Jeanniard

3.5 ha owned and *en fermage*. Morey-Saint-Denis *premier cru* Les Chenevery, Les Genavrières and La Riotte (both the last two *négoce*); Chambolle-Musigny *premier cru* Les Combottes (*négoce*); Pommard *premier cru* Les Saussilles; village Morey-Saint-Denis Vieilles Vignes; village Gevrey-Chambertin.

The lean, *sympa* and forty-ish Alain Jeanniard, having been in electronics, came back to Morey-Saint-Denis in 1999 and has built up his small domaine since then, on the back of some village vines he rents from his family. Yields are low, there is a severe *tri* of the fruit, and 25 to 33 percent new wood is employed. Jeanniard additionally looks after the Mazis-Chambertin and the Clos de la Roche vines of the Hospices de Beaune and acts as a merchant. This is a good address.

Henri Jouan

3.2 ha owned. Clos Saint-Denis (0.36 ha); Morey-Saint-Denis *premier cru* Clos Sorbè; village

Morey-Saint-Denis; village Chambolle-Musigny; village Gevrey-Chambertin in the *lieu-dit* Aux Echézeaux.

Henri Jouan is now in semi-retirement and has been succeeded by his son Philippe, whose first vintage was the 2004. The fruit is de-stemmed, the must vinified at 30°C and the wines given about 20 percent new oak. The style here is for wines of medium body only, which evolve soon, but the two top wines have no lack of intensity and elegance.

★★ Domaine des Lambrays

10.71 ha owned. Clos des Lambrays (8.66 ha); Morey-Saint-Denis Premier Cru; village Morey-Saint-Denis; Puligny-Montrachet *premier cru* in Clos des Caillerets and Les Folatières.

If we ignore the handkerchief-sized morsel belonging to Jean Taupenot-Merme, the Clos des Lambrays is the largest of the Burgundian *grand cru* monopolies. For 25 years it has been managed by the affable and talented Thierry Brouin. Brouin produces three red wines, the young vine wine of the *grand cru* having been downgraded and added to that from the few parcels of *premier cru* owned by the domaine, and two excellent white wines. The red must is given 5 to 7 days cold-soaking, vinification takes place with 80 to 100 percent of the stems, at temperatures up to 35°C, and maturation takes place with 50 to 70 percent new wood. Today, the *grand vin* is labelled *vieilles vignes*.

Georges Lignier et Fils

15 ha owned and *en fermage*. Clos de la Roche (1.05 ha); Clos Saint-Denis (1.49 ha); Charmes-Chambertin (0.50 ha); Bonnes-Mares (0.29 ha); Gevrey-Chambertin *premier cru* Les Combottes; Morey-Saint-Denis *premier cru* Clos des Ormes; Volnay *premier cru tout court*; village Morey-Saint-Denis; village Gevrey-Chambertin; village Chambolle-Musigny; village Marsannay *rouge, rosé et blanc*.

This is in many ways an exasperating domaine. Sometimes the results are fine. Frequently, though, they are rather a disappointment. With just over 2 hectares in the Clos des Ormes, the lion's share, this Lignier is supplier of this wine to some of the *négoce*, and it is often better under their bottlings than under his.

The man himself, Georges, grandson of Georges, a notable Morey figure, lost his father early. Lean, fair, thinning on top, and with piercing blue eyes, he appears thoughtful, somewhat inscrutable. He has now been joined by his nephew Benoît.

The grapes are almost entirely de-stemmed and vinified at up to 34°C after a few days cold-maceration, and the top wines are given 50 percent new oak. The cellar is a rabbit warren, somewhat cramped, but extensive. Why is the wine so irregular? It is a puzzle.

★ Hubert Lignier

2.6 ha owned and *en métayage*. Clos de la Roche (0.33 ha); Charmes-Chambertin (0.05 ha); Morey-Saint-Denis *premier cru* in Les Chaffots, Les Chenevery, Les Faconnières and La Riotte; Gevrey-Chambertin *premier cru* Les Combottes; Chambolle-Musigny *premier cru* Les Baudes; village Morey-Saint-Denis; village Gevrey-Chambertin; village Chambolle-Musigny; village Fixin *blanc*.

Hubert Lignier was born in 1936 and is the elder cousin of Georges Lignier. In 1991 his son Romain took over responsibility for the wines, since when they have improved dramatically. Tragically, Romain died of a brain tumour in 2004. The estate has since been divided.

This Lignier's wines have a higher reputation than those of cousin Georges. Romain was one of the first to realize that there was no point—indeed quite the reverse—in over-extracting and over-oaking. The wines are vinified at temperatures up to 33°C after de-stemming and 5 days cold-soaking. Thirty percent new wood is used. The end result is full, rich, concentrated and succulent. The Faconnières and the Chenevery are blended together as *premier cru vieilles vignes*.

Lucie and Auguste Lignier

5.5 ha owned and *en métayage*. Clos de la Roche (0.67 ha); Charmes-Chambertin (0.06 ha); Morey-Saint-Denis *premier cru* in La Riotte, Les Chaffots, and *Cuvée Romain Lignier* (Les Faconnières) and Les Chenevery); Gevrey-Chambertin *premier cru*

Les Combettes; Chambolle-Musigny *premier cru* Les Baudes; village Chambolle-Musigny; village Gevrey-Chambertin; village Morey-Saint-Denis, including the *lieu-dit* Clos des Sionnières.

Following family difficulties, Kellen Lignier, widow of Romian, set up on her own in 2006, naming the domaine after her two children. These 2006s showed well in October 2007.

★ Lignier-Michelot

9 ha owned, *en fermage/en métayage*. Clos de la Roche (0.30 ha); Morey-Saint-Denis *premier cru* Aux Charmes, Les Chenevery and Les Faconnières; village Morey-Saint-Denis, including the *lieu-dit* En la Rue de Vergy and a *vieilles vignes cuvée*; village Gevrey-Chambertin; village Chambolle-Musigny, including a *vieilles vignes cuvée*.

The youthful Virgile Lignier has been in charge here since 1992 and has gradually increased the amount of wine bottled at the domaine, while simultaneously fine-tuning the quality. The fruit is de-stemmed, cold-soaked for 4–6 days and vinified at temperatures up to 34°C. There is 30 to 50 percent new oak, and bottling occurs after 12 months. These wines are neat, stylish and medium to medium-full bodied.

Michel Magnien
Maison Frédéric Magnien

9.75 ha owned and *en fermage*. Clos de la Roche (0.37 ha); Charmes-Chambertin (0.28 ha); Clos Saint-Denis (0.12 ha); Gevrey-Chambertin *premier cru* in Les Cazetiers and Les Goulots; Morey-Saint-Denis *premier cru* in Les Chaffots and Les Milandes; Chambolle-Musigny *premier* cru Les Sentiers; village Gevrey-Chambertin including the *lieu-dit* Les Seuvrées (*vieilles vignes*) and Aux Echézeaux; village Morey-Saint-Denis, including the *lieux-dits* Les Monts Luisants and Les Très Girard; village Chambolle-Musigny in the *lieu-dit* Les Fremiers.

As well as the extensive range of wines from his own domaine, which he works alongside his father Michel, now retired, Frédéric Magnien will offer you twenty-five to thirty merchant wines, mainly red, and all from the Côte de Nuits. These are made from bought-in fruit.

As you might expect, the two ranges are very similar, distinctly oaky and rather extracted. While others have taken their foot off the pedal in this respect, Frédéric Magnien's foot is firmly down on the floor. In my experience, the results do not age with dignity.

Odoul-Coquard

7.5 ha owned and *en fermage*. Charmes-Chambertin (in the Mazoyères—0.17 ha); Gevrey-Chambertin *premier cru* Aux Combottes; Morey-Saint-Denis *premier cru* Clos La Riotte (*monopole*); Nuits-Saint-Georges *premier cru* Les Argillières; village Morey-Saint-Denis; village Gevrey-Chambertin; village Nuits-Saint-Georges.

Thierry Odoul, forty-plus, originally from Vosne-Romanée, has been in charge of his in-laws' domaine since 1992. The fruit is 100 percent de-stemmed, cold-macerated for 4–5 days and vinified at 30°C maximum, and the wine is aged in 20 to 50 percent new wood for 18 months before bottling. The Clos La Riotte is a plot owned by the village and planted in 1983 with different clones, as a sort of experiment. It is very good indeed. His other wines are also very good. This is an address to note.

★ Christophe Perrot-Minot/Henri Perrot-Minot

13.5 ha owned and *en fermage*. Charmes-Chambertin (0.82 ha); Mazoyères-Chambertin (0.73 ha); Vosne-Romanée *premier cru* Les Beaux Monts and in the *lieu-dit* Champs Perdrix; Nuits-Saint-Georges *premier cru* in Les Cras, Les Murgers and La Richemone; Chambolle-Musigny *premier cru* in Les Baudes, Les Charmes, La Combe d'Orveau, Les Fuées and a *vieilles vignes cuvée*; Morey-Saint-Denis *premier cru* La Riotte; Village Vosne-Romanée; village Morey-Saint-Denis, including the *lieu-dit* En La Rue de Vergy; village Gevrey-Chambertin; village Chambolle-Musigny.

The handsome Christophe Perrot-Minot took over from his father Henri in 1995, since when the estate has slowly increased the amount it bottles itself to 100 percent. In 2000 Christophe took over the 4.5 hectare domaine of André Pernin-Rossin of Vosne-Romanée, considerably increasing the range of wines he offers. This was one of the properties I felt was exaggerating the amount of extraction and new wood in the mid-1990s. There is 100 percent de-stemming, 5 to 7 days cold-soaking, 30 to 50 percent new oak and only one racking, at the time of the unification, before bottling. There is a little merchant wine: Chambertin and Chambertin Clos de Bèze, from Rossignol-Trapet and Damoy, which Christophe Perrot harvests himself.

I am pleased to see a return to the pursuit of elegance and not power. "I want to bring out the fruit," says Christophe today. This is a very good address.

★★ Ponsot

11.25 ha owned and *en métayage*. Owned: Clos-de-la-Roche (3.4 ha); Chapelle-Chambertin (0.70 ha); Morey-Saint-Denis *premier cru* Les Monts-Luisants (*rouge et blanc*); Chambolle-Musigny *premier cru* Les Charmes; village Gevrey-Chambertin "Cuvée de l'Abeille"; village Morey-Saint-Denis "Cuvée des Grives" and "Cuvée des Alouettes"; village Chambolle-Musigny "Cuvée des Cigales." *En métayage*, mainly to the Mercier family (Domaine des Chézeaux): Griotte-Chambertin (0.89 ha); Clos-Saint-Denis (0.60 ha); Clos de Vougeot (0.30 ha); Chambertin (0.20 ha). Formerly *en métayage* elsewhere, but no longer exploited: Latricières-Chambertin (0.32 ha)—up to 1994.

Clonal selection in Burgundy can be said to have started here, Jean-Marie Ponsot having provided some cuttings from very old Pinot Noir from his Clos de la Roche for use as mother plants. Laurent Ponsot, son of Jean-Marie, has been making the wine since 1982. In 2001 he extensively enlarged the winery, which now includes a splendid barrel cellar the end of which is naked rock, and in the following year, he took over the small domaine of Léon Volpato.

This is one of the most individual domaines in the whole of Burgundy: its approach includes picking late, retaining up to 25 percent of the stems, fermenting at high temperatures (but not cold-soaking), using new oak (now), using minimal sulphuring, not racking and bottling late. He uses a vertical press. A further curiosity is the white Monts Luisants. It used to be produced using 20 percent Chardonnay. This

has now been uprooted. So the origin is pure Aligoté, and very old Aligoté at that. It is unique. Overall, the results can be stunning—but not invariably.

Gérard Raphet

12 ha owned and (part of Charmes-Chambertin) *en métayage*. Clos-de-Vougeot (1.47 ha), including a *vieilles vignes cuvée*; Charmes-Chambertin (1.10 ha); Clos de la Roche (0.38 ha); Chambertin, Clos de Bèze (0.21 ha); Gevrey-Chambertin *premier cru* in Lavaux-Saint-Jacques and Les Combottes; Morey-Saint-Denis *premier* cru Les Milandes; village Gevrey-Chambertin; village Morey-Saint-Denis; village Chambolle-Musigny.

Gérard Raphet took over from his father Jean in 2002 and is now in charge at this important domaine. Ten percent of the stems are retained; the wine is fermented for 12 days at a maximum temperature of 32–34°C and bottled after 18 months. Only 5 percent new wood is used, but the remainder of the barrels are recent enough.

The line-up is impressive, and the atmosphere efficient. The results can be very good: rich, full, plummy and succulent. Since Gérard has been in command, the yields have been tightened up, and the proportion of new oak increased. But he has also divided the Clos de Vougeot into two cuvées. He protests that the old-vine bottling represents only 10 percent of the total. But I find an inevitable dilution in the "basic."

★ Louis Rémy

3.5 ha owned. Chambertin (0.32 ha); Latricières-Chambertin (0.58 ha); Clos de la Roche (0.66 ha); Chambolle-Musigny *premier cru* Derrière La Grange; village Morey-Saint-Denis in the *lieu-dit* Aux Chéseaux; village Chambolle-Musigny in the *lieu-dit* Les Fremiers Vieilles Vignes.

Madame Marie-Louise Remy and her daughter Chantal Remy-Rosier are the surviving Remys in the wine business, the Gevrey-based domaine of Madame Remy's brother-in-law Philippe having been sold to the Domaine Leroy in 1989.

At the top of the village, under the Clos-des-Lambrays and facing the Place du Monument, Madame Remy occupies a substantial and attractive mansion, opposite which is a splendid two-level, deep-vaulted cellar which dates from the seventeenth century and is somewhat too extensive, it would appear, for their rather small domaine.

I have had some splendid old Louis Remy wines from the 1940s, 1950s and 1960s, but following Louis's death during the vintage in 1982, quality dropped. Chantal Remy-Rosier is a qualified oenologist, however, and I am pleased to note that things have improved since the 2000 vintage. Yields are low. A small percentage of stems are retained, the *cuvaison* lasts 15 days at temperatures up to 30–32°C, and some one third of the barrels are renewed annually.

★★ *Clos de Tart*

7.53 ha owned.

Owned by the Mommessin family and today run by Sylvain Pitiot, Clos de Tart has emerged in the last decade as one of the truly great wines of Burgundy and, as I have said previously, one which is full and the most masculine of the Morey-Saint-Denis *grands crus*.

Yields are low here, the vineyard having been largely transformed to Cordon de Royat training. The juice is cold-soaked for 6 days, vinified at a maximum temperature of 32°C, with some 20 percent of the stems, and aged for 16–24 months, entirely in new oak. The wine is hand bottled with neither fining nor filtration.

★ *Taupenot-Merme*

12.9 ha owned. Charmes-Chambertin and Mazoyères-Chambertin (1.42 ha); Corton, Rognet (0.43 ha); Morey-Saint-Denis *premier cru* La Riotte; Gevrey-Chambertin *premier cru* Bel Air; Chambolle-Musigny *premier cru* La Combe d'Orveau; Nuits-Saint-Georges *premier cru* Les Pruliers; Auxey-Duresses *premier cru* Les Duresses and Les Grands Champs; village Morey-Saint-Denis; village Gevrey-Chambertin; village Chambolle-Musigny; village Auxey-Duresses *rouge et blanc*; village Saint-Romain *rouge et blanc*; plus a few rows of Clos des Lambrays, hardly enough to make one barrel of wine.

Jean Taupenot hails from Saint Romain, where his twin brother Pierre continues the family exploitation. He married the vivacious and attractive Denise Merme, sister of Madame Perrot-Minot (q.v.), and has since built on her inheritance. The wines are now the responsibility of their children Virginie and Romain.

They vinify after de-stemming and a week's cold-soaking, prefer a long 3-week *cuvaison*, and employ 25 to 40 percent new wood. The Saint-Romain and Auxey-Duresses came from Jean Taupenot's family in 2003. The Corton was acquired in 2005. The wines have improved in recent years. This is now a very good address.

Jacky Truchot-Martin

7 ha owned. Clos-de-la-Roche (0.45 ha); Charmes-Chambertin (0.65 ha); Morey-Saint-Denis *premier cru* Clos Sorbès; Gevrey-Chambertin *premier cru* Les Combottes; Chambolle-Musigny *premier cru* Les Sentiers; village Morey-Saint-Denis; village Chambolle-Musigny.

This 7-hectare domaine was sold in 2005 to François Feuillet of Paris, PDG of Trigano. Along with his other estate, based in Nuits-Saint-Georges, the vines are now cared for, and the wine made by, David Duband of Chevannes (see page 168).

CHAMBOLLE-MUSIGNY

"In the opinion of many," said Dr. Lavalle in 1855—and he has been echoed by just about every other writer on the subject since—"this commune produces the most delicate wines of the Côtes de Nuits."

Delicate, yes; but feeble, no. Chambolle-Musigny's wines may be lighter in structure than those of Vosne-Romanée or Gevrey-Chambertin, but they can and should be every bit as intense. Being less dense, they will show the perfume of the Pinot Noir, not to mention this variety's inherent elegance, more radiantly. Gaston Roupnel talks of silk and lace, and Antony Hanson of "subtle nobility"; Remington Norman writes of the epitome of the finesse of which Burgundy is capable. I too find myself irresistibly seduced, particularly as recent vintages seem to have favoured the commune, and this has been put to good use by an increasing quantity of very good local domaines.

History

Chambolle takes its name from the rushing action of the stream or little river Grône, which comes tumbling out of the Combe de Chamboeuf above the village. When there was a severe thunderstorm, a fresh flood would bubble like boiling water through the vines below: hence Campus Ebulliens, or *champ bouillant*. The village was known as Cambola in 1110 and was dependent on the nearby Gilly-Lès-Cîteaux until 1500, the date inhabitants received authorisation to build a local church. This was completed 6 years later, under the orders of Jean Moisson, an ancestor of the De Vogüé family, and it is one of the richest of the Côte, with wall paintings in the choir, classed as a *monument historique*. It is well worth a visit. Opposite the church is a venerable lime tree, said to have been planted during the time of Henri IV.

Like Morey-Saint-Denis, much of the land was under the direct control of the monks of Cîteaux until sequestered at the time of the French Revolution. Pierre Gros, the Canon of Saint-Denis de Vergy, donated the *Champ de Musigné* to the Cistercian monks in 1110, at the same time that they were establishing the Clos de Vougeot. It has been suggested that the origin of the name is Gallo-Roman: a certain Musinus, perhaps.

The origin of Bonnes-Mares, Chambolle's second *grand cru*, lies in the word *marer*, to cultivate, though it has been suggested that there is a second, more felicitous connection with the *bonnes mères*, the Bernardine nuns of Notre Dame de Tart.

Dr. Lavalle, in 1855, decreed but one *tête de cuvée:* Musigny itself. Bonnes-Mares and the *climats* of Varoilles, Fuées, Cras and Amoureuses were *premières cuvées*. Varoilles lies above Bonnes-Mares and has since lost status, being only partly *premier cru* today, while Fuées and Cras are the extension of this same slope as it turns round to face the south above the village itself. The Amoureuses lies directly below Le Musigny.

Lavalle goes on to say that, while the main road must be considered the lower limit for *bons crus*, one can nevertheless find good wine from the other side of the road, a truth which still holds good today. Two examples are the Bourgogne Bons-Bâtons of Ghislaine Barthod and Michelle and Patrice Rion. He also points out that the soil of the commune in general is not as fertile and therefore does not produce as much wine as in Morey or Vougeot, indeed only 5 *pièces* per hectare in Musigny, though 7 or 8 elsewhere, he says. This premise is still valid today: Chambolle always produces less than Vosne-Romanée or Morey-Saint-Denis. The Combe de Chamboeuf affords an entrance into the Côte for a swathe of hail, and Chambolle, like parts of Nuits, tends to suffer more than most.

Location

The commune of Chambolle-Musigny is roughly square in shape, with the addition of a tongue which flicks out to the south over the vineyards of Musigny and up into the Combe d'Orveau.

Divided into two by the river Grône and the valley at the foot of the Combe de Chamboeuf, part of the land immediately south of the village is on slopes which face north, and these provide village wines. Below the *grand cru* of Bonnes-Mares, which overlaps into Morey-Saint-Denis to the north, below the village itself, and below Le Musigny, stretching down halfway toward the main road, lie the *premiers crus*.

The *terroir* of Chambolle-Musigny is marked by its high percentage of active limestone and its lack of clay. There is also less magnesium in the soil. Only in the northern section of Le Musigny, where it touches a *lieu-dit* suitably called Les Argillières, and on the Morey side of Bonnes-Mares is there a marked percentage of clay—*marnes blanches* in the case of the latter. Elsewhere, the soil is a light, very pebbley, limestone debris, meagre in depth, lying on a base rock of Bathonian and Bajocian limestone. Erosion is a problem, particularly in Musigny itself.

The Vineyard

GRANDS CRUS Chambolle-Musigny possesses two *grands crus*: Bonnes-Mares, of which 1.52 hectares out of 15 lie in the neighbouring commune of Morey-Saint-Denis, and Le Musigny. Including the Morey segment, these two comprise just under 26 hectares and produce an average of 760 hectolitres per year.

PREMIERS CRUS

There are twenty-four *premiers crus*, in whole or in part. Altogether, they cover some 60 hectares and produce 2,050 hectolitres per year. In alphabetical order, they are as follows: Les Amoureuses, Les Baudes, Aux Beaux Bruns (part), Les Borniques, Les Carrières, Les Chabiots, Les Chatelots, La Combe d'Orveau (part), Aux (or Les) Combottes (part), Les Cras, Aux Échanges, Les Feusselottes, Les Fuées, Les Grands Murs, Derrière la Grange (part), Les Groseilles, Les Gruenchers, Les Hauts-Doix, Les Lavrottes, Les Noirots, Les Plantes, Les Sentiers, Les Véroilles (part).

VILLAGE WINE There are some 94 hectares of village land. This produces an average of 4,060 hectolitres per year.

Like Gevrey-Chambertin and Vosne-Romanée, but unlike Morey-Saint-Denis and Vougeot, the appellation Chambolle-Musigny, village or *premier cru*, covers red wine only. There is, however, a little Le Musigny *blanc*.

In general, and as you would expect, the wines of Chambolle-Musigny are at their most sturdy to the north, on the border with Morey-Saint-Denis, and at their most ethereal where the land abuts Vougeot to the south. Nevertheless, however, I find an immediate difference between, say, the Morey of the Roumier's Clos de la Bussière and Robert Groffier's Chambolle-Musigny, Les Sentiers, from the adjacent vineyard, a difference which is more than just a question of different winemaking. And I find less of a difference between Groffier's Sentiers and his

Hauts-Doix, or between Freddy Mugnier's Fuées and his Amoureuses. Wherever they come from, all four wines are archetypal Chambolles: ballerinas, not shot-putters.

The Grands Crus

LE MUSIGNY

SURFACE AREA: 10.86 ha
AVERAGE PRODUCTION: 300 hl
PRINCIPAL PROPRIETORS: De Vogüé (7.12 ha);
★ Jacques-Frédéric Mugnier (1.13 ha); Jacques Prieur (0.77 ha); ★ Joseph Drouhin (0.67 ha); ★ Leroy (0.27 ha); ★ Vougeraie (0.21 ha); ★ Louis Jadot (0.17 ha); ★ Drouhin-Laroze (0.12 ha); Georges Roumier (0.10 ha); Christian Confuron (0.08 ha); ★ Joseph Faiveley (0.03 ha).

Le Musigny is one of the very greatest *climats* in the whole of the Côte d'Or, one of a handful which includes Chambertin and Clos-de-Bèze, La Tâche and Romanée-Conti. This is more than a prince of the blood in the royal house of Burgundy, as Pierre Léon-Gauthier would have it. This is majesty itself; if one is thinking of its texture and character, then it is the queen rather than the king. The other four can fight among themselves for the role of consort.

The vineyard has always consisted of two sections, divided by a path. The northern part, slightly the larger, is Grand Musigny, or simply Musigny. The southern, in the plural, is Les Petits Musignys. This might lead you to expect the latter as being the more morcellated, but no. This part is the monopoly of the Domaine Comte Georges de Vogüé.

In Dr. Lavalle's day, the total comprised 10.05 hectares. In 1929 part of the Chambolle *premier cru* La Combe d'Orveau, further to the south and across another path, was incorporated, adding 0.61 hectares. In 1989 a further four *ouvrées* (0.16 ha) (both of these sections belonging to the Domaine Jacques Prieur) were added on this side.

The *climat* lies between 260 and 300 metres in altitude, the slope varying between 8 and 14 percent. The soil is middle Bathonian oolite upslope, but more exposed Comblanchien limestone debris further down. It is quite different from the *grands crus* of Morey and Gevrey, and indeed of Bonnes-Mares and the rest of Chambolle. There is a red clay you do not find elsewhere. There is also a less high level of active limestone.

Having remained in ecclesiastical hands during the Middle Ages, but always apart from the Clos de Vougeot, and indeed never having been enclosed, the vineyard began to be divided in the seventeenth and eighteenth centuries, and among its owners are to be found the fathers of the Oratory in Dijon, the Grand Prior of Champagne and local parliamentary families such as the Bouhiers and the De Berbuseys. Today's principal owners, the De Vogüé family, are descended from the Bouhiers. They can trace their ownership in the best vines of the Côte back longer than most.

As well as its lion's share of Musigny *en rouge*, the De Vogüé domaine has persisted with planting a small parcel of Chardonnay. Until recent times it was common to mix between 5 and 10 percent of the Chardonnay in among the Pinot Noirs in order to give the wine an extra zip of acidity and to soften it up. Today the De Vogüé domaine keeps its Chardonnay apart, in a little parcel of two thirds of a hectare, and would normally make about six casks of it—but currently this parcel has very young vines, and the produce is sold as Bourgogne *blanc*. It is a full wine, with its own peculiar flavour, nothing like a Corton-Charlemagne or a Montrachet.

Musigny, consequently, is the only *grand cru* with the exception of Corton which can be white as well as red.

At its best the red wine can be quite simply the most delicious wine to be found in Burgundy. Speaking personally, and I'm not the only one who holds this opinion, it is *the* summit of achievement. With its vibrant colour; exquisitely harmonious, complex, profound *bouquet*; blissful balance between tannin, acidity and the most intensely-flavoured fruit—all the *petits fruits rouges* you could possibly imagine; and incomparable breed, depth, originality and

purity on the finish, a great Musigny is heaven in a glass. Would that one could afford to drink it more often!

LES BONNES-MARES

SURFACE AREA: 15.06 ha
AVERAGE PRODUCTION: 466 hl (13.54 in Chambolle; 1.52 in Morey)
PRINCIPAL PROPRIETORS: ★ De Vogüé (2.70 ha); (Drouhin-Laroze (1.49 ha); ★ Georges Roumier (1.39 ha); Bernard Clair/Domaine Fougeray de Beauclair (1.20 ha); ★ Louis Jadot (1.11 ha); Bart (1.03 ha); ★ Robert Groffier (0.97 ha); ★ Vougeraie (0.70 ha); ★ Dujac (0.58 ha); Naigeon (0.50 ha); ★ Bruno Clair (0.41 ha); Peirazeau (0.39 ha); ★ Jacques-Frédéric Mugnier (0.35 ha); ★ Bertheau (0.34 ha); Castagnier/Newman (0.33 ha); ★ D'Auvenay (0.26 ha); Georges Lignier (0.29 ha); Hervé Roumier (0.29 ha); ★ Bouchard Père et Fils (0.24 ha); ★ Joseph Drouhin (0.23 ha); Arlaud (0.20 ha); Charlopin-Parizot (0.12 ha).

Bonnes-Mares is rare among *grands crus*, in that it has shrunk rather than grown over the last century. Curiously, part of the land within the nineteenth-century wall of the Clos de Tart used to be Bonnes-Mares. This anomaly was rectified in 1965.

This left 1.52 hectares within Morey, and the rest in the commune of Chambolle. All of the former, and a little else besides, belonged to the late Bernard Clair, and the majority of this is leased to Domaine Fougeray de Beauclair (the rest has passed to Bernard's son, Bruno). The remainder of this *grand cru* is divided among some thirty-five proprietors, according to Bazin. Some of these must be members of the same family who vinify together. Twenty-five declared a harvest in 2004. Bonnes-Mares seems always to have been divided. One hundred and forty years ago there were already at least seventeen proprietors.

The *climat* lies between 265 and 300 metres above sea level and south of Clos de Tart, and geologically is cut in two diagonally across the slope from the top at the Morey end toward the bottom in the middle of the vineyard. North of this, the soil is heavier and contains more clay, a marl known as *terres rouges*. South toward Chambolle, the soil is lighter in colour and texture, and there are fossilised oysters. This is the *terres blanches*. All over the vineyard the stone and pebble content is high. At the top of the slope, there is little but broken-up limestone on top of the limestone rock. Further down, the surface soil may be as much as 70 centimetres thick. Erosion, however, seems to be less of a problem than in Musigny, though the incline of the slope is similar.

The geological division helps explain the generally held view that the Bonnes-Mares which come from the Morey-Saint-Denis end are bigger and more vigorous than those of the Chambolle proximity. I find that many Bonnes-Mares, when you taste them alongside Clos Saint-Denis and Clos de la Roche in the same cellar, are more muscular, somewhat more dense, four-square and closed-in: masculine wines indeed. There is also often an element of spice, which I find in Clos de Tart, but not in the other Morey *grands crus*.

To compare Bonnes-Mares and Le Musigny in the same cellar—at De Vogüé or *chez* Freddy Mugnier, for example—is equally illuminating. Here the difference is enormous. One can hardly believe that the wines come from the same commune.

Bonnes-Mares, then, is scarcely Chambolle-Musigny. The texture is velvet, even worsted, rather than silk and lace. The wine is full, firm and sturdy, needing its time. There is depth and richness, but not the nuance and breed of one of the really top *grands crus*. The tannic power can be almost too much.

The Premiers Crus

LES AMOUREUSES   (5.40 ha)

The *climat* lies downslope from Le Grand-Musigny on several levels, as the land descends abruptly in a series of small terraces toward Vougeot. A large board on the left, as one takes the little road up to Chambolle, announces "Robert Groffier et Fils—Les Amoureuses." Groffier, with over a hectare, is the largest owner.

This is a vineyard which, like Clos Saint-Jacques in Gevrey-Chambertin, is regarded by most—and priced accordingly—as the equal of a *grand cru*. In Robert Groffier's cellar and elsewhere, I regularly prefer it to the Bonnes-Mares. But Bonnes-Mares it is not. Les Amoureuses is really a sort of younger brother to Musigny itself: perfumed, silky smooth, intense and soft rather than brutal and muscular, and with real finesse.

RECOMMENDED SOURCES
Robert Groffier (Morey-Saint-Denis); De Vogüé; Jacques-Frédéric Mugnier; Georges Roumier; Bertheau; Amiot-Servelle; Moine-Hudelot (all Chambolle-Musigny); Joseph Drouhin; Louis Jadot (both Beaune).

The wines of Les Hauts-Doix (1.75 ha), adjacent but lower down and facing a little toward the north, are less fine, but similar. Robert Groffier's is a good example.

LES CHARMES   (9.53 ha)

Across the road up to Chambolle is the large *climat* of Les Charmes. This is the most familiar *premier cru*, but the vineyard is more morcellated. The number of owners runs into the dozens.

At its best, this is yardstick Chambolle: fresh in expression, ripe, juicy and elegant in its fruit, medium-bodied and simply delicious. It doesn't have the intensity of Les Amoureuses, the hidden depth of Les Cras or Les Fuées or the slight spice and roasted quality of Les Sentiers or Les Baudes. It is simply itself: classic Chambolle-Musigny.

RECOMMENDED SOURCES
Amiot-Servelle; Ghislaine Barthod; Bertheau; Joël Hudelot-Baillet (Chambolle-Musigny); Leroy (Vosne-Romanée); Christian Clerget (Vougeot); Ponsot (Morey-Saint-Denis); Alain Hudelot (Vougeot).

Further up the slope, toward the village, lies Les Feusselottes (4.40 ha); on either side are two separate parcels called Les Plantes (2.57 ha), and to the north you will find Les Combottes (1.55), some of which is not *premier cru*. Above Les Charmes lies Les Chatelots (2.96 ha). All these produce similar wines with the exception of Les Feusselottes, whose wines are more mineral and more black-fruity than the rest.

RECOMMENDED SOURCES
LES FEUSSELOTTES
Dr. Georges Mugneret (Vosne-Romanée).

LES CHATELOTS
Ghislaine Barthod (Chambolle-Musigny).

LES SENTIERS	*(4.89 ha)*
LES BAUDES	*(3.42 ha)*
LES LAVROTTES	*(0.92 ha)*
DERRIÈRE LA GRANGE	*(0.47 ha)*
LES NOIROTS	*(2.85 ha)*
LES GRUENCHERS	*(2.82 ha)*
LES GROSEILLES	*(1.34 ha)*
LES BEAUX-BRUNS	*(1.54 ha in premier cru)*
AUX ÉCHANGES	*(0.93 ha in premier cru: monopoly of Domaine Leymarie-Ceci)*

These are the *premiers crus* which lie under Bonnes-Mares. There is a little bit more muscle here, despite which they are true Chambolles. In addition there is a touch of spice and, in hot summers, more of an element of cooked fruit than elsewhere in the commune. This is a fertile hunting ground for the Chambolle lover.

RECOMMENDED SOURCES
LES SENTIERS
Robert Groffier (Morey-Saint-Denis); Arlaud, Hubert Lignier (both Morey-Saint-Denis).

LES BAUDES
Ghislaine Barthod (Chambolle-Musigny); Séra-fin (Gevrey-Chambertin).

DERRIÈRE LA GRANGE
Amiot-Servelle (Chambolle-Musigny).

LES GRUENCHERS
Dujac (Morey-Saint-Denis); Armelle and Bernard Rion (Vosne-Romanée).

LES GROSEILLES
Digioia-Royer (Chambolle-Musigny).

LES BEAUX-BRUNS
Ghislaine Barthod (Chambolle-Musigny); Denis Mortet, Thierry Mortet (Gevrey-Chambertin).

LES FUÉES	*(4.38 ha)*
LES CRAS	*(3.45 ha)*
LES VÉROILLES	*(0.37 ha)*

Les Véroilles lies above the southern end of Bonnes-Mares, and only recently has part of it been promoted to *premier cru*. This section is the monopoly of Ghislaine Barthod. The remainder was *en friche* at the time of the promotion. Les Fuées and Les Cras end the extension southward of the Bonnes-Mares slope.

This is an area of *premier cru* wine second only to that of Amoureuses. The wines are nicely firm, with a certain backbone and a cool dignity: poised wines with very good fruit and no lack of elegance. I like them very much, indeed.

RECOMMENDED SOURCES
LES FUÉES
Jacques-Frédéric Mugnier, Ghislaine Barthod (Chambolle-Musigny); Joseph Faiveley (Nuits-Saint-Georges); Perrot-Minot (Morey-Saint-Denis).

LES CRAS
Ghislaine Barthod, Georges Roumier (Chambolle-Musigny).

LES VÉROILLES
Ghislaine Barthod (Chambolle-Musigny).

LES CHABIOTS	*(1.50 ha)*
LES BORNIQUES	*(1.43 ha)*

Above Les Amoureuses and on the same line as Le Musigny, if inching just to the north, you would expect something worth a second sip from here. Sadly, much of the area looks more or less derelict, and I know of no good examples of these two *climats*.

LA COMBE D'ORVEAU   *(2.38 ha)*

South of the Petits-Musigny, but on the same line with it, and overlooking the vineyards of Echézeaux on the south-facing side of the Combe, this *premier cru climat* (there is also a bit of village *appellation contrôlée* under this name, from which the Domaine Jean Grivot of Vosne-Romanée produces a very good wine) is little known but can produce some extremely good wine. It is more Echézeaux than Amoureuses, however, with a satisfying core of concentration and depth—but no lack of elegance, either.

RECOMMENDED SOURCES

Bruno Clavelier (Vosne-Romanée); Joseph Faiveley (Nuits-Saint-Georges); Perrot-Minot, Taupenot-Merme (both Morey-Saint-Denis).

The Growers

Bernard Amiot

5.50 ha owned and *en fermage*. Chambolle-Musigny *premier cru* in Les Charmes and Les Chatelots; village Chambolle-Musigny, including the *lieu-dit* Aux Echézeaux.

Chambolle and Morey are villages rich in Amiots, but not all are closely related to each other, and this Amiot is no close cousin of Pierre in Morey (see page 110). Bernard Amiot exploits his domaine, built up since 1962, with his son Frédéric and makes soft, harmonious, ample wines. Sometimes, though, they are a little *too* soft. A small percentage of the stems are retained, maceration lasts about 10–12 days, at temperatures up to 32°C, and the first growths go into new wood until the first racking.

★ Amiot-Servelle

6.77 ha owned. Chambolle-Musigny *premier cru* in Les Amoureuses, Les Charmes, Derrière la Grange, Les Feusselottes and Les Plantes; village Chambolle-Musigny.

Christian Amiot, one of the sons of Pierre of Morey-Saint-Denis, married Elizabeth, daughter of the late Jean Servelle, in the late 1980s, and since the 1990 vintage, what used to be Servelle-Tachot has sailed under new colours.

Quality has improved, too. Christian Amiot is a sensitive winemaker, fully prepared to adapt the recipe according to the nature of the ingredients: no stems, a few days cold-maceration, controlled fermentations and no excess of new oak. The wines now are very good, indeed.

★★ Ghislaine Barthod

6.73 ha owned and *en fermage*. Chambolle-Musigny *premier cru* in Les Baudes, Les Beaux-Bruns, Les Charmes, Les Chatelots, Les Combottes, Les Cras, Les Fuées and Les Véroilles; village Chambolle-Musigny.

Ghislaine Barthod took over winemaking responsibility from her father Gaston (he passed away in 1999) in 1987, and from the 1992 vintage onward, the labels bear her name and not her father's. What has happened here since 1987 is exemplary of modern-day Burgundy. Ghislaine went to wine school. Gaston, though, once a soldier, had no theoretical qualifications. The yield is now much less than it used to be. There is a *table de tri*. There is more control over vinification temperatures; more *pigeage* and less *remontage*; self bottling rather than contract bottling; fining and filtering only when absolutely necessary; and so on.

So for more than 15 years we have had definitely fine quality, rather than merely good, making this cellar a splendid place to compare the nuances between seven different Chambolle first growths. This is the only domaine which has *premier cru* Les Véroilles. In addition, there is some young-vine Combottes, first vinified separately in 2001, and a splendid Bourgogne *rouge* from a *lieu-dit* called Les Bons Bâtons on the other side of the main road. Ghislaine Barthod is married to Louis Boillot (see below). The 2005s are very lovely.

★ François Bertheau

6.18 ha *en fermage*. Bonnes-Mares (0.34 ha); Chambolle-Musigny *premier cru* in Les Amoureuses, Les Charmes and a *premier cru* (from Les Baudes, Les Groseilles and Les Noirots); village Chambolle-Musigny.

François Bertheau has now taken over from his father Pierre at what until 2003 was called Domaine Pierre Bertheau et Fils. Like his father, he is a careful winemaker, and the results are succulent, elegant and classic examples of Chambolle-Musigny. The fruit is de-stemmed, cold-soaked for 3 or 4 days and fermented at a maximum temperature of 30°C. There is 30 percent new wood, and the wine is aged for 18 months before bottling. This is an address which deserves greater recognition. At present the Bertheaus still sell off much of their produce in bulk.

★ Louis Boillot et Fils

7.09 ha owned and *en fermage*. Nuits-Saint-Georges *premier cru* Les Pruliers; Gevrey-Chambertin *premier cru* Les Champonnets and Les Cherbaudes; Pommard *premier cru* Les Croix Noires and Les Fremiers; Volnay *premier cru* Les Angles, Les Brouillards and Les Caillerets; village Gevrey-Chambertin, including the *lieu-dit* Les Evocelles; village Chambolle-Musigny; village Pommard; village Volnay, including the *lieu-dit* Les Grands Poisots; village Beaune in the *lieu-dit* Les Epenots; village Fixin; Côte de Nuits Villages.

In 2002 Louis Boillot split with his brother Pierre, who remains in Gevrey-Chambertin at Domaine Lucien Boillot et Fils, and moved his operation to Chambolle-Musigny, where he lives with his wife, Ghislaine Barthod. The Chambolle cellar was enlarged, and Louis vinified his 2003s there, having made his 2002s in both cellars.

I was never particularly impressed by what the brothers jointly achieved in Gevrey-Chambertin. Too many compromises were being made. On his own, Louis has been able to introduce "small but decisive changes," and quality here is now one-star. The 2005s are his best yet.

Louis Boillot is also a merchant, offering village and *premier cru* wines of Morey-Saint-Denis and Chambolle-Musigny.

Digioia-Royer

3.5 ha owned and *en fermage*. Chambolle-Musigny *premier cru* Les Groseilles and Les Gruenchers; village Chambolle-Musigny, including a *vieilles vignes cuvée*.

Michel and Marie-Joanne Digioia are a charming young couple who still sell much of what they look after off in bulk. What they make themselves is well worth investigating, though the Gruenchers is from young vines and is merely pretty and somewhat superficial. Their recipe is no stems, 15 days *cuvaison*, 10 percent new oak and bottling without filtration.

Gilbert Felletig

12.5 ha owned and *en fermage*. Chambolle-Musigny *premier cru* in Les Carrières, Les Charmes, Les Combottes, Les Feusselottes, Les Lavrottes and Les Plantes, and *premier cru* (from Les Borniques, Les Chabiots, Les Fuées and Les Noirots); Vosne-Romanée *premier cru* from Les Chaumes, Les Petits Monts and Les Reignots, village Vosne-Romanée; village Nuits-Saint-Georges; village Gevrey-Chambertin from the *lieu-dit* La Justice; village Chambolle-Musigny.

Gilbert Felletig took over from his father Henri—the family ancestors came from Romania—in 2000. Since then, the property has been enlarged, and a lot of little details have combined to improve the wine. The equipment is up-to-date, there is more new oak, and the wines are more concentrated. The domaine was further enlarged in 2005, with Gilbert Felletig taking over the lion's share of Michel Modot's vines. So far, the quality is good plus, but my hunch is that even better is in store.

Joël Hudelot-Baillet

8.4 ha owned and *en fermage*. Bonnes-Mares (0.12 ha); Chambolle-Musigny *premier cru* Les Charmes and Les Cras; village Chambolle-Musigny; village Vosne-Romanée.

While Joël Hudelot is still very much with us, responsibility has passed to his son-in-law Dominique Le Guen, who arrived in 1998 and took charge in 2001. More is now sold in bottle, and, as elsewhere, things have been tightened up—lower harvest, installation of a *table de tri*, and so on. Total de-stemming, 8 to 10 days cold-soaking, fermentation at 35°C and up to 50 percent new oak comprise the approach. Currently, the Charmes (70-year-old vines) is to be preferred to the Cras (17-year-old). This is now a very good address.

Michel Modot

6.7 ha owned and *en fermage*. Chambolle-Musigny *premier cru* in Les Charmes and Les Lavrottes; village Chambolle-Musigny.

Michel Modot lost his son in a car accident in the autumn of 2003. In 2005 he decided to wind things up. Much of the estate is now farmed by Gilbert Felletig. This estate was the majority owner in Les Lavrottes. Most of this was replanted in 2000.

Daniel Moine-Hudelot

5.8 ha owned and *en fermage*. Chambolle-Musigny *premier cru* in Les Amoureuses, Les Charmes and Les Feusselottes; village Chambolle-Musigny.

This is an estate over whose future hangs a question mark, for Daniel Hudelot is now of retirement age, as is his brother who works alongside him. The brother has no children, and Daniel, a sole daughter, who is apparently not interested in taking over. Fifteen years ago, this estate owned 0.35 hectares in Le Musigny and 0.17 hectares in Bonnes-Mares, as well as 0.15 hectares of Clos Vougeot. Gradually, these gems have been sold off—the prices were so high that the death duties thereon would have been crippling. The style here is for lightish wines. In good years, there is no lack of elegance or intensity.

★★ Jacques Frédéric Mugnier

13.5 ha owned. Le Musigny (1.13 ha); Bonnes-Mares (0.35 ha); Chambolle-Musigny *premier cru* in Les Amoureuses and Les Fuées; Nuits-Saint-Georges *premier cru* Clos de la Maréchale (*monopole*); village Chambolle-Musigny.

The Mugnier domaine occupies the Château de Chambolle-Musigny, a rather gaunt pile built in 1709 with what was a splendid, if rather sparsely filled, cellar in the basement. The vines used to be farmed by outsiders, but in 1984 Freddy Mugnier returned to take over. For a time, he supplemented his living by working as an airline pilot three days a week.

In 2004 Mugnier took back the family's Clos de la Maréchale monopoly in Nuits-Saint-Georges, which had been leased to Maison Faiveley for 50 years. This increased the size of the domaine from 4 to 13.5 hectares and necessitated the construction of a large extension to the cellar and a new modern *cuverie*.

Frédéric Mugnier's wines are quite different from those of De Vogüé, or indeed those of his neighbour Christophe Roumier. They are lighter and seem at the outset paler in colour. They are less new-oaky. He uses only 20 percent new wood. But they have great purity, intensity and finesse. Note his village wine, a large percentage of which comes from a parcel in the *premier cru* Les Plantes. The Maréchale is no longer somewhat burly, as it used to be in Faiveley's day. It has a touch of Chambolle elegance. Mugnier has T-grafted some vines here to produce a white wine.

★★ Georges Roumier et Fils
Christophe Roumier

12.6 ha owned and *en fermage* (and *en métayage* under the label of Christophe Roumier: wines asterisked). Le Musigny (0.10 ha); Bonnes-Mares (1.39 ha); Corton-Charlemagne (0.20 ha); Chambolle-Musigny *premier cru* in Les Amoureuses, Les Combettes, Les Cras; Morey-Saint-Denis *premier cru monopole* Clos de la Bussière; village Chambolle-Musigny. ★ Ruchottes-Chambertin (2/3 of 0.51 ha), ★ Charmes-Chambertin (half of 0.27 ha).

Jean-Marie Roumier, who did so much to put this domaine on the map, died in 2002. Since 1982, however, the wines had been the responsibility of his son Christophe, one of the most capable and perspicacious of the new generation of Burgundians (Lafon, Grivot, etc.) who all took over their family estates at about this time. Christophe is personally the share-cropper in Ruchottes and Charmes-Chambertin for a M. Bonnefond, under whose label you will occasionally see the identical wine.

Some of the stems are retained, the juice is cold-soaked for a week and fermented at a maximum of 32°C and 15 to 50 percent new oak is employed. It all depends, Roumier will haste to add, on the vintage and the appellation. The wines here are very fine, built to last. The Bonnes-Mares is regularly one of Burgundy's greatest bottles. The 2005s are super here.

Hervé Roumier

5.1 ha owned and *en fermage*. Bonnes-Mares (0.29 ha); Clos de Vougeot (0.27 ha);

Chambolle-Musigny *premier cru* in Les Amoureuses and Les Fuées; village Chambolle-Musigny.

Hervé Roumier, son of Alain, who was for a long time *régisseur* of the Domaine Comte Georges de Vogüé, and elder brother of Laurent (see below), died of cancer in 2004. His widow continues the exploitation, but it is Laurent who now makes the wines. Not surprisingly, they are very similar. The 2002s and 2003s, made by Hervé, had rather more weight than the 2004s.

Laurent Roumier

4 ha owned. Clos de Vougeot (0.60 ha); Bonnes-Mares (0.15 ha); village Chambolle-Musigny.

Laurent Roumier worked alongside Hervé (see above), his elder brother by 8 years, until 1990, since when he has been on his own. A new *cuverie* was installed here in 2004. His wines are persistent and elegant, but a little lightweight.

Hervé Sigaut

9.3 ha owned and *en fermage/en métayage*. Chambolle-Musigny *premier cru* in Les Carrières, Les Charmes, Les Chatelots, Les Fuées, Les Groseilles, Les Gruenchers and Les Noirots; Morey-Saint-Denis *premier cru* in Les Charrières and Les Milandes; village Chambolle-Musigny; village Puligny-Montrachet in the *lieu-dit* Les Enseignières.

Hervé Sigaut and his wife Anne took over from the charming, now 80-year-old Maurice Sigaut in 1990. Today the entire production is sold in bottle. As elsewhere, there have been a number of cumulatively important improvements over the years, in particular the purchase of a sorting table in 2004 and stainless steel vats in a new vinification centre which works by gravity in the same year. This is a good address. I expect it to be an even better one in the near future.

★★★ Comte Georges de Vogüé

12.5 ha owned. Le Musigny (7.12 ha, of which 0.66 ha is Musigny *blanc*); Bonnes-Mares (2.70 ha); Chambolle-Musigny *premier cru* Les Amoureuses (also Les Baudes and Les Fuées, but this is labelled *premier cru* or goes into the village wine); village Chambolle-Musigny.

This famous domaine can trace its ancestry back to the Middle Ages and occupies a renaissance courtyard—the château is no longer inhabited—in the middle of the village. The cellars are substantial and impressive.

The domaine having been through a lean period in the 1970s and early 1980s when the wine was not up to standard, things were taken in hand in the late 1980s, and from 1989 the team of François Millet in the cellar, Jean-Luc Pépin in the office and Éric Bourgogne in the vineyard has not put a foot wrong.

The Domaine de Vogüé owns seven tenths of Le Musigny, including the totality of Les Petits Musignys, and is the largest landholder in Bonnes-Mares, exploiting the southernmost, downslope quarter of this *grand cru*.

The harvest is very low. After total de-stemming, there is no deliberate cold-maceration. The wine is vinified at a maximum of 32°C. The percentage of new oak varies from 15 percent for the village wine to 45 percent for the Musigny and Bonnes-Mares. As mentioned on page 119, there is no Musigny *blanc* for the time being. The vines are too young.

Quality here is consistently very high indeed. These are not wines for the short term, though the delicious village Chambolle, into which goes young vine wine from the greater *climates*, comes forward reasonably quickly in light vintages such as 1997 and 2000. No, the best Vogüé wines need keeping 15 years at least. But they are well worth waiting for.

VOUGEOT

The commune of Vougeot is so dominated by its famous Clos that one tends to forget that there is both village and *premier cru* wine as well as the *grand cru*: not much—only 15.5 hectares—but enough to note. I have to say though, that just as the magic name of Clos de Vougeot is more likely than not to lead to disappointment, this being for the most part a second-division *grand cru* rather than a first-division one such as Le Musigny, Richebourg or Romanée-Saint-Vivant, so I find the *premier cru* wines of the commune to be of minor importance. This is not—as it might be, say, in Fixin—for a want of good growers. So it must be the *terroir*. I feel the authorities, having been saddled with the inescapable fact of decreeing the whole of the Clos as *grand cru*, to be bent rather too far backward to be kind to the rest of the commune.

Location

Just as the Clos itself is notorious for occupying more lower land—all the way down to the main road—than any of the other *grands crus*, so the *premiers crus*, immediately to the north, very nearly run down to the back of the houses in the village, which now, thankfully for its inhabitants, has been bypassed. There is a fault in the land here, a series of small terraces descending like a giant staircase. Above lie the vines of Le Musigny and Les Amoureuses. At the bottom is a small lake, fed by the source of the Vouge River and the stream of the Grône, which comes down from the *combe* above Chambolle-Musigny. The adjacent village Vougeot vines almost seem to be planted in a hole in the ground. Wherever you are, you seem to be looking down on them.

The soil here is very light, a fragile mixture of limestone scree and debris, but it contains rather more sand and alluvial material than most. Drainage can be a problem.

The Vineyard

GRAND CRU The Clos de Vougeot accounts for more than 80 percent of the land in the commune. With 50.59 hectares, it produces around 1,800 hectolitres of wine a year. The wine can only be red.

PREMIERS CRUS There are four: Les Cras, La Vigne Blanche (Le Clos Blanc), Clos de la Perrière and Les Petits Vougeots (in part). The appellation allows both red and white wine. The surface area comprises 11.68 hectares and produces about 350 hectolitres of red and 100 hectolitres of white wine a year.

VILLAGE WINE There are 4.83 hectares of village wine producing about 90 hectolitres of red and 36 hectolitres of white wine a year.

Village and *premier cru* Vougeot *rouge* is a light wine, superficially similar in structure to Chambolle-Musigny. But it lacks both the intensity and the class of a typical Chambolle. Too often, frankly, it's a bit weak. The explanation lies in the sandy structure of the soil. This produces fruit with a tendency to rapidly become overripe, with a consequent lack of grip in the resulting wine.

There are only two white Vougeots regularly seen on the market: that of Domaine de la Vougeraie, successors to L'Heritier Guyot, and that of Domaine Bertagna. Both have improved considerably in the last decade. They are worth seeking out as occasional alternatives to Meursault.

The Grand Cru

CLOS DE VOUGEOT

SURFACE AREA: 50.59 ha
AVERAGE PRODUCTION: 1,800 hl
PRINCIPAL PROPRIETORS: Château de la Tour (5.48 ha); ★ Méo-Camuzet (3.03 ha); Rebourseau (2.21 ha); ★ Louis Jadot (2.15 ha); ★ Leroy (1.91 ha); ★ Grivot (1.87 ha); ★★ Gros Frère et Soeur (1.50 ha); Gérard Raphet (1.47 ha); ★ Vougeraie (1.41 ha); ★ René Engel (1.37 ha); ★ François Lamarche (1.36 ha); ★ Faiveley (1.29 ha); Jacques Prieur (1.28 ha); ★ Drouhin-Laroze (1.03 ha); ★ Alain Hudelot-Noëllat (0.69 ha); ★ S.C. La Livinière (Domaine d'Audhuy) (0.56 ha).

A further forty proprietors/exploitants work over 0.20 hectares of vines, including the following:

Bertrand Ambroise

★ Robert Arnoux

★ Bertagna

★ Bouchard Père et Fils

Capitain-Gagnerot

Philippe Charlopin

Hubert Chauvenet-Chopin

Jérôme Chézeaux

Yvon Clerget

★ Jacky Confuron-Cotéditot

Christian Confuron

★ Jean-Jacques Confuron

★ Joseph Drouhin

R. Dubois

Régis Forey

★ Clos Frantin

Genot-Boulanger

François Gerbet-Castagnier

★ Anne Gros

★★★ Michel Gros

Jean-Michel Guillon

★ Alfred Haegelen

Chantal Lescure

Leymarie-Ceci

Sylvain Loichet

Château de Marsannay

Jean-Marc Millot

★ Mongeard-Mugneret

★ De Montille

★ Denis Mortet

★ Dr. Georges Mugneret

Michel Noellat

Prieuré-Roch

Bernard and Armelle Rion

Daniel Rion

Hervé Roumier

Laurent Roumier

Jean Tardy

★ Thibault Liger-Belair

Tortochot

This is not the largest *grand cru* in Burgundy: Corton and Corton-Charlemagne are quite a bit more substantial. But it is the largest in the Côte de Nuits. Of the twenty-four *grands crus* here, only Clos de Vougeot and Echézeaux could be said to be sizeable.

Like Echézeaux, and like most of Burgundy, the Clos is split up. Today there are some eighty proprietors and 100 different parcels, some of which are detailed and recommended above.

The history of the Clos de Vougeot is exemplary of the history of vinous Burgundy. At the beginning of the twelfth century, the centre of the western world was neither London, nor Paris, nor even Rome, but the Abbey of Cluny in the southern Mâconnais. Founded by the followers of Saint Benedict in AD 910, Cluny was the wealthiest and most powerful religious settlement in Christendom.

Elsewhere in France, however, there were Benedictines who felt that with such power had come a relaxation in the strict monastic virtues laid down by their founding saint. Humility, obedience, silence and even chastity had been forgotten, replaced by rich living, sumptuous eating and drinking, and a worldliness far removed from the original objective. One such concerned Benedictine was Robert, Abbot of Molesmes, a monastery north of Dijon between Langres and Les Riceys. Robert had attempted unsuccessfully to reform the way of life at Molesmes, but he found that only a few of his fellow monks wished to return to the simple life. In 1098, with some twenty companions, he left Molesmes and established a new monastery, a reformed commune, on the flat plains of eastern Burgundy, in a clearing within a forest of oaks and marshy reedlands. From the ancient French word for reed, *cistel*, the name evolved to the Latin *cistercium*. The new order became known as the Cistercians, and the new abbey was named Cîteaux.

But at Cîteaux, the land was unsuitable for the vine. No matter how hard they tried, the monks could not persuade the vine to thrive in the marshy bogs surrounding the abbey. Following the Vouge River upstream, the monks explored the higher ground to the west. Eventually they settled on some uncultivated slopes, bartered with some Burgundian landowners and acquired a few hectares of land. This was the nucleus of the Clos de Vougeot.

The monastery soon started receiving gifts of adjoining land suitable for the vine. The poverty, industry, austerity and saintliness of the Cistercians contrasted well with the opulent high life of the other religious orders. Donors shrewdly decided that the appropriate gesture in this world would be recompensed when it might be needed later, and the vineyard grew. Around 1160, a press house was constructed, but it was not until 1336 that the vineyard took the form we know today, and later still that the famous wall forming the Clos was eventually completed. Finally, in Renaissance times, the château was constructed, affording guest rooms for the abbot and distinguished visitors. The château has been modified several times since, having been completed in 1891 and restored after World War II. It is now the headquarters of the Chevaliers de Tastevin, Burgundy's leading wine promotion fraternity.

Clos de Vougeot, by now a vineyard of some 50 hectares, remained in the ownership of the Cistercians until the French Revolution in 1789 when it was sequestered and put up for sale as a *bien national*. It was decided to sell the Clos as one lot, and on January 17, 1791, ahead of six adversaries, it was acquired by a Parisian banker, one Jean Foquard, for the huge sum of 1,140,600 livres, payable in *assignats* (paper money). Foquard, it appears, never settled his debt, and the authorities turned to Lambert Goblet, the monk cellarist or *magister celarii*, to continue to administer the estate. A year later the vineyard passed to the brothers Ravel, but after the Restoration in 1815, the Clos de Vougeot changed hands yet again, the Ravels and their associates having been continually in dispute over their relative shares and responsibilities over a period of 25 years.

This time the Clos de Vougeot's proprietor was a man of financial substance. Jules Ouvrard took the ownership of this important vineyard with the seriousness that it deserved. He was the local *député* (Member of Parliament) for much of his career. He was a conscientious proprietor, with land in Corton, Chambertin and Volnay, and he was also the owner of La Romanée-Conti, which he vinified at Clos de Vougeot.

After Ouvrard's death in 1860, there was the usual difficulty about inheritance, and this was not finally resolved until the Clos was sold—for 600,000 francs—in 1889. For the first time the land was divided. Originally there were six purchasers—five Burgundian wine merchants and one other—but these six soon became fifteen, and now there are eighty: an average of 0.6 hectares or 250 cases per proprietor.

The Clos de Vougeot is not only one of the largest *grands crus* in Burgundy but also the only one apart from Mazoyères/Charmes-Chambertin whose land runs right down to the main road connecting Nuits-Saint-Georges and Dijon. Not surprisingly, over such a large area, the soil structure is complex, and there are differences in aspect and drainage. Add to these the many different owners, each making an individual wine, and you can see why there are variations from one grower's Clos de Vougeot to another's.

At the top and best part of the Clos, where the vineyard borders the *grands crus* of Grands-Echézeaux to the south and Le Musigny to the north, the soil is a pebbly, oolitic limestone of Bathonian origin. There is little clay. Here there are two unofficial *lieux-dits*—unofficial in the sense that they are not legally recognised as parts of the Clos as are, for instance, the subdivisions of Corton—Le Grand Maupertius and Le Musigni [sic]. Halfway down the slope, the soil becomes marl—that is, a mixture of limestone and clay, but limestone of a different origin, Bajocian; however, there are still pebbles here, so the land drains well. Further down the slope still, the soil is less good; it becomes more alluvial and drains less well.

Understandably, Clos de Vougeot wines from this lower part of the vineyard are criticised. The critics argue that this land is not worthy of its *grand cru* status, pointing out that over the wall to the south, the vineyards are entitled to only the plain Vosne-Romanée appellation. If the Clos had not been one large vineyard, contained within its retaining walls, it would never have been decreed *grand cru* in its entirety.

Tradition has it that the original ecclesiastical proprietors produced three wines: from the top or best land came the Cuvée des Papes, from the middle the Cuvée des Rois and from the lower slopes the Cuvée des Moines, and only this latter one was sold commercially. Some people suggest the division was, in fact, vertical, as you face up the slope, not horizontal. Is the wine from the lower, flatter slope inferior? In practice as well as in principle, yes—but it nevertheless remains more important to choose your grower than the geography within the vineyard. Jean and Étienne Grivot own a large area of Clos de Vougeot, by which I mean almost 2 hectares, but on the lower levels of the *climat*. Yet with old vines—at least half date from 1920—and with meticulous vinification, this is by no means one of the lesser Clos de Vougeot wines. In fact, I would certainly place it in the top ten. Jean Grivot explains that in dry vintages, the upper slopes can become a little parched, though he fairly admits that the lower land can get somewhat humid if the weather turns wet.

At its best, Clos de Vougeot can rank among the greatest Burgundies, alongside Chambertin and the best of Vosne-Romanée. But it rarely does so. Normally, I would consider it in the second division of *grands crus*, comparable with those of Morey and Corton, or indeed its neighbours Echézeaux and Grands-Echézeaux. In style, the wine is plumper, lusher and spicier than Chambertin or La Tâche, less firm, less intensely flavoured and with less definition. It also does not possess the cumulative complexity and fragrance of Musigny. Yet when rich, fullish and generous, with a fruit which is half redolent of soft, red summer berries and half that of blackberries and chocolate, plus undertones of liquorice, burnt nuts and even coffee (a promising sign in a young Burgundy), the wine can be immensely enjoyable. Sadly, because of the vineyard's size and renown and its multiplicity of owners, it is one of the most abused names in the area.

The Premiers Crus

LE CLOS BLANC (3.05 ha)

This *climat*, producing white wine as the name suggests, is the monopoly of Domaine de la Vougeraie (see below).

CLOS DE LA PERRIÈRE (2.26 ha)

Part of Les Petits-Vougeots and a monopoly of Bertagna (see below).

LES PETITS VOUGEOTS (3.49 ha)
LES CRAS (2.99 ha)

Les Petits Vougeots lies upslope, under Musigny, though several metres lower, while Les Cras lies on the other side of Le Clos Blanc, about two thirds of the way down the slope toward the road.

At the Bertagna domaine, which is the only cellar I know where one can compare different *premiers crus* Vougeots of the same colour, I find the Cras firmer and fuller but sometimes also a bit coarser than the Petits-Vougeots, while their Clos de la Perrière, which has more new oak, has the most richness and definition of all. But that is a very small statistical sample. Alain Hudelot-Noëllat, the Domaine Clerget, Fourrier, Ambroise, Jean Mongeard-Mugneret and the Domaine de la Vougeraie are the only other sources for Vougeot in bottle that I know of.

RECOMMENDED SOURCE
Bertagna.

The Growers

★ Bertagna

21 ha owned. Clos Saint-Denis (0.51 ha); Clos de Vougeot (0.33 ha); Corton, Les Grandes Lolières (0.25 ha); Corton-Charlemagne (0.27 ha); Chambertin (0.20 ha); Vougeot *premier cru* in Clos de la

Perrière (*monopole*), Les Cras (*rouge et blanc*) and Les Petits-Vougeots; Nuits-Saint-Georges *premier cru* Les Murgers; Vosne-Romanée *premier cru* Les Beaux-Monts; Chambolle-Musigny *premier cru* Les Plantes; village Vougeot (Clos Bertagna); village Chambolle-Musigny.

The Domaine Bertagna was acquired by the Reh family of Germany (owners of the excellent Trier-based Reichsgraf von Kesselslatt estate) in 1982. But it was not until 1988 that the wine was anything other than uninspiring. Since then, there has been a distinct improvement, particularly since the arrival of Claire Forrestier in 1999 (she left in 2006). The harvest has been reduced, and there is now more cold-soaking and less new wood. The fruit is totally de-stemmed. There is automatic temperature control of the fermentation, keeping the maximum below 32°C, and bottling after 12 to 18 months. These are well-coloured, plump, fleshy wines. The Vougeot *blanc* vines date from 1985. Having ventured into Corton in 1994, the domaine has expanded since into the Hautes-Côtes.

Christian Clerget

6.02 ha owned and *en fermage*. Echézeaux (1.09 ha); Chambolle-Musigny *premier cru* Les Charmes; Vougeot *premier cru* Les Petits Vougeots; village Vosne-Romanée in the *lieu-dit* Les Violettes; village Chambolle-Musigny; village Morey-Saint-Denis.

Things have improved over the last decade here, since Christian Clerget took over from his father Georges and uncle Michel. A new cellar has been constructed. There is a *table de tri*, total de-stemming and not so much the introduction of more new wood, but the more rapid disposal of the old barrels. The results are much more sophisticated. This is a good address.

Christian Confuron et Fils

7 ha owned and *en fermage*. Clos de Vougeot (0.25 ha); Le Musigny (0.08 ha); Bonnes-Mares (0.07 ha); Chambollé-Musigny *premier cru* Les Feusselottes; Nuits-Saint-Georges *premier cru* Les Vaucrains; village Nuits-Saint-Georges *rouge et blanc*; village Chambolle-Musigny; Côte de Nuits Villages.

Philippe Confuron, short, stocky, plump and in his forties and a passionate fisherman ("It's how I relax," he says) is in charge here, and his approach, following his personality, is idiosyncratic. No new oak, very minimal doses of SO_2, and the wines stored higgledy-piggledy in three different *caves* because they remain at three different temperatures, and it simplifies the reception of customers. I like the man. I like the wines. Sophie Meunier of Domaine J.J. Confuron is his cousin.

★ Alain Hudelot-Noëllat

10 ha owned and *en fermage*. Clos de Vougeot (0.69 ha); Romanée-Saint-Vivant (0.48 ha); Richebourg (0.28 ha); Vosne-Romanée *premier cru* in Les Beaumonts, Les Malconsorts and Les Suchots; Nuits-Saint-Georges *premier cru* Les Murgers; Chambolle-Musigny *premier cru* Les Charmes; Vougeot *premier cru* Les Petits Vougeots; village Vosne-Romanée; village Chambolle-Musigny.

Despite occasional inconsistencies in the past, this is definitely one of the top domaines in Burgundy, for when Alain Hudelot's top wines are on song, they are truly magnificent. The vineyards are now ploughed and the vines green harvested, steadily reducing the yields from those produced a decade ago. The vines are old, and the cellar tidy and efficient. Hudelot retains about 10 percent of the stems, believes in a long maceration at up to 32°C and gives his *grands crus* 100 percent new oak. He neither fines nor filters.

These are wines of great flair and concentration: full, opulent and multidimensional. The only weak point is the Vougeot. But that is the soil, not the winemaking of Alain Hudelot.

Château de la Tour

5.48 ha owned. Clos-de-Vougeot (5.48 ha).

The château, a nineteenth-century folly which makes a curious contrast with the medieval/ Renaissance bastion further up the slope, is the second building within the Clos of Vougeot and is the headquarters of the largest owner of the *grand cru*. The joint proprietors are the sisters Jeanne Labet and Nicole d'Echelette, and it is François, Jeanne's son, who is responsible for the wine.

There are five parcels of vines within the Clos, of ages ranging from 23 years to 95, and at times François Labet makes a *vieilles vignes cuvée*. The vines are higher trained than hitherto to increase the size of the leaf canopy. Three quarters or more of the stems are retained. After 7 to 10 days of cold-soaking, the wine is fermented at a maximum of 30°C with frequent *pigeages*, matured in upwards of 50 percent new oak and bottled without fining or filtration.

You would hope for the benefits of economies of scale here. Sadly, I find the result one of the least impressive of Clos de Vougeots.

Pierre Labet

6.8 ha owned. Beaune *premier cru* in Les Couchérias; Savigny-lès-Beaune *premier cru blanc* in Les Vergelesses; village Beaune *rouge et blanc* in the *lieux-dits* Clos des Monsnières and Clos du Dessus des Marconnets; Meursault in the *lieu-dit* Les Tillets.

The wines of François Labet's father Pierre are also made at the Château de la Tour and largely follow the same recipe. The white wine vines are young, very young in the case of the Meursault. I find them thin and superficial.

Leymarie-Ceci

4 ha owned. Clos de Vougeot (0.50 ha); Chambolle-Musigny *premier cru* Aux Echanges (*monopole*); village Vougeot; village Morey-Saint-Denis; village Gevrey-Chambertin.

Jean-Charles Leymarie took over as owner here following his father's death in 2004. He is a merchant in Belgium. The *régisseur* on the spot is Franck Hieramente. Following total de-stemming, the must is cold-soaked and vinified at up to 33°C and the wine given 30 percent or more new wood. These are sturdy wines, clumsy sometimes. They need time.

VOSNE-ROMANÉE AND FLAGEY-ECHÉZEAUX

Vosne-Romanée is the greatest Pinot Noir village on earth. It is the last of the *hors concours* communes of the Côte de Nuits—in the sense that it contains *grand cru climats*—as one travels south toward Nuits-Saint-Georges. It possesses six of the twenty-four great growth vineyards of this part of the Côte. There are a further two in Flagey-Echézeaux.

This may not be as many as Gevrey-Chambertin, which has eight; nor may their combined harvest be as much as that of Corton. But in the eyes of wine connoisseurs—or in their hearts and minds—the wines of Vosne are wines to conjure with: La Romanée-Conti, incomparable and one of the most expensive Burgundies money can buy; La Tâche, often its peer, occasionally its superior; sumptuous Richebourg; silky-smooth Romanée-Saint-Vivant; not to mention a host of delicious *premiers crus*, some of which, like the 1980 vintages of Cros Parantoux after Henri Jayer had breathed magic life into it, are every bit as good as a *grand cru*, and a first-division *grand cru* at that.

But in addition to the fine *climats* and great *terroirs* in Vosne-Romanée, today's village contains a very large number of estates, from the large and majestic to the discreet and modest, which produce excellent wine. Some are long-established. Others have only begun to bottle seriously in the last couple of decades or so. But today, given a successful vintage, the consumer can hardly go wrong.

The Vosne-Romanée style is for wines which are rich, austere, sensual, masculine and aristocratic. The Abbé Courtépée, writing before the French Revolution, said of Vosne-Romanée, "*Il n'y a pas de vins communs*" (There are no common wines in the village). The same could be said today.

History

Vosne-Romanée is mentioned in documents as early as the sixth century, successively as Vaona, Vadona, Vanona and Voone: the word means forest. In AD 890 the priory of Saint-Vivant was founded there by Manasses the First, and this soon attracted gifts of vineyards, notably from Alix de Vergy in 1232. Most of the best vineyards originally belonged either to this establishment, a Clunaic order, or to the Cistercian abbey in nearby Cîteaux.

By the mid-eighteenth century much of the land had been secularised. The Croonembourgs had sold Romanée to the Prince de Conti. La Tâche and a section of Romanée-Saint-Vivant were in private hands. Much of Richebourg, though, still belonged to the church.

The Revolution changed everything. Almost immediately, the church landholdings were sequestered. Rather later, the vineyards belonging to the lords of the *ancien régime* were to follow suit. The aristocratically owned Romanée-Conti and La Tâche were sold off as biens *nationaux* on the same day (April 21, 1794), while the ecclesiastical holdings of Richebourg had been auctioned off 3 years earlier, together with the Clos-de Vougeot, on January 17, 1791. As with the rest of Burgundy, the next century saw most of the *climats* become increasingly subdivided. Only the very greatest, as much by luck as anything else, were able to preserve their unity.

Dr. Lavalle in 1855 divided the vineyards of Vosne-Romanée and Flagey into five levels of quality. Romanée-Conti, Richebourg, La Tâche and La Romanée, along with Grands-Echézeaux, were decreed têtes de *cuvées*, and Romanée-Saint-Vivant and La Grande Rue as *premières* cuvées, along with Malconsorts, Beaux-Monts, Brûlées and Suchots.

In advance of the disciplines of *appellation contrôlée* in the mid-1930s, both Richebourg and La Tâche were enlarged: the former incorporated Les Varoilles (or Véroilles), the latter part of Les Gaudichots, the proprietors having been able to prove that the wines were of equal standing and that a "local, loyal and constant" precedent had been set. Similarly, the southern section of Romanée-Saint-Vivant was absorbed. More recently, La Grande Rue has been upgraded to *grand cru*.

Location

The two communes of Vosne-Romanée and Flagey-Echézeaux lie adjacent to each other between that of Vougeot, to the north, and Nuits-Saint-Georges, to the south. While the village of Flagey, anomalously for Burgundy, lies down beyond the railway line, definitely on the wrong side of the tracks, the sleepy village of Vosne lies in the middle of its vineyards, on the line where *premier cru* gives way to village wine, set well away from the main road. Vosne-Romanée is not a village of much architectural interest. But it is small and tranquil. At one end are a square and the village church, at the other a more imposing *mairie*. Between the two is the Château de Vosne-Romanée, property of the Liger-Belair family. This dates in part from the mid-seventeenth century, but mainly from the end of the eighteenth. The second story was constructed in the 1850s. The village suffered badly at the hands of both Austrian troops in Napoleonic times and German soldiers in 1870. Little remains of the original medieval village. Chambolle, with its steep streets and narrow *culs de sac*, has more charm. Morey, with its wide main street, off which there are many substantial medieval and late Renaissance courtyards, is more imposing.

The Vineyard

It is convenient to take these two communes together. Flagey possesses solely its two *grands crus*: Grands-Echézeaux and Echézeaux. All its other wines are labelled as Vosne-Romanée.

GRANDS CRUS There are eight *grands crus*: Echézeaux, Grands-Echézeaux, La Grande Rue, La Romanée-Saint-Vivant, Richebourg, La Tâche, La Romanée and La Romanée-Conti. These comprise 75 hectares and produce an average of 2,240 hectolitres per annum. Of this, one *climat*, Echézeaux, provides over half. Four of these *grands crus* are the monopoly of a single owner.

PREMIERS CRUS There are twelve in Vosne-Romanée. From south to north, they are Aux Malconsorts, Au-Dessus des Malconsorts, Les Chaumes, Clos des Réas, Les Gaudichots, Aux Reignots, Cros Parantoux, Les Petits Monts, Aux Brûlées, Les Beaux Monts (in part), Les Suchots and La Croix Rameau. There are a further two in Echézeaux, sold as Vosne-Romanée: Les Rouges and En Orveaux. The *premiers crus* total 58 hectares and produce an average of 2,400 hectolitres per annum.

VILLAGE WINE   There is a total of 105 hectares of village vineyard. The average production is 4,700 hectolitres. The appellation Vosne-Romanée covers red wine only.

The Grands Crus

ROMANÉE-CONTI

SURFACE AREA: 1.81 ha
AVERAGE PRODUCTION: 45 hl
PROPRIETOR: Monopoly of the Domaine de la Romanée-Conti, Vosne-Romanée.

This most celebrated *grand cru* in Burgundy is surrounded by La Grande Rue to the south, Richebourg to the north, and Romanée-Saint-Vivant to the east. On these three sides it is bounded by a small stone wall. Merely a path separates Romanée-Conti from La Romanée, its neighbour further up the slope.

Roughly square in shape—a mere 150 metres by 150—and lying precisely in mid-slope at an altitude of between 260 and 275 metres, its incline of about 6 degrees ensures a perfect drainage without any grave danger of erosion and an aspect of marvellous exposure from early morning until dusk.

The soil is *limono-argileux*, a fine sandy-clay mixture, in this case feeble in the sand content, brown in colour and mixed with pebbles and limestone scree. For most of the *climat* this is based on a subsoil of Prémeaux limestone of the lower Bathonian period. At the foot the subsoil is a marl formed by the deposits of small fossilised oysters (*marnes à ostrea acuminate*). There is a depth of barely 50 centimetres of surface soil before one encounters the bare rock. Since 1985, along with the other Domaine de la Romanée-Conti (DRC) vineyards, the land has been cultivated biologically.

LA ROMANÉE

SURFACE AREA: 0.85 ha
AVERAGE PRODUCTION: 31 hl
PROPRIETOR: Monopoly of the Château de Vosne-Romanée, M. Le Comte Liger-Belair. Up to 2001 the *climat* was farmed and the wine made by Régis Forey, Vosne-Romanée. The *élevage*, bottling and marketing of the wine was by Maison Bouchard Père et Fils, Beaune. In 2002 Louis-Michel Liger-Belair took over the responsibility for the vines and the winemaking. After the 2005 vintage, the arrangement with Bouchard Père et Fils came to an end.

The tiny La Romanée, the smallest *appellation contrôlée* in France, lies directly upslope from Romanée-Conti and is separated from it by a path. The altitude ranges from 275 to 300 metres, and the incline is a little steeper, from 9 degrees upward. Further upslope is the *premier cru* Aux Reignots.

The soil structure, however, is similar: again *limono-argileux* feeble in its sand fraction, mixed with pebbles, based on a friable Prémeaux limestone. The depth of surface soil, however, is much less.

Opinions are divided as to whether this was ever part of the Romanée now known as Romanée-Conti. The consensus seems to be that it was not, the *climat* being grouped together from parcels called Aux Echanges and Au-Dessus de la Romanée, some of which belonged to the Domaine Lamy de Samerey before the Revolution, by the Liger-Belair family in the first 30 years of the nineteenth century. The Liger-Belairs have owned it ever since.

How does it differ from Romanée-Conti itself? Or indeed from Richebourg, its neighbour to the north, the closest vines of which belong to the DRC? At its best it is equally perfumed, but it didn't, until the recent change of responsibility, have quite the aristocratic intensity of Romanée-Conti or the sumptuousness of Richebourg. It is an austere wine in its youth, and there is an element of reserve even when it is fully mature. But it is unmistakably of *grand cru* lineage. Since 2002 it has become more aristocratic. It is now truly one of the great wines of Burgundy.

LA TACHE

SURFACE AREA: 6.06 ha
AVERAGE PRODUCTION: 151 hl
PROPRIETOR: Monopoly of the Domaine de la Romanée-Conti.

Vosne-Romanée La Tâche is made up of two *lieux-dits*: La Tâche and La Tâche-Gaudichots. It lies to the south of Romanée-Conti and La Romanée and runs parallel with these two *climats*, being separated from them only by the newest Côte d'Or *grand cru*, La Grande Rue. Lying between 255 and 300 metres in altitude, steeper at the top, flatter at the bottom, but well-drained nevertheless, La Tâche encompasses a number of different soil structures: decomposed limestone of the lower Bathonian period at the top, thinly covered by pebbles and limestone debris, and deeper, richer, more clayey soil at the bottom of the slope, in parts mixed with fossilised oyster deposits.

Since 1985, as with the other DRC vineyards, La Tâche has been cultivated biologically.

RICHEBOURG

SURFACE AREA: 8.03 ha
AVERAGE PRODUCTION: 228 hl
PRINCIPAL PROPRIETORS: ★ Domaine de la Romanée-Conti (3.51 ha); ★ Leroy (0.78 ha); ★ Gros Frère et Soeur (0.69 ha); ★ A.F. Gros (0.60 ha); ★ Anne Gros (0.60 ha); ★ Thibault Liger-Belair (0.55 ha—*en métayage* to Denis Mugneret up to 2001); ★ Méo-Camuzet (0.35 ha); ★ Grivot (0.32 ha); Mongeard-Mugneret (0.31 ha); ★ Hudelot-Noëllat (0.28 ha); ★ Clos Frantin (0.07 ha).

Richebourg lies immediately to the north of La Romanée and Romanée-Conti and upslope from Romanée-Saint-Vivant. It is made up of two *lieux-dits*: Les Richebourgs and Les Véroilles-sous-Richebourg. While the aspect of Romanée-Conti faces due east, that of Richebourg inclines just a little toward the north at its upper end.

Lying at an altitude of between 280 and 260 metres, the gradient is similar to that of Romanée-Conti, as is the soil structure, a pebbly clay-sand mixture with a low sand content, mixed with limestone debris, lying on the rosy Prémeaux rock of the lower Bathonian period.

Originally owned by the monastery of Cîteaux, the majority of Richebourg was sold off as a *bien national* in 1790. By 1855 the owners included MM Frantin (who owned the bulk of Les Véroilles), Marey (already a proprietor before the Revolution), Duvault-Blochet (ancestors of the De Villaines of the DRC), Liger-Belair, Lausseure and Marillier. As with La Tâche and Gaudichots, the proprietors of Les Véroilles were able to prove to the Court of Appeal in Dijon in the 1920s that their wine had been sold as Richebourg and at the same price for long enough to warrant this section being officially included within the *grand cru*.

Richebourg is indisputably the best of the non-monopoly *grands crus* of Vosne. It is fuller, fatter, richer, more intense and generous, but more masculine and long-lasting than Romanée-Saint-Vivant. At its best, it can offer an explosion of flavours: coffee and chocolate when young, violets when mature, all within a velvet-textured cornucopia of small black and red fruits. I count some Richebourgs among the greatest Burgundies I have ever tasted. "Sumptuous," said Camille Rodier more than 60 years ago. How I agree!

ROMANÉE-SAINT-VIVANT

SURFACE AREA: 9.44 ha
AVERAGE PRODUCTION: 233 hl
PRINCIPAL PROPRIETORS: ★ Domaine de la Romanée-Conti (5.29 ha); ★ Leroy (0.99 ha); ★ Domaine de Corton-Grancey/Louis Latour (0.76 ha); ★ Jean-Jacques Confuron (0.50 ha); ★ Hudelot-Noëllat (0.48 ha); ★ Robert Arnoux (0.35 ha); Follin-Arbelet (0.33 ha); ★ Domaine de l'Arlot (0.25 ha); ★ Dujac (0.17 ha); ★ Sylvain Cathiard (0.17 ha).

Romanée-Saint-Vivant is the closest *grand cru* to the village of Vosne-Romanée, its vines running down behind the church at the northern end of the village to the courtyard of the old abbey of Saint-Vivant, now (having been the property of the Marey-Monge family) belonging to the Domaine de la Romanée-Conti.

The incline here is gentle, the altitude between 265 and 250 metres and the exposure to the east. The soil is heavier than it is further up the slope, and there is more of it: a brown clay-limestone mixed with pebbles on a Bajocian marl base.

For 650 years the land was the property of the local abbey, a Clunaic dependency. In the sixteenth century the bottom end of the parcel known as the Clos-des-Quatre-Journaux was detached. This is the section now owned by Dujac, Arnoux, Poisot, Arlot and Cathiard. During the Revolution, the rest was acquired by Nicolas-Joseph Marey of Nuits-Saint-Georges, known as Marey the younger, for 91,000 francs. The Marey-Monge family (as they were to become) sold off part of their inheritance in 1898 to Louis Latour and Charles Noëllat. They retained the rest until 1966, when a lease was granted to the Domaine de la Romanée-Conti. The Neyrand family, heirs of Mlle Geneviève Marey-Monge, last of her line, sold this to the DRC after her death in September 1988, for, it is understood, about 60 million French francs.

Romanée-Saint-Vivant is the lightest, the most delicate and the most feminine of the Vosne *grands crus*. For me there is a distinct resemblance to Musigny. At its best it is an exquisitely perfumed wine, silk where Richebourg is velvet, but no less intense, no less beautiful. While in the DRC line-up the Richebourg is usually superior, elsewhere, at Leroy or Hudelot-Noëllat, this is not always the case. It is a question of personal taste.

LA GRANDE RUE

SURFACE AREA: 1.65 ha
AVERAGE PRODUCTION: 60 hl
PROPRIETOR: Monopoly of the Domaine François Lamarche, Vosne-Romanée.

By official decree of July 8, 1992, La Grande Rue, sandwiched between La Tâche and La Romanée/Romanée-Conti, became the thirty-first *grand cru* of the Côte d'Or.

It shares the same geology and aspect, it occupies the same position on the slope, and prior to the mid-1930s, when the rest became officially *grands crus*, it sold without difficulty at high prices as Romanée La Grande Rue. Dr. Lavalle, in 1855, considered the wine as good as Romanée-Saint-Vivant and Les Véroilles-sous-Richebourg, if not the equal of Richebourg, La Tâche or Romanée-Conti itself. Why then was La Grande Rue not appointed *grand cru* in the first place? Apparently, the Lamarche family, proprietors since 1933, were not sufficiently concerned to insist on it.

The more recent elevation, 56 years later, clearly demonstrated the INAO's attitude to classification in Burgundy. It is the land and not the quality of the wine which is classified. The vines no doubt *could* produce *grand cru* quality. In the 1940s and 1950s they did. But in 1992 they had not done so for more than 20 years. If you compared the average production with that of Romanée-Conti next door, you could see one of the explanations for this. If you visited the region in the autumn just before the harvest and walked along the road that separates the two *climats*, another difference became apparent: the DRC vines were in immaculate condition, with all excess foliage pruned back and all excess bunches of grapes eliminated; the Lamarche vines were all over the place, groaning with fruit. François Lamarche's winemaking was also suspect.

It was a sad state of affairs. Thankfully, since 1998 or so, the quality of the Lamarche wines has considerably improved.

GRANDS-ECHÉZEAUX

SURFACE AREA: 9.14 ha
AVERAGE PRODUCTION: 290 hl
PRINCIPAL PROPRIETORS: ★ Domaine de la Romanée-Conti (3.53 ha); Mongeard-Mugneret (1.44 ha); Jean-Pierre Mugneret/Jean-René Naudant (0.90 ha); Domaine Thénard/Bordeaux-Montrieux (0.54 ha—sold through Maison Remoissenet Père et Fils); ★ Engel (0.50 ha); Henri de Villamont

(0.50 ha); ★ Joseph Drouhin (0.47 ha); ★ Gros Frère et Soeur (0.37 ha); ★ Lamarche (0.30 ha); ★ Clos Frantin (0.25 ha); Jean-Marc Millot (0.20 ha); ★ Robert Sirugue (0.13 ha). In total, there are twenty-one proprietors.

Grands-Echézeaux forms a roughly triangular piece which fits into and squares off the south-west corner of Clos de Vougeot. On the other two sides, it is bounded by the much more extensive Echézeaux. Originally, it belonged to the Abbey of Cîteaux, but unlike the Clos de Vougeot itself, it seems to have led a secular existence since at least the seventeenth century, one of the pre-revolutionary proprietors being the influential Marey family.

Relatively flat, at 260 metres, the brown soil is quite deep, a chalky limestone mixed with clay and pebbles on a Bajocian limestone base.

Generally regarded as superior to Echézeaux, and priced accordingly, Grands-Echézeaux is a richer, more structured wine with greater intensity and definition and a black fruit, gamey flavour: rustic in the best sense. It can be firm, even hard in its youth, less obviously generous than either Echézeaux or the more refined *grands crus* of Vosne-Romanée. It needs time. But the best are clearly as good as the best Clos de Vougeots. And a lot more interesting than the least good.

ECHÉZEAUX

SURFACE AREA: 37.69 ha
AVERAGE PRODUCTION: 1,200 hl
PRINCIPAL PROPRIETORS: ★ Domaine de la Romanée-Conti (4.67 ha); Mongeard-Mugneret (2.50 ha); ★ Emmanuel Rouget (1.43 ha); ★ Lamarche (1.32 ha); ★ Mugneret-Gibourg (1.24 ha); ★ Perdrix (1.15 ha); Jacques Cacheux (1.07 ha); Christian Clerget (1.09 ha); Clos Frantin (1.00 ha); Jean-Marc Millot (0.97 ha); ★ Robert Arnoux (0.90 ha); ★ Joseph Faiveley (0.87 ha); ★ Grivot (0.85 ha); ★ Dujac (0.69 ha); Dominique Mugneret (0.61 ha); Fabrice Vigot (0.60 ha); Bizot (0.56 ha); ★ Engel (0.55 ha); Jayer-Gilles (0.54 ha); ★ Jadot (0.52 ha); ★ Gros Frère et Soeur (0.41—until 2006); ★ Anne Gros (0.41—from 2007) ★ Joseph Drouhin (0.41 ha); ★ Bouchard Père et Fils (0.39); Jacques Prieur (0.36 ha); Daniel Rion (0.35 ha); Jean Tardy (0.35 ha); Naudin-Ferrand (0.34 ha); Philippe Charlopin (0.33 ha); Capitain-Gagnerot (0.31 ha); ★ Régis Forey (0.30 ha); Michel Noëllat (0.29 ha); A.F. Gros (0.26 ha); Alfred Haegelen (0.26 ha); François Confuron-Gendre (0.22 ha); Antonin Guyon (0.20 ha); François Gerbet (0.19 ha); Cécile Tremblay (0.18 ha). In total, there are eighty-four proprietors.

Echézeaux is one of the largest *grands crus* in Burgundy. It lies upslope and to the south of Grands-Echézeaux and the Clos de Vougeot. However, unlike the Clos, it does not run all the way down to the Nationale. The lower slopes are merely village wine, sold as Vosne-Romanée *tout court*. The Vosne-Romanée *premiers crus* of Beaux Monts, Brûlées and Suchots separate Echézeaux from Richebourg and Romanée-Saint-Vivant.

Within Echézeaux there are a number of *lieux-dits*, not seen on labels, but important locally to locate a grower's vines. Above Grands-Echézeaux are Les Poulaillères, where the Domaine de la Romanée-Conti's vines are situated, and Echézeaux-du-Dessus. On the Chambolle-Musigny border lies En Orveaux. At the top of the slope are Les Champs Traversins and Les Rouges-du-Bas. Below the *premier cru* of Les Beaux-Monts (*bas*) are Les Loachausses and Les Criots-en-Vignes-Blanches. Lower down, next to Les Suchots, are Clos Saint-Denis and Les Treux. Lowest still, outside the wall of Clos-de-Vougeot, lies Les Quartiers-de-Nuits.

Naturally in such a large vineyard, the *terroir* varies considerably. At its highest point, the *grand cru* reaches 300 metres; at its lowest, 250. Upslope, the incline is steep (up to 13 degrees), and the surface soil thin, with the underlying rock often visible. The stone here is Bajocian, friable in parts, hard in others, sometimes pure, sometimes with an important clay content. Lower down, the incline is flatter, the soil richer and deeper and the drainage less efficient.

Is there, then, as in Clos de Vougeot, a difference in quality between the different sections? The answer is certainly yes, but to a lesser degree, for the very bottom of the slope is not *grand cru*.

As always in Burgundy, the winemaker's degree of competence is paramount. Moreover, many of the landholders possess a number of different parcels within the conglomerate *climat*.

Echézeaux is, in general, a second-division *grand cru*, without the concentration and finesse of the best. In many cases the customer would be better off with a top *premier cru* wine, though he may not find it any cheaper. The wine is looser-knit than Grands-Echézeaux, with the same aspect of the rustic, but suppler tannins. It can be very good indeed, but it is rarely fine.

The Premiers Crus

With the recent elevation of La Grande Rue to *grand cru*, there are now fourteen *premiers crus* in Vosne-Romanée (and Flagey-Echézeaux). To the south, between the village and the Nuits-Saint-Georges boundary, lie Aux Malconsorts, Les Chaumes and Clos-des-Réas (the last the monopoly of the Domaine Jean Gros). Above La Tâche, La Romanée and Richebourg you will find Les Gaudichots, Aux Reignots, Les Petits Monts and Cros Parantoux. Further north are Aux Brûlées, Les Beaux-Monts, Les Suchots and La Croix Rameau. Part of Les Beaux-Monts is technically in Flagey-Echézeaux, as are En Orveaux and Les Rouges.

Which are the best? As far as I am concerned, there is a first division—Malconsorts, Suchots, Brûlées, Beaux-Monts and Cros Parantoux (plus, because it is so well made, Clos de Réas)—and the rest. Étienne Grivot describes the Suchots as the most aristocratic, the Beaux-Monts as the most classic, and the Brûlées (his faces southeast) as softer and more voluptuous.

From south to north, they are as follows:

AUX MALCONSORTS AND
AU-DESSUS DES
MALCONSORTS   (5.86 ha)

The *climat* lies on the Nuits-Saint-Georges border, indeed marches with Aux Boudots across the boundary. Nevertheless, there is little of Nuits-Saint-Georges about the wine. It is more true to say that Boudots is much more of a Vosne than

a Nuits. Lying as it does next to La Tâche and, it would seem, on identical land, Malconsorts can be a bargain. The wine is less intense and less structured than the *premiers crus* which lie on the northern side of the village. But it can have flair, fat, finesse and a fine perfume.

RECOMMENDED SOURCES
Alain Hudelot-Noëllat (Vougeot); Sylvain Cathiard, Clos Frantin, Lamarche (all Vosne-Romanée); Dujac (Morey-Saint-Denis); De Montille (Volnay).

LES CHAUMES   (6.46 ha)

Downslope from Les Malconsorts lies Les Chaumes. The slope is gentler, the surface soil deeper and richer, and there is more clay and alluvial soil in its composition. The result is wine of a little less depth and personality, a little less style. While I rate Malconsorts as, in its own way, the equal of Beaux-Monts, Brûlées and the other top *premiers crus* on the other side of the village, that cannot be said of Les Chaumes. Properties such as Méo-Camuzet, in their pricing structure, seem to agree.

RECOMMENDED SOURCES
Robert Arnoux, Lamarche, Louis-Michel Liger-Belair, Jean Grivot, Méo-Camuzet, Jean Tardy (all Vosne-Romanée); Daniel Rion (Nuits-Saint-Georges).

CLOS DES RÉAS   (2.12 ha)

This walled triangular vineyard is the monopoly of the Domaine Michel Gros. Though it is located further down toward the valley than all the other *premiers crus*, few would deny that the wine fully merits the title of first growth, and it is a very good one at that. The wine is not a heavyweight, but has the pure fragrance of Pinot Noir at its most elegant.

RECOMMENDED SOURCE
Michel Gros (Vosne-Romanée).

LES GAUDICHOTS   (1.03 ha)

The Domaine de la Romanée-Conti has some Gaudichots, but sells it off in bulk. There are a couple of other proprietors. But the only wines I have ever seen are those of Régis Forey, of Vosne-Romanée, and Thierry Vigot, who lives up in the Hautes-Côtes at Messanges, plus a merchant wine from Nicky Potel. In their hands we have a sturdy beast, not without depth and richness and even concentration, but *sauvage*. It needs time.

RECOMMENDED SOURCES
Forey Père et Fils (Vosne-Romanée); Nicolas Potel (Nuits-Saint-Georges).

AUX REIGNOTS   *(1.62 ha)*

The main grower here is Louis-Michel Liger-Belair, of the Château de Vosne-Romanée. Sylvain Cathiard and Robert Arnoux are the other major participants. Like the Gaudichots, which it adjoins—here we are above La Romanée—the wine has a touch of the rustic. But it is full, rich and substantial, nevertheless.

RECOMMENDED SOURCES
Robert Arnoux, Sylvain Cathiard, Louis-Michel Liger-Belair (all Vosne-Romanée).

LES PETITS MONTS   *(3.67 ha)*

There are not many who produce this wine in bottle. Yet the *climat*, though small, is split between as many as twenty growers. One is the Domaine de la Romanée-Conti, which sells its wine off in bulk. Véronique Drouhin is another: I have had some fine recent vintages from her, vinified by Maison Drouhin in Beaune. The Gerbet sisters exploit 0.59 hectares; Jean Mongeard, 0.30. Another grower is Robert Sirugue, who has 0.56 hectares, and who now produces lovely wines. The *climat* lies above Richebourg.

RECOMMENDED SOURCES
Drouhin (Beaune); Robert Sirugue (Vosne-Romanée).

CROS PARANTOUX   *(1.01 ha)*

This small *premier cru* lies above Richebourg and alongside that bit of Richebourg known as Les Véroilles. Having been allowed to deteriorate into scrub, it was planted by the great Henri Jayer during the war. He owned the larger part of it (0.72 ha). The domaine for which he was share-cropping, Méo-Camuzet, owns the rest. Jayer has now ceded his vines to his heir and nephew, Emmanuel Rouget.

This is a wine of *grand cru* standard, and first-division *grand cru* at that: full, powerful, rich, oaky and splendidly concentrated. An essence of a wine: brutal when young, and velvety, mellow and exotic when mature.

RECOMMENDED SOURCES
Méo-Camuzet (Vosne-Romanée); Emmanuel Rouget (Flagey-Echézeaux).

LES BEAUX MONTS   *(11.39 ha)*

Sometimes contracted to Beaumonts, this is one of the largest of the Vosne-Romanée *premiers crus*. Though it lies upslope and adjacent to Echézeaux and is separated from Richebourg only by the smaller Les Brûlées, it has a distinct personality of its own, which comes in part from its exposure, which inclines partly toward the south, and in part from its soil, which contains marl and clay. It is a nice big wine, but nonetheless perfumed, full of finesse, even lush.

RECOMMENDED SOURCES
Dujac (Morey-Saint-Denis); Alain Hudelot-Noëllat (Vougeot); Bruno Clavelier, Grivot, Leroy (all Vosne-Romanée); J.J. Confuron; Daniel Rion (Nuits-Saint-Georges); Louis Jadot (Beaune).

LES BRÛLÉES   *(4.53 ha)*

Divided by the road which goes up to Concoeur, Les Brûlées marches with Les Beaumonts on one side, facing southeast, and Richebourg on the other, inclining to the northeast. From these schizophrenic origins, there is nevertheless plenty of wine of quality: wine with backbone, richness and depth in a particularly masculine sort of way.

RECOMMENDED SOURCES
Engel, Grivot, Leroy, Méo-Camuzet (all Vosne-Romanée).

LES SUCHOTS   (13.07 ha)

This is another large *premier cru*—the largest in the commune. It lies on the same level as Romanée-Saint-Vivant, on flatter, richer, deeper soil than the Beaux-Monts. Nevertheless, it is less structured than the above. At its best it can, like Romanée-Saint-Vivant, produce wine with a considerable flair and perfume, but there is usually a slightly gamey, rustic touch which betrays the fact that its northern neighbour is Echézeaux.

RECOMMENDED SOURCES
Alain Hudelot-Noëllat (Vougeot); Robert Arnoux, Jacky Confuron-Cotétidot, Grivot (all Vosne-Romanée); Domaine de l'Arlot (Nuits-Saint-Georges); Jadot (Beaune). The Domaine de la Romanée-Conti owns a hectare of vines, which is farmed by Henri Roch, of the Domaine Prieuré-Roch.

LA CROIX-RAMEAU   (0.60 ha)

This small *climat* is an enclave within Romanée-Saint-Vivant which the four joint owners have tried—unsuccessfully so far—to get incorporated into the *grand cru*. Lamarche is one of these owners; Jacques Cacheux is another. The vines of the latter were planted in 1986. The wine is succulent and medium-bodied, but with the flair to merit elevation to *grand cru*.

EN ORVEAUX   (1.79 ha)

Sylvain Cathiard has a plot in this small *climat*, upslope from Echézeaux on the Chambolle side. One can see the proximity: elegance, medium body, intensity.

RECOMMENDED GROWER
Sylvain Cathiard (Vosne-Romanée).

LES ROUGES   (2.62 ha)

We are almost up in the hills here, at 320 metres and above the central part of Echézeaux. One of the few proprietors whose wines I know is the Grivot family, with this parcel coming from their aunt Jacqueline Jayer. It is a more pedestrian wine than their better *premiers crus*: less succulent, a little four-square.

The Growers

★ Robert Arnoux

14 ha owned and *en fermage/en métayage*. Echézeaux (0.90 ha); Clos de Vougeot (0.45 ha—top); Romanée-Saint-Vivant (0.35 ha); Vosne-Romanée *premier cru* in Les Chaumes, Les Reignots and Les Suchots; Nuits-Saint-Georges *premier cru* in Les Corvées-Pagets and Les Procès; village Vosne-Romanée, including the *lieu-dit* Les Maizières; village Nuits-Saint-Georges, including the *lieu-dit* Les Poisets; village Chambolle-Musigny.

Robert Arnoux, who died in 1995 at age sixty-four, was a large and somewhat intimidating man on first acquaintance. He had doubled his exploitation since taking over from his father in the 1950s, and this necessitated frequent extensions—the last in 2005—to the cellar underneath his house, set back from the main Nuits-Dijon highway. He was succeeded by his son-in-law, Pascal Lachaux (b. 1962).

I have had fine quality from this domaine in the past, particularly from his Romanée-Saint-Vivant and his Suchots, old vines at the top of the vineyard. There was then a dip, but since the 1993 vintage, effectively when Pascal Lachaux took over, quality has again been fine. The culture of the vines is biological; yields are low; there is 100 percent de-stemming, 35 to 100 percent new oak and neither fining nor filtration.

Bizot

2.7 ha *en fermage*. Echézeaux (0.56 ha); Vosne-Romanée *premier cru* (from declassified Echézeaux); village Vosne-Romanée, including the *lieux-dits* Les Réas, Les Jachées and a *vieilles vignes cuvée*.

The youthful, handsome Jean-Yves Bizot took over his family's vines a decade ago. Yields are severely cut back, and chaptalisation and sulphur levels are kept to a minimum, if not eschewed altogether. He vinifies at low temperatures, with all the stems, and matures the wines in 100 percent new oak without racking, fining or filtration. This results in wines which appear a bit light at the outset. But they put on both colour and weight as they age. There are classy wines here.

Jacques Cacheux et Fils

6.93 ha owned and *en fermage/en métayage*. Echézeaux (1.10 ha); Vosne-Romanée *premier cru* in Les Suchots and La Croix-Rameau; Chambolle-Musigny *premier cru* in Les Charmes and Les Plantes; village Chambolle-Musigny; village Vosne-Romanée; village Nuits-Saint-Georges Au Bas de Combe.

In 1994 there was a change of generation. Jacques Cacheux (of medium height, shy, gentle, greying, and bespectacled), who had arrived in the village from Cambrai and married the local Lucette Blée in the 1950s, so becoming a *vigneron*, took his retirement. His much taller and darker son Patrice (b. 1958) is now in charge. Patrice's wife is Patricia, *née* Sirugue.

Patrice has changed the vinification techniques employed by his father. The grapes are now totally de-stemmed and cold-soaked for a week. The wine is macerated for a shorter period—a week or so—matured using 30 to 100 percent new wood and bottled without fining or filtering. The object is supple wines for drinking in the medium term. Jacques's wines were fuller and more tannic. Cacheux is one of the first of his peers to bottle his village wines with artificial corks. Quality is now very good here. You have to be careful when vinifying the Croix-Rameau, you will be told, for it has a tendency to produce a wine which is too solid. The vines were 20 years old in 2007.

René Cacheux

3.20 ha owned and *en fermage*. Vosne-Romanée *premier cru* Les Beaumonts and Les Suchots; village Vosne-Romanée; village Chambolle-Musigny.

Two Blée daughters married two Cacheux brothers. Gérald Cacheux, son of René, worked for Armelle and Bernard Rion for 15 years, returning to help his father make his last vintage before he retired in 2004. Father made good wine but sold most of it in bulk. Gerald

is bottling more and more. He has reduced the harvest, he now performs a more severe *triage*, and he has upped the percentage of new wood to one third for the *premiers crus*. This is a promising new(–ish) address.

★★★ Sylvain Cathiard

4 ha owned. Romanée-Saint-Vivant (0.17 ha); Vosne-Romanée *premier cru* in Les Malconsorts, En Orveau, Les Reignots and Les Suchots; Nuits-Saint-Georges *premier cru* in Aux Thorey and Les Murgers; village Vosne-Romanée; village Chambolle-Musigny in the *lieu-dit* Le Clos de l'Orme; village Nuits-Saint-Georges.

Sylvain Cathiard is one of my favourite growers in the whole of Burgundy. He is a quiet man with—poor devil!—a serious stutter, and he must be fifty-ish. There is a touch of genius here in the winemaking, resulting in bottles of exceptional purity and fragrance: Pinot Noir at its most elegant.

The grapes are entirely de-stemmed and macerated for a fortnight at temperatures of up to 33°C, and the *premiers crus* and *grands crus* are given 50 and 100 percent new wood, respectively. These are wines of concentration and complexity. They will keep. This is a splendid address. The 2005s are breathtakingly fine.

Bruno Clavelier

5.86 ha owned and *en fermage*. Corton, Le Rognet (0.34 ha); Vosne-Romanée *premier cru* in Les Beaux-Monts and Les Brûlées; Nuits-Saint-Georges *premier cru* Aux Cras; Chambolle-Musigny *premier cru* La Combe d'Orveau; Gevrey-Chambertin *premier cru* Les Corbeaux; village Vosne-Romanée, including the *lieux-dits* La Combe Brûlée, Les Hauts de Beaumont, Les Hautes Maizières and La Montagne (*monopole*).

Bruno Clavelier (b. 1964), a qualified oenologue, took over the vines of his parents and maternal grandparents (Brosson) in 1987 and has since enlarged this domaine by extending it into Nuits-Saint-Georges and Gevrey-Chambertin, the Corton being the latest addition. His domaine is now officially biodynamic.

The average age of the vines is old here. The fruit is 90 percent de-stemmed, and the wine vinified classically at 28–30°C and matured using a maximum of 35 percent new oak. The wines are not filtered. Full, rich and perfumed: this is quality produce.

★ Jacky Confuron-Cotétidot

7 ha owned and *en fermage/en métayage*. Charmes-Chambertin (0.39 ha); Clos de Vougeot (0.25 ha); Echézeaux (0.22 ha); Mazis-Chambertin (0.08 ha); Vosne-Romanée *premier cru* Les Suchots; Nuits-Saint-Georges *premier cru* in Les Murgers and Aux Vignerondes; Gevrey-Chambertin *premier cru* in Craipillot, Lavaux-Saint-Jacques and Petite Chapelle; village Vosne-Romanée; village Chambolle-Musigny; village Nuits-Saint-Georges; village Gevrey-Chambertin.

The Confuron brothers—Yves, who also looks after the wines of the Courcel domaine in Pommard, and Jean-Pierre, who is also responsible for the wines at Chanson—are in charge here. They have modified the winemaking of their father Jacky. There is still the long cold-soaking, use of all the stems and minimal sulphuring, but now the harvests have been reduced, and there is less *pigeage*, but *cuvaisons* are prolonged to a month or more, and the percentage of new wood has been increased to a third. "It's more of an infusion than an extraction," says Jean-Pierre. They own over 2 hectares in the Suchots, making them the largest landholder. Quality is very good now.

François Confuron-Gendre

10 ha owned and *en fermage/en métayage*. Echézeaux (0.22 ha); Vosne-Romanée *premier cru* in Les Beaumonts, Les Chaumes and Les Brûlées; village Vosne-Romanée; village Nuits-Saint-Georges; village Gevrey-Chambertin.

The 40-year-old François Confuron took over from his father Serge a decade ago and has steadily increased the amount of domaine bottling here ever since. The majority of the stems are removed, and there is no cold-soaking and 10–20 days maceration. Thereafter, about one third new wood is employed. The wines are fresh, stylish and full of fruit. This man is a rising star.

★★ René Engel

7 ha owned. Clos de Vougeot (1.37 ha); Grands-Echézeaux (0.50 ha); Echézeaux (55 a); Vosne-Romanée *premier cru* Les Brûlées; Village Vosne-Romanée.

In the decade and a half after he took over after his father's early death in 1981, Philippe Engel (b. 1955) transformed this domaine from the very good, selling much of its produce in bulk, to the very serious indeed, now bottling everything.

The fruit is completely de-stemmed and given a couple of days to cold-soak before the fermentation starts. Maceration lasts up to 3 weeks, and maturation employs 30 to 50 percent new oak. The result is wine of great intensity, splendid style and individuality and real power to last. This is a fine source.

Tragically, Philippe died of a heart attack at the early age of forty-nine, in May 2005. The 2005s were sold off in bulk. In 2006 the estate was sold to François Pinault, owner, inter alia, of Château Latour.

★ Régis Forey (Domaine Forey Père et Fils)

8 ha owned and *en fermage*. Echézeaux (0.30 ha); Clos de Vougeot (0.30 ha); Vosne-Romanée *premier cru* Les Gaudichots and Les Petits Monts; Nuits-Saint-Georges *premier cru* in Les Perrières and Les Saint-Georges; Morey-Saint-Denis *premier cru* (from Les Blanchards and Clos Baulet); village Vosne-Romanée; village Nuits-Saint-Georges; village Morey-Saint-Denis.

Régis Forey's domaine is half owned, half rented, his own parcels including the Echézeaux and the Vosne-Romanée Les Gaudichots, the latter from which often derives his best wine. A decade ago he moved into a spacious new winery on the road to Flagey. Perhaps coincidentally, his wines began to acquire an extra element of elegance. Since 1995 Forey has diminished the amount of sulphur employed. There is partial de-stemming, a short *maceration à froid* and a *cuvaison* of up to 4 weeks. This results in full, quite muscular wines. They need time. This is now a very good address.

Clos Frantin

See Albert Bichot, Beaune (page 207).

François Gerbet

12 ha owned and *en fermage/en métayage*. Clos de
Vougeot (0.31 ha); Echézeaux (0.19 ha); Vosne-
Romanée *premier cru* Les Petits Monts and Les
Suchots; Chambolle-Musigny *premier cru* Les Plantes;
village Vosne-Romanée, including the *lieu-dit* Aux
Réas. Half of the exploitation is in the Hautes-Côtes-
de-Nuits at Concoeur.

The Gerbet sisters—Marie-Andrée, tall and
blonde, and Chantal, petite and brunette—are in
reality Mesdames Vincent Berthaut (*viticulteur*
in Fixin) and Denis Berin (airline pilot). There
is a third sister who lives in Paris. François, their
father, who arrived and fell in love with a local
girl during the war, retired in 1983.

The recipe here is for de-stalking in most vintages, a *cuvaison* of about a fortnight and up to
75 percent new wood for the top wines and the
separately bottled village Aux Réas. You can find
some good things here (remarkably seductive
2003s for instance), but sometimes the results
can be a bit rigid, with the oak dominating.

★★★ Jean Grivot

15.5 ha owned (the domaine is *fermier* for the Grivot
family vineyard). Richebourg (0.32 ha); Clos de
Vougeot (1.87 ha); Echézeaux (0.85 ha); Vosne-
Romanée *premier cru* in Les Beaux-Monts, Les
Brûlées, Les Chaumes, Les Suchots, Les Reignots
and Les Rouges; Nuits-Saint-Georges *premier cru* in
Aux Boudots, Les Pruliers and Les Roncières; village
Vosne-Romanée, including the *lieu-dit* Les Bossières;
village Nuits-Saint-Georges, including the *lieux-dits*
Les Charmois and Les Lavières; Village Chambolle-
Musigny in the *lieu-dit* La Combe d'Orveau.

Run by Étienne Grivot (b. 1959) and his charming wife Marielle (who is the sister of Savigny's
Patrick Bize), this is one of the great domaines
of Burgundy. Everything is done in the vineyard
with respect for the quality and life of the soil.
Though not biodynamic, the viticulture is as
natural as possible, involving the Plocher energy
system of bringing vigour to the environment.

Entirely de-stemmed, the must is cold-
macerated for a few days, with the length depending on the vintage; vinified at 26–33°C; and kept

in 20 to 50 percent new wood until the first
and only racking. The entire domaine is run to
transform the juice of ripe fruit into wine in as
natural a way as possible.

The wines have been quite brilliant here
since a brief flirtation with the theories of
oenologist Guy Accad in the late 1980s. Year
after year, one of the very finest red Burgundies
at the annual Domaine Familiaux/Institute of
Masters of Wine tasting in London is Grivot's
Vosne-Romanée Les Beaumonts. The 2005s are
excellent.

★★★ Anne Gros

5.8 ha owned and *en fermage*. Richebourg
(0.60 ha); Clos de Vougeot (0.93 ha); Echézeaux
(0.45 ha—from 2007); village Vosne-Romanée; village
Chambolle-Musigny.

The petite, charming and attractive Anne Gros
(b. 1966) has been in charge here since 1988,
this estate—formerly François Gros—having
been detached from the old Louis Gros domaine
in 1963. Prior to her arrival, it disposed of half of
its wine in bulk. Anne is now selling everything
in bottle.

The fruit is entirely de-stemmed, the fermentation temperatures are allowed to climb
up to 32°C, and 90 percent new wood is used for
the *grands crus*. Since 1993 Anne Gros has produced some of the finest wines in all Burgundy.
Quietly confident, she has a sure, perfectionistic touch, and the results are wines of great
refinement, intensity, purity and depth of character. Like her cousins (see below), Anne Gros
has expanded into the Hautes-Côtes. The 2005s
are very lovely.

A.F. Gros

See Parent, Pommard (page 222).

★★ Domaine Gros Frère et Soeur

18.4 ha owned and *en fermage*. Clos de Vougeot
(1.50 ha); Richebourg (0.69 ha); Echézeaux
(0.41 ha—up to 2006); Grands Echézeaux (0.37 ha);
Vosne-Romanée *premier cru* Les Chaumes; village
Vosne-Romanée. There is a large exploitation at
Concoeur in the Hautes-Côtes-de-Nuits.

Bernard Gros (b. 1958), stocky, dark, and moustached, is the younger brother of Michel Gros (see below); he started work at the domaine of his uncle Gustave and aunt Colette in 1980, taking over on Gustave's death in 1984.

Like his brother Michel, Bernard believes in heating up the must to approaching 40°C at the end of the maceration process. Unlike Michel's process, even Bernard's village Vosne gets 100 percent new oak. This makes its presence felt in the wines. They seem chunkier, and as well, like the man himself, they are more exuberant. But perhaps they have less finesse. Currently, the vines are young in this domaine, having been progressively totally replanted since 1984. Even in 2007, the only parcels which average over 20 years of age are the Chaumes and the Grands Echézeaux. There are very good wines here though, nevertheless.

★★★ Michel Gros

19 ha owned and *en fermage*. Clos de Vougeot (0.20 ha); Richebourg (22 a); Vosne-Romanée *premier cru* Aux Brûlées and Clos des Réas (*monopole*); Nuits-Saint-Georges *premier cru* (from Aux Murgers and Aux Vignerondes); village Nuits-Saint-Georges, including the *lieu-dit* Chaliots; village Chambolle-Musigny; village Vosne-Romanée; village Morey-Saint-Denis in the *lieu-dit* En La Rue de Vergy. There is a significant holding in the Hautes-Côtes-de-Nuits.

This is yet another part of the old Louis Gros domaine, first split in 1963 and then further divided between the children of Jean Gros in 1995: son Michel (b. 1956), tall and a little shy, and his pretty, dark-haired sister Anne-Françoise (married to François Parent of Pommard). Michel has in fact been making the wine here since 1975.

The fruit is de-stemmed; the *cuvaison* prolonged to 10–14 days at a maximum of 38°C at the end; and the *grands crus*, and sometimes the Clos des Réas, matured in 100 percent new wood.

I have had great Gros wines in the past. They are very pure and very intense, and have a breed which I find wholly admirable. The Clos

de Vougeot, having been replanted in 1986, is only just now beginning to be properly serious again. But the Clos des Réas is regularly very fine. The wines here are understated, intense and very delicious. I loved the 2005s.

Jean-Pierre and Michel Guyon

8 ha owned and *en fermage*. Echézeaux (0.20 ha); Vosne-Romanée Les Brûlées and En Orveaux; Aloxe-Corton *premier cru* Les Guérets; Savigny-lès-Beaune *premier cru* Les Peuillets; village Vosne-Romanée, including the *lieu-dit* Charmes des Maizières; village Nuits-Saint-Georges; village Gevrey-Chambertin; village Chorey-lès-Beaune, including the *lieu-dit* Les Bons Ores.

The thirty-something Guyon brothers (no relation to any homonyms in Savigny-lès-Beaune) operate from both sides of the Route Nationale No 74, the *cuverie* on the east side being relatively new. I like the style here today. There is still the long maceration, up to 4 weeks on occasion (and sometimes in some of the wines I find this a little too much), but now there is less *pigeage* and a greater selection of the fruit in the first place. As a result, the wines are less sturdy, more refined. This is a good—at the top levels, really very good—address.

Alfred Haegelen-Jayer

4.2 ha owned and *en fermage*. Clos de Vougeot (0.80 ha); Echézeaux (0.26 ha); Nuits-Saint-Georges *premier cru* Les Damodes; village Vosne-Romanée; village Chambolle-Musigny; village Nuits-Saint-Georges.

The charming, diminutive Alfred Haegelen (b. 1939), who hails from Alsace, arrived in Burgundy in 1969 and married Madeleine, a niece of the great Henri Jayer and a sister of Robert Jayer-Gilles of Magny-lès-Villers.

One third of the stems are left, the *cuvaison* lasts 18 days, and one third new oak is used. I like the style of Haegelen's wines. They are full without being robust and are rich and concentrated: indeed this is extremely succulent, nicely long-tasting Pinot Noir. This is a good source, especially for the Clos de Vougeot. But as you will see, Alfred Haegelen is now of retirement age. The last time I saw him, he told me neither his son nor his daughter was interested in the succession.

★ François Lamarche

10 ha owned and *en fermage*. La Grande Rue (1.65 ha—*monopole*); Clos de Vougeot (1.36 ha); Echézeaux (1.32 ha); Grands Echézeaux (0.30 ha); Vosne-Romanée *premier cru* in Les Chaumes, La Croix Rameau, Les Malconsorts and Les Suchots; Nuits-Saint-Georges *premier cru* Les Cras (from 2006); village Vosne-Romanée.

Quality has been steadily improving here since 1992, the date La Grande Rue was finally elevated to *grand cru* status, a task neglected by the older generation in the 1930s. Moreover, after years when one's abiding memory of a visit *chez* Lamarche was the smell of drains in the cellar, this problem was cleared up in 2004.

François Lamarche (b. 1944) and his wife Marie-Blanche run this estate today. There is a sorting table, the fruit is de-stemmed, and after a short cold-soaking, the wine is vinified at a maximum temperature of 30°C. Between 60 and 100 percent new oak is employed.

After producing splendid wines in the 1950s and 1960s, standards declined in the later years of Henri Lamarche, who died at age ninety-three in 1985. Since the 1999 vintage, the Grande Rue has been of *grand cru* status, and the domaine worthy of its star.

★★★ Leroy

22 ha owned. Clos de Vougeot (1.91 ha); Romanée-Saint-Vivant (0.99 ha); Richebourg (0.78 ha); Clos de la Roche (0.67 ha); Latricières-Chambertin (0.57 ha); Chambertin (0.50 ha); Corton-Renardes (0.50 ha); Corton-Charlemagne (0.43 ha); Musigny (0.27 ha); Gevrey-Chambertin *premier cru* Les Combottes; Chambolle-Musigny *premier cru* Les Charmes; Vosne-Romanée *premier cru* in Les Beaux-Monts and Les Brûlées; Nuits-Saint-Georges *premier cru* in Aux Boudots and Aux Vignerondes; Savigny-lès-Beaune *premier cru* Les Narbantons; Volnay *premier cru* Santenots; village Gevrey-Chambertin; village Chambolle-Musigny in the *lieu-dit* Les Fremières; village Vosne-Romanée in the

lieu-dit Les Genaivrières; village Nuits-Saint-Georges in the *lieux-dits* Les Lavières, Aux Allots and Au Bas de Combe; village Pommard in the *lieux-dits* Les Vignots, Les Trois Follots; Auxey-Duresses *blanc*. In addition, Madame Bize-Leroy's other estate, the personally owned Domaine d'Auvenay, has important holdings in Mazis-Chambertin, Bonnes-Mares, Chevalier-Montrachet, Criots-Bâtard-Montrachet, Puligny-Montrachet *premier cru* Les Folatières and Meursault.

This is one of the greatest estates in Burgundy. It is also, at more than €250 per bottle for Chambertin in 2005, almost certainly the most expensive.

Lalou Bize, part owner, and until 1993, joint manager with Aubert de Villaine of the Domaine de la Romanée-Conti, bought the moribund 12-hectare Domaine Charles Noëllat in Vosne-Romanée for 65 million francs in 1988. Part of the finance came from the sale of one third of Leroy S.A. to her Japanese agents Takashimaya. The following year, there was a further acquisition: 19 million francs for the 2.5-hectare Domaine Philippe Remy in Gevrey-Chambertin. More land in Musigny and elsewhere followed the year after, altogether creating one of the most impressive ranges of wine to be seen anywhere in one cellar.

The wines are magnificently impressive too. The old vines have been jealously preserved. The yield is cut to the quick and reduced even further by the domaine's insistence on cultivation according to biodynamic principles. There is no de-stemming, a long *cuvaison* and plenty of new oak. The results are breathtakingly intense, pure and concentrated, and curiously quite different in style from those at the Domaine de la Romanée-Conti, despite the approach being superficially similar.

One thing puzzles me. For several years now, bottling has taken place here after merely a year or less in cask. Lalou Bize says that the wines are ready, and anyway, she has nothing to top up the barrels with. But with others—with cleaner lees than hitherto—bottling later, this policy seems curious.

★★ Comte Liger-Belair

8.9 ha *en fermage/en métayage*. La Romanée
(0.85 ha); Echézeaux (0.60 ha); Vosne-Romanée
premier cru in Les Brûlées, Les Chaumes, Les Petits
Monts, Aux Reignots and Les Suchots; Nuits-Saint-
Georges *premier cru* Les Cras; village Vosne-Romanée
in the *lieux-dits* Clos du Château (*monopole*) and
La Colombière; village Vosne-Romanée; village
Nuits-Saint-Georges.

The youthful Louis-Michel Liger-Belair is both
an agricultural engineer and an oenologist. He
began to take over the family vines in 2000. In
2002 he became responsible for the Reignots
and the Romanée, previously tended by Régis
Forey. But until 2005, part of the latter continued to be matured and bottled by Bouchard
Père et Fils. In 2006 Louis-Michel took over
most of the vines of a M. Lamadon who had
been the estate's share-cropper in the village
Vosne-Romanée.

The vineyard is increasingly worked biodynamically and ploughed with the family's own
horse, Fanny. The grapes are de-stemmed, cold-
macerated for a week and vinified at up to 32°C,
and the wine is stored in new oak.

From the start, Louis-Michel has shown
himself to be a sensible and astute winemaker:
a man of real talent. These are elegant, finely
tuned and very pure wines. The Romanée 2002
was the best Burgundy I sampled out of barrel in the autumn of 2003. His 2005s are even
better.

Fabrice Martin

3.30 ha owned and *en fermage*. Village Vosne-
Romanée; village Nuits-Saint-Georges; village
Gevrey-Chambertin.

This small estate used to be known as Martin-
Noblet, but changed its name when Fabrice
Martin took over the vines of his parents in 2000
and started a serious move toward domaine
bottling. There is total de-stemming and a short
cold-soaking, but only a minimum of new wood,
as Fabrice prefers to promote the flavours of the
fruit. The Vosne-Romanée is the best of the three
wines: a medium-weight, cool, stylish example.

★★ Méo-Camuzet

13.9 ha owned and *en fermage*. Clos de Vougeot
(3.00 ha—2.75 ha exploited); Corton (0.45 a);
Richebourg (0.35 ha); Vosne-Romanée *premier cru*
in Aux Brûlées, Les Chaumes and Cros Parantoux;
Nuits-Saint-Georges *premier cru* in Aux Boudots and
Aux Murgers; village Vosne-Romanée; village Nuits-
Saint-Georges; village Marsannay.

Jean Méo, civil servant and politician, and great-
nephew of Étienne Camuzet, founder of this
estate, was an absentee landlord. Up to 1988 the
bulk of this domaine was leased out to share-
croppers, the most important of which was the
great Henri Jayer.

His son Jean-Nicolas (b. 1964) decided to
take over personally on Jayer's retirement.
With Jean-Nicolas initially aided by his father's
avuncular genius, and still following the latter's
methods—great attention to the initial quality
of the fruit, 100 percent de-stemming, a few
days cold-soaking, long *cuvaisons* at up to 35°C
and plenty of new oak—the results are very fine
here; my only occasional qualm is the amount
of new wood.

Méo-Camuzet Frère et Soeur is an associate
merchant company, specialising in Fixin and
Chambolle-Musigny (*premiers crus* Les Feusselottes and Les Cras).

The last of the share-croppers is Jean Tardy
(see below).

Mongeard-Mugneret

30 ha owned and *en fermage*. Echézeaux (1.82 ha);
Grands-Echézeaux (1.44 ha); Echézeaux "Vieilles
Vignes" (0.68 ha); Clos de Vougeot (0.63 ha);
Richebourg (0.31 ha); Vosne-Romanée *premier cru*
in Les Orveaux, Les Petits Monts and Les Suchots;
Nuits-Saint-Georges *premier cru* Aux Boudots;
Vougeot *premier cru* Les Cras; Savigny-lès-Beaune
premier cru Les Narbantons; Pernand-Vergelesses
premier cru Les Basses-Vergelesses; Beaune *premier
cru* Les Avaux; village Vosne-Romanée, including the
lieu-dit Les Hautes Maizières; village Nuits-Saint-
Georges, including the *lieu-dit* Les Plateaux; village
Gevrey-Chambertin; village Chambolle-Musigny;
village Fixin; village Savigny-lès-Beaune.

The bluff, rotund Jean Mongeard (b. 1929), hitherto madly busy on this committee and that, has now retired. For 15 years, responsibility for the winemaking has been in the hands of his tall, bespectacled son Vincent (b. 1956).

The grapes are de-stemmed (except for the top three wines), allowed to cold-macerate for a few days, vinified at a high temperature and matured using up to 60 percent new oak for the *grands crus* and 40 to 50 percent for the village wines. All this leads to full, sturdy well-coloured wines, with plenty of concentration. I used to find the effect of the oak (from François Frères, who usually produces very high-class barrels) very toasted here, to the detriment of the wine. In 1998 Vincent Mongeard decided to source his own wood, weather it himself, and then have it transformed into casks by Rousseau in Couchey to his own recipe. He (and I) are pleased by the results. The wines are much better than they were 15 years ago.

Dominique Mugneret

6 ha owned and *en fermage/en métayage*. Echézeaux (0.61 ha); Nuits-Saint-Georges *premier cru* Aux Boudots; village Vosne-Romanée; village Nuits-Saint-Georges in the *lieu-dit* Les Fleurières; village Gevrey-Chambertin.

Until the 2001 vintage, Denis Mugneret (b. 1936) and his son Dominique (b. 1961) farmed land *en métayage* for the Liger-Belair family in Richebourg, Clos-de-Vougeot, and Nuits-Saint-Georges, Les Saint-Georges. Denis has now retired, and Dominique is in charge.

The grapes are completely de-stemmed, given a few days cold-maceration, vinified at temperatures up to 32°C and matured in 30 to 75 percent new oak.

Quality has improved here. There is also a merchant's business under the name Christine et Dominique Mugneret.

★ *Gérard Mugneret*

7 ha owned and *en fermage/en métayage*. Echézeaux (65 a); Vosne-Romanée *premier cru* in Les Brûlées and Les Suchots; Nuits-Saint-Georges *premier cru* Aux Boudots; Chambolle-Musigny *premier cru* Les Charmes; Savigny-lès-Beaune *premier cru* Les Gravins; village Vosne-Romanée; village Gevrey-Chambertin.

Gérard Mugneret, a vigorous, welcoming man in his fifties, used to be one of the *métayers* of his late uncle Dr. Georges Mugneret's estate (see below). In 2004, having reached the age of fifty-six, he gave up his interest in their Nuits-Saint-Georges Les Chaignots. "I'll have a bit more spare time," he said. The fruit is totally de-stemmed and given a few days cold-maceration before fermentation (up to 34°C) and a long maceration, and the wine is matured in an average of one third new oak. The results are impressive: pure, focussed, rich and stylish.

★ *Dr. Georges Mugneret*
★ *Mugneret-Gibourg*

8.9 ha owned and *en fermage*.

DR. GEORGES MUGNERET: Clos-de-Vougeot (0.34 ha); Ruchottes-Chambertin (0.64 ha); Echézeaux (1.14 ha); Chambolle-Musigny, *premier cru* Les Feusselottes; Nuits-Saint-Georges *premier cru* in Les Chaignots and Aux Vignerondes.

MUGNERET-GIBOURG: Echézeaux (1.24 ha); village Vosne-Romanée; village Nuits-Saint-Georges.

The charming, hospitable and elegant Mugneret ladies, Jacqueline and her daughters Marie-Christine and Marie-Andrée, produce meticulously crafted wines from the yield of their estate. Most of the Mugneret-Gibourg part is tended *en métayage* by other *vignerons*. So, for instance, they get only half of the Echézeaux; the rest goes to Fabrice Vigot.

The fruit is entirely de-stemmed, cold-macerated for 2 or 3 days and fermented at a temperature of up to 33°C. There is a healthy percentage of new oak: from 20 percent up to 80 percent for the top wines. These wines are full-ish, concentrated, very stylish and extremely well balanced: delicious examples of pure Pinot Noir. This is a fine domaine. The 2005s are lovely.

From 2007 the two vineyard holdings have been amalgamated. In the future, all the wines will be sold as Dr. Georges Mugneret-Gibourg.

Michel Noëllat et Fils

20 ha owned and *en fermage*. Clos de Vougeot (0.47 ha); Echézeaux (0.29 ha); Vosne-Romanée *premier cru* in Les Beaumonts and Les Suchots; Nuits-Saint-Georges *premier cru* Aux Boudots; Chambolle-Musigny *premier cru* Les Feusselottes; village Morey-Saint-Denis; village Chambolle-Musigny; village Vosne-Romanée; village Nuits-Saint-Georges; village Fixin.

Some of this domaine's vines are leased from Michel Noëllat's aunt, Madame Corbet. The vines are old. Some of the stems are occasionally kept. Cold-soaking lasts a few days and is followed by a *cuvaison* of about 18 days. Forty percent or more new oak is used for the *premiers* and *grands crus*.

Quality is good here, but not up to the standard of the superstars of the village, of which there are quite a few.

Bernard and Armelle Rion

7.5 ha owned and *en fermage/en métayage*. Clos-de-Vougeot (0.90 ha); Vosne-Romanée *premier cru* Les Chaumes; Nuits-Saint-Georges *premier cru* in Les Damodes and Les Murgers; Chambolle-Musigny *premier cru* Les Gruenchers; village Vosne-Romanée Vieilles Vignes; village Nuits-Saint-Georges in the *lieu-dit* Les Lavières; village Chambolle-Musigny in the *lieu-dit* Les Echézeaux.

This domaine was formerly called Rion Père et Fils. Bernard Rion (b. 1955) is a cousin of the Rions of Prémeaux. The grapes are entirely de-stemmed, fermented at a high temperature, given long *cuvaisons* and matured using a high percentage of new oak (50 percent for the village and *premiers crus*, the totality for the Clos Vougeot).

These are quite structured wines, which take time to show their full glory. But sometimes I feel they lack flair and elegance.

Bernard and his wife are additionally breeders of bearded collies and other dogs, as well as being professional truffle hunters.

★★★ Romanée-Conti

25.6 ha owned and *en fermage*. La Tâche (6.06 ha—*monopole*); Romanée-Saint-Vivant (5.29 ha); Echézeaux (4.67 ha); Grands-Echézeaux (3.53 ha);

Richebourg (3.51 ha); Romanée-Conti (1.81 ha—*monopole*); Le Montrachet (0.68 ha); plus other land in Vosne-Romanée, the produce of which is sold off in bulk or farmed by others. From time to time (1999, 2002), a Vosne-Romanée *premier cru* Cuvée Duvault-Blochet—named after a former owner—is produced from the younger vines in the *grands crus*.

This is the most famous name in Burgundy, and one of its largest domaines: certainly probably the largest in terms of *grand cru* ownership. Jointly owned by the De Villaine and Leroy/Bize/Roch families, and today administered by the scholarly Aubert de Villaine (b. 1939) and Henri-Frédéric Roch (b. 1962), the DRC, at an unapologetically high price, produces some of the most sought-after wines in the world.

The vineyard is run on sternly *biologique* (if not quite *biodynamique*—there have been tests) lines, with the domaine producing its own rootstock. There is never much in the way of de-stemming here. After a careful *triage* (sorting out of the substandard fruit)—they've been doing this since 1977, the pioneers in Burgundy—the must is left for 6 days at a low temperature and then fermented at up to 34°C, now with mechanical *pigeage* two or three times a day, before being matured entirely in new oak.

Are the wines worth these high prices? For the sublimely individual, poised and intensely flavoured Romanée-Conti itself, and the lusher but equally magical La Tâche, the answer is indisputably yes. For the other wines, where there is competition at less greedy levels, the response is moot. You can often do better elsewhere. And then there is a question of style. The large proportion of stems sometimes leaves an unmistakable taste, particularly in less rich vintages. This is not to the taste of the more modern school of Burgundian winemakers, who have adopted Henri Jayer as their guru. But the beauty of Burgundy is its diversity. There is plenty of room for both. And the DRC at its best produces prodigiously fine wine.

Emmanuel Rouget
(Henri Jayer, Georges Jayer, Lucien Jayer)

7 ha owned and *en fermage/en métayage*. Echézeaux (1.43 ha); Vosne-Romanée *premier cru* in Les

Beaumonts and Cros-Parantoux; village Vosne-Romanée; village Nuits-Saint-Georges; village Savigny-lès-Beaune.

It was only by accident that the genial, bullet-headed Henri Jayer (1922–2006) became a winemaker, and hence a guru. Youngest of three, he was approached during the war by M. Camuzet, mayor of Vosne: "Would you like to look after my vines for me?" So a share-cropping lease was drawn up which was to last until the late 1980s. In the meanwhile, he made the wines of his elder brothers: Georges and Lucien.

Since his retirement, the family vines have been tendered by his nephew Emmanuel Rouget, who lives in the old Gouroux premises in Flagey. A little wine, for friends and for some of France's three-star restaurants, continued to seep out under Jayer's name for many years.

Jayer's reputation, so high today, dates from the time he altered his vinification methods toward the end of the 1970s: total de-stemming, a week-long *macération à froid* before fermentation, lots of new oak, no filtration and hand bottling. And in addition, there was meticulous attention to cleanliness, keeping the wine topped up regularly in cask, and so on.

The result: wines rich in colour and aroma, opulently oaky, full but not aggressively tannic and vibrantly intense in flavour. The Cros Parantoux is the real star, even better than the Echézeaux, of which, long after Henri Jayer's retirement, there were three individual bottlings corresponding to the brothers' three holdings, plus one under the Rouget label.

Emmanuel Rouget, to use a phrase from my youth, is a crazy mixed-up kid. He never replies to letters or telephone messages—I only get to see him by gate-crashing on the back of a visit by his British agent—and it is clear that he finds the responsibility, and perhaps even more, the celebrity, of being Henri Jayer's successor uncomfortable to bear. The wines—especially at the lower levels where perhaps Jayer did not intervene (as he continued to do with the Cros Parantoux)—are unsophisticated. Given the price they sell for and the difficulty of securing them in the first place, one is tempted to say why bother.

★ *Robert Sirugue et ses Enfants*

12 ha owned and *en fermage/en métayage*. Grands-Echézeaux (0.12 ha); Vosne-Romanée *premier cru* Les Petits-Monts; village Vosne-Romanée.

Now that Robert Sirugue (b. 1934) is retired, responsibility has passed to the next generation: son Jean-Louis and his wife Catherine, and daughter Marie-France. This triumvirate took over in 1997, since when the crop has been reduced and a *table de tri* installed. Quality had dropped during the 1980s and 1990s but is now firmly back where it should be. These are lovely wines.

Jean Tardy

5.5 ha owned and *en fermage/en métayage*. Echézeaux (0.35 ha); Clos de Vougeot (0.125 ha); Vosne-Romanée *premier cru* Les Chaumes; Nuits-Saint-Georges *premier cru* Aux Boudots; village Nuits-Saint-Georges in the *lieu-dit* Les Bas de Combe; village Chambolle-Musigny in the *lieu-dit* Les Athets; village Vosne-Romanée in the *lieu-dit* Vigneux; village Fixin.

Jean Tardy and his son Guillaume are the last remaining *métayers*—until 2007—for the Méo-Camuzet domaine in the Clos de Vougeot. The fruit is de-stemmed; allowed to ferment at its own pace, at up to 30°C; and matured using a goodly percentage of new oak, up to 100 percent for the top *climats*. The wines are not kept too long in cask. I like the style here: soft and oaky, rich, balanced and pure, plump and intensely-flavoured, though sometimes lacking a bit of bite.

Fabrice Vigot

5.25 ha owned and *en fermage/en métayage*. Echézeaux (0.60 ha); village Vosne-Romanée, including the *lieu-dit* Les Colombiers; village Nuits-Saint-Georges; village Gevrey-Chambertin.

Fabrice Vigot is the younger brother of Thierry, who lives up in the Hautes-Côtes in Messanges. Until 1988 they worked together, but then

Fabrice, who wanted to produce somewhat more supple wines, decided to go his own way.

He adopts a *biologique* approach in the vineyards, cold-soaks for 5 days, macerates at up to 30°C and uses some 30 percent new oak. There is good Echézeaux, from the Rouges du Bas, but the results with other wines are more uneven. However, in 2004 he invested in a pneumatic press, and in 2006 built himself a new *cuverie*, so I expect a higher standard here. In the Echézeaux, he is the share-cropper for the Domaine Mugneret-Gibourg.

NUITS-SAINT-GEORGES

Situated roughly halfway between Beaune and Dijon, Nuits-Saint-Georges effectively marks the start (or the end, depending which direction you are going) of the Côte de Nuits, the greatest fiefdom of the Pinot Noir in the world. Nuits-Saint-Georges is a large commune, second in size in this part of the world to Gevrey-Chambertin, and the name Nuits-Saint-Georges, easy to recognise, easy to pronounce—and sadly, still, easy to abuse—is familiar to wine lovers all over the world.

The town itself is an industrial conglomeration, rather than a viticultural village, and is the commercial centre of the Côte de Nuits. Here are the *négociants*, the *tonnelleries*, the transport agents, the schools, the banks and the markets. It is a bustling, busy, friendly place, less self-conscious than Beaune. The vineyards stretch on either side of a gap in the Côte, out of which, from Arcenants and L'Étang-Vergy, two villages in the Hautes-Côtes, flows a stream called the Meuzin. On the southern side, the vines continue into the commune of Prémeaux, whose wines are entitled to the Nuits-Saint-Georges appellation. Beyond Clos-de-la-Maréchale, Nuits's southernmost *premier cru*, the land is Côte-de-Nuits-Villages, not village wine, and one is soon across the border into the Côte de Beaune.

The original Nuits was a Gallo-Roman villa further out into the plain. The name, though, has no nocturnal connections. It is more likely a corruption of the Celtic *un win*, a stream in a valley, or otherwise something to do with nuts. In the early Middle Ages, the area was the domaine of Hugues, *sire* of Vergy, who donated much of the land to the local monastery of Saint-Denis and the priory of Saint-Vivant. Slowly a village began to expand further up the valley of the river Meuzin in the site it occupies today. Though it was originally fortified, it lost its strategic importance when the Duchy of Franche-Comté was absorbed into the Kingdom of France in 1678. Nuits-Saint-Georges was no longer a frontier outpost, and the wall surrounding it was slowly dismantled over the succeeding couple hundred years. As a result of this and the fact that the main road thunders right though the centre, Nuits has little of the medieval attraction of, say, Beaune.

Like Beaune, though, it has its own Hospices, a charitable foundation dating from 1692, and it is similarly endowed with vines. The wines are also sold by auction, and this takes place on the Sunday preceding Palm Sunday, following a tasting at the Clos de Vougeot. The Hospices de Nuits possesses 10 hectares, and all the *cuvées* sold at auction come from *premiers crus*.

History

As early as 1023, the date it featured in a donation made to the Chapitre de Saint-Denis de Vergy, the Clos-Saint-Georges, as it was then, was established as the commune's senior vineyard. This was the sole wine of the area regarded as a *tête de cuvée*—and therefore the equal of the Romanées, Richebourg and La Tâche, in Vosne-Romanée, and only these—by Dr. Morelot in 1831. By the time of Dr. Lavalle, writing in 1855, its reputation had slipped to that of what I might call the second division of *grands crus*—Clos des Lambrays and Corton—and was classed as a *tête de cuvée*, alongside Vaucrains, Cailles, Porrets, Pruliers, Boudots, Cras, Murgers and Thorey (the wines of Prémeaux being assessed separately), but at the head of them, a position it continued to occupy in *Le Vin de Bourgogne*, by

Camille Rodier, in 1920. By that time, the town—as it, like most of the other villages of the Côte, had become by then—had appropriated Saint-Georges to tag on as a suffix to its name, in an effort to raise the visibility of the rest of the wines.

One further element of Nuits's glory must not be forgotten. In 1698 Louis XIV, the Sun King, was suffering from what, in some versions of the legend, is described as a fistula, but what Richard Olney, in his *Romanée-Conti*, prosaically insists was gout (the king was fifty at the time). Guy-Crescent Fagon, the king's doctor, prescribed *vieux bourgogne*, in place of the then-fashionable but more acidic champagne. Nuitons will tell you that this Burgundy was a Nuits from the Abbey of Saint-Vivant. Who would be so uncharitable as to ask them for proof? Anyway, the "cure" seems to have done the trick, and the resultant publicity didn't do Burgundy any harm either.

Location

Nuits-Saint-Georges has no *grands crus* but an impressive list of twenty-seven *premiers crus*, plus another nine in Prémeaux. On the Vosne side, the *vignoble* is wide, and the slope gentle, except right at the top under the trees, which is where you will find the first growths. The best known include Aux Boudots, La Richemone, Aux Murgers, Les Damodes and Aux Chaignots.

South of the village, the vineyards begin again, and the slope is narrower, with the main road climbing up at a slant as it continues south toward the village of Prémeaux. Here lie Les Pruliers, Roncière, Les Poirets (or Les Porrets-Saint-Georges), Les Vaucrains, Les Cailles and, the most southerly, Les-Saint-Georges itself. I call this section middle Nuits-Saint-Georges.

Across the border into Prémeaux, the incline is at first steeper, and the vineyard more confined. This is the narrowest section, east to west, of the entire Côte d'Or. Here you will find Clos des Forêts Saint-Georges, Aux Perdrix, Clos des Corvées, Les Argillières and two *monopoles*, both *clos*: Arlot and Maréchale. The aspect of the Clos de la Maréchale is distinctly southeast rather than east, and the slope is once again quite gentle.

The soil structure of the Nuits-Saint-Georges *vignoble* is no less complex than the rest of Burgundy—indeed more so, for it is 6 kilometres as the crow flies from Aux Boudots on the Vosne boundary to the end of the Clos de la Maréchale. To aid us, some major studies of the land have been attempted recently. Over a couple of years at the beginning of the 1990s, a team of geologists and geographers led by M. Lenouf, of the University of Dijon, analysed the soil in each *premier cru*. Following this, a team of professional testers—including Georges Pertuiset, president of the sommeliers of the region; Jean Siegrist of the local INRA; René Naudin, expert in the effects of maturation in oak; local brokers Becky Wasserman and Russell Hone; and others, including the Nuits-Saint-Georges proprietors themselves; and even me, if I occasioned to be in the region—participated in some extensive tastings, *climat* by *climat*, to see if we could isolate in words the effects of these *terroir* differences in the character of each *cru*. Sadly, the results of this latter undertaking were less successful than that provided by the geologists.

North of the town, the subsoil underneath the *premier cru*, like that of Vosne-Romanée, is essentially a Bathonian limestone in origin, covered with a mixture of pebbles, silt, limestone debris and clay. Further down the slope, in the area of the village vines, there is marl of Oligocene origin, covered by clay–sand mixtures, and *limons* of different types, together with pebbles and alluvial matter brought down by the river Meuzin from the Hautes-Côtes. At first the wines have a lot in common with those from neighbouring vineyards across the commune boundary, but the incidence of clay increases as one travels south. The soil becomes richer, and the wines, as a result, have a tendency to be four-square.

In middle Nuits-Saint-Georges, the limestone is Bathonian or the harder Comblanchien. Here and there in the *premiers crus*, the surface soil will contain sand or gravel, moderating the effect of the clay. Erosion is more of a problem here, one solution to which, pioneered by the

Gouges family, is to plant a special ray-grass between the rows of vines. In the village wine areas of this section, the soil is less alluvial than on the other side of village, and the *limons* are higher in their percentage of clay and mixed with Bathonian and Bajocian debris. This is the best part of the commune. In a line beginning with Les Saint-Georges and continuing at 245 to 260 metres above sea level, successively through Les Cailles, Les Poirets (or Porrets), Roncière and finally Les Pruliers, not forgetting Les Vaucrains, which is directly above Saint-Georges, run the greatest wines of Nuits—and true Nuits-Saint-Georges (which, arguably, Boudots on the Vosne-Romanée border is not).

Across into Prémeaux, the soil is very thin on the higher slopes, and the structures very complicated—that of the Clos Arlot being quite different from that of its neighbours north and south. Most of the vineyard here is on rock. Lower down on the flatter land—there is in fact one *premier cru* vineyard, part of Les Grandes Vignes, which lies on the "wrong" side of the main road—the soil is deeper, and there is more clay and marl. In general, the wines here are more sinewy, slightly hard and robust (Clos Arlot being an exception), with less breed, less concentration and less definition.

The authorities were quite correct to deny any vineyard in Nuits-Saint-Georges the status of *grand cru*. At their best they can have depth and finesse, as well as richness and structure, but at *premier cru* rather than *grand cru* level. Moreover, there is always a certain minerally, gamey hint of the rustic (country rather than sophisticated charm, to borrow Anthony Hanson's description of the wines of a grower in Fixin, equally applicable here) and a certain leaden footedness that detracts from the real class, definition and flair. In mitigation, it is fair to point out that as a consequence of the huge popularity of the name, there has been much abuse, and to judge by some of today's *négociant* wines (not the *négociants* mentioned between these covers, I hasten to add), this abuse continues, with Côte-de-Nuits-Villages being passed off as Nuits-Saint-Georges. More sin has been committed in this name than in the name of all the other villages in Burgundy put together. Not everything is the fault of the wines themselves, least of all of the growing number of good individual properties.

The Vineyard

PREMIERS CRUS   There are thirty-seven *premiers crus* in Nuits-Saint-Georges and Prémeaux, in whole or in part. For convenience, I divide these into the three sub-areas I have already outlined.

NORTHERN NUITS-SAINT-GEORGES: Aux Argillas (*Les Argillas* is village Nuits); Aux Boudots; Aux Bousselots; Aux Chaignots; Aux Champs Perdrix (part); Aux Cras; Les Damodes (part); Aux Murgers; En-La-Perrière-Noblot (part); La Richemone; Aux Thorey (part); Aux Vignerondes.

MIDDLE NUITS-SAINT-GEORGES: Les Cailles; Les Chaboeufs; Chaînes Carteaux; Les Crots (part); Les Perrières; Les Poirets (or Les Porrets); Les Poulettes (part); Les Procès; Les Pruliers; Les Hauts Pruliers (part); Roncière; Rue de Chaux; Les Saint-Georges; Les Vallerots (part); Les Vaucrains.

PRÉMEAUX: Les Argillières/Clos des Argillières; Clos Arlot (*monopole*); Clos de la Maréchale (*monopole*); Les Didiers; Les Forêts; Les Grandes Vignes/Clos des Grandes Vignes (part); Aux Corvées/Clos des Corvées; Les Corvées-Pagets/Clos des Corvées Pagets; Aux Perdrix; Les Terres Blanches (part).

Within these, a number of growers boast monopolies over a particular subsection or *clos*. Others are sold under other main names. Among these latter vines can be numbered the following: the Château Gris, a 2.8 hectare enclosure within Les Crots; the Clos-Saint-Marc, which lies within the Corvées and is an exclusivity of Michelle and Patrice Rion; and another part of the Corvées known as the Clos des Corvées, which is operated by the Domaine Prieuré-Roch. Moreover, a couple of vineyards close to Les Saint-Georges itself have slyly, like the town of Nuits, added Saint-Georges to their title, as if it were some magic potion to everlasting success. Thus, Les Poirets or Porrets (despite being separated from it by Les Cailles) and Les Forêts (despite being separated from it by Les Didiers) are more often than not suffixed "-Saint-Georges." It's amazing what you can get away with!

These *premiers crus* cover 142.79 hectares, of which 42.25 hectares lie in Prémeaux, and produce some 5,700 hectolitres of red wine a year.

VILLAGE WINE There are 175.32 hectares of village wine in Nuits-Saint-Georges, of which a mere 11.79 lie in Prémeaux. Production averages 7,000 hectolitres a year.

WHITE WINE Like Morey-Saint-Denis, but unlike most of the other villages in the Côte de Nuits, Nuits-Saint-Georges produces some white wine, both village and *premier cru*. While the separate bottling of white wine is relatively new, and the quantities are certainly rare (*confidentiel* is a nice French translation), it must be remembered that it has always been the practice until the last generation or so to complant a few white grape vines among the reds in order to soften the wine and lend it a bit of vivacity.

The main impetus behind Nuits *blanc*, however, comes from another angle. In the late 1930s, Henri Gouges discovered some mutated Pinot Noir vines which were producing white grapes, took cuttings and propagated them, and in 1947 had enough to produce some wine. Others have borrowed cuttings from him. I call this mutation Pinot Gouges. Others make white wine from Chardonnay or Pinot Beurot or a mixture of all three. There is not much: 2.54 hectares, at the last count, and 102 hectolitres. You have to know your merchant well to be able to get hold of some. But the wine is intriguing. Meursault it isn't, nor Corton either, and it comes in different styles. In most cases it is best at 4–8 years rather than 10-plus. But it is worth investigating.

The Premiers Crus

These are dealt with roughly in a north–south order:

AUX BOUDOTS   (6.30 ha)

This *climat*, perfectly sited at 250–290 metres above sea level, marches with the Vosne-Romanée *premier cru* Les Malconsorts. The soil is a brown limestone mixed with a fine gravel, just a touch of clay and fragments of white oolitic rock, resting on the pink limestone of Comblanchien, here rather more eroded and crumbly than further south.

The wine is altogether more Vosne in character than Nuits. Indeed the vineyards further down the slope, on the other side of the excellent village *climat* Au Bas de Combe, produce village Vosne-Romanée rather than Nuits-Saint-Georges. There is an elegant and a potential silkiness here which is alien to Nuits, and while by no means light, the wine is neither as full and gutsy as a middle Nuits, nor as full and firmly concentrated as a Vosne from, say, Suchots or Beaumonts.

Some years ago, having bought a Boudots and a Malconsorts from the same source, I much amused myself by offering blind samples to professional friends. "Find the commune," I would demand. Or "One is Vosne and the other Nuits. Which is which?" We came to the conclusion I have outlined.

RECOMMENDED SOURCES

Jean Grivot, Leroy, Méo-Camuzet, Denis Mugneret, Gérard Mugneret, Jean Tardy (all Vosne-Romanée); Jean-Jacques Confuron (Nuits-Saint-Georges); Louis Jadot (Beaune)—this from the Domaine André Gagey.

LES DAMODES	(8.55 ha)
AUX CRAS	(3.00 ha)
LA RICHEMONE	(1.92 ha)
AUX MURGERS	(4.89 ha)

Cras, Richemone and Murgers are the next three *climats* on the same level of slope as Aux Boudots, while Les Damodes runs along the top of all four. The soil structure is similar, based on the same Comblanchien pink limestone rock, but there is more gravel, especially in Murgers, and less soil and more broken-up rock in the upper slopes of Les Damodes, where the incline is steeper and there is some sand.

Damodes can be lighter, and Murgers quite meaty, but otherwise, these form a sort of half-way house between Boudots and the yardstick flavours of the northern section of Nuits-Saints-Georges one finds in Aux Chaignots and Aux Vignerondes. While there is a bit of Vosne about them, and therefore an innate elegance, none would be confused with a Malconsorts.

RECOMMENDED SOURCES
LES DAMODES
Alfred Haegelen (Vosne-Romanée); Jean Chauvenet, Joseph Faiveley, Lechenaut, Gilles Remoriquet (all Nuits-Saint-Georges). Robert Jayer-Gilles (Magny-Lès-Villers in the Hautes-Côtes).

AUX CRAS
Bruno Clavelier (Vosne-Romanée).

LA RICHEMONE
Alain Michelot (Nuits-Saint-Georges).

AUX MURGERS
Bertagna, Alain Hudelot-Noëllat (both Vougeot). Sylvian Cathiard, Jacky Confuron, Méo-Camuzet (all Vosne-Romanée).

AUX CHAIGNOTS	(5.86 ha)
AUX VIGNERONDES	(3.84 ha)
AUX BOUSSELOTS	(4.24 ha)
AUX THOREY	(5.00 ha)
EN LA PERRIÈRE NOBLOT	(0.30 ha)
AUX CHAMPS PERDRIX	(0.73 ha)
AUX ARGILLAS	(1.89 ha)

The first four *climats* in the preceding table provide exemplars of northern Nuits-Saint-Georges. Only small parts of Champs Perdrix and En La Perrière Noblot, both being at the top of the slope, are classed as *premier cru*. The bottom of Argillas (Aux Argillas) is *premier cru*, while the land above, as here the land curves round to disappear into the Hautes-Côtes, is merely village (Les Argillas). The best part of Thorey, under the title Clos de Thorey, is a monopoly of the Domaines Antonin Rodet.

Once again, the base rock is Comblanchien limestone, but there is Bajocian *ostrea acuminata* containing fossilised oysters in Les Vignerondes, Aux Bousselots and Aux Argillas,

and in the lower part of those vineyards, the base rock, still pink, is the Bathonian *calcaire de Prémeaux*. There is rather more gravel and pebbles than further north, mixed up with broken white oolite rock, and rather more clay and marl.

The wines here are rich, full and elegant, but nonetheless quite sturdy, not as muscular as they are south of Nuits-Saint-Georges, but not quite as concentrated as the best that section can provide either.

RECOMMENDED SOURCES
AUX CHAIGNOTS
Gérard Mugneret, Dr. Georges Mugneret (both Vosne-Romanée); Robert Chevillon, Joseph Faiveley, Alain Michelot (all Nuits-Saint-Georges).

AUX VIGNES-RONDES
Jacky Confuron, Leroy, Dr. Georges Mugneret (all Vosne-Romanée); Joseph Faiveley, Daniel Rion (both Nuits-Saint-Georges).

AUX BOUSSELOTS
Jean Chauvenet, Robert Chevillon, Philippe Gavignet, François Legros, Gilles Remoriquet (all Nuits-Saint-Georges).

AUX THOREY
Antonin Rodet (Mercurey); Sylvain Cathiard (Vosne-Romanée); Hubert de Montille (Volnay).

AUX CHAMPS-PERDRIX
Alain Michelot (Nuits-Saints-Georges).

EN LA PERRIÈRE NOBLOT
Machard de Gramont (Nuits-Saint-Georges).

AUX ARGILLAS
Philippe Gavignet (Nuits-Saint-Georges).

I now turn to the middle part of the Nuits-Saints-Georges *vignoble*.

LES CROTS	(1.16 ha)
RUE DE CHAUX	(2.12 ha)
LES PROCÈS	(1.34 ha)
LES HAUTS PRULIERS	(0.40 ha)

These small and relatively little-known *climats* lie immediately south of the town of Nuits-Saint-Georges and the road which winds up to the village of Chaux in the Hautes-Côtes (halfway up is a very good vantage point from which to get a panoramic view of the southern Côte de Nuits).

Les Crots, most of which is taken up with the vineyards of the Château Gris, is on a steep escarpment, necessitating terracing for the vines. The soil is superficial and very stony, on a pink Comblanchien bedrock. Underneath, in the Rue de Chaux and Procès, there is more surface soil and more clay, and the Bathonian rock is of two types, white oolite as well as the pink Prémeaux limestone. Les Procès and Les Hauts-Pruliers are stonier.

The wines here have neither the elegance nor the definition of either the best of the northern sector or the top *climats* just a little further down the line. They have colour and weight, but an absence of real grace and flair. Sometimes the tannins can be a bit brutal. There is a lot of difference between a Pruliers and even the best of the Hauts-Pruliers above. There are good honest bottles from the best sources, nonetheless.

RECOMMENDED SOURCES
RUE DE CHAUX
Bertrand Ambroise, Jean Chauvenet, Gilles Remoriquet (all Nuits-Saint-Georges).

LES PROCÈS
Robert Arnoux (Vosne-Romanée).

HAUTS-PRULIERS
Daniel Rion (Nuits-Saint-Georges).

LES PRULIERS	(7.11 ha)
LES RONCIÈRES	(0.97 ha)
LES PORRETS OR POIRETS OR	
PORRETS-SAINT-GEORGES	(7.35 ha)

At 250–270 metres above sea level, at an incline which varies between 8 and 12 percent, these three vineyards are ideally placed, and their wine is second only to Les Saint-Georges itself. With the exception of Les Porrets, there is less clay, however, than in this most famous vineyard or in Les Procès to the north, but there are plenty of stones—more gravel in Les Poirets and the southern part of Les Pruliers, mixed

in with limestone earth of various colours, yellower in the Roncières where the rock is white oolite, and browner in the other two *climats* on either side, where the oolite mixes with pink Prémeaux limestone.

These three wines—and it may derive from the fruity suggestions of the name of Les Pruliers (and Porrets could come from *poirier*, a pear tree)—seem to me to have an impressive, often somewhat cooked fruit flavour: plums mixed with the general soft-fruit aspects of the Pinot Noir. The wines are full, profound, meaty, rich, sinewy and backward, rather tougher in their youth than those from the northern sector. But be patient! They gain a lot in generosity as they soften up. Of the three, Porrets is the most approachable, the most obviously elegant right from the beginning.

RECOMMENDED SOURCES
LES PRULIERS
Jean Grivot (Vosne-Romanée); Robert Chevillon, Henri Gouges, Lechenaut (all Nuits-Saint-Georges).

LES RONCIÈRES
Jean Grivot (Vosne-Romanée); Robert Chevillon, François Legros (both Nuits-Saint-Georges).

LES PORRETS
Joseph Faiveley; Henri Gouges (Clos des Porrets-Saint-Georges); Alain Michelot (all Nuits-Saint-Georges).

LES PERRIÈRES	(2.47 ha)
LES POULETTES	(2.13 ha)
LES CHABOEUFS	(2.80 ha)
LES VALLEROTS	(0.87 ha)
CHAÎNES CARTEAUX	(2.53 ha)

Above Les Porrets, Les Cailles and Les Saint-Georges there is a little gap in the line of the hills, a suspicion of a valley. This means that the steep Chaînes-Carteaux is moved around to face just a little to the north, as is the *climat* of Les Vallerots, only the lowest elements of which are designated *premier cru*. Chaboeufs lies in the middle down, which flows an air current, marginally lowering the microclimate.

Poulettes and Perrières are on the other side, the former above the latter, on quite a steep slope.

The Perrières vineyard, as the name suggests (*perrière* being synonymous with *carrière*, a quarry) is very rocky and stony. There are a number of faults here in the rock, exposing both white oolite and pink Prémeaux limestone. Above, in the Poulettes, the vines are on terraces, and the oolite comes to the fore. In the Chaboeufs there is more clay and more sand, as there is in the Chaînes Carteaux.

With the exception of Les Perrières, which produces a somewhat atypical Nuits-Saint-Georges—lighter, minerally, but elegant—this is not great terrain. That lies further down the slope. Chaboeufs is the best, but again, as in Procès, for instance, the size can overwhelm the fruit, and the tannins can be a bit unsophisticated.

It is in Les Perrières that Henri Gouges has collected his mutated Pinot and produces white wine.

RECOMMENDED SOURCES
LES PERRIÈRES
Jean Chauvenet, Robert Chevillon, François Legros (all Nuits-Saint-Georges); Régis Forey (Vosne-Romanée).

LES CHABOEUFS
Jean-Jacques Confuron, Philippe Gavignet (both Nuits-Saint-Georges).

LES SAINT-GEORGES	*(7.52 ha)*
LES CAILLES	*(7.11 ha)*
LES VAUCRAINS	*(6.20 ha)*

Here, just as the commune, if not the wine, is about to overflow into neighbouring Prémeaux, we have the greatest *climat* in Nuits-Saint-Georges, and two worthy princes of the blood. The three are large vineyards; Les Vaucrains lies upslope at 260–280 metres, Les Cailles directly north of Les Saint-Georges at 245–260 metres.

One of the clues to Les Saint-Georges's supremacy is perhaps the complexity of its soil structure. The Bathonian rock is of all three neighbouring types (Prémeaux, white oolite and Comblanchien). The earth is very stony, so it drains well, though the slope at 7–8 degrees is quite gentle, and the clay is mixed with a little more soil than elsewhere. Across in Les Cailles things are similar, except that there is no Prémeaux stone. There is also more sand. Up above, in the Vaucrains, the soil is not so much gravelly or pebbly as rocky, and with quite large stones at that, but it is quite heavy. Again there is clay and sand. But the rock is mainly oolite.

What this means in terms of wine is that we have two elements in Cailles and Vaucrains which are then blended together in Les Saint-Georges to produce something greater than the sum of its parts. Les Cailles, in Nuits-Saint-Georges terms, is subtle and feminine, with very seductive, composed, soft-fruit flavours. Vaucrains is vigorous and rich and full-bodied, sturdy but not too wild or untameable.

And Les Saint-Georges is the synthesis of the lot. In my experience, it definitely *is* the best wine of the commune. It is simply the most complete, the most complex, and the most profound. When you get the richness of a fine year, and the balance you can find in a top grower's Les Saints-Georges, you *can*, yes, easily get tempted into arguing for its elevation to *grand cru*.

RECOMMENDED SOURCES
LES SAINT-GEORGES
Régis Forey (Vosne-Romanée); Robert Chevillon, Joseph Faiveley, Henri Gouges, Thibault Liger-Belair, Alain Michelot, Gilles Remoriquet (all Nuits-Saint-Georges).

LES CAILLES
Robert Chevillon, Alain Michelot (both Nuits-Saint-Georges).

LES VAUCRAINS
Bernard Ambroise, Jean Chauvenet, Robert Chevillon, Henri Gouges, Alain Michelot (all Nuits-Saint-Georges).

We now cross into the commune of Prémeaux.

LES DIDIERS	*(2.40 ha)*
(*monopole* of the Hospices de Nuits-Saint-Georges)	
LES FORÊTS OR CLOS DES FORÊTS-SAINT-GEORGES	*(7.11 ha)*
(The Clos is the *monopole* of the Domaine de L'Arlot)	
AUX CORVÉES OR CLOS DES CORVÉES	*(5.13 ha)*
(*monopole* of Domaine Prieuré-Roch)	
AUX CORVÉES (CLOS SAINT-MARC)	*(0.93 ha)*
(*monopole* of Michèle and Patrice Rion)	
LES CORVÉES-PAGETS	*(1.48 ha)*
AUX PERDRIX	*(3.49 ha)*
(*monopole* of the Domaine des Perdrix)	
LES ARGILLIÈRES	*(0.22 ha)*
CLOS DES ARGILLIÈRES	*(4.22 ha)*
LES GRANDES-VIGNES OR CLOS-DES-GRANDES-VIGNES	*(2.21 ha)*
(*monopole* of Domaine Thomas-Moillard up to 2004; the Château de Puligny-Montrachet from 2005)	
CLOS DE L'ARLOT	*(5.45 ha)*
(*monopole* of the Domaine de L'Arlot)	
CLOS DE LA MARÉCHALE	*(9.55 ha)*
(*monopole* of Maison Joseph Faiveley up to 2003; J.F. Mugnier from 2004)	
LES TERRES BLANCHES	*(0.91 ha)*

Here we come to the narrowest, and in part, the steepest section of the Côte. The road from Nuits-Saint-Georges runs at an angle up the slope toward Prémeaux and descends within the village, but then climbs up again, so that as you get to the end of the Clos-de-la-Maréchale, you are well above 240 metres. It is therefore a bit surprising that the vineyards opposite should be only Côte-de-Nuits-Villages, not village AC, while on the Nuits side of the village, again on the east side of the road, part of Les Grandes-Vignes has been decreed *premier cru*.

Among these twelve *premiers crus* the soil varies significantly. To the north—in Didiers, Forêts, Corvées, Perdrix and Argillières—it is relatively deep in mid-slope, and brown or yellow-brown, mixed with sand and clay and stones of various origins, mainly oolitic, on a Comblanchien base.

The wines here are sturdy, muscular and masculine. They can have plenty of richness, but they can lack refinement. Didiers perhaps represents a halfway house down from Les

Saint-Georges (my experience is naturally with the Hospices de Nuits *cuvée*, but this can have different *éleveurs*), but otherwise, we are quite a step away from the finesse and nuance of Nuits-Saint-Georges's greatest *climat*.

The soil in Les Grandes-Vignes is similar, but there is a little less clay, the active limestone is higher, and the Bathonian base rock is more complex. My experience comes from both the Thomas-Moillard wine and that of Domaine Daniel Rion, whose vines are village AC. The Clos-des-Corvées, until 1994 a Jadot monopoly (the land is owned by a member of the Thomas family), is similarly sturdy: size without much grace. Like most of the above it is a little obvious.

Many of these *climats* are *monopoles*. The Clos-de-la-Maréchale repeats the soil structure of Forêts and Corvées, but the angle of the slope is flatter, and the orientation more toward the south. There is no denying a suggestion of the rustic in the full, robust character of the wine. It ages well, though.

At the Clos Arlot there is a distinct fault in the rock. Behind the garden of this estate, there is plenty of evidence of quarrying. In front, the vineyard itself is on several levels, with a slope of 35 percent.

All this produces a light wine, notwithstanding Jean Paul de Smet's particular style of winemaking (all the stems and whole grape maceration): from the Clos-des-Forêts he produces something rather more sturdy. Clos Arlot is feminine, the fruit flavours cherry and red currant-like. But quite how much this is the Domaine de l'Arlot thumbprint and how much it is the signature of the *climat* is difficult to tell.

RECOMMENDED SOURCES

LES DIDIERS
Hospices de Nuits (but depends on who does the *élévage*).

CLOS DES FORÊTS
Arlot (Nuits-Saint-Georges).

AUX PERDRIX
Domaine des Perdrix (Nuits-Saint-Georges).

CLOS SAINT-MARC
Michèle and Patrice Rion (Nuits-Saint-Georges).

LES CORVÉES-PAGETS
Robert Arnoux (Vosne-Romanée).

LES ARGILLIÈRES
Daniel Rion (Nuits-Saint-Georges).

CLOS DES GRANDES VIGNES
Château de Puligny-Montrachet (Puligny-Montrachet).

CLOS DE L'ARLOT
Arlot (Nuits-Saint-Georges).

CLOS DE LA MARÉCHALE
J.F. Mugnier (Chambolle-Musigny).

The Growers and the Négociants
Nuits-Saints-Georges

★ Jean Chauvenet

9.56 ha owned and *en fermage/en métayage*. Nuits-Saint-Georges *premier cru* in Aux Bousselots, Les Damodes, Les Perrières, Rue de Chaux and Les Vaucrains; village Nuits-Saint-Georges; village Vosne-Romanée.

Jean Chauvenet's wines are made by his handsome son-in-law, Christophe Drag. The potential yield is controlled from the outset, making green harvesting unnecessary. The fruit is entirely de-stemmed. After a few days of cold-soaking the fermentation is controlled at 28–32°C. Thereafter, maturation takes place in 15 to 25 percent new oak.

Quality has been fine here for a decade or more. The tannins are more sophisticated, the fruit expression richer and classier, the flavours more complex: all because there is more attention to detail, more control and no stems. This is a very good place to study the differences between Nuits *premiers crus*.

Hubert Chauvenet-Chopin

16 ha owned and *en fermage/en métayage*. Clos de Vougeot (0.35 ha); Nuits-Saint-Georges *premier cru* in Aux Argillas, Aux Chaignots, Les Murgers and Aux Thorey; village Nuits-Saint-Georges, including the *lieu-dit* Les Charmottes; village Chambolle-Musigny; village Vougeot; Côte de Nuits Villages (two different *cuvées*).

Over the last 15 years, Hubert Chauvenet has gradually taken over the estate of his father-in-law Daniel Chopin of Comblanchien, adding it to his own domaine, a sizeable property in its own right.

Since the 2001 vintage, everything has been bottled under the Chauvenet-Chopin name. Quality is high here. The fruit is de-stemmed, the must is cold-soaked for a few days, and up to 50 percent of new wood is employed, though less than hitherto, to the wines' advantage. You should pick Vougeot early, says M. Chauvenet. The sandy soils produce fruit which rapidly gets overripe, with a consequent lack of grip.

Chevillon-Chezeaux

8.2 ha owned and *en fermage/en métayage*. Nuits-Saint-Georges *premier cru* in Aux Bousselots (*blanc* as well as *rouge*), Les Champs-Perdrix, Les Crots, Les Forêts and Les Saint-Georges; village Nuits-Saints-Georges, including the *lieu-dit* Les Saint-Julien; village Vosne-Romanée.

Michel Chevillon is the brother of Robert (see below), and Philippe Chezeaux, responsible for the wine, is Michel's son-in-law. The *cuverie* has been enlarged and modernised. But the wine is rather more rustic and lacks concentration in comparison with those of the following domaine. Reducing the yield would be a start.

★ Robert Chevillon

13 ha owned and *en fermage/en métayage*. Nuits-Saints-Georges *premier cru* in Les Bousselots, Les Cailles, Les Chaignots, Les Perrières, Les Pruliers, Les Roncières, Les Saint-Georges and Les Vaucrains; village Nuits-Saint-Georges *blanc et rouge*.

With the sons of Robert Chevillon, Denis and Bertrand, now firmly in charge, this is a splendid domaine with a marvellous palette of *premiers crus* and very old vines—75 years in the case of Les Saint-Georges, Les Cailles and Les Vaucrains. Where else can you sample eight *premier cru* Nuits-Saint-Georges under one roof? A small percentage of stems are retained, there is a brief cold-maceration, the fermentation temperatures are held between 30° and 33°C, and 30 percent new wood is utilised in the maturation. There is nothing special about the recipe, but the results are rich, classy, individual and more opulent than most. And there is that *rara avis*, Nuits-Saint-Georges *blanc*.

Georges Chicotot

6.55 ha owned and *en fermage/ en métayage*. Nuits-Saint-Georges *premier cru* in La Rue de Chaux, Les Pruliers, Les Saint-Georges and Les Vaucrains; village Nuits-Saint-Georges, including the *lieu-dit* Les Charmottes; village Ladoix.

"Jojo" Chicotot is a slight, balding, dark-haired, intense man in his fifties; he looks like a jockey. This is a domaine which believes in long cold-soaking, vinification with whole bunches and no subsequent interference until bottling. The result, though the base wine is fine—or seems to be—is that too often, the wine in bottle shows too much reduction. The Ladoix was acquired in 2005.

Dufouleur Père et Fils

DOMAINE GUY DUFOULEUR: 34 ha. Nuits-Saint-Georges *premier cru* in Chaînes Carteaux, Clos des Perrières, Les Crots and Les Poulettes; Fixin *premier cru* Clos du Chapitre (*monopole*); Nuits-Saint-Georges *premier cru blanc* Clos des Perrières; village Nuits-Saint-Georges; village Morey-Saint-Denis; village Santenay *rouge et blanc* in the *lieu-dit* Clos Genet.

DOMAINE BARBIER ET FILS: 11 ha. Village Gevrey-Chambertin in the *lieu-dit* Les Murots; village Nuits-Saint-Georges in the *lieu-dit* Belle Croix; village Pommard in the *lieu-dit* Les Vaumuriens Hauts; village Savigny-lès-Beaune in the *lieu-dit* Aux Fourches.

The Domaine Guy Dufouleur can date its history back to 1596. In 1848 the merchant business was created. It absorbed the *négociant* side of Domaine Liger-Belair in 1990, bought the Domaine Barbier in 1995 and took over the monopoly of the Fixin Clos du Chapitre from the Gelin family a month later. Still run by members of the Dufouleur family, the house style is in the main for relatively light, but clean and fruity wines for early drinking. The *premiers crus*, particularly the Fixin, are a different matter; these are serious wines.

At the end of 2006, both domaines and the merchant business were taken over by Antonin Rodet of Mercurey.

★★ Joseph Faiveley

119.19 ha owned and *en fermage* (37.21 ha of this is in the Côte d'Or). Chambertin, Clos de Bèze (1.29 ha); Latricières-Chambertin (1.21 ha); Mazis-Chambertin (1.20 ha); Le Musigny (0.03 ha); Clos de Vougeot (1.29 ha); Echézeaux (0.87 ha); Corton, Clos-des-Cortons-Faiveley (*monopole*—3.02 ha); Corton-Charlemagne (0.62 ha); Gevrey-Chambertin *premier cru* in Les Cazetiers, Championnet, Clos des Issarts, Combe au Moine and Craipillot; Chambolle-Musigny *premier cru* in Les Fuées and La Combe d'Orveau; Nuits-Saint-Georges *premier cru* in Aux Chaignots, Les Damodes, Les Porrets-Saint-Georges, Les Saint-Georges and Les Vignerondes; Beaune *premier cru* Clos de l'Écu; village Gevrey-Chambertin, including the *lieu-dit* Les Marchais; village Nuits-Saint-Georges, including the *lieux-dits* Les Argillas and Les Lavières; village Pommard in the *lieu-dit* Vaumuriens; Côte de Beaune Villages. Additionally, there is a large (82-hectare) domaine in the Côte Chalonnaise, based in Mercurey, some of the produce of which is sold under the name of Domaine de la Croix-Jacquelet.

While Maison Faiveley is a *négociant*, François Faiveley and his son Erwan are in the fortunate position of being able to supply 80 percent of their requirements—certainly at the top end of the scale—from their own family domaine. And they intend to keep it that way. They have no wish to expand beyond a point where they feel they cannot personally supervise and guarantee the evolution and quality of every bottle that leaves their cellar door.

Great attention is paid to the quality of the fruit in the first place. *Sélection massale* is essential, as are severe pruning and consequent de-budding to control the quantities produced. This is followed by a painstaking *triage* and fermentation at low temperatures (26–28°C) to preserve the fruit, with an insistence on natural yeasts.

This is one of the greatest sources of quality wine in the whole of Burgundy. The wines are outstandingly clean, rich, balanced and concentrated, and the best are hand bottled without filtration and say so on the label.

In 2006 François Faiveley passed responsibility for the day-to-day administration of the business to his son Erwan. Subsequently, Bernard Hervet, late of Bouchard Père et Fils, was appointed general manager. In 2007 Faiveley acquired the domaines of Annick Parent in Monthelie and Matrot-Wittersheim in Meursault to further extend holdings in the Côte de Beaune.

Philippe Gavignet

11.8 ha owned and *en fermage*. Nuits-Saint-Georges *premier cru* in Les Bousselots, Les Chaboeufs and Les Pruliers; village Nuits-Saint-Georges, including the *lieu-dit* Les Argillas (*rouge et blanc*); Côte-de-Nuits-Villages.

There are a number of Gavignets in Nuits-Saint-Georges. This is the best. Philippe, born in 1961, took over from his father Michel in 1992. He leaves 25 percent of the stems in his *premier cru* vinifications, cold-macerates for 5 to 10 days (the better the wine, the longer the cold-soaking), holds the temperature at 30–32°C and uses between a quarter and a third new wood. There are good, substantial, vigorous wines here, particularly the Pruliers, ex the Château de Bligny. The white Nuits-Saint-Georges is half Chardonnay, half Pinot Gouges.

★★ Henri Gouges

14.69 ha *en fermage* (family owned). Nuits-Saint-Georges *premier cru* in Les Chaignots, Chaines-Carteaux, Clos-de-Porrets-Saint-Georges (*monopole*), Les Perrières (*blanc*), Les Pruliers, Les Saint-Georges and Les Vaucrains; village Nuits-Saint-Georges.

If domaines could be doyens, this would be the doyen of the commune, having bottled and sold its wine direct since the 1920s. Today, two cousins—Pierre, who looks after the vines, and Christian, who tends the wine—are in charge, grandsons of the late Henri, who died in 1967.

Pierre was a pioneer of planting ray-grass to avoid erosion. Subsequently, he found that the wines were richer and more concentrated, as a result of the root system having to delve deeper.

Back in the 1930s, Henri Gouges discovered some Pinot Noir which had mutated and was producing white grapes. Intrigued, he took cuttings and planted them in a corner of the Perrières.

This plot has been gradually expanded. Now there is enough to vinify three casks of Nuits-Saint-Georges *blanc*. The Gouges family have passed on cuttings to their neighbours. I call this strain Pinot Gouges. The wine bears no resemblance to Chardonnay. It is delicious.

The fruit is de-stemmed. There is a brief cold-maceration, and fermentation temperatures are controlled at a maximum of 30°C. The Gouges dislike new oak, preferring to let the fruit and the character of the *terroir* sing out, so only 10 percent is used. The results are magnificent, but not for those who expect plump, vibrant, oaky wines. The Gouges style is for austerity, compactness and a minimum of new oak. Patience is required and expected. The 2005s are excellent.

Hospices de Nuits-Saint-Georges

12.15 ha owned. Nuits-Saint-Georges *premier cru* in Aux Boudots, Les Corvées-Pagets, Les Didiers (*monopole*), Les Murgers, Les Forêts, Rue de Chaux, Les-Saint-Georges, Les Terres Blanches and Les Vignerondes; village Nuits-Saint-Georges; village Gevrey-Chambertin.

Smaller and less well-known than the Hospices de Beaune, but with a rather better track record of quality winemaking in recent years, this is a fine estate. The *premiers crus*, under the names of their donors, are sold by auction on the Sunday prior to Palm Sunday, after a tasting at the Clos-de-Vougeot.

Unlike in Beaune, the Hospices has its own team of *viticulteurs*. In the winery, the fruit is entirely de-stemmed, and vinified at up to 34°C, and the wine is lodged in 100 percent new oak. The current winemaker is Jean-Marc Moron. The quality in the final bottle depends, of course, on who does the subsequent *élevage*. As with its Beaune counterpart, there is a danger of over-oaking.

Dominique Laurent

2.3 ha owned. Village Meursault in the *lieu-dit* Les Forges.

Dominique Laurent—his notice board slyly says Dom. Laurent, leading the innocent to believe he is a domaine—is a recent star in the Côte d'Or firmament. His first vintage was 1992. Formerly a pastry chef, and with the girth to prove it, he was bitten by the wine bug, moved to Nuits, and set about buying up the odd cask here and there from some of the leading growers in the Côte de Nuits. Though the range is wide, quantities are minuscule, the approach is determinedly "hands off," and the wines are for those who like lots of oak (Laurent often racks from new to new—to give his wines, as he puts it, "200 percent" new oak). The wines show impressively in cask, but do not always live up to their early promise when I meet them later in bottle.

Fernand Lecheneaut et Fils

10 ha owned and *en fermage/en métayage*. Clos-de-la-Roche (0.08 ha); Morey-Saint-Denis *premier cru* Clos des Ormes; Nuits-Saint-Georges *premier cru* in Les Damodes and Les Pruliers; Chambolle Musigny *premier cru* Les Borniques; village Nuits-Saint-Georges; village Vosne-Romanée; village Chambolle-Musigny; village Morey-Saint-Denis; village Gevrey-Chambertin; Marsannay.

The brothers Philippe and Vincent Lecheneaut look after their domaine biologically. Following a severe *triage*, there is almost total de-stemming, 3 to 6 days *macération à froid*, fermentation temperatures up to 35°C and from one third to one half (100 percent for the Clos de la Roche) new oak. These are good succulent wines with plenty of dimension.

François Legros

6.5 ha owned and *en fermage/en métayage*. Nuits-Saint-Georges *premier cru* in Les Bousselots, Les Perrières and La Roncière; Vougeot *premier cru* Les Cras; Morey-Saint-Denis *premier cru* in Clos Sorbè, Les Milandes and La Riotte; Chambolle-Musigny *premier cru* Les Noirots; Saint-Aubin *premier cru* Clos du Village (*rouge*) and Les Murgers des Dents de Chien, En Remilly and Sur Gamay (*blanc*); village Nuits-Saint-Georges; village Chambolle-Musigny; village Puligny-Montrachet.

François Legros took over at this family domaine at the age of thirty in 1988. Eleven years later, the estate was substantially enlarged by the addition of the Saint-Aubin parcels through his mother's inheritance. In the same year, Legros constructed a new winery down by Nuits-Saint-Georges's rugby stadium. Hand harvesting, a severe *triage* (the 2003s are fine as a result), 10 days of cold-soaking, total de-stemming and 30 to 50 percent very lightly toasted new wood—Vosge for the Chambolle, Allier for the others—are the order of the day here. The results are good.

★ *Thibault Liger-Belair*

6.75 ha owned and *en fermage/en métayage*. Clos de Vougeot (0.75 ha); Richebourg (0.55 ha); Nuits-Saint-Georges *premier cru* Les Saint-Georges; Vosne-Romanée *premier cru* Les Petits Monts; village Vosne-Romanée in the *lieu-dit* Aux Réas; village Nuits-Saint-Georges in the *lieu-dit* La Charmotte.

Thibault Liger-Belair, cousin of Louis-Michel in Vosne-Romanée, took over the vines of his branch of the family when the leases (with Denis Mugneret and Georges Chicotot and others) ended in 2002. Half the wine is his under the share-cropping arrangement he has with his family. The rest is purchased by his *négociant* company Thibault Liger-Belair Successeurs.

The vineyard is treated biologically, even biodynamically in parts. The fruit is de-stemmed, and the juice cold-soaked, and there is 30 to 40 percent new wood used. The first few vintages show real promise. This is a future star.

Bertrand Machard de Gramont

5.96 ha owned and *en fermage*. Village Nuits-Saint-Georges in the *lieux-dits* Aux Allots, Les Hauts-Pruliers and Les Vallerots; village Vosne-Romanée.

Like the other Machard de Gramont estate in Prissey, this domaine came into existence in 1983. It is run by Bertrand Machard de Gramont and his daughters Marie-Christine and Axelle. The latter, in charge in the vineyard, is gradually replanting a further 2 hectares on terraces in Les Vallerots. Total de-stemming, 4 to 5 days of cold-maceration, 33°C maximum temperature during fermentation and one fifth to one quarter new oak is the usual recipe. These are neat wines, softer but more stylish than *chez* the cousins.

★ Alain Michelot

8 ha owned and *en fermage/en métayage*. Nuits-Saints-Georges *premier cru* in Les Cailles, Les Chaignots, Les Champs-Perdrix, Les Forêts Saint-Georges, La Richemone, Les Saint-Georges and Les Vaucrains; Morey-Saint-Denis *premier cru* Les Charrières; village Nuits-Saint-Georges, including the *lieu-dit* Champs Perdrix and a *vieilles vignes cuvée*; village Morey-Saint-Denis.

Alain Michelot is a large, bluff, friendly individual in his early sixties, his ginger hair and beard now grey, and he works with his daughter Edolie from headquarters off the main road which runs through the middle of Nuits-Saint-Georges. In the last decade things have been tightened up here. No stems; 4 to 5 days maceration; vinification at a maximum temperature of 30°C after 24 hours, at the beginning at 33–34°C; and 30 percent new oak is the recipe. And the results are usually very good. The house style is for round, fruity wines which avoid the toughness of most Nuits-Saint-Georges. Despite being softer than some, the wines keep well.

Jean-Marc Millot

7.15 ha owned and *en fermage*. Clos de Vougeot "Grand Maupertuis" (0.34 ha); Grands-Echézeaux (0.20 ha); Echézeaux (0.97 ha); Vosne-Romanée *premier cru* Les Suchots; village Vosne-Romanée; village Savigny-lès-Beaune; Côte de Nuits Villages, including Clos des Faulques.

The 50-year-old Jean-Marc Millot inherited much of his domaine through his mother, *née* Gouroux, of Flagey-Echézeaux. The winemaking is conservative, in the best sense of the word: low harvests, retaining some of the stems, and maceration for 2 to 3 weeks or more. The wines are full, rich and sturdy. The Grands-Echézeaux is matured in 100 percent new wood and is concentrated and old-viney. It needs time. In 2004 Millot moved his headquarters from the family cellars in Comblanchien to a brand new *cuverie* in Nuits-Saint-Georges. Coupled with a greater attention to *triage* than hitherto, this has led to an immediate rise in quality. This is a future star, I believe.

★ Maison Nicolas Potel

Following the untimely death of his father Gérard in October 1997 and the subsequent sale of the family Domaine de la Pousse d'Or, Nicolas Potel set himself up as a merchant. He vinifies fruit where he can and houses the barrels in a cellar opposite that of Alain Michelot in the middle of the town.

From the start, Nicky Potel's range of wines was impressive, both for its breadth—he seemed to have a knack for securing parcels which had eluded his peers—and for its high quality. The wines are well-coloured, full without being sturdy, rich and succulent, pure and elegant. The contrast with the more manipulated wines of fellow merchant Dominique Laurent, who has the next-door cellar, is telling. The business is now a subsidiary of Labouré-Roi/Cottin Frères.

Domaine Nicolas Potel

12 ha owned and *en fermage*. Beaune *premier cru* in Grèves, Teurons, Pertiusots, Montée Rouge, Clos du Roi; Savigny-lès-Beaune *premier cru* in Hauts Jarrons, Peuillots; village Beaune; village Volnay; village Savigny-lès-Beaune *rouge* and *blanc*; village Santenay *blanc*; Saint-Romain *rouge* and *blanc*; côte de Nuits villages *rouge* and *blanc*.

Nicolas Potel started his own domaine in 2005, extended it in 2006, and went biodynamic in 2007. The first results are promising.

Prieuré-Roch

10.56 ha owned and *en fermage*. Clos de Vougeot (0.63 ha); Chambertin, Clos de Bèze (1.01 ha) (owned by the Domaine Marion); Vosne-Romanée *premier cru* Les Suchots; Nuits-Saint-Georges *premier cru* Clos-des-Corvées (*monopole*); village Vosne-Romanée, including the *lieux-dits* Clos Goillotte (*monopole*), Les Clous and Les Hautes-Maizières.

Henri-Frédéric Roch, *co-gérant* of the Domaine de la Romanée-Conti, believes in retaining all the stems and bottling late, after at least 22 months. Part of the Clos des Corvées 2002 was not bottled until early 2005, as a trial, and I preferred this bottling to the normal one: the wine had a better colour and was richer. Today, there are three different *cuvées* from the 5 hectare Corvées: No 1, Nuits-Saint-Georges *Premier Cru*, and Nuits-Saint-Georges Clos des Corvées.

Yields are low here, and the approach is very *bio*, but I find the wines light and rather too stemmy.

Gilles Remoriquet

8.95 ha owned and *en fermage/en métayage*. Nuits-Saint-Georges *premier cru* in Les Bousselots, Les Damodes, La Rue de Chaux and Les Saint-Georges; Vosne-Romanée *premier cru* Au Dessus des Malconsorts; village Nuits-Saint-Georges including the *lieu-dit* Les Allots.

It is the tall, *sympa*, bespectacled Gilles Remoriquet who is in charge here. Up to 15 percent of the stems; a brief cold-maceration; fermentations up to 32°C at the start, and then prolonged at 28–30°C; and 30 to 40 percent new oak make up the recipe. These are good, rich, meaty wines, typical of Nuits-Saint-Georges. They need time.

Charles Thomas

This domaine was sold to Étienne de Montille and Jeremy Seysses, who have divided the spoils between them, in the summer of 2005.

Prémeaux

Bertrand Ambroise

20 ha owned and *en fermage/en métayage*. Clos de Vougeot (0.17 ha), Corton, Le Rognet (0.50 ha), Corton-Charlemagne (0.20 ha); Nuits-Saint-Georges *premier cru* in Clos des Argillières, La Rue de Chaux and Les Vaucrains; Vougeot *premier cru* Les Cras; Pommard *premier cru* Les Saussilles; Saint-Aubin *premier cru blanc* Murgers des Dents de Chien; village Vosne-Romanée in the *lieu-dit* Les Damodes; village Nuits-Saint-Georges; village Pommard; village Beaune in the *lieu-dit* Saint-Désirée; village Saint-Aubin *blanc*; Côte-de-Nuits-Villages.

Bernard Ambroise's growing domaine—the Clos des Argillières, the Vougeot Les Cras and the Saint-Aubin *premier cru* have all been added in the last decade—has its origins in the vines of his father-in-law Michel Dupasquier, under whose name, up to 1990, much of the stock appeared. These are big wines, with plenty of new oak and plenty of fruit and guts, but I find they lack grace.

Domaine de l'Arlot

14 ha owned. Romanée-Saint-Vivant (0.25 ha); Vosne-Romanée *premier cru* Les Suchots; Nuits-Saint-Georges *premier cru* in Clos-des-Forêts-Saint-Georges (*monopole*), Clos de l'Arlot (*monopole*) *rouge et blanc*; Côte de Nuits Villages in the *monopole* Clos du Chapeau.

In 1987 the insurance group AXA, owners of Bordeaux's Château Pichon-Longueville-Baron and other estates, bought the moribund Clos de l'Arlot and installed Jean-Pierre de Smet, a disciple of Jacques Seysses of the Domaine Dujac, to run it.

The cellar is splendid (so too is the newly renovated château), and Smet's winemaking is meticulous and flexible, following the character of the vintage, but normally with a high percentage of the stems and a minimum of sulphur. This is an address for those who wish to be seduced by Nuits on the light side (especially the Clos l'Arlot itself), not for those who seek hand-to-hand combat. There is also—and in reasonable quantity, for a whole hectare is under vine—a white Nuits-Saint-Georges. This is delicious. Others like the red wines more than I: lean wines with a marked taste of the stems are not to my taste.

Jean-Pierre de Smet retired in 2006. His place has been taken by Olivier Leriche.

Jérôme Chézeaux

12 ha owned and *en fermage*. Clos de Vougeot (0.20 ha); Vosne-Romanée *premier cru* in Les Chaumes and Les Suchots; Nuits-Saint-Georges *premier cru* in Les Boudots, Les Pruliers, Rue de Chaux and Les Vaucrains; village Nuits-Saint-Georges; village Vosne-Romanée.

Opposite Bertrand Ambroise's winery in Prém-eaux, you will find the premises of the forty-something Jérôme Chezeaux, who took over from his father Bernard, who died early, in 1993. Total de-stemming, a brief cold-maceration, 15–21 days *cuvaison*, and 30 percent new oak is the usual recipe here. The portfolio is impressive, and the wines very good: not blockbusters but persistent and classy.

★★ Jean-Jacques Confuron

7 ha owned. Romanée-Saint-Vivant (0.50 ha); Clos de Vougeot (0.52 ha); Vosne-Romanée *premier cru* Les Beaux-Monts; Chambolle-Musigny *premier cru* (from Les Châtelots and Les Feusselottes); Nuits-Saint-Georges *premier cru* in Aux Boudots, Les Chaboeufs; village Chambolle-Musigny; village Nuits-Saint-Georges in the *lieu-dit* Les Fleuriers; Côtes-de-Nuits-Villages.

The origins of this domaine lie with the Noël-lat estate in Vosne-Romanée, and the vines have passed through the female side for a couple of generations since. The owners are Alain and Sophie Meunier, Sophie being *née* Confuron. Quality has been very high here for 20 years or more with low harvests and a firmly *biologique* approach to the viticulture. A small percentage of stems are left, the wine is cold-macerated for 5 days, fermentation temperatures are allowed to rise to 33°C, and between 30 to 80 percent new oak is used. Until 1995, special 100 percent oak cuvées were set aside for the American market. This—thankfully, for the wines were overpowered—has now ceased. The quality of the wine is classy, poised and very fine. Alain Meunier's wine deserves greater recognition. He also has a *négociant*'s licence and a separate cellar in Echevronne with his associate Jacques Féry.

R. Dubois et Fils

22 ha owned and *en fermage*. Clos de Vougeot (0.83 ha); Nuits-Saints-Georges *premier cru* in Les Porêts-Saint-Georges and Clos des Argillières; Savigny-lès-Beaune *premier cru* Les Narbantons; village Chambolle-Musigny in the *lieu-dit* Les Combottes; village Vosne-Romanée in the *lieu-dit* Les Chanlandins; village Nuits-Saint-Georges, including the *lieu-dit* Les Longecourts; village Savigny-lès-Beaune in the *lieu-dit* Les Gollardes; village Beaune "Blanche Fleur"; Côte-de-Nuits-Villages *blanc*.

This is a large family domaine, with all the members of two generations seemingly actively involved, though father Régis officially retired in 2006, and the welcome is warm. Today the winemaker is oenologue Béatrice Dubois, while her brother Raphaël, born 1969, deals with the commercial side. The wine is made without the stems, vinified at about 30°C after a few days cold-soaking, and 20 percent new oak is used. During the *élévage* the wines are aged partly in tank, partly in wood, with the receptacles being interchanged when the wines are racked. I find them quite structured, but somewhat lean and unstylish. Raphaël Dubois set up a parallel business in 2002 under his own name. He buys fruit only, not wine.

Chantal Lescure

18 ha owned. Clos de Vougeot (0.30 ha); Vosne-Romanée *premier cru* Les Suchots; Nuits-Saint-Georges *premier cru* Les Vallerots; Pommard *premier cru* Les Bertins; Beaune *premier cru* Les Chouacheux; village Chambolle-Musigny in the *lieu-dit* Les Mobies; village Nuits-Saint-Georges in the *lieux-dits* Les Creux Fraiches Eaux; village Pommard in the *lieux-dits* Les Chanlins, Les Vaumuriens and Les Vignots; Côte de Beaune *rouge* "Le Clos des Topes Bizot" and *blanc* "La Grande Chatelaine."

This domaine was created in 1983, but until the death of Madame Lescure in 1996, it just produced fruit, the results being turned into wine by Maison Labouré-Roi, though bottled under the Lescure label. Since then, under the direction of François Chavenait, it has been independent, and standards have improved, though there is still room for improvement. The approach in the vineyards is biological. There is a long gentle maceration for 20 days or so, and the wine is matured using 20 to 70 percent new oak.

Machard de Gramont

18.9 ha owned and *en fermage*. Vosne-Romanée *premier cru* Les Gaudichots; Nuits-Saint-Georges *premier cru* Les Damodes; Savigny-lès-Beaune *premier cru* in Les Guettes and Les Vergelesses (*blanc*); Beaune *premier cru* in Les Chouacheux and Aux Coucherias; Pommard *premier cru* Le Clos *blanc*; village Chambolle-Musigny in the *lieu-dit* Les Nazoires; village Nuits-Saint-Georges including the *lieux-dits* Les Argillats, Les Damodes, Les Hauts-Poirets, Les Hauts Pruliers, En La Perrière-Noblot, Les Poulettes and *blanc*; village Gevrey-Chambertin in the *lieu-dit* Les Pressionniers; village Aloxe-Corton; village Chorey-lès-Beaune;

village Savigny-lès-Beaune; village Beaune in the *lieu-dit* Les Epenottes; village Pommard; village Puligny Montrachet in the *lieu-dit* Les Houillères.

Most of this domaine, run by Arnaud Machard de Gramont and his son Alban, has been built up since the family split in 1983. The headquarters, a cavernous farmhouse, is down by the railway line in Prémaux-Prissey. The fruit is de-stalked; macerated for a long time with plenty of *pigeage*; kept up to 24 months in oak, up to 50 percent of which is new; and bottled without fining. The results are well-coloured, full-bodied and rich, but rather brutal and four-square.

★★ Perdrix

10.3 ha owned. Echézeaux (1.15 ha); Nuits-Saint-Georges *premier cru* in Aux Perdrix (*monopole*), Les Terres Blanches *rouge et blanc*; village Nuits-Saint-Georges; village Vosne-Romanée.

This excellent estate is the personal fief of Bertrand Devillard, PDG of Maison Antonin Rodet of Mercurey. The Perdrix itself is consistently one of the very best examples of Nuits-Saint-Georges on the market, and the Echézeaux can be very fine. Supervised by Devillard himself and his Rodet oenologue Nadine Gublin, the man on the spot is Robert Vernizeau. He does a good job.

Château de Prémeaux

10 ha owned and *en fermage*. Nuits-Saint-Georges *premier cru* Les Argillières; village Nuits-Saint-Georges; Côtes de Nuits Villages.

The original château was destroyed in the Revolution. Today's elegant mansion was built to replace it by a Pelletier ancestor. Arnaud Pelletier, tall, early thirties, sporting a goatee, took over from his father Alain in 2004. The culture in the vineyard is *biologique*. Arnaud has reduced the yield and the number of *pigeages* and now picks the fruit into small plastic trays. He retains 10 percent of the stems, cold-soaks for 4 or 5 days and uses 30 percent new wood for the top wines. I didn't like the 2003s, but have enjoyed other recent vintages. Often the two *premiers crus* are blended together.

Protot

2.5 ha owned. Côte de Nuits Villages.

Opposite the entrance to the Domaine de la Vougeraie are the cellars of this small domaine, run by the cheerful Daniel Protot and his father Bernard. Here is yet more proof, if more were needed, that Côte de Nuits Villages can provide excellent value for money.

Daniel Rion et Fils

17.92 ha owned and *en métayage*. Clos-de-Vougeot (0.55 ha); Vosne-Romanée *premier cru* in Les Beaux-Monts and Les Chaumes; Nuits-Saint-Georges *premier cru* in Les Hauts-Pruliers, Les Terres-Blanches (*rouge et blanc*) and Les Vignerondes; village Chambolle-Musigny; village Vosne-Romanée; village Nuits-Saint-Georges, including the *lieux-dits* Les Grandes-Vignes and Les Lavières; Côte de Nuits Villages.

Following the departure of Patrice Rion (see below), his brothers Christophe and Olivier are now in charge here. There is a sorting table. The reds are de-stemmed, cold-soaked for 5 days and vinified at 30–32°C. Fifty percent new oak is used, and bottling occurs after 16 months. The results are competent but rarely exciting.

Michèle and Patrice Rion

6.50 ha owned, under contract, and *en fermage*. Bonnes-Mares (12 a), Chambolle-Musigny, *premier cru* Amoureuses, Fuées, and *premier cru tout court*; Nuits-Saint-Georges *premier cru* in Clos des Argillières and Clos Saint-Marc (*monopole*) and Terres Blanches; Chambolle-Musigny *premier cru* Les Charmes; Village Chambolle-Musigny from the *lieu-dit* Les Cras.

After a fight with his brothers (see Domaine Daniel Rion), Patrice set up on his own domaine in 2000. He also has a *négociant* business. The fruit is de-stemmed and the wine fermented at 32°C, and there is 50 to 100 percent new oak. The winemaking equipment is up-to-date here, and the wines are round and elegant.

Jean-Pierre Tréchutet

9.2 ha owned and *en fermage*. Nuits-Saint-Georges; Côte de Nuits Villages.

The 50-year-old Jean-Pierre Trechutet is the fifth generation to exploit this modest—no *premiers* or *grands crus*—but high-quality estate. In both colours, from generics upward, and even in 2003, the results here are consistently very good. A clue to this success? Old vines and low *rendements*.

★ *La Vougeraie*
34.2 ha owned. Clos de Vougeot (1.41 ha); Mazoyères-Chambertin (0.74 ha); Corton Clos du Roi (0.50 ha); Bonnes-Mares (0.70 ha); Corton-Charlemagne (0.22 ha); Le Musigny (0.21 ha); Vougeot *premier cru* in Le Clos *blanc* (*blanc monopole*) and Les Cras; Gevrey-Chambertin *premier cru* Bel Air; Nuits-Saint-Georges *premier cru* in Les Corvées Pagets and Les Damodes; Beaune *premier cru* in Clos du Roi and Les Grèves; Savigny-lès-Beaune *premier cru* Les Marconnets; village Gevrey-Chambertin, including the *lieux-dits* Les Evocelles and La Justice; village Pommard, including the *lieux-dits* Les Charmots and Les Petits Noizons; village Chambolle-Musigny; village Vougeot in the *lieu-dit* Clos du Prieuré.

In 1999 Pascal Marchand was seduced away from the Comte Armand's Clos des Epeneaux in Pommard by Jean-Claude Boisset, who had decided to pool all the vineyards of the various companies he had acquired over the years into a single entity. The nucleus of Vougeraie is the old Domaine Pierre Ponnelle. Marchand arrived at the time of the harvest. The following year he started transforming the viticulture into biodynamic. The results have been more and more exciting ever since.

Marchand left in March 2006 to set up on his own as a merchant. Pierre Vincent, who had been running Jaffelin, another Boisset business, was brought in to manage the Domaine de la Vougeraie.

COMBLANCHIEN AND CORGOLOIN

THE SOUTHERN CÔTE-DE-NUITS-VILLAGES
The Clos de la Maréchale marks the end of the appellation of Nuits-Saint-Georges. Between here and Ladoix, the first village of the Côte de Beaune, a distance of some 3 kilometres, the Côte is broken up by a series of marble quarries, and the stone, and detritus and dust therefrom, disfigures and dirties the landscape. This is a sort of no-man's-land. But there are some vines. Together with the land of Brochon and Fixin, these are the vineyards of Côte-de-Nuits-Villages (though Fixin has the right to village status as well).

You get the feeling, however, that here, marble quarrying is more important than viticulture. It is above the Nuits-Saint-Georges *premier cru* of Forêts, that they produce the pink limestone of Prémeaux. Here at Comblanchien, it is milky coffee in colour. The stone is popular throughout France. According to Anthony Hanson, it was used to decorate Orly airport. And it is much seen locally, on the counters of the *boulangeries* and *charcuteries* of Nuits-Saint-Georges, for example.

Part of Prémeaux-Prissey produces Côte-de-Nuits Villages in these parts, as do the villages of Comblanchien and Corgoloin. The areas under vine are as follows:

Prémeaux-Prissey	17.27 ha
Comblanchien	58.76 ha
Corgoloin	84.41 ha

This is a total of 160.84 hectares, rather more than half of the total permitted area in theory, and, in fact, as Fixin is mostly bottled as such, constitutes the lion's share of the appellation in bottles.

A list of recommended Côte-de-Nuits Villages sources is given on page 79.

The Growers

★ *D'Ardhuy, Clos des Langres, Corgoloin*
41 ha owned and *en métayage/en fermage*.

S.C. LA JUVINIÈRE: Corton Les Combes (0.10 ha); Corton Les Pougets (0.42 ha); Corton Clos du Roi (0.57 ha); Corton-Charlemagne (0.51 ha); Clos de Vougeot (0.56 ha); Vosne-Romanée *Premier Cru*; Pommard *Premier Cru*; Volnay *premier cru* in Frémiets and Chanlin; Aloxe-Corton *Premier Cru*; Beaune *Premier Cru rouge et blanc*; Savigny-lès-Beaune *premier cru* Les Peuillets; Puligny-Montrachet *Premier Cru*; village Nuits-Saint-Georges; village Pommard; village Volnay; village Aloxe-Corton; village Ladoix; village Savigny-lès-Beaune in the *lieu-dit* Clos de Godeaux;

village Puligny-Montrachet; Côte de Nuits Villages Clos des Langres.

S.C. LES TERRES VINEUSES: Corton Les Hautes Mourottes (0.63 ha); Corton Renardes (2.63 ha); Corton Clos du Roi (0.39 ha); Corton-Charlemagne (0.53 ha); Savigny-lès-Beaune *Premier Cru*; Ladoix *Premier Cru rouge et blanc*; village Meursault; village Gevrey-Chambertin; village Aloxe-Corton; village Savigny-lès-Beaune *rouge et blanc*; village Pernand-Vergelesses; village Ladoix *rouge et blanc*.

S.C. DOMAINE DES CARMES: Savigny-lès-Beaune *Premier Cru*.

S.C. DOMAINE DES GUETTES: Savigny-lès-Beaune *Premier Cru*.

This important domaine, owned by the D'Ardhuy-Santiard family, was reborn in 2003 when the contract that they had with Château Corton-André in Aloxe-Corton came to its end. For the time being, Château Corton-André will still be allowed to purchase some of the wine, but it will be the same wine as that produced by the youthful and talented new *régisseur* Carel Voorhuis.

Based at an ivy-encrusted building in the middle of the Clos des Langres, the most southerly vineyard in the Côte de Nuits, viticulture and viniculture have been transformed under the new regime. Yields have been cut, *triage* is now severe, and the winemaking approach is flexible. For the most part, the fruit is de-stemmed; there is no cold-soaking or use of enzymes; temperatures are allowed to rise to 30–32°C; there are frequent *pigeages*; and there is a variable, 5 to 50 percent, use of new oak. This is a new star.

Chopin et Fils, Comblanchien

13 ha owned and *en métayage*. Nuits-Saint-Georges *premier cru* Les Murgers; village Nuits-Saint-Georges, including the *lieu-dit* Bas de Combe; Côte-de-Nuits Villages (*rouge et blanc*).

Arnaud, grandson of André Chopin, after whom the domaine is named, is in charge here today. He has reduced the harvest and modernised the cellar, and he now sells all his wine in bottle. Some 10 percent of the stems are retained, the wine is vinified at 25–30°C, and there is about 30 percent new wood used. A curiosity is the white Côte-de-Nuits Villages. The best of Chopin's three *cuvées* of Côte-de-Nuits Villages is neat, oaky and very stylish. The wines are good here.

Anne-Marie Gille, Comblanchien

9 ha owned and *en fermage*. Village Nuits-Saint-Georges in the *lieu-dit* Les Brûlées; Côte de Nuits Villages.

This domaine proudly announces that it has existed since 1570. Pierre Gille, son of Henri, who used to be a pilot, and his attractive wife Anne-Marie, who used to be a pharmacist, run the estate today. They took over in 1993 and have enlarged it since then. After total de-stemming, the fruit is cooled for several days before the fermentation is allowed to progress. The Côte de Nuits Villages is vinified in tank and aged in cask. The Nuits-Saint-Georges is matured in one third new wood. The results can be very good. This is an address worth investigating.

Damien and Liselotte Gachot-Monot, Gorgoloin

14 ha owned and *en fermage*. Nuits-Saint-Georges *premier cru* Les Poulettes; village Nuits-Saint-Georges, including the *lieu-dit* Aux Crots; Côte-de-Nuits Villages, including "Les Chaillots" and *blanc*.

The 37-year-old Damien Gachot took over the family domaine, inherited though the female line, in 1993, and built a new *cuverie* and cellar across the road in 2003. He hand harvests, does a lot of *triage*, doesn't tread down too much—wishing to produce supple, fruity wines—and bottles according to the lunar calendar after 16 months. Fragrant, elegant wines are here: another fine source for Côte de Nuits Villages.

★ Gilles Jourdan, Corgoloin

5.3 ha owned and *en fermage*. Côte-de-Nuits Villages, including La Robignotte.

Gilles Jourdan took over from his father Jean in 1977 and has sold everything in bottle since then. There is a manual harvest, 100 percent de-stemming, cold-soaking for 45 days, long fermentations (*pigeages* but no *remontage*) at a maximum of 30°C and an average of 25 percent new oak. This is high-class winemaking: an excellent address. There will be some white Côte-de-Nuits Villages in 2008.

Jean Petitot et Fils, Corgoloin

9.2 ha owned. Aloxe-Corton *premier cru* La Coutière; Village Nuits-Saint-Georges in the *lieu-dit* Les Poisets; Côte-de-Nuits Villages, including the *lieux-dits* Les Vignottes Vieilles Vignes and Les Monts de Boncourt; village Pommard; village Ladoix.

Henri Petitot, approaching forty, made his first vintage in 1990 and took over responsibility in 2002. The Pommard and the Aloxe have been purchased since. You'll find the winery adjacent to a fine and substantial mansion, part of which is eighteenth century, behind Corgoloin's church. This is a major source for top-quality Côte-de-Nuits Villages. The old vine Les Vignottes is excellent.

La Poulette, Corgoloin

11 ha owned and *en fermage*. Nuits-Saint-Georges *premier cru* in Les Chaboeufs, Les Poulettes and Les Vaucrains; Vosne-Romanée *premier cru* Les Suchots; village Nuits-Saint-Georges; Côte-de-Nuits Villages.

The family domaine of François and Françoise Michaut-Audidier has been passed through the female line for over six generations. Most of the harvest is manual. The fruit is de-stemmed, and the wines here are reared partly in cask, partly in *foudre*. This estate has the lion's share of the Poulettes, which lies between Vaucrains and Les Porrets; this is a surprisingly supple wine: good but not brilliant.

Pierre Thibert, Corgoloin

4 ha owned and *en fermage*. Nuits-Saint-Georges *premier cru* Rue de Chaux; village Nuits-Saint-Georges; Chorey-lès-Beaune; Côte-de-Nuits Villages.

Pierre Thibert started from scratch in 1989 and moved to his somewhat artisanal premises in Corgoloin in 1995. The fruit is usually largely de-stemmed after manual harvesting and macerated at temperatures up to 34°C with regular *pigeages*, and there is one third new wood for the Nuits-Saint-Georges before bottling 12 months after the harvest. Quality is good, but variable.

HAUTES-CÔTES-DE-NUITS AND HAUTES-CÔTES-DE-BEAUNE

Above and behind the Côte d'Or in the Hautes-Côtes, the countryside is peaceful and pastoral. There are valleys and plateaux, pastures and woodland, rocky outcrops and gently sloping fields. Up here it is cooler and often more exposed, and the soils are less fine, less complex. Only in carefully selected sites is the aspect suitable for the vine. This is the area known as the Hautes-Côtes.

There have always been vines in the Hautes-Côtes. Before *phylloxera*, there were as many as 4,500 hectares in cultivation, although much was planted with non-"noble" grapes. But then, as elsewhere, the vineyards declined, and as recently as 1968, there were barely 500 hectares of vines.

That was the nadir, but resurrection was already at hand. *Appellation contrôlée*, with the prefix Bourgogne, had been bestowed on the Hautes-Côtes in 1961, and in 1968 a cooperative cellar called Les Caves des Hautes-Côtes—not up the back of beyond but sensibly on the main road outside Beaune where no passer-by could fail to notice it—was established. This now vinifies and sells 25 percent of the combined appellation. Meanwhile, at the research station at Echevronne above Pernand-Vergelesses, suitable clones of the Pinot Noir were being developed, and following a visit to Bordeaux, trials were being carried out with high-trained vines, thus avoiding the worst of the frost, and, because they could be planted further apart for mechanical cultivation, thus economizing on the expense of planting and maintaining new vineyards. Since then, the fortunes of the Hautes-Côtes have blossomed. There are now well over 1,400 hectares under vine, and production in 2005 reached a total of 25,959 hectolitres in the Hautes-Côtes-de-Nuits and 35,134 in the Hautes-Côtes-de-Beaune. Eighty-three percent of this is red and *rosé*.

From a geographical point of view, the two parts of the Hautes-Côtes do not quite correspond with the division between the Côte de Nuits and the Côte de Beaune. The northern section, the Hautes-Côtes-de-Nuits, begins at Ruelle-Vergy above Chambolle and continues to

Echevronne and Magny-lès-Villers. Echevronne is in the Hautes-Côtes-de-Beaune, while the land at Magny is divided between the two. There is then a separate section of the Hautes-Côtes-de-Beaune which begins at Mavilly-Mandelot above Beaune and extends south to Sampigny-lès-Maranges and Cheilly-lès-Maranges near Santenay.

There is a little—17 percent—white Hautes-Côtes wine as such: much is made into Crémant de Bourgogne. In my view, this is less successful than the red wine, tending to be a bit lean. The customer is better off with a Mâcon villages. But it is the red wine, exclusively from the Pinot Noir, which is the cornerstone of the appellation and the key to its deserved recent success. This is a wine to buy in a warm, ripe year like 2003—the wines are then delicious, and some of the best values in Burgundy. Avoid the wines of a cold rainy vintage.

The Growers

Cave des Hautes-Côtes, Beaune

600 ha. 120 *adhérents* (stakeholders). Corton (0.20 ha); Charmes-Chambertin (0.15 ha); Gevrey-Chambertin *premier cru* in Clos du Chapitre and Craipillot; Morey-Saint-Denis *premier cru* Clos Sorbè; Vougeot *premier cru* Les Cras; Nuits-Saint-Georges *premier cru* in Les Aigrots and Montée Rouge; Savigny-lès-Beaune *premier cru* Les Lavières; Pommard *premier cru* Les Charmots; Puligny-Montrachet *premier cru* La Garenne; Saint-Aubin *premier cru* En Remilly; village wines in Gevrey-Chambertin, Morey-Saint-Denis, Nuits-Saint-Georges, Aloxe-Corton, Pernand-Vergelesses (*rouge et blanc*), Savigny-lès-Beaune, Chorey-lès-Beaune, Beaune (*rouge et blanc*), Pommard, Volnay, Monthelie, Auxey-Duresses, Meursault, Saint-Romain (*rouge et blanc*), Chassagne-Montrachet, Santenay (*rouge et blanc*), Maranges and Marsannay.

The Cave des Hautes-Côtes boasts of offering seventy-four different appellations, but a large number of the *cuvées* of their Côte d'Or wines are very small. Naturally, the concentration is on Hautes-Côtes-de-Beaune and Hautes-Côtes-de-Nuits, as well as, increasingly important these days, Crémant de Bourgogne. Some 60 percent

of their Hautes-Côtes vineyards are machine harvested. This is an up-to-date establishment, and the wines are good. As always in the Hautes-Côtes, the consumer is wise to stick with the vintages where there has been a fine Indian summer.

François Charles et Fils, Nantoux

14 ha owned. Volnay *premier cru* Les Fremiets; Beaune *premier cru* in Les Boucherottes and Les Epenottes; village Volnay in the *lieu-dit* Clos de la Cave (*monopole*); village Pommard; village Meursault.

This thriving and expanding domaine is one of the best in the area and is today run by Pascal Charles, son of François. Like many in the Hautes-Côtes he has stopped machine harvesting. There is 25 percent new wood for the better wines.

★ David Duband, Chevannes
François Feuillet

DAVID DUBAND: 9.18 ha owned and *en fermage*. Nuits-Saint-Georges *premier cru* in Les Procès and Les Pruliers; village Nuits-Saint-Georges.

FRANÇOIS FEUILLET: 9.10 ha owned (Duband has half of this under the share-cropping arrangement). Clos de la Roche (0.41 ha); Echézeaux (0.50 ha); Mazoyères-Chambertin (0.65 ha); Gevrey-Chambertin *premier cru* Les Combottes; Chambolle-Musigny *premier cru* Les Sentiers; Morey-Saint-Denis *premier cru* in Les Blanchards, Clos des Ormes, Clos Sorbè and Les Ruchots; Nuits-Saint-Georges *premier cru* in Les Chaboeufs and Aux Thorey; village Gevrey-Chambertin; village Morey-Saint-Denis; village Chambolle-Musigny; village Vosne-Romanée; village Nuits-Saint-Georges.

David Duband's father was a member of the Hautes-Côtes cooperative until he extricated himself in 1991. David took over when his father retired in 1995. When the Parisien François Feuillet bought a small domaine based in Nuits-Saint-Georges, he entrusted young Duband with the share-cropping role. Feuillet bought the estate of Jacky Truchot-Martin of Morey-Saint-Denis in 2005, quadrupling the size of his exploitation. The wines, whether labelled Duband or Feuillet, are identical.

This is up-to-date, classic, modern winemaking. Low yields, a severe *triage*, 100 percent elimination of the stalks, 8 to 10 days cold-soaking, fermentations at 30°C and 40 to 80 percent new oak (the latter less than when I first met him, to the wines' advantage). High quality here—and a nice man.

Féry, Echevronne

10 ha owned. Savigny-lès-Beaune *premier cru* Les Vergelesses; village Vosne-Romanée (from Aux Réas); village Nuits-Saint-Georges (from Charmois and Damodes); village Morey-Saint-Denis; village Savigny-lès-Beaune.

M. Féry is a Lyon lawyer. The vines and the viniculture are supervised by Alain Meunier of the Domaine J.J. Confuron in Prémeaux. There is a joint merchant business under the name Féry-Meunier. Sadly, there is nothing here remotely as exciting as you will find in the J.J. Confuron cellars in Prémeaux.

Henri Gros, Chamboeuf

4 ha owned. Village Vosne-Romanée; Bourgogne Hautes Côtes de Nuits.

There are no Hautes-Côtes vines in Chamboeuf, up above Gevrey-Chambertin. Henri Gros's vines lie above Vosne-Romanée. The wines are fresh, stylish and worthy of notice. He is no relation to the Vosne-Romanée–based Gros family.

Lucien Jacob, Echevronne

19.45 ha owned and *en fermage*. Beaune *premier cru* in Les Avaux, Les Cent-Vignes and Les Toussaints; Savigny-lès-Beaune *premier cru* in Les Peuillets and Les Vergelesses (*blanc et rouge*); Pernand-Verglesses *premier cru*; village Savigny-lès-Beaune (*blanc et rouge*); village Gevrey-Chambertin; village Chambolle-Musigny.

The tall, bearded Jean-Michel Jacob, aided by his wife Christine and his sister Chantal Forey (married to Régis Forey of Vosne-Romanée), runs this expanding and evolving, increasingly *biologique* domaine. There was a new *cuverie*, plus pneumatic press, for the 2001 vintage. From 2002 Jacob made a deliberate decision to reduce his harvest. The fruit is completely destemmed; cold-soaked for 2 or 3 days; and vinified at 32°C for three days, and then at 25–27°C for 6 to 8 days. There is now a modicum of new wood. There are well-made, stylish wines here, getting better year by year. They also sell liqueurs: *crème de cassis, framboise et mûre*.

Gilles Jayer, Magny-lès-Villers

11 ha owned. Echézeaux (54 a); Nuits-Saint-Georges *premier cru* Les Damodes; village Nuits-Saint-Georges in the *lieu-dit* Les Hauts-Poirets; Côtes-de-Nuits-Villages.

Gilles Jayer has now taken over from his father Robert. They are cousins of the Jayers in Vosne-Romanée. Like his father, Gilles is a very firm believer in new oak. But a change has thankfully been made. No longer is it 100 percent for everything, including his Hautes-Côtes. The top wines could take it and were certainly very good, but for the lesser wines, this was definitely an acquired taste: one I did not share. Today, I find the results here more civilised.

★ Olivier Jouan, Arcenant

8.5 ha *en fermage*. Charmes-Chambertin (0.33 ha); Morey-Saint-Denis *premier cru* in Les Charrières, La Riotte (*vieilles vignes*) and Les Ruchots (*vieilles vignes*); village Morey-Saint-Denis in the *lieu-dit* Clos Solon; village Chambolle-Musigny in the *lieu-dit* Les Bussières.

Olivier Jouan, forty-ish, tall, dark and handsome, is a cousin of Henri and Philippe Jouan in Morey-Saint-Denis. He took over the vines of his uncle Michel in 1999 and has extended the estate since, moving from Morey-Saint-Denis to Arcenant in the Hautes-Côtes in 2002. As you can see, this domaine is rich in old vines, and the results are very good indeed. There is more *pigeage* for the Moreys, more *remontage* for the Chambolle and 30 to 50 percent new wood.

Mazilly Père et Fils, Meloisey

18 ha owned and *en fermage*. Beaune *premier cru* in Les Cent Vignes, Les Montrevenots and Les Vignes Franches; Pommard *premier cru* Les Poutures; Savigny-lès-Beaune *premier cru* Les Narbantons; Monthelie *premier cru* Le Clou des Chênes; village

Gevrey-Chambertin; village Beaune; village Pommard; village Volnay; village Meursault.

Frédéric Mazilly and his brother Aymeric have continued to expand the domaine they inherited from their father Pierre a dozen years ago and to fine-tune the quality. This is now one of the best sources of Hautes-Côtes. There is a wide range of other wines too.

Jean-Pierre Mugneret, Concoeur

7 ha owned. Echézeaux (0.90 ha); Nuits-Saint-Georges *premier cru* Les Boudots; village Vosne-Romanée; village Nuits-Saint-Georges.

Jean-Pierre Mugneret has a cellar in Vosne-Romanée, but his main headquarters are up in the Hautes-Côtes next to Concoeur's church. There is a large aquarium in the customer reception part of the cellar. Partial de-stemming only, quite long macerations and 60 to 80 per-cent new wood for the Echézeaux produce well-coloured, succulent, meaty wines with no lack of style. He retired for health reasons after the 2005 vintage. Having no children interested in taking over, he has leased his vines to Jean-René Nudant of Ladoix.

Henri Naudin-Ferrand, Magny-lès-Villers

22 ha owned. Echézeaux (0.34 ha); Ladoix *premier cru* La Corvée; Côte-de-Nuits Villages.

Though Henri still appears on the domaine bro-chure and on some of the labels, this excellent estate is owned by the determined and individ-ual Claire, one of his three daughters. She has been responsible for the wines since 1992, and over the years has been buying the rest of the family's shares, in order to have total control. This exercise was completed in 2004.

The *cuverie* was updated in 1999; now al-most everything moves by gravity, including the bottling. There is a *table de tri*. The white Hautes-Côtes and some of the reds are picked by machine. One red Hautes-Côtes *cuvée* is made by whole grape vinification. I find it rather more rustic than those produced from de-stemmed

fruit. These, whether white or red, are exem-plary: pure, gently oaky, intense and classy.

Agnès and Sébastien Pacquet, Meloisey

6 ha owned and *en fermage*. Village Auxey-Duresses *rouge et blanc*.

Agnès Pacquet took over part of the family estate, formerly rented off, in 2001. The Auxey vines lie on the Saint-Romain side of the commune. The wines are clean, fruity and well made.

Parigot Père et Fils, Meloisey

16 ha owned and *en fermage*. Pommard *premier cru* in Les Charmots and Les Epenots; Beaune *premier cru* Les Aigrots and Les Grèves; Savigny-lès-Beaune *premier cru* Les Peuillets; Chassagne-Montrachet *premier cru blanc* Clos Saint-Jean; village Pommard in the *lieux-dits* Clos de la Chanière, Clos Beauder and Les Vignots; village Volnay in the *lieu-dit* Les Echards; village Savigny-lès-Beaune in the *lieu-dit* Les Peuillets; village Meursault in the *lieu-dit* Le Limouzin and Les Vireuils Dessous.

Régis and Alexandre Parigot, father and son, tend this leading Hautes-Côtes domaine, the stock of which is aged in a combination of *foudres* and *pièces*. Everything is hand harvested here. These are very good wines.

Thierry Vigot, Messanges

3.35 ha owned and *en fermage/en métayage*. Echézeaux (0.40 ha); Vosne-Romanée *premier cru* Les Gaudichots; village Nuits-Saint-Georges in the *lieu-dit* Les Bas de Combe.

In the three *climats* just listed, Thierry Vigot exploits the vines of Mme Gilberte Thomas, while he has his own vines in lesser areas, includ-ing that oddity, a *vin de pays de la Côte d'Or blanc*. Total de-stemming, a few days cold-soaking, vin-ification at 28–30°C and a judicious, but above all flexible, attitude toward the use of new oak is the recipe here. All this takes place in a rather cramped cellar. M. Vigot makes good wine. I am less enthusiastic about his *élevage*. Since 2001 he has sold most of his top wines off in bulk.

The Côte d'Or

THE CÔTE DE BEAUNE

Clos du Roi

Blanches Fleurs

Clos-de-l'Écu

A l'Écu

Les Fèves

Les Bressandes

Les Toussaints

Les Cent Vignes

Les Grèves

Les Teurons

Aux Cras

Les Bas des Teurons

Sur les Grèves

Clos Saint Anne

Clos de la Féguine

Aux Coucherias

Montée Rouge

Champs Pimont

La Mignotte

Les Avaux

Clos des Avaux

Les Seurey

Clos de la Mousse

Les Sizies

Les Tuvilains

Belissand

Les Reversées

Les Aigrots

Les Montrevenots

Le Clos des Mouches

Les Vignes Franches

Pertuisots

Clos Saint-Landry

Les Boucherottes

Les Chouacheux

Les Epenotes

Les Beaux-Fougets

The Growers

Albert Bichot et Cie

Gabriel Bouchard

Bouchard Père et Fils S.A.

Joseph de Bucy

Carré-Courbin

Champy Père et Fils

Chanson Père et Fils

Yves Darviot

Domaine des Croix

Joseph Drouhin, S.A.

Maison Alex Gambal

Emmanuel Giboulot

Camille Giroud, S.A.

Hospices de Beaune

Louis Jadot

Lucien le Moine

Albert Morot

Blair Pethel, Domaine Dublaire

Albert Ponnelle

Jean-Claude Rateau

Remoissenet Père et Fils

Comte Senard

Domaine des Terregelesses

BLIGNY-LÈS-BEAUNE AND TAILLY / 215

Gabriel Fournier, Domaine de la Galopière

Catherine and Claude Maréchal

Ghislaine and Bernard Maréchal-Caillot

Aline and Joël Patriarche

Domaine Saint-Fiacre

POMMARD / 216

History

The Vineyard

The Premiers Crus

Les Petits Epenots

Clos des Epeneaux

Les Grands Epenots

Les Boucherottes

Les Saussilles

Les Pézerolles

En Lagillière

Les Charmots

Les Arvelets

La Platière

La Chanière

Clos Blanc

La Refène

Clos de la Commaraine

Clos de Verger

Les Chanlins-Bas

Les Rugiens-Hauts

Les Rugiens-Bas

Les Jarolières

Les Chaponnières

Les Fremiers

Les Croix Noires

Les Bertins
Les Poutures
Les Combes-Dessus
Clos Micot
The Growers
    Comte Armand
    Domaine du Clos des Epeneaux
    Billard-Gonnet
    Jean-Marc Boillot
    Coste-Caumartin
    De Courcel
    Cyrot-Buthiau
    Jean Garaudet
    Michel Gaunoux
    A.F. Gros
    Jean-Luc Joillot
    Lahaye Père et Fils
    Raymond Launay
    Lejeune
    Moissenet-Bonnard
    François Parent
    Parent
    Château de Pommard
    Daniel Rebourgeon-Mure
    Aleth le Royer-Girardin

VOLNAY / 223
History
Location
The Vineyard
The Premiers Crus
    Clos des Chênes
    Taille Pieds
    Clos de l'Audignac
    En Verseuil
    Clos de la Bousse d'Or
    Clos du Château des Ducs
    Clos de la Cave des Ducs
    La Barre
    Clos des Ducs
    Les Pitures-Dessus
    Les Chanlins
    Les Frémiets
    Les Angles
    Pointes d'Angles
    Les Brouillards
    Les Mitans

Les Grands Champs
En l'Ormeau
La Gigotte
Carelle sous la Chappelle
Les Carelles-Dessous
Champans
Le Ronceret
Les Aussy
Les Lurets
Robardelle
Les Caillerets
En Chevret
Santenots
The Growers
    Marquis d'Angerville
    Bitouzet-Prieur
    Jean Boillot
    Jean-Marc Bouley
    Réyane and Pascal Bouley
    Yvon Clerget
    Michel Lafarge
    Hubert de Montille
    Les Deux Montilles
    Vincent Perrin
    Pousse d'Or
    Roblet-Monnot
    Régis Rossignol-Changarnier
    Nicolas Rossignol
    Rossignol-Jeanniard
    Cécile Tremblay
    Joseph Voillot

MONTHELIE / 231
History
Location
The Vineyard
The Premiers Crus
    Les Champs Fulliot
    Sur la Velle
    Les Vignes Rondes
    Le Meix Bataille
    Le Cas Rougeot
    La Taupine
    Le Clos Gauthey
    Les Riottes
    Le Château Gaillard
    Les Duresses

Bernard Bachelet et ses Fils
Maurice Charleux
Fernand Chevrot
Yvon and Chantal Contat-Grange

Edmond Monnot
Claude Nouveau
Christian Perrault et Fils
Jean-Claude Regnaudot et Fils

CÔTES-DE-BEAUNE VILLAGES

Unlike the Côte-de-Nuits-Villages, the Côte-de-Beaune Villages is not a *terroir*-specific appellation. The Nuits wines come from either the Fixin/Brochon area or from Prémeaux-Prissey, Comblanchien and Corgoloin. Production is in small quantities, and the source is simply the vineyards which are marginally beyond the pale.

Côte-de-Beaune Villages can come from any one, or a combination, of fifteen *communes* and appellations from Ladoix to Maranges. These are Auxey-Duresses, Blagny, Chassagne-Montrachet, Chorey-lès-Beaune, Côtede Beaune, Ladoix, Meursault, Monthelie, Pernand-Vergelesses, Puligny-Montrachet, Saint-Aubin, Saint-Romain, Santenay, Savigny-lès-Beaune and Maranges (i.e., all the *communes* except Aloxe-Corton, Beaune, Pommard and Volnay).

While domaine-bottling growers use the appellation mainly for the production of young vines and other lesser *cuvées* they deem not worthy of the village name (nor the price), *négociants* may buy up wine sold under the village names and then make up their own blends.

The declarations are confusing. Statistics from the Bureau Interprofessionnel des Vins de Bourgogne (BIVB) give a very small figure for the production of Côte-de-Beaune Villages. Looking at the figures produced by the Union Générale des Syndicats (UGS), one can see that this figure corresponds to already amalgamated wine (i.e., where a grower has vinified the produce of two villages together). In the UGS statistics, one also notices that Chorey, for example, has two declarations: one as Chorey-lès-Beaune, the other as Chorey, Côte de Beaune. If we take this latter figure as that which will be bottled as Côte-de-Beaune Villages, we can add up a figure of about 260 hectares of vines and a production of 11,600 hectolitres under this appella-

tion, which includes red wines only. But this figure does not include any contribution from Maranges, which is in the Saône-et-Loire *département* and not included, infuriatingly, in the UGS statistics. Maranges produces a lot of wine bottled as Côte-de-Beaune Villages. The other main villages producing these wines, in order of size of provision, are Chorey-lès-Beaune, Auxey-Duresses, Chassagne-Montrachet, Saint-Romain, Ladoix, Saint-Aubin and Pernand-Vergelesses. The remainder only produce token amounts of Côte-de-Beaune Villages.

The wine—it can only be red—itself is soft, plump and fruity—an unpretentious Pinot Noir for early drinking that fills the gap between Bourgogne Rouge and Hautes-Côtes and the cheapest of the village wines.

CORTON AND THE WINES OF LADOIX, ALOXE-CORTON AND PERNAND-VERGELESSES

The Côte de Beaune begins, if not with a bang, then with a splendid isolated mound, the hill of Corton. This is an egg-shaped escarpment—the egg lying on its flatter side—and on top of it, perched like a toupee, is the Forêt de Corton, owned by Prince Florent de Mérode, *seigneur* of nearby Serrigny. Vines flow down on all suitable sides of this hill, from above Ladoix, facing almost as much north as east, via Aloxe, to above Pernand, facing as much west as south. All this is *grand cru*: the biggest in Burgundy, representing over one third of the total *grand cru* surface area.

Not all of the land, arguably, is of true *grand cru* potential. Certainly, not all the wine produced from it is of *grand cru* standard. But the vines are shared between these three *communes*. So it is logical to include them in a single chapter. And it is equally logical to deal with the *grand cru* first.

CORTON AND CORTON-CHARLEMAGNE

In total, there are some 160.19 hectares of *grand cru* land on the slopes of the Corton hill. Split between the three villages, this represents 22.43 hectares in Ladoix, 120.51 in Aloxe-Corton and 17.26 in Pernand-Vergelesses. Out of the 160.19 hectares, 71.88 *can* produce Corton-Charlemagne: this includes all the Pernand land, 48.57 hectares in Aloxe-Corton, and 6.05 hectares in Ladoix. I say *can*. The growers have the option in the Corton-Charlemagne appellation to plant either Pinot Noir or Chardonnay. And to complicate matters further, they also have the right—though few exercise it—to plant Chardonnay elsewhere on the hill and to produce Corton *blanc* from it. There is, as Hugh Johnson puts it, a slight Alice in Wonderland air about the legislation on the Corton hill.

If you look at a map, you will see that the area marked Corton-Charlemagne is that facing southwest toward the village of Pernand-Vergelesses and across the valley toward Savigny. The red wine area seems to be that overhanging Ladoix and Aloxe-Corton. In reality, some red wine is produced in the lower slopes of the Charlemagne vineyard, whereas white wine—Corton-Charlemagne—is produced all the way around the hill, albeit at the top of the slope.

As a further complexity, the hill is divided into a number of *climats*, which will appear prefixed by Corton on the labels: Corton, Clos du Roi; Corton, Les Bressandes and so on. Le Corton is a *lieu-dit* in its own right. But Corton *tout court* is a mixture of several different *lieux-dits*. And I must also mention the brand of Maison Latour here, a major proprietor in the area: Château Corton-Grancey.

History

Charlemagne, Charles the First and Great, as was befitting of an individual who was Holy Roman Emperor and effectively the ruler of the western civilised world, was a giant of a man.

He towered over his subjects, dominating them as much physically as by the force of his personality. One of his many domaines, and the one producing one of his favourite wines was at Corton—itself named, one interpretation suggests, after an obscure first century Roman emperor named Orthon: Curtis (domaines) d'Orthon—became contracted to Corton. As with certain vineyards in Germany, the story is related that Charlemagne, noticing that the snows always melted first on this particular slope, ordered vines to be planted there, and lo, these produced excellent wine.

At the time the wine was red, but, as Charlemagne grew older and his beard whiter, his wife Luitgarde, ever watchful over the dignity of her spouse, objected to the majesty of her emperor being degraded by red wine stains on his beard and suggested that he switch to consuming white wine. It was commanded that white grapes be planted on a section of the hill: Corton-Charlemagne was born, and it continues still.

According to the Burgundian historian Camille Rodier, that part of the *vignoble* donated by Charlemagne to the *Collégiale* of Saulieu in AD 775 corresponds exactly to the current domaine of the Bonneau du Martray family, owners of one of the largest domaines and one of the best sections of the hill. Other later owners included Modoin, Bishop of Autun, who donated his Corton vines to the cathedral there in AD 858; the Abbots of Cîteaux; the Knights Templar; the Dukes of Burgundy; Charlotte Dumay, who left her land to the Hospices de Beaune in 1534; and the kings of France, whose tenure 400 years ago is still commemorated in the *climat* Corton, Clos du Roi.

The earliest extant document referring to Corton-Charlemagne dates from 1375 and refers to a lease of the "Clos le Charlemagne" by the Chapitre de Saint-Androche-de-Saulieu to a local farmer. A century later, the abbot tried to wriggle out of this contract. In 1620 the lessee was a M. Esmonin. Again, 10 years later, the clergy attempted to have the agreement revoked. In 1791, following the revolution, the land was sold as a *bien national* and valued at 10,800 *livres*.

Legend aside, white wine production from the Chardonnay grape on the hill of Corton is a recent development. André Jullien, in his *Topographie de Tous les Vignobles Connus*, 1824, makes no mention of white Corton. Le Corton is one of his *vins rouges de première classe*, and the reds from Pougets, Charlemagne and Les Bressantes [*sic*] are among those of the *troisième classe*. There is no note of white Aloxe or Pernand at all.

By mid-century, however, Chardonnay had arrived. Dr. Lavalle in his *Histoire et Statistique de la Vigne et Des Grands Vins de la Côte d'Or*, published in 1855, speaks of Pinot Noir on the mid-slope and lower lying ground and what he terms Pinot Blanc on the upper parts. In the 16-hectare section of Corton-Charlemagne lying in the *commune* of Aloxe, MM. Gouveau, De Grancey, Chantrier, Jules Paulet and the Hospices de Beaune are listed as the main proprietors, while in the 19 hectares of land across the border in Pernand, only MM. Bonneau-Véry (now the Bonneau de Martray family) is worthy of note. "*On ne recolte presque que des vins blancs dans ce climat*," he states.

By the end of the century, the owners included Louis Latour, who had acquired the Grancey domaine, and Jules Senard—two families which are still important proprietors in the area. Twenty years later, Camille Rodier brought out the first edition of his classic *Le Vin de Bourgogne*. In the 1948 edition, he writes of the Chardonnay grape being planted more and more widely "over the previous 30 years," in what was by that time formally the appellation of Corton-Charlemagne. (This is a repeat of what he noted in the first edition.) This grape, he wrote, gives white wines a fine golden colour and full flavour, this flavour combining cinnamon and gunflint.

The Aloxe facing slopes, like the Charlemagne side of the hill, were also largely in ecclesiastical hands in the Middle Ages. The monks of the Abbey of Sainte-Marguerite, up in the neighbouring valley of the river Rhoin near Bouilland, were some of the first to exploit the vinous possibilities of the *climat*, having received a donation of land in 1164. The Cistercians were soon to follow, as were the Templars, just as they were on the other side of the hill.

From the beginning of the seventeenth century onward, as the power of the church waned, the land on Corton hill was progressively annexed by the local bourgeoisie, who either bought it outright, or took a simple cash lease rather than a more uncomfortable *métayage* arrangement. During the reign of Louis XV, a number of important acquisitions were made. Two Dijon gentlemen, M. de Vergnette-Lamotte and M. Le Bault, bought a sizeable amount of land from the Abbey at Cîteaux; M. Larbalestier, another local, became proprietor of the vineyards of the Abbey of Sainte-Marguerite; and the brothers Thiroux of Beaune took over the famous *climat* of Clos du Roi. Another arrival was M. du Tillet, squire of the village of Serrigny (as well as Aloxe and Pernand). Le Bault was further to increase his domaine; his wife Jacqueline, as vivacious and intelligent as she was beautiful (there is a fine portrait dating from 1755 by Greuze), was in her own right heiress of 500 *ouvrées* (nearly 21 hectares) in Aloxe. It was the Bault family that constructed Corton-Grancey.

It was through Madame la Belle, as he addressed Jacqueline le Bault, that Voltaire acquired a taste for Corton (and it is to him that we owe our gratitude for his having commissioned the Greuze portrait). Voltaire was an admirer, but Madame was not to be tempted. The one-sided passion was to continue for many years, during which many dozens of bottles of Bault Corton were despatched to Geneva or Ferney or wherever it was that Voltaire was nursing his frustration at the time. Incidentally, the orders were for both red and white wine, in equal quantities. Sadly, however, Voltaire, great man of many talents, was not a real wine lover. He was knowledgeable about wine, as you would expect a man of his catholicity of interests to be, but the nuances of connoisseurship passed him by. To him, wine was merely a beverage.

The French Revolution caused its upsets in Corton as much as elsewhere. Much of the vineyard was declared *biens nationaux*. Other land changed hands as the fortunes of the *ancien régime* families withered, and a newly rich bourgeoisie emerged. It is interesting to note that an *ouvrée* of Clos du Roi was worth half as much again as an *ouvrée* of Corton-Charlemagne. But as the Charlemagne was largely planted in Gamay at that time, one wonders why the premium was not higher.

As we move further into the nineteenth century, a number of familiar names come into the picture. The ubiquitous Jules Ouvrard, proprietor of Clos de Vougeot, the Domaine de la Romanée-Conti and the Domaine de la Pousse d'Or, reconstituted the Clos du Roi, already divided. From the Granceys, Jean Latour bought the château which had formerly belonged to the Baults. The Geisweiler family bought vineyards in Le Corton, Les Renardes and Les Languettes. Other important landowners included August Dubois, mayor of Dijon, and the poet and gentleman of letters Simon Gauthey.

Dr. Lavalle, previously mentioned, divided the red wines into four categories. The *têtes de cuvées* are Le Corton, Clos du Roi, Les Renardes and Les Chaumes (with, he noted, the upper part of Le Corton producing delicious white wine); the *premiers crus* include most of what is now the rest of the *grand cru rouge* vineyard: Les Bressandes, Les Perrières, Les Fiètres, Les Languettes, Les Pougets, Le Meix and La Vigne au Saint. Aloxe wines, he writes, are the firmest and most definitive of all the wines of the Côte de Beaune, and those of Corton itself possess these characteristics to the greatest degree.

When the commission that was to become the INAO delimited the territories of Aloxe, Ladoix and Pernand in 1936, they broadly followed the classification of Dr. Lavalle, adding part of Les Maréchaudes, Les Paulands, Les Vergennes and Le Rognet, on the Ladoix side, and other parcels below the road that runs from Aloxe to Pernand to the *grand cru*. The result is that Aloxe today possesses the least amount of *premier cru* vineyard of all the main Burgundy *communes*. Today there are, as I have said, across the three villages, a total of 160 hectares of land which can produce either Corton or Corton-Charlemagne.

As I have also said, this is too much. The red wines produced on the Pernand side of the hill; those whose origins come from underneath the road that runs round from Aloxe to Pernand (such as La Vigne au Saint and Clos de Meix); and much of what lies in the *commune* of Ladoix and on the lower slopes above the N74 do not produce *grand cru* quality wine. I would like to see all these downgraded to *premier cru*. I also find such Corton Blancs as I encounter similarly not up to the standard of Charlemagne. Again, I would consider *premier cru* a more appropriate designation. It will never happen, of course. But we can live in hope.

The Soil and the Wine

The Chardonnay is planted on the upper slopes in a whiteish coloured marl with a high clay content on a hard limestone rock base—Oxfordian rather than the older Bathonian or Bajocian in the Côte de Nuits. Further down the slope, there is more iron and pebbles but less clay in the soil, and the colour is redder. Here the Pinot produces the better wine, particularly on the more easterly facing slopes above Aloxe and Ladoix. Today, however, growers in Le Corton and elsewhere can get a better price for white wine than for red, and a switch of colour can be noticed. I remember Jean-Marc Voarick once telling me that the next time they come to replace their vines in the Languettes *climat* he would change to Chardonnay rather than continue to grow Pinot.

On the Pernand side of the hill, the soil is flinty, and the white wine will have more austerity and be steelier than that coming from above Aloxe. The whites from Aloxe *climats* are softer and more *flatteur* in their youth, and they develop faster.

This is particularly noticeable in hot vintages producing lush wines, such as 1999. After a few years in bottle, many of the Charlemagnes produced on the Aloxe-Corton side were already drying out, being high in alcohol and low in acidity. Those from the Pernand side, notably that of Domaine Bonneau du Martray, were still fresh and crisp.

The reverse, of course, is true with red wine. Pinots Noirs on the Pernand side just do not get enough sun for long enough in the day—except in exceptional vintages—to get beyond ripeness to real concentration. Those above Aloxe-Corton with the classical aspect and 270–300 metres of altitude, in the middle of the slope, will provide the most perfect examples of red Corton. Clos du Roi is generally considered the best, followed in no particular order by Les Bressandes, Le Corton, Les Perrières, Les Pougets, Les Grèves and Les Renardes.

There are large numbers of separate Corton *lieux-dits*. Those most commonly declared separately are Les Bressandes (the largest), Les Carrières, Les Chaumes, Clos-de-la-Vigne-au-Saint (*monopole* of the Domaine Latour), Clos des Meix (*monopole* of the Domaine du Comte Senard), Clos-des-Cortons-Faiveley (*monopole* of the Domaine Faiveley), Le Clos du Roi, Les Combes, Le Corton, Les Grandes Lolières, Les Grèves, Les Hautes Mourottes, Les Basses Mourottes, Les Languettes, Les Maréchaudes, Les Perrières, Les Pougets, Le Rognet et Corton and Les Vergennes.

Principal Proprietors

CORTON-CHARLEMAGNE: Louis Latour (9.64 ha); ★ Bonneau du Martray (9.50 ha); ★ Bouchard Père et Fils (3.25 ha); ★ Roland Rapet (2.50 ha); Maratray-Dubreuil (1.62 ha); ★ Louis Jadot (1.60 ha); Michel Voarick (1.66 ha); Robert and Raymond Jacob

Corton and Corton-Charlemagne

Surface Area (2005)	160.10 ha
Average Production	
Rouge	3,530 hl
Blanc	2,075 hl
2005 Declaration	
Corton Rouge	93.90 ha
Corton Blanc	3.70 ha
Corton-Charlemagne	51.20 ha

(1.26 ha); Maurice Chapuis (1.20 ha); Michel Mallard (1.20 ha); ★ Pavillon/Bichot (1.20 ha); Dufouleur (1.09 ha); ★ Domaine d'Ardhuy (1.04 ha); Marius Delarche (1.00 ha); Roux Père et Fils (1.00 ha); Vincent Sauvestre (1.00 ha); Pierre Marey et Fils (1.00 ha); ★ Michel Juillot (0.80 ha); Hospices de Beaune (0.70 ha), see below; Doudet-Naudin (0.70 ha); Pierre Dubreuil-Fontaine (0.70 ha); Follin-Arbelet (0.70 ha); ★ Chanson (0.65 ha, Vergennes); ★ Joseph Faiveley (0.62 ha); ★ Simon Bize (0.60 ha); Régis Pavelot (0.60 ha); Nudant (0.60 ha); Pierre and Françoise Lassagne (0.59 ha); Hippolyte Thévenot/ Antonin Guyon (0.55 ha); Dublaire (0.50 ha).

Growers with less than half a hectare whose wines can be recommended include De Montille (currently young vines) (0.45 ha); Leroy (0.43 ha); Rollin Père et Fils (0.42 ha); Capitain-Gagnerot (0.41 ha); Chandon de Briailles (0.39 ha); Jean-Claude Belland (0.36 ha); Bruno Clair (0.34 ha); Joseph Drouhin (0.34 ha); Jean-François Coche-Dury (0.34 ha); Champy (0.33 ha); Jean-Pierre Maldant (0.33 ha); Vincent Girardin (0.30 ha); Genot-Boulanger (0.29 ha); Laleure-Piot (0.28 ha); Bertagna (0.25 ha); Tollot-Beaut (0.24 ha); Jaffelin Père et Fils (0.23 ha); Denis Père et Fils (0.22 ha); Jacques Prieur (0.22 ha); Vougeraie (0.22 ha); Bertrand Ambroise (0.20 ha); Christophe Roumier (0.20 ha); Patrick Javillier (0.17 ha).

The Hospices de Beaune possess 0.38 hectares (*Cuvée* Françoise de Salins) as well as 0.32 hectares of Chardonnay planted in Corton-Vergennes (Corton *blanc Cuvée* Paul Chanson).

CORTON ROUGE: Louis Latour (15.09 ha); Hospices de Beaune (6.40 ha), see below; ★ D'Ardhuy (4.74 ha); ★ Comte Senard (3.95 ha); ★ Prince Florent de Mérode (3.80 ha); ★ Bouchard Père et Fils (3.54 ha); Vincent Sauvestre (3.35 ha); ★ Joseph Faiveley (3.02 ha); Maurice Chapuis (2.80 ha); Baron Thénard (sold by ★ Remoissenet Père et Fils) (2.68 ha); ★ Chandon de Briailles (2.57 ha); Capitain-Gagnerot (2.14 ha); ★ Louis Jadot (2.10 ha); Pousse d'Or (2.03 ha); Hippolyte Thévenot/Antonin Guyon (1.96 ha); Pierre Dubreuil-Fontaine (1.82 ha); ★ Jean-Claude Belland (1.73 ha); Marius Delarche (1.70 ha); Maillard Père et Fils (1.70 ha); Tollot-Beaut (1.51 ha); Cachat-Ocquidant (1.42 ha); ★ De Montille

(1.39 ha); Chevalier Père et Fils (1.30 ha); Roland Rapet (1.25 ha); Michel Gaunoux (1.23 ha); Didier Meuneveaux (1.23 ha); Michel Voarick (1.00 ha); ★ Michel Juillot (1.20 ha); Gaston and Pierre Ravaut (1.00 ha); Baron Thénard (0.90 ha); Doudet-Naudin (0.80 ha); Jean-Pierre Maldant (0.73 ha); Jacques Prieur (0.73 ha); Bruno Colin (0.71 ha); Parent (0.58 ha); Edmond Cornu (0.56 ha); ★ Pavillon/Bichot (0.55 ha); Laleure-Piot (0.53 ha); Bertrand Ambroise (0.50 ha); Denis Père et Fils (0.50 ha); ★ Leroy (0.50 ha); Pierre Marey et Fils (0.50 ha); ★ Vougeraie (0.50 ha).

Growers with less than half a hectare whose wines can be recommended include the following: Genot-Boulanger (0.47 ha); Méo-Camuzet (0.45 ha); Taupenot-Merme (0.43 ha); Follin-Arbelet (0.40 ha); Maratray-Dubreuil (0.40 ha); Régis Pavelot (0.40 ha); Mestre (0.37 ha); Vergelesses (0.35 ha); Bruno Clavelier (0.34 ha); Arnoux Père et Fils (0.33 ha); Champy (0.33 ha); Dupont-Tisserandot (0.33 ha); Lahaye (0.30 ha); Bertagna (0.25 ha); Dom. de la Croix (0.25 ha); Joseph Drouhin (0.25 ha); François Gay (0.21 ha); Michel Gay (0.20 ha); Philippe Bouzereau (0.15 ha); Nudant (0.11 ha).

The Hospices de Beaune offer the following Corton *rouge cuvées*: Charlotte Dumay (3.40 ha, Les Renardes, Les Bressandes, Clos du Roi) and Dr. Peste (3 ha, Les Bressandes, Les Chaumes, Les Voierosses, Clos du Roi, Les Fiètres, Les Grèves).

Corton-Charlemagne is quite a different wine from the *grands crus* of Puligny and Chassagne. There should be a steely backbone, a raciness, which fleetingly suggests a *grand cru* Chablis. There will probably be a higher acidity. There should certainly be a certain austerity and a need for long aging, as much as a decade, before the wine comes around. This will not be because it has the pent-up, concentrated intensity of a Montrachet—it won't quite have that—but because it is a wine of sufficient size, depth and structure to require sufficient time to round off. However, like red Corton, sadly there are more indifferent producers than exciting ones.

The quality of the vintages, too, does not necessarily follow that of the south. The weather pattern may not always be similar, and this will affect both the state of the fruit and the date it will arrive at maximum fruition. Corton-Charlemagne successes follow as much the successful vintages in red Corton and red wines generally as they do the best years for Meursault, Puligny and Chassagne.

As for the red wines, what is the essential character of a Corton *rouge*? Firstly, it is the biggest red wine of the Côte de Beaune. This is not so much a factor of its girth or its tannins—Pommards can make as large an impression—but of its depth, its grip and its necessity to be aged before it is ready. Red Cortons need time to round off and naturally they last well in bottle. When they are young, there is an austerity, almost a hard edge, to a red Corton; the fruit has a herbaceous, leafy aspect to it. You have to wait to get the generosity.

And Corton, in the main, is only a second-division *grand cru* for red wines. Often it is a bit lean. Only the vines from the heart of the appellation, from Clos du Roi and a few of the accompanying *climats*, can aspire to greatness. Only these seem to have the fat underneath the structure which will give rise when fully mature to that magic natural sweetness we look forward to on the finish of a great Burgundy.

LADOIX

Ladoix-Côte de Beaune, it says on the label, as if it might be confused with other Ladoix elsewhere—after all there are several Pouillys—but also because this is one of a number of lesser Côte de Beaune villages which have the option of also selling their wine under the label of Côte-de-Beaune Villages.

Ladoix is the first Côte de Beaune *commune* one reaches as one drives south toward Beaune from Nuits-Saint-Georges. The vineyards begin north of the village up and behind the hamlet of Buisson. There is a road here where you can drive up the valley toward Magny-les-Villers in the Hautes-Côtes. The appellation ends in the middle of the village of Ladoix. One step more and you are technically in the *commune* of Aloxe-Corton. There are even Aloxe-Corton *premiers crus* in the *commune* of Ladoix.

Much of the *vignoble*, then, is the continuation of the hill of Corton, as it turns around almost toward the north. The village wines lie in less well-exposed slopes, lower down on the flatter land, and along the road toward the border with the Côte de Nuits. There is a sprinkling of *premiers crus* on either side of the road to Magny. In 2002 the *premier cru* land was increased by 10 hectares.

It is this road, rather than the artificial line on the map a few hundred metres to the north, which really marks the difference between the Côtes of Nuits and Beaune, for it is here that the geology changes. North is Comblanchien limestone, and south a younger Jurassic rock; Bathonian gives way to the softer, more marly Oxfordian, and the wine, as a result, changes too.

The village itself is jolly and bustling and seems to consist almost entirely of houses which give onto the main road or onto a perpendicular road from the adjoining hamlet of Serrigny. There are a number of good growers, most of them remarkably welcoming. And prices for Ladoix *rouge* and *blanc* (the appellation covers both) are cheap. This is not a village the snobs and label hunters are likely to stop at. The wines are soft and plump, and if only they could be a bit more dependable and a bit less rustic, they would present excellent value for the money. But the locals are making progress all the time.

The Vineyard

PREMIERS CRUS   There are eleven *premiers crus*, in whole or in part. On the northern side, we have Les Buis; Le Clou d'Orge (part); La Corvée (part); and La Micaude. On the Corton side lie Les Hautes Mourottes (part) and Les Basses Mourottes (both of which are also the extension of *grand cru* Corton); Bois Roussot (part); Les Gréchons (part); Les Joyeuses (part); En Naget; and Le Rognet. In total these cover 22.75 hectares. In 2005, 736 hectolitres of red wine and 355 hectolitres of white wine were produced.
VILLAGE WINE   There are 74 hectares of village land under vine. They produce 3,600 hectolitres of wine per year. Much of this is sold as Côte-de-Beaune Villages. In 2005, 3,064 hectolitres of red wine were declared as Ladoix *rouge*, and 550 hectolitres as Ladoix *blanc*.

The Premiers Crus

LES BUIS (red wine only)	*(0.99 ha)*
LE CLOU D'ORGE	*(1.58 ha)*
LA CORVÉE OR LES CORVÉES	*(7.14 ha)*
(*monopole* of the Domaine Capitain-Gagnerot)	
LA MICAUDE	*(1.64 ha)*

The wines from the northern *premiers crus* of Ladoix come from halfway up the slope (240–250 m), are oriented almost due south on a gentle incline and have Comblanchien limestone as their base rock. There is a nice sturdy masculinity about these wines, and usually a better colour and grip than that of those from the hills opposite. But they can be less elegant.

RECOMMENDED SOURCES
LA CORVÉE
Chevalier Père et Fils, Edmond Cornu, André and Jean-Pierre Nudant (Ladoix).

LA MICAUDE (*monopole*)
Capitain-Gagnerot (Ladoix).

LES BASSES-MOUROTTES	*(1.05 ha)*
LE BOIS-ROUSSOT	*(2.45 ha)*
LES GRÉCHONS (white only)	*(4.15 ha)*
LES HAUTES-MOUROTTES	*(0.83 ha)*
LES JOYEUSES	*(0.76 ha)*
EN NAGET (white only)	*(0.54 ha)*
LE ROGNET (white only)	*(0.80 ha)*

These are lighter, softer wines, with red fruit flavours, such as cherry and red currant, rather than black (*cassis*, blackberry). They mature quicker. They can be a bit thin and rustic.

RECOMMENDED SOURCE
LES GRÉCHONS
Chevalier Père et Fils.

Ladoix Leading Domaines

Cachat-Ocquidant et Fils
10.5 ha owned and *en fermage/métayage*.
Corton, Clos de Vergennes (*monopole*) (1.42 ha);

Aloxe-Corton *premier cru* Les Maréchaudes; village Ladoix, including the *lieu-dit* Les Madonnes, Vieilles Vignes; village Aloxe-Corton; village Pernand-Vergelesses.

Jean-Marc Cachat and his son David are in charge here. The domaine has machine harvested since 1994. There is plenty of new oak, and no old wood, which is just as important. These wines are of quite good quality.

Capitain-Gagnerot et Fils

16 ha owned. Corton (1.81 ha); Echézeaux (0.31 ha); Corton, Les Renardes (0.33 ha); Corton-Charlemagne (0.41 ha); Clos-de-Vougeot (0.17 ha); Aloxe-Corton *premier cru* Les Moutottes; Savigny-lès-Beaune *premier cru* Les Charnières (part of Les Lavières); Ladoix *premier cru rouge* La Micaude (*monopole*) and Le Bois-Roussot; Ladoix *premier cru blanc* Les Gréchons and Les Hautes Mourottes; village Ladoix *rouge*; village Ladoix *blanc*; village Aloxe-Corton; village Pernand-Vergelesses.

The attractive Capitain mansion is set back from the main road through Ladoix, an island in a sea of vines. Beyond is the winery. The Capitains, Patrice and Michel, now in their fifties, offer a wide range of wines, and the standard is generally good. "*Rien de grand ne se fait sans passion*" (nothing great is produced without passion) is a family motto. A family tree in the foyer traces the Capitains back to the seventeenth century. There is total de-stemming, a *cuvaison* for 12 to 14 days at 25–28°C (maximum 30°C) and 12.5 percent new wood, but there are no barrels of over 5 years old.

Chevalier Père et Fils

12 ha owned and *en fermage*. Corton, Le Rognet (1.15 ha); Corton-Charlemagne (0.50 ha); Ladoix *premier cru rouge* in Le Clou d'Orge and Les Corvées and *blanc* in Les Gréchons; village Ladoix *blanc*; village Ladoix *rouge*; village Aloxe-Corton; Côte-de-Nuits-Villages.

Claude Chevalier, tall, handsome and in his fifties now, is in charge here; father Georges, who first started bottling in 1959, retired some 10 years ago. Since 2000 there have been a

number of changes for the better here. Yields have been reduced, and the wines are altogether more sophisticated. This is one of the best addresses in the village.

Edmond Cornu et Fils

12.5 ha owned and *en fermage*. Corton, Les Bressandes (0.56 ha); Aloxe-Corton *premier cru* Les Moutottes; Ladoix *premier cru* La Corvée; village Aloxe-Corton; village Savigny-lès-Beaune; village Ladoix, including the *lieu-dit* Les Carrières; village Chorey-lès-Beaune *rouge et blanc*.

The genial, hospitable Edmond Cornu is now retired, and responsibility lies with his son Pierre. The fruit is de-stemmed, there is a 4-day cold-soaking, fermentation takes place at a maximum of 32°C, and there is 10 percent new oak. All this takes place in an air-conditioned *cuverie*. Quality has improved a great deal here in the last decade. The wines are now very good.

Robert and Raymond Jacob

10 ha owned. Corton, Les Carrières (0.24 ha); Corton-Charlemagne (from the Hautes-Mourottes (1.26 ha); Aloxe-Corton *premier cru* Les Valozières; village Aloxe-Corton; village Ladoix *rouge et blanc*.

The Jacob brothers (Raymond is the one with the moustache), no close relation to those in Echevronne, run this estate out of a splendidly large cellar, extended in 1990, in the hamlet of Buisson. The wines, of which the best receive one third new wood, are supple, fruity and for the medium term.

Jean-Pierre Maldant

7.06 ha owned and *en fermage*. Corton (0.73 ha) in Les Grandes Lolières and Les Maréchaudes; Corton-Charlemagne (0.33 ha); Aloxe-Corton *premier cru* in Les Maréchaudes and Les Valozières; Savigny-lès-Beaune *premier cru* in Les Peuillets and Les Fourneaux; village Aloxe-Corton; village Savigny-lès-Beaune; village Ladoix, including the *lieu-dit* Les Chaillots; village Chorey-Lès Beaune *rouge et blanc*.

I first encountered M. Maldant's wines when I scored his Corton-Charlemagne 1985 well at a blind tasting arranged by Claude Chapuis when he was writing his book. I then went to taste *sur place* and found a charming man in his fifties in a small cellar bang in the middle of Ladoix. He vinifies with 30 percent of the stems for his Cortons, but none for the rest, lets the temperature rise as high as 35°C, and uses 10 percent new wood. I like the man. I like his wines.

Michel Mallard et Fils

14 ha owned and *en fermage*. Corton, Les Renardes (0.65 ha); Corton, Les Maréchaudes (0.35 ha); Corton in Le Rognet and Les Lolières (0.30 ha); Ladoix *premier cru* Les Joyeuses; Savigny-lès-Beaune *premier cru* Les Serpentières; Aloxe-Corton *premier cru* in Les Valozières, La Toppe au Vert and Les Petites Lolières; village Ladoix; village Aloxe-Corton; Côte-de-Nuits villages.

Eight years ago, the opinionated Patrick Mallard was not a fan of new wood. Since then, he has constructed a new winery, and a lot has changed here. The harvest is mechanical, after which the fruit is sorted through. This is followed by quite a long (8 days) cold-soaking. There is a long maceration with temperatures raised at the end to 42°C. The wine is matured in 100 percent new oak with a high toast. These are good wines, but not to my taste.

Maratray-Dubreuil

16 ha owned and *en fermage*. Corton, Les Bressandes (0.80 ha); Corton, Les Grandes Lolières (0.42 ha); Corton-Charlemagne (0.40 ha); Corton, Le Clos du Roi (0.40 ha); Ladoix *premier cru blanc* Les Gréchons; Ladoix *rouge* Les Nagets; village Aloxe-Corton; village Ladoix *rouge et blanc*; village Chorey-lès-Beaune.

Next to Jean-Marc Cachat, you will find Marie-Madelaine Maratray and her brother François, both in their thirties. Their mother was *née* Dubreuil-Fontaine of Pernand-Vergelesses. In the yard behind their house is a big modern *chai* with a cellar underneath. Eight percent of the stems are retained, the red wine is fermented at 28–30°C and 10 percent new wood is used. There is good quality here. Again, there has been an improvement in the last decade.

★ *Prince Florent de Mérode*

6 ha owned. Corton, Les Maréchaudes (1.53 ha); Corton, Les Bressandes (1.19 ha); Corton, Clos du Roi (0.57 ha); Corton, Les Renardes (0.51 ha); Aloxe-Corton *premier cru* Les Maréchaudes; village Pommard in the *lieu-dit* Clos de la Platière; village Ladoix *rouge* in the *lieu-dit* Les Chaillots.

Prince Florent de Mérode lives in the Château de Serrigny, a splendid moated castle, in part dating from the Middle Ages. His family has been here since 1700, and his wife is a member of the Luc-Saluces family of Château d'Yquem.

Quality has risen significantly in recent years. Proper temperature control was installed in 2002. Today, the grapes are totally de-stemmed, having been picked over to discard the unripe, rotten and bruised on a *table de tri*. There is a new winemaker, Didier Dubois (his first vintage was 2001), 8 days cold-soaking, 25 to 35 percent new oak, no filtration and bottling by gravity. The wines are now made in a spacious *chai*, converted out of old stables and cowsheds, with an impressive cellar at the end, opposite the Château de Serrigny. More importantly, I feel, the vines are cropped to a lower *rendement*. The Prince de Mérode's wines are well coloured, rich, concentrated, individual and stylish. This is one of the best sources today for a range of quality Corton.

Nudant

17.45 ha owned and *en fermage*. Echézeaux (0.66 ha); Corton, Les Bressandes (0.61 ha); Corton-Charlemagne (0.18 ha); Aloxe-Corton *premier cru* La Coutière; Ladoix *premier cru* in La Corvée and Les Buis; Nuits-Saint-Georges *premier cru* Les Boudots; Ladoix *premier cru blanc* Les Gréchons; village Aloxe-Corton in the *lieu-dit* Les Valozières; village Chorey-lès-Beaune; village Savigny-lès-Beaune; village Ladoix *rouge*; village Nuits-Saint-Georges; village Vosne-Romanée.

In 2005 this estate took over that of Jean-Pierre Mugneret of Concour, part of which they had been share-cropping since 2002. The Nudant premises, now run by Jean-René and his son Guillaume, are on the main road at the north end of the village. The Nudants prefer to machine harvest. It gives them a more precise choice over when to harvest. There are no stems, fermentation temperatures for the red wines are at 30–32°C, and 10 to 20 percent new oak is the rule here. The wines are good. The domaine also produces a single vineyard Bourgogne Rouge, La Chapelle-Notre-Dame, which comes from a 35-year-old vineyard around the exquisite Romanesque chapel which lies under Valozières on the Aloxe side of the village. There is very good quality here.

ALOXE-CORTON

The sleepy little village of Aloxe (pronounced like the fish: Alose, with a z) lies halfway up the hill away from the main road. It possesses neither bar nor village shop. Its inhabitants must make the 6-kilometre journey to Beaune for sustenance or conviviality. What it does have are some of the oldest cellars in Burgundy, dating from monastic times, and several fine buildings decorated with the typically Burgundian tiled roofs in different colours.

The remit of Aloxe's vineyards greedily stretches more than halfway around the hill toward Pernand-Vergelesses, and way back up and behind the village of Ladoix into territory which would much more logically be the fief of that *commune*, giving it the lion's share of the *grand cru* of Corton and the *premier cru* vineyards which lie beneath it. Aloxe-Corton can be red or white, but the proportion of white produced today is insignificant.

Aloxe-Corton, not just because it has adopted the suffix of the famous *grand cru*, is a better-known and rather more expensive wine that Pernand-Vergelesses and Ladoix. The vineyards are in general more favourably placed, oriented toward the south and southeast. The basic limestone is softer here than further north, decomposing into a flaky rock known as *lave*. On top of this, in the *premier cru* vineyards, the soil is quite deep, red in colour and rich in iron. There is a high pebble content, particularly on the Pernand-Savigny side (Les Vercots, Les Guérets,

for example), these stones having been washed down the valley of the river Rhoin, which flows out from the village of Savigny-lès-Beaune.

This *terroir* gives a wine which is well coloured and nicely sturdy; it is a meaty wine with a rich, robust character and plenty of depth. The amount of *premier cru* vineyard, 38 hectares, is small, however. The *grand cru* has absorbed most of the land on the slopes.

The Vineyard

PREMIERS CRUS There are 13 *premier crus*, in whole or in part, some of which are technically in the *commune* of Ladoix. In Aloxe-Corton, we have Les Chaillots (part); Clos des Maréchaudes; Les Fournières; Les Guérets; Les Maréchaudes; Les Meix (Clos du Chapitre); Les Paulands (part); Les Valozières (part); and Les Vercots. In Ladoix, we have much more of the Clos des Maréchaudes and Les Maréchaudes; La Coutière; Les Petites-Lolières; Les Moutottes; and La-Toppe-au-Vert.

Many of these *premiers crus* lie on the lesser, downward slopes of areas which are *grand cru* Corton and share their names. Confusingly, at least one, Paulands, is *grand cru* at the top, *premier cru* in the middle, but only village AC at the bottom.

In total, these comprise 37.59 hectares and produce some 1,400 hectolitres of wine per year. VILLAGE WINE Village Aloxe-Corton runs all the way down to the N74. There are 89.71 hectares producing 4,000 hectolitres of red wine and 23 hectolitres of white wine per year. The white wine is as likely to incorporate some Pinot Beurot (akin to the Pinot Gris) in its *encépagement* as not, and, though rare, is worth pursuing, for it has an interesting, individual flavour.

The Premiers Crus

LES MOUTOTTES	(0.94 ha)
LES PETITES LOLIÈRES	(1.64 ha)
LA COUTIÈRE	(2.52 ha)
LA TOPPE AU VERT	(1.72 ha)
CLOS DES MARÉCHAUDES	(1.41 ha)
LES MARÉCHAUDES	(2.30 ha)
LES PAULANDS	(1.59 ha)

These seven small *premiers crus* comprise those above the village of Ladoix, where the orientation varies between just north of east and southeast. The wines are quite a bit fuller than those of the Ladoix *premiers crus* of this sector, but they are often a bit hard, even a bit lean, even a bit rustic. They lack the depth, succulence and elegance of both the *grands crus* better situated further up the slope and the *premiers crus* to the south. Few of these names are ever seen on their own, except for Les Maréchaudes.

RECOMMENDED SOURCES
LA COUTIÈRE
Nudant (Ladoix).

LES MARÉCHAUDES
Jean-Pierre Maldant (Ladoix).

LES VALOZIÈRES	(6.59 ha)
LES CHAILLOTS	(4.63 ha)
LES FOURNIÈRES	(5.57 ha)
LES MEIX	(1.90 ha)
(Clos du Chapitre)	

Directly under Les Bressandes, Les Perrières and Les Grèves—all part of the best section of Corton—these *premiers crus climats* provide the best of Aloxe-Corton. The wines combine body and richness, together with a minerally spice, which comes from the iron in the soil. They keep well.

RECOMMENDED SOURCES
LES VALOZIÈRES
Jean-Pierre Maldant, Nudant (both Ladoix); Comte Senard (Aloxe-corton).

LES FOURNIÈRES
Tollot-Beaut (Chorey-lès-Beaune).

LES VERCOTS	(4.19 ha)
LES GUÉRETS	(2.56 ha)

These two *premiers crus* lie on the other side of the village toward Savigny-lès-Beaune, are separated from the *grand crus climats* of Clos de Meix and La Vigne-au-Saint by a little dip in the terrain, and are only authorised for village wine. One sees few examples of Vercots, and I cannot remember ever having been offered

pure Guérets, but my impression is of a slightly less sturdy wine than a Valozières, but not necessarily a less rich or less interesting one.

RECOMMENDED SOURCES
LES VERCOTS
Tollot-Beaut (Chorey-lès-Beaune).

Didier Meuneveaux, of Aloxe-Corton, makes a very good *premier cru* blend of Les Guérets and Les Fournières. Patrick Bize, of Savigny's Domaine Simon Bize, produces a very good Aloxe-Corton *village* from Les Suchots, which is nearby.

The Growers

Maurice Chapuis
10 ha *en fermage*. Corton-Charlemagne (1.20 ha); Corton, Les Chaumes (1.15 ha); Corton, Les Perrières (1.05 ha); Corton, Les Languettes (0.60 ha); Aloxe-Corton *premier cru* in Les Fournières, Les Guérets, Les Valozières and Les Vercots; village Aloxe-Corton; village Savigny-lès-Beaune; village Chorey-lès-Beaune *blanc*.

Maurice, son of Louis, has been in charge here since 1985. He uses no stems, 4 days cold-maceration, fermentation temperatures up to a maximum of 33°C and 15 percent new wood. The Chapuis family is conscientious about not overproducing. Having gone through a period when I felt the results should have been better, the early 2000s show the Chapuis domaine to be back where it was 20 years ago.

Bruno Colin
4.43 ha owned and *en métayage/en fermage*. Corton, Les Renardes (0.71 ha); Beaune *premier cru* in Les Avaux and Les Sizies; Savigny-lès-Beaune *premier cru* Les Peuillets; village Aloxe-Corton.

One of the delights of visiting this cellar is that you pass from one old cellar into an even older, vaulted second one, which is said to date from the thirteenth century. Twenty-five percent new oak is used for the Corton here, which in my experience is very good. Beware of the dog, a light milky-coffee Labrador called Popeye. He'll drink all the wine you are prepared to give him!

Chateau de Corton-André

3.93 ha owned. Corton, Le Château (*monopole*) (0.33 ha); Corton, Les Renardes (0.44 ha); Corton-Charlemagne (0.13 ha); Aloxe-Corton *premier cru* in Les Paulands and Les Petites Lolières; village Savigny-lès-Beaune in the *lieu-dit* Clos des Guettottes; village Aloxe-Corton; village Ladoix.

This small domaine—down from 50 hectares a decade ago, when it leased the D'Ardhuy vines—is associated with La Reine Pédauque, owner of the tourist-trapping cellars-to-visit by the northern entrance to the centre of Beaune. The château itself is grand; it dates from the fifteenth century and is surrounded by a park at the foot of the *grand cru* Les Perrières. But elsewhere in the village is a large box of a factory which disfigures the landscape and houses a much larger *négociant* business. This belongs in an industrial estate and should never have been allowed to be built there.

On the face of it, the winemaking is as it should be, but the results are uninspiring. The curious thing is that none of the "home team" seems to realise it. Do they never taste anyone else's wines?

Franck Follin-Arbelet

6 ha owned and *en fermage*. Corton-Bressandes (0.40 ha); Corton-Charlemagne (0.40 ha); Romanée-Saint-Vivant (0.33 ha); Corton (0.30 ha); Aloxe-Corton *premier cru* in Clos du Chapitre and Les Vercots; Pernand-Vergelesse *premier cru* in En Caradeux and Les Fichots; village Aloxe-Corton.

The tall, lean, somewhat unkemptly-bearded Franck Follin took over the vines of his father-in-law André Masson in 1993 and has more than doubled his exploitation since then. He lives along the road to Savigny on the edge of the village, but stores his wines in a fine, cool, vaulted cellar in the centre. He de-stems completely, vinifies up to 35°C, uses from 10 to 75 percent new oak and bottles without filtration. Follin's wines show well in cask, and though I have had some disappointments when I have seen them again in bottle, I now find the results more regular. This is an address to note.

Louis Latour

47.1 ha owned and *en fermage*. Corton (12.59 ha) (mainly sold as Château Corton-Grancey); Corton-Charlemagne (9.64 ha); Corton, Clos-de-la-Vigne-au-Saint (*monopole*) (2.50 ha); Chambertin (0.81 ha); Romanée-Saint-Vivant Les Quatre-Journeaux (0.76 ha); Chevalier-Montrachet, Les Demoiselles (0.51 ha); Aloxe-Corton *premier cru* in Les Chaillots and Les Fournières; Pernand-Vergelesses *premier cru* Ile de Vergelesses; Beaune *premier cru* in Clos du Roi, Les Perrières, Vignes-Franches, Les Grèves (*blanc*) and Aux Cras (*blanc*); Pommard *premier cru* Les Epenots; village Aloxe-Corton; village Pernand-Vergelesses; village Volnay.

Maison Louis Latour is, of course, a major *négociant*. This sizeable domaine, based in Aloxe-Corton, provides about 10 percent of the firm's turnover, perhaps a quarter of its Burgundian requirements.

In recent years the domaine has taken an increasingly biological-ecological approach to viticulture. Yields are low; the fruit is de-stemmed and vinified totally naturally. And, yes, the wines are still subsequently flash-pasteurised. The top reds (though in my experience not the Château Corton-Grancey) and the whites are usually good, even fine. But the lesser reds lack fruit, and the whites can lack concentration and finesse. I find the results puzzlingly inconsistent.

Didier Meuneveaux

6 ha owned and *en fermage/en métayage*. Corton, Les Perrières (0.66 ha); Corton, Les Chaumes (0.31 ha); Corton, Les Bressandes (0.26 ha); Aloxe-Corton *premier cru* in Les Fournières and Les Guérets; Beaune *premier cru* in Les Reversées; village Aloxe-Corton; village Pernand-Vergelesses; village Chorey-lès-Beaune.

Now that Philippe Senard has moved his winery to Beaune, there are even fewer domaines in Aloxe than there used to be. Didier Meuneveaux's estate is one of the very best. The headquarters is a substantial *maison bourgeoise* at the entrance to the village. Yields are low, the fruit is de-stemmed and then cold-soaked for a week, the temperature of the fermentation is allowed to rise to 35°C, and 20 percent new wood or more is used during the maturation. I have been impressed here by the cleanliness and originality of these wines.

Michel Voarick

8.53 ha owned and *en fermage*. Corton, Clos du Roi (0.50 ha); Corton, Les Renardes (0.50 ha); Corton, Les Languettes (0.83 ha) (up to 2002: now replaced with Corton-Charlemagne); Corton-Charlemagne (1.66 ha, from 2003); village Aloxe-Corton; village Pernand-Vergelesses *rouge et blanc*.

Jean-Marc Voarick believes in old-fashioned methods: no de-stemming, one *remontage* and one *pigeage* per day, temperatures up to 35°C and no new wood for the red wines. The cellars are very cold, which is perhaps one of the reasons he bottles late. These are big, brutal wines. They can soften up while the fruit is still there in very rich years. But sometimes the flavours are too rustic, I find. The wines are proportionately better in the best vintages. But I have liked what I have seen of 2002, 2003 and 2004.

PERNAND-VERGELESSES

In Pernand-Vergelesses I sometimes get the feeling that I have been transported to some *vieux village perché* in the south of France. There is as much vertical to it as horizontal. It's a pretty village, full of old houses, sharp corners and steep alleys clinging to the side of a hill which overlooks the western side of the Bois de Corton. Opposite, therefore, is the Charlemagne part of the Corton *vignoble*. Pernand also commands a fine view back over the flatter land toward Beaune.

Apart from Corton and Corton-Charlemagne, the main part of Pernand's vineyard is on the east-facing slopes of the Bon Noël, which separates the village from Savigny-lès-Beaune. There are nine *premiers crus* (up from six in 2002, when three new *climats* were elevated but for white wines only), of which the best is the Ile de Vergelesses. There is rather more communal land up behind the villages than is generally realised,

and here the vines of Pernand flow imperceptibly into those of the Hautes-Côtes. Here also are the remaining vines of Aligoté, for which Pernand used to have a fine reputation. Most of this Aligoté has now been replaced with Chardonnay, for which the growers can command a higher price. Régis Pavelot, though, retains his old vines and makes a very serious example.

Village Pernand-Vergelesses, whether white or red—the former used to represent about a fifth of the total production but is now double that—can be somewhat lean in lesser years, but it is usually good value. The red wine has a little more weight than the average Ladoix or Chorey-lès-Beaune, and is less rustic. Maison Louis Jadot of Beaune produces good examples of both colours from a *premier cru monopole* called La Croix de Pierre, and Bernard Dubreuil-Fontaine and his daughter Christine have the monopoly of the Clos Berthet, one of the new *premiers crus* (the Pinots Noirs were uprooted in 1995, but the Chardonnays remain). White Pernand, when it is good, is cool, crisp and appley with individual, slightly herbal, flowery tones to it. A third good example of this colour is that made by François Germain at the Château de Chorey-lès-Beaune.

The *terroir* under the Bois Noël is relatively similar to that of the Corton hill. Upslope, we find silico-calcerous marl on a limestone base red in colour and rich in iron. Clay makes up about one third of the soil. There are more stones on the lower slopes, though. This is due to the effect of the river Rhoin, which flows through Savigny.

The Vineyard

PREMIERS CRUS The original six *premiers crus*, in whole or in part, are Creux de la Net (part); En Caradeux (part); La Croix-de-Pierre; Les Fichots; Ile-de-Vergelesses; and Les Vergelesses or Les Basses-Vergelesses. The three recent additions, *blanc* only, are Le Clos du Village (monopoly of R. Rapet et Fils); Le Clos Berthet (monopoly of Dubreuil-Fontaine); and Sous Frétille. These cover 56.28 hectares and produce 1,520 hectolitres of red wine and 650 hectolitres of white wine a year.

VILLAGE WINE   There are 72.14 hectares of village wine, and these come from three sectors: above and below the *premiers crus*, on the slopes opposite the Bois de Corton and on either side of the road which continues up the valley toward Echevronne. Not counting any Aligoté which may be planted in village land, the average amount of village wine produced is equally shared between red and white wine at roughly 1,500 hectolitres each per year.

Pernand-Vergelesses *rouge* is also allowed to be sold as Côte-de-Beaune Villages.

The Premiers Crus

ILE DE VERGELESSES   *(9.41 ha)*

Lying at an altitude of between 270 and 285 metres above sea level, on a relatively gentle slope facing exactly to the southeast, with Savigny-lès-Beaune's Les Vergelesses vineyard above and Pernand's Les Vergelesses (or Les Basses-Vergelesses) below, the squashed oval-shaped vineyard of the Ile is ideally placed. It is surely a contender for elevation to *grand cru*.

The wine is individual—clearly better than the other *premiers crus*. It has medium-full body, an intense nose which recalls damson and black-cherry and a distinction and an intensity lacking in neighbouring wines. Yet, compared with the top *premiers crus* of Volnay and Pommard, the wine is cheap. It can be one of Burgundy's bargains.

RECOMMENDED SOURCES
Chandon de Briailles (Savigny-lès-Beaune); Denis Père et Fils, Régis Pavelot, R. Rapet Père et Fils (all Pernand-Vergelesses).

LES VERGELESSES OR LES BASSES-VERGELESSES	*(18.06 ha)*
EN CARADEUX	*(11.58 ha)*
LES FICHOTS	*(11.23 ha)*
SOUS FRÉTILLE (white only)	*(6.22 ha)*
CREUX-DE-LA-NET	*(3.44 ha)*
LA CROIX-DE-PIERRE	*(2.80 ha)*
CLOS BERTHET (white only)	*(1.00 ha)*
CLOS DU VILLAGE (white only)	*(0.57 ha)*

These *climats* can produce well-priced, good, honest bottles—medium-bodied, with both black and red fruit, and usually with good acidity. These are wines for the medium term. You won't pay the earth, so don't expect the moon. The whites are proportionately more interesting.

RECOMMENDED SOURCES
LES VERGELESSES OR LES BASSES-VERGELESSES
Roger Rapet, Laleure-Piot (Both Pernand-Vergelesses); Girard-Vollot, Jean-Marc Pavelot (Both Savigny-lès-Beaunes).

CREUX DE LA NET
Roger Jaffelin (Pernand-Vergelesses).

LES FICHOTS
Roger Jaffelin, Pierre Marey et Fils (Both Pernand-Vergelesses).

EN CARADEUX
Régis Pavelot (Pernand-Vergelesses).

LA CROIX DE PIERRE
Louis Jadot (Beaune).

CLOS BERTHET
Dubreuil-Fontaine (Pernand-Vergelesses).

CLOS DU VILLAGE
R. Rapet et Fils (Pernand-Vergelesses).

SOUS FRÉTILLE
Château De Chorey-lès-Beaune, Marius Delarche, Jaffelin Père et Fils, Pierre Marey et Fils, R. Rapet et Fils, Rollin Père et Fils (all Pernand-Vergelesses).

The Growers

★★★ *Bonneau du Martray*

11 ha owned. Corton-Charlemagne (9.50 ha); Corton *rouge* (1.50 ha).

No other domaine in Burgundy, for even the Domaine de la Romanée-Conti now offers Vosne-Romanée *premier cru* on occasion, sells only *grand cru* wine. The domaine's land on the Corton hill straddles the Pernand-Aloxe border and produces exemplary Corton-Charlemagne, vinified in oak, of course, of which one third is new. In 1994 there was a dual change of generation here, Jean Le Bault de la Morinière, who had inherited the domaine from his aunt, gave way to his son Jean-Charles, and Henri Brochon in the cellar ceded responsibility to his sons Bernard and Jean-Pierre. Since then, the sixteen vineyard parcels have been picked and vinified separately, and the viticulture has become more and more biodynamic. Having reduced the area under Pinot Noir at the bottom of the slope, retaining the oldest vines, and having made other improvements, the red wine, which had tended to be a bit feeble, is now very good. But it is for its white wine, one of the very greatest in all Burgundy, that this domaine gains three stars.

Marius Delarche Père et Fils

8.15 ha owned and *en fermage*. Corton, Les Renardes (1.61 ha); Corton-Charlemagne (1.00 ha); Le Corton (0.90 ha); Pernand-Vergelesses *premier cru rouge* in Ile de Vergelesses and Les Vergelesses; Pernand-Vergelesses *premier cru blanc* in En Caradeux and Sous Frétille; village Pernand-Vergelesses *rouge et blanc*; village Aloxe-Corton.

Philippe Delarche, son of Marius, is in charge here with his son Étienne. There has been much improvement here since 1993 when a new *cave*, working by gravity on three levels, was constructed facing the western side of Corton-Charlemagne. Since 1999 the crop has been reduced, and a *table de tri* introduced. The reds could still get better—they can be a little forward and lightweight. But the whites are now very good indeed.

Denis Père et Fils

12.7 ha owned and *en fermage*. Corton-Charlemagne (0.50 ha); Corton, Les Paulands (0.22 ha); Pernand-Vergelesses *premier cru rouge* in Ile de Vergelesses and Les Vergelesses; Pernand-Vergelesses *premier cru blanc* Sous Frétille; Savigny-lès-Beaune *premier cru*; village Pernand-Vergelesses *rouge et blanc*; village Savigny-lès-Beaune; village Aloxe-Corton; village Chorey-lès-Beaune.

It is the *fils*, Roland and Christophe, who are in charge here, father Raoul being *en retraite*. Total de-stemming, fermenting temperatures at 32°C for red and 20°C for white and between 10 and 25 percent new oak is the recipe here. As the Corton vines are young, it is the Ile which is the pick of the cellar. I have enjoyed recent vintages.

Dubreuil-Fontaine

19 ha owned and *en fermage*. Corton, Les Bressandes (0.77 ha); Corton-Charlemagne (0.69 ha); Corton, Les Perrières (0.60 ha); Corton, Clos du Roi (0.44 ha); Pernand-Vergelesses *premier cru rouge* in Les Fichots and Ile de Vergelesses; Pernand-Vergelesses *premier cru blanc* Clos Berthet (*monopole*) and Sous Frétille; Savigny-lès-Beaune *premier cru* Les Vergelesses; Beaune *premier cru* Les Montrevenots; Aloxe-Corton *premier cru* Les Vercots; Pommard *premier cru* Les Epenots; village Pernand-Vergelesses *rouge* in the *lieu-dit* Clos Berthet (*monopole*); village Pommard; village Volnay.

For nearly a decade, responsibility for the wine has laid on the shoulders of Bernard Dubreuil's daughter Christine Gruère. In my previous book, *Côte d'Or*, I expressed hopes that standards here—they've been bottling longer than most—having jollied along at the "quite good" level, would start to rise. I remain underwhelmed. There are now more than a handful of better domaines in the *commune*.

Jaffelin Père et Fils

10.5 ha owned and *en fermage*. Corton-Charlemagne (0.23 ha); Pernand-Vergelesses *premier cru* in Creux de la Net *rouge et blanc* and Les Fichots; Beaune *premier cru* Belissand; village Pernand-Vergelesses in the *lieu-dit* Clos de Bully; village Savigny-lès-Beaune.

Pierre Jaffelin is responsible here and operates from cellars which lie opposite one of Bonneau du Martray's at the top of the village. The domaine has machine harvested since 1996. Jaffelin cold-soaks for 2 or 3 days and then "lets the wine make itself." He uses one quarter new oak. There are neat, attractive wines here. They possess the lion's share of the Creux de la Net.

Laleure-Piot Père et Fils

9.5 ha owned and *en fermage*. Corton-Charlemagne (0.28 ha); Corton from Le Rognet and Les Bressandes (0.53 ha); Pernand-Vergelesses *premier cru* in Ile de Vergelesses and Les Vergelesses; Pernand-Vergelesses *premier cru rouge et blanc*; Savigny-lès-Beaune *premier cru* Les Vergelesses; village Pernand-Vergelesses *rouge et blanc*; village Aloxe-Corton; village Chorey-lès-Beaune; Côte-de-Nuits Villages.

Here is another domaine which has made considerable strides in the last decade. Jean-Marie and Frédéric Laleure, like others, have installed a *table de tri* in the winery and now pay more attention to controlling the size of the crop. Both the whites and the reds are cold-soaked (the former after pressing). This extracts better fruit and fat, say the Laleures.

Pierre Marey et Fils

10 ha owned and *en fermage*. Corton-Charlemagne (1.00 ha); Corton (0.50 ha); Pernand-Vergelesses *premier cru* Les Fichots; Pernand-Vergelesses *premier cru blanc* Sous Frétille; village Pernand-Vergelesses *rouge et blanc*.

Father Pierre, now in his seventies, and son Éric Marey's *grands crus*, all on the Pernand side, are much morcellated. This is an up-and-coming domaine which makes wines with plenty of personality and a nice touch of oak. "When I was a boy," says Pierre Marey, "there were fifty *petits vignerons* in Pernand. Now there are fourteen."

Régis Pavelot et Fils

8.5 ha owned and *en fermage*. Corton-Charlemagne (0.60 ha); Corton (0.40 ha); Pernand-Vergelesses *premier cru* En Caradeux, Les Fichots, Ile de Vergelesses, Les Vergelesses; Pernand-Vergelesses *premier cru blanc* Sous Frétille; village Pernand-Vergelesses *rouge et blanc*; village Aloxe-Corton.

Luc Pavelot is gradually taking over from father Régis, who is now in his mid-sixties. The cellar looks like a concrete bunker and lies halfway down the slope below that of Roland Rapet. A feature of this domaine is its jealously guarded old vines, including one of the most serious Aligotés to be found in Burgundy. The other wines are very good too.

★ Rapet Père et Fils

18 ha owned and *en fermage*. Corton-Charlemagne (2.50 ha); Corton from Les Pougets and Les Perrières (1.25 ha); Pernand-Vergelesses *premier cru* Ile de Vergelesses and Les Vergelesses; Pernand-Vergelesses *premier cru blanc* in En Caradeux, Sous Frétille and Clos du Village (*monopole*); Beaune *premier cru* Clos du Roi; village Aloxe-Corton; village Savigny-lès-Beaune; village Pernand-Vergelesses *rouge et blanc*.

Since Vincent Rapet joined his father Roland at this important domaine in 1991, quality has slowly but surely been ratcheted up to stellar levels. Some of the stems are sometimes retained, the red wine is fermented at a maximum of 33°C, and about 20 to 30 percent of new wood is used, depending on the appellation and the vintage. "Each year is different. One must adapt." The wines are bottled after a year or so. A new cuverie was constructed in 2003. The canopy has been raised. And the white wines are kept longer on their lees to add to their depth. The Rapets have been making wine here for more than two centuries, and the wines are now very exciting.

Rollin Père et Fils

13 ha owned and *en fermage/en métayage*. Corton-Charlemagne (0.42 ha); Pernand-Vergelesses *premier cru* in Les Fichots, Ile de Vergelesses and Les Vergelesses; Pernand-Vergelesses *premier cru blanc* Sous Frétille; village Pernand-Vergelesses *rouge et blanc*; village Aloxe-Corton.

Simon, the *fils*, tall, dark, lean, bespectacled and in his forties, has now taken over from his father in this modern, efficient *cave* below the village on the road to Echevronne. Up to 20 percent of the stems are used. There are 4 or 5 days cold-soaking before fermentation, a longer maceration than a few years ago, and a quarter new oak in the top wines. Here is yet another estate where there has been a noticeable improvement in quality in the last decade. There are very good wines in both colours now.

SAVIGNY-LÈS-BEAUNE

At the beginning of the valley of the river Rhoin, 6 kilometres northwest of Beaune, lies Savigny, one of the largest of the Côte de Beaune *communes* with 383 hectares of vines. Savigny is a modest little village. Some of the older houses may carry an enigmatic wall inscription such as "*Les vins de Savigny sont nourrissants, théologiques et morbifuges*" (the wines of Savigny are nourishing, theological [whatever that is supposed to mean—causing one to ponder on the meaning of life, I suppose] and will chase away every illness), or something equally inscrutable. These appeared between the seventeenth and nineteenth centuries, but no one knows who the authors were or the reasons behind their execution of these inscriptions.

The village can trace its ancestry back to Gallo-Roman times, when it was known as Saviniaco. But even earlier, the Romans themselves constructed a road through the valley, part of the connection between Autun and Langres, both important settlements at the time. Well-preserved traces of the road still exist. In the eleventh century, Augustine monks built the exquisite Abbey of Sainte-Marguerite up in the valley near Bouilland. Back in Savigny, the imposing château on the edge of the village, today a museum of old motor cars, dates from the beginning of the seventeenth century.

Another communal claim to fame is that it was here in the mid-nineteenth century that the first viticultural tractor was invented, and as a consequence of this, vines were first planted in rows in the surrounding vineyards.

Savigny-lès-Beaune—the *lès*, with an accent, meaning "by" or "near to"—is the most divided *vignoble* in Burgundy. Part of the vineyard lies on the south-facing slope of the Bois de Noël, as it curves round from Pernand-Vergelesses. Opposite, on the northeast-facing flank of Mont Battois—down which the motorway thunders from the Morvan to the plain of Beaune—are the other half of Savigny's *premiers crus*, adjoining those of Beaune. There is, incidentally, a rest site on the motorway above the village called the Aire de Savigny-lès-Galloises, from which there is a splendid panorama toward the hill of Corton. If you stop here, you will find yourself exactly halfway between Lille and Marseilles. The flatter land between the *premiers crus* is village *appellation contrôlée*, as is an important but normally overlooked chunk of vineyard on south-facing higher ground beyond the village.

The soil on the Bois de Noël side consists of gritty, sandy marl covered with ferruginous oolite on the top slopes and red-brown crumbly limestone below. It is not very stony and not very permeable, for the clay content is high. On the Mont Battois slopes, the soil is sandier and even less stony, with deep limestone scree on the flatter land below.

The result, combined with the orientation, is wines which are quite separate in character. From the Pernand side, the wines have medium weight and are elegant and persistent. The Mont Battois slopes opposite give more structured, earthier, more *sauvage* wines, which get rounder and fatter as the slope turns round and approaches the boundary with Beaune.

There is also some white wine, not as much as in Pernand, but of an interesting character and similarly quite different from that of Meursault or the other villages to the south. To some extent this is the *terroir*, but it is also the consequence of the practice here of complanting with the Chardonnay some Pinot Blanc or Pinot Beurot, the latter a sort of Pinot Gris, as used in Alsace. These Pinots ripen well and give good sugar readings but less acidity. More importantly, they add a bit of spice. Growers like Patrick Bize can offer both Bourgogne *blanc* and Savigny *blanc* from various blends of Chardonnay and Pinot. And really good they are, too.

There is plenty of Savigny, and the village offers some very good sources of wine. Moreover, prices are inexpensive compared with those of either Pommard or Volnay. All this adds to the good value—it is a happy hunting ground for those who seek good inexpensive Burgundy.

The Vineyard

PREMIERS CRUS   There are twenty-two *premiers crus* in Savigny-lès-Beaune, in whole or in part. On the Pernand side, we have Champ Chevrey (part of Aux Fourneaux); Les Charnières; La Bataillère (part of Les Vergelesses); Aux Clous; Aux Fourneaux (part); Petits Godeaux; Aux Gravains; Aux Guettes (part); Les Lavières; Aux Serpentières; Les Talmettes (part of Les Vergelesses); Aux Vergelesses; and Les Basses Vergelesses. On the Mont Battois slope will be found La Dominode (part of Les Jarrons); Les Hauts

Jarrons; Les Jarrons; Les Bas Marconnets; Les Hauts Marconnets; Les Narbantons; Les Peuillets (part); Redrescut (or Redrescul); and Les Rouvrettes (part). These cover 144.02 hectares and produce around 5,350 hectolitres per year of red wine and 275 hectolitres of white.

VILLAGE WINE   There are 238.58 hectares of village land in Savigny. Of this, 150 hectares lie in the plain on the east side of the village or on unfavoured slopes. The rest lie further up the valley of the Rhoin. Here you will find the *lieux-dits* of Les Gollards and Les Vermots, and it is from here that I feel that the best of Savigny's village wines derive. There is good Bourgogne, both red and white, from here, too.

The average production of village wine is 8,350 hectolitres of red wine and 1,180 hectolitres of white wine per year.

The Premiers Crus

AUX VERGELESSES	*(15.38 ha)*
LA BATAILLIÈRE	*(1.81 ha)*
LES BASSES VERGELESSES	*(1.68 ha)*
LES TALMETTES	*(3.10 ha)*

The large Vergelesses *climat* and its three subsidiaries, all of which can call their wine Vergelesses, represent Savigny-lès-Beaune's best wine. Here Savigny is at its most refined, with the most intensity and depth. Here it is at its smoothest, its most velvety, its most complete. Savigny-lès-Beaune Les Vergelesses lies in part above Pernand's Ile de Vergelesses and can often be its equal, rather superior to Pernand's (Basses) Vergelesses.

La Bataillière, once a *clos*, but having lost that designation because the walls crumbled, apparently has historically been considered *the* best part. It is really a continuation of the Ile. Today it is the *monopole* of the Domaine Albert Morot of Beaune. Les Talmettes, a little further around the hill under the forest at the top of the slope, makes slightly less distinctive wine.

RECOMMENDED SOURCES

AUX VERGELESSES

Simon Bize (Savigny-lès-Beaune); Lucien Jacob (Echevronne).

LA BATAILLIÈRE

Albert Morot (Beaune).

LES LAVIÈRES	*(17.66 ha)*
AUX FOURNEAUX	*(6.42 ha)*
CHAMP CHEVREY	*(1.48 ha)*
LES CHARNIÈRES	*(2.07 ha)*

These four *climats* lie below Vergelesses and produce a soft, round, more loose-knit wines, but wines with plenty of charm and succulent, plump, red fruit. This is perhaps the easiest Savigny to appreciate, both at the outset and a little later on, for it evolves earlier than most. Les Lavières is superior to Aux Fourneaux.

RECOMMENDED SOURCES

LES LAVIÈRES

Bouchard Père et Fils (Beaune); Camus-Bruchon, Chandon-de-Briailles (both Savigny-lès-Beaune); Tollot-Beaut (Chorey-lès-Beaune); Claude Maréchal (Bligny-lès-Beaune).

AUX FOURNEAUX

Simon Bize, Chandon de Briailles (both Savigny-lès-Beaune).

CHAMP CHEVREY

Tollot-Beaut (Chorey-lès-Beaune).

AUX GRAVAINS	*(6.15 ha)*
PETITS GODEAUX	*(0.71 ha)*
AUX SERPENTIÈRES	*(12.34 ha)*
AUX CLOUX	*(9.92 ha)*
AUX GUETTES	*(14.08 ha)*

Continuing around toward the village, we come to the final group of premiers crus on the Pernand side. These wines are firmer that those of the Lavières and less refined than those of the Vergelesses, but nevertheless, they share many of the same characteristics: Savignys with style rather than raw substance.

RECOMMENDED SOURCES

AUX GRAVAINS

Jean-Marc Pavelot (Savigny-lès-Beaune).

AUX SERPENTIÈRES

Simon Bize, Michel Écard (both Savigny-lès-Beaune).

AUX GUETTES

Simon Bize (Savigny-lès-Beaune) as Clos des Guettes; A.F. Gros (Pommard); Louis Jadot (Beaune).

LES ROUVRETTES	(2.83 ha)
LES NARBANTONS	(9.49 ha)
LES JARRONS	(1.46 ha)
LA DOMINODE	(7.87 ha)
LES HAUTS JARRONS	(4.44 ha)
REDRESCUL	(0.50 ha)
LES HAUTS MARCONNETS	(5.34 ha)
LES BAS MARCONNETS	(2.99 ha)
LES PEUILLETS	(16.17 ha)

These are the Savigny-lès-Beaune *premier crus* which lie under the motorway and Mont Battois. Les Rouvrettes lies nearest to the village. Peuillets marches with Beaune, Clos du Roi (with the motorway separating them); likewise, Marconnets marches with its namesake in the next *commune*.

The wines don't *have* to be tough and *sauvage* here. What one is looking for is a combination of guts and balanced fruit, plus tannins which are properly sophisticated. The best, in my view, come from the Marconnets and that part of Jarrons normally sold as La Dominode. Bruno Clair of Marsannay has a plot of vines planted in 1902 here. This wine gives the lie to anyone who believes that Savigny cannot provide fine wine.

RECOMMENDED SOURCES

LES ROUVRETTES

Girard-Vollot (Savigny-lès-Beaune).

LES NARBANTONS

Camus-Bruchon, Michel Écard, Girard-Vollot (All Savigny-lès-Beaune); Leroy (Vosne-Romanée).

LES JARRONS

Maurice Écard (Savigny-lès-Beaune).

LA DOMINODE

Jean-Marc Pavelot (Savigny-lès-Beaune); Louis Jadot (Beaune); Bruno Clair (Marsannay).

LES MARCONNETS

Simon Bize (Savigny-lès-Beaune).

LES PEUILLETS

Capron-Charcousset, Girard-Vollot, Jean-Marc Pavelot (all Savigny-lès-Beaune).

The Growers

★ Simon Bize et Fils

22 ha owned and *en fermage/en métayage*. Corton-Charlemagne (0.60 ha); Latricières-Chambertin (0.40 ha); Savigny-lès-Beaune *premier cru* in Les Vergelesses (*rouge et blanc*), Aux Fourneaux, Les Serpentières, Les Guettes and Les Marconnets; village Savigny-lès-Beaune, including the *lieux-dits* Les Grands Liards and Les Bourgeots; village Savigny-lès-Beaune *blanc*; village Aloxe-Corton in the *lieu-dit* Les Suchots.

The wines were very good here 20 and 30 years ago, when the late Simon Bize was in charge—I have fond memories of the 1971 Vergelesses—but, after a hiccup in the early 1990s, they are even better now. His son Patrick is one of Burgundy's most sensitive and perfectionistic winemakers, ever seeking to add a touch here and modify a detail there.

Only the younger vines, which for Patrick means anything under 20 years, are de-stemmed here. There is a long *cuvaison*, controlled at 30–33°C, and 50 percent new wood is used. Bize's wines are understated, slow to evolve and a little austere at the start. But they are beautifully poised and clear-cut in their flavours, with the individual characters of the five *premiers crus* visible for all to see. Patrick Bize additionally makes excellent generics, including whites from both Chardonnay and Pinot Beurot. He also offers a little merchant Puligny-Montrachet. This is an address not to be missed.

Camus-Bruchon

9.12 ha owned and *en fermage*. Savigny-lès-Beaune *premier cru* in Aux Gravains, Les Lavières and Les Narbantons; Beaune *premier cru* Clos du Roi; Pommard *premier cru* Les Arvelets; village Savigny-lès-Beaune *blanc et rouge*, including the *lieux-dits* Grands Liards and Pimentiers and a *vieilles vignes* red wine *cuvée*; village Chorey-lès-Beaune.

The grapes are now de-stemmed here, and the must cold-soaked for 8 to 10 days. The fermentation temperatures are allowed to rise to 35°C, and 25 to 30 percent new oak is employed. Lucien Camus is a serious winemaker. His wines are for those who like sturdy bottles and do not mind the occasional rustic touch.

★★ Chandon de Briailles

14 ha owned and *en métayage*. Corton, Les Bressandes (1.74 ha); Corton, Clos du Roi (0.44 ha); Corton, Les Maréchaudes (0.39 ha); Corton-Charlemagne (0.39 ha); Corton *blanc* (0.25 ha); Volnay *premier cru* Les Caillerets; Aloxe-Corton *premier cru* Les Valozières; Pernand-Vergelesses *premier cru* in Ile de Vergelesses and Les Basses-Vergelesses; Savigny-lès-Beaune *premier cru* in Les Lavières and Aux Fourneaux; village Savigny-lès-Beaune, including the *lieu-dit* Aux Fourneaux.

This important property is owned by Aymar and Nadine de Nicolay (pronounced Nicolaï) and their four children, and it is their son François and their youngest daughter Claude who are in charge, together with cellar master Jean-Claude Bouveret, known to one and all, even to himself, for obvious reasons, as Kojak. Progress has been impressive here over the last decade, and this is now a prime source for Ile de Vergelesses (of which they are the largest landholder) and a clutch of excellent Cortons. The domaine has been fully biodynamic since 2005. The fruit is only partially de-stemmed, fermentation temperatures are low, and the percentage of new oak is very low. This results in wines of only medium structure, but they are pure and fragrant and keep well.

Doudet-Naudin

12 ha owned (by Yves Doudet). Corton, Les Maréchaudes (0.80 ha); Corton-Charlemagne (0.70 ha); Savigny-lès-Beaune *premier cru* in Les Guettes and Redrescut; Aloxe-Corton *premier cru* in Les Guérets and Les Maréchaudes; Pernand-Vergelesses *premier cru* Les Fichots; Pernand-Vergelesses *premier cru blanc* Sous Frétille; Beaune *premier cru* in Clos du Roi and Les Cent-Vignes; village Savigny-lès-Beaune in the *lieu-dit* Aux Petits-Liards; village Aloxe-Corton in the *lieu-dit* Les Boutières; village Pernand-Vergelesses *rouge et blanc*.

In the last half-dozen years, there have been some welcome changes at the Domaine Doudet, run by Yves Doudet and his daughter Isabelle.

Yields have been reduced, the vineyards are now ploughed, and viticulture is by *lutte raisonnée*. In 2002 a *table de tri* was added. There is still a way to go, but at least it is a start. In 2005 the estate was almost doubled by the acquisition of the Klein domaine in Pernand-Vergelesses.

Michel Écard

6 ha owned and en *fermage*. Savigny-lès-Beaune *premier cru* in Aux Clous, Les Hauts Jarrons (*blanc*), Les Jarrons, Les Narbantons, Les Peuillets and Les Serpentières; village Savigny-lès-Beaune *rouge et blanc*.

The rotund, bluff, genial Maurice Écard sold half his estate off in 2006 to Maison Béjot of Meusault, who have retained the name. His son Michel exploits the rest. This is a modern, efficient set-up, and somehow you know you have stumbled on a good source of wine even before you have sampled a single cask. There is a sorting table, the fruit is de-stemmed, the *cuvaison* lasts for 12 days at temperatures up to 34°C, and 10 percent new oak is used. The results are plump, fruity wines for the medium term. A good source.

Jean-Michel Giboulot

12 ha *en fermage*. Savigny-lès-Beaune *premier cru* in Aux Fourneaux, Aux Gravains, Les Narbantons, Les Peuillets and Aux Serpentières; village Savigny-lès-Beaune *rouge* (including the *lieu-dit* Les Grands Liards) *et blanc*.

Jean-Michel Giboulot practices the *lutte raisonnée* in his vineyards. In order to keep the yields under control—green harvesting is a last resort—he trains the young vines to the *Cordon du Royat* system. He has also planted ray-grass between his vines to prevent erosion and to reduce the vigour of the vines. There are no stems, the fermentation temperature is warmed up at the end to fix the colour and obtain a maximum of *matière*, and 25 percent new oak is used for the *premiers crus*. There is very good quality here—a considerable improvement from a decade ago.

Jean-Jacques Girard

16.5 ha owned and *en fermage*. Savigny-lès-Beaune *premier cru* in Aux Fourneaux, Les Lavières, Les Peuillets, Les Rouvrettes and Aux Serpentières; Pernand-Vergelesses *premier cru* Les Basses-Vergelesses;

Pernand-Vergelesses *premier cru blanc*; village Savigny-lès-Beaune *rouge et blanc*.

Jean-Jacques Girard's family have been making wine since 1614. Having split with his brother Philippe (the domaine used to be called Girard-Vollot) in 1998, he has now been joined by his son Vincent. He makes Savignys which are a bit hard and sinewy. They need time. But they have gotten more civilised in recent years. He is also a merchant, offering four casks of Corton-Charlemagne, bought in as grapes.

Philippe Girard

9 ha owned and *en fermage*. Savigny-lès-Beaune *premier cru* in Les Lavières, Les Narbantons, Les Peuillets and Les Rouvrettes; village Aloxe-Corton; village Pernand-Vergelesses *rouge et blanc*; village Savigny-lès-Beaune *rouge et blanc*.

Dating from 1998 (see above), this is the other half of the Girard family domaine. Though the fruit is entirely de-stemmed, there is nevertheless a rustic touch here.

Pierre Guillemot

8 ha owned and *en fermage*. Corton, Le Rognet (0.33 ha); Savigny-lès-Beaune *premier cru* in Les Jarrons, Les Narbantons and Les Serpentières; village Savigny-lès-Beaune *rouge et blanc*.

Jean-Pierre Guillemot is in charge here. In 1999 he acquired the Corton when the Château de Bligny estate was wound up. In the last decade standards have improved. There is a greater attention toward the nuances of winemaking and a little more new oak (20 percent for the *premiers crus*). There is good quality here now.

Antonin Guyon

46 ha owned. Charmes-Chambertin (0.90 ha); Corton, Les Bressandes (0.86 ha); Corton-Charlemagne (0.55 ha); Corton, Clos du Roi (0.55 ha); Corton, Les Chaumes (0.33 ha); Corton, Les Renardes (0.22 ha); Aloxe-Corton *premier cru* in Les Fournières, Les Guérets and Les Vercots; Pernand-Vergelesses *premier cru* Les Vergelesses and Les Fichots; Pernand-Vergelesses *premier cru blanc* Sous Frétille; Meursault *premier cru* Les Charmes Dessus; Volnay *premier*

cru, Clos des Chênes; village Chambolle-Musigny, including the *lieu-dit* Clos du Village; village Gevrey-Chambertin; village Savigny-lès-Beaune; village Beaune, including the *lieu-dit* Clos du Charme Gaufriot; village Pernand-Vergelesses *blanc et rouge*; village Chorey-lès-Beaune.

Twenty-three hectares of Hautes-Côtes-de-Nuits in Meuilley make up almost half this estate, whose headquarters occupy imposing premises on the edge of Savigny. The bulk of the rest of the domaine came from Hippolyte Thevenot in 1965 and is still registered as such on the *déclaration*. Dominique Guyon is in charge here, and there are some nice wines, the Volnay, Clos des Chênes, always being one of the best. There is very good quality and no lack of finesse here.

Patrick Jacob-Girard

8.5 ha owned and *en fermage*. Savigny-lès-Beaune *premier cru* Aux Gravains, Les Hauts Jarrons and Les Marconnets; village Savigny-lès-Beaune *rouge et blanc*; village Pernand-Vergelesses.

M. Jacob is no relation to the other Jacobs or Girards. In his late forties he operates from a tidy cellar in the middle of the village, de-stems entirely and prefers 1-year-old wood (which he obtains from an estate in Vosne-Romanée) to new oak. These wines are of quite good quality.

Pierre and Jean-Baptiste Lebreuil

9.5 ha owned and *en fermage*. Savigny-lès-Beaune *premier cru rouge et blanc* in Aux Clous and Les Serpentières; village Savigny-lès-Beaune *rouge et blanc*, including the *lieu-dit* Les Grands Liards; village Aloxe-Corton.

"Domaine Les Guettottes," it says on the label. It was started by Pierre's grandfather in 1935 and expanded by his father in the 1960s, when they embarked on domaine bottling. Jean-Baptiste joined his father in 2000. The harvest is manual. The fruit is de-stemmed, cold-soaked for 5 or 6 days and fermented at temperatures up to 32°C, sometimes warming up to 38°C at the end. Up to a quarter new oak is used. Quality is not bad, but this is not one of the front-runners in the village.

Jean-Michel Maurice, Domaine du Prieuré

11.5 ha owned and *en fermage*. Savigny-lès-Beaune *premier cru* in Les Hauts Jarrons and Les Lavières; village Savigny-lès-Beaune *blanc et rouge*.

The extended Maurice family produces light and quite pleasant wines, intended for drinking in the medium term. But they do not really excite me.

Moret-Nominé

Up above Savigny-lès-Beaune lies Le Hameau de Barboron, a hotel tastefully converted out of an old manoir, in the middle of peace and quiet. Odile Moret runs the hotel; her husband Daniel, on the side, runs a small but high quality merchant business producing only white wines, bought in as fruit. The first vintage was 2000. I recommend it.

★ Pavelot

12 ha owned and *en fermage*. Beaune *premier cru* Les Bressandes; Savigny-lès-Beaune *premier cru* La Dominode, Aux Gravains, Aux Guettes, Les Narbantons and Les Peuillets; Les Serpentières; Pernand-Vergelesses *premier cru* Les Vergelesses; village Savigny-lès-Beaune *blanc et rouge*.

This is one of the best domaines in Savigny. Hugues Pavelot has now joined his equally tall, lean and handsome father, Jean-Marc, and they make a formidable team. Viticulture is by *lutte raisonnée*, 90 percent of the vineyard is ploughed, and there is a *tri* both in the vineyard and in the winery. There is a short period of cold-soaking after total de-stemming, only one racking and 10 to 20 percent new oak. The wines are elegant, plump and understated, letting all the fruit spring out, yet never simple. There is depth here, and they last.

Henri de Villamont

9.5 ha owned. Grands Echézeaux (0.50 ha); Savigny-lès-Beaune *premier cru* Clos des Guettes; Chambolle-Musigny *premier cru* Les Baudes; Chambolle-Musigny *premier cru* (from Groseilles, Feusselottes, Combottes and Chatelots); village Savigny-lès-Beaune.

Henri de Villamont, which belongs to the Swiss company Schenk, occupies imposing premises on the outskirts of Savigny and possesses a domaine which produces some 10 percent of its turnover. Here they aim for the *rendement de base*, do not cold-soak and ferment up to 33°C, warming things up at the end. There is 25 to 33 percent new wood. The wines can be very good in cask, but in my experience, they are less exciting in bottle.

CHOREY-LÈS-BEAUNE

It is only at Chorey-lès-Beaune and at Gevrey-Chambertin—and for precisely the same reason—that *appellation village* vineyards spill significantly over the main highway, the N74, toward the east. Today neither the stream which runs down from the *combe* above Gevrey nor the river Rhoin, which flows out of the Vallée d'Orée from Bouilland down to Savigny and beyond, are major profluent events. But in geological times, they must have been. The mini-canyons they left behind prove it. And over the aeons, considerable limestone debris mixed with sand has been brought down the valley to spread out over suitable vineyard land beyond the usual Burgundian confines. Chorey-lès-Beaune is unique. Most of the *commune*—as well as the village itself—lies on the "wrong" side of the road. It is also the producer of that valuable item, so often overlooked by those in pursuit of the latest perfect score among the *grands crus*: red Burgundy at an affordable price.

There are no first growths in Chorey, nor do you see many wines aggrandising themselves with the mention of a *lieu-dit*. Nearly all the wine is red, and more than half of this is sold as Côte-de-Beaune Villages, the village being the major contributor to the appellation. Chorey-lès-Beaune is a soft, plump, fruit-forward wine, usually ready for drinking a couple of years at most after bottling. Those which come from the Aloxe-Corton side are richer, fuller and fatter than those from vineyards neighbouring Beaune and Savigny. There are some 130 hectares under vines producing red wine, plus another handful planted in Chardonnay; some of the vineyards have actually been demoted from *appellation contrôlée* to generic in recent years, an almost unheard-of thing for Burgundy! Total production, including Côte-de-Beaune Villages, is around 6,000 hectolitres of red wine and 140 hectolitres of white wine per year.

The Growers

Arnoux Père et Fils

20 ha owned and *en fermage*. Corton, Les Rognets (0.33 ha); Beaune *premier cru* in Les Cent-Vignes and En Genêt; Savigny-lès-Beaune *premier cru* Les Guettes and Les Vergelesses; Aloxe-Corton *premier cru*; village Aloxe-Corton; village Pernand-Vergelesses *blanc*; village Savigny-lès-Beaune; village Beaune; Chorey-lès-Beaune.

Distant cousins of the Arnoux of Vosne-Romanée, Pascal and his uncle Rémi run this efficient estate out of a hangar-like *chai* on the edge of the village. The domaine is three times the size it was 20 years ago. Harvesting is manual. The Arnoux retain 10 percent of the stems, vinify the reds at up to 33°C and employ one quarter new oak overall. There are good wines at all levels here, and this is a useful address.

★ Château de Chorey-lès-Beaune
Domaine Germain

17 ha owned and *en fermage*. Beaune *premier cru* in Les Boucherottes, Les Cras, Les Cent-Vignes, Sur Les Grèves (*blanc*), Les Teurons and Les Vignes Franches; Aloxe-Corton *premier cru* Les Valozières; Chorey-lès-Beaune; village Beaune "Cuvée Tante Berthe"; village Pernand-Vergelesses *blanc* in the *lieu-dit* Les Combettes; village Meursault.

Not surprisingly, the Château de Chorey is the most impressive edifice in the village: a properly moated castle, medieval in origin, in a fine park. Benoît Germain, whose first totally independent vintage was 1999, is gradually converting to biodynamic methods in his vineyards. In 2002 he decided to isolate an old vine *cuvée* from parcels of Beaune Les Cras, Teurons and Vignes Franches. Here he retains 30 percent of the stems and matures the wine for two years in new oak. This is the Cuvée Tante Berthe. The remaining wines are made more traditionally,

and frankly, I prefer them. They have very good *terroir* definition. The white Pernand-Vergelesses is delicious, too.

Dubois d'Orgeval

13 ha owned and *en fermage/en métayage*. Beaune *premier cru* in Les Marconnets and Les Teurons; Savigny-lès-Beaune *premier cru* in Les Marconnets and Les Narbantons; Chorey-lès-Beaune; village Savigny-lès-Beaune; village Aloxe-Corton; village Beaune; village Pommard.

The Dubois are a large extended Chorey family. This domaine, which was established in 1985, united local land with the Orgeval's Beaunes and Pommards. Harvesting is by hand. One third or so of the stems are retained, fermentation temperatures are allowed to rise to 35°C, and 20 percent new oak is used for the maturation. The wines are held back until ready for drinking and mainly sold to private clients. They are of quite good quality.

François Gay et Fils

6.38 ha owned and *en fermage*. Corton, Les Renardes (0.21 ha); Savigny-lès-Beaune *premier cru* Les Serpentières; Beaune *premier cru* Clos des Perrières; village Aloxe-Corton; village Savigny-lès-Beaune; Chorey-lès-Beaune.

François Gay, smallish, balding and in his mid-sixties, lives in an isolated house on the edge of the village. His barnlike *chai* hides his garden from much of the village. He has now been succeeded by his son Pascal, who made his first vintage in 2002. A small percentage of the stems are sometimes retained here. There is a 3- or 4-day period of cold-soaking. The fermentation temperatures are allowed to rise to 34–35°C, and 30 percent new wood is used. These are lovely clear-cut wines—very clean and harmonious. It is a very good address.

Michel Gay et Fils

8.5 ha owned and *en fermage*. Corton, Renardes (0.21 ha); Beaune *premier cru* Les Toussaints; Savigny-lès-Beaune *premier cru* in Les Serpentières and Les Vergelesses; village Aloxe-Corton; Chorey-lès-Beaune *rouge et blanc*.

Michel Gay, brother of François, and his son Sébastien run one of the best domaines in the village. Vinification methods are similar to those of François, but the wines are richer and sturdier and need time to develop. They can be very good.

Daniel Largeot

11 ha owned and *en fermage*. Beaune *premier cru* Les Grèves; Chorey-lès-Beaune; village Savigny-lès-Beaune; village Aloxe-Corton.

Daniel Largeot, sixty-something, tall, balding and passionate, gives the initial impression of being somewhat haphazard. So does the appearance of the cellar, which was enlarged in 2000. Deeper investigation shows this to be misleading. This man believes in low *rendements*, *saignées* if necessary, enzymes to help clarify the wine and one quarter new oak for the better *cuvées*. Until 1994 they did not de-stem; subsequently, one third was retained; and now they de-stem completely. Daniel Largeot has now been joined by his son-in-law Rémi Martin.

Sylvain Loichet

3.5 ha owned. Clos Vougeot (0.48 ha); Ladoix *premier cru blanc* Les Gréchons; village Ladoix *blanc*; Côte de Nuits Villages.

The 23-year-old Sylvain Loichet made his first vintage—from vines returned to family hands after the leases had run out—in a warehouse in Comblanchien in 2005. A year later he moved to Chorey. He also has a small merchant business. These are early days, but I have liked what I have tasted.

Maillard Père et Fils

18 ha owned and *en fermage*. Corton, Les Renardes (1.50 ha, of which 0.33 ha produce Corton *blanc*); Corton (0.20 ha); Aloxe-Corton *premier cru* Les Grandes-Lolières; Beaune *premier cru* Les Grèves; village Aloxe-Corton, village Ladoix; village Savigny-lès-Beaune; village Beaune; village Pommard; village Meursault; Chorey-lès-Beaune.

I first ran into the Maillard family—Pascal and his brother Alain are in charge here—and their wines at the *Salon des Jeunes Professionnels* exhibition, which is held during the weekend of *Les Trois Glorieuses*. Subsequent tastings on the spot confirmed this cellar as a good source for sound, consistently made wines which evolve in the medium term. The fruit is de-stemmed, the must is cold-soaked for a few days, and the wine is matured using 25 percent new oak. "We want to bring out all the fruit," say the Maillards.

René Podichard

9 ha owned. Beaune *premier cru* Les Cent-Vignes; Chorey-lès-Beaune *rouge et blanc*; village Savigny-lès-Beaune; village Aloxe-Corton.

There have been Podichards in Chorey since the sixteenth century, says René, a shortish man in his mid-seventies. He is "thinking" about retiring and gradually passing things over to his step-son Jean-Pierre Maldant in Ladoix. This is a neat, tidy set-up in the centre of the village. The wines are good and classy, and the domaine believes in holding the best back until they are ready for drinking. This is a more-than-useful source.

Tollot-Beaut et Fils

24 ha owned and *en fermage*. Corton, Les Bressandes (0.91 ha); Corton (0.60 ha); Corton-Charlemagne (0.24 ha); Aloxe-Corton *premier cru* in Les Vercots and Les Fournières; Beaune *premier cru* in Les Grèves and Clos du Roi; Savigny-lès-Beaune *premier cru* in Les Lavières and Champ-Chevrey (*monopole*); village Aloxe-Corton; village Beaune in the *lieu-dit* Les Blanches-Fleurs; village Savigny-lès-Beaune; Chorey-lès-Beaune.

This is a well-known and very reliable source. The extended Tollot family—those in charge today are the thirty-something Jean-Paul, Olivier and Nathalie Tollot—work hard, do not spend their money on fripperies and keep an immaculate cellar. The wines—with 80 to 100 percent de-stemming; 8- to 12-day *cuvaison* at, for reds, up to 32°C; and between 20 and 60 percent new oak—have a particular signature. They are round, gently oaky and just slightly sweet in character and texture, and they will never disappoint. But like a Bordeaux-classed growth—La Lagune, for example—which never quite gives you super-second excitement, so do the Tollot wines never make the hair on the back of your neck tingle. This is a good source nevertheless, and the Chorey is a good example of basic red Burgundy.

BEAUNE

If Dijon is the departmental capital of the Côte d'Or, Beaune is the wine nerve centre of Burgundy. Inside the old walled city the atmosphere is still largely medieval. The streets are cobbled, the roads narrow and the buildings ancient. Aside from market days, and away from the Place Carnot and the few pedestrianised shopping streets which lie nearby, Beaune is a sleepy, shuttered town, full of hidden alleys, quiet Renaissance courtyards and ecclesiastical remnants of its glorious religious and aristocratic past. There is a fine church, the Collégiale Notre-Dame, whose origin dates from the twelfth century. There is a *Musée du Vin*, housed in a mansion formerly owned by successive Dukes of Burgundy in the fifteenth and sixteenth centuries. The Hôtel de Ville was once an ancient convent; another, the Couvent des Cordeliers, houses one of Beaune's wine firms and is a trap for the unwary tourist. And of course there is the Hôtel Dieu, heart of the Hospices de Beaune, one of the most magnificent wine monuments in the world.

Beaune explodes to life during the weekend of the *Trois Glorieuses*, three extravagant feasts which surround the Hospices de Beaune charity auction on the third Sunday in November. The city teems with people: local growers who have come up to show their wines in the massed throng of the Hôtel de Ville or the rather more sedate surroundings of the *Palais des Congrès*, and tourists, agents, buyers and friends of the local *négociants*, most of whom have their headquarters in the centre of the town, though today their cellars are housed in modern warehouses on the outskirts. Everybody is there. For one hectic week, countless litres of wine are drunk

or sampled and spat; it is impossible to find a parking space for your car, let alone a bed for the night. And then life returns to normal. The traffic whizzes round the *périphérique* without the metre-thick *bastions* which formed the city walls, or avoids Beaune altogether by taking the nearby motorway, and the old medieval centre regains it traditional somnolence.

History

Beaune lies on a natural crossroads. The "navel of Europe" was the extravagant boast of the local mayor, quoted by Christopher Fielden and John Arlott (*Burgundy*, 1976). It was where the old east–west road from Besançon to Autun met the old north–south *route* from Champagne and Dijon to Lyon and Marseilles; there was the added benefit of two natural springs which had their sources in the hills nearby. Colonised by the Romans as Belna or Belno Castrium in AD 40, the influence of Beaune grew as the importance of Autun, the capital of Burgundy in earlier Gallo-Roman days, fell, particularly after the destruction of the latter city by the sons of Clovis in the sixth century. By then, the vine was already important. Gregory of Tours, who wrote a history of France in about AD 570, described the hills as "covered in vines."

Until the Dukes of Burgundy moved to Dijon in the fourteenth century, Beaune was in all senses the capital of Burgundy. In 1395, Philippe Le Hardi published an ordinance prohibiting the plantation of the ignoble Gamay in favour of the noble Pinot, and from then on, the best sites of the Côte d'Or were exclusively planted with members of the Chardonnay or Pinot family, and the wines grew in fame.

The town of Beaune itself owes it character to the splendid pentagular fortified castle which was constructed during the reign of Charles XIII (1483–1498) and to the massive city fortifications which were built during the time of his predecessor Louis XI. This enclosed the town and has effectively preserved its centre. Unlike Dijon, Lyon, Mâcon or any other of the main cities of greater Burgundy, one can still imagine life as it might have been four or five hundred years ago.

Location

Beaune is the Côte d'Or's third largest *commune* after Gevrey-Chambertin and Meursault. The slope of the *premiers crus* extends from the boundary with Pommard at the southern end toward the border with Savigny-lès-Beaune to the north and is divided in half by the road which goes to Bouze in the Hautes-Côtes and along to Bligny-sur-Ouche. The soil structure, based on limestone, is complex. In general, it is thin to the north (Marconnets, Clos du Roi, Fèves, Bressandes), especially on the steeper, upper part of the slope, and the vines have to stretch deep to find their nutrients. These wines are full, firm and even solid at the outset and need time to mature. In the middle (Toussaints, Grèves, Teurons) there is some gravel (as the name Grèves would indicate), and the wine is of medium weight, plump and succulent. Bouchard Père's Vigne-de-l'Enfant-Jésus comes from an enclave in the Grèves. South of the road to Bligny, there is some sand in the inclined *climat* of Montée Rouge and at Aigrots, Pertuisots and the upper part of Vignes-Franches; on mid-slope (Clos des Mouches, Vignes-Franches—from whence comes Louis Jadot's Clos des Ursules—Sizies, Avaux), the soil is very stony and hard to work; and at the southern end and lower down the slope (Boucherottes, Epenotes, Chouacheux), there is more clay and less gravel. Here the soil is deep, and production can be excessive if not restricted. This sector is known as *le puits* (the well) *de Beaune* and produces soft, tender wines which evolve soon.

Though the colour of the soil is mainly a reddish-brown, there are parts where it is a whiteish marl, more suitable for the Chardonnay than the Pinot. On the upper part of the Clos des Mouches, Drouhin have vines which produce their celebrated white Beaune. Upslope in the Grèves, Jadot has Chardonnay. The results of these vines have a flavour which is somewhat spicier than that of a Meursault.

They also tend to evolve sooner. The production of white Beaune, however, is tiny—a mere 1,080 hectolitres or so per annum.

Which are the best *climats*? Beaune can boast 44 which, in whole or part, are classed as *premier cru* (there are no *grands crus*), and no one seems to agree which are the best. Dr. Morelot in 1831 cited Clos de la Mousse (a small vineyard now the monopoly of Bouchard Père et Fils), Teurons, Cras, Grèves, Fèves, Perrières, Cent-Vignes, Clos du Roi and Marconnets, all of which "have the capacity to produce exquisite wines." But he did not give any order of preference. Dr. Lavalle (1855) listed Fèves, Grèves, Crais (now Cras) and Champs-Pimont as *têtes de cuvées*. Camille Rodier, writing in 1920, reported the best as "Fèves, with its finesse and delicate aroma," and went on to note that "Grèves produces a very complete wine, with more body but not without finesse and velvet (*velouté*); Marconnets, on the Savigy border, is closed and solid, full but *bouqueté*. Clos-des-Mouches at the other end adjoining Pommard, is full-bodied, fruity, very elegant. Others (Cras, Champs-Pimont, Clos du Roi, Avaux, Aigrots) are supple and perfumed, and 'easy to drink'"—a familiar phrase for damning with faint praise, I have always thought. He adds Marconnets, Bressandes and Clos-des-Mouches to Dr. Lavalle's top *crus*. Poupon and Forgeot (*The Wines of Burgundy, 1964* and various editions subsequently) list Marconnets, Fèves, Bressandes, Grèves and Teurons as the best sites.

I would certainly agree with the last four of this final five (Marconnets can be too muscular to have real finesse) and would add Avaux, Coucherias, Cras, Vignes Franches and Clos des Mouches, with the rider that, as always in Burgundy, the grower or *négociant* is of equal importance to the actual source. François Germain at the Château de Chorey always has a good range of Beaune *premiers crus*, as does Albert Morot, whose Beaunes come from the 7-hectare family domaine and include Cent-Vignes, Grèves, Toussaints, Bressandes, Marconnets and Teurons. Bouchard Père et Fils are the largest landholders in the *commune* of Beaune, with 48 hectares of *premier crus*.

Chanson are next with 26, including the majority of Fèves, which they sell as Clos des Fèves. The Hospices de Beaune have eight *cuvées* of Beaune and possess 19 hectares. Drouhin have 15.5 hectares, Patriarche 12, Jadot 9, Louis Latour just over 4 and Remoissenet a couple of hectares. As one can see, most of the best land is owned by *négociants*. There are few important grower-only domaines in Beaune that market their wine in bottle.

How do the wines of Beaune compare with the other wines of the Côte? I find the wines of Beaune come mid-way between those of Pommard and those of Volnay. Pommards, particularly those of Rugiens, but equally from the best part of Epenots and elsewhere, are rich and sturdy. They can be somewhat four-square, but there should always be muscle. Volnays, on the other hand, are elegance personified: fragrance, delicacy, subtlety and finesse are the keynotes. The wines of Beaune are varied, as I have indicated above, but they lie somewhere in between. Only rarely, I would suggest, do they reach the quality of the best of these other two *communes*.

The Vineyard

PREMIERS CRUS As I have said, there are forty-four *climats* which, in whole or in part, are entitled to *premier cru* status. In alphabetical order, these are Les Aigrots; Les Avaux; Les Beaux-Fougets (part); Belissand; Blanches Fleurs (part); Les Boucherottes; Les Bressandes (part); Les Cent Vignes; Champs Pimont; Les Chouacheux; Clos-de-l'Écu; Clos de la Féguine (Aux Coucherias); Le Clos de la Mousse; Clos des Avaux; Le Clos des Mouches; Clos des Ursules (Les Vignes Franches); Clos du Roi (part); Clos Landry or Clos Saint-Landry; Clos Sainte-Anne (Sur les Grèves); Aux Coucherias; Aux Cras; A l'Écu (part); Les Epenotes (part); Les Fèves; En Genêt; Les Grèves; Sur les Grèves (part); Les Longes (part); Les Marconnets; La Mignotte; Montée Rouge (part); Les Montrevenots or Montrememots; En l'Orme; Les Perrières; Pertuisots; Les Reversées; Les Seurey; Les Sizies; Les Bas des Teurons; Les Teurons; Les Toussaints; Les Tuvilains; La Vigne de l'Enfant Jésus (Grèves); Les Vignes Franches.

Some of these are very small, and by no means are all regularly seen. In 40 years I have never come across Les Beaux-Fougeots, Les Longes, En l'Orme or Les Seurey, and I have seen Blanches Fleurs only as a village wine. Altogether, these cover 321.66 hectares, of which about 20 are planted with Chardonnay, and produce 11,500 hectolitres of red and 730 hectolitres of white wine per year.

VILLAGE WINE There are officially 128.13 hectares of village land decreed as Beaune *tout court*. No doubt much more land would be suitable: as in the *communes* to the north and south, all that down to the main road. But as the town has expanded, the village land has shrunk. Today only some 98 hectares (8 of which are white) are declared. Annual production is roughly 3,900 hectolitres of red wine and 350 hectolitres of white.

The village red wine, which is possibly supplemented by the lesser, young-vine *cuvées* of first growths, is a supple, early-maturing Pinot Noir of no great consequence. But the better *premiers crus* are quite a different kettle of fish. I describe these below. The white wine follows the same pattern. The village white wines are crisp, today wholly clean and "modern," quite subtle and for early drinking. The *premiers crus*, of which the Clos des Mouches of Drouhin is the leading example, have an interesting spice, as if there were a little Pinot Beurot in the vineyard. These remind me of those of Savigny and Aloxe, where there is more likely to be some Pinot Beurot in the mix, but at a more concentrated level. Jadot's Beaune Grèves is another recommended example.

CÔTE DE BEAUNE Not to be confused with Côte-de-Beaune Villages, this is a 52-hectare appellation covering land up on the hill of the Mont Batois, between the Beaune-Savigny boundary and the route to Bouze. Behind the villas on the hillside, from which you get a splendid view of Beaune and the plain beyond, there are isolated blocks of vines. Why these are not AC Beaune (which can be de-classified to Côte de Beaune, to further complicate matters), I can't imagine. The wines are similar—light, soft and forward—though produced at a higher altitude. Or if not Beaune, why not Hautes-Côtes-de-Beaune? Annual production averages 850 hectolitres of red and 500 hectolitres of white. Only some 30 hectares of the 52 hectares delineated are currently under vine.

The Premiers Crus

I deal with these in a north–south order.

LES MARCONNETS	(9.39 ha)
EN L'ORME	(2.02 ha)
LES PERRIÈRES	(3.20 ha)
EN GENÊT	(4.34 ha)
CLOS DU ROI	(8.41 ha)
BLANCHES FLEURS	(0.36 ha)

Though at the north end of the Côte, the aspect here is properly southeast (a short distance further south, Grèves inclines more directly to the east), and the wines, especially from Marconnets, furthest up the slope, are fullish, plump and rich. There is a robust element as well, and this can sometimes detract from the finesse. Clos du Roi, underneath Marconnets, produces somewhat more earthy wine.

RECOMMENDED SOURCES

LES MARCONNETS

Albert Morot, Roland Remoissenet (both Beaune).

LES PERRIÈRES

François Gay (Clos des Perrières) (Chorey-lès-Beaune).

CLOS DU ROI

Camus-Bruchon (Savigny-lès-Beaune); Tollot-Beaut (Chorey-lès-Beaune); Gabriel Bouchard (Beaune); Robert Ampeau (Meursault).

CLOS-DE-L'ÉCU	(2.37 ha)
A L'ÉCU	(2.65 ha)
LES FÈVES	(4.42 ha)
LES BRESSANDES	(16.97 ha)
LES TOUSSAINTS	(6.42 ha)
LES CENT VIGNES	(23.50 ha)

The slope turns round to incline more directly to the east here, and not all the Cent Vignes, which is practically flat, is probably really of first-growth quality. Bressandes and Fèves at the top

of the slope can produce very good wine, almost on par with Grèves and Teurons. Compared with the wines in the section above, there is an extra roundness, richness and style here, with the same sort of weight as Marconnets, but not the robust *sauvage* touch. The Clos-de-l'Écu is the monopoly of Faiveley of Nuits-Saint-Georges.

RECOMMENDED SOURCES

CLOS DE L'ÉCU

Faiveley *(monopole)* (Nuits-Saint-Georges).

CLOS DES FÈVES

Chanson *(monopole)* (Beaune).

LES BRESSANDES

Domaine des Croix, Louis Jadot, Albert Morot, Jean-Claude Rateau, Roland Remoissenet (all Beaune); Henri Germain (Meursault).

LES TOUSSAINTS

Louis Jadot, Albert Morot, Roland Remoissenet (all Beaune).

LES CENT VIGNES

François Germain, Château de Chorey, Arnoux Père et Fils, René Podichard (all Chorey-lès-Beaune); Domaine des Croix, Louis Jadot, Albert Morot (all Beaune); Vincent Bitouzet (Volnay); René Monnier (Meursault).

LES GRÈVES	(31.33 ha)
LES TEURONS	(21.04 ha)
AUX CRAS	(5.00 ha)
LES BAS DES TEURONS	(6.31 ha)
SUR LES GRÈVES	(2.90 ha)
CLOS SAINT ANNE	(0.73 ha)
CLOS DE LA FÉGUINE	(1.86 ha)
AUX COUCHERIAS	(7.70 ha)

This is where you will find the finest examples of *premier cru* Beaune. Sur les Grèves, in fact, lies above Teurons, not Grèves, while part of the bottom of this *climat* is technically Les Bas des Teurons and is supposed to be inferior (but because in practice, wine made here is labelled simply as Teurons, there is no way the customer can differentiate). Another part of the upper slope is above Teurons is Aux Cras, next to the road up to Bouze and facing south, not east, while Clos Saint-Anne, Clos de la Féguine (a monopoly of Domaine Jacques Prieur of

Meursault) and Aux Coucherias are the upper extensions beyond Aux Cras, as the hillsides turn round to face toward the south.

Cras, Teurons and Grèves, the former a little lighter than the other two, produce Beaune at its most elegant: fullish but properly round, rich and balanced, with plenty of depth. In cellars where they have both, Teurons is often the best, although this also depends on the age of the vines and the precise location of the vines on the slope.

Coucherias is again just a little lighter than Cras, but flowery, elegant and with a pleasant plump fruit. The Jadot wine is a yardstick example. Sur les Grèves seems to be a favoured location in these parts for Chardonnay.

RECOMMENDED SOURCES

LES GRÈVES (*blanc*)
Château de Chorey, Louis Jadot (both Beaune).

LES GRÈVES (*rouge*)
Daniel Largeot, Tollot-Beaut (both Chorey-lès-Beaune); Domaine des Croix, Joseph Drouhin, Louis Jadot, Albert Morot (all Beaune); Bouchard Père et Fils under Vigne-de-l'Enfant-Jésus (Beaune); Michel Lafarge (Volnay); Bernard Morey (Chassagne-Montrachet).

LES TEURONS
Château de Chorey, Bouchard Père et Fils, Louis Jadot, Albert Morot (all Beaune); Régis Rossignol-Chargarnier (Volnay).

AUX CRAS
Château de Chorey.

AUX COUCHERIAS
Jean-Claude Rateau, Louis Jadot (as Clos des Couchereaux) (both Beaune).

MONTÉE ROUGE	(3.75 ha)
CHAMPS PIMONT	(16.25 ha)
LA MIGNOTTE	(2.40 ha)
LES AVAUX	(11.52 ha)
CLOS DES AVAUX	(3.70 ha)
LES SEUREY	(1.23 ha)
CLOS DE LA MOUSSE	(3.37 ha)
LES SIZIES	(8.58 ha)
LES TUVILAINS	(8.94 ha)
BELISSAND	(4.88 ha)
LES REVERSÉES	(4.78 ha)

These are the *climats*, most of them small, which lie on the south side of the road up to Bouze. The slope is very gentle here, and there is quite a distance between the vines at the top (Montée Rouge) and those in Reversées at the bottom.

I have had my best wines here from Les Avaux (though in her *négociant* days at Leroy, Madame Lalou Bize offered a splendid range of Beaune, including Sizies). But the wines here do not seem to have the definition, the flair and the character of Teurons or Grèves. Pleasant, medium weight, round and fruity is the style. These are for the medium term.

RECOMMENDED SOURCES

LES AVAUX
Champy, Louis Jadot (both Beaune).

CLOS DE LA MOUSSE
Bouchard Père et Fils (*monopole*) (Beaune).

LES REVERSÉES
Jean-Marc Bouley (Volnay); Jean-Claude Rateau (Beaune).

LES AIGROTS	(18.64 ha)
LES MONTREVENOTS OR	
MONTREMEMOTS	(8.42 ha)
LE CLOS DES MOUCHES	(25.18 ha)
LES VIGNES FRANCHES	(9.77 ha)
PERTUISOTS	(5.27 ha)
CLOS SAINT-LANDRY OR	
CLOS LANDRY	(1.98 ha)
LES BOUCHEROTTES	(8.54 ha)
LES CHOUACHEUX	(5.04 ha)
LES EPENOTES	(7.69 ha)
LES BEAUX-FOUGETS	(0.27 ha)

These vineyards stretch from the hillsides of Montagne-Saint-Desirée down toward the main road, from a point where the vines face almost due east, as in Les Aigrots, all the way around to due south, as in Les Montrevenots. The slope is very gentle, only rising slowly, even at the top.

Here we are on the border with Pommard. Is there a similarity, as there is in Marconnets with Savigny? I have to say I don't see one, or at most, only at the foot of the slope between Epenotes and some of the weediest Epenots. Vignes Franches and Clos des Mouches (Jadot's Clos des Ursules in the former and Drouhin's example of the latter) are the best wines and *climats*. Here we can expect the same level of quality as Teurons and Grèves, but in a more expansive, opulent, slightly spicy sort of way. But most of the rest, as in the section above, lack excitement.

RECOMMENDED SOURCES

LE CLOS DESMOUCHES (*blanc*)
Joseph Drouhin (Beaune).

LE CLOS DES MOUCHES (*rouge*)
Joseph Drouhin (Beaune).

LES VIGNES FRANCHES
Château de Chorey, Louis Jadot as Clos des Ursules (both Beaune).

PERTUISOTS
Domaine des Croix (Beaune).

LES BOUCHEROTTES
Château de Chorey, Louis Jadot (both Beaune).

LES CHOUACHEUX
Louis Jadot (Beaune).

LES MONTREVENOTS
Jean-Marc Boillot (Pommard).

The Growers

★ **Albert Bichot et Cie**
DOMAINE DU CLOS FRANTIN: 7.53 ha owned and *en métayage*. Echezeaux (1.00 ha); Clos de Vougeot (0.63 ha); Grands Echézeaux (0.25 ha); Chambertin (0.17 ha); Richebourg (0.07 ha); Vosne-Romanée *premier cru* in Les Rouges and Les Malconsorts; village Vosne-Romanée; village Nuits-Saint-Georges; village Gevrey-Chambertin.

DOMAINE DU PAVILLON: 15.63 ha owned and *en fermage/en métayage*. Corton-Charlemagne (1.20 ha); Corton Clos des Maréchaudes (0.55 ha); Aloxe-Corton *premier cru* Clos des Maréchaudes; Beaune *premier cru* Clos des Mouches; Pommard *premier cru* Les Rugiens; Volnay *premier cru* Les Santenots; Meursault *premier cru* Les Charmes; village Beaune; village Pommard in the *lieu-dit* Clos des Ursulines (*monopole*); village Aloxe-Corton; village Meursault.

A new team took over here in 1999, headed by Philippe de Marcilly, as managing director, and Christophe Chauval, on the wine side. A sea change has since occurred. Bichot's merchant wines are now vinified by themselves, alongside the produce of their own two estates. High quality here begins with the 2002 vintage.

Gabriel Bouchard
4 ha owned and *en fermage*. Beaune *premier cru* in Les Cent-Vignes, Clos du Roi; Pommard *premier cru* Les Charmots; village Savigny-lès-Beaune in the *lieu-dit* Les Liards; village Saint-Romain in the *lieu-dit* Les Perrières; village Beaune.

A rabbit warren of cramped cellars in the back streets of Beaune houses this Bouchard domaine, which claims only a scant relationship to better known Bouchards. Space prevents a total *élevage* in cask. After 12 months the wines have to go back into tank. Mixed results are found here.

★★ *Bouchard Père et Fils S.A.*
130 ha owned. Bâtard-Montrachet (0.80 ha); Bonnes-Mares (0.24 ha); Chambertin (0.15 ha); Chevalier-Montrachet (2.54 ha); Clos-de-Vougeot (0.45 ha); Corton-Charlemagne (3.25 ha); Echézeaux (0.39 ha); Le Corton (3.94 ha); Montrachet (0.89 ha); Aloxe-Corton *premier cru*; Beaune *premier cru* in A l'Ecu, Les Aigrots (*rouge et blanc*), Les Avaux, Belissand, Les Boucherottes, Les Bressandes, Les Cent Vignes, Champs Pimont, Clos Saint-Landry (*blanc; monopole*), Clos de la Mousse (*monopole*), Clos du Roi, En Genêt, Les Grèves (Vigne de l'Enfant Jésus), Les Marconnets, Pertuisots, Les Reversées, Les Seurey, Les Sizies (*rouge et blanc*), Sur les Grèves (*blanc*), Les Teurons (*rouge et blanc*), Les Toussaints and Les Tuvilains (*blanc*); Chassagne-Montrachet *premier cru* En Remilly; Gevrey-Chambertin *premier cru* Les Cazetiers; Meursault *premier cru* in Les Bouchères, Charmes, Genevrières, Les Gouttes d'Or, Perrières and Poruzots; Monthelie *premier cru* in Les Champs Fulliot and Les Duresses; Nuits-Saint-Georges *premier cru* Les Cailles; Pommard *premier cru* in Les Chanlins, Les Combes, Les Pézerolles and Les Rugiens; Savigny-lès-Beaune *premier cru* in Les Lavières; Volnay *premier cru* in Les Caillerets, En Chevret, Clos des Chênes, Frémiets, Pitures and Taillepieds; village wine in Aloxe-Corton, Beaune

(*rouge et blanc*), Bouzeron, Chambolle-Musigny, Meursault, including the *lieu-dit* Les Clous, Monthelie, Pommard, Savigny.

Beaune Clos du Château is produced from the lesser and smaller *premier cru cuvées* in both colours. Bouchard Père et Fils are the largest landholders in Meursault Genevrières with 2.65 hectares. Up until 2002 (and then partly until the 2005 vintage), Bouchard Père et Fils were also *éleveurs* and bottlers of the wines of the Château de Vosne-Romanée (see page 133) (La Romanée *monopole*, Vosne-Romanée Aux Reignots), which has now reverted to the Liger-Belair family. They were also responsible until 2003 for the Domaine du Clos-Saint-Marc in Nuits-Saints-Georges (Clos-Saint-Marc *monopole* and Les Argillières). This has now been bought by Patrice Rion of Prémeaux. Finally, they distribute the wine of the Château de Mandelot in the Hautes-Côtes and were pioneers with Aligoté de Bouzeron.

I have had plenty of splendid Bouchard wines of the 1940s, 1950s and early 1960s and would still be happy to chance them today if any of these happened to come my way. But since then, all the way through the time I started writing my magazine *The Vine*, I have found the end results at Bouchard Père et Fils no better than competent, though occasionally there were glimmers on the horizon.

In 1995 Bouchard Père et Fils was acquired by the dynamic Joseph Henriot of Henriot Champagne. His goal was to make the finest wines possible and restore Bouchard's reputation to its former glories. You could sense the sigh of relief! Since then, Philippe Prost, winemaker, and Bernard Hervet, managing director (who left in February 2006), have done just that. More vineyards, particularly in Meursault, were acquired to add to what was already a sizeable domaine. The elegant Château de Beaune, beneath which are impressive cellars, was restored, and the winery was moved from relatively new (1985) premises opposite the château to a new establishment on the road to Savigny in 2005.

The red grapes are largely de-stemmed, the juice briefly cold-soaked and vinified at up to 30°C. There is 30 percent or more new wood for the red wines and a maximum of 30 percent new oak for the whites. Today, not only is the range comprehensive, but the quality is also consistent and fine.

The excellent firm/domaine of William Fèvre in Chablis also belongs to Joseph Henriot.

Joseph de Bucy

Joseph de Bucy, cellar manager for Jean Germain in Meursault, and then briefly for Albert Bichot, set up on his own as a merchant in 1996. The range is limited. The wines are mostly white. They are good, but he has had difficulties selling them.

Carré-Courbin

8.3 ha owned and *en fermage*. Pommard *premier cru* Les Grands Epenots; Volnay *premier cru* in Les Taillepieds, Clos de la Cave des Ducs (*monopole*), Robardelle and Les Lurets; Beaune *premier cru rouge et blanc* Les Reversées; village Volnay, including a *vieilles vignes cuvée*; village Pommard; village Meursault.

Philippe and Maëlle Carré were the two members of the family in charge here, the previous generation having retired. Substantial progress has been made here in recent years, despite the regular hail problems Volnay has suffered in the last 6 years. The wines are very *terroir* specific, and there is an interesting monopoly from an enclave within the village of Volnay itself. Sadly in 2006, in order to resolve financial and inheritance complications, it was decided to put the domaine up for sale. Many of the choicest parcels were acquired by Champy (see below); the rest were leased or sold to other *vignerons*.

Champy Père et Fils

17 ha owned and *en fermage*. Corton (0.33 ha); Corton-Charlemagne (0.33 ha); Beaune *premier cru in* Champs Pimont, Aux Cras, Les Tuvilains; Pernand-Vergelesses *premier cru* in Les Fichots; village Beaune Vieilles Vignes; village Savigny-lès-Beaune, including the *lieu-dit* Aux Fourches; village Chorey-lès-Beaune; village Pernand-Vergelesses, including the *lieu-dit* Clos de Bully; village Auxey-Duresses; village Saint-Romain;

Côte de Beaune villages; plus Volnay Les Taillepieds, Beaune Les Reversées, and so forth, acquired from Domaine Carré-Courbin in 2006 (see above).

Champy is the oldest *négociant* in Burgundy and has archives dating back to 1720. Somewhat moribund, it was acquired by Jadot in the late 1980s, which was interested in the vineyards. Jadot kept these, and some interesting reserves of old bottles dating back to the mid-nineteenth century, but sold the remainder—name and cellars—in 1990 to Henri Meurgey, a well-recognised oenologue and broker, and his son Pierre.

What the more-or-less-retired Henri and Pierre, plus their talented *chef de cave* Dimitri Bazas, offer today is a wide range of well-priced, well-chosen wines ranging from generics upward, but not too far upward. The emphasis is on affordable village Côte de Beaune wines rather than on a glitzy range of *grands crus*. DIVA, handling estate-bottled Burgundy, is another Meurgey concern.

They are gradually moving to a biodynamic approach in the vineyards they lease, vinifying with 0 to 50 percent of the stems at temperatures up to 32°C and using a quarter to a third new oak. There is a happy lack of a Champy signature in their wines, and quality is now good. I have, however, been largely disappointed by the Champy offerings at my annual 10-year-on tastings.

★ Chanson Père et Fils

43 ha owned. Corton, Vergennes *blanc* (0.65 ha); Beaune *premier cru* in Clos des Fèves *(monopole)*, Les Bressandes, Les Grèves, Le Clos des Mouches, Clos des Marconnets, Clos du Roi, Champs Pimont, Les Teurons and A L'Écu; Savigny-lès-Beaune *premier cru* in La Dominode and Les Marconnets; Pernand-Vergelesses *premier cru* Les Vergelesses and En Caradeux *(blanc)*; Santenay *premier cru* Beauregard; Chassagne-Montrachet *premier cru* Les Chenevottes; Puligny-Montrachet *premier cru* Les Folatières; village Chassagne-Montrachet *rouge et blanc*.

Chanson was established in 1750, and sold by the successor, the Marion Family, to Bollinger Champagne in 1999. Bollinger appointed Gilles de Courcel as PDG and Jean-Pierre Confuron

as winemaker. The land holdings are impressive, and, since 2001, the quality has lived up to the potential. Fifty percent of the stems are retained for the red wines, which are vinified at up to 32°C after a week of cold-soaking. Thirty percent new oak is employed. All this takes place in a modern warehouse outside Beaune, but the company's headquarters lie within one of the town's five *bastions*.

Yves Darviot

3 ha owned. Beaune *premier cru* in Les Grèves, Le Clos des Mouches *(rouge et blanc)*; village Beaune *(rouge et blanc)*; plus, as *négociant* wine, bought in as fruit: Beaune *premier cru* Bressandes, Vignes Franches; village Aloxe-Corton.

The children of the 70-year-old Yves Darviot have shown no interest in taking over, so for some years, Guillaume Esmery has been responsible at this well-established domaine/merchant. Esmery keeps back 10 percent of the stems, doesn't like too much new oak and retains a lot of the carbon dioxide in order to be able to get away with minimal sulphating. Bottling takes place after a year. There are very good wines here.

★ Domaine des Croix

5.07 ha owned. Corton-Charlemagne (0.25 ha); Beaune *premier cru* in Les Teurons, Les Cent Vignes, Les Pertuisots, Les Bressandes, Les Grèves; Savigny-lès-Beaune *premier cru* Les Peuillets; village Beaune; village Pommard; village Savigny-lès-Beaune.

Formerly the Domaine Duchet, this estate was acquired by the American Roger Forbes and his associates in 2005 and is run by the talented David Croix, winemaker at Maison Camille Giroud. The 2005s and 2006s are very promising. I expect great things here.

★★ Joseph Drouhin, S.A.

60.7 ha owned and *en fermage*. Chambertin, Clos de Bèze (0.12 ha); Griotte-Chambertin (0.53 ha); Bonnes-Mares (0.23 ha); Le Musigny (0.67 ha); Grands-Echézeaux (0.47 ha); Echézeaux (0.41 ha); Clos de Vougeot (0.91 ha); Corton, Bressandes (0.29 ha); Corton-Charlemagne (0.34 ha); Bâtard-Montrachet (0.90 ha); Chambolle-Musigny *premier cru* in Les Amoureuses and Les Baudes; Chambolle-Musigny *premier cru* (*tout court*) from Les Noirots, Les Hauts Doix, Les Borniques, Les Plantes, Les Combottes; Vosne-Romanée *premier cru* Les Petits Monts; Nuits-Saint-Georges *premier cru* Les Procès; Volnay *premier cru* Le Clos des Chênes; Beaune *premier cru* including Le Clos des Mouches (*rouge et blanc*), Les Grèves, Les Champs Pimont, Les Epenotes; village Chorey-lès-Beaune; village Meursault; Côte de Beaune; plus a domaine of 37.8 hectares in Chablis. Drouhin is also the exclusive distributor of Domaine Marquis de Laguiche in Chassagne-Montrachet (see page 279).

The firm dates from 1880, when Joseph Drouhin took over an already well-established Burgundian house and then acquired the old cellars of the Dukes of Burgundy near the Collégiale Notre-Dame.

This is one of the most perfectionistic and least paternalistic of the Beaune merchants, dealing in nothing but Burgundy and Beaujolais, not even generics. The wines are now made in modern premises on the outskirts of Beaune, under the supervision of Robert Jousset-Drouhin, head of the firm; his son Philippe, who is responsible for the vineyards; and until December 2006, when she retired, chief oenologue Laurence Jobard. They are as good as any in the Côte, equally fine in both colours. Drouhin's daughter Véronique is responsible for the company's Oregon diversification: Domaine Drouhin.

Maison Alex Gambal

Alex Gambal arrived in Beaune in 1993 to work for the broker Becky Wasserman and left 5 years later to set up his own *négociant* business. As yet, this is a modest—150 casks per year—affair, with most of the wines, apart from the *grands crus*, being bought in as grapes. Most of the produce is sold to the United States. I find some of the wines a bit over-oaked. But you can find good bottles here.

Emmanuel Giboulot

9.65 ha owned and *en fermage*. Village Beaune in the *lieu-dit* Lulunne; Saint-Romaine *rouge et blanc*; Côte de Beaune *blanc* in the *lieux-dits* La Grande Chatelaine, Les Pierres Blanches, Combe d'Eve; Rully *premier cru blanc* La Pucelle.

This domaine has been biological since 1970 and biodynamic since 1990. Emmanuel took over from his father in 1985. Low yields, hand harvesting and meticulously clean vinifications lead to lovely pure wines. This is an address to follow.

★ Camille Giroud, S.A.

1.15 ha owned. Beaune *premier cru* in Aux Avaux and Aux Cras.

Camille Giroud has been transformed in recent years and is now the most exciting of the smaller *négociants* in Burgundy. In 2001 the family company was acquired by a consortium of American bankers, who, with Becky Wasserman's help, recruited the talented David Croix as winemaker. His first vintage was 2002. This is a man of great talent. The approach is "traditional," that is, a minimum of new oak and late bottling. Increasingly, purchases are in fruit, and quality is very good indeed. Older vintages, such as those of the pre-1980s, are also very fine. If you can find them, grab them.

Hospices de Beaune

The Hospices de Beaune comprise two charitable institutions, the Hôtel-Dieu, founded in 1443 by Nicolas Rolin, Chancellor of Philippe Le Hardi, Duke of Burgundy, and his wife Guigone de Salins, and the Hospice de la Charité, endowed by Antoine Rousseau and his wife Barbe Deslandes in the seventeenth century. The Hôtel Dieu is a remarkable building in the centre of Beaune and is one the world's great vinous tourist attractions. It is no longer used as a charitable institution for the sick and the poor, but is preserved as a museum. The central feature of the building is a huge dormitory, the Grande Salle or Chambre des Pauvres, its walls lined with curiously wide yet short beds—the inmates slept two to a bed—each with a sight of the altar at the far end so that, though bedridden, they could participate in the services.

The visitor will then pass into a central courtyard, view the medieval kitchens and pantries and then move into a small art gallery, whose central feature is a magnificent *Last Judgement*, commissioned by Rolin and executed by Roger van der Weyden. This is one of the masterpieces of the Northern Renaissance. Rolin and his wife also commissioned a picture of the Virgin from Jan van Eyck. This is in the Louvre.

Over the years, both of these charitable institutions were the fortunate recipients of vineyards, and these holdings now total some 58 hectares, nearly all of it *premier cru* or *grand cru*, and all but three in the Côte de Beaune, making the Hospices one of the largest names in Burgundy. These 58 hectares are split into 41 different *cuvées* which are blends of a number of different *climats* within the same *commune*. They are sold each year under the name of the benefactor, by auction, on the Sunday afternoon (and up to 2005 well into the evening, for it used to be a lengthy, tedious auction *à la chandelle*) of the third weekend in November. In 2005, 789 casks of wine (plus some of the previous year's *eau de vie*) were auctioned. This is not the entirety of the production—the produce of the younger vines is disposed of in bulk to the local *négociants*. The auction is the central event of the weekend of the Trois Glorieuses and traditionally sets the trend of prices for the vintage, although the actual levels paid are grossly inflated.

The wines are sold when they are barely a month old, and as crucial as their initial quantity is the competence of the firm which will look after it subsequently (although since 2005, anyone can bid, but only local merchants may mature and bottle). It is wise to choose a merchant whose name you can trust.

RED WINE CUVÉES

CHARLOTTE DUMAY: Corton, Les Renardes (2.00 ha); Corton, Les Bressandes (1.00 ha); Corton, Clos du Roi (0.40 ha).

DOCTEUR PESTE: Corton, Les Bressandes (1.00 ha); Corton, Les Chaumes et Les Voirosses (1.00 ha); Corton, Clos du Roi (0.50 ha); Corton, Les Fiètres (0.40 ha); Corton, Les Grèves (0.10 ha).

RAMEAU-LAMAROSSE: Pernand-Vergelesses, Les Basses Vergelesses (0.65 ha).

FORNERET: Savigny-lès-Beaune, Les Vergelesses (1.00 ha); Savigny-lès-Beaune, Les Gravains (0.65 ha).

FOUQUERAND: Savigny-lès-Beaune Les Basses Vergelesses (1.00 ha); Savigny-lès-Beaune, Les Talmettes (0.65 ha); Savigny-lès-Beaune, Aux Gravains (0.33 ha); Savigny-lès-Beaune, Aux Serpentières (0.14 ha).

ARTHUR GIRARD: Savigny-lès-Beaune, Les Peuillets (1.00 ha); Savigny-lès-Beaune, Les Marconnets (0.80 ha).

NICOLAS ROLIN: Beaune, Les Cent Vignes (1.40 ha); Beaune, Les Grèves (0.33 ha); Beaune, En Genêt (0.20 ha); Beaune, Les Teurons (0.50 ha); Beaune, Les Bressandes (0.14 ha).

GUIGONE DE SALINS: Beaune, Les Bressandes (1.20 ha); Beaune, Les Seurey (0.80 ha); Beaune, Les Champs Pimont (0.60 ha).

CLOS DES AVAUX: Beaune, Les Avaux (2.00 ha).

BRUNET: Beaune, Les Teurons (0.50 ha); Beaune, Les Bressandes (0.50 ha); Beaune, Les Cent Vignes (0.50 ha).

MAURICE DROUHIN: Beaune, Les Avaux (1.00 ha); Beaune, Les Boucherottes (0.65 ha); Beaune, Les Champs Pimont (0.60 ha); Beaune, Les Grèves (0.25 ha).

HUGUES AND LOUIS BÉTAULT: Beaune, Les Grèves (1.10 ha); Beaune, La Mignotte (0.54 ha); Beaune, Les Aigrots (0.40 ha); Beaune, Le Clos des Mouches (0.33 ha).

ROUSSEAU-DESLANDES: Beaune, Les Cent Vignes (1.00 ha); Beaune, Les Montrevenots (0.65 ha); La Mignotte (0.40 ha).

DAMES-HOSPITALIÈRES: Beaune, Les Bressandes (1.00 ha); Beaune, La Mignotte (1.13 ha); Beaune, Les Teurons (0.50 ha).

DAMES DE LA CHARITÉ: Pommard, Les Petits-Epenots (0.40 ha); Pommard, Les Rugiens (0.33 ha); Pommard, Les Noizons (0.25 ha); Pommard, La Refène (0.35 ha); Pommard, Les Combes-Dessus (0.20 ha).

BILLARDET: Pommard, Les Petits Epenots (0.65 ha); Pommard, Les Noizons (0.50 ha); Pommard, Les Arvelets (0.40 ha); Pommard, Les Rugiens (0.35 ha).

BLONDEAU: Volnay, Les Champans (0.60 ha); Volnay, Taille Pieds (0.60 ha); Volnay, Le Ronceret (0.35 ha); Volnay, En l'Ormeau (0.25 ha).

GÉNÉRAL MUTEAU: Volnay, Le Village (0.80 ha); Volnay, Carelle sous la Chapelle (0.35 ha); Volnay, Les Caillerets Dessus (0.20 ha); Volnay, Frémiets (0.20 ha); Volnay, Taille Pieds (0.20 ha).

JEHAN DE MASSOL: Volnay, Les Santenots (1.25 ha); Volnay (Santenots), Les Plures (0.25 ha).

GAUVAIN: Volnay, Les Santenots (0.65 ha); Volnay (Santenots), Les Plures (0.75 ha).

LEBELIN: Monthelie, Les Duresses (0.88 ha).

BOILLOT: Auxey, Les Duresses (0.50 ha).

MADELAINE COLLIGNON: Mazis-Chambertin (1.75 ha).

CYROT-CHAUDRON: Beaune, Les Montrevenots (1.00 ha).

RAYMOND CYROT: Pommard premier cru (0.65 ha); Pommard (1.10 ha).

SUZANNE CHAUDRON: Pommard (1.37 ha).

CYROT CHAUDRON ET GEORGES KRITTER: Clos de la Roche (0.40 ha).

WHITE WINE CUVÉES

FRANÇOISE DE SALINS: Corton-Charlemagne (0.40 ha).

BAUDOT: Meursault, Les Genevrières Dessus (0.65 ha); Meursault, Les Genevrières Dessous (0.75 ha).

PHILIPPE LE BON: Meursault, Les Genevrières Dessus (0.13 ha); Meursault, Les Genevrières Dessous (0.40 ha).

DE BAHÈZRE DE LANLAY: Meursault, Les Charmes Dessus (0.13 ha); Meursault, Les Charmes Dessous (0.40 ha).

ALBERT GRIVAULT: Meursault, Les Charmes-Dessus (0.50 ha).

JEHAN HUMBLOT: Meursault, Les Poruzots (0.50 ha); Meursault, Les Grands Charrons (0.10 ha).

LOPPIN: Meursault, Les Criots (0.50 ha); Meursault, Les Cras (0.20 ha).

GOUREAU: Meursault, Les Poruzots (0.35 ha); Meursault, Les Peutes Vignes (0.20 ha).

PAUL CHANSON: Corton blanc, Les Vergennes (0.35 ha).

DAMES DE FLANDRES: Bâtard-Montrachet (0.35 ha).

FRANÇOIS POISARD: Pouilly-Fuissé (4.00 ha).

This is a curious set-up. The end results are the responsibility of three separate entities. Firstly, the vines are tended by a disparate collection of locals, each of whom usually has vines of his/her own in the locality. Secondly, the grapes are delivered to the Hospices' up-to-date winery (it was constructed in 1994) on the outskirts of Beaune. Thirdly, the wines, hardly finished, are sold over the Trois Glorieuses weekend, the third in November—the auction is now run by Christie's—but whoever buys them, as I have said, must have them élevés by one of the local merchants, who must take delivery of the casks by January 1.

This results in several anomalies. Having no 1- or 2-year-old casks to work with, all the wines (an exception was made in 2006) are perforce sold by the Hospices in new casks. The wood seems to have an unusually high toast, and in my view, most Hospices wines are over-oaked, even if racked into older wood immediately after they arrive in the merchant's cellars. Thus, for élevage is just as important as winemaking, the same cuvée from two different négociants will produce two different wines.

The wines, too, with exceptions, consistently disappoint. They lack concentration; they are too slight.

It is a crazy way to endeavour to produce fine wines. The system should be revised so that there is one single person in charge, one single team responsible for everything from A to Z. Quite simply, the Hospices de Beaune should be run as any other Burgundian domaine.

★★ Louis Jadot
150.35 ha owned and en fermage.

This is split up between five domaines:
DOMAINE LOUIS JADOT: 42.45 ha.
ROUGE Chambertin Clos-de-Bèze (0.42); Chapelle-Chambertin (0.39); Bonnes-Mares (0.27); Le Musigny (0.17); Echézeaux (0.35); Corton, Grèves (0.44); Clos de Vougeot (2.15); Gevrey-Chambertin premier cru in Clos Saint-Jacques, Les Cazetiers, La Combe Aux Moines, Lavaux-Saint-Jacques, Les Estournelles-Saint-Jacques,

Les Poissenots; Chambolle-Musigny *premier cru* in Les Amoureuses, Les Feusselottes, Les Fuées; Savigny-lès-Beaune in La Dominode, Les Lavières, Les Narbantons, Les Vergelesses; Beaune *premier cru* in Les Aigrots, Les Avaux, Pertuisots, Les Teurons, Les Tuvilains; Pommard *premier cru* Les Rugiens; Pernand-Vergelesses *premier cru* Clos de la Croix de Pierre; Marsannay; village Savigny; village Pommard; village Santenay in the *lieu-dit* Clos de Malte; Côte de Nuits villages.

BLANC Chassagne-Montrachet *premier cru* Abbaye de Morgeot; Puligny-Montrachet *premier cru* in Les Combettes, Les Folatières, La Garenne and Les Referts; Meursault *premier cru* in Les Genevrières and Les Poruzots; Pernand-Vergelesses *premier cru* Clos de la Croix de Pierre; Savigny-lès-Beaune *premier cru* in Les Hauts Jarrons and Les Vergelesses; village Pernand-Vergelesses; village Savigny-lès-Beaune; village Santenay in the *lieu-dit* Clos de Malte; village Marsannay; Côte de Nuits villages; plus 70 hectares in the Beaujolais (Château des Jacques; Château des Lumières).

DOMAINE DES HÉRITIERS LOUIS JADOT: 15.25 ha.
Corton-Charlemagne (1.60); Corton, Les Pougets (1.47); Chevalier-Montrachet, Les Demoiselles (0.52); Corton (0.19); Pernand-Vergelesses *premier cru* Clos de la Croix de Pierre; Beaune *premier cru* in Les Boucherottes, Les Bressandes, Les Chouacheux, Clos des Couchereaux (in Les Coucherias), Clos des Ursules (in Les Vignes-Franches), Les Teurons; Puligny-Montrachet *premier cru* Les Folatières.

DOMAINE GAGEY: 13.45 ha.
Clos-Saint-Denis (0.17); Echézeaux (0.17); Chambolle-Musigny *premier cru* Les Baudes; Nuits-Saint-Georges *premier cru* Les Boudots; Beaune *premier cru* in Les Aigrots, Les Bressandes (*blanc*), Les Cent Vignes, Les Chouacheux, Les Grèves (*blanc)*, Pertuisots, Les Teurons, Les Toussaints, Les Tuvilains; Savigny-lès-Beaune *premier cru* Clos les Guettes (*rouge et blanc*); Puligny-Montrachet *premier cru* Les Champs Gains; village Chambolle-Musigny.

DOMAINE DUC DE MAGENTA: 5.22 ha.
Chassagne-Montrachet *premier cru* Morgeot "Clos-de-la-Chappelle" *rouge et blanc*; Puligny-Montrachet *premier cru* Clos-de-la-Garenne.

DOMAINE DU CHATEAU DE LA COMMARAINE: 4.04 ha.
Pommard *premier cru* in Clos de la Commaraine and Clos Blanc.

In addition there are long-term contracts in the following first growths: Pommard *premier cru* in Clos des Poutures (*monopole*), Grands Epenots, Epenots; Volnay *premier cru* Clos de la Barre (*monopole*), Clos des Chênes; and Meursault *premier cru* Goutte d'Or.

The winemaker here is the candid and enthusiastic Jacques Lardière: a fountain of knowledge and a man of genius. You will learn more about Burgundy in a morning tasting with him than in 5 years trekking around on your own. And you will never be anything less than highly satisfied with his wines—he is a perfectionist. As you sample what is an exhaustive range and make your comments, you will often be told that yes, probably, this *premier cru* (not quite up to snuff) will be downgraded to the village *cuvée*; with this wine he did such-and-such, with another something quite different; and so forth.

Lardière is a flexible winemaker. Some of the *grands crus* (the Chambertin, Clos de Bèze, for instance) are vinified with the stems; others (the Musigny) are not. He is not worried if fermentation temperatures climb as high as 35°C. In most cases he blocks at least part of the malolactic fermentation in his white wines. There is a powerful instinct at work here.

Lucien le Moine

Lucien le Moine was set up in 1999 by the Lebanese Mounir Saouma and his Israeli wife Rotem Brakin. They deal in only *premier* and *grand cru*, bought in as fruit. They use long macerations; 50 percent new oak; and no racking, fining or filtration. The wines are bottled with high levels of carbon dioxide. They taste more Californian than Côte d'Or and are not to my taste. There is bulk and richness—but no elegance.

Albert Morot

7.91 ha owned. Beaune *premier cru* in Les Aigrots
(*rouge et blanc*), Les Bressandes, Les Cent Vignes,
Les Grèves, Les Marconnets, Les Teurons and Les
Toussaints; Savigny-lès-Beaune *premier cru* in "La
Bataillière" and Les Vergelesses.

Once a *négociant*, this family firm, today run by
Geoffroy Choppin de Janvry, now subsists on
its domaine, which contains only *premiers crus*
vines, and operates out of the gauntly gothic
Château de la Creusotte on the road to Bouze-
lès-Beaune. The grapes are de-stemmed and
vinified at a maximum of 32°C after a brief cold-
soaking. They are then given up to 50 percent
new wood, quite toasted. I find this too much,
for underneath, the wines are not rich enough.

Blair Pethel, Domaine Dublaire

0.95 ha owned. Corton-Charlemagne
(0.50 ha); Chassagne-Montrachet, Les Chaumées;
Savigny-lès-Beaune.

Most wine lovers, I imagine, have fantasies
about owning a vineyard. For outsiders, it is
easier said than done. Quality land is difficult
to acquire, and it is expensive. Who looks after
your vines? Who makes your wine? Blair Pethel,
an American financial journalist, bought his
Corton-Charlemagne in 2004 (the wine was
made by Patrice Rion) and in 2006 took over a
cellar and five *ouvrées* in Savigny-lès-Beaune. He
now has a small merchant's operation running
in tandem with the wines of his domaine.

Albert Ponnelle

1 ha owned. Beaune *premier cru* Les Bressandes;
Savigny-lès-Beaune.

The company of Pierre Ponnelle, founded
around 1850, was sold to Jean-Claude Boisset in
1984, and its important vineyard is today part of
the Domaine de la Vougeraie.
 Pierre-Albert Ponnelle set up his own merchant business in 1999 and has since acquired a
small estate. His viticultural approach is deeply
ecological. He trains high, ploughs with horses
and eschews weed killers and all synthetic

products. The *négociant* business is modest and
is based on the wines of the Côte de Beaune,
bought in as fruit as much as possible and reared
in a minimum of new oak. I like the wines.

★ Jean-Claude Rateau

8.8 ha owned and *en fermage/en métayage*. Beaune
premier cru Les Bressandes, Les Coucherias and Les
Reversées; village Beaune, including the *lieux-dits*
Clos des Mariages and Les Prévoles; Côte-de-Beaune.

Jean-Claude Rateau was one of the first of a now-
increasing number of Burgundian *vignerons*
who are *biodynamique*, and as such, he has been
something of a mentor to others. If this makes
him sound like the wise old man of the hills it is
not meant to. He is a vigorous, tall 50-year-old
with a big black mustache, who started with one
biodynamic hectare in 1979. He picks late. Other
parts of his recipe are no stems, no new oak, a
few days cold-soaking and no racking until bottling. His cellar, on two levels, works entirely by
gravity. The results, especially the Reversées, a
fine example of a not particularly well-sited *premier cru*, are very good.

Remoissenet Père et Fils

2.50 ha owned. Beaune *premier cru* in En Genêt, Les
Grèves, Les Marconnets, Les Toussaints.

Courtier as well as *négociant* (for a long time this
firm was the supplier/broker for Nicolas and it
was on the back of this that the merchant business was established). Roland Remoissenet,
today in his seventies, and a shrewd man of
frequent collecting enthusiasms—and a cat
who walks by himself; he is decidedly not part
of the sometimes self-important Beaune *négociant* "mafia"—sold his business to Edward
and Howard Milstein, American bankers, in
May 2006. Canadian agent Todd Halpbern and
the firm of Lous Jadot have minority shares.
Bernard Repolt, late of Maison Jaffelin, is now
managing director. The firm distributes the
wines of the Domaine Baron Thenard (see
page 308) and these—Le Montrachet, Corton
Clos du Roi, Grands Echézeaux—are often the
best wines. Today the problems of supply, with

all of the best growers bottling all their best wines themselves, must be getting increasingly acute, but you can still get some very fine wines, which keep remarkably well, under the Remoissenet label, particularly in white.

Comte Senard

8.70 ha owned. Corton, Clos de Meix (1.65 ha); Corton, Clos du Roi (0.64 ha); Corton, Les Bressandes (0.63 ha); Corton, En Charlemagne *rouge* (0.40 ha); Corton from Les Paulands (0.63 ha); Corton *blanc* from the Clos de Meix (0.45 ha); Aloxe-Corton *premier cru* Les Valozières; Beaune *premier cru* Les Coucherias; village Aloxe-Corton *rouge et blanc*; village Chorey-lès-Beaune.

Philippe Senard lives in Aloxe-Corton but now makes his wines together with his daughter Lorraine, who started by vinifying the whites in 2001 in one of the battlements surrounding Beaune. The Pinot Noir grapes are 70 percent de-stemmed and cold-soaked for a week, and the juice is vinified at 28–30°C. The results are wines which have good fruit and freshness but lack a bit of fat and succulence. The whites are better.

Back in Aloxe there is a little bistro/wine-tasting operation, which is open in the summer.

Domaine des Terregelesses

6.85 ha owned. Corton-Charlemagne (0.35 ha); Savigny-lès-Beaune *premier cru* Les Vergelesses (*rouge et blanc*); village Savigny-lès-Beaune; village Chorey-lès-Beaune *rouge et blanc*; village Beaune.

The Senards also look after the Domaine des Terregelesses on behalf of absentee landlords. The wines are made in the same way as their own.

BLIGNY-LÈS-BEAUNE AND TAILLY

These villages to the south of Beaune in the plain do not possess any *appellation contrôlée* vineyards. But there are a few sources worth noting.

Gabriel Fournier, Domaine de la Galopière

13 ha owned and *en fermage/en métayage*. Aloxe-Corton *premier cru* Les Valozières; village Aloxe-Corton; village Pommard; village Savigny-lès-Beaune; village Ladoix (*rouge et blanc*); village Meursault including the *lieu-dit* Les Chevalières.

Claire and Gabriel Fournier created their domaine in 1982 and now work with their son Vincent. Slowly but surely, the estate has been enlarged, and more and more is sold in bottle. There is quite good quality here.

Catherine and Claude Maréchal

12 ha *en fermage/en métayage*. Savigny-lès-Beaune *premier cru* Les Lavières; village Savigny-lès-Beaune; village Ladoix; village Pommard in the *lieux-dits* La Chanière and Les Vignots; village Auxey-Duresses *rouge et blanc*; village Volnay; village Pommard; village Chorey-lès-Beaune.

Not a very spectacular list of wines here, but they are carefully made in the modern style, for drinking in the medium term. Maréchal, whose father was a mixed farmer, used to be an electrician. He planted his land with clones produced up at the research station at Echevronne, but rejected them because they produced too little. There is a *table de tri*, lit from underneath. Five percent of the stems, a week cold-maceration, controlled vinification at 32°C and one fifth new oak is the formula here. This is a good address.

Ghislaine and Bernard Maréchal-Caillot

8.61 ha owned and *en fermage*. Village Pommard Vieilles Vignes; village Chorey-lès-Beaune; village Savigny-lès-Beaune; village Ladoix (*vieilles vignes rouge, et blanc*).

Bernard Maréchal is the nextdoor neighbour and younger brother of Claude. He set up independently in 1984 and has built up the estate since. While, like Claude above, he does not offer anything illustrious, this is not an address to be ignored. The wines are pure and elegant— very well made.

Aline and Joël Patriarche
Domaine Saint-Fiacre

6.1 ha owned and *en fermage*. Meursault *premier cru* Les Charmes; village Meursault in the *lieux-dits* Les

Clous and Les Narvaux; Monthelie; Rully *blanc*, La Chaponnière, *et rouge*.

The 43-year-old Joël Patriarche is a cousin once removed of Alain in Meursault. He set up in 1987, and in 1997 he re-named the estate after the patron saint of Tailly, where the domaine is based. The white wines are matured using 20 percent new wood, and they are good, even very good, indeed. The reds, 100 percent de-stemmed since 2000, are quite good.

POMMARD

South of Beaune, we come to the best red wines of the Côte de Beaune after the *grands crus* of Corton: Pommard and Volnay. The road forks after you pass the huge factory of the Cave des Hautes-Côtes. Keep to the left and you run along the plain toward Chagny. Turn right and you rise up into the hills toward Autun. This junction marks the transition from Beaune into Pommard; the Autun road—more or less—separates the higher-rising *premiers crus* of Pommard from the low-lying village wine.

The *commune*, roughly square, is divided into two by a stream, the river Dheune, which flows down from Nantoux in the Hautes-Côtes. On the Beaune side, therefore, the slope turns to face the south, while opposite, the aspect is in the reverse direction. Above the village, in contrast to the other *communes*, there is a large expanse of communal vineyard; rather more, indeed, than there is below on the flatter land. Here on the slopes on the Beaune side, the soil is a stony white marl, getting redder and less stony—except in the Epenots—as one descends into the *premiers crus*. On the south side of the village, the incline is steeper, more rocky, and redder in colour—hence the name Rugiens—while lower down in Les Rugiens-Bas, the subsoil is of Argovian limestone covered with a thick band of marly calcareous debris. Yet further down the slope, in the Fremiers and Poutures, the marl is mixed with an iron-rich oolite, while between the two main roads, where once again we are in village land, the soil is very clayey. Only below the Epenots on the Beaune side does the limestone debris contain much in the way of stone and pebbles, and therefore drain well.

The percentage of active limestone in Pommard is high, and it is the reaction between this and the clays, of which Pommard also has more than Volnay and Beaune, which produces the typical fullness and sturdiness which is the Pommard character. Recent research has shown a similarity between these clays, or at least the electro-magnetic properties of their internal surface areas, and those of the villages of the Côte de Nuits.

History

The name Pommard is of malic origin (Pommarium, Pommone or Polmano are the ways it was written a millennium or so ago), and like much of Burgundy, it belonged either to the church or to the Dukes of Burgundy and their vassals in the Middle Ages. The Abbey de Maizières, the Carmelites of Beaune and the Chevaliers of Malta (the Knights of St. Jean of Jerusalem) were all landowners, as were the Counts of Vienne, *seigneurs* of Commarain, commemorated to this day in the name of one of the *premiers crus* and one of the three local châteaux.

The main château, the one actually called the Château de Pommard, was constructed in 1802 in a neo-classical style. It stands in the middle of a huge *clos*, the largest single ownership in Burgundy, between the two main roads.

Once the property of the ubiquitous Marey-Monge family, it belonged from 1936 until recently to the Laplanches. They sold it in December 2003 to Maurice Giraud (see page 222).

Pommard has for long had a high reputation for its wines, though it has never had had any *grands crus* or *têtes de cuvée*. Perhaps this is because, as noted by Dr. Lavalle in 1855, it had, along with Volnay and Beaune, been the most resistant to the "invasion" of Gamay. If we were to contemplate a change in the hierarchy today, I would nominate for elevation part—but part only—of two of the *premiers crus*: Les Rugiens-Bas and the central part of Les Epenots (the Clos des Epeneaux, but neither all of Les Grands Epe-nots nor all of Les Petits-Epenots). Clearly these produce the most distinctive wines of the village.

The Vineyard

PREMIER CRUS In the *commune* of Pommard, there are twenty-eight *premiers crus*, in whole or in part. These are as follows: Les Arvelets; Les Bertins; Les Boucherottes; La Chanière (part); Les Chanlins-Bas (part); Les Chaponnières; Les Charmots; Clos Blanc; Clos de la Commaraine; Clos de Verger; Clos des Epeneaux; Le Clos Micot or Micault; Les Combes-Dessus; Les Croix Noires; Les Grands Epenots; Les Petits Epenots; Les Fremiers; Les Jarolières; En Lagillière (Les Argillières); Les Pézerolles; La Platière (part); Les Poutures; La Refène; Les Rugiens-Bas; Les Rugiens-Hauts (part); Derrière Saint-Jean; Les Saussilles; Le Village. Altogether, these cover 125.19 hectares and produce around 4,500 hecto-litres a year.

VILLAGE WINE There are 211.63 hectares of vil-lage Pommard, producing some 9,400 hectoli-tres a year.

Pommard, like Volnay but unlike Beaune, is an appellation for red wine only.

The Premiers Crus

LES PETITS EPENOTS	(15.14 ha)
CLOS DES EPENEAUX	(5.23 ha)
LES GRANDS EPENOTS	(10.15 ha)

These three *climats* occupy the best land on the Beaune side of the *commune*, with the Petits Epenots closest to the border to the north and the Grands Epenots closest to the village. The slope here is very gentle, but the presence of pebbles in the soil ensures good drainage and contributes to the considerable elegance which you find in a good Epenots once it has softened up. Curiously, because of a fault in the soil, the mother rock is closer to the surface here than it is further upslope in Pézerolles, Argillières and Charmots. There is a lot of iron oxide. Opinions are divided as to which end, Grands or Petits, is the best. Most of the older books on Burgundy favour the former, while present-day opinion

favours the latter. Certainly as you get closer to the village, the wine becomes not only a little fuller, but also sturdier and more four-square. This is because the soil becomes more alluvial. What no one would deny is the superiority of the Clos des Epeneaux in the middle. The monopoly of the Comte Armand today produces some of the best wines in Burgundy. Most of the remain-ing wines simply say Epenots on the label, not differentiating their origin.

RECOMMENDED SOURCES
LES EPENOTS
De Courcel, Moissenet-Bonnard, Parent, Daniel Rebourgeon-Mure (all Pommard); De Montille (Volnay); Pierre Morey (Meursault).

CLOS DES EPENEAUX
Comte Armand (*monopole*).

LES BOUCHEROTTES	(1.50 ha)
LES SAUSSILLES	(3.84 ha)
LES PÉZEROLLES	(5.91 ha)
EN LAGILLIÈRE	(3.99 ha)
(Les Argillières)	
LES CHARMOTS	(9.65 ha)
LES ARVELETS	(8.46 ha)
LA PLATIÈRE	(2.53 ha)
LA CHANIÈRE	(2.78 ha)

These are the *climats* which start above Les Petits-Epenots on the Beaune border and con-tinue round as the slope turns toward the south and the vineyards disappear up the valley toward Nantoux. The incline is steeper here, and the soil is a stony white marl, but deeper than in the Epenots.

Les Pézerolles and Les Charmots (I have rarely seen a wine from Les Argillières in between the two: the Domaine Lejeune in Pommard and Jean Monnier in Meursault are the only sources I am aware of) offer the wines of the greatest finesse in this sector, but they do not have the flair of the top Epenots. They are nicely substantial and occasionally a little robust; usually, as with all Pommards, they are well coloured. As you move into Les Arvelets and the *climats* beyond, the sun does not impinge properly on the vines until later in the morning, and the wines are less rich. The winemaking has to be precise here to avoid a wine which is all substance and no generosity.

RECOMMENDED SOURCES

LES CHARMOTS

Billard-Gonnet, Aleth Leroyer-Girardin, Moissenet-Bonnard (all Pommard).

LES PÉZEROLLES

Moissenet-Bonnard, Parent (both Pommard); Michel Lafarge, Hubert De Montille, Joseph Voillot (all Volnay).

LES SAUSSILLES

Jean-Marc Boillot (Pommard).

CLOS DES BOUCHEROTTES (*monopole*)

Coste-Caumartin (Pommard).

CLOS BLANC	(4.18 ha)
LA REFÈNE	(2.31 ha)
CLOS DE LA COMMARAINE	(3.75 ha)
CLOS DE VERGER	(2.11 ha)

These four vineyards lie immediately to the north of the village, the first three under Les Arvelets and Les Charmots, and produce medium-full bodied wines (though the Clos de Verger is never more than medium in weight) which I find rather ordinary: more village than *premier cru*.

RECOMMENDED SOURCES

CLOS DE LA COMMARAINE

Louis Jadot.

CLOS BLANC

Louis Jadot.

LES CHANLINS-BAS	(4.43 ha)
LES RUGIENS-HAUTS	(6.83 ha)
LES RUGIENS-BAS	(5.83 ha)
LES JAROLIÈRES	(3.24 ha)
LES CHAPONNIÈRES	(2.87 ha)

Here we are upslope on the southern side of the village and, in the last three *climats* listed above, in very classy territory. Even if Les Rugiens-Hauts and Les Chanlins-Bas cannot boast such good wines, the difference is slight, and in any case, as with Epenots, most growers do not differentiate which part of Rugiens their wines come from. But the Rugiens-Bas is the better *climat*.

The vineyards lie on a steep, rocky slope, prone to erosion, with channels and pipelines organised to evacuate the rain efficiently whenever there is a violent storm. The terrain, and the wine, is quite different from that in the Epenots.

The basic difference between a top Rugiens and a top Epenots is one of energy and intensity. A Rugiens will show a rude power, to go its the size and richness, which is missing in the more laid-back, perhaps more elegant, Epenots. Chanlins and Jarolières betray their Volnay proximity and are somewhat hermaphroditic. Chaponnières is the closest to Rugiens.

RECOMMENDED SOURCES

RUGIENS

Billard-Gonnet, Jean-Marc Boillot, De Courcel, Aleth Leroyer-Girardin, Parent (all Pommard); Jean-Marc Bouley, Yvon Clerget, Hubert De Montille, Joseph Voillot (all Volnay).

CHANLINS

Bernard Vaudoisey (Volnay); Monthelie-Douhairet (Monthelie).

JAROLIÈRES

Jean-Marc Boillot (Pommard); Pousse d'Or (Volnay).

CHAPONNIÈRES

Billard-Gonnet, Parent (both Pommard).

LES FREMIERS	(5.13 ha)
LES CROIX NOIRES	(1.28 ha)
LES BERTINS	(3.54 ha)
LES POUTURES	(4.13 ha)
LES COMBES-DESSUS	(2.79 ha)
CLOS MICOT	(2.83 ha)
(or Micault)	

Finally, we come to the *climats* which lie downslope from Rugiens *et al.* The last two of these are actually below the Autun road.

The wines are definitely lighter here, with Fremiers (bordering on Fremiets—notice the difference in spelling) having a real Volnay touch to it. Poutures and Clos Micot can nevertheless be quite sturdy, as can Les Croix Noires. In general, this should be a sector for good, typical Pommards, which, if not as powerfully rich as Rugiens or as intense as Epenots, are usually more satisfying and more complete than those from the Pézerolles-Charmots area. Of course, as always, it depends on the grower.

RECOMMENDED SOURCES

FREMIERS

Coste-Caumartin, De Courcel (both Pommard); Jean-Marc Bouley (Volnay); Monthelie-Douhairet (Monthelie); Louis Boillot Chambolle-Musigny.

CLOS DE POUTURES

Louis Jadot (*monopole*) (Beaune).

CROIX NOIRES

Louis Boillot (Chambolle-Musigny).

The Growers

★★ Comte Armand
Domaine du Clos des Epeneaux

8.54 ha owned. Pommard *premier cru* Clos des Epeneaux (*monopole*—5.24 ha); village Pommard; Volnay *premier cru* Les Frémiets; Auxey-Duresses *premier cru rouge* from Les Duresses and Les Bréterins; village Volnay; village Auxey-Duresses (*rouge et blanc*).

Until 1994 this was an estate which existed on its own single monopoly, but it has now begun to expand. The Count Gabriel, a Parisian lawyer in his fifties, had the perspicacity in 1984, when the standards were not what they should have been, to employ the young French-Canadian Pascal Marchand as his manager and wine-maker. Since then, the improvement has been exponential and has been continued to even greater heights by Benjamin Leroux, who took over in September 1999. The estate has been partly biodynamic since 1997, and totally so since 2001. This Epenots—or perhaps I should say Epeneaux—is of a size and intensity that few others manage to achieve, yet it retains all the inherent finesse of the *climat*.

The Clos, indeed Epenots as a whole, is a geographical curiosity. The surface soil here (20 cm at the top, 50 cm at the bottom) is much less deep than that upslope in the Saussilles and Pézerolles—hence the greater depth and finesse of the wine. It was replanted, after *phylloxera*, but not until the 1930s onward, so Leroux can enjoy picking and vinifying the produce of vines of different ages.

There is a vibrating sorting table. After this the fruit is de-stemmed but, if possible, not crushed. There is no deliberate cold-soaking. Leroux might add extra carbon dioxide when he closes up the vat after the fermentation is over. He is a winemaker of great talent.

Billard-Gonnet

10 ha owned. Pommard *premier cru* in Les Rugiens, Les Chaponnières, Les Charmots, Clos de Verger, plus a *premier cru tout court* from Les Jarolières, Les Poutures, Les Bertins and Les Pézerolles; Beaune *premier cru* Clos des Mouches (*blanc*); village Pommard.

Philippe Billard is a good source for reliable and often extremely good Pommards. The fruit is completely de-stemmed, the juice is fermented at 30–34°C, and there is not so much a lot of new oak in the cellar as an absence of barrels which are too old.

★ *Jean-Marc Boillot*

11 ha owned and *en fermage*. Bâtard-Montrachet (0.18 ha); Beaune *premier cru rouge et blanc* Les Montrevenots; Pommard *premier cru* in Les Rugiens, Les Saussilles and Les Jarolières; Volnay *premier cru* in Les Pitures, Carelle-sous-La-Chapelle and Le Ronceret; Puligny-Montrachet *premier cru* in La Garenne, La Truffière, Les Referts, Le Champ Canet and Les Combettes; village Pommard; village Volnay; village Meursault; village Puligny-Montrachet; village Chassagne-Montrachet.

This is one of the very few quality domaines in Burgundy which is equally as important in Pinot Noir as in Chardonnay in the variety and standard of its winemaking. Jean-Marc is part of the extended Boillot family, with cousins who make wine in Gevrey and Chambolle-Musigny, a brother who makes wine in Volnay and a brother-in-law (Gérard-Boudot, of Domaine Étienne Sauzet) who makes wine in Puligny-Montrachet. Some of his estate comes from his rightful share of this latter source.

Jean-Marc quarrelled with his father and went off to work as winemaker for Maison Olivier

Leflaive, when it was set up in 1984. In 1989 he inherited his red wine vineyards from his grandfather and set up on his own. Two years later his share of his grandmother Sauzet's estate passed into his hands.

The Pinots are de-stemmed totally without, if possible, breaking the skin of the berries. They are given a week-long maceration at ambient temperatures and then vinified at 30°C. There is some 20 to 25 percent new wood for both red and white wine. I have a high respect for what Jean-Marc produces. He told me once that he considers his Pommard, Saussilles, makes better wine in softer vintages, such as 1997 or 2004, than in firmer ones, which is a point to ponder. Boillot also has a *négociant* licence but seems to exercise it only on the white wine front, with wines from the Côte Chalonnaise and extra Pulignys. He also has a 17-hectare domaine in Pic-Saint-Loup in the Languedoc.

Coste-Caumartin

14.5 ha owned and *en fermage*. Pommard *premier cru* in Clos des Boucherottes (*monopole*), Les Fremiers; Beaune *premier cru* Les Chouacheux; village Pommard; village Saint-Romain *blanc*, including the *lieux-dits* Sous Roche and Sous le Château.

Should you feel you are being watched, as you stand in the creepered, medieval Coste-Caumartin courtyard, complete with an old well, then look up. There is a gargoyled ancestor implacably staring down at you from within a mansard window. Despite the grapes being de-stemmed entirely, there is a character about these wines which is unmistakably rustic—in a good sense. Jérôme Sordet, whose ancestors have owned this estate since 1780, can offer you some very good wines at the top levels. His Clos des Boucherottes is excellent.

★ De Courcel

8 ha owned. Pommard *premier cru* in Les Croix-Noires, Les Fremiers, "Grand Clos des Epenots" and Les Rugiens; village Pommard.

Like the Comte Armand, the Courcels are absentee landlords. Gilles de Courcel, the member of the family who takes charge of the domaine,

having worked for many years in Bordeaux, now runs Maison Chanson. The winemaker here is Yves Confuron, one of the sons of Jacky Confuron-Cotétidot of Vosne-Romanée.

The domaine owns a large slice of Epenots, just on the Beaune side of the Clos des Epeneaux, which they label as the Grand Clos des Epenots. But their best wine is their Rugiens, one of the best examples of this top Pommard. This wine is proof that Rugiens should be a worthy contender for *grand cru* status.

Cyrot-Buthiau

7.14 ha owned. Pommard *premier cru* in Les Arvelets, La Chanière and Les Charmots; Santenay *premier cru* Clos Rousseau; Maranges *premier cru* Les Clos Roussots; village Pommard; village Volnay; Côte de Beaune Villages.

Paul Joseph Cyrot, grandfather of the 40-year-old Olivier, who has been running this domaine since 1989, was estate manager at the Clos du Tart and at the Château de Pommard. It was Olivier's father who built up the existing landholdings in the 1960s and 1970s. The grapes are largely de-stemmed and the wines given 30 to 45 percent new oak. Neatly made wines are found here—not too sturdy and with plenty of personality.

Jean Garaudet

5.5 ha owned and *en fermage*. Pommard *premier cru* Les Charmots; Beaune *premier cru* in Belissand and Le Clos des Mouches; village Pommard, including the *lieu-dit* Les Noizons; village Monthelie *rouge et blanc*.

Jean Garaudet is a small, middle-aged man who presides over a spotless *cave* under and behind his house off the main church square in Pommard. This branch of Garaudets is only distantly related to those in Monthelie. Fifteen percent of the stems are used here. There are 5 days of cold-maceration, temperatures are raised to 35°C for the reds, and 30 percent new oak is used. Careful winemaking is obvious here, and the wines prove it. This is a good source.

Michel Gaunoux

10 ha owned. Corton, Les Renardes (1.23 ha); Pommard *premier cru* in Les Grands Epenots (one of the few

domaines to specify this on the label) and Les Rugiens; Pommard *premier cru tout court* from Les Arvelets, Les Charmots and Les Combes-Dessus; village Beaune.

This is one of two top domaines in Burgundy—Ampeau in Meursault is the other—where you are not allowed to taste out of barrel. They are not interested in letting you see the wine until the *élevage* is complete and the wine is in bottle. Even then, unless they have decided to put the wine on the market, they see no reason to pull any corks. Today it is Michel Gaunoux's widow who will receive you, and what you will be offered is a wine of size, power and alcohol. Sometimes there is a lack of grace. But I have had fine old bottles from this cellar. These wines are built to last.

A.F. Gros

7.35 ha owned. Richebourg (0.60 ha); Echézeaux (0.26 ha); Savigny-lès-Beaune *premier cru* Clos des Guettes; (from 2003) Pommard *premier cru* Les Chanlins (young vines), Les Pézerolles; village Vosne-Romanée, including the *lieux-dits* Clos de la Fontaine, Les Maizières and Aux Réas; village Chambolle-Musigny.

Anne-François Gros, daughter of Jean and Jeannine Gros of Vosne-Romanée, is married to François Parent, and it is he who is responsible for all their wines. These are made in a splendid, dry, vaulted cellar, alongside those of François, off the Place Madelaine in Beaune. But they live in Pommard, so I list them here. The wines are good but lack real magic.

Jean-Luc Joillot

14 ha owned and *en fermage*. Pommard *premier cru* in Les Charmots, Les Epenots and Les Rugiens; village Pommard, including the *lieu-dit* Les Noizons; village Beaune in the *lieu-dit* Montagne Saint-Désirée.

The headquarters of Jean-Luc Joillot's domaine lie outside the walls of the Château de Pommard. There is richness and depth here, but sometimes over-extraction.

Lahaye Père et Fils

23 ha owned and *en fermage/en métayage*. Corton, Les Renardes (0.30 ha); Pommard *premier cru*, including

Les Arvelets; Volnay *premier cru* Les Santenots; Beaune *premier cru* Les Montrevenots; Meursault *premier cru* Les Perrières; village Pommard, including the *lieux-dits* Les Trois Follots and Les Vignots; village Beaune in the *lieu-dit* Les Bons Feuvres; village Meursault, including the *lieux-dits* Les Grands Charrons and Les Meix-Chavaux.

This is a large estate which is run by three brothers: Michel, Dominique and Vincent. The winemaking recipe is similar to most, but I have to say I have never found their wines very inspiring. Even the 2002s were no better than quite good.

Raymond Launay

12 ha owned. Chambertin (0.07 ha); Latricières-Chambertin (0.07 ha); Pommard *premier cru* in Les Chaponnières, Clos Blanc and Rugiens; village Pommard, including the *lieu-dit* Les Perrières (Vieilles Vignes and Vignes Centenaires); village Santenay in the *lieu-dit* Clos de Gatsulard (*monopole*); village Ladoix *blanc* in the *lieu-dit* Le Clou d'Orge.

This 12-hectare estate, owned by the daughter of the late Raymond Launay, Ghislaine Francis, was rescued from its financial problems by Maison Boisset, who bought up much of the unsold stock of older vintages and installed Pascal Marchand, late of the Domaine de la Vougeraie, as manager and winemaker in 2002. This arrangement continued for three years. The 2005s, though, were absorbed as must by various Boisset subsidiaries such as Bouchard Aîné. In 2006 the domaine was rented out to the Château de Pommard.

Lejeune

6.7 ha owned and *en métayage*. Pommard *premier cru* in En Lagillière, Les Poutures and Les Rugiens; village Pommard.

François Jullien de Pommerol, formerly oenology professor at Beaune's *Lycée Viticole*, inherited this domaine through his mother. It is named after Maxime Lejeune, his great-grandfather, and measured 50 hectares at his death in 1864.

His semi-carbonic maceration approach to vinification is original for Pinot Noir, but common in the Beaujolais. After a severe *tri*—a vibrating table was introduced in 2002—the whole bunches are hardly trodden down, allowed a few days natural cold-soaking and then fermented and macerated. There is then up to 75 percent new oak. On my last visit I liked the 2004s but was less enthusiastic about the 2002s and 2003s.

Aubert Lefas, François's son-in-law, is in the process of taking over responsibility here.

Moissenet-Bonnard

4.8 ha owned and *en fermage*. Pommard *premier cru* in Les Charmots, Les Epenots and Les Pézerolles; village Pommard in the *lieux-dits* Les Cras and Les Noizons.

This reliable, quality domaine is run by Jean-Louis and Christine Moissenet. Jean-Louis likes to bottle quite early: the wines then express their fruit. This is a very good address. Pézerolles, by the way, comes from the Old French word Pèze: chick peas.

François Parent

4.65 ha owned and *en fermage*. Pommard *premier cru* in Les Arvelets and Les Pézerolles (the latter since 2003 bottled under the A.F. Gros label); Volnay *premier cru* Les Frémiets; Monthelie *premier cru*; Beaune *premier cru* in Les Boucherottes and Les Montrevenots.

François Parent is married to A.F. Gros (see page 142). The wines of both sides are made by him in spacious cellars in Beaune, although they live in Pommard. Meanwhile his sister Anne (Brandicourt-Parent) runs the Domaine Parent (*tout court*), elsewhere in the village (see page 221). The fruit is de-stemmed, the juice cold macerated for 4 to 7 days and vinified at 30°C and the wines given from 30 to 100 percent (for Anne-Françoise's *grands crus*) new wood. The results used to be slightly burly. They are now more refined.

Since 2004 François Parent has bought the harvest of most of the domaine of his cousin Annick in Monthelie. This expands the exploitation by 1.85 hectares and will give him Monthelie *premier cru* Les Champs Fulliot and

Les Duresses, Pommard *premier cru* Les Rugiens and Volnay *premier cru* Les Frémiets.

Parent

10 ha *en fermage/en métayage*. Corton, Les Renardes (0.30 ha); Corton, Le Rognet (0.28 ha); Pommard *premier cru* in Les Croix Noires, Chaponnières, Les Chanlins, Les Epenots and Les Argillières; Beaune *premier cru* in Les Epenotes; Ladoix *premier cru* La Corvée; village Pommard in the *lieux-dits* La Croix Blanche and Les Noizons; village Ladoix.

In 1993 Jacques Parent, father of François, Anne and Catherine, took his retirement; François withdrew and set up on his own, and Anne, now Brandicourt-Parent, and Catherine, now Fagès-Parent, assumed responsibility here. Quality has definitely improved. Jacques Parent's wines were sturdy and soupy, whereas Anne Parent's are perfumed and stylish. Occasionally, I find them over-oaked, though.

Château de Pommard

26 ha owned. Chassagne-Montrachet *premier cru* in Les Caillerets and Les Chaumées; village Pommard; village Chassagne-Montrachet.

In December 2003, Maurice Giraud, a rich businessman from the Savoie, bought the Château de Pommard from the childless psychoanalyst Jean-Louis Laplanche. Giraud promptly installed Philippe Charlopin of Gevrey-Chambertin, who had already been advising Laplanche, as manager. Charlopin has changed everything. Hitherto, the harvest was too early, there was no sorting out, maceration was too long, casks were of poor quality and the wine was hard and rustic. It is now a great deal better. The land occupies most of the triangle between the village, the Beaune-Chagny road and the roundabout where the roads divide. It is reputed to be the largest single holding in Burgundy. Giraud, with Charlopin's help, is now also a *négociant*.

Daniel Rebourgeon-Mure

7.11 ha owned and *en fermage*. Pommard *premier cru* in Le Clos des Arvelets, Les Charmots, Le Clos Micault and Les Grands Epenots; Volnay *premier cru* in Les Caillerets, Les Mitans and Les Santenots; Beaune *premier cru* Les Vignes Franches; village Pommard; village Volnay; village Beaune.

Daniel Rebourgeon is one of Pommard's best winemakers. His tidy, labarithine *cave* now holds a clutch of good Pommards. The style here is not for solid blockbusters but for attractive plump wines which evolve in the medium term. De-stemming is total, the must is then cold-soaked for just under 1 week, and the temperature of vinification is allowed to rise to 34°C. There is 30 percent new wood.

★ Aleth le Royer-Girardin

7 ha *en fermage*. Pommard *premier cru* Les Charmots, Les Epenots and Les Rugiens; Beaune *premier cru* Le Clos des Mouches and Les Montrevenots; Meursault *premier cru* Les Poruzots; village Pommard.

Old vines, low yields and careful winemaking produce the result, in Aleth Le Royer's hands, of one of the best sources in the village. Ten percent of the stems are retained, the must is cold-soaked for just under a week, temperatures are allowed to rise to 35°C, and the wines are given up to 40 percent new oak. They are rich, concentrated and long-lasting.

VOLNAY

Volnay is one of the most delightful wines and one the most rewarding *communes* in the Côte d'Or. There are a large number of very fine and dedicated growers in the village, and the wine they produce is the epitome of elegance and delicacy, the most fragrant and seductively feminine expression of the Pinot Noir in the Côte de Beaune, directly analogous with the wines of Chambolle-Musigny in the Côte de Nuits. Volnay is as removed as it possibly can be from the souped up, "old-fashioned" brews which were fraudulently bottled as non-appellation Burgundy in our parents' days.

History

Volnay is a small village tucked into the top of its slope above the vineyard and away from the main road. The name comes from a Celtic or early Gallic water god, *de Volen*. The village appears in medieval times as Vollenay and was spelled Voulenay by Thomas Jefferson when he toured France just prior to the French Revolution.

Back in the Middle Ages, as with the rest of Burgundy, ownership of most of the land lay in the hands of the church. The Order of Malta had vines in Les Caillerets, Le Champ-de-Caille (quail) as it was known in those days; the Priory of Saint-Etienne in Beaune was represented in Les Frémiets, Le Verseuil, Les Angles and La Carelle. The Abbey de Maizières had a number of parcels in the best *climats*. The Dukes of Burgundy were also land holders, and they and particularly their spouses spent much time here after Hugues IV constructed a château in 1250: the view was excellent, the water was pure, there was abundant hunting in the forests above— and, of course, there was the local wine, though it was more of a pale rusty red colour in those days, what is called *oeil de perdrix* (partridge eye), for white and red grapes were commonly planted and harvested together.

An inventory taken on behalf of Louis XII, King of France, and after the collapse of the Valois Dukes of Burgundy in 1477, inheritor of the land, mentions holdings in a wide number of what are now top *premiers crus*: En Cailleret, Chevret, Champans, Fremiets, L'Ormeau, Bousse d'Or, Clos-Blanc and Taille-Pieds. From then on, Volnay wines' place at the royal table was secure.

Anthony Hanson has a delightful story concerning the Prince de Condé (*Burgundy*, Faber, 1995), which is well worth repeating. This worthy, enchanted with the quality of the wine, had the idea of transplanting some Pinot Noir vines from Volnay to Chantilly, his château in the Oise near Senlis north of Paris. Obviously, the wine did not come up to expectation. When he complained, he was told, "Monseigneur, you should also have taken the soil and the sun."

Domaine bottling in Burgundy can be said to have begun in Volnay. The present Marquis d'Angerville's grandfather was a constant critic of the cynical fraud being perpetrated by local merchants in the 1930s. As a result they refused to accept his wine, and so he was forced to bottle it himself and to look outside the local *négoce* for his markets. He was soon joined by other growers, including his friends Armand Rousseau of Gevrey-Chambertin and Henri Gouges of Nuits-Saint-Georges, who were being similarly shunned. Encouraged by Raymond Baudoin, the French wine writer and consultant to many top restaurants, by the American Frank Schoonmaker, and later by Alexis Lichine, these fine growers were eventually joined by more and more top estates, leading to the situation today, in which almost everyone who makes good wine bottles and sells at least some of it himself or herself, and one expects that some of the Beaune *négociants* are increasingly hard-pressed to find good wine to mature and sell. The tables have well and truly been turned.

Location

Volnay is one of the smaller *communes* of the Côte de Beaune. On one side lies Pommard, on the other the vineyards of Monthelie and Meursault. *Premier cru* vineyards lie on both sides of the Beaune-Autun road, with village wine extending on the northern side all the way down to the Beaune-Chagny highway. There is more village land above the village itself on the steeper slopes.

While the geology is complex, the soils of Volnay are, in general, lighter than they are in Pommard, and it must be this which largely explains the delicacy of the wines. Travelling upslope from the Autun road from left to right (i.e., from south to north), we come first to the Clos des Chênes. This is Bathonian limestone, poor in nutrient, stony, light in colour and on a steep slope which is oriented more toward the south than the remainder of the *premiers crus*. Next, we come to Taille Pieds and a number of individual clos or vineyards collectively decreed to be the *premier cru* Le Village (which I feel is a contradiction in terms) but which sell under their own, often monopoly, labels: De l'Audignac, Verseuil, Bousse d'Or, Clos du Château des Ducs and so on. Here the limestone is of Argovian or Oxfordian origin with, in the last two *climats*, a

layer of gravel, again light in colour and hard to work, particularly upslope in the Clos des Ducs on the other side of the village. Further along still, alongside the Pommard border, there is Bathonian limestone once again in midslope in Frémiets (here spelled with a *t* rather than an *r* at the end, as in Pommard). The limestone is crumbly and the surface soil shallow. Up above, in Les Pitures and Les Chanlins, the limestone is Argovian again, and very stony.

Below Clos des Chênes, we find various Caillerets. On the Meursault side, the slope continues to be steep; the limestone is an Argovian and Oxfordian crumbly *lave*, but it is much redder in colour, stony again and very well exposed. At the top (Clos-des-60-Ouvrées) there is little surface soil. Lower down, it is deeper before we reach the base rock. This band of rock, over which is a reasonable depth of Bathonian scree and debris, as well as a little more clay, continues north through the *climats* of En Chevret, Les Champans and Le Ronceret. Further along, though, in Les Mitans and Les Brouillards, the land becomes heavier, there is more clay, and the wines are sturdier.

Finally, there is an anomaly. Bordering on Les Caillerets and En Chevret, but over the border in the *commune* of Meursault, we have the large *climat* of Santenots. The land here is once again on Bathonian limestone, much harder than the *lave* of the Champans; it is red in colour and quite stony—with larger stones, at that—in parts. There is more clay than in the Caillerets, and it is more suitable for red wine than white. Such Pinot Noir as is made here—and it is almost entirely planted in Pinot—is entitled to the Volnay appellation: Volnay, Les Santenots.

The Vineyard

PREMIERS CRUS There are thirty-five *premiers crus*, in whole or in part, in Volnay. They are as follows: Les Angles; Les Aussy (part); La Barre (Clos de la Barre); Les Brouillards (part); Cailleret-Dessus (Clos-des-60-Ouvrées); En Cailleret; Les Caillerets; Carelle sous la Chapelle; Les Carelles-Dessous (Part); En Champans; Les Chanlins (part); En Chevret; Clos de l'Audignac;

Clos de la Bousse d'Or; Clos de la Cave des Ducs; Clos de la Chapelle; Clos des Chênes (part); Clos des Ducs; Clos du Château des Ducs; Les Frémiets; Les Frémiets (Clos de la Rougeotte); La Gigotte (part); Les Grands Champs (part); Lassolle (part); Les Lurets (part); Les Mitans; En l'Ormeau; Pitures Dessus; Pointes d'Angles; Robardelle (part); Le Ronceret; Taille Pieds; En Verseuil (Clos du Verseuil); Le Village (part).

In the *commune* of Meursault, all the following have right to the appellation Volnay, Santenots: Clos des Santenots; Les Plures or Pitures; Les Santenots Blancs; Les Santenots-Dessous; Les Santenots-du-Milieu; Les Vignes Blanches.

The *premiers crus,* including Santenots, cover 136.28 hectares and produce about 5,200 hectolitres of wine a year.

In November 2005, the INAO decreed a partial simplification of these thirty-five *premiers crus climats,* as has been done in Chablis. Thus Chanlins can henceforward be (optionally) called Pitures-Dessus; L'Ormeau and Les Grands Champs can be Les Mitans; Pointes d'Angles can be Les Angles; Carelle-Dessous can be Carelle sous la Chapelle; and Les Aussy can be labelled Le Ronceret. You will note that this regrouping covers *climats* that are only *premiers crus* in part.

VILLAGE WINE   There are 98.37 hectares of village Volnay. This produces around 4,300 hectolitres of wine a year. Volnay and Volnay *premier cru* are appellations for red wine only.

Which are the best of the *premiers crus*? Lavalle (1855) lists several as *têtes de cuvées,* though curiously, neither Clos des Chênes nor Taille Pieds, and in his preamble, he singles out Les Caillerets and Les Champans, while Les Santenots du Milieu is his sole *tête de cuvée* among the red wines of Meursault. Rodier promotes Taille Pieds, but not Clos des Chênes, to *première cuvée* and earmarks Les Frémiets, Champans and Les Angles, with Les Caillerets noted as the best of all.

For me there are five *climats* which seem to be a head or so above the rest: Les Caillerets, of course; Clos des Chênes; Taille Pieds; Les Champans; and Les Santenots du Milieu. Which of these is *the* best I find a pointless question.

It depends on the grower, on the age of vines and on the vintage, not to mention on personal taste. But it is at the southern end of the *commune* that I find the wines which give me the greatest satisfaction.

The Premiers Crus

CLOS DES CHÊNES   (15.41 ha)

It is at this, the southern end of Volnay—Clos des Chênes, Taille Pieds, Les Caillerets and, indeed, over the border into Les Santenots du Milieu—that one will find Volnay's best wines. They are all subtly, intriguingly, seductively different. Clos des Chênes is a fuller wine than, say, Les Caillerets, but not as full as the Santenots du Milieu, maturing to velvet rather than silk. It is very pure in its expression of fruit, with a good grip of acidity and the ability to keep well. The structure is there, but it is hidden, and there is plenty of finesse. There is a combination of both austerity and lushness, but never a suggestion of anything four-square. The wines from higher up the slope in the large vineyard, and those on the Monthelie side, show less distinction.

RECOMMENDED SOURCES
Bitouzet-Prieur, Jean-Marc Bouley, Bernard Glantenay, Michel Lafarge (all Volnay); Maurice Deschamps (Monthelie); Joseph Drouhin (Beaune).

TAILLE PIEDS	*(7.13 ha)*
CLOS DE L'AUDIGNAC	*(1.11 ha)*
(monopole of the Domaine de la Pousse d'Or)	
EN VERSEUIL (CLOS DU VERSEUIL)	*(0.68 ha)*
(monopole of the Domaine Yvon Clerget)	
CLOS DE LA BOUSSE D'OR	*(2.14 ha)*
(monopole of the Domaine de la Pousse d'Or)	
CLOS DU CHÂTEAU DES DUCS	*(0.57 ha)*
(monopole of the Domaine Michel Lafarge)	
CLOS DE LA CAVE DES DUCS	*(0.64 ha)*
(monopole of the Domaine Carré-Courbin)	
LA BARRE (CLOS DE LA BARRE)	*(1.32 ha)*
CLOS DES DUCS	*(2.41 ha)*
(monopole of the Domaine Marquis d'Angerville)	

Continuing around the slope above the main road, the geology changes slightly, as described previously, and we come to a number of vineyards in private monopoly. Bousse d'Or, by the way, has nothing to do with gold. It comes from *bousse de terre*, local patois for "good earth." Wines from Taille Pieds can be the complete Volnay: fullish in body, beautifully textured, supremely elegant. Those from other *climats* show a little more tannin in their youth, which can sometimes mask the elegance if you fail to take your time while sampling. But they are neither as stout nor as heavy as the wines on the opposite side of the road, in Champans, for instance, and they mature very gracefully indeed. There is a backbone to these wines which ensures a long life, and if they are a little austere in their youth, so what? They're not made for drinking when three years old.

RECOMMENDED SOURCES

TAILLE PIEDS

Marquis d'Angerville, Bitouzet-Prieur, De Montille, Roblet-Monnot, Rossignol-Jeanniard (all Volnay); Comtes Lafon, René Monnier (both Meursault). Jean-François Coche-Dury produces a fine *premier cru tout court* from vines in Les Clos des Chênes and Taille Pieds.

CLOS DE L'AUDIGNAC

Pousse d'Or (*monopole*) (Volnay).

CLOS DU VERSEUIL

Yvon Clerget (*monopole*) (Volnay).

CLOS DE LA BOUSSE D'OR

Pousse d'Or (*monopole*) (Volnay).

CLOS DU CHÂTEAU DES DUCS

Michel Lafarge (*monopole*) (Volnay).

CLOS DE LA BARRE

Louis Jadot (exclusivity) (Beaune).

CLOS DES DUCS

Marquis d'Angerville (*monopole*) (Volnay).

LES PITURES-DESSUS	*(4.08 ha)*
LES CHANLINS	*(2.86 ha)*
LES FRÉMIETS	*(7.40 ha)*
LES ANGLES	*(3.34 ha)*
POINTES D'ANGLES	*(1.23 ha)*
LES BROUILLARDS	*(5.63 ha)*

Wines from Les Chanlins and Les Frémiets show their Pommard vicinity in a certain muscular sturdiness here, and those from Les Angles and Les Brouillards can be a bit four-square. In general, these Volnays lack the flair of the rest of the *commune*. They can nevertheless be thoroughly nice bottles and should not be passed up. But it is correct to expect a small discount.

RECOMMENDED SOURCES

CLOS DES ANGLES

Nicolas Rossignol (Volnay).

LES PITURES

Jean-Marc Boillot (Pommard); Bitouzet-Prieur (Volnay).

LES FRÉMIETS

Marquis d'Angerville, Jean Boillot, Rossignol-Jeanniard (all Volnay).

LES ANGLES

Louis Boillot (Chambolle-Musigny).

LES BROUILLARDS

Louis Boillot (Chambolle-Musigny); Joseph Voillot (Volnay). Régis Rossignol (Volnay) makes a good *premier cru tout court* from vines in Les Angles, Les Brouillards and Les Mitans. Bouchard Père et Fils produces Clos de la Rougeotte from vines in Les Frémiets.

LES MITANS	*(3.98 ha)*
LES GRANDS CHAMPS	*(0.24 ha)*
EN L'ORMEAU	*(4.33 ha)*
LA GIGOTTE	*(0.54 ha)*
CARELLE SOUS LA CHAPPELLE	*(3.73 ha)*
LES CARELLES-DESSOUS	*(1.46 ha)*

Continuing back toward the south, the wines show more definition compared with those from the *climats* above, yet in Les Mitans they can still be quite sturdy. Those from the Carelles are a little lighter in weight, if Yvon Clerget's is anything to go by. The only domaines producing *premier cru* La Gigotte are that of Vincent Perrin and Darviot-Perrin.

RECOMMENDED SOURCES

LES MITANS

De Montille (Volnay).

LA GIGOTTE

Darviot-Perrin (Monthelie).

CARELLE SOUS LA CHAPELLE

Jean-Marc Boillot (Pommard); Jean-Marc Bouley, Yvon Clerget (both Volnay); Paul Pernot (Puligny-Montrachet).

CHAMPANS	*(11.19 ha)*
LE RONCERET	*(1.90 ha)*
LES AUSSY	*(1.70 ha)*
LES LURETS	*(2.07 ha)*
ROBARDELLE	*(2.94 ha)*

Champans and the *climats* underneath it, in many cases of which only a part is graded *premier cru*, produce a rich, fat, quite sturdy wine of more depth and distinction than those in the section above. It doesn't quite have the *élan* of a Taille-Pieds or a Caillerets, but it can nevertheless be a thoroughly rewarding fine Volnay. Champans itself is an excellent *climat*. The Domaine du Marquis d'Angerville is the major landholder with 4 hectares.

RECOMMENDED SOURCES
CHAMPANS

Marquis d'Angerville, De Montille, Joseph Voillot (all Volnay); Monthelie-Douhairet (Monthelie); Comtes Lafon, Jacques Prieur (both Meursault); Jean-Marc Blain-Gagnard (Chassagne-Montrachet).

LE RONCERET

Jean-Marc Boillot (Pommard); Paul Garaudet (Monthelie).

LES CAILLERETS	*(14.36 ha)*
EN CHEVRET	*(6.35 ha)*

These *climats* can produce Volnay at its very best—not quite as structured as Taille-Pieds or Clos des Chênes above the main road, nor as sturdy as both Santenots and Champans can be, but Volnay of real silk, lace and the complexity of all the *petits fruits rouges* you can imagine. The upper sections of this *climat*, where there is the least surface soil, produce wine with more finesse and distinction than the vines further down. It is here in Caillerets-Dessus that you will find the Domaine de la Pousse d'Or's 60 *ouvrées*.

RECOMMENDED SOURCES
CLOS-DES-60-OUVRÉES

Pousse d'Or (*monopole*) (Volnay).

LES CAILLERETS

Bouchard Père et Fils, Ancienne Cuvée Carnot (Beaune); Bitouzet-Prieur, Jean Boillot, Jean-Marc Bouley, Yvon Clerget, Michel Lafarge, Hubert de Montille, Rossignol-Jeanniard, Pousse d'Or, Joseph Voillot (all Volnay); Louis Boillot (Chambolle-Musigny).

EN CHEVRET

Joseph Drouhin (Beaune); Jean Boillot, Nicolas Rossignol (both Volnay).

SANTENOTS	*(22.73 ha)*

The best sector in this large vineyard is the Santenots du Milieu, of which the Domaine Jacques Prieur's Clos des Santenots is part. The lands lower down (Les Santenots-Dessous) and further south (Les Plures) produce more common wine. A top Santenots du Milieu is full, rich and sturdy and will keep well. It is quite a bit less delicate than a Caillerets, and it is not as elegant, but what it lacks in grace (certainly when it is young), it makes up for in richness and depth when the wine matures. There is a lush sensuality about a good Santenots which is most attractive.

RECOMMENDED SOURCES

Leroy (Auxey-Duresses); Robert Ampeau, Comtes Lafon, Matrot, Francois Mikulski, Jacques Prieur (Clos des Santenots) (all Meursault); Nicolas Rossignol (Volnay). The Marquis d'Angerville produces a Meursault Santenots—a white wine—as does the Domaine Monthelie-Douhairet. These are wines more of interest than pleasure. François Mikulski of Meursault makes a red Meursault, Caillerets. I'd say the same for this.

The Growers

★★ *Marquis d'Angerville*

14 ha owned. Volnay *premier cru* in Clos des Ducs *(monopole)*, Champans, Les Frémiets, Taille Pieds and Les Caillerets; Meursault *premier cru* Les Santenots; village Pommard in the *lieu-dit* Les Combes. The Marquis d'Angerville also produces a Volnay *tout court* which I imagine

comes from the young vines and perhaps holdings in other *premiers crus*.

As I explained in the introduction to this chapter, this estate was one of the very first to bottle and market all its wines itself. Today, it is run by Guillaume d'Angerville and his brother-in-law Renaud de Villette; the latter, having understudied under the late Jacques d'Angerville (who died in 2003), takes the more active role in the vineyard and in the cellar. After a *triage* both in the vineyard and in the cellar, the fruit is de-stemmed, cold-soaked briefly and fermented at low temperatures (30°C maximum), with pumping over but no *pigeage*. Only 15 percent new oak is employed.

The Angerville wines are exemplary: pure, *terroir* specific, elegant and intense. At present, the Cailleret vines are youthful.

Bitouzet-Prieur

13.3 ha *en fermage/en métayage*. Volnay *premier cru* in Clos des Chênes, Les Caillerets, Taille Pieds, Les Pitures, Les Aussy and En l'Ormeau; Meursault *premier cru* in Les Perrières, Les Charmes and Les Santenots; Beaune *premier cru* Cent Vignes; village Volnay; village Meursault, including the *lieux-dits* Clos du Cromin and Les Corbins.

This is another of those rare estates which is of equal note for Chardonnay as well as Pinot Noir. Vincent Bitouzet, who is now 57, operates two cellars, making his Meursault on the spot in the *cuverie* of his in-laws, whereas the red wines are vinified back in Volnay. The Pinots are totally de-stemmed, cold-macerated for up to 10 days and then vinified at temperatures up to 32°C. Use of oak is minimal, a fifth for *premiers crus*. These are very good wines. My favourite Volnay is usually the Caillerets.

★ Jean Boillot

13.9 ha owned. Volnay *premier cru* in En Chevret, Les Frémiets and Les Caillerets; Beaune *premier cru* in Clos du Roi and Les Epenotes; Savigny-lès-Beaune *premier cru* in Les Lavières and Les Vergelesses; Meursault *premier cru* Les Genevrières; Puligny-Montrachet *premier cru* in Clos de la Mouchère

(*monopole*), Les Perrières and Les Pucelles; village Puligny-Montrachet.

This is an impressive estate, almost entirely made up of *premiers crus*, with a 3.4-hectare first-growth Puligny monopoly. It is run by Henri Boillot, son of Jean and brother of Jean-Marc of Pommard. The cellars are clean and tidy. The red grapes are entirely de-stemmed, cold-macerated for almost 2 weeks and fermented at up to 32°C, and the wines are given 50 to 70 percent new oak. A similar percentage of new wood is used for the white wine, much of which is fermented and stored in 350-litre (as opposed to 218-litre) casks. The results are fine.

Henri Boillot also has a merchant business, with headquarters in an industrial estate in Meursault. In November 2005 the inheritance problems were finally sorted out between him, Jean-Marc and their sister Jeannine. Henri's intention is to fuse his two businesses together under his own name.

Jean-Marc Bouley

7.16 ha owned and *en fermage/en métayage*. Volnay *premier cru* in Les Carelles, Les Caillerets, Clos des Chênes and En l'Ormeau; Pommard *premier cru* in Les Fremiers and Les Rugiens; Beaune *premier cru* Les Reversées; village Volnay, including the *lieu-dit* Clos de la Cave and a *vieilles vignes cuvée*; village Pommard.

This estate used to be larger, but in 2002 a lease of some 5 hectares came to its end. Bouley was more relieved than disappointed, however. The land was mainly village and generic, and the Bouley cellar was cramped for space. Now joined by his son Thomas, Jean-Marc Bouley has since constructed a new cellar. A new *cuverie* is to follow when finances permit.

Winemaking, the Bouleys insist, must be flexible enough to accommodate different *cuvées* and vintages. In general, a small percentage of stems are retained, there is a brief *macération à froid*, fermentation temperatures are allowed to climb to 32°C, and there is 30 to 50 percent new wood. These are reliably good wines, less oaky and more *terroir* specific than hitherto.

Réyane and Pascal Bouley

11 ha owned and *en fermage*. Volnay *premier cru* in Champans, Le Ronceret, Robardelle, Clos des Chênes and Santenots; village Volnay; village Pommard; village Beaune.

Pascal Bouley's cramped cellar lies across from the church up a little alley. There is 20 to 25 percent new oak but, I fear, a little too much old wood. Results can be spotty. The best wine is the Champans.

Yvon Clerget

5.68 ha *en fermage*. Clos de Vougeot (0.32 ha); Volnay *premier cru* in Les Caillerets, Clos du Verseuil (*monopole*), Les Santenots and Carelle sous la Chapelle; Volnay *premier cru tout court* from Les Chanlins and Les Mitans; Pommard *premier cru* Les Rugiens; Beaune *premier cru* Les Reversées; village Volnay; village Pommard; village Meursault.

Yvon Clerget comes from one of the oldest families in Burgundy. They can trace their ancestry back to 1268. They do total de-stemming here, thermo-regulated vinification at 33°C for reds and 16°C for whites and one quarter to one fifth new oak. I have had some very good wines here, but I find the results inconsistent. There always seems to be one wine in the line-up which is not as good as it should be. The domaine expanded 10 years ago, as Clerget slowly took over land belonging to his late uncle Félix Clerget of Pommard—hence the Clos Vougeot. At present there is no Carelle sous la Chapelle: the vines are too young.

★★★ Michel Lafarge

11.5 ha owned and *en fermage*. Volnay *premier cru* in Les Caillerets, Clos des Chênes, Clos du Château des Ducs (*monopole*) and Les Mitans; Volnay *premier cru tout court* (mainly from Les Chanlins); Beaune *premier cru* in Les Aigrots (*rouge et blanc*) and Les Grèves; Pommard *premier cru* Les Pézerolles; village Volnay, including a "*vendange selectionnée*"; village Meursault, including a "*vendage selectionnée*."

Year after year, Michel Lafarge, now in his late seventies, and his son Frédéric produce some of the most delicious wines in the village, all the way from a splendid Bourgogne *rouge* to the yardstick Clos des Chênes. In all, they produce sixteen *cuvées* from 11.5 hectares—typically Burgundian!

The estate continues to grow. The Caillerets, which belongs to Frédéric personally, arrived in 2001; the Mitans and the Beaune Aigrots followed in 2005. Since 1999 the domaine has been totally biodynamic.

The Lafarges are not tempted by modern fads. When the harvest arrives, Michel casts his mind back to a year which was similar. What did we do then that was correct or incorrect? Flexibility is the key, and this includes the length of the cold-soaking, the temperature of the fermentation, the length of the *cuvaison* and the amount of new wood. The latter percentage is usually 15 to 25. The grapes are always de-stemmed.

They are a lovely family with yardstick wines. The 2005s are brilliant.

★ Hubert de Montille

17.0 ha owned. Clos de Vougeot (0.29 ha); Corton, Le Clos du Roi (0.84 ha); Corton les Pougets (0.55 ha); Corton-Charlemagne (0.45 ha); Vosne-Romanée *premier cru* Les Malconsorts; Pommard *premier cru* in Les Grands Epenots, Les Pézerolles and Les Rugiens; Volnay *premier cru* in Les Brouillards, Les Carelles, Les Champans, Les Mitans and Les Taillepieds; Beaune *premier cru* in Les Grèves, Les Perrières, Les Sizies and Les Aigrots *blanc*; Puligny-Montrachet *premier cru* Le Cailleret.

This is another great Volnay estate, well known for its policy of minimal chaptalisation. This makes for very pure wines, which are perhaps a little lean and austere in their youth, but which grow magnificently. Until recently, this was a small family domaine of 8 or so hectares, which was run in their spare time first by Hubert de Montille, whose real profession was that of a lawyer, and then by his son Étienne, at first a merchant banker, but later the manager of the Château de Puligny-Montrachet. Then in 2005, together with Jacques Seysses, the Montilles bought the Domaine Charles Thomas of Nuits-Saint-Georges and split it between them, with one or two parcels being sold off elsewhere. The wines are now made in a cellar in Meursault. Since 2002 the original estate has been totally *biodynamique*. The new parcels are now being adapted likewise.

The Montille wines, more fragile than most, suffer more from the various treatments which are necessary while the wine is in cask, such as racking or correcting the sulphur level. This means they are often not on form when you sample them out of cask. They also do not always show well at my 4-year-on tasting. After a decade, however, there is rarely a problem.

Alix de Montille, Étienne's sister, makes the Puligny, acquired in 1993 from Chartron.

★ Les Deux Montilles

Alix de Montille and her brother Étienne created a small, almost only-white-wine *négociants* business in 2003. Alix is responsible for the wines, all bought in as grapes, which are made in the old Ropiteau cellars in Meursault. Relations with the suppliers are very proactive. They use 10 to 20 percent new wood, which is just right. I like the wines very much indeed.

Vincent Perrin

7.8 ha owned and *en fermage*. Volnay *premier cru* in Carelles, La Gigotte, Les Lurets, Les Mitans and Robardelle; village Volnay; village Pommard in the *lieu-dit* Chanlins; village Monthelie; village Meursault; village Saint-Romain *blanc*.

The Perrins, 41-year-old Vincent and his wife Marie-Christine, are a charming couple who took charge of their family domaine in 1997 and started bottling seriously with the 1999 vintage. Apart from the Saint-Romain, the vines are old, and the Perrins now plough their vineyards and, to control yields, have adapted the vines to the *Cordon du Royat*. Their method is no stems, 4 to 8 days cold-soaking, fermentation temperatures at 30–32°C and 20 percent new oak. These are neat wines at an address worth noting.

Pousse d'Or

15.5 ha owned and *en fermage*. Corton, Clos du Roi (1.45 ha); Corton, Bressandes (0.48 ha); Volnay *premier cru* in Clos de la Bousse d'Or (*monopole*), Les Caillerets-Clos des 60 Ouvrées (*monopole*) and Les Caillerets, Clos de l'Audignac (*monopole*); Pommard *premier cru* Les Jarolières; Santenay *premier cru* in Les Gravières (*rouge et blanc*) and Clos de Tavannes; Puligny-Montrachet, Le Cailleret.

This is an impressive domaine, not least because all the parcels are of a size to profit by economies of scale. It was created by Gérard Potel in 1964—the Volnay part having once belonged to M. Duvault-Blochet, owner inter alia of the Domaine de la Romanée-Conti in the mid-nineteenth century—and sold after his death in 1997 to Patrick Landanger, who has since added the Cortons and the Puligny-Montrachet le Cailleret (the latter ex Chartron, inevitably).

There is a double sorting table. The grapes are totally de-stemmed, cold-macerated for a week and fermented at 30°C, and the wine is given 30 percent new wood. Gérard Potel, latterly aided by his son Nicky, made glorious wines. Landanger does not have their talent, but the will is here.

★ Roblet-Monnot

6 ha owned. Volnay *premier cru* in Les Brouillards, Les Pitures-Dessus, Robardelle and Les Taillepieds; Pommard *premier cru* Les Arvelets; village Volnay; village Pommard.

The 35-year-old Pascal Roblet lives in Volnay next door to the Lafarges but makes his wine in a cellar in Bligny-lès-Beaune. *Biodynamique* since 1997, Roblet believes in a dense plantation of 12,000 vines per hectare and in training to *Cordon du Royat*. He uses horses in his vineyard, and in his Taillepieds, he does not *rogner* (clip back the foliage) in order, as he puts it, to not only avoid stress to the vines, but also to increase the area of foliage. There is a vibrating sorting table, not a lot of stems (10 percent or so are retained), fermentation temperatures up to 32°C and 20 to 25 percent new oak. I was impressed by his 1999s, but less impressed by subsequent vintages, which I found a little over-extracted; from 2003 onward, however, I think Pascal Roblet has got it right. He is a rising star.

His wife, Cécile Tremblay, has her own domaine (see below). Pascal and Cécile also have a joint white wine domaine called Nerthus. It started in 2004 and consists of 3 hectares of Bourgogne, Auxey-Duresses *premier cru* Le Val and village Puligny-Montrachet.

Régis Rossignol-Changarnier

7.22 ha owned. Volnay *premier cru* (a blend of Les Angles, Les Brouillards and Les Mitans); Beaune *premier cru* Les Teurons; village Volnay; village Pommard; village Savigny-lès-Beaune; village Meursault.

The charming Régis Rossignol, seventyish, has no successors, but he now has a right-hand man, François Laleure. He makes full, rich, sturdy, long-lasting wines from old vines and a low harvest. There is never any de-stemming here. The estate has been selling in bottle since the 1950s. Today—and very successfully, according to M. Rossignol—he is doing experiments with the must-concentrating-by-evaporation Durafroid machine. This is a good source for "old-fashioned" wines.

★ Nicolas Rossignol
Rossignol-Jeanniard

17 ha owned and en *fermage/en métayage*. Volnay *premier cru* in Les Caillerets, En Chevret, Clos des Angles, Frémiets, Le Ronceret, Santenots and Taillepieds; Pommard *premier cru* in Les Chanlins and Les Jarolières; Beaune *premier cru* in Clos des Mouches, Clos du Roi and Les Reversées; Pernand-Vergelesses *premier cru* Les Fichots; Savigny-lès-Beaune *premier cru* in Les Fourneaux and Les Lavières; village Volnay; village Pommard; village Beaune; village Pernand-Vergelesses; village Savigny-lès-Beaune.

Nicolas Rossignol is a young man in a hurry. He has taken over the family domaine (there is more to come from his grandparents), relieved Michel Ampeau of his excess of red wine by taking over his Savignys and started a merchant business to offer white wine. He works his vines by the biodynamic calendar, ploughs the fields and trains high (1.35 m) to maximise the foliage. He may use some of the stems, he sometimes cold-soaks (you have to adapt to the vintage!), he ferments at a maximum of 32°C, and he gives the wines 10 to 50 percent new oak. There was a certain clumsiness about some of the wines when he first started in the late 1990s. But they are lovely now.

Cécile Tremblay

6 ha owned (rented en *métayage* to others); thus, 3 ha exploited. Chapelle-Chambertin (0.38 ha); Echézeaux (0.18 ha); Chambolle-Musigny *premier cru* Les Feusselottes; Vosne-Romanée *premier cru* Les Beaux Monts; village Vosne-Romanée "Vieilles Vignes"; village Morey-Saint-Denis; village Nuits-Saint-Georges.

Cécile Tremblay is the wife of Pascal Roblet (see above). The wines are made on the same lines in the same cellar. She inherited this domaine through the maternal line of her family, back to Édouard Jayer in 1921, and she was able to take over part of it when some share-cropping arrangements ceased after the 2002 vintage. There will be more to come over the next few years. This is a domaine to watch.

Joseph Voillot

10 ha owned and en *fermage*. Volnay *premier cru* in Champans, Les Brouillards, Les Caillerets and Frémiets; Pommard *premier cru* in Les Rugiens, Les Pezerolles, Les Epenots and Clos Micault; Meursault *premier cru* Les Cras; village Volnay; village Pommard; village Meursault.

Trained oenologue, Jean-Pierre Charlot, son-in-law of Joseph Voillot, has cellars both in Pommard and in Volnay, so he could be listed under either village, but I tend to taste here, so I place him in Volnay. The fruit is de-stemmed, cold-soaked briefly and fermented at temperatures up to 33°C. There is 10 to 25 percent new oak. Charlot, a thinker as well as a competent winemaker—and *sympa* to boot, makes very good wines.

MONTHELIE

After Volnay, there is an important break in the Côte. The first vineyards you come to are the continuation of Volnay's Clos des Chênes—

and *premier cru* as well—but then the slope turns and doubles back on itself into the hills of the Hautes-Côtes. Across the valley there is another southeast-facing ridge, and here the *premiers crus* begin again. But these are mainly within the jurisdiction of the next village: Auxey-Duresses.

Between the two, set back from the main Beaune-Autun road, lies the village of Monthelie, intimate, quiet and attractive without even a local bar to interrupt the sequence of houses, courtyards and farmyard outbuildings. It seems that everyone is involved in the wine business in Monthelie. If you don't make wine or work in the vineyards, it's because you are not yet old enough or because you've done your stint and are now *en retraite*.

History

According to the Abbé Courtépée, the origin of the name Monthelie comes from Mont Oloye, suggesting a high place above an important road—the road in this case being the east–west route across Burgundy. In AD 855, in archives in Autun cathedral, it appears as Monthelio. Above the village, there are remains of a lookout camp which dates back beyond the Romans to Neolithic times.

In the early Middle Ages, the land here belonged to the monks of Saint-Symphorien, followed by the Abbaye de Sainte-Marguerite. The Dukes of Burgundy then took over, only for Hugues the First to make a donation to the Abbaye of Cluny in 1078. In the thirteenth century, Pierre de Monthelie gave land to the ecclesiastics of Notre-Dame de Beaune. In 1523 vineyards in the village appear in the registry of the Kings of France.

It has never been either a village or a vineyard of great importance, though. Apart from the chapel belonging to the château, an attractive coloured-tile-roofed building in the middle of the village, now belonging to the Suremain family (q.v.), Monthelie has never had a church. In the nineteenth century, Dr. Lavalle noted one *climat* (Les Champs-Fulliot) of

première ligne, where the wine fetched 75 percent of that of Volnay. Most of the rest of the *commune* was planted with Gamay. All this led to a certain sense of inferiority. When a village notice was put up on the main road in 1927 it rather plaintively had to insist "Monthelie et Ses Grands Vins."

Location

The continuation of the Volnay *côte*, on which lie all but one of Monthelie's eleven *premiers crus*, is limestone of Bathonian origin. The land is quite steep, covered with red earth lower down and a lighter marl higher up. In the valley and climbing up toward Auxey on the opposite side, the soil is an Argovian marl, light in colour and low in calcareous matter. This gives an altogether different wine. While the *premiers crus* on the Volnay side can very justly be said to produce minor Volnay-style wines in character—not as concentrated, not as *fin*, but very pleasant, and often very well priced—the village land underneath is of much less distinction. It is often rustic. It frequently lacks that *sine qua non*: ripe plump fruit. While *premier cru* Monthelie is rather better than *premier cru* Auxey-Duresses, when it comes to village wine, the reverse is often the case. This is not a question of altitude but of exposition and a soil which is too alluvial.

The Vineyard

PREMIERS CRUS   There are fifteen *premiers crus*, in whole or in part, the last four of which were added in 2006. These are as follows: Le Cas Rougeot; Les Champs Fulliot (part); Le Château Gaillard; Le Clos Gauthey; Les Duresses (part); Le Meix Bataille; Les Riottes; La Taupine; Sur la Velle; Les Vignes Rondes; Le Village (part); Les Barbières; Clos des Toisières; Le Clou des Chênes; Les Clous (part). Several of these are small and obscure. All except Les Duresses and Les Clous lie above the village on the extension of the Volnay *côte*. These growths occupy 40.45 hectares and produce about 1,250 hectolitres of red wine and 40 hectolitres of white wine per year.

VILLAGE WINE   There are 99.45 hectares of village Monthelie, producing about 3,700 hectolitres of red wine and 190 hectolitres of white wine a year.

The Premiers Crus

LES CHAMPS FULLIOT	*(8.11 ha)*
SUR LA VELLE	*(6.03 ha)*
LES VIGNES RONDES	*(2.72 ha)*
LE MEIX BATAILLE	*(2.28 ha)*
LE CAS ROUGEOT	*(0.57 ha)*
LA TAUPINE	*(1.50 ha)*
LE CLOS GAUTHEY	*(1.80 ha)*
LES RIOTTES	*(4.50 ha)*
LE CHÂTEAU GAILLARD	*(0.49 ha)*
LES DURESSES	*(6.72 ha)*
CLOS DES TOISIÈRES	*(0.23 ha)*
LE CLOU DES CHÊNES	*(1.50 ha)*
LES BARBIÈRES	*(1.00 ha)*
LES CLOUS	*(3.00 ha)*

These are, roughly in order of descent down the slope and also in order of quality, the *premiers crus* on the Volnay side of the village: Les Champs Fulliot, Le Clou des Chênes and Sur la Velle touch Volnay Clos des Chênes. The exposure here is to the southeast, and then, as one turns round, toward the south. The incline is gentle but significant enough to offer good drainage, and it is a propitious spot to make good wine.

And, yes, you can find it: of medium weight, with good cherry, red currant, strawberry fruit, if not the real complex fragrance of a Volnay, with perfectly satisfactory grip and style. It's not great, but it is good honest Pinot Noir at a reasonable price.

The *premiers crus* Les Duresses and Les Clous touch Auxey's Les Duresses on the opposite side of the valley. The wines are a bit more four-square, a bit earthy and less distinctive, the fruit less poised. But in good hands, it can be well worth noting.

RECOMMENDED SOURCES

LES CHAMPS FULLIOT
Denis Boussey, Maurice Deschamps (both Monthelie); Bouchard Père et Fils (Beaune).

Denis Boussey also produces a very good Les Champs Fulliot *blanc*.

SUR LA VELLE
Éric de Suremain, Château de Monthelie, Éric Boigelot (all Meursault).

LE MEIX BATAILLE
Monthelie-Douhairet (Monthelie).

LES DURESSES
Paul Garaudet (Monthelie); Comtes Lafon (Meursault); Bouchard Père et Fils (Beaune).

The Growers

Denis Boussey

13.5 ha owned and *en fermage*. Volnay *premier cru* Taillepieds; Monthelie *premier cru* Les Champs Fulliot *rouge et blanc*; Meursault *premier cru* Les Charmes; village Monthelie *rouge et blanc*; village Volnay; village Pommard; village Aloxe-Corton in the *lieu-dit* Les Valozières; village Beaune; village Savigny-lès-Beaune *rouge et blanc*; village Meursault; village Puligny-Montrachet.

Denis Boussey shares tractors and other equipment with his brother Éric, who lives opposite. They have worked their vines independently since 1981. Everyone seems to say his whites are better than his reds, he complained to me once. I could only agree at the time. But now, the reds are rather better. Slowly but surely, Denis Boussey is passing things over to his son Laurent. This is a very good source.

Changarnier

6 ha owned. Monthelie *premier cru* in Le Meix Bataille and Les Champs Fulliot; Auxey-Duresses *premier cru* Les Duresses; village Monthelie, including the *lieu-dit* Les Clous *rouge et blanc*; village Meursault.

Following the death of their father in 2004, Claude Changarnier bought out his brother Pierre. Hitherto, it had been Pierre who had been making the wine. The cellar master is now the youthful, bearded Franck Carré. Good wines are here, but my experience of them is limited. There seemed to be quite a lot of new oak in the cellar for the 2005 vintage.

★ Didier Darviot-Perrin

8 ha owned and *en fermage*. Volnay *premier cru* in La Gigotte (*monopole*) and Les Santenots; Beaune *premier cru* Les Bélissands; Chassagne-Montrachet *premier cru* in Les Bondues (*rouge*), Les Blanchots-Dessus (*blanc*) and Clos Saint-Jean (*blanc*); Meursault *premier cru* in Les Charmes, Les Genevrières, Les Perrières and Les Plures; village Volnay; village Beaune; village Pommard; village Monthelie (*rouge et blanc*); village Meursault, including the *lieux-dits* Clos de la Velle, Les Corbins and Les Tessons; village Chassagne-Montrachet (*blanc*).

Didier Darviot produces very pure, stylish wines, true to their origins, from his estate, much of which was inherited through his wife's family (the Perrin-Ponsots of Meursault). Apart from the Monthelies, of which there is not much, the average age of the vines is a respectable 45 years. This is a fine source.

Maurice Deschamps

8.5 ha owned and *en fermage*. Volnay *premier cru* Clos des Chênes; Monthelie *premier cru* Les Champs Fulliot; village Monthelie *rouge et blanc*.

The handsome Maurice Deschamps does not export to the United Kingdom or to the United States, so my experience of his wines in bottle is somewhat limited. The cellar is tidy, the Pinots are de-stemmed, there is some new oak, and, more importantly, there are no very old barrels. His wines are pure and elegant. This is another very good source.

Dubuet-Monthelie

5 ha owned. Monthelie *premier cru* Les Champs Fulliot; village Monthelie *rouge et blanc*; village Meursault.

The 55-year-old Guy Dubuet and his son David, 26, run this emerging domaine at the bottom of the village. They use 20 percent new wood and bottle after 12 months. There are good wines in both colours.

Dupont-Fahn

5 ha owned and *en fermage*. Monthelie *premier cru* Les Vignes Rondes; village Meursault in the *lieux-dits* Les Vireuils, Murger de Monthelie and Pré de Manche; village Puligny-Montrachet in the *lieu-dit* Les Grands Champs; village Auxey-Duresses *rouge*.

Michel Dupont and his American wife Lesley occupy a modern house and cellar close to the main road. He de-stems his grapes, ferments at 30°C and uses 20 percent new wood. The set-up is tidy, *sympa* and efficient. But the wines could be better.

Paul Garaudet

10 ha owned and *en fermage/en métayage*. Monthelie *premier cru* in Les Duresses, Le Meix Bataille, Le Clos Gauthey (all *rouge*) and Les Champs Fulliot (*blanc*); Volnay *premier cru* in Les Pitures and Le Ronceret; village Monthelie *rouge et blanc*; village Volnay; village Pommard; village Meursault; village Puligny-Montrachet.

Paul Garaudet works out of a modern cellar in the middle of the village. The red grapes are de-stemmed, briefly cold-macerated and then fermented at temperatures up to 34°C, followed by up to 30 percent new wood. These are good sturdy wines, but they are without a great deal of elegance. He also looks after some of the vines of Annick Parent (see below). At the time of writing, the Ronceret is young-vines.

★ Monthelie-Douhairet

6 ha owned. Volnay *premier cru* Les Champans; Pommard *premier cru* in Les Chanlins and Les Frémiets; Monthelie *premier cru* in Les Duresses (*rouge et blanc*) and Clos Le Meix Bataille; Meursault *premier cru* Les Santenots (*blanc*); village Volnay; village Monthelie *rouge et blanc*, including the *lieu-dit* Clos le Meix-Garnier (*monopole*).

The late Mlle Armande Douhairet—she died in the spring of 2004 at age 98 or so—was once described by another writer as a *monument historique*. "No," she replied indignantly, "but perhaps part of the natural heritage, somewhat in need of restoration." Over the last decade, François Lechauve, the cellar master, has gradually modernised things. There is a sorting table, an up-to-date crusher/de-stemmer (the fruit is now completely de-stemmed) and the old barrels have been taken out and burnt. New oak is not called for; the domaine buys 1-year-old barrels. Since 2002 there has been neither fining nor filtration. As at the Hospices de Beaune, the new wine is descended warm into the barrels. The wines are still on the full and sturdy side, but now they show elegance as well. Following the death of Madame Monthelie Douhairet, her adopted heir, the 69-year-old André Porcheret, has installed his granddaughter Cataldine Lippo, in place of Lechauve.

Jean and Annick Parent

3.6 ha owned. Pommard *premier cru* in Les Rugiens and Les Chanlins; Volnay *premier cru* En l'Ormeau and Frémiets; Monthelie *premier cru* Sur la Velle, Le Clos Gauthey (*rouge et blanc*), Les Champs Fulliot and Château Gaillard.

Annick Parent and her father run this fine estate, much of which is let out to neighbours on a share-cropping basis. The wines are labelled either as Annick or as J and A Parent. She is a sensitive winemaker, and her wines are rather more elegant and Volnayish than most. Sadly, for health reasons, Annick Parent has had to wind down. From the 2004 vintage, she has made one wine, the white Château Gaillard. The remainder is sold as fruit to the cousins, Domaine Parent of Pommard. In 2007 this domaine was acquired by Faiveley of Nuits-Saint-Geoges.

Éric de Suremain, Château de Monthelie

8.85 ha owned. Monthelie *premier cru* Sur la Velle; village Monthelie; plus Rully *rouge et blanc*.

A splendid environment, with a fine *manoir*, parts of which date back to the fourteenth century, overlooking the vineyards and situated in a little park. But the wines all too often are disappointing: light and rustic.

AUXEY-DURESSES

Auxey (pronounced Aussey) is the next village along the Autun road. But before you reach it, stop the car just outside Monthelie, before the road descends, and look at the view. It is one of the very best in Burgundy. In front of you lies the village of Auxey, sheltering under the Montagne de Bourdon. Further along, the valley widens again, and you can see the vines of Saint-Romain. To your right are the vineyards of Monthelie, to your left the village of Meursault, and beyond it the valley of the Sâone; behind you there is Volnay and the *climat* of Santenots. You really are in the heart of the Côte de Beaune.

The village of Auxey lies in the valley between the aforementioned Montagne de Bourdon and the Mont Mélian, and two of the three sections which comprise the Auxey *vignoble* lie on the slopes of these hills. Those under the Montagne de Bourdon face southeast and then due south, and it is on the first part, before you come to the village, that you will find the *premiers crus*. This is a good site for the Pinot Noir. Opposite, on what is in effect the extension of the Meursault slope, the orientation is northwest, though the slope is gentle. Here the Pinot will not ripen successfully. This is land for Chardonnay, but not for *premier cru*. A kilometre or so further on, under the vineyard of Saint-Romain, is a third slope, facing southeast once again. You will find both varieties, but again no *premiers crus*.

History

Auxey was known in Gallo-Roman times as Aulaciacum, which was slowly but surely contracted to Alcium or Aussey. In the eleventh century, Cistercian monks created a vineyard and installed a water mill in what was then the hamlet of Auxey. The village was subsequently ruled by a succession of *seigneurs*, who left their mark in the shape of the vestiges of at least two châteaux. You can still see what were once the cellars of one of them behind the church. The church itself is fifteenth century and possesses a *tryptique* attributed to Roger van der Weyden.

Like many villages—in Auxey's case in 1928—the village took on as a suffix the name of one of its top *climats*. Like Morey, it did not pick the very best. Les Duresses is not Auxey's top *premier cru*. That honour goes to Clos du Val. But I suppose Auxey du Val is a bit cumbersome.

The Vineyard

The *climat* of Les Duresses, the first and most easterly facing of the *premiers crus*, is, like its namesake in Monthelie to which it is contiguous, of an Argovian limestone base: a stony marl, light in colour, the soil about 25–30 centimetres thick at the top. As you travel on, and the orientation charges toward the south, the soil becomes less calcareous, more marly and harder to work. When you head into Le Val, this tendency is even more exaggerated. This is the end of the *premiers crus*. This geology is continued in the vineyards which follow, but the soil colour gradually changes to red, and it mixes with more scree and limestone debris. The microclimate is colder here, as a result of the forest on the opposite flank, despite the southerly exposure.

On the Mont Mélian slope, the soil is a red-coloured, very stony limestone debris; the rock underneath is more crumbly, and the surface soil is only 15–20 centimetres thick.

PREMIERS CRUS There are nine *premiers crus*, in whole or in part, and these are as follows: Les Bréterins (part); La Chapelle; Climat du Val; Clos du Val; Bas des Duresses; Les Duresses (part); Les Ecussaux (part); Les Grands Champs; Reugne (part). These cover 31.78 hectares and produce around 1,000 hectolitres of red wine and 16 hectolitres of white wine per year.

VILLAGE WINE There are 137.87 hectares of village wine producing 2,500 hectolitres of red wine, including Côte-de-Beaune Villages, and 1,700 hectolitres of white wine a year.

Premier cru Auxey *rouge* can vary from soft, forward, plump wines in the modern style to rather more substantial bottles which sometimes have a tendency to be a bit four-square, even rustic. The former aspiration, in my view, is fine at the village level, but one looks for more substance and depth of wine if one is paying *premier cru* prices. This sort of Auxey is usually a bigger wine than a Monthelie *premier cru*, and, with the weight but without the artisanal aspects,

it used to be rare, but one can now find it more and more. But—for here we are beginning to range into the Hautes-Côtes—there is nevertheless more of a difference in quality between the good years and the not-so-good than there is in, say, Volnay and Pommard.

Auxey-Duresses is also an important village for white wines. These are rather less expensive than village Meursaults but can often be as good, so they are a much better value. They need drinking reasonably soon.

Today, just about all the growers in Auxey-Duresses produce good white wines, and some of these can be really very attractive. Red wine success and consistency are harder to find; there were plenty of good wines in 2005, but not many in 2004. Yet practically all Auxey *premier cru* is red wine. It is curious.

The Premiers Crus

CLOS DU VAL	(0.93 a)
CLIMAT DU VAL	(8.37 ha)
LES DURESSES	(7.92 ha)
LES BRÉTERINS	(1.69 ha)
LA CHAPELLE	(1.28 ha)
REUGNE	(1.98 ha)
BAS DES DURESSES	(2.39 ha)
LES GRANDS CHAMPS	(4.03 ha)
LES ECUSSAUX	(3.18 ha)

I list these in order of my preference, the last three vineyards being those lower down the slope from the first six.

The Clos du Val, a monopoly of one branch of the extended Prunier family, and now divided between Michel Prunier and his first cousin Philippe (Domaine Prunier-Damy), is Auxey's best site, and seems to produce a wine which is quite a lot richer, fatter and more stylish that the other *premiers crus*. The rest of the Val *climat* and its immediate neighbours produce a more substantial wine than the vineyard of Les Duresses.

RECOMMENDED SOURCES
LE VAL
Alain and Vincent Creusefond, Jean-Pierre and Laurent Prunier (both Auxey-Duresses).

CLOS DU VAL

Michel Prunier et Fille, Philippe-Prunier-Damy (both Auxey-Duresses).

LES DURESSES

Jean-Pierre and Christophe Diconne, Pascal Prunier (both Auxey-Duresses).

LES ECUSSAUX

Robert Ampeau (Meursault).

LA CHAPELLE

Henri Latour, Jean and Gilles Lafouge, Jean-Pierre and Laurent Prunier (all Auxey-Duresses).

The Growers

Alain and Vincent Creusefond

13 ha owned and *en fermage*. Auxey-Duresses *premier cru* in Le Val, plus a *premier cru* from Reugne and Les Duresses; Meursault *premier cru* Les Poruzots; village Auxey-Duresses *rouge et blanc*; village Monthelie; village Meursault; village Beaune.

On the main road, as you enter the village from the Monthelie side, you will find the house and cellars of Alain Creusefond, who has been aided since 2003 by his son Vincent. He is a cousin of Michel Prunier, and so part of this important Auxey family. While some in the *commune* produce more successful Chardonnays than Pinots, the Creusefonds are equally competent in both colours. Thirty-five percent new wood is used for the Poruzots.

Jean-Pierre and Christophe Diconne

10.6 ha owned and *en fermage/en métayage*. Auxey-Duresses *premier cru* Les Bréterins, Les Duresses and Les Grands Champs; village Auxey-Duresses *rouge et blanc*; village Meursault, including the *lieux-dits* Les Narvaux and Les Luchets; village Pommard in the *lieu-dit* Les Vignots.

The irrepressible, enthusiastic Jean-Pierre Diconne is one of Burgundy's eccentrics, and the winemaking here is a bit hit and miss. But I have had some good bottles in both colours, and standards have improved since the arrival of his son Christophe. Yields have been reduced, and

there is now 15 to 20 percent new wood for the village and *premier cru* wines.

Jean and Gilles Lafouge

10 ha owned and *en fermage*. Auxey-Duresses *premier cru* in La Chapelle, Le Val and Les Duresses; Pommard *premier cru* Les Chanlins; Village Auxey-Duresses *rouge et blanc*, including the *lieux-dits* Les Vireux (*blanc*), Les Boutonnières and Les Hautés; village Meursault, including the *lieu-dit* Les Meix Chavaux; village Pommard in the *lieu-dit* Les Noizons.

This long-established domaine, located on the back streets of the village, has been bottling more and more of its own wine since the 38-year-old Gilles Lafouge joined his father after wine school and national service a dozen years ago. I've had some good wines here, especially in white. In general, the Lafouge style is for early maturing wines.

Henri Latour et Fils

16.5 ha owned and *en fermage*. Auxey-Duresses *premier cru* from Les Grands Champs and La Chapelle; village Meursault; village Auxey-Duresses *rouge et blanc*; Saint-Romain *rouge et blanc*.

Cousins of the Lafouges, but not of any Latours in the neighbourhood, François and Sylvain Latour, sons of the now retired Henri, are adherents of the lyre system of training, which is tolerated but not encouraged by the authorities. With a *cordon* controlled pruning system, they will explain, there is a much better sanitary condition of the fruit, and they obtain a better sugar level and a better colour. They also plant ray-grass to prevent erosion, are very *biologique* as regards treatments, are very wary about maturing their wines in too much new oak and have cropped 40 hectolitres per hectare for village wine and 30 for *premier cru* over the last decade. This immaculately tidy cellar produces very good wines.

★★ Maison Leroy

With Madame Lalon Bize-Leroy's acquisition in 1988 of the Charles Noëllat domaine in

Vosne-Romanée (see page 144) one suspects buying activity here in Auxey is a shadow of what it was. But substantial stocks of high-quality old Burgundies remain in the cellar. The Leroy style has always been for wines which last well, bought in as wine when the vintage was a good one, and only when the quality was appropriate. Here is a treasure trove, but an expensive one.

Max and Anne-Marye Piguet-Chouet

12 ha owned and *en fermage*. Auxey-Duresses *premier cru* Le Val; Volnay *premier cru*; village Auxey-Duresses *rouge et blanc*; Saint-Romain *rouge et blanc*; village Meursault in the *lieu-dit* Le Pré de Manche; village Beaune; village Volnay; village Pommard.

Now joined by his son Stéphane, Max Piguet runs one of the most reliable domaines in Auxey-Duresses. One hundred percent de-stemming, a week of cold-soaking and 15 to 25 percent new wood produce stylish wines with no hard edges.

Dominique and Anne-Marie Piguet-Girardin

12.5 ha owned and *en fermage*. Auxey-Duresses *premier cru* in Les Grands Champs; Santenay *premier cru* in La Comme and Clos Rousseau; Chassagne-Montrachet *premier cru* Morgeot; Pommard *premier cru* La Chanière; Meursault *premier cru* Les Charmes; village Auxey-Duresses *rouge et blanc*; village Meursault; village Pommard.

Madame Piguet is Vincent Girardin's sister: hence the Santenays and the Chassagne-Montrachet. Dominique Piguet, bespectacled and in his forties, makes very good wines. Quite a lot is sold off in bulk.

Jean-Pierre and Laurent Prunier

9 ha owned and *en fermage*. Auxey-Duresses *premier cru* in Les Duresses and Le Val; Monthelie *premier cru* in Les Clous, Les Champs Fulliot and Sur La Velle; Volnay *premier* cru Clos des Chênes; village Auxey-Duresses *rouge et blanc*; village Pommard; village Beaune; village Meursault; Saint-Romain *rouge et blanc*.

Laurent Prunier, the brother of Pascal Prunier, now in Meursault, took over his share of the family domaine in 1992 and is still enlarging it, the first and second of the *premiers crus* Monthelie being new in 2006. This is a very good source, consistent in both colours.

Michel Prunier et Fille

12 ha owned and *en fermage*. Auxey-Duresses *premier cru* Clos du Val and a *premier cru tout court*; Volnay *premier cru* Les Caillerets; Beaune *premier cru* Les Sizies; village Auxey-Duresses *rouge et blanc*; village Meursault in the *lieu-dit* Les Clous; village Pommard in the *lieu-dit* Les Vignots; village Chorey-lès-Beaune, including the *lieu-dit* Les Beaumonts.

It is hard to think of the diminutive and somewhat self-effacing Michel Prunier as the doyen of his family. But he is certainly the best grower in the village, and the village seems to be largely populated by his relations.

Now joined by his daughter Estelle, Michel Prunier produces my favourite Auxey: his Clos du Val. The fruit is hand harvested and then passed through a sorting table. *Cuvaisons* are relatively short and temperature controlled. The white wines are bottled after 12 months, the reds after 16 to 18.

Philippe Prunier-Damy

15 ha owned and *en fermage*. Auxey-Duresses *premier cru* Clos du Val; Monthelie *premier cru* Les Duresses; village Pommard; village Beaune; village Volnay; village Monthelie; village Meursault; village Auxey-Duresses *rouge et blanc*; Saint-Romain "Sous le Château" *rouge et blanc*.

This domaine used to be called Roger Prunier, the late Roger being Michel's older brother. Philippe took over in 1979. Together, the two domaines share the monopoly of the Clos du Val. There is *lutte raisonnée* in the vineyard. Thirty percent new wood is used here. These are very good wines from a very clean and tidy cellar.

Vincent Prunier

12 ha owned and *en fermage/en métayage*. Puligny-Montrachet *premier cru* Les Garennes; Saint-Aubin *premier cru rouge* Les Combes and *blanc*, En Remilly and La Chatenière; Auxey-Duresses *premier cru* Les Grands Champs; village Meursault; village

Auxey-Duresses *rouge et blanc*; Saint-Romain *rouge*; village Chassagne-Montrachet *rouge*.

Vincent Prunier's parents were not in the wine business, though his grandparents were. He started off in 1988 with 3 hectares. There are some good wines here. The star is the Meursault, a blend of Les Vireuils and Les Clous.

Dominique and Vincent Roy

11.5 ha owned. Auxey-Duresses *premier cru* in Les Duresses and Le Val; Volnay *premier cru* Les Santenots; village Auxey-Duresses *rouge et blanc*; Côte-de-Beaune Villages.

Two bearded brothers in their forties, Dominique and the lean, dark Vincent, run this emerging domaine, situated on the main road at the entrance to the village. Five percent of the stems; vinification controlled at 30°C, using natural yeasts; 20 percent new oak; and no fining after a light kieselguhr filtration is the recipe here. The *cuverie* consists of squat, round stainless steel tanks, equipped with automatic *pigeage* plungers, over concrete vats, which enables *écoulage* by gravity. Behind this room is a fifteenth century cellar dug out of the side of the slope. This is a good address producing soft wines for early drinking. Recent vintages of the Val are especially good.

SAINT-ROMAIN

Saint-Romain is really part of the Hautes-Côtes, but it has enjoyed full village *appellation contrôlée* since 1947. After Auxey-Duresses, the road divides, and the right-hand fork leads you through the Saint-Romain vineyards toward the village, surrounded by cliffs and perched below the remains of an impressive fortified château. The village is on two levels: Saint-Romain-Le-Haut, within what were originally the bailey walls of the castle, with the main village below. Between the two, the traveller will pass the impressive tiers of weathering oak staves of the cooper François Frères.

The soil is varied but more suitable for producing white wine than red, as are the elevation of the vineyards (between 300 and 400 m) and

the ambient temperature. The vines are largely planted on a quite stony calcareous clay; the higher slopes are more marly, the lower terrains more iron-rich and, consequently, redder in colour.

There are no first growths in the *commune*; it is the only one in the Côte de Beaune apart from Chorey not to possess any. The 135 hectares of village land produce about 1,950 hectolitres of red wine (including Côte-de-Beaune Villages) and 1,800 hectolitres of white wine per year.

This is a village which is rather more successful in Chardonnay than in Pinot Noir. The red wines are hardly different from those of the Hautes-Côtes, at their best light, soft, fruity and for early drinking. In a poor year, they are lean and herbaceous. The white wine comes into its own when the vintage is very warm, such as in 2003, and as a result, the Meursaults and Pulignys are alcoholic, heavy and deficient in acidity. In these years, the advantages of Saint-Romain's cooler climate and consequent racier wines is an advantage. But even in lesser years, this can be a good hunting ground for those seeking inexpensive white wine. Most *négociants*—Louis Jadot for example—will offer one.

RECOMMENDED SOURCES
See below.

The Growers

★★★ D'Auvenay

3.67 ha owned. Mazis-Chambertin (0.26 ha); Bonnes-Mares (0.26 ha); Chevalier-Montrachet (0.16 ha); Criots-Bâtard-Montrachet (0.06 ha); Puligny-Montrachet *premier cru* Les Folatières; village Meursault, including the *lieu-dit* Les Narvaux; village Auxey-Duresses *blanc*.

This is Madame Lalon Bize-Leroy's own private domaine, the produce of which is made and sold quite independently of the Domaine Leroy or Leroy the *négociants*. The vineyards are biodynamic. The cellars are *chez elle*, up on the plateau on the road which leads to the N6. It is aboveground, but temperature controlled. There is not much wine, but it is magnificent.

Christophe Buisson

7 ha owned and *en fermage*. Saint-Romain *rouge et blanc*; Beaune *blanc* in the *lieu-dit* Clos Saint-Désirée; Auxey-Duresses; Savigny-lès-Beaune.

The youthful Christophe Buisson moved to Beaune in 1999. (The cellar is still under construction—he is helped by his father who is a builder.) But the address on his labels still says Saint-Romain, so I include him here. He uses hand harvesting. The Saint-Romain is reared partly in wood (one third new) and partly in tank. He has a *table de tri*, and everything works by gravity. The range is modest, but quality is very high.

Germain Père et Fils

13.5 ha owned and *en fermage*. Beaune *premier cru* in Les Aigrots and Les Montrevenots; Saint-Romain *rouge*, Sous-le-Château, *et blanc*; village Pommard; village Beaune; village Meursault; village Auxey-Duresses.

Patrick and Arnaud Germain have taken over responsibility from their father Bernard at this up-and-coming domaine, and the wines have improved as they have progressively used less and less of the stems and increased the proportion of new oak. The whites are now entirely vinified in wood. There is a fine view from the terrace outside the Germains' home on the road up to Ouches.

★ Alain Gras

12 ha owned and *en fermage*. Village Auxey-Duresses *rouge, vieilles vignes, et blanc*; Saint-Romain *rouge et blanc*; village Meursault in the *lieu-dit* Les Tillets.

The youthful, 50-year-old, balding Alain Gras's bastion lies high up in Saint-Romain-Le-Haut, among the ruins of the medieval château and church. The view from close by is impressive. His first vintage was 1982. He took over his father René Gras's exploitation in 1998, doubling his estate, and has been in the vanguard of putting Saint-Romain on the map. These are modern wines. "I want to make *vins de plaisir*," he says. But they do not lack depth. His old-vine (105 years old!) Auxey *rouge* is better than all but a couple of *premiers crus*.

Thierry Guyot

6.7 ha en fermage/*en métayage*. Saint-Romain *rouge et blanc*; village Beaune; village Puligny-Montrachet.

The future of this long-standing biodynamic domaine is unclear as we go to press, Thierry Guyot having split from his brother-in-law Renaud Boyer, who now works at the Château de Puligny-Montrachet. I am told responsibility is passing to a cousin.

Bernard Martenot, Domaine de la Perrière

13 ha owned and *en fermage*. Beaune *premier cru* Les Aigrots; village Meursault *rouge et blanc*; Saint-Romain *rouge et blanc*.

The genial, 50-year-old Bernard Martenot started bottling seriously a decade ago. He practices the *lutte raisonnée*, harvests by hand and uses 20 percent new oak. I was not allowed to taste the full range of 2004s on my last visit, as they were being prepared for bottling, but I can report positively on the 2002s and 2003s.

MEURSAULT

Choose selectively, and you will perceive a natural progression in the Côte de Beaune. First you have the sturdy reds of Pommard, then the more elegant, softer wines of Volnay and, finally, a white wine *commune*: Meursault. Meursault produces almost as much white wine as all the other *communes* put together. It is a large parish—only Gevrey-Chambertin and Beaune have more land under vines—and indeed, it is a sizeable village with a seemingly limitless number of individual growers. For the past 25 years, I have visited twenty-five or so Meursault proprietors a year, usually eliminating three or four from the previous season in order to add new names. I have yet to arrive at the bottom of the list.

History

The name Meursault (Murisault or Murassalt in old documents) is derived according to some authorities from the Latin for "rat jump." But Pierre Forgeot says the name comes from the fortified camp, dating from Bronze Age and Gallo-Roman times, which lies up in the hills above the village. Does the word *mur* (wall) have anything to do with it? The locals prefer the more colourful athletic rodents, an explanation which seems a bit far-fetched to me, but etymology, I fear, is far from being an exact science, and one can idle away a lot of time up its dark and twisted alleys.

Like the majority of *communes* of the Côte d'Or, the history of the parish is closely associated with the church. Even before there was a vine at Clos de Vougeot, the new Cistercian abbey at Cîteaux, founded by the ascetic Robert de Molesmes in 1098 as a breakaway from the more comfortable order of the Benedictines at Cluny, had received a gift of land in Meursault from Duke Odo II of Burgundy. That was in 1102. This was followed by further donations over the next couple of centuries, with the result that Vougeot Meursault became Cîteaux's most important viticultural territory, a situation which persisted until the French Revolution. Moreover, it is Meursault rather than Puligny-Montrachet which is the heart of the Hospices de Beaune's white wine holdings. In 1669 half the land belonging to the local *seigneur*, M. de Massot, was left to this institution.

Though most of Burgundy is equally as entitled to produce red wine as white, the *commune* seems always to have concentrated its production on white wines. Thomas Jefferson was told when he visited the area in 1787 that there was "too much stone" in the soil for red wine production. No doubt the locals would have produced red wine if they could, for the latter was much more popular. Good Volnay sold for 300 francs per cask, but even the best Meursault (Jefferson refers specifically to Goutte d'Or) could fetch only 150. "At Pommard and Voulenay (*sic*) I observed [the local farmers] eating good white bread; at Meursault rye. I asked the reason of the difference. They told me that white wines fail in quality oftener than the red, and remain on hand. At Meursault only white wines are made."

André Jullien (*Topographie de tous les Vignobles Connus*, written in 1815) refers to the Meursault reds of the Santenots *climat* on the Volnay border, producing a wine similar to Volnay in style, and goes on to say that the majority of the *commune*'s production was white wine. These, having left Burgundy, were often sold under the name of Montrachet, he adds. Perrières, Combettes (now, and perhaps then, across the border in Puligny), Gouttes d'Or, Genevrièvres and Charmes, and in that order, he emphasised, were the best vineyards.

Forty years later, as far as the white wines were concerned, Dr. Lavalle accorded the *climat* of Les Perrières the accolade of *tête de cuvée*. Les Genevrières *dessus*, Les Charmes *dessus*, Les Bouchères and Les Gouttes d'Or were deemed *premières cuvées*. By this time, however, prices of the white wines seem to have caught up with the reds. A Perrières would fetch the same price (1,200 francs the *queue* in good years, direct from the press) as a Santenots-du-Milieu.

Today, Les Perrières would head most people's list of the top *climats* in the *commune*, and I would put the best of the various parts of Charmes and Genevrières in second place, some way above the remainder. And I would also add the best of the white wines of Blagny, only considered part of Meursault since the days of *appellation contrôlée*.

The reason for the very large number of domaine bottlers in the village—well over 100, which is over four times that of Puligny-Montrachet and indeed double that of Gevrey, for instance—is twofold. First, unlike in Puligny, where the water table is high, cellars can easily be constructed out of the bedrock beneath the village. The second reason concerns the fluctuations of fashion. Several times in the last 30 years, while Puligny-Montrachet has been in demand, Meursault has been out of favour. The Beaune *négoce* have not wanted to buy. There have been times when Meursault fetched less per bottle than a generic Chablis. So the growers have decided to go it alone.

The Village

The large, sprawling village of Meursault lies in the middle of its *vignoble* and boasts a fine church dating from 1480, whose 57-metre spire can be seen from some distance away. This is found near the remains of a medieval fortress in the town's main square. Surrounding this *place* there are a number of narrow, winding streets and alleys, laid out to no coherent plan, reaching in one direction toward Auxey and Monthelie, and in another down toward the main road and across to Puligny-Montrachet. Within as well as without the village, hidden in their own parks behind secluding gates, there are a number of fine buildings, some dating back to the sixteenth and seventeenth centuries, or beyond. Chief of these is the seventeenth-century Château de Meursault, now the property of Maison Patriarche. Across the main Beaune-Chagny road is the village of L'Hôpital de Meursault, where you can see the ecclesiastical remains of the old leprosarium. It is in Meursault that the third and least stuffy of the Trois Glorieuses banquets, the Paulée, is held at lunchtime on the Monday after the Hospices de Beaune auction in November. Everyone brings and shares his/her own wine, and you are seated on long tables to facilitate this generosity. The last time I attended, I later counted no fewer than fifty-seven tasting notes in my *carnet*, my descriptions becoming progressively more indecipherable and unintelligible as the afternoon progressed!

Location

The *commune* is divided by the village and has two distinct sections. The smaller northern part is an extension of the Monthelie-Volnay *côte* as it falls gently toward the southeast. The soil is based on Bathonian limestone and is a brown stony debris containing both pebbles and clay, more suitable for red wine than white. Here you will find the *climats* of Santenots and Les Plures. The red wine that is produced here is sold as Volnay, Les Santenots, and is discussed in the Volnay chapter.

South of the village the soil is lighter in colour, rocky rather than pebbley, and the aspect is more to the east, even to the northeast directly above the village. The vines lie sheltered under the forest of the Montagne du Chatelet de Montmellian, on one side of which is the hamlet of Blagny and on the other side the village of Auxey-Duresses. It is close to Blagny that the best *climats* are located. The *terroir* here is of Bathonian origin: Callovian limestone, in parts Argovian white marl, covered in broken limestone debris, especially upslope, where there is hardly any surface soil to speak of. In Les Perrières the soil is the lightest and stoniest of all. Beneath this is Les Charmes, similar in the upper part of the *Dessus* (the *Dessus* goes quite a long way down the slope here!). Further down, the earth is much deeper and the incline more gentle.

Next to this there is Les Genevrières, also divided into *Dessus* and *Dessous*. Again, at the top, the surface layer is thin, but the soil is a little redder in colour and deeper further down the slope. Next to this is Les Poruzots, above part of which is Les Bouchères, and on the same level as Les Bouchères is the last of the *premiers crus* in this sector, Les Gouttes d'Or. Again, the vineyards are very stony in the upper sections, but the upper sections are redder in colour and more clayey in consistency. It quite abruptly becomes less fine as we descend the slope.

Of equal importance is the nature of the underlying rock. In the top parts of Les Genevrières and in Les Perrières, the base rock is hard. Further down in Les Genevrières and across the whole of Les Charmes, there is *lave*, a shaly limestone which crumbles easily.

What is the difference between a Meursault, a Puligny and a Chassagne? The soil in Meursault is less humid than that of Puligny, as the water table is lower. Normally, the crop is smaller. This doesn't necessarily mean that the wines are more concentrated—indeed there are as many weak ephemeral wines as in the other *communes*, perhaps more—but at their best (and I am not speaking of the *grands crus* here), the wines have a fatness, a richness and a nutty-butteriness, as distinct as the more peachy and flowery flavours of the two *communes* to the south.

The Vineyard

PREMIERS CRUS   Meursault (and Blagny, for it is convenient to include Blagny here—though the terrain and wines will be discussed in the next chapter) possess thirty *premiers crus* including the various Santenots and Les Plures, which, if red (but they can also be planted in Chardonnay), make Volnay, Les Santenots. These are, in Meursault, as follows: Les Caillerets; Les Charmes-Dessous; Les Charmes-Dessus; Les Chaumes de Narvaux (Genevrières); Les Chaumes des Perrières; Clos des Perrières; Clos Richemont; Les Cras; Les Genevrières-Dessous; Les Genevrières-Dessus; Les Gouttes d'Or; Aux Perrières; Les Perrières-Dessous; Les Perrières-Dessus; Les Plures; Les Poruzots; Les Poruzots-Dessous; Les Poruzots-Dessus; Les Santenots-Blancs; Les Santenots-du-Milieu.

All the above can be red or white. In practice, only the *climats* near Volnay (Santenots, Plures, Les Cras, Clos Richemont) are planted with Pinot Noir. However, while Meursault Les Cras, Meursault Les Caillerets and so forth can be red or white, Meursault Les Santenots can only be white. If red, the wine is Volnay.

In Blagny, all the following have the right to the appellation Meursault-Blagny *premier cru* if planted with Chardonnay: Sous Blagny; Sous le Dos d'Ane; La Jeunelotte; La Pièce sous le Bois; Les Ravelles. For Blagny *rouge*, see the next chapter.

These *premiers crus* cover 133.88 hectares (this figure includes Volnay-Santenots) and produce around 4,100 hectolitres of white wine per year. Some 75 hectolitres of Meursault *premier cru rouge* is also declared.

VILLAGE WINE   There are 304.95 hectares of village Meursault producing some 12,000 hectolitres of white wine and 720 hectolitres of red wine per year.

White Meursault, said Camille Rodier in 1920, is at the same time dry and rich, with a flavour of hazelnuts. For Hubrecht Duijker (*The Great Wines of Burgundy*) it is ripe peaches which have just been picked on a hot day. Meursault, I would suggest, is an ample, sometimes gentle, wholly approachable wine, less sturdy but more opulent than Puligny, with less backbone, too. It can occasionally be a little too fat and heavy, the broadness of the style not being matched by sufficient acidity. The village wines can often be merely empty and anonymous. But all in all, you have something which is round and ripe and fruity, with a rich buttery flavour, which should be supported but not overwhelmed by new oak. And then you will have something with considerable charm.

Moreover, there are the *"deuxièmes crus."* Nowhere in the Côte d'Or is the concept of a *lieu-dit* which is not a *premier cru* more important. Above the *premiers crus* and taking over from them at the same altitude where they leave off, are what used to be termed (by Dr. Lavalle and others) the *deuxièmes*. I see no reason not to avail ourselves of this description.

Up in the hills, going from south (above Les Genevrières) to north, we have Les Narvaux; Les Tillets; Les Clous; Les Casse Têtes; and Les Vireuils. These tend to be steely and racy. The best have no lack of finesse.

In the line of the *premiers crus* after Les Gouttes d'Or, we have Les Grands Charrons; Le Tesson; Les Rougeots; Les Chevalières; Les Luchets; and Les Meix-Chavaux. These are fuller and rounder, but again have rather more distinction than ordinary village wines from lower down the slope or from the opposite side of the village.

In the late 1990s, inaugurated and sponsored by the village of Meursault, a large expanse of land that had been allowed to go wild was cleared, the large rock pulverised and drained. It was then divided up into two-thirds-hectare parcels and sold off to the young *vignerons* of the village, who planted their plots in 1999 or 2000. This land lies upslope from the *premiers crus* Les Bouchères and Les Gouttes d'Or and is called Les Chaumes or Les Chaumes de Narvaux.

The Premiers Crus

LES PERRIÈRES   (13.72 ha)

This is the surface area of all the various Perrières combined (as are the equivalents below) and includes the 0.95-hectare monopoly of the Clos des Perrières, belonging to Domaine Albert Grivault, which the owners, the Bardet family, are attempting to have elevated to *grand cru.*

Essentially there are two parts to the *climat*: that which lies immediately above Les Charmes (Les Perrières *Dessous*) and that which lies further up the slope. In contrast to elsewhere it is the *Dessous* rather than the *Dessus* which is considered the best. Of course, as always, it depends on the grower (Jean-François Coche-Dury has his vines in the upper part, for example).

We are on the Puligny boundary here (next along are Champ Canet and Les Combettes), and not surprisingly, there are Puligny aspects to a wine from the Perrières. It is the most mineral, the most steely and the raciest of the Meursault *premiers crus*. It is floral, but then so are Genevrières and Charmes, but here the flowers are apple blossom and acacia, honeysuckle rather than honey itself, all quite high-toned. Above all, Perrières is perhaps the most elegant and persistent of the *premiers crus*. At its best, it is positively brilliant, certainly comparable to Bâtard or Bienvenues, though perhaps not as fine—and certainly not as powerful—as Chevalier or Montrachet itself.

RECOMMENDED SOURCES
Bouchard Père et Fils (Beaune); Robert Ampeau, Michel Bouzereau, Yves Boyer-Martenot, Jean-François Coche-Dury, Jean-Michel Gaunoux, Henri Germain, Albert Grivault, Comtes Lafon, Latour-Giraud, Matrot, Mestre-Michelot, Pierre Morey, Jacques Prieur, Guy Roulot (all Meursault); Darviot-Perrin (Monthelie); Château de Puligny-Montrachet, (Puligny); Vincent Bitouzet-Prieur (Volnay).

While none of the major *négociants*, except for Bouchard Père et Fils, actually owns land in Les Perrières, the *cuvées* of Joseph Drouhin, Louis Jadot and Olivier Leflaive Frères are usually worth recommending.

LES GENEVRIÈRES   (16.48 ha)

Les Genevrières-Dessus is on the same level as Les Perrières-Dessous and produces better wine than Les Genevrières-Dessous further down the slope. The vineyard does not, however, go all the way down to the Meursault-Puligny road, as does Les Charmes: the *climat* of Le Limouzin lies in between.

Genevrières is an opulent, even exotic wine. It is rounder than Perrières and if not fuller then certainly lusher, less steely and mineral, flashier and spicier. Here the flavours are muskier, and there can be an element of citrus. Yet the result should be neither coarse nor heavy. A Genevrières should still have grip, should still be a wine of class. Virginal, however, it is not.

Is it better than Charmes? This is a question I find impossible to answer. There is certainly more variation in the quality of Charmes, whose lower sections should be excluded from *premier cru* status. But apart from that, it is a question, as always, of which cellar you are in, the age of the vines, the vintage and personal taste. The two wines are very different.

RECOMMENDED SOURCES
Bouchard Père et Fils, Louis Jadot (both Beaune); Guy Bocard, Bernard Boisson, Michel Bouzereau, Yves Boyer-Martenot, Henri Germain, Rémi Jobard, François Jobard, Comtes Lafon, Latour-Giraud, Mestre-Michelot, Michelot Mère et Fille, François Mikulski (all Meursault); Darviot-Perrin (Monthelie).

LES CHARMES   (31.12 ha)

Larger than both Perrières and Genevrières put together, Les Charmes runs all the way down the slope until it reaches the Meursault-Puligny road, across which, in part, the land is not village AC, but plain Bourgogne. It is perfectly valid to argue that the bottom third of Les Charmes should be downgraded to village status.

But that is not to denigrate the wine of the upper part. Here you will find a Meursault of equal interest and elegance to Genevrières and, in my view, one of greater poise and style than Poruzots or Gouttes d'Or. There is an attractive, soft flowery character to a Charmes: peach blossom, delicately nutty, gently honeyed. The wine is less racy than Perrières and less exotically spicy than Genevrières. But it should be just as intense, just as stylish and just as harmonious.

RECOMMENDED SOURCES

Bouchard Père et Fils (Beaune); Robert Ampeau, Vincent Bitouzet-Prieur (Volnay), Guy Bocard, Hubert Bouzereau-Gruère; Michel Bouzereau, Patrick Javillier, Rémi Jobard, François Jobard, Comtes Lafon, Matrot, Matrot-Wittersheim, Mestre-Michelot, Michelot Mère et Fille, François Mikulski, René Monnier, Guy Roulot (all Meursault); Denis Boussey, Darviot-Perrin (both Monthelie).

LES PORUZOTS	*(11.43 ha)*
LES BOUCHÈRES	*(4.41 ha)*
LES GOUTTES D'OR	*(5.33 ha)*

Although Bouchères is rare—the only examples I come across regularly are those of Bouchard Père et Fils, Latour-Giraud and the Château Genot-Boulanger—the two other *climats* are easier to encapsulate. Poruzots and Gouttes d'Or are fullish wines and can be quite firm, but are always a little four-square, even a little *sauvage*. They can have plenty of fruit, depth and, indeed, interest—like Genevrières with a certain opulent spicy touch. But they cannot match either its flair or its complexity.

RECOMMENDED SOURCES

LES PORUZOTS

Bouchard Père et Fils, Louis Jadot (both Beaune); Jean-Paul Gauffroy, François Jobard, Rémi Jobard, Mestre-Michelot, François Mikulski (all Meursault); Olivier Leflaive Frères (Puligny-Montrachet).

LES BOUCHÈRES

Bouchard Père et Fils (Beaune); Château Genot-Boulanger, Latour-Giraud (both Meursault).

LES GOUTTES D'OR

Bouchard Père et Fils (Beaune); Alain Coche, Arnaud Ente, Jean-Michel Gaunoux, François Mikulski, Bernard Millot (all Meursault).

LES CRAS   *(3.55 ha)*

Les Cras is the only first growth on the Volnay side to be planted in any serious way with Chardonnay. Yet I feel this is nevertheless red-wine soil. The white wine, like the occasional Meursault-Santenots curiosity one comes across, never really convinces me. The Domaine Darnat has the monopoly of the 0.63-hectare Clos Richemont within Les Cras and is the leading example, but even here, I prefer their Gouttes d'Or.

BLAGNY   *(23.44 ha)*

This is made up of La Jeunelotte (5.05 ha), La Pièce sous le Bois (11.15 ha), Sous le Dos d'Ane (5.03 ha), Les Ravelles (1.30 ha) and Sous Blagny (2.21 ha), but these separate *lieux-dits* are more commonly used to differentiate between Blagny *premier cru rouges*.

Meursault-Blagny is a full wine, nicely steely and austere, very much a cross between a Puligny and a Meursault, but with more richness and backbone and less minerality than a Perrières. It is a wine which should need time to mature and should keep well. Strangely, you are more likely to come across it under a *négociant* label than directly from a domaine.

RECOMMENDED SOURCES

Robert Ampeau, Vincent Girardin, François Jobard, Matrot, Matrot-Wittersheim (all Meursault); Martelet de Cherisey (Blagny); Philippe Chavy (Puligny-Montrachet); Maison Louis Jadot, Maison Louis Latour (both Beaune); Gilles Bouton (Saint-Aubin).

THE "DEUXIÈMES CRUS"

Here follows a selection of the best cellars for *deuxièmes crus*:

Michel Bouzereau: Les Tessons; Les Grands Charrons.

Jean-François Coche-Dury: Les Vireuils; Les Narvaux; Les Chevalières; Les Rougeots.

Jean-Philippe Fichet: Les Chevalières; Les Tessons.

Henri Germain: Les Chevalières.

Patrick Javillier: Les Tillets; Les Clous; "Tête de Murgers."

Comtes Lafon: Clos de la Barre.

Matrot: Les Chevalières.

Pierre Morey: Les Tessons.

Guy Roulot: Les Tessons; Les Luchets; Les Tillets.

All the above are in Meursault. Note also the selections at Olivier Leflaive Frères and the Meursault Les Narvaux of the Domaine d'Auvenay in Saint-Romain.

The Growers

★ *Robert Ampeau et Fils*

10 ha owned. Puligny-Montrachet *premier cru* Les Combettes; Meursault *premier cru* in Les Perrières, Les Charmesand La Pièce sous le Bois; Volnay *premier cru* Les Santenots; Beaune *premier cru* Clos du Roi; Auxey-Duresses *premier cru* Les Ecusseaux; Blagny *premier cru* La Pièce sous le Bois; village Meursault; village Pommard.

The Ampeaus—Michel has now taken over from his late father Robert—do not sell *en primeur*, holding back the vintage until they deem it ready for drinking. Moreover, you cannot cherry-pick. You must take red as well as white, off-vintages as well as the good years. This is less of an imposition than it might be. Quality is high in both colours, even in the off-vintages, and the wines are built to last. I'd much rather be offered, say, a 1994 from here than a 1995 from many another Meursault establishment. Finding, despite demands that as much red wine as white must be taken, that his customers were still leaving him with too much red wine, Michel Ampeau leased some of this to Nicolas Rossignol of Volnay in 2002.

Raymond Ballot-Minot et Fils
Philippe Ballot-Dancer
Veuve Charles Dancer-Lochardet

11.3 ha owned and *en fermage/en métayage*. Meursault *premier cru* in Les Perrières, Les Genevrières and Les Charmes; Volnay *premier cru* in Les Santenots, Les Taille-Pieds; Pommard *premier cru* in Les Charmots, La Refène, Les Pézerolles and Les Rugiens; Beaune *premier cru* Les Epenotes; Chassagne-Montrachet *premier cru rouge et blanc* Morgeot; village Meursault *rouge et blanc*, including the *lieux-dits* Les Criots and Les Narvaux; village Pommard; village Beaune; village Chassagne-Montrachet *rouge et blanc*.

Philippe Ballot and, since 2002, his son Charles are in charge of an impressive line-up, some of which is sold off in bulk. The vines in some of the *climats* (Les Santenots; Les Rugiens) are still relatively young, but in Les Genevrières, the average age is 60 years. Ballot seems a conscientious winemaker who has recently enlarged his cellar so that he can keep all the best wines for 18 rather than 12 months before bottling, but I confess I find his whites lacking in concentration. Over the last decade he has lost some of his domaine to his nephew Vincent Dancer, of Chassagne-Montrachet.

Guy Bocard

8.5 ha owned and *en fermage/en métayage*. Meursault *premier cru* in Les Genevrières and Les Charmes; village Meursault, including the *lieux-dits* Le Limouzin, Les Grands Charrons, Les Narvaux and Sous La Velle; village Auxey-Duresses; village Monthelie.

Guy Bocard took over from his father in 1988 or so and has gradually increased the amount he is bottling himself ever since. In 1992 he acquired a new pneumatic press. It produces much finer lees, he says, on which he can keep the wines longer. Bocard is hesitant, and rightly so, about using too much new wood, and confines himself to a maximum of one fifth, now bottling after 18 months. These are neat, well-made wines for the medium term.

Éric Boigelot

8 ha owned and *en fermage*. Meursault *premier cru* Les Caillerets; Volnay *premier cru* in Les Santenots and Les Taille Pieds; Monthelie *premier cru* in Les Champs Fulliot, Le Meix Bataille, Sur la Velle and La Taupine; village Monthelie *rouge et blanc*; village

Volnay; village Pommard; village Meursault, including the *lieu-dit* Les Clous.

Éric Boigelot has now completely taken over from his father Jacques, and in 1999 he transferred from Monthelie to a large, modern cellar in Meursault, next to the Damy cooperage.

He has changed his winemaking for the better since 2002. There is now a 3- to 4-day cold-maceration for the red wines. The vinification temperatures are allowed to mount to 34°C, thereafter being maintained at 30°C to finish fermenting the sugars. But overall, there is a shorter maceration than hitherto. The result is more sophisticated tannins. The top whites get 25 percent new oak and are bottled after 11 months. From the 2003 vintage, this is a very good source.

Maison Henri Boillot
See Domaine Jean Boillot, Volnay

Bernard Boisson-Vadot
Domaine Boisson-Morey
5.26 ha owned and *en fermage*. Meursault *premier cru* Les Genevrières; village Meursault, including the *lieux-dits* Les Chevalières and Les Grands Charrons; village Monthelie; village Pommard.

Now joined by his son Pierre, the tubby, balding, bespectacled Bernard Boisson makes round, ample, cheerfully fruity wines that evolve in the medium term. This is a good source.

Jean-Marie Bouzereau
8.5 ha owned and *en fermage/en métayage*. Meursault *premier cru* Les Charmes, Les Gouttes d'Or and Les Poruzots; Puligny-Montrachet *premier cru* Les Folatières; Volnay *premier cru* Les Champans and Les Santenots; Beaune *premier cru* Les Pertuisots; village Meursault, including the *lieu-dit* Les Narvaux; village Volnay; village Pommard.

Cousin of Michel (see below), Jean-Marie Bouzereau, his older brother Vincent and his father Pierre (Bouzereau-Esmonin) look after an 18-hectare estate in common, the wines being divided at labelling time. The cellar is deep, spacious and tidy. Bottling of the whites (with the *crus* getting 25 to 30 percent new wood) takes place after 11 months.

★ Michel Bouzereau et Fils
11 ha owned. Meursault *premier cru* in Les Perrières, Les Genevrières, Les Charmes and Blagny; Puligny-Montrachet *premier cru* in Champ Gain and Le Cailleret; Beaune *premier cru* Les Vignes Franches; Volnay *premier cru* Les Auxy [*sic*]; village Beaune in the *lieu-dit* Les Epenotes; village Meursault, including the *lieux-dits* Le Limouzin, Les Tessons and Les Grands Charrons; village Pommard; village Volnay.

Michel Bouzereau is slowly giving way to his son Jean-Baptiste. A decade ago they installed a pneumatic press. Slowly but surely, there have been similar refinements in the vineyard, as well as the cellar. The vines are ploughed, except in areas where this is impractical. Slowly they are going *biologique*. Fifteen to thirty percent new wood is used for the maturation of the white wines. Since 2002 the bottling date has been extended from 12 months to 16 or more. Some Meursault Perrières was acquired in 2006, but the parcel needs attention: protection against erosion and replacement of missing vines. This is the best of the many Bouzereaus in the *commune*.

Philippe Bouzereau
12 ha owned and *en fermage/en métayage*. Corton Bressandes (0.15 ha); Meursault *premier cru* in Charmes and Perrières; Puligny-Montrachet *premier cru* Champ Gain; Auxey-Duresses *premier cru* Les Duresses; Beaune *premier cru* Les Teurons; village Meursault in the *lieux-dits* Les Grands Charrons, Les Narvaux and Vieux Clos; village Chassagne-Montrachet *rouge et blanc*; village Auxey-Duresses *blanc*; village Beaune.

There are two Philippe Bouzereaus here: father Philippe handed over responsibility to son Philippe in 2006. In 1995 Philippe *père* took over the imposing Château de Cîteaux in the centre of the village. The cellars, medieval and vaulted, are very fine. The château remains uninhabited. Bottling of the better whites takes place after 18 months. These are uneven wines. A merchant enterprise runs in parallel.

Hubert Bouzereau-Gruère

11 ha owned and *en fermage*. Corton, Les Bressandes
(0.15 ha); Meursault *premier cru* in Les Charmes
(often two bottlings, Le Haut and Le Bas) and Les
Genevrières; Chassagne-Montrachet *premier cru*
blanc Les Chaumées; Saint-Aubin *premier cru blanc*
in Les Cortons and Le Charmois; village Meursault,
including the *lieux-dits* Les Chaumes, Le Clou, Les
Tillets, Le Limouzin and Les Grands Charrons; village
Chassagne-Montrachet *rouge et blanc*, including
the *lieu-dit* Les Blanchots-Dessous; village Puligny-
Montrachet; village Santenay.

I have had some good wines from the *sympa*
Hubert Bouzereau, particularly the Charmes-
du-Haut, where the vines were planted in 1957.
These wines are for the medium term. His
daughters Marie-Laure and Marie-Anne are
gradually taking over responsibility here.

★ Yves Boyer-Martenot

8.5 ha owned and *en fermage/en métayage*. Meursault
premier cru in Perrières, Charmes and Genevrières;
Puligny-Montrachet *premier cru* Le Cailleret;
Auxey-Duresses *premier cru* Les Ecusseaux; village
Meursault, including the *lieux-dits* Les Chaumes,
Les Narvaux, L'Ormeau, Le Pré de Manche and Les
Tillets; village Pommard; village Puligny-Montrachet;
village Auxey-Duresses.

The diminutive Yves Boyer makes very good
wines and has now been joined by his son
Vincent and daughter Sylvie. The cellar and
the *cuverie* were further enlarged in 2005, and
there is now a *cave de dégustation* offering light
snacks—cheese, *charcuterie*—run by Sylvie,
who also supervises a small *négociants* business.
The top whites get 30 percent new wood. Bottling of these still takes place after 11 months.
I hope they will move to bottling the *premiers
crus* later.

Buisson-Charles

5.5 ha owned and *en fermage/en métayage*.
Meursault *premier cru* in Les Bouchères, Charmes,
Les Cras and Les Gouttes d'Or; Volnay *premier cru*
Les Santenots; village Meursault, including the *lieu-
dit* Les Tessons and a *vieilles vignes cuvée*; village
Pommard.

Michel Buisson is now 71, and responsibility for
the domaine is now in the hands of Patrick Essa,
husband of his daughter Catherine. There is 20
to 30 percent new wood for the white wines,
which are bottled after 12 to 14 months; they use
one third new oak for the Santenots. This is a
very good source, and it is getting better.

Roger Caillot et Fils

13 ha owned and *en fermage/en métayage*. Bâtard-
Montrachet (0.49 ha); Puligny-Montrachet *pre-
mier cru* in Les Pucelles and Les Folatières; village
Meursault in the *lieux-dits* La Barre, Le Clos du
Cromin and Les Tessons; village Santenay *rouge et
blanc*; village Monthelie *rouge et blanc*.

The pearls of the Caillots' exploitation are in
Puligny, not Meursault, where, inter alia, he
is joint *métayer* with his brother-in-law Pierre
Morey for part of the Poirier family's Bâtard.
This and the *premiers crus* are usually good; the
Santenays and Monthelies are still relatively
young vines. His reds are not as good as his
whites.

Alain Coche-Bizouard
Fabien Coche-Bouillot

9 ha owned and *en métayage*. Meursault *premier cru*
in Charmes and Les Gouttes d'Or; village Meursault,
including the *lieux-dits* Les Chevalières, Le Limouzin,
L'Ormeau and "Lupré" (Les Luchets and Le Pré de
Manche); Auxey-Duresses *premier cru* Les Duresses;
Monthelie *premier cru*; Pommard *premier cru* La
Platière; village Auxey-Duresses *rouge et blanc*; village
Monthelie; village Pommard.

Fabien, Alain Coche's son, has been making the
wines here since 1999 and also operates a *négociant* business under his name. Old vines and
low *rendements* are the order of the day here,
and 25 percent new wood is used. This was one
of the first estates in the village at which the bottling of the white wines did not take place until
18 months after the harvest. The white wines are
very good. The reds are less exciting.

★★ Jean-François Coche-Dury

11.5 ha owned and *en fermage/en métayage*. Corton-
Charlemagne (0.34 ha); Meursault *premier cru* Les

Caillerets, Genevrières and Perrières; Volnay *premier cru* (from Clos des Chênes and Taille Pieds); village Meursault, including the *lieux-dits* Les Chaumes, Les Chevalières, Les Luchets, Les Narvaux, Les Rougeots and Les Vireuils; village Auxey-Duresses *rouge et blanc*; village Monthelie; village Puligny-Montrachet in the *lieu-dit* Les Enseignères; village Pommard in the *lieu-dit* Les Vaumuriens.

Jean-François Coche, tall and thin, a little shy but not a bit diffident when it comes to talking about his wines, is one of the superstars of white Burgundy (people tend to overlook the excellence of his reds) and now works alongside his son Raphaël, a young man who gives every indication of being a worthy successor to his illustrious father. They use one quarter new oak for the white wines and bottle after 20 months. The results are very fine: beautifully pure and *terroir* expressive.

Rudolphe Demougeot

7.5 ha owned and *en fermage/en métayage*. Savigny-lès-Beaune *premier cru* Les Peuillets; Pommard *premier cru* Les Charmots; village Savigny-lès-Beaune; village Beaune, including the *lieu-dit* Les Epenotes and Clos Saint-Désirée (*blanc*); village Pommard; village Auxey-Duresses; village Monthelie; village Meursault.

This is a curious domaine for the *commune* because production is almost entirely of red wines. Viticulture is very firmly *biologique*, respecting the environment, and the wines are carefully made. Despite there being nothing particularly sexy in the line-up, this is a very good address.

★ Arnaud Ente

4.81 ha owned and *en fermage/en métayage*. Meursault *premier cru* Les Gouttes d'Or; Puligny-Montrachet *premier cru* Les Referts; Volnay *premier cru* Santenots; village Meursault, including the *lieux-dits* L'Ormeau, Les Petits Charrons and a *vieilles vignes cuvée*.

The youthful, attractive-looking Arnaud Ente is one of the best growers to have come to the fore in the last decade. He is exigent about keeping the crop down and meticulous about how he makes his wine—no fining, no filtration, not even any racking for the red wines, and *bâtonnage* only when necessary for the whites which are bottled after 12 to 18 months. This is not a very big domaine, but it is a very fine one.

★ Jean-Philippe Fichet

8 ha owned and *en fermage/en métayage*. Puligny-Montrachet *premier cru* Les Referts; village Meursault, including the *lieux-dits* Les Chaumes de Narvaux, Les Chevalières, Les Clous, Les Gruyaches and Les Tessons; village Monthelie *rouge et blanc*; village Auxey-Duresses *rouge et blanc*.

Jean-Philippe Fichet moved into larger premises in 2001 and only finished the renovation there in 2005, but it has given him the space to start a merchants business, based at first on the other half of the vines he share-crops. There is highly competent winemaking here—it is a pity he has only a minuscule bit (four casks) of *premier cru*. The vines are ploughed throughout, there is a *table de tri*, there is one third new oak and bottling of the whites occurs after 18 months. This is a very good address.

Jean-Michel Gaunoux

6 ha owned. Meursault *premier cru* in Les Gouttes d'Or and Les Perrières; Puligny-Montrachet *premier cru* Les Folatières; Volnay *premier cru* Clos des Chênes; village Pommard; village Meursault.

Jean-Michel Gaunoux is a diminutive man in his forties who exploits what he has inherited from his mother and her parents. He shared premises with his father François until 1990 (his father has married again), when he installed himself in an impressively large (and immaculately tidy) cellar in another part of the village. The vineyards are ploughed. The white wines get 15 to 30 percent new oak and are bottled after 15 to 16 months. There are good wines here. Gaunoux is also a merchant in a small way.

Château Génot-Boulanger

27.54 ha owned. Clos de Vougeot (0.43 ha); Corton Les Combes (0.47 ha); Corton-Charlemagne (0.29 ha); Meursault *premier cru* Les Bouchères;

Puligny-Montrachet in Les Folatières and La Garenne; Chassagne-Montrachet *premier cru blanc* in Les Chenevottes, Les Vergers and Clos Saint-Jean; Beaune *premier cru* in Les Grèves and Les Montrevenots; Volnay *premier cru* Les Aussy; Pommard *premier cru* Clos-Blanc; Aloxe-Corton *premier cru* Clos du Chapitre; Savigny-lès-Beaune *premier cru* Aux Vergelesses; Mercurey *premier cru* in Les Saumonts and Sazenay; village Meursault, including the *lieux-dits* Clos du Cromin, Les Meix Chavaux and Les Vireuils; village Volnay; village Pommard; village Chambolle-Musigny; village Savigny-lès-Beaune; village Beaune *rouge et blanc* in the *lieu-dit* Lulunne; village Puligny-Montrachet; village Mercurey.

Château Génot-Boulanger occupies a fine château, opposite which are the equally elegant offices and under which is the *cave*, in the middle of Meursault. There is a bottle cellar in the industrial estate outside the village. Under the direction of owner and manager Francis Delaby, a successor of a grandfather Génot, who died in 2002, as did his father, quality has considerably improved here. The vineyard is ploughed. There is a *table de tri*. There is 25 to 30 percent new wood, and the top whites are bottled after 16 months. This is a good address.

Henri Germain et Fils

7.85 ha owned and *en fermage/en métayage*. Meursault *premier cru* Les Charmes and Les Perrières; Chassagne-Montrachet *premier cru* Morgeot *blanc*; Beaune *premier cru* Les Bressandes; village Meursault, including the *lieux-dits* Les Chevalières, Clos des Mouches (*rouge—monopole*) and Le Limouzin; village Chassagne-Montrachet *rouge*.

Henri Germain is the brother of François, father of Benoît of the Château de Chorey (see page 200), and he set up independently in 1973. His wife is a Pillot of Chassagne, which explains the vineyards further south. His son Jean-François is now responsible for the wines. While the cellar (which they rent—he lives elsewhere) is not particularly cold or deep, the malos are always late to finish here. The Germains are happy to let nature take its course. They don't bottle for 18 months. This is a good source.

★ Vincent Girardin

15.62 ha owned and *en fermage*. Bienvenues-Bâtard-Montrachet (0.47 ha); Corton-Charlemagne (0.30 ha); Bâtard-Montrachet (0.19 ha); Chevalier-Montrachet (0.16 ha); Puligny-Montrachet *premier cru* in Champ Gain, Les Combettes and Les Folatières; Chassagne-Montrachet *premier cru* in Les Chaumées and Abbaye de Morgeot; Saint-Aubin *premier cru* in En Remilly and Les Murgers des Dents de Chien; Santenay *premier cru* in Clos de Tavannes (*blanc*), Beauregard (*blanc*), Les Maladières and Les Gravières; village Meursault in the *lieu-dit* Les Narvaux; village Savigny-lès-Beaune *blanc* in the *lieu-dit* Les Vermots.

Vincent Girardin, now 45, is an example of what can be achieved in Burgundy even with today's high prices of land, and even without a fortune behind you. When I first met him, in 1985 or so, he lived in Santenay-le-Haut and, alongside his three brothers, exploited 3 hectares, his quarter share of the family domaine. Gradually, piece by piece, he began to build up his own estate; he became a merchant. The wines had a tendency at first to be a bit oaky, but they were very good. He outgrew his premises in Santenay and moved to a new temperature-controlled warehouse in the industrial estate in Meursault, and at the same time, in 2002, took over the old Henri Clerc estate in Puligny-Montrachet *en fermage*. The white wines are vinified at 20°C, given 40 percent new wood and bottled after 11 to 17 months. The reds are fermented at 30°C, using half the stems, after 5 days of cold-soaking, and they are not racked until just before bottling. Again, there is 40 percent new oak. The merchant wines are just as fine as the domaine wines.

Albert Grivault

6 ha owned. Meursault *premier cru* Clos des Perrières (*monopole*) and Les Perrières; Pommard *premier cru* Clos Blanc; village Meursault.

The Clos des Perrières vines were planted in 1985, so they are still quite young. But the other vines in this *premier cru* are old. The Bardet family, successors to Albert Grivault, are trying to get the Clos promoted to *grand cru*. Arguably, the whole of Perrières-Dessous merits this. But then, so do Puligny-Montrachet, Les Combettes, Les Caillerets, Les Pucelles and so forth—where does one stop? And the Bardet Perrières is not (or not yet, perhaps) a great wine. The white wines are normally bottled in July, 10 months after the harvest. This is surely far too early.

★ Patrick Javillier

9.5 ha owned and *en fermage/en métayage*. Corton Charlemagne (0.17 ha); Meursault *premier cru* Charmes; Savigny-lès-Beaune *premier cru* Les Serpentières; village Meursault, including the *lieux-dits* Tête de Murgers (Les Casse-Têtes and Les Murgers), Les Clous, Les Tillets and Clos du Cromin; village Puligny-Montrachet; village Aloxe-Corton; village Pernand-Vergelesses; village Savigny-lès-Beaune (*rouge et blanc*).

The engaging and capable Patrick Javillier not only vinifies *climat* by *climat* but even cask by cask, treating each one differently from the other in order to build up something of even greater complexity when the final blend is assembled. As he puts it, "I vinify one part to bring out the fruit, the other to produce the structure." Bottling takes place after 18 months. He makes splendid wines and wines which last well.

★ François and Antoine Jobard

6 ha owned and *en métayage*. Meursault *premier cru* in Charmes, Genevrières, Le Poruzot and La Pièce sous le Bois (bottled as Meursault-Blagny); Blagny *premier cru* La Pièce Sous le Bois; village Meursault, including the *lieux-dits* Les Tillets, Les Chaumes and En La Barre; village Puligny-Montrachet in the *lieu-dit* Le Trézin.

This is one of the great Meursault estates, François being one of the pioneers of domaine bottling, producing wines which are rather severe in their youth but fine and marvellously long-lasting nevertheless. François's son, Antoine, is now part of the team. The white wines are vinified at 25°C and given 15 percent new oak and 22 months in cask before bottling, without any *bâtonnage*. The Blagny is not de-stemmed. This is "old fashioned" vinification. It works.

Rémi Jobard

8 ha owned and *en fermage*. Meursault *premier cru* in Charmes, Genevrières and Les Poruzots; Volnay *premier cru* Les Santenots; Monthelie *premier cru* in Les Champs Fulliot, Sur la Velle and Les Vignes Rondes; village Meursault, including the *lieu-dit* Les Chevalières, En Luraule and Sur la Velle.

Rémi Jobard has now taken over from his father Charles, the brother of François (see above) and in 2003 started a small merchant's business to run parallel with the family estate. Engaging and talented, Rémi Jobard makes very good wines. This is another domaine which has moved its bottling of white wine from 12 to 18 months.

Jobard-Morey

4.25 ha owned. Meursault *premier cru* in Charmes and Les Poruzots; village Meursault, including the *lieux-dits* Les Narvaux and Les Tillets.

Rémi Ehret, son-in-law to the Jobard-Moreys, is the winemaker here. This is not a very large domaine (and it is even smaller now that they have lost their Gouttes d'Or), but quality is high. The entire estate is now ploughed on a regular basis. Each *cuvée* receives one carefully chosen and manufactured new oak cask each year.

★★★ Comtes Lafon

13.8 ha owned. Le Montrachet (0.32 ha); Meursault *premier cru* in Perrières, Charmes, Genevrières and Les Gouttes d'Or; Puligny-Montrachet *premier cru* Le Champ Gain; village Meursault in the *lieux-dits* Clos de la Barre and Désirée; Volnay *premier cru* in Champans, Clos des Chênes and Santenots-du-Milieu,; Monthelie *premier cru* Les Duresses; village Monthelie *blanc*.

Quite simply, this is the best white wine domaine in Burgundy, and it also makes excellent red wines. It is run by the approaching-50-years-old Dominique Lafon and his director Stéphane Thibodaux. Lafon took over in 1982, at a time when the entire estate was rented out *en métayage*, and the white wine vineyards were tended by the excellent Pierre Morey. As the leases ran out, Lafon took back the vines, doubling what the estate had previously had for sale. It was about this time that the Puligny was acquired and the cellars enlarged. In more recent years the domaine has converted to biodynamism. The white wines are only marginally *bâtonné*-ed and lodged in casks which vary from 100 percent new for the Montrachet, to 20 to 50 percent for the *premiers crus* to zero for the village examples. The Pinots are de-stemmed, briefly cold-soaked and vinified at 30–32°C. Bottling takes place after 18 to 22 months. The cellars are deep and cold, so there is no danger of the wines drying out. And the results are truly excellent: the whites are full, fat, rich and gently oaky, the reds full, firm at first—these are masculine Volnays—and long-lasting.

★ Latour-Giraud

10 ha owned. Meursault *premier cru* in Genevrières, Perrières, Les Bouchères, Le Poruzot and Charmes; Puligny-Montrachet *premier cru* Champ Canet; Maranges *premier cru* in La Fussière; Meursault *premier cru rouge* Les Caillerets; Volnay *premier cru* Clos des Chênes; Pommard *premier cru* La Refène; village Meursault, including the *lieux-dits* Le Clos du Cromin, Le Limouzin, Les Narvaux, Les Vireuils and "Cuvée Charles Maxime."

This has been one of the best sources in the village for some time now. The domaine is one of the biggest owners of Meursault Genevrières, with 2.39 hectares. Only Bouchard Père et Fils possesses more. Jean-Pierre Latour is a thoughtful winemaker. In a plentiful vintage such as 1999, for instance, he de-classed the "heads and tails" of the pressing, preserving only the best middle part, and adding the fine lees at the end to prolong the fermentation and get more depth. He uses 25 percent new wood for the *premiers crus* and bottles after 18 months.

★ Latour-Labille et Fils

12 ha owned and *en fermage*. Meursault *premier cru* in Les Poruzots, Les Gouttes d'Or, Charmes, Perrières and Les Cras (*rouge*); Saint-Aubin *premier cru* Les Frionnes; village Meursault *blanc* in the *lieu-dit* Clos des Meix Chavaux, *et rouge*; village Pommard; village Saint-Aubin.

Jean Latour is now 73. Since 1998 his son Vincent has been in charge. Much has changed here in the last few years. The cellars have been temperature controlled, Vincent has introduced 600-litre *demi-muids*, and the fining and filtration are now more delicate. After 12 months Latour racks the wine back into tank, where it lies until bottling takes place in the spring. The white wines get 30 percent new wood. There are fine wines here now.

Martelet de Cherisey

6 ha *en fermage/en métayage*. Puligny-Montrachet *premier cru* Les Chalumaux, La Garenne and Hameau de Blagny; Meursault *premier cru* Blagny; Blagny *premier cru* La Jeunelotte (*monopole*); village Meursault.

This is a small but expanding domaine based in Blagny and on the estate of the late Comtesse de Montlivault. Hélène Martelet, who runs the estate with her husband Laurent, is a granddaughter of the late Countess. The approach is very biological. The whites get 40 to 70 percent new wood and are bottled after 16 to 20 months. This is a very good address.

Matrot

18 ha owned. Meursault *premier cru* in Perrières, Charmes and Blagny; Puligny-Montrachet *premier cru* in Les Chalumaux, Les Combettes and La Garenne; Volnay *premier cru* Les Santenots; Blagny *premier cru* La Pièce sous le Bois; village Meursault *rouge et blanc*; village Auxey-Duresses; village Monthelie.

For legal and inheritance reasons there are two domaines here, though everything is made by Thierry Matrot and his wife Pascale. Some one third is labelled as Pierre Matrot, Thierry's father: this includes all the Blagny, red and white. The larger remainder, Joseph Matrot, is bought by Thierry and Pascale and is now sold under their label: this includes all the Combettes. Other wines can have either label. But it is all the same wine.

Thierry Matrot is a gentle man of a philosophic disposition. All operations are under question and follow the quality and character of the vintage. The vineyards have been tended by the *lutte raisonnée* for 20 years, entirely ploughed, and treatments are biological. For the whites there is a maximum of 20 percent new wood and bottling after 11 months. The red grapes are 90 percent de-stemmed, given 5 days of cold-soaking and vinified at up to 35°C. Again there is little new oak, and bottling takes place after a year. Matrot's wines can be a bit ungainly in their youth, but they keep well. This is a good address.

Matrot-Wittersheim

3.5 ha owned. Meursault *premier cru* in Blagny and Charmes; Volnay *premier cru* Les Santenots; Blagny *premier cru* La Pièce sous le Bois; village Meursault.

Madame Matrot-Wittersheim is Thierry's aunt. Claudine Roussel, who runs this domaine, is her daughter. This small estate was ceded from the above in 2002. The white wines, bottled early, are good. I am less impressed by the reds. In 2007 this domaine was acquired by Faiveley of Nuits-Saint-Geoges.

Château de Meursault

60 ha owned. Meursault *premier cru* from Charmes and Perrières; Puligny-Montrachet *premier cru* Champ Canet; Beaune *premier cru* in Les Cent Vignes, Les Grèves and *premier cru tout court*; Volnay *premier cru* Clos des Chênes; Pommard *premier cru* in Clos des Epenots; village Pommard in the *lieu-dit* Les Petits Noizons; village Meursault; village Puligny-Montrachet; village Beaune; village Aloxe-Corton; village Savigny-lès-Beaune.

The Château de Meursault, an attractive building with extensive dependencies and a magnificently large cellar underneath, all now serving as a very enticing tourist trap, was acquired by André Boisseaux of Maison Patriarche in 1973. A sister establishment is the Château de Marsannay. Jean-Claude Mitanchey directs both. A decade ago, quality was substandard. The wines were artificial in flavour and over-oaked. Standards are better today. I was pleasantly surprised by the 2004s.

Mestre-Michelot

11 ha owned and *en fermage/en métayage*. Meursault *premier cru* in Charmes, Genevrières, Perrières and Les Poruzots; Santenay *premier cru* in La Comme and Les Gravières; village Meursault, including the *lieux-dits* Les Narvaux, Casse Têtes, Le Limouzin and Sur la Velle; village Puligny-Montrachet; village Pommard.

Nearly 40 years ago, when I was studying for the Master of Wine examination, one of my tutors recommended two estates which produced yardstick white Burgundy: Michelot in Meursault and Sauzet in Puligny-Montrachet. Run by Bernard Michelot, the Meursault domaine was twice the size in those days. Now it is run, and has been for 15 years, by Jean-François Mestre, who married Odile Michelot, and Odile's sister Geneviève has gone her separate way and has her establishment across the road (see below). The vineyards are ploughed and tended by *lutte raisonnée*. There is 20 to 25 percent new oak for the white wines, which are bottled after a year. Forty years ago, this was one of Burgundy's top addresses. Today, the wines are good, but they lack flair.

Michelot Mère et Fille

7.17 ha owned. Puligny-Montrachet *premier cru* in Les Folatières and La Garenne; Meursault *premier cru* in Genevrières and Charmes; village Meursault, including the *lieux-dits* Le Clos du Cromin, Limouzin and Les Tillets.

Geneviève Michelot and her daughter Véronique Bernard are the *mère et fille*—1999 was the first vintage. The third element is Véronique's husband Nicolas. Viticulture is by *lutte raisonnée*. There is one third new wood and bottling after 18 months according to the lunar calendar. The wines have more style here than across the road.

★ François Mikulski

8.5 ha owned and *en fermage/en métayage*. Meursault *premier cru* in Les Caillerets (*rouge*), Charmes, Genevrières, Les Gouttes d'Or and Le Poruzot; Volnay *premier cru* Les Santenots; village Meursault *rouge et blanc*, including the *lieux-dits* Charmes de Narvaux, Le Meix Chavaux and Limouzin; village Pommard.

François Mikulski inherited much of his estate from his late uncle, Pierre Boillot, starting in

1972 and ending when he took over the Gouttes d'Or in 2003. This is an intelligent man with a biological approach to viticulture. For his whites, he chooses one quarter new oak, doesn't approve of *bâtonnage* and bottles after 18 months. The red grapes are de-stemmed, cold-soaked for 4 to 6 days and fermented at 30–32°C. There is 30 percent new oak, and they are bottled just before the whites. These are very good wines.

Bernard Millot

8.5 ha owned. Meursault *premier cru* in Les Gouttes d'Or and Perrières; village Meursault in the *lieux-dits* En la Barre, Les Petits Charrons and Les Terres Blanches; village Puligny-Montrachet.

Bernard Millot practices the *lutte raisonnée*, ploughs his vineyards, prunes severely, picks late and bottles his best wines after 18 months. Is this the best source for Gouttes d'Or, Jefferson's favourite Meursault? Millot has 7 *ouvrées*.

Jean Monnier et Fils

15 ha owned. Meursault *premier cru* in Genevrières and Charmes; Pommard *premier cru* in En lagillière, Clos de Cîteaux (*monopole*), Les Fremiers and Les Grands Epenots; Beaune *premier cru* Les Montrevenots; village Meursault, including the *lieux-dits* La Barre, Les Chevalières and Clos du Cromin; village Puligny-Montrachet; village Volnay.

Jean-Claude Monnier and his son Nicolas make a little bit more red that they do white and use about one quarter new oak for the better wines. The domaine seems efficiently run, but in my experience the wines are rarely exciting.

René Monnier

16.5 ha owned and *en fermage*. Meursault *premier cru* Les Charmes; Puligny-Montrachet *premier cru* Les Folatières; Volnay *premier cru* Clos-des-Chênes; Beaune *premier cru* Les Cent-Vignes and Les Toussaints; village Meursault, including the *lieux-dits* Les Chevalières and Le Limouzin; village Chassagne-Montrachet; village Puligny-Montrachet; village Pommard in the *lieu-dit* Les Vignots; village Monthelie; village Santenay in the *lieu-dit* Les Charmes; village Monthelie *rouge et blanc*.

The René Monnier domaine is guarded by a noisy Alsatian and run by Jean-Louis Bouillot and his wife, daughter of the late René Monnier, together with Xavier Monnot, a grandson of René Monnier. There is 100 percent de-stemming for the red wines, two *pigeages* and two *remontages* a day. Temperatures are held at 30°C, and 20 to 35 percent new oak is used. Bouillot recognises the importance of low yields, aiming for 35 to 40 hectolitres per hectare. This is a good source.

★ Pierre Morey
Morey Blanc, S.A.

10.3 ha owned and *en fermage/en métayage*. Bâtard-Montrachet (0.40 ha); Meursault *premier cru* Perrières; Pommard *premier cru* Les Epenots; Volnay *premier cru* Les Santenots; village Meursault including the *lieu-dit* Les Tessons; village Monthelie.

The Morey family were long-time *métayers* for the Domaine des Comtes Lafon. In the early 1990s this came to an end, and Pierre Morey set up a small *négociant* business to compensate for what he could no longer supply. And he was also appointed *régisseur* for the Domaine Leflaive in Puligny-Montrachet. Morey combines these three separate activities with great skill. He is a fine winemaker.

His domaine has been *biologique* since 1992 and *biodynamique* since 1997. There is a vibrating *table de tri* for the red wines, which are vinified with up to 20 percent of the stems, and get, for the *premiers crus*, 50 percent new wood. There is less new wood for the whites, even the Bâtard-Montrachet. But they are bottled 18 months after the vintage.

Morey Blanc is not so called because only white wines are offered but because Pierre's wife was *née* Blanc. Pierre Morey, now aided by his charming daughter Anne, buys in fruit for this *négociant* operation.

★ Alain and Christianne Patriarche

10 ha owned. Meursault *premier cru* in Genevrières, Blagny "La Pièce sous le Bois" and Les Poruzots; Blagny *premier cru* La Pièce sous le Bois; village Meursault, including the *lieux-dits* Les Grands Charrons, Les Tillets and a *vieilles vignes cuvée*.

Alain Patriarche, stocky, bald, with a splendid bass voice, must be in his late fifties. He is one of the doyens of the village. He uses 30 percent new wood, bottles after 12 months and applies a distinctive black label. The wines are rich and concentrated. I like them very much.

Jacques Prieur

20.68 ha owned and *en fermage*. Clos de Vougeot (1.28 ha); Chambertin (0.84 ha); Le Musigny (0.77 ha); Corton Les Bressandes (0.73 ha); Le Montrachet (0.59 ha); Echézeaux (0.36 ha); Corton-Charlemagne (0.22 ha); Chambertin Clos de Bèze (0.15 ha); Chevalier-Montrachet (0.14 ha); Puligny-Montrachet *premier cru* Les Combettes; Meursault *premier cru* in Perrières and Les Santenots; Volnay *premier cru* in Les Champans, Clos des Santenots (*monopole*) and Les Santenots; Beaune *premier cru* in Clos de la Féguine (*rouge et blanc—monopole*), Aux Coucherias, Champs Pimont and Les Grèves; Chambolle-Musigny *premier cru* in La Combe d'Orveau; village Meursault *rouge et blanc* in the *lieu-dit* Clos de Mazeray (*monopole*).

The Domaine Jacques Prieur, half owned by merchant Antonin Rodet of Mercurey, offers one of the greatest ranges of wine in all Burgundy in terms of grand *climats*. It is managed on the spot by Martin Prieur, who is ably assisted by Rodet's chief oenologist Nadine Gublin.

The domaine is increasingly *biologique*. The white wines are vinified at 20–22°C and given from 30 to 100 percent new wood. The better wines are bottled after 18 to 20 months. *Bâtonnage* takes place until the end of the malolactic fermentation. Currently (it is proposed to vinify some of the reds, especially the Clos de Vougeot, by whole grape methods in the future), the Pinots are de-stemmed, cold-soaked for 4 to 6 days, given 30 to 100 percent new oak and one single racking and bottled after 14 to 19 months.

For as long as I have been going to Burgundy, I have been waiting for quality here to be fine, as it is at Rodet and the associated Domaine des Perdrix. Finally, from 2003, I believe they are getting there.

Pascal Prunier-Bonheur

6 ha owned and *en fermage*. Auxey-Duresses *premier cru* Les Duresses; Beaune *premier cru* Les Sizies; Monthelie *premier cru* Les Vignes Rondes; village Auxey-Duresses *rouge et blanc* and *blanc vieilles vignes*; village Monthelie; village Saint-Romain *rouge et blanc*; village Pommard. Having no Meursault, Pascal Prunier buys in as grapes Meursault *premier cru* Les Poruzots and village Meursault in the *lieu-dit* Les Grands Charrons.

With a name such as Prunier, the youthful 41-year-old Pascal not surprisingly hails from Auxey-Duresses. He acquired a modern cellar in Meursault in 1996 and has vinified here since 2000. The white wines get 15 to 30 percent new oak, and the best *cuvées* are bottled after 18 months. They are pure, balanced and classy. The reds are less good.

★★★ Guy Roulot

10.2 ha owned. Meursault *premier cru* in Les Bouchères, Charmes, Perrières and Les Poruzots; village Meursault, including the *lieux-dits* Les Tessons, Clos de Mon Plaisir (*monopole*), Les Luchets, Les Tillets, Les Vireuils and Les Meix-Chavaux; Monthelie *premier cru* Les Champs Fulliot; village Monthelie *rouge*; village Auxey-Duresses *rouge*.

Now increasingly *biodynamique*, this domaine, run by Jean-Marc Roulot, son of Guy, who died prematurely in 1982, and his sister Michèle, has long been one of the superstars of the *commune* and was a pioneer of separately bottling what I term the *deuxièmes crus* of Meursault. For a time in the mid-1990s, Jean-Marc also made the Puligny-Montrachet Les Caillerets of the Domaine de Montille. He is married to Hubert de Montille's daughter Alix.

Jean-Marc has great talent. There is no exaggerated use of new wood here, and over the last decade he has moved from bottling after 12 months to 18 months. The wines are even more *terroir* expressive as a result, and are very pure and very elegant.

Vincent Sauvestre

59 ha owned and *en fermage*. Corton Les Maréchaudes (3.00 ha); Corton Les Vergennes (0.35 ha); Corton

Charlemagne (1.00 ha); Nuits-Saint-Georges *premier cru* in Les Chaboeufs, Les Saint-Georges and Les Vallerots; Aloxe-Corton *premier cru* in Les Maréchaudes and Les Valozières; Savigny-lès-Beaune *premier cru* Les Godeaux, Les Lavières, Les Peuillets and Les Talmettes (*blanc*); Beaune *premier cru* in Les Avaux and Les Grèves; Pommard *premier cru* La Platière; Volnay *premier cru* Les Santenots; village Ladoix *rouge et blanc*; village Savigny-lès-Beaune *rouge et blanc*; village Beaune *rouge et blanc* in the *lieu-dit* Clos des Rouards; village Meursault, including the *lieu-dit* Clos des Tessons; Côte de Beaune *rouge et blanc* in the *lieu-dit* Clos des Mosnières; Côte de Nuits villages; Côte de Beaune villages.

Vincent Sauvestre, born in 1961, took over from his father in 1988, at which time the domaine consisted of just 6 hectares based in Meursault. Since then, he has built an empire which extends from 30 hectares in Chablis, via his extensive holdings in the Côte d'Or, to 32 hectares (the Domaine Sires de Vergy) in the Hautes-Côtes, to the 16-hectare Domaine Roland Sounit in Rully and the 12-hectare Domaine Protheau in Mercurey. There are further estates in Saint-Véran, the Côte du Rhône, Corbières and Provence. He also owns the *négociants* Béjot on the main road in Meursault, through which everything is distributed. In 2005 he acquired the merchants Chartron and Trébuchet in Puligny-Montrachet, and the Domaine Maurice Ecard of Savigny-lès-Beaune in 2006.

Despite all this, there is something of a family atmosphere in the extensive cellars under his name on the road to Monthelie in Meursault, and there are more than one or two very good wines.

BLAGNY

Up in the hills between Meursault and Puligny lies the hamlet of Blagny. It is peaceful up here. Birds sing. The vineyards are divided by hedge-rows and copses and a miracle of wildflowers in the spring, and the village itself is hardly more than a handful of houses centred around the old *manoir*, the property of the late Comtesse de Montlivault. You are leagues away from the hustle and bustle of Beaune.

Blagny is a curious appellation, existing solely for red wines. If white, they become Meursault-Blagny, *premier cru*, or less commonly, Meursault followed by one of the names of the Blagny *premiers crus*. And there is little village Meursault land. Alternatively, because the *commune*'s dividing line runs through the middle, the white wine can be Puligny-Montrachet.

There is rather more communal Puligny up here (the *lieu-dit* of Le Trézin) than there is communal Meursault, and technically the Puligny-Montrachet *premiers crus* of Sous le Puits, La Garenne and Hameau de Blagny are Blagny *premier cru* if they produce red wine.

The vineyard land climbs up to 360 metres. The soil is an Argovian marl, covered in limestone debris. Upslope the colour is red, and there are plenty of pebbles. Lower down it is less pebbley. On the Meursault side, the underlying rock is decayed and crumbly, white in colour, even with a blue tinge. You are facing southeast. On the Puligny side the orientation is more easterly, the soil is deeper and the underlying rock firmer and redder in colour. Here there is the highest predominance of pebbles.

The Vineyard

There are eight *premiers crus*, as follows:

LA JEUNELOTTE	(5.05 ha)
(Meursault)	
LA PIÈCE SOUS LE BOIS	(11.15 ha)
(Meursault)	
SOUS LE DOS D'ANE	(5.03 ha)
(Meursault)	
SOUS BLAGNY	(2.21 ha)
(Meursault)	
SOUS LE PUITS	(6.80 ha)
(Puligny-Montrachet)	
LA GARENNE OR SUR LA GARENNE	(9.87 ha)
(Puligny-Montrachet)	
HAMEAU-DE-BLAGNY	(4.28 ha)
(Puligny-Montrachet)	
LES RAVELLES	(1.30 ha)
(Meursault)	

This area totals 45.69 hectares, 24.74 hectares of which are in Meursault and 20.74 in Puligny-Montrachet. In addition there are 9.73 hectares of village land, 1.77 hectares of which are in Meursault and 7.96 in Puligny-Montrachet. These produce around 220 hectolitres of Blagny *premier cru rouge* and 45 hectolitres of village Blagny *rouge* per year, plus around 400 hectolitres of Meursault *premier cru* Blagny and 60 hectolitres of village Meursault.

Blagny *rouge* is a fairly sturdy, if not robust, wine, a sort of cross between a Chassagne-Montrachet and a Pommard, but a cross of good examples. In its youth it can be dumb and four-square. But given time, it will mellow out to something with no lack of character or depth. It is unfashionable, and therefore cheap. It is certainly considerably more interesting than red Meursault. Like on the hill of Corton, Chardonnay is planted upslope, and Pinot Noir lower down, the best *climats* for red wine being La Pièce sous le Bois and Sous le Dos d'Ane.

RECOMMENDED SOURCES
LA PIÈCE SOUS LE BOIS
Robert Ampeau, François Jobard, Matrot (all Meursault); Paul Pernot (Puligny-Montrachet).

SOUS LE PUITS
Gilles Bouton (Saint-Aubin).

PULIGNY-MONTRACHET

Puligny-Montrachet is the greatest white wine *commune* on earth. Though with a mere 230 hectares of vineyards it is considerably smaller than either of its two neighbours, Meursault and Chassagne-Montrachet, the village can boast two of Burgundy's six white wine *grands crus* in their entirety, Chevalier-Montrachet and Bienvenues-Bâtard-Montrachet, plus roughly half, and, so the authorities would have us believe, the best sections of two others, Bâtard-Montrachet and Le Montrachet itself. Of the six, only Corton Charlemagne and the diminutive Criots-Bâtard-Montrachet do not lie, at least partly, in Puligny-Montrachet.

Puligny's *grands crus* lie at the southern end of the appellation, overlapping into neighbouring Chassagne-Montrachet, and this is where the Chardonnay grape reaches it most regal and supreme expression. Other parts of the world, particularly California and to a lesser extent Australia, can and do produce plenty of competition for village Burgundy. But at *grand cru* level, the best white Burgundies remain unequalled. Elsewhere, the *terroirs* have not yet been found or have not yet been correctly exploited. The top Montrachets, Chevaliers and Bâtards are wines to drink on bended knees, with heartfelt and humble thanks.

History

The origin of the village of Puligny-Montrachet is Gallo-Roman. In the first few centuries after the birth of Christ, vines were first commercially planted in the area and the village was known as Puliniacus. Subsequently, particularly during the Dark Ages, it was the local Benedictine monastery at the Abbey of Maizières, between Dijon and Verdun sur le Doubs, which carried on the traditions of viticulture and viniculture. From time to time, the abbey would receive donations of land. In 1200 Guy de Saint-Sernin ceded half his *dîmes* (tithes) in Puligny and Blagny. In May 1252, the brothers Pierre and Arnolet of Puligny made a number of donations to Maizières, including vines and land on "Mont Rachez." In 1286 Guy Berrier of Chagny also donated a plot of vines "En Mont Raschet." Gradually the Benedictine holdings became of considerable importance.

The fourteenth century was an unhappy time for the inhabitants of Puligny. Famine and pestilence roamed the land, and these difficulties were further compounded locally when Philippe le Hardi, Duke of Burgundy, confiscated the land of the *Seigneur* de Mypont, the lay ruler of Puligny and its immediate locality. In the interregnum, much of the land, formerly under vines, returned to scrub, and the Mypont baronial keep was allowed to crumble into ruins.

In the fifteenth century, a lawyer from Beaune, one Jean Perron, a new member of the *noblesse de la robe*, became *seigneur* of Puligny and Mypont. He had the vineyard slopes replanted and the Château de Puligny—what is today called Le Vieux Château, in the upper part of the village—constructed. In a much renovated and updated form, this château still exists today. But a newer building, nearer to the main road, built around the middle of the nineteenth century but in a Renaissance style, is today's official Château de Puligny-Montrachet.

There is some disagreement about when exactly the fame of Le Montrachet began to surface. Jean-François Bazin (*Montrachet*) echoes the eighteenth century Abbé Courtépée. Compared with the top red wine vineyards of the Côte de Nuits, Le Montrachet is something of a *parvenu* amongst *grands crus*. It was not even *en réputation* in the beginning of the seventeenth century, when 24 *ouvrées* (about a hectare) changed hands for a mere 750 *livres*. According to Dr. Lavalle in 1855, the wines were first mentioned in 1482, by which time the land was already much divided.

Somewhat later, by which time its renown was assured, the majority of the *climat* belonged to the Clermont-Montoizon family. In 1728 the Abbé Arnoux, which published the smallest and slimmest of volumes (if my facsimile copy is an accurate reproduction) on Burgundy in London (but in French) describes Montrachet as "the most curious and most delicate of all in France. A wine of which neither the Latin nor the French vocabulary is capable of describing its *douceur*."

Naturally, Le Montrachet was noted by Thomas Jefferson in his tour of the French vineyards in 1787. The best wines of the Côte, he noted, were Chambertin, Romanée, Clos Vougeot and Montrachet, the first and last at opposite ends. Montrachet sold for 1,200 *livres* the *queue* (a *queue* being two barrels) or 48 francs a bottle. This was the same price as the top three reds he cited. But at the time, the rest of the whites only fetched half that of the equivalent red wines.

The majority of Le Montrachet was sequestered and sold as *bien national* during the Revolution. That of the Clermont-Montoison family measured 100 *ouvrées* (about half the 8 hectares) and was sold in two lots for 35,000 and 37,100 *livres* plus commission, to Henri Pourtalès. The one

holding which seems to have survived the Revolution was that of the Laguiche family, who had married into the Clermont-Montoisons, and this despite the fact that Charles-Amable de la Guiche (as the name was spelled in those days) died on the steps of the guillotine in 1794. Perhaps, and it would not have been a unique ruse for the time, the Pourtalés sale was a bit of a blind.

By the mid-nineteenth century, according to Dr. Lavalle at the time, Le Montrachet was so far in a category of its own that its rating was *Tête de Cuvée, Extra*. Next in line, as *Premières Cuvées* comes ahead of the rest, Chevalier-Montrachet, which is followed by "Blagny-Blanc," Bâtard-Montrachet and Les Combettes, and then Les Platières, Les Referts and Les Charmes.

Les Platières has changed its name since, but given that all the other *climats*, not all of them today *premiers crus*, lie on the Meursault border, I assume that this is where Platières was located. Interestingly, Les Caillerets, Le Clavoillon and Les Pucelles were planted entirely with Pinot Noir at the time, while many of the rocky lands further upslope—Le Champ Canet and Les Folatières, for example—though noted by Lavalle, were very patchily planted. Such vineyards as existed would, in the *phylloxera* times which followed, come to be neglected and turn into *friche*. It would take the arrival of the *concasseur* in the 1950s, a machine which could pulverise the rock into something ploughable and plantable, before these *climats*, and those even further upslope, such as Champs-Gain, would be regained for the Chardonnay vine.

Curnonsky in the 1920s spoke of the five greatest wines of France: the Coulée de Serrant in Savennières, Condrieu and Château Grillet in the Rhône valley, the Vin Jaune of Château Chalon and Le Montrachet. The first three, in the eighteenth century, were sweet wines. So I believe, in the best years at any rate, was Le Montrachet. I have had nineteenth century Montrachets which no longer had any residual sugar to speak of but certainly had a botrytis affected nose and an originally sweet mouth-feel. I think nature was allowed to take its course, as today in Vouvray, and if the weather smiled, so much the better. Remember that almost all Champagne, until Madame Pommery changed the fashion with her Brut 1874, was sweet. That was the *mode* of the times.

Puligny, like Chassagne, appropriated the suffix Montrachet to its name in 1879. The village of Puligny is tight and modest, centred around two squares, the Place du Monument and the Place des Marronniers. There are few shops and no bar, but a pleasant and Michelin-starred restaurant-hotel, suitably called Le Montrachet, with, until his recent departure, a *maître sommelier*, Jean-Claude Wallerand, who was passionate and knowledgeable about wine (something that is not always the case, even in the top restaurants), and who more than once pointed me in the direction of an up-and-coming young *vigneron*.

A noted feature of the village is its very high water table, which makes the construction of underground cellars a costly if not impossible business. Henri Clerc's—which is marginally lower than the road outside—has been flooded on more than one occasion. The solution, as with the Domaine Leflaive and the merchant Olivier Leflaive, is to make sure your above-ground *chai* is temperature controlled, for otherwise, the ambient temperature might dry out the wine in a hot summer.

Puligny-Montrachet, which is now almost entirely white, is a quite different wine from either Meursault or Chassagne-Montrachet. There is a structure, a raciness, a masculinity even, which is missing in the other *communes*. There seems to be more grip, and this gives the wines, however ripe and rich, a reserve which requires longer ageing. It also gives them a personality and breed which you rarely find in Chassagne, and only in Meursault in the three great *premiers crus*, Perrières, Charmes and Genevrières, which lie at the Puligny end of that *commune*. Puligny is where Burgundian Chardonnay is at its most complete.

Location

The *commune* of Puligny-Montrachet lies on either side of and upslope from its village,

the village itself being set back a few hundred metres from the main Beaune-Dijon highway. The *premiers crus* and *grands crus* begin where the incline begins to rise appreciably and when the altitude has reached 240 metres. Vineyard land continues upslope, becoming progressively steeper as the altitude rises. Here and there the vineyards are pockmarked with patches of scrub and piles of larger stones, or the gradient may be interrupted by a series of steplike terraces. The further uphill you get, and above Blagny the vineyard continues to 400 metres (there is a marvellous view from up here), the more meagre the soil becomes, until finally it is just broken-up rock.

Le Montrachet itself lies at 260 metres and overlaps into the *commune* of Chassagne. The *climat* is perfectly exposed, very well drained and protected from the prevailing westerly wind and anything nastier that might whistle down the valley from Saint-Aubin by the hill of Mont Rachet itself. The soil is based on a hard Bathonian limestone topped with light brown limestone debris. There is Bajocian marl at the top of the *climat* and pebbles in the lower part. Overall, it is very stony.

What is so special about Le Montrachet? Scientists have been analysing the soil for ages. Yes, there is some iron here. The limestone is active (less so than in Chevalier above, more so than in Bâtard below). There is some clay (more so than in Chevalier this time, less so than in Bâtard). There is a marked amount of magnesium and of lead—ditto gallium and beryllium. And there are copper, zinc, strontium, titanium, cobalt, tin, molybdenum, vanadium, nickel, chromium and even silver. We know what the presence of some of these trace elements will affect. Chromium is good for fruit-setting, zinc for reducing the acidity and increasing the sugar richness, cobalt for speeding up the maturity and so forth. But no one has come any closer to explaining the miracle of Le Montrachet than the locals themselves: aspect and drainage is the real clue, according to them.

Up above, in Chevalier, the terrain is steeper. The rock is Bajocian marl and rendzina. There is less soil. Below, in Bâtard-Montrachet and its enclaves, Bienvenues-Bâtard-Montrachet and Criots-Bâtard-Montrachet (which, though it lies in the neighbouring *commune* of Chassagne, is convenient to include here), there is more clay, the soil is deeper and richer and there is less fragmented rock and more gravel. Bâtard-Montrachet also overlaps into Chassagne.

The *premiers crus* of Puligny-Montrachet lie in the same line as the *grands crus* and continue upslope on the northern side. Immediately next door, we have Les Caillerets on the same level as Le Montrachet, and Les Pucelles continuing on the other side of the road from Bâtard. It is not so much that the geology changes, though the Caillerets is even more pebbly than its famous neighbour, as that the orientation differs— marginally less to the south, marginally more to the east. Beyond Les Pucelles, within which lies Clos de Meix, we have Clavoillon. Beyond Les Caillerets, and continuing upslope, is Les Folatières. Le Clavoillon has quite deep soil, including some clay. Les Folatières is a large, steep *climat*, prone to erosion. Upslope, and in Les Champs-Gain and Les Truffières, where there are vineyards quite recently rescued from the scrub and planted with vines, the soil is light and red-brown in colour. Midslope, there is white marly Bajocian limestone debris.

Les Perrières, which includes the Clos de la Mouchère, extends from Le Clavoillon. The soil is marly, with plenty of pebbles and other stone fragments, as the name Perrières would suggest. We then come to the Meursault border. Les Chalumaux and Champ Canet are upslope and have red earth with broken up limestone rock on a crumbly limestone base (elsewhere the rock is much harder). Les Combettes and Les Referts marching with Meursault les Charmes: there is very little surface soil in the former, and richer, deeper and more marly terrain in the latter.

The Vineyard

GRANDS CRUS There are five *grands crus* on the Puligny-Chassagne border: Le Montrachet (strictly Montrachet in Puligny and Le Montrachet in Chassagne, though not all labels agree with this); Chevalier-Montrachet; Bâtard-Montrachet; Bienvenues-Bâtard-Montrachet; and Criots-Bâtard-Montrachet. These comprise 32.5 ha and produce an average of 1400 hl per annum.

PREMIERS CRUS Puligny-Montrachet possesses twenty-six *premiers crus* in whole or in part. These are Le Cailleret; Les Chalumaux (part); Le Champ Canet; Le Champ Gain; Au Chaniot (in Les Folatières); Le Clavoillon; Clos de la Garenne; Clos de la Mouchère (in Les Perrières); Clos des Meix (in Les Pucelles); Les Combettes; Les Demoiselles (in Le Cailleret); Les Folatières (part); La Garenne; Hameau de Blagny; La Jaquelotte (in Champ Canet); Les Perrières; Peux Bois (in Les Folatières); Les Pucelles; Sous le Puits; Les Referts; En la Richarde (part) (in Les Folatières); La Truffière.

As mentioned in the previous chapter, the *climats* of Hameau de Blagny, La Garenne and Sous le Puits, if planted with Pinot Noir, produce Blagny *premier cru* and not Puligny *rouge*. Apart from a little *premier cru rouge* from Le Cailleret, all *premier cru* Puligny-Montrachet is white. These *premiers crus* occupy 100.12 hectares and produce about 4,350 hectolitres per year.

VILLAGE WINE There are 114.22 hectares of village land, and this produces about 5,300 hectolitres of white wine and 40 hectolitres of red wine per year.

The Grands Crus

LE MONTRACHET

SURFACE AREA: 8 ha (4.01 lying in Puligny-Montrachet, 3.99 lying in Chassagne-Montrachet)
AVERAGE PRODUCTION: 393 hl
PRINCIPAL PROPRIETORS: ★ Marquis de Laguiche (vinified and marketed by Maison Joseph Drouhin) (2.06 ha); ★ Baron Thénard (mainly *élevé* and sold by Maison Roland Remoissenet et Fils) (1.83 ha); ★ Bouchard Père et Fils (0.89 ha); Regnault de Beaucaron/Guillaume (0.80 ha); ★ Romanée-Conti (0.68 ha); Jacques Prieur (0.59 ha); ★ Comtes Lafon (0.32 ha); ★ Ramonet (0.26 ha); ★ Marc Colin (0.11 ha); ★ Guy Amiot and Mlle Monnot (0.09 ha); ★ Fontaine-Gagnard (0.08 ha); ★ Blain-Gagnard

(0.08 ha); ★ Leflaive (0.08 ha); Lamy-Pillot (0.05 ha); ★ Château de Puligny-Montrachet (0.04 ha).

Le Montrachet is, or should be, Chardonnay at its most perfect, the slowest to mature and the longest lived. Whenever you taste a range of *grands crus*, there is yet another enormous step up after you have sampled the Chevalier—even if the Chevalier itself is twice as good as the Bâtard and the Bienvenues. In Le Montrachet itself, there is an extra element of power, concentration, intensity and grip, such that it makes it sometimes quite impossible to quantify and qualify seriously, even as late as the summer after the vintage, when many a village wine is being polished up for bottling.

Styles vary, as do *négociant* techniques, and you will see from the above that the merchants are in charge of the bulk of this *climat*, for the Beaucaron domaine is the supplier to Jadot, Latour and others, selling its grapes at the time of the vintage for these houses to vinify; but Le Montrachet is always a fuller, richer wine than the other *grands crus*, with a better acidity, as well as great deal more depth and finesse. It can sometimes be a bit top heavy, but it is usually, in my experience, despite the obviously more inflated price, rather more reliable than the other *grands crus*, red or white. There are plenty more disappointing Chambertins than there are Montrachets! It needs at least 10 years to ascend to its best.

Of the important names, Bouchard Père et Fils, Laguiche and Ramonet have their holdings in the Puligny half, while Lafon, Jacques Prieur, the Domaine de la Romanée-Conti, Baron Thénard and the remainder of the Chassagne growers own their vines in the Chassagne section.

CHEVALIER-MONTRACHET

SURFACE AREA: 7.36 ha
AVERAGE PRODUCTION: 255 hl
PRINCIPAL PROPRIETORS: ★ Bouchard Père et Fils (2.54 ha); ★ Leflaive (2.00 ha); ★ Louis Jadot (0.52 ha); ★ Louis Latour (0.52 ha); Jean Chartron (0.47 ha); ★ Château de Puligny-Montrachet (0.25 ha); ★ Michel Niellon (0.22 ha); ★ D'Auvenay (0.16 ha); ★ Michel Colin-Deléger (0.16 ha); ★ Vincent Girardin (0.16 ha); Jacques Prieur (0.14 ha); Vincent Dancer (0.10 ha).

Located upslope from Montrachet, and on much meaner soil, Chevalier-Montrachet never produces to excess, which is one explanation for the quality of its wines, which are clearly superior to Bâtard, Bienvenues and Criots. Chevalier-Montrachet is a full, firm wine, but not four-square, with very good acidity and a masculine reserve. If it doesn't have quite the intensity of Le Montrachet itself, then it certainly has a great deal of depth and elegance, and I think it is this element of breeding, as well as harmony, which sets it above Bâtard and its neighbours. Once again, it is a wine which can be approached with confidence. The majority of the suppliers are consistent and reliable.

BATARD-MONTRACHET

SURFACE AREA: 11.97 ha
AVERAGE PRODUCTION: 514 hl
PRINCIPAL PROPRIETORS: ★ Leflaive (1.81 ha); ★ Ramonet (0.45 ha); Bachelet-Ramonet (0.56 ha); Paul Pernot (0.60 ha); ★ Pierre Morey (0.40 ha); Roger Caillot-Morey (0.47 ha, *en métayage* from Claude-Maxence Poirier); ★ Philippe Brenot (0.37 ha); ★ Jean-Noël Gagnard (0.37 ha); ★ Jean-Marc Blain-Gagnard (0.34 ha); ★ Richard Fontaine-Gagnard (0.30 ha); ★ Hospices de Beaune (0.35 ha); Barolet-Pernot (0.23 ha); ★ Vincent Girardin (0.19 ha); ★ Jean-Marc Boillot (0.18 ha); ★ Etienne Sauzet (0.14 ha); Marc Morey (0.14 ha); Jean Chartron (0.13 ha); Michel Morey-Coffinet (0.13 ha); ★ Romanée-Conti (0.13 ha, sold in bulk); ★ Michel Niellon (0.12 ha); Louis Lequin (0.12 ha); ★ René Lequin-Colin (0.12 ha); ★ Joseph Drouhin (0.09 ha); ★ Château de la Maltroye (0.09 ha); Bouchard Père et Fils (0.08 ha); Bernard Morey (0.075 ha); Jean-Marc Morey (0.075 ha); ★ Château de Puligny-Montrachet (0.04 ha).

Bâtard-Montrachet is a much-fragmented *climat*, producing wines of a range of quality from excellent to beyond the pale. It produces a fatter, more open, more exotic wine than Chevalier-Montrachet, usually with less grip and a more flowery, fleshy, honeyed, spicy richness. It can be four-square. It can also be blowsy. But I find it more consistent across the board than Bienvenues and Criots.

BIENVENUES-BATARD-MONTRACHET

SURFACE AREA: 3.69 ha
AVERAGE PRODUCTION: 178 hl
PRINCIPAL PROPRIETORS: ★ Leflaive (1.16 ha);
★ Ramonet (0.56 ha); ★ Vincent Girardin (0.47 ha);
★ Paul Pernot (0.37 ha); Guillemard-Clerc (0.18 ha, exploited *en fermage*); Bachelet-Ramonet (0.13 ha);
★ Etienne Sauzet (0.12 ha); ★ Louis Carillon (0.11 ha); Jean-Claude Bachelet (0.09 ha); Barolet-Pernot (0.09 ha).

Bienvenues is, roughly speaking, the northeast quarter of Bâtard—downslope, marching with the bottom part of Les Pucelles. The wine has a fatness, a honeyed or honeysuckle fragrance and a certain delicacy: it is feminine where Chevalier is masculine. It can sometimes be rather weak and feeble, and it is a wine whose grapes have a tendency to overripen more readily than most. But when you chance on a fine example you will find the complexity, accessibility and elegant harmony very seductive. It is usually a little cheaper, but not necessarily any worse, than Bâtard-Montrachet.

CRIOTS-BATARD-MONTRACHET

(This *climat* is wholly in Chassagne-Montrachet, but it is included here for readers' convenience.)

SURFACE AREA: 1.75 ha
AVERAGE PRODUCTION: 69 hl
PRINCIPAL PROPRIETORS: ★ Roger Belland (0.61 ha); Charles Bonnefoy (0.20 ha, sold in bulk); ★ Richard Fontaine-Gagnard (0.33 ha); ★ Jean-Marc Blain-Gagnard (0.21 ha); ★ D'Auvenay (0.06 ha); Hubert Lamy (0.05 ha, *en fermage* from Mme Marcelle Perrot); Blondeau-Danne (0.05 ha).

This tiny *grand cru*, one of the smallest appellations in France, lies immediately to the south of Bâtard-Montrachet. Its wine is the most delicate of the five senior *climats* in the vicinity. While the structure may be similar, compared with Bienvenues, the flavours are less honeyed, and the citrus element is expressed as lemon sherbet or as limes. Again there is a flowery touch, but the flowers are less exotically perfumed and cooler, the effect more minerally. Criots can be elegant and exquisite. It can also be a bit empty.

The Premiers Crus

LES DEMOISELLES   (0.60 ha)
LE CAILLERET   (3.33 ha)

Being the extension of Le Montrachet to the north, this is, or should be, the best of the *premiers crus*. The lion's share, despite sales in the 1990s to the Saier family (former owners of Morey-Saint-Denis's Clos des Lambrays), to Hubert de Montille of Volnay and to Michel Bouzereau and Yves Boyer-Martenot of Meursault, still belongs to Jean Chartron. The enclave known as Les Demoiselles consists of the first fifty-six rows of vines on the Montrachet side, underneath the end of Chevalier. At its best, these make exquisite wines: not as powerful as Le Montrachet itself, but of pure breed, excellent grip and beautiful balance.

RECOMMENDED SOURCES
LE CAILLERET
Jean Chartron (Puligny-Montrachet); Hubert de Montille (Volnay); Michel Bouzereau, Yves Boyer-Martenot (both Meursault); Domaine des Lambrays (Morey-Saint-Denis).

LES DEMOISELLES
Guy Amiot-Bonfils, Michel Colin-Deléger (both Chassagne-Montrachet).

LES PUCELLES   (5.13 ha)
CLOS DES MEIX   (1.63 ha)

Downslope, we come to Les Pucelles, another *climat* which can often give you the same lift and delight as you get from a *grand cru*. The Clos des Meix is that part in the middle of the bottom of the *climat*, rather like a bite out of a sandwich. No one seems to declare it as such these days. The largest owner here is the Domaine Lefaive, with over 3 hectares, and this is frequently a very delicious wine, all silk, flowers and fragrance. I look for something feminine here, delicate, soft and honeyed, but with a good intense acidity underneath.

Leflaive, Jean Chartron (Clos de la Pucelle), Paul Pernot (all Puligny-Montrachet); Jean Boillot (Volnay); Marc Morey (Chassagne-Montrachet); plus the *négociant* selections of, for example, Joseph Drouhin (Beaune) and Olivier Leflaive Frères (Puligny-Montrachet).

LE CLAVOILLON (OR CLAVAILLON)   *(5.59 ha)*

Le Clavoillon continues on from Les Pucelles, and is very nearly the monopoly of the Domaine Leflaive, which has 4.79 hectares. The soil is obviously less fine here, with more clay in it, for we have a more four-square wine, which is in my view the least good of Leflaive's *premiers crus*. This is good stuff, but it does not aspire to *grand cru* status.

RECOMMENDED SOURCES
Leflaive (Puligny-Montrachet).

LES (OR EX) FOLATIÈRES   *(17.65 ha)*

This is the largest Puligny-Montrachet *premier cru* and includes the enclaves of En la Richarde, Peux Bois and Au Chaniot, none of which seem to be declared separately. Les Folatières is a fullish, meaty, mineral wine with plenty of weight of fruit and good grip—a typical Puligny *premier cru* in fact. The *climat* lies just above Clavoillon, next to Le Cailleret, but climbing further upslope toward the hamlet of Blagny.

RECOMMENDED SOURCES
Leflaive, Richard Maroslavac, Jean-Luc Pascal, Paul Pernot (all Puligny-Montrachet); Vincent Girardin, René Monnier (both Meursault); D'Auvenay (Saint-Romain); Louis Jadot (Beaune); Domaine des Lambrays (Morey-Saint-Denis); plus the *négociant* selections of, for example, Joseph Drouhin (Beaune) and Olivier Leflaive Frères (Puligny-Montrachet).

CLOS DE LA GARENNE   *(1.53 ha)*

This *climat*, which is quite separate from La Garenne, lies next to Les Folatières, on the north side of the road which climbs up to Blagny, and

is the monopoly of the Duc de Magenta. The wine is made and sold, but under a special label, by Maison Louis Jadot of Beaune. Similar to a good Folatières, it is always one of Jadot's very best Pulignys.

SOUS LE PUITS	*(6.80 ha)*
LA GARENNE	*(9.87 ha)*
LES CHAMP GAIN	*(10.70 ha)*
LA TRUFFIÈRE	*(2.48 ha)*
HAMEAU DE BLAGNY	*(4.28 ha)*

There is, I feel, a pioneering spirit here, much of the land having been converted from scrub by means of major engineering feats of pulverising the rock, clearing the bushes and smoothing out the terrain to make it economic to plant the vine. Sixty years ago, as old photographs will show, this was nature's territory, not man's.

The wines are less fine and less fat than they are further downslope—we are above 300 metres here, rising to 380 and more—and in lighter years they can be a bit thin. But there is usually good acidity, an absence of overripeness and an attractive minerally quality.

RECOMMENDED SOURCES
LA GARENNE
Château de Puligny-Montrachet (Puligny-Montrachet); Marc Colin, Giles Bouton, Larue (all Saint-Aubin/Gamay).

LE CHAMP GAIN
Roland Maroslavac, Jean-Luc Pascal (both Puligny-Montrachet); Vincent Girardin (Meursault); Roger Belland (Santenay); Louis Jadot (Beaune).

LA TRUFFIÈRE
Jean-Marc Boillot (Volnay); Michel Colin-Deléger, Bernard Morey (both Chassagne-Montrachet). See also the *négociant* selections, for example, Olivier Leflaive Frères.

LES CHALUMAUX   *(5.79 ha)*

Incorporating Sous le Courthil, this is a *climat* whose wine I know best in the cellars of Thierry Matrot of Meursault. His example is not as fine as his Combettes, but it has an herbal-flowery personality all of its own. On the basis of this example, I would rate Chalumaux with the second division of Puligny *premiers crus*.

RECOMMENDED SOURCES
Matrot (Meursault).

LE CHAMP CANET	*(4.06 ha)*
LES COMBETTES	*(6.76 ha)*
LES REFERTS	*(5.52 ha)*
LES PERRIÈRES	*(8.41 ha)*

The first three *climats* run down the Meursault boundary, marching with Meursault les Perrières and Meursault les Charmes. Puligny's Perrières occupies the land between Les Combettes and Les Referts and Le Clavoillon, and includes the 3.92-hectare *monopole* of Clos de la Mouchère, belonging to the Domaine Jean Boillot of Volnay. La Jacquelotte, which you will not see declared separately, is part of Le Champ Canet.

The jewel here is not Le Champ-Canet, though that is directly on the line with Meursault Les Perrières, but Les Combettes. Les Combettes is the most complete wine of the four *climats*, a mouthwatering and deliciously elegant combination of Meursault and Puligny, with the steeliness of the latter and the honeysuckle and hazelnut of the former. Le Champ Canet is similar, but not quite as fine or as three-dimensional; Les Referts is fatter, spicier and a little coarser, and Les Perrières, in my experience of Carillon's fine example (the Sauzet domaine's vines are currently relatively young), is the closest to Les Combettes. The Clos de la Mouchère, in the exclusive hands of Henri Boillot of Domaine Jean Boillot, is steely and very elegant.

RECOMMENDED SOURCES
LE CHAMP CANET
Louis Carillon, Étienne Sauzet (both Puligny-Montrachet); Jean-Marc Boillot (Pommard).

LES COMBETTES
Leflaive, Roland Maroslavac, Étienne Sauzet (all Puligny-Montrachet); Vincent Girardin, Matrot (both Meursault); Jean-Marc Boillot (Pommard).

LES REFERTS
Louis Carillon, Étienne Sauzet (both Puligny-Montrachet); Jean-Marc Boillot (Pommard).

LES PERRIÈRES
Louis Carillon, Étienne Sauzet (both Puligny-Montrachet); Jean Boillot (Volnay) as Clos-de-la-Mouchère (*monopole*); plus the *négociant* selections of, for example, Maison Louis Jadot, Maison Roland Remoissenet et Fils (both Beaune); Olivier Leflaive Frères (Puligny-Montrachet).

The Growers

★★★ *Louis Carillon et Fils*

11 ha owned. Bienvenues-Bâtard-Montrachet (0.12 ha); Puligny-Montrachet *premier cru* in Le Champ Canet, Le Champ Gain, Les Combettes, Les Perrières and Les Referts; Chassagne-Montrachet *premier cru* in Les Chenevottes, Clos Saint-Jean and Les Macherelles (*blanc*); Saint-Aubin *premier cru* Les Pitangerets (*rouge*); Mercurey *premier cru* Les Champs Martin; village Puligny-Montrachet; village Chassagne-Montrachet *rouge*; village Mercurey *rouge*.

The Carillon family—it is now François, grandson of Louis, who is in charge of the winemaking with his brother Jacques in the vineyard—have been resident in the village since 1632. Their wines are fine but understated. I quickly learned that it was a mistake to dismiss them for not, when they were in cask, flamboyantly waving a lush personality about, for when I sampled them blind in bottle they always came out near the top. Now I know better, admire them from the outset, and buy lots for myself. Since 1996, like Leflaive, the wines have been decanted into tank after 12 months and bottled 6 months afterward, except for the Bienvenues, which remain in cask. They use 20 percent new oak for all the top wines. François prefers the Referts; I like the Perrières. The Mercureys, which are sold under the name of Jacques et François Carillon, are leased off on a share-cropping basis to Bruno Lorenzon.

Jean Chartron

12 ha owned and *en fermage*. Chevalier-Montrachet Clos des Chevaliers (0.47 ha—*monopole*); Bâtard-Montrachet (0.13 ha); Puligny-Montrachet *premier cru*

in Clos du Cailleret *rouge (monopole) et blanc*, Clos de la Pucelle *(monopole)* and Les Folatières; Saint-Aubin *premier cru* Les Murgers des Dents de Chien; village Puligny-Montrachet; village Chassagne-Montrachet *rouge et blanc* in the *lieu-dit* Les Benoîtres; village Pommard in the *lieu-dit* Les Vaumuriens; village Rully *blanc* in the *lieu-dit* Montmorin.

Up until the summer of 2005, the wines of the domaine Jean Chartron, made by Jean-Michel Chartron, were sold through merchants Chartron and Trébuchet. Chartron and Trébuchet then went bust, and the name was acquired by Vincent Sauvestre, and since then, the Chartrons have had to go it alone and have taken on a lease in Rully. I always found the domaine wines rather better than the merchant wines, which are the responsibility of others and are disconcertingly variable; they still are. Bottling takes place after 9 to 12 months. The red Cailleret, when it is on form, resembles a good Volnay.

Alain Chavy

7 ha owned and *en fermage*. Puligny-Montrachet *premier cru* in Le Clavoillon, Les Folatières, Le Champ Gain and Les Pucelles; Saint-Aubin *premier cru* En Remilly; village Puligny-Montrachet including the *lieu-dit* Les Charmes and Les Enseignères; village Meursault.

In 2003 Alain Chavy and his brother Jean-Louis, responsible for their father's wines at Domaine Gérard Chavy et Fils, went their separate ways. Alain lives in a fine house on the road out of the village toward Chagny with, rare in the village, a proper cellar. These are good wines—and they seem to be improving. Alain Chavy is now bottling after 18 months.

Jean-Louis Chavy

6.5 ha owned and *en fermage*. Puligny-Montrachet *premier cru* in Le Champ Gain, Le Clavoillon, Les Folatières and Les Perrières; Beaune *premier cru* Les Cent Vignes; village Puligny-Montrachet, including the *lieu-dit* Les Charmes.

Following the split (see above), this is the other half of the old Gérard Chavy domaine. Jean-Louis is the elder brother. The white wines are fermented at 25°C and given 20 percent new oak, and the *premiers crus* are bottled after 16 months. As with his brother, I feel things are improving. A bit of sibling rivalry is no bad thing!

Philippe Chavy

8 ha owned and *en fermage/en métayage*. Puligny-Montrachet *premier cru* in Les Folatières and Les Pucelles; Meursault *premier cru* in Blagny, Les Charmes and Sous le Dos d'Ane; Saint-Aubin *premier cru* Les Murgers des Dents de Chien; village Puligny-Montrachet, including the *lieux-dits* Les Corvées des Vignes and Rue Rousseau; village Meursault, including the *lieu-dit* Les Narvaux.

Philippe is cousin to the two Chavys above and has inherited half his father's domaine—the remainder of which is now being exploited by his brother Hubert Chavy-Chouet of Meursault. There used to be a frighteningly hairy dog of dubious ancestry and temperament guarding the premises. Thankfully for the occasional visitor, he is no more. High quality here dates from 2002, when father Albert retired. The vines are ploughed, and Philippe works to the biodynamic calendar. He bottles after 12 months.

Benoît Ente

3.1 ha owned and *en fermage/en métayage*. Puligny-Montrachet *premier cru* in Champ Gain, Les Folatières and Les Referts; village Puligny-Montrachet; village Chassagne-Montrachet.

Benoît Ente, born in 1968, started working with his aunt, Mme David, in 1990. The wine was sold in bulk to Louis Latour. This arrangement came to an end in 1998. That year his vines were badly hailed, so 1999 was effectively his first vintage. These were only quite good. But the improvement since then has been considerable. There is no systematic *bâtonnage*, and he uses 20 to 30 percent new oak, bottling after 12 months. This is an address to watch.

★★★ Leflaive

24.52 ha owned. Le Montrachet (0.08 ha); Chevalier-Montrachet (2.00 ha); Bâtard-Montrachet (1.91 ha); Bienvenues-Bâtard-Montrachet (1.60 ha); Puligny-Montrachet *premier cru* in Le Clavoillon,

Les Combettes, Les Folatières, Les Pucelles; Meursault *premier cru* Sous le Dos d'Ane; village Puligny-Montrachet.

Totally biodynamic since 1997, this famous domaine is run by Anne-Claude Leflaive, with Pierre Morey as *régisseur*. They are a formidable team. A decade ago, quality was not up to the exacting standards we have come to expect. But since 1995, things have been back where they should be: this is the very summit of white Burgundy. They have also replanted their Blagny *rouge* in the Dos d'Ane with Chardonnay and now make solely white wine from this parcel. The vines here are now 10 years old.

The wines are fermented at 18–24°C, given 10 to 40 percent new oak (there is one 500-litre cask for the Montrachet) and after 12 months racked into stainless steel where they wait another 6 months before bottling.

★ *Olivier Leflaive Frères, S.A.*

14 ha owned and *en fermage*. Meursault *premier cru* Les Poruzots; Chassagne-Montrachet *premier cru* Abbaye de Morgeot and Clos Saint-Jean; village Puligny-Montrachet; village Chassagne-Montrachet *rouge et blanc*.

Created in 1984, by Olivier Leflaive, cousin of Anne-Claude above, this merchant, which has since built up its own domaine, showed right from the start that it could produce high quality. Franck Grux took over as winemaker in 1988. They produce a wide range of wines, mainly white, which come forward reasonably soon. This address is recommended.

Roland Maroslavac-Léger

5.13 ha owned and *en fermage*. Puligny-Montrachet *premier cru* in Champ Gain, Les Combettes and Les Folatières; Saint-Aubin *premier cru* Les Murgers des Dents de Chien; village Puligny-Montrachet; village Chassagne-Montrachet.

This is a reliable and now consistent cellar, and it is hosted by the cheerfully hospitable Roland Maroslavac. Some of his holdings are very small (0.16 ha of Combettes, for example), which must pose vinification problems on occasion.

But there are good wines here, especially among his *premiers crus*, which are now bottled after 18 months. Since 2006, this estate only produces white wine.

Stéphane Maroslavac-Trémeau

15.5 ha owned and *en fermage*. Puligny-Montrachet *premier cru* in Champ Gain, Les Folatières, Les Pucelles and Les Referts; Meursault *premier cru* Blagny; village Puligny-Montrachet, including the *lieu-dit* Clos du Vieux Château; village Santenay.

The youngish Jérôme Meunier is *régisseur* here for the widow of Stéphane Maroslavac who died in 2003 and was the father of Roland (see above). Seventy percent of the produce is sold off as fruit or must to the local *négoce*, and most of the rest is sold in bottle to passing private customers. Meunier has fine-tuned things since his arrival. The vineyard is ploughed, the harvest has been reduced to 40 to 45 hectolitres per hectare, there is a pneumatic press, and there is usually only one racking before a now more retarded bottling.

Jean Pascal et Fils

14.56 ha *en fermage/en métayage*. Puligny-Montrachet *premier cru* in Champ Gain, Les Chalumeaux, Les Folatières and Hameau de Blagny; Volnay *premier cru* Les Caillerets; Blagny *premier cru* Sous le Puits; village Puligny-Montrachet, including the *lieu-dit* Les Enseignères; village Blagny; village Meursault; village Volnay; village Pommard; village Auxey-Duresses.

This is a source which has yet to show me anything that sends me into raptures. Jean-Luc, son of Jean Pascal, is in charge. There is 25 to 50 percent new oak for the whites and 20 to 35 percent for the reds, which are entirely destemmed and now cold-soaked, before vinification. Bottling takes place after 9 to 11 months.

★ *Paul Pernot et Fils*

20 ha owned and *en fermage*. Bâtard-Montrachet (0.60 ha); Bienvenues-Bâtard-Montrachet (0.37 ha); Puligny-Montrachet *premier cru* in Les Folatières, Clos de la Garenne and Les Pucelles; Meursault *premier cru* Blagny; Blagny *premier cru* La Pièce sous le Bois; Beaune *premier cru* in Clos du Dessous des Marconnets, Les Reversées and Les Teurons; village

Puligny-Montrachet; village Volnay in the *lieu-dit* Les Carelles; village Pommard in the *lieu-dit* Les Noizons; village Beaune; village Santenay.

This large domaine must be a boon to the Beaune *négoce*, for quality is very high, and Paul Pernot and his three sons only dispose themselves of some 20 percent of the crop in bottle. It is no secret that they have been major suppliers to Maison Drouhin for many years. I have consistent enthusiastic notes of Pernot wines. The whites are given 20 percent new oak and bottled after 11 months, as are the reds.

★ Château de Puligny-Montrachet

20.93 ha owned. Le Montrachet (0.04 ha); Chevalier-Montrachet (0.25 ha); Bâtard-Montrachet (0.04 ha); Puligny-Montrachet *premier cru* in Les Chalumaux, Les Folatières and La Garenne; Meursault *premier cru* in Les Perrières and Les Poruzots; Saint-Aubin *premier cru rouge et blanc* En Remilly; Monthelie *premier cru* Les Duresses; Pommard *premier cru* Les Pézerolles; Nuits-Saint-Georges *premier* cru Clos des Grandes Vignes (*monopole*); village Puligny-Montrachet; village Chassagne-Montrachet; village Meursault; village Saint-Aubin; village Monthelie *rouge et blanc*; village Pommard; Saint-Romain.

The bank Crédit Foncier de France, owner of, among other things, Châteaux Bastor-Lamontagne in Sauternes and Beauregard in Pomerol, acquired the Château de Puligny-Montrachet in 1989 from the Laroche Company of Chablis. They have since built up the domaine from 15 hectares to its present size, acquiring land from Jean Chartron and the Fleurot family, among others. There is a splendid modern vinification centre, a temperature and humidification-controlled cellar and one old-fashioned baby vertical press for the Montrachet.

Quality was humdrum until the arrival as managing director in 2002 of Étienne de Montille. He moved the barrel cellar back to the attractive temperature-controlled vaults underneath the château, started turning the viticultural practices biodynamic and lowered the amount of new wood, as well as the yields. A dramatic improvement has resulted.

★ Étienne Sauzet

8 ha owned. Bâtard-Montrachet (0.14 ha); Bienvenues-Bâtard-Montrachet (0.12 ha); Puligny-Montrachet *premier cru* in Le Champ-Canet, Les Combettes, Les Folatières, Les Perrières, Les Referts; village Puligny-Montrachet; village Chassagne-Montrachet.

Gérard Boudot, married to a granddaughter of the late Étienne Sauzet and brother-in-law of Henri and Jean-Marc Boillot, is one of Puligny's most gifted winemakers. He produced his thirty-second vintage in 2005. He now works with his daughter Émilie and her husband Benoît Riffault. In the late 1990s, he compensated for what he had lost when some of the Sauzet domaine passed to Jean-Marc by acquiring a merchant's licence. Everything is vinified and stored in the same cellar. Splendid wines are here. Only white wines are produced. They are vinified at about 20°C; *bâtonnage* takes place "if necessary." The *premiers crus* and *grands crus* are bottled after 18 months.

SAINT-AUBIN AND GAMAY

The N6 main road cuts a grand swathe through what is technically the *commune* of Chassagne—there are Chassagne vineyards on either side—but what feels like the border between Chassagne and Puligny. Just beyond where the Mont-Rachet hill turns round to face the southwest, you cross over from the terrain of both these villages into that of Saint-Aubin.

The first village you come to, however, will be that of Gamay. At this point, the prevailing aspect of the hills veers round toward the southeast once again. As the N6 thunders off into the Hautes-Côtes, you reach the village of Saint-Aubin.

Up until recently, the *commune* was one of those neglected, out-of-the-way villages of the Côte, producing more red than white wine, much of which went into the Côte-de-Beaune Villages melting pot. It was then discovered as a convenient source of inexpensive white, a sort of halfway house between Puligny and the whites of the Côte Chalonnaise, of a quality nearer to the former but a price nearer to the latter.

Growers then turned to Chardonnay, which they planted in addition to what they already had. In the early 1980s, there were 120 hectares under production, two thirds of which was red wine. Today, there are 156 hectares, and two thirds of what is produced is white wine. Prices, sadly, are no longer the bargains that they were. But a good Saint-Aubin *premier cru*, at two thirds that of village Puligny, can still be a good buy, and it will probably develop sooner.

The soil structure is varied, for we are dealing with two different hills, one on either side of the village of Gamay. The first, the Roche du May, is the continuation of the Mont-Rachet slope, an Argovian marl covered by limestone debris and brown clayey limestone mixtures. Above the village of Saint-Aubin rises the Montagne du Ban. Here the limestone is Callovian, or Callovian mixed with the more marly Argovian in the sector of the *premiers crus*.

The Vineyard

Saint-Aubin is rich—one could argue too rich—in *premiers crus*. The whole of the vineyard between the Puligny border and the village of Gamay is *premier cru*, as is the little bit on the opposite side of the N6 which continues the Chassagne slope. Most of the section between Gamay and Saint-Aubin is also *premier cru*: only when you get beyond the village and the quaintly named vineyard of Derrière Chez Édouard (which reminds me irresistibly of the British expression "It's brighter over Bill's Mum's") is there much village vineyard.

PREMIERS CRUS There are twenty-nine *premiers crus* in Saint-Aubin, in whole or in part. These are Les Castets (part); Les Champlots; Le Charmois; La Chatenière; Les Combes-au-Sud; Les Cortons; En Créot; Echaille; Derrière chez Édouard; Les Frionnes; Le-Bas-de-Gamay-à-l'Est; Sur Gamay; Marinot; En Montceau; Les Murgers des Dents de Chien; Les Perrières; Pitangeret; Le Puits (part); En la Ranché; En Remilly; Sous Roche Dumay; Sur le Sentier du Clou; Derrière la Tour; Les Travers de Marinot; Bas-de-Vermarain-à-l'Est (part); Vignes Moingeon;

Le Village (part); En-Vallon-à-l'Est. The *premiers crus* make up 111.40 hectares and produce 1,500 hectolitres of red wine and 4,000 hectolitres of white wine per year.

VILLAGE WINE Village Saint-Aubin covers a mere 44.42 hectares (less than half that of *premier cru*) and produces 780 hectolitres of red wine, including Côte-de-Beaune Villages, and 1,315 hectolitres of white wine per year.

Both colours are light, soft, crisp wines which evolve in the medium term. Both can be a bit thin and ungenerous in poorer vintages. With the *vignoble* lying at 260–340 metres, we are in more senses than one halfway into the Hautes-Côtes. The ambient temperature is cooler, the fruit needs longer to ripen fully, and, therefore, it is more liable to be caught by rain during the harvest.

In general the white wines are of far greater interest than the reds. The reds are no more than light Chassagnes, not usually too rustic, but with a tendency to attenuate. The white wines, especially those from the *climats* nearest to Chassagne and Puligny (Le Charmois on the Chassagne side, En Remilly, Les Murgers-des-Dents-de-Chien and La Chatenière on the Puligny side) can have plenty of character and deftness, a sort of crisp raciness which can be most attractive. The *climats* above the village of Saint-Aubin itself—Les Frionnes and Les Perrières—have less definition.

RECOMMENDED SOURCES
See below.

The Growers

Jean-Claude Bachelet

9.48 ha owned and *en fermage*. Bienvenues-Bâtard-Montrachet (0.09 ha); Puligny-Montrachet *premier cru* Sous le Puits; Chassagne-Montrachet *premier cru* La Macherelle (*blanc*) and La Boudriotte (*rouge* Blanchot Dessus); Saint-Aubin *premier cru* Les Champlots *et blanc*, Les Frionnes, Les Chanmois, Les Murgers des Dents de Chien, La Chatenière, and En Remilly (*blanc*), and Derrière-La-Tour (*rouge*); village Puligny-Montrachet; village Chassagne-Montrachet *rouge et blanc*.

Benoit and Jean-Baptiste, sons of John Claude, are now firmly in charge here, and quality has improved as a result. Bottling now takes place after 18 months and not two years, sulphur levels have been reduced, and the wines are more stylish. A domaine to watch.

Gilles Bouton

15 ha owned and *en fermage/en métayage*. Puligny-Montrachet *premier cru* in La Garenne and Sous le Puits; Meursault *premier cru* Blagny (in La Jeunelotte); Saint-Aubin *premier cru blanc* in La Chatenière, Les Champlots, Les Murgers des Dents de Chien and En Remilly; Saint-Aubin *premier cru rouge* Les Champlots and En Créot; Blagny *premier cru* Sous le Puits; village Chassagne-Montrachet *rouge et blanc*.

The energetic and *sympa* Gilles Bouton took over the estate of his grandfather Aimé Langoureau in 1977 and has since enlarged it to its present size. In 2005 he constructed a new *cuverie* and bought a new pneumatic press and now performs a more serious *triage* than hitherto. He makes good wine in both colours, the Murgers des Dents de Chien and En Remilly being the best Saint-Aubin *blancs*, the Champlots the best *rouge*. But the pick of his cellar is the Meursault, Blagny and the Blagny *premier cru* (*rouge*) Sous le Puits.

★ Marc Colin et Fils

17.17 ha owned and *en fermage*. Le Montrachet (0.11 ha); Chassagne-Montrachet *premier cru blanc* in En Cailleret, Les Champs Gains, Les Chenevottes and Vide Bourse; Puligny-Montrachet *premier cru* La Garenne; Saint-Aubin *premier cru blanc* in La Chatenière, Les Combes, Le Charmois, Les Cortons, En Créot, Sur Gamay, En Montceau, En Remilly and Sur le Sentier du Clou; Saint-Aubin *premier cru rouge tout court*; village Puligny-Montrachet; village Chassagne-Montrachet *rouge et blanc*; village Saint-Aubin *rouge et blanc*; village Santenay.

Marc Colin has now retired, leaving the family domaine to be run by two of his sons, Damien and Joseph, while the third, Pierre-Yves has gone his separate way. The wines are made in a large modern cellar in Gamay, a couple of dozen metres from the family home, and

have improved considerably over the years. Yields have been reduced, and the viticulture has become more sensitive and the winemaking more precise. Michel Colin-Deléger of Chassagne-Montrachet is a cousin. This is a very good address.

Pierre-Yves Colin-Morey

4.5 ha Chassagne-Montrachet *premier cru blanc* Les Caillerets and Les Chenevottes; Saint-Aubin *premier cru blanc* in En Remilly, La Chatenière, Les Champlots and Les Combes; village Chassagne-Montrachet Les Enseignères; village Saint-Aubin. All white, plus village Santenay *rouge vieilles vignes*, Les Champs Claude.

Pierre-Yves Colin, the eldest son, withdrew from the previous domaine in 2006. In 2001 he set up a merchants business with his wife Caroline Morey. Hitherto he had, since the retirement of his father, been the winemaker. What he produces on his own account is pure, elegant and precise. He is a name to watch. The *négociant* side of the activity deals only in white wines.

★ Hubert Lamy et Fils

16.75 ha owned and *en fermage*. Criots-Bâtard-Montrachet (0.05 ha); Chassagne-Montrachet *premier cru blanc* Les Macherelles; Saint-Aubin *premier cru blanc* in Clos de la Chatenière, Clos de Meix, Derrière chez Édouard, Les Frionnes, Les Murgers des Dents de Chien and En Remilly; Saint-Aubin *premier cru rouge* Les Castets and Derrière chez Édouard; village Puligny-Montrachet in the *lieu-dit* Les Tremblots; village Chassagne-Montrachet (*rouge*); village Saint-Aubin *rouge et blanc* including the *lieu-dit* La Princée; village Santenay in the *lieu-dit* Clos des Hâtes.

Run by Olivier Lamy, son of Hubert, this is, with that of Marc Colin, the best address in the *commune*. The headquarters is a modern cellar on three levels, working as much as possible by gravity, in the village of Saint-Aubin. Since he took over in 1991, Olivier Lamy has increased the density of plantation to 14,000 vines per hectare. In the cellar you will find most of the wines maturing in double-sized *demi-muids* of 600-litre volume. There are delicious wines here.

Sylvain Langoureau

8.5 ha owned and *en fermage*. Puligny-Montrachet *premier cru* Les Chalumaux and La Garenne; Meursault-Blagny *premier cru* La Pièce sous le Bois; Saint-Aubin *premier cru* in Le Bas de Vermarain à l'Est, Derrière chez Édouard, Les Frionnes, En Remilly and Sur le Sentier du Clou; Saint-Aubin *premier cru* tout court; village Saint-Aubin; village Chassagne-Montrachet *rouge et blanc*.

This is an improving domaine. The viticulture is becoming more and more *biologique*, with an emphasis on encouraging the vines to build up their own defence systems. In the *cave* a pneumatic press was acquired in 2001, and more recently, temperature control was installed and the bottle cellar enlarged. Langoureau does not approve of *bâtonnage*. These are good wines.

Larue

15 ha owned and *en fermage/en métayage*. Puligny-Montrachet *premier cru* in La Garenne and Sous le Puits; Chassagne-Montrachet *premier cru rouge* Les Boudriottes; Saint-Aubin *premier cru rouge*; Saint-Aubin *premier cru blanc* in Les Combes, Les Cortons, Les Murgers des Dents de Chien, En Remilly, Sur le Sentier du Clou and *premier cru vieilles vignes*; Blagny *premier cru*; village Puligny-Montrachet; village Chassagne-Montrachet *rouge et blanc*.

Didier and Denis Larue formed a GAEC (a family farming company) to exploit the vineyards they inherited in 1985. When I first came across them, I felt that lack of space was inhibiting their ability to get the best out of their wines. This has now been resolved with a brand new winery in 2000, to which a modern reception centre was added in 2005. Quality is very good quality here now.

Patrick Miolane

8 ha owned. Saint-Aubin *premier cru* Les Perrières; village Chassagne-Montrachet in the *lieu-dit* La Chanière; village Puligny-Montrachet; village Saint-Aubin.

The fortyish, bearded, pig-tailed Patrick Miolane took over his parents' estate in 1998. Yields have

been cut and the winemaking refined since then. These are very good wines now.

Henri Prudhon et Fils

13.13 ha owned and *en fermage/en métayage*. Puligny-Montrachet *premier cru* La Garenne; Chassagne-Montrachet *premier cru* Les Chenevottes; Saint-Aubin *premier cru blanc* in Les Castets, Les Chatenières, Les Murgers des Dents de Chien, Les Perrières, En Remilly, Sur Gamay and Sur le Sentier du Clou; Saint-Aubin *premier cru rouge* Les Frionnes and Sur le Sentier du Clou; village Puligny-Montrachet; village Chassagne-Montrachet; village Saint-Aubin (*rouge et blanc*).

Gérard Prudhon and his sons Philippe and Vincent produce soft, attractive, early-maturing wines. As elsewhere in the village, the whites are more interesting than the reds. In 2006 a new cellar was constructed, and they now intend to build up a merchant's business. This is a good source.

Gérard Thomas

11.28 ha owned and *en fermage*. Meursault *premier cru* Blagny; Puligny-Montrachet *premier cru* La Garenne; Saint-Aubin *premier cru blanc* in La Chatenière, Les Murgers des Dents de Chien and Les Combes; Saint-Aubin *premier cru rouge* Les Frionnes; village Puligny-Montrachet; village Saint-Aubin *rouge et blanc*.

Gérard Thomas works with his daughters Anne-Sophie, who is married to a Prudhon, and Isabelle Humbert. As with others in the village, he produces wines for early drinking, and more interesting whites than reds. Good but not brilliant is how I would describe the quality here.

CHASSAGNE-MONTRACHET

Chassagne Montrachet is the last-but-one important *commune* of the Côte d'Or before the hills fizzle out at Dezize, Cheilly and Sampigny-Lès-Maranges. It is the third of the three great adjacent wine villages after Meursault and Puligny-Montrachet. Divided by the main highway between Chagny and Chalon to the south and Autun and Auxerre to the west and northwest, now to a large extent superseded by the Paris-Lyon motorway, Chassagne produces both red and white wine. Historically, its vineyards have been planted with Pinot Noir. Today, more and more Chardonnay can be found, and it is the white wines which have the greater renown and which achieve the higher prices. This is not just because of the proximity of the *grands crus* of Le Montrachet and Bâtard-Montrachet, both of which *climats* straddle the Puligny-Chassagne *commune* boundary (indeed the smallest and most southerly of the white wine *grands crus*, Criots-Bâtard-Montrachet, falls entirely within Chassagne) nor solely as a result of the current demand for fine white Burgundy. The white wines simply are better. The reds are good full-bodied, stalwart, workhorse examples of the Pinot Noir, somewhat burly, occasionally rustic—similar in a way to those of Pommard or even the less distinctive examples of the Côte de Nuits. The whites, too, are full and firm, less definitive perhaps than those of Puligny, but with a better grip than the majority of Meursaults. When comparing generic examples of the same shipper, I normally find the Chassagne more exciting than the latter, if not the former.

History

As in many places in this part of France, the village has had a turbulent history. It was known as Cassaneas in AD 886, leading Christopher Fielden and John Arlott (*Burgundy, Vines and Wines*) to suggest a connection with a diminutive of the Latin *casa*, a house. And surely the *premier cru* La Romanée has a Roman connection. The local *seigneur* toward the end of the Middle Ages was Jean de Chalons, Prince of Orange. His castle, at the top of the *côte* surrounded by what was then the village of Chaissagne, was besieged by the army of Louis XI at the end of the fifteenth century, for the Prince had sided with Louis's rival, Margaret of Burgundy. After much attrition the locals had to capitulate, and for their mischance in being on the losing side they had their village burned to the ground.

Eventually, a new village sprang up halfway down the slope. This was largely monastic in its origins. The Abbot of Maizières, recognising the vinous value of the local terrain, cleared much of the hillside, planted vines and built a local priory, the Abbaye de Morgeot, to house the brothers who worked on the vineyards. A sister establishment was established by the Abbess of Saint-Jean-le-Grand. Morgeot and Clos-Saint-Jean remain two of the largest and most important *premiers crus*.

Historically, as I have said, Chassagne was a red wine village like most in the Côte d'Or. Montrachet seems always to have been renowned for its white wines, but elsewhere, except in Meursault, what was made was red. Camille Rodier (*Le Vin de Bourgogne*, 1920) quotes a Dr. Ramain, who himself had dug up an inventory belonging to the then Marquis de Laguiche, lord of the village in the eighteenth century and still an important landowner today. This document stipulated that a bottle of the Marquis's (red) Morgeot was worth two bottles of his Montrachet. As Rodier comments, "For a moment God is eclipsed by one of his saints."

Jullien (*Topographie de tous les Vins Connus*, 1816) cites the red wines of Chassagne among those of his third class and notes that the wines of "Morjot," La Maltroie and Clos-Saint-Jean are among his first class, alongside lesser *grands crus* such as Clos-de-Tart and Clos-de-la-Roche in Morey and the *climats* of Musigny and Les Amoureuses in Chambolle. No mention is made of white wines in the village apart from Le Montrachet and its satellites. This dearth of Chardonnay is confirmed by Dr. Lavalle, who wrote one of the most interesting source-books on Burgundy in 1855: "If one excepts the vineyard producing the white wines called Montrachet, one finds only a few *ouvrées* here and there in Pinot Blanc, as in Ruchotte, for example ... everywhere the Pinot Noir is planted in the good sites and Gamay in the poorer soils." However, he also mentions that Chassagne is the *commune* in Burgundy where one finds the Pinot Beurot or Pinot Gris (the so-called Tokay d'Alsace) also a white grape, in the greatest abundance.

The observation quoted above is repeated verbatim (without acknowledgement!) by Camille Rodier. The red wines, in Rodier's view, although less elegant than those of Volnay, have more colour and body. They last well. They have an "indisputable similarity to some of the great wines of the Côte de Nuits."

Yet by the 1930s, there must have been more than just a token amount of Chardonnay outside the *grands crus*. I can remember bottles of the 1940s, though I have never sampled wines of the pre-War period. But Morton Shand, writing in 1929, and even Warner Allen, as late as 1952, make no mention of the Chassagne white, concentrating their purple prose on Le Montrachet itself. It must be said, however, that their knowledge of France's vineyards was largely acquired second-hand, absorbed through the bottle itself. They probably never actually went and talked to a grower on the spot.

Old men with long memories of the village and its wines can remember when it was first decided to move from red wine to white. It was when the vineyards were being replanted after the *phylloxera* epidemic. Was this perhaps, I suggested, because the Chardonnay took to its graft better than the Pinot Noir? This was one of the explanations for why Sancerre, originally a red wine, became white. But they claim no: it was merely a response to a changing fashion. By the time of the introduction of the laws of *appellation contrôlée* in 1936, some 20 to 25 percent of Chassagne's vineyards produced white wine. And, unlike most of the villages in the Côte d'Or, the top vineyards of Chassagne are allowed to produce *premier cru* wine of either colour. Since the Second World War, the move to white has accelerated. The grower Albert Morey remembers that when he bought his plot of Caillerets in 1949 the entire *climat* was planted in Pinot Noir. Today, it produces one of the best Chardonnays in the *commune*. In 1982, 48 percent of the village and the *premier cru* wine was white, but by 1992 the percentages were reversed. Today, over 61 percent—but 75 percent of the *premier cru*

wine—of Chassagne's production comes from the Chardonnay. The cause is self-evident: the white wines sell for 50 percent more.

Location

Chassagne is one of the largest *communes* of the Côte d'Or, with nearly 370 hectares under vines. This is similar to its neighbour Santenay, which is smaller than Meursault, but sizeably larger than Puligny. In addition, one must count the entirety of the diminutive *grand cru* Criots-Bâtard-Montrachet (1.6 ha) and just under half of both Le Montrachet (8 ha) and Bâtard-Montrachet (12 ha).

The soil structure is complex. The rocky subsoil, like most of Burgundy, is basically an oolitic limestone. Here it is Bathonian, the same strata which is found in the Côte de Nuits. At Chassagne you can see a quarry halfway up the slope above the village, as well as the production therefrom of polished slabs of pink, beige or grey marblelike stone in the graveyards and fireplaces of the local growers. At various points in the village, the surface soil, essentially limestone debris, has more or less clay, more or less gravel and more or less chalk (Criot is a corruption of *craie*: chalk); it also changes colour. The heavier *terres rouges* are found further down the slope at Morgeot, while higher up along the line from Embazées through Ruchottes to Caillerets, you will find the lighter *terres blanches*. In general, it is here in the leaner more chalky soils of the upper slopes of the village that the best white wines have their origins.

North of the village, the slope from the top of Clos-Saint-Jean down through Les Vergers and Les Chevenottes to the N6 is gentler, the soil contains both clay and gravel, and the Pinot Noir comes into its own, as it does at Morgeots, though much of this *climat* is now under Chardonnay. Finally round toward the border with the *commune* of Saint-Aubin, across which lies this village's best *climat*, Le Charmois, the higher slopes above Les Chaumées have recently been reclaimed from the scrub. Again this cooler, northeast-facing slope has been found to produce good racy white wines.

As I have said, it is the white wines which are the most distinctive. In general, they are full and firm, more akin to Puligny than to the softer, rounder wines of Meursault. From the top of the slope on the Saint-Aubin side, vineyards such as Les Chaumées produce lightish, racy wines with a touch of peach or crabapple, while lower down, say in Chenevottes, the produce is plumper and sometimes a touch four-square. For the best of the more masculine versions of white Chassagne, you need to go to Morgeot; Cailleret and Les Grandes Ruchottes upslope are flowery, racy and feminine. Embazées and La Romanée are "all in finesse" and lighter still; while in Les Champs-Gain, halfway up the slope, you will get an elegant compromise: fullish, plump, succulent wines. My vote, though, goes to the Cailleret.

The Vineyard

GRANDS CRUS   See Puligny-Montrachet.

PREMIERS CRUS   There are a great many, indeed a record fifty-one, but you will rarely see most of them, for many have the right to be sold under a more familiar name, such as Morgeot. In alphabetical order, they are as follows: Abbaye de Morgeot; Les Baudines; Blanchot-Dessus; Les Boirettes; Bois de Chassagne; Les Bondues; La Boudriotte; Les Brussonnes; En Cailleret; La Cardeuse; Les Champs Gains; La Chapelle; Les Chaumées; Les Chaumes; Les Chenevottes; Clos Chareau; Clos Pitois; Clos Saint-Jean; Les Grands Clos; Les Petits Clos; Les Combards; Les Commes; En Crets; Ez Crottes; Dent de Chien; Les Embazées (or Embrazées); Les Fairendes; La Grande Borne; Les Petites Fairendes; Francemont; Guerchère; Champs Jendreau; Les Macherelles; La Maltroie; La Grande Montagne; Morgeot; Les Murées; Les Pasquelles; Petingeret; Les Places; Les Rebichets; En Remilly; La Romanée; La Roquemaure; Les Grandes Ruchottes; Tête du Clos; Tonton Marcel; Les Vergers; Vide Bourse; Vigne Blanche; Vigne Derrière; En Virondot. These cover 141.25 hectares and produce around 1,400 hectolitres of red wine and 4,500 hectolitres of white wine per year.

VILLAGE WINE   There are 150.08 hectares of village Chassagne-Montrachet. Production averages 3,750 hectolitres of red and 3,200 hectolitres of white wine per year.

Readers will note that over 75 percent of Chassagne-Montrachet *premier cru* is white wine, while just over 45 percent of village wine is this colour. This is logical. Most of the slope, excellent for Chardonnay, is *premier cru*. The lower lying land, more suitable for red wine, is village *appellation contrôlée*.

The Premiers Crus

EN REMILLY	(1.56 ha)
DENT DE CHIEN	(0.64 ha)
BLANCHOT DESSUS	(1.32 ha)
VIDE BOURSE	(1.17 ha)

These are the *premiers crus* on the north side of the N6, and they seem to produce nothing but white wine. Blanchot Dessus lies directly next to Le Montrachet, on slightly lower land. Dent de Chien and En Remilly have been carved out of the rock above, while Vide Bourse lies downslope from Bâtard-Montrachet.

Vide Bourse can produce rather a four-square wine; En Remilly and Dent de Chien are really quite the opposite, all raciness and flowers. Darviot's Blanchot is a serious example, worth catching if you can.

RECOMMENDED SOURCES
EN REMILLY
Michel Colin-Deléger (Chassagne-Montrachet); Philippe Brenot (Santenay).

BLANCHOT DESSUS
Didier Darviot-Perrin (Monthelie); Jean-Noël Gagnard, Michel Anglade-Deléger (both Chassagne-Montrachet).

DENT DE CHIEN
Château de la Maltroye (Chassagne-Montrachet).

VIDE BOURSE
Bernard Morey, Fernand and Laurent Pillot (both Chassagne-Montrachet).

LES CHAUMÉES	(7.43 ha)
LES VERGERS	(9.41 ha)
(including Petangeret, Les Pasquelles)	
LES CHENEVOTTES	(9.26 ha)
(including Les Commes)	
LES BONDUES	(1.73 ha)
(can be sold as Les Chenevottes)	
LES MACHERELLES	(5.19 ha)

On the opposite side of the N6, facing almost due east, lie these *premiers crus*. I list them from the top of the slope downward. Here again, most of the wines are white, the most racy from Chaumées, the richest, but perhaps a little lumpy, from Chenevottes and Macherelles. But this is a good composite site.

RECOMMENDED SOURCES
LES CHAUMÉES (*blanc*)
Michel Colin-Deléger (Chassagne-Montrachet).

LES VERGERS (*blanc*)
Guy Amiot-Bonfils, Michel Colin-Deléger, Richard Fontaine-Gagnard, Michel Niellon, Fernand and Laurent Pillot, Jean and Jean-Marc Pillot, Ramonet (all Chassagne-Montrachet).

LES CHEVENOTTES
Michel Colin-Deléger, Richard Fontaine-Gagnard, Jean-Noël Gagnard, Château de la Maltroye, Bernard Moreau, Jean and Jean-Marc Pillot (all Chassagne-Montrachet).

LES MACHERELLES (*blanc*)
Guy Amiot-Bonfils, Jean and Jean-Marc Pillot (both Chassagne-Montrachet); Hubert Lamy (Saint-Aubin).

LES MACHERELLES (*rouge*)
Jean and Jean-Marc Pillot (Chassagne-Montrachet).

CLOS SAINT-JEAN	(14.16 ha)
(including Les Rebichets, Les Murées)	
LA MALTROIE	(11.61 ha)
(including Les Places, En Crets)	

Clos Saint-Jean lies above the village, under the largest of the quarries, while La Maltroie lies on the other side of the road and houses which connect Chassagne-le-Haut with Chassagne-le-Bas. You would expect Clos Saint-Jean to be preferred for white wine and La Maltroie for red. Curiously, the opposite is the case. There is a little Pinot Noir, which belongs to the village and is vinified in turn by the local growers, in La Maltroie, but otherwise, most of the wines are white, a major exception being those of the Château de la Maltroye (spelled with a *y*) which has the majority of the Clos du Château immediately beneath the mansion.

Moreover, while many growers have replanted their Clos Saint-Jean in Chardonnay, I find it one of the least convincing *premiers crus en blanc*. The wine seems to me to lack both substance and fruit. No doubt the age of the vines comes into it. But I'm convinced this is not the whole explanation. There must be something in the soil which detracts from the character of the Chardonnay. Red Clos Saint-Jean, on the other hand, can be rich, full, juicy and most enjoyable, slightly less heavy and less spicy than Morgeot.

RECOMMENDED SOURCES
CLOS SAINT-JEAN (*rouge*)
Guy Amiot-Bonfils, Richard Fontaine-Gagnard, Jean-Noël Gagnard, Lamy-Pillot, Château de Maltroye, Ramonet (all Chassagne-Montrachet).

LA MALTROIE (*blanc*)
Michel Colin-Deléger, Richard-Fontaine Gagnard, Jean-Noël Gagnard, Château de la Maltroye, Bernard Moreau, Michel Niellon (all Chassagne Montrachet).

LA MALTROIE (*rouge*)
Château de la Maltroye (Chassagne Montrachet).

EN CAILLERET	(19.67 ha)
(including Les Combards, Vigne Derrière)	
LES CHAMPS GAINS	(4.62 ha)
LA GRANDE MONTAGNE	(2.78 ha)
(including Tonton Marcel, En Virondot)	
LES GRANDES RUCHOTTES	(2.13 ha)
(can be sold as La Grande Montagne)	
LA ROMANÉE	(3.35 ha)
(can be sold as La Grande Montagne)	
BOIS DE CHASSAGNE	(4.38 ha)
LES EMBAZÉES OR EMBRAZÉES	(5.19 ha)
(can be sold as Bois de Chassagne)	
LES BAUDINES	(3.60 ha)
(can be sold as Bois de Chassagne)	

These are the *climats* on the *côteaux* above the road that leads down from Chassagne to

Santenay. This is the best section for white Chassagne. The vineyards lie at 250–330 metres, are well exposed but sheltered and face directly southeast. The wines here lose the somewhat clumsy, four-square aspect of other white Chassagnes, and they gain in both raciness and depth. At the Chassagne end (En Cailleret, Les Champs Gains), the wines are fuller and less mineral in character than at the Santenay end (Les Baudines, Les Embazées). This *côteau* is almost entirely planted in Chardonnay.

RECOMMENDED SOURCES

EN CAILLERET
Guy Amiot-Bonfils, Bachelet-Ramonet, Jean-Marc Blain-Gagnard, Richard Fontaine-Gagnard, Jean-Noël Gagnard, Bernard Morey, Marc Morey, Michel Morey-Coffinet, Jean and Jean-Marc Pillot, Paul Pillot, Ramonet (all Chassagne-Montrachet); Marc Colin (Saint-Aubin); René Lequin-Colin (Santenay).

LES CHAMPS GAINS
Guy Amiot-Bonfils, Jean-Noël Gagnard, Michel Niellon, Jean and Jean-Marc Pillot (all Chassagne-Montrachet); Marc Colin (Saint-Aubin).

LA GRANDE MONTAGNE
Richard Fontaine-Gagnard, Lamy-Pillot (both Chassagne-Montrachet).

LES GRANDES RUCHOTTES
Bernard Moreau, Château de la Maltroye, Fernand and Laurent Pillot, Paul Pillot, Ramonet (all Chassagne-Montrachet).

LA ROMANÉE
Bachelet-Ramonet, Château de Maltroye, Michel Morey-Coffinet, Paul Pillot (all Chassagne-Montrachet).

LES EMBAZÉES
Bernard Morey (who spells it Embrazées) (Chassagne-Montrachet).

LES BAUDINES
Bernard Morey (Chassagne-Montrachet).

MORGEOT   (54.23 ha)

The following *climats* can sell their wine as Morgeot: Les Boirettes; La Boudriotte; Les Brussonnes; Champs Jendreau; La Chapelle;

Les Chaumes; Clos Chareau; Clos Pitois; Ez Crottes; Les Fairendes; Francemont; La Grande-Borne; Les Grands Clos; Guerchère; Les Petites Fairendes; Les Petits Clos; La Roquemaure; Tête du Clos; and Vigne Blanche.

This incorporates not only all the *premier cru* land below the Chassagne-Santenay road, around the Abbaye de Morgeot itself, but also the flatter land above the road, where the vineyards lie underneath those described in the previous section. The only *climats* declared separately seem to be Boudriotte and Vigne Blanche, and usually by growers who also offer a Morgeot.

Judging by production figures, the land is equally divided between Chardonnay and Pinot Noir here, with Morgeot being the major source for *premier cru rouge*. The whites, in my experience, can be a bit too fat and heavy-footed for comfort, for this, I believe, is really red wine soil. The reds are sturdy, quite muscular and dense when they are young, and fuller and spicier than Clos Saint-Jean, but they mellow with age and can give some nice bottles when 7 years old or so.

RECOMMENDED SOURCES

MORGEOT (*blanc*)
Bachelet-Ramonet, Jean-Marc Blain-Gagnard, Michel Colin-Deléger, Richard Fontaine-Gagnard, Jean-Noël Gagnard, Jacques Gagnard-Delagrange, Lamy-Pillot, Bernard Moreau, Fernand and Laurent Pillot, Jean and Jean-Marc Pillot, Paul Pillot, Ramonet (all Chassagne-Montrachet); Duc du Magenta/Jadot (Chassagne-Montrachet/Beaune); Henri Germain (Meursault); Vincent Girardin (Santenay).

MORGEOT (*rouge*)
Richard Fontaine-Gagnard, Jean-Noël Gagnard, Lamy-Pillot, Jean and Jean-Marc Pillot, Ramonet (all Chassagne-Montrachet); Duc de Magenta/Jadot (Chassagne-Montrachet/Beaune); Vincent Girardin, René Lequin-Colin (both Santenay).

LA BOUDRIOTTE (*blanc*)
Jean-Marc Blain-Gagnard, Jacques Gagnard-Delagrange, Château de la Maltroye, Ramonet (all Chassagne-Montrachet).

LA BOUDRIOTTE (*rouge*)

Lamy-Pillot, Ramonet (which offers both La Boudriotte and a Clos de la Boudriotte) (both Chassagne-Montrachet); Larue (Saint-Aubin).

The Growers

Guy Amiot-Bonfils

12.45 ha owned and *en fermage/en métayage*. Le Montrachet (0.09 ha); Chassagne-Montrachet *premier cru blanc* in Les Baudines, En Cailleret, Les Champs Gains, Clos Saint-Jean, Les Macherelles, La Maltroie and Les Vergers; Chassagne-Montrachet *premier cru rouge* in Clos Saint-Jean and La Maltroie; Puligny-Montrachet *premier cru* Les Demoiselles; Saint-Aubin *premier cru blanc* En Remilly; village Chassagne-Montrachet *rouge et blanc*; Santenay *rouge* in the *lieu-dit* La Comme Dessus.

Unlike the others in the village who have constructed new cellars and warehouses down on the plain, Guy Amiot and his son Thierry enlarged their own underground cellar. Guy Amiot's father was an absentee landlord and leased much of the land out to neighbours on a *métayage* basis, and so it was not until the late 1990s that Amiot was responsible for every aspect of his wine. The Montrachet and all the reds are bottled unfiltered. This is a very good source.

Michel Anglada-Deléger

3 ha owned and *en fermage*. Chassagne-Montrachet *premier cru* Blanchot-Dessus.

Michel Anglada is brother-in-law to Michel Colin-Deléger, having married Georges Deléger's other daughter. For 20 years he was in the French Air Force, retiring in 1995. He makes one delicious wine. The rest is now sold or rented to Philippe and Bruno, sons of Michel Colin. He describes his winemaking methods as "traditional": no *bâtonnage*, 20 percent new wood and bottling after a year. As a sideline, he runs A.D. Wines, selling fine Burgundy to private clients.

Bachelet-Ramonet

12.7 ha owned. Bâtard-Montrachet (0.56 ha); Bienvenues-Bâtard-Montrachet (0.13 ha); Chassagne-Montrachet *premier cru blanc* in En Cailleret, La Grande Montagne, Les Grandes Ruchottes, Les Morgeots and La Romanée; Chassagne-Montrachet *premier cru rouge* in Clos de la Boudriotte, Clos Saint-Jean and Morgeot; village Chassagne-Montrachet *rouge et blanc*; village Puligny-Montrachet.

This estate used to produce marvellous wines but went rapidly downhill in the 1980s, when Jean Bachelet became old, tired, unwell, and seemingly not up to the task. It is now his son-in-law Alain Bonnefoy who is in charge, and the whites, whose signature had always been an elegant delicacy, have improved. They have always been more interesting than the reds. Ninety percent of this domaine is picked by machine.

★ Jean-Marc Blain-Gagnard

8.17 ha owned and *en fermage*. Le Montrachet (0.08 ha); Bâtard-Montrachet (0.34 ha); Criots-Bâtard-Montrachet (0.21 ha); Chassagne-Montrachet *premier cru blanc* in La Boudriotte, En Cailleret, Clos Saint-Jean and Morgeot; Chassagne-Montrachet *premier cru rouge* in Morgeot and Clos Saint-Jean; village Chassagne-Montrachet *blanc et rouge*; village Pommard.

Jean-Marc Blain is the senior of Jacques Gagnard's sons-in-law, though married to the younger daughter Claudine. He produced his first vintage in 1980. Part of the Bâtard plus the yield of the Montrachet used to be labelled as Edmond Delagrange-Bachelet, his wife's maternal grandfather. Blain's white wines, like those of the rest of the family, concentrate on the finesse and the fruit and are delicate for Chassagnes. But they are all the more attractive as a result. This is a fine source.

Chateau de Chassagne-Montrachet

25 ha owned. Corton Clos des Fiètres (0.40 ha); Chassagne-Montrachet *premier cru rouge* Les Chaumées; Saint-Aubin *premier cru blanc* in Le Charmois and Pitangeret; Saint-Aubin *premier cru rouge* in Le Charmois, Les Frionnes and Pitangeret; village Chassagne-Montrachet *rouge et blanc*; village Beaune.

The origins of the château, now solely visible as part of the impressive *caves*, date from the eleventh century. It has been much knocked about and rebuilt since, most recently and importantly in the eighteenth century. The firm Michel Picard acquired it in 2000. It is now its base. The wines are unexciting. In 2006 Maison Picard bought the 7.5-hectare domaine of Bernard Colin, cousin of the Bruno Colin below.

Bruno Colin

8.31 ha owned and *en fermage*. Puligny-Montrachet *premier cru* La Truffière; Chassagne-Montrachet *premier cru blanc* in La Boudriotte, Les Chaumées, Les Chenevottes, La Maltroie, Morgeot, En Remilly and Les Vergers; Saint-Aubin *premier cru blanc* Le Charmois; Chassagne-Montrachet *premier cru rouge* La Maltroie; Santenay *premier cru* Les Gravières; Maranges *premier cru* La Fussière; village Chassagne-Montrachet *rouge et blanc*; village Santenay.

Alongside his father Michel (see below), Bruno Colin uses the old family *cuverie* and cellar in the heart of the village, which he has recently enlarged. Judging by the 2004 and 2005 vintages, the first two since the family division, quality is every bit as good here as it was in the time Michel was in charge.

Philippe Colin

7 ha owned and *en fermage*. Chevalier-Montrachet (0.08 ha); Chassagne-Montrachet *premier cru blanc* in Les Chaumées, Les Chenevottes, Dent de Chien, Les Embrazées, La Maltroie, Morgeot, En Remilly and Les Vergers; Saint-Aubin *blanc premier cru* in Les Champlots, Le Charmois and Les Combes; Montagny *premier cru* "En Varigny"; Chassagne-Montrachet *premier cru rouge* Morgeot; Maranges *premier cru rouge* La Fussière; Santenay *premier cru rouge* Les Gravières; village Chassagne-Montrachet *rouge et blanc*; village Santenay; village Maranges.

Philippe Colin, the younger of Michel Colin's two sons, operates from the industrial estate below the village. His En Remilly is from a different, older parcel (planted in 1962) than that of Michel. He also buys in or farms parcels which still technically belong to Georges and Robert Deléger or to Michel Anglada (see above), and these are incorporated into the preceding statistics. He is thinking about keeping the wines longer than the 12 to 14 months traditional in the family. It is a question of space.

★ *Michel Colin-Deléger*

0.70 ha owned and *en fermage/en métayage*. Chevalier-Montrachet (0.08 ha); Chassagne-Montrachet *premier cru* En Remilly; Puligny-Montrachet *premier cru* Les Demoiselles.

After the 2003 harvest, the Michel Colin-Deléger domaine was split, with Michel himself retaining the juiciest plums. He is an excellent winemaker; his Demoiselles are rather superior to the other two examples. I regularly buy his En Remilly, too (and wish I could afford more of the Chevalier-Montrachet!).

Michel Coutoux

Michel Coutoux is Michel Niellon's son-in-law. He married Niellon's daughter Françoise in 1991, and since then, he has been Niellon's right-hand man. Niellon is now in his early seventies. In 1997 Coutoux decided to set up a parallel merchant's business. He buys in fruit and must, and he makes only white wines, bottling after 12 months. The wines are generally very good.

★ *Vincent Dancer*

5.15 ha owned. Chevalier-Montrachet (0.90 ha); Chassagne-Montrachet *premier cru blanc* in La Romanée, Tête du Clos (Morgeot) and *rouge* in La Grande Borne (Morgeot); Meursault *premier cru* Les Perrières; Pommard *premier cru* Les Pézerolles; Beaune *premier cru* Les Montrevenots; village Meursault in the *lieux-dits* Les Corbins and Les GrandsCharrons; village Chassagne-Montrachet *rouge et blanc*; village Pommard in the *lieu-dit* Les Perrières.

Vincent Dancer started off with 3.5 hectares in 1996. Now, more has been passed down from his uncle Philippe Ballot in Meursault, and various share-cropping arrangements came to their end in 2004. But nevertheless, he makes 11 wines from 5.5 hectares—very Burgundian! Dancer, however, is a fine winemaker. The domaine went biodynamic in 2006.

Jean and Pierre Duperrier-Adam

5.6 ha owned. Chassagne-Montrachet *premier cru* En Cailleret; Saint-Aubin *premier cru blanc* in Les Perrières and Le Sentier du Clou; village Chassagne-Montrachet; village Puligny-Montrachet.

Jean Duperrier was a math teacher and a weekend *vigneron*. He then had heart problems and was advised to give up the professional side of his life. He works with his son Pierre. This is a very good source for Cailleret, which lies at the bottom of the garden. It is not too oaky, despite being vinified and matured in 100 percent new wood.

★ Richard Fontaine-Gagnard

10 ha owned and *en métayage*. Le Montrachet (0.08 ha); Bâtard-Montrachet (0.30 ha); Criots-Bâtard-Montrachet (0.33 ha); Chassagne-Montrachet *premier cru blanc* in Bois de Chassagne, La Boudriotte, En Cailleret, Les Chenevottes, Clos des Murées, Clos Saint-Jean, La Maltroie, Morgeot, La Romanée and Les Vergers; Chassagne-Montrachet *premier cru rouge* in Clos Saint-Jean and Morgeot; Volnay *premier cru* Clos des Chênes; Pommard *premier cru* Les Rugiens; village Chassagne-Montrachet *rouge et blanc*.

The affable Richard Fontaine, brother-in-law and immediate neighbour of Jean-Marc Blain (see above) can offer you as many as 10 different *premier cru blanc* Chassagnes, a wonderfully educational experience. Like *chez* his brother-in-law, these get some 30 percent new wood and are bottled after a year. I would like to see more Chassagne growers extend this to 18 months. There is fine wine here, though, in both colours.

★ Jean-Noël Gagnard

11 ha owned. Bâtard-Montrachet (0.37 ha); Chassagne-Montrachet *premier cru blanc* in Blanchot-Dessus, En Cailleret, Les Champs Gains, Les Chaumées, Les Chenevottes, Clos de la Maltroie, Morgeot and La Maltroie; Chassagne-Montrachet *premier cru rouge* in Clos Saint-Jean and Morgeot; village Chassagne-Montrachet *rouge*, Cuvée Lestimé, *et blanc*, Les Masures and Les Chaumes; Santenay *premier cru* Clos de Tavannes.

The attractive Caroline Lestimé, Jean-Noël Gagnard's only child, took over when he retired in 1989, but in my view it was not until 1994 that her presence made itself felt. From this vintage onward, the white wine results have been not merely very good but fine. Yields have been reduced, there is a less heavy hand with the sulphur, and bottling now takes place after 18 months. The reds, sadly, remain a bit slight.

★ François and Vincent Jouard

10.42 ha owned. Bâtard-Montrachet (0.13 ha); Chassagne-Montrachet *premier cru blanc* in Les Chaumées, Les Champs Gains, La Maltroie and Morgeot; Chassagne-Montrachet *premier cru rouge* in Clos Saint-Jean and Morgeot; village Chassagne-Montrachet *rouge et blanc*.

The Jouard brothers' domaine emerged in the mid-1990s, with much being leased off to others, and most of their own produce, for cash flow reasons, was sold off in bulk. Now the leases have come to an end, and the Jouards are bottling more and more themselves. They use *lutte raisonnée* in the vineyards and one third new oak for the whites, which are bottled after 12 months. The wines are of fine quality here.

Gabriel and Paul Jouard

10.5 ha owned and *en fermage*. Bâtard-Montrachet (0.04 ha); Chassagne-Montrachet *premier cru* in Les Baudines, Les Chaumées "Clos de la Truffière," Les Morgeots and Vide Bourse; Saint-Aubin *premier cru tout court*; village Chassagne-Montrachet *rouge*, including a *vieilles vignes cuvée*, and *blanc*; village Santenay *rouge et blanc*.

Paul Jouard, cousin of the two Jouards above, joined his father (who died in 2003) in 1992. All his top wines are white, with the last, the Morgeots, having been changed from red in 1990, and they are given 40 to 50 percent new wood. Bottling takes place after just over a year. There are very good wines here. The Vide Bourse (an isolated *premier cru* downslope from Bâtard), as always, is the least advanced, but the best.

Marquis de Laguiche

4.75 ha owned. Le Montrachet (2.06 ha); Chassagne-Montrachet *premier cru* Morgeot (*blanc et rouge*); village Chassagne-Montrachet *blanc*.

This famous estate sells its produce under contract to Maison Joseph Drouhin of Beaune. Is this perhaps the best Montrachet of them all?

Although the vines are looked after by the domaine's own personnel, the viticultural programme is a joint effort between Philippe Drouhin and the Marquis, and it is Drouhin's team which harvests the fruit and makes the wine.

Lamy-Pillot

18.5 ha owned and *en fermage/en métayage*. Le Montrachet (0.05 ha); Chassagne-Montrachet *premier cru blanc* in Les Caillerets, La Grande Montagne, Clos Saint-Jean, Morgeot, plus a *premier cru tout court*; Chassagne-Montrachet *premier cru rouge* in La Boudriotte, Clos-Saint-Jean and Morgeot; Saint-Aubin *premier cru blanc* in Le Charmois, Les Combes and En Créot; Saint-Aubin *premier cru rouge* Les Castets; village Chassagne-Montrachet *rouge et blanc*; village Saint-Aubin *rouge et blanc* Les Pucelles; village Beaune in the *lieu-dit* Les Blanches Fleurs; village Santenay.

Solid, burly, red-faced, and with a handshake like a vice, René Lamy, brother of Hubert of Saint-Aubin, has one of the largest collections of corkscrews I have ever seen: 730 examples, at the last count.

He is now in semi-retirement, and responsibility has passed to his daughters Florence Caillat-Lamy and Karine Cadot-Lamy and their husbands. It is Sébastien Caillat who is responsible for making the wines. Things have been fine-tuned: yields have been reduced, a vibrating *table de tri* was introduced, and there is now proper temperature control of the fermentations and less recourse to sulphur. The wines are now very good.

Duc de Magenta

In 1986 the Duc de Magenta entered into a long-term contract with Jadot (see page 212), which now takes some 80 percent of the yield,

in the form either of grapes (for the red wines) or of must (for the white). Until the harvest, the vines are the responsibility of Magenta and his team; Jadot merely ensures that the harvest is not too excessive.

★ Château de la Maltroye

14.5 ha owned. Bâtard-Montrachet (0.09 ha); Chassagne-Montrachet *premier cru blanc* in Les Baudines, Les Chenevottes, Clos du Château de la Maltroye, Les Dents de Chien, Les Grandes Ruchottes, Les Macherelles, Morgeot (including Les Crêts, Les Fairendes, Vigne Blanche) and La Romanée; Chassagne-Montrachet *premier cru rouge* in La Boudriotte, Clos du Château de Maltroye and Clos Saint-Jean; Santenay *premier cru rouge et blanc* in La Comme and Les Gravières; Chassagne-Montrachet *rouge et blanc*.

In the days of André Cournut, this cellar was a shambles, and the quality of the wines reflected the mess. André's son Jean-Pierre took over in 1995 and put things in order, and the wine has vastly improved. The vines are tended by *lutte raisonnée* and now almost entirely ploughed. Yields are low, fermentation is started in tank before the must is transferred to casks (10 to 100 percent new) and the spotless cellar is temperature controlled. The whites are bottled after 12 months. Quality is now high here.

Cournut also has a wholesale licence and occasionally buys Hospices de Beaune wines.

Bernard Moreau

14.14 ha owned and *en fermage*. Chassagne-Montrachet *premier cru blanc* in Les Champs Gains, Les Chenevottes, Les Grandes Ruchottes, La Maltroie and Morgeot; Chassagne-Montrachet *premier cru rouge* in Morgeot, La Cardeuse (*monopole*); Saint-Aubin *premier cru blanc* En Remilly; village Chassagne-Montrachet (*rouge et blanc*).

Offering more choice in white and more volume in red is how the friendly Bernard Moreau and his sons Alexandre and Benoît explain their domaine. Quality has improved over the last decade. Firstly, *lutte raisonnée* and ploughing is occurring in the vineyards; secondly, a pneumatic press and a *table de tri* have been installed in the winery. One third new wood is used and the whites are bottled after 12 to 15 months. The domaine increased in size by almost 5 hectares by the acquisition of a lease in 2005. These are very good wines.

★ Bernard Morey

15 ha owned and *en fermage*. Bâtard-Montrachet (0.075 ha); Chassagne-Montrachet *premier cru blanc* in Les Baudines, Les Caillerets, Les Embazées (spelled Embrazées), Morgeot and Vide-Bourse; Puligny-Montrachet *premier cru* La Truffière; Santenay *premier cru blanc* Passetemps; Santenay *premier cru rouge* Grand Clos Rousseau; Beaune *premier cru* Les Grèves; Saint-Aubin *premier cru blanc* Le Charmois; Maranges *premier cru* La Fussière; village Chassagne-Montrachet *rouge et blanc*; village Santenay; village Maranges.

Brother of Jean-Marc (see below), the genial Bernard Morey, now working with his sons Vincent and Thomas, moved into a house on the road by the Abbaye de Morgeot, below which is an extensive cellar, some 15 years ago, but he still stores his white wine in cask in the cellars of his father Albert, back in the heart of the village. Very good and very reliable wines in both colours are here: fullish, ample and gently oaky (40 percent new). There is also a flourishing *négociant* business here.

Jean-Marc Morey

8 ha owned and *en fermage*. Bâtard-Montrachet (0.075 ha); Chassagne-Montrachet *premier cru blanc* in Les Caillerets, Les Champs Gains, Les Chaumées and Les Chenevottes; Chassagne-Montrachet *premier cru* in Clos Saint-Jean and Les Champs Gains; Saint-Aubin *premier cru* Le Charmois; Santenay *premier cru rouge* Grand Clos Rousseau; Beaune *premier cru* Les Grèves; village Chassagne-Montrachet *rouge et blanc*; village Santenay *blanc*.

The origins of this domaine lie with that of the Moreys' father Albert, from whom I used to buy in the 1970s. A decade later, the brothers split when Albert reached retirement age. Though the wines are made more or less in the same way (Jean-Marc uses less new oak, however), I don't find things as consistent here as *chez* Bernard, above.

Marc Morey

9.33 ha owned and *en fermage*. Bâtard-Montrachet (0.14); Chassagne-Montrachet *premier cru blanc* Les Caillerets, Les Chenevottes, Morgeot, Les Vergers and En Virondot; Chassagne-Montrachet *premier cru rouge* Morgeot; Puligny-Montrachet *premier cru* Les Pucelles; Saint-Aubin *premier cru blanc* Le Charmois; village Chassagne-Montrachet *rouge et blanc*; village Beaune.

This domaine lies within audible range of the local quarry and is run by Marc Morey's son-in-law Bernard Mollard and his wife Marie-Joseph and daughter Sabine. The cellar was enlarged in 2003. Quality used to be merely good but is now getting better and better. "Perfume and finesse is what I am looking for," I was told. Quite so—with 30 percent new oak for the whites and bottling after 11 months they have it. There is a small merchant's business alongside.

Michel-Morey Coffinet

8.5 ha owned and *en fermage*. Bâtard-Montrachet (0.13 ha); Chassagne-Montrachet *premier cru blanc* in Les Caillerets, Dent de Chien, Blanchot-Dessus, Les Fairendes, En Remilly and La Romanée; Chassagne-Montrachet *premier cru rouge* in Clos Saint-Jean and Morgeot; Puligny-Montrachet *premier cru* Les Pucelles; village Chassagne-Montrachet *rouge et blanc*.

Much of this domaine comes from Fernand Coffinet, Michel Morey's father-in-law; the rest comes from the previous domaine, Michel being the son of Marc. The wines are housed in a magnificent vaulted cellar at the top of the village. Currently, both the Bâtard and the Pucelles are young vines. This is another very good Chassagne source.

★ Michel Niellon

5 ha owned. Chevalier-Montrachet (0.22 ha); Bâtard-Montrachet (0.12 ha); Chassagne-Montrachet *premier cru blanc* in Les Chaumées, Les Chenevottes, Clos Saint-Jean, Les Champs Gains, La Maltroie and Les Vergers; Chassagne-Montrachet *premier cru rouge* in Clos-Saint-Jean and La Maltroie; village Chassagne Montrachet *rouge et blanc*.

Michel Niellon's cellars are almost as small as his domaine. He has two, one underneath his house and the other next to it, and both are exceedingly cramped. The latter, where he keeps the *premiers* crus, can get a bit hot in the summer. He believes in old vines and low *rendements*. Small is beautiful in this case, though I find his *grands crus* proportionately better than his *premiers crus*. At the time of writing, the Vergers are young vines. He bottles after 12 months. I once asked him if he had ever considered bottling later, after 18 months as at Ramonet. The answer was succinct: no.

Fernand and Laurent Pillot

14.9 ha owned and *en fermage*. Chassagne-Montrachet *premier cru blanc* in Les Grandes Ruchottes, Morgeot, Les Vergers and Vide Bourse; Chassagne-Montrachet *premier cru rouge* in Clos-Saint-Jean and Morgeot; Pommard *premier cru* in Les Charmots, Clos de Verger, La Refène and Les Rugiens; Beaune *premier cru* Les Boucherottes; Meursault *premier cru blanc* Les Caillerets; Saint-Aubin *premier cru rouge* Sur le Sentier du Clou; village Santenay; village Puligny-Montrachet; village Chassagne-Montrachet *rouge et blanc*; village Pommard; village Volnay.

Since 1993 this domaine has boasted a total of twenty-three appellations (including generics). Laurent Pillot, son of Fernand, is married to a niece of Pommard's Virgile Pothier-Rieusset, and she brought her family's vineyards with her. A new cellar in the industrial estate was constructed in 1994 and enlarged in 2003. There are very good wines here. As with the following domaine, the arrival of a new generation has had a positive effect.

★ Jean Pillot et Fils

10 ha owned and *en fermage/en métayage*. Chassagne-Montrachet *premier cru blanc* in Les Caillerets, Les Champs Gains, Les Chenevottes, Les Macherelles, Morgeot, Les Vergers and Clos Saint-Jean; Chassagne-Montrachet *premier cru rouge* in Clos Saint-Jean, Les Macherelles and Morgeot; village Chassagne-Montrachet *rouge et blanc*; village Santenay *rouge*; village Puligny-Montrachet.

Jean-Marc Pillot, a trained oenologist, took over responsibilities here from his father Jean in 1995, and at the same time, the domaine relocated to a new, spacious cellar down on the flat land nearer to Chagny. Real progress has been made since. These are very good wines. There is also a merchant's business on the side.

Paul Pillot

12 ha owned and *en fermage*. Chassagne-Montrachet *premier cru blanc* in Les Caillerets, Les Champs Gains, Clos-Saint-Jean, Les Grandes Ruchottes and La Romanée; Chassagne-Montrachet *premier cru rouge* Clos Saint-Jean; Saint-Aubin *premier cru blanc* Le Charmois; village Chassagne-Montrachet *rouge et blanc*.

Paul Pillot is a cousin once removed of the two Pillots above, and half a generation older. He has now been joined by his son Thierry. The wines are good here, if early to develop. I would like to see a shorter crop and a bit more concentration and definition. The Grandes Ruchottes are young vines.

★★★ Ramonet

17 ha owned. Le Montrachet (0.26 ha); Bâtard-Montrachet (0.45 ha); Bienvenues-Bâtard-Montrachet (0.56 ha); Chassagne-Montrachet *premier cru blanc* in Les Boudriottes, Les Caillerets, Les Chaumées, Les Grandes Ruchottes, Morgeot and Les Vergers; Chassagne-Montrachet *premier cru rouge* in Les Boudriottes, Clos de la Boudriotte, Clos-Saint-Jean and Morgeot; Puligny-Montrachet *premier cru* Champ Canet; Saint-Aubin *premier cru blanc* Le Charmois; village Chassagne-Montrachet *rouge et blanc*; village Puligny-Montrachet in the *lieux-dits* Les Enseignères and Les Nosroyes.

Noël and Jean-Claude Ramonet took over from their much-revered grandfather, Pierre ("*Père*"), the creator of this marvellous estate, in 1984. Nothing much has changed, except that today everything is bottled on the spot (previously some buyers employed a local contract bottler).

The beauty of the Ramonet wines is that they are totally individual: more Ramonet than Chassagne. The work is done by instinct, not by the book. And neither Ramonet has had any technical training. Risks are taken, and they do not always come off. But when they do (which is usually), they are brilliant. The Ramonets like to work with a lot of lees, hardly settling out the must. They are also one of the few in Chassagne who bottle after 18 months. These are not wines for the fainthearted. They keep very well indeed.

SANTENAY

With Santenay we come to the last of the important villages of the Côte d'Or. In fact we come to two, for there is Santenay-le-Haut and Santenay-le-Bas with a kilometre between them. Huddling under the Mont de Sène, Santenay-le-Haut is a largely medieval, straggly hamlet of narrow winding streets and ancient patched-up houses. Santenay-le-Bas, on the shores of the river Dheune and the Canal du Centre, which links the Loire with the Sâone, is rather grander and more modern. There are several noble mansions, plus the renovated fortress originally constructed in the fourteenth century for Philippe le Hardi. On the grounds of this castle are two plane trees, said to be the oldest in France, planted by Henri V in 1599. Above the village is the hamlet and thirteenth century chapel of Saint-Jean de Narosse.

The village dates from Gallo-Roman times, when it was known as Santennacum or Santillacum. Archeologists have excavated traces of a temple dedicated to Mercury at the top of the Mont de Sène, which was already a spa by this time. The spring water is said to be extremely salty but beneficial to those suffering from gout and rheumatism.

Because it is a spa, the village has a licence to operate a casino (there is a French law which connects the two). The casino is situated within the thermal complex and was reopened after having been shut for some years, in 1957. Henri Cannard (*Ballades en Bourgogne*) reports that, at least in 1978, it was number two in France, immediately after Vittel and ahead of Vichy.

The Vineyard

Santenay is an important vineyard. Only Gevrey-Chambertin, Beaune and Meursault produce more wine. The vineyards continue the Côte below Chassagne, with the slope gradually shifting its orientation in a gentle "S" shape until the exposure is more south than east, at which point one comes to the border with Maranges and, indeed, the end of the Côte d'Or *département*.

In the northern part of the *commune*, the vineyard soil contains gravel over a marly Argovian limestone—hence the name of Les Gravières for one of the best sites, which lies lower down the slope. Above, in La Comme, the soil is shallower but heavier. There is more clay. Beauregard, which lies next door, is a mixture of the two.

Closer to the village is the *climat* of Passetemps, whose soil is gravelly in character but a touch more alluvial. There is then a gap in the *premiers crus*, with the isolated La Maladière and Beaurepaire above Santenay-le-Bas, where the soil changes to a Bajocian marl, more commonly found in the Côte de Nuits. On the other side of Santenay-le-Haut the soil is richer, heavier and browner in colour, once again based on the hard Bajocian limestone. Here are the *climats* of Grand Clos Rousseau and Les Fourneaux.

PREMIERS CRUS There are thirteen *premiers crus*, in whole or in part. These are as follows: Beauregard; Le Chainey (Grand Clos Rousseau, part); Clos Faubard; Clos des Mouches; Clos de Tavannes; La Comme; Comme-Dessus (part); Les Fourneaux; Les Gravières; Grand Clos Rousseau; La Maladière; Passetemps; Petit Clos Rousseau. These cover 124.29 hectares and produce about 5,400 hectolitres of red wine and 340 hectolitres of white wine per year.

VILLAGE WINE Village Santenay comprises 253.89 hectares and yields about 9,400 hectolitres of red wine and 800 hectolitres of white wine per year. In general Santenay *rouge* comes in two styles: something akin to Chassagne-Montrachet, but earthier, more solid and coarser, from the village *climats* and the southern end of the *commune*, and something lighter and rather more refined from the *premiers crus* at the north end. But even these "lighter" wines have plenty of body. They are Beaune-ish rather than Saint-Romain-ish. They are not expensive, and they are becoming increasingly round, fruity and attractive as vinification techniques control the temperature, abandon the stems and forswear excessive *pigeage*.

The whites, too, have improved. They should be crisp, medium-bodied and fruity, less racy but fuller than Saint-Aubins, perhaps with a touch of spice. They can, of course, be thin and anonymous, and in some cases heavy and rustic, but these examples, thank God, are getting rarer. There has been a lot of progress in Santenay in recent years, and wine lovers could do well to pinpoint the village as a source of good value in both colours.

The Premiers Crus

CLOS DE TAVANNES	*(5.32 ha)*
(can also be sold as Les Gravières)	
LA COMME	*(21.61 ha)*
LES GRAVIÈRES	*(23.85 ha)*
BEAUREGARD	*(17.91 ha)*
CLOS FAUBARD	*(5.14 ha)*
CLOS DES MOUCHES	*(1.57 ha)*
PASSETEMPS	*(11.47 ha)*

This is the better part of the *commune*. There is a local saying that the best wines of Santenay come from east of the belfry. I would add that the closer you are to the Chassagne border (i.e., the most in danger of being out of earshot), the better the wine. According to Claude Muzard, the Clos de Tavannes, the north end of Les Gravières, is the "*grand cru*" of Santenay. This land is propitious for Chardonnay, too, if you choose a good spot at the top of the slope. The red wines range from those which are Volnay-ish, in Les Gravières and Clos de Tavannes, to those which are more solid, Pommard-ish, in La Comme. Both styles have rather more definition and finesse than most Chassagne-Montrachet *premier cru rouge*. Beauregard produces wines of medium weight, a sort of cross between the two but with marginally less flair. The wines of Passetemps are a little less weighty and have less definition still.

RECOMMENDED SOURCES
CLOS DE TAVANNES
Pousse-d'Or (Volnay); Gino Capuano, Lucien Muzard (both Santenay).

LA COMME
Jean-Claude Belland, Roger Belland, Gino Capuano, René Lequin-Colin, Mestre, Prieur-Brunet (all Santenay).

LES GRAVIÈRES
Pousse-d'Or (Volnay); Roger Belland, Gino Capuano, Mestre, Lucien Muzard (all Santenay); Vincent Girardin (Meursault).

BEAUREGARD
Roger Belland (Santenay).

PASSETEMPS
Roger Belland, Philippe Brenot, Mestre (all Santenay).

CLOS-FAUBARD
Mestre (Santenay).

BEAUREPAIRE	*(15.48 ha)*
LA MALADIÈRE	*(13.56 ha)*

These two *climats* produce wines which are medium-full, meaty and sturdy in character. There can be a hot pepperiness about them in their youth. There is good richness and depth, though, and reasonable style: more so than the wines below, less so than the wines above.

RECOMMENDED SOURCES
LA MALADIÈRE
Vincent Girardin (Meursault); Lucien Muzard, Prieur-Brunet (both Santenay).

GRAND-CLOS-ROUSSEAU	*(7.67 ha)*
PETITS-CLOS-ROUSSEAU OR	
CLOS-ROUSSEAU	*(9.84 ha)*
LES FOURNEAUX	*(6.06 ha)*
(can also be sold as Clos Rousseau)	
LE CHAINEY (OR GRAND CLOS ROUSSEAU)	*(0.06 ha)*

These are quite different wines from those produced in Les Gravières and are much closer to Maranges, with which they are contiguous. There is usually a good weight here and a healthy, open, ever-so-slightly rustic aspect to the fruit.

Bernard Morey (Chassagne-Montrachet); Claude Nouveau (Marchezeuil).

CLOS ROUSSEAU

Roger Belland (Santenay); Fernand Chevrot (Maranges).

The Growers

Jean-Claude Belland

12 ha owned and *en fermage*. Chambertin (0.41 ha); Corton, Clos de la Vigne au Saint (0.49 ha); Corton, Les Grèves (0.55 ha); Corton, Les Perrières (0.69 ha); Corton-Charlemagne (0.36 ha); Chassagne-Montrachet *premier cru* Morgeot; Santenay *premier cru* in La Comme and Clos des Gravières; village Aloxe-Corton; village Puligny-Montrachet; village Santenay; village Maranges.

The cramped, damp, mouldy cellars of Jean-Claude Belland lie on the town's main square, the Place Jet d'Eau. Given the domaine's holdings in Corton and Chambertin, it is a pity that the results are unremarkable. Indeed, often the only wines worth noting are the Santenays.

★ Roger Belland

23.9 ha owned. Criots-Bâtard-Montrachet (0.61 ha); Puligny-Montrachet *premier cru* Les Champs Gains; Chassagne-Montrachet *premier cru blanc et rouge* Clos Pitois (*monopole*); Santenay *premier cru* in Beauregard, La Comme and Les Gravières, Maranges *premier cru* in La Fussière; village Santenay *blanc and rouge*, including the *lieux-dits* Les Charmes, Clos Rousseau, Comme-Dessus and Passetemps; village Pommard in the *lieu-dit* Les Cras; village Maranges in the *lieu-dit* Clos Roussot (*sic*).

Roger Belland runs this important domaine with his daughter Julie. The cellar is modern (though there is a more picturesque *caveau de dégustation* under the house); the barrels are all reasonably new (30 percent actually new each year), and the wines are individual and stylish. This is one of the best sources in the village.

Philippe Brenot

5 ha owned and *en métayage*. Bâtard-Montrachet (0.37 ha); Chassagne-Montrachet *premier cru blanc* En Remilly; village Puligny-Montrachet in the *lieu-dit* Les Enseignères; village Chassagne-Montrachet *blanc* in the *lieu-dit* L'Ormeau; Chassagne-Montrachet *premier cru rouge*; Santenay *premier cru* Passetemps; village Santenay in the *lieu-dit* Les Pérolles.

Philippe Brenot is additionally a professor at the Beaune Wine School. He makes particularly good white wines but sells two thirds of the nine *pieces* of Bâtard off in bulk.

Capuano-Ferreri

14 ha owned and *en fermage/en métayage*. Santenay *premier cru* in Clos de Tavannes, La Comme, Les Gravières and Passetemps; village Santenay, including the *lieu-dit* Champ-Claude; Chassagne-Montrachet *premier cru* Morgeot Blanc.

Gino Capuano (his brother-in-law, Jean-Marc Ferreri, is a footballer and sleeping partner in the business) obtains much of his wine through being a share-cropper of the Domaine de l'Abbaye de Santenay (see below). Quality is quite good here.

Françoise and Denis Clair

14.5 ha owned and *en fermage*. Santenay *premier cru* in Beaurepaire, Clos de la Comme, Clos des Mouches and Clos de Tavannes; village Santenay, including the *lieux-dits* Champ Claude and Clos Genet; Saint-Aubin *premier cru* in Les Murgers des Dents de Chien, Les Champlots, Les Frionnes and En Remilly; Puligny-Montrachet *premier cru* La Garenne.

The hospitable Clairs work with their son Jean-Baptiste at this domaine, which lies under the Clos Faubard *climat*. The Saint-Aubins come from Françoise's side of the family. This domaine produces clean, stylish, well-made wines for the medium term.

Michel Clair et Fille
(Domaine Michel Clair
Domaine Anne Clair
Domaine de l'Abbaye de Santenay)

18 ha owned and *en fermage*. Santenay *premier cru* in Clos de Tavannes, La Comme (*rouge et blanc*) and Les

Gravières; village Santenay *rouge et blanc*, including the *lieu-dit* Clos Genet (*rouge*) and Sous la Roche (*blanc*); village Meursault.

From the 2005 vintage, these three domaines, where daughter Anne has increasingly taking over the winemaking, have been regrouped under one name. Much of the land was inherited from grandfather Louis Clair (Domaine de l'Abbaye de Santenay) and was share-cropped. The leases to Domaine Lucien Muzard ran out in 2004, but those to Gino Capuano continue until 2008. Quality is impressive and improving. This is a future star.

Chateau de la Crée

7 ha owned and *en fermage*. Santenay *premier cru rouge* in Beauregard, Beaurepaire, Les Gravières and *blanc* in Clos Faubard; Chassagne-Montrachet *premier cru blanc* in Morgeot; Volnay *premier cru* Clos des Angles; village Meursault, including the *lieux-dits* Les Tillets and Les Grands Charrons; village Santenay, including the *lieux-dits* Clos du Château, Clos de la Confrérie and En Foulot (all *rouge*) and Charmes and En Foulot (both *blanc*); village Volnay; village Pommard; village Maranges.

The Château de la Crée is run by Nicolas Ryhiner and the wine made by Aline Beauné. In May 2005 it was a building site, with the cellars being established and the building itself, which lies in a little park under Santenay-le-Haut, being converted into a deluxe private hotel suitable for conferences. The domaine was much extended in 2005; only three red wines were produced in 2004, and the first vintage was 2004. These were very promising. Watch this space!

Jessiaume Père et Fils

14 ha owned. Santenay *premier cru* Les Gravières (*rouge et blanc*); Beaune *premier cru* Les Cent Vignes; Volnay *premier cru* Les Brouillards; Auxey-Duresses *premier cru* Les Ecusseaux (*rouge et blanc*); village Santenay.

Underneath a spacious vinification and barrel cellar is an extensive rabbit warren of a bottle cellar leading under the courtyard all the way back to the main road. The Jessiaume

family have been here since the 1850s and own 5.5 hectares in Les Gravières. The domaine is run today by Bernard and his sons Marc and Pascal. Sadly, the resultant wine could be rather better than it is at present. Late in 2006 the domaine was acquired by the Scottish millionaire, David Murray, who also owns Château Routas in Provence. The Jessiaume sons remain responsible for the wines on the spot.

Louis Lequin

7 ha owned. Bâtard-Montrachet (0.12 ha); Corton, Les Languettes (0.09 ha); Corton-Charlemagne (0.09 ha); Chassagne-Montrachet *premier cru* Morgeot (*rouge et blanc*); Santenay *premier cru rouge* in Clos Rousseau, La Comme and Passetemps; village Santenay, including the *lieux-dits* Les Charmes, Clos Genet and Les Hâtes; village Pommard; village Nuits-Saint-Georges; village Maranges.

The 58-year-old Louis Lequin and his older brother René (see below) jointly ran the domaine of their late father Jean (Lequin-Roussot) until they went their separate ways after the 1992 harvest. Louis remains at the old Lequin-Roussot premises near the level crossing and now works with his son Antoine. The wines are reliable here, if never very startling. The Corton-Charlemagne is currently young vines.

★ René Lequin-Colin

8.16 ha owned and *en fermage*. Bâtard-Montrachet (0.12 ha); Corton, Les Languettes (0.09 ha); Corton-Charlemagne (0.09 ha); Chassagne-Montrachet *premier cru rouge* Morgeot; Chassagne-Montrachet *premier cru blanc* from Les Caillerets, Morgeot and Les Vergers; Santenay *premier cru* in La Comme and Passetemps; village Nuits-Saint-Georges; village Pommard; village Chassagne-Montrachet *rouge et blanc*, including the *lieux-dits* Les Charrières and Clos Devant; village Santenay *rouge et blanc*, including the *lieux-dits* Les Charmes and Les Hâtes and a *vieilles vignes cuvée*.

Run today by the genial René Lequin and his son François out of modern cellars on the road to Santenay-le-Haut, this is clearly the better of the two Lequin domaines. There is 30 percent new wood for the white wines. The red grapes are entirely de-stemmed, vinified at up to 32°C and given 15 percent new oak. The reds as well as the whites are *bâtonnés*.

Mestre et Fils

18.35 ha owned. Corton from Les Languettes (0.37 ha); Santenay *premier cru rouge* in Clos Faubard, Clos de Tavannes, La Comme, Les Gravières and Passetemps and *blanc*, Beaurepaire, Clos Faubard and Passetemps; Chassagne-Montrachet *premier cru rouge* Morgeot; Chassagne-Montrachet *premier cru blanc* in Tonton Marcel (*monopole*); village Santenay *rouge et blanc*; village Chassagne-Montrachet; village Ladoix *rouge et blanc*; village Aloxe-Corton; village Maranges.

Gérard, Michel and Gilbert Mestre, three of the four sons of Georges Mestre (the fourth, Jean-François, left to take over at Michelot's in Meursault) run this estate and are a reliable source of wines which evolve in the medium term. You'll find them on the main square, at the Place du Jet d'Eau, where they are open 7 days a week. Theirs are good but not great wines.

Jean Moreau

9 ha owned and *en fermage*. Santenay *premier cru rouge* in Beauregard, Clos des Mouches, Clos Rousseau and *premier cru blanc* in Beaurepaire; village Santenay *rouge et blanc*; village Maranges *rouge*; village Pommard Vieilles Vignes; village Meursault in the *lieu-dit* Les Pellands.

Jean-Moreau is now 79, and his domaine is today run by his grandson David and a cousin Emmanuel Nugues. They have been responsible since 2004. Twenty percent of the stems are retained, and the red wines are kept 20 to 24 months in cask. Following Jean's philosophy, there is little new wood in the cellar. There are good wines here, particularly since 2004.

★ Lucien Muzard et Fils

16 ha owned and *en fermage*. Santenay *premier cru rouge* in Beauregard, Clos Faubard, Clos de Tavannes, Les Gravières and La Maladière; Santenay *premier cru blanc* Clos Faubard; village Santenay in the *lieux-dits* Clos des Hâtes, Les Charmes and Champs Claude (*rouge et blanc*); village Chassagne-Montrachet;

village Pommard in the *lieu-dit* Les Cras; village Maranges.

This domaine, now run by the brothers Claude and Hervé Muzard, was until 2004, in part, a share-cropper for the late Louis Clair's Domaine de l'Abbaye de Santenay. The red grapes are de-stemmed, allowed to macerate *à froid* for as much as a week and vinified at a maximum of 32°C. There is up to 30 percent new wood. All the white wines, even the Aligoté, are fermented in barrel. Quality has improved considerably here in recent years, especially since the brothers started vinifying in a new *cuverie* in Dezize-lès-Maranges. This is one of the stars of the village now. There is a small *négociants* business on the side.

Louis Nié, Clos Bellefond

8.5 ha owned. Pommard *premier cru* La Platière; Volnay *premier cru* Les Santenots; Chassagne-Montrachet *premier cru* in Morgeot; Santenay *premier cru* Passetemps; village Santenay in the *lieux-dits* Clos-Bellefond (*monopole*) and Clos Genet.

The headquarters of this estate lie above its monopoly on the edge of the village: a fine château in a park with some impressive mature trees. It is today run by Bernard Chapelle, a grandson of the late Louis Nié. Sadly, the wine does not live up to its setting.

Olivier Père et Fils

10 ha owned and *en fermage*. Santenay *premier cru* Beaurepaire *rouge et blanc*; Savigny-lès-Beaune *premier cru* Les Peuillets; village Santenay in the *lieux-dits* Les Charmes (*rouge*) and Les Bievaux, Les Coteaux Sous les Roches, Clos de Champs Carafe (*blanc*); village Savigny-lès-Beaune *rouge et blanc*.

Antoine Olivier is a bright young man whom I believe is destined to become one of the stars of the commune. He took over from his father in 2003, and has more recently moved down from Santeney-le-Haut to the main village, where he is now installed in the old Girardin premises. He is passionate about Santenay *blanc*, but his reds are good, too. He is also in a small way a merchant, offering, in 2006, *inter alia*, some Nuits-Saint-Georges, Les Damodes.

G. Prieur
Domaine Prieur-Brunet

20 ha owned. Bâtard-Montrachet (0.08 ha); Meursault *premier cru* Charmes; Chassagne-Montrachet *premier cru blanc* Les Embazées; Chassagne-Montrachet *premier cru rouge* Morgeot; Santenay *premier cru rouge* in La Comme and La Maladière; Santenay *premier cru blanc* Clos Rousseau; Beaune *premier cru* Clos du Roi; Pommard *premier cru* La Platière; Volnay *premier cru* Les Santenots; village Meursault, including the *lieux-dits* Les Chevalières and Les Forges; village Santenay, including the *lieux-dits* En Boichot (*blanc*) and Le Foulot (*rouge*).

This well-established domaine can trace its history back to 1804, when a pair of brothers from Change cashed in on the post-revolutionary spoils of the Château Perruchot in Santenay. A more recent event was the marriage between Guy Prieur and Elizabeth Brunet of Meursault. Today, the business is run by Dominique Prieur and his wife Claude Uny-Prieur. This used to be a good source, but it doesn't seem to have moved with the times. It is not in my first division list any longer.

★ Vincent

5 ha owned and *en fermage*. Santenay *premier cru rouge* Beaurepaire, Les Gravières and Passetemps; Auxey-Duresses *premier cru blanc* Les Bréterins; village Auxey-Duresses *blanc* "Les Hautes."

Jean-Claude Vincent and his wife Anne-Marie, a young couple in their thirties, run this increasingly bio estate. They succeeded his grandfather André Bardollet-Bravard in 1997. The red grapes are partly de-stemmed, with the quantity depending on the vintage, and then cold-soaked and vinified at a maximum of 28°C. These get 50 to 80 percent new wood, the whites 30 to 40 percent. There is high quality in both colours here. There is a parallel merchant activity under the name of Vincent-Escalier.

MARANGES

Maranges is where the "Golden Slope" comes to its end. Beyond Santenay, the hills curve round to face due south, and here, shared between three villages, Cheilly, Dezize and Sampigny, which were combined in 1989 to form a single appellation, we have the *vignoble* of Maranges. Administratively, we have crossed the border into the Sâone-et-Loire *département*—which makes life complicated for the writer because wine production details are not included in the Côte d'Or statistics—but this is nevertheless still part of the heart of Burgundy. The Côte Chalonnaise hills are a separate series of outcrops to the southeast.

Prior to the Maranges decree, this was not so much forgotten country as a part of Burgundy which was completely unknown. Most of the wine was red and went into Côte-de-Beaune Villages blends. Since then, people have started to visit Maranges, and for good reason. There is good winemaking, interesting wines and good value here. It is also attractive country.

The Vineyard

A gentle slope, rising up from 240 metres to about 360 metres before you come to the trees, dominates the country to the south, and indeed the village of Cheilly, which lies on the lower land. In one block, shared between the three *communes*, is the *premier cru* land, toward the top of the slope. The soil is varied, a stony, brown limestone, which gets heavier, more clayey and less stony as one journeys downslope. The wine is almost entirely red; it is honest, sturdy and rustic in the best sense, useful for blending with the thinner reds of the lesser villages of the Côte de Beaune, but well worth examining in its own right. It has good acidity, and it keeps well.

PREMIERS CRUS There are ten *premiers crus*, several of which overlap between the three villages.

IN CHEILLY
Clos de la Boutière; Les Clos Roussots (part); La Fussière; En Marange; Les Plantes en Marange.

IN DEZIZE
Les or En Marange(s) (part); Clos de la Fussière; La Croix Moines; La Fussière (part).

IN SAMPIGNY
Le Clos des Loyères; Le Clos des Rois; Les Clos Roussots; Les Maranges (part).

Together, these comprise 82.51 hectares and produce 2,700 hectolitres of red wine per year. Village Maranges occupies 136.77 hectares and produces some 5,400 hectolitres of red wine and 150 hectolitres of white wine per year.

RECOMMENDED SOURCES
See below.

The Growers

Bernard Bachelet et ses Fils

37.5 ha owned and *en fermage*. Chassagne-Montrachet *premier cru rouge et blanc* Morgeot; Meursault *premier cru* Charmes; Pommard *premier cru* Les Chanlins; Maranges *premier cru* La Fussière; Santenay *premier cru* Clos des Mouches; Saint-Aubin *premier cru rouge*; village Puligny-Montrachet; village Meursault in the *lieu-dit* Les Narvaux; village Chassagne-Montrachet *rouge et blanc;* village Santenay; village Gevrey-Chambertin; village Maranges, including the *lieu-dit* Les Clos Roussots.

Vincent, Jean-François and Jean-Louis, forty-something sons of Bernard Bachelet, run this large domaine from the family headquarters in Dezize, but vinification takes place in Chassagne-Montrachet. I have found the standard good and reliable here in both colours.

Maurice Charleux

10 ha owned and *en fermage*. Maranges *premier cru* in Le Clos des Rois and La Fussière; Santenay *premier cru* Clos Rousseau; village Maranges *rouge et blanc*; village Santenay *rouge et blanc*.

Maurice Charleux's cellar is also in Dezize. He took over from his parents in 1970, having worked in the vineyards since he was 14, and now runs the estate with his son Vincent. His style is for a typically sturdy Maranges, vinified with regular *pigeages* for 12 days, but they are neither too dense nor unduly rustic. Indeed, they have been getting steadily better and better. I prefer the Clos des Rois to the Fussière.

Fernand Chevrot

11 ha owned and *en fermage*. Santenay *premier cru* Clos Rousseau; village Maranges *rouge et blanc*.

Fernand Chevrot took on responsibility for the family domaine upon his father's early death in 1967. Now in his late fifties, he is one of the few to make a specialty of the Maranges *blanc*. There are good wines here. The winery is situated under a splendid mansion in the flat lands of Cheilly.

Yvon and Chantal Contat-Grange

7 ha *en fermage*. Maranges *premier cru* in Les Clos Roussots, La Fussière and Les Loyères; village Maranges *rouge et blanc*; village Santenay *rouge et blanc*, including the *lieu-dit* Saint Jean de Narosse.

Neither Yvon Contet nor Chantal Grange is Burgundian. They arrived from the Haute-Savoie in 1981 and have gradually built up this estate, entirely *en fermage*. This is a good source.

Edmond Monnot

11 ha owned and *en fermage*. Maranges *premier cru* in Le Clos des Rois and Les Clos Roussots; Village Maranges in the *lieux-dits* Clos de la Boutière (*monopole*) and Le Clos des Loyères; village Santenay *rouge* in the *lieu-dit* Les Charmes-Dessus; village Santenay *blanc* in the *lieu-dit* Le Chainey.

From Edmond Monnot's terrace in Dezize, there is a splendid panorama down the slopes of the Maranges vineyards to the south (from the Chevrots there is an equally impressive view in the opposite direction). Monnot's wines are perhaps the most elegant of the domaines in the area. He is now assisted by his son Stéphane.

Claude Nouveau

14.25 ha owned and *en fermage*. Santenay *premier cru* Grand Clos Rousseau; Maranges *premier cru* La Fussière; village Santenay, including the *lieu-dit* Les Charmes-Dessus; village Santenay *blanc*; village Maranges.

Claude Nouveau's modern winery is in Marchezeuil, toward Nolay, but I include him here for convenience, rather than in the Hautes-Côtes section, because his vineyard holding is essentially similar to those listed here. His winery is spotless. The reds have good fruit and substance without being rustic; the whites are crisp and elegant. Both are for the medium term. There are very good things here.

Christian Perrault et Fils

12 ha owned and *en fermage*. Maranges *premier cru* in Clos des Loyères, Les Clos des Rois, Les Clos Roussots (including Cuvée Joseph), La Fussière (including a *vieilles vignes cuvée*); village Santenay.

The splendidly bearded Christian Perrault lives on one side of the village of Dezize, has his cellar on the other side and runs his domaine with his son Nicolas. The fruit is de-stemmed and cold-macerated for 15 days, and the wine is matured in *demi-muids* as well as in barrels, 15 percent of which are new. These are decidedly sturdy wines, but, even in 2004, not the most sunny of vintages; there is good fruit underneath, though.

Jean-Claude Regnaudot et Fils

8 ha owned and *en fermage*. Santenay *premier cru* Grand Clos Rousseau; Maranges *premier cru* in Les Clos Roussots and La Fussière; village Santenay; village Maranges.

The 27-year-old Didier Regnaudot is steadily taking over from his 62-year-old father. He has lowered the yield, updated the equipment and generally improved attention to detail. The wines, almost entirely red, are very good now. This is a source to note.

The Côte Chalonnaise

Domaine Maurice Protheau et Fils
Chateau d'Etroyes
Domaine François Raquillet
Domaine Michel and Olivier Raquillet
Maison Antonin Rodet
Château de Chamirey, Mercurey
Château de Rully, Rully
Domaine du Château de Mercey, Maranges
Domaine Hugues and Yves de Suremain
Maison L. Tramier et Fils
Domaine Trémeaux Père et Fils
Domaine Tupinier-Bautista

Givry Leading Domaines
Domaine Guillemette and
   Xavier Besson
Domaine René Bourgeon
Domaine Chofflet-Valdenaire
Propriété Desvignes
Domaine Didier Erker
Domaine du Gardin-Perrotto
Clos Salomon
Domaine Michel Goubard et Fils
Domaine Jean-Marc and Vincent Joblot

Domaine François Lumpp
Domaine Gérard Mouton
Domaine Parize Père et Fils
Pelletier-Hibon
Domaine de la Vernoise
Domaine Jean-Paul Ragot
Domaine Michel Sarrazin et Fils
Domaine Jean Tartraux et Fils
Domaine Bernard Tartraux-Juillet
Domaine Martine Tessier
Domaine Baron Thénard

Montagny Leading Domaines
Domaine Stéphane Aladame
Domaine Arnoux Père et Fils
Chateau de Cary-Potet
Cave des Vignerons de Buxy
Lucien Denizot
Domaine des Moirots
Domaine Jean-Claude Pigneret and
   Sylvie Nugues
Les Chais Saint-Pierre
Chateau de la Saule
Alain Roy-Thevenet

THE CÔTE CHALONNAISE, or Région de Mercurey, to give it its alternative name, has long been a well-known "forgotten area," though this may seem paradoxical. While everyone acknowledges that it is worth investigating, few merchants bother to go prospecting. There are many well-known growers whose wines are hardly ever exported.

The Côte Chalonnaise begins at the southern tip of the Côte de Beaune but on a different ridge of hills slightly to the east. The vineyards lie on the most favoured parts of a series of hummocky slopes, roughly following the line of the D981 road which runs due south from Chagny down to Cluny. The main wine villages, each with its own separate *appellation contrôlée*, are Bouzeron (for Aligoté only) Rully, Mercurey, Givry and Montagny. Total production is small, barely a seventh of that of the Côte d'Or. Up to 1990, unlike the Mâconnais and Chablis,

but like the Côte d'Or, there was no regional appellation for the generic wines of the Côte

Côte Chalonnaise

	MAXIMUM YIELD (hl/ha)	MINIMUM ALCOHOL
Red Wine		
Generic Wines	55	10.0°
Village Wines	45	10.5°
Premiers Crus	45	11.0°
White Wine		
Generic Wines	60	10.5° (Chardonnay) 9.5° (Aligoté)
Village Wines	50 (55 Aligoté de Bouzeron)	11.0°
Premiers Crus	50	11.5°

	SURFACE AREA (ha)		PRODUCTION (hl)	
	ROUGE AND *ROSÉ*	*BLANC*	*ROUGE* AND *ROSÉ*	*BLANC*
Village Wines				
Bouzeron (Aligoté Only)	—	51	—	2,997
Rully	97	155	4,633	7,768
Rully *Premier Cru*	27	64	1,325	3,604
Mercurey	417	61	17,830	3,123
Mercurey *Premier Cru*	149	19	6,172	690
Givry	125	34	6,453	1,934
Givry *Premier Cru*	101	9	4,983	521
Montagny	—	104	—	6,091
Montagny *Premier Cru*	—	202	—	14,282
TOTAL	915	700	41,396	41,010
TOTAL *ROUGE, ROSÉ* AND *BLANC*	1,615		82,406	
Generic Wines				
Bourgogne Côte Chalonnaise	352	123	20,068	7,825

Chalonnaise: they were labelled anonymously as Bourgogne Rouge, Bourgogne Blanc and so on. Since then, there has been a separate appellation, Bourgogne-Côte Chalonnaise. The area covers land in forty-four communes in the Saône-et-Loire, surrounding what has already been delimited as Bouzeron, Rully, Mercurey, Givry and Montagny. This covers red and *rosé* wines from Pinot Noir and white wines from Chardonnay and Aligoté. If made from Aligoté, it must say so on the label.

In addition, although statistics are available only for the whole Saône et Loire and not for just the Côte Chalonnaise, there are other generics produced, including simple Bourgogne, Aligoté, BGO, PTG and Crémant de Bourgogne.

In general, there is little difference between the wines of the Côte Chalonnaise and the lighter wines of the Côte de Beaune. Broadly, the soils are the same: a mixture of different limestones and gravel and limestone mixed with clay. The grape varieties, Pinot Noir and Chardonnay, are used in both regions. The main difference is the microclimate of the vineyards. Lying at somewhere between 220 and 340 metres, their altitude is much the same as that of the Côte d'Or vineyards (though certain authorities would have you believe they are significantly higher), but they are less sheltered from the prevailing westerly wind and, despite being further to the south, need more hours of sun to ripen fully. As a consequence, they are picked later.

The Côte Chalonnaise is not a monocultural vine-growing area. The surface under vine declined considerably after the *phylloxera* epidemic, and though it has increased in the last 20 years, it is still but a shadow of what it was a century ago. There were 600 hectares under vine in Rully in 1860. Today there are 340 (although this is 10 percent more than in 1998). Instead, the vine occupies the particularly favoured sites—sheltered, well-exposed, gently sloping to the east or southeast and on geologically correct, well-drained soil. This is the theory, at any rate. In practice, if a *vigneron* has so many hectares, absolutely every square metre will be planted, whether it is suitable or not, provided the law allows him to. At the same time, the machinations of SAFER, a French bureaucratic body which authorises transfers of land and changes in use, together with the chauvinistic attitude of the local left-wing political parties, mean that it is difficult to increase the area under vine, much of which would be suitable, and hard for outsiders to come in and set themselves up as new domaines. As a result, demand for land always exceeds supply.

THE WEATHER: THE VINTAGES

As I have said, vintage begins later in the Côte Chalonnaise than in the Côte de Beaune: the microclimate is cooler. This disadvantages the Côte Chalonnaise in cool years, or when the climate collapses after the equinox. Equally, there is a gain in torrid seasons such as 2003, or when there is an Indian summer well into October. But by and large, vintages follow those of the Côte d'Or and are addressed in Part Two.

BOUZERON

Travelling south, the first village in the Côte Chalonnaise is Bouzeron. The vines are found on the slopes of a valley which lies parallel with and between those of Santenay and Rully. The area has long been renowned for its Aligoté wine, its reputation having been acknowledged by the Abbé Courtépée in the eighteenth century, and in 1979 a special Bourgogne Aligoté de Bouzeron appellation was established. At the time, there were fewer than 20 hectares of Aligoté in the commune, but this has now grown to 51 hectares.

According to Aubert de Villaine, the doyen of the village as well as co-proprietor of the Domaine de La Romanée-Conti, it is important to choose the right strain of Aligoté. The Aligoté Doré is much superior to the Aligoté Vert and gives a wine of greater perfume and elegance. The soil is also important. Here at Bouzeron, it is marly with a high proportion of limestone, and there is very little surface soil before you strike the bedrock. This helps temper the normally vigorous Aligoté grape, producing a rather more concentrated wine than elsewhere. The best wines come from the slopes on either side of the village, rather than from the plateau closer to Rully, which, at 370 metres, is a little too cool.

Bouzeron Leading Domaine

★ Domaine A. and P. de Villaine

20.6 ha. Mercurey, Les Montots (*rouge*); Rully, Clos Les Saint-Jacques (*blanc*); Bourgogne Rouge "La Digoine," Bourgogne Blanc "Les Clous," Bourgogne Aligoté.

Aubert de Villaine produces some of the best generic wines in Burgundy, and if anything were proof that there is something special in the Bouzeron soil, not just for Aligoté but for Pinot Noir and Chardonnay, it can be found in his wines. Viticulture is *biologique*, and the wines are largely matured in wooden *foudres*. They have all the elegance and concentration of fruit, if not, of course, the volume and staying power, of much more illustrious growths. There are very delicious wines in both colours here.

OTHER ALIGOTÉ DE BOUZERON PRODUCER OF NOTE: Maison Bouchard Père et Fils (Beaune).

→ Bouzeron ←	
Surface Area (2005)	51 ha (Aligoté Only)
Production (2005)	2,997 hl
Grape Varieties	Pinot Noir, Chardonnay, Aligoté
Maximum Yield	
Pinot Noir	45 hl/ha
Chardonnay	50 hl/ha
Aligoté	55 hl/ha
Minimum Alcohol	
Pinot Noir	10.0°
Chardonnay	10.5°
Aligoté	9.5°
Optimum Drinking	1 to 4 Years

	RED	WHITE
Surface Area (2005)		
Premier Cru	27 ha	64 ha
Village	97 ha	155 ha
Production (2005)		
Premier Cru	1,325 hl	3,604 hl
Village	4,633 hl	7,768 hl
Grape Varieties	Pinot Noir	Chardonnay
Maximum Yield	45 hl/ha	50 hl/ha
Optimum Drinking	2 to 6 Years	2 to 4 Years
Minimum Alcohol		
Premier Cru	11.0°	11.5°
Village	10.5°	11.0°

Premiers Crus		*Surface Area (ha)*
Agneux	—	0.40
La Bressande du Château	—	2.61
Les Champs-Cloux	4.62	—
Chapitre	1.64	0.81
Clos du Chaigne à Jean de Fran	—	3.26
Clos Saint-Jacques	—	1.69
Les Cloux	1.19	6.77
La Fosse	1.13	1.90
Grésigny	—	3.22
Les Margotées	—	4.00
Marissou	2.24	4.86
Le Meix Cadot	0.50	5.46
Le Meix Caillet	—	0.36
Molesme	4.22	1.48
Mont Palais	0.89	3.16
Les Pierres	0.18	—
Pillot	—	1.30
Les Préaux	2.81	—
La Pucelle	0.12	6.34
Rabourcé	0.50	7.49
Raclot	—	1.88
La Renarde	1.20	—
Vauvry	1.00	3.53

Note: The twenty-three *premiers crus* above represent 30 percent of the appellation. Minimum alcoholic degrees for *rosé* are the same as for red.

RULLY

The vineyards of Rully begin in the suburbs of Chagny and continue south to the boundary with Mercurey. The Montagne de la Folie divides Rully from the commune of Bouzeron, and at the north end of this ridge, underneath a large water tower which you can see for miles, the Noël-Bouton family at the 13.5-hectare Domaine de La Folie, technically in Chagny rather than Rully, overlooks the excellent *premier cru* of Clos Saint-Jacques.

A few kilometres further on is the village itself, dominated by its one surviving château (there were originally three), behind which is the slope of most of the rest of the *premiers crus*.

Rully owes its name to a Gallo-Roman lord named Rubilius, though there is abundant evidence of local occupation in prehistoric times, and it is probable that it was in the time of Rubilius and his successors that the vine was first seriously cultivated in the area.

Over the years, the village gradually created a reputation for its wines. By the early seventeenth century, the white wine was noted as being that which the vineyards excelled in producing. It was here, in 1822, that the first Burgundian champagne-style wines were produced, and for much of the next century and a half, *mousseux* or *crémant* was the mainstay of the local vinous economy.

Today it is estimated that some 4.5 million bottles of *Crémant de Bourgogne* originate in Rully *caves*. The still wine AC production is some 2 million bottles.

Phylloxera, which arrived in Rully in 1893, plus two world wars and the depression which lasted until the late 1950s, almost served to wipe the wines of Rully off the map. From 600 hectares in 1895, the *vignoble* declined to less than 90 hectares and only 10 active *vignerons* in 1945.

Like the rest of vinous Burgundy, Rully's soils date from the Jurassic Period. While there is some limestone dating from the Bathonian era, most of the local land is marl or limestone-marl, often covered with ferruginous oolite, and dates from the Oxfordian period. As elsewhere, the soils at the top of the slope are white in colour, stonier and more adapted to white wine production than the redder, more clayey soils further down the slope.

Rully produces roughly 65 percent white wine and 35 percent red. The reds are lighter than those of Mercurey and Givry, and rather better, proportionately, in the warmer vintages. In cold years they can be a little ungenerous, though thankfully they are better made these days, since almost every grower now de-stems completely.

More consistently successful are the white wines. I find these more interesting than those of Montagny, their main rival in the Côte Chalonnaise. Their character is lemony-crisp and floral, ripe but lean rather than four-square. With a judicious use of new oak, this can be a major alternative to Saint-Aubin and other similar wines in the Côte de Beaune, and at a fairer price. Those of Paul Jacqueson are outstanding.

Rully Leading Domaines

Domaine Christian Belleville

38 ha. Rully *premier cru* in Chapitre (*blanc et rouge*), Les Cloux (*blanc*), La Fosse (*blanc*), Montpalais (*blanc*), La Pucelle (*blanc*), Rabourcé (*blanc et rouge*); Mercurey *premier cru* Clos l'Évêque (*rouge*); Village Rully, including the *monopole* Les Chauchoux (*rouge*); Village Mercurey; Village Santenay, Chambolle-Musigny, Gevrey-Chambertin.

From a mere 5 hectares he inherited in 1982, Christian Belleville has built up this domaine to its present size and has also established a small chain of hotels in the Côte d'Or and Saône-et-Loire. The wines, sadly, are indifferent. He harvests by machine. The whole set-up is somewhat industrial. He is well situated to attract the passing tourist, however.

Domaine Raymond Bètes

10 ha. Rully *blanc et rouge*.

Raymond Bètes sells off much of the production of this estate in bulk. He offers only village wines. The cellar and the equipment therein are a bit artisanal here, and this is reflected in the quality of the wine.

★ Domaine Jean-Claude Brelière

7.1 ha. Rully *premier cru* in Champs-Cloux (*rouge*), Margotées (*rouge and blanc*), Montpalais (*rouge*), Préaux (*rouge*); Rully *rouge et blanc* ("La Barre").

Jean-Claude Brelière's father founded this estate in 1948. He and his wife Anne took over in 1973. He is not too keen on new oak and keeps some of the wine in tank in order to preserve its freshness. This is one of the few domaines in Rully whose red wines are as good as its whites, two of the reasons being, I am sure, Brelière's target of 40 hectolitres per hectare as a *rendement* for his Pinot Noir and the fact that there is a period of cold-soaking prior to fermentation. Currently, the Champs-Cloux is young vines. The microclimate is warm, and Brelière has recently switched from Chardonnay to Pinot Noir in this *climat*. Quality is very good here. The 2005s are lovely. The Champs-Cloux is the best red. M. Brelière now buys in grapes to supplement his own production.

★ Domaine Michel Briday

14 ha. Rully *premier cru* in Les Pierres, Les Champs-Cloux (*rouge*), Grésigny, La Pucelle (both *blanc*); Mercurey *premier cru* in Clos Marcilly (*rouge*); Rully; Mercurey; Bouzeron Aligoté.

Stéphane Briday, Michel's son, is another of Rully's first-division winemakers. He has been at the helm of this estate since 1998. He often wins a gold medal for his Mercurey, which gets up the nose of the local producers. It is superior to his Rully Champs-Cloux. Of his whites, I prefer the Grésigny. But the Rully Les Pierres in 2005 was delicious.

Jean and Vincent Daux
Domaine de l'Ecette

14 ha. Rully *blanc et rouge*.

Vincent Daux took over from his father Jean in 1997. There are no *premiers crus*, but a single vineyard *cuvée* from the *lieu-dit* Maizières. These are decent wines for the short term—but they are not first division.

André Delorme
★ Domaine de la Renarde

58 ha. Rully *premier cru rouge et blanc* (*assemblage* of different parcels; Givry *premier cru rouge* in Clos du Cellier aux Moines; Givry *blanc* "Virgourdine"; Mercurey *premier cru rouge* (blend of different vineyards); Montagny *premier cru blanc* (various sites vinified together); Village Rully, including the *lieu-dit* Varot, Mercurey; Bouzeron les Cardières; Crémant de Bourgogne.

When the 65-year-old Jean-François Delorme joined his father at the end of the 1950s, the firm produced only sparkling wine. He has built up this sizeable estate since then. It operates on three sites in the village: a winery, a storage and distillation centre and a separate office–*cum*–sales-to-passing-tourists facility. For an enterprise of this size, quality is high. The Rully *premier cru* blends are from older vines than the widely circulated Varot. These are the better wines.

In December 2005 André Delorme sold the business, but not the domaine, to Veuve Ambal, a sparkling wine producer based in Beaune.

★ Domaine Vincent Dureuil-Janthial

17 ha. Rully *premier cru blanc* in Le Chapitre, Le Meix Cadot, Les Margotées; Rully *premier cru rouge* (*tout court*); Village Rully *blanc et rouge* "Maizières"; Puligny-Montrachet *premier cru* in Les Champs Gains; Nuits-Saint-Georges *premier cru* in Clos des Argillières; Nuits-Saint-Georges; Mercurey *rouge*.

Vincent Dureuil, in his mid-thirties, took over the final part of the vines of his father Raymond in 2003, in which year he also bought in a couple of parcels of *premier cru* Rully *rouge* Clos du Chapitre to supplement his red wine production. Since then, he has become, in a small way, a *négociant*. There is high-class winemaking here. He is one of the few in the village who eschews machine harvesting. Since he stopped using herbicides, he told me, he hasn't had to chaptalise. The 2005s are fine.

Domaine Jacques Dury

14.5 ha. Rully *premier cru blanc* in Le Meix Cadot, Marissou and Les Margotées; Rully *blanc et rouge*.

This is an estate which specialises in white wines. These mature in 10 to 15 percent new wood and are very good. Hervé Dury, now in his mid-thirties, joined his father in 1990 after leaving wine school, and he is now in charge.

Domaine de la Folie
Jérôme Noël-Bouton

13.5 ha. Rully *premier cru blanc* in Clos Saint-Jacques and Clos du Chaigne (*monopole*); Rully *blanc* "Clos Roque," "Clos de la Folie"; Rully *rouge* " Clos de Bellecroix," "Clos Roque," "Chaponnières."

The Domaine de la Folie lies at the northern end of Rully, dominated by a water tower. I have known this estate for years, having imported vintages such as 1976 and 1978 when I was a wine merchant. Then it was M. Jérôme Noël-Bouton, who had made his fortune out of one of those brands of gas you buy in a heavy metal container, who received me. Today, it will be his granddaughter, along with *régisseur* Jérôme Desprès. Two thirds of the production is white wine, and it is reared partly in tank, partly in wood. The wines are good, if early maturing. They would be so much better if matured entirely in oak.

★ *Domaine Christophe Grandmougin*

9.7 ha. Rully *premier cru rouge et blanc* in La Fosse, Marissou; Rully *blanc*.

Christophe Grandmougin, young, dark-haired and intense, is one of the finest talents to emerge in the Côte Chalonnaise for some years. His father made very good wine which he sold off in bulk. Christophe is slowly but surely—there is a question of cash flow here—building up his sales in bottle. All bar one hectare of this domaine is on *premier cru* land. These are splendid wines!

Henri and Paul Jacqueson
★ *Domaine de Chèvremont*

11 ha. Rully *premier cru blanc* in Grésigny, Les Margotées, La Pucelle, Raclot; Rully *premier cru rouge* in Les Chaponnières; Mercurey *premier cru rouge* in Les Naugues; Mercurey *rouge* "Les Vaux."

This is the source of the best white wines in the Côte Chalonnaise. The estate was built up by Henri Jacqueson from 1946 onward, and expansion has continued, chiefly in *premier cru* land, since his son Paul took over in 1972. Paul is one of only four (out of twenty or thirty) in the village—there are more in Mercurey and Givry, where harvests are mainly of red grapes—who refuse to pick by machine. Nor did he acidify his 2003s. The 2002s are delicious, and the 2005s and 2006s perhaps even better.

Domaine Ninot
Le Meix Guillaume

15 ha. Rully *premier cru blanc* Grésigny; Village Rully *blanc*; Village Rully *rouge* in "Meix Guillaume,"

"Chaponnières"; Mercurey *premier cru rouge* in Les Crêts, Les Saumonts, Les Velley; Village Mercurey *rouge*.

Pierre-Marie Ninot retired in 2003 and handed over responsibility to his daughter Erell. Viticulture is by *lutte raisonnée*, the soil is ploughed, and there are *tables de tri* both in the vineyard and in the cellar. I have noticed a considerable improvement in quality here in the last couple of years.

Maison Albert Sounit

The Sounits sold their merchants business to a Danish company in 1996 and their vines to the *négociant* Béjot in Meursault (who has retained the name Ronald Sounit). Gérard Bellot is the man on the spot in Rully. A range of merchant Côte Chalonnaise wines is offered. The quality is good.

MERCUREY

Mercurey is a sizeable commune, larger than Gevrey-Chambertin, Meursault or Beaune, the biggest of the Côte d'Or. It produces twice as much as either Nuits-Saint-Georges or Pommard and makes almost entirely red wine. The commune straddles the D978, the main road from Chalon to Autun, and includes the villages of Bourgneuf-Val d'Or and Saint-Martin-sous-Montaigu. The chief vineyards lie on slopes which face as much due south as southeast above (i.e., north of) the village. As there is more wine to distribute, and as a number of well-known Burgundy *négociants*, particularly Faiveley, have vineyards in the commune, this is the Côte Chalonnaise's best-known red wine. It is also the most expensive. Whether the quality is worth the extra money is a moot point.

The village takes its name from Mercurey, the Roman god and winged messenger, who was also the god of commerce. There used to be a Gallo-Roman temple in the *climat* of Clos Voyens, we are told. Now there is a windmill on the site.

Mercurey is the most structured of the Chalonnaise red wines, and this, in leaner

Mercurey

	RED	WHITE
Surface Area (2005)		
Premier Cru	149 ha	19 ha
Village	417 ha	61 ha
Production (2005)		
Premier Cru	6,172 hl	690 hl
Village	17,830 hl	3,123 hl
Grape Varieties	Pinot Noir	Chardonnay
Maximum Yield	45 hl/ha	50 hl/ha
Optimum Drinking	2 to 8 Years	2 to 4 Years
Minimum Alcohol		
Premier Cru	11.0°	11.5°
Village	10.5°	11.0°
Premiers Crus	*Surface Area (ha)*	
Clos des Barraults	3.35	1.39
La Bondue	3.39	0.30
Les Byots	1.17	—
La Cailloute	1.56	0.17
Les Champs Martin	6.97	1.73
La Chassière	2.86	—
Clos du Château de Montaigu	1.90	—
Les Combins	5.18	—
Les Crêts	1.95	1.50
Les Croichots	5.95	0.36
Le Clos l'Évêque	16.14	0.06
Clos Fortoul	2.51	—
Les Fourneaux	1.87	0.40
Clos des Grands Voyens	4.92	—
Griffères	—	0.37
La Levrière	1.32	—
Clos Marcilly	5.38	—
La Mission	—	1.92
Clos des Montaigus	6.55	0.23
Les Montaigus	1.66	—
Clos des Myglands	6.31	—
Les Naugues	2.49	—
Clos de Paradis	5.79	0.82
Les Puillets	2.62	—
Le Clos du Roy	10.06	0.55
Les Ruelles	2.54	—
Les Saumonts	1.86	0.25
Sazenay	7.44	2.20
Clos Tonnerre	2.84	—
Les Vasées	3.44	—
Les Velley	8.44	0.84
Clos Voyens	2.30	0.19

Note: Minimum alcoholic degrees for *rosé* are the same as for red.

years, can take the form of a rather stringy and skeletal character, lacking fruit and flesh. At its best, it is rich and ample though, with a certain earthiness: the best of the Côte Chalonnaise reds. The whites are another matter; like those of Givry, production is meagre, and they show neither the fruit nor the succulence of those of Rully. One has to be careful not to over-oak Mercurey whites. The wood has a tendency to dominate.

Mercurey Leading Domaines

Domaine Bordeaux-Montrieux

4.48 ha. Mercurey *premier cru rouge* in Grand Clos Fortoul (*monopole*); Village Mercurey *rouge*.

Jacques Bordeaux-Montrieux, head of the family which runs the Domaine Baron Thénard in Givry (see page 308), bought up this small, independently run Mercurey domaine in 1944. As with that of Thénard, much of the crop used to be sold as finished wine to Maison Roland Remoissenet Père et Fils in Beaune—Remoissenet was sold in the summer of 2005, but the arrangement continues. The wines are forward and easy to drink, but they lack flair.

★ Domaine Luc Brintet

11 ha. Mercurey *premier cru rouge* in Les Champs Martin, Les Crêts, Les Vasées, La Levrière (*monopole*); Mercurey *premier cru blanc* in Les Crêts; Village Mercurey *rouge et blanc*, including a *vieilles vignes cuvée*; Village Rully *rouge et blanc*.

This is one of the best domaines in Mercurey. Luc Brintet has now had almost two decades at the helm and has gradually been fine-tuning things ever since. The year 2002, for instance, saw the arrival of a new pneumatic press, causing Brintet to be more satisfied with his 2002s than his 1999s.

Domaine Jean-Pierre Charton

8 ha. Mercurey *premier cru rouge* in Les Naugues, Le Clos du Roy; Mercurey *premier cru blanc* in Le Clos du Roy; Village Mercurey *rouge*, vieilles vignes, "Champ Michaut."

The Charton family house is on the main road, with the winery under Jean-Pierre's parents' house up in the vineyards. There are good wines here. Charton is not a believer in lots of new wood. "The more the wood gives at first, the more it takes back later (i.e., in the sense of drying out). But, it depends on the temperature of the *cave*. If it is consistently at 10°C." He also believes in early bottling, which was essential for the 2003s.

★ Domaine des Croix Jacquelet
Joseph Faiveley

81.98 ha. owned and *en fermage* in the Côte Chalonnaise. Mercurey *premier cru rouge* in Clos du Roy, Clos des Myglands (*monopole*); Village Mercurey *rouge*, including the *lieux-dits* La Framboisière and Les Mauvarennes; Village Mercurey *blanc*, including the *lieux-dits* Clos Rochette and Les Mauvarennes; Village Rully *rouge et blanc* in the *lieu-dit* Les Villeranges; Village Givry *rouge et blanc* in the *lieu-dit* Champ Laliot; Montagny *premier cru* Les Las; Village Montagny, including the *lieu-dit* Les Joncs; Bouzeron.

The Faiveley family was one of the first to appreciate the potential importance of the Côte Chalonnaise, and they have built up a sizeable domaine here (second only to the Buxy cooperative).

The same perfectionism is evident here as at Nuits-Saint-Georges. The recipe includes low yields, hand harvesting, a severe *triage*, the use of indigenous yeasts and relatively cool fermentation temperatures. The results are fine. If I have one criticism, it is that I find some of their village wines a little oaky: it makes them a touch rigid.

Domaine de l'Europe
Guy Cinquin and Chantal Côte

2.5 ha. Mercurey *rouge* "Les Closeaux," "Les Chazeaux," including a *vieilles vignes cuvée*.

Balloons are an equal passion for this charming couple. He is from the Beaujolais and spent some time as *régisseur* at the neighbouring Domaine Maurice Protheau. She is from Belgium and is a painter. They set up in 1995. There are good wines here.

Domaine Patrice Guillot

7.5 ha. Mercurey *premier cru rouge* in Clos des Montaigus, Les Velley; Village Mercurey *rouge et blanc*.

Patrice Guillot, his wife and their two young daughters live up in the hills above the vineyards and look after this estate, partly inherited from an uncle. He has been in charge since 1988. These are good wines, despite the Clos des Montaigus being young vines.

Domaine Jeannin-Naltet Père et Fils

8.43 ha. Mercurey *premier cru rouge* in Clos des Grands Voyens, Clos l'Évêque, Les Naugues; Village Mercurey *rouge*.

Thierry Jeannin-Naltet looks after this family domaine situated up on the slopes north of the village, encircled by its vines, chief of which is the 5-hectare monopoly of Clos des Grands Voyens. There is a *table de tri* in the vineyard, and the wines reside in barrel (20 percent new wood) for 18 months before bottling, filtered by Kieselguhr but not fined. Quality is good—the Grands Voyens 2002 is very good—but not exceptional.

Domaine Émile Juillot
Nathalie and Jean-Claude Theulot

11.25 ha. Mercurey *premier cru rouge* in La Cailloute (*monopole*), Les Combins, Les Champs Martin, Les Croichots, Les Saumonts; Mercurey *premier cru blanc* in La Cailloute (*monopole*), Les Champs Martin, Les Saumonts; Village Mercurey *blanc* (including a *vieilles vignes cuvée*); Village Mercurey *rouge*, including Château Mypont.

Tucked in behind the local hotel and one rosette restaurant Le Val d'Or, you will find the headquarters of this reliable estate. It has not had any connection with the Juillot family for some time, the Theulots having bought out Émile Juillot in the 1980s. The viticulture is by *lutte raisonnée*, with ploughing of the younger vines. There are two sorting tables, one in the vineyard and one in the winery, and the red wines are aged using 25 percent new wood. On the tasting table, you will see jars of earth from the Cailloute and the Combins illustrating the soil

differences: the former red friable limestone debris is filled with fossils, the latter grey marl with much more clay. The Combins is the best red wine here. The Cailloute, a monopoly, produces one of Mercurey's top white wines.

★ Domaine Michel Juillot

30 ha. Mercurey *premier cru rouge* in Clos des Barraults, Les Champs Martin, Les Combins, Clos du Roy, Clos Tonnerre; Mercurey *premier cru blanc* in Clos des Barraults, Les Champs Martin; Village Mercurey *rouge et blanc*, including "En Sazenay"; Village Aloxe-Corton "Les Caillettes"; Corton-Perrières (1.20 ha); Corton-Charlemagne (0.80 ha).

This is, and justly so, one of the most respected Côte Chalonnaise domaines. There have been Juillots in the village since 1404, and this, the senior branch, has been bottling longer than most. Laurent Juillot, who took over from his father Michel in 1996, picks his entire domaine by hand and believes in a more Côte d'Or-like density of vines per hectare (10,000), low harvests and a careful *tri* in the vineyard. Thereafter, all the wine—even his Bourgogne Blanc—is reared at least partially in new wood. One must take every step to bring out the *terroir* characteristics of each wine, according to Juillot's maxim. The Clos des Barraults *rouge* I usually find just a bit better than the Champs Martin, but the Clos du Roy, of which the normal harvest is 600 magnums (it is only bottled in magnum), is better still. The Cortons are high-class. The local whites in 2002, however, I found under par, but the 2005s and 2006s are rich and elegant in both colours.

Domaine Laborde-Juillot

You will find the name of this domaine in other, older books on wine. It was an odd affair. Though based in Mercurey (Jean Laborde's father-in-law was Juillot), they had no vines in the village: only in Rully, Givry and Santenay. The domaine was wound up in 2002.

★ Domaine Bruno Lorenzon

5.28 ha. Mercurey *premier cru rouge* in Les Champs Martin, including Cuvée Carline; Mercurey *premier cru blanc* in Les Champs Martin, Les Croichots; Village Mercurey *rouge*.

If the established leading Mercurey domaine is that of Michel Juillot, the rising (or recently risen) star is Bruno Lorenzon. He became independent only in 1995, and for a couple of years, his father's name, Alfred, appeared on the label of some of the stock. At first, he erred on the side of over-extraction and too much new oak. But he soon saw the error of his ways and began vinifying more sensibly, while raising the level of the foliage in the vineyard to maximise photosynthesis and therefore concentration in the wines. This is an excellent address. You might, like me, see no improvement in the Cuvée Carline over the basic Champs Martin. It is oakier and more intense, but is it better? It was the latter I bought in 2002, at two thirds of the price of the former. The whites are fine, too. And the 2005s are delicious in both colours. Lorenzon is also a major partner in a local firm of barrel makers.

Domaine Jean Maréchal

10 ha. Mercurey *premier cru rouge* in Clos des Barraults, Clos l'Évêque and bottled as Cuvée Prestige; Village Mercurey *rouge*, including Les Ormeaux and *vieilles vignes*.

Quentin and Thomas, the tall sons of Jean-Marc Bovagne, himself the son-in-law of the late Jean Maréchal, are now in charge of this domaine, which is well sited on the main road through the village. Fifty percent of the estate is *premier cru*, and formerly most was bottled as Cuvée Prestige. Today, more and more of the first growths are being bottled separately. The Cuvée Prestige now comes from a mixture of Les Byots, Les Champs Martin, Les Naugues and Les Vasées. There is quite good quality here.

Domaine du Meix-Foulot
Agnès de Launay

20 ha. Mercurey *premier cru rouge* in Les Velley, Clos du Château de Montaigu (*monopole*), Les Saumonts; Mercurey *premier cru blanc tout court*; Village Mercurey *rouge et blanc*.

Agnès de Launay, married (her husband works for Maison Jadot) with three boys, took over from her father in 1996. The domaine headquarters is a sort of medieval bastion up in the hills above the village to the south. Agnès doesn't like new oak. Indeed the wines are reared in a mixture of tank and old wood and are bottled late. This is not my style of wine.

★ Domaine L. Menand Père et Fils

10 ha. Mercurey *premier cru rouge* in Les Byots, Clos des Combins (*monopole*), including a *vieilles vignes cuvée*, Les Champs Martin, Les Croichots; Mercurey *premier cru blanc* in Clos des Combins (*monopole*); Village Mercurey *rouge*, including "Les Vaux."

Philippe Menand, a youthful and good-looking man in his thirties, is the seventh generation here, and his arrival (he took over when his father Georges-Claude retired in 1994) has led to a substantial increase in quality here. He practices *lutte raisonnée* in the vineyard, which is ploughed. There are sorting tables in the vines and in the winery. The reds are vinified with a small proportion of the stems after cold-soaking, and the wine is matured using 30 percent new oak. The winery was rebuilt in 2004. There is impressive quality here. The Clos des Combins Vieilles Vignes is a fine example, and in 2005, it was excellent.

Maison Michel Picard
Domaine Émile Voarick
Domaine Levert-Barault
Domaine du Champ Perdrix
Château de Davenay

DOMAINE VOARICK: 62 ha. Mercurey *premier cru rouge* in Clos du Roy, Clos de Paradis; Mercurey *premier cru blanc* in Clos de Paradis; Givry *premier cru rouge* La Grande Berge; Village Mercurey *rouge et blanc*; Village Givry *rouge et blanc*.

DOMAINE LEVERT-BARAULT: 8 ha. Mercurey *premier cru rouge* in Clos des Barraults, Les Champs Martin, Les Combins. Village Mercurey *rouge*.

DOMAINE DU CHAMP PERDRIX: 10 ha. Village Rully *blanc* Les Saint-Jacques.

CHÂTEAU DE DAVENAY: 17 ha. Montagny *premier cru blanc*, including Clos Chaudron; Rully *premier cru blanc* in Le Meix Cadot, Rabourcé; Rully *premier cru rouge* in Le Meix Cadot; Village Montagny; Village Rully *blanc*.

Michel Picard has built up an extensive domaine since he first acquired Voarick in 1991. He is also proprietor of the Château de Chassagne-Montrachet (see page. 276), which is now his headquarters. This is a slick, modern business, properly in the twenty-first century. Sadly, I find the wines disappointing.

Domaine Maurice Protheau et Fils
Chateau d'Etroyes

50 ha. Mercurey *premier cru rouge* in Le Clos l'Évêque, Les Combins, Les Croichots, La Crée (Les Crêts), Les Velley; Mercurey *premier cru blanc* in Les Champs Martin, Le Clos l'Évêque; village Mercurey *rouge et blanc*. Under the name of Domaine des Fromanges, Village Rully *rouge et blanc*.

The Protheau family can trace its history in Mercurey and its wines back to 1720. For most of the last century, they were merchants as well as vineyard holders, but in 1996 it was decided to give this up and concentrate on the wines of their own estate. The man in charge is Maurice's son Philippe. Quality has improved of late, and the *cuverie* is up-to-date. But there is plenty of room for further refinement here.

★ Domaine François Raquillet

11 ha. Mercurey *premier cru rouge* in Les Naugues, Les Puillets, Les Vasées, Les Velley; Mercurey *premier cru blanc* in Les Velley; village Mercurey *rouge*, including a *vieilles vignes cuvée, et blanc*.

François Raquillet took over from his father Jean in the mid-1990s and raised quality here to first-division standards almost immediately. At the same time, the cellar, partly underground and behind the house up in the vineyard, was enlarged and the winemaking equipment upgraded. Today, he also acts in a small way as a merchant, buying in fruit from his neighbours.

Domaine Michel and Olivier Raquillet

6 ha. Mercurey *premier cru rouge* in Les Velley, Sazenay; Mercurey *premier cru blanc* in Sazenay; village Mercurey *rouge et blanc*.

Based in the hamlet of Chamirey, opposite the *château*, this estate has been run by son Olivier, a slightly younger man than his cousin François,

since 1998. The red grapes are not de-stemmed and are matured partly in wood, partly in tank. There is room for improvement here.

★ Maison Antonin Rodet
Château de Chamirey, Mercurey
Château de Rully, Rully
Domaine du Château de Mercey, Maranges

Maison Rodet is based in Mercurey. Their Côte Chalonnaise portfolio consists predominantly of four domaines they either rent or farm: the 31-hectare Château de Rully (*rouge et blanc*); the 37-hectare Château de Chamirey (the personal property of *Président Directeur Général* Bertrand Devillard)—Mercurey *premier cru rouge* Les Ruelles (*monopole*) and village Mercurey *rouge*, Mercurey *premier cru blanc* La Mission (*monopole*) and village Mercurey *blanc*; Givry, Domaine de la Ferté, *premier cru rouge* La Servoisine and village Givry *rouge*; and the 52-hectare Château de Mercey, Mercurey *premier cru rouge*, Sazenay and Bourgogne Hautes-Côtes-de-Beaune, *rouge et blanc*. Supervised by the ebullient Nadine Gublin, oenologue, this is a prime source for well-made wines, which if without quite the character and individuality of the area's superstars, are nevertheless highly reliable.

Rodet's small selection of Côte d'Or wines is also very good. In addition, the firm owns half of Domaine Jacques Prieur in Meursault (see page 255), and the team is responsible for Bertrand Devillard's excellent Domaine des Perdrix (see page 163). At the end of 2002, Rodet acquired the domaine and merchant's business of Dufouleur Père et Fils in Nuits-Saint-Georges and the Nuits-Saint-Georges *premier cru* monopoly of Clos de Thorey. The Château de Rully is well worth a visit. Do not miss the splendid medieval kitchens.

Domaine Hugues and Yves de Suremain

20 ha. Mercurey *premier cru rouge* in La Bondue, Clos l'Évêque, Les Crêts, Les Croichots, Sazenay; Mercurey *premier cru blanc* (*tout court*, mainly from Sazenay); village Mercurey *rouge et blanc*.

The main house and the cellars lie on the main road. Here lives Hugues de Suremain, now well into his eighties. His son lives up in the vines. The next generation, in the name of Loïc, has recently joined the exploitation. Winemaking seems rather old fashioned and haphazard here. The stems are still used, the wine is held as much *en masse* as in barrel, and bottling is late. The 2002s were still held in bulk in May 2004.

Maison L. Tramier et Fils

This merchant is based in Mercurey. In 2003 it took over the lease of part—2 hectares—of the local Château Mi-Pont (village AC). This Pinot Noir is hand harvested, vinified for 10 days and bottled after a year. I found both the 2003 and 2004 soft but a bit anonymous. I thought of young vines, but no: they are of an *age moyen*.

Meanwhile, at least two other locals vinify wines from the Château Mi-Pont. One of them, Michel Juillot, has occasionally bottled the wine separately.

Domaine Trémeaux Père et Fils

10 ha. Mercurey *premier cru rouge* in Les Croichots, Les Naugues; Village Mercurey *rouge*.

Half the production here is sold off in bulk. The rest is mainly held in tank. Up to 2000 there were no oak barrels at all in the cellar. Now small wood accounts for 30 percent of what Gilles Trémeaux keeps. Quality does not impress here. The wines are plump but forward.

Domaine Tupinier-Bautista

11 ha. Mercurey *premier cru rouge* in Sazenay; Mercurey *premier cru blanc* in Sazenay; Village Mercurey *rouge*, including Cuvée Victoria and Cuvée Vieilles Vignes, and *blanc*.

Manuel Bautista took over from his father-in-law Jacques Tupinier in 1997. The reds are cold-soaked for a few days before fermentation. There is 50 percent new wood for the top red wines, and one third for the whites. The wines here are firm and meaty. There is good quality at this address.

GIVRY

Givry lies on the Chagny-Cluny road; it is a bustling small town, both larger and more imposing than either Rully or Mercurey. Its vineyards begin north of the town, in the commune of Dracy-le-Fort, and continue southward before the slopes bend to the west in the *commune* of Jambles. Between Givry and Jambles, you will find the suburban hamlet of Poncey. The heartland of Givry and most of its first growths lie on southeastern-facing slopes immediately above the town. Many of these first growths—Clos Salomon, for instance—are monopolies.

The red wines of Givry can be the most charming and the most stylish of the Côte Chalonnaise, and in structure, they are midway between those of Rully and Mercurey.

The soil here is just beginning to change from that of the marl and chalky limestone of the northern part of Burgundy to the richer, sandier limestone of the Mâconnais. As in Mercurey, however, there is a little clay, and consequently, the wines are predominantly red. Contrary to what is found elsewhere, according to the authoritative book *Terroirs et Vins de France* (ed. Charles Pomerol, 1984), it is the land which has the least clay which produces the best reds of Givry.

There is a little white wine, which like that of Mercurey, for me used to lack both the sap and the style of that of Rully. But since 2004, this has changed. The locals, especially Jean-Marc Joblot and François Lumpp, are beginning to take them seriously.

Givry Leading Domaines

★ Domaine Guillemette and Xavier Besson

7 ha. Givry *premier cru rouge* in Les Grands Prétans, Le Petit Prétan; Village Givry *rouge et blanc*, including La Matrosse, Le Haut Colombier; Beaune *premier cru rouge* Les Champs Pimont.

The Bessons took over in 1989 from parents who didn't consider the potential of what they had and who sold off what they made in bulk. The château—and it is a proper château—and its dependencies lie at the foot of the vines. The wine matures—with 50 percent new wood for the *premiers crus*—in a splendid, high, thirteenth-century vaulted cellar. It is almost like tasting in church. There is very good quality here, particularly in the 2005s.

Givry

	RED	WHITE
Surface Area (2005)		
Premier Cru	101 ha	9 ha
Village	125 ha	34 ha
Production (2005)		
Premier Cru	4,983 hl	521 hl
Village	6,453 hl	1,934 hl
Grape Varieties	Pinot Noir	Chardonnay
Maximum Yield	45 hl/ha	50 hl/ha
Optimum Drinking	2 to 6 Years	2 to 4 Years
Minimum Alcohol		
Premier Cru	11.0°	11.5°
Village	10.5°	11.0°

Premiers Crus	Surface Area (ha)	
Clos de la Barraude	3.40	—
Le Bois Chevaux	9.21	—
Les Bois Gautiers	3.89	—
Cellier aux Moines	10.78	—
Clos Charlé	3.91	—
En Choué	4.96	0.28
Clos du Cras Long	1.74	—
Crauzot	1.13	0.83
La Grande Berge	11.01	0.45
Les Grandes Vignes	2.34	0.15
Les Grands Prétans	5.05	—
Clos Jus	5.56	1.00
Clos Marceaux	2.95	—
Clos Marole	3.92	—
Le Paradis	0.71	—
Petit Marole	0.76	0.30
Le Petit Prétan	0.80	—
La Plante	1.01	0.97
Clos Saint-Paul	2.00	—
Clos Saint-Pierre	2.13	—
Clos Salomon	6.88	—
Servoisine	5.98	0.65
Clos du Vernoy	0.70	—
A Vigne Rouge	2.16	0.45
Le Vigron	0.96	0.80

Note: Minimum alcoholic degrees for *rosé* are the same as for red.

Domaine René Bourgeon

9 ha. Givry *premier cru rouge* in Clos de la Barraude, En Choué; Village Givry *rouge et blanc*, including Clos de la Bridée.

René Bourgeon—slight and friendly but a little shy—has now retired, though it is still likely to be he who will receive the peripatetic journalist in his cellars in Jambles. Son Jean-François and son-in-law Christophe Zaninot—"the boys"—are now in charge, but will be in the vines. There is *lutte raisonnée* in the vineyard and 20 percent new oak in the cellar. These are good wines.

Domaine Chofflet-Valdenaire

12 ha. Givry *premier cru rouge* in En Choué, Clos Jus; Village Givry *rouge et blanc* "Les Galaffres."

Denis Valdenaire is the leading grower in Russilly. He took over from his father-in-law Jean Chofflet in the early 1990s. Every time I visit, there seems to be a further extension to the cellar. The spacious modern *cuverie* serves as a table tennis annexe for Valdenaire and his children at other times of the year. "Why are Givry whites usually less exciting than Rullys?" I asked him. Because generally the Chardonnay here is planted in lower-quality red wine soils, he replied. His are good wines.

Propriété Desvignes

11 ha. Givry *premier cru rouge* in La Grande Berge, Clos Charlé, Clos du Vernoy; Village Givry *rouge*, including Meix au Roi, *et blanc*, including Les Grandes Vignes.

The Desvignes estate is based in Poncey, home to many of Givry's best domaines. Éric Desvignes started working alongside his father in 1983 and took over when the latter retired in 1999. The wines are mostly lodged in tanks or in wooden *foudres*, the Desvignes not being fans of new wood. The 2003s showed well in May 2004, but I was less impressed by the 2002s.

Domaine Didier Erker

6.5 ha. Givry *premier cru rouge* in Les Grands Prétans, Les Bois Chevaux; Village Givry *rouge*, including Les Grands Prétans (not all of which is first growth); Village Givry *blanc* "En Chenèvre."

Didier Erker's family is of Austrian origin, but arrived in France several generations ago. He himself took over this estate from his father-in-law Jean-Auguste in 1996, since when there has been a major move toward domaine bottling. The wine is matured in a modern cellar behind the house beneath the vines in Givry itself. Erker is the only grower who offers both *premier cru* and village wine from Les Grands Prétans. He is a nice man with good wines.

★ Domaine du Gardin-Perrotto
Clos Salomon

8.4 ha. Givry *premier cru rouge* in La Grande Berge and Clos Salomon (*monopole*); Village Givry *blanc*; Montagny le Clou.

This well-reputed domaine for long produced only one wine: the 7 hectare Clos Salomon. Recently, Ludovic du Gardin and Fabrice Perrotto have branched out. The first vintage of the Montagny was 2003, of the Givry *blanc*, 2004. The Grande Berge is a lease. The vineyard is ploughed. Sexual confusion is used to combat grape worm. There is a sorting table in the *cuverie* (sadly, not as common in the Côte Chalonnaise as one would like). The Pinot Noir is cold-soaked and the wine given one third new oak. Clos Salomon is one of the commune's best wines: the 1999 is particularly fine, the 2002 less good, but the 2005 rich and sophisticated.

Domaine Michel Goubard et Fils

32 ha. Givry *premier cru rouge* in La Grande Berge; Village Givry *blanc* "Champ Pourrot."

The Goubard domaine is based in Saint-Désert, on the way to Buxy, and is now run by brothers Pierre-François (in the cellar) and Vincent (in the vines), the domaine having been built up to its present size since 1962 when the brothers' father Michel took over. A new *cuverie* and extension of the bottle cellar was constructed in 2001. This is a well-run and reliable estate.

★ Domaine Jean-Marc and Vincent Joblot

13.5 ha. Givry *premier cru rouge* Clos du Bois Chevaux, Clos Grand Marole, Clos du Cellier aux Moines, Clos de la Servoisine; Givry *premier cru blanc* in Clos de la Servoisine; Village Givry *rouge et blanc*, including Pied de Chaume.

This is Givry's best estate. Why? One of the reasons must be the controlled harvest: 35–42 hectolitres per hectare in 1999, a large vintage elsewhere. A second must be the age of the vines. The Joblot estate has been bottling and exporting longer than most. Twenty years ago

I was critical of Jean-Marc Joblot's excessive use of new oak. I found the 1985 unfailingly rigid in bottle. But today, though three quarters of the barrels are new, the effect is less marked. The wood is more sophisticated, and the wines are richer and more concentrated. There are fine, classy wines here, especially in 1999, 2002 and 2005. The Clos de la Servoisine is the pick of an excellent bunch.

★ Domaine François Lumpp

6.5 ha. Givry *premier cru rouge* in Clos du Cras Long, Clos Jus, Petit Marole; Givry *premier cru blanc* in Petit Marole; Village Givry *rouge*, including Crauzot, Le Pied du Clou; Village Givry *blanc*, including Clos des Vignes Rondes, Crauzot.

François Lumpp is one of my favourite Côte Chalonnaise *vignerons*. He separated from his brother Vincent in 1991, acquired premises on the main (Beaune to Cluny *par le vignoble*) road and immediately started producing high-quality wine. He is one of the few in the commune who takes white wines seriously. The reds (60 percent new wood) are fine too. Lumpp is a craftsman and a master winemaker. *Lutte raisonnée*, ploughing in the vineyards, a sorting table, a short week of cold-soaking: he does it all. He considers his 2002s the finest he has ever made. But I think his 2005s are just as good. The Clos Jus is the star here.

Domaine Gérard Mouton

10 ha. Givry *premier cru rouge* in Clos Charlé, Clos Jus, La Grande Berge, Les Grands Prétans. Village Givry *rouge et blanc*.

Gérard Mouton and his son Laurent produce very good wines, especially from the Clos Jus. The Grands Prétans vines are hardly 10 years old, so the wine is slighter. Viticulture is by *lutte raisonnée*, there is a sorting table, and 35 percent new oak is used for the red *premiers crus*. I would like to be more familiar with this domaine, but on my last two visits, though confirmed well in advance, I have been received by Madame and allowed only to sample a few bottled wines.

Domaine Parize Père et Fils

10 ha. Givry *premier cru rouge* Les Grandes Vignes; Village Givry *rouge et blanc* Champ Nalot.

Laurent Parize took over from his father Gérard in 2002 at this Poncey-based domaine, at which time the cellar was enlarged, enabling all the reds to be aged in cask. This is an engaging and friendly family with good wines, especially the Grandes Vignes, where the 2002 and 2003 are both very good indeed.

Pelletier-Hibon
Domaine de la Vernoise

6.8 ha. Givry *premier cru rouge* in Le Vigron; Village Givry *rouge et blanc*.

Luc Hibon, having married Karine Pelletier, took over his in-laws' 4-hectare estate in 2001 and has since enlarged it. Previously, he had worked for 8 years at the Château de Cary-Potet in Montagny. The couple occupy a modern house with cellar attached, in Poncey. I have been there once, in May 2004. I liked them. I liked their wines.

Domaine Jean-Paul Ragot

8.5 ha. Givry *premier cru rouge* in Clos Jus, La Grande Berge; Village Givry *rouge et blanc*, including Champ Pourrot.

Jean-Paul Ragot's rabbit warren of a cellar will eventually take you to a new *cuverie*, installed in 2003. Despite both the *premiers crus* being young vines, quality is very good here. Maturation is partly in *foudre*, partly in cask, of which 30 percent is new.

Domaine Michel Sarrazin et Fils

30 ha. Givry *premier cru rouge* in Les Grands Prétans, plus a *premier cru tout court*; Givry *premier cru blanc tout court*; Village Givry *rouge*, including Champ Lalot, Clos de la Plétin, Sous la Roche; Village Givry *blanc*, including Les Grognots.

The thirty-something Guy Sarrazin is in charge here at this extensive family domaine, based in Jambles. This is a more industrial operation than most. Harvesting is by machine. Quality is reliable here, but rarely outstanding.

Domaine Jean Tartraux et Fils

6 ha. Givry *premier cru rouge* in Clos Jus, Les Grandes Berges; Village Givry *rouge et blanc*.

The fils is Sylvain, who took charge here upon the retirement of his father in 1996. Bernard Tartraux (see below) is his uncle. The lesser wines are partly matured in tank. The Clos Jus, in 100 percent new oak, is clearly the wine to look out for here.

Domaine Bernard Tartraux-Juillet

6 ha. Givry *premier cru rouge* in Clos Jus, La Grande Berge, Les Grands Prétans; Village Givry *rouge et blanc*.

A couple of hundred metres away from the estate above, you will find the headquarters of the Bernard Tartraux domaine in the back streets of Poncey. I wonder about the *élevage* here. Having tasted rather burly barrel samples of his 2003 *premiers crus* in May 2004, I found two successive bottles of the Clos Jus 2002 to be weak and oxidised. This was not the first time. I have had similar experiences on past visits.

Domaine Martine Tessier

2.7 ha. Givry *premier cru rouge* in Clos Jus, La Grande Berge, Vieilles Vignes; Village Givry *rouge et blanc*.

This small estate is also based in Poncey. Martine Tessier took over from her parents, who sold off their production in bulk, in 1999. There is *lutte raisonnée* in the vineyard and 50 percent new wood for the Grande Berge. I find the white a little neutral, but the village red *primeur* plump and stylish and the Grande Berge very good. This is a domaine to note.

Domaine Baron Thénard

23.15 ha. Givry *premier cru rouge* in Les Boix Chevaux, Le Cellier aux Moines, Clos Saint-Pierre (*monopole*); Village Givry *rouge et blanc*; Chassagne-Montrachet Clos Saint-Jean; Pernand-Vergelesses, Ile de Vergelesses; Corton Clos du Roi (0.90 ha); Grands-Échezeaux (0.54 ha); Le Montrachet (1.79 ha).

The history of this estate begins with the Baron Paul Thénard, who married a local lady in 1842. Control subsequently passed through the female line to the Bordeaux-Montrieux family, and Jacques and his wife Dominique are joint managers today, aided by their son Jean-Baptiste. Until 2005 much of what was produced was sold as wine to Maison Roland Remoissenet Père et Fils of Beaune. It is my understanding that this relationship continues, despite the sale of Remoissenet in April 2005. The Givrys, both under the Thénard and under the Remoissenet label, are round and agreeable, but not first-division stuff.

MONTAGNY

Beyond Givry, there is a gap before one reaches Montagny. The hillsides of Saint-Désert and Moroges can be the source of some useful generic wines. A few kilometres on, one comes to Buxy, the capital of the appellation, which extends over four communes: Montagne, Buxy itself, Jully-Lès-Buxy and Saint-Vallerin.

The name Montagny comes from the Gallo-Roman *montanius*, that is, mountain. In the Middle Ages, a deed was drawn up transferring the land here from the Dukes of Burgundy to the chapter of Saint-Vincent in Chalon. Further south, however, in Jully-Lès-Buxy and Saint-Vallerin, the locals were already directly responsible to the great Abbey of Cluny.

Though today this is exclusively an appellation for white wine, both Pinot Noir and Gamay were widely planted here until as late as the 1950s. Nevertheless, it was white wine for which the commune was renowned, and which sold for a higher price, even back in the 1920s. Progressively from 1950, over a 20-year period, Chardonnay replaced the other grape varieties. Modernisation, improvement of quality and the opening up of foreign markets was led by the cooperative, which today is responsible for two thirds of the appellation. Even today, however, there is only a small number of individual domaines of repute—rather fewer than in Givry, Mercurey and Rully.

For many years, almost all Montagny was sold as "*premier cru.*" This had nothing to do with its geographical source: the wine merely

Montagny

	WHITE
Surface Area (2005)	
Premier Cru	202 ha
Village	104 ha
Production (2005)	
Premier Cru	14,282 hl
Village	6,091 hl
Grape Varieties	Chardonnay
Maximum Yield	50 hl/ha
Minimum Alcohol	
Premier Cru	11.5°
Village	11.0°
Optimum Drinking	2 to 5 Years

Premiers Crus	Surface Area (ha)
Les Bassets	2.54
Les Bonneveaux	2.98
Les Bordes	0.55
Les Burnins	1.96
Les Chaniots	6.37
Le Clos Chaudron	4.42
Les Cloux	0.21
Les Coères	21.06
Les Combes	0.19
Les Gouresses	0.15
Les Jardins	1.40
Les Las	0.39
Le Mont Cuchot	6.89
Les Perrières	0.56
Les Platières	2.69
Les Resses	0.89
Saint-Morille	1.18
Le Vieux Château	6.10
Les Vignes sur le Cloux	2.50
Les Vignes Derrières	1.51
Les Vignes du Soleil	2.00

had to have come from grapes with a minimum potential alcoholic content of 11.5°. Now, the land has been classified, and there are fifty-three slopes deemed *premier cru*, far too large a number. However, in 2004, only twenty-one different first growths were declared. The individually best known, and largest, is Les Coères.

These lie on a series of southeast-facing hills below the village of Buxy in the communes of Montagny, Jully-Lès-Buxy and Saint-Vallerin.

The soil structure is based on limestone rock of various ages in the Jurassic Period. At the top of the slope, the limestone is pure. Lower down, there is both clay and siliceous debris, often mixed with quartz. In parts of the appellation, the soil is quite deep, thicker than elsewhere in the Côte Chalonnaise, and this plays its part in the style of the wine. Only Chardonnay is allowed, so all Montagny is white.

While a lot of standard Montagny is somewhat neutral and four-square, this is potentially the best as well as the most substantial white wine of the Côte Chalonnaise. It is less crisp and flowery than Rully, but fuller, fatter and more honeyed, sometimes nutty and always broader in flavour. Under the label of a good source which is prepared to age the wine in newish wood, a Montagny wine can be every bit as good as a lesser village wine from the Côte de Beaune—and an excellent value.

Montagny Leading Domaines

★ Domaine Stéphane Aladame

7 ha. Montagny *premier cru* in Les Burnins, Les Coères, Les Platières, plus "Cuvée Quintessence" and "Cuvée Sélection," *premier cru tout court*; Village Montagny.

The youthful (born 1974) Stéphane Aladame has come a very long way in a very short space of time. He started in 1992 with 3 hectares he took over from an old-age pensioner. His parents had no connection with the wine business. But Stéphane soon established himself as one of the leading lights of the appellation. He now buys in grapes to keep pace with the rising demand for his wines. Beware, however. Some of his vineyards are planted with a sub-variety of Chardonnay: Chardonnay muscaté. This may not be to your taste. It is not to mine. But the rest are fine, especially so in 2002 and 2005.

Domaine Arnoux Père et Fils

7.5 ha. Montagny *premier cru* in Les Bonnevaux and *premier cru tout court*; Village Montagny.

There are nice old vines in the *premiers crus*, but less so in the village wine. No wood is used. There are good wines from Laurent Arnoux here.

Chateau de Cary-Potet

12 ha. Montagny *premier cru* in Les Bassets, Les Jardins; Village Montagny.

Charles de Besset's château is an impressive edifice just outside Buxy. The wines are forward and quite attractive, but they do not live up to their surroundings.

★ Cave des Vignerons de Buxy

1,000 ha, including 194 ha of Montagny (*premiers crus* in Les Chaniots, Les Coères, Le Mont Cuchot) and 19 ha in Givry (*premiers crus* in Clos de la Barraude (*monopole*), Clos Jus, Clos Marceaux, Les Grands Prétans, Les Bois Gautiers). Other major appellations produced include Rully, Mercurey and Mercurey *premier cru*.

The Cave was founded in 1931. For most of my wine-trade career—and I was a very good customer for its generic Burgundies—the director was Roger Rageot, who was appointed at the age of 26 in 1968 and retired in 2002. We are almost exact contemporaries. He is a good friend. It is Rageot who has put this establishment, and the reputation of Montagny, on the map. The cooperative adherents practice *lutte raisonnée* and use sexual confusion against the grape worm. Today, the director is Rémi Marlin, who instigated the installation of a brand new *cuverie*, capacity 33,000 hectolitres, in 2004. This is a thoroughly admirable set-up.

Lucien Denizot
Domaine des Moirots

12 ha. Montagny *premier cru in* Le Vieux Château; Village Givry *rouge* "Champ Pourrot" and Givry *blanc*.

Christophe Denizot, gently bearded, has been in charge here at the family domaine in Bissey-sous-Cruchaud, north of Montagny, since his father Lucien retired in 2001. The Givrys were acquired in 1996 but were planted in 1973. The wines are now given more time in cask but, being more concentrated than hitherto, can take it. They have been practising *lutte raisonnée* since 1993; there is a *table de tri* and 10 to 15 percent new oak. This is a very good address.

Domaine Jean-Claude Pigneret and Sylvie Nugues
Les Chais Saint-Pierre

7 ha. Montagny *premier cru tout court*.

This couple owns 7 hectares but exploits only 2.5. The rest, including the Montagny, is made by the local cooperative, yet they sell it under their own label—a curious arrangement. The *cave* is in Saint-Désert. The wines are quite good.

Chateau de la Saule
Alain Roy-Thevenet

17 ha. Montagny *premier cru tout court*, including a *vieilles vignes cuvée*; Village Givry *rouge*.

This is Montagny's senior estate, which has sold wine in bottle since Alain Roy's father bought the château in 1960. The building and its wine-making dependencies lie on the flatter land below the village of Montagny. Alain Roy likes to keep things simple and makes only two white wines: a younger vine *cuvée* for early drinking and an oakier *vieilles vignes cuvée* for future reference. He's a charming, welcoming man in his mid-fifties. And his wines are very good.

PART TWO

The Vintages

Vintage Assessments

WHEN I FIRST STARTED to plan *Côte d'Or*, it became obvious to me that in at least one respect it would have to be radically different from my books on Bordeaux. In Bordeaux there are approximately 150 châteaux of *cru classé* quality. Apart from the Graves, each produces a single *grand vin*. Moreover, quantities are large. It is therefore not too difficult to assemble a representative selection, taste them in one or two or three sessions and base a vintage assessment on the results. Additionally, elsewhere in these books, the very same wines had been vertically sampled.

Burgundy, obviously, is different. Most domaines will make a number of wines worthy of note. But quantities are minuscule, and right from the word go, they disappear into the cellars of private consumers, never to be seen again. Assembling a range of even fifty or so, some years after the event, is hard work. To do justice to the 1,500 wines which are perhaps worthy of assessment is almost impossible. To repeat the process until one becomes familiar with the evolution of every single wine is quite outside the bounds of possibility.

I therefore decided it would be ludicrous to base these Vintage Assessments on a single tasting. Even if I assembled all the Burgundies I had tasted over the last six or so years, it would hardly do justice to the range that would be dispersed over the world's wine cellars. Nonetheless, this would be better than nothing, and would have to do.

I therefore set out to sample as many fine Burgundies as possible. In this I have been immeasurably assisted by many dozens of groups of friends and wine lovers' associations. Will you come and talk to us, they asked? Only if it is over a serious range of Burgundy, I generally replied. The response was generous in the extreme. As a result I have probably sampled more fine Burgundy in the last 6 years than most might do in a lifetime. It has been a splendid few years! Here are the results.

The tastings fall roughly into three parts. Firstly, there are the newer vintages (wines not yet safely in bottle have not been noted). Notes on these recent vintages come from a multitude of opportunities in Europe and the United States: private tastings, trade opportunities and the like. The two most important of these are the joint Institute of Masters of Wine/Domaines Familiaux tasting in March two and a half years after the vintage, and a four-day session usually hosted by Bill Baker of Reid Wines a year and four months later. Secondly, there is my Ten Year On yearly celebration. This takes place in Burgundy in June. I invite all the top growers to join me with a sample or two. I arrive with a few cases of champagne, a side or two of smoked salmon and some farmhouse English cheese (far better for red wine than the vast majority of French cheeses!); *le tout Bourgogne* descends on Becky Wasserman's Le Serbet in Bouilland, and we all have a splendid time. It is a celebration, not a competition. But it is a fascinating opportunity to see a range of decade-old wines alongside each other.

Finally, for vintages even older than a decade, I have been deeply indebted to my friend Bob Feinn and his group of New Haven Connecticut-based Burgundy lovers. Thanks to their generosity, I have been able to indulge in wines of vintages as old as 1959 or earlier.

As you will see in my notes (usually the most recent representative comment for all the wines I have had the opportunity of tasting more than once), I have in the main listed those wines sampled since January 1, 2000.

A FURTHER IMPORTANT POINT

Generalising is hazardous—particularly in Burgundy. If you are rating something like the quality of a vintage, or its state of maturity, do you go by the best or by the average? What, indeed, in Burgundy, *is* the average?

I have based my assessments of the vintage as a whole on the premise that those who have been kind enough to invest in a copy of this book are those who take Burgundy seriously and therefore have bought the best (and I don't mean only *grand cru* wine) from the best growers. We all know that this approach does not represent Burgundy in general, but it corresponds to what has been carefully selected by merchants in the United Kingdom, the United States and elsewhere, out of all the dross that is available, to offer to you, their customers.

As I have said, only wines tasted since January 1, 2000, have been noted. I have confined myself to

wines of the Côte d'Or, and those in the main of *premier cru* and *grand cru* quality. My book *Côte d'Or*, published in 1998, contains many notes of top Burgundies of vintages back to 1949 sampled during the 1990s. Some of these may still be relevant.

On the basis of this selection, and my experience when I return to investigate even the meanest of vintages, I can safely say that in every year, there are some surprisingly good wines. Good *terroir* and good winemaking will out. A 2004 may not have the richness of a 2005, nor a 2000 the depth and concentration of a 1999. But it can still be good. Mistakes obviously are made, even in the best of vintages. But if you stick to the best growers, you will nearly always find something which will give you pleasure, even in vintages rated only 11 out of 20.

Readers are invited to access my Web site clive-coates.com for notes on important tastings undertaken since this book went to press.

PLEASE NOTE

1. All tasting notes are of wines safely in bottle, having recovered from bottling, subsequent shipping, and so forth. Cask samples have been excluded.

2. In many cases, I have tasted the wines on a number of occasions. For these wines, I have inserted my most recent tasting note.

3. Regarding the state of maturity comments, a comment such as "drink soon" refers to the wine's state of play in 2008 when this book is to be published. For instance, a note taken in 2004, where I originally wrote "drink now to 2008," has been amended to "drink soon."

4. The marks accorded are out of 20, and can be translated into value judgements as follows:

12.0	Poor
13.0	Not Bad
14.0	Quite Good
15.0	Good
16.0	Very Good

17.0   Very Good Indeed

18.0   Fine Plus

19.0   Very Fine Indeed

20.0   Outstanding

5. In all vintages, however bad, the best growers will produce surprisingly good wine (Burgundy, and the Pinot Noir especially, is particularly favoured in this respect): not so rich and concentrated perhaps, but showing the elegance of the *climat*, and not without complexity and balance. Sadly, the reverse is also true. Even in the very best of vintages the incompetent will ruin what nature has provided.

For this reason, wines are marked within the context of the vintage. A successful result despite the weather needs applauding. A disappointing effort when the sun smiled needs equally to be criticised. My assessment of the vintage as a whole as well as its future development from 2008 onward will be made clear in the preambles to the chapters which follow.

Note: For a preliminary report on the 2007 vintage, see page 823.

2006

After a normal winter and a late spring, the weather in Burgundy was unexceptional in May and June, but then extremely hot in July, occasioning the usual hailstorms. August was cold, wet and dispiriting. In September, good conditions returned again, which continued, with some interruptions, through to the end of the month. The harvest got under way on September 15. In Chablis (which had experienced less rain in August) and in the Côte d'Or, it began on September 18, with the Côte de Nuits following on September 20.

This is a very variable vintage, even harder to generalise about than usual. Normally, in "difficult" years, the wines are proportionately better as one climbs the hierarchy (i.e. the rating of both the estate and the vineyard). In 2006 there were some very successful generic wines—and some very disappointing *grands crus*, even in the cellars of the most highly regarded domaines. In general, however, the Chablis are very good (better than the 2005s), as are the whites of the Côte Chalonnaise, while the whites of the Maconnais and the Côte d'Or are more variable, with some being quite high in alcohol and weak in acidity, and therefore lacking in bite as a result. The best are superior to the 2005s, while the less good are not as interesting as the previous vintage. The reds are better in the Côte de Nuits than in the Côte de Beaune, and best of all in Nuits-Saint-Georges and Vosne-Romanée. Here, the hail experienced in Gevrey-Chambertin in July did no harm, apart from its impact on the yield. The hail which followed in Chambolle in August, however, has left its effect. Some wines are tainted. In general, the red wines have turned out better than the growers expected just after the vintage. They are not up to the standard of the famous 2005s, but they have a decent colour and show attractive fruit and ripe tannins, if, for the most part, not being very high in acidity. They will evolve in the medium term. And there are plenty of highly agreeable wines to be found at the best cellars in Savigny, Pommard and Volnay.

The 2006 vintage is good in the Beaujolais, with some very pleasant fruity wines having been produced; but it is not up to the standard of the 2005 crop.

⇢ Rating for the Vintage ⇠

Red	16.0
White	16.0

⇢ Size of the Crop ⇠
(In hectolitres, excluding generic wine)

	RED	WHITE
Grands Crus	12,738	4,004
Village and Premiers Crus	165,281	63,527
TOTAL	178,019	67,531

2005

A smaller vintage than 2004 but well up on 2003, 2005 was indeed not far from an average-sized crop. And it is a vintage of very high quality indeed. As this book nears its 2007 publication deadline, we are in very early days. While there is not much malic acid in the wines, the malolactic fermentations are in some cases taking their time. In June I tasted the white wines quite comprehensively. I also visited some red wine domaines. I visited a lot more in the autumn. More importantly, I listened to what the growers had to say. I encountered a level of enthusiasm I had not found since 1999. The 1999s are indeed delicious. The 2005s seem even more concentrated. The reds have more structure, based on very ripe tannins. The whites benefit from having the acidity of 2002 to go with their ample fruit.

↦ Rating for the Vintage ↤	
Red	19.0
White	18.5

↦ Size of the Crop ↤		
(In hectolitres, excluding generic wine)		
	RED	WHITE
Grands Crus	13,214	3,692
Village and		
Premiers Crus	175,674	58,817
TOTAL	188,888	62,509

WEATHER CONDITIONS

The winter of 2004–2005 was not especially cold, although there were plenty of days of frost; spring was late in arriving, however, causing a delayed bud-break. Precipitation was low, and this was to become the essential background to the 2005 growing season. The summer was not particularly hot, although there was a heat wave in May, which led to a normal and efficient flowering. There were some hailstorms early in the season, mainly affecting the Côte de Nuits, and a more serious outburst in Santenay and Chassagne on the Sunday evening after July 14, but after that, hardly a drop of rain was experienced in the Côte d'Or until September. At this stage one could see a small potential harvest of healthy but thick-skinned, concentrated berries.

All looked very promising, provided the tannins arrived at maturity at the same time as the sugar–acid ratio was at its optimum. You could see the effect of hydric stress more in the top vineyards on the slope than in the generics on the plain. The leaves around the fruit, at the base of the canopy, were already dried out. Admittedly, it did aid those growers who strip these leaves in the run up to the harvest. Yet, despite the drought, August had been only intermittently warm and sunny, and as September progressed, growers were beginning to get anxious about the lack of water. Happily, rain arrived on Tuesday September 6, as one whole morning of solid, but thankfully not violent, precipitation. Thereafter, the skies cleared, and September became increasingly sunny and warm. The Côte d'Or harvest was all but complete by the weekend of October 1.

The *ban des vendanges* was fixed for Monday, September 12, in the Côte de Beaune and Thursday, September 15, for the Côte de Nuits. Many growers waited a full week before they started harvesting in order to ensure full phenolic ripeness. The weather remained benign, although it began to get cooler at night. There was no need to rush, and the upside was that the acidities were preserved.

The year 2005 seems to be one of consistently high quality from Marsannay to Maranges—and into the Côte Chalonnaise as well—and in both colours. It is also a vintage for the long term.

2004

Although it was clear from the outset that 2004 was a very good white wine vintage, faces were long in red wine cellars in the autumn following the harvest, when one arrived to sample the 2003s. A lean acidity dominated the 2004 wines. They appeared to have no flesh, let alone softness and charm. Six months later, opinions had changed, but only slightly. It was not until after the *grandes vacances*, following a racking which degassed the carbon dioxide, that smiles began to be seen on growers' faces. The 2004s took a long time to evolve. *Malos* were late, and there was a lot of malic acidity. By October 2005, however, it was clear that there was fruit, if not a great deal of structure. Following bottling, these red wines continued to fatten out to their advantage. There is no lack, particularly in the Côte de Nuits, of purity, elegance and *terroir* definition. In both colours, this is a more than satisfactory vintage for the medium term.

→ Rating for the Vintage ←	
Red	14.0–16.0
White	16.5

→ Size of the Crop ← (In hectolitres, excluding generic wine)		
	RED	WHITE
Grands Crus	12,547	4,078
Village and Premiers Crus	164,592	67,053
TOTAL	177,139	71,131

WEATHER CONDITIONS

The summer of 2004 was inauspicious, causing problems of oïdium (downy mildew) to be added to concerns preventing a vine eager to compensate for having produced only half a normal crop in 2003. The latter was resolved by an even more draconian approach to de-budding and deflowering than usual (plus green harvesting for those too lazy to attack the vines at the outset). The oïdium was to have its effect on the cleanliness of the lees of the resulting wine, thus compromising the *élevage*.

In the meanwhile, however, the quality of the vintage had been mightily improved by fine weather in September. This resulted in very fragrant wines of medium body, with high acidities but delicious perfumes in the whites, but, as I have said, rather dour reds (at least at first).

WHERE ARE THE BEST WINES?

- Overall, 2004 was not as abundant a vintage as 2001 and 2000. But individual yields varied greatly. While the top estates restricted their crops, some of their less exigent neighbours produced much more than they should have. The white wine harvest was only a cellar-full short of that of 1999, a full 10 percent more abundant than 2000 and 2001. Some of these wines will doubtless prove no more than ephemeral.

- Nevertheless, the 2004 vintage is better in white than it is in red. There are some fine 2004 whites in the top estates, especially in Meursault and in Corton-Charlemagne.

- The red wine vintage is better in the Côte de Nuits than in the Côte de Beaune (once again, Volnay was hailed on), and it gets progressively better the further up the Côte de Nuits one is. Thus, as in 2001 and 2000, the best wines come from Gevrey-Chambertin.

WHEN WILL THE WINES BE AT THEIR BEST?

The lesser whites, such as those from Rully, Auxey-Duresses and Pernand-Vergelesses will drink well from the summer of 2007 onward, as will many white village wines from the senior communes. Drink these soon. Drink *premier cru* whites from the top estates from 2008–2009 and *grands crus* a year or two later. Few wines, even at this level, will last much beyond their tenth birthdays.

Equally, many of the lesser reds from the Côte Chalonnaise and the Côte de Beaune will be at their best drunk young when they are still full of fresh fruit. Start drinking the best reds from 2008, leaving the *premiers and grands crus* of the Côte de Nuits until 2010–2011. The very best Côte de Nuits will last until the last half of the next decade.

2003

It was the hottest summer ever, the earliest vintage since records began and the smallest harvest since 1984. This was not so much as a result of hydric stress, although this certainly played its part, but because of spring frost and subsequent hail damage. All in all, 2003 was a very extraordinary year, which produced very un-Burgundian wine. Most of the white wines are heavy, oily and flat, reminding one of old style Châteauneuf-du-Pape. Many of the reds— more in the Côte de Beaune than in the Côte de Nuits—taste of the Midi, or of California. They are burnt, spicy, alcoholic and overrich, and they also lack acidity. Having said that, I must acknowledge that even in Burgundy, there are those who like this vintage better than I, as do many American wine critics. *A chacun son goût!*

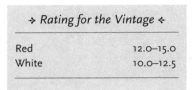

→ Rating for the Vintage ←

Red	12.0–15.0
White	10.0–12.5

→ Size of the Crop ←
(In hectolitres, excluding generic wine)

	RED	WHITE
Grands Crus	9,093	2,884
Village and		
Premiers Crus	117,896	43,142
TOTAL	126,989	46,026

WEATHER CONDITIONS

The last few months of 2003 were wet. This moisture would turn out to be a godsend, for even in the dry heat that the subsequent summer would bring, only in the most exposed vineyards of young vines would the vines suffer from a lack of water. After a cold start to the year, the weather conditions soon warmed up. Budbreak occurred early in March. This meant that when there were two nights of severe frost in mid-April, the results were devastating. Almost the entire Côte d'Or was affected. Many growers pointed out that they lost much more as a result of frost than as a result of the drought which followed. An important consequence—more serious for the whites than the reds—was that much of the 2003 harvest would be based on second-generation fruit.

Early, and in increasing heat, the flowering passed off normally, ushering in a summer which would be unprecedentedly warm, with temperatures rising to 42°C and above in August. Not only did much of the fruit shrivel up, but it also suffered damage from two savage thunderstorms, one on June 12 and the other on July 20. Hail damage was widespread.

The most intelligent growers, such as Michel and Frédéric Lafarge, realised early on that the fruit needed to be protected: that one should cut back the foliage less, and certainly not de-leaf around the fruit. But nevertheless, they were in a quandary. By August 20, 80 days rather than the habitual 100 after the flowering, the fruit was ripe from a sugar point of view, and acidities were disappearing through the floor. But the polyphenols were not yet mature, despite the short crop. This was particularly true in those vineyards with the least water-retentive clay and the warmest exposures, and where the vines, being young, had no extensive root systems. Here the evolution of the tannins was blocked.

Picking times vary enormously. The Lafarges picked early; they are very happy they did so, for their wines have almost normal acidities. Others waited until the end of the month, by which time there had been some much-welcomed rain, and temperatures had abated. Many picked in the mornings only and then hastened to cool the musts down.

Once into September the weather ameliorated. It became much colder at night. By this time, however, most, if not all, of the Côte de Beaune had been collected, as well as quite a portion of the Côte de Nuits. The few who were left, like Laurent Ponsot, were able to benefit greatly.

But the winemakers' problems were by no means over with the end of the harvest. There was the question of how to make and *élevé* the wine. There were no references. Usually a vintage will resemble an earlier one. Wise old heads will remember what they did right and where they went wrong. But 2003 (although some, mistakenly, cited 1947) had no parallels.

Should one acidify? Most did. Should one reduce the *bâtonnage*, reduce the amount of new oak, or bottle earlier? Opinions varied. The best advice, in retrospect, was "treat the 2003s classically and they'll become more classic." This turned out to be true.

WHERE ARE THE BEST WINES?

- Where not too frosted, the generic Bourgognes, red and white, have greatly benefited from the 2003 heat.

- Old vines and soils which are more clayey and water retentive produced better wines.

- *Terroirs* which often have a tendency to produce rather firm, austere wines were favoured this year.

- For whites, cooler areas such as Saint-Romain, Pernand-Vergelesses and Saint-Aubin were favoured.

- Chassagnes are better than Pulignys. Pulignys are better than Meursaults.

- The so-called Meursault Deuxièmes Crus—including Chevalières, Grands Charrons, Les Clous, Tillets, and Tessons—are better than the *premiers crus*.

- Corton-Charlemagne, and after that Chevalier-Montrachet, is the best of the *grands crus*.

- The Côte de Nuits reds are more successful than those of the Côte de Beaune.

- Thus the best red 2003s will be found in Santenay, Chassagne-Montrachet, Pommard, Savigny-lès-Beaune, Corton, Nuits-Saint-Georges, and, especially, Gevrey-Chambertin.

- The Hautes-Côtes are good in both colours.

WHEN WILL THE WINES BE AT THEIR BEST?

By the time this book hits the shelves in the spring of 2008, I fear that many of the whites will be beginning to lose what little freshness they had in the first place. If you've got them, drink them soon. The same comments apply to the village wines of the Côte de Beaune. The better reds vary enormously, as can quickly be seen from the colours: some are already brown, and others are still fresh, but in all cases the colours are very deep. Quite un-Burgundian!

There are some very pleasant reds, especially from the Côte de Nuits, which, if a bit overripe, are really quite fresh and enjoyable. These will come on stream in 2008 or so and last, perhaps, 5 years. The rest are flatter and more rustic; these should be consumed as soon as they soften.

TASTING NOTES

WHITES

Auxey-Duresses, Vieilles Vignes, 2003
Domaine Pascal Prunier-Bonheur
Fat but racy. This is very good for a 2003. Just about ready. (February 2006)

NOW TO 2010   16.0

Bâtard-Montrachet, 2003
Domaine Leflaive
Ripe but too four-square. Full bodied but lacks freshness. Hot at the end. (March 2006)

DRINK SOON   13.5

Chassagne-Montrachet, Les Embrazées, 2003
Domaine Bernard Morey

Not too heavy. Gently oaky. Medium-full body. Decent freshness. Positive finish. Good. (March 2006)

NOW TO 2009   15.0

Chassagne-Montrachet, En Morgeot, 2003
Domaine René Lamy-Pillot

Good nose. Gently oaky. Not a bit sulphury. Fullish body. Plump and succulent. Unexpectedly classy both for Lamy-Pillot and 2003. Very good plus. (November 2005)

NOW TO 2010   16.5

Chassagne-Montrachet, Les Ruchottes, 2003
Domaine Ramonet

No acidification. Rich, full, exotic and opulent. Concentrated. Not too alcoholic. A fat wine, but with good acidity and freshness for the vintage. Will come forward soon. Very good indeed for the vintage. (November 2005)

NOW TO 2012   17.0

Corton-Charlemagne, 2003
Domaine Bonneau du Martray

While the nose leaves something to be desired—there is a little built-in sulphur—the palate is rich, concentrated and really quite fresh for 2003, and the finish is good. (March 2006)

NOW TO 2012   17.0

Meursault, Charmes, 2003
Domaine des Comtes Lafon

Reasonably fresh. Gently oaky. Plump. Decent length. A good effort. (March 2006)

DRINK SOON   15.0

Meursault, Genevrières, 2003
Domaine des Comtes Lafon

Bottled March 2005. Youthful colour. Fat nose but not too heavy. More classic than I had expected after its showing in cask. Still not quite recovered from the bottling. Fullish, rich, but a little tight. Decent grip and positive follow-through but a bit hot at the end. Very good for the vintage. But not my style of wine. (September 2005)

2008 TO 2014   16.0

Meursault, Perrières, 2003
Château de Puligny-Montrachet

Cool and splendidly mineral for a 2003. Surprisingly good grip. Fullish body. Complex. Good length. Fine for a 2003. (June 2005)

NOW TO 2012   17.5

Meursault, Santenots, 2003
Domaine du Marquis d'Angerville

Not a bit too four-square (white from red wine soil) on the nose, surprisingly. Cool and juicy on the palate. Surprisingly good. Really quite fresh, even at the end. (March 2006)

DRINK SOON   16.0

Puligny-Montrachet, Les Chalumaux, 2003
Château de Puligny-Montrachet

Picked in refridgerated trucks. Bottled after 8 months. Clean and fresh. Surprisingly cool and full of fruit. It lacks a bit of bite nevertheless. Very good for what it is. (June 2005)

NOW TO 2010   16.0

Puligny-Montrachet, Le Clavoillon, 2003
Domaine Leflaive

A little four-square on the nose. Medium-full body. Ripe. But it lacks zip. Quite good at best. (March 2006)

DRINK SOON   14.0

Puligny-Montrachet, Les Folatières, 2003
Domaine des Lambrays

Bottled in June. Spicy nose. Slightly exotic, even a little blowsy. Slightly oaky. A little heavy on the palate. Lacks subtlety and breed. Only fair. (September 2004)

NOW TO 2014   13.5

Puligny-Montrachet, Les Referts, 2003
Domaine Jean-Marc Boillot

Fullish, oaky nose. Quite a solid wine. Good grip. Ripe and long on the palate. Fullish body. Good plus. (March 2006)

NOW TO 2010   15.5

Puligny-Montrachet, Les Referts, 2003
Domaine Étienne Sauzet
A little flat on the nose. Forward. Some fruit.
Quite good. (March 2006)
DRINK SOON   14.0

REDS
Aloxe-Corton, 2003
Domaine Robert and Raymond Jacob
A lovely ripe example. Fullish body. Good soft
tannins. Very good acidity. Rich. Fat. Very good.
(February 2006)
2008 TO 2014   16.0

Aloxe-Corton, Les Chaillots, 2003
Domaine Louis Latour
Not too pruney. Indeed, decent freshness. Ripe
and decent follow-through and finish. (January 2005)
2009 TO 2014   15.0

Aloxe-Corton, Les Fournières, 2003
Domaine Tollot-Beaut et Fils
Full colour. Slightly stewed, spicy nose. Rather
sweet and ungainly on the attack, and the finish
is a little hot. But quite good. (March 2006)
2008 TO 2014   14.0

Aloxe-Corton, Les Valozières, 2003
Domaine du Comte Senard
Lightish colour for the vintage. Quite an evolved
nose but quite sound. Not very 2003-ish. Light
to medium body. No tannin. Quite fresh but
rather slight. Quite good. (March 2006)
NOW TO 2010   14.0

Auxey-Duresses, Clos du Val, 2003
Domaine Philippe Prunier-Damy
At first a little flatter than his 2003 Monthelie
Les Duresses. But good follow-through. Ripe and
ample on the palate. Good plus. (February 2006)
NOW TO 2010   15.5

Auxey-Duresses, Les Duresses, 2003
Domaine Pascal Prunier-Bonheur
Medium colour and weight. Sllightly astringent.
Clumsy. Not special. (February 2006)
NOW TO 2010   13.0

Beaune, Premier Cru, 2003
Domaine Louis Latour
Perrières and Clos du Roi. Fullish, ample, quite
spicy. Decent freshness. Quite good. (January 2005)
2009 TO 2014   14.0

Beaune, Bressandes, 2003
Domaine Jean-Claude Rateau
Spicy but in a good, positive, fresh sense. More
caramel than sultanas. Medium-full body. Good
tannins. Very good for what it is. (February 2006)
2008 TO 2013   16.0

Beaune, Clos du Dessus des Marconnets, 2003
Domaine Labet-Dechelette
Light, thin and attenuated. Very poor. (March 2006)
DRINK UP   11.0

Beaune, Clos de l'Écu, 2003
Domaine Joseph Faiveley
Good colour. Quite a firm, tannic nose. But a good
cool ripeness underneath. Complex and elegant
and with plenty of depth. Nothing too hot about
this at all. This is very good indeed. (March 2006)
2009 TO 2018   17.0

Beaune, Clos des Mouches, 2003
Domaine Yves Darviot
Bottled after 10 months. Quite spicy but fresh
and stylish for the vintage. Medium to medium-
full body. Ripe. Good balance. Nice and fresh.
Very good. (February 2006)
2009 TO 2020   16.0

Beaune, Clos des Mouches, 2003
Domaine Joseph Drouhin
Good colour. Quite a full, firm nose. Good tan-
nins. Quite full. Rich and meaty. Needs time.
Good plus. (March 2006)
2009 TO 2015   15.5

Beaune, Aux Cras, 2003
Domaine Germain Père et Fils/
Château de Chorey-lès-Beaune
Good colour. Quite fresh, civilised nose.
Medium-full body. Good grip. Balanced

and stylish. Long and positive. Very good. (March 2006)

2008 TO 2015   16.0

Beaune, Grèves, 2003
Domaine Tollot-Beaut et Fils

Slightly cooked but not too much so. Indeed better on the nose than the palate. Ripe, rich, full and succulent. Quite oaky. Good. (March 2006)

2008 TO 2014   15.0

Beaune, Les Sizies, 2003
Domaine Hubert de Montille

Good colour. Good nose. Not a bit too hot or sweet. Ripe. Rich. Medium-full body. Good tannins. Balanced and stylish. Very good. (March 2006)

2008 TO 2015   16.0

Bonnes Mares, 2003
Domaine Georges Roumier et Fils

Fullish colour. Very lovely nose. Profound, fresh, succulent and multidimensional. A lot of class. On the palate it starts well but then tails off a bit. The finish lacks energy. A pity. Very good indeed at best. (March 2006)

2008 TO 2016   17.0

Chambertin, 2003
Domaine Armand Rousseau

Not a huge colour. Very subtle, concentrated, gently intense nose. Splendid concentration. Ripe and sweet but not overripe or southern. Medium-full body. Very fresh, very classy and very harmonious. A brilliant effort. (March 2006)

2009 TO 2020+   20.0

Chambertin, 2003
Domaine Jean Trapet Père et Fils

Medium-full colour. Ripe nose. Quite soft and succulent. Not a tannic monster. Medium-full body. Very good grip. Good depth and class. Longer, more vigorous and more positive than their 2003 Chapelle and Latricières. But fine plus at best. (March 2006)

2009 TO 2020   18.0

Chambolle-Musigny, Les Cras, 2003
Domaine Georges Roumier et Fils

Good colour. Ripe nose. Like their 2003 Morey-Saint-Denis Clos de la Buissière, a little cooked. Medium-full body. No aggressive tannins. Decent fruit but a slight lack of freshness and style. (March 2006)

2008 TO 2016   16.0

Chambolle-Musigny, Derrière la Grange, 2003
Domaine Louis Rémy

Very good colour. Good fresh nose. Rich, fat and very ripe on the palate but not a bit too southern. Difficult to find Chambolle but very good indeed. (February 2006)

NOW TO 2012   17.0

Chapelle-Chambertin, 2003
Domaine Cécile Tremblay

This is really quite civilised. Ripe, full bodied, ample and delicious for a 2003. (February 2006)

2008 TO 2014   17.5

Charmes-Chambertin, 2003
Domaine Denis Bachelet

Medium to medium-full colour. Exotic nose. Lovely rich, voluptuous fruit. Clean and fresh for a 2003. Medium body. Not a lot of tannin. Not a lot of nuance or dimension either. But balanced for the vintage. Very good. (April 2006)

2009 TO 2015   16.0

Château de Monthelie, Sur la Velle, 2003
Domaine de Suremain

Good colour. Sweet-sour nose. A little burnt. Fullish body. Quite rich. Decent grip and decent length. Quite soft tannins. Good. (March 2006)

2008 TO 2014   15.0

Clos de la Roche, 2003
Domaine Dujac

Good colour. A bit reduced on the nose. Medium-full body. Quite fresh. But not a great deal of depth and dimension. Rather dull. If reasonably stylish. Good plus. (March 2006)

2008 TO 2016   15.5

Clos de la Roche, Cuvée Vieilles Vignes, 2003
Domaine Ponsot

Magnum. Fine colour. Rich, full, succulent nose. Very ripe, but not overripe. Full body. Ripe tannins. Surprisingly good acidity. Positive finish. This is a very fine example. (March 2006)

2009 TO 2018   18.5

Clos de Vougeot, 2003
Domaine René Engel

Fine colour. Full, concentrated nose. Not too Midi at all. Full and rich on the palate. Very good tannins. Exotic of course. But really quite civilised. Fine. (February 2006)

2009 TO 2014   17.5

Clos de Vougeot, 2003
Domaine Jean Grivot

Full colour. Fat, oaky nose. A certain amount of slightly astringent tannin on the attack. Rich, cleaner finish. No lack of depth or acidity. Quite fresh fruit. Very good indeed for the vintage. (March 2006)

2010 TO 2020   17.0

Clos de Vougeot, Château de la Tour, Vieilles Vignes, 2003
Domaine Labet-Dechelette

Medium-full colour. Decently fresh and decently plummy on the nose. Medium-full body. Some tannin. A little pruney but some depth and a positive finish. Good plus. (March 2006)

2009 TO 2018   15.5

Corton, 2003
Domaine Bonneau du Martray

Good colour. Positive, meaty nose. Rich and full. Not too cooked. Medium-full body. Good attack. But a slight lack of subtlety on the follow-through and a bit hot at the end. Good plus. (March 2006)

2008 TO 2015   15.5

Corton, Bressandes, 2003
Domaine Chandon de Briailles

Medium colour. A touch of the stems on the nose but rather more substance than the Ile de Vergelesses. Medium body. Ripe. Fresh.

Harmonious. Very good long, positive finish. Very good indeed. (March 2006)

2008 TO 2018   17.0

Corton, Bressandes, 2003
Domaine Tollot-Beaut et Fils

Good colour. The nose is much less stewed than with their Aloxe Fournières. Medium-full body. A little sweet, but neither too hot nor too pruney and with a positive finish. Very good plus. (March 2006)

2009 TO 2018   16.5

Corton, Clos des Cortons, 2003
Domaine Joseph Faiveley

Very good colour. Very rich nose. Quite oaky, too. Full body. Some tannin. But fresh, concentrated, stylish and profound. But the oak dominates a bit on the finish. Fine. (March 2006)

2010 TO 2020+   17.5

Corton, Clos des Meix, 2003
Domaine du Comte Senard

Medium-full colour. Fresh, ripe nose. Juicy and succulent and not a bit cooked. Medium-full body. Forward but balanced and stylish. Very good plus. (March 2006)

NOW TO 2015   16.5

Corton, Clos du Roi, 2003
Domaine du Comte Senard

Good colour. Fresh nose. Good substance and depth. Rather more to it than with their Aloxe Valozières. Medium body. Not a lot of tannin. But rich and with plenty of depth and character. Nicely fresh, too. Very good indeed. (March 2006)

2008 TO 2018   17.0

Corton, Le Clos du Roi, 2003
Domaine Michel Voarick

Rich, fat and exotic on the nose. Not too stewed or pruney on the palate. Fullish body. Good tannins. A bit too southern for my liking, but a very good example of the vintage. (February 2006)

2008 TO 2014   16.0

Corton, Les Perrières, 2003
Domaine Maurice Chapuis

Good colour. Not a bit too southern on the nose. Quite spicy on the palate. A suggestion of prunes. Medium-full body. A little tannin. Decent acidity. Slightly bitter at the end. At least some class. Good for what it is. (February 2006)

2008 TO 2013   15.0

Corton, Les Renardes, 2003
Domaine Bruno Colin

Somewhat stewed and rustic on the nose. Even a little oxidised. Better on the palate. Fresher and plumper but a little attenuated all the same. Drink soon—as soon as it is ready. (February 2006)

2008 TO 2010   13.5

Corton, Le Rognet, 2003
Domaine Bertrand Ambroise

Not a bit too extracted or too boisé, nor too roasted. Full body. Very good tannins. Very good acidity. Fresh and stylish. Fine. (February 2006)

2009 TO 2020   17.5

Gevrey-Chambertin, Les Cazetiers, 2003
Domaine Dupont-Tisserandot

Rich and concentrated. Unmistakably 2003 but very good grip. Really quite long, fresh and attractive. Good plus. (February 2006)

2008 TO 2012   15.5

Gevrey-Chambertin, Clos du Fonteny, 2003
Domaine Bruno Clair

Fullish colour. Nicely austere on the nose. Medium-full body. Not a lot of depth and concentration. It is balanced and pretty but a little fragile. Forward. (March 2006)

NOW TO 2012   15.5

Gevrey-Chambertin, Clos Saint-Jacques, 2003
Domaine Armand Rousseau

Medium-full colour. A little oak. Soft and succulent on the nose. Nice and cool. This is very lovely. Fresh, fullish bodied, intense and harmonious. It has all the ripeness of the vintage but none of the detractions. Excellent grip. Very long. Very classy. Very good indeed. (March 2006)

2008 TO 2020   17.0

Grands Echézeaux, 2003
Domaine Joseph Drouhin

Good colour. Very lovely nose. Intense and concentrated. Very classy. Not a bit cooked. Fullish body. A little new oak. Rich and persistent. Lovely balance. Very fine. (March 2006)

2009 TO 2020+   18.5

Ladoix Rouge, 2003
Domaine Robert and Raymond Jacob

Good colour. This is a lot better than their 2004. Medium-full body. Ripe, succulent and juicy. Good grip. Unexpectedly stylish. Very good for what it is. (February 2006)

NOW TO 2012   15.0

Latricières-Chambertin, 2003
Domaine Louis Rémy

Full, rich and full of fruit. Nicely cool. Good tannic structure and very good grip. Fine plus. (February 2006)

2009 TO 2015   18.0

Latricières-Chambertin, 2003
Domaine Jean Trapet Père et Fils

Medium-full colour. Just a touch more spicy on the nose than their 2003 Chapelle-Chambertin. And not quite as much depth on the palate. Very good acidity though. Positive at the end. Fine, too. (March 2006)

2008 TO 2018   17.5

Mazis-Chambertin, 2003
Domaine Joseph Faiveley

Good colour. Fullish, rich, succulent nose. Some oak but not too much. Nice and fresh. Full bodied, rich, vigorous and very harmonious. Excellent grip. Lovely finish. Great class. This is very fine. (March 2006)

2009 TO 2020+   18.5

Monthelie, Les Duresses, 2003
Domaine Philippe Prunier-Damy
Good colour. Rich, full, fat and very civilised. Lovely fruit on the palate. Very good. (February 2006)
NOW TO 2010   16.0

Morey-Saint-Denis, Clos de la Buissière, 2003
Domaine Georges Roumier et Fils
Good colour. Good plummy, rich nose. Quite fresh. Good structure. The flavour is just a little cooked, but the tannins seem civilised and the follow-through is fresh. Good plus. (March 2006)
2008 TO 2016   15.5

Morey-Saint-Denis, Clos des Ormes, 2003
Domaine Georges Lignier et Fils
Medium colour for the vintage. Not too exotic. Not very elegant. But quite fresh. Not bad. (February 2006)
NOW TO 2010   14.0

Musigny, 2003
Domaine Jacques-Frédéric Mugnier
Good colour. Very fine nose. Ripe but not a bit overripe. Fresh and classy. Intense and lovely. Fullish body. Intense, balanced and very, very subtle. Splendid finish. Excellent. (March 2006)
2008 TO 2020+   19.5

Nuits-Saint-Georges, 2003
Domaine Bertrand Ambroise
Huge colour. Very rich jammy-chocolaty fruit. But this has good tannins and very good grip. There is balance and substance. Very good. (February 2006)
2009 TO 2015   15.0

Nuits-Saint-Georges, Vieilles Vignes, 2003
Domaine Jean-Pierre Truchetet
Village wine. Three different plots. Good colour. Very good nose. Cool and classy. Not a bit too méridional. Good backbone. Ripe tannins. Needs time. Lovely finish. Very good plus. (February 2006)
2009 TO 2020   16.5

Nuits-Saint-Georges, Aux Boudots, 2003
Domaine Méo-Camuzet
Good colour. Slightly reduced on the nose at first. Rich, succulent and not a bit too cooked underneath. Fullish body. Oaky, juicy and a little sweet. But good grip. What it lacks compared to the very best is a bit of zip and personality. Very good indeed. (March 2006)
2009 TO 2020   17.0

Nuits-Saint-Georges, Clos de la Maréchale, 2003
Domaine Joseph Faiveley
Good colour. Now just about mature. Soft but earthy nose. Just a little tannin to resolve but just about ready. Medium to medium-full body. Plenty of fruit and good acidity if no great depth and concentration. Good positive finish. Good plus. (March 2006)
NOW TO 2012   15.5

Nuits-Saint-Georges, Clos Des Porrets Saint-Georges, 2003
Domaine Henri Gouges
Good colour. Quite firm on the nose but very good freshness and style. Fullish body. Good tannins. Nicely cool fruit. Rich and positive. Very good finish. Fine. (March 2006)
2010 TO 2020+   17.5

Nuits-Saint-Georges, Les Pruliers, 2003
Domaine Philippe Gavignet
Good colour. Rich. Some new wood not apparent in their 2004s. One hundred percent new oak, but not too excessive. Good grip. Really quite fresh, seductive and sophisticated. Fine for the vintage. (February 2006)
2009 TO 2015   17.5

Nuits-Saint-Georges, Les Pruliers, 2003
Domaine Jean Grivot
Very good colour. Rich nose. A touch of oak, but it seems to have more energy as well as substance compared to his 2003 Vosne-Romanée Suchots. Fullish body. Good vigour. Very good

depth and lovely fruit. Excellent grip. This is very fine. (March 2006)

2010 TO 2020+ 18.5

Nuits-Saint-Georges, Rue de Chaux, 2003
Domaine Bertrand Ambroise

Full and tannic on the palate. But not too roasted or pruney. Rich. Fresh. Long. Very good plus. (February 2006)

2009 TO 2017 16.5

Nuits-Saint-Georges, Les Saint-Georges, 2003
Domaine Henri Gouges

Very good colour. Even firmer, more backward nose than that of his Clos des Porrets Saint-Georges. But lovely depth and character. Not a bit hot. Fullish body. Quite some tannin. Rich. Backward. Very good grip. Potentially fine plus. (March 2006)

2012 TO 2025+ 18.0

Pernand-Vergelesses, Ile de Vergelesses, 2003
Domaine Chandon de Briailles

Fullish colour. Soft nose. Not too cooked. Medium to medium-full body. Ripe and subtle. Harmonious. Quite cool. Finishes well. Very good. (March 2006)

2008 TO 2016 16.0

Pommard, Les Chanlins, 2003
Domaine Monthelie-Douhairet

A bit lighter and less intense than their 2003 Volnay Champans. But fresh and stylish. Good plus. (February 2006)

2008 TO 2014 15.5

Pommard, Les Grands Epenots, 2003
Domaine Michel Gaunoux

Medium-full colour. A bit pruney on the nose. Medium-full body. Decent fruit, but the background is a bit unstylish. Fair. (March 2006)

2008 TO 2014 13.5

Pommard, Les Rugiens, 2003
Domaine Michel Gaunoux

Medium-full colour. Fresher than his 2003 Pommard Grands Epenots. But again on the

palate it is a little stewed and unstylish. Quite good. (March 2006)

2008 TO 2014 14.0

Pommard, Les Rugiens, 2003
Domaine Hubert de Montille

Good colour. Good nose. Rich, full, cool and stylish. Fullish body. A meaty wine. Harmonious and positive. Fresh at the end. Fine. (March 2006)

2009 TO 2020 17.5

Richebourg, 2003
Domaine Anne Gros

Very fine colour. Not a bit hot or alcoholic (13.6°) nor lacking acidity. Rich, full bodied, fine and civilised. Very promising. (February 2004)

2010 TO 2020 18.5

Savigny-lès-Beaune, La Dominode, 2003
Domaine Bruno Clair

Quite good colour. A bit dried out on the nose. Lightish and rather attenuated on the palate. Ready. Not special. (March 2006)

NOW TO 2010 13.0

Savigny-lès-Beaune, Aux Vergelesses, 2003
Domaine Simon Bize et Fils

Quite good colour. Quite fresh on the nose. Almost sweet on the palate. Medium body. Not much tannin. Best at the end. Ripe but not too cooked or cloying. Good. (March 2006)

2008 TO 2014 15.0

Savigny-lès-Beaune, Les Vergelesses, 2003
Domaine Labet-Dechelette

Soft nose. A bit slight perhaps but not too flabby. A bit hot on the palate though. And the finish lacks grace. (March 2006)

DRINK SOON 12.5

Volnay, Premier Cru, 2003
Domaine Régis Rossignol-Changarnier

As 2003s go, this goes a long way. Rich and fat. Not too southern. Very good acidity. Medium-full body. Long. Very good indeed. (February 2006)

2008 TO 2016 17.0

Volnay, Champans, 2003
Domaine du Marquis d'Angerville
Deep colour. Exotic fruit. Big and concentrated. Somewhat over the top. Not too tannic but very rich and a bit overblown. Quite good. (June 2005)
2008 TO 2012   14.0

Volnay, Champans, 2003
Domaine Monthelie-Douhairet
Good colour. Very fresh and plump on the nose. Fullish body. Very delicious. Lovely finish. Fine. (February 2006)
2009 TO 2020   17.5

Volnay, Clos des Chênes, 2003
Domaine Michel Lafarge
Good colour. Lovely nose. Really quite subtle and Volnay-ish. Medium-full body. Fresh. Harmonious and succulent. Long and complex. Very lovely. Fine plus. (March 2006)
2009 TO 2020   18.0

Volnay, Clos des Ducs, 2003
Domaine du Marquis d'Angerville
Good colour. Quite a cool, classy nose. A bit more cooked on the palate. But decent length. But their 2003 Volnay Taillepieds is fresher and rather better. Good plus. (March 2006)
2008 TO 2015   15.5

Volnay, Santenots du Milieu, 2003
Domaine des Comtes Lafon
Good colour. Rich, full nose. Fat and classy. Medium-full body. Good tannins. Stylish, balanced fruit. Plenty of subtance here and good fresh character. Lovely finish. Fine. (March 2006)
2009 TO 2020   17.5

Volnay, Taillepieds, 2003
Domaine du Marquis d'Angerville
Good colour. Stylish nose. Lovely positive fruit. Good class and intensity. Medium-full body. Fresh. Ripe. Lots of depth here. Fine plus. Much better than their 2003 Clos des Ducs. (March 2006)
2009 TO 2020   18.0

Volnay, Taillepieds, 2003
Domaine Hubert de Montille
Good colour. Cool, classy nose. Not a bit cooked. Medium-full body. Good tannins. Good grip. Not quite the intensity and depth of d'Angerville's but positive and long. Very good plus. (March 2006)
2008 TO 2018   16.5

Volnay, Taillepieds, 2003
Domaine Roblet-Monnot
Good colour. Very good depth and style for a 2003. Medium-full body. Good ripe tannins. Very good grip for the vintage. Really quite Volnay-ish. Very good plus. (February 2006)
2008 TO 2013   16.5

Vosne-Romanée, Les Petits Monts, 2003
Domaine Robert Sirugue et ses Enfants
Very good colour. Rich. Full. Very good tannins. Lots of depth. Lovely bramble fruit flavours. Fine for the vintage. (February 2006)
2009 TO 2016   17.5

Vosne-Romanée, Les Suchots, 2003
Domaine Jacques Cacheux et Fils
The *plus tendre* of his 2003s, he says. Medium weight. Slightly too soft and jammy. Lots of fruit. Decent length. But merely good. Will evolve fast. (February 2006)
NOW TO 2011   15.0

Vosne-Romanée, Les Suchots, 2003
Domaine Jacky Confuron-Cotétidot
Good colour. Quite closed on the nose. Fullish body. Spicy and gamey but decent acidity. A little too southern for my taste but good for the vintage. (February 2006)
2008 TO 2015   15.0

Vosne-Romanée, Les Suchots, 2003
Domaine Jean Grivot
Very good colour. A touch of new oak on the nose. But nicely cool, rich and profound. On the palate not a great deal of structure or, indeed, vigour, but ripe and balanced. Very good indeed. (March 2006)
2008 TO 2019   17.0

Vosne-Romanée, Les Suchots, 2003
Domaine Alain Hudelot-Noëllat

Fine colour. Mocha-chocolate nose. Medium to medium-full body. Ripe but soft tannins. Ample fruit. Not cooked for a 2003. This is fine.
(March 2006)
2008 TO 2015   17.5

2002

The 2002 red Burgundies, while not at the top levels in the same league as the great 1999s (or indeed the 2005s), are already proving to be very popular in the marketplace. The red wines have a good colour, a refreshing acidity, a medium-full body, and lots of plump fruit and ripe tannins. They are relaxed wines. There is a French phrase, sometimes applied to people, *"bien dans sa peau,"* which literally means "comfortable within one's skin" or at ease with oneself. This is an apt description of the 2002s. The vintage is fine at the generic level. The village and *premiers crus* are also delicious. It is only at top *grand cru* level that there is a clear difference vis-à-vis 1999. But subtract 1999 (and 2005) from the equation, and we have a year which is as good as anything else produced in recent memory. The vintage is also geographically consistent. Although some will suggest that the Côte de Beaune is better than the Côte de Nuits, I do not agree. There are some lovely wines in Nuits-Saint-Georges and Chambolle-Musigny. For the third year in succession, according to Jacques Lardière of Jadot, Gevrey-Chambertin is the best commune.

The white wines, too, are extremely good, perhaps even better than the reds. There is a refreshing acidity which brings out wonderfully elegant complex fruit. This is coupled with good weight and the potential to age well. All in all, this is a highly successful vintage.

WEATHER CONDITIONS

It was a severe winter, very cold—but dry—both before and after Christmas. I remember it being minus 8.5°C at 8:30 A.M. in Savigny-lès-Beaune several mornings in a row. This was followed by a mild February and March, allowing an easy bud-break, but this was succeeded by a cool May. This retarded the flowering, but fine weather after June 13 meant that this turned out successfully, although the crop would not be excessive. The next 10 weeks were dry, but not too hot. Thankfully, there were no hailstorms.

August was warm and still dry, and this led to a situation in the early days of September where the development of the fruit—the Chardonnays more than the Pinots—was somewhat blocked. Then there was rain. This did no harm except in Ladoix, where it was somewhat excessive and thus reduced the concentration of the Cortons and such Charlemagnes as come from the top of this side of the hill. This rainy period was soon followed by fine weather. Beginning in mid-September a cool north wind set in, accompanied by clear skies and cold nights. These conditions were similar to those of 1996, except that the crop in 1996 was larger, and the weather had not been so fine in August. Volumes were reduced, and concentration and potential alcohol levels were accelerated by this drying wind. The harvest began on September 15 and was over by October 1. The fruit was healthy but not, in some cases, completely ripe. The best growers

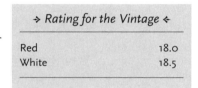

→ Rating for the Vintage ←	
Red	18.0
White	18.5

→ Size of the Crop ←		
(In hectolitres, excluding generic wine)		
	RED	WHITE
Grands Crus	13,114	3,726
Village and Premiers Crus	170,522	62,385
TOTAL	183,636	66,111

waited a few days, benefiting from the continuing good weather, and then eliminated on the sorting table the berries that were not fully concentrated. It was hardly necessary to chaptalise. After October 1 the weather deteriorated, affecting the quality of the Hautes-Côtes.

At first, there was quite a high level of malic acid, and the *malos* were slow to complete; as a result, the 2002s were a bit aggressive. It was only after the *malos* had finished, and carbon dioxide levels had started to decline—or were reduced by those who rack at the end of the summer—that the 2002s began to show their texture. They are wines of roundness and succulence as well as of pure fruit. At first there was somewhat less *terroir* definition than in the 1999s at the same stage, and although, according to Christian Gouges, this aspect would improve, I feel, as Marie-Andrée Mugneret (Domaine Dr. Georges Mugneret) has indicated, that the expression of the 2002s will always be more about Pinot Noir than exactly were the wines come from. It boils down to the weather pattern. A great vintage, which by definition is one of wines which speak loudly of their origins, is the product of a fine August (*août fait le moût*) as well as a fine September. August 2002 was good, but not brilliant. And the first two weeks of September were inclement as well. Many growers, despite *malos* which in some cases had not finished by the time of the 2003 harvest, decided to bottle early "to preserve the fruit."

WHERE ARE THE BEST WINES?

The wines of 2002 are very consistent. There are lovely wines in both colours throughout the Côte d'Or and throughout the Côte Chalonnaise. Only in the Hautes-Côtes, although even here mainly highly satisfactory wines can be found, is the pattern less even. Stick to the best growers, and you can hardly go wrong.

WHEN WILL THE WINES BE AT THEIR BEST?

This is a fine vintage for the lesser wines, and many, including Bourgogne *Rouge*, Côte-de-Beaune

Villages, and Marsannay, are now ready. The lesser village wines such as Santenay will follow soon after, with Côte de Beaune *premiers crus* emerging from 2008. Even the Côte de Nuits *premiers crus* will be ready by 2010, while the top *grands crus* still need a decade. That said, because of the nature of the tannins, I think the vintage will not go as deep into its shell in the interim as some. The 2002s will be more pleasant to drink in their adolescence than many.

TASTING NOTES

WHITES
Bâtard-Montrachet, 2002
Maison Henri Boillot
Good depth on the nose. Not too oaky. Medium-full body. Ripe and balanced. Not quite the depth and dimension for fine. But very good indeed. (June 2006)

2009 TO 2918   17.0

Bâtard-Montrachet, 2002
Domaine Jean-Noël Gagnard
Magnum. Rich colour. Very lovely rich nose. Full, fat, concentrated and profound. Very lovely rich, balanced fruit. Ripe and gently oaky. Vigorous. Excellent. (January 2006)

2010 TO 2025   19.0

Bâtard-Montrachet, 2002
Hospices de Beaune
Bottled by Antoine de Varenne. Not over-oaky at all. Full, rich and plump. Very fine concentrated fruit. Still youthful. Very lovely. Very fine. (January 2005)

2009 TO 2021   18.5

Bâtard-Montrachet, 2002
Domaine Leflaive
Firm, full, backward nose. Slightly adolescent. Full, rich and meaty. Very good grip. Lots of depth. Needs time. Doesn't sing as much as their Bienvenues-Bâtard-Montrachet today. But very fine. (June 2006)

2012 TO 2022   18.5

Bâtard-Montrachet, 2002
Domaine Pierre Morey

Full and backward but poised and elegant on the nose. Fullish body. Very lovely fruit. Vigorous, harmonious, multidimensional and very, very stylish. Very fine plus. (June 2006)

2012 TO 2025   19.0

Bâtard-Montrachet, 2002
Domaine Ramonet

Full, rich and rather less adolescent than their Bienvenues-Bâtard-Montrachet. Very lovely nose. Full body. Backward. Very, very concentrated. Very lovely fruit. Pure, classy, long and complex. Very fine plus. (June 2006)

2012 TO 2025   19.0

Bâtard-Montrachet, 2002
Domaine Étienne Sauzet

Very classy, composed nose. Very elegant, concentrated fruit. Medium-full body. Delicate but intense. Poised, balanced and multidimensional. Very lovely. (June 2006)

2010 TO 2025   19.0

Bienvenues-Bâtard-Montrachet, 2002
Domaine Louis Carillon et Fils

Very, very lovely fruit on the nose. Splendidly elegant and complex. Subtle. Medium-full body. Ripe and rich. Very good minerally background. Very long. Very fine. (June 2006)

2010 TO 2020   18.5

Bienvenues-Bâtard-Montrachet, 2002
Maison Vincent Girardin

Quite oaky. Rather more blowsy than most 2002s on the nose. Not the greatest of concentration or vigour on the palate. But decent class and balance. Very good at best. Quite forward. (January 2006)

NOW TO 2014   16.0

Bienvenues-Bâtard-Montrachet, 2002
Maison Olivier Leflaive Frères

Ripe, quite soft on the nose. A quite forward wine, without the concentration and depth of a real *grand cru*. Yet balanced, elegant, attractive and not short. Very good. (June 2006)

2009 TO 2017   16.0

Bienvenues-Bâtard-Montrachet, 2002
Domaine Leflaive

A richer, ampler, fuller wine than Carillon's. Equally fine. The oak is a little more marked (but not a bit excessive). Very rich. Very profound. Still youthful. Great intensity. Very fine. (June 2006)

2010 TO 2020   18.5

Bienvenues-Bâtard-Montrachet, 2002
Domaine Ramonet

Rich, fat, youthful nose. Backward on the palate. Full, very concentrated and very profound. Still a bit adolescent. Lots of depth and vigour. Needs time. Very fine. (June 2006)

2012 TO 2025   18.5

Chassagne-Montrachet, 2002
Domaine Bichot

Medium body. Ripe, civilised, balanced and attractive. Good plus for what it is. (October 2004)

NOW TO 2014   15.0

Chassagne-Montrachet, 2002
Domaine du Marquis de Laguiche/
Maison Joseph Drouhin

Ripe, gently oaky, very succulent on both nose and palate. Fullish body. Lovely fruit. Very fine grip. Excellent harmony. Long and very stylish. Fine. (October 2005)

NOW TO 2017   17.5

Chassagne-Montrachet, Abbaye de Morgeot, 2002
Maison Olivier Leflaive Frères

Soft nose. Quite forward. Flowery and fragrant. Medium body. Balanced and positive at the end. Nicely fresh and pure. Ready. Very good. (June 2006)

NOW TO 2011   16.0

Chassagne-Montrachet, Blanchot-Dessus, 2002
Domaine Anglada-Deleger
Fullish, ripe, concentrated nose. Medium-full body. Good crisp acidity. Plenty of depth and class. Long, vigorous finish. Fine. (June 2006)
NOW TO 2018   17.5

Chassagne-Montrachet, Les Caillerets, 2002
Domaine Guy Amiot et Fils
Fragrant nose. Nice flowery fruit. Medium-full body. Good ample, balanced fruit. A slight lack of real flair but very good. (June 2006)
NOW TO 2015   16.0

Chassagne-Montrachet, Les Caillerets, 2002
Domaine Blain-Gagnard
Stylish nose. Nicely steely. Medium to medium-full body. Very good crisp, peachy fruit. Long and harmonious. Fine. (June 2006)
NOW TO 2018   17.5

Chassagne-Montrachet, Les Caillerets, 2002
Domaine Marc Colin et Fils
Full, rich and concentrated. Very lovely fruit. Plenty of depth and grip. Lots of vigour. Clean and pure. Very long on the palate. Fine. (April 2006)
2009 TO 2016   17.5

Chassagne-Montrachet, Les Caillerets, 2002
Domaine Richard Fontaine-Gagnard
Fullish, ample nose. Good weight and harmony. Medium-full body. Good grip. Good fruit. Not the intensity of Blain-Gagnard but long and very good plus. (June 2006)
NOW TO 2016   16.5

Chassagne-Montrachet, Les Champs Gain, 2002
Domaine Guy Amiot et Fils
Soft, ripe, flowery nose. Medium body. Quite advanced. Pleasant but lacks a bit of bite and flair. Quite good plus. (June 2006)
NOW TO 2011   14.5

Chassagne-Montrachet, Les Chaumées, 2002
Domaine Michel Colin-Deléger et Fils
Still a little closed on the nose. But good fragrant fruit. Medium-full body. Good crisp acidity.

Plenty of depth and concentration. Long. Very good indeed. (June 2006)
NOW TO 2015   17.0

Chassagne-Montrachet, Les Chenevottes, 2002
Domaine Michel Colin-Deléger et Fils
Slightly less high toned on the nose than their 2002 Chassagne-Montrachet Chaumées. More herbal. Not quite the zip of the Chaumées but good weight, plenty of fruit, and nicely long and positive. Very good plus. (June 2006)
NOW TO 2015   16.5

Chassagne-Montrachet, Les Chenevottes, 2002
Domaine Bernard Morey
Domainee. Youthful colour. Mellow, ripe, gently oaky nose. Good concentration. Good depth. Medium to medium-full body. Balanced and succulent. Good style. Long and positive. Very good. Needs a year or two. (March 2005)
NOW TO 2014   16.0

Chassagne-Montrachet, Les Chenevottes, 2002
Domaine Marc Morey et Fils
Ripe, ample, fullish nose. Medium-full body. Good grip. Fragrant peachy fruit. Long. Very good. (June 2006)
NOW TO 2015   16.0

Chassagne-Montrachet, Les Grandes Ruchottes, 2002
Domaine Fernand and Laurent Pillot
Lovely nose. Poised, harmonious and classy. Medium-full body. Concentrated, rich, profound and very fragrant. This is long and lovely. Fine plus. (June 2006)
2009 TO 2019   18.0

Chassagne-Montrachet, Les Macherelles, 2002
Domaine Guy Amiot et Fils
Decent weight and depth of fruit on the nose. But on the palate it lacks a bit of grip and concentration. Medium body. Just a touch short. (June 2006)
NOW TO 2010   14.0

Chassagne-Montrachet, Maltroye, 2002
Domaine Jean-Noël Gagnard
Still quite reticent on the nose. Clean, full, concentrated and with very good acidity. Lovely

peachy fruit. Elegant and profound. Very good indeed. (March 2005)

NOW TO 2017   17.0

Chassagne-Montrachet, Morgeot, 2002
Domaine Michel Colin-Deléger et Fils

Full nose. Quite rich. Good grip. Medium fruit. Very good ripe, balanced fruit. Not a bit four-square. Good depth. Lovely finish. Very good indeed. (June 2006)

NOW TO 2017   17.0

Chassagne-Montrachet, Morgeot, 2002
Domaine Louis Latour

Good ripe, balanced fruit on the nose. Medium to medium-full body. Ample and agreeable but it lacks a little personality and depth. Positive at the end though. Good. (June 2006)

NOW TO 2012   15.0

Chassagne-Montrachet, Morgeot, 2002
Domaine Fernand and Laurent Pillot

Good ripe nose. No lack of depth. Medium-full body. Good grip. Stylish and complex. Long and positive. Very good indeed. (June 2006)

NOW TO 2016   17.0

Chassagne-Montrachet, Morgeot, Clos de la Chapelle, 2002
Domaine Duc de Magenta/Maison Louis Jadot

Profound nose. Very high quality fruit here. Balanced and concentrated. Fullish body. Splendidly intense. Lots and lots of depth. Excellent grip. Marvellous finish. This is really fine. (March 2005)

NOW TO 2018   18.0

Chassagne-Montrachet, Morgeot, Clos Pitois, 2002
Domaine Roger Belland

Fragrant, flowery nose. Forward. Medium body. A slight lack of depth, concentration and grip. Quite good at best. (June 2006)

NOW TO 2010   14.0

Chassagne-Montrachet, Morgeot, Vigne Blanche, 2002
Château de la Maltroye

Gently oaky. Rich, ripe, profound and very beautiful. Fullish body. Very good grip. Lots of concentration. Very classy. Still needs time. Fine plus. (March 2005)

NOW TO 2018   18.0

Chassagne-Montrachet, En Remilly, 2002
Domaine Michel Colin-Deléger et Fils

A bit closed-in on the nose. Medium-full body. Racy and minerally. Lovely poised, fragrant fruit. Elegant and persistent. Fine finish. Fine quality. (June 2006)

NOW TO 2018   17.5

Chassagne-Montrachet, La Romanée, 2002
Domaine Vincent Dancer

Nicely steely on the nose. Very pure and well balanced. Lovely fruit here. Medium-full body. Good grip and concentration. Long and complex. Fine. (June 2006)

2009 TO 2019   17.5

Chassagne-Montrachet, La Romanée, 2002
Maison Olivier Leflaive Frères

Good weight and minerality on the nose. Softer, more forward, slightly less weight and slightly looser-knit than Vincent Dancer's. But harmonious and with good grip and persistence. Elegant too. Very good indeed. (June 2006)

NOW TO 2017   17.0

Chassagne-Montrachet, Les Ruchottes, 2002
Domaine Ramonet

Quite developed for what it is. Rich, ample and full bodied. Rich and succulent. Very good balance. Quite a meaty, ripe wine but fine quality. (June 2006)

NOW TO 2015   18.0

Chassagne-Montrachet, Tête du Clos, 2002
Domaine Vincent Dancer

Poised, fragrant nose. Medium-full body. Ripe. Good vigour and depth. Good grip. Balanced. Long. Very good plus. (June 2006)

NOW TO 2015   16.5

Chassagne-Montrachet, Les Vergers, 2002
Domaine Michel Colin Père et Fils

Just a touch four-square on the nose. There isn't quite the zip and flair here, compared with Colin's other wines. Yet it is medium-full body, there is good grip and the finish is positive. Very good. (June 2006)

NOW TO 2013   16.0

Chassagne-Montrachet, Les Vergers, 2002
Domaine Marc Morey et Fils

This is really quite developed on the nose. Alarmingly so on the palate. It is already a bit tired. Medium body. Disappointing. (June 2006)

DRINK UP   12.0

Chassagne-Montrachet, Les Vergers, 2002
Domaine Fernand and Laurent Pillot

Slightly four-square on the nose. But good weight and grip on the palate. Medium-full body. Ripe and peachy. Positive at the end. Stylish at the end. Very good. (June 2006)

NOW TO 2013   16.0

Chassagne-Montrachet, Vide Bourse, 2002
Domaine Fernand and Laurent Pillot

Fullish on the nose. A little four-square. Ripe and ample. Medium-full body. Decent fruit. But a little pedestrian. There is a lack of zip and complexity. Good at best. Yet the finish is positive. (June 2006)

NOW TO 2013   15.0

Chassagne-Montrachet, En Virondot, 2002
Domaine Marc Morey et Fils

Lightish, flowery nose. Forward on the palate. This lacks both depth and concentration. It is pleasantly fresh at the moment, but that's all it has, and it won't last. (June 2006)

DRINK SOON   13.0

Chevalier-Montrachet, 2002
Domaine Bouchard Père et Fils

Full colour. Very fine quality. Lots of depth and lovely fruit here. Fullish body. Profound. Very classy. This has a great deal of vigour, depth and class. Really excellent. (June 2006)

2012 TO 2025   19.5

Chevalier-Montrachet, 2002
Domaine Michel Colin-Deléger et Fils

Classy nose. Still youthful. Fresh and medium-full on the palate. At first a little hidden. But complex and classy underneath. Vigorous. Very pure fruit. Lovely balance. Very fine. (June 2006)

2010 TO 2020   18.5

Chevalier-Montrachet, 2002
Domaine Leflaive

Splendidly concentrated, youthful, crisp nose. Full and rich. This has a lot of class and depth. Yet to drink it now isn't too infanticidal. Very lovely fruit. Long. Intense and vigorous. Excellent. (April 2002)

NOW TO 2020   18.5

Chevalier-Montrachet, Clos des Chevaliers, 2002
Domaine Jean Chartron

Elegant nose. But not the power of Bouchard's. Medium-full body. Harmonious. Subtle and complex. Ripe and very stylish. Very long at the end. Fine plus. (June 2006)

2010 TO 2020   18.0

Corton Blanc, 2002
Domaine du Comte Senard

Lovely, stylish nose. Not a bit four-square which Corton Blancs often are. Medium-full body. Ripe, rich attack. Then it tails off a bit. It is fresh. But it lacks concentration, weight and zip. (March 2005)

NOW TO 2010   15.0

Corton-Charlemagne, 2002
Domaine Bertagna

Magnum. Good crisp nose. Properly steely on the palate. Full bodied, concentrated, intense and classy. The oak is just right. This is fine plus. (June 2006)

2010 TO 2020   18.0

Corton-Charlemagne, 2002
Domaine Simon Bize et Fils

The nose is a bit hidden. Better on the palate. Medium-full body. Good grip. Gently oaky. Good depth. Very good plus. (June 2006)

2009 TO 2018   16.5

Corton-Charlemagne, 2002
Domaine Bonneau du Martray

Very concentrated nose. Still youthful. Very lovely on the palate. Full body. Beautifully balanced. Very classy. Multidimensional. Very fine finish. Very fine plus. (June 2006)

2012 TO 2025   19.0

Corton-Charlemagne, 2002
Domaine Bouchard Père et Fils

Magnum. Fragrant, minerally nose. Medium-full body. Classy ripe fruit. Good grip. Classic. Fine. (June 2006)

2009 TO 2019   17.5

Corton-Charlemagne, 2002
Domaine Chapuis

Slightly more developed than most of these Corton-Charlemagnes on the nose. Ripe and stylish though. Medium-full body. Attractive ripe, balanced fruit. Long and positive at the end. Very good plus. (June 2006)

2009 TO 2018   16.5

Corton-Charlemagne, 2002
Domaine Jean-François Coche-Dury

Rich, ripe, steely nose. Full and very concentrated. Just very lightly oaky. Rich and intense. Very long on the palate. Lots of depth. Very fine. (June 2006)

2010 TO 2020   18.5

Corton-Charlemagne, 2002
Domaine Marius Delarche

Quite a forward example. Ripe. Medium-full body. It lacks the grip and steeliness of a Corton-Charlemagne but is ripe and balanced. Good but not great. (June 2006)

NOW TO 2015   15.0

Corton-Charlemagne, 2002
Domaine Joseph Faiveley

Ripe, rich nose. Not too oaky. A bit more oaky on the palate though. Medium-full body. Good fruit. Balanced if not that concentrated. The oak comes through at the end. Very good at best. (June 2006)

2009 TO 2016   16.0

Corton-Charlemagne, 2002
Domaine Patrick Javillier

Magnum. Elegant, flavour-steely nose. Very good depth and class. Full body. Vigorous, minerally and splendidly balanced. Profound. Youthful. Very fine. (June 2006)

2010 TO 2020   18.5

Corton-Charlemagne, 2002
Domaine Michel Juillot

Ripe nose. Medium to medium-full body. Not as concentrated or as intense as some. More developed. Balanced and attractive though. But I am looking for more depth. Good. (June 1006)

2009 TO 2016   15.0

Corton-Charlemagne, 2002
Domaine Louis Latour

Quite a full example on the nose. A touch of built-in sulphur. Ripe, rich and fruity. But a lack of flair and depth. (June 2006)

2010 TO 2018   15.0

Corton-Charlemagne, 2002
Maison Olivier Leflaive Frères

Ripe, gently oaky nose. Quite forward. But quite classic. Medium-full body. Nice and steely. Good vigour. Balanced, complex and stylish. Very good indeed. (June 2006)

2009 TO 2019   17.0

Corton-Charlemagne, 2002
Maison Morey-Blanc

Lovely fruit on the nose. Sophisticated and harmonious. Fullish. Classic. Concentrated and profound on the palate. This is very long, very elegant and very complex. Very fine. (June 2006)

2010 TO 2020   18.5

Corton-Charlemagne, 2002
Domaine du Pavillon/Albert Bichot

Nicely steely on the nose. Still a little closed. Fullish and quite concentrated. Fine quality fruit. Balanced, ripe and rich on the palate. Not the depth of the very best, but a fine example. (July 2006)

2009 TO 2016   17.5

Corton-Charlemagne, 2002
Domaine Rapet Père et Fils

Lovely flowery-steely nose. Intense and ripe. Medium-full body. Long and complex on the palate. Very good concentration. This is fine plus. (June 2006)

2010 TO 2020   18.0

Criots-Bâtard-Montrachet, 2002
Domaine Roger Belland

Fragrant nose. Stylish. Very good fruit. A subtle example. Medium-full body. Very pure. The oak is very understated. Long and complex. Fine. (June 2006)

2010 TO 2020   17.5

Criots-Bâtard-Montrachet, 2002
Maison Camille Giroud

Fullish, rich, stylish, vigorous nose. Lots of quality here. The oak is just right. Fullish on the palate. Complex and very classy. Lovely finish. Very fine. (June 2006)

2010 TO 2020   18.5

Criots-Bâtard-Montrachet, 2002
Domaine Louis Jadot

Delicate, understated, but intense and very, very elegant. Lovely balance. Lots of personality. Very fine finish. Very complex. (October 2005)

NOW TO 2020   18.5

Meursault, 2002
Domaine Pierre Morey

Ripe, quite opulent and concentrated for a village example. Classy fruit. Quite backward. No undue oak. This has depth and concentration on the palate. Very good for a village wine. (March 2005)

NOW TO 2014   15.5

Meursault, Premier Cru, 2002
Château de Meursault

Quite a developed nose. Fullish, ripe and balanced but a lack of zip, concentration and flair. Quite good at best. (July 2006)

NOW TO 2011   14.0

Meursault, Blagny, 2002
Domaine François and Antoine Jobard

Restrained nose. Ripe, rich, concentrated and backward. Fullish body. Just a touch of oak. Very good grip. A lot of depth. Will need time but very good indeed. (June 2006)

2009 TO 2018   17.0

Meursault, Blagny, Château de Blagny, 2002
Domaine Louis Latour

Full, ripe, even a touch of residual sugar on the palate. Good grip though. Not too sulphury. Round. Lacks a little zip but good plus. (March 2006)

NOW TO 2010   15.5

Meursault, Blagny, 2002
Domaine Matrot-Wittersheim

Quite forward but fresh, very gently oaky, rich and concentrated. Nice and minerally. Not a bit heavy. Elegant. Very good plus. Better still in a year. (March 2005)

NOW TO 2012   16.5

Meursault, Blagny, 2002
Domaine Alain and Christian Patriarche

Closed-in still. Full and rich on the palate. Ripe and ample but a little adolescent still. Lovely fruit. A keeper. Very good indeed. (February 2006)

2009 TO 2020   17.5

Meursault, Blagny, La Jeunelotte, 2002
Domaine Martelet de Cherisey

Ripe, ample, rich and quite developed. Quite full. Good class but lacks a little power and real class. Very good if not great. Ready. (March 2005)

NOW TO 2009   16.0

Meursault, Les Bouchères, 2002
Domaine Latour-Giraud

Medium colour. Some evolution on the nose. A touch of sulphur. Fullish and a little four-square. Good fruit. But not the greatest class or dimension. Good rather than fine. (April 2005)

NOW TO 2012   15.0

Meursault, Les Bouchères, 2002
Maison Morey-Blanc

Backward. Lovely ripe, rich fruit on the nose.
Classy. Fullish body. Gently oaky. Ample and
profound. Excellent balance. Needs time. Fine.
(July 2006)

2009 TO 2020   17.5

Meursault, Les Caillerets, 2002
Domaine Fernand and Laurent Pillot

Fresh. Quite accessible. Medium body. Slightly
four-square. But decent fruit and freshness on
the palate. But it lacks a little dimension. Quite
good plus. (July 2006)

NOW TO 2010   14.5

Meursault, Charmes, 2002
Domaine Vincent Bitouzet-Prieur

Ample, ripe and balanced. Clean. Good. But it
lacks the personality and finesse for very good.
Needs another year. (February 2006)

NOW TO 2014   15.0

Meursault, Charmes, 2002
Maison Henri Boillot

Full, quite broad nose. Quite oaky. Medium to
medium-full body. Good grip. Stylish but not
the greatest depth or concentration or dimension. (July 2006)

NOW TO 2012   15.0

Meursault, Charmes, 2002
Domaine Bouchard Père et Fils

Quite developed on the nose. Gentle, quite
forward, medium bodied on the palate. It
has balance and charm. Good plus. Ready.
(July 2006)

NOW TO 2010   15.5

Meursault, Charmes, 2002
Domaine Louis Jadot

Very good fruit, plus elegance and grip on
the nose. Very well balanced on the palate.
Medium-full body. Lovely fruit. Long and very
good indeed. (July 2006)

NOW TO 2018   17.0

Meursault, Charmes, 2002
Domaine des Comtes Lafon

Surprisingly delicate on the nose. Ripe, charming, balanced and persistent. Very elegant and
understated. Very good indeed. (July 2006)

NOW TO 2017   17.0

Meursault, Charmes, 2002
Maison Olivier Leflaive Frères

Forward nose. Quite high toned. Medium body.
Flowery. Decently balanced but not much depth
or vigour. Quite good. Ready. (July 2006)

NOW TO 2010   14.0

Meursault, Charmes, 2002
Maison Morey-Blanc

Quite backward on the nose. Good depth and
fruit here. Medium-full body. Ripe and balanced.
Very good follow-through. Elegant. Lovely finish. Very good indeed. (July 2006)

NOW TO 2018   17.0

Meursault, Les Charmes, 2002
Domaine du Pavillon/Albert Bichot

Good, racy, flowery nose. There is style here.
Medium to medium-full body. Crisp, ripe and
fruity on the palate. Elegant. Even complex.
Long on the finish. Very good indeed. Just about
ready. (July 2006)

NOW TO 2012   17.0

Meursault, Clos de la Barre, 2002
Domaine des Comtes Lafon

Village wine. Fullish, ample and concentrated.
Not too oaky. Good grip and definition. Very
impressive for what it is. (March 2005)

NOW TO 2014   16.0

Meursault, Genevrières, 2002
Domaine Bouchard Père et Fils

Ripe, round, ample, quite full nose. Good
weight. Good grip. Good class. Rather more
character and vigour than their Charmes. Very
good indeed. (July 2006)

NOW TO 2016   17.0

Meursault, Genevrières, 2002
Domaine Michel Bouzereau et Fils

Quite accessible but good depth of fruit on the nose. Round and ample. Developed. Fruity but without the grip of some. Merely good. Ready. (July 2006)

NOW TO 2011   15.0

Meursault, Genevrières, 2002
Domaine Louis Jadot

The nose is a bit closed. Ripe fruit. Medium-full body. Good energy. I would have liked a bit more zip. Will develop. Very good plus. (July 2006)

NOW TO 2015   16.5

Meursault, Genevrières, 2002
Domaine François and Antoine Jobard

Plenty of depth and concentration on the nose. Backward. Medium-full body. Ripe and balanced. But it doesn't have the dimension of their 2002 Meursault Blagny. Very good. (July 2006)

NOW TO 2015   16.0

Meursault, Genevrières, 2002
Domaine des Comtes Lafon

The nose is still a bit closed. Rich, fullish, ample and concentrated on the palate. Very good grip. This is showing much better than their 2002 Meursault Charmes. Very profound. Very long. Fine plus. (July 2006)

2010 TO 2020   18.0

Meursault, Genevrières, 2002
Maison Olivier Leflaive Frères

Good depth here on the nose. Rather more backbone and energy than their 2002 Meursault Charmes. Medium-full body. Lovely fruit. Good vigour and good style. Long. Very good indeed. (July 2006)

NOW TO 2018   17.0

Meursault, Genevrières, 2002
Maison Morey-Blanc

Lots of classy, concentrated wine on the nose here. Fullish body. Very gently oaky. Very lovely fruit. Lots of vigour and depth. Fine finish. Fine plus. (July 2006)

2010 TO 2020   18.0

Meursault, Les Gouttes d'Or, 2002
Domaine Bouchard Père et Fils

Lovely fragrant, high-toned nose, but no lack of weight behind it. Quite backward. Medium-full body. Good grip. A vigorous wine with plenty of depth. Very good indeed. (July 2006)

NOW TO 2016   17.0

Meursault, Gouttes d'Or, 2002
Domaine Louis Jadot

Delicate colour. Fine nose. Fat and opulent. Slightly earthy. Good but not brilliant class. Better on the palate. Juicy and crisp. Quite forward. Very good plus. (October 2005)

NOW TO 2014   16.5

Meursault, Les Gouttes d'Or, 2002
Domaine Louis Latour

Good medium-full, succulent nose. More open than Bouchard Père et Fils's 2002 Gouttes d'Or. Good grip. Classy fruit. Long. Very good indeed. (July 2006)

NOW TO 2016   17.0

Meursault, Perrières, 2002
Maison Henri Boillot

Nicely minerally on the nose. Not much oak at all. Fullish body. Classic. Classy. Lovely fruit and very good balance. Lots of energy. This is fine. (July 2006)

2009 TO 2019   17.5

Meursault, Perrières, 2002
Domaine Bouchard Père et Fils

Closed-in nose. But a lot of depth and class here. Fullish body. Lovely ripe fruit. Harmonious and very elegant. Lovely finish. Fine plus. (July 2006)

2009 TO 2020   18.0

Meursault, Perrières, 2002
Domaine Michel Bouzereau et Fils
Some development on the nose. And not the fine-grained class of some. Quite forward. Medium to medium-full body. More elegant than the nose would suggest. Succulent, balanced and accessible. Just about ready. Very good. (July 2006)
NOW TO 2014   16.0

Meursault, Perrières, 2002
Château de Puligny-Montrachet
Minerally. Ripe, rich and fullish bodied. Still needs time. Harmonious and classy. Very good plus. (June 2005)
NOW TO 2014   16.5

Meursault, Perrières, 2002
Domaine Jean-François Coche-Dury
Quite a broad nose. Still youthful though. Indeed a little closed. Quite full on the palate. Very classy. Splendidly mineral. Very good grip. Harmonious and classic. Lots of energy. Fine plus. (July 2006)
2010 TO 2020   18.0

Meursault, Perrières, 2002
Domaine Vincent Dancer
Steely, classy nose. Lots of lovely fruit here. This is a lovely wine. Medium-full body. Very lovely fruit. Great style and depth. Very, very long. Very fine. (July 2006)
2010 TO 2020   18.5

Meursault, Perrières, 2002
Domaine Joseph Drouhin
Quite developed on the nose. It lacks the grip of some. Forward. A bit weak. Decent fruit but no flair. Fully ready. Disappointing for Drouhin. Quite good at best. (July 2006)
NOW TO 2010   14.0

Meursault, Perrières, 2002
Domaine des Comtes Lafon
Lovely nose. Complete, quite backward and very classy. Medium-full body. Very good fruit. Harmonious and still to show its real depth. But certainly fine. (July 2006)
2010 TO 2020   17.5

Meursault, Perrières, 2002
Maison Olivier Leflaive Frères
Succulent, ripe, balanced fruit on the nose. Quite forward. Indeed just about ready. But properly steely, harmonious and elegant. Very good indeed. (July 2006)
NOW TO 2015   17.0

Meursault, Perrières, 2002
Domaine Pierre Morey
Full nose. Backward. One of the fullest and certainly the least advanced of the 2002 Perrières. Excellent fruit and depth. Lots of class. Lots of energy. Very fine. (July 2006)
2010 TO 2020   18.5

Meursault, Perrières, 2002
Château de Puligny-Montrachet
Closed-in on the nose. Good class and *terroir* definition. Medium-full body on the palate. Good if not very good grip. A slight lack of personality perhaps. Very good. (July 2006)
2009 TO 2016   16.0

Meursault, Perrières, 2002
Domaine Guy Roulot
Very lovely nose. Poised, elegant and complete. Very lovely fruit. Medium-full body. Quite accessible. Marvellous harmony. Everything in place. Very complex. Very long. Very fine. (July 2006)
2009 TO 2020   18.5

Meursault, Poruzots, 2002
Domaine Louis Jadot
Some development on the nose. But good style here. Yet on the palate a little neutral. Decent fruit but not a lot of grip or depth. Only quite good. (July 2006)
NOW TO 2010   14.0

Meursault, Poruzots, 2002
Domaine François and Antoine Jobard
Fullish, backward, classy nose. Medium-full body. Gently oaky. Plenty of depth and very good grip. Lovely finish. This is fine. (July 2006)
2009 TO 2019   17.5

Meursault, Poruzots, 2002
Château de Puligny-Montrachet

Just a touch four-square on the nose. Medium-full body. Decent fruit and grip. But no great depth, complexity or class. Positive finish though. So good plus. (July 2006)

NOW TO 2014   15.5

Meursault, Sous le Dos d'Ane, 2002
Domaine Leflaive

Meursault-Blagny in all but name. The vines are a little youthful (10 years old or so). So decent classy fruit but no great depth on the nose. Medium to medium-full body. Balanced. Very pure. Long and elegant. Finishes well. Very good. (July 2006)

NOW TO 2016   16.0

Meursault, En Luraule, 2002
Domaine Joseph Drouhin

Fragrant, stylish, fruity nose. Medium weight. Balanced, neatly made, complex and elegant on the palate. Lovely long finish. Just about ready. Very good. (July 2006)

NOW TO 2012   16.0

Meursault, Narvaux, 2002
Domaine Joseph de Bucy

Ripe, racy, minerally and stylish. But ready now. Good. (March 2005)

NOW TO 2009   15.0

Meursault, Les Tessons, 2002
Domaine Michel Bouzereau et Fils

Quite an evolved, nutty nose. It lacks a little zip. Medium body. It could have done with a bit more vigour and grip but balanced and fruity, elegant and attractive. Good plus. (April 2006)

NOW TO 2010   15.5

Meursault, Tillets, 2002
Domaine Alain and Christian Patriarche

Still youthful. Ample, ripe and quite substantial. Very fine depth. Lots of vigour. Long and complex. Very good indeed for a village wine. This is for keeping. (February 2006)

NOW TO 2014   16.0

Montrachet, 2002
Domaine Guy Amiot et Fils

No great weight or concentration and a little built-in sulphur on the nose. Medium-full body. Elegant and fruity. A fine wine. But not the depth and flair for a Montrachet. (June 2006)

2010 TO 2020   17.5

Montrachet, 2002
Maison Camille Giroud

Magnum. Full, rich, abundant, classy nose. Very good grip. Lovely concentrated fruit. Full body. Excellent depth. Classy and balanced. Very, very long and vigorous. Very fine indeed. (June 2006)

2012 TO 2025   19.5

Montrachet, 2002
Domaine Louis Jadot

Very backward. This doesn't sing at all. There is some very fine fruit. And the wine is very full with a lot of grip. Vigorous. Intense and concentrated. Very fine. But is it great? (June 2006)

2012 TO 2025   18.5

Montrachet, 2002
Domaine des Comtes Lafon

Marvellous nose. Full, rich, super-concentrated and super-classy. On the palate while very fine it is not quite up to the promise of the nose. Is this just a question of time? We'll see. Pretty splendid nonetheless. (June 2006)

2012 TO 2022   19.5

Montrachet, 2002
Domaine du Marquis de Laguiche/
Maison Joseph Drouhin

Quite developed on the nose for a four-year-old Montrachet. Very pure, complex and stylish nonetheless. Fullish body. Ripe. Splendidly balanced. Very subtle. Very elegant. Very long. Very fine indeed. (June 2006)

2012 TO 2025   19.5

Montrachet, 2002
Maison Olivier Leflaive Frères

Stylish if not very big and concentrated on the nose. Lovely fruit. No lack of intensity. But fine rather than great. (June 2006)

2010 TO 2020   17.5

Montrachet, 2002
Domaine Ramonet

Full, rich, backward, high-quality nose. Full body. Rich and intense. Very, very concentrated. Splendid depth, dimension and harmony. This is excellent. (June 2006)

2012 TO 2025   20.0

Le Montrachet, 2002
Domaine de la Romanée-Conti

Still very, very firm and closed-in, both on the nose and on the palate. Full body. Marvellous concentrated fruit. Very pure. Nicely dry. Not a bit too oaky. Rich and profound. Splendidly balanced and superbly long on the palate. Excellent. (July 2006)

2012 TO 2035   20.0

Morey-Saint-Denis, Les Monts Luisants (Blanc), 2002
Domaine Dujac

Pretty. Balanced. Elegant. Forward. Young vines still? Decently long and complex at the end. (March 2005)

NOW TO 2010   15.0

Morey-Saint-Denis, Clos des Monts Luisants (Blanc), 2002
Domaine Ponsot

Full, rich, quite powerful wine. High acidity. A wine for food. Lots of character. Very individual. Still very young. (June 2005)

NOW TO 2020   16.5

Pernand-Vergelesses, En Caradeux, 2002
Domaine Rapet Père et Fils

Good depth. Very nice pure, fruity character. Quite distinct from Meursault/Puligny. Good acidity. Plenty of vigour. Stylish. Quite full. Very good. (May 2005)

NOW TO 2015   16.0

Pernand-Vergelesses, Les Combottes, 2002
Château de Chorey

Village *appellation contrôlée*. Quite oaky. Ripe and succulent. Balanced. Slightly obvious but attractive. (March 2005)

NOW TO 2010   13.0

Puligny-Montrachet, 2002
Domaine Leflaive

Fullish body. Very good grip. Ripe. Backward for a village wine. Concentrated, too. Lots of interest here. Very good. (March 2005)

NOW TO 2017   16.0

Puligny-Montrachet, Le Cailleret, 2002
Domaine Michel Bouzereau et Fils

Fresh nose. Some weight behind it, but no real flair. Medium-full body. Decent fruit and balance. A little anonymous but a positive finish. Quite good plus. (June 2006)

NOW TO 2012   14.5

Puligny-Montrachet, Clos du Cailleret, 2002
Domaine des Lambrays

Fullish, concentrated, profound nose. High acidity here. Fullish body. Exciting, very elegant fruit with a lot of depth behind it. Vigorous. Finely balanced. This is very fine. (June 2006)

2010 TO 2020   18.5

Puligny-Montrachet, Le Cailleret, 2002
Domaine Hubert de Montille

Laid-back, slightly herbal nose. A softer wine than that of the Lambrays, but delicious fruit. Very complex and harmonious. Very long. Lovely. Fine plus. (June 2006)

2009 TO 2018   18.0

Puligny-Montrachet, Les Chalumaux, 2002
Château de Puligny-Montrachet

Not as much character and definition as their Puligny La Garenne 2002. Fruity and balanced. Medium weight. Good plus. (June 2004)

NOW TO 2010   15.5

Puligny-Montrachet, Champ Canet, 2002
Domaine Louis Carillon et Fils

Lovely peachy fruit on the nose. Good weight. Very pure. Intensely flavoured. Very elegant. Lovely balance. Very long and complex at the end. Very fine. (June 2006)

2009 TO 2020   18.5

Puligny-Montrachet, Champ Canet, 2002
Maison Olivier Leflaive Frères

Lightish and quite forward but harmonious and stylish on the nose. Just about ready now, but good depth and grip. Nicely peachy. Very well balanced. Very good plus. (June 2006)

NOW TO 2014   16.5

Puligny-Montrachet, Champ Canet, 2002
Domaine Étienne Sauzet

Good structure and plenty of elegant, balanced fruit on the nose. Medium-full body. Round, ripe and concentrated. This has plenty of depth and vigour. Lovely long finish. Fine plus. (June 2006)

2009 TO 2018   18.0

Puligny-Montrachet, Les Champs Gains, 2002
Domaine Roger Belland

Quite forward, flowery nose. Attractive fruit if no great weight. Fully ready. Ripe if without great depth or grip. A pleasant wine. Quite good. (June 2006)

NOW TO 2011   14.0

Puligny-Montrachet, Champ Gain, 2002
Domaine Louis Jadot

Good depth here on the nose. Lots of fruit and good concentration. Medium-full body. Good grip. Plenty of substance. Long, vigorous and complex. Very good plus. (June 2006)

2009 TO 2017   16.5

Puligny-Montrachet, Champ Gain, 2002
Maison Olivier Leflaive Frères

A bit light weight on the nose. Light-medium body. Pleasant fruit but no real concentration or grip. Fully ready. (June 2006)

NOW TO 2010   14.0

Puligny-Montrachet, Le Clavoillon, 2002
Domaine Leflaive

Good fullish, fresh nose. But, as always, something a little four-square about it, especially after their Combettes. On the palate this is medium-full bodied, ripe and round. Plenty of depth. Very good indeed. (June 2006)

2009 TO 2016   17.0

Puligny-Montrachet, Clos de la Mouchère, 2002
Domaine Jean Boillot et Fils

Rather dumb on the nose. Not too oaky though. Fullish bodied, ripe and rich. Lovely peachy fruit. Very well balanced. Profound and intense. Fine plus. (June 2006)

2010 TO 2020   18.0

Puligny-Montrachet, Les Combettes, 2002
Domaine Jean-Marc Boillot

A ripe, quite accessible nose. Good grip but not hard. A little oak. Medium to medium-full body. Lovely fruit. Still a little raw. More energy on the follow-through than on the attack it seems. This is long and vigorous. Fine. (June 2006)

2010 TO 2020   17.5

Puligny-Montrachet, Les Combettes, 2002
Domaine Louis Carillon et Fils

Lots of depth and concentration on the nose. Still youthful. A slightly riper and fuller but broader-based wine than their 2002 Puligny Champ Canet. More backward. At present it is the Champ Canet which shows more flair. But this could be equally as good. (June 2006)

2009 TO 2018   17.5

Puligny-Montrachet, Les Combettes, 2002
Domaine Louis Jadot

Quite an evolved colour. The nose seems a little flat. Better on the palate, though, by quite some way. Yet evolving quite fast. Quite full bodied. A touch of oak. Very ripe and luscious. Balanced. Very good plus. (March 2005)

NOW TO 2014   16.5

Puligny-Montrachet, Les Combettes, 2002
Domaine Leflaive

Refined, closed-in nose. Very lovely pure fruit here. Medium-full body. Finely poised. Very intense. Excellent grip. This is very lovely. Marvellous finish. Give it time. (June 2006)

2010 TO 2020   18.5

Puligny-Montrachet, Les Combettes, 2002
Domaine Jacques Prieur

Some evolution on the colour. Rich, round, cedary nose. Very ripe. Quite full. Very good depth and concentration. Quite a lot of oak, yet not aggressively so. Lovely ripe fruit, almost exotic, but balanced by good acidity. Very good indeed. (March 2005)

NOW TO 2017   17.0

Puligny-Montrachet, Les Combettes, 2002
Domaine Étienne Sauzet

Lots of depth and concentration on the nose. Still needs time. Splendid flowery-mineral fruit on the palate. Medium-full body. A profound, intense, youthful wine. Lovely finish. (June 2006)

2010 TO 2020   18.5

Puligny-Montrachet, Les Folatières, 2002
Domaine Jean Chartron

Soft nose. Quite developed but stylish. Medium to medium-full body. Lovely peachy fruit. Very good balance. This has plenty of depth and class. Fine. (June 2006)

NOW TO 2017   17.5

Puligny-Montrachet, Les Folatières, 2002
Château de Puligny-Montrachet

Fragrant, flowery but complex and profound on the nose. Medium-full body. Ample. Very well balanced. Good concentration. This is fine plus. (June 2006)

2009 TO 2019   18.0

Puligny-Montrachet, Les Folatières, 2002
Domaine Joseph Drouhin

Lovely ripe nose, with good depth behind it. Elegant too. Quite full. Very lovely fruit and excellent balance. Vigorous and intense and classy. Long at the end. Very fine. (June 2006)

2009 TO 2020   18.5

Puligny-Montrachet, Les Folatières, 2002
Domaine Benoit Ente

Ripe, rich, concentrated and classy. Quite full bodied. Youthful. Lots of lovely fruit. Very well balanced. Still closed. Very pure peachy fruit. Long. Very good indeed. (June 2005)

2009 TO 2020   17.0

Puligny-Montrachet, Les Folatières, 2002
Domaine Louis Jadot

Firm, full nose. Lots of depth and vigour. A fullish, backward wine. Very lovely concentrated fruit. Lots of breed here and a fine vigorous finish. This is very fine. (June 2006)

2010 TO 2020   18.5

Puligny-Montrachet, Les Folatières, 2002
Domaine des Lambrays

A backward nose, but lots of depth and quality here. Medium-full bodied, ample, peachy, concentrated and very well balanced. Lovely long, elegant finish. Perhaps their 2002 Caillerets just has the edge. Very fine. (June 2006)

2010 TO 2020   18.5

Puligny-Montrachet, Les Folatières, 2002
Domaine Louis Latour

Rather closed-in on the nose. Quite full body. Good depth and grip. Good peachy fruit. The finish is better than the attack. Just a touch four-square. So very good indeed but not fine. Needs time. (June 2006)

2009 TO 2017   17.0

Puligny-Montrachet, Les Folatières, 2002
Maison Olivier Leflaive Frères

Open, forward nose but attractively balanced fruit. Medium body. Fully ready. Balanced and charming on the palate. But a little lightweight. Good plus. (June 2006)

NOW TO 2012   15.5

Puligny-Montrachet, Les Folatières, 2002
Domaine Leflaive

Fullish nose. Still backward. Lots of depth and intensity. Fullish body. Ample, succulent and concentrated. Very lovely fruit. Very fine balance and a lovely finish. Very fine. (June 2006)

2010 TO 2020   18.5

Puligny-Montrachet, La Garenne, 2002
Domaine Gilles Bouton

Ripe, round, balanced, stylish and quite rich. Very good fruit and style. Reasonably forward, but peachy and with good depth and energy. Very good plus. (April 2006)

NOW TO 2012   16.5

Puligny-Montrachet, La Garenne, 2002
Château de Puligny-Montrachet

Crisp. Balanced. Minerally. Good grip and more weight and definition than some. Very stylish. Very good. (June 2004)

NOW TO 2011   16.0

Puligny-Montrachet, Clos de la Garenne, 2002
Domaine Duc de Magenta/Maison Louis Jadot

Still quite closed-in on the nose. Lovely, classy fruit and splendid concentration, though. Fullish body. This is still very youthful. But a splendid wine in potential. Excellent depth and concentration. Splendid harmony and intensity. Very fine at the very least. (June 2006)

2010 TO 2020   18.5

Puligny-Montrachet, Les Perrières, 2002
Domaine Louis Carillon et Fils

Fragrant, classy nose. Lovely peachy fruit. Medium-full body. Intense and concentrated. Very pure. Lots of vigour. This is very lovely. Multidimensional. Splendidly long finish. Very fine. (June 2006)

2010 TO 2020   18.5

Puligny-Montrachet, Les Perrières, 2002
Domaine Étienne Sauzet

A little anonymous on the nose at present. This doesn't have the intensity or precision of Carillon's Perrières. Medium-full body. Yet balanced and most attractive. Very good indeed. (June 2006)

NOW TO 2016   17.0

Puligny-Montrachet, Les Pucelles, 2002
Domaine Jean Boillot et Fils

Still a little closed-in on the nose but good ripe fruit here. Quite full bodied. Good grip and concentration. This has plenty of depth and energy. Long and classy at the end. Fine plus. (June 2006)

2010 TO 2019   18.0

Puligny-Montrachet, Les Pucelles, 2002
Maison Olivier Leflaive Frères

Not the weight of the Domaine Leflaive or Jean Boillot's on the nose. But balanced, pure and with no lack of attraction. Rather more forward. This is a clean, balanced wine with a good finish. But it pales by comparison. Very good plus. (June 2006)

NOW TO 2016   16.5

Puligny-Montrachet, Les Pucelles, 2002
Domaine Leflaive

A little closed-in on the nose. But very lovely, gentle, vigorous, balanced, ripe fruit on the nose. Quite full. Very good grip and very lovely, pure, intense fruit. Still youthful. But very lovely indeed. Very concentrated. Lots of energy. Excellent finish. (June 2006)

2010 TO 2020   19.0

Puligny-Montrachet, Les Referts, 2002
Domaine Louis Carillon et Fils

Round, ripe nose. Not as refined as his Champ-Canet, but good succulence and balance. Medium to medium-full body. Quite forward. Nicely crisp, though, and positive at the end. Very good. (June 2006)

NOW TO 2014   16.0

Puligny-Montrachet, Sous le Puits, 2002
Domaine Louis Latour

Stylish nose. Good weight. It lacks a bit of flair and nuance, but that is the *climat*, which doesn't really merit being *premier cru*. Well-made. Decent depth, fruit and balance. Good. (June 2006)

NOW TO 2019   15.0

Puligny-Montrachet, La Truffière, 2002
Domaine Michel Colin-Deléger et Fils

A little dumb on the nose. Good fruit and depth underneath. Medium to medium-full body. Ripe, racy and elegant. Very good concentration. Good style and intensity. Lovely long finish. Fine. (June 2006)

2009 TO 2019   17.5

Saint-Aubin, La Chatenière, 2002
Domaine Marc Colin

Soft, stylish, crisp and peachy on the nose. Lovely balance. Medium body. Just about ready. Ripe. Good depth. Very good for what it is. (March 2005)

NOW TO 2010   16.0

Saint-Aubin, La Garenne, 2002
Domaine Marc Colin

Ripe, quite rich nose. Good depth for a Garenne. Medium weight. Crisp and peachy. Quite complex. Very harmonious. Nicely pure. Very good. Better still in a year. (March 2005)

NOW TO 2013   16.0

Saint-Aubin, En Remilly, 2002
Château de Puligny-Montrachet

Still very youthful. Quite full. Plenty of depth. Good acidity. Very stylish Puligny-style finish. Very good for what it is. (June 2005)

NOW TO 2012   15.0

Vougeot, Le Clos Blanc, 2002
Domaine de la Vougeraie

A much more complete wine than their Vougeot Clos du Prieuré 2002. Much more relaxed too. Fullish body, ample, balanced and with plenty of ripe fruit laced with a little Pinot Beurot. Very good indeed. (September 2004)

NOW TO 2015   17.0

Vougeot, Clos du Prieuré, 2002
Domaine de la Vougeraie

Not as relaxed as their 2002 Clos Blanc, although bottled a full year ago. Racy, minerally and ripe underneath. Medium to medium-full body. Good acidity. Good plus. (September 2004)

NOW TO 2012   15.5

REDS

Aloxe-Corton, 2002
Domaine Robert and Raymond Jacob

Lots of finesse. Medium to medium-full body. Very well balanced and nice classy fruit. A delicious example. (February 2006)

NOW TO 2016   16.0

Aloxe-Corton, Les Chaillots, 2002
Domaine Louis Latour

Medium body. Not a lot of strength or dimension, but decent fruit and style. Quite forward. (January 2005)

NOW TO 2011   13.5

Aloxe-Corton, Clos du Chapitre, 2002
Domaine Follin-Arbelet

Medium-full colour. Slightly tarty and perfumed on the nose. Better on the palate. Medium body. Somewhat raw and astringent tannins. It lacks class but decent fruit. Not bad. (July 2006)

NOW TO 2011   13.0

Aloxe-Corton, Les Fournières, 2002
Domaine Tollot-Beaut et Fils

Good colour. Rich, substantial, meaty and slightly oaky on the nose. A little four-square and not very stylish. But quite good. (March 2004)

NOW TO 2014   14.0

Aloxe-Corton, Les Guérets, 2002
Maison Camille Giroud

Medium-full colour. Good, rich, fresh nose. Plenty of depth here. Medium-full body. Fresh, plump and ripe. Not a very stylish wine, but balanced and with a good, positive finish. Good. (July 2006)

2009 TO 2015   15.0

Aloxe-Corton, Le Suchot, 2002
Domaine Simon Bize et Fils

Good colour. Slightly rustic, stemmy nose. Ripe. Medium to medium-full body. Good grip. Finishes better than it starts. Good. (March 2005)

NOW TO 2016   15.0

Aloxe-Corton, Les Vercots, 2002
Domaine Tollot-Beaut et Fils

Medium to medium-full colour. Rather humdrum nose. No high tones. Medium body. Boring. Sweet. Very dull. (July 2006)

NOW TO 2011   13.0

Auxey-Duresses, 2002
Domaine Pascal Prunier-Bonheur

A little bit more oaky than his 2004, but no new oak. Decent grip. Good for what it is. (February 2006)

NOW TO 2010   15.0

Auxey-Duresses, Vieilles Vignes, 2002
Domaine Pascal Prunier-Bonheur

Very, very good and now fully ready. (February 2006)

NOW TO 2010   16.5

Auxey-Duresses, Premier Cru, 2002
Domaine du Comte Armand

Medium-full colour. Quite soft, succulent, fruity nose. Medium to medium-full weight. Ripe tannins. Good grip. Not the greatest class, but long and positive. Good. (July 2006)

NOW TO 2014   15.0

Auxey-Duresses, Les Duresses, 2002
Domaine Jean and Gilles Lafouge

A lightish but quite elegant wine, with decent fruit and no hard edges. More or less ready. Quite good. (February 2006)

NOW TO 2010   14.0

Auxey-Duresses, Les Duresses, 2002
Domaine Pascal Prunier-Bonheur

Lightish in colour and in weight. Soft, stylish and balanced. A little slight on the palate, but stylish and positive at the end. Forward. Quite good. (February 2006)

NOW TO 2011   14.0

Beaune, Vieilles Vignes, 2002
Maison Champy

Good colour. Ripe and succulent on the nose. Lovely fruit. Quite approachable already. Good grip and style. Very good for what it is. (March 2006)

2009 TO 2014   16.0

Beaune, Premier Cru, 2002
Domaine Louis Latour

Clean, full bodied, plump and succulent. Lovely fruit. Long and satisfying. (January 2005)

NOW TO 2016   16.0

Beaune, Bressandes, 2002
Domaine Jean-Claude Rateau

Good colour. 14°. The last plot harvested. Profound, elegant nose. Lots of depth and dimension here. A meaty, fullish, backward wine. Quite spicy. Will be gamey. Good tannins. Good grip. Slightly adolescent at present. Long on the palate. Very good. (July 2006)

2009 TO 2019   16.0

Beaune, Cent Vignes, 2002
Domaine Duchet

Fullish colour. Quite a soft, supple nose for a 2002 of this standing. Medium to medium-full weight. Stylish, clean and fragrant. Very good grip. Very stylish. Lovely finish. Very good. (June 2006)

NOW TO 2018   16.0

Beaune, Champimonts, 2002
Maison Champy

Fullish colour. Rich, ripe nose. Good freshness and style. Medium-full body. A little tannin. Juicy, fresh and stylish. Good grip. Long and positive. Very good. (July 2006)

2009 TO 2019   16.0

Beaune du Château, 2002
Domaine Bouchard Père et Fils

Medium to medium-full colour. Good positive, plump, fruity nose. Medium to medium-full body. Quite spicy/caramelly in flavour. Clean. Good grip. Good length. Good plus. (July 2006)

2009 TO 2018   15.5

Beaune, Les Chouacheux, 2002
Domaine Coste-Caumartin

Good colour. Ample, generous nose. Lovely red fruit flavours. Medium-full body. Lots of depth and concentration. A little tannin. Very good finish. Very good plus. (March 2005)

NOW TO 2020   16.5

Beaune, Clos des Couchereaux, 2002
Domaine Louis Jadot

Medium-full colour. Elegant, fragrant nose. Good depth and finesse here. Medium-full body. Intense, stylish and harmonious. Lovely long finish. Very good indeed. (July 2006)

2010 TO 2020   17.0

Beaune, Clos des Fèves, 2002
Domaine Chanson Père et Fils

Fullish colour. Positive, succulent nose. Fullish. Some tannin. Needs time. The attack is a little solid, but the finish is better. Good fruit. Decent style. But good at best. (July 2006)

2009 TO 2017   15.0

Beaune, Clos des Mouches, 2002
Maison Chanson Père et Fils

Surprisingly forward, but no lack of depth, intensity and class. Pure. Very little evidence of oak. Crisp at the end. Very good. (October 2004)

NOW TO 2010   16.0

Beaune, Clos des Mouches, 2002
Domaine Yves Darviot

Bottled after 18 months. Good colour. Rich, quite sturdy nose. Very good fruit. Good depth and grip. Firmer than a lot of 2002 Beaunes. But nicely fat as well. Rich finish. Really stylish. Very good plus. (February 2006)

2009 TO 2018   16.5

Beaune, Clos des Mouches, 2002
Domaine Joseph Drouhin

Medium colour. Very stylish nose. Fragrant. Round. Elegant and harmonious. Medium to medium-full body. Good acidity. Complex. Lovely finish. Very good. (July 2006)

NOW TO 2019   16.0

Beaune, Clos de la Mousse, 2002
Domaine Bouchard Père et Fils

Medium-full colour. Ripe nose. Soft. No hard edges. Medium body. A little sweet. But good enough acidity. Lacks a bit of zip and nuance. Quite good plus. (July 2006)

NOW TO 2014   14.5

Beaune, Clos du Roi, 2002
Domaine Chanson Père et Fils

Full colour. Classy nose. A bit more closed-in than most of these Beaunes. But very good depth. Fullish body. Quite concentrated. Very good grip. Lovely, stylish fruit. Quite backward but long, complex and elegant. Nicely fresh. Very good plus. (July 2006)

2009 TO 2020   16.5

Beaune, Clos des Ursules, 2002
Domaine Louis Jadot

Full colour. Just a touch of sulphur on the nose. Slightly adolescent. Ripe and opulent on the palate. Spicy. Fullish body. Very good tannins.

Energetic and succulent. Long and lovely at the end. Very good indeed. (July 2006)

2010 TO 2025   17.0

Beaune, Aux Coucherias, 2002
Domaine Labet-Dechelette

Lightish colour. Anemic nose. Slight and sweet, letting the oak dominate. Medium body. Slightly astringent on the palate. Disappointing. (March 2005)

NOW TO 2009   13.0

Beaune, Aux Coucherias, 2002
Domaine Jean-Claude Rateau

The only example of white from this *climat*. Lovely fresh, subtle nose. This is still young. Medium-full body. Quite succulent. Yet good vigour underneath. Lots of dimension. Individual. Very good. (February 2006)

NOW TO 2012   16.0

Beaune, Les Cras, Vieilles Vignes, 2002
Domaine Germain Père et Fils/
Château de Chorey-lès-Beaune

Good colour. Full, rich and oaky on the nose and palate. Concentrated and profound. Plenty of class and lots of dimension. Very good. (March 2005)

NOW TO 2020   16.0

Beaune, Les Grèves, 2002
Maison Nicolas Potel

Medium colour. Fresh, ripe, succulent nose. Good quality fruit. Fullish body. Some tannin. Very good grip. This has depth. Needs time. Long. Classy. Very good plus. (July 2006)

2010 TO 2020   16.5

Beaune, Les Grèves, 2002
Domaine Tollot-Beaut et Fils

Medium to medium-full colour. Somewhat nondescript on the nose. A bit evolved. A bit thin. Medium body. Slightly confected. A touch sweet. Four-square. Lacks distinction. (July 2006)

NOW TO 2011   13.0

Beaune, Grèves, Vigne de l'Enfant Jésus, 2002
Domaine Bouchard Père et Fils

Good purple colour. Quite full. Round and rich. Good grip. Pure and elegant. Not great tannic structure but sufficient backbone here. Medium-full body. Lovely fruit on the attack. Good substance. Very good grip. Lots of depth and class. Long and positive. Very good indeed. (July 2006)

2009 TO 2020   17.0

Beaune, Les Montrevenots, 2002
Domaine Germain Père et Fils/
Château de Chorey-lès-Beaune

Good subtance. A little spicy. Good tannins. This has good depth and style. Quite good plus. (February 2006)

NOW TO 2012   14.5

Beaune, Les Reversées, 2002
Maison Camille Giroud

Full, backward colour. Backward, rich and concentrated nose. Good grip. Plenty of depth. Fullish body. Concentrated and fresh. Ripe and classy. Still a bit of tannin. But plenty of depth and dimension. Very good indeed. (July 2006)

2010 TO 2020   17.0

Beaune, Vignes Franches, 2002
Domaine Louis Latour

Full colour. Rich, full, quite firm but very succulent nose. Fullish body. A little tannin. Quite chunky. Good grip. Still needs time. Long. Very good. (July 2006)

2009 TO 2018   16.0

Beaune, Clos du Dessus des Marconnets, 2002
Domaine Labet-Dechelette

Village *appellation contrôlée*. Slightly weak on the nose. Light but fresh on the palate. Quite stylish. Reasonably positive at the end. (March 2005)

DRINK SOON   13.5

Bonnes Mares, 2002
Domaine Drouhin-Laroze

Medium-full colour. Rich, meaty and with a touch of new oak. Fullish body. Ripe, succulent and seductive. Very good grip. Not too oaky. More refined than hitherto. Lovely long, complex finish. Very good indeed. (July 2006)

2012 TO 2030   17.0

Bonnes Mares, 2002
Domaine Joseph Drouhin

Medium-full colour. Full, quite firm, rich nose. Fragrant and classy. Fullish body. Rich and concentrated. Lots of breed. Intense and vigorous on the follow-through. Great class. Fine plus. (July 2006)

2014 TO 2030   18.0

Bonnes Mares, 2002
Domaine Louis Jadot

Medium-full colour. Ripe, slightly adolescent nose. Quite structured. Lots of depth. Full body. Some tannin. Backward. Lovely fruit. Very good grip. Quite a lot of wine here. Lots of finesse too. (July 2006)

2015 TO 2030   17.5

Bonnes Mares, 2002
Domaine Jacques-Frédéric Mugnier

Light colour. Delicate but very complex, subtle and refined nose. Medium weight. Deceptively so, for there is plenty of substance here. All in lace and finesse and nuance. Very, very long. Fine. (July 2006)

2012 TO 2030   17.5

Bonnes Mares, 2002
Maison Nicolas Potel

Medium to medium-full colour. Ripe nose. But not the complexity and refinement of Jadot or Drouhin. Medium to medium-full body. Balanced, clean and stylish. Good length. Very good indeed. (July 2006)

2012 TO 2028   17.0

Bonnes Mares, 2002
Domaine Georges Roumier et Fils

Medium-full colour. Splendidly firm, rich nose. Lots of depth and quality here. Understated. Full body. Rich. Concentrated. This is backward and very fine. (July 2006)

2015 TO 2030   19.0

Bonnes Mares, 2002
Domaine Comte Georges de Vogüé

Full colour. Full, rich, backward, oaky nose. Very Vogüé. Very impressive. Full body. Good ripe tannins. Very good grip. Lots of class and vigour. Very lovely fruit. Very fine. (July 2006)

2014 TO 2030   18.5

Chambertin, 2002
Maison Camille Giroud

Full colour. Classy nose. Not a blockbuster, but pure and concentrated. Medium-full body. Ripe and succulent. Good grip. This is fine plus but lacks the flair of the very best. (July 2006)

2012 TO 2035   18.0

Chambertin, 2002
Domaine Héritiers Louis Latour

Full colour. Dull nose. No excitement. No *grand cru* quality here. Medium to medium-full body. Rather astringent. No distinction. (July 2006)

2010 TO 2016   14.0

Chambertin, 2002
Domaine Armand Rousseau

Medium-full colour. Even more exciting on the nose than their Clos de Bèze. Rich, fullish, ample, gently oaky, with very, very classy fruit. Fullish body. The complete Burgundy, as so often. Amazing depth, concentration, harmony and distinction. Brilliant! (July 2006)

2012 TO 2040   20.0

Chambertin, 2002
Domaine Jean Trapet

Fullish colour. Rich, quite spicy on the nose. Lots of concentration. Quite a lot of new wood here compared with the Latricières, and no more concentration or depth. Stylish, though. Balanced and complex, and long on the palate. Very fine. (March 2005)

2012 TO 2030   18.5

Chambertin, Clos de Bèze, 2002
Domaine Bruno Clair

Full colour. Very pure, refined fruit on the nose. Ripe and succulent. Medium-full body. Very good tannins and grip. Lovely fruit. Lots of energy. Really classy. Very lovely finish. Very, very long. This is very fine plus. (July 2006)

2012 TO 2035   19.0

Chambertin, Clos de Bèze, 2002
Domaine Pierre Damoy

Full colour. Ripe, ample nose. Somewhat evolved. A hint of reduction. Full body. Good tannins. Good grip. Not a bit astringent. Slightly adolescent, but fine and energetic underneath. Very good fruit. Fine plus. (July 2006)

2014 TO 2030   18.0

Chambertin, Clos de Bèze, 2002
Domaine Drouhin-Laroze

Full colour. Ample, rich, succulent, oaky nose. Medium-full bodied, round and ripe, but without the grip and distinction of the best. Decent follow-through and finish. Fine at best. (July 2006)

2012 TO 2030   17.5

Chambertin, Clos de Bèze, 2002
Domaine Joseph Faiveley

Full colour. Rich nose. But very concentrated and backward. Somewhat austere. Full bodied, tannic and muscular. A bit over-extracted? Will it soften? Very good? (July 2006)

2015 TO 2028   16.0

Chambertin, Clos de Bèze, 2002
Domaine Louis Jadot

Fullish colour. Splendidly rich and concentrated on the nose. A very profound wine here. Full body. Very good tannins. Excellent intensity and vigour. Very classy fruit and very good grip. Backward. But potentially very fine indeed. (July 2006)

2015 TO 2035   19.5

Chambertin, Clos de Bèze, 2002
Domaine Prieuré-Roch

Full colour. Medium-full, ample, stemmy nose. A little sweet. Lacks distinction. Loose-knit on the palate. Hollow and empty on the attack. Some fruit. Decent finish. Not bad plus. (July 2006)

DRINK SOON   13.5

Chambertin, Clos de Bèze, 2002
Domaine Armand Rousseau

Full colour. Excellent fruit and concentration on the nose. A lovely wine. Full, fat and ample.

Gently oaky. Very concentrated and classy. Splendid fruit. Even better than Bruno Clair's. (July 2006)

2012 TO 2035   19.5

Chambolle-Musigny, 2002
Domaine Virgile Lignier

Good colour. Fragrant, stylish and complex on the nose. Medium to medium-full body. Just a little tannin. Ripe, plump and very attractive. Fine, long finish. Very good, especially for a village wine. (March 2005)

NOW TO 2020   16.0

Chambolle-Musigny, Premier Cru, 2002
Domaine Joseph Drouhin

Medium to medium-full colour. Fragrant, stylish nose. Round and harmonious. Medium-full body. Lovely balance. Good intensity. Very good fruit. Long and elegant. Very good indeed. (July 2006)

2011 TO 2025   17.0

Chambolle-Musigny, Les Amoureuses, 2002
Domaine Jacques-Frédéric Mugnier

Medium colour. Very delicate, very intense and very lovely on the nose. But almost too delicate. Medium to medium-full body. This is even better than the Fuées, even more subtle and intense. Very long and very fine. (July 2006)

2012 TO 2030   18.5

Chambolle-Musigny, Les Amoureuses, 2002
Domaine Comte Georges de Vogüé

Fullish colour. Very rich and concentrated. Quite full. Definitely oaky. But not too much so on the nose. A total contrast to Mugnier's. Medium-full body. Great breed and depth. Marvellous fruit. Very sophisticated tannins. Very long. Multidimensional. Excellent. (July 2006)

2015 TO 2030   19.0

Chambolle-Musigny, Les Baudes, 2002
Domaine Louis Jadot

Medium-full colour. Ripe nose. But not the greatest elegance or fragrance as yet. Slightly adolescent. Medium-full body. Decent fruit

and better at the end than on the attack. But it doesn't really sing today. (July 2006)

2012 TO 2025   15.0

Chambolle-Musigny, Aux Beaux Bruns, 2002
Domaine Ghislaine Barthod

Fullish colour. Rich and ripe and slightly robust on the nose. Medium-full body. Decently absorbed tannins. Good fruit. Tarty but nice. Not the greatest of elegance but very good. (July 2006)

2012 TO 2025   16.0

Chambolle-Musigny, Les Charmes, 2002
Domaine Ghislaine Barthod

Medium-full colour. Lovely nose. Real class and depth. Harmonious, fragrant, complex and impressive. Fullish body. Rich and ample. Very long and complex. Very lovely. Impressive quality. Fine plus. (July 2006)

2012 TO 2030   18.0

Chambolle-Musigny, Les Charmes, 2002
Domaine Michèle and Patrice Rion

Medium-full colour. Ripe and plump on the nose. Medium-full body. Nicely cool and fresh. Balanced, stylish and long. Very good indeed. Better than their 2002 Les Cras. (July 2006)

2011 TO 2025   17.5

Chambolle-Musigny, Clos de l'Orme, 2002
Domaine Sylvain Cathiard

Medium-full colour. Very lovely, poised, fragrant nose. Lots of depth as well as very lovely complexity and character here. Medium to medium-full body. Intense and concentrated. Very harmonious. Very, very long and lovely. This is very fine, and it is only a village *appellation contrôlée*. (July 2006)

2012 TO 2030   18.0

Chambolle-Musigny, La Combe d'Orveau, 2002
Domaine Bruno Clavelier

Medium-full colour. Slightly lumpy on the nose. It lacks distinction. Adolescent. Medium-full body. Somewhat reduced. A bit astringent as a result. It doesn't impress. (July 2006)

2009 TO 2015   13.0

Chambolle-Musigny, Les Cras, 2002
Domaine Ghislaine Barthod

Medium-full colour. Quite cool, austere and fullish for a Chambolle. Lots of depth and class, though. Fullish body. Marvellous fruit. Lots of depth and class. Intense and long. Fine plus. (July 2006)

2012 TO 2030   18.0

Chambolle-Musigny, Les Cras, 2002
Domaine Michèle and Patrice Rion

This is not a *premier cru*: village *appellation contrôlée*. Medium-full colour. Plump, ripe, stylish nose. Medium to medium-full weight. Ample and balanced. Nice and cool. Classy. Long. Very good plus. (July 2006)

2011 TO 2025   16.5

Chambolle-Musigny, Les Cras, 2002
Domaine Georges Roumier et Fils

Medium-full colour. Lovely fragrant but fullish, masculine, persistent nose. Great poise and class. Medium-full body. Very lovely, almost exotic, ripe fruit. Excellent grip. Very long and persistent finish. Fine. (March 2005)

2011 TO 2030   17.5

Chambolle-Musigny, Aux Échanges, 2002
Maison Nicolas Potel

Medium-full colour. Soft, fragrant, attractively fruity nose. Medium-full body. Good style. Quite intense. Classy and balanced. Very good plus. (July 2006)

2012 TO 2025   16.5

Chambolle-Musigny, Les Feusselottes, 2002
Domaine Daniel Moine-Hudelot

Medium colour. Some development. Sweet and a bit weak. Light and weedy on the palate. Already a bit attenuated. No. (July 2006)

DRINK UP   11.0

Chambolle-Musigny, Les Fuées, 2002
Domaine Jacques-Frédéric Mugnier

Medium to medium-full colour. Lightish nose. But very flowery and fragrant. Almost ethereal. Medium to medium-full body. Graceful,

intense, complex and very classy on the palate. Very lovely pure fruit. Very, very long. Fine plus. (July 2006)

2012 TO 2030   18.0

Chambolle-Musigny, Les Groseilles, 2002
Domaine Digioia-Royer

Medium-full colour. Plump, ripe, attractive nose. Medium-full body. Ample, balanced, classy and long on the palate. Nicely fresh. Most impressive. Fine. (July 2006)

2012 TO 2025   17.5

Chambolle-Musigny, Les Gruenchers, 2002
Domaine Fourrier

Medium-full colour. Plump, ripe, balanced nose. High quality here. Plenty of depth. Medium-full body. Ripe and quite concentrated. Plump and graceful. Nicely cool on the follow-through. Classy. Fine. (July 2006)

2012 TO 2025   17.5

Chambolle-Musigny, Les Véroilles, 2002
Domaine Bruno Clair

Medium to medium-full colour. Soft, very stylish, crisp, medium-weight nose. Medium body. Lacks a little substance but ripe, elegant and long on the palate. Good. (March 2006)

NOW TO 2018   15.0

Chapelle-Chambertin, 2002
Maison Camille Giroud

Medium colour. Discreet nose. Less oaky than their Latricières-Chambertin. Fullish body. Balanced. Very good fruit. Not quite the same flair at present, but very good intensity and drive underneath. Fine too. (July 2006)

2012 TO 2030   17.5

Chapelle-Chambertin, 2002
Domaine Ponsot

Medium-full colour. Classy nose. Understated, ripe, complex and individual. Medium to medium-full body. Balanced. Subtle. Long. Lovely finish. Very good indeed. (July 2006)

2012 TO 2028   17.0

Chapelle-Chambertin, 2002
Domaine Jean Trapet

Medium to medium-full colour. Good meaty, plummy nose. Balanced and stylish. Medium-full weight. Fresh and succulent, but not the greatest richness and concentration. Very good plus. (March 2005)

2010 TO 2025   16.5

Charmes-Chambertin, 2002
Domaine Hervé Arlaud

Fullish colour. Good weight and depth but with a touch of reduction on the nose. Fullish body. Some tannins. A touch of astringency. Good classy, intense fruit underneath. Long. Very good indeed. (July 2006)

2014 TO 2028   17.0

Charmes-Chambertin, 2002
Domaine Denis Bachelet

Medium to medium-full colour. Splendid nose. Quite closed. It has gone into its shell. But lots of depth. Very high quality. Infanticide to drink now. Doesn't show very well today. But lovely rich, balanced, profound fruit. (April 2006)

2012 TO 2030   18.5

Charmes-Chambertin, 2002
Domaine Bouchard Père et Fils

Medium-full colour. Ample, ripe nose. Good depth and class. On the palate a little adolescent. Fullish body. Good grip. Ripe tannins. At present it doesn't show much finesse, but at least very good plus. (July 2006)

2012 TO 2028   16.5

Charmes-Chambertin, 2002
Domaine Bernard Dugat-Py

Full colour. Very rich and concentrated on the nose. Some extraction. Full bodied, rich and tannic. Quite a brutal attack. But a splendidly rich, concentrated, black-fruity follow-through. Fine plus. (July 2006)

2014 TO 2030   18.0

Charmes-Chambertin, 2002
Domaine Claude Dugat

Full colour. Firm, full, rich and concentrated on the nose. Some extraction. Plenty of wine here. Full body. Very concentrated. Very rich. Backward. Very, very long. Potentially fine plus. (July 2006)

2014 TO 2030   18.0

Charmes-Chambertin, 2002
Domaine Dupont-Tisserandot

Full colour. Firm, full, rich nose. Some extraction. Full body. Good fruit but slightly lacking grip. So it is ample but a little short. Slightly raisinny. Good plus. (July 2006)

2012 TO 2025   15.5

Charmes-Chambertin, 2002
Domaine Louis Jadot

Medium-full colour. Concentrated, backward nose. Lots of depth and quality. Fullish body. Slightly adolescent. Good grip. Ample fruit. Needs time. Very good indeed. (July 2006)

2014 TO 2030   17.0

Charmes-Chambertin, 2002
Maison Frédéric Magnien

Medium to medium-full colour. Firm, full, rich and concentrated. Not too over-extracted. A bit dense on the palate. Medium-full body. Decent fruit and grip but a little four-square. No uplift at the end. Good plus. (April 2006)

2012 TO 2020   15.5

Charmes-Chambertin, 2002
Domaine Ponsot

Medium to medium-full colour. Lightish but intense nose. Medium body. Not a lot of tannin. Ample, intense and individual. Classy. Long on the palate. Very good indeed. (July 2006)

2012 TO 2028   17.0

Charmes-Chambertin, 2002
Maison Nicolas Potel

Medium to medium-full colour. Fruity but slightly anonymous on the nose. Medium-full body.

Fresh. Good fruit and harmony. Not the greatest personality or depth but very good plus. (July 2006)

2012 TO 2025   16.5

Charmes-Chambertin, 2002
Domaine Gérard Raphet

Medium-full colour. Some development. Opulent and spicy on nose and palate. Medium-full body. Quite soft already. Very ripe. Very good grip. Long and classy. Lovely finish. Fine plus. (October 2005)

2011 TO 2030   18.0

Charmes-Chambertin, 2002
Domaine Armand Rousseau

Fullish colour. Ripe and succulent on the nose. More to it than usual. Medium-full body. Good tannins. Ripe, quite round and accessible. Long finish. This is very good indeed. (July 2006)

2012 TO 2028   17.0

Charmes-Chambertin, Mazoyères, 2002
Domaine de la Vougeraie

Fullish colour. Juicy, concentrated, fresh nose. Good style. Black fruity. Fullish bodied. Ample. A touch oaky. Youthful. Very good grip. Long and classy. Fine. (July 2006)

2012 TO 2030   17.5

Château de Monthelie, Sur la Velle, 2002
Domaine Éric de Suremain

Lightish colour. A little slight. Not special. Forward. (March 2005)

DRINK SOON   12.0

Chorey-lès-Beaune, 2002
Domaine Germain Père et Fils/
Château de Chorey-lès-Beaune

Very good colour. Ample, rich and concentrated. Unexpectedly so for a Chorey. Gently oaky. Fullish body. Quite firm. Plenty of depth. Lovely fruit. Very good. (March 2005)

NOW TO 2015   16.0

Chorey-lès-Beaune, 2002
Domaine Tollot-Beaut et Fils

Good colour. Rich and spicy on the nose. More oaky than the Château de Chorey. Ripe and

plump. Medium-full body. Good richness on the follow-through. Good plus. (March 2005)

NOW TO 2014   15.0

Clos des Lambrays, 2002
Domaine des Lambrays

Medium-full colour. Fresh, elegant, harmonious, ripe nose. Most attractive. Medium to medium-full body. Very finely poised, ripe fruit. Long, complex and intense. Lovely finish. Fine plus. (July 2006)

2012 TO 2028   18.0

Clos de la Roche, 2002
Domaine Dujac

Fullish colour. Ripe, gently stemmy, classy, fresh nose. Medium-full body. Intense. Very well balanced. Complex. Long. Fine plus. (July 2006)

2012 TO 2028   18.0

Clos de la Roche, Vieilles Vignes, 2002
Domaine Ponsot

Fullish colour. Very profound, rich, concentrated nose. This is splendid. Fullish body. Chocolaty. Excellent depth. Very fine fruit. Essence of wine here. Excellent. Still very young. Very fine plus. (March 2006)

2012 TO 2030   19.0

Clos de la Roche, 2002
Domaine Louis Rémy

Medium-full colour. Ripe, rich, opulent nose. Medium to medium-full body. Fruity attack but then a bit hollow. Clean but lacks dimension and concentration. Forward. Good plus at best. (July 2006)

2010 TO 2020   15.5

Clos Saint-Denis, 2002
Domaine Hervé Arlaud

Full colour. Plenty of depth and character here. Rich and opulent. Fullish body. Very good tannins. Rich fruit. Voluptuous. Long, complex and stylish at the end. Fine. (July 2006)

2012 TO 2028   17.5

Clos Saint-Denis, 2002
Maison Champy
Medium-full colour. Somewhat rustic on the nose. Medium body. Evolved. Coarse. Poor. (July 2006)
NOW TO 2012   12.0

Clos Saint-Denis, 2002
Domaine Dujac
Medium-full colour. Lovely, gentle fruit on the nose. A touch of the stems. Balanced. Cool. Fresh and elegant. Just a little softer and less rich than their Clos de la Roche. Fine. (July 2006)
2012 TO 2026   17.5

Clos Saint-Denis, 2002
Maison Nicolas Potel
Medium-full colour. Ample, ripe, attractive, stylish nose. Medium-full body. Good tannins. Fresh, quite concentrated fruit. Good energy. Long on the finish. Very good indeed. (July 2006)
2011 TO 2025   17.0

Clos de Tart, 2002
Domaine Mommessin
Full colour. Lovely full, rich nose. Quite backward. Full body. Sophisticated tannins. Lots of drive and energy. Profound, rich and harmonious. Very, very long. Excellent. (July 2006)
2015 TO 2030   19.0

Clos de Vougeot, 2002
Domaine Bertagna
Full colour. Plump, fresh and ripe on the nose. Classy and profound. Well made. Fullish bodied, rich and quite meaty. Nicely cool and stylish. Long. Not quite the flair for fine but very good indeed. Finishes well. (July 2006)
2012 TO 2025   17.0

Clos de Vougeot, 2002
Domaine Bouchard Père et Fils
Medium to medium-full colour. Ripe, quite elegant nose. Soft and plump. Medium-full body. Ripe and attractive, but no real class or dimension. Slightly hot. Very good plus. (July 2006)
2012 TO 2022   16.5

Clos de Vougeot, 2002
Domaine Chanson Père et Fils
Full colour. Some stems on the nose (from Jacky Confuron?). Medium-full body. Rich. Sweet. Stemmy. Not my taste but decent fruit, balance and length. Very good plus. (July 2006)
2012 TO 2025   16.5

Clos de Vougeot, 2002
Domaine Jérôme Chézeaux
Medium-full colour. Youthful nose. Good depth. Quite closed. Plenty of wine here. Rich, full, oaky and concentrated on the palate. Very good grip. Lots of dimension. Lots of class. Very long at the end. This is very fine, even for a 2002. (October 2005)
2012 TO 2030   18.5

Clos de Vougeot, 2002
Domaine Drouhin-Laroze
Medium-full colour. Rich, ripe, profound and slightly jammy/oaky on the nose. Medium-full body. Plump and attractive. Reasonably balanced. Ripe and positive. Very good indeed. (July 2006)
2012 TO 2028   17.0

Clos de Vougeot, 2002
Domaine René Engel
Medium-full colour. Smooth, silky, plump, well balanced nose. Plenty of class here. Very faint hint of the stems (yet 100 percent destemmed). Medium-full body. Soft, round and subtle. Long. Fine. (July 2006)
2012 TO 2025   17.5

Clos de Vougeot, 2002
Domaine Forey Père et Fils
Full colour. Rich and ripe, full and plump on the nose. Old-viney concentration. Soft, ripe and plump on the palate. Fullish body. Very integrated. Lovely finish. Long. Fine. (July 2006)
2012 TO 2025   17.5

Clos de Vougeot, 2002
Domaine du Clos Frantin/Albert Bichot
Medium-full colour. Rich, ripe and succulent on the nose. Fullish, meaty and concentrated.

Backward. Good depth. Very good, rich fruit. Very good indeed. Perhaps fine. Needs time. (July 2006)

2014 TO 2028   17.0

Clos de Vougeot, 2002
Domaine Jean Grivot

Medium-full colour. Lots of character, lots of depth and very high quality on the nose. A little adolescent at first. Full bodied, concentrated and vigorous. Excellent fruit. Long and lovely. Very fine. (July 2006)

2015 TO 2030   18.5

Clos de Vougeot, Le Grand Maupertuis, 2002
Domaine Anne Gros

Fine colour. Lovely full, rich nose. Great class here. Fullish body. Profound and aristocratic. Subtle and multidimensional. Excellent fruit. Very, very long on the palate. Excellent. (July 2006)

2013 TO 2030   19.0

Clos de Vougeot, 2002
Domaine Louis Jadot

Fullish colour. Full, rich but backward nose. Got better as it evolved. Quite a big, even muscular wine. But good grip and vigour. Very good fruit. Long. Fine. Needs time. (July 2006)

2015 TO 2030   17.5

Clos de Vougeot, Vieilles Vignes, 2002
Domaine Labet-Dechelette, Château de la Tour

Medium colour. Fruity and balanced but slightly weedy for a 2002 *grand cru* on the nose. Evidence of the stems, too. Medium body. Good balance. Quite rich. This is very good. But it should be a lot better. (March 2005)

2010 TO 2025   16.0

Clos de Vougeot, 2002
Domaine Lamarche

Fullish colour. Fresh, full nose, with a hint of chocolate ice cream. Ripe, plump and succulent. Fullish body. Fresh. Virile. Some oak. Lovely fruit. Long and complex. This is fine plus. (July 2006)

2014 TO 2030   18.0

Clos de Vougeot, 2002
Domaine Thibault Liger-Belair

Medium-full colour. Fresh, plump, oaky nose. Medium-full body. Fresh and balanced. Classy and complex yet by no means a blockbuster. Fine. (July 2006)

2012 TO 2028   17.5

Clos de Vougeot, 2002
Domaine Méo-Camuzet

Full colour. Firm, backward nose. Took time to come out of the glass. When it did, I saw opulence, plenty of substance and rich, balanced, succulent fruit. Lovely long, stylish finish. Fine plus. (July 2006)

2012 TO 2030   18.0

Clos de Vougeot, 2002
Domaine Denis Mortet

Full colour. Rather dense and over-extracted on the nose. This is a bit ungainly, and a retrograde step on 2000–2001. Full body. Sweet. Oaky. Commercial. Lovely fruit. Very good grip. But fine rather than great. (July 2006)

2015 TO 2030   17.5

Clos de Vougeot, 2002
Maison Nicolas Potel

Medium to medium-full colour. Ripe and succulent on the nose if with no real depth or finesse. Medium-full body. Fresh. Attractive fruit. Long and positive. Very good indeed. (July 2006)

2012 TO 2025   17.0

Clos de Vougeot, 2002
Domaine Prieuré-Roch

Medium-full colour. Slightly reduced on the nose. Better on the palate. Medium-full body. Good grip. Not too stemmy. Decent fruit. Slightly raw. Good at best. (February 2006)

2009 TO 2014   15.0

Clos de Vougeot, 2002
Domaine Daniel Rion et Fils

Fullish colour. Plump, accessible, juicy-fruity, cherry-flavoured nose. Quite oaky. Medium to medium-full body. Very soft. Very succulent. Very attractive. Fresh and quite classy. But a typical and a little one-dimensional. (March 2005)

NOW TO 2020   18.0

Clos de Vougeot, 2002
Domaine de la Vougeraie

Full colour. Very impressive, classy, old-viney, concentrated nose. Lovely black fruit flavours. Full bodied, rich, ample and ripe. Very good grip. Balanced and long and very stylish. Fine plus. (September 2004)

2012 TO 2025+   18.0

Corton, 2002
Domaine Bonneau du Martray

Good colour. Rich, meaty nose. Fat and concentrated. Just a little oaky. Lots of depth and class. Fullish body. Good tannins. Balanced and fragrant. Very good grip. Fine. (March 2005)

2009 TO 2020+   17.5

Corton, 2002
Domaine Follin-Arbelet

Medium-full colour. Slightly rustic nose. Medium body. Not much tannin. Slightly astringent. This lacks distinction. Not bad plus. (July 2006)

NOW TO 2013   13.5

Corton, 2002
Domaine Tollot-Beaut et Fils

Medium-full colour. Ripe but spicy and slightly leaden-footed nose. Medium body. Sweet. Lacks freshness, nuance and finesse. Quite good. (July 2006)

NOW TO 2016   14.0

Le Corton, 2002
Domaine Bouchard Père et Fils

Medium colour. Soft, fragrant, classy nose. Medium to medium-full body. But good grip, style and intensity. Forward. Not hard. Very good indeed. But not the depth and concentration of fine. (July 2006)

NOW TO 2016   17.0

Corton, Les Bressandes, 2002
Domaine Chandon de Briailles

Medium colour. Ripe, rich, fragrant, stylish nose. Medium-full body. Good vigour and depth. Classy and persistent. Lots of dimension. Lovely finish. Fine. (July 2006)

2009 TO 2020+   17.5

Corton, Les Bressandes, 2002
Domaine Prince Florent de Mérode

Medium to medium-full colour. Quite full nose. Rich and fruity. Good elegance. Fresh. Fullish body. Succulent. Ripe. Good intensity. This is classy and very good, especially at the end. (July 2006)

2009 TO 2020   16.0

Corton, Les Bressandes, 2002
Domaine du Comte Senard

Good colour. Plump, succulent nose. Plenty of vigour. Plenty of fruit. This is rather more structural than usual and a lot more classic. Very lovely, complex, classy fruit. Long and intense. Very fine. (March 2005)

2009 TO 2020+   18.5

Corton, Les Bressandes, 2002
Domaine Tollot-Beaut et Fils

Medium-full colour. Ripe. Rather more stylish than the ordinary Corton on the nose. Nevertheless, a little chunky and graceless. (July 2006)

2009 TO 2016   14.5

Corton, Château Corton-Grancey, 2002
Domaine Louis Latour

Medium colour. Soft, ripe nose. But not much depth or distinction. Medium body. Sweet. Evolved. Decent acidity but not much structure nor grip, nor class. Agreable but not a bit *grand cru* quality. Quite good. (July 2006)

NOW TO 2014   14.0

Corton, Clos des Cortons Faiveley, 2002
Domaine Joseph Faiveley

Fullish colour. A bit closed-in on the nose. Slightly austere on the attack. Fullish body. Some tannin. But good depth and concentration of fruit underneath. Vigorous. Rich and classy. Just needs time. Fine plus. (July 2006)

2012 TO 2030   18.0

Corton, Clos des Maréchaudes, 2002
Domaine du Pavillon/Albert Bichot

Very good colour. Fat, roasted, caramelly nose. Fullish body. Good tannins. A little astringent at present, but good energy and astringent underneath. This is closing in. Good depth and class, though. Very good indeed (if not fine). (October 2004)

2011 TO 2025   17.0

Corton, Clos du Roi, 2002
Domaine Chandon de Briailles

Medium-full colour. Fragrant, fresh nose. Evidence of the stems. Medium body. Not much tannin. Gentle, charming and quite stylish. Quite positive. But it lacks real depth. Good plus. (July 2006)

NOW TO 2016   15.5

Corton, Clos du Roi, 2002
Domaine Prince Florent de Mérode

Medium-full colour. Ripe, rich, fresh, concentrated nose. A medium-full, rich, succulent example. Good depth. Good class. Long and positive. Very good plus. (July 2006)

2009 TO 2020   16.5

Corton, Le Clos du Roi, 2002
Domaine de la Pousse d'Or

Medium to medium-full colour. Quite fat and succulent on the nose. Quite rich. Medium to medium-full body. A certain lack of vigour and juiciness on the palate. It tails off to leave a bit of astringency at the end. Unexciting for what it is. (February 2006)

NOW TO 2014   15.0

Corton, Clos du Roi, 2002
Domaine du Comte Senard

Good colour. Quite full, firm, rich nose. Plenty of depth. Quite earthy on the palate. Some tannin. More backward than his Bressandes,

and it doesn't sing as much today. But fine. (March 2005)

2010 TO 2025   17.5

Corton, Clos du Roi, 2002
Domaine du Baron Thénard/
Maison Roland Remoissenet

Medium-full colour. No great distinction here on the nose. Ripe but not very fresh or elegant. Evolved. Pedestrian. Already a bit astringent. Forward. No. (July 2006)

DRINK SOON   12.0

Corton, Le Clos du Roi, 2002
Domaine Michel Voarick

Rich, full, succulent, not a bit too tough. Lovely fruit. Complex, persistent and very classy. Splendid finish. This is very fine. (February 2006)

2009 TO 2025   18.5

Corton, Les Grandes Lolières, 2002
Domaine Bertagna

Medium-full colour. Fragrant, fruity nose. If no great weight. Sweet and spicy. Medium body. Decent fruit. Decent acidity. Unexciting. (July 2006)

2010 TO 2020   14.5

Corton, Les Grèves, 2002
Domaine Louis Jadot

Medium-full colour. Still youthful. Ripe and full on the nose. Still a little closed. On the palate quite firm but not aggressively hard. Fullish body. Very good grip. Lovely fruit. Concentrated and profound. Quite round. Lots of depth. Long and classy. Fine quality. (March 2006)

2010 TO 2020+   17.5

Corton, Les Perrières, 2002
Domaine Maurice Chapuis

Medium weight. Lovely fruit. A very good elegant, harmonious but not very powerful wine. It will develop soon. But undoubted complexity and class. Long at the end. Very good plus. (February 2006)

2009 TO 2019   16.5

Corton, Les Pougets, 2002
Domaine Louis Jadot
Fullish colour. Ripe, full, rich and plump. Yet rather oxidised on the nose. Assuming this last aspect is not typical, a concentrated wine, full bodied, profound and potentially very fine. A second bottle was rich, full, raw, oaky and youthful. Good grip. Fine. (July 2006)
2010 TO 2025   18.5

Corton, Les Renardes, 2002
Domaine Bruno Colin
Medium to medium-full body. Lovely fragrant, stylish nose. Good fresh fruit. Plump. Stylish. Balanced. Long and subtle. Very good indeed. (February 2006)
NOW TO 2020   17.0

Corton, Les Renardes, 2002
Domaine Michel Gaunoux
Good colour. Good stylish, fragrant fruit on the nose. Fullish bodied, rich and balanced, but a bit four-square on the palate. Yet rich and intense on the follow-through. Fine plus. (March 2005)
2010 TO 2025   18.0

Corton, Le Rognet, 2002
Domaine Bertrand Ambroise
Full, firm and rich. Oaky but not excessively so. Good tannins underneath. Plenty of wine here. Long. Fine. (February 2006)
2010 TO 2020+   17.5

Echézeaux, 2002
Domaine Arnoux Père et Fils
Full colour. Like his Suchots, just delicately reduced on the nose. Full and plump underneath. Lots of depth and concentration on the palate. This is full bodied, intense, long and classy. Lovely finish. Fine plus. (July 2006)
2009 TO 2025   18.0

Echézeaux, 2002
Domaine Bouchard Père et Fils
Medium-full colour. Higher-toned nose than Jadot's. Less rich. More fragrant though. Medium body. Balanced, succulent and long. Positive. Elegant. Very good indeed. (July 2006)
2010 TO 2025   17.0

Echézeaux, 2002
Domaine Jacky Confuron-Cotétidot
Medium colour. Some evolution. Stylish but stemmy nose. Concentrated and old viney. Medium body. Very good acidity. Good concentration. Ripe and rich. Not my style but rich, fresh, even sweet at the end. (July 2006)
2009 TO 2025   15.5

Echézeaux, 2002
Domaine René Engel
Medium to medium-full colour. Lovely, classy round, soft, fragrant nose. Ripe, plump and multidimensional. Medium body. Quite round now. Fresh and rich and complex. Lots of vigour and energy. Fine. (July 2006)
2009 TO 2025   17.5

Echézeaux, 2002
Domaine Forey Père et Fils
Full colour. Slightly tight, but fresh, fruity nose. Good depth and class. Slightly four-square on the palate. It lacks a bit of acidity, so a little astringent. Quite good at best. (July 2006)
2009 TO 2025   14.0

Echézeaux, 2002
Domaine du Clos Frantin/Albert Bichot
Medium-full colour. Very ripe, even slightly pommadé on the nose. Fullish, fresh but slightly concocted. Fullish body. Quite oaky. A little sweet. Good grip though. A meaty wine. Very good indeed. (July 2006)
2009 TO 2022   17.0

Echézeaux, 2002
Domaine Jean Grivot
Fullish colour. Backward. Closed-in. But profound nose. Needs time. This is intense, fullish and very lovely. Excellent grip. Lovely fruit. (July 2006)
2009 TO 2025   18.5

Echézeaux, 2002
Domaine A.F. Gros

Medium-full colour. Good fruit on the nose. Ripe. Not too solid or ungainly. Quite fresh too. Medium body. A little tannin. Not enough concentration or dimension. Yet balanced. (July 2006)

NOW TO 2015   15.5

Echézeaux, 2002
Domaine Louis Jadot

Medium-full colour. Decent fresh style on the nose but a little ungainly. Full and rich, but adolescent on the palate. On the palate there is plenty of substance here. But tannic and tough. The wine is promising underneath. Very good (plus?). (July 2006)

2012 TO 2025   16.0

Echézeaux, 2002
Maison Nicolas Potel

Fullish colour. Fresh, high-toned, aromatic, fragrant nose. Fresh. Slightly lumpy but quite stylish. Good depth. This is attractive. Very good. (July 2006)

2011 TO 2026   16.0

Echézeaux, 2002
Domaine de la Romanée-Conti

Quite light and forward compared to my expectation. Ripe. But not a lot of backbone. Decent length. Fragrant and elegant. But not special. (November 2005)

2009 TO 2015   16.0

Echézeaux, 2002
Domaine Emmanuel Rouget

Fullish colour. Concentrated nose. Rich fruit, but somewhat closed-in and flat. Lacks high tones. Fullish body. Ripe. No great nuance and class. Sweet and sensual. A bit four-square. Good. Could have been better. (July 2006)

2009 TO 2025   15.0

Fixin, Clos Marion, 2002
Domaine Fougeray de Beauclair

Medium to medium-full colour. Slightly loose-knit nose. But ample and fruity if no great style.

Medium body. No tannins to absorb. Slightly one-dimensional. A decent wine but no great depth or elegance or dimension. Quite forward. (March 2005)

NOW TO 2014   14.0

Gevrey-Chambertin, Mes Favorites, 2002
Domaine Alain Burguet

Good colour. Lovely, rich nose. Good structure. Very good depth. Typically Gevrey. Medium-full body. A touch of oak. Very blackberry and black-curranty. Good tannins. Very good grip. As usual excellent for a village wine. (March 2005)

2010 TO 2025   17.0

Gevrey-Chambertin, Vieilles Vignes, 2002
Domaine Denis Bachelet

Fine, full colour. Creamy rich on the nose. Lovely ripe tannins. This is fullish bodied, profound and classy. A real delight. (September 2005)

2011 TO 2027   17.0

Gevrey-Chambertin, Premier Cru, 2002
Domaine Claude Dugat

Very good colour. Very black currant-leafy on the nose. A little like a young Hermitage. Slightly raw at present. Full body. Backward. Some tannin. Slightly austere at the moment. But the finish is most impressive. Very good indeed. (July 2006)

2014 TO 2028   17.0

Gevrey-Chambertin, Les Corvées, 2002
Domaine Bichot

Rather more sophisticated than their 2003. Riper, fuller and more complete. Much better tannins. Good grip. Long. A very good example of a village wine. (October 2004)

NOW TO 2020   15.5

Gevrey-Chambertin, Les Cazetiers, 2002
Domaine Bruno Clair

Medium-full colour. Even more classy than his Fonteny on the nose. Very lovely fruit. Poised and classy. This bottle is corked but one can see a very fine wine underneath, bigger than his Clos de Fonteny. But with more depth and dimension and class. (July 2006)

2012 TO 2030   18.0

Gevrey-Chambertin, Les Cazetiers, 2002
Domaine Joseph Faiveley

Medium-full colour. Ample, ripe, classy and succulent on the nose. Backward on the palate. Fullish body. Some tannin. Very good grip. Round, succulent and vigorous at the end. Fine. (July 2006)

2014 TO 2030   17.5

Gevrey-Chambertin, Les Cazetiers, 2002
Domaine Philippe Naddef

Much more civilised than his Marsannay 2002. Not over-oaked or hard. Fullish body. Firm. Very good fruit. Lots of depth and class. Well balanced. Very good plus. Long. (May 2004)

2010 TO 2020   15.5

Gevrey-Chambertin, Les Cazetiers, 2002
Domaine Armand Rousseau

Medium-full colour. Quite firm on the nose. Still youthful. More so than Faiveley's Cazetiers, which is a bit surprising. Medium-full body. Toffee flavours. This is slightly astringent and doesn't really convince. Very good at best. (July 2006)

2012 TO 2022   16.0

Gevrey-Chambertin, Champeaux, 2002
Domaine Denis Mortet

Full colour. Rich and concentrated. Full and classy on the nose. Some oak. Fullish on the palate. Not over-extracted but certainly very oaky. Rich, vigorous and concentrated. Very good plus. (July 2006)

2013 TO 2028   16.5

Gevrey-Chambertin, Clos du Fonteny, 2002
Domaine Bruno Clair

Good colour. Rich, still slightly austere nose. Lovely fruit. Medium-full body. The usual Clair slightly lean style. But long and classy. Ripe tannins. Very good plus. (July 2006)

2009 TO 2020+   16.5

Gevrey-Chambertin, Clos Saint-Jacques, 2002
Domaine Bruno Clair

Full colour. Quite a bit fuller and more concentrated than the Cazetiers. This is youthful but rich, fullish, vigorous and profound. Medium-full body. Elegant, complex and harmonious. Very good vigour. This is very fine. (July 2006)

2010 TO 2030   18.5

Gevrey-Chambertin, Clos Saint-Jacques, 2002
Domaine Louis Jadot

Medium-full colour. Splendidly rich, concentrated nose. Very lovely fruit. Full body. Very ripe tannins. Fresh, complex and very elegant. This is very lovely. Very fine long finish. (July 2006)

2013 TO 2030   19.0

Gevrey-Chambertin, Clos Saint-Jacques, 2002
Domaine Armand Rousseau

Fullish colour. Very lovely nose. Great concentration. Great poise. Fabulous fruit. Fullish body. Sumptuous. Balanced. Rich and profound. Some oak. Very lovely fruit. Great intensity and class. Very impressive. (July 2006)

2012 TO 2040   19.0

Gevrey-Chambertin, Aux Combottes, 2002
Domaine Dujac

Medium-full colour. Very Dujac on the nose: ripe, stylish and individual. Fresh. Evidence of the stems. Medium to medium-full body. Good class and intensity. Balanced. Very good plus. (July 2006)

2012 TO 2025   16.5

Gevrey-Chambertin, Les Corbeaux, 2002
Domaine Denis Bachelet

Fullish colour. Rich, firm nose. Lovely, slightly austere cassis fruit. Still a little closed. Fullish body. Very lovely fragrant, ripe fruit. Good tannins. Good acidity. Lots of class and depth. Really lovely. (June 2006)

2010 TO 2025   17.5

**Gevrey-Chambertin,
Estournelles-Saint-Jacques, 2002
Domaine Humbert Frères**

Medium-full colour. Plump, succulent, stylish nose. Good definition. Good class. Medium to medium body. Intense and elegant. Very good fruit. Very good grip. This is by no means a blockbuster, but long, complex and fine. (July 2006)

2012 TO 2030   17.5

**Gevrey-Chambertin, Fonteny, 2002
Domaine Joseph Roty**

Fullish colour. Very good old-viney concentration but quite oaky nose. Fullish body. Super-concentrated. Old viney. Fine grip. Lots of energy. Very fine. (July 2006)

2012 TO 2030   18.5

**Gevrey-Chambertin, Fonteny, 2002
Domaine Christian Sérafin**

Medium to medium-full colour. Ample, ripe, quite oaky nose. Medium-full body. Plump. Accessible. Very good tannins. Very good grip. Long and succulent. Very good plus. (July 2006)

2012 TO 2025   16.5

**Gevrey-Chambertin, Lavaux-Saint-Jacques, 2002
Domaine Bernard Dugat-Py**

Full colour. Rich, full, ample, old-viney, concentrated nose. Some oak. But a lot of depth here. Full body, but very ripe tannins. Quite a big wine nevertheless. Full bodied and intense. This is very impressive. (July 2006)

2015 TO 2030+   18.0

**Gevrey-Chambertin, Lavaux-Saint-Jacques, 2002
Domaine Claude Dugat**

Medium-full colour. Closed-in but good quality nose. Rather tight at present. Better on the palate. Fullish bodied, rich, balanced and composed. Backward but fine. (July 2006)

2015 TO 2030   17.5

**Gevrey-Chambertin, Lavaux-Saint-Jacques, 2002
Domaine Bernard Maume**

Medium to medium-full colour. Lumpy and reduced on the nose. Medium body. A bit astringent. Unbalanced and rather rustic in its fruit. (July 2006)

DRINK SOON   12.0

**Gevrey-Chambertin, Lavaux-Saint-Jacques, 2002
Domaine Denis Mortet**

Full colour. Quite modern, oaky nose. Ripe and rich. Very oaky. Not too extracted. Ripe and succulent on the follow-through. Long and intense. Fine plus. (July 2006)

2015 TO 2030   18.0

**Gevrey-Chambertin, Petite Chapelle, 2002
Domaine Dupont-Tisserandot**

Full colour. Rather raw and appley on the nose. Some volatile acidity. Better as it evolved. Fullish body. Slightly rigid. Yet good tannins and good grip. Rich, full bodied and ample if slightly austere. Less malic nevertheless and a bit ungainly. (July 2006)

2012 TO 2022   14.0

**La Grande Rue, 2002
Domaine Lamarche**

Medium-full colour. Cool, clean, ripe, individual nose. Very good fruit. Full body. Rich. Meaty. Very good grip. Balanced. Good tannins. Quite a big wine. Fine. (July 2006)

2014 TO 2030   17.5

**Grands Echézeaux, 2002
Domaine Joseph Drouhin**

Medium-full colour. Ripe, fragrant, elegant nose. Medium-full body. Good grip. Ripe and elegant. Soft, rich and complex. Long. Lovely. Fine plus quality. (July 2006)

2012 TO 2028   18.0

**Grands Echézeaux, 2002
Domaine René Engel**

Medium to medium-full colour. Ripe, fat, concentrated nose. Lovely fruit here. Medium-full body. Rich and intense. Very well-covered tannins. Classy. Balanced. Very long. Very fine. (July 2006)

2012 TO 2028   18.5

Grands Echézeaux, 2002
Domaine du Clos Frantin/Albert Bichot

Medium-full colour. Some oak on the nose. But very good fruit and depth. Full body. Very good grip. Good tannins. A wine with depth and backbone. Long succulent finish. Fine. (July 2006)

2012 TO 2028   17.5

Grands Echézeaux, 2002
Domaine de la Romanée-Conti

Medium-full colour. Spicier and fuller than the Echézeaux on the nose. Rather less developed. Full bodied, concentrated and intense. Excellent grip. Lots of wine here. Quite powerful at the end. Very fine. (July 2006)

2013 TO 2030   18.5

Grands Echézeaux, 2002
Domaine Robert Sirugue et ses Enfants

Medium-full colour. Quite firm, but rich and potentially opulent on the nose. Fullish body. Spicy/earthy flavours. Good backbone and grip. Long. Very good plus. (July 2006)

2012 TO 2025   16.5

Griotte-Chambertin, 2002
Domaine Joseph Drouhin

Medium-full colour. Fragrant, high-toned, succulent nose. Lovely fruit. Medium-full body. Quite round already. Fresh and flowery. Elegant and complex. Fine plus. (July 2006)

2012 TO 2030   18.0

Griotte-Chambertin, 2002
Domaine Claude Dugat

Fullish colour. Rich, full, concentrated nose. Less extraction than their Charmes. Classy. Impressively profound. Full body. Very good tannin. Very good grip. Rich and tannic. Backward. Potentially very fine. (July 2006)

2015 TO 2030   18.5

Latricières-Chambertin, 2002
Domaine Joseph Faiveley

Full colour. Splendidly rich and opulent on the nose. Creamy-rich, old-vine character. Full body. Backward palate. Some tannin. Rich, concentrated and classic. Very lovely style. Very fine plus. (March 2005)

2012 TO 2030   19.0

Latricières-Chambertin, 2002
Maison Camille Giroud

Medium-full colour. Classy nose. Fresh and oaky. Fullish body. Well balanced. Lovely fruit. Good energy. Good definition. Long. Fine. (July 2006)

2012 TO 2030   17.5

Latricières-Chambertin, 2002
Domaine Louis Rémy

Medium colour. Ripe, round, ample nose. Medium-full body. Good fruit. Good grip. Ripe tannins. Slightly four-square and a bit overblown, but very good. (July 2006)

2012 TO 2025   16.0

Latricières-Chambertin, 2002
Domaine Jean Trapet

Medium-full colour. Rather more depth, class and interest than their Chapelle-Chambertin. Fullish body, vigorous and concentrated. This is very promising. Lots of class, too, on the palate. Balanced. Multidimensional. Very fine. (March 2005)

2012 TO 2030   18.5

Marsannay, 2002
Domaine Philippe Naddef

Good colour. Quite a sizeable wine for a Marsannay. Some tannin and also some new oak. This makes it slightly bitter at present. Medium to medium-full body. On the palate there is very good fruit underneath and good grip. Good for what it is. (May 2004)

NOW TO 2012   15.0

Marsannay, Clos du Roy, 2002
Domaine Sylvain Pataille

Very clean, well-made, silky-smooth wine. Round but vigorous. Medium body. Now lovely to drink, but it will still keep well. Very good. (September 2004)

NOW TO 2009   15.5

Marsannay, Les Longeroies, 2002
Domaine Bruno Clair

Medium to medium-full colour. Very lovely pure Pinot on the nose. Medium body. Very ripe, almost sweet. But balanced, succulent and very stylish. Long finish. Very lovely. A splendid example of what it is. (March 2005)

NOW TO 2020   15.5

Mazis-Chambertin, 2002
Domaine Joseph Faiveley

Medium-full colour. Quite rich and full, but a little tough on the nose. Fullish body. Tannic. Slightly raw. This masks the fruit. But the follow-through is rich and opulent. Very good or better. But a bit austere at present. (July 2006)

2014 TO 2030   16.0

Mazis-Chambertin, 2002
Domaine Bernard Maume

Fullish colour. Rich and fat but rather rustic on the nose. Fullish body. Not a lot of tannin. Opulent but not very clean or classy. Quite good. (July 2006)

2012 TO 2022   14.0

Mazis-Chambertin, 2002
Domaine Philippe Naddef

Good colour. Rich, profound, concentrated and oaky. Lots of depth. Lots of quality. Fullish body. Firm. Lots of black fruit. Very good grip. Long. Very good indeed. (May 2004)

2011 TO 2026   17.0

Monthelie, 2002
Domaine Pierre Morey

Ripe, earthy, with a touch of oak. Good grip. Medium body. Good for what it is. (March 2005)

NOW TO 2013   14.0

Monthelie, Les Duresses, 2002
Domaine des Comtes Lafon

Medium colour. Not a lot of weight but very stylish fruit on the nose. Crisp, pure and balanced. Soft and fragrant on the palate. Very clean. Long. Ready. Lovely for what it is. (July 2006)

NOW TO 2012   15.5

Monthelie, Les Duresses, 2002
Domaine Annick Parent

Medium to medium-full colour. Soft, fragrant, stylish nose. Medium weight. Still a little raw but very elegant, ripe fruit. Clean and balanced. Long. Very good for what it is. (March 2005)

NOW TO 2014   16.0

Monthelie, Les Champs Fulliot, 2002
Domaine Guy Dubuet-Monthelie et Fils

Cool but ripe and stylish. Medium body. A little tannin. A little lean. But nicely pure. No attenuation. Positive finish. Will round off. (February 2006)

NOW TO 2015   14.5

Monthelie, Sur la Velle, 2002
Domaine Éric Boigelot

Lightish colour. A little thin and attenuated. No. (February 2006)

DRINK SOON   12.5

Morey-Saint-Denis, 2002
Domaine Dujac

Medium-full colour. Fragrant nose. Signs of the stems. Ripe, opulent, fresh and rich on the palate. Good energy and intensity. Long and impressive. Very good indeed for a village wine. (March 2005)

2009 TO 2025   16.0

Morey-Saint-Denis, Vieilles Vignes, 2002
Domaine Hubert Lignier

Fullish colour. Fullish, quite oaky but old-viney and concentrated nose. Fullish body. Ample. Balanced. Attractive and promising. Long and stylish. Fine. (July 2006)

2012 TO 2025+   17.5

Morey-Saint-Denis, Premier Cru, 2002
Domaine des Lambrays

In bottle six months. Medium colour. Some cassis on the nose but a slight lack of generosity, even bitterness on nose and palate. Medium body. Slightly attenuated although not lacking grip. What it lacks is sex appeal. This may be the recent bottling. (September 2004)

2009 TO 2020   15.0

Morey-Saint-Denis, Les Chenevery, 2002
Domaine Virgile Lignier

Good colour. Ripe nose. Some new oak. No great concentration but composed and stylish. Medium to medium-full body. A little tannin. Rich. Good vigour. Elegant. Long. Very good plus indeed. (March 2005)

NOW TO 2022   17.0

Morey-Saint-Denis, Clos de la Buissière, 2002
Domaine Georges Roumier et Fils

Full colour. Ripe, full, spicy but backward nose. Fullish body. Some tannin. As always, especially compared with his Chambolle Les Cras, a touch rustic. But meaty, spicy and very good. (March 2005)

2011 TO 2025   16.0

Morey-Saint-Denis, Clos Sorbè, 2002
Domaine Louis Jadot

Medium to medium-full colour. Ample, ripe, succulent nose. Elegant too. But quite soft and forward. Medium to medium-full body. Good tannins. Good grip. This is balanced and positive. Finishes well. Very good plus. (July 2006)

2011 TO 2022   16.5

Morey-Saint-Denis, Les Faconnières, 2002
Domaine Lignier-Michelot

Medium-full colour. Quite soft, fragrant, stylish nose. Medium to medium-full body. Not a great deal of tannin. Very ripe fruit, but balanced and long on the palate. A seductive wine. Very good plus. (July 2006)

2010 TO 2020   16.5

Morey-Saint-Denis, Les Ruchots, 2002
Domaine Hervé Arlaud

Medium-full colour. Ripe, quite firm, but plump fruit on the nose. Medium-full body. Good tannins. Good depth. Good vigour. Juicy and long on the palate, and nicely stylish. Very good indeed. (July 2006)

2012 TO 2025   17.0

Musigny, 2002
Domaine Joseph Drouhin

Fullish colour. Very lovely nose. Splendid fruit. Real finesse on the nose. Fullish body. Harmonious, clean, intense and vigorous. Absolute knockout! Brilliant! (July 2006)

2014 TO 2035   20.0

Musigny, 2002
Domaine Jacques-Frédéric Mugnier

Medium-full colour. Very exquisite fruit on the nose. Rich, succulent and very finely poised. This is very intensely concentrated, yet not a bit heavy. Essence of wine, indeed, and really fine elegance. Very, very long and very, very lovely. (July 2006)

2012 TO 2030   20.0

Musigny, 2002
Domaine Comte Georges de Vogüé

Full colour. Opulent and oaky, but also malic on the nose. Big, oaky, modern and most impressive. But is it as classy as Mugnier's or Drouhin's? Slightly solid? Needs time. (July 2006)

2015 TO 2035   19.0

Le Musigny, 2002
Domaine de la Vougeraie

Fullish colour. Stunning nose: a cornucopia of ripe, rich, succulent fruit. Medium-full body. Excellent grip. Really aristocratic character, balance and finesse. Multidimensional and very, very intense. More Mugnier (next to whose vines the Vougeraies lie) than Vogüé. Quite brilliantly lovely. They made two and one-half casks. (September 2004)

2012 TO 2040   20.0

Nuits-Saint-Georges, 2002
Domaine Bichot

Slightly corky but medium bodied, juicy, freshly balanced and quite stylish. (October 2004)

NOW TO 2015   14.0

Nuits-Saint-Georges, 2002
Domaine Henri Gouges

Fullish colour. Lovely rich, positive nose. Very stylish and full of interest for a village wine. Medium-full body. Some tannin. Good grip. Lots of dimension. Very good indeed for what it is. (March 2005)

2020 TO 2025   16.0

Nuits-Saint-Georges, 2002
Domaine Louis Jadot

Medium-full colour. A little development. Ripe, slightly spicy nose. No aggressive tannins. Medium-full bodied, ample and stylish. Very good grip. Lots of fruit and complexity. This is a very fine example of a village wine. Lovely finish. (April 2006)

2009 TO 2020+   16.5

Nuits-Saint-Georges, Vieilles Vignes, 2002
Domaine Jean Pierre Truchetet

Good colour. A little closed on the nose. Medium-full weight. Good grip. Plenty of concentrated, ripe fruit. Very pure. Long and classy. A very good example. (February 2006)

NOW TO 2019   16.0

Nuits-Saint-Georges, Au Bas de Combe, 2002
Domaine Jean Tardy et Fils

Medium to medium-full colour. Ripe and succulent, sweet and oaky on the nose. Medium to medium-full body. Quite rich. Good concentration. Stylish and balanced. Lots of charm. Fresh. Clean. Very good. (March 2005)

NOW TO 2017   15.5

Nuits-Saint-Georges, Premier Cru, 2002
Domaine Thibault Liger-Belair

Medium-full colour. Rich, full, oaky nose. Medium-full body. Good fruit and grip if not that concentrated. But rather overwhelmed by the oak. Good. (July 2006)

2012 TO 2025   15.0

Nuits-Saint-Georges, Aux Boudots, 2002
Domaine Jean Grivot

Fullish colour. Youthful, closed-in, tight nose. But very good depth underneath. Fullish body. Backward. Lots of depth. Rather adolescent. But very good indeed. Lovely finish. (July 2006)

2012 TO 2030   17.0

Nuits-Saint-Georges, Aux Boudots, 2002
Domaine Louis Jadot

Medium-full colour. Firm, full, rich, gently oaky nose. High class. Fullish bodied, rich and

concentrated. Very lovely fruit. Lots of depth. Excellent balance. This is fine plus. A lovely example. (July 2006)

2012 TO 2030   18.0

Nuits-Saint-Georges, Aux Boudots, 2002
Domaine Méo-Camuzet

Full colour. Rich, quite oaky nose. Some tannin. Plenty of depth. Fullish body. Very well balanced. Fresh and ripe. No undue oak on the palate. Intense and concentrated. This is fine. Just a touch four-square perhaps, but this should go. (July 2006)

2012 TO 2030   17.5

Nuits-Saint-Georges, Les Cailles, 2002
Domaine Bouchard Père et Fils

Medium-full colour. Somewhat closed on the nose. But good depth and concentration underneath. Some good fruit here. But some weakness too. Medium-full body. Curate's eggy. Curious. Better as it developed. (July 2006)

2012 TO 2020   15.5

Nuits-Saint-Georges, Les Cailles, 2002
Maison Patrice Rion

Fullish colour. Ample, ripe and succulent on the nose. Perhaps not the greatest of class. Medium-full body. Slightly astringent. Decent fruit and balance. But it doesn't really sing. Quite good. (July 2006)

2012 TO 2020   14.0

Nuits-Saint-Georges, Aux Chaignots, 2002
Domaine Robert Chevillon

Medium-full colour. Fat, rich, plump nose. Medium-full body. Open and attractive. Ripe, rich and harmonious. Good class and depth. Very good indeed. Not quite the concentration for fine. (July 2006)

2011 TO 2025   17.0

Nuits-Saint-Georges, Aux Chaignots, 2002
Domaine Joseph Faiveley

Medium-full colour. A little strained and weedy on the nose: somewhat attenuated. Thin and astringent on the palate. Medium to medium-full body. Disappointing. (July 2006)

2010 TO 2015   12.5

Nuits-Saint-Georges, Aux Chaignots, 2002
Domaine Henri Gouges

Medium-full colour. Firm nose. Rich, concentrated and backward. Fullish body. Some tannin. Lovely fruit and depth. Classy. Long and well balanced on the follow-through. Needs time. Fine. (July 2006)

2014 TO 2030   17.5

Nuits-Saint-Georges, Aux Chaignots, 2002
Domaine Alain Michelot

Good, full colour. Rich, full, aromatic on the nose. Very cassis, blackberry nose. Very good acidity. Bigger, fatter and more concentrated than the 1999. A little tannin. Richer. More substantial. A lot of depth. Lovely acidity. This is fine. (March 2005)

2010 TO 2020+   17.5

Nuits-Saint-Georges, Clos des Argillières, 2002
Domaine Bertrand Ambroise

Rich, ripe, full, not too oaky on the nose. Medium-full body. Good tannins. Not a great deal of depth underneath but good plus. (February 2006)

NOW TO 2019   15.5

Nuits-Saint-Georges, Clos des Corvées, 2002
Domaine Prieuré-Roch

Good colour. Good richness and concentration on the nose. Old-vine fruity. Medium-full body. Some tannins. This has depth and vigour. Only marginally stemmy. Very good plus. (February 2006)

2011 TO 2019   16.5

Nuits-Saint-Georges, Clos des Corvées
Pagets, 2002
Château de Premeaux

Good colour. Lovely aromatic nose. Quite forceful. Slightly spicy. Yet decent acidity. Good depth. Finishes very well. Very good plus. (February 2006)

2009 TO 2019   16.5

Nuits-Saint-Georges, Clos des Porrets
Saint-Georges, 2002
Domaine Henri Gouges

Fullish colour. Rich, full nose. Very lovely fruit. Not a bit too brutally tannic. Full body. Quite substantial. Some tannin, of course. Lovely black fruit. Very good grip. Still very youthful. Fine but needs time. (July 2006)

2014 TO 2030   17.5

Nuits-Saint-Georges, Les Damodes, 2002
Domaine Jean Chauvenet

Fullish colour. Ripe, gently oaky, stylish nose. Medium-full body. Good depth. Balanced. Ripe, complex and elegant. Very good plus. (July 2006)

2012 TO 2025   16.5

Nuits-Saint-Georges, Les Damodes, 2002
Domaine Jayer-Gilles

Fullish colour. Very oaky, and of high toast at that, on the nose. Fullish body. Some tannin. Good acidity. Way too much oak. Not bad. (July 2006)

2012 TO 2020   13.5

Nuits-Saint-Georges, Les Damodes, 2002
Domaine de la Vougeraie

Fullish colour. Ripe and pure and rich on the nose. Medium-full body. Ripe and stylish. Fresh and harmonious. Long and complex. Very good indeed. (July 2006)

2012 TO 2025   17.0

Nuits-Saint-Georges, Aux Murgers, 2002
Domaine Sylvain Cathiard

Fullish colour. Quite a firm, tannic, closed-in wine on the nose. Medium-full body. A little tannin. Ample and accessible, but a slight lack of flair for fine. Very good plus. (July 2006)

2011 TO 2020   16.5

Nuits-Saint-Georges, Les Perrières, 2002
Domaine Jean Chauvenet

Fullish colour. Stylish, accessible nose with a touch of oak, and, like the Damodes, good but not the greatest concentration. Medium-full body. Attractive fruit. Balanced. Long. Very good indeed. (July 2006)

2011 TO 2025   17.0

Nuits-Saint-Georges, Les Procès, 2002
Domaine Joseph Drouhin

Medium to medium-full colour. Stylish nose. Quite profound. Good clean fruit. Medium-full body. Balanced. Elegant fruit. Not too tough. Long and accessible. Very good indeed. (July 2006)

2010 TO 2020   17.0

Nuits-Saint-Georges, Les Pruliers, 2002
Domaine Philippe Gavignet

Good colour. Lovely pure, plump nose. Very harmonious. Very complex. A rich wine. On the palate fullish bodied, profound and intense. Very classy. Very long. Fine. (February 2006)

2011 TO 2025   17.5

Nuits-Saint-Georges, Les Pruliers, 2002
Domaine Henri Gouges

Fullish colour. Similar to the Clos des Porrets on the nose. But a little denser and more backward. Full body. Tannic. Backward. Quite tough. But very promising at the end. (July 2006)

2013 TO 2025   17.0

Nuits-Saint-Georges, Les Pruliers, 2002
Domaine Jean Grivot

Medium-full colour. Not as inspired as his Boudots on the nose. Less weight, concentration and excitement. But good, ripe fruit here. On the palate medium-full body. Some tannin. Good fruit but lacks a little real flair. Very good plus. (July 2006)

2012 TO 2025   16.5

Nuits-Saint-Georges, Les Saint-Georges, 2002
Domaine Joseph Faiveley

Medium-full colour. Rich, full, quite backward nose. Full body. Some tannin. Very good grip and depth of fruit. Long. Needs time. Much better than their Chaignots. Fine. (July 2006)

2012 TO 2025   17.5

Nuits-Saint-Georges, Les Saint-Georges, 2002
Domaine Henri Gouges

Full colour. Splendidly rich and concentrated on the nose. Backward though, of course. A very lovely wine. Full bodied and tannic but rich, concentrated and vigorous. Very, very long and multidimensional. Very fine. (July 2006)

2013 TO 2030   18.5

Nuits-Saint-Georges, Les Vaucrains, 2002
Domaine Jean Chauvenet

Full colour. Lovely fruit. Plenty of depth and concentration. Impressive nose here. The best of the Chauvenets. Fullish body. Very good concentration. Lovely fruit. Complex and classy. Very long. Fine plus. (July 2006)

2012 TO 2025   18.0

Nuits-Saint-Georges, Les Vaucrains, 2002
Domaine Henri Gouges

Full colour. Backward, closed-in nose. But not too brutal. Fullish body. Some tannin. Rich, full bodied and concentrated. Needs time. A true Vaucrains. Very long. Fine. (July 2006)

2015 TO 2030   17.5

Nuits-Saint-Georges, Les Vaucrains, 2002
Maison Nicolas Potel

Fullish colour. Classy nose. Very pure. Lovely fruit. Not as brutal as Vaucrains often is. On the palate medium-full. Lovely fruit on the attack. Very good grip. Long, complex and classy. Fine. (July 2006)

2012 TO 2025   17.5

Pernand-Vergelesses, Ile de Vergelesses, 2002
Domaine Chandon de Briailles

Medium colour. Fragrant, stylish, persistent nose. A little light and an absence of concentration and vigour on the palate. Elegant but forward. Yet an intense, elegant finish. Very good. (March 2005)

NOW TO 2015   16.0

Pernand-Vergelesses, Ile de Vergelesses, 2002
Domaine Rémi Rollin

Fragrant nose. Good fruit and a nice juicy style. Medium body. Fresh. Good tannins. Elegant and if just a little lean, no lack of attractive fruit. Positive finish. Good plus. (April 2006)

NOW TO 2015   15.5

Pommard, Premier Cru, 2002
Domaine Bouchard Père et Fils
Medium colour. Soft nose. Not a lot of distinction or character. Better on the palate. Medium-full body. Ripe. Good grip and energy. Slightly ungainly at present but good plus. (July 2006)

2010 TO 2020   15.5

Pommard, Clos des Boucherottes, 2002
Domaine Coste-Caumartin
Premier cru. Good colour. Rich, full, backward nose. Fullish. Some tannin. Splendidly concentrated fruit. Lots and lots of depth. Fine. (March 2005)

2010 TO 2025   17.5

Pommard, Chanlins, 2002
Domaine Monthelie-Douhairet
Good colour. Ripe, fat and meaty on both nose and palate. Medium-full body. Very lovely, succulent fruit. Splendid balance. Really stylish. Fine. (February 2006)

2011 TO 2025   17.5

Pommard, Les Charmots, 2002
Domaine Gabriel Billard
Lightish colour. Soft, ripe, slightly spicy nose. No great class but ample and decently ripe tannins. A touch sweet. Medium to medium-full body. Quite forward for what it is. Quite good. (March 2005)

NOW TO 2015   14.0

Pommard, Clos des Epeneaux, 2002
Domaine du Comte Armand
Fullish colour. Closed-in nose. Lots of depth. Full. Backward. High quality. Full bodied and complex on the palate. Lovely. Very fine tannins. Very concentrated fruit. Very, very long. Excellent. (July 2006)

2012 TO 2030   18.5

Pommard, Clos Micault, 2002
Domaine Bichot
Medium-full body. Some tannin. Ripe and black fruity. Good grip. Quite intense. Good style. Still very youthful. Very good. (October 2004)

2009 TO 2019   16.0

Pommard, Les Fremiers, 2002
Domaine Louis Boillot
Fullish colour. Stylish, ample, fruity nose. Good depth and freshness. Medium-full body. Plump. Fresh. Balanced. Positive. Very good. (July 2006)

2009 TO 2018   16.0

Pommard, Les Fremiers, 2002
Domaine de Courcel
Fullish colour. Ripe, plump and classy on the nose with a touch of the stems. Medium-full body. Balanced, clean and classy. Long. Lots of charm. Very good. (July 2006)

2010 TO 2020   16.0

Pommard, Grand Clos des Epenots, 2002
Domaine de Courcel
Full colour. A touch of the stems here. Rich and succulent. Medium-full body. Concentrated and harmonious. Profound and succulent. Very well made. Long. Very good indeed. (July 2006)

2010 TO 2020+   17.0

Pommard, Les Grands Epenots, 2002
Domaine Michel Gaunoux
Medium to medium-full colour. Ripe but a little lacking in zip and vigour on the nose. Medium to medium-full body. Lacks hightones. Decent grip but not quite enough richness and zip. Good plus at best. (March 2005)

NOW TO 2015   15.5

Pommard, Les Grands Epenots, 2002
Maison Vincent Girardin
Fullish colour. A bit tight still on the nose. But good depth if a little raw at present. On the palate very blackberry fruity. Medium to medium-full body. Fresh. Not the greatest of finesse but balanced and good plus. (July 2006)

2009 TO 2018   15.5

Pommard, Les Jarolières, 2002
Domaine Jean-Marc Boillot
Fullish colour. Full, rich, fat nose. A slight touch of reduction at first. Medium-full body. Fresh, ripe and balanced. Positive and classy. Lovely finish. Very good indeed. (July 2006)
2010 TO 2020+   17.0

Pommard, Les Perrières, Vieilles Vignes Centenaires, 2002
Domaine Launay
Fine, full colour. Still very vigorous. Rich, creamy nose. Classy, vigorous and balanced. Full body. Still some tannin. Still a little bitter. But plenty of depth and potential if no great class. Good plus. (September 2005)
2009 TO 2017   15.5

Pommard, Les Pézerolles, 2002
Domaine A.F. Gros
Medium-full colour. Round, ripe nose. Not too solid. Medium weight. Quite rich. Good grip. A little closed-in at present but good quality. (July 2006)
2009 TO 2018   15.0

Pommard, Les Pézerolles, 2002
Maison Nicolas Potel
Medium-full colour. Soft and succulent on the nose. Medium-full body. Just a little tannin. Good fresh fruit. Quite complex. Balanced and complex. Long on the palate. Very good. (July 2006)
2010 TO 2020   16.0

Pommard, Les Poutures, 2002
Domaine Louis Jadot
Medium-full colour. Rich, full, backward nose but with a curious high-toned flavour. Strange sweet-sour character. Medium body. Rather stewed. A bad bottle? (July 2006)
2009 TO 2015   13.0

Pommard, Les Rugiens, 2002
Domaine de Courcel
Medium-full colour. Ripe, rich, fat and succulent, with a slight touch of the stems. A bit fuller,

more tannic, more backward than his Clos des Epenots. Less distinctive. But very good plus. (July 2006)
2010 TO 2020   16.5

Pommard, Les Rugiens, 2002
Domaine Hubert de Montille
Medium to medium-full colour. Plump, fruity nose. Medium to medium-full body. Pleasantly fruity on the palate, but not much dimension or individuality. Decently positive finish so good plus. (March 2005)
NOW TO 2015   15.5

Richebourg, 2002
Domaine Jean Grivot
Fullish colour. Closed-in on the nose. Very splendid fruit underneath. Full bodied. Fat. Very, very rich. Backward. Some tannin. Very fine grip. Slightly adolescent but lovely potential. Very fine plus. (July 2006)
2014 TO 2030   19.0

Richebourg, 2002
Domaine Anne Gros
Fine colour. Rather more closed-in on the nose than her Clos de Vougeot. Still a bit austere. Underneath, the wine is excellent. Full bodied, intense and vigorous. Very lovely fruit indeed. Aristocratic. Profound. Complete. (July 2006)
2015 TO 2030   19.5

Richebourg, 2002
Domaine Méo-Camuzet
Full colour. A little reduction on the nose at first. But this soon blew away. A rich, sumptuous example: not a bit too oaky. Full bodied. Youthful. Very good tannins. Rich, vigorous and classy finish. (July 2006)
2014 TO 2030   19.0

Richebourg, 2002
Domaine de la Romanée-Conti
Fullish colour. Firm nose. A bit raw, even slightly vegetal on the nose. At the moment this is quite

brutal. But there is a lot of substance here. Full bodied, vigorous and powerful. Multidimensional. Excellent. Needs time. (July 2006)

2015 TO 2040   19.5

La Romanée, 2002
Domaine Liger-Belair/
Maison Bouchard Père et Fils

Fullish colour. Very lovely fragrant nose. Very poised, aristocratic fruit. Medium-full body. Very intense. A mouth-filling wine which is very long, complex and very harmonious. Sadly I did not sample this against the wine fully *élevé*-d by Liger-Belair, but I see my note is almost identical. Very fine indeed. (July 2006)

2012 TO 2030   19.5

La Romanée, 2002
Domaine du Vicomte Liger-Belair

First vintage. Not as full a colour as the Reignots. Slightly closed-in but fabulous, Musigny-ish nose (Musigny-ish as in Mugnier, not Vogüé). Not as full as his Reignots but twice as fragrant, intense, concentration of fruit and depth. Multidimensional. Aristocratic. Quite excellent. (June 2005)

2012 TO 2030   20.0

Romanée-Conti, 2002
Domaine de la Romanée-Conti

Fullish colour. Ethereal nose with a touch of Christmas cake. Very, very lovely. Subtle and multidimensional. Fullish body. Very lovely complex fruit. Splendidly together and balanced. Lovely long, lingering finish. Marvellous. (July 2006)

2013 TO 2040   20.0

Romanée-Saint-Vivant, 2002
Domaine Arnoux Père et Fils

Full colour. Full, rich and concentrated on the nose. Plenty of depth and class here. Full body. Ample and voluptuous. Very finely balanced. Good tannins. Long and satisfying. Very fine. (July 2006)

2014 TO 2030   18.5

Romanée-Saint-Vivant, 2002
Domaine Sylvain Cathiard

Magnum. Fullish colour. High-class nose. Rich, intense, very splendid fruit. Fullish body. Yet silky. Very fresh. Very complex and really sophisticated. This is very, very lovely. Goes on and on for ages at the end. Splendid quality. (July 2006)

2012 TO 2030   19.5

Romanée-Saint-Vivant, 2002
Maison Champy

Fullish colour. Plump nose. Quite ripe and rich. But not very elegant. Fullish bodied, ample, reasonably balanced on the palate. Rich and complex. Not great but fine. (July 2006)

2014 TO 2028   17.5

Romanée-Saint-Vivant, 2002
Domaine Follin-Arbelet

Medium-full colour. Quite rich nose. Some structure. Lacks real refinement. The fruit is a little boiled-sweety. Fullish body. Decent fruit. Decent grip. But somewhat pedestrian for this *climat*. (July 2006)

2012 TO 2028   16.5

Romanée-Saint-Vivant, 2002
Domaine de la Romanée-Conti

Fullish colour. Rich but silky on the nose. Ample and almost Musigny-ish in character. Fullish body. Still very young on the palate. Harmonious and succulent. Complex and intense. Very classy. Very lovely. (July 2006)

2012 TO 2030   19.0

Romanée-Saint-Vivant, Les Quatre
Journeaux, 2002
Domaine Louis Latour

Medium to medium-full colour. Ripe, fullish nose. A touch of tabac. Somewhat four-square. Medium-full body. Good ripe attack, but the follow-through lacks flair. Merely very good. (July 2006)

2012 TO 2028   16.0

Ruchottes-Chambertin, Clos des Ruchottes, 2002
Domaine Armand Rousseau

Fullish colour. Lovely nose. Pure and concentrated. Cool and complex. Admirably correct. Medium-full body. Ripe tannins. Lovely balance. Classy, subtle and profound. Very long. Fine plus. (July 2006)

2012 TO 2030   18.0

Savigny-lès-Beaune, 2002
Domaine Simon Bize et Fils

Clean. No undue oak. Balanced and stylish. Fresh and very good for what it is. (March 2005)

NOW TO 2010   16.0

Savigny-lès-Beaune, Premier Cru, 2002
Domaine Bouchard Père et Fils

Medium to medium-full colour. Balanced, fruity but dull nose. Medium body. Fruity on the palate. But boring. No distinction here. (July 2006)

NOW TO 2011   13.5

Savigny-lès-Beaune, Clos des Guettes, 2002
Domaine Louis Jadot

Clean and crisp. Flowery and elegant. Very gently oaky. Stylish. Medium body. Now just about ready. Good plus. (May 2005)

NOW TO 2009   15.5

Savigny-lès-Beaune, La Dominode, 2002
Domaine Bruno Clair

Good colour. Slightly herbaceous on the nose. The tannins are a bit hard. Yet on the palate a touch over-evolved. Is this bottle sick still? Medium-full body. I would like to see this again. (March 2005)

(SEE NOTE)

Savigny-lès-Beaune, Les Marconnets, 2002
Domaine Simon Bize et Fils

Good colour. Slightly stemmy on the nose. A little astringent on the palate. Fat but earthy. Rich and balanced though. Good. (March 2005)

NOW TO 2016   15.0

Savigny-lès-Beaune, Les Narbantons, 2002
Domaine Mongeard-Mugneret

Fullish, meaty, oaky nose. Lacks a bit of elegance. Medium to medium-full on the palate.

A bit one-dimensional but reasonably balanced and reasonably ripe. Quite good. (April 2006)

NOW TO 2013   14.0

La Tâche, 2002
Domaine de la Romanée-Conti

Full colour. Fat, rich nose. Not as raw as the Richebourg but nevertheless still very young. Full body. Still an infant. Lots of wine here. Very ample and with lots of vigour and depth. Splendid finish. Excellent. (July 2006)

2015 TO 2040   20.0

Volnay, 2002
Maison Camille Giroud

Medium colour. Fresh, fragrant and stylish. Medium weight. Good acidity. Pure. Elegant, even complex. Quite forward but very good for what it is. (March 2005)

NOW TO 2012   16.0

Volnay, Cuvée Général Muteau, 2002
Hospices de Beaune (Emerin)

Medium-full colour. Quite marked by the oak on the nose. Ripe, fat and fruity underneath. Full body. A little tannin. Oaky and four-square. A little short. Chunky and boring. (July 2006)

2010 TO 2020   13.5

Volnay, Premier Cru, 2002
Domaine du Marquis d'Angerville

Medium colour. Lovely fragrant nose. Rich, cherry-raspberry. Gentle but persistent. Medium weight. Fresh. Balanced. Elegant. Positive. Very good. Quite forward. (March 2005)

NOW TO 2014   15.0

Volnay, Premier Cru, 2002
Domaine Régis Rossignol-Changarnier

Medium colour. Corked but a decently ripe, slightly chunky wine underneath. (July 2006)

2009 TO 2018   15.0

Volnay, Premier Cru, 2002
Domaine Nicolas Rossignol

Good colour. Vigorous nose. Lots of fruit, depth and succulence. Very Volnay. Fullish bodied, ripe, intense, profound and long on the palate. Lovely long finish. Fine. (February 2006)

2010 TO 2025   17.5

Volnay, Les Brouillards, 2002
Domaine Louis Boillot

Medium-full colour. Fragrant nose. Classy fruit. Very Volnay. Supple and succulent. Medium-full body. Good tannins. Ripe and fresh. Fruity and long with lots of charm. Very good plus. (July 2006)

2009 TO 2019   16.5

Volnay, Caillerets, 2002
Domaine Vincent Bitouzet-Prieur

Medium to medium-full colour. Lovely fragrant nose. Good energy. Medium to medium-full weight. Elegant. Balanced. Complex. Long. This is very good plus. (February 2006)

NOW TO 2020   16.5

Volnay, Les Caillerets, 2002
Domaine Bouchard Père et Fils

Medium-full colour. Rich, gently oaky nose. Soft fruit. Ripe. Very good tannins. Medium-full body. Very stylish and complete. Good acidity. Nicely intense at the end. Very good indeed. (July 2006)

2009 TO 2025   17.0

Volnay, Les Caillerets, 2002
Domaine Chandon de Briailles

Medium-full colour. Soft, ripe, succulent nose with a touch of the stems. Soft and ripe. But a little lacking grip. Pleasant but it lacks depth and distinction for what it is. (July 2006)

NOW TO 2016   14.0

Volnay, La Carelle, 2002
Maison Camille Giroud

Fragrant, complex and stylish. Medium body. Not a lot of tannin but very good intensity and grip. Classy. Very Volnay. Very good indeed. (June 2005)

NOW TO 2016   17.0

Volnay, Carelle sous la Chapelle, 2002
Domaine Jean-Marc Boillot

Fullish colour. Chunky nose. A touch reduced at present. But good ripe fruit underneath. Fullish

body. A bit of tannin. A bit astringent today but good grip. At least very good, I think. (July 2006)

2009 TO 2018   16.0

Volnay, Carelle sous la Chapelle, 2002
Domaine Hubert de Montille

Medium colour. Light but fragrant and classy nose. But only medium body. Ripe, fresh and fruity but not concentrated enough. Good plus. (July 2006)

2009 TO 2017   15.5

Volnay, Champans, 2002
Domaine du Marquis d'Angerville

Medium-full colour. Closed-in but classy nose. Fullish. Ample. Some tannin. But very composed and integrated. Quietly successful. Good grip. Ripe. Long. Stylish. Very good indeed. (July 2006)

2010 TO 2020   17.0

Volnay, Champans, 2002
Domaine des Comtes Lafon

Medium-full colour. Rich, ripe, fullish, succulent, classy nose. Plenty of depth. Fullish body. Good tannins. Balanced but slightly four-square. Not the nuance of Angerville's. Needs time. (July 2006)

2010 TO 2020   16.0

Volnay, Champans, 2002
Domaine Monthelie-Douhairet

Good colour. Ripe, meaty nose. Good weight and depth. Medium-full body. Lovely stylish Pinot fruit. Balanced and vigorous. Very pure. Very long. Fine. (February 2006)

2010 TO 2025   17.5

Volnay, Clos du Château des Ducs, 2002
Domaine Michel Lafarge

Medium-full colour. Rich, backward nose. Lots of depth and concentration. Backward. Still a bit raw. Fullish body. Very good tannins. Very good grip. Lovely fruit. Needs time. (July 2006)

2010 TO 2025   17.0

Volnay, Clos des Chênes, 2002
Château de Meursault

Fullish colour. Solid, slightly four-square nose. But ripe if not much finesse. Fullish body.

Slightly chunky. Some tannin and astringency. Lacks nuance. Quite good. (July 2006)

2009 TO 2014   14.0

Volnay, Clos des Chênes, 2002
Domaine Michel Lafarge

Medium-full colour. Very lovely nose. Rich, ample and gently oaky. Elegant and complex. A true Volnay. Very fragrant and very concentrated. Yet not a blockbuster. Very delicious fruit. This is really fine. (July 2006)

NOW TO 2020+   18.0

Volnay, Clos des Chênes, 2002
Domaine des Comtes Lafon

Fullish colour. Slightly chunky on the nose. Not the finesse and purity of their 2002 Santenots du Milieu. The least good of Lafon's Volnays. Medium-full body. Not the greatest grip or nuance. Fruity. Good plus at best. (July 2006)

2009 TO 2015   15.5

Volnay, Clos des 60 Ouvrées, 2002
Domaine de la Pousse d'Or

Not an enormous colour. And quite evolved for a 2002. Medium body only. Not much tannin. Decent fruit and grip. But no real flair. Merely good. (February 2006)

NOW TO 2014   15.0

Volnay, Clos des Ducs, 2002
Domaine du Marquis d'Angerville

Medium-full colour. Quite firm, closed but profound nose. Full bodied, rich and backward. Very well made. Lovely balance. Super fruit. Very long and complex. This is really fine. (July 2006)

2009 TO 2025   18.0

Volnay, Frémiets, 2002
Domaine du Marquis d'Angerville

Medium to medium-full colour. Fragrant, balanced and really quite intense on nose and palate. Medium to medium-full body. Fresh. Persistent. Very good indeed. (July 2006)

NOW TO 2020   17.0

Volnay, Les Mitans, 2002
Domaine Hubert de Montille

Medium colour. Ripe, succulent nose. No hard edges. A touch of the stems. Medium body. Not a lot of tannin. Good grip. Stylish and fruity. Long. Very good. (July 2006)

2009 TO 2018   16.0

Volnay, Les Mitans, 2002
Domaine Vincent Perrin

Medium-full colour. Ripe, open, stylish nose. Nicely individual fruit. Very myrtille. Medium-full body. Some tannin to resolve and a bit adolescent at the moment. But the grip is there, and the finish is stylish and complex. Not brilliant but very good. (February 2006)

NOW TO 2018   16.0

Volnay, Les Mitans, 2002
Maison Nicolas Potel

Medium colour. Slightly raw and ungainly on the nose. But decent fruit underneath. Medium to medium-full body. A touch four-square. Good fruit and balance. Positive finish. Good. (July 2006)

2009 TO 2018   15.0

Volnay, En l'Ormeau, 2002
Domaine A and J Parent

Medium colour. Slightly weedy-stemmy nose. Better on the palate. Slightly sweet. But medium to medium-full body. Good grip. Good. (July 2006)

2009 TO 2016   15.0

Volnay, Pitures, 2002
Maison Nicolas Potel

Medium-full colour. Richer, fatter, sweeter and more succulent than his 2002 Mitans. Good plump fruit. Medium to medium-full body. Lovely fruit. Succulent, fresh and pure. Very stylish and very complex. Fine. (July 2006)

2009 TO 2020   17.5

Volnay, Les Santenots, 2002
Domaine Éric Boigelot

Medium to medium-full colour. Not a lot on the nose. It lacks a bit of succulence, but decent fruit and freshness on the palate. But the astringency is lurking. Only fair. (February 2006)

NOW TO 2011   13.5

Volnay, Santenots, 2002
Maison Vincent Girardin

Fullish colour. Just a touch reduced on the nose. But ripe and rich enough. Fullish and succulent. Medium to medium-full body. Ripe. Decently balanced. But slightly astringent. Will be very good, I think. (July 2006)

2009 TO 2020   16.0

Volnay, Les Santenots du Milieu, 2002
Domaine des Comtes Lafon

Fullish colour. Rich, full, oaky nose. Lots of depth here. Quite full. Plenty of concentration. Some tannin. Vigorous and very promising. Backward. Lovely finish. Fine plus. (June 2005)

2010 TO 2025   18.0

Volnay, Taillepieds, 2002
Domaine du Marquis d'Angerville

Fine colour. Even more classy on the nose than his Champans 2002. Excellent fruit. Real depth, complexity and finesse. Very fine tannins. Very gentle touch of oak. Very, very lovely long finish. (June 2005)

2010 TO 2025+   18.5

Volnay, Taillepieds, 2002
Domaine Vincent Bitouzet-Prieur

Medium-full colour. Less ample than their 2002 Volnay Caillerets. But more structure. Less easy to enjoy at present. Medium-full body. Good tannins. Good vigour and nice rich fruit underneath. Needs time. Very good plus. (February 2006)

2010 TO 2020   16.5

Volnay, Taillepieds, 2002
Domaine Bouchard Père et Fils

Medium colour. Quite a soft nose. But very classy, ripe fruit. No hard edges. Medium to medium-full weight. Very Volnay. Intense and fragrant. Long and complex. Lots of finesse. Fine. (July 2006)

2009 TO 2020+   17.5

Volnay, Taillepieds, 2002
Domaine Carré-Courbin

Medium-full colour. Medium weight on the nose. Soft, fruity and charming. Medium body. A bit lacking grip. Slightly astringent. Fruity but forward. (July 2006)

DRINK SOON   14.0

Volnay, Taillepieds, 2002
Domaine Hubert de Montille

Medium to medium-full colour. Soft nose. A little weak and feeble. Better on the palate. Medium to medium-full body. Decent grip. But a little skinny. Good plus at best. (March 2005)

NOW TO 2015   15.5

Volnay, Taille Pieds, 2002
Maison Nicolas Potel

Good colour. Marvellous fruit. Concentrated and oaky. Very classy. Medium-full body. Very succulent. Lots of depth. Long and fine. (March 2002)

NOW TO 2026   17.5

Volnay, Taillepieds, 2002
Domaine Roblet-Monnot

Very good colour. Very lovely, pure, intense, complex nose. Excellent fruit on the palate. Fullish body. Harmonious. Very classy. Very long. Fine. (February 2006)

2010 TO 2025   17.5

Vosne-Romanée, 2002
Domaine du Clos Frantin/Albert Bichot

Good colour. Ripe, black-fruity nose. Rich and meaty. Full and backward. Very good grip. Slightly austere now but very good depth. Promising finish. Needs time. Very good. (October 2004)

2010 TO 2020+   16.0

Vosne-Romanée, 2002
Maison Camille Giroud

Good colour. Very clean and stylish. Very good grip. Medium to medium-full body. Good pure, fragrant Vosne-Romanée fruit. Long. Very good for what it is. (September 2005)

NOW TO 2016   15.0

Vosne-Romanée, 2002
Domaine Jean Grivot

Full, vigorous colour. Still youthful. Lots of depth on the nose. Rich, ample and very elegant. Splendid for a village example. Fullish body. Good tannins. Still needs a couple of years. Very lovely fruit. Long. Fine for what it is. (April 2006)

2009 TO 2020+   16.5

Vosne-Romanée, 2002
Domaine Dominique Mugneret

Good colour. Finely balanced. Very ripe fruit. Generous and succulent. Good weight and plenty of dimension. Medium-full body. Ripe tannins, just about absorbed. Classy. Lots of depth. Very good, especially for a village wine. (March 2005)

2009 TO 2023   16.0

Vosne-Romanée, Premier Cru, Cuvée Duvault-Blochet, 2002
Domaine de la Romanée-Conti

Medium-full colour. Lovely fragrant nose. Quite high volatile acidity. Essentially soft, especially by comparison to the rest of the *rouges*. Quite forward. Medium to medium-full body. Good acidity. Round and succulent. Classy. Long and positive. (July 2006)

2009 TO 2020   17.0

Vosne-Romanée, Les Beaux Monts, 2002
Domaine Bertagna

Fullish colour. Soft, stylish, accessible nose. Very clean fruit. Medium-full body. This is very pure and very harmonious. Lovely complex fruit. Very long. More accessible than Grivot's. Equally good. (July 2006)

2012 TO 2030   18.0

Vosne-Romanée, Les Beaux Monts, 2002
Domaine Bruno Clavelier

Medium to medium-full colour. Accessible nose. Stylish, balanced fruit. Reasonable if not great concentration and depth. Medium-full weight. Somewhat pedestrian compared to Grivot's

and Bertagna's. Slightly astringent. Lacks real finesse, depth and harmony. (July 2006)

2012 TO 2020   14.0

Vosne-Romanée, Les Beaux Monts, 2002
Domaine Jean Grivot

Full colour. Still closed-in on the nose but potentially very fine. This is quite lovely. Very concentrated. Marvellously fresh, complex fruit. Very intense and persistent. Really elegant. Really fine. (July 2006)

2012 TO 2025   19.0

Vosne-Romanée, Les Beaux Monts, 2002
Maison Nicolas Potel

Medium-full colour. Clean, accessible, attractive nose. Good depth and harmony. Nice and fresh. Medium-full body. Easy to enjoy. Open. Balanced. Stylish. Very good plus. (July 2006)

2012 TO 2025   16.5

Vosne-Romanée, Aux Brûlées, 2002
Domaine René Engel

Medium to medium-full colour. Ripe nose. Lovely fruit and balance. Very elegant. Very seductive. Medium-full body. Balanced, ripe, rich and harmonious. Very intense. Very fresh. Splendid finish. This is lovely. Fine plus. (July 2006)

2012 TO 2030   18.0

Vosne-Romanée, Aux Brûlées, 2002
Domaine Michel Gros

Medium to medium-full colour. A little sulphur on the nose at present. But stylish, accessible fruit underneath. Medium-full body. Ripe and quite concentrated. Good tannins. Very good harmony and depth. Splendid finish. Lovely style. Fine. (July 2006)

2012 TO 2030   17.5

Vosne-Romanée, Aux Brûlées, 2002
Domaine Méo-Camuzet

Full colour. Fullish and tannic, even tough and extracted on the nose. Better on the palate. Fullish, but the tannins are absorbed. Fine concentrated fruit. Plenty of depth.

Harmonious. Vigorous. Powerful, indeed. Fine.
(July 2006)

2014 TO 2030   17.5

Vosne-Romanée, Les Chaumes, 2002
Domaine Lamarche

Medium-full colour. Good class and concentration on the nose. Good depth for Chaumes. Gently oaky. Medium-full body. Mocha flavours. Good concentrated, stylish fruit. Harmonious. Attractive. Very good plus. (July 2006)

2012 TO 2025   16.5

Vosne-Romanée, Cros Parentoux, 2002
Domaine Méo-Camuzet

Very good colour. Full, rich, meaty nose. Slightly less oaky than his 2002 Vosne-Romanée Brûlées. Full body. Splendid ripe, rich fruit. A more profound, more complete wine. Splendid finish. Very fine. (July 2006)

2014 TO 2030   18.5

Vosne-Romanée, Aux Malconsorts, 2002
Domaine Sylvain Cathiard

Medium-full colour. Very lovely, complex, classy fruit on the nose. Marvellously multidimensional. This is quite brilliant! Very, very concentrated and intense. Fullish but by no means a blockbuster. Splendid harmony. Very, very long and lingering at the end. (July 2006)

2012 TO 2030   19.0

Vosne-Romanée, Aux Malconsorts, 2002
Domaine du Clos Frantin/Albert Bichot

Medium-full colour. Classy, concentrated nose. Fullish, ripe, rich and concentrated on the palate. Harmonious. Still needs time to resolve its tannins. Not quite the refinenement for fine but very good indeed. (July 2006)

2012 TO 2025   17.0

Vosne-Romanée, Aux Malconsorts, 2002
Maison Nicolas Potel

Medium-full colour. Ripe, rich and concentrated on the nose. Lovely fruit. Lots of dimension. Ample, fullish bodied, ripe wine on the palate.

Attractive fruit. Fresh and balanced. Long. Fine.
(July 2006)

2012 TO 2025   17.5

Vosne-Romanée, Les Petits Monts, 2002
Domaine F. Gerbet et Filles

Fullish colour. No undue oak. Ripe and fruity. Medium to medium-full body. Fresh and balanced. Long. Very good. (July 2006)

2010 TO 2017   16.0

Vosne-Romanée, Les Petits Monts, 2002
Domaine Louis Jadot

Fullish colour. Refined, cool, slightly closed-in nose. Very good grip. Will get more generous as it evolves. Not exactly opulent at present but very classy fruit. Fullish body. Complex. Long. Fine. (October 2005)

2011 TO 2027   17.5

Vosne-Romanée, Les Petits Monts, 2002
Domaine Robert Sirugue et ses Enfants

Good colour. Slightly closed in on the nose. Cool, concentrated, rich and very pure Pinot on the palate. Quite full. Lovely elegant style. A profound wine. Fine. (February 2006)

2011 TO 2025   17.5

Vosne-Romanée, Aux Reignots, 2002
Domaine Sylvain Cathiard

Medium-full colour. Clean, classy, slightly austere on the nose. Medium to medium-full body. Very ripe, absorbed tannins. Lovely fruit. Not too austere on the follow-through. Very long at the end. Fine. (July 2006)

2012 TO 2025   17.5

Vosne-Romanée, Les Reignots, 2002
Domaine Bouchard Père et Fils

First vintage. Full colour. Very youthful still. Just a little reduction on the nose. This, of course, blew away after a while. Fullish body. Very rich. Very good grip. Excellent tannins. This is rounder than other Reignots or Petits Monts, but it has the same vibrant acidity. Lots of depth. Lots of class. Fine plus. (June 2005)

2011 TO 2025   18.0

Vosne-Romanée, Les Suchots, 2002
Domaine Arnoux Père et Fils

Full colour. Fat, rich, ripe and fullish on the nose with a faint reductive echo. Slightly adolescent on the palate. Clumsy. Some sulphur. Difficult to assess. As it developed in the glass, one could discern a full bodied, backward but very concentrated wine. Very long and multidimensional. Fine plus. (July 2006)

2013 TO 2030   18.0

Vosne-Romanée, Les Suchots, 2002
Domaine Jacky Confuron-Cotétidot

Medium-full colour. Slightly closed on the nose, but fresh and fragrant. Medium-full body. Lots of depth and grip. Plenty of ripe fruit. Complex. Stylish. Very good indeed. (February 2006)

2011 TO 2025   17.0

Vosne-Romanée, Les Suchots, 2002
Domaine Louis Jadot

Fullish colour. Very fine nose. Very pure essence of Pinot fruit. Fullish body. Very good tannins. Excellent grip. Most attractive fruit. Long. Plenty of substance here and plenty of vigour. Very fine. (July 2006)

2013 TO 2030   18.5

Vougeot, Clos de la Perrière, 2002
Domaine Bertagna

Good colour. Ripe, rich and fragrant on the nose. Plenty of dimension here. Medium to medium-full body. Very succulent. Lovely fruit. Good acidity. Long and elegant. Very good plus. (February 2006)

2010 TO 2025   16.5

Vougeot, Les Cras, 2002
Domaine de la Vougeraie

Medium-full colour. Plump nose. Slightly earthy. Medium to medium-full body. Not a great deal of tannin. Good acidity. Slightly raw at present. Will get more generous as it ages. Ripe and stylish though. Good plus. (March 2005)

2009 TO 2020   15.5

2001

Somewhat surprisingly, although the whites are good but not great, the 2001 red Burgundy harvest has turned out to be really very good, especially in the Côte de Nuits. There is more substance, definition and character than in the 2000s, although the 2002s are more regular and even better. In the 2001s there is a most appealing fresh, pure fruit, well balanced by a good acidity. The tannins are ripe, and the wines speak of their origins. They will evolve in the medium to long-term, with the very best requiring a minimum of 10 years from the time of the harvest.

WEATHER CONDITIONS

Generally speaking, 2001 was a wet, cool and cloudy year in Burgundy. February and March were both rainy but mild; April and May—all but the last few days of the latter month—were rainy and cool. The flowering was late and drawn out, and although the weather was reasonably warm for the first time in the year, the humidity left by all this wet weather produced outbreaks of mildew. It also caused *mille-randage*, which reduced the size of the crop.

July was miserably cold and wet, only heating up in the last 10 days of the month. This resulted in a hailstorm on August 2 which severely reduced the crop in Volnay, Monthelie and the vineyards on the Auxey-Meursault border. The effect in parts of the Côte Chalonnaise was even worse, especially in Bouzeron. The last half of August was warm, but most of the first three weeks in September were once again grey and cool, although reasonably dry.

The *ban des vendanges* fixed the first date of the harvest as Monday, September 17, in the Côte de Beaune and Thursday, September 20, in the Côte de Nuits. This was before the fruit was fully ripe, especially in those vineyards not green harvested, but no one was forced to start on that date. Although some of the less thoughtful rushed to pick, the better growers waited. There was a little rain on September 19, and rather more on September 26–27, but mainly at night. But in between it was windy, drying up the fruit, and after September 28, it became much warmer and sunnier.

Even though the weather conditions were not ideal, the vines' leaves remained green, right up until the middle of the harvest. Photosynthesis was continuing to take place, making up for a blockage in this progress toward maturity occasioned by the cool weather earlier. Moreover, the wind helped concentrate the fruit, even if it was not initially very sunny.

While some of the Pinot Noir vineyards in the Côte de Beaune had been picked earlier, with the growers waiting for the white wine grapes to mature fully, much of the Côte de Nuits was not cleared until after September 28 in the best of the vintage conditions. This was a year that favoured the late pickers. This is the main explanation not only for why it was a better year in red than in white, but also for why the Côte de Nuits was more successful than the Côte de Beaune. The other explanation is that there was a crucial difference in precipitation between the northern and the southern sectors of the Côte d'Or during the harvest and in the weeks running up to it. However, once picking did begin, it was essential to clear the vines quickly before the grapes turned. Some doubled the number of pickers in order to get all the fruit into the winery at its best.

Triage, of course, was vital. Unlike the 1999 vintage, which was marvellously healthy, but like that of 2000, there was, in 2001, an ever-present danger of rot. Sorting tables are now becoming more and more efficient. They vibrate, shaking off excess water. They have wind tunnels which dry fruit that is moist. They can be lit from underneath, assisting in the elimination of fruit which may have changed colour but may not be fully ripe. The fruit is then de-stemmed (except in some top domaines such as the Domaine de la Romanée-Conti) but hardly crushed at all, and then poured onto a second sorting table. Here it can be examined again, berry by berry. This ensures that only the perfect fruit is vinified.

In many cases in 2001, the next step was a *saignée*: the bleeding off of excess juice, not only to improve the solid–liquid ratio, but also to eliminate the oxidizing enzymes, a helpful action in years such as 2001.

As with the 2000s, 2001 was not a year for over-extraction, over-oaking or over-chaptalisation. Despite the good acidities, the wines were essentially quite fragile. By this I do not mean that they were weak, but that the balance—and therefore the inherent elegance—risked being easily compromised by overmanipulation. Equally, this was a vintage for early bottling to preserve the freshness of the fruit.

WHERE ARE THE BEST WINES?

For red wines, the vintage is better in the Côte de Nuits than in the Côte de Beaune, and better in the Côte de Beaune than in the Côte Chalonnaise. Hail damage halved the harvest in some *climats* in Volnay, almost wiped out Bouzeron and had severe effects in Rully and in parts of Mercurey. The vines which survived were nevertheless unsettled as a result. Even putting these villages aside, the Savignys are proportionally better than the Santenays. There are some fine Cortons. Nuits-Saint-Georges is a village which has produced lovely 2001s, and these are better, proportionately speaking, than those in Vosne-Romanée and Chambolle-Musigny where one or two wines are just a little *tendre*. The vintage is at its best in Gevrey-Chambertin.

As far as the whites are concerned, Meursault has produced some of the best wines.

> ### ✦ Rating for the Vintage ✦
>
> | | |
> |---|---|
> | Red | 14.0–16.0 |
> | White | 14.5 |

> ### ✦ Size of the Crop ✦
> (In hectolitres, excluding generic wine)
>
> | | RED | WHITE |
> |---|---|---|
> | Grands Crus | 13,955 | 3,935 |
> | Village and Premiers Crus | 174,216 | 60,185 |
> | TOTAL | 188,171 | 64,120 |

The harvest here is always lower than in Chassagne-Montrachet or Puligny-Montrachet. This is not a great year for Côte Chalonnaise *blanc*. The very best whites will be found in Corton-Charlemagne.

WHEN WILL THE WINES BE AT THEIR BEST?

Except for the grandest bottles, the whites are now ready. Drink them soon. Also, drink most of the village wines from all the way up and down the Côte d'Or, and the lightest of the *premiers crus*. Hold the firmer *premier* and *grand cru* wines until 2009 or so, or later. But there will not be many which will be better at 15 years old than at 10.

TASTING NOTES

WHITES

Bâtard-Montrachet, 2001
Domaine Jean-Marc Boillot
Magnum. Fullish, rich, youthful colour. Full, rich, ample, harmonious nose. Lots of depth and quality. Not a bit heavy. Balanced, ripe and complex. Very elegant. Lovely finish. Very long. (June 2004)
NOW TO 2014   18.5

Bâtard-Montrachet, 2001
Domaine Jean-Noël Gagnard
Magnum. Full, rich, fat but quite developed on the nose. Similar on the palate. Ripe. Fullish body. Reasonably fresh. But it lacks a bit of elegance and zip. Merely very good. (June 2006)
NOW TO 2011   16.0

Beaune, Clos des Mouches, 2001
Domaine Yves Darviot
Good nutty nose. This is quite classy. Medium-full body. Plenty of depth for the vintage. Good acidity. Nicely concentrated. This is very good. (March 2003)
NOW TO 2011   16.0

Chassagne-Montrachet, 2001
Domaine Duperrier-Adam
Good fruit. Nice style. Ripe. Medium body. This is clean and balanced. A very good example. (June 2003)
NOW TO 2009   15.0

Chassagne-Montrachet, 2001
Château de la Maltroye
Ripe, rich and stylish. Good depth, especially for what it is and 2001. *À point*. Not the greatest of grip. Drink soon. (October 2003)
DRINK SOON   14.0

Chassagne-Montrachet, Les Caillerets, 2001
Domaine Jean-Noël Gagnard
Ripe, gently oaky, very stylish nose. Impressive fruit. Excellent grip. Fullish body. Very clean, pure and very intense. This is most lovely. Very fine for the vintage. (October 2003)
NOW TO 2014   18.5

Chassagne-Montrachet, Les Chaumées, 2001
Domaine Ramonet
Lean but with good, classy fruit. Plenty of substance and depth. Just needs another year to round off a little. Very good. (March 2005)
NOW TO 2012   16.0

Chassagne-Montrachet, Clos de la Boudriotte, 2001
Maison Vincent Girardin
Medium colour. Fresh, if not very substantial on the nose. Medium body. Not much tannin or dimension, but an attractive bottle for drinking soon. (July 2005)
NOW TO 2011   14.0

Chassagne-Montrachet, Clos Saint-Jean, 2001
Maison Vincent Girardin
Medium to medium-full colour. Fresh nose. Plump, rich and positive. Medium body. Good acidity. Ripe and stylish. Very good for what it is. (March 2004)
NOW TO 2015   16.0

Chassagne-Montrachet, Les Grandes Ruchottes, 2001
Château de la Maltroye
Magnum. Fresh colour. Ripe, fresh, elegant, fully developed and gently oaky. Ample. Rich. Balanced. No great concentration or austerity, but no lack of grip or depth, especially for a 2001. Long. Very good indeed. But now ready. (September 2005)
NOW TO 2011   17.0

Chassagne-Montrachet, Morgeot, 2001
Domaine Joseph Faiveley

Soft and mellow. Ripe and positive. But a little too oaky for my taste. Good though. (June 2006)
NOW TO 2012   15.0

Chassagne-Montrachet, Morgeot, 2001
Maison Faiveley

Soft and mellow. Ripe and positive, but a little too oaky for my taste. Good. (June 2006)
NOW TO 2012   15.0

Chassagne-Montrachet, Morgeot Vigne Blanche, 2001
Château de la Maltroye

Fullish colour. Ripe and aromatic on the nose. Medium-full body. Balanced. *À point.* Round and ripe. Fresh and nutty. Good grip. Lots of depth and class. Very fine for the vintage. (March 2005)
NOW TO 2010   18.5

Chassagne-Montrachet, Les Ruchottes, 2001
Domaine Ramonet

Leaner than the 2002. More forward. Medium to medium-full body. Clean, stylish and balanced. Nicely floral. Decent depth. Very good style. Very good. (May 2005)
NOW TO 2010   16.0

Corton Blanc, 2001
Domaine Maillard Père et Fils

From the Renardes. Thirty-three ares. Eighty percent new wood. Some oak but plenty of fruit and depth. Supple. Fullish bodied. Very good grip. The vines are still young. A very marly parcel in the middle of the Renardes. This is very good indeed. From 2007. (February 2003)
NOW TO 2014   17.0

Corton Blanc, 2001
Domaine du Comte Senard

Stylish but it lacks a little depth and grip. Good fruit. Not a bit four-square. Positive finish nevertheless. Very good. (March 2004)
NOW TO 2012   16.0

Corton-Charlemagne, 2001
Domaine Bonneau du Martray

Ripe, round, stylish and very pure. Medium to medium-full body. Essentially gentle. But lovely fruit. Nice and fresh if not by any means a blockbuster. Long. Classy. Very fine for the vintage. (June 2005)
NOW TO 2012   18.5

Corton-Charlemagne, 2001
Domaine Bouchard Père et Fils

A little subdued on the nose. But ripe and rich and with plenty of depth. Minerally with personality on the palate. Very good grip. Good substance and lots of class. Long and complex. Fine. (June 2003)
NOW TO 2018   17.5

Corton-Charlemagne, 2001
Domaine Doudet-Naudin

A little lacking in depth and character for what it is. Medium-full. Some depth and decent grip. But it doesn't add up to anything very interesting. (February 2003)
NOW TO 2010   14.0

Corton-Charlemagne, 2001
Domaine Joseph Faiveley

Ample, rich and ripe. Heaps of fruit. Lots of depth and structure. This is intense and very fine. Already showing very, very well. Good, ripe acidities but no enormous length and energy. Lovely finish. Fine but not great. (June 2003)
2009 TO 2021   17.5

Criots-Bâtard-Montrachet, 2001
Domaine Richard Fontaine-Gagnard

Ripe, classy and ample. Medium-full body. Lovely fruit. Concentrated and complex on the palate. Very fine, peachy flavours. Lots of depth and class. Very fine finish. Just about ready. (April 2005)
NOW TO 2011   18.5

Meursault, Blagny, 2001
Domaine Martelet de Cherisey

Delicate, flowery but very stylish nose. Very good acidity. Indeed a little lean. But good depth. Medium body. Needs a year. Very good for the vintage. (September 2004)

NOW TO 2010   16.0

Meursault, Les Charmes, 2001
Domaine Joseph Faiveley

Deep colour. Rich, well-matured nose. Very oaky. Medium-full body. Rather over the top. (June 2006)

DRINK SOON   13.5

Meursault, Charmes, 2001
Domaine des Comtes Lafon

Rich, fat, stylish and profound on the nose. Complex. The oak is exactly right. Not a blockbuster, but supple and lovely. Really fine for the vintage. (March 2004)

NOW TO 2015   17.5

Meursault, Clos de la Barre, 2001
Domaine des Comtes Lafon

Ripe, full, nicely vigorous nose. Gently oaky. Good fruit. Good depth. Very good. (March 2004)

NOW TO 2012   16.0

Meursault, Genevrières, 2001
Domaine des Comtes Lafon

Slightly more evolution in the colour than the 2002. Soft, flowery nose. Less definition than the 2002 but clean and stylish. Medium-full body. The attack is gentle and fruity. The follow-through shows more depth and a touch of oak. Ripe and balanced. Very good. But it will evolve soon. Lacks a little personality. (September 2005)

NOW TO 2013   16.0

Meursault, Genevrières, 2001
Domaine Latour-Giraud

Good depth for a 2001. Rich and youthful. Fully mature. Good grip. Quite full. Ample. Lovely fruit. Aromatic and balanced. Fine for the vintage. Long finish. À point. (March 2006)

NOW TO 2011   17.5

Meursault, La Jeunelotte, 2001
Domaine Martelet de Cherisey

Slightly broader and more minerally than their Puligny Hameau de Blagny 2001, tasted alongside.

Good grip. Medium-full body. Still a little firm. Long, harmonious and fine plus. (October 2003)

NOW TO 2014   18.0

Meursault, Perrières, 2001
Maison Chanson Père et Fils

Not a lot on the nose. But nicely peachy and minerally on the palate. Medium to medium-full body. Good style. Good depth. Good grip. Long. Very good indeed. (October 2004)

NOW TO 2012   17.0

Meursault, Perrières, 2001
Domaine Guy Roulot

Very good grip, depth and *terroir* expression for the vintage. Lean. Minerally. Good acidity. Unexpected dimension. Less opulent than Lafon's. Very classy. Very good indeed for 2001. (October 2004)

NOW TO 2011   17.0

Meursault, Les Tessons, 2001
Domaine Pierre Morey

Slightly adolescent. But ripe, fullish and plump. Quite good but not brilliant. (March 2004)

NOW TO 2009   14.0

Meursault, Les Vireuils, 2001
Domaine Jean-François Coche-Dury

Full and ample. Ripe and with plenty of depth. Unexpectedly rich for the vintage. Indeed very good. Vigorous and just about à *point*. (February 2005)

NOW TO 2009   16.0

Montrachet, 2001
Domaine des Comtes Lafon

Fine, discreet and concentrated, and very fine indeed on the nose. Fullish body. Ample. Lots of depth and intensity. Excellent grip. Very lovely fruit. This is a really excellent wine and not just for a 2001 white. Crisp, cool, elegant and multidimensional. Very long and complex and profound. (June 2005)

2009 TO 2025   20.0

Le Montrachet, 2001
Domaine de la Romanée-Conti

Ripe but slightly restrained nose. Succulent and balanced but without any great drive. Lovely ripe fruit nevertheless. And decent grip. Quite forward. Good style. Fine. (September 2005)

NOW TO 2017   17.5

Puligny-Montrachet, 2001
Domaine Louis Carillon et Fils
Slight touch of sulphur. Good structure. Good depth. Good. (March 2005)

NOW TO 2011   15.0

Puligny-Montrachet, 2001
Domaine Leflaive
Delicate but ripe and stylish on the nose. Medium body. Fully ready. Enjoy it while it is fresh. (March 2004)

NOW TO 2010   16.0

Puligny-Montrachet, Les Caillerets, 2001
Domaine Hubert de Montille
A much classier and more distinctive wine than at the Master of Wine tasting. Readily impressive for the vintage. Lovely fruit. Very good balance. Ready now. (June 2004)

NOW TO 2009   17.5

Puligny-Montrachet, Le Clavoillon, 2001
Domaine Leflaive
Rich, concentrated nose. As usual just a touch four-square. Ripe and full on the palate. Not the greatest concentration but lovely, abundant, balanced fruit. Very good indeed for the vintage. Just about ready. (June 2006)

NOW TO 2014   17.0

Puligny-Montrachet, Les Demoiselles, 2001
Domaine Michel Colin-Deléger et Fils
Quite a developed colour. Soft nose. Not a lot of concentration or grip. Fresh, ripe and fruity if no great depth. Yet stylish and reasonably long on the palate. Very good plus for the vintage. (November 2005)

DRINK SOON   16.5

Puligny-Montrachet, Les Folatières, 2001
Domaine des Lambrays
Some evolution on the colour. Fine nose. Elegant, fresh, gently oaky and peachy ripe. Medium-full body. Very good plus. (September 2004)

NOW TO 2010   16.5

Puligny-Montrachet, Les Folatières, 2001
Château de Puligny-Montrachet
Decent definition. Less depth than their 2002. But there is class here as well as attractive fruit. A little bland, but very good for the vintage. (June 2004)

DRINK SOON   15.0

Puligny-Montrachet, Hameau de Blagny, 2001
Domaine Martelet de Cherisey
Delicate, understated, stylish nose. Very pure and clean. Round and soft and fresh. This is gentle but lovely and really quite intense at the end. Fine. (October 2003)

NOW TO 2013   17.5

Saint-Aubin, Les Murgers des Dents de Chien, 2001
Domaine Christophe Guillo/Domaine de Meix
Clean, stylish, fruity and with good depth for the vintage. Very delicate oaky background. This is very good indeed for the vintage. (October 2003)

DRINK SOON   17.0

Saint-Romain Blanc, Sous le Château, 2001
Domaine Coste-Caumartin
Soft, ripe nose. Good weight and depth. Plenty of interest for a Saint-Romain. Nice and dry and steely. Good length. Positive finish. Very good plus for what it is. (October 2003)

DRINK SOON   15.0

Savigny-lès-Beaune Blanc, 2001
Domaine Arnoux Père et Fils
Vinified in wood. This again is ripe and stylish. Good oaky depth. Crisp and clean. Well balanced. Very good. (February 2003)

DRINK SOON   16.0

Savigny-lès-Beaune Blanc, 2001
Domaine Simon Bize et Fils
Plump, ripe and fresh. Good substance. Plenty of interest. Good. (March 2004)

DRINK SOON   15.0

Savigny-lès-Beaune Blanc, Aux Clous, 2001
Domaine Pierre and Jean-Baptiste Lebreuil
Gently oaky. Quite fruity and stylish. But a little too light and forward. (February 2003)

DRINK SOON   13.0

Savigny-lès-Beaune Blanc, Redrescul, 2001
Domaine Doudet-Naudin
Monopole. First harvest. Young vines. Not bad.
Slightly ungainly. But it is early days. (February 2003)
DRINK UP   13.0

Vougeot, Le Clos Blanc, 2001
Domaine de la Vougeraie
Slightly leaner than both 2000 and 2002;
lighter, too. But no lack of fruit, balance or inter-
est. Very good for the vintage. (September 2004)
NOW TO 2011   16.0

Vougeot, Clos du Prieuré, 2001
Domaine de la Vougeraie
On the light side but agreeable, balanced fruit,
and of course, its own un-Côte-de-Beaune indi-
viduality. Good. Ready. (September 2004)
DRINK SOON   15.0

REDS

Aloxe-Corton, 2001
Domaine Daniel Largeot
Like his Savigny-Lès-Beaune 2001, a touch astrin-
gent. Not quite enough grip. Lacks high tones.
But the fruit is attractive. This is quite soft and for-
ward. Ten to 25 percent new wood. (February 2003)
NOW TO 2010   13.5

Aloxe-Corton, 2001
Domaine Pierre et Jean-Baptiste Lebreuil
On the light side, but fruity and charming. A bit
slight at the end. Quite good. (February 2003)
NOW TO 2009   13.5

Aloxe-Corton, 2001
Domaine René Podichard
Good fruit. A slight lack of grip in the middle.
(February 2003)
NOW TO 2009   13.0

Aloxe-Corton, Les Chaillots, 2001
Domaine Louis Latour
This is a little concocted. Slightly pruney. Yet
decent volume and acidity. A lack of real style.
Only quite good. (January 2005)
NOW TO 2012   14.0

Aloxe-Corton, Les Fournières, 2001
Domaine Tollot-Beaut et Fils
Medium-full colour. Meaty nose. Quite oaky.
Medium-full body. Ample and positive. Good
grip. Good tannins. Not the greatest of class
but long on the palate. Good. (March 2004)
NOW TO 2015   15.0

Aloxe-Corton, Les Maréchaudes,
Vieilles Vignes, 2001
Domaine Doudet-Naudin
Slightly earthy. Some minerality. Some tannin.
Slightly ungainly and astringent. Not a lot of
style. From 2005. (February 2003)
NOW TO 2009   13.0

Beaune, 2001
Domaine Maillard Père et Fils
Delicious, ripe and succulent. Lovely example.
Very well balanced. Lots of charm. Heaps of
fruit. (February 2003)
NOW TO 2011   15.0

Beaune du Château, Premier Cru, 2001
Domaine Bouchard Père et Fils
A mixture of several *premiers crus*. Light, soft,
but fragrant and fruity. Fully ready. Nice and
fresh. No great dimension. But stylish enough.
Good. (May 2005)
NOW TO 2010   15.0

Beaune, Cuvée "Tante Berthe,"
Premier Cru, 2001
Domaine Germain Père et Fils/
Château de Chorey-lès-Beaune
Good colour for the vintage. Quite strongly oaky
on the nose. Rich, full and sweet. Medium to
medium-full body. Getting soft. Ripe and posi-
tive. Good grip and personality. A bit too oaky
for my taste. Good though. (June 2006)
NOW TO 2015   15.0

Beaune, Premier Cru, 2001
Domaine Louis Latour
This is also a bit feeble. Yet fresher than their Aloxe-
Corton Les Chaillots 2001, which I tasted alongside.
Decent fruit. *À point*. Quite good plus. (January 2005)
NOW TO 2012   14.5

Beaune, Les Aigrots, 2001
Domaine Albert Morot
Medium colour. Light, slightly stretched nose. Some oak on the palate. A little stewed. Only fair. (July 2005)
NOW TO 2014   13.0

Beaune, Les Boucherottes, 2001
Domaine A.F. Gros
Medium colour. Ample nose with a touch of oak. Medium weight. Decent acidity but it lacks richness. Quite good. The finish is positive. (July 2005)
NOW TO 2016   14.0

Beaune, Les Bressandes, 2001
Domaine Chanson Père et Fils
Medium to medium-full colour. Slightly pinched nose. Slight touch of oak. Medium weight. Decent style and balance, but slightly anonymous. Quite good. (July 2005)
NOW TO 2015   14.0

Beaune, Les Bressandes, 2001
Domaine Albert Morot
Medium colour. Slightly nondescript nose. Slightly stewed on the palate. Some oak. Not much depth. Only fair. (July 2005)
NOW TO 2014   13.0

Beaune, Les Cent Vignes, 2001
Domaine René Monnier
Medium colour. Earthy nose. Decent weight and richness, but rather coarse on the palate. Artisanal. Medium to medium-full body. (July 2005)
NOW TO 2012   12.0

Beaune, Les Cent Vignes, 2001
Domaine Albert Morot
Medium to medium-full colour. Another earthy nose. Light and astringent on the palate. It lacks fruit. Fair at best. (July 2005)
NOW TO 2012   13.0

Beaune, Les Cent Vignes, 2001
Domaine René Podichard
Ripe but not proportionately as good as his Savigny-Lès-Beaune 2001. Slightly hollow in the middle. (February 2003)
NOW TO 2010   14.0

Beaune, Champimonts, 2001
Domaine Chanson Père et Fils
Medium to medium-full colour. Ample nose. Good richness. Medium to medium-full body. Ripe and balanced. Cool. Quite stylish. Quite good plus. (July 2005)
NOW TO 2016   14.5

Beaune, Les Chouacheux, 2001
Domaine Chantal Lescure
Medium colour. Slight lack of personality and richness on the nose. But better on the palate. Medium to medium-full body. Decent fruit and balance. Lacks a bit of elegance. Quite good though. (July 2005)
NOW TO 2014   14.0

Beaune, Clos du Dessus des Marconnets, 2001
Domaine Labet-Dechelette
Thin, diffuse and evolved. The oak dominates. No. (March 2004)
DRINK UP   12.0

Beaune, Clos des Fèves, 2001
Maison Chanson Père et Fils
Decent colour. Ripe and round. Medium to medium-full. Balanced and succulent. Ripe tannins. What it lacks is a bit of finesse. Decent finish. Just a little tannin to resolve. Quite good. (July 2005)
NOW TO 2011   14.0

Beaune, Clos des Marconnets, 2001
Domaine Chanson Père et Fils
Medium colour. Earthy nose. A little astringent. Decent grip. But a lack of style. Medium weight. (July 2005)
NOW TO 2013   13.0

Beaune, Clos des Mouches, 2001
Domaine Chanson Père et Fils
Medium to medium-full colour. Quite stylish but slightly watery all the way through. Forward. Medium body. Only fair. (July 2005)
NOW TO 2013   13.0

Beaune, Clos des Mouches, 2001
Domaine Joseph Drouhin
Medium colour. Light but fragrant nose. Lacks a bit of energy. Medium body. One-dimensional. Some style undeniably. But only quite good. (July 2005)
NOW TO 2014   14.0

Beaune, Clos du Roi, 2001
Domaine Tollot-Beaut et Fils
Medium colour. Slight touch of reduction on the nose. But decent weight here, if no great style. Medium to medium-full body. Some richness. Good positive finish. A good commercial brew.
(July 2005)
NOW TO 2015   15.0

Beaune, Clos des Ursules, 2001
Domaine Louis Jadot
Good colour. Still quite closed-in on the nose. Medium-full body. Fragrant, balanced and very stylish on the palate. Lovely long finish. This is very good plus. (March 2004)
NOW TO 2015   16.5

Beaune, Les Coucherias, 2001
Domaine Labet-Dechelette
Medium colour. Slightly weedy nose. Quite ripe on the palate. Medium body. Decent grip. But it lacks a bit of style. Quite good at best.
(March 2004)
NOW TO 2012   14.0

Beaune, Les Cras, Vieilles Vignes, 2001
Domaine Germain Père et Fils/
Château de Chorey-lès-Beaune
Good colour. Rich, full, ample, oaky nose. Fullish body. Very good tannins. Very good grip. Lots of lovely fruit on the palate. This is impressive. (March 2004)
NOW TO 2017   16.5

Beaune, Grèves, Vigne de l'Enfant Jésus, 2001
Domaine Bouchard Père et Fils
Medium to medium-full colour. Slightly adolescent at present on the nose. Ripe and

stylish. Medium to medium-full body. If the nose is a bit pinched, the wine on the palate shows much better. Good substance. Some tannin. Good acidity. Less succulent than the 2002 but will last just as well. Very good plus.
(March 2004)
NOW TO 2018   16.5

Beaune, Les Grèves, 2001
Domaine Yves Darviot
Medium colour. Ripe, fragrant nose. If no great richness or depth, at least positive and balanced. Medium weight. Not much tannin. Fresh, clean and elegant. Decent Beaune fragrance. Just about *à point*. Good. (May 2005)
NOW TO 2011   15.0

Beaune, Les Grèves, 2001
Domaine Michel Lafarge
Medium colour. Some brown at the rim. Somewhat neutral on the nose. Light. Quite fruity. The attack is a bit insipid, but the finish is better. But only fair. (September 2005)
NOW TO 2009   13.5

Beaune, Les Grèves, 2001
Domaine Albert Morot
Medium colour. Some fruit on the nose and depth on the palate. A touch of oak. Better than the rest of the Morot wines. Quite good.
(July 2005)
NOW TO 2016   14.0

Beaune, Les Grèves, 2001
Domaine Tollot-Beaut et Fils
Medium colour. Broad-flavoured, oaky nose. Quite rich on the palate. Good grip. Competent if not exciting. Good finish. Quite good plus.
(July 2005)
NOW TO 2016   14.5

Beaune, Grèves, 2001
Domaine Daniel Largeot
A touch of new wood here. Fresh. Medium body. It lacks a little grip and depth. But, once again, attractive fruit. (February 2003)
NOW TO 2011   14.0

Beaune, Les Marconnets, 2001
Domaine Albert Morot

Medium to medium-full colour. The oak dominates the fruit. Medium weight. Quite ripe on the aftertaste. Not bad. (July 2005)

NOW TO 2013   13.0

Beaune, Les Reversées, 2001
Domaine Jean-Marc Bouley

Medium to medium-full colour. Ripe but a bit four-square on the nose. Some oak on the palate. Medium to medium-full body. A decent bottle. Quite good. (July 2005)

NOW TO 2014   14.0

Beaune, Les Reversées, 2001
Domaine Nicolas Rossignol

Medium-full colour. Quite a stewed nose. Better on the palate. Good weight. Some tannin. Good grip. Rich, black cherry-flavoured without undue oak. Will keep. Good. (July 2005)

2009 TO 2018   15.0

Beaune, Les Teurons, 2001
Domaine Bouchard Père et Fils

Medium colour. Decent weight and richness, but a little reduced on the nose. Balanced. Medium to medium-full body. Not a great deal of concentration or power, but quite neatly made. Decent finish. Quite good plus. (July 2005)

NOW TO 2015   15.0

Beaune, Les Teurons, 2001
Domaine Chanson Père et Fils

Medium to medium-full colour. Fruity but rather nondescript nose. Medium weight. Rather chunky and astringent. No charm. (July 2005)

NOW TO 2014   13.0

Beaune, Les Teurons, 2001
Domaine Albert Morot

Medium to medium-full colour. Tight, oaky, slightly astringent nose. Medium to medium-full body. Quite rich. But a little lumpy. (July 2005)

NOW TO 2014   13.5

Beaune, Les Toussaints, 2001
Domaine Albert Morot

Medium to medium-full colour. Rather coarse, astringent nose. Medium to medium-full body. A bit thin, short and dry on the palate. Unexciting. (July 2005)

NOW TO 2012   12.5

Bonnes Mares, 2001
Domaine Hervé Arlaud

Medium-full colour. Ripe, fullish, rich nose. Rather more substantial than their Clos Saint-Denis. Fullish body. Good class and depth. Very good fruit. Good grip. Very good indeed. (July 2005)

2010 TO 2025   17.0

Bonnes Mares, 2001
Domaine Drouhin-Laroze

Medium-full colour. Quite sturdy, ripe, oaky nose. Fullish. Abundant. Slightly astringent at the end. It is very long and very vigorous. Very good fruit. Quite oaky. Fine. (July 2005)

2009 TO 2020   17.5

Bonnes Mares, 2001
Domaine Joseph Drouhin

Medium-full colour. Fragrant nose. Ripe, medium-full, velvety rich and concentrated. On the palate very good grip. Persistent, classy and abundant. Lovely finish. Fine. (July 2005)

NOW TO 2025   17.5

Bonnes Mares, 2001
Domaine Dujac

Full colour. Rich, fat, balanced and stylish. Very Dujac. Much better than their Clos Saint-Denis. Medium-full body. Harmonious, persistent, classy and complex. Lovely finish. Fine plus. (July 2005)

2009 TO 2025   18.0

Bonnes Mares, 2001
Domaine Fougeray de Beauclair

Full colour. Ripe, plump, rich nose. Fullish. Old viney. Good grip. Still youthful. Lovely follow-through. Impressive but it tails off a bit. Needs

time. A classy example. Very good indeed.
(July 2005)
2010 TO 2025   17.0

Bonnes Mares, 2001
Maison Frédéric Magnien
Fullish colour. Dense, oaky, slightly over-
extracted nose. Medium-full body. Astringent.
Lacks zip. A bit astringent at the end. Boring.
(July 2005)
2009 TO 2016   13.0

Bonnes Mares, 2001
Domaine Jacques-Frédéric Mugnier
Good colour. Plump nose. Slight austerity.
Slight leanness. Medium-full body. Cool. Good
tannins. Classy and subtle. Long. Fine plus.
(June 2005)
2010 TO 2025   18.0

Bonnes Mares, 2001
Maison Nicolas Potel
Fullish colour. Decent nose, but a lack of real
class and personality. Medium to medium-full
body. Ripe, but lacks zip and concentration.
Boring. (July 2005)
NOW TO 2017   14.0

Bonnes Mares, 2001
Domaine Georges Roumier et Fils
Full colour. Backward nose. Needs time.
Ungainly at present. Closed-in and awkward.
But very good tannins. Lovely pure fruit.
Plenty of substance here. Doesn't sing today.
But certainly fine at least. Just needs time.
(July 2005)
2012 TO 2025   17.5

Bonnes Mares, 2001
Domaine Comte Georges de Vogüé
Full colour. Lovely fragrant, composed, classy,
gently oaky nose. Much more approachable
than Roumier's. Fullish body. Very lovely pure,
cool fruit. Good tannins. This is very high class.
Marvellously long follow-through. Very fine
plus. (July 2005)
2010 TO 2025   19.0

Bonnes Mares, 2001
Domaine de la Vougeraie
Fullish colour. Rich, full, nicely oaky and profound on the nose. Very promising! Medium-
full body. Still very youthful. Ripe, rich, cool and
balanced. Nicely reserved. Very long and classy.
Very fine. (July 2005)
2010 TO 2025   18.5

Chambertin, 2001
Domaine Bertagna
Rich, full, slightly aromatic nose. Lots of depth
and flesh. Lots of intensity at the end. Very
classy too. This is very fine for the vintage.
(February 2006)
2010 TO 2020+   18.5

Chambertin, 2001
Domaine Pierre Damoy
Full colour. Very corky. Undrinkable. (July 2005)
(SEE NOTE)

Chambertin, 2001
Domaine Denis Mortet
Full colour. Quite an evolved nose. Not the greatest depth or class underneath. On the palate
medium-full body. Lacks a bit of grip. Slightly
astringent. Not too over-extracted but boring.
(July 2005)
2009 TO 2020   15.0

Chambertin, 2001
Domaine Jacques Prieur
Good colour. Ripe nose. But no great depth or
power. And on the palate it is strangely weak
and anemic. Yet their Musigny and other 2001
reds are really quite good. Odd. (July 2005)
NOW TO 2012   13.5

Chambertin, 2001
Domaine Rossignol-Trapet Père et Fils
Full colour. Ripe, rich but quite soft on the nose.
Classy though. Medium-full body. Decent depth
and fruit, but in terms of Chambertin, a little
lacking concentration. Very good at best. The
finish is clean and positive though. (July 2005)
2009 TO 2020   16.0

Chambertin, 2001
Domaine Armand Rousseau

Fullish colour. Profound, backward, rich and concentrated on the nose. Even better than his Clos de Bèze. Fullish body. Complete. Gently oaky. Ripe, rich and marvellously poised and balanced. About as good as you'll get in 2001. (July 2005)

2010 TO 2030   20.0

Chambertin, 2001
Domaine Jean Trapet Père et Fils

Good colour. Full and concentrated but not enough so for a *grand cru*. This is not a lot more profound than their 2001 Latricières. Fullish body. Very good grip. Fine plus to very fine. (July 2005)

NOW TO 2020+   18.0

Chambertin, Clos de Bèze, 2001
Domaine Bouchard Père et Fils

Medium-full colour. Slightly sweaty nose. Better as it evolved. But slightly tight and astringent nevertheless. Medium-full body. Decent grip. But clumsy. Very good at best. (July 2005)

2010 TO 2020   16.0

Chambertin, Clos de Bèze, 2001
Domaine Bruno Clair

Medium-full colour. Ripe, slightly austere and lean nose. Very clean and pure. Very Bruno Clair. Very classy. Rich, fullish bodied, composed and balanced. Cool and very lovely. Very, very long. Excellent. (July 2005)

2010 TO 2025   19.0

Chambertin, Clos de Bèze, 2001
Domaine Pierre Damoy

Full colour. This is very rich and concentrated. Backward. Lots of depth. Full and rich. Gently oaky. Cool and balanced. Long and very fine. But it lacks just a little personality. (July 2005)

2010 TO 2025   18.5

Chambertin, Clos de Bèze, 2001
Domaine Drouhin-Laroze

Fullish colour. Fat, rich, oaky nose. Fullish, ample and classy. Good grip. Lovely fruit. Long

and intense at the end. This has lots of class and dimension. Very fine plus. (July 2005)

2010 TO 2025   19.0

Chambertin, Clos de Bèze, 2001
Domaine Joseph Faiveley

Fullish colour. Rich nose. Backward. Very classy. Lots of depth. Fullish body on the palate. Lovely finish. Seems very fine. (June 2003)

2011 TO 2025   18.5

Chambertin, Clos de Bèze, 2001
Maison Camille Giroud

Fullish, immature colour. Good breed on the nose. Ripe and concentrated, but quite accessible. Medium to medium-full body. Rich, oaky and succulent. Very good grip and depth for the vintage. Lots of dimension. Lots of energy. A very fine example of a 2001. (June 2006)

2009 TO 2020   18.5

Chambertin, Clos de Bèze, 2001
Maison Frédéric Magnien

Full colour. Over-extracted and slightly oxidised on the nose. Lots of oak. Clumsy, sweet and astringent at the end. Tastes like all his wines. (July 2005)

2009 TO 2020   13.5

Chambertin, Clos de Bèze, 2001
Maison Nicolas Potel

Fullish colour. Clean, classy, pure, rich, concentrated nose. Lots of depth and quality here. On the palate this is equally impressive. Lovely fruit and very intense. Fullish body. Pure, balanced and very long. (July 2005)

2010 TO 2025   19.0

Chambertin, Clos de Bèze, 2001
Domaine Armand Rousseau

Full colour. Rich, concentrated, closed-in nose. A backward wine. Full body. Very well-covered tannins. Lots of structure. But very, very rich and concentrated. Excellent grip. Marvellous class. Excellent. (July 2005)

2010 TO 2025   19.5

Chambolle-Musigny, 2001
Domaine Jacques-Frédéric Mugnier

Medium colour. Lovely fragrant nose. A bit light but very intense. Lots of very classy fruit. Medium body. Concentrated. Rich. Lots of substance here. Very long and very impressive, especially for a village example. (March 2004)

NOW TO 2020   16.5

Chambolle-Musigny, Vieilles Vignes, 2001
Domaine Digioia-Royer

Medium to medium-full colour. Fragrant and succulent on the nose. Good style. Medium-full bodied, pure and persistent. Lovely fruit. Fine. (July 2005)

2009 TO 2020   17.5

Chambolle-Musigny, Premier Cru, 2001
Domaine Jean-Jacques Confuron

Medium to medium-full colour. Slightly reduced. But good size and depth. Medium-full body. Lacks a little class because of the reduction. Decent balance and follow-through. Good at best. (July 2005)

2009 TO 2020   15.0

Chambolle-Musigny, Premier Cru, 2001
Domaine Joseph Drouhin

Medium to medium-full colour. Fragrant nose. Ripe but just a touch raw. Medium to medium-full body. Lovely fruit. Quite high acidity. Elegant and potentially very good indeed. But it needs 2 or 3 years to round off. (October 2005)

NOW TO 2020   17.0

Chambolle-Musigny, Les Amoureuses, 2001
Domaine Robert Groffier

Medium to medium-full colour. Fragrant, classy, persistent nose. Medium-full bodied, concentrated and silky smooth. Very persistent. Very lovely pure fruit. Long and very fine. (July 2005)

2009 TO 2025   18.5

Chambolle-Musigny, Les Amoureuses, 2001
Domaine Georges Roumier et Fils

Medium to medium-full colour. Rather tight compared with Mugnier and de Vogué. But the quality is here. Similar to his Cras, a bit closed-in. But splendid concentration and potential.

Lovely cool, classy fruit. Very long. Excellent harmony. Very fine at least. (July 2005)

2010 TO 2025   18.5

Chambolle-Musigny, Les Amoureuses, 2001
Domaine Comte Georges de Vogüé

Medium to medium-full colour. Very classy nose. Very lovely fruit. Lots of depth. Medium-full body. Great poise and class. Excellent grip. Very lovely pure, classy fruit. Lots of dimension. Very, very long and lovely. (July 2005)

2010 TO 2025   19.0

Chambolle-Musigny, Les Baudes, 2001
Domaine Joseph Drouhin

Good colour. Ripe, very stylish, gently oaky nose. Very elegant fruit. This has lots of attraction. Seductive, plump, rich and succulent. Already quite round. No hard edges. Very good acidity. This has lots of class and depth. Long, ripe and profound at the end. Fine quality. (July 2005)

NOW TO 2018   17.5

Chambolle-Musigny, Les Baudes, 2001
Domaine Christian Sérafin

Medium-full colour. Fullish, rich, oaky nose. Medium-full, ripe, balanced, oaky wine on the palate. Slightly raw at present but plenty of depth and quality. Very good indeed. (July 2005)

2010 TO 2025   17.0

Chambolle-Musigny, Charmes, 2001
Domaine Ghislaine Barthod

Medium to medium-full colour. Soft, fragrant, classy nose. Lovely on the palate. Soft and succulent. But good depth, backbone and grip. Very classy. Very well made. Fine. (July 2005)

2010 TO 2025   17.5

Chambolle-Musigny, Charmes, 2001
Domaine Michel Magnien

Medium to medium-full colour. Big, slightly overblown, slightly oxidised, oaky nose. Ripe. Medium to medium-full body. No great depth or concentration. But a pleasant bottle. Not over done. (July 2005)

2010 TO 2020   16.0

Chambolle-Musigny, Charmes, 2001
Domaine Gérard Mugneret

Medium to medium-full colour. Lovely fresh nose. More sprightly than his Vosne Suchots. Ripe, even sweet fruit. Medium-full body. Good grip. Slightly raw but long on the palate. Very good indeed. (July 2005)

2009 TO 2020   17.0

Chambolle-Musigny, Charmes, 2001
Domaine Ponsot

Medium colour. Subtle, balanced, individual nose. A laid-back, subtle wine. Medium-full body. Very fresh and very clean. Intense at the end. Fine. (July 2005)

2009 TO 2025   17.5

Chambolle-Musigny, Aux Combottes, 2001
Domaine Michel Magnien

Medium to medium-full colour. Ample, full but slightly reduced nose. A bit over-extracted. Stewed and sweet. Not my style. (July 2005)

NOW TO 2014   12.0

Chambolle-Musigny, Les Cras, 2001
Domaine Ghislaine Barthod

Medium to medium-full colour. Slightly closed but profound, pure and very fine on the nose. Fullish body. Great purity, class and energy on the palate. A lovely example. Very splendid fruit and grip. Fine plus. (July 2005)

2010 TO 2025   18.0

Chambolle-Musigny, Les Cras, 2001
Domaine Georges Roumier et Fils

Medium-full colour. Big, masculine, backward nose. Some tannin. Fullish. Adolescent. Very good grip and concentration. This is not on form, but it is potentially fine at least. The finish is most impressive. (July 2005)

2011 TO 2025   17.5

Chambolle-Musigny, Aux Échanges, 2001
Maison Nicolas Potel

Medium to medium-full colour. Quite fragrant nose. Quite classy too. A touch bland but medium to medium-full, ripe and stylish. Medium to medium-full body. Good grip. Very good plus. (July 2005)

2009 TO 2020   16.5

Chambolle-Musigny, Les Feusselottes, 2001
Domaine Dr. Georges Mugneret

Medium colour. Ripe, succulent and fresh on the nose. Medium-full bodied, balanced, sprightly and with very lovely fruit. Long and complex. Fine. (July 2005)

2009 TO 2020   17.5

Chambolle-Musigny, Les Fuées, 2001
Domaine Louis Jadot

Medium to medium-full colour. A little pinched on the nose. But rather closed-in. Ripe, rich and with good vigour on the palate. Medium to medium-full body. Lacks the nuance of the best, but classy fruit and good energy. Very good indeed. (July 2005)

2009 TO 2020   17.0

Chambolle-Musigny, Les Fuées, 2001
Domaine Jacques-Frédéric Mugnier

Medium colour. Stylish nose. Slightly closed but lots of depth. Fullish body. Rich and concentrated. Very good grip. Lots of class. Lots of intensity. This is very special. (July 2005)

2010 TO 2025   18.5

Chambolle-Musigny, Les Fuées, 2001
Maison Nicolas Potel

Medium-full colour. Ripe, succulent nose. Very lovely fruit here. Good structure. Ripe tannins and very good grip. Lots of depth and class. Fine. (July 2005)

2010 TO 2025   17.5

Chambolle-Musigny, Les Gruenchers, 2001
Domaine Digioia-Royer

Medium-full colour. Not a lot on the nose at first. Yet clean and stylish. A pretty, well-made wine without a great deal of depth and grip. Young vines. Pretty. Very good. (July 2005)

NOW TO 2018   16.0

Chambolle-Musigny, Les Gruenchers, 2001
Domaine Jean-Claude Fourrier

Medium colour. Full, rich and fragrant on the nose. Medium body. A delicate wine on the palate. Not a blockbuster. Yet clean, pure and stylish. Very good indeed. (July 2005)

NOW TO 2020   17.0

Chambolle-Musigny, Les Gruenchers, 2001
Maison Alex Gambal

Medium to medium-full colour. Slightly reduced on the nose. A bit clumsy on the palate and slightly astringent at the end. Medium to medium-full body. Decent grip. But a lack of class. Quite good at best. (July 2005)

NOW TO 2014   14.0

Chambolle-Musigny, Les Hauts-Doix, 2001
Domaine Robert Groffier

Medium to medium-full colour. Fragrant, stylish and very lovely fruit on the nose. Round and rich. Medium-full body. So ripe it is almost sweet. Lovely. (July 2005)

2009 TO 2020   17.5

Chambolle-Musigny, Les Sentiers, 2001
Domaine Hervé Arlaud

Medium to medium-full colour. Lovely fragrant, fresh nose. Lots of depth. Medium to medium-full body. Gently oaky. Ripe, rich and succulent. Very good finish. Very good indeed. (July 2005)

NOW TO 2020   17.0

Chambolle-Musigny, Les Véroilles, 2001
Domaine Ghislaine Barthod

Medium to medium-full colour. Corked. But slightly more austere than his Cras on the nose. Yet rich on the palate. Nicely full and abundant. Very good indeed, I think. (July 2005)

2010 TO 2020   17.0

Chambolle-Musigny, Les Véroilles, 2001
Domaine Bruno Clair

Medium-full colour. Classy nose. Slightly austere but lovely fruit. Medium to medium-full. Ripe. Good acidity. Not the greatest concentra-

tion and weight on the palate, but long, classy and complex. Lovely long finish. Very good indeed. (March 2004)

NOW TO 2018   17.0

Chapelle-Chambertin, 2001
Domaine Pierre Damoy

Fullish colour. Full, concentrated, slightly backward but classy nose. Composed, fresh, classy and cool. Fullish body. Balanced. Persistent. Fine. (July 2005)

2010 TO 2020   17.5

Chapelle-Chambertin, 2001
Domaine Ponsot

Medium-full colour. Cool, pure, slightly austere but very classy nose. On the palate it lacks a little personality at present. But it has depth underneath. And class too. (July 2005)

2009 TO 2020   17.5

Chapelle-Chambertin, 2001
Domaine Jean Trapet Père et Fils

Good colour. Still a little hard on the nose. Slightly tough. Some tannin. Better on the palate. Medium-full body. Good grip. Ripe but firm. Long, complex and classy. Very good indeed. (March 2004)

2009 TO 2020   17.0

Charmes-Chambertin, 2001
Domaine Hervé Arlaud

Medium to medium-full colour. Rich, fat, concentrated nose. Good base of oak. Classy fruit here. Medium-full body. Stylish and energetic. Very good fruit. Long. Fine. (July 2005)

2009 TO 2025   17.5

Charmes-Chambertin, 2001
Domaine Denis Bachelet

Splendid colour. Deep, rich and vigorous. Splendidly concentrated nose. Backward. Full bodied. Not a bit aggressive though. Marvellous concentration and intensity of fruit. Real class. Very harmonious. Very fine. (April 2006)

2010 TO 2020+   18.5

Charmes-Chambertin, 2001
Domaine Philippe Charlopin

Fullish colour. Ripe and rich if without great style and personality on the nose. Ripe and mocha-flavoured on the palate. Fullish body. Good grip and vigour. But not quite the elegance for fine. (July 2005)

2010 TO 2020   17.0

Charmes-Chambertin, 2001
Domaine Bernard Dugat-Py

Very full colour. Rich, full, concentrated and backward on the nose. Lots of substance here. Fullish body. Some tannin. Lots of depth. Very profound, intense fruit. Splendid finish. Very, very long. Even better than Bachelet's 2001 Charmes. (April 2006)

2012 TO 2030   19.0

Charmes-Chambertin, 2001
Maison Vincent Girardin

Fullish colour. Slightly overblown nose. Ripe but clumsy. Better on the palate. Plump. Medium-full body. No lack of grip. Rich. Very good indeed. (July 2005)

2020 TO 2025   17.0

Charmes-Chambertin, 2001
Domaine Humbert Frères

Full colour. Ripe but no greater depth or class than the best of their premiers crus. On the palate medium to medium-full bodied, but very intense and persistent. Subtle, pure, clean and very well balanced. Long. Lovely. (July 2005)

2010 TO 2025   18.0

Charmes-Chambertin, 2001
Domaine Louis Jadot

Medium-full colour. Ripe and fruity with a touch of *tabac* on the nose. Medium-full body. Good grip. Good, plump fruit. Fresh at the end. Long and classy, too. Fine. (April 2006)

2010 TO 2022   17.5

Charmes-Chambertin, 2001
Maison Frédéric Magnien

Fullish colour. Sweet, oaky, slightly stewed nose. Medium-full. Oaky. Rich and full on the palate. But over-extracted. (July 2005)

NOW TO 2014   13.0

Charmes-Chambertin, 2001
Maison Nicolas Potel

Fullish colour. Soft and ripe but not very serious on the nose. Medium body. No great backbone. Slightly bland. Good but not great. Quite forward. (July 2005)

NOW TO 2016   15.0

Charmes-Chambertin, Très Vieilles Vignes, 2001
Domaine Joseph Roty

Full colour. Splendidly rich nose. Substantially better than his 2000. Fat, ripe and creamy. Fullish body and accessible. Very good grip. The finish is intense and very classy. This is very fine. (April 2006)

2011 TO 2025   18.5

Charmes-Chambertin, 2001
Domaine Armand Rousseau

Medium to medium-full colour. Surprisingly drinkable already. Medium weight, slightly tight on the nose. Medium body on the palate. Ripe. No great depth or concentration. But that is the vintage. No hard edges. The tannins are fully absorbed. Decent finish. (April 2006)

NOW TO 2014   16.0

Château de Monthelie, Sur la Velle, 2001
Domaine Éric de Suremain

Medium to medium-full colour. Ripe nose. Good, classy tannins. Medium to medium-full body. Round and sophisticated. Very good depth. Very good for what it is, especially given the 2001 weather problems. (March 2004)

NOW TO 2015   15.5

Chorey-lès-Beaune, 2001
Domaine Arnoux Père et Fils

Good fruit here. Ripe and stylish. Quite soft but not too *tendre*. Good. Needs a year. (February 2003)

NOW TO 2011   15.0

Chorey-lès-Beaune, 2001
Domaine Germain Père et Fils/
Château de Chorey-lès-Beaune

Good colour. Nicely balanced *petits fruits rouges* on the nose. Just a little thin and forward on the palate. Ripe and stylish though. (March 2004)

NOW TO 2012   14.0

Chorey-lès-Beaune, 2001
Domaine René Podichard

Owner is thinking about retiring. Passing things on to Jean-Luc Maldant (stepson). Good, individual style. Ripe. Good depth, grip and substance. Very good. (February 2003)

NOW TO 2013   15.5

Chorey-lès-Beaune, 2001
Domaine Tollot-Beaut et Fils

Good colour. Slight touch of caramel on the nose. Quite oaky. Medium to medium-full body. The palate is a little sweet and artificial, but ripe and generous enough. (March 2004)

NOW TO 2015   14.0

Chorey-lès-Beaune, Les Beaumonts, 2001
Domaine Daniel Largeot

Only partly whole-grape fermented now. Ripe, soft and perfumed. Medium body. Good follow-through. (February 2003)

NOW TO 2011   15.0

Clos des Lambrays, 2001
Domaine des Lambrays

Medium to medium-full colour. Some development. Fragrant nose. Soft, ripe, almost sweet. Quite forward. Medium-full body. Classy, intense and harmonious. Fine. (July 2005)

NOW TO 2020   17.5

Clos de la Roche, 2001
Domaine Guy Castagnier

Medium-full colour. Rather artisanal on the nose. Lacks concentration and depth. Medium body. Slightly astringent. Uninteresting. (July 2005)

NOW TO 2013   13.0

Clos de la Roche, 2001
Domaine Dujac

Good colour. Ample, rich, ripe, stylish nose. Lovely balance and very pure. Medium-full body. Good acidity. All the usual, slightly lean Dujac style. Very long. Fine plus. (March 2004)

NOW TO 2020   18.0

Clos de la Roche, Cuvée Vieilles Vignes, 2001
Domaine Ponsot

Magnum. Good colour. Very good fruit on the nose. Medium-full body. Slightly austere but the tannins just about absorbed. Complex. Delicious. (March 2006)

2010 TO 2020+   18.5

Clos Saint-Denis, 2001
Domaine Hervé Arlaud

Full colour. Fragrant, poised and stylish on the nose. Medium-full body. Good style. Quite rich. Not quite the depth, vigour and grip of a great wine, but long, complex and classy. Very good indeed. (July 2005)

NOW TO 2020   17.0

Clos Saint-Denis, 2001
Domaine Bertagna

Full colour. Very good, rich, ripe fruit on the nose with a gentle touch of oak. Fullish body. Very ripe but balanced fruit. Good oaky base. Long, complex and very lovely. Fine plus. (July 2005)

2010 TO 2025   18.0

Clos Saint-Denis, 2001
Domaine Dujac

Full colour. Lovely ripe, cool, fragrant nose. Only a touch of the stems. On the palate this is a touch flat and astringent after some of the other Clos Saint-Denis wines. Good fruit, but it lacks a little zip. Disappointing for Dujac. Very good at best. (July 2005)

NOW TO 2015   16.0

Clos Saint-Denis, 2001
Domaine Heresztyn

Very good colour. Slightly closed-in and a touch of reduction on the nose. Very lovely fullish, ample palate. Good tannins. Ripe and intense. Very good grip. This is most impressive. Very, very long, lingering finish. Very fine. (October 2003)

2011 TO 2027   18.5

Clos Saint-Denis, 2001
Maison Lucien le Moine

Full colour. Maderised nose. Undrinkable. Coarse, over-oaked and over-extracted. (July 2005)

(SEE NOTE)   10.0

Clos de Tart, 2001
Domaine du Clos de Tart

Full colour. Firm, rich, concentrated, backward nose. Excellent attack. Cool, rich, full and concentrated. Vigorous and very, very lovely. This is most impressive. Lovely long, rich, complex finish. Very fine indeed. (July 2005)

2010 TO 2025   19.0

Clos de Vougeot, 2001
Domaine Bouchard Père et Fils

Medium to medium-full colour. Ripe, round and stylish on the nose. Medium-full body. Good grip. Rich and vigorous. Good depth but a slight lack of class. Finishes well. Very good. (July 2005)

2010 TO 2025   16.0

Clos de Vougeot, 2001
Domaine Guy Castagnier

Medium-full colour. Meaty but slightly rustic on the nose. Medium-full body. Some oak. Slightly astringent at the end. But good energy. Quite good. (July 2005)

2009 TO 2016   14.0

Clos de Vougeot, 2001
Domaine Jean-Jacques Confuron

Fullish colour. A touch of oak on the nose. Good, concentrated fruit. Fullish body. Good tannins. Very good grip. Rich, profound and positive. Lovely long finish. This is fine. (July 2005)

2010 TO 2025   17.5

Clos de Vougeot, 2001
Domaine Joseph Drouhin

Fullish colour. Succulent, aromatic nose. Classy. Medium-full body. Ripe, ample fruit. Well-covered tannins. Lovely balance. Long. Lovely. (July 2005)

2009 TO 2025   17.5

Clos de Vougeot, 2001
Domaine du Clos Frantin/Albert Bichot

Fullish colour. Rich but quite sturdy nose. Better than their Échezeaux but not as good as their Grands Échezeaux. Ripe, fullish bodied, balanced and positive. Very good, but it lacks a little class. (July 2005)

2010 TO 2020   16.0

Clos de Vougeot, 2001
Maison Alex Gambal

Fullish colour. Ample and full of fruit on the nose. Decent fruit but not a great deal of grip. So slightly astringent at the end. Medium to medium-full body. Quite good only. (July 2005)

2009 TO 2020   14.0

Clos de Vougeot, 2001
Maison Vincent Girardin

Medium-full colour. Full, ample nose. A little closed-in. Medium-full on the palate. A little tannin. A little oak. This is intense and classy. Still youthful. Lots of depth and dimension. Lovely finish. Fine plus. (March 2004)

2009 TO 2025   18.0

Clos de Vougeot, 2001
Domaine Jean Grivot

Medium-full colour. Ripe, rich, full, classy nose. Still youthful. Some tannin. Medium-full body. Good vigour and intensity. Lots of dimension. Lots of finesse. Not a blockbuster, but very lovely and long at the end. Very fine. (July 2005)

2009 TO 2020   18.5

Clos de Vougeot, Le Grand Maupertuis, 2001
Domaine Anne Gros

Fullish colour. Lovely classy, concentrated nose. Fullish body. Very concentrated on the palate.

Super-ripe tannins and very good grip. Lots of wine here. Super. (July 2005)

2010 TO 2025　　　　　　　　　　　　　18.0

Clos de Vougeot, Le Grand Maupertuis, 2001
Domaine Michel Gros

Fullish colour. Ample, rich nose. Very stylish. Very lovely fruit here. Excellent balance. A little more approachable and succulent than Anne Gros's example. Very lovely finish. (July 2005)

2010 TO 2025　　　　　　　　　　　　　18.0

Clos de Vougeot, Musigni, 2001
Domaine Gros Frère et Soeur

Fullish colour. Ample, rich, blackberry and oak nose. Not quite the class of the other two Gros examples, but fullish and vigorous. This is just a little overblown. Quite oaky too. Fullish body. Decent finish though; at best very good. (July 2005)

2010 TO 2025　　　　　　　　　　　　　16.0

Clos de Vougeot, 2001
Domaine Alain Hudelot-Noëllat

Full colour. Ripe, succulent nose. Quite forward yet fullish enough. Ample. Ripe. Quite soft. Plump and very good. (July 2005)

2009 TO 2020　　　　　　　　　　　　　16.0

Clos de Vougeot, Château de la Tour, Vieilles Vignes, 2001
Domaine Labet-Dechelette

Good colour. Slightly weedy on the nose. Medium to medium-full body. Quite ripe and pleasant, but a certain lack of class and energy. Forward. (March 2004)

NOW TO 2015　　　　　　　　　　　　　15.0

Clos de Vougeot, 2001
Domaine Méo-Camuzet

Good colour. Full, rich, very oaky nose. Fullish on the palate, too. Concentrated. Very good grip. This is still very young. But it has very good intensity at the end. Fine plus. (June 2004)

2010 TO 2030　　　　　　　　　　　　　18.0

Clos de Vougeot, 2001
Domaine Dr. Georges Mugneret

Medium to medium-full colour. Good, rich, fragrant nose. Medium-full body. Quite oaky. Poised. Lovely fruit. Excellent balance. Lovely style. Fine. (July 2005)

2010 TO 2025　　　　　　　　　　　　　17.5

Clos de Vougeot, 2001
Maison Nicolas Potel

Full colour. Ample, succulent nose. Ripe. Medium-full bodied. Balanced and classy. No hard edges. Long and positive. Very good indeed. (July 2005)

2010 TO 2025　　　　　　　　　　　　　17.0

Clos de Vougeot, 2001
Domaine Jacques Prieur

Medium-full colour. Cool, quite firm, fullish, classy nose. Medium to medium-full weight. A bit more interest than the Échezeaux. Slightly more richness and spice. More dimension, too. Long. Classy. Fine. (July 2005)

2010 TO 2020　　　　　　　　　　　　　17.5

Clos de Vougeot, 2001
Domaine Prieuré-Roch

Evolved colour. On the light and weedy side. Even more dilute than their 2001 Vosne-Romanée Les Suchots. (February 2006)

DRINK SOON　　　　　　　　　　　　　11.0

Clos de Vougeot, 2001
Domaine de la Vougeraie

A very subtle, classy wine. Medium-full colour. Lovely, slightly austere nose. It has the intellectual, slightly minerally character of 2001. Medium-full body. Some tannin. Very good grip. Individual fruit. Long, complex and classy. Fine. (July 2005)

2010 TO 2020　　　　　　　　　　　　　17.5

Corton, 2001
Domaine Bonneau du Martray

Good colour. Quite full on the nose and palate, but round, succulent and fat on the follow-through. Good fruit. Balanced and classy. Very good follow-through. Good mouth-feel. Long. Fine. (June 2005)

2009 TO 2019   17.5

Corton, Cuvée Dr. Peste, 2001
Hospices de Beaune/Maison Morey-Blanc

Medium colour. Fragrant nose. Not a block-buster, but elegant and persistent. On the palate a little lumpy. Quite oaky. The tannins are a bit burly. Good grip. Good but not great. (July 2005)

2010 TO 2020   15.0

Corton, 2001
Domaine Tollot-Beaut et Fils

Medium to medium-full colour. Good caramel, roasted nuts, gingerbread nose and a touch of oak. Medium-full body. Quite rich. Stylish and complex. Good backbone. Ripe tannins. Long and positive. Very good indeed. (March 2005)

NOW TO 2017   17.0

Corton, Les Bressandes, 2001
Domaine Chandon de Briailles

Very light colour. Ample, aromatic, ripe nose. Quite forward. Medium to medium-full body. Ripe tannins. Silky smooth. Long. Lovely. (July 2005)

NOW TO 2020   17.5

Corton, Les Bressandes, 2001
Domaine Antonin Guyon

Medium to medium-full colour. Closed-in but ripe nose. Decent substance. A bit lumpy although quite rich. Medium-full body. Good grip. Slightly four-square. Quite good plus. (July 2005)

2010 TO 2018   14.5

Corton, Les Bressandes, 2001
Domaine Maillard Père et Fils

Medium-full colour. Slightly vegetal on the nose. Medium body. No richness. Decent grip but unexciting. (July 2005)

NOW TO 2014   12.5

Corton, Les Bressandes, 2001
Domaine de la Pousse d'Or

Medium colour. Decent depth and substance on the nose although lacking a bit of personality.

Medium-full body. Rich and meaty. Plenty of depth. Got better and better in the glass. Very good plus. (July 2005)

2010 TO 2020   16.5

Corton, Les Bressandes, 2001
Domaine Jacques Prieur

Medium-full colour. Slightly cooked on the nose. Good substance. Fresher on the palate. Medium-full bodied, ripe, oaky and quite rich. Good balance. This has class. Good long, positive finish. Fine. (July 2005)

2009 TO 2020   17.5

Corton, Les Bressandes, 2001
Domaine Tollot-Beaut et Fils

Medium to medium-full colour. Slightly over-extracted and bitter on the nose. Quite oaky. Medium-full body. Some tannin. Some astringency. Ripe and meaty. Not really stylish but quite good. (July 2005)

2010 TO 2020   14.0

Corton, Clos des Cortons Faiveley, 2001
Domaine Joseph Faiveley

Good colour. Rich. Very good acidity. Ripe, intense, long and complex. Very good acidity. This is very lovely. Very individual. Very fine. (July 2005)

2010 TO 2025   18.5

Corton, Clos Rognet, 2001
Domaine Méo-Camuzet

Medium-full colour. Rich, ripe, oaky and four-square on the nose. Fullish, rich, ripe and fresh. A bit disjointed, but the fruit is clean and elegant. All the elements are here. Very good indeed but needs time. (July 2005)

2010 TO 2020   17.0

Corton, Clos du Roi, 2001
Domaine Chandon de Briailles

Medium colour. Lovely, stylish, ripe, fragrant nose. Lots of depth. Splendid balance. Soft. Medium weight. Yet persistent. Fine. (July 2005)

NOW TO 2020   17.5

Corton, Clos du Roi, 2001
Domaine Antonin Guyon

Lightish colour. A little green on the nose. Light to medium body. Some fruit on the palate. But a little astringent. Only quite good. (July 2005)

NOW TO 2014   14.0

Corton, Clos du Roi, 2001
Domaine de la Pousse d'Or

Medium to medium-full colour. Decent weight and fruit on the nose. Slightly jammy perhaps. Good depth, substance and grip on the palate. More class than the Bressandes. Long. Meaty. Very good indeed. (July 2005)

2010 TO 2020   17.0

Corton, Clos du Roi, 2001
Domaine du Comte Senard

Good colour. Balanced, fruity, stylish nose. Medium to medium-full body. Ripe, fresh and balanced. Good tannins. Plenty of dimension. The follow-through is ample. Very good plus. (March 2004)

NOW TO 2017   16.5

Corton, Les Maréchaudes, 2001
Domaine Chandon de Briailles

Medium colour. Ripe, fragrant and stylish on the nose. Not the depth or elegance of the Bressandes and the Clos du Roi though. Soft, elegant and persistent. Very good indeed. (July 2005)

NOW TO 2018   17.0

Corton, Les Maréchaudes, Vieilles Vignes, 2001
Domaine Doudet-Naudin

A certain astringency here. But decent fruit. Slightly unbalanced. A little stewed. Doesn't sing. From 2008. (February 2003)

NOW TO 2014   14.0

Corton, Renardes, 2001
Domaine Michel Gaunoux

Good colour. Fat, rich nose. Slightly *sauvage*. Medium-full body. Some tannin, not all of

it very stylish. A meaty example. Good plus. (March 2004)

NOW TO 2015   15.5

Corton, Renardes, 2001
Maison Camille Giroud

Good colour. Ripe, elegant, laid-back nose. Not a bit hard. Medium-full body. Lovely tannins. Very good grip. Smooth and velvety. Very well balanced. Long. Impressive. Very stylish for a Corton. Fine plus. (September 2005)

2010 TO 2025+   18.0

Corton, Les Renardes, 2001
Domaine Maillard Père et Fils

One and one-tenth hectares. Good colour. Rich and concentrated. Pure. Lots of fruit. Good backbone, but the tannins are very ripe. Lovely grip. Very concentrated. Fine. (February 2003)

2009 TO 2020   17.5

Echézeaux, 2001
Domaine Joseph Faiveley

Medium to medium-full colour. Quite firm, but crisp nose. Medium to medium-full body. This lacks zip and class. Slightly oxidised. Unexciting. (July 2005)

NOW TO 2013   13.0

Echézeaux, 2001
Domaine du Clos Frantin/Albert Bichot

Medium to medium-full colour. Soft, ripe nose. Quite forward. Slightly astringent. Medium body. Lacks class. A meagre wine. (July 2005)

NOW TO 2013   13.0

Echézeaux, 2001
Maison Alex Gambal

Medium-full colour. Ripe, succulent, stylish nose. Decent structure. Decent fruit. Not really *grand cru* class. But not too bad. (July 2005)

2009 TO 2016   14.0

Echézeaux, 2001
Domaine Jean Grivot

Medium-full colour. Good weight and richness on the nose. Like the Beaumont, this is not exactly a very meaty wine, but it has good depth, harmony and very classy fruit. It is a little fatter. Very good indeed. (July 2005)

2009 TO 2020   17.0

Echézeaux, 2001
Domaine A.F. Gros

Fullish colour. Fresh, plump nose. Ripe. Medium-full body. Quite rich and meaty. Not the most exciting wine but good plus. Finishes positively. (July 2005)

2009 TO 2018   15.5

Echézeaux, 2001
Domaine Louis Jadot

Medium to medium-full weight. No great size or depth, but very pure. Good tannins, if not a lot of them. Fresh, ripe, stylish fruit. Shows very well. Very good indeed. (June 2003)

NOW TO 2016   17.0

Echézeaux, 2001
Maison Frédéric Magnien

Medium to medium-full colour. Oaky nose. A little over-macerated. Good fruit and grip underneath. But rather over-balanced. Medium-full body. Quite good at best. (July 2005)

2010 TO 2020   14.0

Echézeaux, 2001
Domaine Mugneret-Gibourg

Full colour. Rich, ample, well-balanced nose. Ripe, fullish, concentrated and harmonious. This has very good fruit. Cool and blackcurranty. Long on the palate. Very good indeed. (July 2005)

2010 TO 2020   17.0

Echézeaux, 2001
Domaine Jacques Prieur

Fullish colour. Rich nose. Some oak. No lack of tannin. On the palate there is decent balance, but not a lot of depth and dimension. Medium-full body. Attractive fruit. Very good indeed. (July 2005)

2009 TO 2020   17.0

Echézeaux, 2001
Domaine de la Romanée-Conti

Good colour. Very lovely soft, ripe, succulent fruit on the nose. Quite oaky. Plummy. Plump. Medium bodied. Very good grip and intensity. Very pure and complex. Even delicate. But that is all to its own good. Very good indeed. (September 2005)

NOW TO 2020   17.0

Fixin, Clos Marion, 2001
Domaine Fougeray de Beauclair

Monopole. Medium-full colour. Lightish but fresh, plump nose. Lightish and slightly lean on the palate. Not much tannin. This is a bit thin, but it is reasonably fresh and fruity. Forward. Not bad. (October 2003)

DRINK SOON   13.5

Fixin, Clos Napoléon, 2001
Domaine Pierre Gelin

Medium to medium-full colour. A touch dry and pinched on the nose. Medium body. A little tannin. Slight lack of ripeness, richness and charm. Fair at best. Will it round off? (March 2005)

NOW TO 2010   13.5

Gevrey-Chambertin, Vieilles Vignes, 200
Domaine Denis Bachelet

Good colour. Lovely nose. Gently oaky. Rich and succulent. Medium to medium-full body. Good acidity. Fresh, fruity, complex and delicious. Very elegant. Good length. Very good. (March 2005)

NOW TO 2014   16.0

Gevrey-Chambertin, Vieilles Vignes, 2001
Domaine Alain Burguet

Village wine. Medium colour. Fullish, rich nose. Plenty of depth here. Gently oaky. Rich. Fullish body. Very good grip and very lovely style. Long and elegant. Very good indeed. (July 2005)

2010 TO 2025   17.0

Gevrey-Chambertin, Vieilles Vignes, 2001
Domaine Heresztyn

Good colour. Gingerbread on the nose. Medium weight. Fresh. Balanced. Decently complex. Long. Very good plus. (Octrober 2003)

NOW TO 2019   16.5

Gevrey-Chambertin, Premier Cru, 2001
Domaine Bernard Maume

Medium colour. Ripe nose. Ample, round and rich. Slightly weedy on the palate though. Sweet but no zip. No class. (July 2005)

NOW TO 2014   13.5

Gevrey-Chambertin, Les Cazetiers, 2001
Domaine Bruno Clair

Medium colour. Rich, oaky, ripe and succulent on the nose. This is very lovely on the palate. Medium-full body. Excellent harmony. Very fine fruit. Long, complex, fresh and delicious. Fine plus. (July 2005)

2010 TO 2025   18.0

Gevrey-Chambertin, Les Cazetiers, 2001
Domaine Dupont-Tisserandot

Medium-full colour. Ripe and oaky on the nose. Medium-full body. Concentrated, meaty and old viney. Nice, cool fruit. Good grip. Long and intense. This is very good indeed. (July 2005)

NOW TO 2020   17.5

Gevrey-Chambertin, Les Cazetiers, 2001
Domaine Joseph Faiveley

Medium to medium-full colour. Not a lot of power and concentration on the nose. Slightly green. Rather astringent on the palate. Bland and unstylish. Only fair. (July 2005)

NOW TO 2012   13.0

Gevrey-Chambertin, Les Cazetiers, 2001
Domaine Michel Magnien

Medium to medium-full colour. Slightly four-square on the nose. Some oak here. Slightly cooked and astringent. No joy here. Fair. (July 2005)

NOW TO 2013   13.0

Gevrey-Chambertin, Les Cazetiers, 2001
Domaine Armand Rousseau

Medium colour. Ripe, soft and succulent on the nose. Medium body. No hard edges. Quite forward. Fresh. Balanced. Full of fruit. Easy to drink. Lovely finish. Very good indeed. (July 2005)

NOW TO 2015   17.0

Gevrey-Chambertin, Les Cazetiers, 2001
Domaine Christian Sérafin

Medium to medium-full colour. Classy nose. Gently oaky. Rich and succulent. Fullish body. Plenty of vigour. Rich and ample. Long. Very good indeed. (July 2005)

2009 TO 2020   17.0

Gevrey-Chambertin, Les Champeaux, 2001
Domaine Denis Mortet

Very fine colour. Rich, concentrated nose. Lots of depth. Some oak. Fullish body. Very ripe tannins. Very good grip. Fresh. Lots of individuality. Inherently soft. Much less extracted. Delicious fruit. Very good indeed. (September 2005)

NOW TO 2020   17.0

Gevrey-Chambertin, Cherbaudes, 2001
Domaine Fourrier

Medium colour. Round and rich, concentrated and full of fruit. An ample wine on the nose. Ripe, succulent, balanced and nicely fat on the palate. Very good acidity. Lovely finish. Fine. (July 2005)

2010 TO 2020+   17.5

Gevrey-Chambertin, Clos Saint-Jacques, 2001
Domaine Bruno Clair

Medium colour. Soft nose. Not as big or as intense as his Cazetiers. But fruity and stylish. Soft. Medium to medium-full weight. Rich and delicious. Subtle. Very long. Very fine. (July 2005)

2010 TO 2025   18.5

Gevrey-Chambertin, Clos Saint-Jacques, 2001
Domaine Sylvie Esmonin

Medium-full colour. Rich, fat, oaky and meaty. Full and ample. A little bit over-oaked and not enough subtlety underneath. But very ripe fruit and good balance. Very good. (July 2005)

2010 TO 2025   16.0

Gevrey-Chambertin, Clos Saint-Jacques, 2001
Domaine Louis Jadot

Medium-full colour. Firm, rich, backward nose. Very cool, classy, concentrated fruit. This is full

and high class. Lovely fruit. Very good grip. Long and delicious. Very intense. Very fine. (July 2005)
2010 TO 2025   18.5

Gevrey-Chambertin, Clos Saint-Jacques, 2001
Domaine Armand Rousseau
Medium colour. Very fine refined nose. Lots of depth. Very subtle. Fine but not great. Doesn't quite have the grip and intensity. This is succulent and ample. But no better than fine today. (July 2005)
2009 TO 2020   17.5

Gevrey-Chambertin, Combe au Moine, 2001
Domaine Fourrier
Medium colour. Elegant nose. Slightly more high toned than his Cherbaudes. Lighter but stylish. Good grip. Very good plus. (July 2005)
2009 TO 2020   16.5

Gevrey-Chambertin, Aux Combottes, 2001
Domaine Hervé Arlaud
Medium colour. Cool, slightly austere but very classy nose. Medium-full body. Ripe. Quite pronounced acidity. But good style underneath. (July 2005)
2009 TO 2020   16.5

Gevrey-Chambertin, Aux Combottes, 2001
Domaine Dujac
Fullish colour. Rich, fragrant, Chambolle-ish on the nose. Medium-full. Intense. Balanced. Very lovely fruit. Lots of depth. This is very lovely. Excellent grip. Lovely ripe fruit at the end. Very, very long finish. Fine. (March 2004)
NOW TO 2020+   17.5

Gevrey-Chambertin, Les Corbeaux, 2001
Domaine Denis Bachelet
Medium to medium-full colour. Ripe, rich, ample and very stylish on the nose. Lots of depth. Rich and concentrated. Backward and profound. Very lovely. (July 2005)
2010 TO 2025   17.5

Gevrey-Chambertin, Craipillot, 2001
Domaine Humbert Frères
Medium colour. Rich, full, succulent, gently oaky nose. Medium to medium-full

body. Intense. Lovely fruit. Very long. Fine. (July 2005)
2009 TO 2020+   17.5

Gevrey-Chambertin, Estournelles-Saint-Jacques, 2001
Domaine Humbert Frères
Medium to medium-full colour. Subtle nose. Ripe, fragrant and classy. Profound, rich, concentrated and very lovely indeed. Ripe and concentrated. Fullish body. Lots of depth. Fine plus. (July 2005)
2010 TO 2025   18.0

Gevrey-Chambertin, Fonteny, 2001
Domaine Christian Sérafin
Medium-full colour. Rich and oaky on the nose. Lovely fruit. Fullish bodied, ample, ripe, slightly obvious but very well made. Very good indeed. (July 2005)
2010 TO 2025   17.0

Gevrey-Chambertin, Lavaux-Saint-Jacques, 2001
Domaine Bernard Dugat-Py
Full colour. Very big, oaky, concentrated nose. Is this too much over the top? Big. Very concentrated. Very fine grip and class though. Is this really what Burgundy should be? Yet I have to say it is impressive. Fine but not special. (July 2005)
2012 TO 2025   17.5

Gevrey-Chambertin, Lavaux-Saint-Jacques, 2001
Domaine Humbert Frères
Medium-full colour. A bit taught on the nose. Needs time to soften. Yet good class. An ampler, richer but more backward version of their Estournelles. Just as fine. (July 2005)
2011 TO 2025   18.0

Gevrey-Chambertin, Lavaux-Saint-Jacques, 2001
Domaine Bernard Maume
Medium-full colour. Animal and fat on the nose. Touch of game. Medium body. Slightly astringent. Rather coarse. (July 2005)
NOW TO 2014   13.0

Gevrey-Chambertin, Lavaux-Saint-Jacques, 2001
Domaine Denis Mortet
Medium-full colour. A little closed still but very pure fruit. Not over-extracted at all. Just a little modern because of the oak. But rich, concentrated, vigorous and energetic. Very good indeed. (July 2005)
2010 TO 2025   17.0

Gevrey-Chambertin, La Perrière, 2001
Maison Frédéric Magnien
Medium-full colour. Coarse, slightly oxidised and reduced nose. No joy here. Flat and nondescript. High acidity. Not much succulence or class. (July 2005)
2010 TO 2020   14.0

Gevrey-Chambertin, Petite Chapelle, 2001
Domaine Humbert Frères
Medium-full colour. Soft, sexy and gently succulent on the nose. Slightly less energy than their Estournelles or Lavaut, but ample, pure, fresh and ripe. Subtle, long finish. Very good plus. (July 2005)
NOW TO 2020   16.5

Gevrey-Chambertin, Poissenot, 2001
Domaine Humbert Frères
Medium-full colour. Less interest than their Petite Chapelle, but soft and elegant. Quite forward. Medium body. Slightly one-dimensional after their other wines, but stylish and good plus. (July 2005)
NOW TO 2014   15.5

La Grande Rue, 2001
Domaine François Lamarche
Medium-full colour. Firm, slightly closed-in, classy nose. Very good concentrated fruit here. Fullish body. Some oak. Vigorous and concentrated. Very good grip. This is elegant and fine plus. (July 2005)
2010 TO 2025   18.0

Grands Echézeaux, 2001
Domaine Joseph Drouhin
Good colour. Ripe, intense, round and full of fruit on the nose. Gently oaky. Medium-full

body. Good grip. This has a lot of finesse and is well balanced. Fine plus. (March 2004)
2009 TO 2025   18.0

Grands Echézeaux, 2001
Domaine du Clos Frantin/Albert Bichot
Medium-full colour. Much bigger, fresher and richer than their Échezeaux. Medium-full body. Good tannins. Concentrated, persistent and classy. Lovely finish. Fine. (July 2005)
2010 TO 2025   17.5

Grands Echézeaux, 2001
Domaine Gros Frère et Soeur
Fullish colour. Rich, full, oaky nose. Very good concentration. Full body. Lots of depth. Quite a backward example. Fine. (July 2005)
2010 TO 2025   17.5

Grands Echézeaux, 2001
Domaine François Lamarche
Medium-full colour. Slightly chloriny on the nose. It is also a little corked. The wine seems to lack zip. Medium-full body. Dull. Second bottle: rich, full and concentrated. Lots of depth. Just a touch of oak. This is a very lovely wine. It has real dimension. Classy and long on the finish (2011 to 2025; 18.5). (July 2005)
2009 TO 2020   14.0

Grands Echézeaux, 2001
Domaine de la Romanée-Conti
Slightly less colour than the Echézeaux. Firmer nose. More depth and concentration but more austere. The acidity is more dominant, the fat less so. But there is more weight here. At present it is the Echézeaux which sings. But this is fine quality. Fine. (September 2005)
2010 TO 2022   17.5

Grands Echézeaux, 2001
Domaine du Clos Frantin/Albert Bichot
Medium to medium-full colour. Decent fruit on the nose although no great class. Slightly dirty. Quite fresh. Medium-full body. Not special. (July 2005)
2009 TO 2020   13.0

Griotte-Chambertin, 2001
Domaine Ponsot
Medium-full colour. Rich, fat, cool nose. Medium-full. Rich and slightly austere. Classy. Long and complex. Very good plus. (July 2005)
2010 TO 2020   16.5

Latricières-Chambertin, 2001
Domaine Drouhin-Laroze
Medium-full colour. Good ripe, succulent fruit on the nose. Fullish. Classy. Slightly astringent at the end. Cool. Lacks a little richness. But certainly fine. (July 2005)
2010 TO 2020   17.5

Latricières-Chambertin, 2001
Domaine Joseph Faiveley
Good colour. Fresh, quite substantial, rich nose. Medium-full body. Some tannin. Fatter than their Mazis 2001. Ripe, rich and succulent. Fine. (June 2003)
2009 TO 2020   17.5

Latricières-Chambertin, 2001
Domaine Ponsot
Medium-full colour. Slightly closed-in but classy, balanced fruit on the nose. Medium-full body. Ripe and oaky. Rich and balanced. Long and complex. Lovely. Very good indeed. (July 2005)
2010 TO 2025   17.0

Latricières-Chambertin, 2001
Domaine Jean Trapet Père et Fils
Good colour. Richer, firmer and more vigorous than their 2001 Chapelle-Chambertin. Full body. Nicely concentrated. Good grip. Lovely ripe fruit. Very stylish. Fine. (March 2004)
NOW TO 2020   17.5

Marsannay, Les Longeroies, 2001
Domaine Bruno Clair
Good colour. Plump, ripe, fresh, stylish and fruity on the nose. This is delicious. Medium body. Crammed with fruit on the palate. Good zip. Plenty of dimension. (March 2004)
NOW TO 2014   15.5

Mazis-Chambertin, 2001
Domaine Bernard Dugat-Py
Full colour. Rich, concentrated, ripe and oaky on the nose. Full bodied, rich, fat and concentrated on the palate. Quite extracted. Lots of new oak. A bit of an effort to drink. Will it soften properly? I think so. (July 2005)
2012 TO 2025   18.0

Mazis-Chambertin, 2001
Domaine Dupont-Tisserandot
Full colour. Closed-in nose. Rich, concentrated and backward. Quite extracted. But good depth and grip. Full bodied and meaty. Rich and very good indeed. Needs time. (July 2005)
2012 TO 2025   17.0

Mazis-Chambertin, 2001
Domaine Joseph Faiveley
Good colour. Slightly austere on the nose and palate. Medium-full weight. Excellent grip. Intense, elegant and very long on the palate. Not an enormous amount of tannin. Very good indeed. (March 2004)
2009 TO 2025   17.0

Mazis-Chambertin, 2001
Domaine Bernard Maume
Fullish colour. Clumsy nose. Fullish but a bit astringent. Lacks richness. Nothing exciting. (July 2005)
2009 TO 2020   14.0

Mazoyères-Chambertin, 2001
Maison Frédéric Magnien
Fullish colour. Rather purer and cleaner than their Charmes. But all too similar on the palate. Less grip. Less body. More astringency. No. (July 2005)
NOW TO 2013   12.5

Monthelie Rouge, 2001
Domaine Pierre Morey
Good colour. Fresh, plump nose. Good style and no lack of depth. Slightly sauvage at the end, but good for what it is. (March 2004)
NOW TO 2011   14.0

Monthelie, Sur la Velle, 2001
Domaine Annick Parent

Medium colour. Slightly diffuse on the nose. Light, stylish and fruity on the palate. Fresh. No lack of interest. Positive finish. Good plus. (October 2003)

DRINK SOON   15.5

Morey-Saint-Denis, 2001
Domaine Dujac

Good colour. Fragrant nose. Fresh and intense. Very good fruit. Very good acidity. Medium weight. Not quite as concentrated or as intense on the palate as I would have liked, but certainly very good. Very elegant. (March 204)

NOW TO 2017   16.0

Morey-Saint-Denis, Premier Cru, 2001
Domaine des Lambrays

Medium colour. Very lovely nose. Surprisingly elegant and accessible. Medium to medium-full body. Ripe, balanced, minerally and subtle. This is individual, and very lovely for what it is. (September 2004)

2010 TO 2020   17.0

Morey-Saint-Denis, Premier Cru, Cuvée des Alouettes, 2001
Domaine Ponsot

Medium colour. Soft, aromatic, very pure, cool fruit on the nose. Medium-full body. Rich, balanced, vigorous and stylish. Very good indeed. (July 2005)

2010 TO 2020   17.0

Morey-Saint-Denis, Aux Charmes, 2001
Domaine Lignier-Michelot

Medium to medium-full colour. Light but fragrant nose. Balanced and fresh. But lightish. Good fruit but just a little weedy. Forward. Quite good plus. (July 2005)

NOW TO 2014   14.5

Morey-Saint-Denis, Les Charrières, 2001
Domaine Alain Michelot

Medium to medium-full colour. A bit slight on the nose. Medium body. Fresher than Lignier-

Michelot's Charmes. Good fruit. Ripe. Well made. Long. Very good. (July 2005)

NOW TO 2016   16.0

Morey-Saint-Denis, Clos de la Buissière, 2001
Domaine Georges Roumier et Fils

Medium to medium-full colour. Slightly robust nose. Fullish and ripe underneath. Fullish body on the palate. Some tannin. Rich but meaty. Lacks a bit of style but very good. (July 2005)

2011 TO 2020   16.0

Morey-Saint-Denis, Clos Sorbè, 2001
Maison Frédéric Magnien

Medium to medium-full colour. Oaky nose but rather weak structure behind it. Stewed and attenuated. Unexciting. (July 2005)

NOW TO 2011   12.5

Morey-Saint-Denis, Les Faconnières, 2001
Domaine Lignier-Michelot

Medium to medium-full colour. Still youthful. Lightish but fragrant, balanced, stylish nose. Good depth on the palate. Medium body. Harmonious and stylish. Fresh. Long. Not that concentrated. But very good. (June 2006)

NOW TO 2014   16.0

Morey-Saint-Denis, Les Milandes, 2001
Domaine Heresztyn

Medium-full colour. Fat nose but somewhat reduced. Slightly corked, too. Medium-full body. Good concentration. A decent wine at least. (July 2005)

2009 TO 2016   15.0

Morey-Saint-Denis, Les Milandes, 2001
Domaine Christian Sérafin

Medium-full colour. Rich, stylish, concentrated and oaky on the nose. Fullish bodied, rich and oaky. Meaty and succulent. Good grip. Very well made as usual. Very good indeed. (July 2005)

2010 TO 2025   17.0

Morey-Saint-Denis, Les Ruchots, 2001
Domaine Hervé Arlaud

Medium-full colour. Soft, but ripe and quite stylish nose. Slightly earthy on the palate. This has good fruit, but a lack of zip and freshness. Medium body. Quite good only. (July 2005)

NOW TO 2014   14.0

Morey-Saint-Denis, Les Ruchots, 2001
Maison Frédéric Magnien

Medium to medium-full colour. Rich, meaty and oaky nose. Clumsy on the palate. Medium to medium-full body. A little astringent. Not very attractive. (July 2005)

2009 TO 2020   14.0

Morey-Saint-Denis, En la Rue de Vergy, 2001
Domaine Bruno Clair

Ripe. Good substance. Plump, fruity and gently oaky. Compared with most Côte de Beaunes, this shows very well. Good. (March 2004)

NOW TO 2010   15.0

Musigny, 2001
Domaine Joseph Drouhin

Medium-full colour. Just a little tight on the nose at first. Medium-full body. Ripe and vigorous. Clean and classy. Very long. Very well-covered tannins. Intense. Very fine plus. (July 2005)

2010 TO 2025   19.0

Musigny, 2001
Domaine Louis Jadot

Splendidly rich and ripe. Fullish bodied, very concentrated and ample for a 2001. Lovely fruit. Only in bottle 3 months, but it seems very fine. (June 2003)

NOW TO 2020   19.0

Le Musigny, 2001
Domaine Jacques-Frédéric Mugnier

Fine colour. Ample, ripe, gently oaky nose. Intense, classy and multidimensional. Lovely fruit. Very harmonious. Medium-full body. Quite fat. Very fine expression of Musigny. Impeccably balanced. Great length and complexity. Excellent. (June 2006)

2014 TO 2030   20.0

Musigny, 2001
Domaine Jacques Prieur

Very good colour. Rich, full, ample, quite structured nose. Fullish. Lovely plump, fresh fruit.

It doesn't have the depth and flair of Vogüé's, nor the distinction, but it has class and plenty of succulence. Fine plus. (July 2005)

2010 TO 2025   18.0

Musigny, 2001
Domaine Comte Georges de Vogüé

Full colour. Much more closed-in than their Bonnes Mares. Impressive concentration and finesse though. Fullish body. A little adolescent. Some oak. Very good grip. Intense and potentially lovely. (July 2005)

2010 TO 2025   19.0

Nuits-Saint-Georges, 2001
Domaine Henri Gouges

Very good colour. Rich nose. Slightly *sauvage*. Medium to medium-full body. This is a typical village Nuits. More substance than sophistication, but it has depth and balance. Good plus. (March 2004)

NOW TO 2015   15.5

Nuits-Saint-Georges, Premier Cru, 2001
Domaine Michel Gros

Medium colour. Ample, ripe, succulent nose. A touch of oak. Medium-full body. Good tannins. Lovely fruit. Very good grip. Long and lovely. (July 2005)

2011 TO 2025   17.5

Nuits-Saint-Georges, Aux Boudots, 2001
Domaine Jean-Jacques Confuron

Medium-full colour. Rich, oaky nose. Lots of depth here. Medium-full body. Ripe, round, rich and concentrated. Lovely elegance and lovely balance. Lots of vigour and depth. Fine plus. (July 2005)

2011 TO 2025   18.0

Nuits-Saint-Georges, Les Boudots, 2001
Domaine Jean Grivot

Good colour. Rich and ripe. Good substance on the nose. Less evolved than most wines in this flight. Slightly more *sauvage* than his 2001 Beaux Monts. Fullish body. Some tannin. Very good grip and depth. Needs time. (July 2005)

2009 TO 2020+   17.0

Nuits-Saint-Georges, Aux Boudots, 2001
Domaine Méo-Camuzet
Medium to medium-full colour. Ripe and oaky. Quite rich. Medium-full body. Good tannins. Ample, succulent and with very good grip. This is very good indeed. (July 2005)
2011 TO 2025   17.0

Nuits-Saint-Georges, Aux Boudots, 2001
Maison Nicolas Potel
Medium colour. Fragrant but light nose. Medium body. Stylish. But a little one-dimensional. Decent balance, but a lack of concentration and depth. Good at best. (July 2005)
2009 TO 2017   15.0

Nuits-Saint-Georges, Aux Boudots, 2001
Domaine Jean Tardy et Fils
Medium colour. Soft nose. Not much depth and grip. A bit weak, in fact. Good on the palate though. Some tannin. Medium to medium-full body. Slightly one-dimensional but an attractive wine. Very good. (July 2005)
2010 TO 2020   16.0

Nuits-Saint-Georges, Les Cailles, 2001
Domaine Bouchard Père et Fils
Medium-full colour. Stylish nose. Round and ripe. Very good fruit. Sturdy. Masculine. Medium-full body. Quite tannic. Backward. Slightly austere but plenty of depth. Very good indeed. (July 2005)
2012 TO 2025   17.0

Nuits-Saint-Georges, Les Cailles, 2001
Domaine Alain Michelot
Fullish colour. Good depth and intensity on the nose. Lots of dimension and style. Not as rich or as concentrated as Bouchard's. Nor as much personality on the palate. Fragrant but very good at best. (July 2005)
2010 TO 2020   16.0

Nuits-Saint-Georges, Les Chaboeufs, 2001
Domaine Jean-Jacques Confuron
Medium-full colour. Slightly soft and weak on the nose. Not a patch on his Boudots. Slightly anonymous on the palate. Medium to medium-full body. Good acidity. Lacks a bit of richness and concentration. Good plus. (July 2005)
2010 TO 2020   15.5

Nuits-Saint-Georges, Aux Chaignots, 2001
Domaine Robert Chevillon
Medium-full colour. Slightly overblown nose. Lacks zip. Medium body. Soft, sweet and fragrant. More forward than some. Decent fruit. Good length. Very good. (July 2005)
2010 TO 2020   16.0

Nuits-Saint-Georges, Aux Chaignots, 2001
Domaine Henri Gouges
Medium-full colour. Big, full, rich, backward nose. Full. Some tannin. Backward. Rich. Needs time. Lots of depth underneath. Very good indeed. (July 2005)
2012 TO 2025   17.0

Nuits-Saint-Georges, Aux Chaignots, 2001
Domaine Alain Michelot
Medium-full colour. Good style if not a lot of depth on the nose. Medium-full body. Elegant, balanced and fragrant. This is most attractive. Very good indeed. (July 2005)
2010 TO 2020   17.0

Nuits-Saint-Georges, Aux Chaignots, 2001
Domaine Dr. Georges Mugneret
Medium-full colour. Decidedly oaky on the nose. Medium-full body. Ample and exotic. But very good acidity and lovely fruit. A seductive example. Long. Fine. (July 2005)
2011 TO 2025   17.5

Nuits-Saint-Georges, Aux Chaignots, 2001
Domaine Gérard Mugneret
Medium-full colour. Fragrant nose. Medium weight. Medium-full body. Ripe and succulent. Not the greatest depth or concentration, but balanced and amply fruity. Very good indeed. (July 2005)
2009 TO 2020   17.0

Nuits-Saint-Georges, Chaînes Carteaux, 2001
Domaine Henri Gouges
Medium colour. Slightly tight on the nose, but good grip and fruit. Medium-full body. Ripe and ample. Good tannins. Good grip. This is most attractive. (July 2005)
2011 TO 2025   16.5

Nuits-Saint-Georges, Château Gris, 2001
Domaine Lupé-Cholet
Medium to medium-full colour. Slightly tight on the nose. Doesn't appear to have a lot of grip underneath. Accessible, abundant and very stylish and balanced on the palate. Medium to medium-full body. Positive. Very good indeed. (July 2005)
2010 TO 2025   17.0

Nuits-Saint-Georges, Clos des Porrets
Saint-Georges, 2001
Domaine Henri Gouges
Good colour. Impressive nose. Rich, full and plummy. Lots of depth. Full body. Backward. Very good, ripe tannins. Very fine grip, too. The fruit is profound. Lovely finish. This is fine plus. (March 2004)
2009 TO 2025+   18.0

Nuits-Saint-Georges, Les Damodes, 2001
Domaine Jean Chauvenet
Medium to medium-full colour. Slightly bland on the nose. Medium body. Easy to enjoy. Ripe. Some oak. Decent grip. But essentially one-dimensional. (July 2005)
2009 TO 2020   16.0

Nuits-Saint-Georges, Les Murgers, 2001
Domaine Bertagna
Decent colour. Quite a soft nose. But fresh, clean and fruity. Medium weight. Positive. Elegant. But not the dimension of their 2004 which is very good plus. Quite forward. (February 2006)
NOW TO 2015   16.0

Nuits-Saint-Georges, Aux Murgers, 2001
Domaine Méo-Camuzet
Good colour. Rich, oaky nose. Medium-full and ripe. Easy to enjoy. Balanced and stylish on the palate. It doesn't have the concentration of the *premiers crus* of Gouges, but it is long and very good plus. (March 2004)
2009 TO 2020   16.5

Nuits-Saint-Georges, Aux Perdrix, 2001
Domaine des Perdrix
Medium-full colour. Rich, full, concentrated and a little oaky on the nose. Full, rich, tannic and ample. Quite a meaty example. Good grip. A bit adolescent today. Needs time. Fine. (July 2005)
2012 TO 2025   17.5

Nuits-Saint-Georges,
Les Porêts-Saint-Georges, 2001
Domaine Alain Michelot
Medium-full colour. Ample nose. But a lack of zip and elegance. Medium body. Soft. Easy to drink. What it lacks is depth and concentration and drive. Pleasant though. (July 2005)
NOW TO 2015   14.0

Nuits-Saint-Georges, Clos des Porrets
Saint-Georges, 2001
Domaine Henri Gouges
Medium-full colour. Backward and tannic, but rich and ripe on the nose. Firm, full and closed-in. This has lots of depth and class. But it needs time. Very good indeed. (July 2005)
2012 TO 2025   17.0

Nuits-Saint-Georges, Les Procès, 2001
Domaine Joseph Drouhin
Medium-full colour. Bland nose. Some evolution. Lacks real depth. Medium to medium-full body. Elegant and fruity on the palate. Better acidity than was apparent at first. This has character. Very good. (July 2005)
2009 TO 2019   16.0

Nuits-Saint-Georges, Les Pruliers, 2001
Domaine Robert Chevillon
Medium-full colour. Light but fragrant nose. Not a great deal on the palate. Decent fruit, but a little short. (July 2005)
NOW TO 2012   14.0

Nuits-Saint-Georges, Les Pruliers, 2001
Domaine Henri Gouges
Fullish colour. Full, rich and backward. Higher toned than the Clos des Porrets. Medium-full body. Has it enough acidity? Ripe. Not really a blockbuster, but rich and full bodied. Very good. (July 2005)
2010 TO 2020   16.0

Nuits-Saint-Georges, Les Pruliers, 2001
Domaine Jean Grivot
Medium colour. Decent fruit, but a slight absence of weight and succulence on the nose. On the palate hardly medium weight. A touch of astringency. A bit feeble really. A disappointment. (July 2005)
NOW TO 2010   13.0

Nuits-Saint-Georges, La Richemone, 2001
Domaine Alain Michelot
Medium-full colour. Quite oaky on the nose. Medium to medium-full weight. Ripe and succulent. But a little bland on the palate. Medium-full body. Decent depth but not a very exciting personality. (July 2005)
NOW TO 2016   14.0

Nuits-Saint-Georges, Rue de Chaux, 2001
Domaine Jean Chauvenet
Medium-full colour. Fragrant nose. Decent balance and concentration if no great style. Rich. Medium-full body. Meaty. Ripe. Good grip. Good depth. Long. Very good indeed. (July 2005)
2010 TO 2023   17.0

Nuits-Saint-Georges, Rue de Chaux, 2001
Maison Antonin Rodet
Medium to medium-full colour. Lovely clean, rich, pure nose. Quite firm but not a bit too sturdy. Full body. Rich. Very good tannins. This is surprisingly fine for this *climat*. Long. Backward. Lovely. (July 2005)
2012 TO 2025   17.5

Nuits-Saint-Georges, Les Saint-Georges, 2001
Domaine Robert Chevillon
Medium colour. Rich nose. But a touch reduced. Medium-full weight. A little tannin. Ripe and

quite sweet. Not the greatest of finesse but good. (July 2005)
2009 TO 2016   15.0

Nuits-Saint-Georges, Les Saint-Georges, 2001
Domaine Joseph Faiveley
Medium colour. Full, concentrated nose. Tannic and backward. Full, tough, ripe, rich and oaky. Needs time. Good grip. Difficult to judge. Very good indeed, I think. (July 2005)
2012 TO 2025   17.0

Nuits-Saint-Georges, Les Saint-Georges,
Hospices de Nuits, Cuvée Sire de Vergy, 2001
Domaine Joseph Faiveley
Fullish colour. Ripe nose. Quite oaky. Less austere than the Vaucrains of Gouges. Rounder and more succulent at present. More austere on the palate. Just what it should be, but not as concentrated as that of Gouges. Good grip and stylish fruit. Fine. (September 2004)
2010 TO 2025   17.5

Nuits-Saint-Georges, Les Saint-Georges, 2001
Domaine Henri Gouges
Good colour. Backward nose but very, very rich and concentrated. Splendid fruit here. A big tannic wine, but very harmonious and unexpectedly classy. Splendid follow-through: ample, rich, balanced and very fine. (July 2005)
2009 TO 2025+   18.5

Nuits-Saint-Georges, Les Saint-Georges, 2001
Maison Frédéric Magnien
Medium to medium-full colour. Big, oaky, extracted nose. Quite sweet. Underneath all this mass there is not a very big wine. Decent fruit and decent grip. Quite fresh and classy. But dominated by the oak. (July 2005)
2009 TO 2018   14.0

Nuits-Saint-Georges, Les Saint-Georges, 2001
Domaine Alain Michelot
Medium-full colour. Ripe, oaky, rich and abundant on the nose. High-class fruit here. Medium-full body. Some tannin. Ripe, rich,

succulent and very seductive. Good grip. Long. Lovely. Fine plus. (July 2005)

2011 TO 2025   18.0

Nuits-Saint-Georges, Les Saint-Georges, 2001
Maison Antonin Rodet

Medium to medium-full colour. Fresh, pure, clean but austere nose. Medium-full body. Ripe and chocolaty. Rich. Good grip. Long. Very good indeed. (July 2005)

2010 TO 2025   17.0

Nuits-Saint-Georges, Les Vallerots, 2001
Domaine Chantal Lescure

Fullish colour. Slightly sturdy and lumpy on the nose. No great finesse here. On the palate this is astringent and very poor. Ripe fruit underneath. But badly made. (July 2005)

NOW TO 2012   12.0

Nuits-Saint-Georges, Les Vaucrains, 2001
Domaine Jean Chauvenet

Medium-full colour. Medium to medium-full weight on the nose. Just a little stewed. Medium to medium-full body. Slightly bland. Lacks vigour and dimension. Pleasant but not exceptional. Lacks class. (July 2005)

NOW TO 2014   13.5

Nuits-Saint-Georges, Les Vaucrains, 2001
Domaine Robert Chevillon

Fullish colour. Quite an overblown nose. Lacks grip. Like their Saint-Georges, this has perfectly pleasant, sweet fruit, but no real grip or finesse. (July 2005)

2009 TO 2016   15.0

Nuits-Saint-Georges, Les Vaucrains, 2001
Domaine Henri Gouges

Full colour. Firm, full nose. Quite tannic, but the tannins are well covered. Quite austere. Fullish bodied and tannic on the palate. Good acidity. This is a backward example. But there is a lot of depth here. Potentially fine, at the very least. Lots of concentrated fruit. Fine plus. (July 2005)

2013 TO 2033   18.0

Nuits-Saint-Georges, Les Vaucrains, 2001
Maison Nicolas Potel

Medium colour. Slightly heavy footed on the nose. No finesse. Medium body. Rather astringent on the palate. Spurious sweetness of fruit. Slightly astringent at the end. (July 2005)

NOW TO 2012   12.5

Nuits-Saint-Georges, Les Vignerondes, 2001
Domaine Joseph Faiveley

Good colour. Lovely nose. Rich and oaky. Composed and profound. Very stylish. Fullish body. Some tannin. Good depth and lovely fruit. Long and complex. Very good indeed. (March 2004)

2009 TO 2020+   17.0

Pernand-Vergelesses, Les Fichots, 2001
Domaine Doudet-Naudin

A certain freshness at the beginning but a bit of astringency in the back. Decent fruit. Quite good. (February 2003)

NOW TO 2011   14.0

Pernand-Vergelesses, Ile de Vergelesses, 2001
Domaine Chandon de Briailles

Medium colour. Light but fragrant, elegant nose. On the palate the fruit is stylish, but the whole thing is a little weedy and one-dimensional. Quite good. (March 2004)

NOW TO 2011   14.0

Pommard, Vieilles Vignes, 2001
Domaine Philippe Pacalet

Medium colour. Medium weight. Slightly sweaty nose at first. Cleaner as it evolved. Medium body. Decent acidity. Not a great deal of tannic structure. But quite fragrant and fruity, as well as spicy from the new oak. Already quite soft. Ripe and pleasant if not that concentrated. But good for what it is. (May 2003)

NOW TO 2010   15.0

Pommard, Premier Cru, 2001
Domaine Philippe Billard-Gonnet

Medium colour. Fragrant, balanced and stylish on the nose. Medium body. Quite forward. Slightly short yet decent fruit. Not bad plus. (July 2005)

NOW TO 2013   13.5

Pommard, Les Arvelets, 2001
Domaine A.F. Gros

Medium colour. Soft nose. Some fruit but not much backbone. Medium-full body. Good grip. Good tannins. Positive. Lacks a little personality but quite good plus. (July 2005)

NOW TO 2015   14.5

Pommard, Les Bertins, 2001
Domaine Chantal Lescure

Medium colour. Ripe if a little unstylish on the nose. Medium to medium-full body. Slightly astringent and stewed. Artisanal. No. (July 2005)

NOW TO 2012   12.5

Pommard, Les Chanlins, 2001
Domaine Annick Parent

Medium-full colour. Ripe and fragrant with good weight on the nose. Medium body. Decent fruit and balance. But nothing exciting here. Just a little less astringent than some. (July 2005)

NOW TO 2013   13.5

Pommard, Les Chanlins, 2001
Domaine Nicolas Rossignol

Medium-full colour. Rich, fat, ripe and impressive on the nose. Rather thin and astringent on the palate though. Lacks grip and richness at the end. (July 2005)

NOW TO 2014   13.5

Pommard, Les Chaponnières, 2001
Domaine Philippe Billard-Gonnet

Medium-full colour. Slightly four-square on the nose. Good fruit as it developed. Rather lumpy on the palate. Unexciting. (July 2005)

NOW TO 2013   13.0

Pommard, Les Charmots, 2001
Maison Olivier Leflaive Frères

Medium colour. Decent weight and fruit on the nose. Medium to medium-full weight on the palate. Slightly lean fruit. But not astringent nor soupy. Positive at the end. At least clean if not very generous. Quite good. (July 2005)

NOW TO 2014   14.0

Pommard, Les Charmots, 2001
Domaine Moissenet-Beaumard

Medium-full colour. Nicely plump fruit and good weight on the nose. Medium-full body. Quite rich on the attack. Then it tails off. Astringent at the end. (July 2005)

NOW TO 2014   13.0

Pommard, Clos des Arvelets, 2001
Domaine Daniel Rebourgeon-Mure

Medium colour. A meaty nose. Slightly astringent. Better on the palate. Medium-full body. Good grip. Slightly hot on the aftertaste. Quite good. (July 2005)

NOW TO 2015   14.0

Pommard, Clos des Epeneaux, 2001
Domaine du Comte Armand

Medium-full colour. Lovely fragrant, classy fruit on the nose. Medium to medium-full body. Ripe and complex. A touch of toffee and gingerbread. Not the usual blockbuster but fragrant, elegant, harmonious and complex. Some evolution already. Fine. (June 2005)

NOW TO 2015   17.5

Pommard, Les Epenots, 2001
Maison Lucien le Moine

Medium colour. Soupy, sweet, slightly oxidised and totally un-Burgundian. Stewed. Astringent. Undrinkable. (July 2005)

(SEE NOTE)   10.0

Pommard, Les Epenots, 2001
Maison Olivier Leflaive Frères

Medium colour. Light nose. Some fruit but not enough substance, it seems. Yet medium to medium-full body. Balanced and elegant. Good grip. Long. Very good. (July 2005)

NOW TO 2017   16.0

Pommard, Les Epenots, 2001
Domaine Moissenet-Beaumard

Medium-full colour. Quite elegant, fruity, balanced nose. Some oak. Medium-full body. Rich.

Fat. Succulent. Good grip. Lovely long finish. Very good indeed. (July 2005)

2009 TO 2020   17.0

Pommard, Les Epenots, 2001
Domaine François Parent

Medium colour. Soupy-sweet on the nose. Some oak. Similar palate. Astringent. No. (July 2005)

NOW TO 2012   11.0

Pommard, Les Grands Epenots, 2001
Domaine Pierre Morey

Medium colour. Fragrant, stylish nose. But is it a little weak? On the palate rather short, dilute and astringent. Watery. But as it evolved, it seemed to put on weight. Elegant and very good. (July 2005)

NOW TO 2015   16.0

Pommard, Les Jarolières, 2001
Domaine Nicolas Rossignol

Medium-full colour. Plump, ripe nose. Good weight. On the palate, though, thin and astringent. (July 2005)

NOW TO 2013   13.0

Pommard, Les Pézerolles, 2001
Domaine A.F. Gros

Medium colour. Rather weak on the nose. Decent palate. Some fruit. But no great depth or personality. Medium body. (July 2005)

NOW TO 2014   13.5

Pommard, Les Pézerolles, 2001
Domaine Michel Lafarge

Medium colour. Soft nose. Lacks a bit of energy. Medium body. Some fruit. Better than his Volnays this year. (July 2005)

NOW TO 2014   13.5

Pommard, Les Pézerolles, 2001
Domaine Hubert de Montille

Medium to medium-full colour. Good meaty nose. The attack has more to it than does the 2001 Rugiens, and the follow-through is rather more positive. But good at best. (July 2005)

NOW TO 2013   15.0

Pommard, Les Rugiens, 2001
Domaine Philippe Billard-Gonnet

Medium-full colour. Fat, ripe nose. Slightly over the top and overripe. Rich on the palate. Curious. Is this a representative bottle? Second bottle: ripe and generous and oaky. Fullish body. Very good. (July 2005)

NOW TO 2016   16.0

Pommard, Les Rugiens, 2001
Domaine Bouchard Père et Fils

Medium colour. Some weight and depth on the nose. But a lack of real elegance. Medium body. Rather short. No. (July 2005)

NOW TO 2011   12.5

Pommard, Les Rugiens, 2001
Domaine Jean-Marc Bouley

Medium colour. Lightish, rather anonymous nose. A bit short. Medium body. Slightly four-square. A bit raw and lumpy. Unexciting. (July 2005)

NOW TO 2014   13.0

Pommard, Les Rugiens, 2001
Domaine de Courcel

Medium to medium-full colour. Ripe, succulent nose. Good style. Medium body. Now getting soft. A touch of sandalwood. Good fruit. But essentially a little lean. Best with food. Richer on the finish. Very good. (March 2005)

NOW TO 2015   16.0

Pommard, Les Rugiens, 2001
Domaine Michel Gaunoux

Medium colour. A bit light and diffuse on both the nose and the palate. The finish is quite stylish and fragrant. But the net result is quite good plus at best. (March 2004)

NOW TO 2012   14.5

Pommard, Rugiens, 2001
Maison Vincent Girardin

Medium-full colour. Ripe, not quite as structured on the nose as his 2001 Volnay Santenots, but ample and spicy. Medium body. Round, but not a great deal of depth and concentration, nor grip. Good at best. (March 2004)

NOW TO 2011   15.0

Pommard, Les Rugiens, 2001
Domaine Hubert de Montille

Medium to medium-full colour. Fat on the nose. Plump and oaky. Decent attack, but then it tails off a bit. Fruity, but a lack of depth and grip. Quite good. (March 2004)

NOW TO 2012   14.0

Pommard, Les Rugiens, 2001
Domaine Annick Parent

Medium colour. Rich, oaky nose. A meaty wine. Medium-full body. Rich if a little four-square. Good grip. Slightly adolescent. Quite good. (July 2005)

NOW TO 2015   14.0

Pommard, Les Rugiens, 2001
Domaine François Parent

Medium colour. Lightish but quite fragrant nose. Medium body. Decent balance and style. But not very exciting. (July 2005)

NOW TO 2013   13.5

Richebourg, 2001
Domaine Jean Grivot

Full, immature colour. Rich nose. Plenty of quality, richness and depth. Very high-class fruit. Medium-full body. Ripe tannins. Very lovely quality. Multidimensional. Very fine indeed in potential. (April 2006)

2010 TO 2030   19.5

Richebourg, 2001
Domaine Gros Frère et Soeur

Full colour. Lovely, rich, ample, succulent fruit on the nose. A touch of oak, too. Medium-full body. Quite evolved, and a little astringent at the end. Not quite enough grip. Disappointing for what it is. (July 2005)

2010 TO 2025   15.0

Richebourg, 2001
Domaine A.F. Gros

Fullish colour. Rich, quite oaky nose. Full, ample, rich and ripe. Lots of grip. This is a

delicious wine. Nice and cool, and composed. Really quite stylish. Very fine. (July 2005)

2011 TO 2025   18.5

Richebourg, 2001
Domaine Anne Gros

New label. Medium-full colour. Splendid fruit on the nose. Real flair and concentration. Medium-full body. More obviously tannic structure than the 2002. Very good grip. Slightly less rich. Certainly less plump. But more spice. Plenty of energy and distinction. Lovely long, complex finish. Very fine plus. (July 2005)

2011 TO 2025   19.0

Richebourg, 2001
Domaine Alain Hudelot-Noëllat

Medium to medium-full colour. Higher toned on the nose. Not too exaggerated oak. On the palate this shows ample fruit, but not the energy, class and grip that the label would suggest. Slightly bland. Very good at best. (July 2005)

2009 TO 2020   16.0

Richebourg, 2001
Maison Dominique Laurent

Medium-full colour. Rich and oaky on the nose. Ripe and medium-full bodied on the palate, but the oak dominates. The wine underneath has good fruit but isn't concentrated enough to take the oak. Good at best. (July 2005)

2009 TO 2020   15.0

Richebourg, 2001
Domaine de la Romanée-Conti

Good colour. Firm, rich, backward, profound nose. Slightly austere, like their 2001 Grands Echézeaux. But lots of very classy wine here. Medium-full body. Good, ripe tannins, although by no means a blockbuster. Nice long finish. Lots of finesse. This will keep well. (September 2005)

2011 TO 2025+   18.0

Romanée-Conti, 2001
Domaine de la Romanée-Conti

Not a great deal of colour. Delicate nose. Subtle but not exactly rich or profound. Improved in the glass. Medium to medium-full body. A strange combination of high acidity and overripeness takes the class away nonetheless. Lacks real succulence. Fine at best. (September 2005)

2010 TO 2022   17.5

Romanée-Saint-Vivant, 2001
Domaine Jean-Jacques Confuron

Medium-full colour. Very lovely, perfumed fruit on the nose, with just a touch of oak. Fullish body. Composed, harmonious, intense and lovely. Very good fruit. Very long and complex. Real class and depth. Very fine. (July 2005)

2010 TO 2025   18.5

Romanée-Saint-Vivant, 2001
Maison Camille Giroud

Fullish colour. Lush, fragrant nose. Very elegant, balanced fruit. Medium-full body. Very good grip. Velvety rich. Very classy. Lovely finish. Very fine. (June 2005)

2009 TO 2020+   18.5

Romanée-Saint-Vivant, 2001
Domaine Alain Hudelot-Noëllat

Medium to medium-full colour. Ripe and aromatic on the nose. Medium-full body. Ample, fresh and balanced. This is classy and composed. I find it more interesting than his Richebourg. Fine plus. (July 2005)

2010 TO 2025   18.0

Romanée-Saint-Vivant, 2001
Domaine de la Romanée-Conti

Good colour. I get a lot of the stems on the nose here and not much else. Medium body. More fruit as it developed, with a decently positive finish. But, all in all, a little lean. Very good plus at best. (September 2005)

2009 TO 2020   16.5

Ruchottes-Chambertin, 2001
Domaine Dr. Georges Mugneret

Full colour. Rich, fullish, oaky on the nose. Fullish body. Very lovely fresh fruit. Lots of class and vigour. Long and complex. Fine plus. (July 2005)

2009 TO 2025   18.0

Ruchottes-Chambertin, Clos des Ruchottes, 2001
Domaine Armand Rousseau

Medium-full colour. Cool, classy nose. Medium-full body. No hard edges. Good class and grip. Ripe. Fresh. Still a little closed. Long. Fine. (July 2005)

2009 TO 2020   17.5

Santenay, Clos de la Confrérie, 2001
Maison Vincent Girardin

Good colour. Soft, ripe, generous nose. Medium body. Still a little tannin. A lot more definition than most Volnays. More class too. Very good fruit. Fresh. Positive at the end. Very good. (March 2004)

NOW TO 2015   16.0

Savigny-lès-Beaune, 2001
Domaine Daniel Largeot

Decent fruit. Just a little more substance and tannin than his Chorey-Lès-Beaune Les Beaumonts 2001. Not a lot different though. (February 2003)

NOW TO 2010   14.0

Savigny-lès-Beaune, 2001
Domaine Pierre and Jean-Baptiste Lebreuil

On the light side, but quite stylish. Decent freshness. (February 2003)

NOW TO 2010   13.5

Savigny-lès-Beaune, 2001
Domaine René Podichard

Lovely old-vine fruit. Long. Complex. Very good. (February 2003)

NOW TO 2014   16.0

Savigny-lès-Beaune, Aux Clous, 2001
Domaine Pierre and Jean-Baptiste Lebreuil

Medium colour. Again a bit on the light side. Forward, but fresh and ample. Good, stylish fruit here. Good. (February 2003)

NOW TO 2010   15.0

Savigny-lès-Beaune, Les Golardes, 2001
Domaine Fougeray de Beauclair
Soft, ripe and stylish. Now ready. Medium body.
Decent class. More succulent than some. Quite
good plus. (March 2005)
DRINK SOON   14.5

Savigny-lès-Beaune, Aux Grands Liards, 2001
Domaine Simon Bize et Fils
Medium colour. Slight touch of the stems on the
nose and a slight lack of fruit. Medium weight. Bal-
anced. Subtle. Good for a village wine. (March 2004)
NOW TO 2012   15.0

Savigny-lès-Beaune, Les Grands Liards, 2001
Domaine Pierre and Jean-Baptiste Lebreuil
Riper and fresher than their basic Savigny 2001.
But a slight touch of the rustic. (February 2003)
NOW TO 2011   14.0

Savigny-lès-Beaune, Aux Guettes, 2001
Domaine Doudet-Naudin
Young vines (planted 1996). Surprisingly deep
colour. Some tannin. Not stewed though. Quite
fat and quite fresh if no great complexity. Quite
good. (February 2003)
NOW TO 2011   14.0

Savigny-lès-Beaune, Les Marconnets, 2001
Domaine Simon Bize et Fils
Good colour. Rich, full, meaty nose. Good tan-
nins. Lots of fruit. Medium-full body. Succulent
and ripe. Long. Good. (March 2004)
NOW TO 2015   15.0

Savigny-lès-Beaune, Aux Petits Liards,
Vieilles Vignes, 2001
Domaine Doudet-Naudin
Ripe. Slightly hard but of reasonable style. Good
substance. Not bad. (February 2003)
DRINK SOON   13.0

La Tâche, 2001
Domaine de la Romanée-Conti
Medium-full colour. Ripe, plump nose. Rich
but not as firm as the Richebourg. Nor, it would

appear at first, any more depth. Yet rather more
opulent than the Romanée-Conti, as always.
Medium-full body. Slightly austere acidity. As
it developed, plenty of real concentration, and
long and positive at the end. Very fine plus.
(September 2005)
2012 TO 2025+   19.0

Volnay, Premier Cru, 2001
Domaine du Marquis d'Angerville
Medium colour. Fragrant nose. Slightly astringent
and weedy on the palate. Decent balance. Medium
body. Only quite good. Not really enough to it.
(March 2004)
NOW TO 2012   14.0

Volnay, Les Caillerets, 2001
Domaine du Marquis d'Angerville
Medium colour. Fragrant nose. Not a great block-
buster but elegant. Medium body. Forward. No
great weight, but positive, elegant, even intense.
Very stylish, long finish. Very good. (July 2005)
NOW TO 2015   16.0

Volnay, Les Caillerets, Ancienne
Cuvée Carnot, 2001
Domaine Bouchard Père et Fils
Medium colour. Rather common on the nose.
Fruity but lacks real Volnay elegance. Medium
weight. No real personalilty. Slightly bitter at the
end. (July 2005)
NOW TO 2014   13.0

Volnay, Les Caillerets, 2001
Domaine Jean-Marc Bouley
Medium colour. Some oak on the nose. A little
stewed. Medium to medium-full body. Slightly
astringent at the end. Ungainly. (July 2005)
NOW TO 2014   13.0

Volnay, Les Caillerets, 2001
Domaine Rossignol-Jeanniard
Medium colour. Quite ripe if no great elegance
on the nose. Slightly souped-up. Soft but bor-
ing. Medium weight. (July 2005)
NOW TO 2014   13.0

Volnay, Champans, 2001
Domaine du Marquis d'Angerville
Medium colour. Soft, but ripe and elegant on the nose. Slightly more weight than his Caillerets. Good grip. Good depth and class. Slightly less fragrant though. Good plus. (July 2005)
NOW TO 2015   15.5

Volnay, Clos des Angles, 2001
Domaine Rossignol-Jeanniard
Medium colour. Slight touch of reduction on the nose. A little sweetness to the fruit underneath. Medium to medium-full body. Positive. Balanced. Stylish. Good follow-through. Good. (July 2005)
NOW TO 2016   15.0

Volnay, Clos de la Barre, 2001
Domaine Louis Jadot
Medium colour. Decent style, personality and fruit here. Medium body but not astringent. Positive finish. Forward. (July 2005)
NOW TO 2014   14.0

Volnay, Clos de la Chapelle, 2001
Maison Nicolas Potel
Medium colour. Not much on the nose. Rather thin and astringent on the palate. Nothing here. (July 2005)
NOW TO 2012   13.0

Volnay, Clos du Château des Ducs, 2001
Domaine Michel Lafarge
Medium-full colour. Ripe and ample on the nose. But rather astringent and reduced on the palate. Dry finish. Unexciting. (July 2005)
NOW TO 2012   13.0

Volnay, Clos des Chênes, 2001
Domaine Jean-Michel Gaunoux
Medium colour. Rather sweaty nose. Rather dilute at the end. Medium weight. Quite fruity in the middle. But empty. (July 2005)
NOW TO 2013   13.0

Volnay, Clos des Chênes, 2001
Domaine Antonin Guyon
Medium colour. Pleasant fruit on the attack, but short and dilute on the follow-through. Boring. (July 2005)
NOW TO 2013   13.0

Volnay, Clos des Chênes, 2001
Domaine Michel Lafarge
Good colour. Lightish nose. More to it on the palate. Medium weight. Good grip. This still needs time. It is a bit on edge at present. Good fruit. But a slight lack of velvet. (March 2004)
NOW TO 2015   15.0

Volnay, Clos des Ducs, 2001
Domaine du Marquis d'Angerville
Medium to medium-full colour. This has a lot of depth and class. Lovely fruit. Plenty of dimension. Medium to medium-full body. Profound, complex and balanced. Good dimension. Long and positive. Very classy. Fine. (July 2005)
NOW TO 2018   17.5

Volnay, Frémiets, 2001
Domaine du Marquis d'Angerville
Medium colour. Fragrant nose. A touch of sweet herbs. Flowers and peppermint on the palate. Rather more style, depth and definition than his basic 2001 Volnay *premier cru*. Medium to medium-full body. Balanced. Really good given the hail difficulties here. (July 2005)
NOW TO 2015   15.5

Volnay, Le Ronceret, 2001
Domaine Nicolas Rossignol
Medium-full colour. Rich, meaty nose. Good, ample wine here. Fullish body. Not too over-extracted. Pommard-ish rather than Volnay, but good, positive finish. Good. (July 2005)
2009 TO 2016   15.0

Volnay, Santenots, 2001
Domaine Sylvie Esmonin
Medium colour. Strangely herbal scented, but not in an attractive way on the nose. Slightly

reduced. Slightly weak and rather astringent on the palate. It tails off. No. (July 2005)

NOW TO 2010 11.0

Volnay, Santenots, 2001
Maison Vincent Girardin

Medium-full colour. Full, rich and meaty on the nose. Medium-full body. Fresh, complex and classy on the palate. Plenty of depth. Good, positive follow-through. This is very good. (July 2005)

NOW TO 2015 16.0

Volnay, Santenots, 2001
Maison Morey-Blanc

Medium colour. Slightly dilute on the nose. Light, sweet, fragrant and forward. Decent enough finish. Quite good. (July 2005)

NOW TO 2011 14.0

Volnay, Santenots, 2001
Domaine Rossignol-Jeanniard

Medium to medium-full colour. Slightly over-extracted on the nose. Slightly reduced too. Medium-full body. Rather lumpy and astringent. No enjoyment here. (July 2005)

NOW TO 2012 12.5

Volnay, Santenots du Milieu, 2001
Domaine des Comtes Lafon

Medium to medium-full colour. Decent fruit on the nose. Slightly four-square. Decent weight, but not enough grip or personality. Better and better as it developed. Good plus. (July 2005)

NOW TO 2014 15.5

Volnay, Taillepieds, 2001
Domaine du Marquis d'Angerville

Medium colour. Peppermint on the nose. Medium to medium-full body. Fragrant, ripe and stylish. Good, positive follow-through. This has class and personality. Good plus. (July 2005)

NOW TO 2015 15.5

Volnay, Taillepieds, 2001
Domaine Hubert de Montille

Medium colour. Rather dilute on the nose. Short and dilute on the palate. Thin and astringent. Slightly rancid. No. (July 2005)

NOW TO 2011 12.5

Vosne-Romanée, Les Beaumonts, 2001
Domaine Bertagna

Medium colour. Soft nose. Good fruit. But perhaps a little bland. Better on the palate. Good intensity if not a blockbuster. Ripe. Persistent. Medium to medium-full body. Very good indeed. (July 2005)

2009 TO 2020 17.0

Vosne-Romanée, Les Beaumonts, 2001
Domaine Jean-Jacques Confuron

Medium colour. Soft nose, especially compared with his Nuits. Round and fruity, but not much depth. Slightly corky. On the palate medium to medium-full body. Very good, ripe fruit. Fresh and stylish. Very good indeed. (July 2005)

2010 TO 2020 17.0

Vosne-Romanée, Les Beaux Monts, 2001
Domaine Jean Grivot

Good colour. Lovely nose. Rich, full, ample and very elegant. Medium-full body. Ripe and plump. Good tannin. Still a little adolescent compared with some. Lovely fruit. Very harmonious. Long. Lovely finish. Fine. (July 2005)

2009 TO 2020+ 17.5

Vosne-Romanée, Les Brûlées, 2001
Domaine René Engel

Medium-full colour. Some development. Aromatic, spicy, gently oaky nose. Medium-full body. Ample nose. Not the greatest of grip and concentration, but attractive and accessible. Not short by any means. Ample and generous. Warm finish. Very good plus. (March 2004)

NOW TO 2016 16.5

Vosne-Romanée, Aux Brûlées, 2001
Domaine Michel Gros

Medium-full colour. Rich, full and stylish on the nose. Very pure. Full, rich, concentrated and very well balanced. Great elegance and purity. Lots of depth and dimension. This is super. Very lovely finish. (July 2005)

2010 TO 2025   18.5

Vosne-Romanée, Les Chaumes, 2001
Domaine Bouchard Père et Fils

First vintage. Medium-full colour. Less development than in his village wines. Good depth, fruit and substance, but a little raw and unformed at present. Medium-full body. Lovely ripe tannins. Very cool, classy, plummy fruit. Very gently oaky. Lovely harmony. Fine. (June 2005)

2009 TO 2020   17.5

Vosne-Romanée, Les Chaumes, 2001
Domaine Jean Tardy et Fils

Medium colour. Fragrant nose. Light but stylish. Medium body. Ripe, fresh and balanced. Good depth. For what it is, better than his Boudots. Long. Very good indeed. (July 2005)

NOW TO 2018   17.0

Vosne-Romanée, Clos du Château, 2001
Domaine Bouchard Père et Fils

Medium to medium-full colour. Rather more fragrant on the nose than his Vosne-Romanée Colombière. A little fuller, too. Riper and more succulent. Soft tannins. Ripe and very intense. Long and vigorous. Velvety and lovely. Very good for a village wine. (June 2005)

NOW TO 2016   16.0

Vosne-Romanée, Clos de la Colombière, 2001
Domaine Bouchard Père et Fils

Medium colour. Stylish, positive nose. Light, but ripe and positive. Medium weight. Attractive and balanced. Good intensity. Long. Lots of character. Nearly ready. Good plus. (September 2005)

NOW TO 2012   15.5

Vosne-Romanée, Clos des Réas, 2001
Domaine Michel Gros

Medium-full colour. Light, fruity nose if without great depth. But plenty of elegance. Medium to medium-full body. Pure, very elegant Pinot fruit. Fragrant. Subtle. Long. Very good indeed. (July 2005)

2010 TO 2020   17.0

Vosne-Romanée, Aux Malconsorts, 2001
Domaine du Clos Frantin/Albert Bichot

Medium-full colour. Lovely, cool Pinot fruit on the nose. Balanced and classy. Profound and very pure. Impressive depth and finesse on the palate. Full bodied, rich and concentrated. Long. Very fine. (July 2005)

2010 TO 2025   18.5

Vosne-Romanée, Les Malconsorts, 2001
Maison Camille Giroud

Good colour. Rich, fat, old-viney nose. Sumptuous fruit. Not a bit aggressive. Ripe, succulent and classy. Medium-full body. Ripe tannins. Very good grip. Long and very classy. Very Vosne. A noble wine. Very concentrated. Fine plus. (June 2004)

2011 TO 2028+   18.0

Vosne-Romanée, Aux Malconsorts, 2001
Domaine François Lamarche

Medium to medium-full colour. Ripe and elegant. Cool and balanced on the nose. On the palate this is medium to medium-full bodied, quite concentrated, long and classy. But it doesn't have the depth of the Clos Frantin. Fine though. Lovely finish. (July 2005)

2010 TO 2025   17.5

Vosne-Romanée, Aux Malconsorts, 2001
Maison Nicolas Potel

Medium-full colour. A little sturdy and burly on the nose. Slightly tough. Needs time. On the palate this is only medium to medium-full bodied, and it lacks concentration and depth. Ripe, but one-dimensional and slightly ungainly. (July 2005)

2010 TO 2020   15.0

Vosne-Romanée, Les Suchots, 2001
Maison Lucien le Moine

Medium-full colour. Over the top, oxidised nose. Very curious and un-Burgundian. Sweet. Disgusting. (July 2005)

NOW TO 2010   10.0

Vosne-Romanée, Les Suchots, 2001
Domaine Gérard Mugneret

Medium colour. Soft and succulent on the nose. No great grip, depth or concentration. Indeed, there is a suspicion of astringency at the end. But soft, enjoyable, supple and fruity. Very good. (July 2005)

NOW TO 2016   16.0

Vosne-Romanée, Les Suchots, 2001
Domaine Prieuré-Roch

Medium colour. Quite some evolution. Not much nose. Some fruit. Less evidence of the stems than in more recent vintages. But lightish. Slightly astringent at the end. Yet fresh. Not much here though. (February 2006)

DRINK SOON   13.0

Vougeot, Clos de la Perrière, 2001
Domaine Bertagna

Medium to medium-full colour. Nice, pure Pinot on the nose. Ripe and soft. Round and rich. Clean. Medium to medium-full body. Good tannins. Gently oaky. Rich finish. Very good indeed. (July 2005)

2009 TO 2025   17.0

Vougeot, Les Cras, 2001
Domaine de la Vougeraie

Medium to medium-full colour. Good depth on the nose. Rich, concentrated and backward. Fullish. Vigorous. Good tannins. Ripe and very well balanced. Lots of depth. Lovely finish. Fine. (July 2005)

2010 TO 2025   17.5

2000

In quantity, 2000 was a good crop—anything over 250,000 hectolitres is a highly satisfactory harvest. But in quality, as opposed to almost every other vintage in the last 10 years, 2000

only rates as quite good. The reds lack power and concentration, although they are rather better in the Côte de Nuits than in the Côte de Beaune. The whites are ripe but are evolving fast. There is an absence of zip.

WEATHER CONDITIONS

The early months of the year were warm (February was wet, and March was dry) leading to an early bud-break. April was cool—but not so cold that there was any frost damage—and inclement; but after the middle of May, the weather improved. The vines flowered rapidly and uniformly in the first week of June, promising a large and early harvest.

We then came to July. This was cold and miserable, one of the coolest in recent years—and with no lack of rain. Nevertheless, the evolution of the fruit remained ahead of previous vintages. August was warm, setting a platform for a potential quality which, despite the rain in September, would not be washed out entirely. *Août*, as the French say, *fait le moût*: August makes (decides of the quality of) the must.

The *ban des vendanges* was ordained to be Monday, September 11, in the Côte de Beaune. The fruit in the top *climats*, where the harvest was not excessive, was in a very fine state of health and readiness. On the late afternoon and evening of September 12, there was a thunderstorm which unleashed between 25 and 75 millimetres of rain in the Côte de Beaune.

This storm had a decisive and divisive impact on the quality of the reds. Much less rain fell in the Côte de Nuits: much less had fallen before this downpour, and much less was to fall thereafter. While the rest of the month remained unsettled, it was both drier and cooler in the Côte de Nuits. The fruit could continue to ripen. Indeed, in many cases, the Côte de Nuits fruit attained potential levels of alcohol of 13° or over, even 14°, as in 1997. Importantly, there was much less rot, especially where yields had been reduced. The Côte de Nuits benefited from the fact that, in general, its growers harvest later. The poor growers in the Côte de Beaune, however, were confronted with the onset of botrytis.

As ever, however, there are mesoclimatic differences. It rained less in the Côte de Beaune north of the motorway (i.e., in Savigny, Chorey, Pernand and Aloxe) than further south. Less precipitation, too, was experienced in Monthelie and in Auxey-Duresses. The sector from the southern half of Beaune to the northern vineyards of Volnay, plus Santenay, seemed to have gotten the worst of it.

The 2000 vintage is an illustration of how much progress has been made in Burgundy in the last 20 to 30 years. A generation ago, a vintage such as 2000 would have been only fair in the Côte de Nuits, and a disaster in the Côte de Beaune. That it was not owes much to the growers' courage in cutting down the potential crop by means of short pruning, removal of excess buds and eventual green harvesting; their dedication in eliminating all but the ripest, healthiest fruit, to the extent in many cases of discarding 50 percent of the harvest; and subsequently, their intelligence in working with the wine on its lees so that it could enrich itself and put on both weight and vigour during its life in cask.

From the start, opinions were more bullish about the whites than the reds. Many growers produced better whites because they had to harvest their red grapes first, this enabling the Chardonnays to achieve maximum ripeness, for they were not fully ripe on the day of the *ban des vendanges*. The analyses were good. On paper, the wines seemed superior to those of 1999, provided one had not over-cropped. They had good grip and no lack of depth. There was no shortage of individual wines, indeed entire cellars, where the 2000s appeared to be superior to the 1999s.

Sadly, although there are many honourable exceptions, the 2000s today lack a bit of definition, while the 1999s seem to be getting better and better. Yet there are many very attractive bottles, drinkable now.

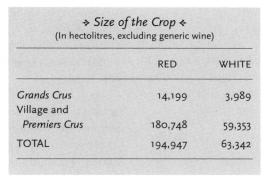

→ Rating for the Vintage ←	
Red	13.5–15.5
White	15.5

→ Size of the Crop ← (In hectolitres, excluding generic wine)	RED	WHITE
Grands Crus	14,199	3,989
Village and Premiers Crus	180,748	59,353
TOTAL	194,947	63,342

WHERE ARE THE BEST WINES?

- Meursault and Chassagne-Montrachet are better than Puligny-Montrachet.
- There is less of a difference in quality between the white *premiers* and *grands crus* than usual. Proportionately, 2000 *grands crus blancs* are disappointing.
- Of the red wines, the Côte de Nuits is a lot more successful than the Côte de Beaune, with Gevrey-Chambertin being the best commune of all. Here we have very good *terroir* definition.
- There was hail in Marsannay on August 25, but this does not seem to have done the wines any harm.
- The Hautes-Côtes-de-Nuits and the Hautes-Côtes-de-Beaune north of the motorway benefited from a reduced crop, owing to poorer flowering later than in the Côte d'Or, and to the better weather at the end of September and early October.

WHEN WILL THE WINES BE AT THEIR BEST?

The lesser wines, generics and Côte Chalonnaise, Marsannay and most of the Côte de Beaunes at village level need drinking soon or very soon. With the exception of a few Savigny, Beaune and Pommard *premiers crus*, as well as Corton, this applies to the rest of the Côte de Beaune. The Côte de Nuits is a different matter. Most wines are ready, but there is no hurry to drink them up. *Grands crus*, even some *premiers crus*, will still improve. The best will still be fresh when they are 10 years old. But I fear few will still be vigorous in 2015.

TASTING NOTES

WHITES

Bâtard-Montrachet, 2000
Domaine Joseph Drouhin

Composed and classy on the nose. Rich and full but not four-square. Very Bâtard on the palate. Full bodied, rich, quite alcoholic and slightly chunky. But good grip underneath. Good fruit. Long. Youthful. Fine. (September 2002)

NOW TO 2018   17.5

Bâtard-Montrachet, 2000
Domaine Jean-Noël Gagnard

Firm, youthful, oaky and adolescent on the nose, but of fine quality underneath. A little sulphur. Ample, rich and meaty on the palate. This has a lot of depth and very good grip. Long. Very lovely. It needs time. Very fine. (September 2002)

NOW TO 2018   18.5

Bâtard-Montrachet, 2000
Maison Vincent Girardin

Good substance and depth. Good grip and fruit. A lack of real personality perhaps. Fullish bodied, ripe and with decent grip. But compared with some just a little pedestrian. Everything is here in place, but a slight lack of character. Fine though. (September 2002)

NOW TO 2018   17.5

Bâtard-Montrachet, 2000
Domaine Vincent et François Jouard

Rich nose. And a little four-square with it. Full body. Concentrated. Lots of depth. Plenty of rich, fat, ample fruit. Good but not excellent grip and zip. Lacks just a little high tones. Very good indeed. (June 2002)

NOW TO 2017   17.0

Bâtard-Montrachet, 2000
Maison Olivier Leflaive Frères

Full nose. Peaches, pears and angelica. Quite oaky on the palate. Not a wine of great volume or concentration. But quite stylish and with decent grip. Very good indeed. (January 2003)

NOW TO 2012   17.0

Bâtard-Montrachet, 2000
Domaine Leflaive

Broad nose. A touch of oak. Quite evolved. Smells of popcorn. Medium-full body. Ripe and balanced. Not the greatest of class and depth. Slightly four-square because the fruit is a bit pedestrian. Very good but not brilliant. (March 2006)

NOW TO 2010   16.0

Bâtard-Montrachet, 2000
Château de la Maltroye

This is quite different. Very ripe, almost tropical, exotic nose. Underneath very closed-in. Full bodied. Firm. Excellent grip. Splendidly long, multidimensional finish. Lots of class. Still very youthful. This is very fine. (January 2003)

NOW TO 2020   18.5

Bâtard-Montrachet, 2000
Domaine Pierre Morey

As always with this wine, and indeed with other Bâtards, while full, rich and with good grip, it is not yet showing its class. Very good depth though. Potentially fine plus. (September 2002)

NOW TO 2018   18.0

Bâtard-Montrachet, 2000
Domaine Paul Pernot et Fils

Some evolution on both nose and colour. On the palate an understated wine. Medium-full body. Subtle and complex. Not a blockbuster. Just about ready. Ripe and balanced. Lovely long finish. Needs a year or so. Fine plus. (March 2005)

NOW TO 2013   18.0

Bâtard-Montrachet, 2000
Domaine Ramonet

Almost exotic on the nose. Youthful, full bodied, rich and exotic on the palate. Flamboyant. A wine for keeping. But great depth, personality and class. This is very fine plus. (September 2002)

NOW TO 2020   19.0

Bâtard-Montrachet, 2000
Domaine Étienne Sauzet

Lovely nose. Gently oaky. Rich, fullish bodied, ripe and harmonious. Subtle and classy. Quite ample. Not the greatest grip. I think their Bienvenues is better. Decent length at the end though. This is fine, too. (September 2002)

NOW TO 2016   17.5

Bâtard-Montrachet, 2000
Maison Verget

Rather weak and feeble. This is a disgrace for the *climat*. Very weedy on the palate and very short. Drink up if at all. (September 2002)

DRINK UP   12.0

Bienvenues-Bâtard-Montrachet, 2000
Domaine Bachelet-Ramonet

Good nose: rich and cool. This is decent but slightly lean on the palate. It lacks a bit of depth, and it is a little slight. Good acidity though. Very good at best. (September 2002)

NOW TO 2013   16.0

Bienvenues-Bâtard-Montrachet, 2000
Domaine Jean-Claude Bachelet

Clean but a certain lack of depth, grip and concentration. Stylish but forward and a little lightweight on the nose. Good acidity. Quite classy. But quite forward. It lacks a bit of concentration on the follow-through. Not short though. Very good plus. (September 2002)

NOW TO 2014   16.5

Bienvenues-Bâtard-Montrachet, 2000
Domaine Louis Carillon et Fils

Lots of drive and intensity here on the nose. Excellent class. Lovely minerally touches. Very harmonious. Subtle and poised. Long and complex. This is still youthful. Very lovely finish. Fine plus. (September 2002)

NOW TO 2016   18.0

Bienvenues-Bâtard-Montrachet, 2000
Domaine Leflaive

Very good, crisp, peachy nose. Good class and intensity. Fullish body. Lots of depth. Great class and intensity. Very long and lovely. Very fine plus. A wine for keeping. (September 2002)

NOW TO 2017+   19.0

Bienvenues-Bâtard-Montrachet, 2000
Domaine Paul Pernot et Fils

Lovely, rich nose. Sandalwood and flowers. Medium-full body. Good grip. Cool. Very lovely. Lots of depth here. This will last well. Very fine. (September 2002)

NOW TO 2016+   18.5

Bienvenues-Bâtard-Montrachet, 2000
Domaine Ramonet

Full, backward, meaty and concentrated. A most impressive nose. Rich, ample and a bit adolescent on the palate at present. Lots of fruit. Excellent grip. A wine which will last. Potentially very fine. (September 2002)

2008 TO 2018+   18.5

Bienvenues-Bâtard-Montrachet, 2000
Domaine Étienne Sauzet

Lovely nose. Very concentrated fruit. Flowery, peachy and very well balanced. Quite a forward example. Lovely fruit. Long finish. Fine. (September 2002)

NOW TO 2016   17.5

Chassagne-Montrachet, 2000
Domaine Jean-Noël Gagnard

Gently oaky. Plump, peachy and fresh. Medium-full body. Very clean. Fragrant. Very good indeed for what it is. (March 2003)

NOW TO 2010   15.5

Chassagne-Montrachet, 2000
Domaine Jean-Marc Pillot

Good substance. Good depth. Quite rich. Very good fruit. Very good for what it is. (February 2003)

DRINK SOON   16.0

Chassagne-Montrachet, L'Estimée, 2000
Domaine Jean-Noël Gagnard

Lightish, reasonably fresh colour. Not too rustic. But not a wine of much depth, interest and class, even in 2000. Lacks backbone. Forward. (March 2003)

DRINK SOON   13.5

Chassagne-Montrachet, Abbaye de Morgeot, 2000
Maison Olivier Leflaive Frères

Rich, ample, ripe and lush on both nose and attack. Slightly four-square but decent acidity. Good plus. (January 2003)

NOW TO 2010 15.5

Chassagne-Montrachet, Les Baudines, 2000
Domaine Bernard Morey

Ripe and pleasantly oaky. Good acidity. Stylish. Quite tropical. Nicely steely underneath. Good. (September 2002)

NOW TO 2014 15.0

Chassagne-Montrachet, Blanchots Dessus, 2000
Domaine Anglada-Deleger

A slightly perfumed touch on the nose. Medium to medium-full body. Balanced. Peachy. Some evolution. Strange flavour but not unclean. Slightly exotic. Good length. But curiously attractive. Very good. (June 2005)

NOW TO 2010 16.0

Chassagne-Montrachet, Blanchot-Dessus, 2000
Domaine Darviot-Perrin

Very stylish on the nose. Splendidly racy. Lovely ripe fruit. Excellent grip. This has a lot of depth. Ready sooner than the 1999 though. Fine. (September 2002)

NOW TO 2016 17.5

Chassagne-Montrachet, Blanchot-Dessus, 2000
Domaine Jean-Noël Gagnard

A little reduced on the nose. Medium weight. Not quite enough zip and character. Clean but a little dull. Quite good. (September 2002)

NOW TO 2010 14.0

Chassagne-Montrachet, En Cailleret, 2000
Domaine Bachelet-Ramonet

Soft, fragrant and very stylish. Lovely fruit. Fine grip. This is fresh, ripe, long and lovely. Fine plus. (September 2002)

NOW TO 2016 18.0

Chassagne-Montrachet, En Cailleret, 2000
Domaine Marc Colin

Good rich, racy nose. This is stylish and has good depth. Not quite the grip on the palate though. Sadly, it tails off a bit at the end. Good at best. (September 2002)

NOW TO 2013 15.0

Chassagne-Montrachet, En Cailleret, 2000
Domaine Duperrier-Adam

This is clean and stylish. Fresh and fruity. More subtle at the end than it seems at first. Good depth. Very good plus. (September 2002)

NOW TO 2015 16.5

Chassagne-Montrachet, Les Caillerets, 2000
Domaine Jean-Noël Gagnard

As usual, Jean-Noël Gagnard's best wine, but a bit ungainly at present. Full bodied, concentrated, rich and meaty. Excellent grip. Very elegant. Plenty of dimension at the end. It needs time. Will keep well. Fine. (September 2002)

NOW TO 2016+ 17.5

Chassagne-Montrachet, En Cailleret, 2000
Maison Vincent Girardin

Good structure on the nose. Meaty, rich and racy. On the palate this is peachy and has good depth and style. It finishes long and positively. Very good plus. (September 2002)

NOW TO 2016 16.5

Chassagne-Montrachet, En Cailleret, 2000
Domaine Morey-Coffinet

This is a little pedestrian on the nose. It lacks elegance. A little SO_2. It lacks fruit. It lacks grip. Ugly. (September 2002)

DRINK SOON 12.5

Chassagne-Montrachet, En Cailleret, 2000
Domaine Bernard Morey

Ripe and rich. Not quite as racy as it could be perhaps, but there is more to it on the follow-through than the attack would suggest. Rich. Good depth. Good grip. Very good plus. (September 2002)

NOW TO 2016 16.5

Chassagne-Montrachet, Les Champs Gain, 2000
Domaine Jean-Noël Gagnard

This has a little more to it than does his Blanchot-Dessus. Subtle and stylish. Long. It got better and better in the glass. Very good. (Sepember 2002)

NOW TO 2014   16.0

Chassagne-Montrachet, Les Champs Gain, 2000
Domaine Michel Niellon

Good colour. Full nose. A little more sulphur than most people use today. It makes it a little heavy and four-square. Better on the palate. Good grip. Plenty of substance and fruit. But good rather than fine. (September 2005)

NOW TO 2014   15.0

Chassagne-Montrachet, Les Chaumées, 2000
Domaine Michel Colin-Deléger et Fils

Lovely stylish, steely nose. Peaches and cream. Medium body. Lovely fruit. Very gentle suggestion of oak. Ripe. Good, positive follow-through. Very stylish. Very good indeed. (September 2002)

NOW TO 2016   17.0

Chassagne-Montrachet, Les Chaumées, 2000
Domaine Jean-Noël Gagnard

Slightly fuller and richer than Michel Colin's example. Not quite the grip, personality or fruit though. A touch of oak. It finishes well. Plenty of depth. Very good. (September 2002)

NOW TO 2016   16.0

Chassagne-Montrachet, Les Chaumées, 2000
Domaine Vincent and François Jouard

Soft, oaky, stylish and fruity. Very fragrant, peachy-vanilla flavours. Reasonable grip and acidity. Medium to medium-full body. Quite intense at the end which is the best part. The attack is a touch weak. Long on the finish, though, and elegant. Very good. (March 2003)

NOW TO 2010   16.0

Chassagne-Montrachet, Les Chaumées, 2000
Maison Olivier Leflaive Frères

Medium weight. Flowery and fresh on the attack. A slight lack of extra dimension after that, but this is good plus and still a bit raw. (January 2003)

NOW TO 2010   15.5

Chassagne-Montrachet, Les Chenevottes, 2000
Domaine Michel Colin-Deléger et Fils

Rather racier and more interesting than Jean-Noël Gagnard's example. Good fruit. Good grip. But good plus rather than better. A slight lack of personality compared, say, with his Chaumées. (September 2002)

NOW TO 2014   15.5

Chassagne-Montrachet, Les Chenevottes, 2000
Domaine Joseph Drouhin

Soft, ripe, quite forward, stylish but just a little bland on the nose. Better on the palate. This is round and has no lack of fruit or grip. More to it at the end than seems at the start. Very good. (September 2002)

NOW TO 2015   16.0

Chassagne-Montrachet, Les Chenevottes, 2000
Domaine Jean-Noël Gagnard

Medium weight. Slightly closed on the nose. A little sulphur here. Decent Granny Smith–type fruit but not the style of other wines from this stable. Quite good. (September 2002)

NOW TO 2012   14.0

Chassagne-Montrachet, Les Chenevottes, 2000
Château de la Maltroye

Classy nose. Ripe and succulent, clean and with a slight touch of oak. Quite delicate though. Lovely fruit on the palate. Good intensity. Good acidity. Not exactly rich, but very pure and plenty of dimension. Very good indeed. (April 2005)

NOW TO 2012   17.0

Chassagne-Montrachet, Les Chenevottes, 2000
Domaine Bernard Morey

The best of the Chenevottes. The wine with the most depth and concentration. Good grip. Peachy. Positive and stylish at the end. Very good plus. (September 2002)

NOW TO 2016   16.5

Chassagne-Montrachet, Clos du Château de la Maltroye, 2000
Château de la Maltroye

Rich, profound and concentrated. Quite closed at the outset. Lots of depth. Good, oaky base. Both fat and minerally at the same time. Excellent grip. Long. Very youthful. Fine plus. (January 2003)

NOW TO 2015   18.0

Chassagne-Montrachet, Clos de la Maltroie, 2000
Domaine Jean-Noël Gagnard

Ripe, fresh and stylish. Medium-full body. A very good example which again will last well. Not quite the quality of fruit of Bernard Morey's though. (September 2002)

NOW TO 2015   16.0

Chassagne-Montrachet, Clos Saint-Jean, 2000
Domaine Michel Niellon

A little coarse. Not much fruit here. And a bit too much SO_2. Not bad at best. (September 2002)

NOW TO 2010   13.0

Chassagne-Montrachet, Les Embrazées, 2000
Domaine Borgeot

A little SO_2 on the nose. Light, but quite clean and stylish on the palate. A hint of oak. Quite racy. Good but forward. Peachy. (March 2003)

DRINK SOON   15.0

Chassagne-Montrachet, Les Embrazées, 2000
Maison Vincent Girardin

Good rich, positive nose. Some oak. Open and accessible. The follow-through is not as interesting, nor does it have as much depth. But clean and competent. Good. (September 2002)

NOW TO 2014   15.0

Chassagne-Montrachet, Les Embrazées, 2000
Domaine Bernard Morey

Ripe, fullish bodied and gently oaky. Good grip and definition. Quite racy. This has style and depth. Ripe and rich. Plenty of character. Very good plus. (June 2003)

NOW TO 2012   16.5

Chassagne-Montrachet, Les Fairendes, 2000
Domaine Morey-Coffinet

Quite racy and peachy on the nose. Some oak. Good, fat, ample example. Good grip. Quite an opulent example on the palate. Good plus. (September 2002)

NOW TO 2015   15.5

Chassagne-Montrachet, Francemont, 2000
Maison Verget

A bit bland and blowsy on the nose. Very dull and dilute on the palate. Too forward, too. A disgrace! (September 2002)

DRINK SOON   10.5

Chassagne-Montrachet, La Grande Montagne, 2000
Domaine Bachelet-Ramonet

Delicate, but racy and stylish on the nose. Lovely fruit. Delicately oaky. Good grip. This is very good. (September 2002)

NOW TO 2015   16.0

Chassagne-Montrachet, Les Grandes Ruchottes, 2000
Château de la Maltroye

Hidden at first. This is concentrated and steely. Really profound. Fat and rich again. Very lovely fruit. Full bodied. Backward. Fine plus. (January 2003)

NOW TO 2015   18.0

Chassagne-Montrachet, Les Grandes Ruchottes, 2000
Domaine Fernand and Laurent Pillot

Rich, full, complete nose. Lots of depth here. This is *grand cru* quality. Very good depth. Plenty of substance here. Rich. Very long. Very fine. (September 2002)

NOW TO 2018   18.5

Chassagne-Montrachet, Les Macherelles, 2000
Domaine Bernard Morey

Not the greatest of Bernard Morey's wines, but then not the greatest of *climat* either. Yet thoroughly competent. Medium-full body. Ripe, balanced and stylish with a positive finish. Will keep well. Good plus. (September 2002)

NOW TO 2015   15.5

Chassagne-Montrachet, La Maltroie, 2000
Domaine Bernard Morey

Ripe, rich and opulent on the nose. Ripe and fullish bodied. Good depth. Attractive fruit. This has a good structure. It will last well. Very good plus. (September 2002)

NOW TO 2016   16.5

Chassagne-Montrachet, Morgeot, 2000
Domaine Bacheley-Legros

This is a very well-made wine, with the oak just so. Ripe, fruity and elegant. But medium bodied only and quite accessible already. Very good. But not a wine for a 10-year span. (February 2003)

DRINK SOON   16.0

Chassagne-Montrachet, Morgeot, 2000
Domaine Coutoux

Somewhat reduced on the nose. Decent fruit on the palate underneath. A good basic but no better. (September 2002)

NOW TO 2010   14.0

Chassagne-Montrachet, Morgeot, 2000
Domaine Jean-Noël Gagnard

Somewhat sulphury on the nose and dilute on the palate. Dull. Not bad plus. (September 2002)

NOW TO 2010   13.5

Chassagne-Montrachet, Morgeot, 2000
Domaine Duc de Magenta/Maison Louis Jadot

Lovely clear-cut, very stylish fruit on the nose. Rich, fullish bodied and positive. Quite accessible now, but very long. Lovely fruit. Will keep well. Fine. (September 2002)

NOW TO 2016   17.5

Chassagne-Montrachet, Les Morgeots, 2000
Domaine Vincent and François Jouard

From Les Fairendes. Good, ample, rich nose. But not too heavy. Fullish and plump. Good

depth. Lots of fruit. Ripe and rich at the end with a touch of citrus and spice. Good grip. Long finish. Very good. (June 2002)

NOW TO 2012   16.0

Chassagne-Montrachet, Morgeots, 2000
Domaine René Lamy-Pillot

Quite an evolved nose. Soft, fat, slightly blowsy. On the palate medium body. Decent grip and nice, ripe fruit, but not a wine of great distinction. À point now. A little built-in sulphur. Good plus. (October 2005)

NOW TO 2010   15.5

Chassagne-Montrachet, Morgeot, 2000
Domaine Bernard Morey

Good nose. Fullish, rich and balanced. Not as finely fruity as the Jadot/Magenta but very good acidity. Long, elegant and positive. Will last well. Very good plus indeed. (September 2002)

NOW TO 2016   16.5

Chassagne-Montrachet, Morgeot, 2000
Domaine Fernand and Laurent Pillot

Cleaner and more positive on the nose than most of these Morgeots. Good depth and fruit. It could have done with a bit more grip. But quite long. Good plus. (September 2002)

NOW TO 2015   15.5

Chassagne-Montrachet, Morgeot,
Vieilles Vignes, 2000
Maison Vincent Girardin

Soft, fullish, quite oaky nose. Ripe and succulent. Plenty of fruit. Decent length. Medium-full body. Ample and attractive. Ready. Very good. (June 2005)

NOW TO 2010   16.0

Chassagne-Montrachet, Morgeot,
Clos Pitois, 2000
Domaine Roger Belland

Fullish body. Just a little four-square. But rich and meaty. Plenty of depth. No lack of style. Good plus. (February 2003)

NOW TO 2012   15.5

Chassagne-Montrachet, Morgeot, Les Fairendes, Vieilles Vignes, 2000
Domaine Vincent and François Jouard

Medium-full bodied, crisp, fresh and fruity. Medium-full depth. Good but not the greatest concentration, but neat, clean and elegant. Very good. (November 2002)

NOW TO 2010   16.0

Chassagne-Montrachet, Morgeot, Vigne Blanche, 2000
Château de la Maltroye

This is fat, rich, fullish bodied, round and slightly spicy. Plenty of depth. Plenty of class. Complex at the end. Very good indeed. (January 2003)

NOW TO 2012   17.0

Chassagne-Montrachet, En Remilly, 2000
Domaine Michel Colin-Deléger et Fils

A little SO$_2$ here. Slightly weak on the palate. This doesn't sing the way it did in cask. Forward. A pity. Not bad plus. (September 2002)

NOW TO 2007   13.5

Chassagne-Montrachet, La Romanée, 2000
Domaine Bachelet-Ramonet

Good, steely fruit on the nose. Ripe, oaky and opulent on the palate. Decent structure. Quite exotic. Good length. A positive example. Very good plus. (September 2002)

NOW TO 2016   16.5

Chassagne-Montrachet, La Romanée, 2000
Domaine Vincent Dancer

Good, fresh, lemon-sherbet nose. Ripe and racy on the attack. It tails off a bit afterward. But good, if quite forward. (September 2002)

NOW TO 2011   15.0

Chassagne-Montrachet, La Romanée, 2000
Maison Vincent Girardin

Fullish, ample, balanced nose. This has good depth. Good structure. A little oak. Plenty of drive and intensity. This is very good indeed. It will last well. (September 2002)

NOW TO 2016   17.0

Chassagne-Montrachet, La Romanée, 2000
Château de la Maltroye

Ample nose. Good depth and structure. Better follow-through than most of the Château de la Maltroye's examples. Slightly cooked fruit though. Good plus. (September 2002)

NOW TO 2014   15.5

Chassagne-Montrachet, La Romanée, 2000
Domaine Morey-Coffinet

Plump, fruity, succulent, stylish and well balanced. But already à point. This is a most attractive wine, but it isn't for the long term. The 1999 is better. Very good. (January 2004)

NOW TO 2010   16.0

Chassagne-Montrachet, Les Ruchottes, 2000
Domaine Ramonet

Compared to the 1999, this is rather more loose knit and ready now. A sort of cross between 2001 and 1999. Fruity, ripe and balanced, but it lacks a little thrust. Very good plus. (May 2005)

NOW TO 2012   16.5

Chassagne-Montrachet, Tête du Clos, 2000
Domaine Vincent Dancer

Light, pretty and forward. Good fruit. Stylish. For early drinking. But attractive. Good. (September 2002)

NOW TO 2010   15.0

Chassagne-Montrachet, Les Vergets, 2000
Domaine Michel Colin-Deléger et Fils

Crisp and clean on the nose. Ripe, stylish and generously fruity on the palate. A lovely example for this lesser *climat*. Very well made. Long and complex at the end. Very good plus. (September 2002)

NOW TO 2016   16.5

Chassagne-Montrachet, Les Vergets, 2000
Domaine Genot-Boulanger

Light, but stylish and fruity on the nose. Similar palate. This has balance and interest, even length if no great depth or structure. An attractive wine. Very good. (September 2002)

NOW TO 2014   16.0

Chassagne-Montrachet, Les Vergets, 2000
Domaine Marc Morey

Good nose. Decent structure. Ripe and balanced. Slightly flat on the follow-through though. It lacks a bit of nuance. Not short though. Good. (September 2002)

NOW 2014   15.0

Chassagne-Montrachet, Les Vergets, 2000
Domaine Fernand and Laurent Pillot

A round, ripe, quite opulent nose. Good attack. Decent on the palate. It could have done with a bit more grip. Not short though. Good plus. (September 2002)

NOW TO 2016   15.5

Chassagne-Montrachet, Les Vergets, 2000
Domaine Ramonet

Fullish, rich, backward nose. A masculine wine. Not the greatest of zip. But ripe and quite opulent. It will last well. Good plus. (September 2002)

NOW TO 2016   15.5

Chassagne-Montrachet, Vide Bourse, 2000
Domaine Bernard Morey

Good grip on the nose. Full bodied, but racy and peachy. Similar to Pillot's Vide Bourse, not quite enough at the end but reasonably positive. Good length. Good style. Very good plus. (September 2002)

NOW TO 2016   16.5

Chassagne-Montrachet, Vide Bourse, 2000
Domaine Fernand and Laurent Pillot

Ripe, rich, full, positive nose. Good grip. On the palate slightly less positive, but a very good example nonetheless. (September 2002)

NOW TO 2015   16.0

Chassagne-Montrachet, En Virondot, 2000
Domaine Marc Morey

Rather pedestrian all the way through. Decent structure and balance. But no style. Not short. Just a little coarse. Not bad plus. (September 2002)

NOW TO 2015   13.5

Chevalier-Montrachet, 2000
Domaine Bouchard Père et Fils

Rather closed-in on the nose. Lots of lovely fruit on the palate. Full bodied, firm and concentrated. Very good grip. The finish is most impressive. Marvellously intense and powerful. Rich, vigorous and quite delicious. This is potentially at least fine plus. (September 2002)

2008 TO 2018   18.0

Chevalier-Montrachet, 2000
Domaine Michel Colin-Deléger et Fils

Rich, fullish, nutty and oaky nose. Quite accessible. Ample, full bodied, abundantly rich on the palate. Very good grip for a 2000. Still youthful on the follow-through. Just needed a little more zip to be great. Just very slightly top-heavy. Real depth. Only just ready. Very fine. (June 2006)

NOW TO 2015   18.5

Chevalier-Montrachet, 2000
Domaine Vincent Dancer

Overblown on the nose if not slightly oxidised. This is rather disappointing. Medium to medium-full body. Decent acidity. But not special. A bad bottle. (September 2002)

DRINK UP   14.0

Chevalier-Montrachet, 2000
Domaine Georges Deléger

Fullish, rich, classy and profound on the nose. Splendid fruit. Very lovely balance. Refined, multidimensional. Excellent. (September 2005)

2009 TO 2020   19.5

Chevalier-Montrachet, 2000
Domaine Leflaive

Very lovely complete nose. This is really excellent. Marvellously concentrated fruit with a touch of oak. This is almost perfect. Beautiful balance. Great style. Very, very long, complex and classy. Very fine indeed. (September 2002)

2009 TO 2020   19.5

Chevalier-Montrachet, 2000
Domaine Michel Niellon

Firm, rich and old viney, but a bit of sulphur at present on the nose. Adolescent. Full bodied, rich and quite alcoholic. Even burly. Lots of substance here. Very concentrated fruit. Quite how stylish, it is difficult to say. Fine plus at least. (September 2002)

2010 TO 2020   18.0

Chevalier-Montrachet, 2000
Château de Puligny-Montrachet

Light and feeble. Corked, too. But not a very good wine anyway. (September 2002)

(SEE NOTE)

Chevalier-Montrachet, 2000
Domaine Étienne Sauzet

Quite honeyed together with orange blossom on the nose. But stylish and balanced. Delicate. Lovely fruit. Medium-full body. Excellent acidity. Long. Very fine. (September 2002)

NOW TO 2019 — 18.5

Corton-Charlemagne, 2000
Domaine Bonneau du Martray

Crisp, very stylish, steely and minerally. Youthful. Medium-full body. Very composed. Gently oaky. Already delicious but best kept a year or two. (April 2005)

NOW TO 2017 — 18.5

Corton-Charlemagne, 2000
Domaine Bouchard Père et Fils

After the examples of Drouhin and Jadot, this is a little dead on the nose. It lacks the depth and the vigour on the palate. Good fruit and good grip. But a little lacking grand cru character. Yet it got better and better in the glass. Fine plus. (September 2002)

NOW TO 2016 — 18.0

Corton-Charlemagne, 2000
Domaine Bruno Clair

Ripe and quite oaky on the nose. Nicely austere. This is medium-full bodied with very good concentration and intensity. Lovely fruit. Very long. Lots of dimension. Fine plus. (January 2003)

NOW TO 2012 — 18.0

Corton-Charlemagne, 2000
Domaine Doudet-Naudin

Fragrant. Quite ripe. Gently oaky. Quite oaky. Quite decent, but no real flair or depth. Quite good at best. (February 2003)

NOW TO 2012 — 14.0

Corton-Charlemagne, 2000
Domaine Joseph Drouhin

Slightly reduced on the nose. Very lovely fruit here. Concentrated and steely. Composed and harmonious. Fullish body. Just a hint of oak (rather less than Jadot). Lovely, minerally Chardonnay. Very long. Fine, potentially. (September 2002)

NOW TO 2020 — 17.5

Corton-Charlemagne, 2000
Domaine Joseph Faiveley

Rich, full, fine colour. Not too dominated by the oak. Ripe. Good grip. Now mellow but yet with plenty of vigour. Slightly spicy because of the wood, which is certainly evident. Fine. (June 2006)

NOW TO 2015 — 17.5

Corton-Charlemagne, 2000
Domaine Genot-Boulanger

This is soft, forward and accessible. Ripe, stylish and balanced. But it doesn't show much grand cru character. Very good at best. (September 2002)

NOW TO 2013 — 16.0

Corton-Charlemagne, 2000
Domaine Louis Jadot

Full, rich, oaky nose. This is firm, ripe and concentrated. Still very young. Rich. Lots of energy and depth though. Full bodied and vigorous. Very good grip at the end. It needs time. Fine plus. (September 2002)

2008 TO 2020 — 18.0

Corton-Charlemagne, 2000
Domaine Patrick Javillier

Rich, full, steely and austere. Very good potential. Youthful. Very lovely fruit. A serious example in the Bonneau du Martray mode. Very fine. (September 2004)

2008 TO 2020+ — 18.5

Corton-Charlemagne, 2000
Domaine Pierre Morey et Fils

In many ways I could say the same about this as I said about his Pernand Sous Frétille 2000.

But more depth and character. Long. Very good indeed. (February 2003)

NOW TO 2015   17.0

Corton-Charlemagne, 2000
Maison Morey-Blanc

A little sulphur on the nose. Fullish, steely, ripe but closed-in. Difficult to assess. The fruit seems good, and the grip is there. Good style. Good length. Very good indeed. (September 2002)

NOW TO 2019   17.0

Corton-Charlemagne, 2000
Domaine Rapet Père et Fils

Good fresh, stylish, gently oaky nose. Nice and minerally. Medium-full weight. Good depth and class. Ripe and subtle. Long and really quite intense. Fine plus. (January 2003)

NOW TO 2018   18.0

Corton-Charlemagne, 2000
Domaine Rollin Père et Fils

Not really a great deal here on the attack. But what there is, is clean, balanced and fruity. The follow-through shows a bit more personality. Decent grip and steeliness at the end. But very good at best. (September 2002)

NOW TO 2015   16.0

Corton-Charlemagne, 2000
Domaine Georges Roumier et Fils

Very, very lovely nose. Cool, composed, flowery and steely. Absolutely classic. Fullish weight. Very good oaky base. Excellent grip. Ample, ripe, rich fruit. This is excellent. Really very long. Very fine indeed. But it needs time. (September 2002)

2008 TO 2020   19.5

Corton-Charlemagne, 2000
Domaine Tollot-Beaut et Fils

Slightly fat, some sulphur and a bit blowsy on the nose. It lacks sophistication. Better on the palate. Forward. It lacks a bit of grip and concentration. Boring for a *grand cru*. Quite good. (September 2002)

NOW TO 2012   14.0

Corton-Charlemagne, 2000
Maison Verget

Forward and rather overblown. A bit sweet and a bit diffuse. Light for a Corton-Charlemagne. Not too short but a bit weak. Quite good. (September 2002)

NOW TO 2010   14.0

Corton-Charlemagne, 2000
Domaine Michel Voarick

Not much flair here. Slightly heavy and sulphury. A distinct lack of zip. Oak underneath. This will get flabby. (February 2003)

NOW TO 2011   14.0

Corton-Charlemagne, 2000
Domaine de la Vougeraie

Good oak here. Stylish, subtle fruit, too. This is ripe and balanced. Quite soft for a *grand cru*. Easy to enjoy. The fruit is balanced and sophisticated. The finish is very long and lovely. Fine plus. (September 2002)

NOW TO 2016   18.0

Meursault, 2000
Domaine Arnaud Ente

A soft, flowery, quite forward, peachy example. Good fresh acidity. Positive and stylish. Good plus. (September 2002)

NOW TO 2012   15.5

Meursault, 2000
Domaine des Comtes Lafon

A ripe, gently oaky, ample, medium-full-bodied example. Lots of personality. Plenty of depth. Good grip. It will last well. Very good. (September 2002)

NOW TO 2015   16.0

Meursault, Blagny, La Jeunelotte, 2000
Domaine Martelet de Cherisey

Quite firm and backward on the nose. Good grip. This is a little ungainly, but the fruit is ripe, and the wine has depth and a positive finish. Good. (September 2002)

NOW TO 2014   15.0

Meursault, Blagny La Pièce sous le Bois, 2000
Domaine Sylvain Langoureau

A little sulphur on the nose. Quite forward. Decent fruit. Rather clumsy. Not enough grip. Fair at best. (September 2002)

DRINK SOON   13.0

Meursault, Les Bouchères, 2000
Domaine Latour-Giraud

Ripe and full. Just on the verge of being over-ripe. Quite backward. A slight touch of citrus. Very good depth and grip though. Very good. (September 2002)

NOW TO 2016   15.5

Meursault, Charmes, 2000
Domaine Michel Bouzereau et Fils

Lovely flowery nose. This is very elegant. Not too firm but neither too ephemeral. Very well balanced. Very good grip on the palate. This is fine. (June 2003)

NOW TO 2015   17.5

Meursault, Charmes, 2000
Domaine Yves Boyer-Martenot

Soft and ripe on the nose. Quite gentle, but has not as yet been in bottle very long. On the palate this is cool and composed, quite concentrated and certainly classy. Flowery and plump. But will develop quite soon. Good balance. Good plus. (June 2002)

NOW TO 2010   15.5

Meursault, Charmes, 2000
Domaine Coche-Bizouard

A little ungainly on the nose compared with Michel Bouzereau's but less evolved. Medium-full body. Good depth and grip on the palate. Still quite firm. Lovely long finish. This is fine. (September 2002)

NOW TO 2016   17.5

Meursault, Charmes, 2000
Domaine Darviot-Perrin

Subtle, understated, steely nose. Very lovely. Very pure. Medium to medium-full body. Rich, ripe and flowery. This again is a lovely example. Fine. (September 2002)

NOW TO 2016   17.5

Meursault, Charmes, 2000
Domaine des Comtes Lafon

Full, firm, but rich and composed on the nose. Good oaky base. Lovely flowery fruit. Very typically Charmes. A complete wine. Full bodied, concentrated and intense. Delicious. Excellent grip. This will last and last. Very fine plus. (September 2002)

2008 TO 2020   19.0

Meursault, Charmes, 2000
Domaine Latour-Giraud

Quite a sizeable, backward wine on the nose. Full bodied and slightly rigid, but good fruit, grip and depth underneath. Very long. Very good indeed. It needs time. (September 2002)

NOW TO 2018   17.0

Meursault, Charmes, 2000
Maison Olivier Leflaive Frères

Not a lot on the nose, but ripe and nutty on the palate. Medium to medium-full body. Good grip. This has good depth and freshness. Still needs a few years. Slightly raw at present. Good plus. (January 2003)

NOW TO 2010   15.5

Meursault, Charmes, 2000
Domaine Michelot Mère et Fille

Deeper colour than most. Just a little oxidised but not too much. Slightly edgy. Medium-full body. Good acidity. There is something a little rigid at present. But the wine has good fruit. Good plus at least. (September 2002)

NOW TO 2014   15.5

Meursault, Charmes, 2000
Domaine René Monnier

Some substance but not much flair on the nose. A little sulphur. A little four-square too. Some fruit. But only quite good. It lacks real class. (September 2002)

NOW TO 2012   14.0

Meursault, Charmes, 2000
Maison Morey-Blanc

Light, weedy and ephemeral. Decent fruit and acidity underneath. But not enough depth. Forward. Not bad. (September 2002)

NOW TO 2010   13.0

Meursault, Charmes, 2000
Domaine Guy Roulot

Slightly closed on the nose. Still youthful. Very lovely fruit though. Medium to medium-full body. Excellent grip. This is a classic. Lovely concentrated, complex fruit. Long and complex. Very fine. (September 2002)

NOW TO 2020   18.5

Meursault, Chevalières, 2000
Domaine Coche-Bizouard

Stylish, balanced, fruity nose. Medium weight. Good depth and grip. Still youthful. But no lack of personality. Good. (September 2002)

NOW TO 2012   15.0

Meursault, Clos de la Barre, 2000
Domaine des Comtes Lafon

Very good nose. Lots of depth. A slight touch of oak. Rich and ripe. Firm, oaky and long lasting. This is delicious. As always, it will beat many a *premier cru*. Very classy. Very good indeed. (September 2002)

NOW TO 2018   17.0

Meursault, Clos de Cromin, 2000
Domaine Patrick Javillier

Lots of depth here. Rich and profound. Backward. Very good harmony. Lots of fruit. Very good. It needs time. (September 2002)

NOW TO 2014   16.0

Meursault, Clos des Perrières, 2000
Domaine Albert Grivault

Better than his basic. Rich and nicely steely on the nose. Decent fruit and depth, and some oak on the palate. Not brilliant but very good. (September 2002)

NOW TO 2011   16.0

Meursault, Désirée, 2000
Domaine des Comtes Lafon

Something a bit scented and tarty on the nose. Not enough grip. Flat on the finish.

This is a bit of a disappointment. Not bad. (September 2002)

DRINK SOON   13.0

Meursault, Les Durots, 2000
Domaine Pierre Morey

Good colour. Good, plump nose. Good fruit on the palate. The tannins are ripe, but the wine is a little four-square. Good finish though. (March 2003)

NOW TO 2010   14.5

Meursault, Genevrières, 2000
Domaine Bouchard Père et Fils

Ripe, stylish and very Genevrières on the nose, with its touch of citrus peel. Full bodied, ample, rich and meaty. This has plenty of substance, depth and grip. It needs time. Slightly rigid at present. Quite exotic and new worldly. Fine. (September 2002)

NOW TO 2016   17.5

Meursault, Genevrières, 2000
Domaine Michel Bouzereau et Fils

Accessible, succulent, with very good, ripe fruit on the nose. Nicely opulent. Medium to medium-full body. Decent acidity, but the finish is just a little diffuse. Very good though. (September 2002)

NOW TO 2014   16.0

Meursault, Genevrières, 2000
Domaine des Comtes Lafon

Youthful colour. Ripe nose. Slightly fatter and with rather more character than the 2001. Plenty of depth. Fullish body. Composed, ripe and quite rich. Good grip. Still youthful. Minerally, classic and still a little closed. Plenty of vigour and dimension on the aftertaste. Long. Very good indeed. (September 2002)

NOW TO 2017   17.0

Meursault, Genevrières, 2000
Domaine Latour-Giraud

Rich, fullish nose. Very good fruit and depth. Medium-full body. Now just about ready. Rich and plump on the palate. Harmonious and classy. Lovely finish. Fine. (April 2005)

NOW TO 2012   17.5

Meursault, Genevrières, 2000
Domaine Michelot Mère et Fille

Slightly more colour than most. A bit oxidised on the nose. More so on the palate. Fruity but flat. No future. A bad bottle? (September 2002)

DRINK UP — 12.0

Meursault, Genevrières, 2000
Domaine Moret Nomine

Watery, oxidised, dirty and unpleasant. No. (September 2002)

(SEE NOTE) — 10.0

Meursault, Genevrières, 2000
Maison Morey-Blanc

Firm nose. Backward. Slightly rigid as well as closed-in. Decent fruit but a certain lack of style. This is ripe but essentially clumsy. Only fair. (September 2002)

NOW TO 2011 — 13.5

Meursault, Les Gouttes d'Or, 2000
Domaine Coche-Bizouard

Ripe, ample, stylish and balanced. Lovely, flowery fruit. Good depth. Long and positive. This is very good plus. (September 2002)

NOW TO 2016 — 16.5

Meursault, Les Gouttes d'Or, 2000
Domaine Darnat

Flat, coarse and lumpy. Some built-in sulphur. No. (September 2002)

DRINK UP — 11.0

Meursault, Les Gouttes d'Or, 2000
Domaine Arnaud Ente

Good grip. Nicely peachy. A bit corked but not so much as to hide what is at least a good plus example. Very good acidity, similar to his basic Meursault. Very good. (September 2002)

NOW TO 2016 — 16.0

Meursault, Les Gouttes d'Or, 2000
Domaine Jean-Michel Gaunoux

Hard and cheap on the nose. Rather too much sulphur and not enough style. Good acidity. Quite firm. But a bit edgy. Not bad. (September 2002)

DRINK SOON — 13.0

Meursault, Les Gouttes d'Or, 2000
Domaine des Comtes Lafon

Light but flowery. Decent fruit but not the greatest depth and style. Good acidity. Forward. Quite good plus. (September 2002)

NOW TO 2011 — 14.5

Meursault, Les Gouttes d'Or, 2000
Domaine Bernard Millot

Rather too much built-in sulphur on the nose. Underneath a decent wine with medium body and good fruit. But only not bad plus. (September 2002)

DRINK SOON — 13.5

Meursault, Les Grands Charrons, 2000
Domaine Vincent Dancer

Soft, gently oaky, forward but stylish nose. Quite concentrated. Very attractive fruit. Ripe and elegant. Very good. (September 2002)

NOW TO 2011 — 15.0

Meursault, Les Gruyaches, 2000
Domaine Jean-Philippe Fichet

Fuller and firmer than his Tessons. Slightly more four-square. But attractive fruit and good grip. Good plus too. (September 2002)

NOW TO 2012 — 15.5

Meursault, Les Meix Chavaux, 2000
Domaine Franck Grux

Soft, ripe, forward and fruity. Good style. It lacks a bit of grip and depth, but quite good. (January 2003)

DRINK SOON — 14.0

Meursault, Narvaux, 2000
Domaine Borgeot

Slightly pedestrian nose. A touch of built-in sulphur. Better on the palate. Clean and crisp. Good fruit if not much elegance. Balanced. Good. (March 2003)

NOW TO 2009 — 15.0

Meursault, Les Perrières, 2000
Domaine Bouchard Père et Fils

Flowery on the nose, but is it a little diffuse? Ripe and balanced on the palate. But more

Meursault Charmes in character than Perrières. This is stylish, long and very good indeed. (September 2002)

NOW TO 2015   17.0

Meursault, Les Perrières, 2000
Domaine Yves Boyer-Martenot

A little more vigour and grip on the nose than their Charmes. Very good depth on the palate. It seems to have more life and concentration than the Charmes. Very impressive on the follow-through. Properly minerally, as it should be. Lots of potential for ageing. Very good indeed. (June 2002)

NOW TO 2017   17.0

Meursault, Les Perrières, 2000
Domaine Jean-François Coche-Dury

Quite a deep colour, surprisingly. Cool, classy nose. Concentrated and classic. Full bodied, concentrated, intense and composed on the palate. Very, very lovely. This is well-nigh perfect. Marvellous depth. Brilliant. A great wine! (September 2002)

NOW TO 2020   20.0

Meursault, Les Perrières, 2000
Domaine Coutoux

Rather an un-Meursault nose. Very curious. Not entirely clean. A burnt touch from the oak underneath. Rigid. Ungainly. Good grip. Not bad. (September 2002)

DRINK SOON   13.0

Meursault, Les Perrières, 2000
Domaine Vincent Dancer

Quite pleasant and stylish, but a little on the light side. Yet decent length. Good fruit. But forward. Good plus. (September 2002)

DRINK SOON   15.5

Meursault, Les Perrières, 2000
Domaine Darviot-Perrin

Properly steely and minerally. Composed. Pure and discreet. This is very lovely. Medium-full body. Excellent balance. Very long. Very classy. Very fine. (September 2002)

NOW TO 2018   18.5

Meursault, Les Perrières, 2000
Domaine Joseph Drouhin

This has a lovely nose. Understated and intense. Medium to medium-full body. Concentrated and minerally. Very fine fruit and harmony. Long. Very classy. Very fine. (September 2002)

NOW TO 2018   18.5

Meursault, Les Perrières, 2000
Domaine Jean-Michel Gaunoux

Better than his Goutte d'Or, but similarly rigid. Good acidity but a little ungainly. Good fruit. Medium-full body. Certainly quite good. But will it get any better? (September 2002)

NOW TO 2010   14.0

Meursault, Les Perrières, 2000
Domaine Albert Grivault

Soft and sulphury on the nose. Cleaner on the palate. Decent fruit and decent acidity, but rather rigid and unstylish. Forward. Fair. (September 2002)

DRINK SOON   13.5

Meursault, Les Perrières, 2000
Domaine Louis Jadot

Less open on the nose than Drouhin's. More oaky on the palate. Very concentrated. Very intense. Very lovely steely character. Long. Fine plus. (September 2002)

NOW TO 2018   18.0

Meursault, Les Perrières, 2000
Domaine des Comtes Lafon

While not as totally brilliant as Coche-Dury's (or indeed as good as the Charmes this year) this is balanced, concentrated and complete. Lovely fruit. Fullish body. Very good grip. Long and most impressive. Very fine. (September 2002)

NOW TO 2018   18.5

Meursault, Les Perrières, 2000
Domaine Latour-Giraud
Fresh, concentrated, pure and minerally. Fullish body. Very well balanced. Very stylish. This has a lot of depth and class. Long and lovely. Fine quality. (October 2003)
NOW TO 2016   17.5

Meursault, Les Perrières, 2000
Maison Olivier Leflaive Frères
Good, steely nose. Medium-full body. Virile. Very good grip. Minerally and racy as it should be. Fine finish. Very good indeed. (October 2003)
NOW TO 2012   17.0

Meursault, Les Perrières, 2000
Domaine Moret Nomine
Ripe, but forward and slightly diffuse on the nose. Medium body. Quite fruity. Certainly clean, but it tails off. Quite stylish, but not enough grip and concentration. Good at best. (September 2002)
NOW TO 2011   15.0

Meursault, Les Perrières, 2000
Domaine Pierre Morey
Rather more closed-in and adolescent today than the 1999. But on the palate also minerally, profound and elegant. The fruit and the grip are both there. Full bodied, rich, fat and indeed concentrated. Still very youthful. Not quite the intensity of the 1999 but fine for the vintage. (March 2003)
NOW TO 2014   17.5

Meursault, Perrières, 2000
Domaine Guy Roulot
Full, rich, ripe and steely. Very lovely pure, slightly closed-in fruit. Excellent grip. Excellent fruit. Even better than his Charmes. Very long. This is really very fine. (September 2002)
NOW TO 2018   19.0

Meursault, Le Porusot, 2000
Domaine Latour-Giraud
Quite an orange colour. This is not too overblown on the palate. Decent peachy flavours and good acidity. But slightly raw. And it lacks style. Quite good. (September 2002)
NOW TO 2010   14.0

Meursault, Rougeots, 2000
Maison Verget
Reasonable weight and class on the nose. Some oak. Forward. Nicely sweet-sour character. Good acidity. Medium body. Very good for a village example. (March 2003)
DRINK SOON   15.5

Meursault, Santenots, 2000
Domaine du Marquis d'Angerville
Gently oaky, fragrant, medium body. Good freshness. Not a bit heavy or rigid. Indeed elegant and individual. Flowery. Very good. (June 2003)
NOW TO 2009   16.0

Meursault, Tessons, 2000
Domaine Jean-Philippe Fichet
Slightly raw, but good depth and grip on the nose, and with a stylish touch of oak. Good, elegant, medium-bodied wine. Very good grip. Positive. Long finish. Good plus. (September 2002)
NOW TO 2012   15.5

Meursault, Tessons, 2000
Domaine Pierre Morey
Firm, rich, quite profound, but youthful and closed-in on the nose. Some sulphur (?) sugar. Underneath there is good depth. But it is difficult to see the class. Quite good. (September 2002)
NOW TO 2014   14.0

Meursault, Tête de Murger, 2000
Domaine Patrick Javillier
This is even better than his Clos du Cromin. Full body. Very good grip. Lovely fruit. Lots of depth, even concentration. Very good persistence. Very good. (September 2002)
NOW TO 2014   16.0

Meursault, Les Tillets, 2000
Domaine Patrick Javillier

Slightly adolescent but fullish and very fresh. Youthful. Very good potential. Nicely mineral. Very good for what it is. (September 2004)

NOW TO 2012   15.5

Le Montrachet, 2000
Domaine Bouchard Père et Fils

Full, very rich and very closed on the nose. Lots of wine here. Excellent grip. Full bodied, concentrated, vigorous and very youthful. But excellent potential. Very, very lovely, rich fruit. Very, very long. Splendid. This is very fine indeed. (September 2002)

2010 TO 2020+   19.5

Le Montrachet, 2000
Domaine Marc Colin

A little light and also a touch overblown on the nose. Much better on the palate. Rich, full bodied, creamy, old viney and concentrated. Excellent grip. This is very lovely. Very long and classy. Fine plus but not great. (September 2002)

2009 TO 2019   18.5

Le Montrachet, 2000
Maison Vincent Girardin

Quite high toned—lemon sherbet—on the nose. Medium to medium-full weight. Decent grip. But not really the depth and sheer aristocracy of the *climat*. Fine but not great. (September 2002)

NOW TO 2016   17.5

Le Montrachet, 2000
Domaine du Marquis de Laguiche/
Maison Joseph Drouhin

This is very classy and very composed, and not as backward as some on the nose. Medium-full body. Ripe, classy and very harmonious. Very lovely fruit. Excellent grip. Long. Very, very lovely. Real finesse. Super. (September 2002)

2009 TO 2019   19.5

Montrachet, 2000
Maison Olivier Leflaive Frères

This has the volume and concentration Olivier Leflaive's Bâtard lacks. Rich and full bodied. Very good grip. Lots of substance here. Still very youthful. Fine plus. (September 2003)

2008 TO 2018   18.0

Le Montrachet, 2000
Domaine Jacques Prieur

Fat, rich and concentrated. A little closed. Plenty of depth. But not a lot of distinction. Lots of substance here. But not the class or character of what it should be. Developed considerably in the glass. After an hour and a top up, unmistakably fine. (August 2002)

NOW TO 2012   17.5

Le Montrachet, 2000
Domaine de la Romanée-Conti

Slightly heavy on the nose at this stage. Quite a big, muscular wine. Full of fruit. Showing a little sulphur. And not the greatest length or zip. Quite powerful at the end. Fine but not great. (November 2002)

DRINK SOON   18.0

Le Montrachet, 2000
Maison Étienne Sauzet

A little more new oak than in Girardin's example. Good weight. Good richness. Fullish body. Decent but not the greatest grip. Ample, but it lacks a bit of personality, for a Le Montrachet, this is dull. (September 2002)

NOW TO 2016   17.0

Pernand-Vergelesses, En Caradeux, 2000
Domaine Rapet Père et Fils

Lightish in colour. Fragrant and flowery, and gently oaky and stylish on both nose and palate. Quite different from a Meursault/Puligny/Chassagne. Medium body. But quite intense. Fresh, balanced and elegant. Very clean. Good plus. (January 2003)

DRINK SOON   15.5

Pernand-Vergelesses, Sous Frétille, 2000
Domaine Pierre Marey et Fils
Good fruit. It lacks a little character, but clean if slightly four-square. (February 2003)
DRINK SOON   13.5

Puligny-Montrachet, 2000
Domaine Bouchard Père et Fils
A fine example of a village wine. Clean and pure. Lovely fruit. Balanced. Medium to medium-full body. Lots of depth. Very good. (March 2003)
NOW TO 2009   16.0

Puligny-Montrachet, 2000
Domaine Gérard Chavy et Fils
Clean. Crisp. Very peachy. Lovely style. Very good indeed for what it is. Ready. (February 2003)
NOW TO 2010   17.0

Puligny-Montrachet, Les Caillerets, 2000
Domaine Hubert de Montille
Still reticent. But very classy. Rich but restrained. Harmonious and discreetly peachy. Medium-full body. Fine. (February 2005)
NOW TO 2017   17.5

Puligny-Montrachet, Les Chalumaux, 2000
Domaine Sylvain Langoureau
Some SO$_2$. Decent fruit, but a bit short. Clean. Forward. Boring. (September 2002)
DRINK SOON   13.5

Puligny-Montrachet, Les Chalumaux, 2000
Maison Olivier Leflaive Frères
Soft, flowery nose. A bit light, but decent grip and quite stylish. Fresh at the end. This has charm. But it is essentially quite delicate. Good plus. (January 2003)
DRINK SOON   15.5

Puligny-Montrachet, Les Chalumaux, 2000
Domaine Martelet de Cherisey
Good fruit and depth. Ripe. Good grip. This is stylish, and rather more interesting and positive than most examples. It will last well. Very good plus. (September 2002)
NOW TO 2015   16.5

Puligny-Montrachet, Champ Canet, 2000
Domaine Jean-Marc Boillot
Full, slightly "hot," but good substance and depth here, even concentration. Very good grip. Plenty of fruit. Plenty of quality. Better than his Referts. Long. It will last well. (September 2002)
NOW TO 2016+   17.0

Puligny-Montrachet, Champ Canet, 2000
Domaine Louis Carillon et Fils
Splendid, ample fruit on the nose. Ripe, balanced and stylish. More substance than Sauzet's, less than Jean-Marc Boillot's. Plump and succulent, concentrated and balanced on the palate. Very lovely. Fine plus. (September 2002)
NOW TO 2016   18.0

Puligny-Montrachet, Champ Canet, 2000
Domaine Latour-Giraud
Crisp, racy, decently substantial and stylish on the nose. Ripe and elegant on the palate. Positive. Very good. (September 2002)
NOW TO 2016   16.0

Puligny-Montrachet, Champ Canet, 2000
Maison Olivier Leflaive Frères
Good nose. Ripe, balanced, positive and elegant. On the palate medium-full body, plenty of depth and grip. This still needs time. Splendidly peachy and long on the palate. Very good indeed. (January 2003)
NOW TO 2012   17.0

Puligny-Montrachet, Champ Canet, 2000
Domaine Étienne Sauzet
Lovely nose. This is ripe, quite delicate, but complex and with a lot of finesse. The palate is also very impressive. Again delicate, especially after Jean-Marc Boillot's example, but lovely nonetheless. Fine. (September 2002)
NOW TO 2015   17.5

Puligny-Montrachet, Champ Gain, 2000
Maison Vincent Girardin
Quite forward. Decent fruit. Lighter in weight than other Girardin Pulignys. Stylish and balanced. Good plus. (September 2002)
NOW TO 2012   15.5

Puligny-Montrachet, Le Clavoillon, 2000
Domaine Gérard Chavy et Fils

A slight touch of sulphur on the nose. A similar lack of high tones when compared to that of Leflaive, but rather less concentrated and rather more blowsy. This is uninspiring. Quite good at best. (September 2002)

NOW TO 2010   14.0

Puligny-Montrachet, Le Clavoillon, 2000
Domaine Leflaive

As usual a little four-square on the nose. Not as interesting as their Folatières. As so often, it lacks high tones. Fullish bodied and rich though. And plenty of substance here. Very good plus. Will keep well. (September 2002)

NOW TO 2016   16.5

Puligny-Montrachet, Clos du Cailleret, 2000
Domaine des Lambrays

Full bodied and rich, and with more concentration and personality than their Folatières, and a touch more oak. Excellent grip and finish. A very fine example. Bravo! (January 2003)

NOW TO 2020   18.5

Puligny-Montrachet, Clos de la Garenne, 2000
Domaine Joseph Drouhin

Fullish, rich, fat and fruity, and with very good grip. This is profound and concentrated. Very lovely. Fine plus. (September 2002)

NOW TO 2016   18.0

Puligny-Montrachet, Les Combettes, 2000
Domaine Jean-Marc Boillot

Fullish and ripe, but just a little flat on the attack. The finish is better. Reasonable grip and depth. Still a bit adolescent. But it doesn't quite sing. Merely very good. (September 2002)

NOW TO 2016   16.0

Puligny-Montrachet, Les Combettes, 2000
Domaine Louis Carillon et Fils

Ripe, rich, concentrated and succulent on the nose. Subtle, clean and positive on the palate. Ripe. Very good grip. This is fine plus. (September 2002)

NOW TO 2016   18.0

Puligny-Montrachet, Les Combettes, 2000
Domaine Roland Maraslovac

A bit tight at the start, but after it developed in the glass, one had a fullish wine with no lack of class and distinction. Plenty of depth. Still needs time. Very good indeed. (June 2003)

NOW TO 2014   17.0

Puligny-Montrachet, Les Demoiselles, 2000
Domaine Guy Amiot et Fils

Soft, stylish fruit. Balanced but delicate. Just a whiff of sulphur. This has quality, but it lacks a bit of concentration and zip. Very pleasant but not enough depth for what it is. Very good at best. (September 2002)

NOW TO 2015   16.0

Puligny-Montrachet, Les Enseignères, 2000
Maison Vincent Girardin

Ripe, peachy, positive nose. This is very good for a village example. Not the greatest of grip, but fresh and stylish. Good. (September 2002)

NOW TO 2012   15.0

Puligny-Montrachet, Les Enseignères, 2000
Maison Verget

Slightly over the top and blowsy on the nose. Similar on the palate. No depth. No grip. No style. (September 2002)

DRINK SOON   11.0

Puligny-Montrachet, Les Folatières, 2000
Domaine Roger Caillot

Good, positive, classy nose. Good depth here. Quite fat. Medium-full weight. Good richness and class. Good follow-through. Plump, balanced and long. Fine. (April 2005)

NOW TO 2012   17.5

Puligny-Montrachet, Les Folatières, 2000
Domaine Gérard Chavy et Fils

Good colour. Ripe and fruity. Good concentration and style. A very good example, if quite forward. Elegant and nicely peachy. Good plus. (September 2002)

NOW TO 2012   15.5

Puligny-Montrachet, Les Folatières, 2000
Domaine Joseph Drouhin

This is very well made. Lovely steely fruit. Ripe and balanced. Good intensity. Medium-full body. Subtle. Long. Very good indeed. (September 2002)

NOW TO 2016   17.0

Puligny-Montrachet, Les Folatières, 2000
Domaine Genot-Boulanger

Rather better than I thought in cask—in most cases it is the opposite. Good concentration. Good grip and very stylish, peachy fruit. This is very good indeed. (September 2002)

NOW TO 2016   17.0

Puligny-Montrachet, Les Folatières, 2000
Domaine des Lambrays

This is very lovely. Full and rich, with lots of mouthfeel. Yet not a bit heavy. Balanced and concentrated with a good, peachy, steely acidity. Long and youthful. Fine. (January 2003)

NOW TO 2016   17.5

Puligny-Montrachet, Les Folatières, 2000
Domaine Leflaive

Fullish, firm, profound and backward. But very good fruit on the nose. Good ample, ripe wine. Decent acidity. Fullish body. Fine. Still very young. Will last well. (September 2002)

NOW TO 2016   17.5

Puligny-Montrachet, Les Folatières, 2000
Domaine René Monnier

Slightly four-square. Ripe and quite stylish. Good grip and depth. Decent fruit. It lacks a little nuance. Very good though. Will last well. (September 2002)

NOW TO 2016   16.0

Puligny-Montrachet, Les Folatières, 2000
Domaine Moret-Nominé

Rather blowsy and oxidised on the nose. A bit weak on the palate. Fruity but forward. Some style. Not too loose. Quite good. (September 2002)

NOW TO 2010   14.0

Puligny-Montrachet, Les Folatières, 2000
Domaine Paul Pernot et Fils

Lovely peachy, orange-blossom fruit on the nose. Medium-full body. Ripe, balanced, concentrated and intense. This has a lot of style. Long and lovely. Excellent finish. Fine plus. (September 2002)

NOW TO 2016   18.0

Puligny-Montrachet, Les Folatières, 2000
Maison Étienne Sauzet

The Folatières is a bought-in Sauzet. This is not as good as his domaine wines. Fresh and fruity, but no depth or concentration. Not short. Just rather raw and rather dull. Quite good at best. (September 2002)

NOW TO 2012   14.0

Puligny-Montrachet, La Garenne, 2000
Domaine Sylvain Langoureau

Better than his Chalumaux. Less sulphur. More fruit. Similarly forward though. A decent example for drinking soon. (September 2002)

NOW TO 2010   14.0

Puligny-Montrachet, La Garenne, 2000
Domaine Larue

Not much on the nose. Decent acidity and style, but a bit lightweight. The finish is positive though. Quite good plus. (September 2002)

NOW TO 2013   14.5

Puligny-Montrachet, La Garenne, 2000
Domaine Étienne Sauzet

Light, but balanced and stylish. Fruity, fragrant and forward. Nothing much here. But what there is is pretty. Quite good. (September 2002)

NOW TO 2011   14.0

Puligny-Montrachet, Les Garennes, 2000
Maison Olivier Leflaive Frères

Just a little weak both on nose and palate. Not enough grip, nor enough volume. The fruit is pretty, and the wine is not short. But quite good at best. (January 2003)

DRINK SOON   14.0

Puligny-Montrachet, Hameau de Blagny, 2000
Domaine Martelet de Cherisey

Soft, fruity, stylish and balanced on the nose. Somewhat light and forward, but good. (September 2002)

NOW TO 2012   15.0

Puligny-Montrachet, Hameau de Blagny, 2000
Maison Antonin Rodet

Light and soft. A little dilute and neutral on the nose. Clean and crisp. But not enough depth for a *premier cru*. Quite stylish and not too short nevertheless. (August 2002)

DRINK SOON   15.0

Puligny-Montrachet, Les Perrières, 2000
Domaine Louis Carillon et Fils

Delicious. Pure, steely and beautifully ripe. Balanced and harmonious. Medium-full body. Very long and complex. Very classy. Fine. (June 2003)

NOW TO 2014   17.5

Puligny-Montrachet, Les Perrières, 2000
Domaine Gérard Chavy et Fils

Just a little blowsy on the nose. But good fruit and style. Slightly weak. Slightly short. But pleasant. Forward. Quite good. (September 2002)

NOW TO 2009   14.0

Puligny-Montrachet, Les Perrières, 2000
Maison Vincent Girardin

This has plenty of depth, style and very good acidity. Ample, rich and backward. Very elegant. Plump and rich. Long. It will last well. Fine. (September 2002)

NOW TO 2016   17.5

Puligny-Montrachet, Les Pucelles, 2000
Domaine Jean Boillot et Fils

Medium weight. *À point*. Succulent and peachy. Gently oaky. Plenty of character. Well balanced. Very good plus if not the depth and vigour for fine. (May 2004)

NOW TO 2010   16.5

Puligny-Montrachet, Les Pucelles, 2000
Domaine Gérard Chavy et Fils

A soft, ripe, very charming, very flowery and fruity nose. Forward. A little flat and short at the end. For early drinking. Quite good plus. (September 2002)

DRINK SOON   14.5

Puligny-Montrachet, Les Pucelles, 2000
Maison Joseph Drouhin

This is lovely. Really stylish, cool, balanced, ripe fruit. Good structure. Subtle. Long. This will last. Very classy. Fine plus. (September 2002)

NOW TO 2016   18.0

Puligny-Montrachet, Les Pucelles, 2000
Domaine Leflaive

Fullish, rich, stylish, concentrated and backward. Excellent grip. This is a positive and intense wine, built to last. Really good grip, and concentration and vigour on the palate. Very fine. (September 2002)

NOW TO 2016+   18.5

Puligny-Montrachet, Les Referts, 2000
Domaine Jean-Marc Boillot

Ripe, rich and opulent on the nose. Fullish body. Fresh, balanced and positive. Slightly hot on the palate. Very good though. (September 2002)

NOW TO 2016   16.0

Puligny-Montrachet, Les Referts, 2000
Domaine Louis Carillon et Fils

This is very lovely and rather superior to their Perrières today. Full bodied, rich and firm. Very, very well mannered and harmonious. Very, very lovely fruit. Super. Fine plus. (September 2002)

NOW TO 2016   18.0

Puligny-Montrachet, Les Referts, 2000
Domaine Benoit Ente

Rather anonymous on the nose. Flat and dilute on the palate. Not blowsy though. Some style at least. Quite good. (September 2002)

NOW TO 2010   14.0

Puligny-Montrachet, Les Referts, 2000
Domaine Jean-Philippe Fichet

Good, fresh, quite firm nose. Decent fruit on the palate if not much nuance. But well made. Good grip. Will still develop. Good plus. (September 2002)

NOW TO 2015   15.5

Puligny-Montrachet, Les Referts, 2000
Maison Vincent Girardin
Good firm, stylish nose. Ripe and balanced. Not the depth of fruit of his Perrières, but long, positive and very good plus.
NOW TO 2016   16.5

Puligny-Montrachet, Les Referts, 2000
Maison Louis Jadot
Ripe and stylish if not quite the thrust on the nose that I had hoped for. Medium-full body. Very good fruit. Decent acidity. On the follow-through just a little overripe, and it lacks a bit of grip. Fullish in substance and a positive finish though. Good plus. (September 2002)
NOW TO 2012   15.5

Puligny-Montrachet, Les Referts, 2000
Domaine Étienne Sauzet
Fullish, rich, balanced and stylish. Rather more substance than other Sauzet wines here. Good depth. Positive finish. Very good indeed.
(September 2002)
NOW TO 2016   17.0

Puligny-Montrachet, Sous le Puits, 2000
Domaine Jean-Claude Bachelet
Good structure and depth for this *climat*. Decent acidity. A touch of oak. Quite appley. But good. It finishes positively. (September 2002)
NOW TO 2014   15.0

Puligny-Montrachet, Sous le Puits, 2000
Maison Verget
Better than their Enseignères, but similarly weak and blowsy. Ripe but very forward. Not bad plus. (September 2002)
NOW TO 2010   13.5

Puligny-Montrachet, La Truffière, 2000
Domaine Michel Colin-Deléger et Fils
This has got what Bernard Morey's wine lacks: the grip. Fullish body. Lots of intensity at the end. Very classy. Lots of depth and class. Lovely style. Very long. Fine. (September 2002)
NOW TO 2016   17.5

Puligny-Montrachet, La Truffière, 2000
Domaine Bernard Morey
Good, ample fruit if not quite the grip of acidity here. Decent substance and good style. Not short. But no better than very good.
(September 2002)
NOW TO 2015   16.0

Saint-Aubin, Le Charmois, 2000
Domaine Bernard Morey
Bernard Morey's 2000s are consistently good, and this is no exception. Fullish body. Fresh and peachy. Plenty of depth and class. Long, ripe and very good plus. (October 2002)
NOW TO 2010   16.5

Saint-Aubin, Le Charmois, 2000
Domaine Jean-Marc Morey
Soft, ripe, flowery-peachy, elegant nose. Medium weight. Good fruit. Balanced, clean and stylish. Very good. (October 2002)
NOW TO 2010   16.0

Saint-Aubin, Clos de la Chatenière, 2000
Domaine Hubert Lamy et Fils
Magnum. Fragrant, flowery, peachy nose. Good depth, and plenty of class and interest. Medium to medium-full body. Long. Elegant. Now *à point*. Very good. (September 2004)
NOW TO 2010   16.0

Saint-Aubin, Les Murgers des
Dents de Chien, 2000
Domaine Hubert Lamy et Fils
Crisp and clean. Ready for drinking. Very classy. Very minerally. Lovely style and plenty of depth. Very good. (June 2004)
DRINK SOON   16.0

Saint-Aubin, En Remilly, 2000
Domaine Larue
Amply fruity. Good depth and volume. Ripe and stylish. This is a very good example with a gentle touch of wood and a long, positive finish.
(March 2003)
DRINK SOON   15.5

Vougeot, Clos Blanc, 2000
Domaine de la Vougeraie
The first truly fine example of the wine from this
climat. Very individual. Gently oaky. Fresh. Yet
fullish bodied. Elegant and nutty. Fine. (June 2004)
NOW TO 2009   17.5

REDS

Aloxe-Corton, 2000
Domaine François Gay et Fils
Ripe, slightly chocolaty fruit. Good depth. Very
stylish and very positive at the end. (February 2003)
NOW TO 2010   16.0

Aloxe-Corton, 2000
Domaine Daniel Largeot
A slight astringency. Fruity but it lacks fresh-
ness. (February 2003)
DRINK SOON   12.0

Aloxe-Corton, 2000
Domaine Maillard Père et Fils
Good style, depth and quality of fruit for what it
is. Clean. Good personality. Good. (February 2003)
NOW TO 2010   15.0

Aloxe-Corton, 2000
Domaine Michel Voarick
This has good fruit and substance. And more
depth than most at this level. Not that stylish,
but fresh and harmonious. Good. (February 2003)
NOW TO 2011   15.0

Aloxe-Corton, Les Fournières, 2000
Domaine Tollot-Beaut et Fils
Very good colour. Quite a firm nose. And quite a
lot of tannin on the palate. It is even a bit stewed.
Good fruit and good grip. But the astringency
dominates. Will this soften? (March 2003)
NOW TO 2012   15.0

Aloxe-Corton, Les Grandes Lolières, 2000
Domaine Maillard Père et Fils
Premier cru. Good crisp fruit. Gently oaky. Good
substance. Fresh, succulent and charming.
Quite forward but good plus. (February 2003)
NOW TO 2010   15.5

Aloxe-Corton, Les Maréchaudes, 2000
Domaine Doudet-Naudin
Some fruit. But no style or balance. Short. No.
(February 2003)
DRINK UP   11.5

Aloxe-Corton, Les Moutottes, 2000
Domaine Capitain-Gagnerot
Above Ladoix. Better colour. Better substance.
This is fruity, fragrant and elegant. Nicely bal-
anced. Fresh. Good plus. (February 2003)
NOW TO 2010   15.5

Beaune, Bressandes, 2000
Domaine Albert Morot
Medium to medium-full colour. Not much
depth on the nose. Less to it than the Teurons.
Diffuse follow-through. A bit thin. (July 2004)
DRINK SOON   12.0

Beaune, Cent Vignes, 2000
Domaine Albert Morot
Medium-full colour. Quite succulent, ripe nose.
Good depth. Some substance. Not a lot of class but
a decent follow-through. Quite good. (July 2004)
NOW TO 2010   14.0

Beaune, Champs Pimont, 2000
Domaine Jacques Prieur
Good, quite rich, peachy nose. Not too heavy
nor too square. Quite full and honeyed on the
palate. Just a little hot but good plus. No lack of
depth. (August 2002)
NOW TO 2009   15.5

Beaune, Clos des Avaux, 2000
Maison Antonin Rodet
Good colour. Fullish, plump, balanced and succu-
lent. Medium to medium-full body. Very good style
and length. Lovely finish. Very good. (August 2005)
NOW TO 2014   16.0

Beaune, Clos des Perrières, 2000
Domaine François Gay et Fils
Quite firm for a 2000. Good grip and depth.
Lovely fruit. This is very good. (February 2003)
NOW TO 2014   16.0

Beaune, Clos du Roi, 2000
Domaine Tollot-Beaut et Fils
Medium colour. Some development. Light, fragrant nose. Ripe and fruity. Medium body. Decent acidity. Quite stylish if no real depth or dimension. Positive at the end though. Quite good. (July 2004)
NOW TO 2010   14.0

Beaune, Clos des Ursules, 2000
Domaine Louis Jadot
Medium-full colour. Rich nose. Good weight. Medium body. Ripe and positive on the palate. Good grip. Some succulence. Good. (July 2004)
NOW TO 2012   15.0

Beaune, Coucherias, 2000
Domaine Pierre Labet
Good colour. Decent, plump nose. A bit sweet, a bit astringent and a bit thin on the palate. Spurious. (March 2003)
DRINK SOON   13.5

Beaune, Les Cras, 2000
Domaine Germain Père et Fils/
Château de Chorey-lès-Beaune
More freshness and fragrance than last time out, if I remember correctly. Rich, full, ripe and abundant on the nose. Medium body. Fresh, round and ample. Very good. (September 2004)
DRINK SOON   16.0

Beaune, En Genêt, 2000
Domaine Arnoux Père et Fils
A *premier cru* above Clos du Roi. Balanced, fresh and elegant. Good depth. Very good style. Plenty of depth for a 2000. (February 2003)
NOW TO 2013   15.5

Beaune, Grèves, 2000
Domaine Bouchard Père et Fils
Medium colour. Fragrant nose. Good class and balance. But a bit watery and fruitless on the palate. Dilute. Lacks charm. (July 2004)
DRINK SOON   12.5

Beaune, Les Grèves, 2000
Domaine Michel Gay
Good depth and style. Succulent and quite concentrated. Very good indeed for a 2000. (February 2003)
NOW TO 2013   17.0

Beaune, Grèves, 2000
Domaine Michel Lafarge
The vines are 75 years old. Medium to medium-full, youthful colour. Ripe nose. Stylish. Not much tannin, but good structure and good balance. Medium to medium-full body. No aggressivity. Quite forward but elegant, and not lacking intensity and smoothness. The charm is beginning to come out now. It got better and better in the glass. Good plus. (September 2004)
NOW TO 2012   15.5

Beaune, Grèves, 2000
Domaine Daniel Largeot
This is quite fresh. But only medium body. Nicely fruity. But quite forward, even for a 2000. Stylish though. Positive finish. (February 2003)
DRINK SOON   14.0

Beaune, Grèves, 2000
Domaine Albert Morot
Medium to medium-full colour. Decent fruit on the nose. Lacks a bit of fruit and succulence on the palate. Medium body. Reasonably positive follow-through and finish. Quite good. (July 2004)
NOW TO 2010   14.0

Beaune, Grèves, 2000
Domaine Charles Thomas
Medium-full colour. Chunky nose. Some caramel, some chocolate. Lacks a bit of fruit and succulence on the palate. Not bad at best. (July 2004)
DRINK SOON   13.0

Beaune, Montrevenots, 2000
Domaine Vincent Dancer
Medium-full colour. Fresh, light nose. Fresh palate. A little obviously chaptalised. Will get astringent. Nothing special here. (July 2004)
DRINK SOON   12.0

Beaune, Pertuisots, 2000
Domaine Devevey

Medium-full colour. A little thin on the nose. Thin and fruitless on the palate. Poor. (July 2004)

DRINK SOON   11.5

Beaune, Teurons, 2000
Domaine Albert Morot

Medium colour. Some development. Light, spicy nose. Light fruity palate. Not much to it. Will get astringent. Not bad. (July 2004)

DRINK SOON   13.0

Beaune, Les Toussaints, 2000
Domaine Michel Gay

A little astringency here. But good fruit underneath. Lacks a little grip and style. Quite good. (February 2003)

NOW TO 2010   14.0

Beaune, Les Vignes Franches, 2000
Domaine Germain Père et Fils/
Château de Chorey-lès-Beaune

Medium to medium-full colour. Some development. Soft nose. A bit one-dimensional, but some fruit and not unstylish. Light on the palate. Quite ripe but not much depth. Decently positive finish. Quite good. Ready. (September 2005)

NOW TO 2009   14.0

Bonnes Mares, 2000
Domaine Bouchard Père et Fils

Medium-full colour. The nose is a bit hidden. Fullish. Some tannin. Somewhat four-square. It lacks a little flair. Good fruit and decent grip. But a bit adolescent. Good plus. (July 2004)

NOW TO 2017   15.5

Bonnes Mares, 2000
Domaine Drouhin-Laroze

Medium to medium-full colour. Rich, succulent nose. Fullish and ample. But closed-in. On the palate this is ripe and well balanced. Medium-full body. Slightly rigid. Very good but not brilliant. But better than expected. (July 2004)

NOW TO 2020   16.0

Bonnes Mares, 2000
Domaine Robert Groffier

Very good colour. Splendidly concentrated on the nose, especially for a 2000. Still a little austere at first. Full body. Some tannin. A bit closed-in. Excellent fruit. Very good grip. Most impressive. Marvellous finish. (October 2002)

NOW TO 2020   19.0

Bonnes Mares, 2000
Domaine Louis Jadot

Medium-full colour. Rich, ample, full but generous nose. This is very lovely. Full bodied, rich, fat and complete. Good tannin. Opulent but with very, very good grip. Fresh and very stylish. Super. (July 2004)

2010 TO 2025   18.5

Bonnes Mares, 2000
Domaine Jacques-Frédéric Mugnier

One-third new oak. Good backbone. Plums rather than raspberries. A little unresolved tannin. Good acidity. I find this more promising than his Amoureuses today. But the Amoureuses is more elegant. (June 2003)

2008 TO 2020+   18.5

Bonnes Mares, 2000
Domaine Georges Roumier et Fils

Medium-full colour. Rich, backward nose. Good attack. But a slight lack of vigour in the middle. Ripe and succulent. Ample, ripe and seemingly good grip. Yet it doesn't convince. Very good plus at best. (July 2004)

NOW TO 2020   16.5

Bonnes Mares, 2000
Domaine Comte Georges de Vogüé

Medium-full colour. High toned, but intense and classy on the nose. Very good intensity. Medium-full body. Succulent, pure, ripe and vigorous. This is fine, but it's not as fine as Jadot's example this year. Fine, long, complex, classy finish though. (September 2005)

2009 TO 2024   17.5

Chambertin, 2000
Domaine Bouchard Père et Fils

Fullish colour. Less clumsy than the Clos de Bèze. Fullish. Good grip. Not brilliant, but at least balanced and classy. Medium-full on the palate. A slight lack of concentration and intensity. But fine nevertheless. (July 2004)

2009 TO 2024   17.5

Chambertin, 2000
Maison Frédéric Esmonin

Fullish colour. Some development. Quite solid but a little unforthcoming on the nose. Not entirely physiologically ripe in the tannic department. Full body. Plenty of good, ripe, concentrated fruit. But a certain lack of real flair. Slightly four-square. Fine plus though. (July 2004)

2009 TO 2025   18.0

Chambertin, 2000
Domaine Armand Rousseau

Fullish colour. Full, rich, ripe, concentrated and multidimensional. Lovely fresh fruit. On the palate this is very, very lovely. I'm tempted to give it 20. Splendidly virile and concentrated. Splendid fruit. Real class. Really vigorous. Very, very long. Excellent. (July 2004)

2012 TO 2025   19.5

Le Chambertin, 2000
Domaine Jean and Jean-Louis Trapet

After a rather disappointing 2001, this is unexpectedly delicious. Rather more alive. Rich, fullish for the vintage. Fragrant and concentrated. Splendid for a 2000. A real surprise! (May 2005)

NOW TO 2020   19.0

Chambertin, Clos de Bèze, 2000
Domaine Bouchard Père et Fils

Fullish colour. Rich but a little reduced on the nose. Slightly clumsy. Full and ripe underneath. Good grip. Slightly ungainly. It may resolve itself. Very good plus. (July 2004)

2009 TO 2020   16.5

Chambertin, Clos de Bèze, 2000
Domaine Bruno Clair

Fullish colour. Good, cool, classy nose. Ripe and rich, balanced and with plenty of dimension. As always, with Clair, a cool, refined wine. This lacks a little weight and grip. But fine quality. (July 2004)

NOW TO 2022   17.5

Chambertin, Clos de Bèze, 2000
Domaine Prieuré-Roch

Medium to medium-full colour. Some evolution. Some depth, grip and concentration. But rather too gamey and coarse, especially on the palate which is weedy and astringent as well. Disappointing. (February 2006)

DRINK SOON   11.0

Chambolle-Musigny, 2000
Domaine Jacques-Frédéric Mugnier

Magnum. Some development. À point now. Soft, fragrant, intense, classy and positive on nose and palate. Lovely fragrant fruit. Good balance. Good length. Very good plus. (September 2005)

DRINK SOON   16.5

Chambolle-Musigny, 2000
Domaine Comte Georges de Vogüé

Good colour. Still very fresh. Ripe, fragrant nose. Medium body. No hard edges. Good freshness. Lovely fruit and balance. Long, positive and stylish. Very good. Just about ready. (September 2005)

NOW TO 2015   16.0

Chambolle-Musigny, Les Amoureuses, 2000
Domaine Jacques-Frédéric Mugnier

Medium colour. Some development. Light but intense nose. A touch of the stems it seems. On the palate a bit lightweight, but lovely, intense fruit. Balanced. Classy. Very lovely. (July 2004)

NOW TO 2020+   18.0

Chambolle-Musigny, Les Amoureuses, 2000
Domaine Georges Roumier

Medium-full colour. Rich nose. But not a lot of fragrance or complexity. Medium-full body. Slightly adolescent. Perhaps the Cras is, too. But this doesn't convince. Ripe and plump, but a little one-dimensional. Very good at best. (July 2004)

NOW TO 2020+   16.0

Chambolle-Musigny, Les Amoureuses, 2000
Domaine Comte Georges de Vogüé

Medium to medium-full colour. Fragrant and intense on both nose and palate. Medium-full body. Lacks a little sweetness and charm at present, but this will come as it rounds off. Very concentrated and very lovely. Long and classy. (June 2006)

2009 TO 2019   17.5

Chambolle-Musigny, Les Baudes, 2000
Domaine Joseph Drouhin

Medium to medium-full colour. Fragrant nose. Stylish. Very Chambolle. Medium body only. Oaky, but fresh and intense. Long and complex on the palate. Lovely fruit. Very good finish. Very good indeed. (July 2004)

NOW TO 2018   17.0

Chambolle-Musigny, Les Baudes, 2000
Domaine Hubert Lignier

Medium-full colour. Ripe, oaky, vigorous nose. Good substance. Medium-full body. Plump and fat. Very good fruit. Very good grip. Slightly adolescent but with lots of vigour. Very good indeed. (July 2004)

NOW TO 2020   17.0

Chambolle-Musigny, Les Beaux Bruns, 2000
Domaine Ghislaine Barthod

Fullish colour. Good, plump nose. Plenty of vigour here. Ripe and plump. Medium to medium-full body. Some tannin still to resolve. Very good grip. Long. Very good indeed. (July 2004)

NOW TO 2020   17.0

Chambolle-Musigny, Les Beaux Bruns, 2000
Domaine Denis Mortet

Fullish colour. Rich, full, modern nose. But not over-extracted. On the palate quite meaty, but without the balance and fragrance it should have. Only quite good. (July 2004)

NOW TO 2016   14.0

Chambolle-Musigny, Les Charmes, 2000
Domaine Ghislaine Barthod

Medium to medium-full colour. Lovely nose. A bit closed-in compared with some, but plump, ripe and fruity. Medium-full body. Clean, ample, pure and generous. Very good quality. No lack of vigour. Fine. (July 2004)

NOW TO 2020+   17.5

Chambolle-Musigny, Les Charmes, 2000
Domaine Gérard Mugneret

Medium to medium-full colour. Still youthful. Fresh and elegant if not very profound on the nose. Very good on the palate. Some structure. Good grip. Medium to medium-full body. Lovely fruit. Long. Good dimension for a 2000. Gentle base of oak. Very good plus. (June 2005)

NOW TO 2015   16.5

Chambolle-Musigny, Les Charmes, 2000
Domaine Daniel Rion

Medium-full colour. Good nose. Fresh and plump with a touch of mint. Ripe. Medium to medium-full body. Plenty of fruit. Good follow-through. Lacks a little flair but very good. (July 2004)

NOW TO 2018   16.0

Chambolle-Musigny, La Combe d'Orveau, 2000
Domaine Bruno Clavelier

Medium to medium-full colour. Ripe and slightly chunky on the nose. The tannins are a little rude here, and the wine is a touch clumsy. Decent fruit and depth. Good finish. But merely good. (July 2004)

NOW TO 2018   15.0

Chambolle-Musigny, Les Cras, 2000
Domaine Michèle and Patrice Rion

Medium colour. Soft and fragrant but forward on the nose. Medium body only, but fresh and balanced. Good style. Good length. Positive finish. Good plus. (July 2004)

NOW TO 2017   15.5

Chambolle-Musigny, Les Cras, 2000
Domaine Georges Roumier et Fils

Medium-full colour. The nose is a bit ungainly at present. On the palate there is plenty of balanced, complex, plump fruit. Good tannins. No lack of substance. But the Chambolle fragrance is buried

under the wine's adolescence. Long though. Surely, at least very good indeed. (March 2003)
NOW TO 2020   17.0

Chambolle-Musigny, Les Fuées, 2000
Domaine Joseph Faiveley
Medium to medium-full colour. Some development. Soft, elegant and succulent, but not much power. Yet profound and intense. Medium body. Lovely fruit. Long if not complex enough for fine. Not at all oaky. Very stylish. Very good indeed. (June 2006)
NOW TO 2014   17.0

Chambolle-Musigny, Les Fuées, 2000
Domaine Jacques-Frédéric Mugnier
Good colour. Very lovely, intense fruit. Rich and profound. Very good grip. Plenty of vigour and energy. Cool and very classy. Fine. (June 2003)
NOW TO 2016   17.5

Chambolle-Musigny, Les Groseilles, 2000
Domaine Digioia-Royer
Medium colour. Soft, fragrant, fresh nose. Quite forward. Medium body. Balanced. Cool. A bit slight but well made. Good positive finish. (July 2004)
NOW TO 2012   15.0

Chambolle-Musigny, Les Hauts-Doix, 2000
Domaine Joseph Drouhin
Medium colour. Some development. Ripe, intense, stylish, fresh nose. Medium-full body. Very good grip. This is long and complex, vigorous and classy. Lovely finish. Fine. (July 2004)
NOW TO 2020   17.5

Chambolle-Musigny, Les Hauts-Doix, 2000
Domaine Robert Groffier
Medium-full colour. Ripe, fragrant, stylish nose. Good weight and depth. Medium-full body. Very rich. Almost sweet. Concentrated and intense. Very long. Fine. (July 2004)
NOW TO 2020+   17.5

Chambolle-Musigny, Les Sentiers, 2000
Domaine Robert Groffier
Full colour. Rich, fat, slightly spicy nose. A touch of gingerbread which is not found in the Haut-Doix. A rich, concentrated, almost sweet palate. Medium-full body. Good intensity. Very good indeed. (July 2004)
NOW TO 2020+   17.0

Chambolle-Musigny, Les Véroilles, 2000
Domaine Bruno Clair
Lightish colour. Light but fragrant on nose and palate. Medium body. Slightly lean. Classy fruit. But a lack of fat. Good plus. (July 2004)
NOW TO 2018   15.5

Chapelle-Chambertin, 2000
Domaine Louis Jadot
Fullish colour. Full, rich, youthful, oaky nose. Lots of depth. Very fresh. Fullish on the palate. Lovely finish, balanced, high-class fruit. Very good grip. This is very lovely. Fine plus. (July 2004)
2009 TO 2025   18.0

Charmes-Chambertin, 2000
Domaine Hervé Arlaud
Good fullish colour. Some development. Open, ripe nose. Medium weight. Ample and attractive if slightly one-dimensional. Medium to medium-full body. Good acidity. Slightly raw. Not the greatest class, but that is the vintage. Positive at the end. Very good plus. (April 2006)
2009 TO 2020   16.5

Charmes-Chambertin, 2000
Domaine Denis Bachelet
Very good, firm, fresh colour. Full for the vintage. Splendidly rich for a 2000. Ripe, positive, stylish and balanced. "This is the sort of wine I like to make," says Denis Bachelet. Lovely fruit. Absolutely no lack of succulence or depth. Medium-full body. Complex, classy and multidimensional. Excellent. Just about ready. (June 2006)
2008 TO 2017   19.5

Charmes-Chambertin, 2000
Domaine Jacky Confuron-Cotétidot
Medium colour. High toned. Accad-type nose. High in acidity. High in greenness. Not very classy. Thin and astringent on the palate. Decent fruit behind it but no succulence. Dry at the end. (July 2004)
NOW TO 2010   14.0

Charmes-Chambertin, 2000
Domaine Bernard Dugat-Py

Very full, immature colour. Fullish, very ripe, plummy nose. A little tannin. Backward. Not too dense. Lots of wine here. Really concentrated for a 2000. Not quite the sheer class of Claude Dugat's but very fine nonetheless. (April 2006)

2011 TO 2020   18.0

Charmes-Chambertin, 2000
Domaine Claude Dugat

Full, youthful colour. Restrained. Understated. Quietly composed and very classy. Medium-full body. Creamy rich and concentrated. Very good depth and grip. Very, very lovely. (April 2006)

2009 TO 2020   19.0

Charmes-Chambertin, 2000
Domaine Dujac

Medium to medium-full colour. Some development. Very Dujac. Ripe, almost sweet. Open and fresh. Medium to medium-full body. Just about ready. Long, positive and classy. Fine. (April 2006)

NOW TO 2020   17.5

Charmes-Chambertin, 2000
Domaine Bernard Maume

Medium to medium-full colour. Some development. Fragrant. Good grip. Lovely fruit and very stylish on the nose. Slightly rustic on the finish after a very promising attack. The aftertaste is a little astringent. Very good indeed. (July 2004)

2010 TO 2025   17.0

Charmes-Chambertin, 2000
Maison Nicolas Potel

Medium-full colour. Still youthful. Accessible, fragrant nose with a touch of coffee. Medium-full body. Ripe. Just a little tannin. Very good fruit and grip. Clean, vigorous and positive. Very fresh. Fine plus. (April 2006)

2009 TO 2020   18.0

Charmes-Chambertin, Très Vieilles Vignes, 2000
Domaine Joseph Roty

Medium to medium-full colour. Still very fresh. Rich, ample, quite meaty nose. This is now ready. Medium to medium-full body. The fruit

is a little boiled sweety, but there are no hard edges here and a decent grip. Pity about the soupy-ness. Quite good. (March 2003)

NOW TO 2010   14.0

Charmes-Chambertin, 2000
Domaine Armand Rousseau

Medium to medium-full colour. Some development. Lacks a bit of grip and depth. Sweet. Medium body. A bit diffuse and weedy on the palate. Forward and one-dimensional. Unexciting. (July 2004)

NOW TO 2017   14.0

Charmes-Chambertin, Mazoyères, 2000
Domaine de la Vougeraie

Fullish colour. Rich, fat, oaky and succulent. This is positive and very well made. Not a blockbuster, but ripe and meaty. Very fresh and very classy. Long on the palate. Lovely finish. Fine. (July 2004)

NOW TO 2025   17.5

Château de Monthelie, 2000
Domaine de Suremain

Light to medium colour. Fragrant nose, but light and short on the palate. It will get astringent. Not bad plus. (March 2003)

DRINK SOON   13.5

Chorey-lès-Beaune, 2000
Domaine Arnoux Père et Fils

A little lighter than the 2001, but fresh and good for what it is. (February 2003)

DRINK SOON   15.0

Chorey-lès-Beaune, 2000
Domaine François Gay et Fils

Eighteen months in wood. Slightly raw still. But again, the fruit is ample and stylish. Good positive finish. (February 2003)

NOW TO 2010   14.5

Chorey-lès-Beaune, 2000
Domaine Michel Gay

This is a good, meaty example. Good colour. Good substance. Both fruity and balanced if, like the 2001, not very classy. (February 2003)

DRINK SOON   13.5

Chorey-lès-Beaune, 2000
Domaine Germain Père et Fils/
Château de Chorey-lès-Beaune
Very good colour. Just a touch reduced at first. Slightly astringent as a result. Decent fruit. Medium body. Tollot-Beaut's is better. Quite good. (March 2003)
NOW TO 2009   14.0

Chorey-lès-Beaune, 2000
Domaine René Podichard
Good fruit. Lovely style. Very succulent. Ripe, long and stylish. Very good, indeed, for what it is. (February 2003)
NOW TO 2011   16.0

Chorey-lès-Beaune, 2000
Domaine Pierre Thubert
This is rather better than their 2001. Fresh. Reasonable substance. Ample and fruity. Stylish and long. Very good. (February 2003)
NOW TO 2011   15.5

Chorey-lès-Beaune, 2000
Domaine Tollot-Beaut et Fils
Medium to medium-full colour. Good depth. No lack of structure for a 2000 Chorey. Fresh and attractive. Positive finish. This is very good for what it is. (March 2003)
NOW TO 2011   15.0

Clos des Lambrays, 2000
Domaine des Lambrays
Medium to medium-full colour. Medium weight on the nose. Plump and stylish if no great weight or grip. Good, medium-full body. Succulent fruit on the palate. Good grip. Ample, positive and stylish. Fine. Very good finish. (September 2004)
NOW TO 2015   17.5

Clos de la Roche, 2000
Domaine Dujac
Medium colour. Lovely, fragrant, typically Dujac nose. A bit on the light side on the palate, especially compared with his Clos Saint-Denis. Yet balanced and stylish. Long and composed. Very good indeed. (July 2004)
NOW TO 2020   17.0

Clos de la Roche, Vieilles Vignes, 2000
Domaine Hubert Lignier
Medium-full colour. Rich, full, slightly more modern than some. Good, oaky base. High quality. Fullish bodied, oaky, rich, fresh. Very good grip. This is fragrant, intense and very classy. Lovely finish. Fine plus. (July 2004)
2009 TO 2025   18.0

Clos de la Roche, Cuvée Vieilles Vignes, 2000
Domaine Ponsot
Magnum. Medium colour. Soft, fragrant nose. Not a great deal of weight. More to it on the palate. Delicious fruit. Really quite concentrated. Balanced. More succulent than his 2001. Less spice. Very fine. (March 2006)
2009 TO 2018   18.5

Clos de la Roche, 2000
Domaine Louis Rémy
Medium to medium-full colour. Ample nose. Not rustic. Good acidity. Slightly edgy perhaps. Medium-full body. Good, ripe tannins. But a little astringent on the palate. Decent fruit. Good length. Very good but lacks the flair of great. It collapsed in the glass. (July 2004)
NOW TO 2017   14.5

Clos de la Roche, 2000
Domaine Armand Rousseau
Medium-full colour. Ripe, ample, plump and succulent on the nose. Some development. Medium to medium-full weight. Looser knit than some, similar to his Charmes. Plump and fruity. Stylish. Evolving soon. Not the flair of the best. Very good but not great. (July 2004)
NOW TO 2017   16.0

Clos Saint-Denis, 2000
Domaine Dujac
Medium-full colour. Rather more colour than the Clos de la Roche. Fatter, fuller and plumper on the nose. Rich. Fullish body. Ample. Altogether

better. Nicely fat and succulent. Very good grip. Long. Very lovely. (July 2004)

NOW TO 2025　　　　　　　　　　　　　　18.0

Clos Saint-Denis, 2000
Domaine Louis Jadot

Medium-full colour. Fragrant nose. Quite accessible. Stylish and well balanced. Medium-full body. Balanced. Classy. Generous. Very good vigour at the end. Very lovely harmony and splendid fruit. (July 2004)

NOW TO 2025　　　　　　　　　　　　　　18.0

Clos de Tart, 2000
Domaine Mommessin

Fullish colour. Full, muscular nose. Some tannin. Rather too beefy and astringent for comfort. Fullish weight. Slightly astringent. Good grip. Rich. Needs time. But I fear that it is a bit too big for its boots. (July 2004)

2010 TO 2020　　　　　　　　　　　　　　15.0

Clos de Vougeot, 2000
Domaine Robert Arnoux

Medium-full colour. Gently oaky. Good fruit and grip on the palate. Fullish, ripe, rich, vigorous and concentrated. Old viney. Excellent acidity. This is a fine wine. Long on the palate. Very good finish. (July 2004)

NOW TO 2012　　　　　　　　　　　　　　17.5

Clos de Vougeot, 2000
Domaine Jérôme Chézeaux

Medium colour. Ripe, succulent nose. Clean, positive and classy. Medium to medium-full body. Good depth and grip. Plenty of substance and dimension. Good finish. Very good indeed. (October 2005)

NOW TO 2018　　　　　　　　　　　　　　17.0

Clos de Vougeot, 2000
Domaine Jacky Confuron-Cotétidot

Medium to medium-full colour. High-toned nose. Stemmy. Good acidity but not much style. Light and weedy on the palate. Astringent at the end. Poor. (July 2004)

NOW TO 2010　　　　　　　　　　　　　　12.5

Clos de Vougeot, 2000
Domaine Joseph Drouhin

Medium-full colour. Fragrant nose. Cherries and chocolate. Good quality and very good harmony. Lovely fruit. Very well made and relaxed. Medium-full body. Very well balanced. Ripe. Essentially gentle. Long. Very good indeed. (July 2004)

NOW TO 2020　　　　　　　　　　　　　　17.0

Clos de Vougeot, 2000
Domaine René Engel

Medium-full colour. Some development. Spicy nose. Some secondary flavours now. Aromatic. Gently oaky. As with all Engel's 2000s, a bit more forward than most. Ripe and stylish. Medium to medium-full body. Long. Lovely. (July 2004)

NOW TO 2020　　　　　　　　　　　　　　17.5

Clos de Vougeot, 2000
Domaine Joseph Faiveley

Medium-full colour. Some oak. Ripe, succulent nose. Good depth here. Fullish, fat, concentrated and rich. Vigorous and with lots of dimension. A bit more structure than Arnoux's. Fine, too. (July 2004)

2009 TO 2024　　　　　　　　　　　　　　17.5

Clos de Vougeot, 2000
Domaine Jean Grivot

Fullish colour. Aromatic, vigorous, ripe nose. Individual. Medium-full body. A little tannin. Very fresh. Very lovely fruit. Very consistent. Very long. Great flair. Fine plus. (July 2004)

NOW TO 2024　　　　　　　　　　　　　　18.0

Clos de Vougeot, 2000
Domaine Jean-Michel Guillon

Medium to medium-full colour. Firm nose. A little dry perhaps. Some tannin but not too astringent. Decent fruit. Decent grip. Medium to medium-full body. Lacks a bit of flair but good. (July 2004)

NOW TO 2017　　　　　　　　　　　　　　15.0

Clos de Vougeot, 2000
Domaine Alfred Haegelen-Jayer

Medium-full colour. Plump nose but a little reduced. It lacks class. Medium to medium-full

body. A bit clumsy in the middle and dry at the end. There is fruit here, and decent acidity. But it is all a bit artisanal. (July 2004)
NOW TO 2017   13.5

Clos de Vougeot, Château de la Tour, 2000
Domaine Labet-Dechelette
Medium-full colour. Ripe, fruity nose. But a little lacking depth. Medium to medium-full body. Some fruit but a little astringent. Quite plump and sizeable on the follow-through. Decent length. But very good at best. (March 2003)
NOW TO 2016   16.0

Clos de Vougeot, 2000
Domaine Méo-Camuzet
Fullish colour. A little closed-in. Fullish. A little tannin. Some oak. Very good fruit. Firm, backward and full bodied. Some tannin. Good grip. The fruit underneath is very good indeed. (July 2004)
2010 TO 2024   17.0

Clos de Vougeot, 2000
Domaine Denis Mortet
Fullish colour. Juicy, modern, fresh and stylish on the nose. Well made in a modern sort of way. Very ripe. Lacks a little grip and freshness at the end. Fullish bodied on the attack. Ample and ripe. Very good. (July 2004)
NOW TO 2018   16.0

Clos de Vougeot, 2000
Domaine Dr. Georges Mugneret
Medium to medium-full colour. Slightly attenuated on the nose. Fresher on the palate. But although fruity, succulent and balanced, it doesn't really convince. Medium to medium-full body. Good plus. (July 2004)
NOW TO 2017   15.5

Clos de Vougeot, 2000
Domaine Jacques Prieur
Medium to medium-full colour. Slightly raw on both nose and palate. Not a lot of concentration or distinction. A lack of richness and succulence on the palate. Slightly rigid. Difficult to see anything exciting here. One-dimensional. No great intensity or length at the end. After 30 minutes it was really rather thin. (August 2002)
NOW TO 2012   14.0

Clos de Vougeot, 2000
Domaine Charles Thomas
Medium-full colour. Clumsy nose. Medium-full body. Some undue astringency. A little extracted. The wine is a bit ungainly anyway. (July 2004)
NOW TO 2012   13.5

Corton, 2000
Domaine Bonneau du Martray
Medium colour. Ripe, succulent nose. Decent depth. Medium-full body. Good acidity. This is rich, but slightly hot. Good but not brilliant. Decent fruit. (July 2004)
NOW TO 2014   15.0

Corton, 2000
Domaine Follin-Arbelet
Medium to medium-full colour. Slightly thin on the nose. Some fruit but a lack of weight. This lacks style on the palate. The finish is weedy and ugly. (July 2004)
DRINK SOON   12.5

Le Corton, 2000
Domaine Bouchard Père et Fils
Medium to medium-full colour. Good class on the nose. Fragrant and full of fruit. Only medium body. But stylish and balanced. Slightly lightweight for a Corton but good plus. (July 2004)
NOW TO 2012   15.5

Corton, Bressandes, 2000
Domaine Chandon de Briailles
Medium to medium-full colour. Riper, richer and less stemmy than the Clos du Roi. Nevertheless rather short. (July 2004)
DRINK SOON   12.5

Corton, Les Bressandes, 2000
Domaine Edmond Cornu et Fils
Fine colour. Impressive nose. This is really very fine for a 2000. Full. Very good tannins. Rich and concentrated. Very fine grip. A wine of real

style and complexity. Excellent for what it is. (February 2003)

2008 TO 2020   17.5

Corton, Bressandes, 2000
Domaine Joseph Drouhin

Medium to medium-full colour. Fragrant, delicate but balanced and elegant nose. A bit weedy on the palate. But quite classy, quite harmonious and quite long. Quite good. (July 2004)

NOW TO 2010   14.0

Corton, Les Bressandes, 2000
Maison Vincent Girardin

Very good colour. Surprisingly rich and meaty (in a classy sense) on the nose. Most impressive. Fullish body. Some tannin. Very concentrated and with excellent grip. This is very lovely. Lots of vigour and energy. Lots of class. (October 2002)

NOW TO 2018   18.5

Corton, Bressandes, 2000
Domaine Antonin Guyon

Medium-full colour. Rich, ripe nose. Not as oaky as their Clos du Roi. Not as classy, but decent weight, grip and fruit. Less good on the finish. Quite good. (July 2004)

NOW TO 2010   14.0

Corton, Les Bressandes, 2000
Domaine Didier Meuneveaux

Good colour. Ripe fruit. Good acidity. Medium to medium-full body. Fresh and succulent. This is very, very good for the vintage. (February 2003)

NOW TO 2018   17.0

Corton, Les Bressandes, 2000
Domaine du Comte Senard

Good colour. Fresh, plump nose. Medium-full body. A little tannin. This is ripe and vigorous, with good acidity and depth. Long. Fine. (March 2003)

NOW TO 2018   17.5

Corton, Bressandes, 2000
Domaine Tollot-Beaut et Fils

Medium-full colour. Slightly extracted nose. A bit clumsy. Thin, vegetal, astringent and undrinkable. (July 2004)

DRINK SOON   10.5

Corton, Clos des Cortons Faiveley, 2000
Domaine Joseph Faiveley

Good colour. Fullish but slightly closed-in nose. Medium to medium-full. Some fruit but a touch rigid still. Some oak. Good energy. Medium-full body. Decent grip. Decent follow-through. But it doesn't really sing. No undue oak though. Very good plus. (June 2006)

NOW TO 2015   16.5

Corton, Clos Rognet, 2000
Domaine Méo-Camuzet

Very good colour. Full, quite oaky nose. Medium-full body on the attack. Some tannin. Good, fresh fruit. It tails away a little on the palate, but it is not short, just a little one-dimensional. Good freshness. Very good indeed. (March 2003)

NOW TO 2016   17.0

Corton, Clos du Roi, 2000
Domaine Chandon de Briailles

Medium colour. Ripe, fragrant, slightly lean nose, showing some of the stems. Slightly sweet. Light and rather weedy on the palate. Will get astringent. (July 2004)

DRINK SOON   12.0

Corton, Clos du Roi, 2000
Domaine Antonin Guyon

Medium-full colour. Ripe, succulent, oaky nose. This has merit. Good weight. Good grip. Fresh. Succulent. Positive. Long. Very good plus. (July 2004)

NOW TO 2018   16.5

Corton, Clos du Roi, 2000
Domaine Michel Voarick

Stylish, balanced, plump and fresh. Not enormous depth, but balanced, long and fine for the vintage. (February 2003)

NOW TO 2018   17.0

Corton, Clos des Vergennes, 2000
Domaine Cachat-Ocquidant et Fils

Monopole. Supple and round. A good effort. This has fruit, charm and a positive finish. Good. (February 2003)

NOW TO 2014   15.0

Corton, Les Languettes, 2000
Domaine Maurice Chapuis

A good example of what it is, especially Languettes, which is better in Chardonnay. Only a light-medium colour. But balanced and fresh. Not weedy. Good follow-through. Plump and fruity. More to it than it seems at first sight. Good length. Supple and succulent. Very good indeed. (February 2003)

NOW TO 2015   17.0

Corton, Les Maréchaudes, 2000
Domaine Doudet-Naudin

This has a bit more energy. But it is still a bit astringent. Decent fruit. Decent depth. Disappointing for what it is nevertheless. Quite good. (February 2003)

NOW TO 2013   14.0

Corton, Pougets, 2000
Domaine Louis Jadot

Medium colour. Quite full, firm and ripe on the nose. Good depth. But on the palate rather a dog's dinner. Clumsy. Slightly astringent. Unbalanced. Not bad at best. (July 2004)

DRINK SOON   13.0

Corton, Les Renardes, 2000
Domaine François Gay et Fils

Lots of stylish fruit here. Real class. A lot of depth. A really fine example. Nothing Renardes-ish here. Long. From 2007. (February 2003)

NOW TO 2017   17.5

Corton, Les Renardes, 2000
Domaine Michel Gay

Ripe and plump. Proportionately not as good as his Beaune Grèves. It lacks a little flair. But a decent example. (February 2003)

NOW TO 2014   16.0

Corton, Les Renardes, 2000
Maison Antonin Rodet

Good colour. A bit tight on the nose. Quite rich on the attack. Good depth, style and dimension. Medium to medium-full body. Nicely cool and

with ripe, well-covered tannins. Stylish. Very good indeed. (August 2002)

NOW TO 2015   17.0

Corton, Le Rognet, 2000
Domaine Chevalier Père et Fils

This is soft and velvety. Good substance. A little tannin. Ripe and with very acidity. Long and classy. Fine. (February 2003)

NOW TO 2015   17.5

Corton, Rognet, 2000
Domaine Bruno Clavelier

Medium-full colour. Modern nose. Ugly and over-macerated. Over-oaked. A weedy wine underneath. (July 2004)

DRINK SOON   11.5

Corton, Le Rognet, 2000
Domaine Michel Mallard et Fils

This is very fine for a 2000. Full, oaky, rich and meaty. Very good grip and depth. Lots of dimension. Plenty of fruit. Long. (February 2003)

2010 TO 2020   18.0

Echézeaux, 2000
Domaine Bouchard Père et Fils

Medium-full colour. Some tannin. A little backward. But good fruit on the attack. Fullish body. Good fruit. Good grip. Ripe. Long. Very good. (July 2004)

2009 TO 2026   16.0

Echézeaux, 2000
Domaine René Engel

Medium-full colour. Ripe, forward, aromatic nose. Very good fruit and style. Medium to medium-full body. Generous. Balanced. Long. Very stylish. Lovely. (July 2004)

NOW-2018   17.5

Echézeaux, 2000
Domaine Joseph Faiveley

Medium-full colour. Some development. Ripe, slightly spicy nose. Medium body. Not as exciting as their 2000 *premier cru* Gevrey les

MAPS

GENERAL LEGEND

A.O.C. Grands Crus Rouge

A.O.C. Grands Crus Rouge
(or, sometimes, grand crus blanc)

A.O.C. Grands Crus Blanc

A.O.C. Grands Crus Blanc
(or, sometimes, grand crus rouge)

A.O.C. Premiers Crus Rouge

A.O.C. Premiers Crus Rouge
(or, sometimes, premier crus blanc)

A.O.C. Premiers Crus Blanc

A.O.C. Premiers Crus Blanc
(or, sometimes, premier crus rouge)

A.O.C. Villages Rouge

A.O.C. Villages Rouge
(or, sometimes, villages crus blanc)

A.O.C. Villages Blanc

A.O.C. Villages Blanc
(or, sometimes, villages crus rouge)

A.O.C. Villages
(Marsannay rosé)

A.O.C. Villages

Woods

Contour Lines (20 meter intervals)

Lakes, Ponds

Rivers, Canals

Site or Appellation Border

Sub Commune Border

Commune Border

Department Border

Roads, Lanes

Railroad (S.N.C.F.)

Tamisot Site

Egriselle Hamlet

Fixin Neighboring Commune

Yonne Department

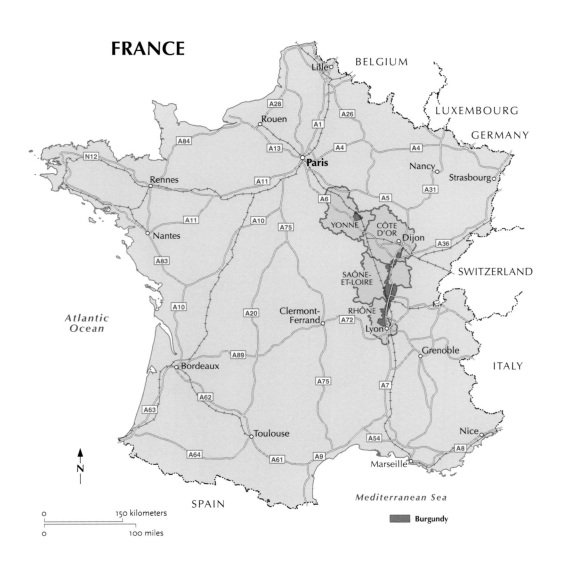

FRANCE

BELGIUM

Lille

LUXEMBOURG

GERMANY

A28

Rouen

A26

A1

Paris

A13

A4

A4

Nancy

Strasbourg

A84

N12

Rennes

A11

A6

A5

A31

A11

A10

A75

YONNE

CÔTE
D'OR

Dijon

A36

Nantes

SAÔNE-
ET-LOIRE

SWITZERLAND

A83

Atlantic
Ocean

A10

A20

Clermont-
Ferrand

A72

RHÔNE

Lyon

A89

Bordeaux

Grenoble

ITALY

A62

A75

A7

A63

Nice

Toulouse

A54

A8

A64

A61

A9

Marseille

SPAIN

Mediterranean Sea

Burgundy

0 ———— 150 kilometers

0 ———— 100 miles

N

THE BURGUNDY REGION

| 50 kilometers |
| 25 miles |

N

Yonne

A6

Chablis o Tonnerre
Auxerre o   **Chablis and**
          Auxerrois

Côte d'Or

A31

RN74

A6   Dijon o

Nuits-Saint-Georges   **Côte de**
                       Nuits

RN74

Côte de   A31
Beaune
Beaune o   A36

Autun o   A6

D981

Côte
Chalonnaise
          Châlon-sur-Saône

Saône et Loire

D981

Mâconnais   A6

Mâcon o

Beaujeu
o

Beaujolais
Villefranche-sur-Saône o

A6

Lyon
o

A7

A47

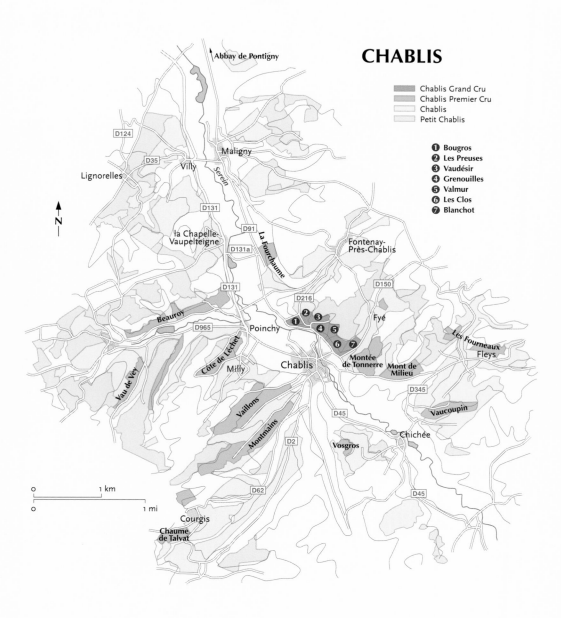

CHABLIS

Chablis Grand Cru
Chablis Premier Cru
Chablis
Petit Chablis

❶ Bougros
❷ Les Preuses
❸ Vaudésir
❹ Grenouilles
❺ Valmur
❻ Les Clos
❼ Blanchot

Abbay de Pontigny

D124

D35
Villy
Maligny
Lignorelles

Serein

D131

la Chapelle-
Vaupelteigne
D91
D131a

La Fourchaume

Fontenay-
Près-Chablis

D131
D216
D150

Beauroy
D965
Poinchy
❷ ❸
❶ ❹ ❺
❻ ❼
Fyé

Côte de Léchet
Milly
Chablis
Montée
de Tonnerre
Mont de
Milieu

Les Fourneaux
Fleys

Vau de Vey
Vaillons
D45
D345

Montmains
D2
Vaucoupin

Vosgros
Chichée

D62
D45

Courgis
Chaume
de Talvat

N

0   1 km
0   1 mi

CHABLIS GRAND CRU

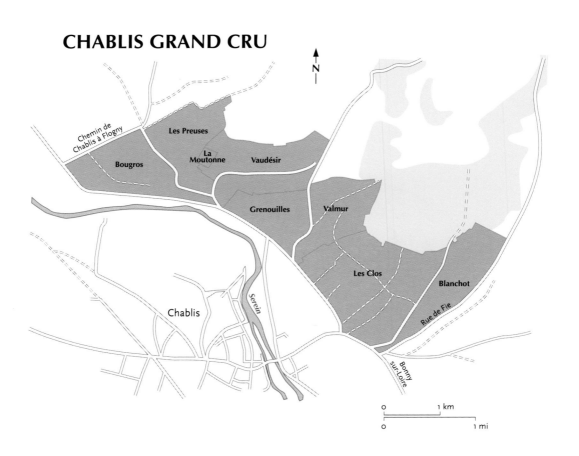

N

Chemin de
Chablis à Flogny

Les Preuses

Bougros

La
Moutonne

Vaudésir

Grenouilles

Valmur

Les Clos

Blanchot

Rue de Fie

Chablis

Serein

Bonny
sur-Loire

0   1 km
0   1 mi

CHABLIS SATELLITES IN YONNE

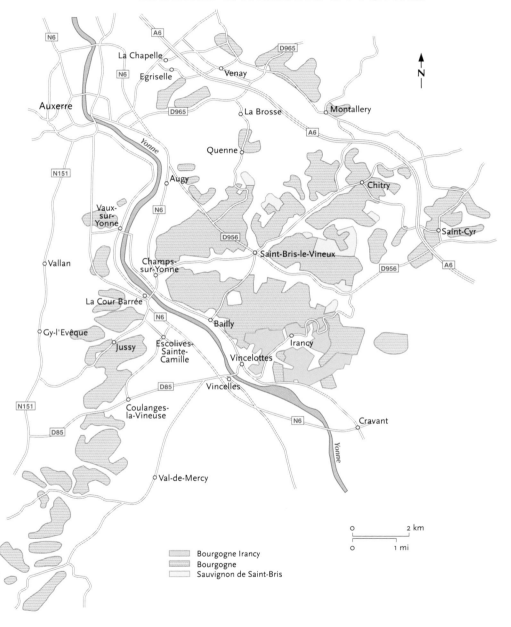

Bourgogne Irancy
Bourgogne
Sauvignon de Saint-Bris

2 km
1 mi

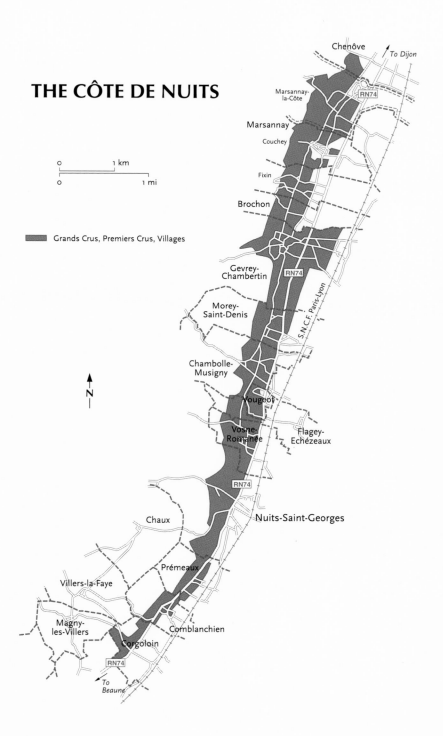

THE CÔTE DE NUITS

Chenôve

To Dijon

Marsannay-
la-Côte

RN74

Marsannay

Couchey

Fixin

Brochon

Gevrey-
Chambertin

RN74

Morey-
Saint-Denis

S.N.C.F. Paris-Lyon

Chambolle-
Musigny

Vougeot

Vosne-
Romanée

Flagey-
Echézeaux

RN74

Chaux

Nuits-Saint-Georges

Prémeaux

Villers-la-Faye

Magny-
les-Villers

Comblanchien

Corgoloin

RN74

To
Beaune

1 km

1 mi

■ Grands Crus, Premiers Crus, Villages

N

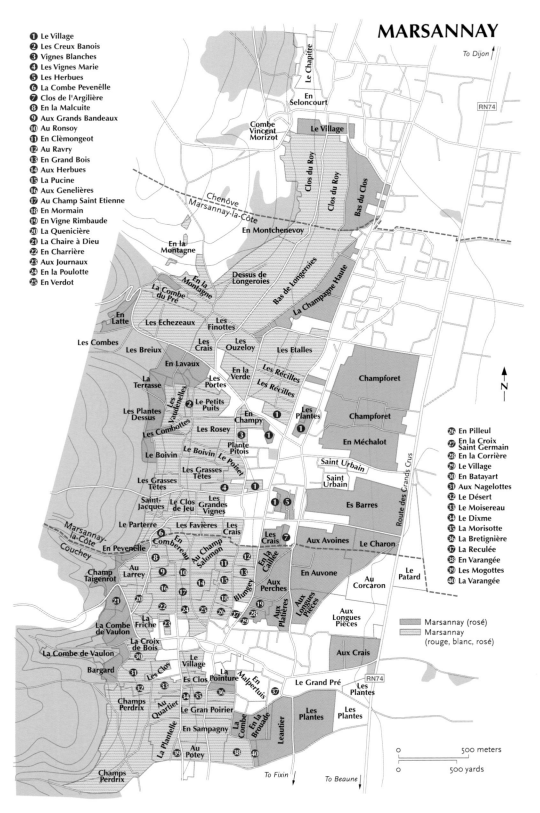

MARSANNAY

To Dijon

RN74

1. Le Village
2. Les Creux Banois
3. Vignes Blanches
4. Les Vignes Marie
5. Les Herbues
6. La Combe Pevenêlle
7. Clos de l'Argilière
8. En la Malcuite
9. Aux Grands Bandeaux
10. Au Ronsoy
11. En Clèmongeot
12. Au Ravry
13. En Grand Bois
14. Aux Herbues
15. La Pucine
16. Aux Genelières
17. Au Champ Saint Etienne
18. En Mormain
19. En Vigne Rimbaude
20. La Quenicière
21. La Chaire à Dieu
22. En Charrière
23. Aux Journaux
24. En la Poulotte
25. En Verdot

26. En Pilleul
27. En la Croix Saint Germain
28. En la Corrière
29. Le Village
30. En Batayart
31. Aux Nagelottes
32. Le Désert
33. Le Moisereau
34. Le Dixme
35. La Morisotte
36. La Bretignière
37. La Reculée
38. En Varangée
39. Les Mogottes
40. La Varangée

Le Chapître
En Seloncourt
Combe Vincent Morizot
Le Village
Clos du Roy
Clos du Roy
Bas du Clos
Chenôve
Marsannay-la-Côte
En Montchenevoy
En la Montagne
Dessus de Longeroies
Bas de Longeroies
La Champagne Haute
En la Montagne
La Combe du Pré
En Latte
Les Echezeaux
Les Finottes
Les Combes
Les Breiux
Les Crais
Les Ouzeloy
Les Etalles
En Lavaux
En la Verde
Les Récilles
Les Récilles
Champforet
La Terrasse
Les Portes
Les Plantes Dessus
Les Vaudenelles
Le Petits Puits
En Champy
Les Plantes
Champforet
Les Combottes
Les Rosey
En Méchalot
Le Boivin
Le Boivin
Plante Pitois
Le Poisot
Saint Urbain
Les Grasses Têtes
Les Grasses Têtes
Saint Urbain
Saint-Jacques
Le Clos de Jeu
Les Grandes Vignes
Es Barres
Le Parterre
Les Favières
Les Crais
Marsannay-la-Côte
En Pevenêlle
Les Crais
Aux Avoines
Le Charon
Couchey
En Combereau
En Champ Salomon
En la Caille
Aux Avoines
Champ Taigenrot
Au Larrey
En Auvone
Le Patard
Au Corcaron
Aux Perches
Aux Longues Pièces
Aux Longues Pièces
La Friche
La Combe de Vaulon
La Croix de Bois
La Combe de Vaulon
Aux Platières
Aux Crais
Bargard
Le Village
Les Clos
Es Clos
Pointure
En Malpertuis
Le Grand Pré
Les Plantes
Champs Perdrix
Au Quartier
Le Gran Poirier
Les Plantes
Les Plantes
En Sampagny
La Combe
En la Brouade
Leautier
La Plantelle
Au Potey
Champs Perdrix
To Fixin
To Beaune

N

Route des Grands Crus

Marsannay (rosé)
Marsannay (rouge, blanc, rosé)

0   500 meters
0   500 yards

FIXIN

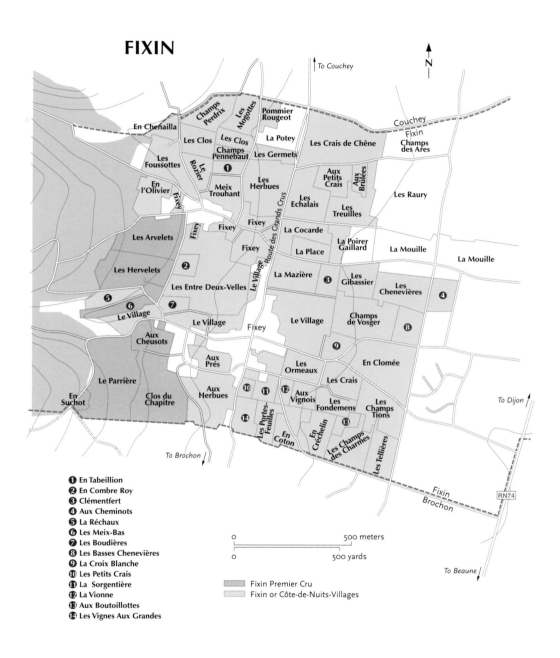

To Couchey

N

Champs Perdrix

Les Mogottes

Pommier Rougeot

En Chenailla

Les Clos

Les Clos

La Potey

Les Crais de Chêne

Couchey
Fixin

Champs Pennebaut

Les Germets

Champs des Ares

Les Foussottes

Le Rozier

❶

En l'Olivier

Fixey

Meix Trouhant

Les Herbues

Aux Petits Crais

Aux Brûlées

Les Raury

Les Echalais

Les Treuilles

Les Arvelets

Fixey

Fixey

Fixey

La Cocarde

La Poirer Gaillard

La Mouille

Fixey

La Place

La Mouille

❷

Les Hervelets

La Mazière

Les Gibassier

Les Chenevières

❹

Les Entre Deux-Velles

Le Village

Route des Grands Crus

❺

❻

❼

Le Village

Champs de Vosger

❽

Aux Cheusots

Le Village

Fixey

Le Village

❾

Aux Prés

En Clomée

Le Parrière

Les Ormeaux

Les Crais

En Suchot

Clos du Chapitre

Aux Herbues

❿

⓫

⓬

Aux Vignois

Les Fondemens

Les Champs Tions

To Dijon

⓮

Les Portes-Feuilles

⓭

En Coton

En Créchelin

Les Champs des Charmes

Les Tellières

To Brochon

Fixin
Brochon

RN74

To Beaune

❶ En Tabeillion
❷ En Combre Roy
❸ Clémentfert
❹ Aux Cheminots
❺ La Réchaux
❻ Les Meix-Bas
❼ Les Boudières
❽ Les Basses Chenevières
❾ La Croix Blanche
❿ Les Petits Crais
⓫ La Sorgentière
⓬ La Vionne
⓭ Aux Boutoillottes
⓮ Les Vignes Aux Grandes

0   500 meters
0   500 yards

▨ Fixin Premier Cru
▨ Fixin or Côte-de-Nuits-Villages

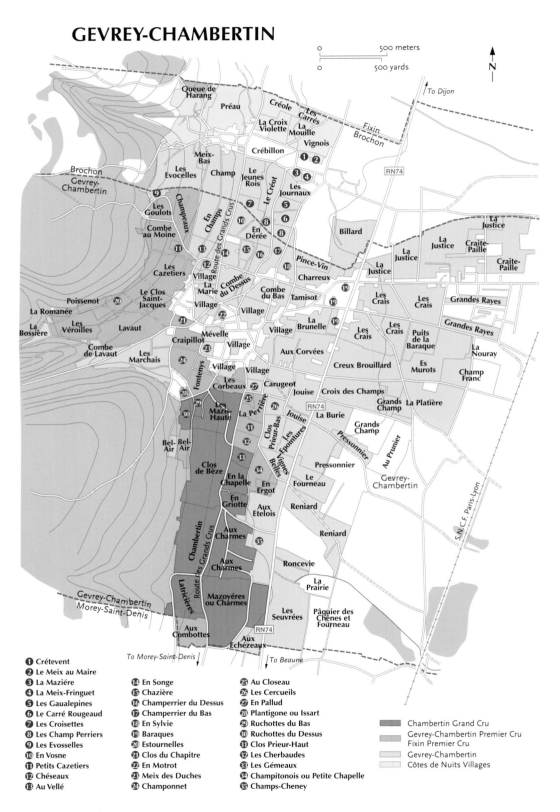

GEVREY-CHAMBERTIN

❶ Crétevent
❷ Le Meix au Maire
❸ La Maziére
❹ La Meix-Fringuet
❺ Les Gaualepines
❻ Le Carré Rougeaud
❼ Les Croisettes
❽ Les Champ Perriers
❾ Les Evosselles
❿ En Vosne
⓫ Petits Cazetiers
⓬ Chéseaux
⓭ Au Vellé
⓮ En Songe
⓯ Chazière
⓰ Champerrier du Dessus
⓱ Champerrier du Bas
⓲ En Sylvie
⓳ Baraques
⓴ Estournelles
㉑ Clos du Chapitre
㉒ En Motrot
㉓ Meix des Duches
㉔ Champonnet
㉕ Au Closeau
㉖ Les Cercueils
㉗ En Pallud
㉘ Plantigone ou Issart
㉙ Ruchottes du Bas
㉚ Ruchottes du Dessus
㉛ Clos Prieur-Haut
㉜ Les Cherbaudes
㉝ Les Gémeaux
㉞ Champitonois ou Petite Chapelle
㉟ Champs-Cheney

Chambertin Grand Cru
Gevrey-Chambertin Premier Cru
Fixin Premier Cru
Gevrey-Chambertin
Côtes de Nuits Villages

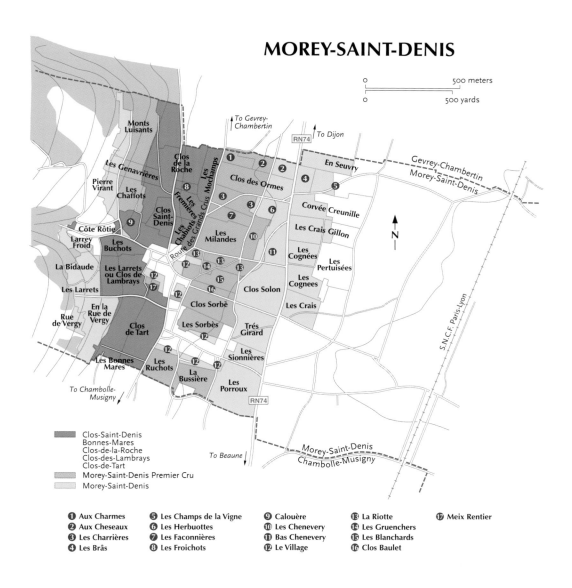

MOREY-SAINT-DENIS

500 meters

500 yards

To Gevrey-
Chambertin

RN74   To Dijon

Gevrey-Chambertin
Morey-Saint-Denis

Monts
Luisants

Les Genavrières

Pierre
Virant

Les
Chaffots

Côte Rôtie

Larrey
Froid

Les
Buchots

La Bidaude

Les Larrets
ou Clos de
Lambrays

Les Larrets

Rue
de Vergy

En la
Rue de
Vergy

Clos
de la
Roche

Les
Fremières

Clos
Saint-
Denis

Les
Chabiots

Route des Grands Crus

Les
Millards Mochamps

Clos des Ormes

Les
Milandes

Clos de Tart

Clos Sorbè

Les Sorbès

Les Bonnes
Mares

Les
Ruchots

La
Bussière

Les
Sionnières

Les
Porroux

En Seuvry

Corvée Creunille

Les Crais Gillon

Les
Cognées

Les
Pertuisées

Les
Cognees

Clos Solon

Les Crais

Trés
Girard

N

S.N.C.F. Paris-Lyon

To Chambolle-
Musigny

RN74

Clos-Saint-Denis
Bonnes-Mares
Clos-de-la-Roche
Clos-des-Lambrays
Clos-de-Tart

Morey-Saint-Denis Premier Cru

Morey-Saint-Denis

To Beaune

Morey-Saint-Denis
Chambolle-Musigny

❶ Aux Charmes
❷ Aux Cheseaux
❸ Les Charrières
❹ Les Brâs
❺ Les Champs de la Vigne
❻ Les Herbuottes
❼ Les Faconnières
❽ Les Froichots
❾ Calouère
❿ Les Chenevery
⓫ Bas Chenevery
⓬ Le Village
⓭ La Riotte
⓮ Les Gruenchers
⓯ Les Blanchards
⓰ Clos Baulet
⓱ Meix Rentier

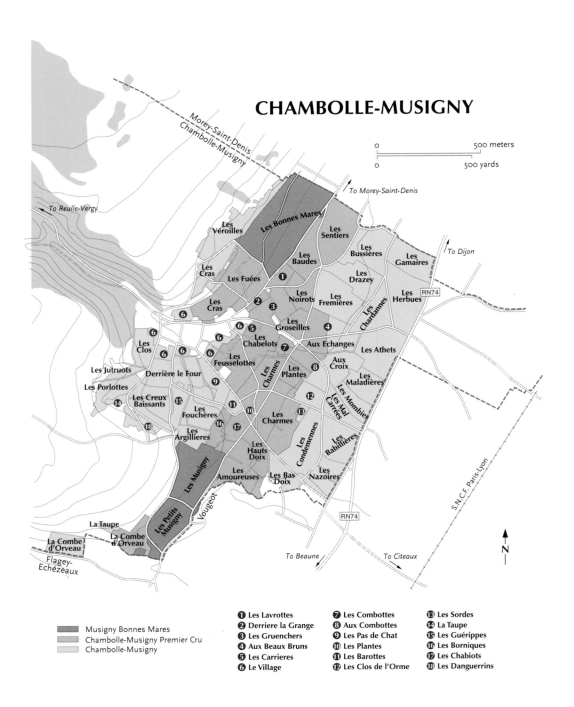

CHAMBOLLE-MUSIGNY

To Reulle-Vergy

Morey-Saint-Denis
Chambolle-Musigny

To Morey-Saint-Denis

To Dijon

500 meters

500 yards

Les Véroilles

Les Bonnes Mares

Les Sentiers

Les Bussières

Les Gamaires

Les Baudes

Les Cras

Les Fuées

❶

Les Drazey

Les Cras

❷ ❸

Les Noirots

Les Fremières

Les Chardannes

Les Herbues

RN74

❻

Les Groseilles

❹

Les Clos

❻

❻

❻

Les Chabelots

❺

❼

Aux Echanges

Les Athets

Les Feusselottes

Les Charmes

Les Plantes

❽

Aux Croix

Les Jutruots

Derrière le Four

❾

Les Maladières

Les Mombies

Les Porlottes

Les Creux Baissants

⓮

⓯

Les Fouchères

⓫

❿

⓭

Les Charmes

⓬

Les Clos de l'Orme

Les Mal Carrées

⓲

⓰ ⓱

Les Argillières

Les Hauts Doix

Les Condemennes

Les Babillières

Les Musigny

Les Amoureuses

Les Bas Doix

Les Nazoires

Vougeot

S.N.C.F. Paris-Lyon

La Taupe

Les Petits Musigny

RN74

La Combe d'Orveau

La Combe d'Orveau

Flagey-Echézeaux

To Beaune

To Citeaux

N

Musigny Bonnes Mares
Chambolle-Musigny Premier Cru
Chambolle-Musigny

❶ Les Lavrottes
❷ Derriere la Grange
❸ Les Gruenchers
❹ Aux Beaux Bruns
❺ Les Carrieres
❻ Le Village

❼ Les Combottes
❽ Aux Combottes
❾ Les Pas de Chat
❿ Les Plantes
⓫ Les Barottes
⓬ Les Clos de l'Orme

⓭ Les Sordes
⓮ La Taupe
⓯ Les Guérippes
⓰ Les Borniques
⓱ Les Chabiots
⓲ Les Danguerrins

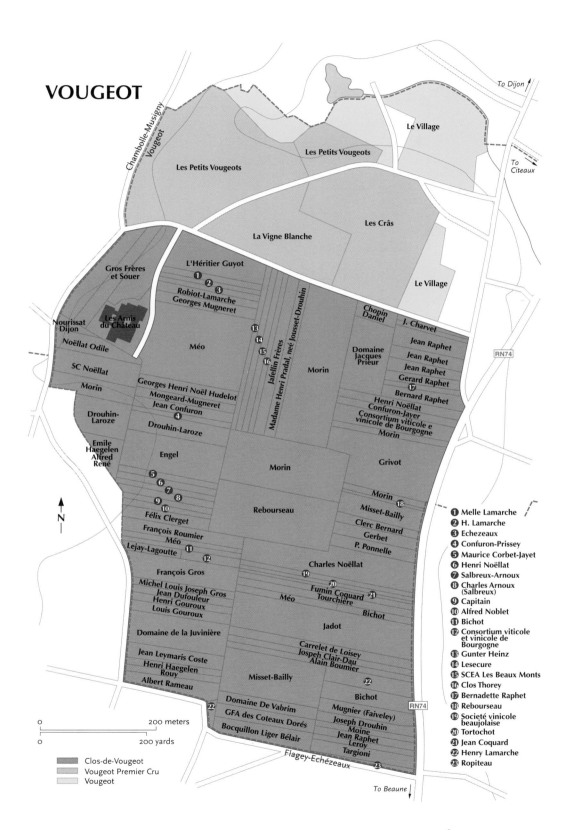

VOUGEOT

To Dijon

Chambolle-Musigny

Vougeot

Les Petits Vougeots

Le Village

Les Petits Vougeots

To Citeaux

Les Crâs

La Vigne Blanche

Le Village

L'Héritier Guyot

Gros Frères
et Souer

❶ ❷ ❸

Robiot-Lamarche
Georges Mugneret

Les Amis
du Château

Chopin
Daniel

J. Charvet

Nourissat
Dijon

Noëllat Odile

⑬

⑭

Méo

⑮

⑯

Domaine
Jacques
Prieur

Morin

Jean Raphet

Jean Raphet

Jean Raphet

Gerard Raphet

RN74

SC Noëllat

Morin

Georges Henri Noël Hudelot

Mongeard-Mugneret

Jean Confuron

❹

Drouhin-Laroze

Bernard Raphet

⑰

Henri Noëllat
Confuron-Jayer
Consortium viticole e
vinicole de Bourgogne
Morin

Drouhin-
Laroze

Emile
Haegelen
Alfred
René

Engel

❺

❻

❼

❽

❾

⑩

Félix Clerget

François Roumier
Méo

Lejay-Lagoutte

Morin

Rebourseau

Grivot

Morin

⑱

Misset-Bailly

Clerc Bernard
Gerbet
P. Ponnelle

⑪

⑫

François Gros

Michel Louis Joseph Gros
Jean Dufouleur
Henri Gouroux
Louis Gouroux

Charles Noëllat

⑲

⑳

Fumin Coquard
Tourchière

㉑

Méo

Bichot

Jadot

Domaine de la Juvinière

Jean Leymaris Coste

Henri Haegelen
Rouy

Albert Rameau

Misset-Bailly

Carrelet de Loisey
Joseph Clair-Dau
Alain Boumier

㉒

Bichot

㉒

Domaine De Vabrim

GFA des Coteaux Dorés

Bocquillon Liger Bélair

Mugnier (Faiveley)

Joseph Drouhin
Moine
Jean Raphet
Leroy
Targioni

RN74

Flagey-Echézeaux

㉓

To Beaune

Madame Henri Pradal, neé Jousset-Drouhin

Jalellin Frères

| 0 | 200 meters |
| 0 | 200 yards |

❶ Melle Lamarche
❷ H. Lamarche
❸ Echezeaux
❹ Confuron-Prissey
❺ Maurice Corbet-Jayet
❻ Henri Noëllat
❼ Salbreux-Arnoux
❽ Charles Arnoux
(Salbreux)
❾ Capitain
⑩ Alfred Noblet
⑪ Bichot
⑫ Consortium viticole
et vinicole de
Bourgogne
⑬ Gunter Heinz
⑭ Lesecure
⑮ SCEA Les Beaux Monts
⑯ Clos Thorey
⑰ Bernadette Raphet
⑱ Rebourseau
⑲ Societé vinicole
beaujolaise
⑳ Tortochot
㉑ Jean Coquard
㉒ Henry Lamarche
㉓ Ropiteau

Clos-de-Vougeot
Vougeot Premier Cru
Vougeot

FLAGEY-ECHÉZEAUX AND VOSNE-ROMANÉE

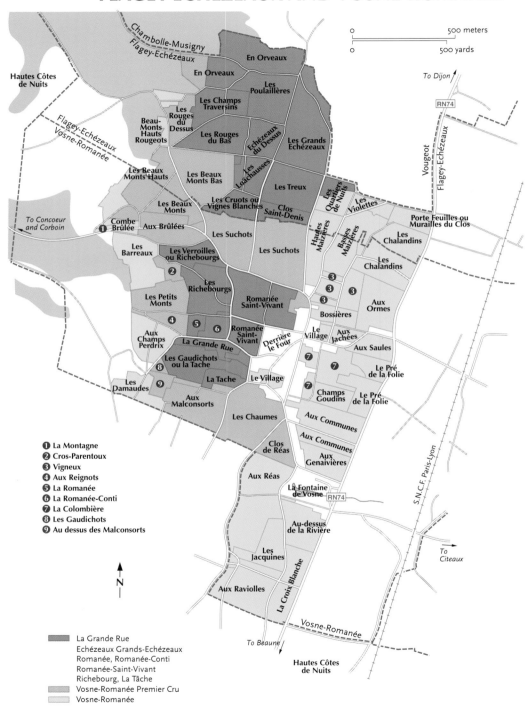

500 meters

500 yards

Chambolle-Musigny
Flagey-Echézeaux

Hautes Côtes
de Nuits

En Orveaux

En Orveaux

Les
Poulaillères

To Dijon

RN74

Flagey-Echézeaux
Vosne-Romanée

Les Champs
Traversins

Les
Rouges
du
Dessus

Beau-
Monts
Hauts
Rougeots

Les Rouges
du Bas

Echézeaux
du Dessus

Les Grands
Echézeaux

Vougeot

Flagey-Echézeaux

Les Beaux
Monts Hauts

Les Beaux
Monts Bas

Les
Loächausses

Les Treux

Les
Quartiers
de Nuits

Les
Violettes

To Concoeur
and Corboin

Les Beaux
Monts

Les Cruots ou
Vignes Blanches

Clos
Saint-Denis

Porte Feuilles ou
Murailles du Clos

Combe
Brûlée

Aux Brûlées

Les Suchots

Hautes
Maizières

Basses
Maizières

Les
Chalandins

Les
Barreaux

Les Verroilles
ou Richebourgs

Les Suchots

Les
Chalandins

Les
Richebourgs

Romanée-
Saint-Vivant

Aux
Ormes

Les Petits
Monts

Bossières

Aux
Champs
Perdrix

Romanée-
Saint-Vivant

La Grande Rue

Derrière
le Four

Le
Village

Aux
Jachées

Aux Saules

Les Gaudichots
ou la Tache

Le Village

Champs
Goudins

Le Pré
de la Folie

Le Pré
de la Folie

Les
Damaudes

La Tache

Aux
Malconsorts

Les Chaumes

Aux Communes

Aux Communes

Aux
Genaivières

Clos
de Réas

Aux Réas

La Fontaine
de Vosne

RN74

S.N.C.F. Paris-Lyon

Au-dessus
de la Rivière

To
Cîteaux

❶ La Montagne
❷ Cros-Parentoux
❸ Vigneux
❹ Aux Reignots
❺ La Romanée
❻ La Romanée-Conti
❼ La Colombière
❽ Les Gaudichots
❾ Au dessus des Malconsorts

Les
Jacquines

Aux Raviolles

La Croix Blanche

N

Vosne-Romanée

To Beaune

Hautes Côtes
de Nuits

La Grande Rue
Echézeaux Grands-Echézeaux
Romanée, Romanée-Conti
Romanée-Saint-Vivant
Richebourg, La Tâche

Vosne-Romanée Premier Cru

Vosne-Romanée

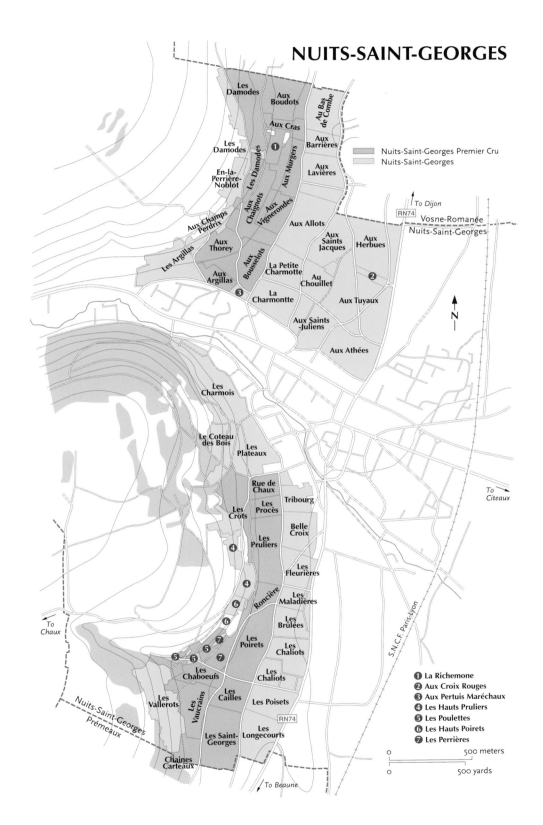

NUITS-SAINT-GEORGES

Les Damodes
Aux Boudots
Au Bas de Combe
Aux Cras
Aux Barrières
Les Damodes
Aux Murgers
Aux Lavières
En-la-Perrière-Noblot
Aux Chaignots
Aux Vignerondes
Aux Allots

Nuits-Saint-Georges Premier Cru
Nuits-Saint-Georges

To Dijon
RN74
Vosne-Romanée
Nuits-Saint-Georges

Aux Champs Perdrix
Aux Thorey
Les Argillas
Aux Argillas
Aux Bousselots
La Petite Charmotte
Au Chouillet
La Charmontte
Aux Saints-Juliens
Aux Saints Jacques
Aux Herbues
Aux Tuyaux

N

Aux Athées

Les Charmois

Le Coteau des Bois
Les Plateaux

Rue de Chaux
Les Crots
Les Procès
Tribourg
Belle Croix
Les Pruliers
Les Fleurières
Roncière
Les Maladières
Les Brûlées
Les Poirets
Les Chaliots
Les Chaboeufs
Les Chaliots
Les Cailles
Les Poisets
Les Vallerots
Les Vaucrains
Les Saint-Georges
Les Longecourts
Chaines Carteaux

To Citeaux

To Chaux

S.N.C.F. Paris–Lyon

RN74

❶ La Richemone
❷ Aux Croix Rouges
❸ Aux Pertuis Maréchaux
❹ Les Hauts Pruliers
❺ Les Poulettes
❻ Les Hauts Poirets
❼ Les Perrières

Nuits-Saint-Georges Prémeaux

To Beaune

0   500 meters
0   500 yards

PRÉMEAUX

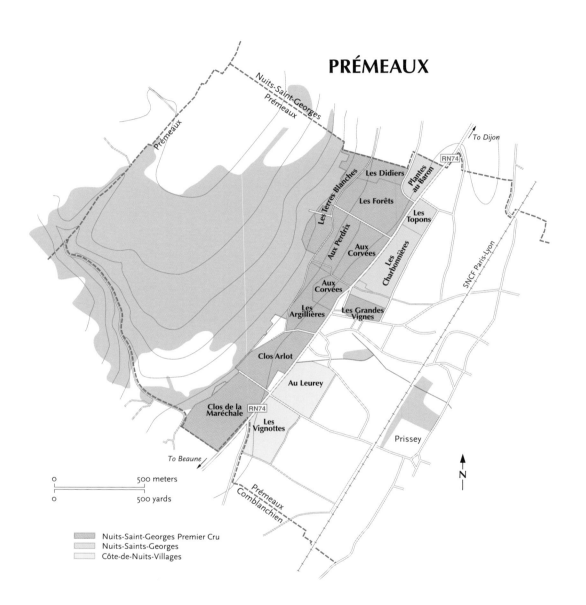

Nuits-Saint-Georges
Prémeaux

Prémeaux

To Dijon

RN74

Les Didiers

Plantes au Baron

Les Terres Blanches

Les Forêts

Aux Perdrix

Les Topons

Aux Corvées

Les Charbonnières

Aux Corvées

Les Grandes Vignes

Les Argillières

SNCF Paris-Lyon

Clos Arlot

Au Leurey

Clos de la Maréchale

RN74

Prissey

Les Vignottes

To Beaune

Prémeaux
Comblanchien

N

0   500 meters

0   500 yards

▓ Nuits-Saint-Georges Premier Cru
▓ Nuits-Saints-Georges
▓ Côte-de-Nuits-Villages

COMBLANCHIEN AND CORGOLOIN

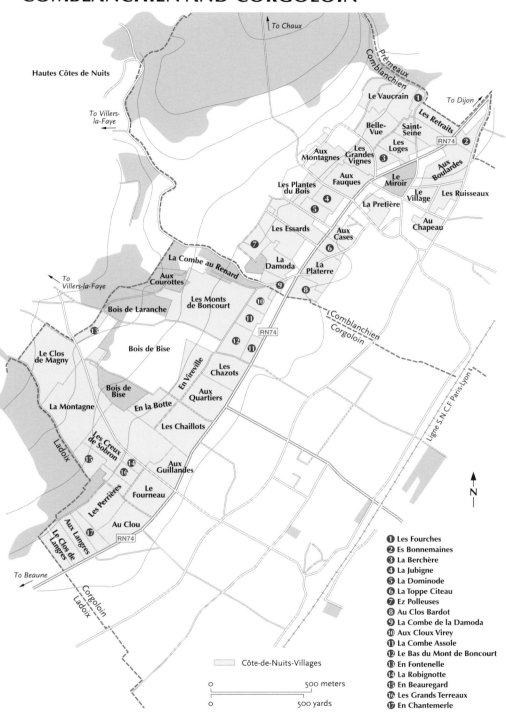

Hautes Côtes de Nuits

To Chaux

To Villers-la-Faye

To Dijon

Prémeaux

Comblanchien

Le Vaucrain ❶

Les Retraits

RN74

Belle-Vue

Saint-Seine

Les Loges

❷

Aux Montagnes

Les Grandes Vignes

❸

Aux Fauques

Le Miroir

Aux Boulardes

Les Plantes du Bois

❹

La Pretière

Le Village

Les Ruisseaux

❺

Au Chapeau

Les Essards

Aux Cases

❻

❼

La Damoda

La Platerre

La Combe au Renard

Aux Courottes

❾

❽

Bois de Laranche

Les Monts de Boncourt

❿

⓫

Comblanchien

Corgoloin

RN74

⓬

⓫

Le Clos de Magny

Bois de Bise

En Vireville

Les Chazots

⓭

Bois de Bise

Aux Quartiers

En la Botte

La Montagne

Les Chaillots

Les Creux de Sobron

Ladoix

⓯

⓮

⓰

Aux Guillandes

Les Perrières

Le Fourneau

Au Clou

⓱

RN74

Aux Langres

Le Clos de Langres

To Beaune

Corgoloin

Ladoix

N

Ligne S.N.C.F Paris-Lyon

❶ Les Fourches
❷ Es Bonnemaines
❸ La Berchère
❹ La Jubigne
❺ La Dominode
❻ La Toppe Citeau
❼ Ez Polleuses
❽ Au Clos Bardot
❾ La Combe de la Damoda
❿ Aux Cloux Virey
⓫ La Combe Assole
⓬ Le Bas du Mont de Boncourt
⓭ En Fontenelle
⓮ La Robignotte
⓯ En Beauregard
⓰ Les Grands Terreaux
⓱ En Chantemerle

Côte-de-Nuits-Villages

0   500 meters

0   500 yards

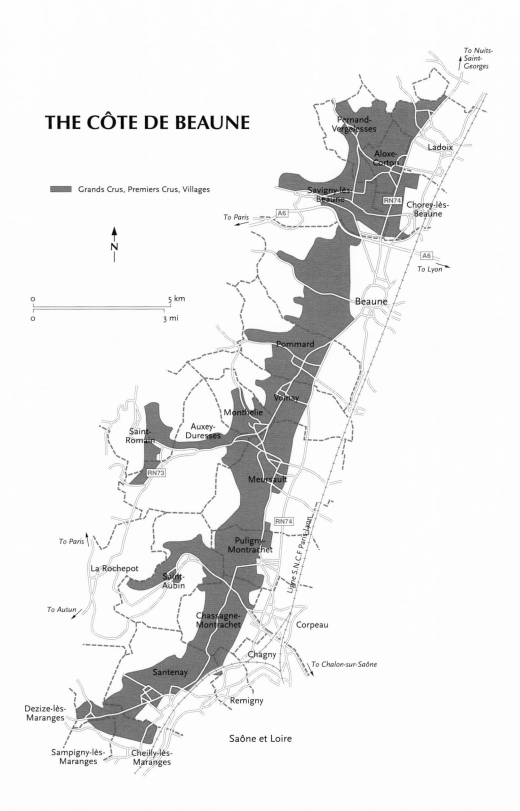

THE CÔTE DE BEAUNE

Grands Crus, Premiers Crus, Villages

N

0   5 km
0   3 mi

To Nuits-Saint-Georges

Pernand-Vergelesses

Aloxe-Corton

Ladoix

Savigny-lès-Beaune

RN74

Chorey-lès-Beaune

To Paris

A6

A6

To Lyon

Beaune

Pommard

Volnay

Monthelie

Auxey-Duresses

Saint-Romain

RN73

Meursault

RN74

To Paris

Puligny-Montrachet

La Rochepot

Saint-Aubin

Ligne S.N.C.F Paris-Lyon

Chassagne-Montrachet

Corpeau

To Autun

Chagny

To Chalon-sur-Saône

Santenay

Remigny

Dezize-lès-Maranges

Saône et Loire

Sampigny-lès-Maranges

Cheilly-lès-Maranges

LADOIX

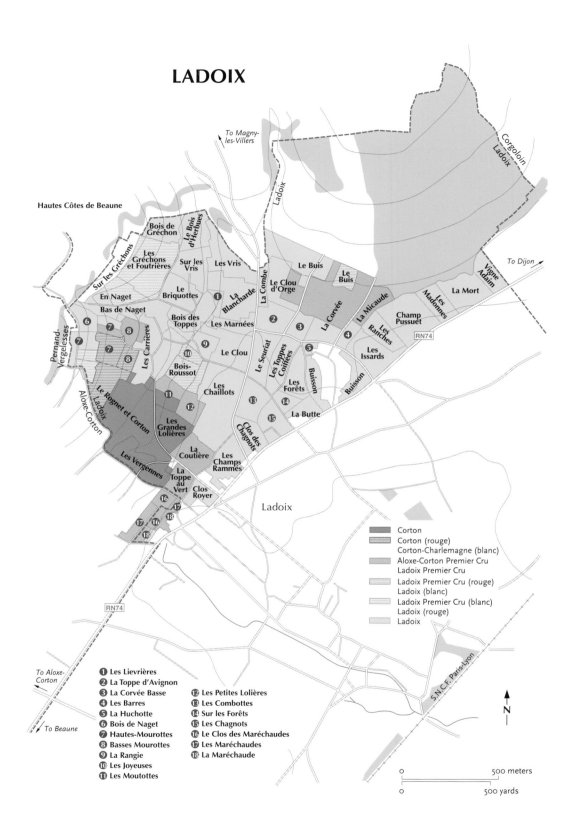

To Magny-
les-Villers

Corgoloin
Ladoix

To Dijon

Hautes Côtes de Beaune

Bois de
Gréchon

Le Bois
d'Herbues

Les
Gréchons
et Foutrières

Sur les
Vris

Les Vris

Le Buis

Le Buis

Vigne
Adam

Sur les Gréchons

La Combe

Les
Madonnes

La Mort

En Naget

Le
Briquottes

La
Blancharde

Le Clou
d'Orge

La Micaude

La Corvée

Champ
Pussuet

Bas de Naget

❶

❷

❸

Les
Ranches

RN74

Pernand Vergelesses

❻

❼

❽

Bois des
Toppes

Les Marnées

❹

Les
Issards

❼

❼

❽

Les Carrières

❾

Le Clou

Le Seuriat

Les Toppes
Coiffées

❺

Buisson

Bois-
Roussot

❿

Les
Forêts

Buisson

Le Rognet et Corton

⓫

Les
Chaillots

⓭

⓮

Ladoix

⓬

⓯

La Butte

Aloxe-Corton

Les Grandes
Lolières

Clos des
Chagnots

La
Coutière

Les
Champs
Rammés

Ladoix

Les Vergennes

La
Toppe
au
Vert

Clos
Royer

⓰

⓱

⓱

⓰

⓲

⓲

Corton
Corton (rouge)
Corton-Charlemagne (blanc)
Aloxe-Corton Premier Cru
Ladoix Premier Cru
Ladoix Premier Cru (rouge)
Ladoix (blanc)
Ladoix Premier Cru (blanc)
Ladoix (rouge)
Ladoix

RN74

S.N.C.F. Paris-Lyon

To Aloxe-
Corton

❶ Les Lievrières
❷ La Toppe d'Avignon
❸ La Corvée Basse
❹ Les Barres
❺ La Huchotte
❻ Bois de Naget
❼ Hautes-Mourottes
❽ Basses Mourottes
❾ La Rangie
❿ Les Joyeuses
⓫ Les Moutottes

⓬ Les Petites Lolières
⓭ Les Combottes
⓮ Sur les Forêts
⓯ Les Chagnots
⓰ Le Clos des Maréchaudes
⓱ Les Maréchaudes
⓲ La Maréchaude

To Beaune

N

0   500 meters

0   500 yards

ALOXE-CORTON

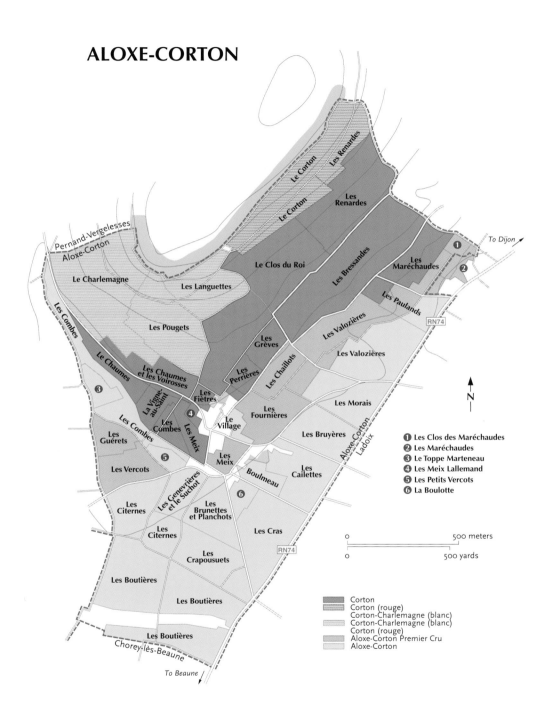

Pernand-Vergelesses
Aloxe-Corton

Le Corton

Les Renardes

Les Renardes

Le Corton

Le Clos du Roi

Les Bressandes

Les Maréchaudes

❶

To Dijon

❷

Le Charlemagne

Les Languettes

Les Paulands

Les Combes

Les Pougets

Les Valozières

RN74

Les Grèves

Les Valozières

Le Chaumes

Les Chaumes
et les Voirosses

Les Chaillots

Les
Perrières

La Vigne-
au-Saint

Les
Fiètres

Les Morais

❸

Le
Village

Les
Fournières

❹

Les Combes

Les
Combes

Les Meix

Les Bruyères

Aloxe-Corton

Ladoix

Les
Guérets

❶ Les Clos des Maréchaudes

❺

Les
Meix

Boulmeau

Les
Cailettes

❷ Les Maréchaudes
❸ Le Toppe Marteneau

Les Vercots

Les Genevrières
et le Suchot

❻

❹ Les Meix Lallemand
❺ Les Petits Vercots
❻ La Boulotte

Les
Citernes

Les
Brunettes
et Planchots

Les
Citernes

Les Cras

N

Les
Crapousuets

RN74

0   500 meters

Les Boutières

0   500 yards

Les Boutières

	Corton
	Corton (rouge)
	Corton-Charlemagne (blanc)
	Corton-Charlemagne (blanc)
	Corton (rouge)
	Aloxe-Corton Premier Cru
	Aloxe-Corton

Les Boutières

Chorey-lès-Beaune

To Beaune

PERNAND-VERGELESSES

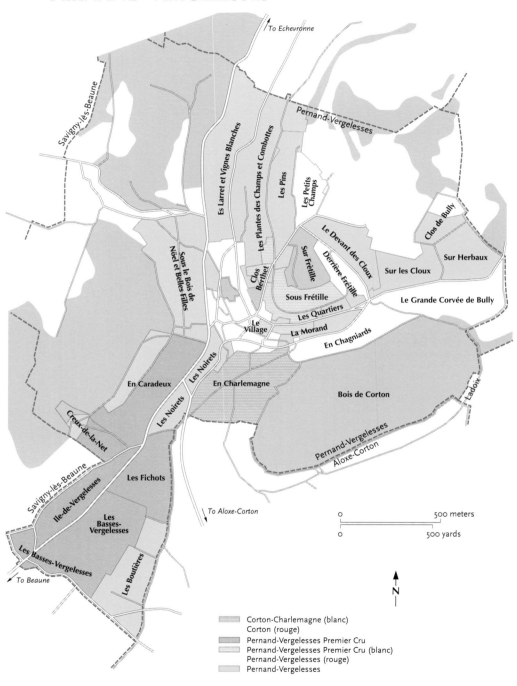

To Echevronne

Savigny-lès-Beaune

Pernand-Vergelesses

Es Larret et Vignes Blanches

Les Plantes des Champs et Combottes

Les Pins

Les Petits Champs

Clos de Bully

Sous le Bois de Noël et Belles Filles

Le Devant des Cloux

Sur Frétille

Derrière Frétille

Clos Berthet

Sur les Cloux

Sur Herbaux

Sous Frétille

Le Grande Corvée de Bully

Les Quartiers

Le Village

La Morand

En Chagniards

Les Noirets

En Caradeux

En Charlemagne

Bois de Corton

Les Noirets

Ladoix

Creux-de-la-Net

Savigny-lès-Beaune

Pernand-Vergelesses

Aloxe-Corton

Les Fichots

Ile-de-Vergelesses

To Aloxe-Corton

Les Basses-Vergelesses

Les Basses-Vergelesses

Les Boutières

To Beaune

N

0	500 meters
0	500 yards

Corton-Charlemagne (blanc)
Corton (rouge)
Pernand-Vergelesses Premier Cru
Pernand-Vergelesses Premier Cru (blanc)
Pernand-Vergelesses (rouge)
Pernand-Vergelesses

SAVIGNY-LÈS-BEAUNE

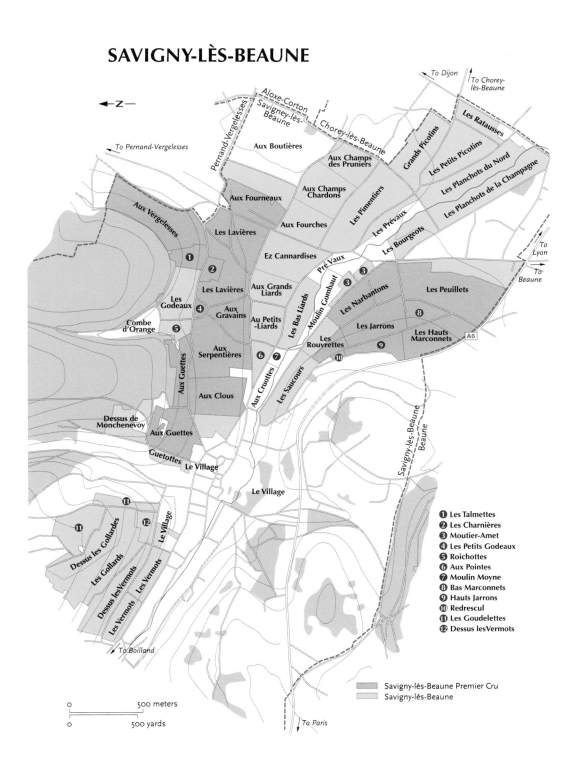

← —N—

To Dijon
To Chorey-
lès-Beaune

Pernand-Vergelesses
Aloxe-Corton
Savigny-lès-Beaune
Chorey-lès-Beaune

To Pernand-Vergelesses

Aux Boutières

Les Ratausses

Grands Picotins
Les Petits Picotins
Les Planchots du Nord
Les Planchots de la Champagne

Aux Champs
des Pruniers

Aux Champs
Chardons

Aux Fourneaux

Les Pimentiers

Les Prévaux

Aux Vergelesses

Les Lavières

Aux Fourches

Les Bourgeots

To
Lyon

Ez Cannardises

Pré Vaux

To
Beaune

❶

❷

❸

❸

Les Lavières

Aux Grands
Liards

Les Bas Liards

Moulin Combaut

Les Narbantons

Les Peuillets

Les
Godeaux

❹

Aux
Gravains

❽

Combe
d'Orange

❺

Au Petits
-Liards

Les Jarrons

Les Hauts
Marconnets

Les
Rouvrettes

❾

A6

❻ ❼

Aux
Serpentières

❿

Aux Guettes

Aux Cruottes

Les Saucours

Aux Clous

Dessus de
Monchenevoy

Aux Guettes

Savigny-lès-Beaune
Beaune

Guetottes

Le Village

Le Village

❶ Les Talmettes
❷ Les Charnières
❸ Moutier-Amet
❹ Les Petits Godeaux
❺ Roichottes
❻ Aux Pointes
❼ Moulin Moyne
❽ Bas Marconnets
❾ Hauts Jarrons
❿ Redrescul
⓫ Les Goudelettes
⓬ Dessus lesVermots

⓫

⓬

Le Village

⓫

Dessus les Gollardes

Les Gollards

Dessus lesVermots

Les Vermots

Les Vermots

Les Vermots

To Boilland

Savigny-lès-Beaune Premier Cru
Savigny-lès-Beaune

o   500 meters

o   500 yards

To Paris

CHOREY-LÈS-BEAUNE

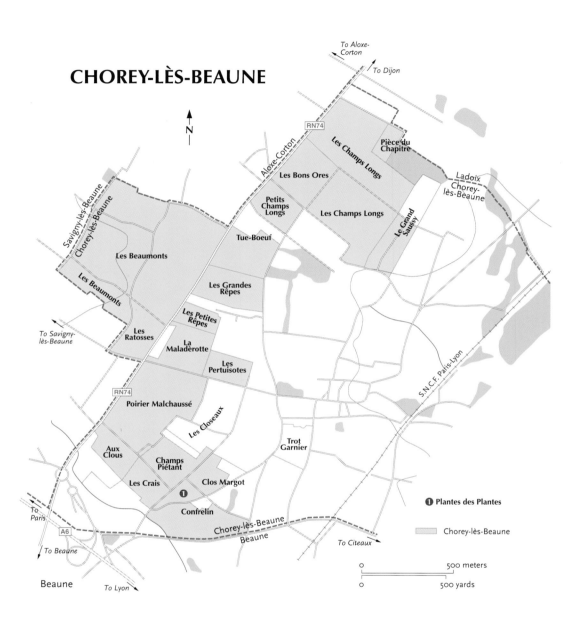

To Aloxe-Corton

To Dijon

N

RN74

Aloxe-Corton

Pièce du Chapitre

Les Champs Longs

Ladoix Chorey-lès-Beaune

Savigny-lès-Beaune

Chorey-lès-Beaune

Les Bons Ores

Petits Champs Longs

Les Champs Longs

Le Grand Saussy

Tue-Boeuf

Les Beaumonts

Les Grandes Rêpes

Les Beaumonts

Les Petites Rêpes

To Savigny-lès-Beaune

Les Ratosses

La Maladerotte

Les Pertuisotes

RN74

Poirier Malchaussé

Les Closeaux

S.N.C.F. Paris-Lyon

Aux Clous

Trot Garnier

Champs Piétant

Les Crais

Clos Margot

To Paris

A6

Confrelin

Chorey-lès-Beaune

Beaune

To Citeaux

To Beaune

Beaune

To Lyon

❶ Plantes des Plantes

Chorey-lès-Beaune

0   500 meters

0   500 yards

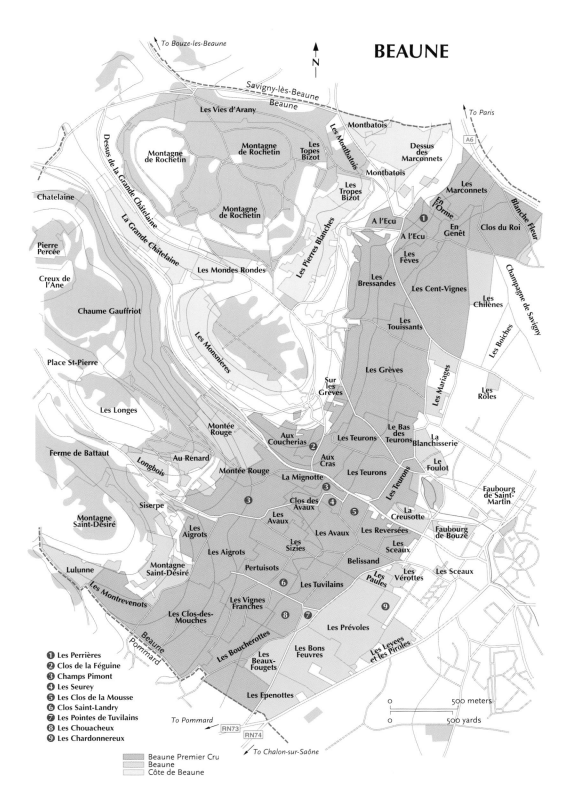

BEAUNE

To Bouze-les-Beaune

Savigny-lès-Beaune
Beaune

To Paris

A6

Les Vies d'Arany

Montbatois

Montbatois

Dessus des Marconnets

Montagne de Rochetin

Montagne de Rochetin

Les Topes Bizot

Les Montbatois

Montbatois

Les Marconnets

Chatelaine

Les Tropes Bizot

A l'Ecu

En l'Orme

❶

En Genêt

Clos du Roi

Blanche Fleur

Montagne de Rochetin

A l'Ecu

Pierre Percée

Les Pierres Blanches

Les Fèves

Les Mondes Rondes

Les Bressandes

Les Cent-Vignes

Champagne de Savigny

Creux de l'Ane

Les Chilènes

Chaume Gauffriot

Les Touissants

Les Boiches

Les Monsnières

Les Grèves

Les Mariages

Place St-Pierre

Sur les Grèves

Les Rôles

Les Longes

Montée Rouge

Le Bas des Teurons

La Blanchisserie

Ferme de Battaut

Aux Coucherias

❷

Les Teurons

Longbois

Au Renard

Aux Cras

Le Foulot

Montée Rouge

Les Teurons

Les Teurons

Faubourg de Saint-Martin

La Mignotte

❸

Siserpe

❸

Clos des Avaux

❹

La Creusotte

Montagne Saint-Désiré

Les Avaux

❺

Les Aigrots

Les Avaux

Les Reversées

Faubourg de Bouze

Lulunne

Les Aigrots

Les Sizies

Les Sceaux

Les Sceaux

Montagne Saint-Désiré

Pertuisots

Belissand

Les Paules

Les Vérottes

Les Montrevenots

❻

Les Tuvilains

❾

Les Vignes Franches

Beaune

Pommard

Les Clos-des-Mouches

❽

❼

Les Prévoles

Les Boucherottes

Les Bons Feuvres

Les Levees et les Piroles

Les Beaux-Fougets

❶ Les Perrières
❷ Clos de la Féguine
❸ Champs Pimont
❹ Les Seurey
❺ Les Clos de la Mousse
❻ Clos Saint-Landry
❼ Les Pointes de Tuvilains
❽ Les Chouacheux
❾ Les Chardonnereux

Les Epenottes

To Pommard

RN73

RN74

To Chalon-sur-Saône

0   500 meters

0   500 yards

Beaune Premier Cru
Beaune
Côte de Beaune

POMMARD

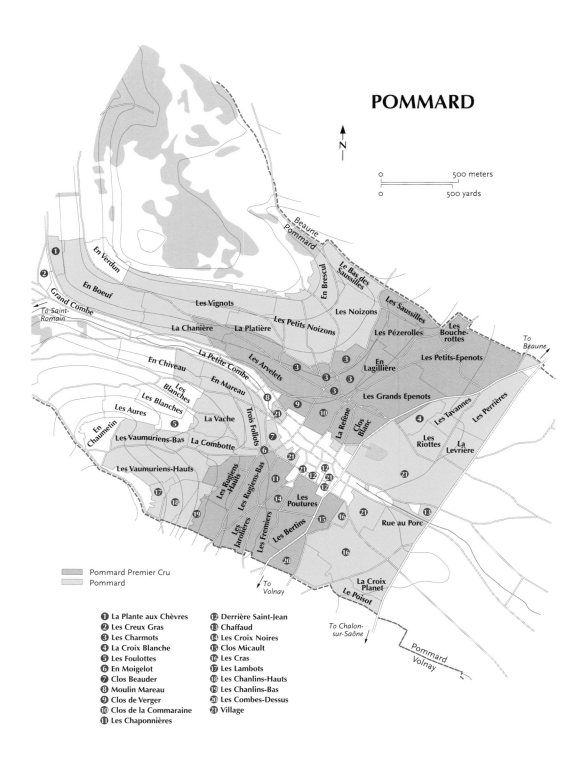

N

0	500 meters
0	500 yards

En Verdun
En Boeuf
Grand Combe
To Saint-Romain
Les Vignots
La Chanière
La Platière
Les Petits Noizons
Les Noizons
Les Pézerolles
Les Bouche-rottes
Les Saussilles
Le Bas des Saussilles
En Brescul
Beaune Pommard
To Beaune
Les Petits-Epenots
En Lagillière
La Petite Combe
Les Arvelets
En Chiveau
En Mareau
Les Blanches
Les Blanches
Les Aures
En Chaumelin
Les Vaumuriens-Bas
La Vache
La Combotte
Trois Follots
Les Grands Epenots
La Refène
Clos Blanc
Les Tavannes
Les Perrières
Les Riottes
La Levrière
Les Vaumuriens-Hauts
Les Rugiens-Hauts
Les Rugiens-Bas
Les Chaponnières
Les Poutures
Rue au Porc
Les Jaroliières
Les Fremiers
Les Bertins
Les Croix Noires
Clos Micault
Les Cras
Les Combes-Dessus
To Volnay
La Croix Planet
Le Poisot
To Chalon-sur-Saône
Pommard Volnay

Pommard Premier Cru
Pommard

❶ La Plante aux Chèvres
❷ Les Creux Gras
❸ Les Charmots
❹ La Croix Blanche
❺ Les Foulottes
❻ En Moigelot
❼ Clos Beauder
❽ Moulin Mareau
❾ Clos de Verger
❿ Clos de la Commaraine
⓫ Les Chaponnières
⓬ Derrière Saint-Jean
⓭ Chaffaud
⓮ Les Croix Noires
⓯ Clos Micault
⓰ Les Cras
⓱ Les Lambots
⓲ Les Chanlins-Hauts
⓳ Les Chanlins-Bas
⓴ Les Combes-Dessus
㉑ Village

VOLNAY

N

| 0 | 500 meters |
| 0 | 500 yards |

Sur Roches

Chanlins

Paux Bois

En Vaut

La Bouchère

Pitures-Dessus

Clos des Ducs

Frémiets

To Pommard

La Cave

❶

❶

Les Angles

La Barre

Les Brouillards

❷

❸

Pommard Volnay

To Beaune

Les Grands Poisots

❶

Bousse d'Or

Les Mitans

Les Serpens

Les Buttes

❶

❶

En l'Ormeau

Les Grands Champs

Les Petit Poisots

❻

Taillepieds

❹

Carelle sous la Chapelle

La Gigotte

Les Famines

Ez Blanches

Clos des Chênes

Clos des Chênes

En Champans

❺

Le Ronceret

❼

Les Pasquiers

Monthélie

Clos des Chênes

En Cailleret

❼

Ez Echards

❽

Caillerets Dessus

Les Aussy

❽

En Chevret

Les Lurets

❾

Cros Martin

Robardelle

RN74

To Auxey-Duresses

To Meursault

Les Lurets

Volnay Meursault

❶ Le Village
❷ Pointes d'Angles
❸ Les Combes
❹ En Verseuil
❺ Carelles-Dessous
❻ Beau Regard
❼ Les Pluchots
❽ Les Petits Garnets
❾ Les Jouères

Volnay Premier Cru

Volnay

To Chalon-sur-Saône

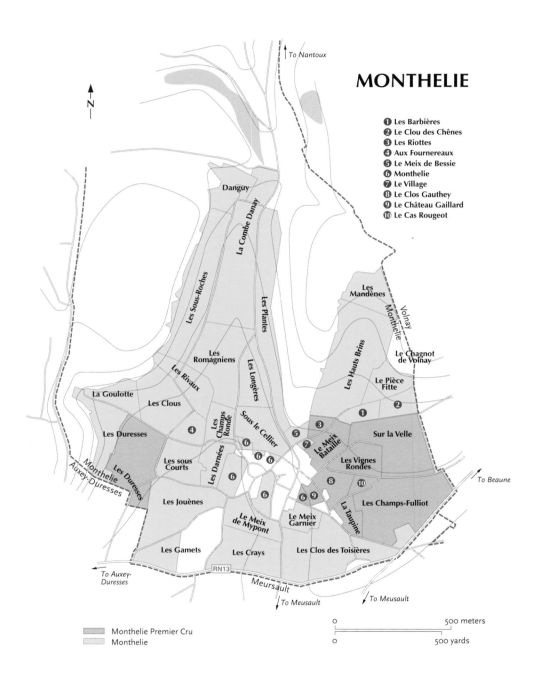

MONTHELIE

1 Les Barbières
2 Le Clou des Chênes
3 Les Riottes
4 Aux Fournereaux
5 Le Meix de Bessie
6 Monthelie
7 Le Village
8 Le Clos Gauthey
9 Le Château Gaillard
10 Le Cas Rougeot

To Nantoux

N

Danguy

La Combe Danay

Les Sous-Roches

Les Plantes

Les Mandènes

Volnay
Monthelie

Les Hauts Brins

Le Chagnot
de Volnay

Les
Romagniens

Les Rivaux

Les Longères

Le Pièce
Fitte

La Goulotte

Les Clous

Les
Champs
Ronde

Sous le Cellier

2

1

Les Duresses

4

5

3

7

Le Meix
Bataille

Sur la Velle

Les sous
Courts

Les Darnées

6

6

6

Les Vignes
Rondes

Monthelie
Auxey-Duresses

Les Duresses

6

8

10

Les Jouènes

6

6

9

Les Champs-Fulliot

La Taupine

Le Meix
de Mypont

Le Meix
Garnier

To Beaune

Les Gamets

Les Crays

Les Clos des Toisières

RN13

To Auxey-
Duresses

Meursault

To Meusault

To Meusault

Monthelie Premier Cru
Monthelie

0   500 meters
0   500 yards

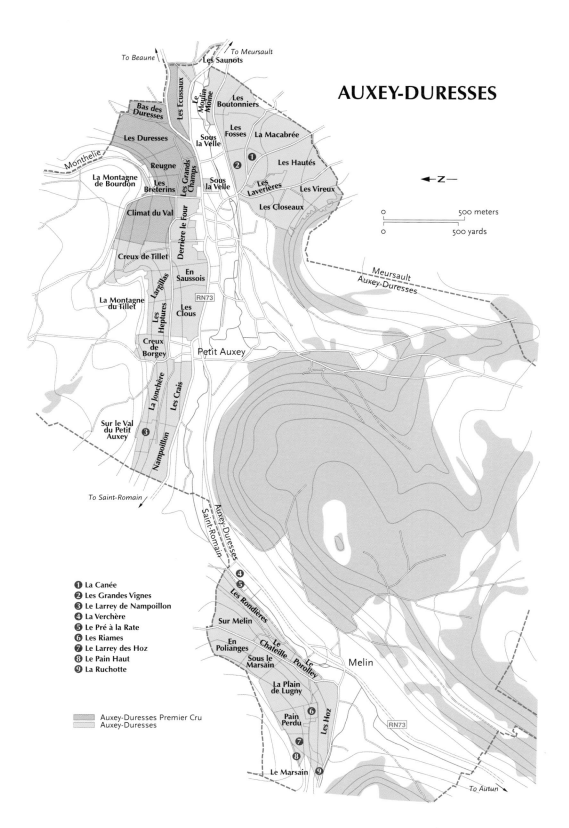

AUXEY-DURESSES

To Beaune

To Meursault

Les Saunots

Les Écussaux

Le Moulin Moine

Les Boutonniers

Bas des Duresses

Les Duresses

Sous la Velle

Les Fosses

La Macabrée

Monthélie

Reugne

Les Grands Champs

Sous la Velle

❶ La Canée

❷ Les Grandes Vignes

Les Hautés

La Montagne de Bourdon

Les Bréterins

Les Laverières

Les Vireux

Climat du Val

Derrière le Four

Les Closeaux

←–N–→

Creux de Tillet

500 meters

En Saussois

500 yards

La Montagne du Tillet

Langillas

RN73

Les Heptures

Les Clous

Meursault
Auxey-Duresses

Creux de Borgey

Petit Auxey

La Jonchère

Les Crais

Sur le Val du Petit Auxey

❸

Nampoillon

To Saint-Romain

Auxey-Duresses
Saint-Romain

❶ La Canée
❷ Les Grandes Vignes
❸ Le Larrey de Nampoillon
❹ La Verchère
❺ Le Pré à la Rate
❻ Les Riames
❼ Le Larrey des Hoz
❽ Le Pain Haut
❾ La Ruchotte

❹

❺

Les Rondières

Sur Melin

En Polianges

Le Chateille

Le Porolley

Melin

Sous le Marsain

La Plain de Lugny

Auxey-Duresses Premier Cru
Auxey-Duresses

Pain Perdu

❻

Les Hoz

RN73

❼

❽

Le Marsain

❾

To Autun

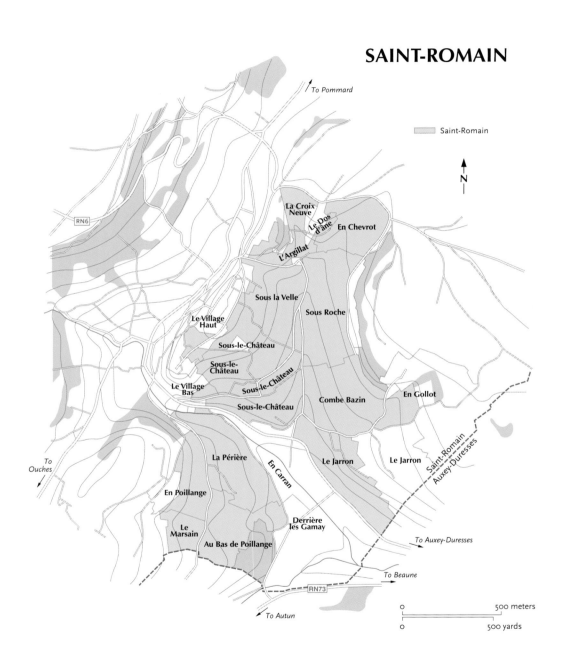

SAINT-ROMAIN

To Pommard

Saint-Romain

N

La Croix
Neuve

Le Dos
d'âne

En Chevrot

L'Argillat

RN6

Sous la Velle

Sous Roche

Le Village
Haut

Sous-le-Château

Sous-le-
Château

Sous-le-Château

Le Village
Bas

Sous-le-Château

Combe Bazin

En Gollot

To
Ouches

La Périère

En Carran

Le Jarron

Le Jarron

Saint-Romain
Auxey-Duresses

En Poillange

Derrière
les Gamay

Le
Marsain

Au Bas de Poillange

To Auxey-Duresses

To Beaune

RN73

To Autun

0   500 meters

0   500 yards

MEURSAULT

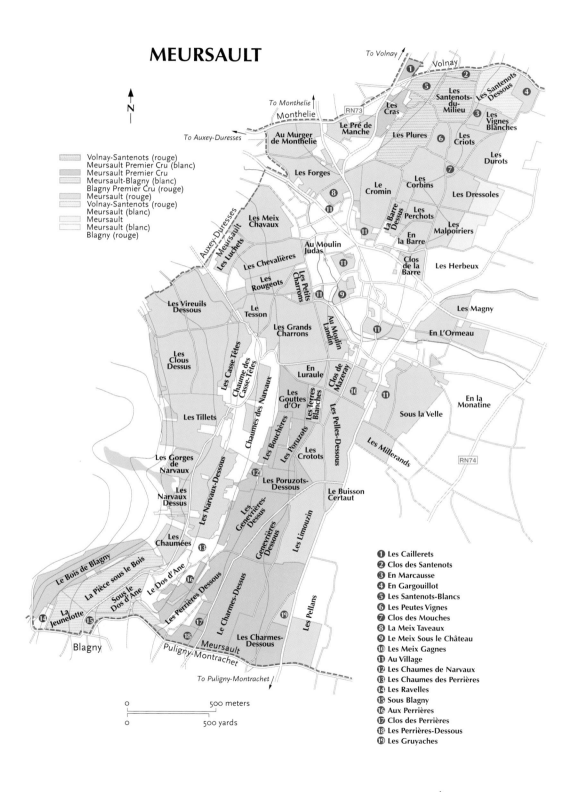

N

To Volnay

Volnay

To Monthelie

Monthelie

RN73

To Auxey-Duresses

Au Murger
de Monthelie

Le Pré de
Manche

Les Cras

Les Santenots-
du-
Milieu

Les Santenots
Dessous

Les Vignes
Blanches

Les Plures

Les Criots

Les Durots

Les Forges

Le
Cromin

Les
Corbins

Les Dressoles

La Barre
Dessus

Les
Perchots

Les
Malpoiriers

En
la Barre

Les Meix
Chavaux

Au Moulin
Judas

Clos
de la
Barre

Les Herbeux

Auxey-Duresses

Meursault

Les Luchets

Les Chevalières

Les
Rougeots

Les Petits
Charrons

Les Magny

En L'Ormeau

Les Vireuils
Dessous

Le
Tesson

Les Grands
Charrons

Au Moulin
Landin

Les
Clous
Dessus

Les Casse Têtes

Chaume des
Casse-Têtes

En
Luraule

Clos de
Mazeray

En la
Monatine

Les Tillets

Chaumes des Narvaux

Les
Gouttes
d'Or

Les Terres
Blanches

Les Pelles-Dessous

Sous la Velle

Les Bouchères

Les Poruzots

Les
Crotots

Les Gorges
de
Narvaux

Les Millerands

RN74

Les Narvaux-Dessous

Les
Narvaux
Dessus

Les Poruzots-
Dessous

Le Buisson
Certaut

Les
Genevrières-
Dessus

Les
Chaumées

Genevrières
Dessous

Les Limouzin

Le Bois de Blagny

La Pièce sous le Bois

Sous le
Dos d'Ane

Le Dos d'Ane

Les Perrières Dessous

Le Charmes-Dessus

Les Pellans

La
Jeunelotte

Blagny

Les Charmes-
Dessous

Meursault

Puligny-Montrachet

To Puligny-Montrachet

0   500 meters

0   500 yards

Volnay-Santenots (rouge)
Meursault Premier Cru (blanc)
Meursault Premier Cru
Meursault-Blagny (blanc)
Blagny Premier Cru (rouge)
Meursault (rouge)
Volnay-Santenots (rouge)
Meursault (blanc)
Meursault
Meursault (blanc)
Blagny (rouge)

1 Les Caillerets
2 Clos des Santenots
3 En Marcausse
4 En Gargouillot
5 Les Santenots-Blancs
6 Les Peutes Vignes
7 Clos des Mouches
8 La Meix Taveaux
9 Le Meix Sous le Château
10 Les Meix Gagnes
11 Au Village
12 Les Chaumes de Narvaux
13 Les Chaumes des Perrières
14 Les Ravelles
15 Sous Blagny
16 Aux Perrières
17 Clos des Perrières
18 Les Perrières-Dessous
19 Les Gruyaches

PULIGNY-MONTRACHET

o |———————————| 500 meters
o |———————————| 500 yards

N ↑

Blagny

Sous le Puits

❶

Les
Chalumaux

Le Trézin

Hameau
de Blagny

❷

Champ-
Canet

To Meursault

La Garenne ou
sur la Garenne

❷

❸

Meursault
Puligny-Montrachet

Champs-Gain

❹

Les Combettes

Les Referts

To Meursault

Les
Charmes

Ez Folatières

❹

Les Perrières

Corvées
des Vignes

Mont Rachet

Clavoillon

Les Levrons

❺

Peux
Bois

Au
Chaniot

Les
Grands
Champs

Les Petits
Nosroyes

Les
Nosroyes

❻

Les Reuchaux

En la
Richarde

❼

Derrière
la Velle

To Beaune

Brelance

Au Paupillot

Saint-Aubin
Puligny-Montrachet

Les Caillerets

Les Pucelles

Voitte

❾

Chevalier-Montrachet

❽

La Rue aux Vaches

Meix
Pelletier

Les
Gageres

Montrachet

Les Meix

Le
Village

Bâtard-Montrachet

Bienvenues-
Bâtard-
Montrachet

Rue Rousseau

Les
Enseignères

Le Village

To Chassagne-
Montrachet

Les
Aubues

Noyer
Bret

Les Tremblot

Chassagne-
Montrachet

Les Houlières

RN74

Puligny-Montrachet

Montrachet
Chevalier-Montrachet
Bâtard-Montrachet
Bienvenues-Bâtard-Montrachet
Puligny-Montrachet Premier Cru
Puligny-Montrachet Premier Cru (blanc)
Blagny Premier Cru (rouge)
Puligny-Montrachet
Puligny-Montrachet (blanc)
Blagny (rouge)

To Chalon-
sur-Saône

❶ Sous le Courthil
❷ Les Truffières
❸ Le Jaquelotte ou Champ Canet
❹ Clos de la Garenne
❺ La Rousselle
❻ Champ Croyon
❼ Les Petits Grands Champs
❽ Clos des Meix
❾ Les Boudrières

SAINT-AUBIN AND GAMAY

Saint-Aubin Premier Cru
Saint-Aubin

0   500 meters
0   500 yards

N

To Puligny-
Montrachet

Meursault-
Saint-Aubin

Puligny-Montrachet

En Vermarain
à l'Est

Bas de Vermarain
à l'Est

Bas de Vermarain
à l'Ouest

En
Créot

② ①

③

Les Champlots

Vignes
Moingeon

En
Gouin

④

Gamay

Hautes-Côtes de Beaune

En la
Ranche

Es Champs

Les
Frionnes

⑤

Sous
Roche
Dumay

⑥

⑦

⑧

Les
Perrières

La Chatenière

Sur Gamay

⑪

⑨

⑬

⑫

Saint-Aubin

En Choilles

⑩

Les Murgers-
des-Dents-
de-Chien

Les
Castets

⑭

Les
Cortons

⑳ ⑱

⑰

Les Pucelles

⑭

RN6

En Remilly

Au Bas
de
Jorcul

⑯

Le Blanc

⑮

Les Argillers

Champ Tirant

⑲

⑯

RN6

En Vollon à l'Est

Les Combes-au-Sud

Le Charmois

Pitangeret

To La Rochepot

Saint-Aubin-
Chassagne-
Montrachet

To Lyon

To Paris

① En Vesveau
② Sous les Foires
③ La Fontenotte
④ Derrière-La Tour
⑤ En Montceau
⑥ Les Travers de Marinot
⑦ Sur le Sentier du Clou
⑧ Marinot
⑨ Echaille
⑩ Le-Bas-de-Gammay-à-l'Est
⑪ Le Puits
⑫ Derrière Chez Édouard
⑬ Les Travers de chez Edouard
⑭ Le Village
⑮ Le Bas de Monin
⑯ En l'Ebaupin
⑰ Les Vellerottes
⑱ Tope Bataille
⑲ La Traversaine
⑳ En Jorcul

CHASSAGNE-MONTRACHET

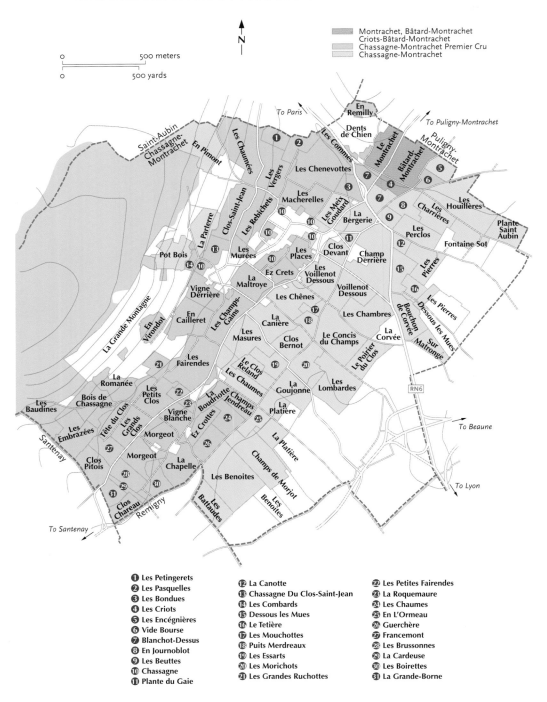

N

| 0 | 500 meters |
| 0 | 500 yards |

Montrachet, Bâtard-Montrachet
Criots-Bâtard-Montrachet
Chassagne-Montrachet Premier Cru
Chassagne-Montrachet

❶ Les Petingerets
❷ Les Pasquelles
❸ Les Bondues
❹ Les Criots
❺ Les Encégnières
❻ Vide Bourse
❼ Blanchot-Dessus
❽ En Journoblot
❾ Les Beuttes
❿ Chassagne
⓫ Plante du Gaie

⓬ La Canotte
⓭ Chassagne Du Clos-Saint-Jean
⓮ Les Combards
⓯ Dessous les Mues
⓰ Le Tetière
⓱ Les Mouchottes
⓲ Puits Merdreaux
⓳ Les Essarts
⓴ Les Morichots
㉑ Les Grandes Ruchottes

㉒ Les Petites Fairendes
㉓ La Roquemaure
㉔ Les Chaumes
㉕ En L'Ormeau
㉖ Guerchère
㉗ Francemont
㉘ Les Brussonnes
㉙ La Cardeuse
㉚ Les Boirettes
㉛ La Grande-Borne

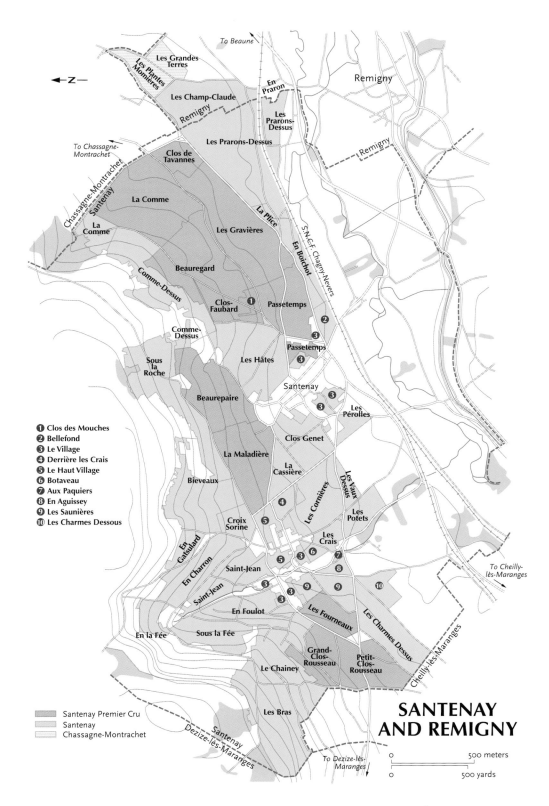

← —Z—

To Beaune

Les Grandes Terres

Les Plantes Momières

Remigny

En Praron

Les Champ-Claude

Remigny

Les Prarons-Dessus

To Chassagne-Montrachet

Les Prarons-Dessus

Remigny

Chassagne-Montrachet

Santenay

Clos de Tavannes

La Comme

La Plice

Les Gravières

La Comme

S.N.C.F. Chagny-Nevers

En Boichot

Beauregard

Comme-Dessus

Clos-Faubard

❶

Passetemps

❷

Comme-Dessus

Passetemps

Sous la Roche

Les Hâtes

❸

Beaurepaire

Santenay

❸

Les Pérolles

❸

❶ Clos des Mouches
❷ Bellefond
❸ Le Village
❹ Derrière les Crais
❺ Le Haut Village
❻ Botaveau
❼ Aux Paquiers
❽ En Aguissey
❾ Les Saunières
❿ Les Charmes Dessous

La Maladière

Clos Genet

La Cassière

Bièveaux

Les Cormières

Les Vaux Dessus

❹

Croix Sorine

❺

Les Potets

Les Crais

En Gatsulard

❺

❼

❽

Saint-Jean

❸

❾

❾

❿

En Charron

❸

Saint-Jean

❸

En Foulot

Les Fourneaux

Les Charmes Dessus

En la Fée

Sous la Fée

Grand-Clos-Rousseau

Petit-Clos-Rousseau

Cheilly-lès-Maranges

To Cheilly-lès-Maranges

Le Chainey

Santenay Premier Cru
Santenay
Chassagne-Montrachet

Les Bras

Santenay

Dezize-lès-Maranges

SANTENAY AND REMIGNY

0   500 meters

0   500 yards

To Dezize-lès-Maranges

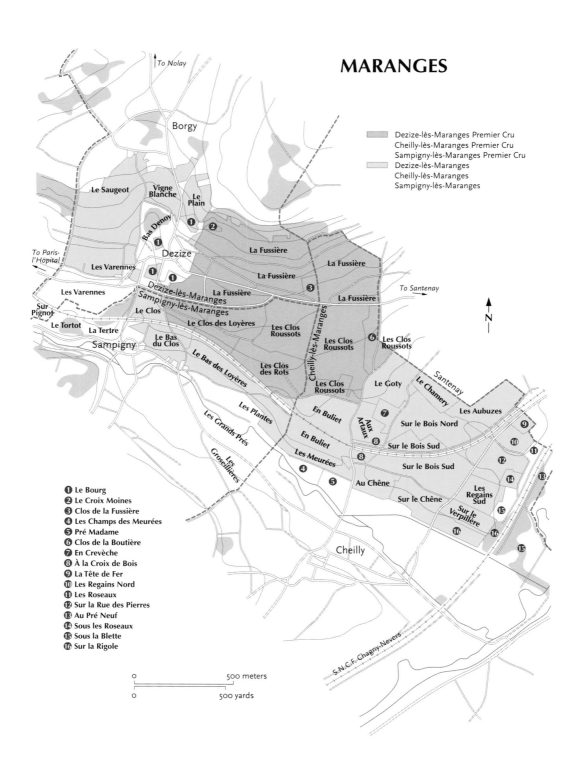

MARANGES

Legend:
- Dezize-lès-Maranges Premier Cru
- Cheilly-lès-Maranges Premier Cru
- Sampigny-lès-Maranges Premier Cru
- Dezize-lès-Maranges
- Cheilly-lès-Maranges
- Sampigny-lès-Maranges

To Nolay

Borgy

Le Saugeot

Vigne Blanche

Le Plain

Bas Denoy

❶

❷

To Paris-l'Hôpital

Dezize

La Fussière

Les Varennes

La Fussière

La Fussière

❸

La Fussière

Les Varennes

To Santenay

Dezize-lès-Maranges

La Fussière

Sampigny-lès-Maranges

Sur Pignot

Le Clos

Le Tortot

Le Clos des Loyères

Les Clos Roussots

❻

Les Clos Roussots

La Tertre

Sampigny

Le Bas du Clos

Les Clos Roussots

Cheilly-lès-Maranges

Le Bas des Loyères

Les Clos des Rots

Les Clos Roussots

Le Goty

Le Chamery

Santenay

Les Aubuzes

Les Plantes

En Buliet

Aux Arlaux

Sur le Bois Nord

❼

❾

Les Grands Prés

En Buliet

❽

Sur le Bois Sud

❿

Les Meurées

Sur le Bois Sud

⓫

Les Groseillières

❹

Au Chêne

⓬

❺

Sur le Chêne

Les Regains Sud

⓮

⓭

Sur le Verpillère

⓯

❶ Le Bourg

⓰

⓰

❷ Le Croix Moines

❸ Clos de la Fussière

⓯

❹ Les Champs des Meurées

Cheilly

❺ Pré Madame

❻ Clos de la Boutière

❼ En Crevèche

❽ À la Croix de Bois

❾ La Tête de Fer

❿ Les Regains Nord

⓫ Les Roseaux

⓬ Sur la Rue des Pierres

⓭ Au Pré Neuf

⓮ Sous les Roseaux

⓯ Sous la Blette

⓰ Sur la Rigole

S.N.C.F. Chagny-Nevers

| 0 | | 500 meters |
| 0 | | 500 yards |

THE CÔTE CHALONNAISE

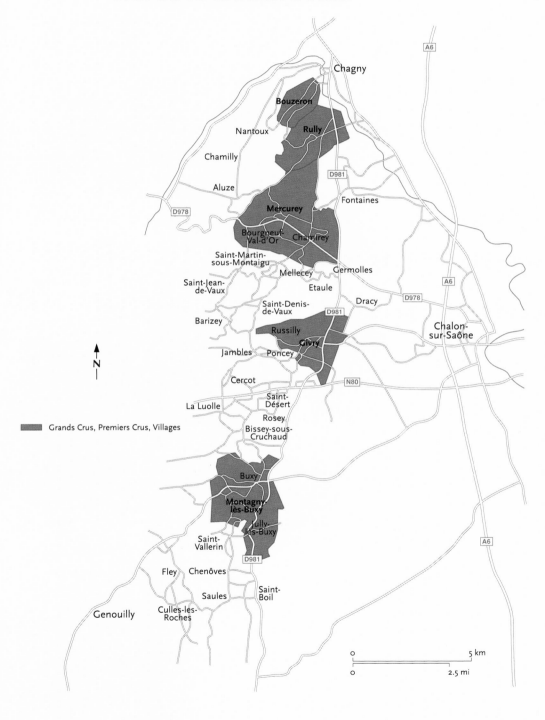

Chagny

Bouzeron

Nantoux

Rully

Chamilly

Aluze

D981

D978

Mercurey

Fontaines

Bourgneuf-
Val-d'Or

Chamirey

Saint-Martin-
sous-Montaigu

Mellecey

Germolles

Saint-Jean-
de-Vaux

Etaule

A6

Saint-Denis-
de-Vaux

Dracy

D978

Barizey

D981

Russilly

Givry

Chalon-
sur-Saône

Jambles

Poncey

N

Cercot

Saint-
Désert

N80

La Luolle

Rosey

Bissey-sous-
Cruchaud

▬ Grands Crus, Premiers Crus, Villages

Buxy

**Montagny-
lès-Buxy**

Jully-
lès-Buxy

Saint-
Vallerin

A6

Fley

Chenôves

D981

Saules

Saint-
Boil

Genouilly

Culles-les-
Roches

o ————— 5 km

o ————— 2.5 mi

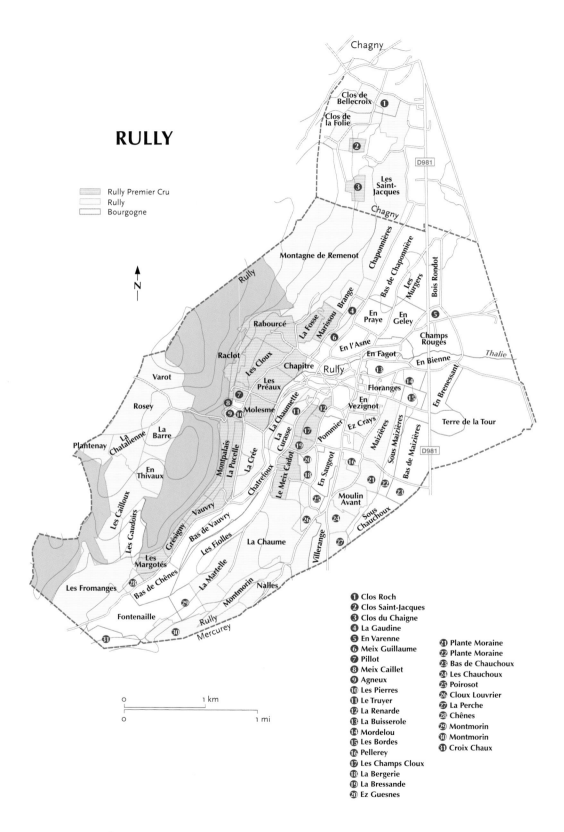

RULLY

Rully Premier Cru
Rully
Bourgogne

N

Chagny

Clos de
Bellecroix ❶

Clos de
la Folie

❷

D981

Les
Saint-
Jacques

❸

Chagny

Montagne de Remenot

Chaponnières

Bas de Chaponnière

Les
Murgers

Bois Rondot

La Fosse

Marissou Brange

Rabourcé

En
Praye

En
Geley

❺

En l'Asne

Champs
Rouges

Raclot

Les Cloux

Chapitre

Rully

❹

❻

En Fagot

En Bienne

Thalie

Varot

Les
Préaux

Floranges

❽

Mordelou

Rosey

❼

Molesme

❾❿

❶❶

La Chaumette

❶❷

En
Vezignot

Ez Crays

Maizières

Sous Maizières

Bas de Maizières

En Brenessant

Terre de la Tour

Plantenay

La
Chatalienne

La
Barre

Montpalais

La Pucelle

La Crée

Chatrefoux

La Curasse

Le Meix Cadot

Pommier

En Saugeot

❶❻

Pellerey

En
Thivaux

❶❼

❶❾

❷❶

❷❷

❷❸

Les Cailloux

Les Gaudoirs

Grésigny

Vauvry

Bas de Vauvry

Les Fiolles

La Chaume

❶❽

❷❺

Villerange

❷❻

❷❹

Moulin
Avant

Sous
Chauchoux

Les
Margotés

❷❽

Bas de Chênes

La Martelle

Montmorin

Nalles

❷❼

Les Fromanges

❷❾

Fontenaille

Rully

Mercurey

❸❿

❸❶

0   1 km

0   1 mi

❶ Clos Roch
❷ Clos Saint-Jacques
❸ Clos du Chaigne
❹ La Gaudine
❺ En Varenne
❻ Meix Guillaume
❼ Pillot
❽ Meix Caillet
❾ Agneux
❿ Les Pierres
⓫ Le Truyer
⓬ La Renarde
⓭ La Buisserole
⓮ Mordelou
⓯ Les Bordes
⓰ Pellerey
⓱ Les Champs Cloux
⓲ La Bergerie
⓳ La Bressande
⓴ Ez Guesnes

㉑ Plante Moraine
㉒ Plante Moraine
㉓ Bas de Chauchoux
㉔ Les Chauchoux
㉕ Poirosot
㉖ Cloux Louvrier
㉗ La Perche
㉘ Chênes
㉙ Montmorin
㉚ Montmorin
㉛ Croix Chaux

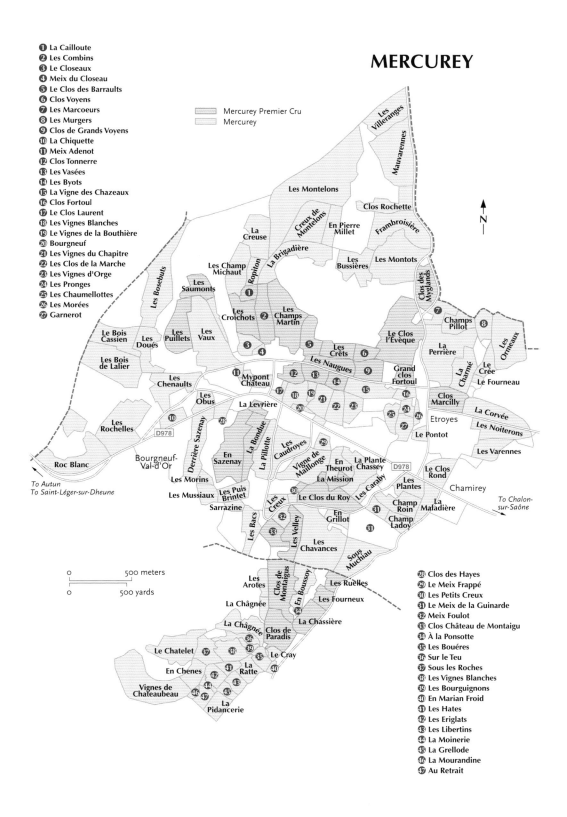

MERCUREY

1 La Cailloute
2 Les Combins
3 Le Closeaux
4 Meix du Closeau
5 Le Clos des Barraults
6 Clos Voyens
7 Les Marcoeurs
8 Les Murgers
9 Clos de Grands Voyens
10 La Chiquette
11 Meix Adenot
12 Clos Tonnerre
13 Les Vasées
14 Les Byots
15 La Vigne des Chazeaux
16 Clos Fortoul
17 Le Clos Laurent
18 Les Vignes Blanches
19 Le Vignes de la Bouthière
20 Bourgneuf
21 Les Vignes du Chapitre
22 Les Clos de la Marche
23 Les Vignes d'Orge
24 Les Pronges
25 Les Chaumellottes
26 Les Morées
27 Garnerot

Mercurey Premier Cru
Mercurey

28 Clos des Hayes
29 Le Meix Frappé
30 Les Petits Creux
31 Le Meix de la Guinarde
32 Meix Foulot
33 Clos Château de Montaigu
34 À la Ponsotte
35 Les Bouéres
36 Sur le Teu
37 Sous les Roches
38 Les Vignes Blanches
39 Les Bourguignons
40 En Marian Froid
41 Les Hates
42 Les Eriglats
43 Les Libertins
44 La Moinerie
45 La Grellode
46 La Mourandine
47 Au Retrait

500 meters
500 yards

GIVRY

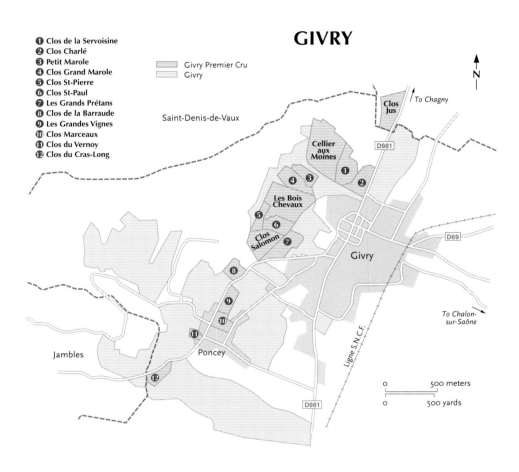

1 Clos de la Servoisine
2 Clos Charlé
3 Petit Marole
4 Clos Grand Marole
5 Clos St-Pierre
6 Clos St-Paul
7 Les Grands Prétans
8 Clos de la Barraude
9 Les Grandes Vignes
10 Clos Marceaux
11 Clos du Vernoy
12 Clos du Cras-Long

Givry Premier Cru
Givry

Saint-Denis-de-Vaux

Clos Jus

To Chagny

D981

Cellier aux Moines

Les Bois Chevaux

Clos Salomon

Givry

D69

Ligne S.N.C.F.

To Chalon-sur-Saône

Jambles

Poncey

D981

0   500 meters
0   500 yards

N

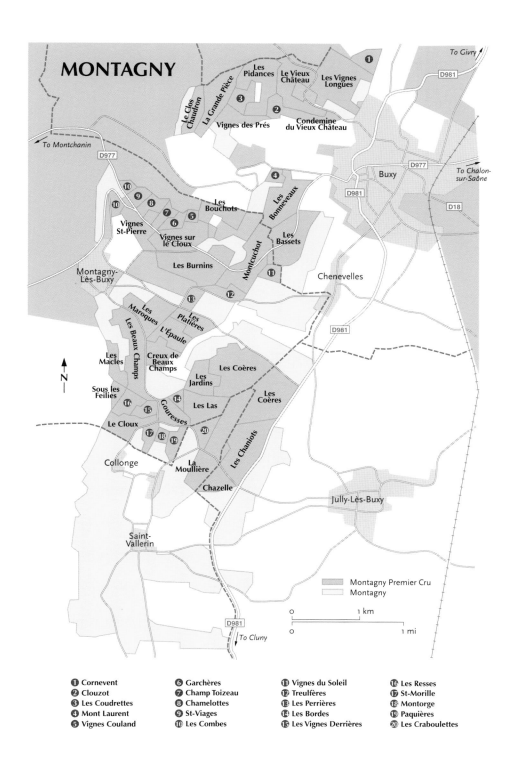

MONTAGNY

To Givry

D981

Les Pidances

Le Vieux Château

Les Vignes Longues

Le Clos Chaudron

La Grande Pièce

Vignes des Prés

Condemine du Vieux Château

To Montchanin

D977

Buxy

D977

To Chalon-sur-Saône

D981

D18

Mont Laurent

Les Bouchots

Les Bonneveaux

Vignes St-Pierre

Vignes sur le Cloux

Montcuchot

Les Bassets

Les Burnins

Montagny-Lès-Buxy

Chenevelles

Vignes du Soleil

Les Maroques

Les Platières

L'Épaule

Les Beaux Champs

Les Macles

Creux de Beaux Champs

Les Coères

Les Jardins

Les Las

Les Coères

Sous les Feilies

Gouresses

Le Cloux

Collonge

La Moullière

Les Chaniots

Chazelle

Jully-Lès-Buxy

Saint-Vallerin

N

Montagny Premier Cru

Montagny

0   1 km

0   1 mi

D981

To Cluny

- ❶ Cornevent
- ❷ Clouzot
- ❸ Les Coudrettes
- ❹ Mont Laurent
- ❺ Vignes Couland
- ❻ Garchères
- ❼ Champ Toizeau
- ❽ Chamelottes
- ❾ St-Viages
- ❿ Les Combes
- ⓫ Vignes du Soleil
- ⓬ Treulfères
- ⓭ Les Perrières
- ⓮ Les Bordes
- ⓯ Les Vignes Derrières
- ⓰ Les Resses
- ⓱ St-Morille
- ⓲ Montorge
- ⓳ Paquières
- ⓴ Les Craboulettes

Cazetiers by a long way. Medium body. Slightly one-dimensional. Accessible. (June 2006)

NOW TO 2011   14.5

Echézeaux, 2000
Domaine A.F. Gros

Medium-full colour. Firm, ripe, slightly clumsy nose. Rich, round, decent grip. Medium-full body. Good fruit. More refined as it evolved. Balanced. Very good. (July 2004)

2009 TO 2021   16.0

Echézeaux, 2000
Domaine Louis Jadot

Medium colour. Adolescent nose. Firm. Ungainly. Full, tannic, but rich underneath. Good grip. Not really showing very well at present but very good potential at least. (July 2004)

2010 TO 2020   16.0

Echézeaux, 2000
Domaine Jayer-Gilles

Fullish colour. Rich, full, lovely but very oaky nose. Full body. Very fresh so not too heavy or astringent. You have to admit it is well made, even if not to one's style. Long. Very good indeed. (July 2004)

2009 TO 2021   17.0

Echézeaux, 2000
Domaine François Lamarche

Medium-full colour. Plump, spicy nose. Good depth and concentration. Classy, old-viney fruit. Fullish bodied. Just a little astringent. But this would be less noticeable with food. Positive finish. Fine. (July 2004)

2009 TO 2021   17.5

Echézeaux, 2000
Domaine Jean-Marc Millot

Medium-full colour. Slightly earthy and barnyardy nose at first. Medium-full body. Ripe, plump and accessible. Not much tannin. Fresh, stylish and balanced. Good long finish. Quite forward but very good indeed. (April 2005)

NOW TO 2014   17.0

Echézeaux, 2000
Domaine Daniel Rion

Medium-full colour. Slightly minty on the nose. Medium weight. A little thin. A little ungainly. Decent balance though. Quite good. (July 2004)

NOW TO 2016   14.0

Echézeaux, 2000
Domaine de la Romanée-Conti

Slightly more colour than the Grands Echézeaux. Some oak on the nose. But no stems. Ripe, gentle, fresh and elegant. Quite forward. Lovely fruit on the palate. Medium to medium-full body. Balanced. Long. Subtle. Delicious. (July 2004)

NOW TO 2020   17.5

Echézeaux, 2000
Domaine Emmanuel Rouget

Fullish colour. Rich, ample, some accessibility, some development. Ample, generous, classy, very poised. Very lovely fruit. Good, oaky base. Long. Lovely. (July 2004)

NOW TO 2025   18.5

Gevrey-Chambertin, Vieilles Vignes, 2000
Domaine Denis Bachelet

Light-medium colour. Fully mature. Ripe and succulent, and intense on nose and palate. Balanced and classy. Medium to medium-full body. Excellent grip. Very fine for what it is. Quite forward. (July 2004)

NOW TO 2020   17.0

Gevrey-Chambertin, 2000
Domaine Bouchard Père et Fils

Medium to medium-full colour. Plump, rich, soft and smooth. Not much tannin. Good freshness and grip though. Medium body. Stylish. Decent length. Good for what it is but slightly one-dimensional. Quite forward. (March 2003)

DRINK SOON   15.0

Gevrey-Chambertin, Mes Favorites, 2000
Domaine Alain Burguet

Full colour. Medium weight. Soft, pleasant attack. More to it on the follow-through.

Good, positive, pure, elegant finish. Good plus. (March 2006)

NOW TO 2010   15.5

Gevrey-Chambertin, Vieilles Vignes, 2000
Domaine Heresztyn

Good colour. Just about ready. Full, firm and rich. Good depth. Still a little austere but will improve. Plenty of substance. Very good for what it is. (October 2003)

NOW TO 2010   16.0

Gevrey-Chambertin, 2000
Maison Antonin Rodet

Good colour. Ripe and spicy on the nose. Slightly artificial fruit at first and a touch of sulphur. Better on the palate. Slightly cool but not too lean. Quite well put together and well balanced. The tannins are ripe, and the finish is positive. Good. (August 2002)

NOW TO 2012   15.0

Gevrey-Chambertin, 2000
Domaine Jean Trapet Père et Fils

Medium colour. Good, plump nose. Plenty of depth and interest here. Medium-full body, fresh, plump and balanced. Lovely fruit. This is very good for a village wine. (March 2003)

NOW TO 2019   16.0

Gevrey-Chambertin, Les Cazetiers, 2000
Domaine Bruno Clair

Medium-full colour. Some development. Light and fragrant. Plenty of depth underneath. On the palate a little too light. Fragrant and stylish though. A very pretty wine. (July 2004)

NOW TO 2012   14.5

Gevrey-Chambertin, Les Cazetiers, 2000
Domaine Joseph Faiveley

Medium to medium-full colour. Lovely, fragrant nose. Ripe, even rich. Accessible and classy. Medium to medium-full body. Long. Fine quality. (June 2006)

NOW TO 2015   17.5

Gevrey-Chambertin, Les Cazetiers, 2000
Domaine Armand Rousseau

Medium to medium-full colour. Light nose. Agreeable but lacks real depth. Medium body. Not much backbone. The wine is quite concentrated, and there is very good acidity. Long. Very good indeed. (July 2004)

NOW TO 2020   17.0

Gevrey-Chambertin, Les Champeaux, 2000
Domaine Bernard Maume

Fullish colour. Some development. Quite chunky. Not a bit too much so. This is cleaner and more stylish than I expected. Not too clumsy. Very good plus. (July 2004)

NOW TO 2020   16.5

Gevrey-Chambertin, Les Champeaux, 2000
Domaine Denis Mortet

Medium-full colour. A ripe, plump, civilised nose. Medium-full body. Ample. Fresh. Balanced. Long. Plenty of grip. Very good indeed. (July 2004)

NOW TO 2025   17.0

Gevrey-Chambertin, Les Cherbaudes, 2000
Domaine Fourrier

Medium to medium-full colour. Some development. Oaky and stylish on the nose, with good balance and depth. Ripe, fragrant, fresh and stylish. Fullish body. Good intensity. Very good. (July 2004)

NOW TO 2020   16.0

Gevrey-Chambertin, Clos du Fonteny, 2000
Domaine Bruno Clair

Medium-full colour. Lovely clean, pure, ripe, fragrant Pinot on the nose. Medium-full body. Very poised and classy. No enormous tannin but very good grip. This is very lovely. (March 2003)

NOW TO 2025   17.5

Gevrey-Chambertin, Clos de la Justice, 2000
Domaine Pierre Bourée

Light-medium, evolved colour. Evolved and rustic on the nose. Rather weedy on the palate.

Good acidity leaving it fresh though. Not bad. (July 2004)

DRINK SOON   13.0

Gevrey-Chambertin, Clos Prieur, 2000
Domaine Jean-Michel Guillon

Medium-full colour. Nicely rich on the nose. Some oak. Good depth and grip. Medium body and a little disappointing after the nose. A bit slight. Stylish and fresh. Not short. But for what it is, I expected a bit more. It tails off a bit. (March 2003)

DRINK SOON   14.5

Gevrey-Chambertin, Clos Saint-Jacques, 2000
Domaine Bruno Clair

Medium to medium-full. Full and rich. Quite different from his Cazetiers. Full bodied and meaty. Rich, abundant, balanced and with very good grip. Very classy. Fine plus. (July 2004)

2009 TO 2025   18.0

Gevrey-Chambertin, Clos Saint-Jacques, 2000
Domaine Sylvie Esmonin

Medium-full colour. A slight touch of oak. Ripe and fresh. Delicious fruit. Medium-full body. Lovely, stylish fruit. Open and accessible. Very cool. Excellent follow-through. This is fine plus. (July 2004)

NOW TO 2020+   18.0

Gevrey-Chambertin, Clos Saint-Jacques, 2000
Domaine Fourrier

Medium to medium-full colour. Some evolution. Is there a touch of the stems here? Ripe and ample. But less concentrated and classy than the other Clos Saint-Jacques. Very good but a little astringent on the palate. The aftertaste lacks the quality of Rousseau's and Clair's. (July 2004)

NOW TO 2012   16.0

Gevrey-Chambertin, Clos Saint-Jacques, 2000
Domaine Louis Jadot

Medium to medium-full colour. Good fruit. Good style on the nose. Ripe, ample and with good depth on the palate. Medium-full body.

Just a little tannin. Just a touch of oak. Plenty of dimension. Balanced. Fine plus. (April 2005)

2008 TO 2020   18.0

Gevrey-Chambertin, Clos Saint-Jacques, 2000
Domaine Armand Rousseau

Medium colour. Soft, oaky, ripe nose. Medium body. No tannin. Not a lot of structure but pleasantly fruity. Lovely now. Good follow-through. Ample. Balanced and classy. Fine for the vintage. Drinking well now. (May 2005)

NOW TO 2015   17.5

Gevrey-Chambertin, La Combe au Moine, 2000
Domaine Fourrier

Medium-full colour. Fragrant, stylish nose. Concentrated, cool, crisp and well made on the palate. Fullish weight. Good energy. Very good fruit. Very good finish. Fine. (July 2004)

NOW TO 2025   17.5

Gevrey-Chambertin, Les Corbeaux, 2000
Domaine Denis Bachelet

Medium-full colour. Some development. Very sophisticated on the nose. Lovely fruit. Very finely balanced. Medium-full body. Classy. Very, very long and very lovely. Very long. (July 2004)

2009 TO 2030   18.5

Gevrey-Chambertin, Estournelles-Saint-Jacques, 2000
Domaine Frédéric Esmonin

Medium to medium-full colour. Elegant, concentrated and pure on the nose. Ethereal. Quite different from the Lavaux but even better. A lot of depth and a lot of class. Long and complex. Very fine. (July 2004)

NOW TO 2028+   18.5

Gevrey-Chambertin, Estournelles-Saint-Jacques, 2000
Domaine Louis Jadot

Medium to medium-full colour. Rich, full, ripe and quite meaty on the nose. A more austere, less evolved wine than the Esmonin. But very fine nonetheless. Full, simple, concentrated and balanced. Very long. Very lovely finish. Very fine. (July 2004)

2009 TO 2028+   18.5

Gevrey-Chambertin, Les Evocelles, 2000
Domaine de la Vougeraie

Medium-full colour. Some development. Soft and fruity on the nose. Very good balancing acidity. Soft. Fresh on the palate. Delicious. Fine. (July 2004)

2009 TO 2025   17.5

Gevrey-Chambertin, Les Fontenys, 2000
Domaine Joseph Roty

Medium-full colour. Ripe but oaky and a little rigid on the nose. Fullish bodied and ample. Quite chunky. Very good depth though. Lots of concentration. Some tannin, but the tannins are ripe. Finishes well. (July 2004)

2010 TO 2025   18.0

Gevrey-Chambertin, Les Goulots, 2000
Domaine Fourrier

Medium-full colour. Some development. Quite a robust nose. Good size, though, and good grip. Lovely pure fruit on the palate. This is very good indeed. (July 2004)

NOW TO 2025   17.0

Gevrey-Chambertin, Lavaux-Saint-Jacques, 2000
Domaine Pierre Bourée

Medium, evolved colour. Ripe but not much style on the nose. Medium body. Flat. Uninteresting. (July 2004)

DRINK SOON   13.0

Gevrey-Chambertin, Lavaux-Saint-Jacques, 2000
Domaine Claude Dugat

Medium-full colour. Quite modern. Oaky, quite extracted nose. Not too much so. Good depth. Fullish body. Good tannins. Lots of concentration. Very good depth. This is a keeper. All in place. Fine plus. (July 2004)

NOW TO 2025+   18.0

Gevrey-Chambertin, Lavaux-Saint-Jacques, 2000
Domaine Frédéric Esmonin

Medium, evolved colour. Fresh nose. Ample. Stylish. Cool and accessible. Medium-full body. Good tannins. Good acidity. This has old-viney fruit and lots of depth. Classy. Very good indeed. (July 2004)

DRINK SOON   17.0

Gevrey-Chambertin, Lavaux-Saint-Jacques, 2000
Domaine Denis Mortet

Full colour. Rich, fat, concentrated and intense on the nose. Lots of lovely ripe fruit here. Not quite the grip of Dugat's, but ample, rich and not a bit short. Full body. Intense. Long. Fine plus. (July 2004)

NOW TO 2025+   18.0

Gevrey-Chambertin, En Reniard, 2000
Domaine Alain Burguet

Medium-full colour. Ripe, plump, raspberry-flavoured Pinot on the nose. Quite supple. Good acidity. Good depth and class for a 2000. Medium body only on the palate. Quite fruity. Good grip yet a little astringent. Slightly one-dimensional and a touch lean. Quite good. (March 2003)

NOW TO 2011   14.0

La Grande Rue, 2000
Domaine François Lamarche

Fullish colour. Rich, full, generous, oaky nose. Lots of depth and high quality. Not a bit adolescent. Fullish. Very clean and very pure. Very good acidity. Medium-full body. Very fresh, complex fruit and a lot of it on the palate. Just a bit of tannin to resolve. Very fine plus. (July 2004)

2009 TO 2025   19.0

Grands Echézeaux, 2000
Domaine Joseph Drouhin

Medium-full colour. Classy fruit on the nose. Plump, ripe, fresh and balanced. Similar on the palate. Medium to medium-full body. Very good intensity. Lots of classy, harmonious fruit.

Complex, long and fragrant. Very Drouhin. Very lovely. Very classy. Very long. (July 2004)

NOW TO 2020+   18.0

Grands Echézeaux, 2000
Domaine René Engel

Medium to medium-full colour. Some development. Seems more evolved than the plain Echézeaux. Open, accessible, spicy fruit. Very ripe. Medium body. Long and complex. Even more depth. Lovely. (July 2004)

NOW TO 2025   18.0

Grands Echézeaux, 2000
Domaine de la Romanée-Conti

Ripe, rich nose. Some tannin to evolve here. Lots of ripe fruit. Good intensity. Lovely black fruit flavours. This is bigger, more concentrated, and really remarkably good this year. Lots of dimension. Long. Impressive. Good substance. Fine. (November 2005)

2009 TO 2020   17.5

Griotte-Chambertin, 2000
Domaine Joseph Drouhin

Medium-full colour. Fragrant, harmonious, very classy nose. And enough substance too. Not lightweight. Very lovely fruit. Medium-full body. Intense, concentrated and very fresh. Lovely long, gentle wine. Very relaxed. Very fine. (July 2004)

NOW TO 2025   18.5

Griotte-Chambertin, 2000
Domaine Fourrier

Medium-full colour. Ample nose but without the depth, zip and flair it should have at this level. This would be all right at the village or lesser *premier cru* level. Medium to medium-full body, and balanced and fruity. But it lacks class and depth. Merely good. (July 2004)

NOW TO 2017   15.0

Ladoix, 2000
Domaine François Gay et Fils

Good colour. Lovely plump fruit. Not a bit rustic. Good weight. Good substance. Nicely

plump and succulent. Very good. Ready. (February 2003)

NOW TO 2011   16.0

Ladoix, Vieilles Vignes, 2000
Domaine Edmond Cornu et Fils

This is really good for a 2000. Rich, fat and quite full. Succulent and balanced. Long. Very good. (February 2003)

NOW TO 2011   15.5

Ladoix, La Corvée, 2000
Domaine Chevalier Père et Fils

Good colour. Ripe, plump and positive. Good structure and plenty of fruit. Succulent and charming. Very good indeed for what it is. (February 2003)

NOW TO 2013   16.5

Ladoix, Les Gréchons, 2000
Domaine Chevalier Père et Fils

White. Lovely fruit. Individual style. Not quite the vivacity of their 2001. But richer and more concentrated. Very good plus. (February 2003)

NOW TO 2013   16.5

Ladoix, Les Joyeuses, 2000
Domaine Michel Mallard et Fils

Fuller and richer than his Savigny, Serpentières, 2000. Good colour. Plenty of depth and substance. Lovely fruit. Good backbone and tannin. Ripe and long. Very good indeed. (February 2005)

NOW TO 2012   16.5

Ladoix, Les Madonnes, Vieilles Vignes, 2000
Domaine Cachat-Ocquidant et Fils

Decent colour. Soft and light, but balanced and charming. It even has good length. Positive finish. (February 2003)

NOW TO 2010   15.0

Ladoix, La Micaude, 2000
Domaine Capitain-Gagnerot

Light and soft. Plenty of fruit. Not too hollow. But nevertheless a bit slight. Just about ready. (February 2003)

DRINK SOON   13.5

Latricières-Chambertin, 2000
Domaine Louis Rémy

Medium to medium-full colour. A little dry and rustic on the nose. Medium-full body. Quite fresh, but a little astringent at the end. Attenuated, too. Only fair. (July 2004)

NOW TO 2012   13.0

Marsannay, 2000
Maison Champy

Very good colour. Plump and stylish. Soft and full of fruit. Medium body. Mellow and just about *à point*. Fresh. Most agreeable. (October 2002)

DRINK SOON   16.0

Marsannay, Les Longeroies, 2000
Domaine Bruno Clair

Good colour. Surprisingly good nose. Plenty of depth and interest here. No great weight, but good, ripe, intense and stylish fruit. A lovely example. (March 2003)

DRINK SOON   14.5

Mazis-Chambertin, 2000
Maison Champy

Medium-full colour. A little development. Slightly attenuated on the nose. Not much class. Doesn't convince. Medium body. A bit weedy on the palate. Astringency lurks. No. (July 2004)

NOW TO 2014   13.0

Mazis-Chambertin, 2000
Domaine Bernard Dugat-Py

Full colour. Rich, chocolaty nose. Lots of concentration. Lots of maceration, too. Not over-extracted on the palate. Fullish body. Rich and concentrated. This has good backbone, very good grip and lots of depth. Very fine. (April 2005)

2009 TO 2022   18.5

Mazis-Chambertin, 2000
Domaine Joseph Faiveley

Medium-full colour. Fresh and not too rigid on the nose. Not a lot of oak. Good freshness. Medium body. Not a lot of depth and volume.

But what there is, is classy and balanced. Very good indeed. (July 2004)

NOW TO 2017   17.0

Mazis-Chambertin, 2000
Maison Vincent Girardin

Medium-full colour. Round, ripe, gently oaky nose. Medium to medium-full weight. Ample and round. Good acidity and good depth for the vintage. Very good indeed. (April 2005)

2008 TO 2018   17.0

Mazis-Chambertin, 2000
Domaine Bernard Maume

Fullish colour. Rather rustic on the nose. Lumpy and barnyardy. Medium-full body. Dry and common. Some acidity. A bit astringent. Only quite good. (July 2004)

NOW TO 2018   14.0

Morey-Saint-Denis, 2000
Domaine Dujac

Medium colour. Ripe, plump and unaggressive on the nose. Medium to medium-full body. Fresh and ample. Just a little tannin. Very good fruit. Long. Very good. (March 2003)

NOW TO 2015   16.0

Morey-Saint-Denis, Premier Cru, 2000
Domaine Dujac

Medium-full colour. Rich, full and plump on the nose. Plenty of depth here. Medium-full body. Good tannins. Plenty of vigour and lots of class. Complex and long. Very good indeed. (March 2003)

NOW TO 2018   17.0

Morey-Saint-Denis, Premier Cru, Vieilles Vignes, 2000
Domaine Hubert Lignier

Medium-full colour. Ripe, vigorous, oaky nose. Lots of depth. Medium-full body. Good grip. Cool, complex and stylish. Profound and multidimensional. Lots of energy here. This is very good indeed.

NOW TO 2020+   17.0

Morey-Saint-Denis, Aux Chezeaux, 2000
Domaine Hervé Arlaud
Medium-full colour. Ripe, round, slightly spicy nose. Good energy. Medium body. Good grip. No lack of depth. Long. Very good. (July 2004)
NOW TO 2018   16.0

Morey-Saint-Denis, Clos de la Buissière, 2000
Domaine Georges Roumier et Fils
Medium-full colour. Plump, medium-full, stylish nose. Not as rustic as it used to be. On the palate medium-full body. A slightly hard-rustic aspect to the tannins. But rich, ample and well balanced. Long, juicy finish. Very good plus. (March 2003)
NOW 2020   16.5

Morey-Saint-Denis, Les Loups, 2000
Domaine des Lambrays
Medium to medium-full colour. Some development. Soft, sweet, forward nose. Quite fresh. Evidence of the stems. Medium body. Good class and intensity. Good grip. Balanced. Good plus. (July 2004)
NOW TO 2015   15.5

Morey-Saint-Denis, Les Milandes, 2000
Domaine Heresztyn
Medium-full colour. Fresh, vigorous nose. Good, ripe fruit here. Medium to medium-full body. Ample, juicy, stylish fruit. Good grip. Very good plus. (July 2004)
NOW TO 2019   16.5

Morey-Saint-Denis, En la Rue de Vergy, 2000
Domaine Bruno Clair
Light-medium colour. Soft, fresh, stylish. A bit lightweight, but balanced and quite intense. Quite good. (July 2004)
NOW TO 2011   14.0

Musigny, 2000
Domaine Jacques-Frédéric Mugnier
Medium-full colour. Splendid fragrant nose. Intense, pure, complex and very lovely. Great finesse. Very pure Pinot. Very Musigny. Very Mugnier. Medium-full body. Intense, complex fruit despite being light and forward. Balanced. Very concentrated fruit at the end. Very lovely long finish. A great 2000. (June 2005)
2009 TO 2025   19.0

Musigny, 2000
Domaine Jacques Prieur
Medium-full colour. Ripe, quite classy nose. Good fragrant fruit. But not the greatest richness or class. Slightly closed still. So we shall see. But I don't think this is anything special, even for 2000. But it did improve in the glass. Much better than their Clos de Vougeot 2000. Very good indeed for the vintage. (August 2002)
NOW TO 2014   17.0

Musigny, 2000
Domaine Comte Georges de Vogüé
Medium-full, elegant but slightly austere. A bit one-dimensional compared with better vintages, but lovely fruit. The class of the *climat* shows. Fine plus for the vintage. (March 2005)
2008 TO 2018   18.0

Le Musigny, 2000
Domaine de la Vougeraie
Good colour. Very lovely nose. Splendidly elegant, intense, ripe and fragrant. Marvellous fruit. Medium to medium-full body. Impeccably balanced. Very long. Already very delicious. Very lovely. (September 2004)
NOW TO 2018   19.5

Nuits-Saint-Georges, Premier Cru, 2000
Domaine Michel Gros
Medium-full colour. Some development. Ripe nose. Fresh. Good depth. Medium to medium-full body. Balanced. Stylish. Good grip. Ripe and with plenty of vigour. Very good plus. (July 2004)
NOW TO 2017   16.5

Nuits-Saint-Georges, Les Boudots, 2000
Domaine Jean Grivot
Fullish colour. Backward nose. Slightly hard and lean at first. Very lovely on the palate though. Splendid complexity and intensity. Medium-full

body. The tannins are very ripe, and the fruit is very rich and well balanced. Long and complex. Lovely. Fine plus. (March 2003)

NOW TO 2021   18.0

Nuits-Saint-Georges, Aux Boudots, 2000
Domaine Louis Jadot

Medium colour. Some development. Ripe and succulent on the nose. Medium-full body. Ripe, ample, rich and balanced. Good class. Very good plus. Finishes positively. (July 2004)

NOW TO 2017   16.5

Nuits-Saint-Georges, Aux Boudots, 2000
Domaine Méo-Camuzet

Fullish colour. Plump, oaky nose. Quite firm on the palate. Very good, slightly chocolate and mocha aspects. Very good grip. This is fullish bodied, very long and with lots of dimension. Classy, too. Very good tannins. Fine. (March 2003)

NOW TO 2021   17.5

Nuits-Saint-Georges, Les Boudots, 2000
Domaine Denis Mugneret

Full colour. Rich, opulent nose. Fullish body. Some tannin. Rich and very ripe indeed. Fat. Lots of depth. Essentially soft, plump and generous. Lots of finesse. Fine. (April 2005)

NOW TO 2015   17.5

Nuits-Saint-Georges, Les Boudots, 2000
Domaine Jean Tardy et Fils

En métayage with Méo-Camuzet. Good colour. Ripe, rich and gently oaky on the nose and palate. Medium-full body. Plump and quite forward but no lack of fruit or depth. Generous at the end. Good plus. (October 2002)

NOW TO 2012   15.5

Nuits-Saint-Georges, Aux Brûlées, 2000
Domaine Henri Gille Père et Fils

This is better within its context than their 2001. Good substance. Good drive and balance. Vigorous, stylish fruit. Long and positive. Very good. (March 2003)

NOW TO 2015   16.0

Nuits-Saint-Georges, Les Cailles, 2000
Domaine Bouchard Père et Fils

Medium-full colour. Round nose. Attractive fruit. Quite evolved. Very good on the palate. Good energy. Ripe tannins. Ample fruit. Long. Very good plus. (July 2004)

NOW TO 2017   16.5

Nuits-Saint-Georges, Les Cailles, 2000
Domaine Robert Chevillon

Medium-full colour. Quite an evolved nose. A touch of oak. Succulent fruit here. Medium body. Good fruit. A lack of grip and freshness though. But positive on the finish. Good plus. (July 2004)

NOW TO 2012   15.5

Nuits-Saint-Georges, Les Chaignots, 2000
Domaine Joseph Faiveley

Medium to medium-full colour. Some development. Soft nose. Fruity. Quite evolved. Decent fruit. Medium body. Lacks a bit of energy. Well balanced and not short. Good. (July 2004)

NOW TO 2012   15.0

Nuits-Saint-Georges, Les Chaignots, 2000
Domaine Gérard Mugneret

Medium to medium-full colour. Stylish nose. Good grip and depth. Medium to medium-full body. Balanced. Fresh. Elegant at the end. Good vigour. Very good plus. (July 2004)

NOW TO 2017   16.5

Nuits-Saint-Georges, Clos des Corvées, 2000
Domaine Prieuré-Roch

Medium colour. Quite evolved. Medium weight. Lacks zip. Bur round and fruity. Ready. Not bad. But lacks sophistication. (February 2006)

NOW TO 2010   13.0

Nuits-Saint-Georges, Clos des Forêts, 2000
Domaine de l'Arlot

Medium colour. Ample, fresh, succulent nose. Lots of fruit here. Only a touch of the stems. Good acidity. Medium to medium-full body. Some tannin to resolve. Very good. (July 2004)

NOW TO 2017   16.0

**Nuits-Saint-Georges, Clos des Porrets
Saint-Georges, 2000
Domaine Henri Gouges**

Medium to medium-full colour. Plump, accessible nose. No enormous depth or concentration, but good fruit. Medium to medium-full body. A little tannin. Ripe, balanced and positive. This is very good indeed for the vintage. Just about ready. (June 2006)

NOW TO 2014   17.0

**Nuits-Saint-Georges, Clos Saint-Marc, 2000
Domaine Bouchard Père et Fils**

Full colour. Good substance and depth on the nose. Quite a meaty wine. But quite evolved. It lacks a bit of zip. The tannins still need to resolve. The Cailles is better. Good. (July 2004)

NOW TO 2015   15.0

**Nuits-Saint-Georges, Clos de Thorey, 2000
Domaine Charles Thomas**

Medium-full colour. Chunky nose. Slightly lactic. Rather astringent and fruitless on the palate. Lacks balance. Will not improve. (July 2004)

NOW TO 2010   12.5

**Nuits-Saint-Georges, Aux Cras, 2000
Domaine Bruno Clavelier**

Medium-full colour. Rather coarse on the nose. Smells and tastes of diesel fuel. Medium body. A bit astringent. Unattractive. (July 2004)

NOW TO 2010   11.0

**Nuits-Saint-Georges, Les Damodes, 2000
Domaine Jean Chauvenet**

Medium to medium-full colour. Fresh, ripe nose. Good class. Good fruit. Good depth, if not very structured. Medium to medium-full body. Ripe, rich and succulent. Almost sweet. Just a little tannin. Positive, attractive finish. Very good plus. (October 2005)

2008 TO 2018   16.5

**Nuits-Saint-Georges, Aux Murgers, 2000
Domaine Méo-Camuzet**

Medium-full colour. Some development. Quite sizeable on the nose. A touch of oak. Good depth. This attack is oaky and chunky, but a bit flat. More grip behind it. But it lacks balance. (July 2004)

NOW TO 2012   14.0

**Nuits-Saint-Georges, Aux Perdrix, 2000
Domaine des Perdrix**

Medium to medium-full colour. Classy nose. Ripe. Very good grip and balance. Lots of character. Slightly softer, but more succulent, charming and accessible than the Saint-Georges of Rodet. Less substance but equally as good. (August 2002)

NOW 2015   16.5

**Nuits-Saint-Georges, Les Perrières, 2000
Domaine Robert Chevillon**

Medium to medium-full colour. A little development. Ripe, succulent, fresh and classy on the nose. On the palate medium to medium-full body. Quite fresh. Attractive fruit. Positive finish. Very good. (July 2004)

NOW TO 2017   16.0

**Nuits-Saint-Georges, En la Perrière Noblot, 2000
Domaine Machard de Gramont**

Soft, ripe and supple. Medium body. It lacks a little grip but very pleasant. Rather more forward. Quite sophisticated. Good fruit. Good. (February 2003)

NOW TO 2014   15.0

**Nuits-Saint-Georges, Les Perrières, 2000
Domaine Jean Chauvenet**

Medium-full colour. Nicely minerally, medium-weight, stylish, balanced fruit on the nose. Medium-full body. Some tannin. Good depth. Lots of character. Long and potentially succulent. Very good grip. Very good indeed. (October 2005)

2008 TO 2020   17.0

**Nuits-Saint-Georges, Les Poulettes, 2000
Domaine de la Poulette**

A little light. Not too weedy, but certainly soft and feminine. Good fruit and depth. Long and quite classy. Good plus. (February 2003)

NOW TO 2012   15.5

Nuits-Saint-Georges, Les Pruliers, 2000
Domaine Robert Chevillon

Medium to medium-full colour. Plump nose. Good weight. Good structure. Slightly cooked, but nevertheless, one can see a very good wine here. Perhaps with just a bit more energy than the Perrières. Long finish. (July 2004)

NOW TO 2020   16.5

Nuits-Saint-Georges, Les Pruliers, 2000
Domaine Henri Gouges

Medium-full colour. Plummy nose. Medium-full body. Balanced. Not as much to it as the Clos des Porrets. Still a little closed. Quite rich. Good fruit. Balanced. Very good. (July 2004)

NOW TO 2018   16.0

Nuits-Saint-Georges, Les Pruliers, 2000
Domaine Jean Grivot

Medium-full colour. Clean, positive, distinctive nose. Very lovely fruit. Very good grip. Medium-full body. Ripe and balanced. Complex. Classy. Very good indeed. (July 2004)

NOW TO 2020   17.0

Nuits-Saint-Georges, Les Richemones, 2000
Domaine Charles Thomas

Fullish colour. Some development. Tough tannins on the nose. Ungainly. A bit over-macerated. A stewed wine which lacks grip. Ugly. It will get attenuated. (July 2004)

NOW TO 2010   11.0

Nuits-Saint-Georges, Rue de Chaux, 2000
Domaine Pierre Thubert

Rich nose. Oaky. Classy and profound for a 2000. Some oak. Very good depth and class on the palate. Balanced. Long. Very good indeed. (February 2003)

NOW TO 2015   16.5

Nuits-Saint-Georges, Les Saint-Georges, 2000
Domaine Joseph Faiveley

Fullish colour. Firm nose. Backward. A touch of oak. Medium-full body. A little tannin. Fresh, plump, gentle, balanced fruit. Classy, long and complex at the end. Fine. (March 2003)

NOW TO 2016   17.5

Nuits-Saint-Georges, Les Saint-Georges, 2000
Domaine Henri Gouges

Fullish colour. Full, rich, concentrated nose. Lots of depth here. Fullish. Still tannic. Still backward. The follow-through is rich, concentrated and very promising. Fine. (July 2004)

2009 TO 2024   17.5

Nuits-Saint-Georges, Les Saint-Georges, 2000
Domaine Denis Mugneret

Medium-full colour. Good, fragrant, elegant nose. Not too tough nor a blockbuster. Medium to medium-full body. Succulent, balanced and stylish. Good grip. Very clean. This is very good plus. (October 2003)

NOW TO 2017   16.5

Nuits-Saint-Georges, Les Saint-Georges, 2000
Maison Antonin Rodet

Very good colour. Fullish, rich nose for a 2000. Still youthful. On the palate some tannin. A little lean, hard and ungenerous still, but this will go. The follow-through is fullish and properly ample. Good length. Very good plus. (August 2002)

2008 TO 2016   16.5

Nuits-Saint-Georges, Les Vaucrains, 2000
Domaine Jean Chauvenet

Fullish colour. Rich, full, meaty but not too aggressive nose. This has concentration. Gently oaky. Full body. Some tannin. Ample, concentrated and very profound on the palate. Fine grip. This has lots of dimension. Fine. (October 2005)

2010 TO 2020+   17.5

Nuits-Saint-Georges, Les Vaucrains, 2000
Domaine Henri Gouges

Fullish colour. Lovely fruit here. Very cassis. Fullish. Tannic and backward. A big, really quite structured wine for a 2000. Ample and rich. Lots of substance here. As fine as the Saint-Georges. Lots of depth. But the tannins need time to resolve. (July 2004)

2009 TO 2020   17.5

Pernand-Vergelesses, Ile de Vergelesses, 2000
Domaine Chandon de Briailles

Medium-full colour. Very lovely, pure Pinot nose. Intense elegant fruit. Medium-full body. No hard edges. Good depth and structure. Fragrant, long and complex. Very good plus. (March 2003)

NOW TO 2015   16.5

Pernand-Vergelesses, Ile de Vergelesses, 2000
Domaine Marius Delarche

Ripe and full of fruit. On the light side, but elegant, fresh and poised. Quite good within the context. A little slight. (February 2003)

NOW TO 2010   14.0

Pernand-Vergelesses, Ile de Vergelesses, 2000
Domaine Denis Père et Fils

Decent depth and substance on the attack. Then it tails off. Not enough grip. Nor dimension. Forward. Quite stylish, though, it has to be said. (February 2003)

DRINK SOON   13.5

Pernand-Vergelesses, Les Vergelesses, 2000
Domaine Jean-Marc Pavelot

Medium colour. Light, fragrant nose. Soft and fruity on the palate. Good acidity but not too lean. Medium body. Fresh. Stylish. No great depth, but attractive and *à point* now. (March 2005)

DRINK SOON   15.5

Pommard, 2000
Maison Antonin Rodet

Good colour. Ample, quite oaky nose and attack. Medium body. Ripe but not a lot of succulence. Decent balance but a slight lack of charm. Quite good. (August 2002)

DRINK SOON   14.0

Pommard, Charmots, 2000
Maison Olivier Leflaive Frères

Medium colour. Ripe nose. Rather weak, thin and nondescript on the nose. Will get attenuated. Poor. (July 2004)

DRINK SOON   12.5

Pommard, Clos des Epeneaux, 2000
Domaine du Comte Armand

Medium-full colour. Rich nose with a touch of oak. Medium-full body. Still a little tannin. Ample and with good roundness for a 2000 Côte

de Beaune. Long and positive. Plump and succulent on the finish. Very good plus. (April 2005)

NOW TO 2014   16.5

Pommard, Epenots, 2000
Domaine de Courcel

Medium to medium-full colour. Quite developed. Fully evolved nose. Has weight and attraction. But already astringent on the palate. Spurious. (July 2004)

DRINK SOON   10.5

Pommard, Epenots, 2000
Maison Olivier Leflaive Frères

Medium to medium-full colour. A slightly edgy, sweet-sour nose. Thin. Very poor. No class. (July 2004)

DRINK SOON   10.5

Pommard, Les Jarolières, 2000
Domaine Jean-Marc Boillot

Good colour. Fresh, stylish nose. Very clean, and quite fat and succulent for the vintage. Medium to medium-full body. Good fruit. Surprisingly fresh and ample for a 2000 Côte de Beaune. Very good plus. Just about ready. (June 2006)

NOW TO 2013   16.5

Pommard, Les Pézerolles, 2000
Domaine Hubert de Montille

Light colour. Light but fragrant nose. But very watery. Nothing much on the palate. Decent acidity and class. But very slight. (July 2004)

DRINK SOON   12.0

Pommard, Rugiens, 2000
Domaine Bouchard Père et Fils

Medium-full colour. Touch of mint on the nose. Weak and watery on the palate. No. (July 2004)

DRINK SOON   11.0

Pommard, Rugiens, 2000
Domaine de Courcel

Medium colour. Quite developed. Thin, attenuated nose. Weak and feeble. Already astringent. (July 2004)

DRINK SOON   11.0

Pommard, Rugiens, 2000
Maison Olivier Leflaive Frères

Medium-full colour. Quite a positive, fruity nose. Rather fluid on the palate. But at least something here. (July 2004)

DRINK SOON   13.0

Pommard, Les Rugiens, 2000
Domaine Hubert de Montille

Medium colour. Fresh nose. But a slight lack of dimension and fat. On the palate a bit light and short. Forward. Quite pretty, even elegant, but not a lot of substance here. (July 2004)

DRINK SOON   14.0

Pommard, Rugiens, 2000
Domaine Charles Thomas

Medium-full colour. Nothing much on the nose. Some style and fruit on the palate. A bit astringent but better than most. (July 2004)

DRINK SOON   13.5

Pommard, Les Vignots, 2000
Domaine Leroy

Medium colour. Quite developed. Evolved nose. Lacks depth and grip. Light, feeble and astringent on the palate. Poor. (July 2004)

DRINK UP   11.0

Richebourg, 2000
Domaine Jean Grivot

Fullish colour. Quite closed-in on the nose. Much less accessible than the rest of this flight. Medium-full body. Very, very concentrated. Excellent vigour. Some tannin. Still a little adolescent. Very, very lovely potential. (July 2004)

2010 TO 2025   19.0

Richebourg, 2000
Domaine Anne Gros

Surprisingly good colour. Soft nose. A little light but no lack of fruit, elegance, harmony or succulence. Medium to medium-full body. This is excellent for the vintage. Surprisingly voluminous. Fresh and balanced. Ripe and classy. Very lovely. (February 2004)

2012 TO 2025   19.0

Richebourg, 2000
Domaine de la Romanée-Conti

Good colour. Slightly bigger but slightly browner than the Romanée-Saint-Vivant. Rich, fat, vigorous nose. Plenty of depth. Medium-full body. Some tannin. Ripe. Good grip. Plenty of depth and dimension. Ample black fruit flavours. Long. Very fine plus. (July 2004)

2009 TO 2025   19.0

La Romanée, 2000
Domaine Bouchard Père et Fils

Fullish colour. Rich nose. Browner than La Tâche. Soft, light and quite forward on the nose. Quite firm and hidden. Some oak. Good grip. Fullish. Some tannin. High class and harmony. Very good vigour and very elegant fruit. Needs time. But lots of concentration and lots of elegance. Very fine. (July 2004)

2010 TO 2025   18.5

Romanée-Conti, 2000
Domaine de la Romanée-Conti

Good colour. Browner than La Tâche. Soft, light and quite forward on the nose. This lacks a bit of vigour. Elegant fruit, balanced and not a bit short or lacking depth. Long on the palate. But very fine plus rather than great. (July 2004)

NOW TO 2020   19.0

Romanée-Saint-Vivant, 2000
Domaine Robert Arnoux

Fullish colour. Ripe, rich, succulent, fat and creamy on the nose. Good attack. Generous. Medium-full body. Very ripe, very seductive. Good balance. But not the greatest grip, nor that of Cathiard's Romanée-Saint-Vivant. Fine plus. (July 2004)

NOW TO 2020   18.0

Romanée-Saint-Vivant, 2000
Domaine Sylvain Cathiard

Fullish colour. Very, very lovely nose. Splendidly poised and elegant. Quite delicious fruit. Laid-back. Medium-full body. Very ripe tannins. Excellent grip. Marvellous balance. Very, very fresh and clean. Multidimensional. Splendid. (July 2004)

NOW TO 2025   19.5

Romanée-Saint-Vivant, 2000
Domaine de la Romanée-Conti

Good colour. Soft, round, ripe and oaky on the nose. Perhaps it lacks a little energy. Medium to medium-full body. Quite evolved. Lacks a bit of the usual depth and dimension. Not as good as the Grands Echézeaux. Stylish, nevertheless. Fine. (July 2004)

NOW TO 2020   17.5

Ruchottes-Chambertin, 2000
Domaine Frédéric Esmonin

Fullish colour. Full, rich, cool, old-fashioned in the best sense. Lots of depth. Medium-full body. Fresh. Lovely concentrated fruit. Complex. Balanced. Long. Lovely, cool wine. Fine plus. (July 2004)

2009 TO 2025   18.0

Ruchottes-Chambertin, 2000
Domaine Dr. Georges Mugneret

Fullish colour. Concentrated. Clean. Pure and very lovely on the nose. Ripe and rich, full and vigorous. Very fine fruit. Lovely balance. This is the best of the Ruchottes. Very long at the end. Full. Rich. Complex and lovely. (April 2005)

NOW TO 2025   18.5

Ruchottes-Chambertin, 2000
Domaine Georges Roumier

Fullish colour. Slightly more rustic, especially at the end. Evidence of the stems here. Medium-full body. Ripe, quite rich but a bit astringent. Slightly loose knit in its fruit. Just a little lacking class. (July 2004)

NOW TO 2015   16.0

Ruchottes-Chambertin, Clos des Ruchottes, 2000
Domaine Armand Rousseau

Medium-full colour. Slightly more evolved. Rich and ripe. Decent dimension. Very good depth. Better on the palate than on the nose. Medium-full body. Fresh. Complex. Classy. Rather better than his Charmes and Clos de la Roche. Long and succulent. Fine plus. (April 2005)

2009 TO 2025   18.0

Savigny-lès-Beaune, 2000
Domaine Arnoux Père et Fils

Good colour. A bit more substance and depth than the Chorey-lès-Beaune 2000. Good structure. Good acidity. Plenty of substance here. Positive finish. Good. (March 2003)

NOW TO 2012   15.0

Savigny-lès-Beaune, 2000
Domaine Henri de Villamont

A little slight and a little artificial. But fruity and balanced. More to it at the end than first appears. Quite good. (February 2003)

NOW TO 2011   14.0

Savigny-lès-Beaune, Aux Grands Liards, 2000
Domaine Simon Bize et Fils

Not a lot of colour. Quite developed on the nose. Slightly animal. Medium body. Ripe. Good grip. No hard edges and good intensity. Plenty of character. Very good for what it is. (March 2003)

NOW TO 2012   15.0

Savigny-lès-Beaune, Les Grands Liards, 2000
Domaine Pierre and Jean-Baptiste Lebreuil

Not too light for a 2000 and quite fresh. But not much backbone. (February 2003)

NOW TO 2010   14.0

Savigny-lès-Beaune, Les Grands Picotins, 2000
Domaine du Prieuré/Jean-Michel Maurice

Less artificial than his 2001 but a bit too light. Will get astringent. (February 2003)

DRINK SOON   12.0

Savigny-lès-Beaune, Les Fourneaux, 2000
Domaine Simon Bize et Fils

Medium colour. A little more structure than the Grands Liards. A little unresolved tannin. Good fruit and grip underneath. A lovely example. Good plus. (March 2003)

NOW TO 2013   15.5

Savigny-lès-Beaune, Aux Fourneaux, 2000
Domaine Jean-Michel Giboulot

Medium body. Plump and fruity. Good freshness. Nice style. Quite forward. (February 2003)

NOW TO 2010   14.0

Savigny-lès-Beaune, Aux Guettes, 2000
Domaine Machard de Gramont

Better class than their 2001. Full. Good fruit. Good balance. Plenty of substance. Long. Very good indeed. (February 2003)

2009 TO 2015   16.5

Savigny-lès-Beaune, Clos des Guettes, 2000
Domaine Henri de Villamont

This is much better than his Savigny *tout court*. More genuine. Ripe. Good depth and personality. (February 2003)

NOW TO 2011   14.5

Savigny-lès-Beaune, Les Jarrons, 2000
Domaine Pierre Guillemet

Some oak (20 percent new) here. Ripe and fresh, and with very good depth for the vintage. Good structure. Ripe and positive. Very good. (February 2003)

NOW TO 2012   16.0

Savigny-lès-Beaune, Les Lavières, 2000
Domaine Chandon de Briailles

Medium colour. Fresh, plump, succulent nose. Very good fruit. Ripe tannin. Medium to medium-full body. Good grip. This is stylish. Lovely finish. (March 2003)

NOW TO 2013   15.5

Savigny-lès-Beaune, Les Lavières, 2000
Domaine Philippe Girard

Good fruit here. Quite fresh and stylish. This is good. (February 2003)

NOW TO 2011   15.0

Savigny-lès-Beaune, Les Marconnets, 2000
Domaine Patrick Jacob-Girard

Not too lightweight for the vintage. But forward nevertheless. Decent fruit. Quite good. (February 2003)

NOW TO 2010   14.0

Savigny-lès-Beaune, Les Peuillets, 2000
Domaine Philippe Girard

Clean, but light, forward and a bit neutral. (February 2003)

NOW TO 2010   13.0

Savigny-lès-Beaune, Aux Serpentières, 2000
Domaine François Gay et Fils

Plenty of depth here. Good tannins. Still needs 2 years. Classy and quite substantial. (February 2003)

NOW TO 2013   15.5

Savigny-lès-Beaune, Aux Serpentières, 2000
Domaine Michel Gay

Ripe, fresh and succulent. Plenty of character, and nice and fresh. Very good. (February 2003)

NOW TO 2012   16.0

Savigny-lès-Beaune, Aux Serpentières, 2000
Domaine Jean-Michel Giboulot

Fuller, richer and with more depth than his Fourneaux. This is stylish and very good. (February 2003)

NOW TO 2011   16.0

Savigny-lès-Beaune, Aux Serpentières, 2000
Domaine Pierre Guillemet

His largest *premier cru*. Ripe and fresh. Good substance. Very good acidity. Stylish and long. This is very good. (February 2003)

NOW TO 2012   16.0

Savigny-lès-Beaune, Aux Serpentières, 2000
Domaine Michel Mallard et Fils

Not too oaky. Soft and succulent. Good depth and grip. This has a long, positive finish. Very good, provided you like new oak. (February 2003)

NOW TO 2011   16.0

Savigny-lès-Beaune, Les Vergelesses, 2000
Domaine Michel Gay

Firmer and richer than his Savigny Serpentières. Good grip and substance. Long. Very good plus. (February 2003)

NOW TO 2013   16.5

La Tâche, 2000
Domaine de la Romanée-Conti

Good colour. Gingerbread spice on the nose. Firm. Some tannin. Slightly astringent. A little hard at present. Good substance. Very good depth. Lovely complex fruit and very good acidity. This is rather better than the Romanée-Conti today. Long. Lovely. (July 2004)

2010 TO 2028   19.5

Volnay, 2000
Domaine des Comtes Lafon
Good size for what it is. Pure and ripe if not very succulent or rich fruit. Medium weight. Good acidity. A very good example of a village wine. (October 2003)
NOW TO 2010   16.0

Volnay, Premier Cru, 2000
Domaine du Marquis d'Angerville
Pitures and L'Ormeau. Lightish colour. Soft, fruity and forward on the nose. Light. *À point*. Quite fresh. Nice and ripe. But a bit one-dimensional. Good for what it is. A pretty wine. (June 2005)
NOW TO 2010   14.0

Volnay, Caillerets, Ancienne Cuvée Carnot, 2000
Domaine Bouchard Père et Fils
Medium-full colour. Decent substance on the nose. But it tails off on the palate. Medium body. Lacks style. Not bad plus at best. (July 2004)
DRINK SOON   13.5

Volnay, Les Caillerets, 2000
Domaine Bouchard Père et Fils
Medium to medium-full colour. Fresh, fruity and positive, but not much concentration and depth on the nose. Medium body. Not much tannin. Good definition. Good acidity. No lack of dimension. Really very good for the vintage. Plenty of interest on the follow-through. (March 2004)
NOW TO 2014   16.0

Volnay, Champans, 2000
Domaine du Marquis d'Angerville
Medium to medium-full colour. Ripe and fruity, and fragrant and elegant on the nose. Only medium weight. Good style though. Balanced. Classy and positive. Good, long finish. Quite good. (July 2004)
NOW TO 2013   14.0

Volnay, Clos des Angles, 2000
Maison Olivier Leflaive Frères
Medium-full colour. A little lean and herbal on the nose. Cheap and thin on the palate. (July 2004)
DRINK SOON   11.0

Volnay, Clos de la Barre, 2000
Domaine Louis Jadot
Medium-full colour. Ripe, round, stylish nose. Medium weight. Reasonable depth and dimension. Positive. Long. Good plus. (July 2004)
NOW TO 2010   15.5

Volnay, Clos du Château des Ducs, 2000
Domaine Michel Lafarge
Medium to medium-full colour. Stylish, fragrant nose. Very good weight. Medium body. Lacks ripeness and richness. Tails off. Quite good at best. (July 2004)
DRINK SOON   14.0

Volnay, Clos des Chênes, 2000
Domaine Antonin Guyon
Medium-full colour. Lightweight on the nose. Thin. Already astringent on the palate. No. (July 2004)
DRINK SOON   11.0

Volnay, Clos des Chênes, 2000
Domaine Michel Lafarge
Medium to medium-full colour. Soft nose. Decent fruit but not much of it. Medium body. Now just about ready. Quite supple and attractive. But not much dimension. Quite good at best. (June 2006)
NOW TO 2010   14.0

Volnay, Clos des Ducs, 2000
Domaine du Marquis d'Angerville
Medium-full colour. Rich, full, even fat and concentrated on the nose. Ample and rich on the palate. But hollow in the middle. It fell apart in the glass. (July 2004)
DRINK SOON   14.0

Volnay, Clos des Santenots, 2000
Maison Olivier Leflaive Frères
Medium to medium-full colour. Some development. Some succulence on the nose. Medium body. Rather weedy, especially at the end. Quite stylish though. (July 2004)
DRINK SOON   12.0

Volnay, Frémiets, 2000
Domaine du Comte Armand
Medium to medium-full colour. A bit light-weight on the nose but decently fragrant. Too light on the palate though. No depth. Yet not too short. Not bad. (July 2004)
DRINK SOON   13.0

Volnay, Frémiets, 2000
Maison Olivier Leflaive Frères
Medium to medium-full colour. Decent weight and fruit on the nose. A lot better than their Pommards. Not exactly clean though. Medium body. Some grip and fat. Not bad plus. Will it get astringent? (July 2004)
NOW TO 2010   13.5

Volnay, Mitans, 2000
Domaine Hubert de Montille
Medium colour. Some development. Decent fruit on the nose. But no real depth. It lacks just a little succulence on the palate. Light, forward but quite pretty. There is decent acidity but a slight lack of grip in the middle. Slightly one-dimensional. Slightly feeble at the end. (July 2004)
DRINK SOON   13.0

Volnay, Robardelle, 2000
Domaine Philippe Carré-Courbin
Medium-full colour. Rich and quite succulent on the nose. Fresh. Medium body. Not astringent. Quite clean and stylish. Quite good plus. Positive at the end. (July 2004)
DRINK SOON   14.5

Volnay, Santenots, 2000
Maison Vincent Girardin
Good colour. Rich, full and fragrant. Exceptionally so for a 2000. Ample. Persistent. Elegant and fine for the vintage. À point. (March 2006)
NOW TO 2015   17.5

Volnay, Santenots, 2000
Domaine Joseph Matrot
Medium-full colour. Slightly lean on the nose. Medium to medium-full body. Riper on the palate than the nose would suggest. Elegant. Fresh. Good grip. No lack of succulence. Good, positive finish. Very good. (April 2005)
NOW TO 2012   16.0

Volnay, Santenots du Milieu, 2000
Domaine des Comtes Lafon
Good, full, vigorous colour. This is a great deal better than most Côte de Beaune 2000s and rather better than last time out. Slightly lean at present and no great depth. But good fruit. Give it 2 years. A very respectable example. (October 2005)
NOW TO 2014   15.5

Volnay, Taillepieds, 2000
Domaine du Marquis d'Angerville
Medium-full colour. A bit light and thin on the nose. Some substance here on the palate. Decently positive. The finish is better than most. Quite good. (July 2004)
NOW TO 2010   14.0

Volnay, Taillepieds, 2000
Domaine Bouchard Père et Fils
Medium to medium-full colour. Lacks a little class on the nose. Medium body. Rather astringent and fruitless. No. (July 2004)
DRINK SOON   12.0

Volnay, Taillepieds, 2000
Domaine Hubert de Montille
Medium colour. Light nose. Not much here. Rather empty. No. (July 2004)
DRINK UP IF AT ALL   10.0

Vosne-Romanée, 2000
Domaine Sylvain Cathiard
Good colour. Really quite full for a 2000. Splendid nose. Rich, fullish and quite oaky. Medium to medium-full body. The tannins are supple and sophisticated, and all but absorbed. The wine is round and rich, balanced, seductive, long and positive. Very good indeed for a village wine. (March 2003)
NOW TO 2014   16.0

Vosne-Romanée, 2000
Domaine Jean Grivot
Medium-full colour. Ripe, clean, pure nose. No lack of depth. Medium to medium-full body. Just a touch of tannin and a certain hard edge to it at present. If this goes, this is certainly good plus. Good grip and good length. (March 2003)
NOW TO 2015   15.5

Vosne-Romanée, Les Beaux Monts, 2000
Domaine Bruno Clavelier
Medium to medium-full colour. A clean wine on the nose. Stylish and balanced, too. Ripe and fresh. Stylish if without the dimension of some. Good plus. (July 2004)
NOW TO 2017   15.5

Vosne-Romanée, Les Beaux Monts, 2000
Domaine Jean Grivot
Medium-full colour. Very lovely style on the nose. Cool, ripe, composed and classy. Medium-full body. Intense. Very subtle. Long. Fresh. Fine. (July 2004)
NOW TO 2020   17.5

Vosne-Romanée, Les Beaumonts, 2000
Domaine Alain Hudelot-Noëllat
Medium to medium-full colour. Rich, plump nose. Slightly clumsy. But good fruit. Not the greatest flair, but plummy, fresh, balanced and positive. Easy to enjoy. Very good.
NOW TO 2017   16.0

Vosne-Romanée, Les Brûlées, 2000
Domaine Bruno Clavelier
Medium colour. Some development. Diesel fuel again on the nose. But most of his wines taste like this this year. The wine behind is quite plump. Could have been good. (July 2004)
DRINK SOON   11.0

Vosne-Romanée, Les Brûlées, 2000
Domaine René Engel
Medium colour. Some development. Ripe and stylish. Fragrant nose. Lovely fruit. Well matured. Spicy. Ready. Balanced and attractive. Long and positive. (July 2004)
NOW TO 2015   16.5

Vosne-Romanée, Les Brûlées, 2000
Domaine Michel Gros
Medium-full colour. Firmer than the Clos de Réas. Rich, plump, stylish and harmonious. Vigorous. Ripe. Very good energy. Fullish. Long. Fine plus. (July 2004)
2009 TO 2024   18.0

Vosne-Romanée, Les Brûlées, 2000
Domaine Méo-Camuzet
Medium to medium-full colour. Quite closed on the nose. Good depth here. Rich and meaty. Full bodied. Concentrated and vigorous. Good grip. Fullish body. Plenty of depth and style. Fine. (July 2004)
2009 TO 2024   17.5

Vosne-Romanée, Les Chaumes, 2000
Domaine Bouchard Père et Fils
Medium-full colour. Rich and fragrant, and very seductive on the nose. Really elegant. Medium body. Soft and pretty well ready. Lovely fruit. Very good grip. Very elegant. Really lovely. Fine quality. (September 2005)
NOW TO 2015   17.5

Vosne-Romanée, Les Chaumes, 2000
Domaine Méo-Camuzet
Fullish colour. Good fruit. Rich if a little solid. Good grip though. Not too four-square. Fullish body. Balanced. Doesn't have the flair of his Brûlées but very good plus. (July 2004)
2009 TO 2021   16.5

Vosne-Romanée, Clos du Château, 2000
Maison Bouchard Père et Fils
Slightly fuller colour. Slightly more substance on the nose and palate compared with their 2000 Vosne la Colombière. Medium to medium-full colour. A little tannin. Very good grip. Lots of style. Very pure. Very intense. Very, very long. Fine. (July 2004)
NOW TO 2013   17.5

Vosne-Romanée, Clos des Réas, 2000
Domaine Michel Gros
Medium colour. Soft, fragrant nose. Stylish and quite developed. But good freshness. Medium-full

body. Good grip, class and depth. Stylish and balanced. Long. Very good indeed. (July 2004)

2009 TO 2020   17.0

Vosne-Romanée, La Colombière, 2000
Maison Bouchard Père et Fils

No enormous colour or weight. But very fresh, concentrated, intense and fragrant on the nose and palate. Very, very lovely pure fruit. Excellent balance. Very, very ripe. Ready now. (June 2004)

NOW TO 2010   17.0

Vosne-Romanée, Les Hautes Maizières, 2000
Domaine Prieuré-Roch

Rather better colour than their 2000s. Evolved, gamey nose. A fully mature wine with some tertiary flavours. Medium body. Fresh but slightly astringent. Quite fruity, but it lacks elegance. Fair. (February 2006)

NOW TO 2010   13.0

Vosne-Romanée, Aux Malconsorts, 2000
Domaine Sylvain Cathiard

Full colour. Still youthful. Splendidly rich nose for a 2000. Sweet and succulent. Crisp, balanced, complex and classy. Just about ready. Medium-full body. Ripe, round and balanced. The tannins are now soft. Very lovely. Unexpectedly rich and velvety, especially for the vintage. Very fine. (October 2005)

NOW TO 2010   18.5

Vosne-Romanée, Les Malconsorts, 2000
Domaine Charles Thomas

Fullish colour. Slightly attenuated. Ripe. Clumsy. Lacks grip. Slightly over-extracted? Not too much so, but a distinct lack of grip and interest. Superficial. (July 2004)

NOW TO 2010   12.5

Vosne-Romanée, Les Petits Monts, 2000
Domaine Joseph Drouhin

Medium colour. Fragrant, very classy nose. Soft but lovely fruit. Similar on the palate. Medium to medium-full body. Very lovely. Very long. Fine. (July 2004)

NOW TO 2020+   17.5

Vosne-Romanée, Les Reignots, 2000
Domaine Robert Arnoux

Medium-full colour. Ripe, intense and classy on the nose. Medium-full body. Ripe and balanced. Concentrated and fresh. This is fine. Lovely long finish. (July 2004)

NOW TO 2019   17.5

Vosne-Romanée, Les Reignots, 2000
Maison Bouchard Père et Fils

Medium-full colour. Some development. Good, quite plummy fruit on the nose. Fullish body. Decent balance. A lack of real dimension though. And suspicions of astringency at the end. Very good at best. (July 2004)

NOW TO 2018   16.0

Vosne-Romanée, Les Reignots, 2000
Domaine Sylvain Cathiard

Medium-full colour. Some development. Lovely nose. Intense. Classy. Balanced and composed. Gently oaky. Concentrated. Medium-full body. Lots of vigour. Very long. Very lovely. Fine plus. (July 2004)

NOW TO 2020+   18.0

Vosne-Romanée, Les Suchots, 2000
Domaine Robert Arnoux

Fullish colour. Splendidly concentrated on the nose. Real depth. Even an old-vine creaminess. Very lovely. Fullish on the palate. Very concentrated fruit. Excellent balance. Classy, complex and very long. Very fine. (July 2004)

2009 TO 2025   18.5

Vosne-Romanée, Les Suchots, 2000
Domaine Alain Hudelot-Noëllat

Medium-full colour. Some development. Slightly looser knit than some on the nose. Decent, plump fruit but with a lot of depth. Medium-full body. Good grip. Finishes with more intensity, balance, class and fruit than it seems to have on the nose. Very good plus. (July 2004)

NOW TO 2020   16.5

Vosne-Romanée, Les Suchots, 2000
Maison Louis Jadot

Medium-full colour. Ripe and succulent with a touch of oak on the nose. A bit more adolescent than Arnoux's or Hudelot's. More closed-in. Full bodied. Rich, fat and concentrated. Lots of depth. Lovely long, complex finish. (July 2004)

2010 TO 2025   18.0

Vougeot, Les Cras, Premier Cru, 2000
Domaine de la Vougeraie

Medium to medium-full colour. Plump, ripe and well made on the nose. Fresh and stylish. Medium to medium-full weight. Good grip. This is elegant and has plenty of dimension. Not a bit weak. Very good plus. (July 2004)

NOW TO 2020   16.5

1999

The year 1999 saw a vast harvest: the most abundant since 1982. What is interesting is that the white wine harvest was 24 percent greater than that of 1982, but the red wine yield was 11 percent less. This is evidence of the gradual move toward producing white wine in Chassagne-Montrachet, Saint-Aubin and some other communes (see Appendix 5). The year 1982 remains the only vintage where a quarter of a million hectolitres of red wine were produced in the Côte d'Or.

Yet despite this abundance, 1999 is a splendid vintage in both colours. It is also consistent up and down the hierarchy as well as geographically. Nature gave the Burgundians a golden opportunity in 1999. Thankfully, most did not waste it.

WEATHER CONDITIONS

One thing was obvious from the outset: nature was insisting on pulling out all the stops. The sortie of prospective bunches of fruit was enormous. Barring disaster, the crop would be huge.

The spring and early summer were mild, indeed quite warm at times, and humid. For the second year in succession, oïdium (downy mildew) presented a problem, as did the more usual mildew. Nevertheless, the flowers successfully set into fruit at the beginning of June, indicating an early harvest.

The remainder of June, the whole of July and the beginning of August were cool, but not too wet. But then from about August 15, a four-week period of very fine weather set in—not the heat wave of 1998, but just a succession of long sunny, warm days. All the cryptogamic threats to the fruit were dried up. The grapes ripened and expanded in size. Growers went up and down the rows of vines not just once but two or three times cutting out the less-advanced bunches. Everything, despite the size of the crop—which was looking larger and larger as one neared the harvest, despite the *vendanges vertes*—was looking increasingly promising.

Thankfully, for otherwise the tannins would have remained blocked, there was a brief interruption for rain at the beginning of September, which ensured that the phenolic elements in the fruit ripened at the same rate as the sugar readings increased.

There was no point in waiting since these sugars were already indicating alcoholic degrees of 13° plus, so as soon as the *ban des vendanges* was announced (September 18 for the Côte d'Or), almost everyone rushed out to pick.

A week later there was rain, but at first this was intermittent and mainly at night. It takes four or five days after heavy precipitation for

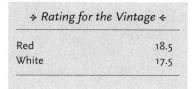

⤞ Rating for the Vintage ⤝

Red	18.5
White	17.5

⤞ Size of the Crop ⤝
(In hectolitres, excluding generic wine)

	RED	WHITE
Grands Crus	15,297	4,187
Village and Premiers Crus	208,830	67,051
TOTAL	224,127	71,238

the berries to become rain inflated; since most growers had more or less finished harvesting, this did not have a serious effect. Indeed, the fruit was in a magnificent state of health, and—despite the size of the crop—of ripeness and concentration, too. With high-class fruit in the first place, the winemakers' task is made easy: one can vinify as one wishes. No compromises have to be made. This was the case in 1999.

Winemakers, as I have said, had an easy vintage, or so it seemed, in 1999. The fruit was in such a state of health that it hardly needed any *triage*, the separating of the good from the not-so-good. Sugar levels were high, necessitating minimal or zero chaptalisation. Acidities were good, and moreover ripe. The phenolic elements were mature, too. And the wine had the sort of structure which could take any amount (save excess) of new oak the cave had decided to use.

What made growers hesitant was the size of the crop. Many growers *saignéed*. Others used one of the new concentrating machines. Some could have—in retrospect, should have—extracted more. But most got it right. At first the wine was not very expressive, but by November 1999, when I was there to sample the 1998s, most producers seemed enthusiastic. As time went on, and *malos* in general, along with the whites, were long to complete, opinions rose. And despite the size of the harvest, there was no lack of *terroir* definition.

The white wines from this year are full, rich and abundant. If they do not have quite the grip of the 2002s, they make up for it in energy and abundance. Both vintages are fine. Which one prefers depends on the mood, the dish and one's personal taste. Most are drinking beautifully now.

The red wines are full and intensely rich. This fruit has given a velvety succulence to the village wines of Pommard and Nuits-Saint-Georges, which normally have a tendency to be rather tough and solid, even dense and rustic. There is plenty of tannic power behind the richness.

A number of wines, quite naturally, have retired into their shells. Some of the initial puppy-fat of the primary fruit has gone: the secondary and tertiary flavours of the mature wine have yet to appear. Hence it is the tannin which sticks out a bit.

Nevertheless, there is an exciting richness and vigour running through the wines. The tannins are ripe; the wines have volume and grip; and the vast majority have finesse as well as balance. As I pointed out at the outset, the Pommards and Nuits-Saint-Georges are better mannered than usual. The vintage is at its best in the Côte de Nuits, but that is what you would expect: here are all but one of the red wine *grands crus*.

WHERE ARE THE BEST WINES?

With the marginal exceptions of some Cortons, both red and white, this is a very consistent vintage.

WHEN WILL THE WINES BE AT THEIR BEST?

All white wines up to *grand cru* level are fully ready now, and even some *grands crus* have reached their peak. Drink the wines up to village level soon, although many still have plenty of vigour in them. The rest can safely be kept until their tenth birthday or beyond.

The village red wines of the Côte de Beaune are now à point. *Premiers crus* still, for the most part, require 2 more years. As far as the Côte de Nuits is concerned, one should postpone drinking these wines for 2 years more (i.e., village wines from now to 2009, *premiers crus* from 2010 to 2011 and then the *grands crus* from 2012 onward). All balanced reds will last very well indeed.

TASTING NOTES

WHITES

Auxey-Duresses Blanc, 1999
Domaine V. de MacMahon

Niece of Duc de Magenta. Most goes to Jadot. Full, rich and opulent. Very ample. Quite unlike the usual leanness of Auxey. Good grip underneath. Unexpectedly concentrated and good quality. (October 2003)

DRINK SOON   15.0

Bâtard-Montrachet, 1999
Domaine Roger Caillot

Quite evolved, both in the colour and on the nose. Rich, full, ripe and opulent, but not too exotic, and with good grip and depth. This is now *à point*. Fullish bodied, balanced, clean and generous. Plenty of plump, attractive fruit. Seductive. Finishes long and fresh. Fine. (October 2002)

NOW TO 2010   17.5

Bâtard-Montrachet, 1999
Domaine Jean-Noël Gagnard

Rich, full, backward and concentrated on the nose. Some oak. Full bodied. Rich and honeyed. Excellent grip. Really very lovely. Intense and powerful. Very fine plus. (September 2004)

NOW TO 2015+   19.0

Bâtard-Montrachet, 1999
Domaine Louis Jadot

Rich, fat, oaky, stylish nose. Lots of depth here. Fullish body. A little oak. Accessible. Very good class, freshness and intensity. Long and complex. Intense. Very lovely. (September 2001)

NOW TO 2015+   19.0

Bâtard-Montrachet, 1999
Domaine Leflaive

Very fine, closed-in nose. Just a touch of SO2. Made for the long term. Adolescent. Very lovely concentrated fruit. Very fine grip. Fullish body. Very Bâtard. Very fine. (September 2001)

NOW TO 2015+   18.5

Bâtard-Montrachet, 1999
Château de la Maltroye

Clean and rich. Lots of definition. Marvellous fruit here. Fullish body. Oaky. Excellent grip. This is very classy and marvellous balanced. A racy example of a Bâtard. Very fine plus. (September 2001)

NOW TO 2015+   19.0

Bâtard-Montrachet, 1999
Domaine Paul Pernot et Fils

A bit more evolution than some. Plump. Honeysuckle flavours. Nice and ripe. Good grip underneath. On the palate this is accessible, fruity and very seductive. But it doesn't have the grip and intensity of the best. Very good indeed. (September 2001)

NOW TO 2012   17.0

Bâtard-Montrachet, 1999
Maison Verget

Clean, ripe, fresh nose. But lacking a little dimension. On the palate rather forward. A little thin even for what it is. Clean and stylish but good plus at best. Young vines? (September 2001)

NOW TO 2010   15.5

Beaune, Clos Saint-Landry Blanc, 1999
Domaine Bouchard Père et Fils

Round, ripe and nutty. Only average acidity though. Decent depth. But slightly fat at the end. Quite good. (March 2003)

DRINK SOON   14.0

Beaune, Grèves, Le Clos Blanc, 1999
Domaine Gagey/Maison Louis Jadot

This is delicious. Very ripe. Medium-full. Excellent fruit. Very good grip. Plump and appley-peachy. Very good indeed. (October 2002)

NOW 2009   17.0

Beaune, Les Teurons, 1999
Domaine Bouchard Père et Fils

Ripe, fragrant, melony-lemony. Just a little oak on the nose. Rich on the palate. Fullish body. Plenty of depth. Long. Good plus. (September 2001)

NOW TO 2010   15.5

Bienvenues-Bâtard-Montrachet, 1999
Domaine Louis Carillon et Fils

Very, very lovely nose. Concentrated, delicate, intense and very elegant. Marvellous laid-back fruit, and complexity and depth. Real class. Very long. Very subtle. Very lovely. Really persistent and pure. Very fine plus. (September 2001)

NOW TO 2020   19.0

Bienvenues-Bâtard-Montrachet, 1999
Domaine Paul Pernot et Fils

Rich, fat and ample. Not as pure or as classy as Carillon's. Rather more evolved, indeed too much so in the glass as it developed. Honeyed, but it lacks grip. Some SO2, too. (September 2001)

NOW TO 2009   15.0

Bienvenues-Bâtard-Montrachet, 1999
Maison Roland Remoissenet et Fils

Fragrant nose. It smells of lemon sherbet. Fullish body. A little four-square. Ripe and even rich. But a lack of flair. Merely good. (September 2001)

NOW TO 2010   15.0

Chassagne-Montrachet, 1999
Domaine Borgeot

Domaine in Remigny. Ripe but slightly four-square nose. Medium-full, ample, fruity and attractive. Not a bit too heavy on the palate. Good, peachy fruit. Good acidity. Ample. Long. Very good for what it is. (March 2002)

DRINK SOON   15.5

Chassagne-Montrachet, 1999
Domaine du Marquis de Laguiche/Maison Joseph Drouhin

Seriously good stuff. Full, oaky, very concentrated, very ripe nose. Rich and voluptuous on the palate, yet with very good grip and depth. Very good indeed. (February 2003)

NOW TO 2016   17.0

Chassagne-Montrachet, Abbaye de Morgeot, 1999
Maison Olivier Leflaive Frères

Stylish, fragrant, ripe and peachy. Just a touch of residual sugar. Medium-full body. Good concentration. Quite accessible. Good acidity. Fresh. Attractively fruity. Ripe. Long. Very good indeed. (March 2002)

NOW TO 2012   17.0

Chassagne-Montrachet, Les Baudines, 1999
Domaine Bernard Morey

Surprisingly mellow and ripe for an upslope *climat*. Good, fat, oaky style. Fullish body. Very clean. Nicely racy on the palate. Long. Very classy. (September 2001)

NOW TO 2012   17.0

Chassagne-Montrachet, Blanchot-Dessus, 1999
Domaine Darviot-Perrin

Pure, racy nose. Lots of depth here. Backward but concentrated. Marvellous depth and concentration. Splendid fruit. Really good grip. Youthful and racy, but very fine. (September 2001)

NOW TO 2015   18.5

Chassagne-Montrachet, Caillerets, 1999
Domaine Marc Colin

Slightly reduced but ample on the nose. Full, fat, oaky and plump. But good depth and class. Lovely fruit. Good length on the finish. Very good plus. (September 2001)

NOW TO 2012   16.5

Chassagne-Montrachet, Les Caillerets, 1999
Domaine Jean-Noël Gagnard

Fully mature. Clean, crisp, plump and succulent. Lovely fruit. Very well balanced. Harmonious and very long. Very classy. Fine. (January 2004)

NOW TO 2010   17.5

Chassagne-Montrachet, Les Caillerets, 1999
Domaine Morey-Coffinet

Rich, full, sensuous nose. Gently oaky. Plenty of depth. Fullish, opulent but very well balanced. Lots of substance here. Very good grip. Very good indeed. (October 2002)

NOW TO 2013   17.0

Chassagne-Montrachet, Caillerets, 1999
Domaine Bernard Morey

Rich, full, classy and ample—and nicely minerally. Rather more to it than the Baudines. Rich and gently oaky. Fullish weight. Very intense. Long, balanced, peachy fruit. Fine. (September 2001)

NOW TO 2012   17.5

Chassagne-Montrachet, Les Caillerets, 1999
Domaine Jean Pillot et Fils
Delicate but classy and intense on the nose.
Medium-full. Clean, pure, crisp and full of
fruit on the palate. Just about ready. Lots of
depth. Balanced, poised and long on the follow-
through. Lovely. Fine. (March 2005)
NOW TO 2012   17.5

Chassagne-Montrachet, Les Champs Gain, 1999
Domaine Jean-Noël Gagnard
Ripe, stylish and flowery if without perhaps quite
the depth of their Caillerets. Slightly less concentration and dimension, but a most attractive
example nevertheless. Very stylish. Very well balanced. Very good plus. (September 2001)
NOW TO 2012   16.5

Chassagne-Montrachet, Les Champs Gain, 1999
Domaine Vincent and François Jouard
Flowery and stylish. Elegant and clean, if without
the depth of some. Medium weight. Not quite
the intensity for fine, but if forward, very stylish
and good harmony. Very good. (September 2001)
NOW TO 2010   16.0

Chassagne-Montrachet, Les Champs Gain, 1999
Domaine Michel Niellon
A bit of sulphur on the nose. Full, fat and rich,
but a bit "hot." It seems a bit clumsy on the
palate. Very ripe but a bit four-square. Good
though. (September 2001)
NOW TO 2010   15.0

Chassagne-Montrachet, Les Champs Gain, 1999
Domaine Jean Pillot et Fils
Full, rich, fat and complex. Plenty of wine here.
Good grip. This is very good if a touch neutral in
comparison with some. Perhaps a little closed-
in. Very good plus. (September 2001)
NOW TO 2012   16.5

Chassagne-Montrachet, Les Chaumées, 1999
Domaine Jean-Noël Gagnard
Soft and flowery, but a little more four-square
and lacking the zip of Jean-Noël Gagnard's other
wines. Gently oaky. Good, stylish, and with fullish

weight on the palate. Balanced. Good drive and
definition. Very good plus. (September 2001)
NOW TO 2012   16.5

Chassagne-Montrachet, Les Chaumées,
Clos de la Truffière, 1999
Domaine Vincent and François Jouard
Fragrant, racy and stylish on the nose. Good,
flowery aspects if only medium weight. Nice and
racy on the palate. Persistent. Even intense. This
has lovely style. Very long. Very good indeed.
(September 2001)
NOW TO 2012   17.0

Chassagne-Montrachet, Les Chaumées,
Clos de la Truffière, 1999
Domaine Michel Niellon
Somewhat sulphury on the nose. Fullish
weight. A bit four-square on the palate. Good
grip but slightly hot at the end. Good at best.
(September 2001)
NOW TO 2010   15.0

Chassagne-Montrachet, Les Chenevottes, 1999
Domaine Michel Colin-Deléger et Fils
Good, plump wine. Ripe and balanced if no
great intensity or dimension. Medium-full body.
Slightly lacking personality if clean and ripe.
Good at best. (September 2001)
NOW TO 2010   15.0

Chassagne-Montrachet, Les Chenevottes, 1999
Domaine Jean-Noël Gagnard
A little heavier and more four-square than
their Chaumées. Medium-full body. Ripe and
balanced, but a slight lack of real character
and flair. Good, long, clean finish. Good plus.
(September 2001)
NOW TO 2011   15.5

Chassagne-Montrachet, Les Chenevottes, 1999
Château de la Maltroye
Lovely nose. Flowery and peachy, and very good
acidity. Not a bit four-square. Very elegant indeed.
Very good personality for Chenevottes. Ripe, bal-
anced, racy finish. Very good plus. (September 2001)
NOW TO 2012   16.5

Chassagne-Montrachet, Les Chenevottes, 1999
Domaine Michel Niellon

Richer, meatier and much better balanced than their Chaumées. Good weight. Very good zip. Ample and ripe, but not quite the style and zip. Good plus. (September 2001)

NOW TO 2010   15.5

Chassagne-Montrachet, Les Chenevottes, 1999
Domaine Jean Pillot et Fils

Ripe, fresh, fullish and stylish on the nose. Not a bit four-square. Lovely fruit here. Fullish body. Very good grip. This is excellent for what it is. Really long, concentrated, old viney and intense. Fine. (September 2001)

NOW TO 2012   17.5

Chassagne-Montrachet, Clos de la Boudriotte, 1999
Domaine Ramonet

Medium to medium-full colour. Ripe and fat, and unexpectedly stylish on the nose, with a touch of spice. Medium to medium-full body. A little tannin but not a bit tough. Very good acidity. Long. Very good plus. (February 2003)

NOW TO 2016   16.5

Chassagne-Montrachet, Clos du Château de la Maltroye, 1999
Château de la Maltroye

Lovely racy fruit here. Peachy and minerally. Very stylish. Full body. Old-vine concentration in a creamy-rich sense. Some oak. This is very lovely. Backward but fine plus. (September 2001)

NOW TO 2015   18.0

Chassagne-Montrachet, Clos de la Maltroie, 1999
Domaine Jean-Noël Gagnard

This is less impressive than the other Jean-Noël Gagnard wines on the nose. A bit flat and sulphury. Medium body. No grip. No depth. Disappointing. Young vines? (September 2001)

DRINK SOON   13.0

Chassagne-Montrachet, Clos Saint-Jean, 1999
Domaine Michel Niellon

Sulphury and four-square on the nose. Not much style here. Thin. Dead. Not for me. (September 2001)

(SEE NOTE)   11.0

Chassagne-Montrachet, Les Embrazées, 1999
Maison Vincent Girardin

Full, fresh nose. Gently oaky, rich and fat. Medium-full body. Racy and minerally. Good depth and class. Will still improve: it is just a little tight at the moment. Very good indeed. (September 2005)

NOW TO 2017   17.0

Chassagne-Montrachet, Les Fairendes, 1999
Domaine Michel Morey-Coffinet

A touch of sulphur on the nose. But decent fruit on the palate. A little tight on the palate. Good depth though. Medium-full body. Good plus. (September 2001)

NOW TO 2010   15.5

Chassagne-Montrachet, Francemont, 1999
Maison Verget

Rather flat and evolved on the nose. Lemony. Medium body. It lacks depth and real grip. Flat. Uninteresting. Forward. (September 2001)

DRINK SOON   13.0

Chassagne-Montrachet, Les Grandes Ruchottes, 1999
Château de la Maltroye

Rich, full, fat and classy on the nose. Fullish body. Oaky, ripe and intense. Lots of depth. Very lovely fruit. Fine. (September 2001)

NOW TO 2012   17.5

Chassagne-Montrachet, Les Grandes Ruchottes, 1999
Domaine Bernard Moreau

Soft, fruity, ripe and classy on the nose. Medium-full body. Gently oaky. Very lovely fruit. Intense and beautiful. Essentially gentle, but very long and very complex. Fine. (September 2001)

NOW TO 2011   17.5

Chassagne-Montrachet, Les Houillères, 1999
Maison Olivier Leflaive Frères
Village wine. Decent fruit. Not quite the back-bone of a true Chassagne. Quite forward. Good style. Quite good plus. (February 2003)
DRINK SOON   14.5

Chassagne-Montrachet, Les Macherelles, 1999
Domaine Jean Pillot et Fils
Ripe and fragrant, full and positive on the nose. Fullish body. Just a touch four-square. Good grip. Ripe but no better than very good. Good finish though. (September 2001)
NOW TO 2011   16.0

Chassagne-Montrachet, La Maltroie, 1999
Domaine Vincent et François Jouard
Quite austere on the nose. Firm. Good grip. Medium to medium-full weight. This is going to need more time than their Chaumées. Less fruit and succulence at the moment, but more vigour at the end. Very good plus. From 2004/2005.
(January 2001)
NOW TO 2013   16.5

Chassagne-Montrachet, La Maltroie, 1999
Domaine Bernard Moreau
Fragrant, clean, peachy nose. But not a lot of weight behind it. Ripe. Medium body. Intense and classy. A lovely example. Almost as good as his Grandes Ruchottes. Very good indeed.
(September 2001)
NOW TO 2011   17.0

Chassagne-Montrachet, La Maltroie, 1999
Domaine Michel Niellon
Less sulphury than some of his wines. Clean and fruity if no great depth. Medium-full body. Exotic. But a little diffuse at the end. A little SO2 at the end. Only quite good.
(September 2001)
NOW TO 2009   14.0

Chassagne-Montrachet, Morgeot, 1999
Domaine Michel Colin-Deléger et Fils
A bit tight on the nose. Fullish bodied but a touch of sulphur. A little four-square. Not one of

Colin-Deléger's greatest. Quite substantial, but it lacks flair. Decent grip though. Not bad plus.
(September 2001)
NOW TO 2009   13.5

Chassagne-Montrachet, Morgeot, 1999
GAEC Des Vignerons (Guy Fontaine and
Jacky Vion)
Rich, full, oaky and exotic. Fat and ample. Good grip. Still very young. Almost too tropical. Not too heavy. Very ripe. Very good. (January 2003)
NOW TO 2012   16.0

Chassagne-Montrachet, Morgeot, 1999
Domaine Jean-Noël Gagnard
A touch of sulphur on the nose, but ripe and stylish and vigorous underneath. This is a bit disappointing. Too much sulphur. Slightly astringent. (September 2001)
DRINK SOON   13.0

Chassagne-Montrachet, Morgeot, 1999
Domaine Vincent Girardin
Ripe, fullish, succulent nose. Good style here. Ample and generous. Lovely style. Fullish body. Very good grip. Long. Fine. (September 2001)
NOW TO 2012   17.5

Chassagne-Montrachet, Morgeot, Clos de la
Chapelle, 1999
Domaine Duc de Magenta/Maison Louis Jadot
Backward but full. Very clean. Splendid ripeness. Great style and depth. Perhaps it lacks a little grip, but full bodied, ripe, rich and long. This is very lovely at the end. Backward. Real depth. Fine plus. (September 2001)
NOW TO 2015   18.0

Chassagne-Montrachet, Morgeot Vigne
Blanche, 1999
Château de la Maltroye
Ample, fullish nose and palate. Very lovely, clean, concentrated fruit. A lot of intensity and depth. Very pure. Very good grip. This is fine.
(October 2001)
NOW TO 2015   17.5

Chassagne-Montrachet, En Remilly, 1999
Domaine Michel Colin-Deléger et Fils

Quite closed, but lots of grip, depth and class. A concentrated, intense wine. Fullish body. Backward. Really marvellous fruit. Excellent grip. This is very classy. Very profound. Lovely. But needs time. Fine plus. (September 2001)

NOW TO 2015   18.0

Chassagne-Montrachet, En Remilly, 1999
Domaine Michel Morey-Coffinet

Very lovely nose. More accessible than Colin-Deléger's example. Lovely peachy fruit. Balanced and stylish. Medium-full body. Ripe, fragrant and peachy. Good but not brilliant depth. Fresh and very good plus though. (September 2001)

NOW TO 2010   16.5

Chassagne-Montrachet, La Romanée, 1999
Château de la Maltroye

Slightly dead on the nose. I would have expected more from this domaine and this *climat*. Perhaps merely closed. Not one of their greatest. Good grip. Decent fruit. Quite racy. Decent length. Good but not great. (September 2001)

NOW TO 2009   15.0

Chassagne-Montrachet, La Romanée, 1999
Domaine Morey-Coffinet

Better than the 2000. Richer, more depth, more concentrated. An ample wine with good grip and plenty of future. Will still improve. Fine. (January 2004)

NOW TO 2016   17.5

Chassagne-Montrachet, Les Ruchottes, 1999
Domaine Ramonet

Will still improve. Fullish, rich, concentrated and balanced. Very lovely fruit. Real depth. Lots of character. Lovely harmony. Fine plus. (May 2005)

NOW TO 2020   18.0

Chassagne-Montrachet, Les Vergers, 1999
Domaine Marc Morey

Clean, fragrant and stylish on the nose. Medium weight. Good concentration. Fullish body. Ripe and balanced. Good intensity. This is backward, but concentrated and impressive for the *climat*. Very good indeed. (September 2001)

NOW TO 2011   17.0

Chassagne-Montrachet, Vigne Blanche, 1999
Château de la Maltroye

A little bit of lemon and lanolin on the nose. Not the greatest of grip and depth. Weak, thin and short. Disappointing. (September 2001)

DRINK SOON   13.0

Chassagne-Montrachet, En Virondot, 1999
Domaine Marc Morey

Ripe and rich. Slightly fuller and more racy than their Vergers. Good class and depth. On the palate a bit less good with less grip, less succulence. Slightly astringent. Only "good." (September 2001)

NOW TO 2010   15.0

Chevalier-Montrachet, 1999
Domaine Bouchard Père et Fils

Very classy, rich, mineral nose. Still very vigorous. Still very closed-in. Fullish body. Rich. Very lovely fruit. Great class and very lovely harmony. Excellent grip. Very, very long. Very fine indeed. (March 2004)

2012 TO 2030   19.0

Chevalier-Montrachet, 1999
Domaine Michel Colin-Deléger et Fils

Still very closed-in on the nose. This is excellent. Very, very full and concentrated. Splendidly noble fruit. Very fine grip. Gently oaky. Lots of depth and dimension. Very classy and quite lovely. (September 2004)

2009 TO 2025   18.5

Chevalier-Montrachet, 1999
Maison Vincent Girardin

Developed colour. Rich, concentrated, very ripe, almost abundant nose. But very good acidity. Ripe and opulent on the palate. Nutty, fat and very rich. Almost sweet. Fine but there is something a little lumpy. It lacks a bit of style. (March 2004)

2009 TO 2025   17.5

Chevalier-Montrachet, 1999
Domaine Leflaive

Like their Bâtard, but even less evolved. A little built-in sulphur. But rich, full and classy underneath. Hidden, but I don't think it quite has the poise of Jadot's or Colin-Deléger's Chevalier-Montrachets. Very lovely nevertheless, but more adolescent. (September 2001)

NOW TO 2015   19.0

Chevalier-Montrachet, 1999
Maison Jean-Marc Pillot

Very fine nose. Lovely racy fruit. Excellent grip. Classy and multidimensional. Ripe. Fullish body. A little more evolved than some. Yet very closed. Very fine grip. This is very fine. (September 2001)

NOW TO 2012   18.5

Chevalier-Montrachet, La Cabotte, 1999
Domaine Bouchard Père et Fils

Marvellous poise of fresh, flowery, peachy fruit on the nose. Full body. Rich, fat, ample and oaky. Lovely balance. Great elegance and intensity. Excellent finish. Very fine plus. (September 2001)

NOW TO 2012   19.0

Chevalier-Montrachet, Les Demoiselles, 1999
Domaine Louis Jadot

Closed-in on the nose. Very concentrated. Excellent fruit. Great class. A marvellous wine. On the palate this is quite brilliant. Splendid concentration and intensity. Great finesse. Splendid grip. The complete example. (March 2004)

NOW TO 2020   19.5

Corton Blanc, 1999
Domaine du Comte Senard

Attractive fruit on the nose, with a touch of oak. Good, ample, balanced style. A little firm. Fullish body. Slightly four-square. Very good rather than fine. (March 2002)

NOW TO 2015   16.0

Corton-Charlemagne, 1999
Domaine Bonneau du Martray

Excellent, very pure, splendidly ripe nose. Yet with all the racy austerity of Corton-Charlemagne.

Full body. Marvellous fruit. Very concentrated. Still rather tight. Excellent potential. Very fine. (March 2002)

NOW TO 2027   18.5

Corton-Charlemagne, 1999
Domaine Bouchard Père et Fils

This is quite a lot richer and more concentrated than the 2000. Very good grip. Fullish body and very fine fruit. Gently oaky. Properly minerally nevertheless. Rich, complex, ripe and very long. Fine plus. (June 2003)

2009 TO 2025   18.0

Corton-Charlemagne, 1999
Domaine Bruno Clair

Elegant and rich. Lacks a little energy, but clean and stylish. Medium body. Very good but not great. Young vines? *À point.* (March 2006)

NOW TO 2014   16.0

Corton-Charlemagne, 1999
Domaine Jean-François Coche-Dury

Richer, rounder and more evolved on the nose than the 2002. On the palate very minerally. Medium to medium-full body. Very ample, ripe, peachy fruit. Very intense and long on the palate. Yet very restrained and composed. Rather more youthful on the palate than the nose. But the oak is more pronounced than in the 2002. Richer and fuller than the 2002. Multidimensional. Excellent. Will still improve. (June 2005)

NOW TO 2020   19.0

Corton-Charlemagne, 1999
Domaine Joseph Drouhin

Ripe and flowery, but does it lack a little weight and depth? Good weight on the palate. Lovely balance. Some oak. A lovely example. Lots of grip and dimension. Very fine. (September 2001)

NOW TO 2018   18.5

Corton-Charlemagne, 1999
Domaine Joseph Faiveley

Rich and fat. Really opulent. Quite evolved. Full bodied and very, very vigorous on the palate.

Splendid, concentrated fruit. Very fine acidity. Very fine. (June 2003)

2009 TO 2025   18.5

Corton-Charlemagne, 1999
Domaine Follin-Arbelet

A little reduced but ripe, concentrated and quite oaky on the nose. Fat. Some evolution. Rich. Very oaky on the palate. Seductive and quite forward for a Corton-Charlemagne. Very good but not great. (September 2001)

NOW TO 2012   16.0

Corton-Charlemagne, 1999
Maison Vincent Girardin

Lovely rich, ripe, gently oaky nose. Full body. Very good acidity. Excellent crisp, peachy fruit. Ripe and delicious. Very fine. (October 2001)

NOW TO 2020   18.5

Corton-Charlemagne, 1999
Domaine Michel Juillot

Over-evolved and oxidised on the nose. This is rather flat on the palate. Very ripe—almost to the point of being overripe. Lovely, plump fruit. But a little over the top, and as a result, it lacks style. Good merely. (September 2001)

NOW TO 2011   15.0

Corton-Charlemagne, 1999
Domaine Louis Latour

Medium-full colour. Still fresh. Ripe nose. No over-oak extraction. Rich but good acidity. Full body. Clean. No undue sulphur. Long and lovely. Will still improve. This is fine plus. (October 2005)

NOW TO 2017   18.0

Corton-Charlemagne, 1999
Domaine Rapet Père et Fils

Still a little closed on the nose. A touch of built-in sulphur. Rich, full and nicely minerally. Not quite the flair of their 2002 but very good grip. A much more exotic wine. Yet properly Corton-Charlemagne. Balanced and long. Fine. Now ready. (October 2005)

NOW TO 2012   17.5

Corton-Charlemagne, 1999
Domaine Rollin Père et Fils

Clean nose but not a lot of depth behind it. Clean and pleasant on the palate, but rather one-dimensional in comparison with the rest of the Corton-Charlemagnes. Medium weight. Good at best. (September 2001)

NOW TO 2011   15.0

Corton-Charlemagne, 1999
Domaine Charles Thomas

Quite a deep colour. Rich, fat, meaty wine with a touch of oak. Good grip. Plenty of depth. This is quite developed, but it is ample and very good indeed. Not quite the grip for fine. (October 2001)

NOW TO 2010   17.0

Corton-Charlemagne, 1999
Maison Verget

Quite honeysuckley and otherwise perfumed on the nose. But not a lot of class. On the palate a bit evolved. Some oak. A lack of grip. Very good but basically a little neutral. (September 2001)

NOW TO 2011   16.0

Meursault, 1999
Domaine Pierre Morey

Village wine. Stylish, rich, gently oaky nose. Lots of depth. Ripe. Medium-full body. Lovely balance. Very classy. Very good for what it is. Will still improve. (March 2002)

NOW TO 2009   15.0

Meursault, Cuvée Maurice Chevalier, 1999
Maison Roland Remoissenet et Fils

Heavy, slightly sulphury nose. Rather neutral on the palate. Some grip, but not enough fruit, class and interest. (September 2001)

DRINK SOON   13.5

Meursault, Blagny, 1999
Domaine Joseph Matrot

Rich, full, buttery nose. A touch of sulphur. Full body. Backward. But good depth here. Good grip too. Good. (September 2001)

NOW TO 2012   15.0

Meursault, Les Bouchères, 1999
Domaine Latour-Giraud

Clean, ripe and succulent nose. Good depth on the palate. Fullish body. Complex and classy. Very good. (September 2001)

NOW TO 2012   16.0

Meursault, Casse-Têtes, 1999
Domaine Michel Tessier

This is still recovering from the bottling. Firm. Full. Just a faint touch of sulphur. Slightly rigid. But there is depth here. Lovely acidity. Very fresh. Fine, positive finish. Very good. From 2004. (January 2001)

NOW TO 2012   16.0

Meursault, Charmes, 1999
Domaine Philippe Ballot-Millot et Fils

Medium weight. Quite forward, but some fruit and style on the nose. A little diffuse at the end. Plump and fruity. Not very complex. Not very long. Quite good at best. (September 2001)

DRINK SOON   14.0

Meursault, Charmes, 1999
Domaine Michel Bouzereau et Fils

Ripe—almost over-ripe. A little botrytis on the nose? This makes it a little spicy and a little astringent on the palate. It takes away the purity. Not bad plus. (September 2001)

NOW TO 2008   13.5

Meursault, Charmes, 1999
Domaine Yves Boyer-Martenot

Firm, rich nose. Lots of depth. Just a touch of oak. Full body. Ripe and steely. Complex and classy. Youthful. Very good finish. (September 2001)

NOW TO 2012   16.5

Meursault, Charmes, 1999
Domaine Alain Coche-Bizouard

A little diffuse on the nose, like his Goutte d'Or, but softer and more supple. Decent fruit and a touch of oak. Better on the palate. Quite rich and complex. Good depth and class. Long and positive at the end. (September 2001)

NOW TO 2011   15.5

Meursault, Charmes, 1999
Maison Vincent Girardin

Classy, supple, soft and aromatic on the nose. Very good fruit and definition. Very clean and well balanced. Medium-full body. Lovely fruit. Long and pure. Very good. (September 2001)

NOW TO 2011   16.0

Meursault, Charmes, 1999
Domaine des Comtes Lafon

Rich, fullish, closed-in. Lovely ripe fruit. Classy and multidimensional. Very intense. Still very young. But very impressive. Fine plus. (March 2002)

NOW TO 2020   18.0

Meursault, Charmes, 1999
Domaine Latour-Giraud

Plump, flowery nose. Medium-full body. Ripe and gently oaky. Good depth and style. Very good acidity. Plenty of vigour on the finish. This is fine plus. (October 2001)

NOW TO 2013   17.5

Meursault, Charmes, 1999
Domaine Joseph Matrot

Odd flavours on the nose. A touch of sulphur. Full body. Somewhat adolescent. A bit four-square on the palate. Good fruit and grip though. Finishes well. (September 2001)

NOW TO 2012   15.0

Meursault, Charmes, 1999
Domaine Michelot Mère et Fille

Rich, ripe, fullish, plump, succulent nose. A little diffuse on the palate and a touch of sulphur. Slightly thin and short at the end. Boring, in fact. (September 2001)

DRINK SOON   13.5

Meursault, Charmes, 1999
Domaine François Mikulski

Rather better than his Poruzots. Fullish body. Firm, backward and concentrated. Very good ripe fruit. Youthful. Balanced. Individual. Good grip. Good plus. (September 2001)

NOW TO 2010   15.5

Meursault, Chevalières, 1999
Domaine Jean-Philippe Fichet

Stylish nose. Pure, balanced and crisp. Lovely on the palate. Ripe and peachy. Very clean and harmonious. Medium-full body. Very good, especially for a wine that is not a *premier cru*.

NOW TO 2012   16.0

Meursault, Clos de la Barre, 1999
Domaine des Comtes Lafon

Youthful colour. Youthful, plump, gently oaky nose. Fullish body. Very good grip. Still not quite yet ready. Lots of energy and depth. Long. Fine. Better in a year. (May 2005)

NOW TO 2015   17.5

Meursault, Les Clous, 1999
Domaine Bouchard Père et Fils

Crisp, stylish nose. Medium weight. Ripe, racy, steely and finely balanced. Understated. Complex. Lovely finish. This is very good indeed for what it is. (March 2002)

DRINK SOON   16.0

Meursault, Désirée, 1999
Domaine des Comtes Lafon

Ripe, fat and slightly spicy. Rich. Fullish bodied. Good grip. Slight hint of botrytis. Lacks a little real zip and elegance. Very good but not fine. (May 2005)

NOW TO 2010   16.0

Meursault, Genevrières, 1999
Domaine Philippe Ballot-Millot et Fils

Good nose. Plenty of attractive fruit here. Slightly oaky. Good depth. A bit lightweight on the palate. It tails off. Clean though. Forward. Not bad plus. (September 2001)

DRINK SOON   13.5

Meursault, Genevrières, 1999
Domaine Bernard Boisson-Vadot

Pretty but lightweight nose. Pleasant wine. But light, short and forward. Not much here. (September 2001)

DRINK UP   13.0

Meursault, Genevrières, 1999
Domaine Bouchard Père et Fils

Youthful colour. Full, rich, mature, quite oaky nose. Lush, rich and concentrated on the palate. Full body. Ample. No evidence of overripeness. Good acidity. Elegant and fine. (December 2005)

NOW TO 2012   17.5

Meursault, Genevrières, 1999
Domaine Michel Bouzereau et Fils

This again, like their Charmes, is a bit overripe on the nose. Better than the Charmes though. Not too hard. But a little diffuse. It lacks real grip. Quite good. (September 2001)

NOW TO 2009   14.0

Meursault, Genevrières, 1999
Domaine Yves Boyer-Martenot

Rather hard on the nose. A little oxidised. Other odd flavours. Better on the palate. Cleaner. This is firm and backward. A little hard and four-square though. Balanced but it lacks flair. Will it improve? (September 2001)

NOW TO 2010   14.5

Meursault, Genevrières, Cuvée Baudot, 1999
Maison Marc Colin/Hospices de Beaune

Full and rich on the nose. Surprisingly, not a bit over-oaked. Medium-full body. Not quite the concentration it should have had. But good ripeness and style. Reasonable grip. Ample and with good definition. Very good. (October 2001)

NOW TO 2012   16.0

Meursault, Genevrières, 1999
Domaine Louis Jadot

Rich, concentrated, quite opulent nose. Very Genevrières in style. Gently oaky. Backward. Fullish body. Citrussy. Very lovely, long finish. Very good indeed. (September 2001)

NOW TO 2012   17.0

Meursault, Genevrières, 1999
Domaine des Comtes Lafon

Good, youthful colour. Lovely nose. There is a concentration and an intensity here which the 2002 and 2000 lack, good as they are. Rich, even fat, but cool, balanced and succulent. The attack is quite opulent. Much more so than the 2000. But it has very good grip and vigour at the same time. Very long. Lots of dimension. Excellent. (September 2005)

NOW TO 2020+   19.0

Meursault, Genevrières, 1999
Domaine Latour-Giraud

Lovely nose. Quite rich and concentrated. Lovely acidity. Fullish, complex and harmonious. Lots of depth. Now à point. This is fine. (March 2003)

NOW TO 2010   17.5

Meursault, Genevrières, 1999
Domaine Michelot Mère et Fille

A little built-in sulphur here. It seems to lack grip. Difficult to see how much personality there is. Rather short and forward on the palate. (September 2001)

DRINK UP   13.0

Meursault, Genevrières, 1999
Domaine François Mikulski

The wine is a bit tight at present. But there is good volume and depth underneath. Youthful. Full and a little sturdy. It lacks a little grace, but it is certainly good. And as it evolves, will become very good at the least. The wine has both depth and balance. (December 2001)

NOW TO 2012   16.0

Meursault, Genevrières, 1999
Domaine Michel Tessier

Very young still. But full, very concentrated and a lot of depth here. Very lovely fruit. Rich and expansive, but excellent grip. This is fine plus. This will keep very well. (January 2001)

NOW TO 2012   18.0

Meursault, Gouttes d'Or, 1999
Domaine Bouchard Père et Fils

Good depth here. Ripe and rich. Lovely fruit. Clean and classy. Not quite the interest of Latour-Giraud's Bouchères. Slightly hard end to it. But this is a phase. Good plus. (September 2001)

NOW TO 2009   15.5

Meursault, Gouttes d'Or, 1999
Domaine Alain Coche-Bizouard

Slightly diffuse nose. A touch of sulphur. Some oak. Just a bit adolescent really. A little hard on the palate. It lacks a bit of fruit and charm. Fullish body. Quite good. (September 2001)

NOW TO 2009   14.0

Meursault, Gouttes d'Or, 1999
Domaine Jean-Michel Gaunoux

A little sweet-sour and vegetal. Slightly hard on the nose. Somewhat oxidised. Astringent on the palate. No. (September 2001)

(SEE NOTE)   10.0

Meursault, Les Gouttes d'Or, 1999
Domaine des Comtes Lafon

Fresh, ripe, fullish, vigorous and stylish. Gently oaky. Lots of depth. Delicious to drink now but will last well. (September 2005)

NOW TO 2010+   17.0

Meursault, Perrières, 1999
Domaine Philippe Ballot-Millot et Fils

Clean nose and good fruit, but not enough concentration, grip or depth. Too fluid and superficial. A touch of sulphur, too. Nothing much on the palate. Rather weak and short. (September 2001)

DRINK UP   12.0

Meursault, Perrières, 1999
Domaine Bouchard Père et Fils

Ripe, racy, fullish and concentrated on the nose. Very good depth and class here. Full body. Quite ripe in its fruit. But good grip. This is backward but of fine quality. It needs time. Splendidly long finish. (October 2004)

NOW TO 2015   17.5

Meursault, Perrières, 1999
Domaine Michel Bouzereau et Fils

Plump nose. Not the greatest of class though. Not too overripe, which his other wines are. But slightly flabby on the finish. Plump, medium-full attack. But a little coarse afterwards. Quite good at best. (September 2001)

NOW TO 2010   14.0

Meursault, Perrières, 1999
Domaine Yves Boyer-Martenot
Classy. Firm and concentrated. Good depth.
Very good grip. Quite full. Firm and backward.
A little adolescent. Very good underneath. This
is not showing its best. Lovely long, stylish, pure
finish though. (September 2001)
NOW TO 2012   16.5

Meursault, Perrières, 1999
Domaine Jean-François Coche-Dury
Very clean. Very pure. Very minerally. Racy. Very
well balanced. Fullish body. Very poised. Very
lovely fruit. Fine. (September 2001)
NOW TO 2015   17.5

Meursault, Perrières, 1999
Domaine Vincent Dancer
Interesting, ripe nose. A touch of angelica. A
medium weight, plump wine. A gentle wine.
It lacks a little depth and complexity. But quite
good plus. (September 2001)
NOW TO 2009   14.5

Meursault, Les Perrières, 1999
Domaine Darviot-Perrin
Ripe, elegant and very persistent. Steely. Very
lovely fruit. Long and complex. Laid-back and
delicious. This has a very promising, lovely finish. Fine. (September 2001)
NOW TO 2015   17.5

Meursault, Perrières, 1999
Maison Joseph Drouhin
Clean, pure, harmonious and classy on the
nose. Soft and plump, yet balanced and steely.
Very good fruit. Poised and elegant. Very good
plus. (September 2001)
NOW TO 2012   16.5

Meursault, Perrières, 1999
Domaine Jean-Michel Gaunoux
Rather sulphury on the nose. Nothing much on
the palate. Astringent. Poor. (September 2001)
DRINK UP   12.0

Meursault, Les Perrières, 1999
Maison Vincent Girardin
Quite evolved nose but cleaned up after a while.
Quite full. Gently oaky. Rich, fat and creamy.
Lots of depth. Lacks just a bit of zip perhaps,
but very good indeed. (January 2005)
NOW TO 2009   17.0

Meursault, Perrières, 1999
Domaine Albert Grivault
Ripe nose. Elegant if no great grip or concentra-
tion. Light, soft, forward and pleasant. A little
short. Quite good at best. (September 2001)
DRINK SOON   14.0

Meursault, Perrières, 1999
Domaine des Comtes Lafon
Fullish, nicely steely nose. Still quite firm. This
is a typical Perrières and a typical 1999. Still
youthful. Full body. Concentrated and minerally. Very good grip. Very long and complex. Will
still improve. Fine plus. (June 2006)
NOW TO 2016   18.0

Meursault, Perrières, 1999
Domaine Latour-Giraud
Rich, ripe, concentrated nose. Lots of depth
here. Backward but very good depth here. Good
grip. The finish is fine. This is very good plus.
(September 2001)
NOW TO 2012   16.5

Meursault, Perrières, 1999
Domaine Joseph Matrot
Slightly closed but not too sulphury. Full and
rich. Plenty of depth. Slightly adolescent on the
palate. Built to last. Good, although not great
concentration and grip, but very good indeed.
(October 2002)
NOW TO 2011   17.0

Meursault, Les Perrières, 1999
Domaine Pierre Morey
Maison Morey-Blanc. Splendidly steely, miner-
ally, concentrated nose. Not a bit adolescent as
I might have expected at this stage from Pierre

Morey. Fullish body. Rich. Lovely fruit. Very good grip. Fine plus. (September 2002)

NOW TO 2016   18.0

Meursault, Perrières, 1999
Domaine Pierre Morey

Backward, but very concentrated and very lovely. Rich, full and profound. This is an exciting wine. Fine fruit. Excellent depth. Very good grip. Long and backward. Perhaps the best of all the Perrières. Very fine. (September 2001)

NOW TO 2015   18.5

Meursault, Perrières, 1999
Domaine Guy Roulot

Elegant, pure and racy. Very lovely fruit. Very typical Perrières. It doesn't have the backbone of Pierre Morey's example, but it is very clean, very lovely, very long, very classy and very complex. This is fine. (September 2001)

NOW TO 2012   17.5

Meursault, Perrières, Clos des Perrières, 1999
Domaine Albert Grivault

Slightly broader and fatter than the Perrières. It lacks a little grip. Shorter and weaker than the above on the palate. Uninspiring. (September 2001)

DRINK SOON   13.0

Meursault, Le Porusot-Dessus, 1999
Domaine Rémi Jobard

Fresh colour. Ripe, round, classy and fruity. Medium to medium-full body. Balanced. Good grip. Pure and harmonious. A very laid-back wine. Delicious now. Very good indeed. (October 2004)

NOW TO 2010   17.0

Meursault, Poruzots, 1999
Maison Vincent Girardin

Gently oaky, ripe and succulent on the nose. Medium-full body. This is appley-peachy, nicely supple and quite stylish. Good plus. (September 2001)

NOW TO 2010   15.5

Meursault, Poruzots, 1999
Domaine Latour-Giraud

Slightly four-square on the nose. I prefer their Bouchères. Similar palate. It lacks suppleness. Good acidity. But it lacks charm. Quite good. (September 2001)

NOW TO 2009   14.0

Meursault, Poruzots, 1999
Domaine François Mikulski

Youthful colour. Fullish, complex nose. Lots of depth of fruit here. Excellent balance. Rich. Concentrated. Classy. Fine quality. (May 2005)

NOW TO 2012   17.5

Meursault, Rougeots, 1999
Maison Verget

Medium weight. Quite open. Plump and fruity. A gentle wine. *Tendre* for a 1999. Medium body. Not a lot of grip or depth. Quite forward. Very pleasant balanced, crisp finish. Good style. Good. (March 2002)

NOW TO 2009   15.0

Meursault, Les Tessons, 1999
Domaine Pierre Morey

Fuller, richer, but more hidden than his 1999 village Meursault. Very stylish nose. Racy and minerally. Good attack. Fullish on the palate. Impressive follow-through. A lot of depth. Excellent balance. Very classy. Very long. Very good. (March 2002)

NOW TO 2014   16.0

Meursault, Tessons, Clos de Mon Plaisir, 1999
Domaine Guy Roulot

Very ripe, quite well-developed nose. Even a touch flabby. Rather better on the palate. Medium to medium-full body. Mature. Good acidity. Nice peach and crab-apple flavour. I would have liked a bit more grip and energy. But certainly good. A second bottle was properly steely, slightly lean, very fresh, very classy and fine (17.5; Now to 2014). (June 2006)

DRINK SOON   15.0

Le Montrachet, 1999
Domaine Bouchard Père et Fils

Very lovely nose. Marvellous fruit. Not too closed-in. Very classy. Splendidly ripe without being overripe. Very luscious. Full, fat, rich and very lovely. An ample example. Great class. Splendid grip. This is excellent, but the Marquis de Laguiche's listed below is even better. (Septemer 2001)

NOW TO 2020　　　　　　　　　19.5

Le Montrachet, 1999
Domaine Marc Colin

A little closed on the nose. Rich and concentrated, but slightly clumsy. Still rather adolescent. Lovely fruit. Some oak. Good depth. Fine grip. But the class of Montrachet is absent. Very good plus merely. (September 2001)

NOW TO 2015　　　　　　　　　16.5

Le Montrachet, 1999
Domaine Louis Jadot

Half bottle. Superb nose. Marvellously rich and concentrated. Multidimensional and profound. Powerful. Very classy fruit. Full, vigorous and long. Excellent. Still very youthful. Very fine plus. (June 2006)

2010 TO 2020　　　　　　　　　19.0

Le Montrachet, 1999
Domaine du Marquis de Laguiche/
Maison Joseph Drouhin

Ripe, flowery and fragrant. Splendid honeysuckle nose. Not as full or as closed as Bouchard's, but equally complex and elegant. Really excellent on the palate. Fullish body. Backward. Excellent grip. Marvellous intensity and complexity of fruit. Multidimensional. Very long. Great class. Magnificent! (September 2001)

NOW TO 2020　　　　　　　　　20.0

Le Montrachet, 1999
Maison Louis Latour

Quite a deep colour. Rich, oaky, quite evolved nose. A touch of built-in sulphur. This is not impressive at all. Bad storage? (March 2005)

DRINK SOON　　　　　　　　　13.0

Le Montrachet, 1999
Domaine du Baron Thénard/
Maison Roland Remoissenet

Somewhat overripe and heavy on the nose. Very rich fruit. But almost sweet in its attacks. Rich, full and meaty, but not very elegant on the palate. Very good grip. A tough, backward wine. But not that exciting. Good plus. (September 2001)

NOW TO 2015　　　　　　　　　15.5

Nuits-Saint-Georges, La Perrière, 1999
Domaine Henri Gouges

Rich and individual. Very little new oak if any. Lots of depth. Lovely fruit. Peach, fondant and a touch of oak on the palate. Full bodied, rich and very well balanced. Quite delicious. Ready. (March 2002)

NOW TO 2010　　　　　　　　　17.5

Pernand-Vergelesses, Ile de Vergelesses, 1999
Domaine Chandon de Briailles

Blanc. Still a little closed. Ripe and stylish. The vines are still young, and the wine doesn't have a great deal of depth. But it is most attractive. Good plus. (June 2002)

NOW TO 2010　　　　　　　　　15.5

Puligny-Montrachet, 1999
Domaine Jean-Marc Boillot

Classy nose. Fresh. Clean. Full of fruit. ripe and stylish. Medium-full body. This is now just about ready. Lovely. Complex, harmonious and long on the palate. (March 2003)

NOW TO 2010+　　　　　　　　　16.0

Puligny-Montrachet, 1999
Domaine Louis Carillon et Fils

Peachy nose. Good depth. Medium body. Elegant. Understated. Nicely crisp. This is quite forward, in that it is more or less ready now. Lovely fruit. Good depth and complexity. Very good indeed for a village wine. Will still improve. (March 2002)

NOW TO 2008　　　　　　　　　16.0

Puligny-Montrachet, 1999
Domaine Leflaive

Good, ripe, stylish nose. No lack of depth or energy. This is a most impressive wine for a village example. Rich and concentrated. Very gently oaky. Excellent grip. Above all, real style. Very good plus. (March 2002)

NOW TO 2015   16.5

Puligny-Montrachet, 1999
Domaine Paul Pernot et Fils

Clean, fresh, plump and peachy. Delicious. Better acidity than some of his *premiers crus*. Nice and crisp. Good plus. (October 2001)

NOW TO 2009   15.5

Puligny-Montrachet, 1999
Domaine de la Vougeraie

Slightly herbal on the nose. Slightly full and evolved on the palate. Good depth though. Good grip. Plenty of substance here. Very good.
(February 2003)

NOW TO 2010   16.0

Puligny-Montrachet, Caillerets, 1999
Domaine Michel Bouzereau et Fils

Pleasant but a bit lightweight, fruity nose. It lacks a bit of grip on the palate. Medium body. But it tails off a bit. Slightly hot at the end. Quite good. (September 2001)

NOW TO 2009   14.0

Puligny-Montrachet, Le Cailleret, 1999
Domaine Hubert de Montille

Marvellously poised, elegant nose. Very lovely fruit. Ripe and gently oaky. Fullish, concentrated and intense. Very closed. Very vigorous. Splendid balance. This is an excellent example. Very fine. (June 2002)

NOW TO 2020   18.5

Puligny-Montrachet, Les Caillerets, 1999
Domaine Jean-Marc Pillot

Stylish nose but a slight lack of intensity compared with his domaine wines. Not as much depth or concentration as the Chassagne Caillerets, for instance. But clean and pure. Very good

plus, but from this *climat* should have been better. (March 2005)

NOW TO 2009   16.5

Puligny-Montrachet, Les Chalumaux, 1999
Maison Champy

Good, oaky background. Good style and personality. Round, composed, ripe and balanced. Very good indeed. (June 2001)

NOW TO 2014   17.0

Puligny-Montrachet, Champ Canet, 1999
Domaine Jean-Marc Boillot

Quite structured but not a bit heavy. Fullish body. Very good grip. Plenty of fruit. Quite classy. Very good plus but not fine. (June 2003)

NOW TO 2012   16.5

Puligny-Montrachet, Champ Canet, 1999
Domaine Latour-Giraud

Gently fruity, quite stylish nose. No great weight underneath but attractively balanced. Peachy, long and complex. Clean finish. Very good.
(September 2001)

NOW TO 2011   16.0

Puligny-Montrachet, Champ Canet, 1999
Maison Olivier Leflaive Frères

Ripe, rich, intense nose. Plenty of concentration here. Fullish body. Good, oaky base. Good grip. Reasonably forward. This is very good indeed.
(October 2001)

NOW TO 2012   17.0

Puligny-Montrachet, Champ Gain, 1999
Domaine Louis Carillon et Fils

Pure, fruity, soft and elegant if with no great weight on the nose. Medium body. Composed, harmonious, classy and complex. Fine for a second-division *premier cru*. (September 2001)

NOW TO 2011   17.5

Puligny-Montrachet, Champ Gain, 1999
Domaine Benoit Ente

Quite evolved, but plump and fruity on the nose. Even more so on the palate. Some fruit but a bit overripe. Medium body. Fat but

it lacks grip. And not entirely clean either.
(September 2001)

DRINK SOON   13.0

Puligny-Montrachet, Le Clavoillon, 1999
Domaine Gérard Chavy et Fils

A little thin on the nose. It lacks fat, grip and
style. It lacks a bit of grip and concentration on the palate. Medium body. It tails off.
(September 2001)

DRINK SOON   13.5

Puligny-Montrachet, Le Clavoillon, 1999
Domaine Leflaive

Good colour. Gently fruity on the nose. But
rather more depth on the palate. Like many
1999s at this point, it has retired into its shell a
bit. But this is not a bad thing. Rich, balanced,
long and stylish. Long, complex, classy finish.
Very good plus. (March 2002)

NOW TO 2015   16.5

Puligny-Montrachet, Clos de la Garenne, 1999
Domaine Duc de Magenta/Maison Louis Jadot

Ripe, profound, backward nose. Lots of depth.
Slightly oaky. Lots of class. Full, concentrated,
clean and really lovely. Marvellous balance.
Very long. *Grand cru* quality here. Very fine.
(September 2001)

NOW TO 2015   18.5

Puligny-Montrachet, Les Combettes, 1999
Domaine Jean-Marc Boillot

Fragrant, honeysuckle flavours on the nose.
Good grip. But a gentle example. Medium body.
Soft and plump. Stylish and complex. Long and
subtle. Really intense. (September 2001)

NOW TO 2012   16.5

Puligny-Montrachet, Les Combettes, 1999
Domaine Louis Carillon et Fils

Vigorous. Quite full. Lots of depth and energy.
The wine has plenty of grip and fine, complex fruit. The oak is just right. Fine. Will still
improve. (March 2004)

NOW TO 2020   17.5

Puligny-Montrachet, Les Combettes, 1999
Domaine Étienne Sauzet

Very lovely nose. Lots of grip, depth, class and complexity. Rather more backward than Jean-Marc
Boillot's. Backward. Very concentrated. Medium-
full body. Very classy. Excellent. (September 2001)

NOW TO 2014   18.5

Puligny-Montrachet, Les Demoiselles, 1999
Domaine Guy Amiot et Fils

Plump nose. Quite full. Good depth and fat.
Backward. Some built-in sulphur, and not
enough grip and concentration. Yet the finish is
good. It lacks real flair though. (September 2001)

NOW TO 2010   14.0

Puligny-Montrachet, Les Demoiselles, 1999
Domaine Michel Colin-Deléger et Fils

Quite an evolved colour and nose. Full, concentrated, rich, fat and spicy. But a touch of oxidation. A bad bottle. A second bottle was much
fresher, classier, crisper and better. Youthful,
full bodied, rich and concentrated on the palate. Profound and very lovely. Very discreetly
oaky. Long. This is very fine. (June 2005)

NOW TO 2020   18.5

Puligny-Montrachet, Les Folatières, 1999
Domaine Gérard Chavy et Fils

A little built-in sulphur. Not enough grip and
concentration. Quite pleasant on the palate. But
it lacks flair, and it finishes a bit "hot." Unexciting really. (September 2001)

DRINK SOON   13.0

Puligny-Montrachet, Les Folatières, 1999
Domaine Benoit Ente

Sadly, rather more evolved than his Champ
Gain. The nose here is rather coarse, too. On
the palate this is really very undistinguished.
Hot finish, too. (September 2001)

DRINK UP   11.5

Puligny-Montrachet, Les Folatières, 1999
Domaine Michelot Mère et Fille

Some sulphur on the nose here, hiding the wine
from view. Not bad, at least, underneath. But

not the depth and flair Folatières should have. Hot finish. (September 2001)

DRINK SOON 13.0

Puligny-Montrachet, Les Folatières, 1999
Maison Paul Pernot et Fils

Peaches and cream on the nose. Good acidity. Ripe and stylish. Not quite enough grip on the palate. But if forward, at least plump and enjoyable. Good plus. (September 2001)

NOW TO 2009 15.5

Puligny-Montrachet, La Garenne, 1999
Domaine Denis Clair

Lightish but fruity nose. Quite stylish and clean too. Quite forward, but reasonable complexity and flair. Medium weight. Good. (September 2001)

NOW TO 2009 15.0

Puligny-Montrachet, Les Garennes, 1999
Domaine Didier Larue

A touch reduced, and a lack of real grip and depth. Rather bland on the palate. Medium weight. One-dimensional and a little short. Reasonably clean and stylish though. Quite good. (September 2001)

DRINK SOON 14.0

Puligny-Montrachet, Les Perrières, 1999
Domaine Louis Carillon et Fils

Very pure on the nose. Only just about ready. Very lovely complex, harmonious fruit. Good concentration. Lovely flowery finish. Fine. (November 2005)

NOW TO 2012 17.5

Puligny-Montrachet, Les Perrières, 1999
Domaine Gérard Chavy et Fils

Rather too much built-in sulphur on the nose. Heavy and astringent on the palate. Difficult to enjoy. (September 2001)

DRINK UP 12.0

Puligny-Montrachet, Les Perrières, 1999
Domaine Étienne Sauzet

Gentle, racy/minerally, plump, citronelle nose. Very stylish. Complex and concentrated on the palate. Very good grip. Lots of character. Fine. (September 2001)

NOW TO 2012 17.5

Puligny-Montrachet, Les Pucelles, 1999
Domaine Bouchard Père et Fils

Quite a developed colour. The nose is, too. Slightly blowsy. Ripe and rich on the palate. Some acidity. But this is ageing fast. A second and third bottle were similar. Got worse and worse in the glass. (April 2006)

(SEE NOTE)

Puligny-Montrachet, Les Pucelles, 1999
Domaine Leflaive

Firm, slightly reduced nose. This is still young. Good depth. Quite masculine. But ripe, and with good concentration and grip. Fragrant as it developed. Fine at least. (January 2005)

NOW TO 2020 17.5+

Puligny-Montrachet, Les Referts, 1999
Domaine Jean-Marc Boillot

Quite tropical fruit on the nose. Rich. A little more residual sugar compared with some. Quite full. Good grip and concentration on the palate. Exotic. Gently oaky. Good vigour and length. Fine. (March 2002)

NOW TO 2015 17.5

Puligny-Montrachet, Les Referts, 1999
Domaine Louis Carillon et Fils

Fresh colour. Ripe and rich. Good concentration. Pure, fragrant and delicious. Quite delicate and extremely good acidity. Intense and classy. Medium-full body. Fine. Just about ready. (May 2005)

NOW TO 2012 17.5

Puligny-Montrachet, Les Referts, 1999
Maison Vincent Girardin

Plump nose. Just a touch four-square, but fresh and ripe. Good weight and grip. Similar palate. It lacks a bit of zip and flair, but good.

NOW TO 2010 15.0

Puligny-Montrachet, Les Referts, 1999
Domaine Étienne Sauzet

Slightly more weight and more earthy but less flowery than his Perrières. Well made. Good fruit. Not the distinction of his Perrières, but good. (September 2001)

NOW TO 2010 15.5

Puligny-Montrachet, Sous le Puits, 1999
Maison Verget

Pleasant, peachy fruit. No great weight but decently balanced. Plump but a little short. Clean but forward. Quite good at best. (September 2001)

NOW TO 2008   14.0

Puligny-Montrachet, Les Trézins, 1999
Domaine Marc Colin

Ripe, clean, quite forward nose. Plump and exotic, but not botrytised. This has good depth for what it is. Good weight, too. In fact surprisingly good. Good grip. Positive finish. (October 2001)

NOW TO 2008   15.0

Puligny-Montrachet, La Truffière, 1999
Domaine Michel Colin-Deléger et Fils

Nicely minerally on the nose. Quite backward. Just a little SO2. Concentrated, racy, fullish and lovely. Lots of depth here. Fine, long finish. (September 2001)

NOW TO 2012   17.5

Puligny-Montrachet, La Truffière, 1999
Domaine Bernard Morey

Rich, fat, racy and stylish on the nose. This is most promising. More accessible than Michel Colin-Deléger's. Lovely fruit. Minerally and super. Even better than Michel Colin-Deléger's 1999 Truffière. (September 2001)

NOW TO 2014   18.0

Saint-Aubin, En Remilly, 1999
Domaine Guy Amiot et Fils

Fullish and ripe. *À point.* Quite a rich, substantial wine for a Saint-Aubin. Plenty of fruit and depth. Long. Very good. (June 2003)

NOW TO 2009   16.0

Saint-Aubin, En Remilly, 1999
Domaine Hubert Lamy et Fils

Soft, ripe, stylish and quite forward. Already delicious to drink. Good depth. Gently oaky. Very good acidity. Lovely fruit. Crisp and stylish. This is very good. (December 2001)

DRINK SOON   16.0

REDS

Aloxe-Corton, Les Fournières, 1999
Domaine Tollot-Beaut et Fils

Good colour. Stylish nose. Not too oaky. Good freshness and personality. Medium body. Good fruit. Stylish and charming. Very good. (March 2002)

NOW TO 2014   16.0

Aloxe-Corton, Les Maréchaudes, 1999
Domaine Doudet-Naudin

This is too astringent in the middle. And the fruit isn't that special either. (February 2003)

DRINK UP   11.0

Aloxe-Corton, Les Moutottes, 1999
Domaine Edmond Cornu et Fils

Good colour. Round on the nose. Ripe. Slightly barnyardy. Medium body. Not much tannin. Not a lot of grip, class or depth. But round and quite pleasant. Reasonable finish. Quite good. (April 2005)

NOW TO 2009   14.0

Beaune, Les Beaux Fougets, 1999
Domaine Rodolphe Demougeot

Old vines. Splendid colour. Lots of wine here. Rich, fat and ample. Very elegant. Long. Very good for what it is. (June 2000)

NOW TO 2010   16.0

Beaune, Les Bressandes, 1999
Domaine Louis Jadot

Medium-full colour. Medium-full, rich, succulent and meaty on the nose. Good weight. A little tannin. Very good grip. Very good plus. (March 2005)

NOW TO 2017   16.5

Beaune, Cent Vignes, 1999
Domaine Albert Morot

Medium colour. A little thin on the nose. Good acidity, but not enough succulence and charm. Medium body. Quite stylish if a little reserved. It finishes better than it starts. Balanced, long and intense. Good. (June 2003)

NOW TO 2017   15.0

Beaune, Les Champs Pimont, 1999
Maison Champy

Lovely rich, succulent nose. Fresh. Medium-full. Good tannins. This is clean, vigorous and classy. Very good plus. (January 2001)
NOW TO 2010   16.5

Beaune, Champs Pimont, 1999
Domaine Jacques Prieur

Decent colour. Slightly soupy on both nose and palate. Medium-full body. The tannins are round and ripe. The wine is quite substantial but quite subtle. No hard edges. But unremarkable. No class. (November 2002)
NOW TO 2010   14.0

Beaune, Chouacheux, 1999
Domaine Chantal Lescure

Medium-full colour. A good meaty wine on the nose. Fullish and quite chunky. It needs time. On the palate rather lumpy and four-square at first. A little tannin still. Dull. Over-extracted. (June 2003)
NOW TO 2014   13.0

Beaune, Clos du Dessus des Marconnets, 1999
Domaine Labet-Dechelette

Good colour. Ripe oaky nose. Medium body. Decent fruit but a little one-dimensional, and the oak rather dominates. Only fair. (March 2002)
NOW TO 2009   13.5

Beaune, Le Clos des Mouches, 1999
Domaine Joseph Drouhin

Quite concentrated on the nose. It seems to have gone into its shell. Full, rich and concentrated. Lovely fruit. Very good grip. Backward too. This is impressive. (October 2002)
NOW TO 2014   17.0

Beaune, Clos des Ursules, 1999
Domaine Louis Jadot

Medium-full colour. Gently oaky, and nicley lush and stylish on the nose. Lovely fruit. Medium-full body. Sophisticated. Very well-covered tannins. Complex, long and classy. Lovely finish. Very good indeed. (October 2002)
NOW TO 2025   17.0

Beaune, Aux Cras, 1999
Domaine Germain Père et Fils/
Château de Chorey-lès-Beaune

Fullish colour. Very lovely nose. Complete. Rich and ample. Concentrated. Fresh. Gentle oaky background. Delicious, complex, profound fruit. Very good grip. Very good tannic structure. Splendid. (September 2002)
NOW TO 2020+   17.5

Beaune, Les Cras, 1999
Maison Camille Giroud

Medium-full colour. Almost sweet nose. Pure raspberry jam. Better as it evolved. Fullish bodied, meaty and with some tannin. This has good depth. Long at the end. Will last well. But a little dirty at the end. (June 2003)
2009 TO 2021   15.5

Beaune, Les Epenots, 1999
Domaine Rodolphe Demougeot

Village *appellation contrôlée*. Round, ripe and juicy. Medium body. Good style. Quite round and rich. Good for what it is. Youngish vines here. (June 2000)
NOW TO 2010   15.0

Beaune, Les Epenots, 1999
Maison Nicolas Potel

Good full colour. Lovely, very Volnay nose and attack. On the palate not quite the depth and intensity, but for Epenotes a lot of character. Lots of charm. Very good plus. (October 2001)
NOW TO 2014   16.5

Beaune, Grèves, Vigne de l'Enfant Jésus, 1999
Domaine Bouchard Père et Fils

Fullish colour. Still youthful. Lovely nose. Quite mellow. Yet vigorous. Plump and full of fruit. Harmonious and stylish. Medium-full body. Still quite firm on the palate. Very fresh. Long and fine quality. (January 2004)
NOW TO 2024   17.5

Beaune, Les Grèves, 1999
Maison Champy

Fullish colour. Quite oaky. Now a little evolution on the nose. Ample, ripe and rich on the palate. Lots of depth and dimension. Already very enjoyable. Yet medium-full bodied and quite structured. This is very good. (March 2003)

NOW TO 2020   16.0

Beaune, Grèves, 1999
Domaine Joseph Drouhin

Medium-full colour. Very good fruit here. Pure and harmonious. Medium to medium-full body. Clean, fresh and very well balanced. Intense and very classy. Very long. Very good indeed. (June 2003)

NOW TO 2023   17.0

Beaune, Grèves, 1999
Domaine Louis Jadot

Quite firm and oaky on the nose. Lovely, peachy nose. Appley fruit. Full body. Plenty of depth. It needs time. Very good. (September 2001)

NOW TO 2012   16.0

Beaune, Grèves, 1999
Domaine Michel Lafarge

Medium-full colour. Still youthful. Slightly closed-in on the nose. Good fragrance as it developed. Medium-full body. Very good tannins. Slightly chocolaty. Good grip. Ample and full of fruit. It shows well. (June 2005)

NOW TO 2020   16.0

Beaune, Grèves, 1999
Maison Nicolas Potel

Medium-full colour. Stylish, balanced, concentrated and old viney, with an attractive, oaky touch on the nose. Medium body. A little astringent on the palate. Slightly over-extracted? Good fruit underneath and good grip, too. Better at the end. Good plus. (June 2003)

NOW TO 2018   15.5

Beaune, Grèves, 1999
Domaine Jacques Prieur

Medium-full colour. Quite chunky on the nose. But good grip and good fruit. Fullish body. A little cooked. But decent, stylish character. Just a touch four-square. Good grip at the end. It lacks a bit of class though. Quite good plus. (June 2003)

NOW TO 2018   14.5

Beaune, Grèves, 1999
Domaine de la Vougeraie

Full colour. Still very youthful. Quite a chunky, fullish wine on the nose. Still unresolved tannins. Medium-full body. Ripe, balanced and succulent if still a little tough. Good plus but not great. Not enough complexity or class. (June 2005)

NOW TO 2018   15.5

Beaune, Marconnets, 1999
Domaine Albert Morot

Medium colour. Chunkier than the Cent Vignes. But again a lack of fat. It lacks a bit of flair, too. Four-square. Slightly dull at first, but the follow-through is better. Quite good. (June 2003)

NOW TO 2014   14.0

Beaune, Les Montrevenots, 1999
Domaine Vincent Dancer

Very young vines. Second year of production. A little bit more substance than his Bourgogne *Rouge* 1999, but a little raw and astringent. Very stylish fruit underneath and good grip. Very good for what it is. (June 2000)

DRINK SOON   15.0

Beaune, Sizies, 1999
Domaine Michel Prunier

Medium-full colour. Weedy and a little rustic on the nose. Quite sweet. Light and weedy on the palate. Thin and forward. Poor. (June 2003)

DRINK SOON   11.0

Beaune, Les Teurons, 1999
Domaine Bouchard Père et Fils

Medium-full colour. Rich, ripe, fullish nose. A meaty wine. Fullish body. Some tannin. A little backward. But succulent and vigorous. Good grip. It needs time. Very good for what it is. (June 2003)

NOW TO 2018   15.5

Beaune, Les Teurons, 1999
Domaine Germain Père et Fils/
Château de Chorey-lès-Beaune

Very good colour. Ripe, plump nose. Slightly leaner than the Clos des Mouches of Drouhin. But fresh, poised and succulent. Medium-full body. Gently oaky. Profound and complex. A super example. Lovely long finish. Real vigour here. Very good indeed. (March 2002)

NOW TO 2020   17.0

Beaune, Les Teurons, 1999
Domaine Louis Jadot

Medium-full colour. Classy, concentrated nose. Lovely fruit. Rich and complex. Fullish body. Lovely fruit on the palate. Very fine concentration. This is ample, harmonious and very elegant. Lovely finish. Very good indeed. (June 2003)

2009 TO 2024   17.0

Beaune, Les Teurons, 1999
Domaine Albert Morot

Medium-full colour. Fragrant nose. High toned. Good acidity. Ripe underneath. Medium body. Pleasant, but not quite enough depth and concentration. Balanced and stylish though. Very good finish. Good. (June 2003)

NOW TO 2014   15.0

Beaune, Les Teurons, 1999
Domaine Rossignol-Trapet Père et Fils

Medium-full colour. Good, plummy nose. But a little reduced. Slightly clumsy even when this blew off. Medium to medium-full body. Slightly astringent. Some fruit but a bitter touch in the middle. It lacks class. (June 2003)

NOW TO 2012   13.0

Beaune, Toussaints, 1999
Domaine Albert Morot

Medium-full colour. Fuller and richer than their Grèves, but not as classy on the nose. Less grip. More bland. Medium body. Average attack. Then it tails off. Dull. (June 2003)

NOW TO 2012   13.5

Beaune, Les Vignes Franches, Vieilles Vignes, 1999
Domaine Germain Père et Fils/
Château de Chorey-lès-Beaune

Good colour. A little closed on the nose. Full, rich, profound and old viney on the palate. Lovely fruit. Still some tannin to resolve, but

balanced, long and classy. Very good indeed. (September 2002)

NOW TO 2020+   17.0

Bonnes Mares, 1999
Domaine Bart

From the Chambolle side above Domaine de Vogüé. Very good, classy fruit here. Plenty of depth and style if without the concentration and grip for really fine. Medium-full body. Long. Positive. Very good indeed. (January 2002)

NOW TO 2023   17.0

Bonnes Mares, 1999
Domaine Bouchard Père et Fils

Fullish colour. Firm, rich, full and closed-in on the nose. A slight touch of reduction. But classy and profound. Full bodied. Good tannins and very good grip. This is very fine. (June 2003)

2010 TO 2030   18.5

Bonnes Mares, 1999
Domaine Dujac

Medium-full colour. Rich, full and classy. Not too much of the stems. Abundant, oaky, rich and concentrated on the palate. Very fine grip. Long and intense. Very fine. Better than his Clos de la Roche this year. (June 2003)

2009 TO 2029   18.5

Bonnes Mares, 1999
Domaine Fougeray de Beauclair

Fullish colour. Fullish, rich, quite oaky nose. Not over-macerated though. Fullish body on the palate. Good grip. Quite spicy: chocolate and mocha. Some tannin but not a great deal of it. Long, intense and stylish. Elegant and juicy but not enough concentration to support 100 percent new oak. Fine nevertheless. (September 2002)

NOW TO 2025   17.5

Bonnes Mares, 1999
Domaine Robert Groffier

Fullish colour. Still youthful. A touch of reduction on the nose. Fullish body. Quite rich. Not quite the fat and succulence on the follow-through of the very best, but balanced and really quite pure. Certainly not short. Fine. (March 2006)

2009 TO 2020   17.5

Bonnes Mares, 1999
Domaine Georges Roumier et Fils

Full colour. Closed-in but brilliant nose. Marvellous, laid-back, concentrated fruit. Great class. Multidimensional. Full bodied, youthful and concentrated. Even a little tight. Marvellous fruit. Very fine grip. Very, very long, complex and classy. Excellent. Needs time. (March 2005)

2012 TO 2028   19.0

Bonnes Mares, 1999
Domaine Comte Georges de Vogüé

Medium-full colour. Closed-in on the nose. Rich, fat, oaky and opulent. But quite firm at present. Still a bit shy, but this has excellent concentration and intensity. The follow-through is quite terrific. Super! (June 2003)

2010 TO 2030   19.0

Bonnes Mares, 1999
Domaine de la Vougeraie

Full colour. Classy nose. Plenty of depth and very good fruit. Medium-full body. Not as concentrated or as profound as Roumier's or de Vogüé's, but classy, long and positive. Fine plus. (June 2003)

2009 TO 2028   18.0

Chambertin, 1999
Domaine Bouchard Père et Fils

Fine colour. Lovely poised nose. Slightly hidden at present. Fullish but not massive. The tannins are well covered. Sweet and ripe. Very good grip. This is very stylish, but it doesn't quite have the vigour and concentration it should have. Most attractive, balanced fruit, nevertheless, and good intensity. Fine plus. (November 2002)

NOW TO 2020   18.0

Chambertin, 1999
Domaine Camus Père et Fils

This has rather more concentration—as it should have—than his Mazis. Fullish body.

Quite reserved. But not a lot of structure or austerity. Ample and fruity. Good depth. Lacks real grip and concentration at the end for a Chambertin. Forward. Very pleasant but not serious. (January 2002)

NOW TO 2017   17.0

Chambertin, 1999
Domaine Joseph Drouhin

Medium-full colour. Not a blockbuster but splendid, black-fruity nose and fine intensity. On the palate it lacks a bit of intensity. It is ripe and classy, but slightly weak for a *grand cru*. Fine plus at best. (June 2003)

2009 TO 2028   18.0

Chambertin, 1999
Domaine Ponsot

Medium-full colour. Round and very ripe on the nose. It lacks a little nuance and dimension on the palate. Medium-full body. Ripe and balanced. It just lacks a little something. Very good indeed at best. (June 2003)

2009 TO 2028   17.0

Chambertin, 1999
Domaine Jacques Prieur

Full colour. Weak and coarse for a Chambertin on the nose. This is really poor. Dilute and dirty. Ugh! (June 2003)

(SEE NOTE)   11.0

Chambertin, 1999
Domaine Rossignol-Trapet Père et Fils

Full colour. Ripe and plump but not exactly very elegant on the nose. It is also a bit reduced. Medium-full body. It lacks the grip and concentration. But the fruit is decent and quite intense. The finish is very good. Very good plus. (June 2003)

2009 TO 2025   16.5

Chambertin, 1999
Domaine Armand Rousseau

Medium-full colour. The complete nose. Perfect combination of oak and very, very classy, concentrated fruit. Brilliant. This is just about as good as it gets. Rich and ripe. Fat and succulent. Profound and impeccably balanced. Very, very long on the palate. Brilliant! (March 2006)

2010 TO 2030   20.0

Chambertin, 1999
Domaine Jean Trapet Père et Fils

Full colour. Full, concentrated, profound and classy on the nose. Fullish body. Some tannin. Good grip. Very good concentrated, stylish fruit. Does it have the flair of Rousseau's? But long, complex, elegant and very fine. (June 2003)

2009 TO 2028   18.5

Chambertin, Clos de Bèze, 1999
Domaine Bart

Good colour. Lovely nose. This is altogether fuller, richer and more concentrated than his Bonnes Mares 1999. Both from old vines though. Full bodied. Gently new oaky. Fat and vigorous. Very ripe. Splendid fruit. Very good long follow-through. Fine plus. (January 2002)

2009 TO 2029   18.0

Chambertin, Clos de Bèze, 1999
Domaine Bouchard Père et Fils

Medium-full colour. Ample, structured, ripe, rich nose. Still quite closed. Full bodied. No undue tannins. Very good grip. Classy, balanced, intense and lovely. Very long and very fine at the end. (June 2003)

2010 TO 2030   18.5

Chambertin, Clos de Bèze, 1999
Domaine Bruno Clair

Full colour. Splendidly concentrated and very classy on the nose. Very lovely. Fullish body on the palate. Good tannins. Very fine grip. Very lovely, stylish fruit. Long, intense and very classy. (June 2003)

2009 TO 2028   19.0

Chambertin, Clos de Bèze, 1999
Domaine Pierre Damoy

Full colour. Quite firm on the nose. Not as oaky, it seems, as his Chapelle-Chambertin. Good depth and concentration. Slightly rigid. Fullish body. It needs time. A little tannin. The finish is good, and there is plenty of fruit. (June 2003)

2009 TO 2028   18.0

Chambertin, Clos de Bèze, 1999
Domaine Joseph Faiveley

Medium to medium-full colour. Rich, full, meaty and backward on the nose. Lots of quality here. Full bodied, concentrated, youthful but also very well balanced. Splendid fruit. Great intensity at the end. Very fine. (June 2003)

2009 TO 2028   18.5

Chambertin, Clos de Bèze, 1999
Domaine Pierre Gelin

Sixty acres. This is very fine. Full colour. Very rich, concentrated, backward nose. Full bodied, tannic and very concentrated on the palate. Excellent grip. There is a lot of substance here. But a lot of class as well. Very fine. Needs time. (January 2002)

2010 TO 2040   18.5

Chambertin, Clos de Bèze, 1999
Domaine Robert Groffier

Fullish colour. Ample, rich and fruity on the nose. Medium to medium-full body. Ripe and intense. Very lovely, fragrant fruit. There is a Musigny touch here. Very fine. (June 2003)

2009 TO 2028   18.5

Chambertin, Clos de Bèze, 1999
Domaine Armand Rousseau

Fullish colour. Rich, concentrated, oaky and profound on the nose. Fullish body. Gently oaky. Excellent fruit. Very splendid depth and a lovely long finish. High class. (June 2003)

2009 TO 2028   19.0

Chambolle-Musigny, 1999
Domaine Bouchard Père et Fils

Full colour. Fragrant nose. Very good depth. More raw than tannic. But slightly adolescent. Some tannin on the palate. Slightly rigid. A little lumpy. Certainly good. But better? We need time to see. (October 2001)

NOW TO 2017   15.0

Chambolle-Musigny, 1999
Domaine Marchand-Guillot

Ripe, juicy, succulent and very attractive. Medium to medium-full body. Intense and classy. Very good, especially for a village wine. Lovely long finish. (January 2002)

NOW TO 2015   16.0

Chambolle-Musigny, 1999
Domaine Jacques-Frédéric Mugnier

Medium to medium-full colour. Just about mature. Very pure nose. Very Chambolle. Very classy. Very long. Understated. Intense. Lovely finish. (March 2006)

NOW TO 2015   17.0

Chambolle-Musigny, 1999
Domaine François Perrot

Good style and substance. But like the 2000, just a little meagre. Yet long on the palate and pretty cold. The finish is positive and more generous. Good at least. (January 2002)

NOW TO 2013   15.0

Chambolle-Musigny, 1999
Domaine Gérard Seguin

Rather better colour. Good depth, though a bit closed. This has more to it than the Gevrey-Chambertin Vieilles Vignes 1999. Nicely rich. Good length. Positive all the way through. (January 2002)

NOW TO 2015   15.5

Chambolle-Musigny, 1999
Domaine Thibault Père et Fils

This is good, too, although like the 2000, it doesn't have quite the depth of the Gevrey. Ripe and balanced. Plump. Good positive finish. Good plus. (June 2002)

NOW TO 2012   14.5

Chambolle-Musigny, 1999
Domaine Comte Georges de Vogüé

Very lovely Chambolle nose. Good substance, but the tannins are very well covered. Fragrant, ripe and very classy. Excellent for a village example. Long, complex and lovely. Already most enjoyable. (March 2003)

NOW TO 2015   16.5

Chambolle-Musigny, Premier Cru, 1999
Domaine Jean-Jacques Confuron

Medium-full colour. Lovely, soft, fragrant, oaky nose. Very Chambolle. Fullish body. Rich and full of fruit. Very good tannins. Complex and classy. Very good acidity. Very harmonious. Fine. (April 2003)

NOW TO 2024   17.5

Chambolle-Musigny, Premier Cru, 1999
Domaine Comte Georges de Vogüé

Medium-full colour. Very lovely fruit on the nose. Rich, plump, very well balanced and stylish. Medium-full body. Rich and concentrated. Gently oaky. Very long, very harmonious and very classy. Fine plus. (June 2003)

2009 TO 2025   18.0

Chambolle-Musigny, Les Amoureuses, 1999
Domaine Joseph Drouhin

Full colour. Marvellous fruit on the nose. Rich, ripe and succulent. Great class. Slightly more austere on the palate than Girardin's but most impressive on the follow-through. Concentrated, very pure, classy and fine plus. (June 2003)

2010 TO 2028   18.0

Chambolle-Musigny, Les Amoureuses, 1999
Maison Vincent Girardin

Full colour. Fullish, ample, generous nose. This is very lovely and very Amoureuses. Fullish body. Very silky. Very good grip. Lovely fruit. Very impressive. (June 2003)

2010 TO 2028   18.0

Chambolle-Musigny, Les Amoureuses, 1999
Domaine Robert Groffier

Very full colour. Very lovely fruit if not quite the fat of Vogüé's or the intensity of Drouhin's. Medium-full body. Ripe but not the depth. Lovely fruit though. Very ample and harmonious. Fine. (June 2003)

2009 TO 2025   17.5

Chambolle-Musigny, Les Amoureuses, 1999
Domaine Jacques-Frédéric Mugnier

Medium-full, mature-ish colour. Splendidly fragrant, intense nose. Medium body. And now already quite soft. Lots of depth and persistence though. The finish is really splendid. Great class. Very fine. (March 2006)

NOW TO 2025   18.5

Chambolle-Musigny, Les Amoureuses, 1999
Domaine Georges Roumier et Fils

Very full colour. Splendidly rich on the nose. Really excellent fruit. Not as firm as their Cras. Fatter, more concentrated and more succulent. This is very impressive indeed. Full bodied, balanced and complete. Very powerful and intense at the end. Very fine. (June 2003)

2010 TO 2028   18.5

Chambolle-Musigny, Les Amoureuses, 1999
Domaine Comte Georges de Vogüé

Full colour. Quite brilliant on the nose. Rich, very concentrated, very classy and very harmonious. Marvellous fruit. Fullish body. Not as powerful as Roumier's but just as fine in balance and fruit. This is very, very lovely. Very fine. (June 2003)

2010 TO 2028   18.5

Chambolle-Musigny, Les Athets, 1999
Domaine Jean Tardy et Fils

Good, full colour. Quite oaky on the nose. Almost too oaky on the palate. Fullish body and concentration. Fat and rich, and with very good grip and depth. The finish is very good, especially for a village wine. (October 2001)

NOW TO 2018   16.0

Chambolle-Musigny, Les Babillaires, 1999
Domaine Philippe Leclerc

This is ripe and rich. A little softer than the Gevrey village. Fullish bodied, oaky and opulent. Very good again. (January 2002)

NOW TO 2019   15.5

Chambolle-Musigny, Les Baudes, 1999
Domaine Joseph Drouhin

Medium-full colour. Round, ripe, balanced and stylish on the nose. Medium-full body. Rich, concentrated, balanced and intense.

Lots of substance here. Long and stylish. Very good indeed. Not quite the class for fine. (June 2003)

2009 TO 2025   17.0

Chambolle-Musigny, Les Baudes, 1999
Domaine François Perrot

A little fuller, fatter and richer than his Chambolle Charmes. Older vines. More depth. Lots of substance here. Finely poised. Long, complex and classy. Fine. (January 2002)

NOW TO 2027   17.0

Chambolle-Musigny, Les Baudes, 1999
Domaine Sérafin Père et Fils

Fullish colour. Quite oaky, but ripe and concentrated, with plenty of depth on the nose. On the palate the oak dominates a bit. Medium-full body. Good grip. Quite stylish. Slightly extracted. Decent finish. Very good. (June 2003)

2009 TO 2025   16.0

Chambolle-Musigny, Les Beaux Bruns, 1999
Domaine Denis Mortet

Full colour. A little sturdier than some on the nose. A touch of oak. A bit modern. But good stuff. Rich and ripe, and with a decent grip. A little overdone nevertheless. Very good at best. (June 2003)

2010 TO 2024   16.0

Chambolle-Musigny, Charmes, 1999
Domaine Ghislaine Barthod

Full colour. A slight lack of fruit on the nose. A little green. Better on the palate. Richer and riper. But it doesn't really have the richness and the succulence. Good plus at best. (June 2003)

2010 TO 2024   15.5

Chambolle-Musigny, Charmes, 1999
Maison Vincent Girardin

Fullish colour. Very lovely nose. Rich, elegant and quite oaky. Lots of dimension. Medium-full body. Very harmonious. Excellent grip. Very complex. Fine. (October 2001)

NOW TO 2020   17.5

Chambolle-Musigny, Charmes, 1999
Domaine François Perrot

Delicious. Clean and nicely cool. Medium to medium-full body. Classy and intense. Ripe and fragrant. Very Chambolle. Long and very good indeed. (January 2002)

NOW TO 2020   17.0

Chambolle-Musigny, La Combe d'Orveau, 1999
Domaine Bruno Clavelier

Fullish colour. It doesn't have the poise of some of the rest of the *premiers crus*. Fruity but slightly raw. Medium body. Not the greatest concentration, follow-through or class. Good at best. (June 2003)

NOW TO 2018   15.0

Chambolle-Musigny, La Combe d'Orveau, 1999
Domaine Grivot

Not the *premier cru*. Medium-full colour. Ripe, poised, rich and still a little closed. Medium-full body. It lacks a little distinction but very well made. Balanced and long. Very good. (June 2003)

2009 TO 2021   16.0

Chambolle-Musigny, La Combe d'Orveau, 1999
Domaine Taupenot-Merme

Good colour. Ripe but a slight leanness behind it. Slightly attenuated in the middle. Doesn't quite sing. (January 2002)

NOW TO 2014   14.0

Chambolle-Musigny, Les Cras, 1999
Domaine Ghislaine Barthod

Good colour. Firm, fullish nose. High quality. Lots of depth. A little tannin poking out a bit. Super fruit. On the palate medium-full bodied, balanced and profound. Long and rich. Harmonious, intense and classy. Lovely finish. Fine. (March 2004)

2009 TO 2025   17.5

Chambolle-Musigny, Les Cras, 1999
Domaine Michèle et Patrice Rion

Very good colour. Lovely gently oaky nose. Very classy. Still very youthful. Good grip. Medium-full body. Just a little tannin. Slightly raw but very good quality. Very good indeed. Not quite the richness for fine. (September 2002)

NOW TO 2020   17.0

Chambolle-Musigny, Les Cras, 1999
Domaine Georges Roumier et Fils

Fullish colour. Firm, closed-in nose. Rich, full and firm. Quite a big wine for a Chambolle. Full bodied, rich and tannic on the attack. Very ripe and concentrated on the follow-through. Very classy, very long and even quite powerful. Fine. (June 2003)

2010 TO 2028   17.5

Chambolle-Musigny, Derrière le Four, 1999
Domaine Georges Seguin

Medium-full colour. Stylish nose. Quite forward. Medium weight. On the palate a little weak. But decent fruit and grip if slightly one-dimensional. Good plus. (June 2003)

NOW TO 2017   15.5

Chambolle-Musigny, Les Feusselottes, 1999
Domaine Dr. Georges Mugneret

Fullish colour. Delicious fruit on the nose. Fragrant, but with good substance. Fullish body. Very good tannins. Balanced, poised and gently oaky. Very fresh. Very well made. Long and elegant. Fine. (June 2003)

2009 TO 2025   17.5

Chambolle-Musigny, Les Fuées, 1999
Domaine Ghislaine Barthod-Noëllat

Very good colour. Quite firm on the nose for a Chambolle but rich, intense and succulent underneath. Medium-full body. Slightly raw on the attack. Ripe but a little reserved on the follow-through. Lovely fruit though. Most attractive finish. Very good indeed. (October 2002)

NOW TO 2022   17.0

Chambolle-Musigny, Les Fuées, 1999
Domaine Joseph Faiveley

Fullish colour. Quite closed on the nose. But stylish and fragrant. Fullish body. Very good fruit. Backward though. It only really sings on the aftertaste. Classy, long, impressive and fine. (June 2003)

2010 TO 2028   17.5

Chambolle-Musigny, Les Fuées, 1999
Domaine Jacques-Frédéric Mugnier

Very good colour. Still immature. Rich, full, quite sturdy for Frédéric Mugnier. Backward, too. On the palate marvellously profound and classy. Very good, ripe tannins. Lovely fruit. Very complex. Long and lovely. Very fine. (September 2005)

2009 TO 2025   18.5

Chambolle-Musigny, Les Grands Mures, 1999
Maison Frédéric Magnien

Premier cru. Medium-full colour. Still very youthful. Quite oaky on the nose. Somewhat over-macerated on the palate. Full flavoured. Good acidity. Medium-full body. Lacks a little richness as well as grace. It may get better as it ages. (March 2005)

2010 TO 2018   14.5

Chambolle-Musigny, Les Hauts-Doix, 1999
Domaine Robert Groffier

Very good colour. A little reduction on the nose. Medium-full body. Smooth. Very good acidity. Lovely fruit underneath. It should be at least very good plus. We'll see. (September 2002)

NOW TO 2019   16.5

Chambolle-Musigny, Les Véroilles, 1999
Domaine Bruno Clair

Medium-full colour. Good class and depth on the nose. Intense and classy on the palate. Not too lean. Good, concentrated in its cool, very Clair-type way. Ripe at the end. Very good indeed. (October 2002)

NOW TO 2020+   17.0

Chapelle-Chambertin, 1999
Domaine Pierre Damoy

Full colour. Still immature. Fragrant nose. Stylish Pinot. Ripe and harmonious. Still quite backward. But lots of quality and depth. Very lovely fruit here. Slightly raw but intense. Very elegant. Very, very lovely. Very good energy. Very fine. (April 2006)

2009 TO 2030+   18.5

Chapelle-Chambertin, 1999
Domaine Louis Jadot

Medium-full colour. Quite closed on the nose. Rich, ripe and concentrated. Good grip. Fullish body. Quite meaty. Good substance and acidity, but a slight lack of character. Slightly one-dimensional fruit. Very good at best. (June 2003)

2009 TO 2025   16.0

Chapelle-Chambertin, 1999
Domaine Ponsot

Medium-full colour. Ripe, abundant, stylish fruit on the nose. Medium-full body. Good grip. Fresh, lush, intense and elegant. Long on the finish. Not a blockbuster though. Fine. (June 2003)

2009 TO 2025   17.5

Chapelle-Chambertin, 1999
Domaine Jean Trapet Père et Fils

The nose is more elegant than the Latricières. Cooler. More-distinguished cassis fruit. Full body. Very good tannin. Excellent grip. This is very stylish, intense, complex and multidimensional. Very long. Lovely. Fine plus. (June 2003)

NOW TO 2028   18.0

Charmes-Chambertin, 1999
Domaine Hervé Arlaud

Fullish colour. Quite firm, good class and depth here on the nose. Fullish body. Rich, balanced and fresh. Good concentration. Good elegance. This is a fine example. (June 2003)

2009 TO 2025   17.5

Charmes-Chambertin, 1999
Domaine Denis Bachelet

Full, immature colour. Very lovely nose. Delicately concentrated. Very classy, profound fruit. Medium-full body. Getting soft. Intense, profound and complex. Excellent harmony. Very fine plus. (April 2006)

NOW TO 2020   19.0

Charmes-Chambertin, 1999
Domaine Camus Père et Fils

Good colour. Rich. Slightly pruney on the nose. Not too much dead leaves. Ripe and exotic.

Medium-full body. Good acidity. Ample and juicy. Not much finesse, but long and enjoyable. Good plus. (January 2002)

NOW TO 2012   15.5

Charmes-Chambertin, 1999
Domaine Claude Dugat

Very full colour. Full and gently oaky, but very concentrated and intense on the nose. Still quite firm. A little tough still. Fullish body. Quite tannic. Quite oaky on the palate. Backward. Very fine fruit underneath. Long. Splendid. (March 2005)

2012 TO 2025+   18.5

Charmes-Chambertin, 1999
Domaine Bernard Dugat-Py

Very full, immature colour. Not entirely clean on the nose. Slightly reduced and sweaty. Slightly corky. Nevertheless, one can see great concentration and fruit. Not too extracted. Very good grip. Splendid fruit. Very fine. Needs time. (April 2006)

2010 TO 2030   18.5

Charmes-Chambertin, 1999
Domaine Dujac

Medium-full colour. Some development. Ripe. Quite rich. Accessible. A bit more backbone than their 2000. More intensity, too. Balanced. Just about ready. Very good plus. (April 2006)

NOW TO 2020   16.5

Charmes-Chambertin, 1999
Domaine Gilles Duroché

Medium-full colour. Plump, attractive, open nose if no great depth underneath. This soon left a weak, slightly dry wine, of little merit. Astringent at the end. No. (June 2003)

2009 TO 2011   13.0

Charmes-Chambertin, 1999
Domaine Geantet-Pansiot

Magnum. Medium to medium-full, immature colour. Stylish. Quite spicy nose. Good depth and vigour. Medium-full body. Just about ready. Fresh and succulent. Lovely fruit. Long and classy. Fine. (April 2006)

NOW TO 2020   17.5

Charmes-Chambertin, 1999
Maison Vincent Girardin

Full colour. Luscious fruit on the nose. Impressive purity, balance and class. Fullish body on the palate. Very harmonious. Fine fruit. Not as concentrated as Claude Dugat's. Not as tannic. But a lovely example. Very elegant. Very complex. Very long. (April 2006)

2010 TO 2025   18.0

Charmes-Chambertin, 1999
Domaine Huguenot Père et Fils

Good colour. Rather tight on the nose. Not too solid on the palate. Not quite as exciting as the Fonteny. Ripe and balanced, but not as complex or as long on the palate. Very good plus. From 2007. (January 2002)

NOW TO 2020   16.5

Charmes-Chambertin, 1999
Maison Frédéric Magnien

Fullish colour. Still youthful. Very dense. Almost inky on the nose. Full body. Dense tannins. Rather too solid. Over-extracted. A pity. Very good fruit underneath. (April 2006)

2010 TO 2020   14.0

Charmes-Chambertin, 1999
Domaine Bernard Maume

Medium-full colour. A little development. Quite solid if not dense and chunky on the nose. Fullish body. Slightly raw and ungainly. No real finesse. But very good in its chunky sort of way. (April 2006)

2010 TO 2020   16.0

Charmes-Chambertin, 1999
Domaine Odoul-Coquard

Seventeen acres in the Mazoyères. Good colour. Medium-full weight. Ripe and balanced, but a slight lack of real depth, personality and class. A very good wine. But no better than his *premiers crus*. (January 2002)

NOW TO 2010   16.0

Charmes-Chambertin, 1999
Domaine Henri Rebourseau

1.31 hectare in the Charmes rather than the Mazoyères. Full, fat, tannic and gently oaky.

Lots of wine here. Very rich and concentrated. Very good grip. An ample wine with plenty of energy at the end. This is fine. (January 2002)

2009 TO 2025   17.5

Charmes-Chambertin, 1999
Domaine Henri Richard

Fine colour. Rich, full, firm nose. Good tannins. Very good acidity. Ample fruit. Quite oaky. Full bodied and firm on the palate. Good grip. Very rich and stylish. Fine plus. (January 2002)

2009 TO 2029   18.0

Charmes-Chambertin, Très Vieilles Vignes, 1999
Domaine Joseph Roty

Full, youthful colour. Splendidly concentrated nose. Very impressive. Just a touch of oak. Coffee aspects. Fullish body. Concentrated. Round. Not quite as impressive on the nose as on the palate, but very long and very opulent. Very fine. (March 2006)

2011 TO 2030   18.5

Charmes-Chambertin, 1999
Domaine Armand Rousseau

Medium to medium-full colour. Now just about ready. Soft, ripe nose. Full of charm. No hard edges. Medium to medium-full body. Good grip. Ample fruit. Very seductive. Long. Very fresh at the end. Very good plus. (April 2006)

NOW TO 2020   16.5

Charmes-Chambertin, 1999
Domaine Taupenot-Merme

Good substance. Rich, ample, balanced and classy. Good tannins. Plenty of vigour here. Not quite the extra for very fine. But certainly fine. (January 2002)

NOW TO 2025   17.5

Charmes-Chambertin, 1999
Domaine des Varoilles

Good colour. Fine nose. Pure, clean and nicely austere. Medium-full body. Good grip. This is stylish, poised and elegant. Velvety ripe tannins.

Good energy. Ripe and very satisfying. Long and fine. (January 2002)

NOW TO 2028   17.5

Charmes-Chambertin, 1999
Domaine de la Vougeraie

Fullish colour. Ripe, plump, soft and seductive on the nose. Medium-full body. Good fruit. Good grip. This has complexity and depth. Long. Complex. Fine. (June 2003)

2009 TO 2025   17.5

Chorey-lès-Beaune, 1999
Domaine Dubois d'Orgeval

Good colour. Ripe and plump. Good fruit. Medium weight. Good. (February 2003)

DRINK SOON   15.0

Chorey-lès-Beaune, 1999
Domaine Michel Gay

A bit of evolution and, in a rustic sense, edgy. (February 2003)

DRINK UP   11.0

Chorey-lès-Beaune, 1999
Domaine Germain Père et Fils/
Château de Chorey-lès-Beaune

Good colour. Ripe, fragrant nose. Supple and succulent. Plenty of character. Medium body. Very ripe indeed, almost to the point of being sweet. Crammed with fruit. Just a little tannin. Very good acidity. Altogether delicious. Very good for what it is. (March 2002)

NOW TO 2010   15.0

Chorey-lès-Beaune, 1999
Domaine René Podichard

This again is very good indeed. Quite big for a Chorey. Still some tannin to resolve. Long. Classy. (February 2003)

NOW TO 2011   15.5

Chorey-lès-Beaune, 1999
Domaine Pierre Thubert

After the 2000, a bit light and weedy. Will get astringent. Curiously uneven quality here. (February 2003)

DRINK UP   11.0

Chorey-lès-Beaune, 1999
Domaine Tollot-Beaut et Fils

Good colour. A little more substance than the Château de Chorey wine. More oaky, too. Indeed, quite markedly oaky on the palate. Medium body. Not much tannin. Ripe and rich. Good for what it is but not as exciting as the Château de Chorey's. (March 2002)

NOW TO 2011   14.5

Clos des Lambrays, 1999
Domaine des Lambrays

Good colour. Very lovely, rich, plump, full, fresh nose. Very elegant. Medium-full body. Poised, subtle and harmonious. Long and complex. Fine. (September 2004)

2010 TO 2028   17.5

Clos de la Roche, 1999
Domaine Hervé Arlaud

Medium-full colour. Ripe, rich and nicely plump on the nose. Medium-full body. Quite rich. Good fruit, and decent balance and concentration. This is very good indeed. (June 2003)

2009 TO 2025   17.0

Clos de la Roche, 1999
Domaine Dujac

Full colour. Quite soft, impressively concentrated, intense nose. Very good grip. Medium-full body. Very smooth and harmonious. Fine acidity. Intense and classy. Very Dujac. Very long. Very fine. (March 2005)

2009 TO 2025   18.5

Clos de la Roche, 1999
Domaine Leroy

Very full, immature colour. Abundant, ripe nose. Accessible and almost sweet. Yet very profound. Fullish body. Rich, opulent and expansive. Lovely fruit. Very good grip. Not the class of some, but that is Clos de la Roche. Long. Fine plus. (March 2006)

2012 TO 2030   18.0

Clos de la Roche, 1999
Domaine Hubert Lignier

Fullish colour. Rich, full, ample, gently oaky nose. Fullish body. Old-viney fruit. Complex and concentrated. This is ample, intense and lovely. Fine quality. (June 2003)

2009 TO 2025   17.5

Clos de la Roche, Cuvée Vieilles Vignes, 1999
Domaine Ponsot

Magnum. Full, youthful colour. The nose is a little adolescent. Backward. Concentrated, youthful and full bodied. Needs time. A little lumpy. But this will go. Will last a long time. (March 2006)

2012 TO 2040   18.5

Clos Saint-Denis, 1999
Domaine Hervé Arlaud

Full colour. Good, full nose, if without the nuance of their Clos de la Roche. Medium-full body. Good fruit. Decent grip. Very good plus. (June 2003)

NOW TO 2021   16.5

Clos Saint-Denis, 1999
Domaine Joseph Drouhin

Fullish colour. Good fruit. Very supple and complex. Does it lack a bit of richness? It seems to lack a bit of grip. It slightly lacks concentration on the nose, and it is astringent on the palate. A bad bottle. Yet it threw off much of this in the glass. (June 2003)

NOW TO 2014   13.0

Clos Saint-Denis, 1999
Domaine Heresztyn

Good colour. Lovely plump, balanced, succulent, classy fruit on the nose. Fullish body. Very good, ripe tannins. Fine grip. Clean, pure and definitive. This is elegant, fragrant and delicious. Fine. (October 2002)

NOW TO 2020   17.5

Clos Saint-Denis, 1999
Domaine Louis Jadot

Fullish colour. Full, ample, rich, concentrated and balanced on the nose. A lot of depth here. One of the bigger wines of this series of Morey *grands crus*. Oaky, too. A little more backward. Rich, full bodied, ample and fine. (June 2003)

2010 TO 2028   17.5

Clos Saint-Denis, 1999
Domaine Ponsot
Fullish colour. Rich and concentrated. Lovely old-viney fruit on the nose. Rich and fragrant. Fullish body. Very complex. This has very lovely harmony. Very intense. Fine plus. (June 2003)
2009 TO 2028   18.0

Clos de Tart, 1999
Maison Mommessin
Full colour. Still youthful. A big wine. Full, tannic, rich and profound. But backward. Full bodied. Quite structured. Excellent fruit. Very good grip. Very youthful but very impressive, especially at the end. Very fine. (March 2006)
2015 TO 2035   18.5

Clos de Vougeot, 1999
Domaine Jérôme Chézeaux
Medium-full colour. Slightly sweaty/vegetal nose. Curious. Medium weight. Almost bitter. A second bottle was similar. No. (October 2005)
(SEE NOTE)

Clos de Vougeot, 1999
Domaine René Engel
Very full colour. Just a little pinched on the nose. Slightly reduced, too. But became very classy on aeration. Fullish body, rich and lovely on the palate. Indeed better the Grands Échezeaux perhaps. Complete, very long and classy. (June 2003)
2010 TO 2028   18.5

Clos de Vougeot, 1999
Domaine Joseph Faiveley
Medium-full colour. Ripe, stylish, gently oaky nose. Rich and lovely. Full bodied, firm and tannic. Very good grip. Lots of depth here. Lovely intense, virile finish. Fine plus. (June 2003)
2010 TO 2028   18.0

Clos de Vougeot, 1999
Domaine Jean Grivot
Very good colour. Quite austere on the nose. But nothing too hard or harsh. Lovely, cool Pinot fruit. Medium-full body. Not as fat or as abundant as that of Anne Gros. Excellent grip. Very lovely damson fruit. Very complex and classy. Fine plus. (June 2003)
2009 TO 2035   18.0

Clos de Vougeot, Le Grand Maupertuis, 1999
Domaine Anne Gros
Very full colour. Very lovely nose. Rich, complete, profound and gently oaky. Fullish body. Very harmonious. Multidimensional and very pure. Super-concentrated fruit and excellent grip. Brilliant! (March 2006)
2010 TO 2040   19.5

Clos de Vougeot, Château de la Tour, 1999
Domaine Labet-Dechelette
Good colour. Ripe nose. But not the depth and interest of Méo-Camuzet's or Grivot's. Medium body. A little oak. Balanced and fruity, but no real depth or *grand cru* dimension. Very good at best. (March 2002)
NOW TO 2010   16.0

Clos de Vougeot, 1999
Domaine François Lamarche
Full colour. Decent fruit on the nose, but it lacks dimension and real class. Astringent and pedestrian on the palate. Medium to medium-full body. Unexciting. (June 2003)
NOW TO 2015   14.0

Clos de Vougeot, 1999
Domaine Chantal Lescure
Very full colour. Good, ripe nose, but a bit tight and ungainly. Some oak. Medium-full body. Slightly astringent. Good fruit, but it lacks class. Raw and coarse. (June 2003)
2009 TO 2019   14.0

Clos de Vougeot, 1999
Domaine Méo-Camuzet
Full colour. Ample, rich, slightly earthy, quite oaky nose. Medium-full body. Very good tannins. Fresh, ripe, classy and with a good intensity on the follow-through. Lovely finish. Fine plus. (March 2005)
2010 TO 2025   18.0

Clos de Vougeot, 1999
Domaine Méo-Camuzet
Full colour. Some evolution. Quite a lot of new oak. Rich, fat and exotic. Fullish body. Good tannins. Ripe, succulent, rich and complete. Lots of depth. Long. Fine plus. (September 2003)
2010 TO 2030   18.0

Clos de Vougeot, 1999
Domaine Dr. Georges Mugneret
Fullish colour. Lovely nose. Rich, full and gently oaky. Medium-full body. Plump, balanced, fresh and attractive. This finishes well. Long and fine.
(June 2003)
2009–2024   17.5

Clos de Vougeot, 1999
Domaine Henri Rebourseau
Full colour. Quite a full, tannic wine on the nose. Full, oaky and tannic on the palate. Very good grip. Very good fruit. Quite a substantial wine here. Long. Fine. (January 2002)
2011 TO 2025   17.5

Clos de Vougeot, 1999
Maison Antonin Rodet
Very full colour. Very high-class nose. Gently oaky. A lot of depth. Fullish body. Plump, oaky and well balanced on the palate. It just lacks a little dimension, but fresh, classy and fine. (June 2003)
2009 TO 2025   17.5

Clos de Vougeot, Grand Maupertuis, 1999
Domaine Jean Tardy et Fils
Full colour. Rich and oaky on both nose and palate. Ripe, balanced, fresh and attractive. But a slight lack of dimension and originality. Very good indeed at best. (June 2003)
2009 TO 2020   17.0

Clos de Vougeot, 1999
Domaine des Varoilles
Good colour. Rich, fat and seductive on the nose. No lack of substance and depth. Lovely fruit. Fullish body. Some tannin. Slight toffee flavours. This is a more masculine wine than their Charmes. Quite a lot bigger. But rich and stylish, and with very good depth. Fine too.
(January 2002)
NOW TO 2025   17.5

Clos de Vougeot, 1999
Domaine de la Vougeraie
Full colour. Slightly diffuse compared with the rest of the Clos de Vougeots on the nose. Soft on the palate. Forward. Some fruit but no definition. Not much better than the *premier cru*.
(June 2003)
NOW TO 2017   15.0

Corton, 1999
Domaine Bonneau du Martray
Good colour. Lovely plummy fruit on the nose. Full and firm. Very good tannin. Very good grip on the palate. This has a lot of depth. Still a bit closed. Lovely finish. Fine plus. (March 2002)
2009 TO 2030   18.0

Corton, 1999
Domaine Capitain-Gagnerot
Mainly from the Grandes Lolières. This is succulent, balanced and fruity. But light for a Corton and a 1999. Elegant, nevertheless, and quite long. But it doesn't have any backbone.
(February 2003)
NOW TO 2012   15.0

Le Corton, 1999
Domaine Bouchard Père et Fils
Fullish colour. Closed on the nose. Rich, concentrated and highly impressive on the palate. Fullish body. Very good tannins. Still a little austere. Lots of depth. The finish gets better and better. Fine plus. (March 2002)
NOW TO 2024   18.0

Corton, Les Bressandes, 1999
Domaine Chandon de Briailles
Full colour. Plump nose. Evidence of the stems. Ripe, almost sweet, but a lack of fat in the mouth. Quite stylish. This is better than their Clos du Roi. It is fatter and more succulent. Long and quite stylish. Very good. (June 2003)
NOW TO 2018   16.0

Corton, Les Bressandes, 1999
Domaine Antonin Guyon

Medium-full colour. Rich and oaky, rather more oaky than his Clos du Roi. Stylish and balanced. Less coarse on the palate too. This is medium-full bodied, has plenty of fruit and has a decent, clean, long finish. Very good. (June 2003)

NOW TO 2020   16.0

Corton, Les Bressandes, 1999
Domaine Jacques Prieur

Full colour. Quite a chunky nose. A little dry. A little coarse. Medium to medium-full body. Ripe but unbalanced. Decent acidity, but dry and solid on the palate. Better as it evolved. (June 2003)

NOW TO 2012   15.0

Corton, Clos des Cortons Faiveley, 1999
Domaine Joseph Faiveley

Fullish colour. Excellent nose. Real class, depth and definition. Very profound and very lovely. Full bodied, rich, concentrated and very well balanced. Very backward. But very high quality. Excellent. (June 2003)

2011 TO 2030   19.0

Corton, Clos du Roi, 1999
Domaine Chandon de Briailles

Medium-full colour. Ripe and sweet. Slight touch of the stems. Good acidity. On the palate medium-full bodied, slightly lean. It lacks fat. It lacks sex appeal. Slightly astringent at the end. (June 2003)

NOW TO 2015   14.0

Corton, Clos du Roi, 1999
Maison Vincent Girardin

Good fullish colour. Firm, rich, ripe, backward, plummy nose. Full-bodied palate. Ample, rich and succulent. Very good tannins. Plenty of depth. This has a lovely, classy follow-through. Lots of vigour. Fine plus. (March 2003)

NOW TO 2024   18.0

Corton, Clos du Roi, 1999
Domaine Antonin Guyon

Medium-full colour. Plump and rich on the nose. Good depth. Good style. On the palate a little too chunky. It lacks harmony. Medium-full body. Decent acidity. But unexciting. (June 2003)

NOW TO 2015   14.0

Corton, Clos du Roi, 1999
Domaine du Comte Senard

Good colour. Slightly lean, spicy nose. Not as complex as the Bressandes of Chandon de Briailles. Medium body. Plenty of fruit and interest, and no lack of balance or length. But not really of *grand cru* depth. Very good at best. (March 2003)

NOW TO 2016   16.0

Corton, Clos du Roi, 1999
Domaine Charles Thomas

Full colour. Corked, but I think a wine without much class. Very full colour. Ripe, rich, chunky and solid, but with good concentration. Underneath, there is rich fruit here. Fullish body. Good grip. Just needs time. Very good indeed. (June 2003)

2010 TO 2024   17.0

Corton, Le Clos du Roi, 1999
Domaine de la Vougeraie

Good colour. Rich, classy, quite firm nose. Fullish body. Good depth. Very good, quite concentrated fruit. Plenty of class. Long. Very good indeed. (September 2004)

2010 TO 2020+   17.0

Corton, Clos des Vergennes, 1999
Domaine Cachat-Occquidant et Fils

Monopole. Good colour. This is singularly dull. And the oak leaves it a bit astringent. Medium body. Very flat. Lacks grip. Not even much ripe fruit. No. (February 2003)

DRINK SOON   12.0

Corton, Les Languettes, 1999
Domaine Michel Voarick

Good colour. Impressively rich, fragrant, elegant nose. Very lovely Pinot Noir. Fullish body. Vigorous. Still some tannin. Quite firm for a Languettes. Still needs time. Very good indeed. (February 2003)

2009 TO 2020   17.0

Corton, Les Maréchaudes, 1999
Domaine Doudet-Naudin
This is quite serious. But despite the energy, it is difficult to see the definition. Good at best. (February 2003)
NOW TO 2011   14.5

Corton, Maréchaudes, 1999
Domaine Chandon de Briailles
Full colour. This is a lot more animal and stemmy than the Bressandes. Not nearly as stylish. It also lacks a bit of grip. Medium body. Slightly thin. Astringent at the end. Not much here. (June 2003)
NOW TO 2012   13.5

Corton, Pougets, 1999
Domaine Louis Jadot
Medium-full colour. Classy and profound on the nose. Real depth here. Backward. Full bodied, rich, complex and classy. Very lovely quality here. Splendid fruit. Excellent. Very, very long. This is very fine plus. (June 2003)
2010 TO 2030   19.0

Corton, Renardes, 1999
Domaine Maillard Père et Fils
Full colour. Rich, fat, clean and ripe on the nose. Not a blockbuster though. Medium-full body. Ripe, balanced and stylish. This has good length and complexity. Very good plus. (June 2003)
2009 TO 2024   16.5

Corton, Le Rognet, 1999
Domaine Bertrand Ambroise
Full colour. Medium-full weight on the nose. Not too oaky or aggressive as in earlier Ambroise wines. Indeed, very good poised, cool fruit. On the palate the tannins are a little stewed. But there is good Pinot Noir and grip. Lacks a little real class though. But very good indeed. (March 2005)
2010 TO 2020   17.0

Corton, Le Rognet, 1999
Domaine Chevalier Père et Fils
A good, sturdy example. Fullish. Some tannin. Good grip. But a bit rudely put together. Slightly rustic at the end. (February 2003)
NOW TO 2014   14.0

Corton, Rognet, 1999
Domaine René Durand
Fullish colour. Quite chunky on the nose, but ripe and fresh. Medium body. Decent fruit. But light and slightly short. Just dull, especially after the attack. A pity. Quite good. (June 2003)
NOW TO 2014   14.0

Corton, Le Rognet, 1999
Domaine Michel Mallard et Fils
The first year he was fully equipped to do what he wanted to do. This lacks a bit of grip. Succulent and ripe. But it tails off. Will get astringent. Only very good. (February 2003)
NOW TO 2011   15.5

Echézeaux, 1999
Domaine Robert Arnoux
Medium-full colour. Ripe, concentrated, stylish nose. Lots of depth and class here. Fullish body. Quite meaty, but very good grip and tannins. Lovely fruit. Lots of vigour and potential. Plenty of depth. Fine. (October 2003)
2009 TO 2025   17.5

Echézeaux, 1999
Domaine Jean-Yves Bizot
Very good colour. Still very youthful. Rich, ripe, slightly austere, profound nose. Fullish. Ripe tannins. Intense. Pure. Very classy. Very good grip on the palate. Needs some time to absorb the tannins. But rich and lots of depth. Very lovely, especially at the end. Fine plus. (April 2006)
2009 TO 2029   18.0

Echézeaux, 1999
Domaine Joseph Drouhin
Medium to medium-full colour. Lovely, intense fruit on the nose. Delicious Pinot Noir on the palate. Very well balanced. Medium-full body. Integrated, velvety and classy. Very long. Very lovely. Fine. (June 2002)
2009 TO 2025   17.5

Echézeaux, 1999
Domaine René Engel
Fullish colour. Lovely fruit. Ripe and succulent on the nose. Medium-full body. A little raw still,

but rich, ripe, complex and profound. A lovely long, vibrant finish. At least fine. (June 2003)

2009 TO 2027   17.5

Echézeaux, 1999
Domaine Joseph Faiveley

Medium-full colour. More backward than some. Cool, rich and structured on the nose. Full body. Very stylish. Some tannin, though, which dominates the attack. The follow-through is very promising. Long and lovely. Fine plus. (June 2003)

2010 TO 2027   18.0

Echézeaux, 1999
Domaine Louis Jadot

Medium to medium-full colour. Ripe, stylish, succulent nose. Not as big as it might be. But youthful. Good energy. Medium-full body. Very good grip. This has elegance at the end. Very good indeed. (June 2003)

2009 TO 2022   17.0

Echézeaux, 1999
Domaine Jayer-Gilles

Full colour. Ample, black-curranty and very oaky nose. Fullish body. Some tannin. Quite a lot of oak. Ripe and plump, and with good grip. Not over-oaked but just about at the limit. Could have been both richer and more concentrated. Good, positive finish though. Very good indeed. (March 2005)

2009 TO 2020   17.0

Echézeaux, 1999
Domaine Henri Jayer

Fullish colour. Rich, concentrated and quite tannic nose. Very high-class fruit here. Splendid on the palate. Fullish body. Old viney, rich, ripe and with impressive grip. Long. Very lovely. Very fine. (March 2005)

2010 TO 2025+   18.5

Echézeaux, 1999
Domaine François Lamarche

Fullish colour. Slightly tight on the nose. It lacks a bit of class. Good fruit though. Medium-full body. Decent acidity. Ripe and quite intense,

and good length. But one finds it lacks a little class. Merely very good. (June 2003)

2009 TO 2021   16.0

Echézeaux, 1999
Maison Dominique Laurent

Fullish colour. Rich, concentrated and oaky on the nose. Fullish bodied, rich and succulent on the palate. Some tannin. Plenty of concentration. This has very good intensity. Long. A fine example. (June 2003)

2010 TO 2028   17.5

Echézeaux, 1999
Domaine Jean-Marc Millot

Good colour. Elegant, oaky nose. Ripe and succulent. Rich and well balanced. Medium-full body. Lovely fragrant fruit. Not a blockbuster but good grip. Long. Fine plus. (October 2002)

NOW TO 2024   18.0

Echézeaux, 1999
Domaine Mugneret-Gibourg

Medium-full colour. Rich, fat, gently oaky, fullish nose. Fullish bodied, ripe and classy. Good tannins. Still a little raw. Very good fruit. Very good grip. This is going to be at least fine. Lovely finish. (June 2003)

2009 TO 2027   17.5

Echézeaux, 1999
Domaine des Perdrix

Full colour. Rich, full and concentrated on the nose. Less grip and zip on the palate than the nose indicated. Picked a little overripe. Fullish body. Good tannins. Decent acidity. Very good plus. But it doesn't sing today. (June 2003)

2009 TO 2019   16.5

Echézeaux, 1999
Domaine Jacques Prieur

Full colour. Slightly clumsy and slightly reduced on the nose. Good fruit underneath. On the palate medium body. A bit astringent and lumpy. It lacks a bit of zip as well. Ungainly. Decent acidity but a bit of a disappointment. Merely good. (June 2003)

2009 TO 2021   15.0

Echézeaux, 1999
Domaine Daniel Rion et Fils

Good colour. Rich, mellow, classy nose. Ripe. Nicely, stylishly perfumed. Medium-full body. Very good grip. Classy, balanced and intense. Fine plus. (October 2002)

2009 TO 2025   18.0

Echézeaux, 1999
Domaine de la Romanée-Conti

Fine colour. Rich, quite tannic nose. Quite a substantial wine. Profound and delicious fruit. Not a bit too heavyweight. Excellent grip. This is very concentrated and very lovely. Very long on the palate. Fine plus. (July 2003)

2011 TO 2030   18.0

Echézeaux, 1999
Domaine Emmanuel Rouget

Fullish colour. Still youthful. Some new oak on the nose. A little tight. But ripe and juicy underneath. Fullish body. Quite concentrated. Some oak on the palate. Ripe and succulent. Good energy. Needs time. Fine plus. (March 2006)

2011 TO 2028   18.0

Echézeaux, Les Rouges du Bas, 1999
Domaine Méo-Camuzet

Fine colour. Splendidly rich nose. Very ripe, aromatic fruit hiding the backbone. Fullish body. Fine acidity. Very, very rich. Fine plus. (March 2001)

2009 TO 2025   18.0

Fixin, 1999
Domaine Vincent and Denis Berthaut

Quite a light colour. This I think has been bottled a bit late—May to June 2001. Slightly tight and a little astringent. The nose is a bit rustic. Only quite good. Forward. (January 2002)

DRINK SOON   14.0

Fixin, 1999
Domaine Régis Bouvier

An elegant wine. Firm underneath but not *sauvage*. Very good grip. Lovely, cool fruit. Good plus. (January 2002)

NOW TO 2012   15.5

Fixin, 1999
Caveau Saint-Vincent/Michel Defrance

A bit more substantial than his 2000. More tannin and depth. A bit more rustic. Slightly hard at the end for the moment. But good also. (January 2002)

NOW TO 2012   15.0

Fixin, 1999
Domaine Clos Saint-Louis

Fuller, riper and a little more tannic than the 2000. But quite soft again. This is the house style. Good fruit. Quite elegant. Quite good. (January 2002)

NOW TO 2011   14.0

Fixin, 1999
Domaine Pierre Gelin

This is full, rich, concentrated and very good indeed for a village wine. Lovely concentrated fruit. It is quite sturdy but not a bit hard. Excellent fruit. (January 2002)

NOW TO 2020   16.0

Fixin, 1999
Domaine Alain Guyard

Good fat. Ripe and rich. Ample and generous. Medium to medium-full body. Good substance but no hard edges. Good. (January 2002)

NOW TO 2012   15.0

Fixin, 1999
Domaine du Vieux Collège

Good fruit. A certain dryness at the end from the tannins. Not quite astringent. But it is quite soft and marked by the oak. Juicy. An attractive wine if not very *type* Fixin. Quite good. (January 2002)

NOW TO 2011   14.0

Fixin, Les Arvelets, 1999
Domaine Vincent et Denis Berthaut

Medium colour. Ripe. Medium to medium-full body. Good grip. Plenty of fruit. Quite intense. Yet quite forwarded nonetheless. Good plus. (January 2002)

NOW TO 2011   15.5

Fixin, Les Champeaux, 1999
Domaine du Vieux Collège
This is sophisticated. Medium-full, rich and gently oaky. Good backbone. Ripe and balanced. Complex and fresh. Very good. (January 2002)

NOW TO 2012   16.0

Fixin, Les Clos, 1999
Domaine Vincent and Denis Berthaut
Quite light in colour. But good succulence here. Soft and quite *tendre*. More elegant, too. Decent depth. Quite good plus. (June 2002)

NOW TO 2012   16.0

Fixin, Clos Napoléon, 1999
Domaine Pierre Gelin
Lovely rich, ample fruit on the nose. Fullish. Lots of depth. Very good grip. This is rich and opulent. Yet quite firm and tannic. Very good, indeed, if not fine. (January 2002)

NOW TO 2025   17.0

Fixin, Clos de la Perrière, 1999
Domaine Joliet Père et Fils
They have cleaned up their act here. Good colour. Fullish. Not a bit *sauvage*. The tannins are mellow, the wine surprisingly ready to drink. Lovely quite red, fruity fruit. Balanced. Long. Very good. (June 2004)

NOW TO 2017   16.0

Fixin, Les Crais, 1999
Domaine Vincent and Denis Berthaut
This has a bit more to it than their 1999 Fixin les Clos. Again, the colour is a bit light. But this has more fruit and a better acidity. Good style. Good. (January 2002)

NOW TO 2011   15.0

Fixin, Crêt de Chêne, 1999
Domaine René Bouvier
Again, very good, old-viney fruit. Long, concentrated and virile. Fullish body. Lovely vigorous finish. (January 2002)

NOW TO 2013   15.5

Fixin, Hervelets, 1999
Domaine Bart
Good colour. Quite substantial. Quite austere but not too *sauvage*. Some tannin. Ripe and fresh. Good grip. This is good plus. (January 2002)

NOW TO 2014   15.5

Fixin, Hervelets, 1999
Domaine Clos Saint-Louis
Good colour. Quite a full, rich nose. As with the 2000, this shows the difference between village and *premier cru*. Medium-full body. Good grip. Thirty percent new wood, which is exactly right. Fresh. Quite concentrated. Very good style. Long. Very good. (January 2002)

NOW TO 2018   16.0

Fixin, Hervelets, 1999
Domaine Derey Frères
This is rather more rustic than most. A proper Fixin. Medium-full body. Tannic. *Sauvage*. Yet no lack of fruit. Not too hard. Good. (January 2002)

NOW TO 2012   15.0

Fixin, Hervelets, 1999
Domaine Pierre Gelin
First vintage of new purchase. Medium body. Very good grip. Stylish, long and complex. This has a lot of depth and concentration. Yet not a bit tough. Lovely finish. Very good. (January 2002)

NOW TO 2020   16.0

Fixin, Hervelets, 1999
Domaine du Vieux Collège
Much more typical than the village wine. Slightly brutal. Tannic. *Sauvage*. Slightly dry at the end perhaps. Quite good. (January 2002)

NOW TO 2013   14.0

Gevrey-Chambertin, 1999
Domaine Régis Bouvier
Ample, stylish, balanced, cool and really quite concentrated for a village wine. Lovely fruit. Very good depth. Good. (January 2002)

NOW TO 2018   16.0

Gevrey-Chambertin, 1999
Domaine Camus Père et Fils

Slightly stemmy. A little earthy and dead-leafy. Underneath, decent fruit. But not exciting. (January 2002)

DRINK SOON   13.0

Gevrey-Chambertin, 1999
Domaine Collot

Sturdy at first. Medium-full body. Good tannins. Good fruit. The tannins are ripe, and the wine has balance and depth. Very good for a village example. (January 2002)

NOW TO 2014   15.0

Gevrey-Chambertin, 1999
Domaine Derey Frères

Ripe and rich. Fat and succulent. Elegant. Very good for a village wine. (January 2002)

NOW TO 2014   15.0

Gevrey-Chambertin, 1999
Domaine Jean Fournier

Not as exciting, proportionately, as the 2000. It lacks a bit of weight and fat. Somewhat light and neutral. Forward. From 2004. (January 2002)

DRINK SOON   13.0

Gevrey-Chambertin, 1999
Domaine Robert Groffier

Fullish colour. Lovely succulent, ripe nose. Great charm. Medium to medium-full body. Excellent grip and depth. Very long. Real length. Very good, indeed, for a village wine. (October 2001)

NOW TO 2018   16.5

Gevrey-Chambertin, 1999
Domaine Alain Guyard

Rich, substantial, velvety and seductive. Lovely fruit here. Long. This is very good for what it is. (January 2002)

NOW TO 2014   15.5

Gevrey-Chambertin, 1999
Domaine Odoul-Coquard

Comes from the other side of the Route Nationale. Only medium body. Yet fresh and fruity, and reasonably stylish and balanced. Quite good again. But forward. (January 2002)

NOW TO 2010   14.0

Gevrey-Chambertin, 1999
Domaine Henri Richard

Ample, rich, full, concentrated and slightly spicy. Quite sturdy but good depth. Just needs time. Ripe tannins. Good style. Very good. (January 2002)

NOW TO 2015   15.5

Gevrey-Chambertin, 1999
Domaine Thibault Père et Fils

Good colour. Full and rich. Some tannin. Slightly hard, but this is not a fault in this wine. It just needs more time. Ripe, stylish and long. Very good. (January 2002)

NOW TO 2014   15.5

Gevrey-Chambertin, 1999
Domaine Jean Trapet Père et Fils

Rich, spicy and quite substantial. Not exactly elegant. But ripe and with good grip. Some tannin. Medium-full body. Good concentration. Good plus but not the elegance for better. Quite a meaty example. (January 2002)

NOW TO 2013   15.5

Gevrey-Chambertin, 1999
Domaine Alain Voegeli

Still quite austere. Good colour. The nose is a little closed. But the wine is rich and full bodied on the palate. Some tannin. Backward. Yet generous underneath. Lots of vigour. Very good. Needs time. (January 2002)

NOW TO 2015   15.5

Gevrey-Chambertin, Vieilles Vignes, 1999
Domaine Denis Bachelet

Fine, fullish colour. Just beginning to show signs of maturity. Very lovely nose. Succulent. The tannins are softening. Very ripe and rich. Composed, elegant and very lovely. Medium-full body. Very classy. Very harmonious. Slightly oaky. Lots of dimension. Naturally sweet at the end. Seductive and sensual. Delicious. Just about ready. (June 2006)

NOW TO 2018   17.0

Gevrey-Chambertin, Mes Favorites, Vieilles Vignes, 1999
Domaine Alain Burguet

Good colour. Cool, rich, concentrated, and very ripe, yet very fresh and well balanced on the nose. Medium-full body. Good grip. A little tannin to resolve. Quite concentrated. Well made and as reliable as usual. Very good indeed. (October 2002)

NOW TO 2020+   17.0

Gevrey-Chambertin, Vieilles Vignes, 1999
Domaine Marchand-Guillot

Medium-full body. Slightly reserved. But good concentration. Slightly sturdy character. Very good follow-through. Rich. Very good fruit. Good grip. Very good. (January 2002)

NOW TO 2016   16.0

Gevrey-Chambertin, Premier Cru, 1999
Domaine Claude Dugat

Full colour. Very classy nose. Full, firm, rich and concentrated. Some oak. This is most impressive. It has even more grip and depth. Very ripe. Very long. Very impressive. (June 2003)

2010 TO 2030   18.0

Gevrey-Chambertin, Premier Cru, 1999
Domaine Bernard Dugat-Py

Full colour. Rich, full, oaky and quite extracted on the nose. Full body. Some tannin. Meaty. Very good depth and grip. Fine. (June 2003)

2010 TO 2025   17.5

Gevrey-Chambertin, Bel Air, 1999
Domaine Taupenot-Merme

Fullish. Rather more obvious tannins than the Riotte. Good grip. This is a little austere, but that is not a bad thing. Ripe and stylish. Long. Very good indeed. (January 2002)

NOW TO 2024   17.0

Gevrey-Chambertin, Les Cazetiers, 1999
Domaine Bruno Clair

Full colour. Cool, laid-back, classy and rich. Slightly lean, as always with Bruno Clair, but with lots of class. Medium-full body. Very concentrated. More to it than the Fonteny. Very lovely fruit. Long, complex and classy. Very fine finish. Fine. (June 2003)

2009 TO 2025   17.5

Gevrey-Chambertin, Les Cazetiers, 1999
Domaine Joseph Faiveley

Good colour. Slightly austere on the nose. Very pure. Fullish body. Some tannin. Excellent, slightly austere but really concentrated palate. Very good grip. This has purity and length. Very lovely. (April 2003)

2011 TO 2030   18.0

Gevrey-Chambertin, Les Cazetiers, 1999
Domaine Louis Jadot

Medium-full colour. Lovely nose. Really ripe and concentrated. Lots and lots of depth. Not as oaky as some. Fullish body. Round. Very, very harmonious. Lots of lovely old-viney fruit. Very fine, long, succulent finish. Very long. Fine. (June 2003)

2009 TO 2025   17.5

Gevrey-Chambertin, Les Cazetiers, 1999
Domaine Philippe Leclerc

Full, concentrated and profound. Quite tannic. Very good acidity. This has very lovely fruit. It is quite oaky but not too much so. Very good indeed. Even fine. (January 2002)

NOW TO 2028   17.0

Gevrey-Chambertin, Les Cazetiers, Vieilles Vignes, 1999
Domaine Philippe Naddef

Full colour. Full, rich and not too over-oaked. Lots of fruit and depth. Very impressive. A bit solid and tannic on the palate. Slightly over-extracted. Good wine underneath. Good length. But slightly tough. Very good at best. (June 2003)

2011 TO 2025   16.0

Gevrey-Chambertin, Les Cazetiers, 1999
Domaine Armand Rousseau

Medium to medium-full colour. Splendidly Rousseau. Soft, caramelly and not a bit overdone. Very seductive. More evolved than most. Medium-full body. Slightly less intense and concentrated than Bruno Clair's or Jadot's, but lovely class and balance. Very good indeed. (June 2003)

2009 TO 2025   17.0

Gevrey-Chambertin, Les Cazetiers, 1999
Domaine Sérafin Père et Fils

Fullish colour. A touch of reduction, but rich, full and oaky. Quite masculine, it seems. Potentially the best of Sérafin's wines. But slightly adolescent. Excellent grip, though, and very lovely fruit. Fine. (June 2003)

2010 TO 2025   17.5

Gevrey-Chambertin, Champeaux, 1999
Domaine Jean-Claude Fourrier

Medium-full colour. Rich, full, ample nose. This is classy and profound. Slightly less lean than his Clos Saint-Jacques. Sexier but not as classy. Nor on the palate as complex or as harmonious. Medium-full body. Lovely fruit. Good finish. But not as complex. Very good indeed. (June 2003)

2009 TO 2025   17.0

Gevrey-Chambertin, Champeaux, 1999
Domaine Philippe Leclerc

Very fine fruit here. Not a bit too oaky. Ripe and succulent. Fullish body. An ample wine. Very good grip. Long. Very good plus. (January 2002)

NOW TO 2024   16.5

Gevrey-Chambertin, Champeaux, 1999
Domaine Denis Mortet

Full colour. Big, rich, full and oaky. Not as much definition or class as his Lavaux-Saint-Jacques. Fullish body. Some tannin. Ripe and meaty. Slightly over-extracted. It needs time. Good fruit and succulence, but a little structured. Very good plus. (June 2003)

2010 TO 2028   16.5

Gevrey-Chambertin, Champerrier, 1999
Domaine François Perrot

Good colour. Rich, substantial and old viney. Good tannins. Plenty of depth here. Lovely, slightly austere fruit and very good grip. *Premier cru* quality. Very good plus. A *vin de garde*. (January 2002)

NOW TO 2020   16.5

Gevrey-Chambertin, Champonnet, 1999
Domaine Joseph Faiveley

Fullish colour. Rich, full and closed-in on the nose. But not overdone in any way. Lots of depth. Fullish body. Some tannin. Backward. Ripe and succulent underneath. Long and very classy. Very good indeed. (June 2003)

2010 TO 2026   17.0

Gevrey-Chambertin, Champonnet, 1999
Domaine Heretsztyn

Full colour. Cool and classy. Ripe but not lean. But not a bit over-extracted or over-oaked. Balanced and very stylish. Medium-full body. Very clean, very pure and very impressive. This is a lovely, classy, harmonious example. Fresh. Long. Very good indeed. (June 2003)

2009 TO 2025   17.0

Gevrey-Chambertin, En Champs, 1999
Domaine Philippe Leclerc

Good concentration and depth. This is not too oaky. Rich and concentrated. Lovely fruit. Full, rich and concentrated. This is long and satisfying. Old vines here, and it shows. This is very good. (January 2002)

NOW TO 2024   16.0

Gevrey-Chambertin, Cherbaudes, 1999
Domaine Jean-Claude Fourrier

Medium colour. Fragrant nose. Fullish, ample and succulent. Good grip. Medium to medium-full body. Very good plus. (June 2003)

2010 TO 2025   16.5

Gevrey-Chambertin, Clos des Meix des Ouches, 1999
Domaine des Varoilles

Village wine. A monopole. Good colour. Fresh Pinot fruit. Good character. Medium-full body.

Ripe and succulent. This is stylish and very good. (January 2002)

NOW TO 2016   16.0

Gevrey-Chambertin, Clos de Meixvelles, 1999
Domaine Pierre Gelin

A monopole. Medium to medium-full body. Good grip. Quite sturdy, but there is good, rich fruit here, and the wine is balanced and stylish. Good plus. (January 2002)

NOW TO 2015   15.5

Gevrey-Chambertin, Clos Prieur, 1999
Domaine Pierre Gelin

Rather more new wood here. Medium-full body. Rich and concentrated. Rather more sophisticated fruit than the Gevrey Clos de Meixvelles. Ripe, balanced and classy. Very good plus. (January 2002)

NOW TO 2025   16.5

Gevrey-Chambertin, Clos Prieur, 1999
Domaine Rossignol-Trapet Père et Fils

Fullish colour. Ripe, oaky and succulent on the nose. Quite oaky on the palate. Good, full, ample wine. Lovely style. This is very fine. (June 2003)

2009 TO 2025   18.0

Gevrey-Chambertin, Clos Prieur, 1999
Domaine Jean Trapet Père et Fils

Fullish colour. Slightly anonymous on the nose. Slightly four-square. Medium-full body. Fresh, backward and concentrated. Lots of intensity here. This has a lot of depth. Very good. (June 2003)

2009 TO 2025   16.0

Gevrey-Chambertin, Clos Saint-Jacques, 1999
Domaine Bruno Clair

Good colour. Very fine, pure, poised, fragrant, classy nose. Lots of depth and perfume here. This is very lovely. Not a blockbuster, but very fine and concentrated. Real intensity. Splendid balance. Real class. Very vigorous at the end. Very fine plus. (March 2002)

NOW TO 2035   19.0

Gevrey-Chambertin, Clos Saint-Jacques, 1999
Domaine Sylvie Esmonin

Fullish colour, more evolved than most. Quite new oaky. Ripe and succulent nose. Fullish body. Concentrated, rich and harmonious. This is rather better than hitherto. Just about at the limit of the oak. Good grip. Lovely, fine finish. Fine. (September 2002)

NOW TO 2028   17.5

Gevrey-Chambertin, Clos Saint-Jacques, 1999
Domaine Jean-Claude Fourrier

Fullish colour. Stylish nose. Leaner than Rousseau's, more like Bruno Clair's style but with very lovely fruit. Medium-full body. Ripe, succulent, stylish and very well balanced. Fresh and long. Very fine. (June 2003)

2009 TO 2025   18.5

Gevrey-Chambertin, Clos Saint-Jacques, 1999
Domaine Louis Jadot

Medium-full colour. Closed-in on the nose, but real depth and quality here. Concentrated. Backward. Impressive. Slightly dense on the attack. Adolescent. It seems to lack a little drive. So the finish is slightly flat. Curious. Very good at best today. (April 2005)

2009 TO 2019   16.0

Gevrey-Chambertin, Clos Saint-Jacques, 1999
Domaine Armand Rousseau

Full colour. Very, very lovely, classy nose. Essence of fruit. Very, very pure, rich and full. Not as firm or as tough as Claude Dugat's Lavaux-Saint-Jacques. But even more concentrated and pure. Full body. Slightly less obviously tannic. Immensely vigorous on the follow-through. Very, very pure and clean. Excellent. (April 2005)

2010 TO 2035   19.5

Gevrey-Chambertin, Clos Tamisot, 1999
Domaine Pierre Damoy

Soft and gently oaky on the nose. Round, rich and generous. Not a blockbuster, but elegant, fragrant and long. Very good. (January 2002)

NOW TO 2016   16.0

Gevrey-Chambertin, Clos des Varoilles, 1999
Domaine des Varoilles

Lovely nose. Nicely austere. Good fruit. Not a bit lean. Lots of depth. Lots of finesse here. This is even better than the Gevrey-Chambertin la Romanée 1999. Lovely fruit. Medium-full body. Very good tannins. Good intensity. Long and positive at the end. Very good indeed. (January 2002)

NOW TO 2021   17.0

Gevrey-Chambertin, Combe du Dessus, 1999
Domaine Denis Mortet

Village *appellation contrôlée*. Full colour. Quite a lot of extraction and new oak evident. Rich, full bodied, ripe, almost sweet. Good tannins. Not too muscular. Attractive. Easy to enjoy. Very good. (August 2002)

NOW TO 2018   16.0

Gevrey-Chambertin, Combe au Moine, 1999
Domaine Joseph Faiveley

Good colour. Fragrant nose. Quite soft already. Medium body. Fresh and balanced, but not the greatest depth or vigour. Good plus. (March 2006)

NOW TO 2018   15.5

Gevrey-Chambertin, Combe au Moine, Vieille Vigne, 1999
Domaine Jean-Claude Fourrier

Medium-full colour. Slightly reserved on the nose. Medium-full body. Good ripe fruit. The tannins are soft. The wine is classy. It is a little cool at present. Stylish, long, intense and pure, but not rich enough for fine. Very good indeed. (October 2002)

NOW TO 2022   17.0

Gevrey-Chambertin, Combe au Moine, 1999
Domaine Philippe Leclerc

Less structure than his Gevrey Cazetiers 1999. Very good intensity. Oaky but not too much so. Good richness. Very good grip and fine intensity on the palate. Long. Very good indeed. (January 2002)

NOW TO 2024   17.0

Gevrey-Chambertin, Aux Combottes, 1999
Domaine Dujac

Fullish colour. Typical Dujac character. Very lovely ripe nose. Almost sweet. Medium-full body. Ripe tannins. Good grip. Stylish, clean and vibrant. Long on the palate. Fine. (June 2003)

2009 TO 2025   17.5

Gevrey-Chambertin, Aux Combottes, 1999
Domaine Odoul-Coquard

Good colour. Two-thirds old vines, one-third 10 years old. Lovely nose. A bit more new oak here than in his Morey-Saint-Denis Clos la Riotte. Fullish body. Very ripe tannins. Very ample and seductive. Rich on the palate. Almost sweet. Oaky and a bit obvious. But very good all the same. (January 2002)

NOW TO 2018   15.0

Gevrey-Chambertin, Les Corbeaux, 1999
Domaine Denis Bachelet

Full colour. Very lovely fruit here. Clean, pure and very, very classy. This has splendid harmony. Fullish body. Splendid fruit. Very, very complex flavours. A little tannin. This has great class and depth. Very good length. Fine plus. (June 2003)

2009 TO 2030   18.0

Gevrey-Chambertin, Les Corbeaux, 1999
Domaine Philippe Rossignol

This is a bit light for a *premier cru*. But it has elegance and very good fruit. Ripe. Long. Good depth. (January 2002)

NOW TO 2012   16.0

Gevrey-Chambertin, Les Corbeaux, 1999
Domaine Sérafin Père et Fils

Full colour. Slightly more four-square than his Cazetiers. Good fruit and balance, but a little lumpy. Fullish body. Some tannin. Good grip. But the fruit isn't that classy. This is very good at best. (June 2003)

2009 TO 2025   16.0

Gevrey-Chambertin, Craipillot, 1999
Domaine Gérard Seguin

This is rather too light and feminine for a *premier cru* of this village. Ripe and fruity. Oaky. Elegant. But I would have liked a bit more punch. Quite good at best. (January 2002)

NOW TO 2010   14.0

Gevrey-Chambertin, Clos Fonteny, 1999
Domaine Bruno Clair

Medium-full colour. Slightly lean after Roty's example, but rich, ripe and stylish. Very pure, as always. Medium-full body. Very ripe tannins. Very good grip. This is stylish, long and complex. Very classy. Very good plus. (June 2003)

2009 TO 2025   16.5

Gevrey-Chambertin, Fonteny, 1999
Domaine Huguenot Père et Fils

Good colour. Full nose. Good vigour and grip. A hint of mint. Gently oaky. Rich, full and fat. Very stylish. Lovely fruit. Very long on the palate. Very complex. Fine. (January 2002)

NOW TO 2025   17.5

Gevrey-Chambertin, Fonteny, 1999
Domaine Joseph Roty

Medium-full colour. Rich, fat, concentrated, old viney and impressive. Not too oaky. This is lovely. Full bodied, rich, fat and concentrated. Lots of vigour and intensity. Heaps of wine here. Fine plus. (June 2003)

2010 TO 2028   18.0

Gevrey-Chambertin, Fonteny, 1999
Domaine Sérafin Père et Fils

Medium-full colour. Ripe, rich and not too over-extracted or oaky. In fact, very delicious. Fullish body. Good tannins. Ripe. Good grip. Slightly rigid at present but very good plus. Long at the end. (June 2003)

2010 TO 2025   16.5

Gevrey-Chambertin, Les Goulots, 1999
Domaine Jean-Claude Fourrier

Medium-full colour. Rich, full and oaky on the nose. Vigorous, full bodied and rich on the palate. Ripe, positive and intense. Very healthy and sweet at the end. Fine. (June 2003)

2009 TO 2025   17.5

Gevrey-Chambertin, Lavaux-Saint-Jacques, 1999
Domaine Claude Dugat

Very good colour. Aromatic nose. A touch of mocha. Densely knit flavours. Rich, succulent, fat and impressive. A lot of concentration here. Full body. Very good tannins. Splendidly rich and concentrated on the palate. Great drive, vigour and class. Most impressive. Lovely finish. Very classic Gevrey. Very fine. (April 2003)

2012 TO 2032   18.5

Gevrey-Chambertin, Lavaux-Saint-Jacques, 1999
Domaine Harmand-Geoffroy

Medium-full colour. Soft nose. Ripe and gentle. But quite stylish. Medium to medium-full body. Good grip. Not the greatest elegance on the palate—it is a little hot and forced—but a decent finish. It may relax as it evolves. Good plus. (June 2003)

2009 TO 2020   15.5

Gevrey-Chambertin, Lavaux-Saint-Jacques, 1999
Domaine René Leclerc

This is rather too thin. Underneath is some very good fruit. But there is a lack of grip, vigour and backbone. (January 2002)

NOW TO 2009   13.5

Gevrey-Chambertin, Lavaux-Saint-Jacques, 1999
Domaine Denis Mortet

Full colour. Quite a big wine, but not, I think, over-extracted. Rich, fat and plump underneath. This is ripe, rich and ample. Full bodied, rich and satisfying. Slightly tougher and less integrated tannins than Bernard Dugat-Py's. But long and succulent underneath. Fine. (June 2003)

2010 TO 2028   17.5

Gevrey-Chambertin, Lavaux-Saint-Jacques, 1999
Domaine Armand Rousseau

Full colour. Some extraction. But rich and full, oaky and succulent. Full body. Good tannins. Very good grip. Lots of old-viney concentration. A modern wine. But very impressive. Very intense at the end. Fine plus. (June 2003)

2011 TO 2028   18.0

Gevrey-Chambertin, Lavaux-Saint-Jacques, 1999
Domaine Gérard Seguin

Rather more depth and structure, but again, a lack of real fat and substance. Too thin at the

end. A bit more to it than the Gevrey Craipillot 1999 but not much. Quite good at best.
(January 2002)
NOW TO 2010   14.0

Gevrey-Chambertin, Motrot, 1999
Domaine Denis Mortet
Full colour. Modern but in a slightly over-extracted sense. Rich and meaty. Fullish body on the palate. Lots of depth. Very good indeed.
(June 2003)
2010 TO 2025   16.5

Gevrey-Chambertin, La Perrière, 1999
Domaine Heresztyn
Good colour. The nose is still a bit unformed. Good style and depth on the palate. Ripe and balanced. Soft tannins. Good. (October 2002)
NOW TO 2012   15.0

Gevrey-Chambertin, La Perrière, 1999
Domaine Marchand-Guillot
Medium to medium-full body. Lovely, ample fruit. Very ripe and seductive. But not quite the grip or concentration to give it real depth or staying power. But good. Forward.
(January 2002)
NOW TO 2013   15.0

Gevrey-Chambertin, Petite Chapelle, 1999
Domaine Bruno Clair
Medium-full colour. Fragrant but very stylish on the nose. Ripe, succulent and gently accessible. Medium body. Some tannin. Stylish and balanced. More forward than most. This is very good indeed. (June 2003)
2009 TO 2025   17.0

Gevrey-Chambertin, Petite Chapelle, 1999
Domaine François Perrot
Most of the vineyard was planted in 1986 and 1990. One-quarter old vines. Good colour. Medium-full body. Very good, nicely cool fruit. An elegant wine with good tannins and plenty of depth. Long and stylish. Very good plus.
(January 2002)
NOW TO 2025   16.5

Gevrey-Chambertin, Petite Chapelle, 1999
Domaine Jean Trapet Père et Fils
Full colour. Ample, rich nose. Good fruit and depth. Slightly rigid perhaps. A slight touch of reduction. But a fine acidity. Ripe and concentrated. Long and complex at the end.
(June 2003)
2009 TO 2025   15.0

Gevrey-Chambertin, Les Platières, 1999
Domaine Philippe Leclerc
Good colour. Rich and full, but quite oaky. Not too rustic though. Good fruit. Good grip. Good concentration. This just needs time. Very good if you like oaky wines. (January 2002)
NOW TO 2019   15.5

Gevrey-Chambertin, Poissenot, 1999
Domaine Humbert Frères
Quite a light colour. Quite delicate on the nose, but very lovely, classy fruit here. Medium weight. Only a little tannin. I would have hoped for a bit more backbone. But good depth, grip, balance and class. (January 2002)
NOW TO 2020   16.0

Gevrey-Chambertin, La Romanée, 1999
Domaine des Varoilles
Good substance. Very good grip. Generous and fruity. This has more charm than it used to 10 years ago. Ripe. Quite rich. Smooth and elegant. Good grip and intensity at the end. Long. Very good plus. (January 2002)
NOW TO 2021   16.5

Gevrey-Chambertin, Au Velle, 1999
Domaine Denis Mortet
Fullish colour. Rich, fat and stylish on the nose. Fine but modern. Slightly one-dimensional on the palate compared to the two wines above. But ripe and quite powerful. Very good indeed. (June 2003)
2010 TO 2025   16.5

La Grande Rue, 1999
Domaine François Lamarche
Full colour. Good depth and class here on the nose. This is definitely fine. Nice, cool and

plummy. A lot better than the Clos de Vougeot. Full bodied and quite tannic, but pure, balanced and old viney. It needs time. Fine plus. (June 2003)

2010 TO 2028   18.0

Grands Echézeaux, 1999
Domaine René Engel

Full colour. Lots of depth here on the nose. Very classy fruit. Lovely style. Less raw than their Echézeaux. More complete. Lots of depth. Backward but very fine. Marvellous finish. (June 2003)

2010 TO 2028   18.5

Grands Echézeaux, 1999
Domaine de la Romanée-Conti

Fine colour. Slightly more marked by the oak on the nose than the Echézeaux. Richer, more concentrated and more serious on the palate. Full body. Very good tannins and grip. Quite lovely intensity of fruit. This is very, very long and very fine. Super! (May 2005)

2012 TO 2032   18.5

Griotte-Chambertin, 1999
Domaine Joseph Drouhin

Full colour. Very classy nose. Intense and ripe. Rich and abundant. Medium-full body. Concentrated, ripe, intense and classy. Very long. Very lovely. This is fine plus. (June 2003)

2009 TO 2025   18.0

Griotte-Chambertin, 1999
Domaine René Leclerc

Good colour. A little reduced on the nose. Medium body on the palate. Quite ripe. Balanced. Long. Fresh. Plump. Reasonable style and length, but very good at best. Essentially a little weak. (October 2002)

NOW TO 2017   16.0

Griotte-Chambertin, 1999
Domaine Ponsot

One hectare belonging to M. Mercier since 1982 (Domaine de Chezeaux). Half was then planted. Ponsot takes two thirds of the crop. Medium-full colour. Some development. Fragrant nose. No new oak of course. Very pure. Very good

acidity. Medium to medium-full body. Very individual. Lovely fruit. By no means a blockbuster. But very long. Fine. (March 2006)

2009 TO 2025   17.5

Ladoix, Vieilles Vignes, 1999
Domaine Edmond Cornu et Fils

This is very good: fullish, ripe, classy, balanced and succulent. Really quite concentrated. Really lovely. (February 2003)

NOW TO 2012   16.0

Ladoix, Le Clos Royer, 1999
Domaine Michel Mallard et Fils

First year in his new *cuverie*. Bought the parcel from Bouchard Père et Fils. Very good colour. This is full and chunky, even a bit solid. But it has depth, concentration and grip. Very good. Needs time. (February 2003)

2010 TO 2017   15.0

Ladoix, La Corvée, 1999
Domaine Chevalier Père et Fils

Ripe and plump. But less sophisticated than the 2000. Slightly raw at the end. (February 2003)

NOW TO 2010   13.0

Ladoix, Les Madonnes, Vieilles Vignes, 1999
Domaine Cachat-Ocquidant et Fils

Good colour. Quite an earthy sort of flavour. Not very oaky except for the tannins from it. Medium to medium-full body. It lacks a bit of real class and charm. Quite good. (February 2003)

NOW TO 2010   14.0

Latricières-Chambertin, 1999
Domaine Simon Bize et Fils

Good colour. This is very much better than it showed a year ago. Rich fruit. Juicy and concentrated. Lots of depth. This is stylish. Very good grip. Very long. Very fine. (December 2001)

2009 TO 2030   18.5

Latricières-Chambertin, 1999
Domaine Camus Père et Fils

Not a very pronounced colour. Light, attenuated and slightly dry on the nose. Better on the palate. Decent style, too. Better than the Charmes. Soft, plump and balanced. Positive finish. Very good plus. (January 2002)

NOW TO 2013 16.5

Latricières-Chambertin, 1999
Domaine Jean Trapet Père et Fils

Medium-full colour. Slightly reduced on the nose. Ripe and stylish, with good grip and intensity on the palate. Medium-full body. This is better than their Chapelle. Long. Fine. (June 2003)

2009 TO 2025 17.5

Maranges, La Fussière, 1999
Domaine Latour-Giraud

Full colour. Robust nose. A meaty wine, with soft tannins and good acidity. Will get rounder and richer as it develops. Good for what it is. (October 2001)

NOW TO 2009 14.0

Marsannay, 1999
Domaine Huguenot Père et Fils

A full, firm, rich, fat example. Good tannins. Plenty of depth. Not a bit *primeur*. This has not lack of concentration. A big wine for a Marsannay but not brutal. Very good, given it is the basic. From 2005. (January 2002)

NOW TO 2010 14.5

Marsannay, 1999
Domaine Méo-Camuzet

Good colour. Lovely fragrant fruit on both nose and palate. Medium body. Not too much oak. Rich, balanced and stylish. Very good, indeed, for what it is. Will last well. (March 2001)

NOW TO 2012 15.0

Marsannay, Boisvin, 1999
Domaine Collotte

Not that concentrated. But ripe, rich and succulent. This has good grip. Good plus. (January 2002)

NOW TO 2009 14.0

Marsannay, Champs Perdrix, 1999
Domaine Derey Frères

Good substance. A little tannin. Ripe and succulent. Stylish. Good depth. Very good for what it is. (January 2002)

NOW TO 2010 14.5

Marsannay, Les Champs Perdrix, 1999
Domaine Huguenot Père et Fils

Lovely nose. This is an excellent *cuvée*. Very fine fruit. Very well poised. Ripe. Medium-full body. Just a little tannin. Very long. Very good, indeed, for what it is. (January 2002)

NOW TO 2010 15.0

Marsannay, Champs Salomon, 1999
Domaine René Bouvier

Quite chunky but not rustic. Good depth. Very good grip. Very good. (January 2002)

NOW TO 2010 14.5

Marsannay, Le Clos, 1999
Domaine René Bouvier

A monopole. Three hectares in Couchey. Fresh, concentrated, flowery and individual. Long and complex. Very good again. But the Vieilles Vignes has even more interest. (January 2002)

NOW TO 2010 14.5

Marsannay, Le Clos du Jean, 1999
Domaines Collotte

The most concentrated of the three (Clos Salomon and Boisvin). Lovely fruit. This has a lot of depth. Very stylish, too. The best of the three Marsannays. Very good. (January 2002)

NOW TO 2010 14.5

Marsannay, Clos du Roi, 1999
Domaine Régis Bouvier

Not as concentrated as his Marsannay Longeroies Vieilles Vignes 1999. But the fruit is more distinguished, and there is better balance than in the Longeroies. Very lovely. (January 2002)

NOW TO 2025 17.0

Marsannay, Clos du Roi, 1999
Domaine René Bouvier
Big, chunky and tannic. This is a bit tight. Plenty underneath. But it has gone into its shell. Very good. (January 2002)
NOW TO 2011   14.5

Marsannay, Clos du Roi, 1999
Domaine Jean Fournier
Yet more depth and interest. This has a bit of tannin and some fat. Very good. (January 2002)
NOW TO 2009   14.5

Marsannay, Clos Salomon, 1999
Domaine Collotte
Lots of depth here. Rich, fat and ripe. Medium-full body. This is very good. (January 2002)
NOW TO 2009   14.5

Marsannay, Les Échezeaux, 1999
Domaine Marc Brochet
Rather more concentration and personality than the Etalles. Good fruit. Ripe. Balanced. Even complex. Very good for what it is. (January 2002)
NOW TO 2009   14.5

Marsannay, Les Echézeaux, 1999
Domaine Jean Fournier
On the light side. Agreeable. Forward. (January 2002)
NOW TO 2010   15.0

Marsannay, Les Echézeaux, 1999
Domaine Huguenot Père et Fils
Ripe, fullish, opulent and very well balanced. Shows very well. Long. A lovely example. Very well mannered. (January 2002)
NOW TO 2010   15.0

Marsannay, Les Étalles, 1999
Domaine Marc Brochet
On the light side, but good grip and plump, succulent fruit. Finishes positively. Good. (January 2002)
NOW TO 2009   14.0

Marsannay, Les Étalles, 1999
Domaine Alain Guyard
Nice, juicy fruit here. Medium body. A good example. Plenty of personality at the end. (January 2002)
NOW TO 2009   14.0

Marsannay, Les Favières, 1999
Domaine du Vieux Collège
Good substance and tannin. A bit *sauvage*. But good depth and richness underneath. Long. Medium-full body. Very good. (January 2002)
NOW TO 2010   14.5

Marsannay, Les Finottes, 1999
Domaine Bart
Fat and rich. Fullish and succulent. Very good harmony and no lack of class. A very good example. (January 2002)
NOW TO 2009   14.0

Marsannay, Les Genelières, 1999
Domaine Alain Guyard
Rich, rocky soil at the top of a slope. A little more depth and substance. A little tannin. Good also. Perhaps his Etalles 1999 has more finesse. This is more classic. (January 2002)
NOW TO 2009   14.0

Marsannay, Les Longeroies, Vieilles Vignes, 1999
Domaine Régis Bouvier
Very good substance. A little tannin. Ample, fat and concentrated. Will still need a few years. Rich. Lovely. (January 2002)
NOW TO 2009   15.0

Marsannay, Les Longeroies, 1999
Domaine Bruno Clair
Good colour. Lightish but stylish, open, plump nose. Quite forward. Just about ready. Lots of charm. Light to medium body. Positive and harmonious. Good for what it is. (March 2002)
DRINK SOON   14.0

Marsannay, Les Longeroies, 1999
Domaine Collot

Lots of fruit. Ripe and rich. Good substance. Long. Subtle. Very good. (January 2002)

NOW-2009   14.5

Marsannay, Les Longeroies, 1999
Domaine Jean Fournier

Good personality. On the light side but good, plump fruit. Forward but good. (January 2002)

DRINK SOON   14.0

Marsannay, Les Longeroies, 1999
Domaine du Vieux Collège

Slight aspect of the rustic as a result of the stems. But good ripe, rich, ample fruit. Good plus. (January 2002)

NOW TO 2009   14.0

Marsannay, Ouzeloy, 1999
Domaine René Bouvier

Shows well. Very good ripe, fresh fruit. Full-ish body. Plenty of depth. Long and very good. (January 2002)

NOW TO 2011   14.5

Mazis-Chambertin, 1999
Domaine Camus Père et Fils

Good colour. Firm nose. Some stems but not too much undergrowth. Quite oaky on the palate. Fullish, ample, ripe and concentrated. This is very good indeed. But it lacks real flair and bite. Very easy to drink. Smooth and ripe. (January 2002)

NOW TO 2014   17.0

Mazis-Chambertin, 1999
Domaine Claude Dugat

Very full colour. Very lovely nose. Rich, full, fat and very concentrated. Not too much so, though. And oaky as well, although less than his Charmes. A big wine. Full bodied and tannic. But concentrated and rich. Hugely fruity. But is it too much? I don't think so. On the verge but not over it. (April 2005)

2010 TO 2030   18.5

Mazis-Chambertin, 1999
Domaine Bernard Dugat-Py

Very full colour. Full, quite solidly concentrated nose. No lack of oak. Not as tight as Claude Dugat's Charmes-Chambertin. And with slightly more profound, classy fruit. But full bodied, closed-in, intense and very lovely. Excellent grip. This is splendid. (March 2005)

2012 TO 2025+   19.0

Mazis-Chambertin, 1999
Domaine Dupont-Tisserandot

Good colour. Nice, meaty nose. Ample and rich with a touch of spice. Medium-full bodied and succulent on the palate. Good tannins. Not great (*grand cru*) personality, style or depth, but very good indeed. (October 2002)

NOW TO 2022   17.0

Mazis-Chambertin, 1999
Domaine Frédéric Esmonin

Medium-full colour. Slightly solid on the nose. Slightly dry and monolithic. Rich, full bodied, fat and tannic on the palate. Quite meaty. Good grip. This has a long, positive finish. But a slight lack of flair. Very good indeed though. (June 2003)

2009 TO 2025   17.0

Mazis-Chambertin, 1999
Domaine Joseph Faiveley

Medium-full colour. Slightly closed-in. But high-quality fruit and concentration here. Medium-full body. Very good tannins. Cool, intense and concentrated. Lovely fruit. Complex. Very long. Fine plus. (April 2005)

2009 TO 2025   18.0

Mazis-Chambertin, 1999
Maison Vincent Girardin

Full colour. Rich, round, gently oaky nose. Plenty of depth and interest here. Fullish body. Good backbone. Very good, concentrated, old-viney fruit. Lots of depth and class. Long. Fine. (April 2005)

2009 TO 2025+   17.5

Mazis-Chambertin, 1999
Domaine Harmand-Geoffroy

Very full colour. Quite oaky, and the fruit underneath is fresh and ripe but not too concentrated, so the oak tends to dominate. Medium-full body. Not too oaky on the palate. But it lacks a bit of style and grip. Merely good. (June 2003)

NOW TO 2025   15.0

Mazis-Chambertin, 1999
Domaine Bernard Maume

Medium-full colour. Some development. Quite a spicy nose. Even a touch of the rustic. Medium-full body. Ripe, ample and succulent. No lack of finesse. Slightly burly at the end, but balanced and very good indeed. (April 2005)

2009 TO 2024   17.0

Mazis-Chambertin, 1999
Domaine Philippe Naddef

Very full colour. Full, rich and meaty. Quite oaky but not too much so. Certainly very concentrated. Ripe on the palate. Quite full bodied. This has a bit too much new wood and tannins. Good grip. Slightly over the top. Very good plus. (April 2005)

NOW TO 2025   16.5

Mazis-Chambertin, 1999
Domaine Armand Rousseau

Rather weak-looking colour. Ripe nose. Quite forward. Potentially attenuated. Medium body. Ripe but weak-kneed. One-dimensional. Lacks grip, vigour, depth and concentration. Only fair. A bad bottle? (April 2005)

NOW TO 2011   13.0

Mazoyères-Chambertin, 1999
Domaine Henri Richard

Fine colour. A little more rustic than the Charmes. Rich, full and tannic. Very good grip. Very good, ripe fruit. But a slightly fiery, peppery aspect. Slightly more astringent than their Charmes. Very good plus. (January 2002)

NOW TO 2020   16.5

Monthelie, 1999
Domaine Bouchard Père et Fils

Bouchard's own domaine. Good colour. Ripe, plump, succulent, attractive nose. Medium body. Ample. Fresh and balanced. Quite forward. Good fruit. Good style. Quite good plus. (October 2001)

DRINK SOON   14.5

Monthelie, 1999
Domaine Jean Garaudet

Very good colour. Vigorous, meaty and slightly rustic on the nose. Medium-full body. Spicy. Quite soft underneath. Good fruit and acidity. Good with robust food. (October 2002)

NOW TO 2011   14.0

Monthelie, 1999
Domaine Pierre Morey

Good colour. Lovely Volnay-ish, stylish nose. Pure and well balanced. Medium body. Just a little tannin. Good, oaky base. Very long on the palate. Unexpectedly complex. Splendid for a village example. (March 2002)

NOW TO 2011   15.5

Monthelie, La Combe Danay, 1999
Domaine Rodolphe Demougeot

A touch of reduction but ripe, fresh and pleasant. Quite good. (June 2000)

DRINK SOON   14.0

Monthelie, Sur la Velle, 1999
Domaine Jacques and Annick Parent

Good colour. Lovely fragrant nose. Medium weight. Very elegant. Very succulent. A little tannin. Ripe and balanced. Volnay-ish. Very elegant. Good complexity. Very good. (June 2002)

NOW TO 2017   16.0

Morey-Saint-Denis, 1999
Domaine des Lambrays

Medium-full colour. Ripe, laid-back, stylish nose. Very good succulence. Very good grip. Cool, composed fruit. Medium to medium-full body. Still a little austere. Concentrated though. Very harmonious and elegant. Long and very lovely. Fine. (October 2001)

NOW TO 2021   17.5

Morey-Saint-Denis, 1999
Domaine Odoul-Coquard

From the Gevrey side. Good colour. Good substance. Perhaps it lacks a little finesse, but fruity and ample. Just slightly hot at the end. Quite good. (January 2002)

NOW TO 2010   14.0

Morey-Saint-Denis, Premier Cru, 1999
Domaine Dujac

Medium colour. A little evolution. Gently perfumed, sandal-woody oak on the nose. Very good fruit. Medium-full body. Not a bit stemmy. Good grip. Very long. Very classy. Chambolle-ish. Very good indeed. (September 2002)

NOW TO 2019   17.0

Morey-Saint-Denis, Premier Cru, 1999
Domaine des Lambrays

Fine colour. Very rich nose. Fullish, quite structured and with good acidity. Still some tannin. Good fruit. Quite sophisticated but not as much as their 2001. Slightly four-square. Good plus. (September 2004)

2009 TO 2019   15.5

Morey-Saint-Denis, Premier Cru, Vieilles Vignes, 1999
Domaine Hubert Lignier

Full colour. Concentrated and old viney. Rich and gently oaky. Lots of depth. Medium-full body. Rich and succulent. Lovely concentrated fruit. Very harmonious. Plenty of vigour. Lovely fresh wine. (June 2003)

2010 TO 2028   17.5

Morey-Saint-Denis, Aux Cheseaux, 1999
Domaine Hervé Arlaud

Full colour. Ripe, succulent, balanced, quite concentrated fruit on the nose. More expansive than the Ruchots. Richer, and with better balance and grip. This has a lot of depth. Lovely finish. Fine. (June 2003)

2009 TO 2028   17.5

Morey-Saint-Denis, Clos de la Buissière, 1999
Domaine Georges Roumier et Fils

Medium-full colour. Plump, agreeable nose. Not a bit robust or solid, just good depth. Fullish bodied on the palate. Just a touch solid on the palate. But good fruit and grip. Very good. (June 2003)

2009 TO 2025   16.0

Morey-Saint-Denis, Les Loups, 1999
Domaine des Lambrays

Full colour. Fragrant if not that concentrated on the nose. Ripe. A little stemmy. Slightly corky on the palate. Medium body. Ripe but not that exciting. Good intensity though. Good plus. (June 2003)

NOW TO 2020   15.5

Morey-Saint-Denis, Les Millandes, 1999
Domaine Sérafin Père et Fils

Very full colour. Classy nose. Ripe and rich. A little oaky. Lovely fruit. Fullish body. Quite oaky on the palate—perhaps a little too much. But balanced and succulent anyway. Very good plus. (June 2003)

2010 TO 2025   16.5

Morey-Saint-Denis, Clos la Riotte, 1999
Domaine Odoul-Coquard

The vines belong to the village. He makes the wine *en fermage*. Planted in 1983 with different clones as a sort of experiment. A monopole. Good colour. Fat, plump and fruity on the nose and attack. Good intensity. No hard edges. Ripe and seductive. Good grip. Long. Very good indeed. (January 2002)

NOW TO 2015   17.0

Morey-Saint-Denis, la Riotte, 1999
Domaine Taupenot-Merme

Old-vine richness and creaminess. Fullish body. Very lovely fruit. Very good grip and intensity. Very classy. This is a fine example. (January 2002)

NOW TO 2020   17.5

Morey-Saint-Denis, Les Ruchots, 1999
Domaine Hervé Arlaud

Fullish colour. Slightly tight on the nose. But good fruit underneath. Medium-full body. Ripe and balanced on the palate. Good tannins. Good ripeness. Long. Very good plus. (June 2003)

2009 TO 2025   16.5

Morey-Saint-Denis, En la Rue de Vergy, 1999
Domaine Régis Bouvier

Medium-full body. Gently oaky. Rich and ripe. Lots of personality and depth. Splendid, opulent fruit at the end. Very good plus. (January 2002)

NOW TO 2020   16.5

Musigny, 1999
Domaine Joseph Drouhin

Fullish colour. Some development. Marvellous fruit on the nose. Complex, aristocratic, very subtle and fragrant. On the palate medium-full body. Just a little tight on the attack but splendidly succulent on the aftertaste. Real concentration and intensity. Very fine indeed. (March 2006)

2009 TO 2028   19.5

Musigny, 1999
Domaine Jacques-Frédéric Mugnier

Full colour. Very lovely fruit on the nose. Soft but very intense. Ripe, rich, very well balanced and classy. Medium-full body. Brilliant fruit. Marvellous balance. Very, very long and subtle. Delicious. (June 2003)

2009 TO 2028   19.0

Musigny, 1999
Domaine Jacques Prieur

Full colour. Slightly ungainly on the nose. There is good fruit underneath though. But it is a bit corked. But I don't think the wine is special anyway. (June 2003)

(SEE NOTE)

Musigny, 1999
Domaine Comte Georges de Vogüé

Full colour. Marvellous nose. Rich, concentrated, classy and profound. Quite brilliant. Full bodied, tannic, backward, immensely concentrated and with great depth of character. Marvellous intensity of fruit. Very, very long and complex and classy. Perfect! (June 2003)

2015 TO 2040   20.0

Musigny, 1999
Domaine de la Vougeraie

Full colour. Soft, aromatic, ripe fruit on the nose. Very good class. I don't thinnk this has the grip of the Bonnes-Mares, but it has nevertheless some very, very lovely fruit. Medium-full body. Quite long. Fine. (June 2003)

2009 TO 2028   17.5

Nuits-Saint-Georges, 1999
Domaine Odoul-Coquard

From two parcels. Will isolate the Argillas from 2001. The best of the three 1999s. Plump, rich and positive. Not hot. Good fruit. Ripe tannins. Good structure. Ripe and long on the palate. Good. (January 2002)

NOW TO 2012   15.0

Nuits-Saint-Georges, Les Argillières, 1999
Château de Premeaux

Fine colour. Ripe, medium weight nose. Slightly vegetal. Not exactly very rich or concentrated. A touch of oak. Quite elegant. Medium body. Quite stylish. Just a little tannin. Decently balanced but not a great deal of depth. Good plus at best. Better as it evolved in the glass. (March 2002)

NOW TO 2010   15.5

Nuits-Saint-Georges, Aux Boudots, 1999
Domaine Jean-Jacques Confuron

Fullish colour. Classy, succulent, gently oaky nose. Fullish. Slight touch of caramel and vanilla. Good, ripe tannins. Good grip. This is poised, harmonious and full of finesse. Nothing aggressive here. Long and complex. Rich and profound. Fine. (March 2003)

NOW TO 2020   17.5

Nuits-Saint-Georges, Aux Boudots, 1999
Domaine Jean-Jacques Confuron

Full colour. Attractive, rich, oaky nose. Fullish body. Very good grip and nicely oaky on the palate. Plump, ripe and most attractive. Lovely long finish. Fine quality. (June 2003)

2010 TO 2025   17.5

Nuits-Saint-Georges, Les Boudots, 1999
Domaine Jean Grivot

Medium-full colour. Very impressive nose. Rich, full, ample and classy. Still very young. Fullish body on the palate. Very good grip and very ripe tannins. But it is the excellence of the expression of the fruit which really impresses. Very classy. Multidimensional. Fine plus. (March 2003)

2010 TO 2025   18.0

Nuits-Saint-Georges, Aux Boudots, 1999
Domaine Méo-Camuzet

Full colour. Oaky nose. Rich and succulent. Medium-full body. Less sturdy than the Murgers. A better expression of fruit. And good elegance at the end. Fine. (June 2003)

2010 TO 2025   17.5

Nuits-Saint-Georges, Les Boudots, 1999
Domaine Gérard Mugneret

Fullish colour. Fresh, gently oaky, very stylish nose. Medium-full body. Ripe. Perhaps not quite the depth of J. J. Confuron's, but balanced and nicely fresh. Very good indeed. (March 2003)

NOW TO 2018   17.0

Nuits-Saint-Georges, Aux Boudots, 1999
Domaine Jean Tardy et Fils

Fine, full colour. Quite a lot of oak on the nose. Fat, fullish, seductive wine. Easy to drink. Good but not great concentration and intensity, but seductive. Very good, but not the greatest class and individuality. (October 2001)

NOW TO 2021   16.0

Nuits-Saint-Georges, Aux Brûlées, 1999
Domaine Henri Gille Père et Fils

Ripe and rich. Very good tannins. Lovely fruit. Fullish body. Succulent, long, complex and classy. This is very good indeed for what it is. (February 2003)

2009 TO 2018   16.0

Nuits-Saint-Georges, Les Cailles, 1999
Domaine Bouchard Père et Fils

Fullish colour. Plenty of depth and concentration here on the nose. High quality. Full bodied, rich, backward and tannic. Lots of depth on the palate. Vigorous at the end. Fine. (June 2003)

2011 TO 2028   17.5

Nuits-Saint-Georges, Aux Chaignots, 1999
Domaine Joseph Faiveley

Medium-full colour. Rather closed still on the nose. Ripe. Fullish. Good grip. Still a bit raw. Fullish body. Best at the end. Good fruit and plenty of depth. But very good rather than fine. (June 2003)

2010 TO 2025   16.0

Nuits-Saint-Georges, Les Chaignots, 1999
Domaine Henri Gouges

Impressive quality. Good colour. Lovely fruit. Rich and fat. Very good tannins. Lovely balance. Very classy for a Nuits-Saint-Georges. Not a bit dense or muscular. Clean and classy. Very long and complex. Fine. (June 2004)

2009 TO 2025   17.5

Nuits-Saint-Georges, Aux Chaignots, 1999
Domaine Alain Michelot

Medium-full colour. Ripe, aromatic nose. Succulent. Fresh. Good class. Medium-full body. Not a lot of tannin. Very good acidity. Round and sweet. Very stylish and very concentrated. Lovely finish. Very good indeed. (March 2005)

NOW TO 2020   17.0

Nuits-Saint-Georges, Aux Chaignots, 1999
Domaine Dr. Georges Mugneret

Medium-full colour. Rich, succulent, oaky nose. Very attractive. Medium to medium-full body. Ripe and accessible—more so than most. Not the greatest of depth and concentration, but very good plus. (June 2003)

2009 TO 2020   16.5

Nuits-Saint-Georges, Les Chaignots, 1999
Domaine Gérard Mugneret

Fullish colour. Very fine fruit on the nose. Really Vosne-ish. Concentrated. Fullish body. Lovely plump and generous wine. Long and fresh. Classy. Fine.

NOW TO 2020   17.5

Nuits-Saint-Georges, Chaînes Carteaux, 1999
Domaine Louis Jadot

Medium-full colour. Slightly raw on the nose. Very good fruit on the palate. Quite full. Good acidity.

Ample, ripe, complex and harmonious. Very good follow-through. Very good plus. (June 2003)

2010 TO 2025   16.5

Nuits-Saint-Georges, Chaînes Carteaux, 1999
Domaine Bernard Serveau

Medium colour. Slightly lean on the nose. A bit meagre, too. Medium to medium-full body. Better on the palate. Good fruit here. Good acidity too. It lacks a little flair but quite good plus. (October 2002)

NOW TO 2010   14.5

Nuits-Saint-Georges, Clos l'Arlot, 1999
Domaine de l'Arlot

Medium-full colour. Ripe nose. Some stems. Medium body. Not a lot of tannin. Fresh and fruity. Balanced. But too stemmy for my taste. Good for what it is. (June 2003)

NOW TO 2020   15.0

Nuits-Saint-Georges, Clos des Forêts, 1999
Domaine de l'Arlot

Medium-full colour. Quite a bit richer and fatter and therefore less stemmy than the Clos de L'Arlot. Fullish body. A lot more depth and concentration. Good grip. Very good plus. (June 2003)

2009 TO 2024   16.5

Nuits-Saint-Georges, Clos des Porrets
Saint-Georges, 1999
Domaine Henri Gouges

Full colour. Still a little dense and immature on the nose. Rich. Full. Slightly tannic. Yet the fruit is classy, concentrated and fragrant. Lots of depth. Plummy. Virile. Lots of succulence potentially. Very good indeed. (May 2005)

2009 TO 2025   17.0

Nuits-Saint-Georges, Clos des Porrets
Saint-Georges, 1999
Domaine Henri Gouges

Good colour. Full, backward, rich, plummy nose. Fullish body. Good tannins. Slightly spicy. Good grip. Still closed, but impressively long and complex at the end. Fine. (March 2002)

NOW TO 2020   17.5

Nuits-Saint-Georges, Clos des Porrets
Saint-Georges, 1999
Domaine Henri Gouges

Fullish colour. Lovely pure, vibrant nose. Very classy for a Nuits. Splendidly intense, fragrant fruit. Fullish body. Very good tannins. Succulent and classy. Very finely balanced. Complex, long and of fine quality. (October 2002)

NOW TO 2028   17.5

Nuits-Saint-Georges, Aux Cras, 1999
Domaine Bruno Clavelier

Full colour. Slight touch of diesel on the nose. Medium-full body. Balanced, cool and reasonably concentrated. But the bizarre smell persists. A rogue bottle? Good plus otherwise. (June 2003)

NOW TO 2020   15.5

Nuits-Saint-Georges, Aux Cras, 1999
Maison Nicolas Potel

Full colour. Good fruit with some oak on the nose. Not as concentrated as some. Fullish body. Decent attack. Balanced and fruity. But it doesn't have the depth of the best. Very good. (June 2003)

2009 TO 2022   16.0

Nuits-Saint-Georges, Les Fleurières, 1999
Domaine Jean-Jacques Confuron

Village *appellation contrôlée*. Good colour. Quite an earthy nose, with a suggestion of reduction. Good fruit. Medium to medium-full body. Ripe and ample. Not a great deal of grip. But soft and succulent, and will develop quite soon. Good plus. (September 2002)

NOW TO 2016   15.5

Nuits-Saint-Georges, Aux Murgers, 1999
Domaine Bertagna

Full colour. Splendidly rich, oaky nose. Lots of depth and quality here. Full body. Very good tannins. Ample and succulent. Very good grip. This has lots of plump, sophisticated fruit. Fine plus. (October 2002)

2009 TO 2028   18.0

Nuits-Saint-Georges, Aux Murgers, 1999
Domaine Sylvain Cathiard
Full colour. Ripe, concentrated, slightly austere nose. Good depth but backward. Fullish body. The tannins are ripe, and the wine has very good balance and lovely fruit. It finishes long and complex. Fine. (June 2003)
2012 TO 2025   17.5

Nuits-Saint-Georges, Aux Murgers, 1999
Domaine Arnaud Chopin et Fils
Full colour. Ripe, sturdy nose. Good concentration underneath. Medium-full body. Fresh and attractive. Some tannin. Good depth. This is long, stylish and complex. Very good indeed. (June 2003)
2010 TO 2025   17.0

Nuits-Saint-Georges, Aux Murgers, 1999
Domaine Méo-Camuzet
Full colour. Backward, rich, concentrated, oaky nose. Quite a sturdy wine on the palate. Good grip. No lack of oak. It needs time. Still quite tannic. Good, positive finish. Very good indeed. (June 2003)
2010 TO 2025   17.0

Nuits-Saint-Georges, Aux Perdrix, 1999
Domaine des Perdrix
Fullish colour. Stylish, fruity, quite profound nose. Gently oaky. Full, balanced and rich. Good grip. This has plenty of personality and quality. It finishes very well. Very good indeed. (June 2003)
2010 TO 2025   17.0

Nuits-Saint-Georges, En la Perrière Noblot, 1999
Domaine Machard de Gramont
This is fullish, quite tannic, quite firm still. But with good concentration and richness if no enormous class. Good grip. Meaty. Needs time. Good plus. (February 2003)
2010 TO 2016   15.5

Nuits-Saint-Georges, Les Porrets Saint-Georges, 1999
Maison Antonin Rodet
Full colour. Mellow, ripe, oaky nose. Fullish bodied, rich, oaky and opulent. Good tannins.

Very good grip. This is seductive, long and fine. (June 2003)
2010 TO 2025   17.5

Nuits-Saint-Georges, Les Poulettes, 1999
Domaine de la Poulette
Quite different. Dry on the nose to the point of austerity. Medium body. Some tannin. A bit over-extracted. Yet good fruit and grip underneath. Slightly astringent. Quite good. (February 2003)
NOW TO 2012   14.0

Nuits-Saint-Georges, Les Procès, 1999
Maison Joseph Drouhin
Medium colour. Ripe, round, soft, succulent nose. Fully ready but by no means over-evolved. Medium to medium-full body. Lovely fruit. Balanced, round and ripe. Lovely fruit. Soft and fragrant. Fine. (July 2006)
NOW TO 2012   17.5

Nuits-Saint-Georges, Les Pruliers, 1999
Domaine Henri Gouges
Full colour. Very lovely plummy fruit on the nose. On the palate full bodied, backward and tannic, but with very good grip and concentration, and lovely fruit all the way through. Long. Very classy. Fine. (June 2003)
2010 TO 2028   17.5

Nuits-Saint-Georges, Les Pruliers, 1999
Domaine Jean Grivot
Full colour. Attractive fruit on the nose and a touch of oak. Fullish body. Very good tannins. Lovely concentrated fruit. Very good balancing acidity. This is cool, classy and complex. Fine plus. (June 2003)
2010 TO 2025   18.0

Nuits-Saint-Georges, Les Pruliers, 1999
Domaine Philippe and Vincent Lécheneaut
Medium-full colour. Fullish, sturdy, rich nose. But good tannins. Full body on the palate. Rich and quite sturdy. Very good, rich fruit. Very good acidity. Quite accessible already. Stylish and profound. Fine. (March 2002)
NOW TO 2025   17.5

Nuits-Saint-Georges, Les Pruliers, 1999
Domaine Taupenot-Merme
This is a little meagre. Some substance. Some tannin. Good fruit on the attack but not as ample as it should be on the follow-through. Is this a phase? (January 2002)

NOW TO 2020   15.5

Nuits-Saint-Georges, Rue de Chaux, 1999
Domaine Pierre Thubert
This is very good. Not a blockbuster though. Gently oaky. Ripe, rich, balanced and stylish. A feminine example for 1999. Long, complex and elegant. Perhaps a little light. Within its context not as good as the 2000 but very good plus. (February 2003)

NOW TO 2012   15.5

Nuits-Saint-Georges, Les Saint-Georges, 1999
Domaine Joseph Faiveley
Full colour. Rich nose. Real depth and concentration. Lots of energy. Full body. Still some tannin. Very good grip. Ripe tannins. No robustness. Long. Fine. (June 2003)

2009 TO 2025   17.5

Nuits-Saint-Georges, Les Saint-Georges, 1999
Domaine Henri Gouges
Good, full colour. Still youthful. Full, firm nose but not hard. Rich and concentrated. Lots of depth and a great deal of class. Full body. Very good, ripe tannins. A profound, concentrated wine. Very lovely fruit. Complex, balanced and classy. Long. Lovely. Fine plus. (September 2003)

2011 TO 2035   18.0

Nuits-Saint-Georges, Les Saint-Georges, 1999
Maison Lucien le Moine
Full colour. This is a modern wine. Rich, oaky, fat, full but very berry fruit. Dominique Laurent-ish. Not over-macerated though. Very seductive. Fine, perhaps. But not to my taste. (January 2002)

(SEE NOTE)   17.5

Nuits-Saint-Georges, Les Saint-Georges, 1999
Maison Antonin Rodet
Full colour. Good weight on the nose. Concentrated fruit and a touch of oak. Fullish body.

Very good tannins. Just a touch of oak. Classy and succulent. Quite accessible. This is long and very impressive. Fine plus. (June 2003)

2010 TO 2028   18.0

Nuits-Saint-Georges, Les Vaucrains, 1999
Domaine Henri Gouges
Full colour. Closed-in nose. Slightly tough. Lots of depth. Concentrated and backward. As always, quite backward and sturdy. The tannins show. But the finish is impressive. It needs time. Fine. (June 2003)

2012 TO 2025   17.5

Nuits-Saint-Georges, Les Vaucrains, 1999
Maison Dominique Laurent
Very good colour. Full, concentrated nose. Quite structured. Currently a little tough. Quite marked by the oak. Full and rich. Lots of depth and quality. But quite modern. Needs time. Exactly how elegant is it? Is it a little dry at the end? (October 2002)

2010 TO 2020   17.0

Nuits-Saint-Georges, Aux Vignerondes, 1999
Domaine Joseph Faiveley
Medium-full colour. Good fruit here. Quite reserved. Medium-full body. A little tannin. It seems to be just a little hard and fruitless compared with most. But it needs time. Merely good. (June 2003)

2010 TO 2020   15.0

Pernand-Vergelesses, 1999
Maison Champy
Clean, fresh and stylish. Gently oaky. Good substance. This has unexpected depth, class and interest. Good. (October 2001)

DRINK SOON   15.0

Pernand-Vergelesses, 1999
Domaine Germain Père et Fils/
Château de Chorey-lès-Beaune
Fresh, ripe and succulent. Gently oaky. Very good grip. Unexpected depth and quality for what it is. Really stylish. Just about ready. (March 2002)

DRINK SOON   14.5

Pernand-Vergelesses, 1999
Domaine Michel Voarick

Good colour. Plenty of depth, fruit, class and interest. Fullish for a Pernand-Vergelesses village. Still a bit of tannin. But the tannins are ripe and round. Lots of depth. Rich at the end. Very good, indeed, for what it is. (February 2003)

NOW TO 2011   15.5

Pernand-Vergelesses, Clos de la Croix de Pierre, 1999
Domaine Louis Jadot

Perfumed, cherry-raspberry fruit. Balanced. Very stylish. Medium to medium-full body. Lovely finish. Very classy. (March 2005)

NOW TO 2014   15.5

Pernand-Vergelesses, Ile de Vergelesses, 1999
Domaine Chandon de Briailles

Good colour. Very stylish, fragrant nose. Not a blockbuster. Nicely ripe in a slightly lean sort of way. Good grip. Complex, long and individual. Very good plus. (March 2002)

NOW TO 2014   15.5

Pernand-Vergelesses, Ile de Vergelesses, 1999
Domaine Marius Delarche

This is not nearly as good as his 2001. Just like the 2000, it is a bit hollow. More to it, of course, but it lacks real substance. Yet the fruit is balanced and elegant. (February 2003)

DRINK SOON   14.0

Pernand-Vergelesses, Ile de Vergelesses, 1999
Domaine Denis Père et Fils

Proportionately not nearly as good as their 2000. Pleasant fruit but no backbone. Indeed a bit hollow. Forward. Only fair. (February 2003)

DRINK SOON   13.0

Pommard, 1999
Domaine Rodolphe Demougeot

From a *lieu-dit* which gives a high harvest. This is *saignée*-d regularly to concentrate the juice. A round, forward, supple example. Good fruit but not much depth. Stylish and balanced, but drink soon. Quite good. (June 2000)

NOW TO 2010   14.0

Pommard, Bertins, 1999
Domaine Chantal Lescure

Good colour. Muddy, astringent, far too extracted nose. Raw and unpleasant. Similar palate. No. (June 2003)

NOW TO 2009   10.0

Pommard, La Chanière, 1999
Domaine Maillard Père et Fils

Village *appellation contrôlée*. Rich, full, but not too sturdy. Ripe and substantial, but neither austere nor dense. Lovely fruit. Very good grip. A very good example. (February 2003)

NOW TO 2014   15.0

Pommard, Les Chanlins, Vieilles Vignes, 1999
Maison Vincent Girardin

Fine colour. One bottle slightly tough and slightly reduced. Full, rich and quite tannic. On the palate fullish, ripe and with very good acidity. Good, well-covered tannins. Lots of depth. Still young. Good concentration. Finishes very well. A typical good, chunky Pommard. Needs time. (October 2002)

NOW TO 2019   16.0

Pommard, Les Chaponnières, 1999
Domaine Philippe Billard-Gonnet

Medium-full colour. Fragrant, balanced and not too solid on the nose. Most attractive. Medium-full body. Ripe, balanced, supple and quite intense at the end. Long and classy. Very good plus. (June 2003)

NOW TO 2020   16.5

Pommard, Les Chaponnières, 1999
Maison Vincent Girardin

Good colour. Good, ripe fruit and a touch of oak on the nose. Fullish, meaty and chunky, but with very good grip. All this needs is time. Long and succulent. Very vigorous. Very good indeed. (June 2003)

2009 TO 2025   17.0

Pommard, Charmots, 1999
Maison Olivier Leflaive Frères

Good colour. Medium weight. Ripe nose. Not the greatest of depth, but the balance is correct.

On the palate it is a bit weedy for a 1999 Pommard, and a little astringent at the end. Disappointing. (June 2003)

NOW TO 2010   13.0

Pommard, Clos Blanc, 1999
Maison Antonin Rodet

Medium-full colour. Rich, full and meaty on the nose, but classy and succulent, too. Fullish body. Plenty of depth. Ripe and persistent. Classy. This is very good indeed. (June 2003)

2009 TO 2025   17.0

Pommard, Clos des Epeneaux, 1999
Domaine du Comte Armand

Full colour. Rich and opulent, but firm and tannic on the nose. Full bodied, tannic, closed and backward at first on the palate. But hugely rich and concentrated underneath. The tannins are very ripe. Black fruit flavours. Lots of substance here. Fine plus. But does it have the nuance of the best Volnays? It is not as intense. (February 2003)

2010 TO 2028   18.0

Pommard, Clos de Verger, 1999
Domaine Philippe Billard-Gonnet

Good colour. Lighter on the nose than some, but balanced and fruity. Medium to medium-full body. A little astringent. Not enough grip. The finish is better though. Quite good. (June 2003)

NOW TO 2016   14.0

Pommard, Croix Noires, 1999
Domaine de Courcel

Medium-full colour. Vinified with the stems, says the nose. Fruit but slightly weedy. Light on the palate. Forward. Decent fruit but no dimension. (June 2003)

NOW TO 2009   13.0

Pommard, Epenots, 1999
Maison Vincent Girardin

Good colour. Lots of oak on the nose. It hides the wine underneath. Slightly reduced. This is very hard to judge. I think the base wine is good. But has it been over-oaked? Possibly. (June 2003)

2009 TO 2015   11.0

Pommard, Epenots, 1999
Domaine Pierre Morey

Good colour. Quite a chunky nose but good class underneath. Good fruit too. Fullish body. Rich tannin and ripe. Not quite enough personality for better than very good though. (June 2003)

NOW TO 2020   16.0

Pommard, Epenots, 1999
Maison Nicolas Potel

Medium-full colour. Old viney, rich, creamy, ripe and succulent. Most impressive. Medium-full body. Balanced, ripe, profound and intense. This is long and very elegant. Lovely finish. Very good indeed. (June 2003)

2009 TO 2024   17.0

Pommard, Epenots, 1999
Maison Antonin Rodet

Good colour. Fresh, high-toned nose. Plump, ripe and slightly chunky, but good class. Ripe, ripe, fullish bodied and chunky. Some tannin. Good grip. Long at the end. Very good. Needs time. (June 2003)

2010 TO 2025   16.0

Pommard, Epenots, 1999
Domaine le Royer Girardin

Good colour. Abundant, ripe, concentrated nose. Very impressive. Splendidly rich on the palate. Old-viney depth here. Full body. Some tannin but very good grip. Potentially fine. Will need time. A big wine. (June 2003)

2010 TO 2028   17.5

Pommard, Frémiets, 1999
Domaine de Courcel

Good colour. Richer and fatter than the Croix Noires. Much less stemmy. Quite ripe on the palate. Juicy. Medium to medium-full body. Balanced, supple and stylish. It finishes well. Very good. (June 2003)

NOW TO 2019   16.0

Pommard, Grand Clos des Epenots, 1999
Domaine de Courcel

Good colour. Rich, ripe and succulent, with some evidence of the stems on the nose. On the palate medium-full bodied, slightly astringent and lacking a bit of flair, but the finish is better and very long. But merely very good. (June 2003)
NOW TO 2020 16.0

Pommard, Les Grands Epenots, 1999
Domaine Michel Gaunoux

Good colour. Ripe, ample, plump nose. Full-ish body. Some tannin. Vigorous and with very good grip. Quite backward but very promising. Concentrated and classy. Plenty of dimension here. Fine. (March 2002)
NOW TO 2025 17.5

Pommard, Grands Epenots, 1999
Domaine Hubert de Montille

Medium to medium-full colour. Good nose but not quite the depth of the Pézerolles. Rather drier and weedier. Medium to medium-full body. It doesn't have the grip or the concentration. A bit weak. Quite good at best. (June 2003)
NOW TO 2016 14.0

Pommard, Jarollières, 1999
Domaine Jean-Marc Boillot

Good colour. Full, rich and with some oak. Black cherry–flavoured nose. Quite a meaty example. Medium-full body. Some tannin. Very good acidity. Long and intense. Very good plus. (June 2003)
2009 TO 2022 16.5

Pommard, Les Perrières, 1999
Domaine Jean-Michel Gaunoux

The vines lie under the Epenots. Elegant and rich. Not a blockbuster. Ripe, round and stylish. Lovely ripe fruit. Very good for what it is. (June 2000)
2009 TO 2022 16.5

Pommard, Les Petits Noizons, 1999
Domaine de la Vougeraie

Medium-full colour. A little development. Soft, quite spicy, slightly toffee-flavoured on the nose. Quite approachable on the palate. Medium to medium-full body. The tannins are now soft. Good freshness. A slight absence of real style, but accessible and enjoyable. (June 2006)
NOW TO 2015 15.5

Pommard, Les Pézerolles, 1999
Domaine Ballot Millot

Good colour. Stylish fruit on the nose. Silky and old viney. Medium to medium-full weight. This is rich and stylish on the attack. A slight lack of real grip, so it tails off just a little. But very good. (June 2003)
NOW TO 2028 16.0

Pommard, Les Pézerolles, 1999
Domaine Philippe Billard-Gonnet

Medium-full colour. Rich, full and slightly oaky on the nose. This is a little closed and adolescent on the attack. Better on the finish. Fullish body. Rich, balanced and succulent. Very good plus. (June 2003)
NOW TO 2020 16.5

Pommard, Les Pézerolles, 1999
Domaine Vincent Dancer

Very good colour. Rich. Quite oaky. Good Pommard size and density, but not chunky. Ripe, plump, nicely concentrated fruit. Very good. (June 2000)
NOW TO 2015 16.0

Pommard, Les Pézerolles, 1999
Domaine Michel Lafarge

Good colour. Ripe and succulent on the nose. Good depth. Old viney. Not a bit solid, yet full bodied and meaty. Plump and ripe. Long. Very good plus. (June 2003)
NOW TO 2020 16.5

Pommard, Les Pézerolles, 1999
Domaine Hubert de Montille

Medium colour. Fragrant nose. Stylish, ripe fruit here. Not a bit too solid. Medium-full body. Ripe and intense. Very good grip. Not a blockbuster, but quite long. intense and classy. Very good. (June 2003)
NOW TO 2023 16.0

Pommard, Les Rugiens, 1999
Domaine Ballot Millot
Full colour. Fresh, plump and fruity on the nose. Fullish but not too chunky. Rich. Very good grip. This is succulent and with very good length. Very good indeed. (June 2003)
2009 TO 2023   17.5

Pommard, Les Rugiens, 1999
Domaine Bouchard Père et Fils
Medium-full colour. Rich and full. Backward. Fat, plump and impressive. Lots of depth here. Full bodied, tannic, meaty and with very good depth. This is backward but impressive. Lovely long, intense finish. Fine. (June 2003)
2010 TO 2025   17.5

Pommard, Les Rugiens, 1999
Domaine de Courcel
Medium-full colour. Some stems. Not enough backbone and richness on the nose. I find this better than their Epenots, but just. Medium-full body. Ripe and succulent on the palate. Good acidity. Long and positive. Very good plus. (June 2003)
NOW TO 2020   16.5

Pommard, Les Rugiens, 1999
Maison Vincent Girardin
Full colour. Firm, full, oaky and concentrated on the nose. Old viney and very profound. Excellent fruit. Fullish body. Rich. Very good tannins. Fine grip. This is really fine plus. Splendidly elegant and complex at the end. (March 2002)
NOW TO 2020   16.5

Pommard, Les Rugiens, 1999
Maison Olivier Leflaive Frères
Medium to medium-full colour. Rich, succulent, well-integrated wine. Velvety and ripe. Medium to medium-full body. Rather better than their Charmots. Good fruit. Fresh acidity. Ripe tannins. Long finish. Very good plus. (June 2003)
NOW TO 2020   16.5

Pommard, Les Rugiens, 1999
Domaine Hubert de Montille
Full colour. Fatter and richer than most of the Montille wines. And all the better for it.

Medium-full body. Supple, succulent and stylish. Very good acidity. Very good plus. (June 2003)
NOW TO 2020   16.5

Pommard, Les Rugiens, 1999
Domaine Annick Parent
Full colour. Fresh and individual. Rich, balanced and very stylish. Full body. Very rich, very tannic, ripe and full of energy. This is multidimensional. But it needs time. Excellent finish. Fine plus. (June 2003)
2009 TO 2028   18.0

Pommard, Rugiens, 1999
Maison Nicolas Potel
Good colour. Splendidly rich nose. Ample, concentrated and full but not burly. Fullish body. Very concentrated on the palate. Very good tannins. Excellent depth and grip. Vigorous. Classy and profound. Fine finish. Fine quality. (October 2002)
NOW TO 2028   17.5

Pommard, Les Rugiens, 1999
Domaine Charles Thomas
Fullish, immature colour. Rich nose. Ample. Some oak. Nicely full and firm, but with very good grip. The tannins are ripe, and there is plenty of depth. Good energy. Long. Fine. (May 2002)
NOW TO 2030   17.5

Pommard, Saucilles, 1999
Domaine Jean-Marc Boillot
Good colour. Very similar to the Jarollières on the nose. A little riper perhaps. A touch less fat on the palate and a little more astringent. But once again, positive at the end. Good plus. (June 2003)
2009 TO 2018   15.5

Pommard, Les Vignots, 1999
Domaine Rodolphe Demougeot
Some reduction but nevertheless rich, ripe and succulent. Good grip. Good intensity. Long. Promising. Fine for a village example. (June 2000)
NOW TO 2025   17.5

Richebourg, 1999
Domaine Jean Grivot

Full colour. Very different from that of Anne Gros but very fine as well. Cool, fullish bodied and backward. Very concentrated. Very intense. Lovely grip. Very long. Very exciting. (June 2003)

2010 TO 2030   20.0

Richebourg, 1999
Domaine Anne Gros

Very fine colour. Marvellous nose. Full, concentrated, rich, profound, very elegant and complex. Still very young. Full body. Excellent grip. Very concentrated. Very fine tannins. This is clearly superior to the more recent vintages. Splendid fruit. Very, very long and multidimensional. A great wine! (February 2004)

2012 TO 2042   20.0

Richebourg, 1999
Domaine Méo-Camuzet

Very good colour. Quite a sturdy, oaky, tannic nose. This is a big wine. Splendid fruit underneath. Fullish bodied, certainly quite oaky. Rich, abundant and opulent. Concentrated and very finely balanced. A much more masculine wine than the Confuron's Romanée-Saint-Vivant. A little tight at the end but lots of vigour here. Very fine. (May 2003)

2011 TO 2038   18.5

Richebourg, 1999
Domaine Mongeard-Mugneret

Medium-full colour. Rather stemmy and rustic on the nose. There isn't much class here. Rather disappointing for Richebourg. Medium to medium-full body. A little thin. Not much grip. Will get attenuated. This is a bit of a disgrace. Forward. (March 2005)

DRINK SOON   13.0

Richebourg, 1999
Domaine de la Romanée-Conti

Full, youthful colour. Rich, very intense, full, ripe, even sweet on the nose. Neither undue stems nor new oak. Very, very fragrant. Very lovely. Fullish body. Balanced, long and intense.

The usual voluptuous element I associate with Richebourg. Really quite concentrated. Very fine. Needs time. (March 2006)

2011 TO 2030   18.5

La Romanée, 1999
Domaine Bouchard Père et Fils

Medium-full colour. A little development. Fullish and a little lumpy on the nose compared with the Liger-Belair wines today. Quite sturdy. Good grip. Fine but not the class and nuance of what is being produced today—or the best of the vintage. It needs time. (March 2006)

2011 TO 2025   17.5

Romanée-Conti, 1999
Domaine de la Romanée-Conti

Very fine colour. More delicate on the nose than La Tâche. Feminine like the Romanée-Saint-Vivant. Very beautiful, ripe, harmonious fruit. Fullish body. Excellent acidity. Cool and poised. Rich and intense. Complex and very, very aristocratic. Terrific! (July 2003)

2012 TO 2035   20.0

Romanée-Saint-Vivant, 1999
Domaine Robert Arnoux

Fullish colour. Rich, full, opulent, seductive nose with a touch of oak. Very high quality here. Full body. Very, very rich and ripe fruit on the palate. Balanced and intense. Not a bit too extracted or over-oaky. Just very lovely indeed. (June 2003)

2010 TO 2030   18.5

Romanée-Saint-Vivant, 1999
Domaine Sylvain Cathiard

Fullish colour. Marvellous fragrant nose. This is a beautiful bottle. Balanced, gentle, soft but intense. Fullish body. Gently oaky. Excellent grip. This has very lovely, pure fruit and is very long on the palate. Very lovely. (June 2003)

2010 TO 2030   19.0

Romanée-Saint-Vivant, 1999
Domaine Jean-Jacques Confuron

Medium-full colour. Round, rich, ample and concentrated on the nose. Quite accessible.

Very classy. Not a blockbuster but quite delicious. Excellent fruit. Lovely harmony. Very gently oaky. Everything in place. Very seductive. Very classy. Very fine. (March 2005)

2009 TO 2025   18.5

Romanée-Saint-Vivant, 1999
Domaine Alain Hudelot-Noëllat

Full colour. Rich and ripe on the nose. Not quite the intensity and class of some of the other Romanée-Saint-Vivants though. Medium-full body. Abundant. Lovely fruit. Balanced and opulent. Very fine. (June 2003)

2009 TO 2028   18.5

Romanée-Saint-Vivant, 1999
Maison Louis Jadot

Medium-full colour. Still youthful. Fragrant nose. Lots of lovely plump, balanced, elegant fruit. Quite approachable. Very high quality. This is very intense and very elegant. Very subtle and multidimensional. Fullish body. Not so much tannin as just a little raw. Very fine plus. (March 2006)

2011 TO 2030   19.0

Romanée-Saint-Vivant, 1999
Domaine de la Romanée-Conti

Fine colour. Very refined nose. This is brilliantly silky smooth. Fullish body. Very intense. Very poised. Lovely balance. Complex and utterly beguiling. Very, very long on the palate again. (July 2003)

2011 TO 2030   19.0

Romanée-Saint-Vivant, 1999
Domaine Charles Thomas

Full colour. Quite tough on the nose. It smells of yeast extract. Good, more civilised on aeration. Some oak. Still rather tough on the palate. Astringent and lumpy. Over-extracted. I don't think much of this. (June 2003)

2010 TO 2030   14.0

Ruchottes-Chambertin, 1999
Domaine Dr. Georges Mugneret

Fullish colour. Rich, succulent, very classy nose. Fullish body. Very harmonious. Fullish body on the palate. Very lovely, classy fruit. Slightly cool. Yet ample and generous. Finely balanced and very profound. Excellent. (April 2005)

2009 TO 2025+   18.5

Ruchottes-Chambertin, Clos des Ruchottes, 1999
Domaine Armand Rousseau

Medium-full colour. Good, quite firm, classy nose. Lots of depth. Medium-full body. Not the greatest of concentration. Quite fresh. Ripe and stylish. Very good plus but not brilliant. (June 2003)

NOW TO 2021   16.5

Santenay, En Bievau, 1999
Domaine Bart

A good, fragrant village example. Plump. Ripe. Stylish. Medium body. Positive finish. Good tannins. (January 2002)

NOW TO 2010   14.5

Santenay, Beauregard, 1999
Domaine Roger Belland

Good colour. Fresh, rich nose. Slightly herbal in an interesting sort of way. Fullish body, but the tannins are soft. The wine is succulent, balanced and vigorous. Already very drinkable. Lovely fruit. Rich at the end. Very good, indeed, for what it is. (May 2004)

NOW TO 2015   16.5

Santenay, Beaurepaire, 1999
Domaine Sorine et Fils

Medium to medium-full, mature colour. Ripe, fragrant nose. Medium-full body. Round, succulent, ripe fruit. Balanced and attractive. Very good for what it is. Now ready. (October 2005)

NOW TO 2013   15.5

Santenay, Clos Genêt, 1999
Maison Champy

Soft. Lightish. *À point*. Not a lot of weight, but neat, fruity and ready now. (October 2003)

DRINK SOON   14.0

Santenay, Clos de Malte, 1999
Domaine Louis Jadot

Good colour. Fresh, ripe and succulent on the nose. Medium body. Little tannin. Now soft. A generous, agreable wine. No great depth, but pleasant and stylish. (March 2005)

NOW TO 2010　　　　　　　　　　　15.0

Santenay, Clos Rousseau, 1999
Domaine Lénaic Legros

Very good colour. Rich, full and sturdy on the nose. Some tannin. Good, caramelly spice. Fullish body. Good grip. Slightly earthy but a good example. (June 2002)

2009 TO 2020　　　　　　　　　　15.0

Santenay, La Comme, 1999
Château de la Maltroye

Fruity in an apple, pear and greengage sense. Medium body. Not a lot of grip or concentration. Pleasant and forward, but a little lightweight. (September 2001)

DRINK UP　　　　　　　　　　　13.0

Savigny-lès-Beaune, 1999
Domaine Maillard Père et Fils

Ripe. Spicy. Good weight. A bit more evolution, and not as fresh or stylish as their Pommard Chanière 1999. But good. (February 2003)

NOW TO 2011　　　　　　　　　　14.0

Savigny-lès-Beaune, Les Bourgeots, 1999
Domaine Simon Bize et Fils

Good colour. Spicy, stemmy nose. Broad and ripe. Even riper on the palate. Medium to medium-full body. Balanced, fresh and stylish. Not as stemmy on the palate as on the nose. Good. (March 2002)

NOW TO 2012　　　　　　　　　　15.0

Savigny-lès-Beaune, Les Bourgeots, 1999
Domaine Rodolphe Demougeot

Excellent colour. Rich, fruity and succulent. A delicious little example. Fullish body. Good, ripe tannins. Very good fruit. Old vines here. Very good for a village wine. (June 2000)

NOW TO 2012　　　　　　　　　　15.0

Savigny-lès-Beaune, La Dominode, 1999
Domaine Bruno Clair

Good colour. Rich, full, old-viney, slightly oaky nose. Very ripe on the palate. Medium to medium-full body. Succulent. Some tannin. This is still quite closed. The finish is firm, but elegant, long and very delicious. Very good plus. (March 2002)

NOW TO 2020　　　　　　　　　　16.5

Savigny-lès-Beaune, La Dominode, 1999
Domaine Louis Jadot

Good colour. Somewhat reduced at first on the nose. A little rigid on the palate. Needs time to soften. At present it is a little four-square. Medium-full body. Good grip. Good fruit. Needs time. (October 2002)

NOW TO 2018　　　　　　　　　　15.5

Savigny-lès-Beaune, Les Dominodes, 1999
Domaine Jean-Marc Pavelot

Fullish colour. Lovely ripe, stylish nose. Succulent and with good depth. Medium-full body. Good tannins. These are evident, but round and ripe. Still quite sturdy and firm. But very good depth and class. Very typical. Very good. (June 2006)

2009 TO 2020　　　　　　　　　　16.0

Savigny-lès-Beaune, Aux Fourneaux, 1999
Domaine Jean-Michel Giboulot

Soft, round and just about ready. A slight rawness/astringency, though, which shows awkwardly. Good fruit. But I expected a bit more. (February 2003)

NOW TO 2010　　　　　　　　　　13.5

Savigny-lès-Beaune, Les Grands Liards, 1999
Domaine Pierre and Jean-Baptiste Lebreuil

No enormous colour. Too light. Will get weedy. (February 2003)

DRINK UP　　　　　　　　　　　11.0

Savigny-lès-Beaune, Aux Guettes, 1999
Domaine Machard De Gramont

A typical—but good—sturdy Savigny. Ripe. Fullish body. Good tannins. Very good acidity. Still a little tough, but long and positive. Very good. (February 2003)

NOW TO 2014　　　　　　　　　　15.5

Savigny-lès-Beaune, Les Marconnets, 1999
Domaine Simon Bize et Fils

Even better colour than his Bourgeots. Rich nose. Much less stemmy. Lots of depth. Medium-full body. Some tannin. Excellent grip. Ample and rich. Fat and succulent. Elegant and complex. Very good. (March 2002)

NOW TO 2016   16.0

Savigny-lès-Beaune, Les Marconnets, 1999
Domaine Patrick Jacob-Girard

Decent substance, although not that full. Ripe, meaty and spicy. Not that elegant though. (February 2003)

NOW TO 2010   14.5

Savigny-lès-Beaune, Les Marconnets, 1999
Domaine De La Vougeraie

Fullish colour. Sturdy nose. Not too robust but a typical Savigny. Good fruit. Good grip. Fullish body. Slightly four-square but a good wine. (September 2004)

NOW TO 2018   15.0

Savigny-lès-Beaune, Les Narbantons, 1999
Domaine Maurice Écard

Medium colour. Rich and old viney. Touches of caramel and chocolate on the nose. Ripe and balanced. Medium to medium-full body. Round tannins. No hard edges. Good depth. Good plus. (October 2001)

NOW TO 2013   15.5

Savigny-lès-Beaune, Les Narbantons, 1999
Domaine Leroy

Fullish colour but a little evolution. Quite full and solid. Some tannin. Ripe. Very good grip. Slightly burly. Still very youthful. Good depth though. Very good for what it is. (June 2005)

NOW TO 2020   16.0

Savigny-lès-Beaune, Les Narbantons, 1999
Domaine Jean-Marc Pavelot

Very good colour. Very good nose. Lots of energy and depth. Medium-full body. Concentrated and multilayered. Lots of substance here. Some tannin. Very good grip. Quite

powerful. Yet not a bit *sauvage*. Fine for what it is. (January 2002)

NOW TO 2027   16.0

Savigny-lès-Beaune, Les Peuillets, 1999
Domaine Rodolphe Demougeot

Good colour. Lovely ripe, black cherry fruit. Rich, fat and very luscious. Old vines again. The tannins are ripe. The wine is long and stylish. Very good. (June 2000)

NOW TO 2013   15.5

Savigny-lès-Beaune, Aux Petits Liards, 1999
Domaine Doudet-Naudin

Evolving fast. Some oxidation here. Ripe but unstylish. (February 2003)

DRINK SOON   11.0

Savigny-lès-Beaune, Aux Serpentières, 1999
Domaine Jean-Michel Giboulot

More than fifty-year-old vines. This has good depth. Still some tannins. Rich and fullish body. Needs time. Very good grip. Lots of style. Very good plus. (February 2003)

NOW TO 2012   16.0

Savigny-lès-Beaune, Aux Serpentières, 1999
Domaine Pierre Guillemet

Good colour. A fullish, rich, nicely meaty wine. Very good grip. A little adolescent at present. But good, ripe tannins. Very good depth. Long and stylish. Very good. (February 2003)

NOW TO 2014   15.5

Savigny-lès-Beaune, Les Vergelesses, 1999
Domaine Simon Bize et Fils

Not as much colour or as fat as his Marconnets, but rather more definition and style on the nose. Medium-full body. Some tannin. Rather more closed. Lovely style and lots of depth on the palate. It needs time. Very long and positive at the end. Very good plus. (March 2002)

NOW TO 2020   16.5

La Tâche, 1999
Domaine de la Romanée-Conti

Very fine colour. Super-concentrated nose. Quite splendid. It speaks volumes. Superb on the palate. Full bodied, rich, harmonious, concentrated and multidimensional. Splendid depth, intensity and real class. The finish goes on and on for ages. Perfect! (July 2003)

2015 TO 2040 20.0

Volnay, Vieilles Vignes, 1999
Maison Nicolas Potel

Medium-full colour. Lovely, classy fruit. Very fragrant. Medium-full body. Very harmonious. Sweet, fresh, pure and very fragrant. Very Volnay. For a village wine this is very good indeed. (October 2001)

NOW TO 2014 17.0

Volnay, Les Caillerets, 1999
Domaine Bouchard Père et Fils

Jeroboam. Very youthful colour. Lovely nose. Fresh, fragrant, full of fruit and classy. The palate is similar. Quite full. No lack of grip. Ample and old viney. Soft, round and succulent. Ripe and elegant. Long finish. Fine. (April 2005)

NOW 2010 17.5

Volnay, Les Caillerets, 1999
Maison Champy

Quite restrained on the nose. Rich, subtle, very well balanced and stylish palate. Very Volnay. Medium-full body. Very good indeed. Less evolved than the Beaune Champs Pimont 1999, tasted alongside. (January 2000)

NOW TO 2018 17.0

Volnay, Caillerets, Clos des 6o Ouvrées, 1999
Domaine de la Pousse d'Or

Medium-full colour. Slightly reduced on the nose. Slightly lumpy on the palate. Rather austere which is not a bad thing, but four-square too. Good follow-through though. The fruit is classy, and the wine is balanced. But some of the tannins are a bit astringent, and the acidity is a little raw. Merely good. (October 2001)

NOW TO 2010 15.0

Volnay, Les Caillerets, 1999
Domaine Michel Prunier

Medium-full colour. Ripe but no great class. Quite succulent. Medium to medium-full body.

Quite rich, quite mellow and generous. Good grip. Some evolution. Good. (June 2003)

2009 TO 2019 15.0

Volnay, Carelle, 1999
Maison Camille Giroud

Medium-full colour. Rather forced and ungainly. Not much class here. Medium-full body. Dry and tannic on the palate. Bottled a bit late, I suspect. Decent wine underneath. But no attraction. (June 2003)

NOW TO 2015 13.5

Volnay, Champans, 1999
Domaine du Marquis d'Angerville

Full colour. Rich, full and chocolaty, and with rather more weight than his Fremiets. Impressive. Full bodied, backward, rich and meaty. Lot of depth here. Great class. Really fine. (June 2003)

2009 TO 2028 18.0

Volnay, Champans, 1999
Maison Vincent Girardin

Full colour. Just a touch of reduction on the nose. Rich and full underneath. Slightly over-extracted perhaps. Good fruit and grip. Slightly chunky though. Slightly ungainly. Medium-full body. Good. (June 2003)

2009 TO 2020 15.0

Volnay, Champans, 1999
Domaine des Comtes Lafon

Full colour. Fullish, rich, almost opulent nose. Lots of depth here. A big wine with some tannin. Backward. Excellent grip. Long and satisfying. It needs time. Not the flair of Angerville's Champans though. (June 2003)

2010 TO 2025 17.5

Volnay, Champans, 1999
Maison Olivier Leflaive Frères

Medium-full colour. Ripe, succulent, balanced and attractive on the nose. On the lightish side perhaps. Medium body. Balanced and fruity. But it lacks depth and energy. Slightly one-dimensional. Good at best. (June 2003)

NOW TO 2016 15.0

Volnay, Champans, 1999
Domaine Monthelie-Douhairet

Good colour. Quite sturdy on the nose, but rich and ripe underneath. Fullish body. Good tannins. Meaty and succulent. Good grip. This has depth, class and good vigour. Finishes well. Very good plus. (October 2002)

NOW TO 2024   16.5

Volnay, Champans, 1999
Domaine Hubert de Montille

Medium-full colour. Slightly thin and lean on the nose. It lacks charm. A little hint of astringency. This is better than his *premier cru* though. There is good depth and class here. It will get better as it rounds off. Very good. (June 2003)

NOW TO 2020   16.0

Volnay, Champans, 1999
Domaine Jacques Prieur

Full colour. Good nose. Rich and meaty. Plenty of class and depth. Fullish, ample, rich and succulent. Good structure. Good acidity. Long and satisfying. This is very good indeed. (June 2003)

2010 TO 2025   17.0

Volnay, Les Champans, 1999
Domaine Joseph Voillot

Good colour. Fragrant, stylish, medium-weight nose. Lovely ripe fruit on the palate. Rich, succulent and very elegant. Excellent grip. Very Volnay. Fine. (March 2002)

NOW TO 2018   17.5

Volnay, Clos des Angles, 1999
Maison Olivier Leflaive Frères

Fullish colour. Medium weight. Ripe, fresh, clean and balanced on the nose. This is harmonious, fresh and fruity. The attack is very good. It lacks the depth for better than this. But attractive. (June 2003)

NOW TO 2018   16.0

Volnay, Clos des Angles, 1999
Maison Nicolas Potel

Full colour. Ripe, medium-full, succulent and seductive on the nose. Slightly more macerated than the Olivier Leflaive and slightly rigid as a result. Less harmonious. But good. (June 2003)

2009 TO 2019   15.0

Volnay, Clos de la Barre, 1999
Domaine Louis Jadot

Medium-full colour. Medium weight. Good depth and fruit. Good reserves underneath. Medium-full body. Slightly four-square. Good grip but slightly ungenerous. Quite good plus. (June 2003)

NOW TO 2018   14.5

Volnay, Clos du Château des Ducs, 1999
Domaine Michel Lafarge

Fullish colour. Slightly adolescent on the nose. A little closed-in and unforthcoming. This doesn't sing today. There is good substance, grip and plenty of fruit. But it lacks zip. To be seen again. (February 2002)

2010 TO 2025 (SEE NOTE)

Volnay, Clos des Chênes, 1999
Domaine Bouchard Père et Fils

Fullish colour. Rich, full, backward nose. Good depth here. Full, rich, oaky and profound. Very good fruit. Lots of energy. Very long. Very classy. This is a lovely, fine example. (June 2003)

2010 TO 2026   17.5

Volnay, Clos des Chênes, 1999
Domaine Pascal Bouley

Full colour. Rich, fat nose. This is classy and concentrated. Some tannin. A full wine. Still an infant. Very good grip. The tannins are ripe, and the wine is very well balanced. The fruit is very elegant. Lots of dimension. This is fine. (October 2001)

2009 TO 2029   17.5

Volnay, Clos des Chênes, 1999
Domaine Jean-Michel Gaunoux

Fullish, rich, ripe and concentrated. Very lovely fruit here. Good grip. Long, intense and succulent. Good grip. Very stylish. Very good indeed. (June 2000)

NOW TO 2018   17.0

Volnay, Clos des Chênes, 1999
Domaine Antonin Guyon

Full colour. Rich nose. Good fruit and depth.
Medium-full bodied, balanced, rich and harmonious. This is seductive. Perhaps not the greatest class but very good. (June 2003)

2009 TO 2021   16.0

Volnay, Clos des Chênes, 1999
Domaine Michel Lafarge

Fullish colour. A little closed-in on the nose at first. Rich underneath. Fullish body. Some tannin. Splendid concentration but still very youthful. Lovely Volnay fruit. Good grip. Long. Very elegant. Lovely finish. Fine. (March 2006)

2009 TO 2025+   17.5

Volnay, Clos des Chênes, 1999
Domaine des Comtes Lafon

Full colour. Full, quite solid, backward nose. Slightly adolescent. Fullish, ample, ripe and rich. But it doesn't have the depth or grip of the Santenots. Does it lack zip? Merely very good. (June 2003)

2010 TO 2024   16.0

Volnay, Clos des Chênes, 1999
Domaine René Monnier

Fullish colour. Fullish, spicy nose. Good fruit. Fullish bodied, ample, rich and balanced. This has very good depth. Even some class. Very good plus. (June 2003)

2009 TO 2022   16.5

Volnay, Clos des Chênes, 1999
Maison Nicolas Potel

Good colour. Ample, abundant, very lovely nose. Splendid concentration. Pure and rich. Very classy and harmonious. Good tannins. Fullish body. Some oak. Very lovely fruit. Very charming. Super-intense finish. Very seductive. Fine. (October 2001)

2009 TO 2029   17.5

Volnay, Clos des Ducs, 1999
Domaine du Marquis d'Angerville

Fullish colour. Full, rich, meaty, backward nose. Slightly corky. Underneath it is fat, ripe, concentrated and classy. Rather more backward, tannic and substantial than his other wines. Surely fine plus. (June 2003)

2010 TO 2025   18.0

Volnay, Clos des Santenots, 1999
Domaine Jacques Prieur

Fullish colour. Slightly forced on the nose. Good fruit and depth though. Medium-full body. Pinched and ungainly. Stewed and coarse. This is cheap stuff. (June 2003)

NOW TO 2014   12.5

Volnay, Frémiets, 1999
Domaine du Marquis d'Angerville

Medium-full colour. Lovely classy, aromatic nose. Very laid-back. Lovely fruit. Medium-full body. Very integrated. Lovely fruit and well balanced. Long, intense and classy. Very good indeed. (June 2003)

NOW TO 2020   17.0

Volnay, Les Frémiets, 1999
Domaine du Comte Armand

Good colour. Lovely, rich nose. The oak is just about right. Profound and classy. Medium-full body. Very lovely fruit. Very harmonious. This has a lot of depth. Very Volnay. Very good indeed. (September 2002)

NOW TO 2020   17.5

Volnay, Frémiets, 1999
Maison Champy

Medium to medium-full colour. Some development. Soft on the nose. Medium body. It lacks a bit of grip and depth. Pretty but a little simple. Forward. (October 2001)

NOW TO 2009   14.5

Volnay, Frémiets, 1999
Maison Olivier Leflaive Frères

Medium-full colour. Some development. Pleasant, indeed elegant, and fragrant, fruity nose. But not a lot underneath. Medium body. Good fruit but slightly one-dimensional. Yet quite balanced and stylish. Good. (June 2003)

NOW TO 2016   15.0

Volnay, Frémiets, 1999
Domaine Annick Parent

Full colour. Good depth on the nose but slightly reduced. Underneath, good substance and grip. But a lack of style and some astringency. If it throws this off, it could be good. (June 2003)

NOW TO 2016   14.0

Volnay, La Gigotte, 1999
Domaine Vincent Perrin

Medium-full colour. Fragrant, soft nose. Quite elegant. Good fruit. But light and fruity. A bit thin really. Not too bad on the palate. Good acidity. This is quite stylish. Quite good. (June 2003)

NOW TO 2015   14.0

Volnay, Mitans, 1999
Domaine Vincent Perrin

Medium-full colour. Soft, fruity nose. Fragrant and stylish. But quite forward. Medium to medium-full body. Clean and balanced. This is complex and long. But quite forward. Good plus. (June 2003)

NOW TO 2018   15.5

Volnay, Mitans, 1999
Domaine Hubert de Montille

Medium-full colour. Stylish nose. Quite ripe but not a great deal of weight. Medium body. Slightly lean. Good class and balance. It will improve and get more generous as it ages. Good plus today. (June 2003)

NOW TO 2018   15.5

Volnay, Premier Cru, 1999
Domaine Michel Lafarge

Chanlins and Mitans. Fullish colour. Still immature. Very good fruit but still quite closed-in on the nose. On the palate medium-full body, very well integrated tannins and very good grip. Lovely elegant, laid-back fruit. Stylish. Quite concentrated. Good intensity. Long and very good plus. (September 2004)

NOW TO 2020   16.5

Volnay, Premier Cru, 1999
Domaine Hubert de Montille

Medium to medium-full colour. Light, quite fragrant but a little lean on the nose. Medium body. Good acidity. Not a lot of tannin. Stylish and balanced. This will get more generous as it evolves. Positive at the end. Good. (June 2003)

NOW TO 2020   15.0

Volnay, Santenots, 1999
Domaine Michel Buisson

From Les Poutures. Medium weight. Ripe, rich and succulent. No great structure or tannin, but elegant and quite complex. (June 2000)

NOW TO 2011   15.0

Volnay, Santenots, 1999
Domaine Joseph Matrot

Medium to medium-full colour. Still youthful looking. Soft, fragrant and elegant, but not very intense or powerful nose. Medium body. Quite soft already. Delicate. Good intensity on the palate. Elegant. But a slight lack of drive and vigour. Just about ready. Very good plus. (May 2005)

NOW TO 2012   16.5

Volnay, Clos des Santenots, 1999
Domaine Jacques Prieur

Full, immature colour. Still very young. The tannin is a bit tight and hard, and the palate is a bit rigid. Medium-full body. Good grip. Nice and fresh. But it lacks Volnay style. It seems both a little spicy and sweet as well as a bit hard. Needs time. For the moment only "quite good." (November 2002)

NOW TO 2012   14.0

Volnay, Santenots du Milieu, 1999
Domaine des Comtes Lafon

Full colour. Full, rich and oaky on the nose. Masculine where Lafarge's Clos des Chênes is feminine, big as that is. More black fruity. Full body. Quite a lot of tannin. Fine grip. Quite marked oak. Very fresh. Very lovely fruit. Long, complex and multifaceted. Very fine. (February 2003)

2012 TO 2030   18.5

Volnay, Taillepieds, 1999
Domaine du Marquis d'Angerville

Medium-full colour. Rich, full, ripe and meaty on the nose. High-class fruit. Fullish body. Rich, ripe and succulent. This is very lovely. Very long and stylish. Fine plus. (June 2003)

2010 TO 2028   18.0

Volnay, Taillepieds, 1999
Domaine Hubert de Montille

Medium-full colour. This is a lot better than most of the Montille wines today. Rich and fat. Good structure. Lots of depth and elegance. It is lighter than Angerville's and not as concentrated. But balanced and intense. Very good indeed. (June 2003)

NOW TO 2022   17.0

Volnay, Taillepieds, 1999
Maison Nicolas Potel

Medium-full colour. Rich, full, almost jammy, almost overripe nose. Fullish body. Some tannin. Good fruit and grip. Slightly adolescent but good depth here, and the finish is promising. Very good plus. (June 2003)

2009 TO 2022   16.5

Volnay, Taillepieds, 1999
Domaine Roblet-Monnot

Very good colour. Rich, ample, ripe nose. Lots of succulence. A bigger wine than their 2002. Very lovely harmonious fruit. Very good tannins. Profound. No hard edges but still very youthful. Fine plus. (February 2006)

2010 TO 2025+   18.0

Vosne-Romanée, 1999
Domaine René Engel

Medium to medium-full colour. Ripe, rich, balanced and classy on the nose. Youthful. Medium-full body. Fragrant. Still some tannin. Very good grip. Lots of depth for a village wine. Lovely finish. Fine for what it is. (June 2004)

NOW TO 2017   16.0

Vosne-Romanée, 1999
Domaine Gros Frère et Soeur

Medium-full colour. A little tight on the nose. Ample and very elegant on the palate. Very good acidity. Ripe tannins. Medium to medium-full body. Very good for what it is. (October 2001)

NOW TO 2015   15.0

Vosne-Romanée, 1999
Domaine Alain Guyard

From Aux Réas. A bit lightweight. Good fruit and style, but not enough vigour. Not short. But slightly superficial. (January 2002)

NOW TO 2012   14.0

Vosne-Romanée, 1999
Domaine Emmanuel Rouget

Medium to medium-full colour. Fragrant on the nose, but not a great deal of depth or personality. Medium body. A little tannin. Pleasant but quite forward. Easy to drink. Finishes positively but no better than quite good plus. (October 2002)

NOW TO 2010   14.5

Vosne-Romanée, Les Barreaux, 1999
Domaine Anne Gros

Village *appellation contrôlée*. Medium-full colour. Ripe and chunky, especially for a Vosne, at first. More stylish later. Medium-full body. Not the substance the nose would suggest. Lovely fruit though. Some new oak. Very good acidity. Just a little ungainly but improved in the glass. Very good plus. (September 2002)

NOW TO 2018   16.5

Vosne-Romanée, Les Beaumonts, 1999
Domaine Jean Grivot

Very full colour. Backward but not too tannic. Very pure. Excellent fruit. Very, very concentrated and very, very classy. This is unmistakably of *grand cru* quality. Full body. Some tannin. Very concentrated and very lovely indeed. Really profound. Very, very long and lovely on the palate. An aristocratic wine. (March 2002)

2010 TO 2025   19.0

Vosne-Romanée, Les Beaumonts, 1999
Domaine Alain Hudelot-Noëllat

Medium-full colour. Fresh, ripe, rich and accessible on the nose. Very fruity. Clean and classy. Medium-full body. Not the greatest concentration, but balanced, accessible and stylish. Very good plus. (June 2003)

NOW TO 2020   16.5

Vosne-Romanée, Les Beaumonts, 1999
Domaine Daniel Rion et Fils
Good colour. Just a hint of reduction on the nose. Fullish body. Very ripe. Lovely, classy fruit. Very fresh. Long and complex. Very harmonious. Very long and lovely at the end. Fine. (October 2002)

NOW TO 2025   17.5

Vosne-Romanée, Les Beaux Monts, 1999
Domaine Bruno Clavelier
Full colour. Richer than his Brûlées. Fatter and plumper, too. Fullish body. Rich and ample. Very well balanced. Long and lovely. This is fine beyond a doubt. (June 2003)

2009 TO 2025   17.5

Vosne-Romanée, Les Beaux Monts, 1999
Domaine Jean Grivot
Very good colour. Very lovely nose. Totally pure. Extremely concentrated and quite concentrated. This is very impressive. Indeed, *grand cru* quality. Rich. Full body. Very harmonious and very classy. Quite marvellous! (March 2002)

2009 TO 2035   19.0

Vosne-Romanée, Les Brûlées, 1999
Domaine René Engel
Good colour. Ripe, succulent nose. Medium-full body. Just about ready. The tannins are now rounding off. Opulent, beautifully balanced, profound fruit. Long and complex. Fresh. Very fine. (June 2006)

2009 TO 2025   18.5

Vosne-Romanée, Aux Brûlées, 1999
Domaine Jean Grivot
Fullish colour. Very lovely pure fruit on the nose. Poised and very classy. Fullish body. Ripe. Very good tannins. Fine grip and lovely succulence. Long, complex, intense and very impressive. (June 2003)

2009 TO 2028   18.0

Vosne-Romanée, Aux Brûlées, 1999
Domaine Gérard Mugneret
Good, fullish colour. Plump, ripe and succulent on the nose. A hint of oak. Medium-full body. Very good acidity. A little tannin still. Ample and rich. Lacks the distinction and complexity for great, but fine. (June 2003)

2009 TO 2024   17.5

Vosne-Romanée, Aux Brûlées, 1999
Domaine Bruno Clavelier
Medium-full colour. Ripe, plump nose. A slight reduction. Medium-full body. Slightly raw. Very good acidity. At present it lacks just a little fat, and the finish is a little four-square. But very good, I think. (June 2003)

2009 TO 2024   17.5

Vosne-Romanée, Les Chaumes, 1999
Domaine Robert Arnoux
Full colour. Lovely, classy nose. Real essence of Pinot. Fullish, very rich and old viney. Splendid harmony. Fullish bodied and intense. Really fine for a Chaumes. Very, very long. Lovely. Fine plus. (October 2002)

NOW TO 2027   18.0

Vosne-Romanée, Les Chaumes, 1999
Domaine Méo-Camuzet
Very good colour. Excellent fruit on the nose. Poised, classy, harmonious and very aromatic. Medium-full body. Very good oak integration. Excellent grip. Very lovely ripe, rich, fragrant wine. Very good indeed. (March 2001)

2009 TO 2024   17.0

Vosne-Romanée, Clos des Réas, 1999
Domaine Michel Gros
Full, youthful colour. Firm, slightly closed-in nose. Rich and profound. Full body. Very composed. Rich and multidimensional. Lovely stylish fruit. This is classy, intense and long on the palate. Fine. (December 2003)

2010 TO 2030+   17.5

Vosne-Romanée, Cros Parantoux, 1999
Domaine Méo-Camuzet
Fullish colour. Quite oaky on the nose. Impressively rich, full, succulent fruit underneath. But a firm, quite backward wine. Fullish body. Rich, succulent and oaky. Not the depth and

concentration of the best of Grivot or Arnoux, but a fine wine. (March 2003)

2009 TO 2022   17.5

Vosne-Romanée, Les Gaudichots, 1999
Maison Nicolas Potel

Fine colour. Still quite closed on the nose. But although full and backward, no hard edges. Full body. Very classy. Lots and lots of depth and concentration. This is splendid. Very, very long. Needs time. (September 2005)

2009 TO 2025   18.5

Vosne-Romanée, Aux Malconsorts, 1999
Domaine Sylvain Cathiard

Full colour. This is very lovely on the nose. Very pure fruit. Lots of depth and class. Gently oaky. Very laid-back. Complex and classy. Fullish body. Lovely harmony. Really long and elegant. Fine plus. (June 2003)

2009 TO 2028   18.5

Vosne-Romanée, Aux Malconsorts, 1999
Domaine François Lamarche

Full colour. Good, plump nose. Medium-full body. Slightly astringent, and a slight lack of fat and class. Decent balance though. Not short. Good plus. (June 2003)

NOW TO 2017   15.5

Vosne-Romanée, Aux Malconsorts, 1999
Domaine Charles Thomas

Full colour. Quite sturdy on the nose. Good, solid, quite tannic wine but with plenty of richness underneath. This is going to need time. Full body. Quite tannic. Very good acidity. Quite austere. But lovely, cool fruit. Long, complex and classy. Fine plus. (March 2003)

2010 TO 2025   18.0

Vosne-Romanée, Premier Cru, Cuvée
Duvault-Blochet, 1999
Domaine de la Romanée-Conti

Medium-full colour. Lovely classy, fragrant nose. Evidence of the stems but in a rich sense. Fullish body. Now getting round and soft. No obtrusive tannin. Fragrant. Balanced. Very classy.

Very long. Very profound. Just about ready. Fine. (May 2005)

NOW TO 2025   17.5

Vosne-Romanée, Les Reignots, 1999
Domaine Sylvain Cathiard

Fullish colour. Ample, rich, oaky nose. Very poised. Very elegant. Fullish on the palate. Fine tannins. Lovely fruit. Harmonious. Long and most impressive. Long finish. Fine plus. (June 2003)

2009 TO 2028   18.0

Vosne-Romanée, Les Suchots, 1999
Domaine Pierre André

Full colour. Decent fruit but not much depth on the nose. Clean, ripe, quite stylish, quite full-bodied wine on the palate. This is quite balanced and positive. Good plus. (June 2003)

2009 TO 2025   15.5

Vosne-Romanée, Les Suchots, 1999
Domaine de l'Arlot

Medium-full colour. Rich, ripe, stemmy nose. Medium-full body. On the palate it lacks a little life and zip. Decent fruit but not much depth. Disappointing really. (June 2003)

NOW TO 2015   14.0

Vosne-Romanée, Les Suchots, 1999
Domaine Robert Arnoux

Good colour. Very lovely nose. Creamy rich. Splendidly balanced. Vigorous, complex and very classy. Fullish body. Very good tannins. Lovely fruit here. Multidimensional. Very harmonious. Very vigorous and intense. Great style. Very fine. (March 2003)

2009 TO 2025   18.5

Vosne-Romanée, Les Suchots, 1999
Domaine Jean Grivot

Full colour. Great class on the nose. Very poised fruit. Splendid concentration and balance. Backward. Fullish body. Very fine balance. Lovely fruit. This is long and lovely. Very cool and classy. Fine plus. (June 2003)

2010 TO 2028   18.0

Vosne-Romanée, Les Suchots, 1999
Domaine Alain Hudelot-Noëllat

Medium-full colour. Ample with a slight touch of spice on the nose. Good personality and depth. Not quite the grip of the Beaumonts. But rich and ample, and just as long. Very good plus. (June 2003)

2009 TO 2022   16.5

Vosne-Romanée, Les Suchots, 1999
Domaine Chantal Lescure

Full colour. Ripe but chunky on the nose. Medium-full body. Quite ripe. Slightly clumsy. But decent grip and good fruit. Good. (June 2003)

2010 TO 2025   15.0

Vosne-Romanée, Les Suchots, 1999
Domaine Dr. Georges Mugneret

Full colour. Plenty of depth, class and concentration on the nose. Very impressive. Fullish body. Ripe and balanced. Cool and complex. Lovely fruit. Long and impressive. Fine plus. (June 2003)

NOW TO 2022   18.0

Vougeot, Clos du Prieuré, 1999
Domaine de la Vougeraie

Good colour. Fragrant, Chambolle-ish character on nose and palate. Medium to medium-full body. Fresh acidity. Good, succulent fruit. Finishes well. (September 2004)

2009 TO 2018   15.5

Vougeot, Les Cras, 1999
Domaine Jean Mongeard-Mugneret

Medium colour. Light and fragrant, and quite high acidity on the nose. Medium body. Cool and not over-oaked on the palate. Good length. But not a lot of real depth and succulence. Very good. (October 2002)

NOW TO 2017   16.0

Vougeot, Les Cras, 1999
Domaine de la Vougeraie

Full colour. Ample nose. But not a lot of style. Slightly animal and soft. Medium to medium-full body. Ripe and fruity, but the tannins are a little ungainly. Decent acidity. Good at best. (June 2003)

NOW TO 2017   15.0

1998

As in 1997 the climatic conditions in 1998 were uneven. This produced a crop of moderate size, marginally below the 5-year average at the time, but one with a curious difference in quality between red and white. The red wines are quite tannic, without the richness or concentration that would follow in 1999; yet for the most part, they are balanced and thoroughly satisfactory. They are evolving well. The whites, although initially fruity, attractive and seemingly decently balanced have in many cases evolved rapidly. Only a few suggest that you should hold on to them for very much longer.

WEATHER CONDITIONS

The year 1998 got off to a bad start. Easter Monday brought severe frost to the Côte d'Or. While this blighted especially the eventual harvest in Meursault and Puligny, the effects were also felt in Gevrey-Chambertin, Morey-Saint-Denis, Chambolle-Musigny, in Vosne-Romanée but to a lesser extent in Nuits-Saint-Georges, and in the Côte de Beaune, and in Volnay, Pommard and Beaune. Curiously, the hill of Corton and the slopes of Savigny and Chassagne-Montrachet and Santenay in the south seem to have escaped lightly. Because the frost was early, the best exposed vineyards on the slope were hit the hardest. Overall, the red wine production was on par with that of 1997, but in 1998 there was much less production in the *premiers* and *grands crus*, and more in the village wines.

After this frost, the weather in May was fine and warm, and the flowering commenced in good conditions. After the second week in June, however, the weather deteriorated, prolonging the completion of the flowering in the Côte de Nuits, and causing both *coulure* and *millerandage*. This further reduction in the crop is particularly apparent in Gevrey-Chambertin and in Chambolle-Musigny, and many growers have been unable to vinify all their *premiers crus* separately, instead producing only a simple *premier cru tout court*.

July continued the pattern of cool, rainy weather. But with the arrival of August, the conditions changed. For those on holiday, sunbathing by their pools, it was fine, even too hot. For the young vines, with inadequate root systems, and those bunches of grapes most exposed to the sun, it was a disaster. The fruit literally shrivelled up. To compound the problem, in those bunches half-grilled by the sun, a return to humid conditions in early September brought with it the threat of rot.

Happily, the rain then held off until September 26. The weather conditions during the harvest itself were fine, except at the very end, and nearly all the fruit, from *grand cru* down to generic, was picked in dry, sunny conditions. All that was needed—a simple but in 1998 most essential "all"—was to sort through the grapes and eliminate the inadequate ones before fermentations were allowed to begin.

WHERE ARE THE BEST WINES?

The white wines are at their least successful where the frost damage was at its most draconian: in the Meursault *premiers crus* and the *climats* above them and in Puligny-Montrachet, Folatières and the *premiers crus* further upslope. It was here that the oïdium and August heat presented the greatest problems. 1998 is a very good vintage for Corton-Charlemagne. The reds are consistent from Chambolle-Musigny to Volnay. Gevrey-Chambertins, by contrast, are a little disappointing.

> ### → Rating for the Vintage ←
>
> | | |
> |---|---|
> | Red | 16.0 |
> | White | 14.5 |

> ### → Size of the Crop ←
> (In hectolitres, excluding generic wine)
>
> | | RED | WHITE |
> |---|---|---|
> | Grands Crus | 111,907 | 3,605 |
> | Village and Premiers Crus | 168,473 | 51,340 |
> | TOTAL | 180,380 | 54,945 |

WHEN WILL THE WINES BE AT THEIR BEST?

The 1998 Chardonnays were never blockbusters. They are now 9 years old. Only the most vigorous will age much longer, though most should still be attractive. Enjoy them now.

The village red wines, and most of the *premiers crus* of the Côte de Beaune, are now *à*

point. The rest, and those of the Côte de Nuits, will follow soon. Leave the best *premiers* and *grands crus* until 2009 or so. Most reds should keep well into their second decade.

For the results of my Ten Year On tasting, to be held in June 2008, please see my Web site clive-coates.com.

TASTING NOTES

WHITES

Bâtard-Montrachet, 1998
Domaine Jean-Noël Gagnard
Ripe, flowery and gently oaky. Not the power, nor the depth of the 1999. But brisk and stylish. Soft, succulent and peachy on the palate. Medium-full body. Certainly fresh enough. Good dimension at the end. Fine for the vintage. Quietly successful. (January 2002).
NOW TO 2015   17.0

Bâtard-Montrachet, 1998
Domaine Étienne Sauzet
Magnum. Quite a developed colour. Some evolution on the palate. This is a bit flat and boring. It lacks zip. And the finish is slightly tired and flabby. Good at best.
(October 2003)
DRINK SOON   15.0

Bienvenues-Bâtard-Montrachet, 1998
Domaine Louis Jadot
Fresh, crisp, minerally but honeyed. Good depth, class and grip. Very gently oaky. Delicious. Fullish body. Still plenty of life ahead of it. (April 2005)
NOW TO 2010+   18.5

Chassagne-Montrachet, La Boudriotte, 1998
Maison Vincent Girardin
Very good colour. Lovely succulent nose. This is ample and very rich. Medium body. No great

grip or structure but fat and ripe and most enjoyable for the short to medium term. Very juicy. Good positive finish. (October 2000)

DRINK SOON   15.5

Chassagne-Montrachet, Les Caillerets, 1998
Domaine Jean-Noël Gagnard

Delicious, cool, minerally nose. Very delicate oakiness. À point. Ripe, crisp and flowery. Medium body. This is fine for the vintage. (January 2005)

DRINK SOON   17.5

Chassagne-Montrachet, Champgains, 1998
Domaine Vincent and François Jouard

A touch of built-in sulphur on the nose. Quite developed, both in the colour and on the nose. Fresh, medium to medium-full bodied, but still a bit sulphury on the palate. This reduces the quality. Good acidity. Even a bit firm. But it lacks grace. Only fair. (June 2004)

NOW TO 2010   13.0

Chassagne-Montrachet, Les Embrazées, 1998
Domaine Bernard Morey

Stylish, fullish, nutty nose. Good grip and plenty of depth. Nice touch of oak. Peachy. Medium-full body. Positive and elegant. Plenty of dimension. This is a fine example. More "serious" than many 1998 Meursaults and Pulignys. (March 2000)

NOW TO 2010   17.5

Chassagne-Montrachet, Les Grandes Ruchottes, 1998
Chateau de la Maltroye

Quite an evolved colour for a wine which is only 3 years old (other bottles in the bin were already far too old). A bit closed on the nose. A ripe, clean, exuberant and juicy example on the palate. Classy and with plenty of depth. Very good long, vigorous finish for the vintage. Very good plus. (December 2002)

DRINK SOON (SEE NOTE)

Chassagne-Montrachet, La Maltroie, Vieilles Vignes, 1998
Domaine Vincent and François Jouard

Fullish, ripe and rich. Good acidity. Nice and fresh. Flowery, clean and appley in a good sense.

Peachy, too. This is elegant and has good depth. Very good plus. (December 2000)

DRINK SOON   16.5

Chassagne-Montrachet, Morgeot, 1998
Domaine Duc de Magenta/Maison Louis Jadot

Delicious, fresh, gently oaky, appley-peachy nose. Not a bit heavy. Very elegant. Fullish on the palate. Surprisingly good. Slight malic acidity. Round, ripe and fresh. Long and stylish. Just about ready. Fine. (December 2001)

NOW TO 2009   17.5

Chassagne-Montrachet, En Remilly, 1998
Domaine Michel Morey-Coffinet

Mature but fresh colour. Ripe nose. More depth, concentration and volume than his Chassagne la Romanée 1998. Fullish body. Quite fat. Good acidity. Good personality and virility. Quite concentrated peachy fruit. Long and complex. Lovely finish. Fine plus for the vintage. (May 2005)

NOW TO 2011   18.0

Chassagne-Montrachet, La Romanée, 1998
Domaine Michel Morey-Coffinet

Mature but fresh colour. Round, quite developed, floral-peachy nose. Ripe and attractive but no real grip or concentration. Fully ready. Medium-full body. Decent acidity. Clean and quite fresh on the palate. Good fruit. Lacks a bit of vigour and dimension but stylish. Very good indeed for the vintage. (May 2005)

DRINK SOON   17.0

Chassagne-Montrachet, La Romanée, 1998
Domaine Paul Pillot

This is a little tendre. Supple, fruity and ripe. Good style and reasonable depth. Very good for the vintage. (June 2000)

DRINK SOON   16.0

Chassagne-Montrachet, Les Ruchottes, 1998
Domaine Ramonet

Elements of sur-maturity here. Medium to medium-full weight. A lack of class and depth compared with other recent vintages. Quite good at best. A little short. (May 2005)

DRINK SOON   14.0

Chevalier-Montrachet, 1998
Domaine Bouchard Père et Fils

Youthful colour. Minerally on the nose. Less developed than Jadot's. Gently oaky. Medium-full body. Profound and classy. Lovely balance. Intense and very concentrated. Very long. Very fine. Will still improve. (October 2004)

NOW TO 2020   18.5

Chevalier-Montrachet, 1998
Domaine Leflaive

Rich, full, concentrated and high class. Lots of vigour and energy for 1998. Ripe. À point. Lovely long finish. Very fine. (March 2006)

NOW TO 2016   18.5

Chevalier-Montrachet, 1998
Domaine Ramonet

Ripe but a touch of sulphur on the nose. Well matured. Not a lot of energy. Medium body. For Chevalier and Ramonet this is really rather weak and simple. It lacks drive and concentration. Fully ready. (September 2005)

DRINK SOON   15.0

Chevalier-Montrachet, La Cabotte, 1998
Domaine Bouchard Père et Fils

Very rich and full. Very concentrated indeed. Montrachet-ish. Intense. Very good grip. Still very youthful and now slightly adolescent. Not as exciting within the context of the vintage as their Corton-Charlemagne, but very fine. (June 2002)

NOW TO 2020   18.0

Chevalier-Montrachet, Les Demoiselles, 1998
Domaine Louis Jadot

Some development on the colour and on the nose. Some oak. Full bodied, rich, pure, fat and mature. Good acidity. But Bouchard's is better today, more profound. Nevertheless, fine plus. (October 2004)

NOW TO 2018   18.0

Corton-Charlemagne, 1998
Domaine Bonneau du Martray

Soft, ripe and stylish. Good depth and class. Just a little oak. Medium-full body. Good vigour. Very fine for what it is. (November 2005)

NOW TO 2012   18.5

Corton-Charlemagne, 1998
Domaine Bouchard Père et Fils

Youthful colour. Crisp, clean and classically minerally. Better on the palate than on the nose. Barely oaky. Clean and medium-full bodied on the follow-through. Fragrant and long. Very high class for a 1998. Lovely. Just about ready. (September 2005)

NOW TO 2010+   19.0

Corton-Charlemagne, 1998
Domaine Roland Rapet

Fullish bodied. Gently oaky. Rich. Minerally. Classic. Very good grip and vigour. This is very lovely, especially for the vintage. Fine plus. (October 2005)

NOW TO 2015   18.0

Corton-Charlemagne, 1998
Domaine Georges Roumier et Fils

The parcel lies up at the top on the Pernand side, opposite the church. He has to pick very late. 20.4 ares. Cool and crisp. Lovely stylish, delicate wine. Good acidity. Medium-full body. Very ripe and harmonious. Very lovely fruit. Quite delicious. À point now. (June 2003)

NOW TO 2014   19.0

Meursault, 1998
Domaine des Comtes Lafon

Quite a developed colour. Fruity, reasonably balanced, but fully à point and a bit neutral. It lacks vigour and depth. Decent class and a reasonably positive finish. Quite good. (February 2005)

DRINK SOON   14.0

Meursault, Blagny, 1998
Domaine Louis Latour

Crisp. Ripe. Fullish body. Decent grip and depth. But not a lot of class. À point. Good plus. (October 2005)

DRINK SOON   15.5

Meursault, Genevrières, Cuvée Baudot, 1998
Hospices de Beaune/Maison Marc Colin

Rich nose. Not too oaky. Good depth and class. Good grip. Medium weight. Not a lot of vigour or vivacity on the palate. But pleasant fruit. Decent length. Very good. (October 2001)

DRINK SOON   16.0

Meursault, Genevrières, 1998
Domaine des Comtes Lafon

A very small harvest as a result of hail. Quite a developed colour. Quite evolved on the nose, too. Ripe and flowery with a slight faded vegetal aspect. Even a touch oxidised as it developed. Lightish. The fruit is beginning to lose its freshness. Some acidity but no richness or vitality. Loose-knit at the end. Medium body. Quite pleasant but only fair. (September 2005)

DRINK SOON   13.0

Meursault, Genevrières, 1998
Domaine Michel Tessier

It lacks a bit of concentration. Otherwise decent but quite evolved. Only average. (October 2002)

DRINK SOON   13.5

Meursault, Les Perrières, 1998
Domaine Jean-Michel Gaunoux

Rich, fat and firm for a 1998. Positive. Gently oaky on the nose. On the palate, this is all very pleasant, but a little superficial. The follow-through is better. Quite intense. Reasonable grip. Some length. But not that special. It lacks real grip and concentration. (June 2000)

NOW TO 2009   14.0

Monthelie, Le Chateau Gaillard, 1998
Domaine A and J Parent

Monopole. Soft, round and slightly tendre. On the follow-through, a little sweet. Pleasant and forward. But not a stayer. Lacks a little acidity. But no lack of personality. (August 2000)

DRINK SOON   14.0

Le Montrachet, 1998
Domaine de la Romanée-Conti

Rich, fat, with just a touch of built-in sulphur on the nose. Now a bit in its shell. On the palate, this is full bodied, ripe and spicy. Good acidity. Plenty of vigour. Lovely fruit. Lots of depth. Very intense. Very long and very classy. It got better and better in the glass. Very fine. (July 2002)

NOW TO 2012   19.0

Nuits-Saint-Georges, La Perrière, 1998
Domaine Henri Gouges

This is a very lovely example. Quite un-Chardonnay-ish. Lean. Good acidity. Slight aspects of passion fruit but very fresh and crisp, and not exotic. Lots of depth. Real 1998 succulence with a good grip behind it. Better still in 3-years. Fine. (August 2000)

NOW TO 2010   17.5

Puligny-Montrachet, 1998
Domaine Étienne Sauzet

Plenty of personality for a 1998. Very fresh. Lovely fruit. Fine for a village example. Balanced. Vigorous. Very good. (May 2001)

DRINK SOON   16.0

Puligny-Montrachet, Les Chalumaux, 1998
Maison Champy

Soft, plump and flowery. Good style. Clean and balanced and with more depth than Chalumaux usually has. Forward, though. Ready now. (January 2001)

DRINK SOON   15.5

Puligny-Montrachet, Champ Canet, 1998
Domaine Étienne Sauzet

Classy, complex nose. Lots of nuance. Medium to medium-full. Quite delicate. À point. Not a lot of grip on the palate but reasonable length and class. But the finish is a little tired. (February 2003)

DRINK SOON   16.0

Puligny-Montrachet, Les Demoiselles, 1998
Domaine Michel Colin-Deléger et Fils

Quite a developed colour. On the palate, too. This should be drunk quite soon. But full, ripe and with decent concentration and grip. Slight lack of class. It declined in the glass. Very good but not special. (September 2005)

DRINK SOON   16.0

Puligny-Montrachet, Les Folatières, 1998
Domaine Joseph Drouhin

Quite an evolved colour. Not a lot on the nose. Fullish on the palate. A little anonymous. But clean and balanced. No real age. Just a bit neutral. (March 2006)

DRINK SOON   14.0

Puligny-Montrachet, Les Pucelles, 1998
Domaine Bouchard Père et Fils

This is lovely. Rich, plump, fullish and gently oaky. A round, ripe, peachy wine with a lot of depth, class and vigour. Very fine. (November 2000)

NOW TO 2010   18.5

Puligny-Montrachet, Les Referts, 1998
Domaine Jean-Marc Boillot

Lovely fresh, succulent fruit. It doesn't seem to have been disturbed by the climatic conditions. Good acidity but essentially a soft, plump wine for quite early drinking. Very ripe. But very fresh. Very good indeed. (March 2000)

DRINK SOON   17.0

Puligny-Montrachet, Les Referts, 1998
Domaine Louis Jadot

Soft and gently oaky. Ripe almost to the point of being overripe. Reasonable but not great grip and class. Now just about ready. Very good for the vintage. Best drunk quite soon. Will get flabby in the end. (October 2002)

DRINK SOON   16.0

Puligny-Montrachet, Les Referts, 1998
Domaine Étienne Sauzet

Somewhat bland at first on the nose and palate, but better underneath. It is very good. Lots of depth. But it could have had more grip. A little one-dimensional but very good for the vintage. (October 2001)

DRINK SOON   16.0

Puligny-Montrachet, La Truffière, 1998
Domaine Michel Colin-Deléger et Fils

Rich, plump, balanced nose. Good depth for 1998. Ripe and quite evolved. Creamy-apricotty

on the palate. Round. Not lacking grip. Ample and stylish. Very good indeed. (October 2001)

DRINK SOON   17.0

REDS

Beaune, Boucherottes, 1998
Domaine Louis Jadot

Medium-full colour. Quite firm on the nose with a suspicion of the rustic. Medium to medium-full body. The tannins are not as sophisticated as those of the Clos des Avaux. Good fruit and acidity. But it doesn't have the same flair or dimension. Quite good plus. (June 2002)

NOW TO 2015   14.5

Beaune, Les Bressandes, 1998
Domaine Albert Morot

Medium colour. Some development. Soft nose. Not a great deal of depth or grip underneath. Medium body. This is quite fruity but essentially a little feeble. Pleasant but forward. Quite good. (June 2002)

NOW TO 2010   14.0

Beaune, Cent Vignes, 1998
Domaine Albert Morot

Medium-full colour. Good full, firm nose with plenty of depth. This is a lot better than their Bressandes. Medium to medium-full body. Like his Bressandes, it lacks a bit of grip and concentration. Good fresh, plummy fruit, though. Nice and pure. But no better than good. (June 2002)

NOW TO 2015   15.0

Beaune, Les Chouacheux, 1998
Domaine Louis Jadot

Medium-full colour. Good plump nose. Rich and ripe and well balanced. Medium body. Good grip but not a lot of fat or tannin. The follow-through is ample and vigorous. This is good plus. (June 2002)

NOW TO 2015   15.0

Beaune, Clos des Avaux, 1998
Maison Champy

Not a lot of colour. Light, plump nose. Fresh and ripe. Not a lot of structure. Quite forward.

Balanced. Seductive. Good long finish. Very good. (January 2001)

NOW TO 2013   16.0

Beaune, Clos des Avaux, 1998
Domaine Louis Jadot

Medium colour. Soft, plump, attractively balanced, pure Pinot nose. Medium-full body. Good tannins and a hint of oak. Very good grip. Firmer than the nose would suggest. Lovely fruit. Plenty of depth. Very good. (June 2002)

NOW TO 2020   16.0

Beaune, Clos des Coucherias, 1998
Domaine Louis Jadot

Medium-full colour. Lovely nose. Very rich. Some oak. A lot of class and depth here. Medium-full body. Quite a bit more succulent than the Jadot Chouacheux. Ripe, rich, round and plump. Very good style and intensity. Long. Very good plus. (September 2002)

NOW TO 2018   16.5

Beaune, Le Clos des Mouches, 1998
Domaine Joseph Drouhin

Medium to medium-full colour. Just a hint of reduction. But otherwise an ample, rich wine on the nose. Medium-full body. Good ripe tannins. It could have done with a bit more grip and concentration. But stylish and long enough. Good plus. (June 2002)

NOW TO 2017   15.5

Beaune, Le Clos des Mouches, 1998
Domaine Aleth le Royer-Girardin

Very good colour. Rich, full nose. Good oak. Very good ripe tannins. Very lovely fruit. Concentrated and expansive. Long and satisfying. Very good plus. (January 2002)

NOW TO 2020   16.5

Beaune, Clos de la Mousse, 1998
Domaine Bouchard Père et Fils

Medium-full colour. Ripe, quite firm nose. But plenty of succulence. Rich, fresh and fullish bodied. Very fine fruit. Very good acidity. Ripe

tannins. Still needs time but very classy. Fine. (March 2003)

NOW TO 2021   17.5

Beaune, Clos Saint-Landry, 1998
Domaine Bouchard Père et Fils

Ripe. Spicy. Not the greatest of acidity. Medium body. Quite forward. Just a little heavy. Not bad plus. (October 2000)

DRINK UP   13.5

Beaune, Clos des Ursules, 1998
Domaine Louis Jadot

Fullish colour. Backward nose but rich and full. Plenty of depth here. Full bodied, rich and succulent. Good fruit. Good grip. Quite backward. Very good potential. Very good plus. (June 2002)

NOW TO 2020   16.5

Beaune, Aux Cras, 1998
Domaine Germain Père et Fils/Chateau de Chorey-lès-Beaune

Medium to medium-full weight. Slightly more austere and tough nose than the 1999. Not more tannic, but the tannins are less ripe. Good fruit and grip. Medium to medium-full body. Positive. Very good. (September 2002)

NOW TO 2018   16.0

Beaune, Epenottes, 1998
Domaine Charles Thomas

Full colour. Rich, firm nose. A little more extracted than most of these Beaunes. Quite solid on the palate. Fullish body. But not overdone. Good grip. A wine built to last. At present it lacks a little charm. But this will come. Good plus. (June 2002)

NOW TO 2020   15.5

Beaune, Grèves, 1998
Domaine Albert Morot

Medium-full colour. Good depth here on the nose. Still closed-in. Medium-full body. As with all these Morot wines, there is a lack of succulence here, and the wine is a little lean. The tannins show. Will it get more charm as it ages? I am unconvinced. Good at best. (June 2002)

NOW TO 2018   15.0

Beaune, Grèves, 1998
Domaine Tollot-Beaut et Fils
Fullish colour. Ripe, rich and quite substantial on the nose. Medium-full body. Some oak. A good wine, but a touch anonymous. Yet balanced and correct. (June 2002)
NOW 2018   15.0

Beaune, Grèves, Vigne de l'Enfant Jésus, 1998
Domaine Bouchard Père et Fils
Medium-full colour. Still youthful-looking. Ripe but a touch rigid on the nose. Good weight and depth underneath. Fullish body. Good backbone and grip. Ample, ripe, stylish and balanced. Very good grip. Some tannin to resolve. This is fresh and very stylish. Long. Very good indeed for the vintage. (November 2003)
NOW TO 2020+   17.0

Beaune, Les Marconnets, 1998
Domaine Dubois d'Orgeval
This is less astringent than the Beaune Teurons 1998 but a little rustic. Again, a little overdone perhaps, but the finish is better. Quite good plus. (February 2003)
NOW TO 2012   14.5

Beaune, Marconnets, 1998
Domaine Albert Morot
Medium colour. A rather more succulent nose than the other Morot wines above. Medium-full body. Some tannin, which sticks out a bit. Good grip and no lack of depth. It finishes well. Good plus. (June 2002)
NOW TO 2018   15.5

Beaune, Montrevenots, 1998
Domaine Vincent Dancer
Medium to medium-full colour. Lightish nose. A little thin. Light, spicy and quite developed on the palate. Decent grip. But a touch concocted. Hot finish. Not bad. (June 2002)
NOW TO 2011   13.0

Beaune, Sizies, 1998
Domaine Michel Prunier
Medium-full colour. High-toned nose. Quite sweet and perfumed. On the palate, it is a little rigid. But the fruit is there, if not very concentrated. Medium to medium-full body. Decent acidity. It lacks sophistication, though. Quite good. (June 2002)
NOW TO 2015   14.0

Beaune, Les Teurons, 1998
Domaine Dubois d'Orgeval
Quite sturdy on the attack. The tannins stick out a little. Slightly astringent and slightly over-extracted. (February 2003)
NOW TO 2010   13.0

Beaune, Les Teurons, 1998
Domaine Albert Morot
Medium-full colour. Quite a firm nose. Decent attack, but the tannins stick out a bit. Not enough grip and richness. Medium to medium-full body. Quite good at best. (June 2002)
NOW TO 2015   14.0

Beaune, Toussaints, 1998
Domaine Albert Morot
Medium-full colour. Similar on the nose to the Teurons, but more succulent. Again, a little ungenerous and astringent. After the nose, the palate doesn't show a lot better than the Teurons. A little better grip, though. Good. (June 2002)
NOW TO 2018   15.0

Beaune, Les Vignes Franches, 1998
Domaine Germain Père et Fils/
Chateau de Chorey-lès-Beaune
Fullish, rich, oaky and succulent. Still needs to be kept but ripe and full of fruit. Balanced and elegant. No hard edges. Very good indeed. (October 2003)
NOW TO 2015   17.0

Beaune, Vignes Franches, 1998
Maison Vincent Girardin
Fullish colour. Rich, ripe and concentrated on the nose. Medium-full body. Rich and juicy. Good acidity but no hard edges. Good depth. Very good. (June 2002)
NOW TO 2018   16.0

Bonnes Mares, 1998
Domaine Bouchard Père et Fils

Medium-full colour. Ripe and succulent on the nose. Classy fruit. Harmonious and fragrant. Medium-full body. Good grip. Lots of succulent fruit. This is long and multidimensional. Fine. (June 2002)

NOW TO 2018   17.5

Bonnes Mares, 1998
Domaine Dujac

Medium to medium-full colour. Rich and chocolaty. Even better than his Clos Saint-Denis and Clos de la Roche. Lovely fruit here. Fullish body. Very, very concentrated and intense. Very lovely. Harmonious and profound and multidimensional. Very fine. (June 2002)

NOW TO 2025   18.5

Bonnes Mares, 1998
Domaine Fougeray de Beauclair

Good colour. Rich, fat, slightly sweet nose. Good tannins but not quite as sophisticated as they might be. But attractive ripe, plump, balanced fruit. Some structure. Good acidity. Ripe and succulent. This is a fine example. (October 2002)

NOW TO 2015   17.5

Bonnes Mares, 1998
Domaine Louis Jadot

Very good colour. Rich, ripe, concentrated and gently oaky on the nose. This is very stylish. Fullish body. Ample and intense. Very lovely ripe, rich fruit. Marvellous balance. This is really lovely. Very long. Fine plus. (June 2002)

NOW TO 2025   18.0

Bonnes Mares, 1998
Domaine Jacques-Frédéric Mugnier

Medium colour. Very lovely strawberry/raspberry fruit on the nose. Light and fragrant but intense and classy. Medium-full body. Pure and finely poised. Very ripe. But excellent grip. This is long and fine. But a delicate wine. Is it too light? (June 2002)

NOW TO 2018   17.5

Bonnes Mares, 1998
Domaine Georges Roumier et Fils

Medium-full colour. Quite firm on the nose. But with splendid, rich fruit as well as a good touch of oak. Fullish body. Quite firm and masculine. Rich and chocolaty. Good depth. It needs time. Fine plus. (June 2002)

2010 TO 2025   18.0

Bonnes Mares, 1998
Domaine Comte Georges de Vogüé

Medium-full colour. A little reticent on the nose. But some splendid fruit and a lot of depth here. Closed-in at present. At present the fruit seems a little artificial. Medium-full body. Good tannins. A bit adolescent. Good grip. It got more and more sophisticated as it evolved. Very fine plus. (June 2002)

2010 TO 2025   19.0

Chambertin, 1998
Domaine Bernard Dugat-Py

Full colour. Very, very concentrated, oaky nose. Lovely and succulent. Impressive! This is very Dugat, which some will consider untypical. But it is not over-extracted. In this case, unlike his other wines, I think it is too astringent on the palate. There is not enough grip. Merely very good. (June 2002)

NOW TO 2018   16.0

Chambertin, 1998
Domaine Leroy

Youthful colour. Quite full. Quite firm on the nose; a bit closed, like all these 1998s. Oaky. Rich, ripe and fragrant. Good acidity. Very seductive. Really fine for the vintage. (April 2000)

2009 TO 2015   17.5

Chambertin, 1998
Domaine Ponsot

Fullish colour. Ripe nose. Good fruit. But a little pinched. This is rather sweet and attenuated. Old tea aspects. A lack of grip as well as style. (June 2002)

NOW TO 2020   11.0

Chambertin, 1998
Domaine Armand Rousseau

Fullish colour. This is concentrated, classy and much more together than his Clos de Bèze. This is lovely. Fullish bodied, ripe, fresh and ample. Good ripe fruit. Plenty of depth. Very fine, but again not great. (June 2002)

2010 TO 2025   18.5

Chambertin, 1998
Domaine Jean Trapet Père et Fils

Fullish colour. Some development. Like with all the Trapet wines, quite oaky in a quite firm and spicy sort of way. On the palate this is a bit hard and charmless. Some astringency. Merely good. The Latricières-Chambertin shows better today. (June 2002)

2010 TO 2020   15.0

Chambertin, Clos de Bèze, 1998
Domaine Bouchard Père et Fils

Medium-full colour. Rich nose. A bit closed-in. Good depth and richness, though. Full body. Tannic. Rich and concentrated and with good grip. The tannins are a bit dominant at present, but there is plenty of substance underneath. Fine, but not great. (June 2002)

2010 TO 2020   17.5

Chambertin, Clos de Bèze, 1998
Domaine Pierre Damoy

Medium-full colour. Plump nose. Some depth but not the greatest of concentration, it seems. Medium-full body. Not really very rich or concentrated, nor with enough distinction. Like with his Chapelle-Chambertin, I am not convinced. Merely very good. (June 2002)

NOW TO 2018   16.0

Chambertin, Clos de Bèze, 1998
Domaine Joseph Drouhin

Medium-full colour. Rich, ripe, intense nose. Not a blockbuster. But plenty of fruit and class here. Good new oaky touches. On the palate though, it is a little weak. It is no more than pretty, and it lacks grip at the end. A bit of a disappointment. (June 2002)

NOW TO 2018   15.0

Chambertin, Clos de Bèze, 1998
Domaine Joseph Faiveley

Fine colour. Marvellous nose. Profound, concentrated, multidimensional and full of succulent fruit. Full body. Structured but no hard tannins. Very good grip. Very, very rich and concentrated. Intense and lovely. Very, very long and very classy. (June 2003)

NOW TO 2025   19.0

Chambertin, Clos de Bèze, 1998
Domaine Louis Jadot

Fullish colour. Good vigorous, profound, oaky nose. Lots of depth. But then it seems to tail off and fall apart. On the palate there is ripe fruit but the net effect is one of astringency. It is very good at best. (June 2002)

NOW TO 2018   16.0

Chambertin, Clos de Bèze, 1998
Domaine Armand Rousseau

Fullish colour. Slightly raw on the nose. There is depth and oakiness underneath. Better on the palate. Rich, ripe and oaky. It is a bit astringent, though. Decent grip. This is fine. But it is not great. (June 2002)

2010 TO 2020   17.5

Chambertin, Clos de Bèze, 1998
Domaine Charles Thomas

Full colour. Rich, fat, concentrated nose. Lovely concentrated cassis-blackberry fruit. No hard edges. Succulent. Crisp and delicious. Lots of depth here. On the palate, still quite a lot of tannin, giving it an austere edge. Very good acidity. Give it time. Full body. Very fine finish. It needs ten years. (October 2001)

2011 TO 2030   18.5

Chambolle-Musigny, 1998
Domaine Jacques-Frédéric Mugnier

Village wine. Medium to medium-full colour. Some evolution. Very lovely fragrant nose. Very Chambolle. On the palate there is good weight. Some tannin and good acidity. It is a bit closed-in at present. Lovely fruit. Balanced and very elegant. Long. A fine example of a village wine. (September 2004)

NOW 2020   16.0

Chambolle-Musigny, 1998
Domaine Georges Roumier et Fils

Fullish colour. Rich, fresh and lovely. Good structure. Very good grip. Still youthful. Still a little tannic. Very vigorous. Fine for a village wine. (October 2002)

NOW 2014   16.0

Chambolle-Musigny, Les Amoureuses, 1998
Domaine Jacques-Frédéric Mugnier

Medium-full colour. Quite developed nose. Seems quite soft and ready already. Medium to medium-full body. Subtle, fragrant and very pure. Lovely ripeness. Very good intensity. More to it than what appears on the attack. But forward for a 1998 and could do with a bit more power. Very good plus, but not fine. (September 2005)

NOW TO 2015   16.5

Chambolle-Musigny, Les Amoureuses, 1998
Domaine Comte Georges de Vogüé

Good, fresh-looking colour. Very lovely, pure, elegant, fragrant Pinot on the nose. Medium-full body. Gently oaky. Still a little tannin to resolve. Just a touch bitter at present. Lovely ample fruit though. Very good acidity. Ripe, stylish and very lovely. Very fine for the vintage. (May 2002)

NOW TO 2028   18.5

Chambolle-Musigny, Aux Beaux Bruns, 1998
Domaine Ghislaine Barthod

Medium-full colour. Ripe and rich on the nose. Lovely Chambolle fruit. Medium-full body. Ripe and rich. Sophisticated tannins. Ample at the end. This is fine. (June 2002)

NOW TO 2020   17.5

Chambolle-Musigny, Aux Beaux Bruns, 1998
Domaine Denis Mortet

Full colour. Rich and very oaky on the nose. Almost over the top. Fullish bodied, and not too tannic on the palate. Very good grip. Opulent,

long and impressive. But not really a true Chambolle. Fine, though. (June 2002)

2010 TO 2025   17.5

Chambolle-Musigny, Charmes, 1998
Domaine Pierre Bertheau

Medium to medium-full colour. Lovely, stylish, poised nose. Medium to medium-full body. Succulent, fresh, juicy and harmonious on the palate. This is long and impressive. Fine. (June 2002)

2010 TO 2025   17.5

Chambolle-Musigny, Charmes, 1998
Domaine Daniel Rion et Fils

Medium-full colour. Classy nose. Pure and fresh. There is a slight vegetal character to the fruit here. Slightly austere. Medium to medium-full body. A little tannin. Very good but not the flair of some. (June 2002)

NOW TO 2018   16.0

Chambolle-Musigny, La Combe d'Orveau, 1998
Domaine Bruno Clavelier

Medium to medium-full colour. Good plump nose. Just lacking a little style. Medium-full body. Good depth. Balanced and succulent. Quite classy. Very good plus. (June 2002)

NOW TO 2020   16.5

Chambolle-Musigny, Les Cras, 1998
Domaine Ghislaine Barthod

Medium-full colour. Ripe and rich on the nose. Ample fruit and good concentration. Some tannin and structure, but very good depth and intensity. Long. A fine example. (June 2002)

NOW TO 2019   17.5

Chambolle-Musigny, Les Cras, 1998
Domaine Pascal and Michel Rion

Medium-full colour. Stylish on the nose, if without the depth of Ghislaine Barthod's or the succulence and grip at the end. Good attack. The finish is long and multi-layered. Fine. (June 2002)

NOW TO 2018   17.5

Chambolle-Musigny, Les Cras, 1998
Domaine Georges Roumier et Fils
Good full colour. Still youthful. Full, clean and rich. Just a touch of softness. Good tannins. Very good grip. Ripe, vigorous and concentrated on the palate. Very seductive. Very lovely fruit. Surprisingly approachable but delicious. Fine. (June 2003)
NOW TO 2020   17.5

Chambolle-Musigny, Les Feusselottes, 1998
Maison Louis Jadot
Medium-full colour. Fragrant and bright. The wine is very good and full of interest, but it hasn't quite enough grip. Lots of lovely fruit, though. (June 2002)
NOW TO 2018   16.0

Chambolle-Musigny, Les Fuées, 1998
Domaine Ghislaine Barthod
Full colour. Slightly looser-knit and more forward than her Chambolle-Musigny les Cras. A little more developed. Slightly astringent on the palate. But the fruit is essentially ripe, rich and concentrated. Very good at best. (June 2002)
NOW TO 2012   16.0

Chambolle-Musigny, Les Fuées, 1998
Maison Louis Jadot
Full colour. Very good fruit on the nose. Classy, clean and pure. Quite structured. Gently oaky. This is very lovely. Fullish body. Lots of pure Pinot here. Fragrant. Fine. (June 2002)
NOW TO 2020   17.5

Chambolle-Musigny, Les Fuées, 1998
Domaine Jacques-Frédéric Mugnier
Medium-full colour. Very fragrant and classy on the nose. Ripe and intense and harmonious. Medium to medium-full body. Just a little tannin. Quite approachable. Very long and complex and intense. Really lovely. Very seductive. Fine. (June 2002)
NOW TO 2016   17.5

Chambolle-Musigny, Les Véroilles, 1998
Domaine Ghislaine Barthod
Fullish colour. Fullish body. A rich, succulent wine. Ripe, full bodied and oaky on the palate.

Ample. Sweet fruit. Good depth. Not as good as her Cras, but equal with the Fuées. Very good. (June 2002)
NOW TO 2018   16.0

Chapelle-Chambertin, 1998
Domaine Pierre Damoy
Fullish colour. The nose doesn't really convince me. There is fruit but not real grip or definition. Ripe on the palate. But a little pinched. Medium to medium-full body. At first it lacked class and zip. But it improved on aeration. Very good. (June 2002)
NOW TO 2018   16.0

Chapelle-Chambertin, 1998
Domaine Ponsot
Medium-full colour. Some brown. Ripe. Some evolution and spice on the nose. Medium-full body. Soft tannins. Good acidity. Not quite the energy, nor the class of their Griotte 1998 but fine quality. Long and vigorous. Ready. (June 2005)
NOW TO 2015   17.5

Chapelle-Chambertin, 1998
Domaine Jean Trapet Père et Fils
Fullish colour. Good full, rich nose. Fullish bodied, rich, ample and concentrated on the palate. Good tannins. Lots of depth and vigour here. Long and admirable at the end. Very good indeed. (June 2002)
2010 TO 2025   17.0

Charmes-Chambertin, 1998
Domaine Hervé Arlaud
Medium to medium-full colour. Light nose. Not a lot of depth. A little more to it on the palate. Medium body. Ripe and quite rich. Not much tannin. But good style. Very good. (June 2002)
NOW TO 2018   16.0

Charmes-Chambertin, 1998
Domaine Denis Bachelet
Full, firm nose. Some adolescent tannins on the nose. This needs time. It doesn't sing today. On the palate rather better. But a bit strict

nevertheless. Fullish bodied. Balanced. Fruity in a slightly austere way, but with lots of depth and class. Very good concentration. But better still in 2009. (June 2006)

2009 TO 2020+   18.0

Charmes-Chambertin, 1998
Domaine Claude Dugat

Full colour. Still youthful. Rich, slightly austere fruit on both nose and palate. Fullish body. Lots of energy. A little raw but potentially fine. Long and intense. Very fine. Needs time. (April 2006)

2010 TO 2025+   18.5

Charmes-Chambertin, 1998
Domaine Bernard Dugat-Py

Full colour. Full, rich, oaky nose. Plenty of concentration. Full bodied and tannic on the palate. Lots of oak. But good grip underneath. Rich and meaty. This is fine plus. (June 2002)

2010 TO 2025   18.0

Charmes-Chambertin, 1998
Domaine Dujac

Medium-full colour. Elegant nose. Fresh and poised. Gently oaky. Good rich fruit. Quite sweet on the palate. Good energy. Medium-full body. Ripe tannins. This is persistent and fine plus. (June 2002)

NOW TO 2025   18.0

Charmes-Chambertin, 1998
Domaine Louis Jadot

Full colour. Some development. Rich, rich, aromatic, slightly caramelly nose. No hard edges. Fullish body. Very fresh. Lovely clean, pure fruit. Very good grip. Long. Fine plus. (April 2006)

NOW TO 2020   18.0

Charmes-Chambertin, 1998
Maison Antonin Rodet

Medium-full colour. Ample nose. Plump, ripe, rich and accessible. Medium-full body. Good fresh fruit. This is succulent, balanced and stylish. Good tannins. Positive. Fine long finish. (June 2002)

NOW TO 2020   17.5

Charmes-Chambertin, 1998
Domaine Armand Rousseau

Medium-full colour. Succulent nose. Soft and easy to appreciate. Decent attack. But a slight lack of concentration at the end. Medium to medium-full body. Some tannin. Good grip and good style. But very good plus at best. It lacks a little definition. (April 2006)

NOW TO 2018   16.5

Chassagne-Montrachet, Clos de la Boudriotte, 1998
Domaine Ramonet

Medium colour. Fresh, spicy-cherry flavoured. Fresh. Medium body. Not much tannin. Round and ripe and very stylish. Good plus. Ready quite soon. (June 2003)

NOW TO 2014   15.5

Clos des Lambrays, 1998
Domaine des Lambrays

Medium-full colour. Fragrant nose. Not a blockbuster but lively and fruity. Ripe on the palate. Medium body. Just a little tannin. Good intensity and class. Good acidity. This has a lot of charm. Very good indeed. (June 2002)

NOW TO 2016   17.0

Clos de la Roche, 1998
Domaine Dujac

Medium-full colour. Some development. Good plump nose. Ripe and gently oaky. Balanced and stylish. This is very Dujac. A little sweet. Good intensity and grip. Soft ripe tannins. Good long finish. Fine plus. (June 2002)

NOW TO 2018   18.0

Clos de la Roche, 1998
Domaine Leroy

Good colour. Ample, oaky, seductive nose. Good depth if not much austerity. Medium-full body. It lacks a bit of grip and intensity. Very good but not brilliant. (April 2000)

NOW TO 2013+   16.0

Clos de la Roche, 1998
Domaine Hubert Lignier

Fullish colour. Ripe, oaky nose. Slightly four-square. Corked. But one can see a full, rich, oaky, quite profound wine. This is fine plus, I think. (June 2002)

2010 TO 2025   18.0

Clos de la Roche, Cuvée Vieilles Vignes, 1998
Domaine Ponsot

Magnum. Fullish, vigorous colour. Cool, but not lean on the nose. Plums rather than blackberries. Medium-full body. Some tannin. Sweet on the palate. The tannin dominates a bit but very ripe underneath. Very fine. (March 2006)

2009 TO 2025+   18.5

Clos Saint-Denis, 1998
Domaine Dujac

Medium-full colour. It seems both a little firmer and a little fresher on the nose than their Clos de la Roche which is not the way these two wines usually age. Medium-full body. Good grip. Lots of vigour and energy. Very stylish. Fine finish. Better than the Clos de la Roche today. Very fine. (June 2002)

NOW TO 2018   18.5

Clos de Tart, 1998
Domaine Mommessin

Full colour. Rich, full, meaty nose. Some oak. Full bodied, rich and quite profound on the palate. Not overly tannic. There is plenty of substance here. It just needs time. Very good indeed. (June 2002)

2010 TO 2025   17.0

Clos de Vougeot, 1998
Domaine Robert Arnoux

Fullish colour. Rich, full and oaky on the nose. Lots of depth and quality here. Full bodied, ample and succulent. Very good grip. Very plump. This is most impressive. Lovely finish. Fine. (June 2002)

2010 TO 2025   17.5

Clos de Vougeot, 1998
Domaine Jacky Confuron-Cotétidot

Medium-full colour. Less of the stems than in other Confuron-Cotétidot's wines. But a touch

of sulphur. More stems on the palate. Sweet but weedy. No class. Forward, too. (June 2002)

NOW TO 2012   13.0

Clos de Vougeot, 1998
Domaine René Engel

Medium-full colour. Some development. Ripe, rich, round and opulent on the nose. A lot of attraction here. Soft and seductive on the palate. Rich and persistent. Medium to medium-full body. Lots of dimension. Fine plus. (June 2002)

NOW 2020   18.0

Clos de Vougeot, 1998
Domaine Joseph Faiveley

Very good colour. Full, rich and slightly ungainly, but a lot of depth and concentration on the nose. Medium-fullish body. Some tannin. Very classy fruit here. Very good grip and depth. This is longer and more stylish on the palate than Jadot's. Lovely finish. Certainly fine. Serious stuff. (June 2002)

NOW TO 2025   17.5

Clos de Vougeot, 1998
Maison Vincent Girardin

Good colour. Ripe, rich, fat and full of fruit. Medium-full body. Balanced, stylish and concentrated. Classy. Fine. (March 2002)

NOW TO 2026   17.5

Clos de Vougeot, 1998
Domaine Anne Gros

Fullish colour. Marvellous perfume on the nose. Intense and classy. Very lovely indeed on the palate. Rich, fullish bodied and very intense. Impeccably balanced. Generous and rich finish. Very fine plus. (June 2002)

NOW TO 2025   19.0

Clos de Vougeot, 1998
Domaine Alain Hudelot-Noëllat

Medium-full colour. Lovely rich, full nose. This has a lot of depth. Fullish bodied and ample. Fresh, if without the grip of Anne Gros's. This is a splendidly fruity example. Very well balanced. Fine. (June 2002)

NOW TO 2025   17.5

Clos de Vougeot, 1998
Domaine Louis Jadot

Very good colour. Rich, ripe, ample and a little adolescent at present on the nose. Fullish body. Some tannin. Very rich and ripe on the attack. Good class and depth on the palate. But not quite enough for fine. Good grip. Quite long at the end. The Faiveley has more classy fruit and better grip. Very good indeed. (June 2002)

NOW TO 2020   17.0

Clos de Vougeot, 1998
Domaine François Lamarche

Medium-full colour. Good oaky, exotic spice nose. Nothing coarse here. A lot of depth. On the palate, a little astringent. But good depth and decent class. Medium-full body. Decent grip. Very good indeed. (June 2002)

NOW TO 2018   17.0

Clos de Vougeot, 1998
Domaine Leroy

Medium-full colour. Rich, round, ripe nose. Lovely sweet fruit. Medium-full body. Gently oaky. Chambolle-ish. No great structure, but ripe and intense. Very seductive. Finishes long. Fine. (April 2000)

NOW TO 2015   17.5

Clos de Vougeot, 1998
Domaine Denis Mortet

Full colour. Just a touch reduced. Full, rich, sturdy and possibly a little overdone in maceration. Full body. Rich and oaky. Some tannin. This is sweet and ample, but it lacks a bit of class. Plenty of vigour but very good plus at best. (June 2002)

2010 TO 2025   16.5

Clos de Vougeot, 1998
Domaine Dr. Georges Mugneret

Medium-full colour. A little evolution. Good, quite firm, oaky nose. Rich and opulent. Medium body only. It lacks a little depth and concentration, though it's balanced and classy. It could have had more grip. Very good. (June 2002)

NOW TO 2016   16.0

Clos de Vougeot, 1998
Domaine Jacques Prieur

Fullish colour. Ripe but slightly vegetal on the nose. A little weedy on the palate. Quite ripe, but no real depth. Reasonable class. But not on top of the wine. Quite good. (June 2002)

NOW TO 2017   14.0

Clos de Vougeot, 1998
Domaine Laurent Roumier

Medium-full colour. Rather rustic on the nose. Medium to medium-full body. Some fruit and decent balance, but not much class and depth. Rather disappointing for what it is. Not much tannin. Dry and stemmy at the end. A bit short. (March 2003)

NOW TO 2012   14.0

Clos de Vougeot, 1998
Domaine Charles Thomas

Fullish colour. Ripe but chunky on the nose. Open and succulent, but does it lack a bit of grip? On the palate, a little astringent. Medium-full body but a bit dry. Good at best. (June 2002)

NOW TO 2018   15.0

Corton, 1998
Domaine Bonneau du Martray

Good colour. Rich, plump, raspberry-flavoured nose. Some tannin. Fragrant. Medium-full body. Ripe and balanced and vigorous. Very elegant. Fine. (June 2002)

NOW TO 2015   17.5

Corton, 1998
Domaine Follin-Arbelet

Medium colour. Lightish nose. Not much substance here. Decent fruit on the palate. More to it than it seems at first. Decent structure, too. Slightly adolescent. But it finishes well. Good plus. (June 2002)

NOW TO 2020   15.5

Corton, 1998
Domaine Tollot-Beaut et Fils

Medium colour. The nose is a bit light, and on the palate it is a bit pinched. It also lacks grip.

The attack is anonymous, then there is a little astringency, and the finish is a bit attenuated. Only fair. (June 2002)

NOW TO 2014   13.5

Le Corton, 1998
Domaine Bouchard Père et Fils
Fullish colour. A little shitty on the nose (first bottle). A second bottle was clean, fullish bodied, pure and vibrant. Good acidity. Slightly adolescent underneath, but fragrant and long. Very good plus. Surely more finesse to come. (October 2000)

NOW TO 2012   15.5

Corton, Les Bressandes, 1998
Domaine Chandon de Briailles
Medium colour. Soft nose. Slightly boiled-sweet fruit. Medium body. Not a lot of structure for a Corton. Decent fruit and acidity. But it lacks a bit of distinction. Good at best. (June 2002)

NOW TO 2016   15.0

Corton, Les Bressandes, 1998
Domaine Follin-Arbelet
Medium to medium-full colour. Pinched nose. Slightly reduced. Rather coarse. On the palate this is quite appley in flavour. There is a good structure and grip. But a lack of richness and charm. Quite good plus. (June 2002)

NOW TO 2014   14.5

Corton, Les Bressandes, 1998
Domaine Tollot-Beaut et Fils
Medium-full colour. Slightly dry, papery nose. Undistinguished. A bit better on the palate. Medium-full body. Some oak. Slightly astringent. Decent fruit and grip. Not brilliant, but good plus. (June 2002)

NOW TO 2018   15.5

Corton, Clos des Cortons Faiveley, 1998
Domaine Joseph Faiveley
Good colour. Full, fat, firm, rich, opulent nose. Lots of class here. Fullish weight on the palate. Very good, well covered tannins. Lots of concentrated fruit and very good acidity. This is profound and aristocratic. Really classy. Super. (June 2002)

2010 TO 2025+   18.5

Corton, Clos du Roi, 1998
Domaine Chandon de Briailles
Medium colour. Some development. Rich, medium-full, ample nose. This has class. Like the other Chandon wines, this is a bit weak and short on the palate. But it is the best of their three Cortons. Good plus. (June 2002)

NOW TO 2018   15.5

Corton, Clos du Roi, 1998
Domaine Prince Florent de Mérode
Medium-full colour. Good weight and fat on the nose. Fullish, succulent and with no lack of class. Medium to medium-full body on the palate. A little weak for a *grand cru*. Forward, too. Not much tannin. Decent acidity. Quite fruity. Round, ripe and quite succulent. This has charm, if no real depth. Good grip, though. For a *grand cru*, not special. Very good at best. (March 2002)

NOW TO 2012   16.0

Corton, Clos du Roi, 1998
Domaine Charles Thomas
Fullish colour. Some development. Fullish nose. Good tannins. Plenty of depth. On the palate this is quite rich. But though medium-full bodied, it lacks succulence. Some fruit but no better than good plus. (June 2002)

NOW TO 2018   15.5

Corton, Maréchaudes, 1998
Domaine Chandon de Briailles
Medium colour. Some development. Plump nose. But no real distinction. Like their Corton Bressandes, this is reasonably balanced, but it lacks depth, richness and flair. Quite good plus. (June 2002)

NOW TO 2014   14.5

Corton, Les Perrières, 1998
Maison Vincent Girardin
Fine colour. Rich, intense, black cherry nose. Plump, oaky and ripe. Fullish body. Lovely fruit. Very good balance. Very impressive finish. This is intense and very lovely. (March 2002)

NOW TO 2026   17.5

Corton, Les Perrières, 1998
Domaine Marc Morey

Medium-full colour. Quite rich on the nose. This has depth. A bit closed still. Fresh, medium-full bodied, meaty wine. This has attractive fruit. It has good balance and is properly positive. Very good. (June 2002)

NOW TO 2020   16.0

Corton, Pougets, 1998
Domaine Louis Jadot

Fullish colour. Full nose. Backward but concentrated and classy. Quite black fruity. Rich, full bodied, concentrated, oaky and profound on the palate. This has proper depth and weight. Fine. (June 2002)

2010 TO 2025   17.5

Corton, Les Renardes, 1998
Maison Vincent Girardin

Fullish colour. Firm, rich, slightly dense on the nose. A touch of CO_2 in some bottles. Black cherry and plum/damson fruit. Good tannin. Very good grip. A little dumb at first. Expansive at the end. Lovely fruit. Ample and elegant. Fine quality. (March 2002)

NOW TO 2018   17.5

Corton, Les Renardes, 1998
Domaine Leroy

Youthful but not that deep in colour. Youthful nose. Abundant fruit. Good acidity and structure. Slightly raw at present. Recently bottled, so a touch of sulphur. Medium-full body. Ripe and gently oaky. Good grip. Not a great deal of tannin. Plenty of depth and intensity, though. Very good indeed. (April 2000)

NOW TO 2016   17.0

Echézeaux, 1998
Domaine Bouchard Père et Fils

Medium-full colour. Plump and ripe without the greatest of concentration and depth. Fullish body. Good fruit. Decent on the palate. Fresh and with good tannin. But overall, it is no better than very good. (June 2002)

NOW TO 2018   16.0

Echézeaux, 1998
Domaine Jacky Confuron-Cotétidot

Medium colour. Weedy, stemmy nose. Rather sour-evolved too. Similar on the palate. Weak. Poor. (June 2002)

DRINK SOON   12.0

Echézeaux, 1998
Domaine Joseph Drouhin

Fullish colour. Gentle, stylish Pinot nose. Good fruit. Good depth. But by no means a blockbuster. Medium-full body. Lovely balance. Elegant and intense. This has a very fine grip and lovely fruit. Fine. (June 2002)

NOW TO 2020   17.5

Echézeaux, 1998
Domaine René Engel

Full colour. A little development. Oaky nose. Quite soft and accessible for a 1998. Medium-full body. A little tannin. Good grip. Nice ripe, quite creamy, complex fruit. The finish is long, classy and profound. Fine plus. (September 2004)

NOW TO 2025   18.0

Echézeaux, 1998
Domaine Joseph Faiveley

Full colour. Ripe nose. Vosne-ish. Very good rich fruit. Plenty of depth and structure here. Quite a lot of tannin. Full bodied, rich and meaty, even robust, on the palate. Does it lack a little class? It certainly has plenty of weight. Very good plus. (September 2002)

2009 TO 2020   16.5

Echézeaux, 1998
Domaine Jean Grivot

Fullish colour. This is rich, concentrated, oaky and profound on the nose. A multidimensional wine of great beauty for an Échezeaux. Very impressive. Fullish weight on the palate. Opulent, ripe and rich. Very lovely balanced, concentrated fruit. This is very fine. (June 2002)

2010 TO 2020   18.5

Echézeaux, 1998
Domaine Louis Jadot

Full colour. Quite firm on the nose. The tan-nins show a bit. Better on the palate. Full body. Proper Côte de Nuits black fruit masculinity. Very good grip and depth. Long and lovely and promising. This is fine plus. (October 2002)

NOW TO 2020+   18.0

Echézeaux, 1998
Domaine François Lamarche

Fullish colour. Ample and plump on the nose, but a lack of real class. Slightly four-square on the palate. A bit chunky. Decent fruit under-neath. Good at best. (June 2002)

NOW TO 2018   15.0

Echézeaux, Vieilles Vignes, 1998
Domaine Mongeard-Mugneret

Medium-full colour. Sweet toffee liquorice nose. Not a bit hard. Medium-full body. Meaty. Ripe. Good grip. Not the greatest distinction, but vigorous and very good. Just about ready. (October 2005)

NOW TO 2015   16.0

Echézeaux, 1998
Domaine Mugneret-Gibourg

Medium-full colour. Ripe, rich, gently oaky and finely balanced on the nose. This is really lovely. It is succulent, ripe, complex, classy and bal-anced. Much better than their Clos de Vougeot. Very fine finish. (June 2002)

2010 TO 2025   17.5

Echézeaux, 1998
Domaine des Perdrix

Medium-full colour. Quite a high-toned nose. Good fruit underneath. But on the palate, a lack of grip and depth. This is uninspiring. (June 2002)

NOW TO 2014   13.5

Echézeaux, 1998
Domaine Daniel Rion

Medium-full colour. Still youthful but some development. Round, ripe, quite classy nose.

Medium-full body. Some tannin. Good grip. Lacks a little style but balanced. Very good but not great. (September 2005)

NOW TO 2017   16.0

Echézeaux, 1998
Domaine Jacques Prieur

Fullish colour. Better than their Clos de Vou-geot, but quite weedy nevertheless. Ripe, but with neither grace nor grip. Some fruit. But as much astringent. Yet decent acidity. Better than the Domainee des Perdrix's example, at least. Quite good. (June 2002)

NOW TO 2014   14.0

Echézeaux, 1998
Domaine de la Romanée-Conti

Medium-full colour. Fresh, ripe, succulent, classy and well balanced. No undue stemmy fla-vours. Soft and quite persistent. Both red and black fruit here. On the palate just a touch of new wood. Medium-full body. Very well inte-grated tannins. Good grip and vigour. Long and, above all, very elegant and harmonious. Fine. (July 2002)

NOW TO 2020+   17.5

Echézeaux, 1998
Domaine Emmanuel Rouget

Medium to medium-full colour. Slightly dense and four-square on the nose. Lots of oak. Almost sweet. This seems a bit over-extracted to me. It lacks class and freshness. Yet decent length. Good. (June 2002)

NOW TO 2018   15.0

Fixin, Les Crais, 1998
Domaine Vincent and Denis Berthaut

A lightish style. Slightly astringent at the end and without a lot of fat. Not too short though. Quite succulent. (January 2002)

NOW TO 2011   14.0

Gevrey-Chambertin, Premier Cru, 1998
Domaine Bernard Dugat-Py

Full colour. Rich, full and oaky on the nose. Plump, fullish bodied, ripe and oaky on the palate. No undue maceration. In fact, nicely concentrated, long and balanced. Plenty of dimension. Fine. (June 2002)

2010 TO 2025   17.5

Gevrey-Chambertin, Les Cazetiers, 1998
Domaine Bouchard Père et Fils

Medium-full colour. Quite fragrant and high-toned. Good freshness. Only medium to medium-full weight. It doesn't quite have either the concentration or the class for fine. But ample and oaky, and with good length. Very good indeed. (June 2002)

NOW TO 2020   17.0

Gevrey-Chambertin, Les Cazetiers, 1998
Domaine Bruno Clair

Medium-full colour. Very classy, slightly lean fruit on the nose. Very typical of Bruno Clair. Lovely. Medium to medium-full weight. Poised, concentrated, intense and classy. Lots of depth on the follow-through. Fine. (June 2002)

NOW TO 2025   17.5

Gevrey-Chambertin, Les Cazetiers, 1998
Domaine Armand Rousseau

Medium-full colour. Some development. Ample, rich, fat nose. This has old-vine fruit and plenty of depth. Ample, plump and medium-full bodied on the palate. Very good fruit. Plenty of concentration. Good grip. Very good indeed. (June 2002)

NOW TO 2020   17.0

Gevrey-Chambertin, Les Cazetiers, 1998
Domaine Christian Sérafin

Full colour. Finely concentrated. Some oak. Plenty of depth on the nose. A fullish, oaky wine. No undue structure. Old viney. Very good fruit. Positive and intense at the end. Lots of vigour. Fine. (June 2002)

2010 TO 2025   17.5

Gevrey-Chambertin, En Champeaux, 1998
Domaine Denis Mortet

Surprisingly full and immature colour. The nose is rather more hidden than on the 1999, but there is a lot more depth and richness. Good, but not excessive, oaky base. No hardness. Medium-full body. Ripe tannins. Very good acidity. Stylish and complex. Long. Impressively complex and classy. This is very good indeed. (May 2002)

NOW TO 2015   17.0

Gevrey-Chambertin, Cherbaudes, 1998
Domaine Lucien Boillot Père et Fils

Full colour. Fresh and plump, if not very distinguished on the nose. Medium to medium-full weight. Plump and fruity. Very good, if no great grip or distinction. Easy to drink. Very good. (June 2002)

NOW TO 2018   16.0

Gevrey-Chambertin, Clos du Fonteny, 1998
Domaine Bruno Clair

Medium-full colour. Lightish and lean, as is Bruno Clair's style. But elegant and quite intense. A bit light and weedy on the attack. But good depth and class in the middle, and plenty of depth and drive. Very good plus. (June 2002)

NOW TO 2018   16.5

Gevrey-Chambertin, Clos de la Justice, 1998
Domaine Pierre Bourée et Fils

Spicy, open, evolved. Fruity. Easy to drink. Quite elegant. But slightly attenuated at the end. Only fair. (January 2002)

NOW TO 2010   13.0

Gevrey-Chambertin, Clos Saint-Jacques, 1998
Domaine Bruno Clair

Medium-full colour. Not, on the nose, quite as good and succulent as his Cazetiers this year. Elegant, and succulent enough, but only medium-full bodied and quite stemmy on the palate. Good richness, though, and good grip. But no better than fine. (June 2002)

NOW TO 2020   17.5

Gevrey-Chambertin, Clos Saint-Jacques, 1998
Domaine Michel Esmonin et Fille

Medium to medium-full colour. High-toned nose. Plump. But not the greatest of depth. Ripe, almost sweet, on the palate. Touches of chocolate. This has medium body only, but it is intense and concentrated. Very good. (June 2002)

NOW TO 2016   16.0

Gevrey-Chambertin, Clos Saint-Jacques, 1998
Domaine Louis Jadot

Medium-full colour. A slight touch of volatile acidity over a very fine, ripe, concentrated nose. On the palate this is very concentrated and stylish. Very rich. Lots of dimension. This has enormous intensity. Very, very long and lovely. Excellent. Very fine. (April 2005)

2010 TO 2025   18.5

Gevrey-Chambertin, Clos Saint-Jacques, 1998
Maison Dominique Laurent

Medium-full colour. Slightly dense on the nose. Not over-oaked but a bit clumsy. Medium to medium-full body. Slightly rustic. Some oak on the palate. Slightly unsettled. Lacks class. Merely good. (April 2005)

NOW TO 2013   15.0

Gevrey-Chambertin, Clos Saint-Jacques, 1998
Domaine Armand Rousseau

Medium-full colour. Splendidly ripe, rich, ample and poised on the nose. Real dimension here. Ample, ripe, balanced and fullish bodied on the palate. An elegant yet opulent example. Lovely finish. Fine plus. (April 2005)

2010 TO 2020

Gevrey-Chambertin, Aux Combottes, 1998
Domaine Dujac

Full colour. A little development. Ripe, classy and individual. More accessible than most. A medium weight, very smooth, quite oaky, almost sweet, wine. Long. Fine. (June 2002)

NOW TO 2020   17.5

Gevrey-Chambertin, Les Corbeaux, 1998
Domaine Denis Bachelet

Medium-full colour. Lovely nose. Clean and pure and quite backward. But very intense. Very classy on the palate. Medium-full body. Good tannins. Finely poised. Lovely fruit. Long and very complex. Very impressive. Fine. (June 2002)

2010 TO 2020   17.5

Gevrey-Chambertin, Les Corbeaux, 1998
Domaine Bruno Clavelier

Medium-full colour. This is very stylish on the nose. Lovely pure fruit. Finely poised. On the palate this is fresh, balanced and well-made. Not the concentration of Denis Bachelet's Corbeaux. Very good indeed, though. (June 2002)

NOW TO 2018   17.0

Gevrey-Chambertin, Les Corbeaux, 1998
Domaine Christian Sérafin

Medium-full colour. Rich and oaky on the nose. But a bit more four-square than his Cazetiers. Here the new wood takes over a bit too much. Medium to medium-full body but a little over-done. Merely quite good. (June 2002)

NOW TO 2015   14.0

Gevrey-Chambertin, Craipillot, 1998
Domaine Jacky Confuron-Cotétidot

Medium-full colour. Some development. High-toned, light, stemmy nose. Medium body. Quite fresh. But no real depth or dimension. It tails off a bit. Ripe and plump but no better than good. (June 2002)

NOW TO 2016   15.0

Gevrey-Chambertin, Estournelles-Saint-Jacques, 1998
Maison Antonin Rodet

Very good colour. Opulent nose. Just on the verge of being oxidised. The second bottle was fresher: firmer, more vigorous. Full bodied, rich, concentrated and very succulent on the follow-through. This is very lovely. An opulent wine. (October 2000)

NOW TO 2015   17.5

Gevrey-Chambertin, Evocelles, 1998
Domaine Lucien Boillot Père et Fils

Full colour. Rich, full and oaky on the nose. Nicely ample. Plenty of substance here. Full body. Some tannin. Lovely concentrated fruit and very good depth. This is very good, indeed surprisingly so. Lovely fruit at the end. (June 2002)

2010 TO 2020   17.0

Gevrey-Chambertin, Fonteny, 1998
Domaine Joseph Roty

Medium-full colour. Good intensity. Almost sweet fruit on the nose. Medium to medium-full body. Very exotic. Coffee, chocolate, mocha and other flavours. Good grip. Medium to medium-full body. Intense. Very good indeed. (June 2002)

NOW TO 2018   17.0

Gevrey-Chambertin, Fonteny, 1998
Domaine Christian Sérafin

Fullish colour. Here the fruit is almost over-oaked. As with his Corbeaux, the new oak dominates. Good fruit but not enough grip and concentration. The wood is rather perfumed, too. Quite good. (June 2002)

NOW TO 2015   14.0

Gevrey-Chambertin, Lavaux-Saint-Jacques, 1998
Domaine Bernard Dugat-Py

Full colour. Rich, full, oaky and exotic on the nose. Rich, fruity and concentrated. Oaky, but the oak is integrated. Excellent depth. Fullish body. Fine plus. (June 2002)

2010 TO 2020   18.0

Gevrey-Chambertin, Lavaux-Saint-Jacques, 1998
Domaine Humbert Frères

Medium-full colour. Just a little development. On the nose, quite soft, sweet and accessible. On the palate, medium to medium-full body. No hard edges. Feminine for a Lavaux, indeed for a Gevrey. But fragrant, harmonious and classy. Now ready. Very good indeed. (May 2004)

NOW TO 2012   17.0

Gevrey-Chambertin, Lavaux-Saint-Jacques, 1998
Domaine Bertrand Maume

Fullish colour. Ripe, full and sturdy on the nose. A bit coarse on the palate. Medium-full body. Decent grip. But it doesn't sing. Quite good at best. (June 2002)

NOW TO 2015   14.0

Gevrey-Chambertin, Lavaux-Saint-Jacques, 1998
Domaine Denis Mortet

Full colour. Opulent, like the Dugat-Py example, but not the same amount of concentration or depth on the nose. This is sweet, rich, concentrated and impressive. Good grip. Very exotic. Lovely. Fine. (September 2002)

2010 TO 2020   17.5

Gevrey-Chambertin, Petite Chapelle, 1998
Domaine Bruno Clair

Medium colour. Lightish nose. But plump and stylish. Fruity, but a little astringent on the palate and a little weak at the end. Unexciting. (June 2002)

NOW TO 2015   13.0

Gevrey-Chambertin, Petite Chapelle, 1998
Domaine Jean-Michel Guillon

Medium to medium-full colour. A little development. Quite evolved on the nose with a touch of the stems. Ripe and gently oaky but not a great deal of depth or style. Medium weight. Already quite evolved on the palate. Little tannin. Decent acidity. Spicy. Attractive fruit. Fresh. Quite complex. The feminine touch of the climat is evident. But by no means a blockbuster. Good length. Good plus. (March 2002)

NOW TO 2012   15.5

Gevrey-Chambertin, Petite Chapelle, 1998
Domaine Humbert Frères

This is very well made. Fullish, rich and not a bit overdone, letting all the lovely lacy fruit of Petite-Chapelle come out. Ripe, fresh and persistent. Very well balanced. Great finesse. Long and subtle. Fine. (November 2002)

NOW TO 2018   17.5

La Grande Rue, 1998
Domaine François Lamarche

Fullish colour. Full, firm and rich on the nose. Slightly rigid. Some oak. High quality here. Nothing rustic about it. Full and rich and meaty: more La Tâche than La Romanée. Good grip. Slightly adolescent, but lots of fine wine here. (October 2002)

2010 TO 2025   18.0

Grands Echézeaux, 1998
Domaine Joseph Drouhin

Medium to medium-full colour. Rich, gently oaky nose. Quite succulent. Accessible. Medium-full body. Good tannins. Very good grip. This is ripe, concentrated and classy. Long. Lovely fruit. Lovely intense finish. Very fine. (June 2002)

2010 TO 2025   18.5

Grands Echézeaux, 1998
Domaine René Engel

Fullish colour. A little development. Lovely ripe, oaky nose. Not a bit aggressive. Quite round already. Lots of class and depth. Medium-full body. Cool and distinguished. Multidimensional. Splendid finish. Super fruit. Very fine. (June 2005)

NOW TO 2020+   18.5

Grands Echézeaux, 1998
Domaine de la Romanée-Conti

Medium-full colour. Richer, more profound and more classy than their Échezeaux. Good grip. Very lovely fruit. More black fruity than red fruity. A bigger, more tannic and more closed-in wine than the Échezeaux. Fullish body. Good grip. Rich and intense on the follow-through. Lots of dimension. Fine plus. (July 2002)

2010 TO 2025   18.0

Griotte-Chambertin, 1998
Domaine Joseph Drouhin

Good full colour. Now with some signs of maturity. A broader, slightly more loose-knit fruit flavour on the nose. No hard tannins, though. Smooth, ripe and slightly caramel-spiced. Medium-full body. Rich, fat and quite meaty. Good grip. This is a lovely example. Very long. Lots of depth. Very fine for the vintage. (July 2003)

NOW TO 2024   18.5

Griotte-Chambertin, 1998
Domaine Ponsot

Fullish, vigorous colour. Ample, rich, cool, plump fruit on the nose. Medium-full body. Rich. Very good tannins. Good grip. Getting there. Classy. Very long on the palate. (June 2005)

NOW TO 2017   18.0

Latricières-Chambertin, 1998
Domaine Joseph Faiveley

Good colour. Quite firm on the nose, but rich and succulent underneath. Fullish body. Some tannin. Good structure. Very good grip. This has ample, plummy fruit and plenty of zip and style. Very lovely finish. Very seductive. Fine. (September 2002)

2009 TO 2020+   18.0

Latricières-Chambertin, 1998
Domaine Leroy

Fullish colour. Delicious fresh, fragrant fruit on the nose. Fullish. Very fresh on the palate. Very elegant. This is a particularly lovely example. Medium-full body. Balanced. Complex. Positive. Lovely. Very fine. (April 2000)

NOW TO 2018   18.5

Latricières-Chambertin, 1998
Domaine Jean Trapet Père et Fils

Medium-full colour. Quite oaky on the nose. Ripe and rich on the palate. Quite sturdy tannins. Medium-full body. Slightly hard all the way, though. Will this soften? I think this is better than their Chapelle. The finish is longer and more vigorous. Fine. (June 2002)

2010 TO 2025   17.5

Mazis-Chambertin, 1998
Domaine Bernard Dugat-Py

Full colour. Rich, full and oaky nose. A full-bodied, concentrated, old-viney, intense wine on the palate. Lots of depth. Ripe tannins. Long and impressive. Very fine. (June 2002)

2010 TO 2025   18.5

Mazis-Chambertin, 1998
Domaine Joseph Faiveley

Medium-full colour. Still very youthful. Ripe, rich, civilised, succulent nose. Fullish body. Good tannins. Very good grip. Lots of depth and class here. Lots of dimension. Lovely ample, vigorous follow-through. Fine plus. (April 2005)

NOW TO 2020   18.0

Mazis-Chambertin, 1998
Domaine Harmand-Geoffroy

Good colour. Quite oaky on the nose, with a touch of reduction. Fullish. Some tannin. A little robust. Good grip and vigour. Quite rich.

Finishes well. Concentrated and intense. Very good indeed. (October 2002)

NOW TO 2015   17.0

Mazis-Chambertin, 1998
Hospices de Beaune

Made by Alain Corcia for Troigros. Full colour. Full, rich, not-too-oaky nose. Good depth and dimension here. Very rich and fat. Full body. Some tannin. Oaky. Lovely blackberry flavour. Almost sweet. Very creamy, old viney. Backward. Potentially very fine. (April 2005)

2010 TO 2025+   19.0

Mazis-Chambertin, 1998
Maison Antonin Rodet

Good colour. Rich, opulent nose. Ripe and fleshy. Fullish and very seductive. On the palate this has very lovely rich fruit. Good acidity. Softer tannins. Good length. Classy. Fine plus. (October 2000)

NOW TO 2010   18.0

Mazis-Chambertin, 1998
Domaine Armand Rousseau

Light to medium colour. Light, slightly boiled-sweet, fruity nose. No great depth. Light, fresh, fruity on the palate. Not short, but one-dimensional. Forward. Disappointing. (April 2005)

NOW TO 2010   13.0

Monthelie, Chateau Gaillard, 1998
Domaine Annick Parent

Very gently oaky. Quite rich, crisp and minerally. Balanced and integrated. Good depth and class. Long and positive. Flowery. Very good, especially for what it is. (May 2005)

DRINK SOON   16.0

Morey-Saint-Denis, Clos de la Buissière, 1998
Domaine Georges Roumier et Fils

Medium-full colour. Ample, succulent, fullish nose. This example is corked, but one can see a wine of medium-full size with good fruit and grip. Rich and slightly robust. A clean bottle

would certainly be very good plus at the very least. (June 2002)

2010 TO 2020   16.5

Morey-Saint-Denis, Monts Luisants, 1998
Domaine François Thomas

Medium-full colour. Slightly lean on the nose. Not enough fruit on the palate. Medium-full body. Decent quality but unexciting. It lacks depth. Quite fresh at the end, so it is not too astringent. Quite good plus. (June 2002)

NOW TO 2016   14.5

Morey-Saint-Denis, La Riotte, 1998
Domaine Odoul-Coquard

Medium-full colour. Slightly hard and fruitless on the nose. Similar on the palate. This lacks concentration and finishes a bit anonymous. Dull. (June 2002)

NOW TO 2012   13.5

Morey-Saint-Denis, En la Rue de Vergy, 1998
Domaine Bruno Clair

Medium colour. A touch lean on the nose. But soft, medium body. Nicely intense and ripe on the palate. A gentle example. Not the depth or richness for *premier cru* perhaps (which they are trying for) but classy, long and good plus. (October 2002)

NOW TO 2009   15.5

Morey-Saint-Denis, Premier Cru, Vieilles Vignes, 1998
Domaine Hubert Lignier

Medium-full colour. Ripe, plump and oaky on the nose. Lovely fruit on the palate. Good energy. Fullish body. Ripe, succulent and long on the finish. Fine. (June 2002)

2010 TO 2020   17.5

Musigny, 1998
Domaine Leroy

Fine colour. The nose is very lovely here. Very Musigny. Multidimensional. The palate is even better. Rich and oaky. Medium to medium-full body. Succulent, harmonious and seductive.

Lovely long finish. Very fine for the vintage. (April 2000)

NOW TO 2018   18.5

Musigny, 1998
Domaine Jacques-Frédéric Mugnier

Medium-full colour. Much better colour than his Bonnes Mares. Fragrant and intense on the nose. Medium-full body. Ripe. Very good tannins. Very good acidity. This is very classy and very lovely. Long. Very fine indeed. (September 2002)

NOW TO 2025   19.5

Musigny, 1998
Domaine Jacques Prieur

Medium-full colour. Ripe and plump on the nose. But slightly four-square. All the way through to the middle palate, this is just what you would wish. But then it tails away a bit. Medium-full body. Ripe, classy and succulent. But fine, rather than great. Not short. (June 2002)

NOW TO 2018   17.5

Musigny, 1998
Domaine Comte Georges de Vogüé

A wine of great appeal. Fullish, still some tannins, but richer and more intense than 1991 or 1993. Exquisite balance. Very high class fruit. Great breed. Lovely harmony. Good grip. Already lots of charm. Very fine indeed for the vintage. (March 2005)

2010 TO 2030   20.0

Nuits-Saint-Georges, Les Argillières, 1998
Domaine Bouchard Père et Fils

Medium-full colour. Ripe, rich, meaty nose. Fullish body, rich and plentiful. Good depth. Good structure. Good grip. Plenty of substance here. Fresh and positive at the end. Very good plus. (June 2002)

2010 TO 2025   16.5

Nuits-Saint-Georges, Aux Boudots, 1998
Domaine Jean Grivot

Half bottle. Good colour. Rich, quite oaky nose. Lots of depth and finesse. Not a bit ready, of course. But very promising. Fullish body. Ripe

tannins. Very good grip. Real style and dimension. Excellent balance. Lots of substance here. Fine plus, at the very least. (July 2005)

2009 TO 2025+   18.0

Nuits-Saint-Georges, Aux Boudots, 1998
Domaine Louis Jadot

Medium colour. Ripe, ample nose. Good depth and class, if not quite the distinction of Grivot's. Fullish body. Balanced and with very good style. Lovely long follow-through. A poised wine. Fine. (June 2002)

2010 TO 2025   17.5

Nuits-Saint-Georges, Aux Boudots, 1998
Domaine Méo-Camuzet

Medium-full colour. Full and rich with a touch of oak on the nose. Plenty of depth. Full body. Good fruit. Not a bit overdone. Very good grip. This again is harmonious, classy, long and positive. Fine. (June 2002)

2010 TO 2025   17.5

Nuits-Saint-Georges, Aux Brûlées, 1998
Domaine Henri Gille Père et Fils

Much more sophisticated. Good structure. Ripe tannin. Lovely fruit. Very good grip. This is very good indeed. Really quite vigorous. (February 2003)

NOW TO 2020   16.0

Nuits-Saint-Georges, Aux Chaignots, 1998
Domaine Dr. Georges Mugneret

Medium-full colour. Ripe, rich, fullish and ample on the nose. Fresh. Fullish body. Good class. Good structure again. Ripe and rich. Well-made. Very good indeed. (June 2002)

2010 TO 2022   17.0

Nuits-Saint-Georges, Clos des Argillières, 1998
Domaine Daniel Rion et Fils

Medium-full colour. Some development. A suggestion of attenuation on the nose. Medium body. Fruity but a little weak. Forward. But at least it isn't too short. Only quite good. (June 2002)

NOW TO 2015   14.0

Nuits-Saint-Georges, Clos des Corvées, 1998
Domaine Prieuré-Roch

Premier cru. Monopole. Medium colour. Some evolution. Rather dry and flabby on the nose. This shows traces of attenuation. Light and weedy on the palate. A bit of a disgrace for what it is. Sour at the end. Not short but undistinguished. (July 2001)

DRINK SOON   13.0

Nuits-Saint-Georges, Clos des Corvées Pagets, 1998
Domaine Robert Arnoux

Fullish colour. Quite firm and tannic on the nose. It needs time. Not too extracted though. Despite the wine being corked, one can see that there is good distinction, proper balance and plenty of depth here. Very good plus, I'm sure. (June 2002)

2010 TO 2022   16.5

Nuits-Saint-Georges, Clos des Forêts Saint-Georges, 1998
Domaine de l'Arlot

Medium-full colour. A little feeble on the nose. An absence of richness and depth. Medium body. Only a little tannin. The fruit is quite ripe, even a little boiled-sweety in flavour. Decent acidity. But not much concentration, succulence or style. Quite good at best. (June 2002)

NOW TO 2012   14.0

Nuits-Saint-Georges, Clos des Porrets Saint-Georges, 1998
Domaine Henri Gouges

Medium-full colour. Reserved nose. Very lovely fruit. Full, but no excessive or aggressive tannins. Very pure on the palate. It needs time. Medium-full body. Good vigour. Quietly composed. Long. Fine. (October 2002)

2010 TO 2025   17.5

Nuits-Saint-Georges, Aux Cras, 1998
Domaine Bruno Clavelier

Fullish colour. Perfumed nose. It lacks a little distinction. This is rather weedy and astringent.

It lacks grip. Medium body. No future. Is this a bad bottle? (June 2002)

NOW TO 2010   12.5

Nuits-Saint-Georges, Les Damodes, 1998
Domaine Jean Chauvenet

Medium-full colour. Some fruit, but a little concocted on the nose. Medium-full body. Less artificial on the palate. Good acidity. It lacks a little distinction but has good depth and length. Good plus. (June 2002)

NOW TO 2020   15.5

Nuits-Saint-Georges, Les Damodes, 1998
Domaine Joseph Faiveley

Fullish colour. Full, rich and manly on the nose, without being a bit brutal. Full body. Some tannin. A little austere on the attack. Good grip. Perhaps not quite rich enough, but certainly balanced and stylish. It will get more generous as it evolves. Very good plus. (June 2002)

NOW TO 2020   16.5

Nuits-Saint-Georges, Les Hauts Pruliers, 1998
Domaine Daniel Rion et Fils

Fullish colour. Just a little vegetal on the nose. Better on the palate. Medium-full body. Ripe. Good energy. Decent fruit. It lacks a little distinction though. Very good at best. (June 2002)

NOW TO 2018   16.5

Nuits-Saint-Georges, Aux Perdrix, 1998
Domaine des Perdrix

Medium-full colour. Quite firm but good depth here. Fullish body. Oaky and rich. A little closed-in, but with very good depth and grip. Long and intense at the end. This is fine. (June 2002)

2010 TO 2025   17.5

Nuits-Saint-Georges, Poisets, 1998
Domaine Robert Arnoux

Medium-full colour. Good class and good substance. Less firm than the Clos des Corvées Pagets, so easier to judge. Ripe and succulent. Medium-full body. Fresh. Not as concentrated or as profound, but well made. Long and positive. Very good plus. (June 2002)

NOW TO 2020   16.5

Nuits-Saint-Georges, Les Porrets, 1998
Maison Antonin Rodet

Medium-full colour. This is very fine on the nose. Pure and concentrated. Balanced and classy. Very oaky. Fullish body. Lovely ample fruit here. Very well balanced and with an excellent, long finish. Very classy and very long. Fine. (June 2002)

2010 TO 2025 17.5

Nuits-Saint-Georges, Les Procès, 1998
Domaine Joseph Drouhin

Medium colour. Good class. Not very Nuits-Saint-Georges-ish. Medium-full body. Accessible, ripe, balanced and stylish on the palate. Fresh and positive at the end. Very good plus. (June 2002)

NOW TO 2018 16.5

Nuits-Saint-Georges, Les Pruliers, 1998
Domaine Lucien Boillot Père et Fils

Fullish colour. Just a touch rustic on the nose. Better on the palate. Medium-full body. Quite accessible. Good fresh, plump fruit. Balanced. Good tannins. Positive finish. Very good plus. (June 2002)

NOW TO 2018 16.5

Nuits-Saint-Georges, Les Pruliers, 1998
Domaine Robert Chevillon

Medium colour. Ripe and succulent on the nose. Soft, fruity, plump and quite forward. Medium to medium-full body. Good length. This is a typical Chevillon wine. Very good. Quite evolved though. (June 2002)

NOW TO 2018 16.0

Nuits-Saint-Georges, Les Pruliers, 1998
Domaine Henri Gouges

Medium-full colour. Slightly austere, but with very distinguished, plummy fruit on the nose. Not quite with the distinction of his Clos des Porrets, but ripe, balanced, fullish bodied, stylish and long. Lovely. Fine. (June 2002)

2010 TO 2025

Nuits-Saint-Georges, Les Pruliers, 1998
Domaine Jean Grivot

Medium-full colour. Some oak. But lovely intense fruit to match it on the nose. Fullish

body. Quite oaky on the palate. Very good concentration. Lovely balance. Excellent fruit. This, again, is fine. (June 2002)

2010 TO 2025 17.5

Nuits-Saint-Georges, La Richemone, 1998
Domaine Charles Thomas

Fullish colour. It seems a bit green on the nose. Oxidised, too. Fullish bodied, but flat and astringent on the palate. Yet there is good grip. A good bottle could be very good at least and would need time. (June 2002)

2010 TO 2025 10.0

Nuits-Saint-Georges, Les Roncières, 1998
Domaine Robert Chevillon

Medium colour. Evolved. Good soft, quite fruity nose. Quite accessible. Medium body. Only a little tannin. It lacks a little definition and grip. A pleasant example. But quite good only. (June 2002)

NOW TO 2016 14.0

Nuits-Saint-Georges, Les Saint-Georges, 1998
Domaine Joseph Faiveley

Fullish colour. Rich, full, even a little solid, but not too tannic. Full bodied, masculine and tannic on the palate. Very good grip. This has a lot of depth and concentration. It is a little brutal, but there is a lot of potential here. Lovely finish. Fine. (June 2002)

2009 TO 2025 17.5

Nuits-Saint-Georges, Les Saint-Georges, 1998
Domaine Henri Gouges

Medium-full colour. Firm nose. Quite closed. Quite austere. Fullish bodied, tannic and masculine on the palate. Hard at first, but the follow-through is more generous. Plenty of depth and class. Long finish. Fine plus. (September 2003)

2010 TO 2025 18.0

Nuits-Saint-Georges, Les Saint-Georges, 1998
Maison Antonin Rodet

Medium-full colour. I am not convinced by the nose: there is something a bit weak here. This cleared up on aeration. Some new wood apparent. Fullish body. Quite chunky. Not as concentrated as Gouges's, but ripe and sylish and long. Very good indeed. (June 2002)

2010 TO 2025

Nuits-Saint-Georges, Les Vaucrains, 1998
Domaine Jean Chauvenet

Full colour. Full, firm and quite chunky on the nose. Solid, but with plenty of depth underneath. On the palate it seems to lack a little fruit and grip. I am not sure this isn't too astringent for its own good. As it evolved, I became more confident about its future. Very good plus. (June 2002)

2010 TO 2025   16.5

Nuits-Saint-Georges, Les Vaucrains, 1998
Domaine Robert Chevillon

Medium to medium-full colour. Lush for what it is on the nose. Good depth on the palate. More substance than his other wines. More evolved than most of the reds. Ample. Good depth. Very good plus. (June 2002)

NOW TO 2018   16.5

Nuits-Saint-Georges, Les Vaucrains, 1998
Domaine Henri Gouges

Full colour. Full, backward, solid nose. Big and tannic on the palate. But very good grip to accompany it. Rich at the end. Ample, classy, balanced and concentrated. It just needs time. Fine. (June 2002)

2010 TO 2025   17.5

Pommard, Les Arvelets, 1998
Domaine Camus Bruchon

Medium colour. Strong nose but a bit farmyardy. Good acidity but a little astringent on the palate. Medium body. It lacks both richness and charm. Not bad plus. (June 2002)

NOW TO 2010   13.5

Pommard, Clos des Epeneaux, 1998
Domaine du Comte Armand

Medium-full colour. Backward on the nose. Plenty of depth, though. Quite substantial. Lots of wine here. Not as agressively backward as I

expected. Medium-full body. Rich, meaty attack. The tannins come out at the end. I don't think this has quite enough zip. Only good. It needs time. (June 2002)

2010 TO 2025   15.0

Pommard, Epenots, 1998
Domaine de Courcel

Medium-full colour. Rich nose. Almost sweet. Good succulence. Good substance. The best of the three De Courcel wines. Rich and meaty. A touch of oak. Very good grip and depth. Lovely long finish. Very good indeed. (June 2002)

NOW TO 2025   17.0

Pommard, Epenots, Vieilles Vignes, 1998
Maison Vincent Girardin

Very good colour. Firm, backward, fullish bodied. Some tannins. This is rich and balanced, but it needs time. Lots of depth. Fine quality. (October 2000)

NOW TO 2015   17.5

Pommard, Epenots, 1998
Domaine Louis Jadot

Full colour. Full, rich, backward and tannic on the nose. Plenty of depth here. Full and rich on the palate, too. Lots of concentration. Very good grip. The tannins are excellent. Very long and very sophisticated. Lovely finish. (June 2002)

NOW TO 2025   17.5

Pommard, Frémiets, 1998
Domaine de Courcel

Fullish colour. Very stylish nose. Lovely fruit. No lack of depth. Medium to medium-full body. Looser-knit than their Epenots, but an attractive example. Fresh and succulent. Just a little unimpressive at the end, though not short. Good plus. (June 2002)

NOW TO 2018   15.5

Pommard, Les Grands Epenots, 1998
Domaine Hubert de Montille

Medium colour. Like his Volnay Champans, this is a little lean and ungenerous on the nose. On the palate, a little riper, but again, it doesn't really convince. Medium body. Good grip. Stylish, but a little lacking in richness. Quite good plus. (June 2002)

NOW TO 2012   14.5

Pommard, Jarollières, 1998
Domaine Jean-Marc Boillot

Full colour. Meaty nose. Rich and full. Slightly four-square at present. Fullish bodied on the palate. Ripe but quite tannic. Has it got enough grip? It is not short, though. Good plus. (June 2002)

NOW TO 2019   15.5

Pommard, Les Pézerolles, 1998
Domaine Vincent Dancer

Fullish colour. Decent substance on the nose, but just a shade rustic. Medium body. Decent attack, but then a bit short and empty. Young vines? Not bad. (June 2002)

NOW TO 2008   13.0

Pommard, Poutures, 1998
Domaine Louis Jadot

Medium-full colour. Firm, backward nose. At present just a touch hard, but there is good depth underneath. On the palate, this is not as sophisticated as their Pommard Epenots. Slightly astringent at the end. A lack of zip in the middle. But positive. Good. (June 2002)

NOW TO 2016   15.0

Pommard, Les Rugiens, 1998
Domaine Bouchard Père et Fils

Fullish colour. Rich, concentrated and ample on the nose. Good substance. Ripe tannins. Full bodied. Fat. Just a touch of oak. Some tannin. Quite a meaty wine. Ripe and succulent. Very good plus. (June 2002)

NOW TO 2020   16.5

Pommard, Les Rugiens, 1998
Domaine Yvon Clerget

Fullish colour. Nicely fat and succulent on the nose. Ripe and quite substantial. Good rich fruit here. Quite a big wine. Some tannin. But good energy underneath. Very good plus. (June 2002)

NOW TO 2020   16.5

Pommard, Les Rugiens, 1998
Domaine de Courcel

Medium-full colour. This seems a little bland after the other Courcel wines on the nose. Rather weak on the palate. Attenuated and short. A bit of a disgrace. A bad bottle? (June 2002)

DRINK SOON   12.5

Pommard, Les Rugiens, 1998
Maison Vincent Girardin

Good colour. The nose is very ripe and classy. Not a bit too tough. Yet full and concentrated. Fullish body. Excellent grip, intensity, class and harmony. A delicious example. Very long. Very lovely. For a Pommard Rugiens, this is really excellent! (October 2002)

NOW TO 2026   18.0

Pommard, Les Rugiens, 1998
Domaine Hubert de Montille

Medium colour. Better than his Grands Epenots on the nose. But it lacks a little richness, nevertheless. On the palate, this has good structure and tannin but not quite enough richness and fat. Good grip. Still youthful. It may improve. But good plus is the best I can mark it today. (June 2002)

NOW TO 2014   15.5

Pommard, Les Rugiens, 1998
Domaine Annick Parent

Fullish colour. Still vigorous, stylish nose. Lovely fruit. Just a touch of oak. Fullish body. Still a little unresolved tannin. Very attractive and fresh. Still needs time. But long and complex and classy. Very good plus. (September 2005)

NOW TO 2020   16.5

Pommard, Les Rugiens, 1998
Domaine Charles Thomas

Fullish colour. Full and solid and backward on the nose. Plenty of substance here. Fullish body. A little dry and tannic. Decent grip and depth. But it doesn't quite sing. Good plus. (June 2002)

NOW TO 2018   15.5

Richebourg, 1998
Domaine Jean Grivot

Very good colour. Splendid nose. Great concentration. Lots of depth. Aristocratic and backward. Full, rich and quite tannic. Still quite closed. Very good grip. Very classy fruit. A splendid example. Austere but fine. Marvellous finish. (September 2002)

2009 TO 2025+   19.5

Richebourg, 1998
Domaine Anne Gros

Very good colour. Just a suggestion of brown. Fullish nose. Rich, exotic and spicy. A touch of caramel and mocha at present. Cedary flavours as it developed. Fullish body. Some tannin. Very good acidity. Nice ripe, cool fruit on the palate. Plenty of substance and depth. It needs to be kept while the tannins soften up. Very fine. (February 2004)

2010 TO 2030   18.5

Richebourg, 1998
Domaine Alain Hudelot-Noëllat

Medium-full colour. Even better than his Romanée-Saint-Vivant. Very lovely nose. Amazing depth, poise, class and concentration. Very splendid fruit. Fullish bodied, rich and very harmonious. Excellent. (June 2002)

2010 TO 2025   19.0

Richebourg, 1998
Domaine Leroy

Fullish colour. Rich, succulent, seductive nose. Gently oaky. Good balance. Fullish body. Very lovely fruit. Excellently balanced. This is very fine. (April 2000)

NOW TO 2020   18.5

Richebourg, 1998
Domaine Denis Mugneret et Fils

Good colour. Fresh, quite firm nose. Good depth and class. Nicely virile. Full, rich, fat and creamy. Old viney. Very good grip. Ripe tannins. Lots of energy. Excellent long, classy finish. This is very fine indeed. (September 2005)

NOW TO 2025   19.0

Richebourg, 1998
Domaine de la Romanée-Conti

Medium-full colour. A little more depth than their Romanée-Saint-Vivant. Fullish, plump nose. Quite black cherry in flavour. Plus a touch of new oak. Rather more vigour than the Romanée-Saint-Vivant. Fullish body. Rich, concentrated, oaky and succulent. Lots of depth. This is very impressive. It has the vigour the Romanée-Saint-Vivant lacks. Good structure. Very well integrated tannins. Long and complex. Very fine plus. (June 2002)

2010 TO 2025+   19.0

La Romanée, 1998
Domaine Bouchard Père et Fils

Fullish, immature colour. Lovely rich, aromatic nose. Not as concentrated as the 1999, but with a lot more vigour and style than the 1997. Medium-full body. Some tannin. Reasonable grip and depth, but not the greatest of class or individuality. Good fruit. Very good indeed. (March 2003)

NOW TO 2018   17.0

Romanée-Conti, 1998
Domaine de la Romanée-Conti

Medium-full colour. Very lovely nose. Ethereal and subtle. Very great finesse. Very splendidly balanced. Very lovely fruit. This is a medium-full bodied wine. Very individual. But by no means a blockbuster. Very well integrated tannins. Multidimensional. Very, very classy. Lovely, and very long and intense at the end. Marvellously put together. Very fine indeed. (July 2002)

2010 TO 2025   19.5

Romanée-Saint-Vivant, 1998
Domaine Robert Arnoux

Good colour. Impressively concentrated nose. Lovely fruit. Cool and composed. Intense and gently oaky. Needs time. Quite closed in. Full body. Splendidly rich, sumptuous fruit. Excellent tannins. Very good grip. This is very complex, very long and very impressive. Will last well. Very fine plus. (September 2002)

NOW TO 2038   19.0

Romanée-Saint-Vivant, 1998
Domaine Sylvain Cathiard

Magnum. Fine colour. Very lovely pure Pinot fruit on the nose. Very ripe and elegant. Fullish body. Ripe tannins. Intense. Very good grip. Complex. Long. Very classy. Very fine definition. Splendid finish. Very fine indeed. (June 2004)

NOW TO 2030+   19.5

Romanée-Saint-Vivant, 1998
Domaine Follin-Arbelet

Good colour. A little neutral on the nose. On the palate this is a disappointment. Rather thin and weedy. A little artificial sweetness. The tannins are unripe. For Romanée-Saint-Vivant this is a disgrace. I tasted this wine on two separate occasions: indentical notes. The importers obtained a second bottle after I had reported that the first had been uninspiring. (June 2002)

NOW TO 2010   13.0

Romanée-Saint-Vivant, 1998
Domaine Alain Hudelot-Noëllat

Medium-full colour. Lush and ripe and succulent. Not as concentrated or as oaky as Arnoux's. But ample, round, rich and very seductive on both nose and palate. Very good grip. A lovely plump, quite profound, fullish wine. Serious stuff. Splendid aftertaste. Very, very long. Very fine. (September 2002)

NOW TO 2020   18.5

Romanée-Saint-Vivant, 1998
Domaine Leroy

Medium-full colour. Lush, concentrated and cedary on the nose. Very classy. Very seductive. Fullish structure. Balanced and very succulent. A very lovely example. Very ripe tannins. But not the structure of 1995 or 1996. Yet intense, long and lovely. (April 2000)

NOW TO 2018   18.0

Romanée-Saint-Vivant, 1998
Domaine de la Romanée-Conti

Corney and Barrow tasting. Medium-full colour. Very lovely fragrant nose. This is decidedly Musigny-ish. Subtle, intense, multi-layered and very sophisticated. At first, on the palate, you wonder if there is enough grip. There is certainly a slight lack of intensity. But the flavours are very well balanced and very classy. I just wish it had a bit more thrust. Very fine, though. (June 2002)

NOW TO 2020   18.0

Ruchottes-Chambertin, 1998
Domaine Dr. Georges Mugneret

Medium-full colour. Some development. Ripe, rich, fresh, profound nose. Very elegant. Medium-full body. Poised. Succulent. Very harmonious. Long and complex. Very civilised. Lovely finish. Fine plus. (April 2005)

NOW TO 2020+   18.0

Saint-Aubin, Derrière Chez Édouard, 1998
Domaine Hubert Lamy et Fils

Lots of interest and individuality. Good grip. Good structure. Lovely, slightly lean Pinot fruit. This is very good. Just about ready. (September 2004)

NOW TO 2012   15.5

Santenay, Beaurepaire, 1998
Domaine Joseph Drouhin

Half bottle. Medium weight, fresh and plump. A fragrant, if youthful, Pinot Noir. No hard edges. Easy to enjoy. (March 2001)

DRINK SOON   15.0

Santenay, Les Gravières, 1998
Domaine Michel Colin-Deléger et Fils

Medium colour. Plump, slightly austere Pinot nose. Does it need a little more generosity? Medium body. Ripe and stylish. Not a great deal of oak or depth on the attack, but better on the follow-through. Classy and expansive. Good. (January 2002)

NOW TO 2014   15.0

Santenay, Les Gravières, 1998
Maison Vincent Girardin

Fine colour. Rich, full, quite tannic, meaty nose. Quite full. Still quite some tannin on the palate. Good depth. It doesn't have the intensity or richness of a 1999, but there is good style and fruit here. Needs time. Very good. (March 2002)

NOW TO 2018 16.0

Savigny-lès-Beaune, Les Lavières, 1998
Domaine Claude Maréchal

A little lean for a Savigny, but still young. It will benefit from rounding off. No great depth or concentration. But clean and quite good. (March 2001)

NOW TO 2010 14.0

Savigny-lès-Beaune, Les Narbantons, 1998
Domaine Dubois d'Orgeval

A good, quite meaty but stylish example. Ripe. Good tannins. Good grip and style. (February 2003)

NOW TO 2011 15.0

Savigny-lès-Beaune, Les Narbantons, 1998
Domaine Leroy

Fine colour. Full, rich, concentrated and succulent on the nose. This is quite structured but not overly tannic. Marvellous fruit. Very ripe. Lots of depth and quality here. Very good grip. (September 2002)

NOW TO 2020+ 18.5

Savigny-lès-Beaune, Les Narbantons, 1998
Domaine Jean-Marc Pavelot

Good full colour. Rich, elegant, meaty nose. Medium-full body. Just a little tannin here, but ripe, balanced and succulent. Slightly hard at the end. But this will resolve itself. Very good plus. (February 2003)

NOW TO 2014 16.5

Savigny-lès-Beaune, Les Peuillets, 1998
Domaine Jean-Marc Pavelot

Very good colour. Lovely fresh, elegant nose. Medium-full body. Very good tannins. Soft and ripe. Medium depth. Very attractive. (October 2002)

NOW TO 2009 15.0

La Tâche, 1998
Domaine de la Romanée-Conti

Medium-full colour. It seems a little less concentrated, a little less definitive than the Richebourg on the nose. Better on the palate. But there is less grip and succulence. The tannins show a bit. The wine isn't short. Indeed, the follow-through is ample and balanced and vigorous. But there is something missing in the middle here. Very fine, but I prefer the Richebourg this year. (June 2002)

2010 TO 2025 18.5

Volnay, 1998
Domaine Michel Lafarge

Straight-up delicious. Now getting mellow. Clean, pure and classy. Medium body. Very good indeed for what it is. (June 2003)

NOW TO 2015 16.0

Volnay, Premier Cru, 1998
Domaine Michel Lafarge

Good colour. Rich, quite firm, succulent nose. Very lovely plummy fruit. Medium to medium-full body. A little tannin. Still a little austere on the attack, but rich, classy and harmonious at the end. Very good. (June 2001)

NOW TO 2020 16.0

Volnay, Caillerets, Ancienne Cuvée Carnot, 1998
Domaine Bouchard Père et Fils

Good colour. Similar to the Taillepieds 1998. Softer, more aromatic nose. Seems plumper. Less tannin but better balance. Seems richer. Less acidity but better grip. Medium to medium-full body. Longer and classier. More complex. Fine. (June 2002)

NOW TO 2018 17.5

Volnay, Les Caillerets, 1998
Domaine du Marquis d'Angerville

Medium to medium-full colour. Stylish, perfumed, laid-back and very lovely nose. Real Volnay here. Medium-full body. Excellent balance. Intense and fragrant. Very classy and very long. Very lovely. Fine plus. (June 2002)

NOW TO 2025 18.0

Volnay, Les Caillerets, 1998
Domaine Michel Prunier

Medium to medium-full colour. Some development. Quite fragrant, but a little pinched on the nose. On the palate, this lacks a little sophistication, but the class of the *terroir* shows. Medium-full body. Very good balance. Good ripe fruit. Positive and long on the finish. Very good. (June 2002)

NOW TO 2020   16.0

Volnay, Carelle sous la Chapelle, 1998
Domaine Jean-Marc Boillot

Medium-full colour. Fat, rich and succulent on the nose. Very good ripe fruit. A fullish, meaty wine for a Volnay. Ripe. Good tannins. Quite substantial. It will need time. Good concentration and good grip. Very good indeed. (June 2002)

NOW TO 2025   17.0

Volnay, Champans, 1998
Domaine du Marquis d'Angerville

Medium-full colour. Splendid nose. Very, very ripe and rich. Marvellous depth. This seems to be bigger and more concentrated than his Volnay Taillepieds. On the palate, this is very lovely. Harmonious and persistent. Great finesse. Loads of definition. Very, very long. Very fine. (June 2002)

NOW TO 2025   18.5

Volnay, Champans, 1998
Maison Vincent Girardin

Full colour. Full, rich and quite substantial on the nose. Full bodied and oaky. Still very youthful. Lovely plump fruit though. Very well covered tannins and lots of energy. Fine plus. (June 2002)

NOW TO 2025   18.0

Volnay, Champans, 1998
Domaine des Comtes Lafon

Medium-full, youthful colour. Rich fruit on the nose. Stylish, ripe and succulent. Medium-full body. Still a little tannin. Fresh, balanced, plump and attractive. Very good indeed. (June 2003)

NOW TO 2026   17.0

Volnay, Champans, 1998
Domaine Hubert de Montille

Medium colour. Still fresh. Raspberries and roses come springing out of the glass. Very

Volnay. Medium body. Now softening. No hard edges. Very elegant. Long finish. Very good plus. (June 2004)

NOW TO 2016   16.5

Volnay, Clos de la Barre, 1998
Domaine Louis Jadot

Full colour. Medium weight nose. Fragrant and classy. Lots of depth. Medium-full body. Still reserved. But underneath, rich, concentrated, classy and long and definitive. Very promising. Very good indeed. (October 2002)

NOW TO 2020   17.0

Volnay, Clos du Chateau des Ducs, 1998
Domaine Michel Lafarge

Full colour. Real depth and concentration, succulence and grip here on the nose. Fullish body. Very good concentration. Less showy than some. This has gone a little into its shell. But all the elements are here. Very good grip. Very long and complex. Fine. (June 2002)

NOW TO 2020   17.5

Volnay, Clos des Chênes, 1998
Domaine Jean-Michel Gaunoux

Medium to medium-full colour. Soft, ripe, oaky nose. Good style. Only medium body, though, and the follow-through is a bit attenuated. Slightly astringent at the end. Fair at best. (June 2002)

NOW TO 2010   13.5

Volnay, Clos des Chênes, 1998
Domaine Michel Lafarge

Full colour. Quite firm but full and concentrated nose. Fullish body. Not a bit too hard or austere. But slightly more so than his Clos des Chenes 1999. Some tannin. Very good grip. Lots of vigour. Excellent finish. Very fine for a 1998. (March 2006)

2009 TO 2025+   18.5

Volnay, Clos des Chênes, 1998
Domaine Nicolas Potel

Good colour. Slightly hidden on the nose. But very lovely, classy fruit on the palate. Full and rich. Very good tannins. Very classy. Excellent grip. Nicely austere. Plenty of backbone. Very fine indeed. (January 2002)

NOW TO 2025   19.5

Volnay, Clos des Chênes, 1998
Domaine Charles Thomas

Medium-full colour. Not as tough as the other Charles Thomas's wines. Ripe and rich. Good depth and class. Fullish body. Still a little tannin. Good fruit and good grip. Plenty of subtance here. Plenty of dimension. Very good indeed. (June 2002)

NOW TO 2020   17.0

Volnay, Clos du Verseuil, 1998
Domaine Yvon Clerget

Fullish colour. Good depth and class and succulence on the nose at first. But it lost this on aeration. The wine on the palate is rather coarse and rather astringent. Unexciting. Not bad at best. (June 2002)

NOW TO 2010   13.0

Volnay, Frémiets, 1998
Domaine du Comte Armand

Fullish colour. Some development. This is classy on the nose. Accessible and succulent. On the palate rather more backward, but very lovely rich, old-viney fruit. Fat, as well as tannic. Better than the Clos des Epeneaux this year. Fine. (June 2002)

2010 TO 2025   17.5

Volnay, Santenots, 1998
Maison Vincent Girardin

Full colour. Rich, substantial, fat, even chocolaty nose. Full bodied, rich, succulent and balanced on the palate. A fine example with lots of vigour and intensity at the end. Fine. (June 2002)

2010 TO 2025   17.5

Volnay, Santenots, 1998
Maison Antonin Rodet

Full colour. Rich, full and ample on the nose. Plenty of class and depth here. On the palate this is ripe and plummy. Medium-full body.

Good ripe tannins. Good style. Good length. It just lacks a little generosity. But very good indeed. Lots of class. (June 2002)

NOW TO 2020   17.0

Volnay, Les Santenots du Milieu, 1998
Domaine des Comtes Lafon

Medium-full colour. Quite soft on the nose. A touch adolescent. Some sous-bois touches. The tannins are less absorbed than in the 1999. Quite accessible. Ripe and stylish as it developed. Lovely fruit. The tannins are visible but well integrated. Medium-full body. Balanced. Very stylish. Long. Fine plus for the vintage. (June 2002)

NOW TO 2020   18.0

Volnay, Taillepieds, 1998
Domaine du Marquis d'Angerville

Medium-full colour. Fuller and firmer than the other d'Angerville wines. Marvellously classy, concentrated fruit. Still backward. On the palate fullish bodied, fragrant, ripe and intense. Very classy and very long. Fine plus. (June 2002)

NOW TO 2020   18.0

Volnay, Taille Pieds, 1998
Domaine Bouchard Père et Fils

Good colour. Lovely plump nose, but medium to medium-full body only. Some tannin. Medium concentration but good acidity. The wine is not as rich as the 1999, but it is balanced, elegant and full of interest, nevertheless. Very good indeed for the vintage. (June 2002)

NOW TO 2018   17.0

Volnay, Taillepieds, 1998
Domaine Hubert de Montille

Fullish colour. Slightly austere on the nose, but good depth and class. Medium-full body. Nicely austere and ripe at the same time. Fresh, plump and classy. This is individual and fine. (June 2002)

NOW TO 2020   17.5

Vosne-Romanée, Les Beaumonts, 1998
Domaine Emmanuel Rouget

Medium colour. Some development. Fresh nose, though. Quite pure fruit. Accessible. On the palate, as well as being a bit corky, it is a little dry and a bit hollow at the end. It tails off. Quite good. (June 2002)

NOW TO 2012   14.0

Vosne-Romanée, Les Beaux Monts, 1998
Domaine Bruno Clavelier

Medium-full colour. Good ripe, classy nose. Not a blockbuster, but balanced and attractive. On the palate, good grip, medium-full body; balanced, ripe and positive. Long. Very good indeed. (June 2002)

NOW TO 2020   17.0

Vosne-Romanée, Les Beaux Monts, 1998
Domaine Jean Grivot

Fine colour. Marvellous nose. Rich, profound and aristocratic. Fullish body. Good tannins. This has lots of depth. Real vigour and grip. Very good tannins. A keeper, but a splendid example. Multidimensional and very classy. (January 2002)

2009 2030   18.5

Vosne-Romanée, Les Beaumonts, 1998
Domaine Alain Hudelot-Noëllat

Medium-full colour. Ripe, rich and quite concentrated on the nose. Medium to medium-full colour. Lovely fruit. Good balance. Plenty of grip. This is rich at the end, and positive, too. Long. Very good plus. (June 2002)

NOW TO 2020   16.5

Vosne-Romanée, Les Beaux Monts, 1998
Maison Louis Jadot

Medium colour. Some development. Not a blockbuster, but balanced and classy on the nose. On the palate, only medium bodied and a little astringent. It has good fruit and decent length. But it lacks a bit of zip. Good plus, at best. (June 2002)

NOW TO 2016   15.5

Vosne-Romanée, Les Beaumonts, 1998
Domaine Daniel Rion et Fils

Very good colour. Just a touch of oak on the nose. Good richness. Medium-full structure. Nicely opulent and accessible. No hard edges. Ripe and fruity and uncomplicated. Lovely

succulent fruit. This is classy. Very long finish. Fine. (September 2002)

NOW TO 2020   17.5

Vosne-Romanée, Beaux Monts, 1998
Domaine Charles Thomas

Medium-full colour. Now a little developed. Something a little hard and undergrowthy on the nose. Oxidised as it developed. This tastes older than it is. It lacks a bit of grip and freshness. Medium-full body. A little unresolved tannin. Not enough succulence. A disappointment. (2005–2008.) Another bottle had a fresher colour and nose. Medium weight. Ample, rich and beginning to be easy to drink. Ripe. Decent acidity. Medium to medium-full body. A little tannin but not a lot. Appealing, positive finish. Very good. (May 2002)

NOW TO 2014   16.0

Vosne-Romanée, Aux Brûlées, 1998
Domaine Bruno Clavelier

Medium to medium-full colour. Decent nose. But not as fresh or as classy as his Beaux Monts. Fullish body. Nicely plump. Good fruit and grip. It finishes well. Very good plus. (June 2002)

NOW TO 2020   16.5

Vosne-Romanée, Aux Brûlées, 1998
Domaine Méo-Camuzet

Full colour. Full, very oaky wine. Typically Méo-Camuzet in style. Quite full bodied. Marked by the new wood. Yet not overly tannic. There is good concentrated fruit underneath and good acidity. But the oak is too much. Very good at best. (June 2002)

NOW TO 2020   16.0

Vosne-Romanée, Les Chaumes, 1998
Domaine Robert Arnoux

Medium-full colour. Lovely rich, concentrated nose. Medium-full body. Good fresh, concentrated fruit. Good grip. This is long, rich and definitive. Very good indeed. (June 2002)

NOW TO 2020   17.0

Vosne-Romanée, Les Chaumes, 1998
Domaine François Lamarche
Medium-full colour. Ample nose. Just a little sweaty, but quite classy. Ample and old viney. Medium-full body. Good acidity. The ingredients are here but they are not properly put together. Good at best. (June 2002)
NOW TO 2016   15.0

Vosne-Romanée, Les Chaumes, 1998
Domaine Daniel Rion et Fils
Fullish colour. Strangely vegetal on the nose. Light and evolved on the palate. A little attenuated. And there is a lack of acidity. Unexciting. (June 2002)
NOW TO 2010   12.5

Vosne-Romanée, Les Chaumes, 1998
Domaine Jean Tardy et Fils
Medium-full colour. Stewed, sweet, artificial nose. Too astringent already. Medium to medium-full body. Very astringent on the palate. Over-evolved. And yet there is at least some grip underneath. Curious. (June 2002)
NOW TO 2014   13.0

Vosne-Romanée, Clos des Réas, 1998
Domaine Michel Gros
Fullish, youthful colour. Plenty of depth and structure here. Good grip on the nose. Nothing hard or dry about the tannins. Medium-full body. Not as fat, as well as not as rich, as the 1999, but with very good depth and structure. Slightly raw at present. Very good indeed. (December 2003)
NOW TO 2020   17.0

Vosne-Romanée, Les Damodes, 1998
Domaine Fougeray de Beauclair
Village wine above Malconsorts. Medium body. A little sweet and attenuated. It lacks real flair. Decent balance, but only fair. (October 2002)
NOW TO 2009   13.5

Vosne-Romanée, Aux Malconsorts, 1998
Domaine Syvain Cathiard
Fullish colour. Still youthful. Ripe, poised, harmonious and very classy fruit. Medium-full body. Very good tannins. Fresh. Complex. Long and lovely. Not a blockbuster. But very good grip. Fine plus. (June 2006)
NOW TO 2023   18.0

Vosne-Romanée, Les Petits Monts, 1998
Domaine Véronique Drouhin
Medium colour. Some development. Slightly lean, but refined, succulent and juicy on the nose. No under-tannic structure. Medium to medium-full body. Fresh and positive. Very good fruit. Very well balanced. Long and classy. Lovely intensity at the end. Very good indeed. (June 2002)
NOW TO 2025   17.0

Vosne-Romanée, Les Petits Monts, 1998
Domaine Robert Sirugue
Medium to medium-full colour. Good fresh fruit on the nose. Quite oaky. Clean and stylish, if with no great depth or complexity. Quite forward. Good plus. (December 2003)
NOW TO 2012   15.5

Vosne-Romanée, Aux Reignots, 1998
Domaine Robert Arnoux
Medium-full colour. Good depth and class in a slightly lean way on the nose. Fresh. This is just a little dry on the palate. A slight lack of grip. Medium to medium-full body. Good fruit and a positive aftertaste, though. Very good. (June 2002)
NOW TO 2018   16.0

Vosne-Romanée, Aux Reignots, 1998
Domaine Bouchard Père et Fils
Medium to medium-full colour. Rich, fat, classy nose with a good oaky underpinning. Fullish bodied on the palate. Lots of succulent fruit. Very good grip. This is complex and positive. Very well made. Fine. (June 2002)
2010 TO 2025   17.5

Vosne-Romanée, Les Suchots, 1998
Domaine Robert Arnoux
Medium-full colour. Fullish, very concentrated, old-viney nose. Rich and succulent. On the palate, a little closed. But ripe, rich, concentrated

and classy. Complex and long. Very promising. Fine plus. (June 2002)

2010 TO 2025 18.0

Vosne-Romanée, Les Suchots, 1998
Domaine Sylvain Cathiard

Medium-full colour. Very lovely nose. Gently oaky. Rich and ripe. Lots of depth and lots of class. Fuller than his Vosne-Romanée Malconsorts. A little more tannin. Very good grip, though. Lots of depth. This is intense and multidimensional. Very fine. (June 2002)

2010 TO 2025 18.5

Vosne-Romanée, Les Suchots, 1998
Domaine Jean Grivot

Fullish colour. Very lovely nose. Richer and fatter than Sylvain Cathiard's. Oaky and succulent. A splendid example. On the palate, bigger and rather more backward. But real depth. Very, very long. Very well balanced. Very classy. Very fine. (June 2002)

2010 TO 2025 18.5

Vosne-Romanée, Les Suchots, 1998
Domaine François Lamarche

Medium colour. Some development. Ripe and ample on the nose, but without any great class or definition. On the palate, a little astringent. Decent fruit. Some grip, but not really positively put together. Very good at best. (June 2002)

NOW TO 2018 16.0

1997

This was marginally the smallest vintage—especially low in red but average in white—between 1991 and 2003. As was the case in 1998, this vintage was the product of wide fluctuations in climatic conditions, resulting in vines which were *perturbées* (disturbed) and so could not settle down and ripen properly, despite generally promising weather in August and September. The whites are small wines, lacking substance, acidity and concentration. The reds were abundantly rich and ripe, but again

lacked grip and tannic structure, and so have evolved fast and have speedily lost their interest. Some vintages—1991, 2001, 2004—have evolved better than we had thought originally. Others—and 1997 is a major example—have moved in the opposite direction.

WEATHER CONDITIONS

It was a curious year. Thankfully, the weather pattern was not as extreme as in Bordeaux, but followed its general lines: early budding, early start to a protracted flowering, and an uneven summer. The bad flowering affected the volume of Pinot Noir red wine more than it did the Chardonnays, but it paradoxically brought these to fruition before the whites. August was hot and dry, and the development of the Chardonnays was bloqué. The end of the month brought the rain, which was needed, but then a hot and basically very dry September accelerated the path to maturity, at the same time narrowing the window of optimum opportunity when the fruit would be at its best.

The harvest began around September 10, the earliest date since 1982 and 1976. In many cases, contrary to the usual pattern, not only were the red wines collected before the whites, but the generic white wines were picked before the *crus*. The acidities threatened to be low, and a little chaptalisation here would make up for a lack of sugar in the grapes. The best growers, with the best plots, however, decided to wait.

Thankfully, while it was warm, it was also dry. There was but one morning of light showers during the harvest. What happened was that the grapes began to concentrate. And this concentration took place without any tendency to sur-maturity and botrytis. By September 20 the harvest was in full swing, and it began to be noticed that it would take 350 kg of fruit—as opposed to 300 kg—to fill one barrel. The concentration had a further effect: it allowed the later-maturing fruit to catch up. Yet it continued to be vitally necessary to analyse each parcel, or even bits of a parcel, in order to determine the best day to harvest it.

For the Chardonnay crop in the Côte d'Or, there would be the following interlocking problems:

- The crop was large (overall, only 4 percent less than the huge 1996 crop).

- As a result of the extended flowering, ripeness was uneven, not only between one plot and another, but also within each plot.

- Potential for acidity was low, yet at the beginning of September, sugar levels were only moderate.

- The weather in September was very warm during the day and during the night. This would not just shorten the optimum harvesting period but also mean that fruit arriving in the winery would have to be cooled quickly in order not to lose aromas.

→ Size of the Crop ←
(In hectolitres, excluding generic wine)

	RED	WHITE
Grands Crus	12,076	3,727
Village and Premiers Crus	159,606	54,752
TOTAL	171,684	58,479

The red wine harvest, as a result of *coulure* and *millerandage*, was proportionately very much smaller, similar to that of 1995. This shortfall was felt all the way up and down the slope, from *grand cru* to generic wine. In retrospect, this was a godsend. Fermentation problems would have been all the more exaggerated if the crop had been of 1996 proportions.

As far as the red wine crop is concerned, the relevant factors included these:

- Yields were low; the grapes were tiny and black in colour, but thankfully in abundant health.

- Alcohol levels were high: 13° or above.

- pHs were high; acidity levels were low.

- The fruit was arriving at ambient temperatures of up to 27°C. Given that the fermentation process itself is capable of producing

10° of heat, cooling systems would have to be super-efficient to enable the must to be cooled and maintained for the usual few days of cold-soaking (where this is practised) to fix the colour, and subsequently for the usual prolonged *cuvaison* to take place. Not everyone was so equipped.

- Subsequently, many malolactic fermentations occurred very shortly after the sugar-alcohol fermentation rather than, as is usual in Burgundy, in the spring.

The problem in 1997, even more than usual, was to get the balance right. First, the acidities were dangerously low. As I have pointed out above, it was difficult to achieve the usual four or five days of cold-soaking. Second, fermentations were unduly fast. Lots of the resultant CO_2 was boiled off. Those who shortened the maceration produced wines which lacked depth and backbone. Those who prolonged it risked producing stewed wines.

WHERE ARE THE BEST WINES?

The whites are consistent, despite the climatic and winemaking difficulties. One cannot generalise that one commune is superior to another. The best domaines are proportionately better than the also-rans, but this itself is normal.

- Corton-Charlemagne is perhaps where the vintage is at its best.

- This was a good year for Pommard and Nuits-Saint-Georges. The sometimes rugged character of these communes is softened by the character of the vintage.

- Paradoxically the Volnays and Chambolle-Musignys are also good. The Vosnes, Gevreys and Marsannays are more uneven.

WHEN WILL THE WINES BE AT THEIR BEST?

The short answer is now, and don't hang on to them for too long. Some of the lesser wines in both colours are already a bit tired. Just about all the white wines need drinking soon, and most reds should be drunk by 2011 to 2012.

For the results of my Ten Year On tasting, see my Web site clive-coates.com.

TASTING NOTES

WHITES

Bâtard-Montrachet, 1997
Domaine Jacques Gagnard-Delagrange
Very ripe on the nose, almost to the point of being overripe. Certainly a citrus flavour. On the palate we have a splendid grip. Lots of concentration, and rich and very pure fruit. The palate is less sweet, less *agrumes*. Lots of depth. Delicious. Fine plus. (March 2000)

NOW TO 2010   18.0

Bâtard-Montrachet, 1997
Domaine Jean-Noël Gagnard
Better on the nose than the 1998. More depth. Better acidity. Rather more ageing potential. Unexpectedly full, rich and fresh. Very good grip. A great success. There can't be many 1997s as good as this. Excellent fruit and harmony. Long, complex and lovely. This will last very well. Very fine for the vintage. (January 2002)

NOW TO 2018   18.5

Bienvenues-Bâtard-Montrachet, 1997
Domaine Leflaive
Rich, full, backward nose. Lots of depth here. Plenty of substance. Very lovely, cool fruit. Subtle, elegant and balanced. This is very lovely, especially for a 1997. Very good grip. Very long. Fine plus. (February 2003)

NOW TO 2016   18.0

Bienvenues-Bâtard-Montrachet, 1997
Domaine Paul Pernot et Fils
Youthful colour. Ripe nose, fragrant, stylish and balanced if no great grip. Medium-full bodied,

fresh and ample on the palate. Seems fully ready. Good, positive finish. But essentially gentle. Fine for the vintage. (July 2001)

DRINK SOON   17.5

Chassagne-Montrachet, Premier Cru, 1997
Domaine Jacques Gagnard-Delagrange
Half bottle. Good colour. Lots of fruit. Fresh and stylish. Yet already soft and delicious now. Plump, meaty and very Chassagne. (June 2000)

DRINK SOON   15.0

Chassagne-Montrachet, Les Blanchots Dessus, 1997
Domaine Darviot-Perrin
Fresh colour. Lean, mineral nose, but not very expressive. Medium weight. Very good acidity. Fresh. Stylish. Plenty of interest. Underneath, an almost Chablis-like richness. Still very youthful. Good depth and concentration. Very good plus. (March 2005)

NOW TO 2010   16.5

Chassagne-Montrachet, Les Bondues, 1997
Domaine Darviot-Perrin
Good colour for the vintage. Attractive nose. There is good depth and structure for a 1997. Medium to medium-full body. Some tannin. Rich, balanced and stylish. This is delicious for what it is. Hats off to Darviot! Very good. (July 2000)

NOW TO 2009   16.0

Chassagne-Montrachet, Le Cailleret, 1997
Domaine Hubert de Montille
Lovely style on the nose. Gently oaky. Lots of distinction. Medium body. Fully ready. Needs drinking soon. Fine for the vintage. (January 2005)

DRINK SOON   17.5

Chassagne-Montrachet, Les Champs Gain, 1997
Domaine Jean-Noël Gagnard
A touch clumsy on the nose. A little built-in sulphur which blew off soon afterward. On the palate, though, this is medium bodied and had a

good oak base, good fruit, balance and style. As with lots of 1997s a bit weak-kneed, but a very good example. (September 2002)

DRINK SOON 16.0

Chassagne-Montrachet, Les Champs Gain, 1997
Domaine Michel Niellon

Fresh, clean, fullish, vigorous and classy. Now *à point*. Good depth. Nothing heavy or sulphury here. Very good indeed. (July 2004)

NOW TO 2013 17.0

Chassagne-Montrachet, Les Chaumées, 1997
Domaine Michel Colin-Deléger et Fils

Quite a deep colour. This is a classy wine which has not been protected properly. Soft and flowery but now rather evolved. The nose is not special by any means. The palate a little better. Poor. A rogue bottle? (June 2001)

DRINK SOON 12.5

Chassagne-Montrachet, Les Grandes Ruchottes, 1997
Domaine Bachelet-Ramonet

The colour is quite evolved, as is the nose. Indeed, on the palate it is a little flat and oxidised. Some botrytis. Underneath, there is no lack of acidity. But it isn't very impressive. Better on the palate than the nose. (October 2001)

DRINK UP 13.0

Chassagne-Montrachet, La Maltroie, 1997
Domaine Michel Colin-Deléger et Fils

Nice and ripe. Good acidity. Plenty of depth and style. Competent winemaking here if not a great bottle. (March 2000)

DRINK SOON 16.0

Chassagne-Montrachet, La Maltroie, 1997
Domaine Bernard Morey

Medium-full colour. Ripe and oaky but slightly *tendre*, with an aftertaste of orange peel. Round and oaky, ripe and fruity on the palate. Very good but lacks a little grip. (March 2002)

DRINK SOON 16.0

Chassagne-Montrachet, Morgeot, 1997
Domaine Jean-Noël Gagnard

Rich nose. Full, concentrated and with plenty of fruit. Good depth. Decent grip. Ripe fruit. Quite a substantial wine which still has plenty of vigour. Slightly four-square but very good for the vintage. Just about ready. (June 2004)

NOW TO 2012 16.0

Chassagne-Montrachet, Morgeot, 1997
Maison Vincent Girardin

Good rich nose. Stylish, fresh and balanced. Medium-full body. Good grip and concentration. Succulent, fresh and peachy on the palate. Positive finish. Plenty of vigour still. This is very good indeed. (September 2002)

DRINK SOON 17.0

Chassagne-Montrachet, Morgeots, Clos de la Chapelle, 1997
Domaine Duc de Magenta/Maison Louis Jadot

Very good colour. Rich, but full and austere on both nose and palate. This is a good example. Plenty of depth, but not much charm as yet. Good depth. Will keep well. Very good. (December 2001)

NOW TO 2010 16.0

Chassagne-Montrachet, En Remilly, 1997
Domaine Michel Colin-Deléger et Fils

Crisp, ripe and elegant. Medium body. Good intensity and depth. Lovely fruit. Very poised. Not the greatest of concentration or extraction. But balanced and elegant. Very good plus. (June 2000)

DRINK SOON 16.5

Chassagne-Montrachet, Les Ruchottes, 1997
Domaine Ramonet

A lot better than the 1998. Surprisingly, an acidity almost similar to that of 1996. Slightly lean. Medium to medium-full body. Good, slightly austere, clean finish. Very good. (May 2005)

NOW TO 2010 16.0

Chevalier-Montrachet, 1997
Domaine Bouchard Père et Fils

Some development on the colour. Just a little flat on the nose, as are many 1997s, and a little evolved on the palate, too. Medium to medium-full body. Good, but essentially it lacks freshness and grip. Quite ample though. Better with food. Good, long, positive finish. Finishes rather better than it starts. Very good indeed. (October 2005)

NOW TO 2010   17.0

Corton-Charlemagne, 1997
Domaine Bonneau du Martray

Lighter than the 1998. Less concentration. Less depth and less class. Softer, clean and pleasant, but more forward and less vigour than the 1998. Very good but not fine. (November 2005)

NOW TO 2009   16.0

Corton-Charlemagne, 1997
Domaine Bouchard Père et Fils

Slightly less fresh as well as a little bit more lush and evolved than the 1998 on the nose. Medium-full body. Ripe and attractive if without the zip and intensity of the 1998. Long, classy, balanced and satisfying. Certainly fine. (June 2000)

NOW TO 2010   17.5

Corton-Charlemagne, 1997
Domaine Joseph Faiveley

At first this comes across as a rather simple, if elegant, wine. It's almost too discreet. Only medium body. Gently oaky, ripe and fruity, but without a great deal of power. Underneath, it is classy and subtle. And it is balanced and complex. But fully ready now and without enormous bite. Very clean though. Nicely cool. (December 2001)

DRINK SOON   16.5

Corton-Charlemagne, 1997
Domaine Louis Jadot

Youthful, crisp, steely and full on the palate. Slightly four-square. But plenty of depth and quality. Slightly rigid. But very good. Long and positive. Better with food. Fine for the vintage. (April 2005)

NOW TO 2009   17.5

Corton-Charlemagne, 1997
Domaine Régis Pavelot

Fresh and elegant but in a slightly lean way. Only medium body. Elegant, but not quite

the concentration and depth of a *grand cru*. (July 2000)

DRINK SOON   16.0

Meursault, 1997
Domaine des Comtes Lafon

Ripe, rich but slightly adolescent nose. Less so on the palate. Juicy and succulent. Clean, balanced and fullish. Lots of depth and style. Excellent for a village example. Lovely pure fruit. (February 2005)

NOW TO 2010   15.5

Meursault, Charmes, 1997
Domaine François Mikulski

Unexpectedly rich and concentrated for a 1997, with very good supporting acidity. Clean, fullish bodied and stylish. Will still improve. A lot of depth here. Lovely finish. Fine quality. (June 2001)

NOW TO 2010+   17.5

Meursault, Charmes, 1997
Domaine Michel Tessier

A little built-in sulphur. Ripe and decent acidity. Quite stylish. Quite advanced. Quite good. (October 2002)

DRINK SOON   14.0

Meursault, Clos de la Barre, 1997
Domaine des Comtes Lafon

First bottle: very oxidised. Second bottle: absolutely as it should be. Ripe, fresh and gently oaky. Full of interest. Ripe. Quite minerally. Very good. Surely this is the best village Meursault that you can get. (June 2004)

NOW TO 2010   16.0

Meursault, Genevrières, 1997
Domaine François Jobard

A little SO2 on the nose. Firm. Quite austere. Very good acidity. Slightly adolescent. Full bodied for the vintage. Good depth. Good grip. Plenty of enjoyment on the follow-through. Persistent. Full flavoured. Fine for the vintage. (March 2000)

NOW TO 2010+   17.5

Meursault, Genevrières, 1997
Domaine des Comtes Lafon

Soft, ripe nose. À point. No great depth or zip. Mild. Soft. A touch of sulphur built into the wine. Medium to medium-full body. Not a lot of acidity. Nor much real cleanliness and class. Very good for the vintage though. (N.B.: variable bottles here.) (June 2005)

DRINK SOON   16.0

Meursault, Les Gouttes d'Or, 1997
Domaine Arnaud Ente

A little sulphury on the nose. Ripe. Gently oaky. It lacks a little zip. Medium body. Quite pleasant. (June 2000)

DRINK SOON   15.0

Meursault, Les Gouttes d'Or, 1997
Domaine Jean-Michel Gaunoux

Quite a developed colour and nose. A touch oxidised. Not nearly as good as his Perrières. Good acidity. Medium body. Better on the palate. More vigour and more freshness. Quite good. (September 2002)

DRINK SOON   14.0

Meursault, Gouttes d'Or, 1997
Domaine des Comtes Lafon

Rich, ripe, spicy nose. Very good acidity on the palate for a 1997. No lack of class either. Very good fruit. Ample. Full bodied. Lots of succulence. Very good plus. (November 2005)

NOW TO 2009   16.5

Meursault, Perrières, 1997
Domaine Jean-Michel Gaunoux

Crisp, concentrated and with just the right oakiness. This is plump, fruity and à point. Especially good for 1997. Plenty of vigour. Fine. (August 2002)

DRINK SOON   17.5

Meursault, Perrières, 1997
Domaine des Comtes Lafon

Quite a deep colour now. But no undue age. Ripe, fullish and oaky. Good vigour for the vintage. Plenty of depth. Now à point. Good grip and minerality. Very good, indeed, for the vintage. (September 2004)

NOW TO 2009   17.0

Meursault, Poruzots, 1997
Domaine François Jobard

Somewhat restrained with a touch of SO2. Full and rich underneath. Still youthful. Ample. Gently oaky. Plenty of depth and high quality. This is rather fine. Lovely finish. Old-viney and concentrated. Fine. (June 2001)

NOW TO 2015+   17.5

Le Montrachet, 1997
Domaine des Comtes Lafon

Quite an evolved colour. More so than the Perrières 1997. Quite evolved on the nose, too. Oaky but a little diffuse. Very opulent. Ample, rich, plump fruit. Fresh but not very vigorous. The wine has only a little dimension and complexity at the end. I get more pleasure from the Perrières. Peter Wasserman says a previous bottle was better. (September 2004)

DRINK SOON   16.0

Le Montrachet, 1997
Domaine de la Romanée-Conti

Very fresh and crisp on the nose. Still quite closed on the palate. Full, rich and quite opulent. Broad and spicy underneath. This is a big example but rather adolescent at present. Decent acidity. But all a bit closed-in. Very fine but not great. (June 2001)

NOW TO 2015   18.0

Puligny-Montrachet, 1997
Maison Olivier Leflaive Frères

A little simple, a little forward, but fresh and pretty. Quite good for what it is. Ready. (October 2000)

DRINK SOON   14.0

Puligny-Montrachet, Le Cailleret, 1997
Domaine Hubert de Montille

This is not as powerful or as classy as the 1994. The acidity is softer. Medium body. Classy fruit. Quite fresh. Less concentration and backbone. À point now. Flowery. Plump. Quite long.

Fresher than the 1994, of course, but less oaky. Very good indeed. (September 2001)

DRINK SOON 17.0

Puligny-Montrachet, Les Chalumaux, 1997
Maison Champy

Quite rich, a little scented and quite evolved on the attack, but good acidity. Cleaner and crisper as it evolved. Minerally. Medium body. Stylish. Good balance. But not the greatest depth. Fresh at the end. (June 2001)

DRINK SOON 16.0

Puligny-Montrachet, Les Champs Gain, 1997
Domaine des Comtes Lafon

This is not to the standard of Lafon's Meursaults, but is better than the 1996. Ripe. Slightly four-square. Good acidity. Good but not brilliant. (June 2000)

DRINK SOON 15.0

Puligny-Montrachet, Le Clavoillon, 1997
Domaine Leflaive

Still young. But fat, rich and succulent. Full bodied. Plenty of depth. On the palate rich and satisfying. Lots of intensity. Ripe at the end. Very good indeed. (October 2000)

NOW TO 2009 17.0

Puligny-Montrachet, Les Perrières, 1997
Domaine Étienne Sauzet

Very evolved nose. Even slightly oxidised. Better on the palate but no great shakes. Some fruit. Decent acidity. Drink soon. (October 2005)

DRINK SOON 13.5

Puligny-Montrachet, Les Pucelles, 1997
Maison Vincent Girardin

Good freshness. Ripe and stylish. Decent grip, depth and substance. This has a lot of class for a 1997. Holding up well. Long. Fine plus. (June 2003)

DRINK SOON 18.0

Puligny-Montrachet, Les Referts, 1997
Domaine Étienne Sauzet

Good depth and vigour on the nose for a 1997. Attractive, gently oaky fruit. Balanced and fresh.

Long and positive. Will still last well. Very good indeed. (September 2004)

NOW TO 2009 17.0

Puligny-Montrachet, La Truffière, 1997
Domaine Bernard Morey

Ripe, stylish nose, although not very pronounced. Laid-back on the palate. Good depth. Elegant and persistant. Very clean and pure. Very good. (November 2000)

DRINK SOON 16.0

Saint-Aubin, Les Castets, 1997
Domaine Hubert Lamy et Fils

Good depth for a 1997 Saint-Aubin. Soft, plump and balanced. Really quite complex. Good for what it is. (July 2000)

DRINK UP 14.5

Saint-Aubin, Clos de la Chatenière, 1997
Domaine Hubert Lamy et Fils

Fuller, richer and somehow more complete than his Saint-Aubin En Remilly. Lovely balance, with very good fruit with an exotic touch. Real depth. More powerful. Still racy and mineral nevertheless. Very good indeed. (June 2001)

DRINK SOON 17.0

Saint-Aubin, En Remilly, 1997
Domaine Hubert Lamy et Fils

Brisk, supple and nicely racy. Medium body. Now ready. Very stylish. Elegant. A mineral wine. (June 2001)

NOW TO 2009 16.0

REDS

Beaune, Les Boucherottes, 1997
Domaine des Héritiers Louis Jadot

Good colour. Full, ample nose. Good grip. Medium-full body. This has plenty of energy and depth. Just about ready. Very good. (October 2002)

NOW TO 2009 16.0

Beaune, Clos des Couchereaux, 1997
Domaine Louis Jadot

Medium-full colour. Lovely fresh nose. Very stylish. Ripe and balanced. Medium to medium-full body. A little tannin. Still a little raw. But underneath there is very fresh, elegant, complex fruit. Medium body and plenty of depth. Long and harmonious. Very good plus. (March 2000)

NOW TO 2010　　　　　　　　　　　　　16.5

Beaune, Clos des Mouches, 1997
Domaine Aleth le Royer-Girardin

Good colour for the vintage. Ripe, succulent nose. Just a suggestion of oak. Medium body. Good grip. Nice and fat, and very stylish. Just a little raw. Plenty of grip and intensity. Very good for the vintage. (July 2000)

NOW TO 2010　　　　　　　　　　　　　16.0

Beaune, Aux Cras, Vieilles Vignes, 1997
Domaine Germain Père et Fils/
Château de Chorey-lès-Beaune

One of the best 1997s I have had recently. Fine colour. No trace of brown. Very fresh. Very fine acidity. Fullish body. Concentrated. Very fresh, especially for the vintage. Because of the old vines, potentially voluptuous. Yet was very brutal, even tannic 2 or 3 years ago. Very good indeed. (June 2003)

NOW TO 2012+　　　　　　　　　　　　17.0

Beaune, Les Epenots, 1997
Maison Pierre Bourée et Fils

This is soft but not attenuated. Good acidity. Good class. *À point.* (January 2002)

DRINK SOON　　　　　　　　　　　　　15.0

Beaune, Epenottes, 1997
Domaine Charles Thomas

Good fullish, fresh colour. Ripe, ample and fruity on the nose. Medium body. Decent acidity. This is rich and quite structured for the vintage. Not a lot of class but good depth. Good plus. (May 2002)

NOW TO 2010　　　　　　　　　　　　　15.5

Beaune, Les Grèves, 1997
Maison Champy

Medium colour. Slightly adolescent on the nose. Somewhat earthy on the palate. Medium body. Decent acidity. But it lacks a bit of charm and class. The tannins are a bit unsophisticated.

Quite good. A second bottle was much fresher, though still with a certain lack of charm and class (15.0/20). (January 2001)

DRINK SOON　　　　　　　　　　　　　14.0

Beaune, Grèves, Vigne de l'Enfant Jésus, 1997
Domaine Bouchard Père et Fils

Medium colour. Just about mature. Round, soft, spicy and sweet on the nose. But not a great deal of grip. Medium body. Pleasant but a little flat on the follow-through. It lacks zip. Medium to medium-full body. Soft. Plump. Ready. Good. Drink soon. (November 2003)

DRINK SOON　　　　　　　　　　　　　15.0

Beaune, Les Teurons, 1997
Domaine Bouchard Père et Fils

Good colour. Ripe, succulent and almost sweet on nose and palate. Medium body. Not much structure. Now mellow and almost opulently ready to drink. Great charm. Abundant fruit. Even class and length. Very good plus. (January 2003)

NOW TO 2009　　　　　　　　　　　　　16.5

Beaune, Les Teurons, 1997
Domaine Germain Père et Fils/
Château de Chorey-lès-Beaune

Medium colour. A little combined SO2 on the nose. Ripe but a little flat. Medium body. A little one-dimensional at the end. Quite good plus. Should have been better. (August 2000)

DRINK SOON　　　　　　　　　　　　　14.5

Beaune, Vignes Franches, 1997
Domaine Germain Père et Fils/
Château de Chorey-lès-Beaune

Fullish colour. Lovely rich, ample nose. Plums and raspberries. A touch of oak. Fullish body. Some tannin still. But plenty of depth and very lovely fruit. Vigorous and intense. Very good. (September 2004)

NOW TO 2018　　　　　　　　　　　　　15.5

Bonnes Mares, 1997
Domaine Comte Georges de Vogüé

Fullish colour. Now a little sign of maturity. Quite firm nose for a 1997. Rich. Very good acidity. Medium-full body. A little tannin still on the palate. Good, cool fruit. Lots of elegance. Long and complex. Very fine. (May 2002)

NOW TO 2020   18.5

Le Chambertin, 1997
Domaine Joseph Drouhin

This is a little slight for what it is. Good fruit, but not a lot of grip, concentration or depth. Slightly astringent at the end. Medium body. Ripe and succulent but not really *grand cru* quality. (March 2002)

NOW TO 2011   15.5

Chambertin, 1997
Domaine Leroy

Fine colour for the vintage. Exceptionally lovely fruit on the nose. A cornucopia of *petits fruits rouges et blancs*. On the palate medium body. Just a little tannin. Very ripe. Gently oaky. Seductive. Voluptuous. Fine. (April 2002)

NOW TO 2013   17.5

Chambertin, Clos de Bèze, 1997
Domaine Pierre Damoy

Medium colour. Ripe, round and fruity. Medium body. Not a great deal of power or backbone. Not feeble in acidity, but a lack of austerity and depth of flavour. Very ripe but slightly superficial. Exotic. Very good but not great. (January 2002)

NOW TO 2014   16.0

Chambolle-Musigny, 1997
Domaine Jacques-Frédéric Mugnier

Medium colour. Splendidly elegant, supple, fruity nose. Marvellously classy fruit if not great structure. Very pure. Medium body. Just a little tannin. Very good acidity. Long and intense. Very lovely for a village wine. (June 2001)

NOW TO 2013   16.0

Chambolle-Musigny, 1997
Domaine Georges Roumier et Fils

Good colour. Succulent, rich nose. Sweet, even. Almost a touch of toffee. On the palate this is medium bodied. Very good grip and lots of luscious fruit. Soft and supple, but fresh. Rich

without being hard. Very 1997. A lovely example. (March 2000)

NOW TO 2013   16.0

Chambolle-Musigny, Premier Cru, 1997
Domaine Comte Georges de Vogüé

Fullish colour for the vintage. Youthful too. Reticent nose. Good weight, depth and freshness. Very lovely, stylish, really quite concentrated fruit, too. This is a splendid example. Lush, succulent fruit, but unexpectedly good virility and backbone for a 1997. Very classy, too. Just about ready. Fine. (June 2006)

NOW TO 2015   17.5

Chambolle-Musigny, Les Amoureuses, 1997
Domaine Pierre Bertheau

Good colour. Fragrant nose. Good acidity. Still youthful. Medium-full body. Pure and stylish. Not very oaky. A little lean but very good plus. (November 2000)

DRINK SOON   16.5

Chambolle-Musigny, Les Amoureuses, 1997
Domaine Jacques-Frédéric Mugnier

Medium-full colour. Very lovely, understated, fragrant nose. Very Chambolle. Splendid fruit, depth and class. Medium-full body. Ripe, intense and succulent, but very fresh and well balanced. A gentle wine, nicely oaky, long and full of charm. Lovely. Fine plus for the vintage. (September 2002)

NOW TO 2012   18.0

Chambolle-Musigny, Les Amoureuses, 1997
Domaine Comte Georges de Vogüé

Full colour. Round, ripe, cedary and slightly caramel-spicy nose. Medium-full body. Good freshness. Good, ripe fruit. Quite austere for a 1997. Plenty of depth. Very good indeed but not the class of a usual Amoureuses. That is the vintage. Long, though, at the end. (September 2004)

NOW TO 2020   17.5

Chambolle-Musigny, Les Fremières, 1997
Domaine Leroy

Medium to medium-full colour. Fully mature looking. Ripe. Oaky. Good freshness and succulence.

Balanced and stylish. Full of charm. Good length. This is showing very well. Long, positive finish. Just about ready. Very good. (June 2005)

NOW TO 2012   16.0

Charmes-Chambertin, 1997
Domaine Claude Dugat

Medium-full colour. Some maturity. Nutty nose. Ripe and aromatic. Medium-full body. Sweet. Ample. Plump. But it lacks a little zip. Just about ready. Very good plus. (April 2006)

NOW TO 2012   16.5

Charmes-Chambertin, 1997
Domaine Bernard Dugat-Py

Very full colour. Slightly cooked nose. Some tannin. Fullish body. Good backbone. Very good acidity. This still needs time. Very fresh and long, with lots of depth for the vintage. But collapsed in the glass (17.0, then 15.0). (April 2006)

NOW TO 2015+   15.0

Charmes-Chambertin, 1997
Domaine Geantet-Pansiot

Medium-full colour. Some maturity. Very spicy nose. Weak-kneed. Lacks class. Medium body. Cloying. No. (April 2006)

DRINK UP   12.0

Charmes-Chambertin, 1997
Maison Dominique Laurent

Fullish colour. Some maturity. Fresh, chunky and spicy. A little cooked, but decent grip and class. Fullish body. Positive. Plenty of vigour. Fine. (April 2006)

NOW TO 2017   17.5

Charmes-Chambertin, Très Vieilles Vignes, 1997
Domaine Joseph Roty

Medium-full colour. Quite fresh looking. Good, fresh, plump nose. Very ripe and rich, but not too cooked or jammy. This is very lovely. Not as big as Dugat-Py's, but equally fresh, elegant and positive. Long. Lovely fruit. Very fine indeed. À point but will still keep well. (April 2006)

NOW TO 2015   19.5

Chorey-lès-Beaune, 1997
Domaine Daniel Largeot

As long ago as this, there was 30 percent stems and also more macération à froid. Decent colour. But rather hollow in the middle. Decent acidity for a 1997 but no succulence. (February 2003)

NOW TO 2012   13.5

Clos des Lambrays, 1997
Domaine des Lambrays

Medium weight. Fresh and very elegant. A touch of the stems. Good grip for 1997. Elegant, too. Fine. (December 2003)

NOW TO 2012   17.5

Clos de la Roche, 1997
Domaine Hervé Arlaud

Medium colour. Some development. Soft, fragrant nose. Attractive, but a little slight for a grand cru, it seems. The palate confirms this. The wine is medium bodied. It is balanced and elegant. Not a bit short. A little sous bois. But essentially soft centred and quite forward. But this is 1997. Very good plus for the vintage. (June 2002)

NOW TO 2010   16.5

Clos de la Roche, 1997
Domaine Leroy

Good colour. Soft, plump nose. Pleasant, ripe, oaky wine. But without much depth or staying power. Good acidity. But only average quality. (April 2000)

NOW TO 2010   15.0

Clos de la Roche, Cuvée Vieilles Vignes, 1997
Domaine Ponsot

Laurent Ponsot produced lovely 1997s and is very proud of them. Medium to medium-full, mature colour. Coffee, mocha and sweetness on the nose. No lack of acidity. Medium to medium-full body. Lovely ripe tannins. Good structure. Fine, succulent fruit. Generous and sexy. Plump. Very long. Very complex. Just about ready. Very fine plus. (June 2005)

NOW TO 2015   19.0

Clos Saint-Denis, 1997
Domaine Heresztyn

Very good colour for a 1997. Lovely, elegant nose. Understated. Gently oaky. Very fresh, ripe, classy fruit. Medium to medium-full body. Good substance, grip and freshness for a 1997. Long, complex and classy. Lovely. Fine plus for a 1997. (September 2002)

NOW TO 2012   18.0

Clos de Tart, 1997
Maison Mommessin

Medium-full colour. Quite sturdy on the nose for a 1997. Good grip. Good concentration. Good depth. Medium-full body. Good resolved tannins. Very good acidity. Nice plummy flavour. Plenty of substance here. Will get classier as it ages. Fine. (June 2002)

NOW TO 2018   17.5

Clos de Vougeot, 1997
Domaine René Engel

A lot better than most 1997s. Full, fresh colour. Lively nose. Rich and succulent. Fullish body. Very good acidity. Fragrant and profound. Only just ready. (May 2004)

NOW TO 2012   17.5

Clos de Vougeot, 1997
Domaine Alain Hudelot-Noëllat

Medium-full colour. Some maturity now. Rich, rich, ample nose. Good grip and therefore elegance. Medium-full body. Slightly spicy. Already soft and fully ready for drinking. Quite rich. Quite vigorous. Elegant and positive at the end. Fine. (October 2005)

NOW TO 2015   17.5

Clos de Vougeot, 1997
Domaine Louis Jadot

Full colour. Quite firm on the nose. Very good depth and class. Splendidly fresh for a 1997. A touch of oak. Rich and vigorous. Profound and concentrated. Lovely, energetic finish. Fine plus. (October 2002)

NOW TO 2018   18.5

Clos de Vougeot, 1997
Domaine Leroy

Good colour for a 1997. Soft and spicy on the nose. A little superficial. All high toned. Medium body. Little structure. Somewhat empty on the follow-through. Good but not great. (April 2000)

DRINK SOON   15.0

Clos de Vougeot, 1997
Domaine Méo-Camuzet

Medium to medium-full colour. Some rather dry, astringent tannins on the nose. The palate is similar. This lacks a bit of grip. Disappointing. (March 2001)

DRINK SOON   14.0

Clos de Vougeot, 1997
Domaine Henri Rebourseau

Good colour. Slightly stewed and tannic on the nose. Underneath, medium body. Ripe but with a hard edge. Decent grip. But not much class. Slightly astringent at the end which will get more pronounced. Only fair. (October 2000)

DRINK SOON   13.0

Le Corton, 1997
Domaine Bouchard Père et Fils

Good colour. Closed at first. Tannic. It took time to come out of the glass. Fullish body. Very rich. Very good concentration. Splendid class and acidity. This is a lovely, vigorous example. Very fine. (June 2003)

NOW TO 2020   18.5

Corton, Les Bressandes, 1997
Domaine Chandon de Briailles

Very good colour. Very lovely nose. Rich, plummy with a touch of confit. Very ripe. But distinguished as well. Fullish body. Very fine grip. Marvellous fruit. Concentrated and stylish. Really very seductive and very lovely. Excellent for what it is. (October 2000)

NOW TO 2014   18.0

Corton, Les Renardes, 1997
Domaine Leroy

Still a fresh colour. Lovely nose. Interesting black cherry and slightly resinous touches on the nose.

Medium to medium-full body. A little tannin. But more in the sense of the wine being a little raw. Ripe. Good acidity. Not exactly very stylish but very good. Finishes positively. (June 2005)
NOW TO 2017   16.0

Echézeaux, 1997
Domaine Louis Jadot

Full, vigorous colour. Soft and rich but at present not a lot of personality on the nose. Fullish body. Plump and succulent. Very good acidity for the vintage. Good structure, too. Surprisingly long and vigorous. Fine for the vintage. (October 2002)
NOW TO 2017   17.5

Gevrey-Chambertin, Vieilles Vignes, 1997
Domaine Alain Burguet

Fullish colour. Rich, full, meaty nose. Not too tannic but plenty of wine here. Nicely fresh and stylish. Very ripe. Almost sweet. Quite smooth and velvety now. Just about ready. As usual, very good plus. (June 2004)
NOW TO 2012   16.5

Gevrey-Chambertin, Vieilles Vignes, 1997
Domaine Geantet-Pansiot

Fresh, upfront, vigorous but now-drinkable example. Medium-full body. Ample. Juicy. Very good for what it is if no great finesse. (October 2001)
NOW TO 2010   15.5

Gevrey-Chambertin, Vieilles Vignes, 1997
Domaine Heresztyn

Good colour. Stylish, ripe and attractive. Medium-full body. Plenty of depth and character. This is a very good example. Positive at the end. (October 2000)
DRINK SOON   15.5

Gevrey-Chambertin, Vieilles Vignes, 1997
Domaine Christian Sérafin

Ripe, stylish and oaky. Very good depth. Succulent but balanced. Plenty of character. More to it than with most village wine. Fresh and complex. Very good plus. (December 2001)
DRINK SOON   16.5

Gevrey-Chambertin, Les Cazetiers, 1997
Domaine Bruno Clair

Medium to medium-full colour. Soft nose. A touch of tabac. Quite evolved. Slightly weak at the end. Slight suspicion of attenuation. Decent fruit. Some acidity. But it lacks depth and class. Slightly vegetal. Only fair. (June 2001)
NOW TO 2009   13.0

Gevrey-Chambertin, Champeaux, 1997
Maison Pierre Bourée et Fils

Very much the sort of soft, slightly dry, slightly attenuated style one expects. Slightly attenuated. No real grip or concentration. Very 1997. (January 2002)
DRINK SOON   13.5

Gevrey-Chambertin, En Champeaux, 1997
Domaine Denis Mortet

Good purple colour. Naturally a little less intense than the 1998. Ample, rich, quite oaky nose. Lovely, plump, juicy fruit. Medium-full body. Fat. Reasonable acidity. It may get a little astringent in due course, but you'll be able to drink this soon before it gets too dry. Ample fruit. Nicely cool and not jammy. Very good. (May 2002)
DRINK SOON   16.0

Gevrey-Chambertin, Clos Saint-Jacques, 1997
Domaine Michel Esmonin et Fille

Good colour. Soft, but ripe and rich on both nose and palate. Plump, balanced and very good. But not the greatest of nuance and complexity. Decent length nevertheless. (October 2002)
NOW TO 2009   16.0

Gevrey-Chambertin, Clos Saint-Jacques, 1997
Domaine Louis Jadot

Medium-full colour. Now a touch of brown. Fresh, aromatic nose. Not a lot of depth. Forward and fruity. Round and ripe. Medium-full body. Good acidity. Not a lot of backbone, of course. But not a bit short and no lack of freshness. Easy to enjoy. Ready. (November 2002)
NOW TO 2014   17.0

Gevrey-Chambertin, Clos Saint-Jacques, 1997
Domaine Armand Rousseau

Medium-full colour. Now just about mature. Rich, oaky, fat, slightly reduced nose. Medium to medium-full body. Succulent. Good acidity. Stylish. Not great but very good indeed. (April 2005)

NOW TO 2012   17.0

Gevrey-Chambertin, Combe au Moine, 1997
Domaine René Leclerc

Medium to medium-full colour. Fresh. Ripe, spicy, sweet nose. Medium body. Soft. Quite stylish. Decent grip. Really very good for what it is. Unexpectedly so. (March 2006)

NOW TO 2011   17.0

Gevrey-Chambertin, Les Combottes, 1997
Domaine Dujac

Good colour. Still vigorous. Round, ripe nose. Evidence of the stems as well as the oak. Open and accessible. Even sweet. Medium-full body. Very good grip. Ripe tannins. This is stylish, generous and very long for a 1997. Fine. (October 2005)

NOW TO 2015   17.5

Gevrey-Chambertin, Les Corbeaux, 1997
Domaine Denis Bachelet

Good colour. A little development. Ripe, lush nose. Decent acidity. Not the greatest of dimension, but elegant and balanced enough. Medium to medium-full body. Soft tannin. Just about absorbed. Good fruit. Just about ready. Very good plus. (June 2006)

NOW TO 2015   16.5

Gevrey-Chambertin, Estournelles-Saint-Jacques, 1997
Domaine Frédéric Esmonin

Good colour. A little unsophisticated on the nose and palate, but good depth,backbone and grip. Medium-full body. Ripe and rich. Plenty of wine here and not over-extracted. Good plus. (March 2003)

NOW TO 2015   15.5

Gevrey-Chambertin, Lavaux-Saint-Jacques, 1997
Domaine Denis Mortet

Fine colour for the vintage. Mortet deliberately picked early, and the result is a wine with grip, very good freshness and very good support. A *vin de garde* for a 1997. Ripe, cool, composed and delicious. Fine plus for the vintage. (September 2002)

NOW TO 2014   18.0

Gevrey-Chambertin, Vieilles Vignes, 1997
Domaine Alain Burguet

Full, immature colour. Quite a sturdy nose. Fullish body. Some tannins. A touch clumsy, but good grip. If it lacks a little class, it makes up for it in balance and freshness. Plump and plummy. Very good. Still needs time. (June 2006)

2009 TO 2018   16.0

Latricières-Chambertin, 1997
Maison Dominique Laurent

Full, youthful colour. Somewhat robust and unrefined on the nose. Medium-full body. Soft and sweet on the palate. Not a lot of acidity but not too short. Good but not great. (April 2005)

NOW TO 2010   15.0

Latricières-Chambertin, 1997
Domaine Leroy

Medium colour only. Some development. Good, firm nose. A bit closed. On the palate a slight lack of personality as well as real grip. I find this a bit anonymous. (April 2000)

NOW TO 2011   15.5

Latricières-Chambertin, 1997
Maison Roland Remoissenet et Fils

Only a medium colour. Rather weak on the nose and dilute on the palate. Forward. Ready. Not much of either depth or class. Merely light and pleasant. (October 2000)

DRINK SOON   13.5

Mazis-Chambertin, 1997
Domaine Bernard Maume

Medium-full, mature colour. Succulent, rich, slightly oaky, ripe nose. Civilised on the palate.

Medium to medium-full body. Not a lot of grip, so slightly astringent at the end. But ripe and stylish. Very good and reasonably fresh. (April 2005)

NOW TO 2010 16.0

Monthelie, 1997
Domaine Pierre Morey

Good colour for the vintage. Plump, attractive, succulent nose. Just a touch of oak. Good fruit on the attack. Just a little lean at the end, but the wine is so ripe it doesn't matter too much. Good balance. Quite good. (July 2000)

DRINK UP 14.0

Morey-Saint-Denis, Premier Cru, Vieilles Vignes, 1997
Domaine Hubert Lignier

Good fresh, full colour. Just a little mature. Quite a lot of new oak (two thirds) on the nose. Rich, fullish bodied and succulent. Plenty of depth and vigour. Medium-full body. Fresh. Good acidity. Now soft. Now just about ready. Long. Very good indeed. (June 2003)

NOW TO 2010 17.0

Musigny, 1997
Domaine Leroy

Full colour for the vintage. Subtle, complex fruit on the nose. Medium-full. Good acidity. Some structure. But somehow incomplete. Fine for the vintage though. Very lovely fruit. (April 2000)

NOW TO 2009 17.5

Musigny, 1997
Domaine Jacques-Frédéric Mugnier

Medium-full, youthful colour. Very, very delicious, elegant, fragrant, composed nose. Marvellous fruit. On the palate medium-full body. Such lovely succulence and ripe tannins that it seems the wine is already soft textured and almost ready for drinking. Yet it will last and last, and get better and better. Great class. Multidimensional. Very long. Very fine indeed. (September 2005)

2009 TO 2030 19.5

Musigny, Vieilles Vignes, 1997
Domaine Comte Georges de Vogüé

Fullish colour. Now a little sign of maturity. Softer nose than the Bonnes Mares but more intense. Still a bit young and informed though. A little adolescent at present. Ripe and complete though. Medium-full body. Plenty of substance here. Lovely fruit. Very, very long at the end. Very fine, indeed, for the vintage. (May 2002)

NOW TO 2020 19.5

Nuits-Saint-Georges, Aux Allots, 1997
Domaine Leroy

Full colour. Ripe and fragrant but essentially soft on the nose. Fullish body. Some tannin. Decent freshness and acidity. But a touch dense. The tannins are a bit robust, and the wine lacks grace and charm. Slightly astringent at the end. Quite good. (June 2004)

NOW TO 2012 14.0

Nuits-Saint-Georges, Les Boudots, 1997
Domaine Jean Grivot

Medium colour. Some development. Soft, ripe, almost sweet nose. No great backbone, but classy and balanced. Medium body. Not a lot of tannin. You could drink this now. Plump and *gouleyant*. Excellent freshness. Will keep well. Fine for what it is. (November 2001)

NOW TO 2010 17.5

Nuits-Saint-Georges, Aux Boudots, 1997
Domaine Gérard Mugneret

Good colour. Just a hint of reduction. Rich and classy. Very good fruit and grip. Medium-full body. Excellent fruit and lovely grip on the palate. This is composed. You can see the Vosne proximity. Good, oaky base. Long and very classy. Fine plus. (June 2001)

NOW TO 2018 18.0

Nuits-Saint-Georges, Les Chaignots, 1997
Domaine Joseph Faiveley

Medium colour. Now fully mature. Soft, gingerbread nose. Medium to medium-full body. Good freshness and vigour. Ripe. Balanced. Stylish. *À point*. No great depth, but decent class and complexity. Finishes positively. Very good plus for the vintage. (February 2005)

NOW TO 2011　　　　　　　　　　　　16.5

Nuits-Saint-Georges, Aux Chaignots, 1997
Domaine Gérard Mugneret

Magnum. Good colour. Very ripe cherries on the nose. Decent acidity. A slight lack of fat as well as backbone. But ripe enough. Just about ready. Slightly one-dimensional. Good plus at best. (January 2003)

DRINK SOON　　　　　　　　　　　　15.5

Nuits-Saint-Georges, Aux Chaignots, 1997
Domaine Nicolas Potel

Very good colour. Lovely rich, balanced, succulent, gently oaky nose. Good substance, but the tannins are ripe and gentle. Although not really at its best until 2002 or so, very enjoyable. Long and positive at the end. Very good indeed. (April 2000)

DRINK SOON　　　　　　　　　　　　17.0

Nuits-Saint-Georges, Les Lavières, 1997
Domaine Leroy

Village wine. Good colour. Rich, chocolaty nose. Full. Quite some tannin for a 1997. Meaty. Sturdy. Good, full, rich wine underneath. Plenty of depth, concentration and intensity. Lots of wine here and very good class. Needs time. Still quite a lot of tannin. Ripe, long finish. Very good plus. (June 2001)

NOW TO 2015　　　　　　　　　　　　16.5

Nuits-Saint-Georges, Les Perrières, 1997
Domaine Robert Chevillon

Soft, succulent, ripe, almost sweet. But not really enough definition. A bit light. A bit simple for a 1997. Good but not great. (December 2001)

DRINK SOON　　　　　　　　　　　　15.0

Nuits-Saint-Georges, Les Saint-Georges, 1997
Domaine Henri Gouges

Medium colour. Now developed. Soft, ripe nose. Plenty of succulent, almost sweet fruit, but not a lot of depth underneath. Medium body. Quite fresh. Decent fruit. Not a bit short. Indeed,

warm and spicy underneath. But all a bit one-dimensional. And a slight lack of class and *terroir* definition. Very good at best. (September 2003)

DRINK SOON　　　　　　　　　　　　16.0

Nuits-Saint-Georges, Les Saint-Georges, 1997
Hospices De Nuits/Domaine Georges Faiveley

Good colour. Succulent, vigorous nose. Fresh and stylish. Medium-full body. Now quite smooth. But a good backbone and no lack of grip. Ripe, round and positive at the end. Nicely long and stylish. Fine for the vintage. (October 2005)

NOW TO 2014　　　　　　　　　　　　17.5

Nuits-Saint-Georges, Les Vaucrains, 1997
Domaine Alain Michelot

Good, full, youthful colour. Good oak base. A rich, fat, medium-full wine. Good grip and depth for the vintage. Succulent and creamy rich. This is very good plus. Ready. (March 2003)

NOW TO 2012　　　　　　　　　　　　16.5

Nuits-Saint-Georges, Les Vaucrains, 1997
Maison Nicolas Potel

Good colour. Lovely nose. Very rich. Quite sturdy but not a bit sauvage. Very damson plum fruit. Full body. Some tannin. Still very youthful. A little tough, even, but underneath excellent fruit and concentration. Lovely finish. Intense and harmonious. Fine plus. (June 2001)

NOW TO 2018　　　　　　　　　　　　18.0

Pommard, Clos des Epeneaux, 1997
Domaine du Comte Armand

Full colour. Ample, rich, fat, voluptuous nose. Medium-full body. Still a little tannin. This was picked very late when the tannins were properly ripe, so there is very good backbone here. Good depth. Alive and vigorous. Much fresher than most. Fine. Will still improve. (May 2005)

NOW TO 2016　　　　　　　　　　　　17.5

Richebourg, 1997
Domaine Anne Gros

Fullish colour. Just a little mature. Slightly overripe nose. But good grip, depth and class for a 1997. Just a little raw still. Fullish on the palate.

Lovely fruit underneath. Very fine for what it is but not a great wine. Too spicy. Not elegant enough. (October 2005)

NOW TO 2017   18.0

Richebourg, 1997
Domaine Leroy

Medium-full colour. Fat, open, slightly sulphury nose. Better on aeration. Medium body. Some structure. Lots of fruit. Decent grip. This is a lot better than most Leroy 1997s. (April 2000)

DRINK SOON   17.0

Richebourg, 1997
Domaine de la Romanée-Conti

Good colour. Fine grip. Fat, rich and succulent. This has a lot of concentration for the vintage. Nice and cool. Very good grip. Very fine. (June 2001)

NOW TO 2017   18.0

La Romanée, 1997
Domaine Bouchard Père et Fils

Medium-full colour. Some hints of maturity. Very ample, rich nose. Good acidity, but not a lot of backbone or style. Perfumed, luscious, exotic fruit here. Medium body. Spicy sweet but without a great deal of class. It lacks a little freshness and purity. Very good at best. (March 2003)

NOW TO 2013   16.0

Romanée-Saint-Vivant, 1997
Domaine Joseph Drouhin

Medium-full colour. Fully mature. Delicious. Fragrant. Medium to medium-full body. Intense. Very lovely Pinot fruit. Not the greatest concentration and vigour, nor complexity. But that is the vintage. Soft, sweet and easy to drink. Fine for the vintage. À point. (September 2005)

NOW TO 2012   18.0

Romanée-Saint-Vivant, 1997
Domaine Alain Hudelot-Noëllat

Medium-full colour. Fresh, ripe, quite succulent but not very voluminous on the nose. Good freshness. Medium body. This is stylish but not that profound. But fine for a 1997. (April 2001)

NOW TO 2010   17.5

Romanée-Saint-Vivant, 1997
Domaine Leroy

Full colour. Some development. Ripe, soft, exotic nose. Good freshness. No undue oak. Medium-full body. Now getting soft. Not the greatest of elegance but fine for the vintage. Ready soon. (September 2005)

NOW TO 2014   17.5

Romanée-Saint-Vivant, 1997
Domaine de la Romanée-Conti

Medium to medium-full colour. A little development. Impressive nose. Rather more depth than Leroy's and Drouhin's. Lovely fruit. Very classy. As 1997s go, this is excellent. It has much more to it than the rest. Good grip. Plenty of depth. Very impressive. Real length for once. Very fine plus. (March 2002)

NOW TO 2020   19.0

Ruchottes-Chambertin, 1997
Domaine Frédéric Esmonin

Medium-full colour. Quite a lot of extraction on the nose. Good depth and grip. Slightly adolescent at present. Nicely austere. Very good acidity. Not a lot of tannin but good structure for the vintage. Plenty of depth on the palate. As it developed, it got richer and richer. Excellent finish for a 1997. Fine. (October 2001)

NOW TO 2012   17.5

Ruchottes-Chambertin, 1997
Domaine Dr. Georges Mugneret

Medium-full colour. Now mature. Soft nose. Full of fruit if without great class or depth. Medium body. Slightly attenuated. Not much backbone. Decent fruit and even class, but a slight disappointment. (April 2005)

NOW TO 2010   15.5

Santenay, Beauregard, 1997
Maison Nicolas Potel

Medium colour. A little development. Lacks a little personality on the nose. But ripe, cool and well balanced. Good acidity. Slightly raw on the palate. Medium body. Quite good but not exciting. (August 2000)

DRINK SOON   14.0

Santenay, Clos des Hâtes, Vieilles Vignes, 1997
Domaine Hubert Lamy et Fils

Light-medium colour. Fragrant, juicy nose. Light-medium body. No tannin but good balance. Slightly raw but can be enjoyed now. Ripe and full of fruit. Good for what it is. (July 2000)

DRINK UP   14.5

Savigny-lès-Beaune, La Dominode, 1997
Domaine Jean-Marc Pavelot

Fullish colour. Rich nose, but good acitidy. Ripe tannins. Good substance. Medium to medium-full body. Clean. Fresh. Stylish. Ripe and plump. Just about *à point*. Long and positive. Very good. (September 2005)

NOW TO 2012   16.0

Savigny-lès-Beaune, Les Guettes, 1997
Domaine Jean-Marc Pavelot

Plump, ripe, fresh and attractive. Medium body. Not for keeping. Stylish now. Not much tannin. Good plus. (June 2004)

NOW TO 2010   15.5

Savigny-lès-Beaune, Les Lavières, 1997
Domaine Louis Jadot

Full colour. Rich, earthy, meaty nose. Lots of depth. Fullish. Very good class, even intensity. Good substance. Very good grip. Long. Just about ready. Fine for what it is. (October 2002)

NOW TO 2012   17.0

Savigny-lès-Beaune, Les Montchenevoy, 1997
Domaine Javillier-Guyot

Succulent. Very stylish. *À point*. Lovely. (July 2000)

DRINK SOON   15.0

Savigny-lès-Beaune, Les Narbantons, 1997
Domaine Leroy

Good colour. Now just about mature. Round, ripe nose. Good fruit but lacks just a little zip. Some tannin. A little stewed, bitter and astringent. It lacks charm. Not bad plus at best. It may round off. Give it a year. (September 2004)

NOW TO 2010   13.5

Savigny-lès-Beaune, Les Serpentières, 1997
Domaine Simon Bize et Fils

Good colour. Not so much the stems, but a bit of paper on the nose. Fruity attack. Tails off slightly though. Long enough but not very complex. Good but not brilliant. (July 2000)

DRINK SOON   15.0

Savigny-lès-Beaune, Aux Serpentières, 1997
Domaine Maurice Écard

Softer than the Leroy Narbantons. Stylish. *À point*. Very good fruit. Ripe and generous. Very good. (June 2002)

NOW TO 2010   16.0

Savigny-lès-Beaune, Aux Serpentières, 1997
Domaine Patrick Javillier

Medium colour. Ripe nose. Good Pinot. Plenty of depth and style. Just a little unresolved tannin on the nose, but good fruit and character on the palate. Just about ready. Medium body. Not that concentrated. But very *gouleyant*. Quite good plus. (January 2002)

NOW TO 2010   16.0

La Tâche, 1997
Domaine de la Romanée-Conti

Medium colour. Still youthful. Light fresh nose. Lovely fruit. Very stylish. Slightly reserved behind. But ripe and accessible now. Medium body. Good grip. This has got a lot more to it than most. Lots of class, too. Very fine. (October 2000)

NOW TO 2013   18.0

Volnay, Les Caillerets, Ancienne Cuvée Carnot, 1997
Domaine Bouchard Père et Fils

Good colour. No undue development. Plump, ripe and seductive. But a slight lack of grip. Juicy and succulent. No lack of freshness. Medium to medium-full body. Plenty of depth and definition for a 1997. Good, long finish. Fine. (March 2004)

NOW TO 2010   17.5

Volnay, Champans, 1997
Domaine des Comtes Lafon

Much more purple than Lafarge's 1997 Volnay Clos du Château des Ducs. Fresh, raspberry, perfumed nose. Quite full but not sturdy. Balanced and elegant. But on the palate not as elegant as all that. It lacks a bit of freshness. Medium body. Decent length. Ripe but good plus at best. (June 2004)

NOW TO 2012   15.5

Volnay, Clos de la Barre, 1997
Domaine Louis Jadot

Full colour. Some development. Mellow, full but soft, almost exotic nose. Splendid voluptuous fruit on the palate. Good freshness. Quite full bodied. Nicely fat. Very good depth. Long. Fine for the vintage. (October 2002)

NOW TO 2014   17.5

Volnay, Clos du Château des Ducs, 1997
Domaine Michel Lafarge

Some evolution on the colour. Very classy nose. Soft but intense. Velvety and harmonious. Medium body. Good tannins. Fresher than most. Lovely long, intense finish. Very good indeed. (June 2004)

NOW TO 2015   17.0

Volnay, Clos des Chênes, 1997
Domaine Michel Lafarge

Medium-full colour. Some development. Ripe nose. Fresh. Plump. Attractive. Medium to medium-full body. Now à point. Decent acidity if not a lot of depth or concentration. Good, positive finish. Very good indeed. (March 2006)

NOW TO 2014   17.0

Volnay, Clos des Chênes, 1997
Domaine des Comtes Lafon

Good colour. Medium-full weight. Ripe, succulent and quite forward. Stylish, fragrant Volnay nose. Good depth. Good acidity. Classy and complex. Very good indeed. (June 2001)

NOW TO 2009   17.0

Volnay, Frémiets, 1997
Domaine Annick Parent

Surprisingly deep colour. Now some signs of maturity. Aromatic, spicy-sweet nose. Very ripe. Good structure and depth. Very good grip for a 1997. The Volnay silkiness is taking over. Classy. Very good. (September 2004)

NOW TO 2014   16.0

Volnay, Santenots du Milieu, 1997
Domaine des Comtes Lafon

Good colour. Quite open on the nose. But a little austere as 1997s go. Fullish body. Just a little tannin. Very good grip. Will be better still in a year. Long and stylish. Sweet and smooth. Fine for 1997. (November 2005)

NOW TO 2015   17.5

Volnay, Taillepieds, 1997
Domaine du Marquis d'Angerville

Medium-full, fresh colour. Round, soft, fragrant nose. Ripe but not the greatest energy or depth. Medium body. Proper, elegant Volnay fruit. Complex and most attractive. Absolutely à point now. Good finish. For a 1997 certainly a fine example. But in real terms, although very charming, not a profound Burgundy. (April 2005)

NOW TO 2009   17.5

Volnay, Taillepieds, 1997
Domaine Bouchard Père et Fils

Good colour. Aromatic, opulent, sweet and generous on the nose. Medium-full body. Fine acidity for the vintage. Lots of depth and grip. Plenty of dimension and elegance at the end because of this. Fine. (June 2003)

NOW TO 2015   17.5

Volnay, Taillepieds, 1997
Domaine Hubert de Montille

Rather more depth, grip and better acidity than one might have expected. Good tannins. Generous, rich and splendidly balanced. Fuller and more substantial, too. Very good, indeed, for the vintage. (December 2001)

NOW TO 2014   17.0

Vosne-Romanée, 1997
Domaine René Engel

Medium colour. Ripe nose if perhaps with a slight lack of zip. Round, succulent and attractive

on the palate. Finishes positively. Good plus.
(October 2000)
DRINK SOON   15.5

Vosne-Romanée, Les Beaumonts, 1997
Domaine Leroy

Good, fresh colour. Quite oaky on the nose.
Ripe and lush. Medium-full body. Concentrated.
Good acidity for a 1997. Generous and vigorous.
It doesn't have quite the finesse for fine but very
good indeed. (June 2005)
NOW TO 2014   17.0

Vosne-Romanée, Les Beaux Monts, 1997
Domaine Daniel Rion

Fullish, fresh colour. Fresh, youthful and juicy,
yet without a great deal of depth. A touch dry.
On the palate medium body. Not a lot of tannin
if any at all. Stylish. Balanced. No backbone.
Good grip. A very good 1997. (October 2000)
DRINK SOON   16.0

Vosne-Romanée, Aux Brûlées, 1997
Domaine René Engel

Good colour. Rich nose. Some tannin. Rather
better grip than the 1997 village wine, tasted
alongside. Good depth. Good style. Medium-
full body. Very well balanced. This is classy. Very
good indeed. (October 2000)
NOW TO 2009   17.0

Vosne-Romanée, Aux Brûlées, 1997
Domaine Méo-Camuzet

This is much better than the Clos de Vougeot.
Good colour. Lovely, plump nose. Medium
weight. Well balanced. Fresh and plump. Very
attractive. Very good indeed. (March 2001)
NOW TO 2014   17.0

Vosne-Romanée, Les Chaumes, 1997
Domaine Robert Arnoux

Good, fresh colour. Good, fresh, plump nose,
especially for the vintage. Medium weight. Very
good acidity. Lovely, plump fruit. Smooth and
seductive. Very good finish. This is very good
indeed. (October 2005)
NOW TO 2011   17.5

Vosne-Romanée, Clos Goillotte, 1997
Domaine Prieuré-Roch

A monopoly. Village *appellation contrôlée*. Medium
colour. Quite evolved. Rather weak on the nose.
Not yet attenuated but low in acidity. Medium
body. Some fruit. But not much depth. Forward.
Rather one-dimensional. Not much class either.
Not bad plus. (July 2001)
DRINK SOON   13.5

Vosne-Romanée, Clos des Réas, 1997
Domaine Michel Gros

Medium-full colour. Some maturity now. Fruity
and spicy on the nose. But not a lot of expression
because there is not a lot of zip. Medium body.
Not much tannin. Better acidity than it shows on
the nose. Indeed ripe and attractive. Ready soon.
Very good, indeed, for the vintage. (December 2003)
DRINK SOON   17.0

Vosne-Romanée, La Croix Rameau, 1997
Maison Dominique Laurent

Medium to medium-full colour. Good depth here
on the nose. Fatter than his Vosne les Rouges. But
more tannin. Ripe and concentrated. Some oak. A
plumper, richer wine than the Rouges. But more
tannin. More structure. Good plus. (January 2001)
NOW TO 2010   15.5

Vosne-Romanée, Les Malconsorts, 1997
Domaine Sylvain Cathiard

One of the best 1997s of the vintage because of
the really excellent acidity. This allows the fruit
and richness of the vintage to come sailing out.
Medium to medium-full body. No hard tannins.
Very seductive. Lovely finish. Fine plus. (June 2004)
NOW TO 2010+   18.0

Vosne-Romanée, Aux Malconsorts, 1997
Domaine Louis Jadot

Fullish colour. Rich, full, aromatic nose. Lovely
fruit but lacks a touch of zip. Medium-full body.
Ripe and ample. Decent freshness. Succulent
and positive at the end. Very good, indeed, but
not the flair of their Échezeaux or Clos Vougeot.
(October 2002)
NOW TO 2014   17.0

Vosne-Romanée, Aux Reignots, 1997
Domaine Bouchard Père et Fils
Soft, ripe, classy if no great depth or strength. Gently oaky. Medium body. Balanced. Charming. Quite forward. Decent follow-through. Very good. (June 2000)

DRINK SOON   16.0

Vosne-Romanée, Les Rouges, 1997
Maison Dominique Laurent
Série rare. Medium colour. Sweet, rich, round nose. Medium body. Seems a little lean but fresh. No hard edges. Good follow-through. More sweetness on the finish than on the attack. A touch of coffee. Essentially softer and forward. Good. (January 2001)

NOW TO 2012   15.0

Vosne-Romanée, Les Suchots, 1997
Maison Dominique Laurent
Série rare. Medium to medium-full colour. Still a little tight on the nose. Perfumed. Rich and intense. Closed-in but lots of depth. This is proper *premier cru* quality. Concentrated. Lots of quality fruit here. Nicely austere. Complex, subtle and classy. Fine. (January 2001)

NOW TO 2014   17.5

1996

This year produced a bounteous harvest, even more abundant than 1990, although it would be superseded by 1999. It was the product of a summer which was sunny and dry, although not ever very hot. This produced wines with quite dominant acidities, in some cases, as it turned out, rather lean at the lower levels. The situation is proportionally a great deal better as you move up the hierarchy, where there is plenty of character, elegance and vigour in the wines, both red and white, and good *terroir* definition. At first, even though the white 1995s were considered to have the edge, most plumped for 1996 in red. Eleven years later, with the 1995 reds having progressed so satisfactorily (see the next chapter), and with some of the better reds having retained their austerity but losing their fruit, I am among those who have changed their minds. I prefer the 1995 reds. Moreover, as noted on page 0000, the evolution of many of the white wines, owing to cork and premature oxidation problems, has lead to dozens of disappointments.

The premature oxidation of the 1996s was exacerbated by the fact that the *malos* were late to get under way and slow to finish. So instead of being sulphured bit by bit from, say, June onward, many did not get their first dose until September. This meant that much of this sulphur had not combined with the wine when it was bottled. As a result the wines were underprotected.

WEATHER CONDITIONS

After a winter which began cold but turned milder, March and April were very dry months, leading to a delayed bud-break during the first fortnight in April. May was cool, overcast and wet, but this led to a smooth acceleration of a vegetative cycle, and when the sun and the warm weather began at the beginning of June, the vines were able to flower within the period of a week, very rapidly and very successfully. Suddenly, instead of being a week behind, we were 5 days ahead of schedule. The fruit setting was also rapid and without incident, despite a return to cooler temperatures at the end of June.

July was statistically normal—fine and sunny, without thunderstorms—and the fine

→ Rating for the Vintage ←	
Red	16.5
White	15.5

→ Size of the Crop ← (In hectolitres, excluding generic wine)		
	RED	WHITE
Grands Crus	14,548	3,874
Village and Premiers Crus	190,154	56,908
TOTAL	204,702	60,779

weather continued into the first half of August despite a drop in temperatures. Throughout the summer, the north wind was dominant. This had the benefit of reducing the risk of oïdium and mildew, but it meant cool nights, however hot and sunny it might have been during the day.

By the end of August the state of the fruit was again below the norm, but September, while not being particularly warm, was very dry and very sunny. The precipitation for the month was one-third of the norm: 23 mm as opposed to 67. The vines caught up, and the berries increased in sugar without increasing too much in volume; when the vintage started (officially on September 18 for white wines, on September 20 for reds), the cycle was again 5 or 6 days ahead. The harvest continued in good weather save for 2 hours of rain on one day and a morning's-worth on September 27.

The rest of the time, right through until November 1, was dry, and the net effect was to produce fruit at harvest time in a state of health that was unprecedented. "They looked like table grapes," said one grower. "I have been making wine for 33 years. I have never seen grapes so healthy," said another.

Some *vignerons*, in retrospect, picked too early. The fruit seemed ripe on September 18, so why wait? Those who did wait say the potential alcohol figures increased without a corresponding fall in the level of acidity. All the elements were concentrating, and you can see the proof in the dry extract statistics. Dominique Lafon was one of these, pointing out a wide variation from plot to plot in the state of maturity. He commenced with his Montrachet on the nineteenth, stopped twice for a couple of days, and did not finish until October 2: 14 days rather than 7.

WHERE ARE THE BEST WINES?

- Beware of the many white wines which have oxidised prematurely (see above and p. 0000).
- Very good white wines can be found in Chassagne-Montrachet and in Saint-

Aubin. The wines are also fine in Corton-Charlemagne.

- Generic wines, many village wines and those from the cooler *climats* are now rather too lean. The acidity has taken over.
- The Côte de Nuits red wines are better and more consistent than those of the Côte de Beaune.
- Red wines are successful throughout the Côte de Nuits, with the marginal exception of Gevrey-Chambertin. The vintage is particularly good in Nuits-Saint-Georges.

WHEN WILL THE WINES BE AT THEIR BEST?

The vintage is now 11 years old, but there are a number of red *grands* and *premiers crus* which still need time. As far as the white wines are concerned, we have the problem of rogue corks, but the rest, *premier cru* and above, will continue to give much pleasure for 5 years or so. Beyond that it will be a question of wine and storage. The reds, too, are fresh and full of zip, even at village level. The best will still have much to offer even in 2020. At the outset, the 1996s, which showed a lot of elegance even if with high acidities, were preferred to the 1995s, which showed quite a lot of tannin. The former vintage has aged less well than the latter. The large crop is sometimes evident. The acidity shows and there is, especially in the Côte de Beaune, sometimes a lack of generosity. I now prefer the 1995s.

TASTING NOTES

WHITES

Auxey-Duresses, 1996
Domaine du Comte Armand
Ripe, stylish and fresh. Good fruit and personality. Very good for what it is. Good positive finish.
(June 2006)
NOW TO 2010   16.0

Bâtard-Montrachet, 1996
Domaine Jean-Marc Boillot
Magnum. This has a lot of depth and class. Good concentration. Very fresh. Rich but very

good grip. Fullish body. Complex. But now à point. Very elegant. Very fine. (June 2003)

NOW TO 2015   18.5

Bâtard-Montrachet, 1996
Domaine Jean-Noël Gagnard

Very lovely nose. Concentrated, full, pure and profound. Still very young. Fullish body on the palate. High but by no means excessive (or vegetal) acidity. Because of the depth and concentration of the wine, this will still improve. As it gets soft, it will get more and more opulent. At present the finish is a little raw. Fine for the vintage. (January 2002)

NOW TO 2020   17.5

Bâtard-Montrachet, 1996
Domaine Ramonet

A certain age on the colour. And more developed on the nose and palate than one would expect for a grand cru. But not oxidised. Medium-full body. Fat and ripe, even a touch overripe. Good grip. Fully ready. Fine but not great. (October 2005)

NOW TO 2012   17.5

Beaune, Sur les Grèves, 1996
Domaine Germain Père et Fils/
Château de Chorey-lès-Beaune

Round, ripe nose. Good depth and vigour. Medium to medium-full body. Not as interesting or as fresh as his 1996 Pernand-Vergelesses. But good. (June 1996)

NOW TO 2009   15.0

Bienvenues-Bâtard-Montrachet, 1996
Domaine Leflaive

Rather more evolved than I would have liked. But not too much so. There is plenty of fruit here, but it is beginning to dry out. Fullish body. Still elegant, but it will go downhill from here. (June 2006)

DRINK SOON   16.0

Chassagne-Montrachet, Les Baudines, 1996
Domaine Bernard Morey

Rich, full nose. Good freshness. This is holding up very well. Full, rich and ample on the palate.

Long, classy and complex. Fine. Can still be kept. (April 2006)

NOW TO 2010   17.5

Chassagne-Montrachet, La Boudriotte, 1996
Domaine Ramonet

Soft nose. But no undue age. Medium-full body. Ripe. Succulent. Classy. Persistent. Lots of energy. Fine. (July 2003)

NOW TO 2015   17.5

Chassagne-Montrachet, Les Caillerets, 1996
Domaine Jean-Noël Gagnard

Fresh nose. Fullish. But a little four-square. This is more like the wines Caroline Lestimé's father used to produce. Good but it lacks flair. (June 2006)

NOW TO 2010   15.0

Chassagne-Montrachet, Les Caillerets, 1996
Domaine Michel Morey-Coffinet

Youthful colour. Just a touch of oak on the nose and palate. Fresh. Indeed a bit lean. But ripe and stylish if without enormous depth. Medium-full body. Good fruit. No sign of collapse here as in other 1996s. Positive at the end. No hurry to drink. Very good. (May 2005)

NOW TO 2010   16.0

Chassagne-Montrachet, Les Chenevottes, 1996
Domaine Michel Colin-Deléger et Fils

Well-matured colour. On the nose and the palate equally so. Even a bit oxidised. But still enjoyable. Ripe and sweet. Rich and balanced. Better with food. Needs drinking soon. Good but not brilliant. (March 2006)

DRINK SOON   15.0

Chassagne-Montrachet, Les Chenevottes, 1996
Domaine Jean-Noël Gagnard

Magnum. This has good richness, but it is well balanced with the good acidity of the vintage. Yet slightly four-square nevertheless. A beefy wine. Crisp. Less depth than his Champs Gain 1995 but not exactly mellow or concentrated. Slight lumpy. Lacks nuance and real class. A wine to be drunk with food. Very good. (June 2002)

DRINK SOON   16.0

Chassagne-Montrachet, Clos de la Boudriotte, 1996
Maison Vincent Girardin

Medium-full colour. Ripe nose. Fragrant. Slightly raw but approaching maturity. Medium to medium-full body. Just a little tannin. Still a little lean. But good style and fruit underneath. Needs to round off and get more generous. Good. (March 2003)

NOW TO 2016   15.0

Chassagne-Montrachet, Clos Saint-Jean, 1996
Domaine Guy Amiot et Fils

Medium colour. Fresh and with a touch of spice. Medium body. Good acidity. Ripe and juicy, but slightly astringent at the back. Give it 2 years. Good, positive finish. It could have been more concentrated. Good plus. (January 2001)

NOW TO 2010   15.5

Chassagne-Montrachet, Clos de la Truffière, 1996
Maison Vincent Girardin

Quite developed on the nose. A touch of oxidation but still drinkable. Fullish body. Fat and ripe. Quite good. (April 2006)

DRINK UP   14.0

Chassagne-Montrachet, Les Grandes Ruchottes, 1996
Domaine Fernand and Laurent Pillot

Fresh colour. Ripe, elegant nose. Slightly more depth and concentration than their 1996 Chassagne Vide Bourse. On the palate a wine with a lot of character and distinction. Medium-full body. Still quite firm. Even a little closed at first. Profound. Gently oaky. Balanced. Vigorous. Peachy fruit. This is fine plus. Still lots of life ahead of it. (May 2005)

NOW TO 2012   18.0

Chassagne-Montrachet, La Maltroie, 1996
Domaine Michel Colin-Deléger et Fils

The nose is still a little hidden. Good, subtle oak base. Much more open on the palate. A wine of intensity, even power. Fullish body. Very good

grip. Lovely fruit. Very good, indeed, if not quite the interest for fine. (March 2000)

NOW TO 2009   17.0

Chassagne-Montrachet, Les Masures, 1996
Domaine Jean-Noël Gagnard

A delicious example of a village wine and a 1996. Medium weight. Flowery. Balanced. Stylish. Very clean and clear-cut. Long. Fine for what it is. À point but no hurry to drink. (September 2005)

NOW TO 2010+   16.0

Chassagne-Montrachet, Morgeot, 1996
Domaine Blain-Gagnard

Fresh colour. Nutty nose. Quite developed. But fresh on the palate. Good acidity. Nice, peachy fruit. Long and positive at the end. Very good. (April 2006)

DRINK SOON   16.0

Chassagne-Montrachet, Morgeot, 1996
Domaine Jacques Gagnard-Delagrange

Some evolution on the colour. Ripe, fresh but at first reticent on the nose. Medium-full body. Slightly lean on the attack. Good depth underneath. But a bit austere nevertheless. Better with food: more succulent. Very good, indeed, for a 1996. (October 2005)

NOW TO 2010   17.0

Chassagne-Montrachet, Morgeot, 1996
Domaine Jean-Noël Gagnard

Medium to medium-full colour. Soft, plump, well-matured nose. Medium body. Reasonably fresh and stylish. Some depth. Decent finish. Good plus. (June 2006)

NOW TO 2010   15.5

Chassagne-Montrachet, Morgeot, Vieilles Vignes, 1996
Maison Vincent Girardin

Quite a well-matured colour. Fullish, fresh, oaky and with plenty of fruit at first. Not a lot of depth, but not too bad at all as it developed. Rather rigid, rampant acidity though. Best with food. Very good plus. (September 2005)

NOW TO 2010   16.5

Chassagne-Montrachet, Morgeot, 1996
Domaine Louis Jadot

Youthful colour. This is just about ready but will still improve. Full, rich, concentrated and high class. Excellent grip, of course. But long, multi-dimensional and profound on the palate. Very good indeed. Plenty of future. (February 2002)

NOW TO 2009　　　　　　　　　　　　　17.0

Chassagne-Montrachet, Morgeot, 1996
Domaine Bernard Morey

Quite a fat nose but quite evolved, too, despite good backing acidity. Better than his 1996 Chassagne Vide Bourse. Medium-full body. Some oak. Decent fruit but no great depth, concentration or class, or indeed grip on the palate. Very good at best. Slightly too much acidity at the end. Drink quite soon. (October 2005)

DRINK QUITE SOON　　　　　　　　　　16.0

Chassagne-Montrachet, Morgeot,
Clos de la Chapelle, 1996
Domaine Duc de Magenta/Maison Louis Jadot

No undue colour. Rich, fresh and concentrated. Lots of depth on the nose. À point but still very vigorous on the palate. Fullish body. Good acidity. Balanced. Fine. (July 2003)

NOW TO 2015　　　　　　　　　　　　　17.5

Chassagne-Montrachet, La Romanée, 1996
Domaine Morey-Coffinet

Marked by the acidity. A bit edgy. The colour is rather too deep, too. This is going to get even worse as it evolves further. (January 2004)

DRINK UP　　　　　　　　　　　　　　13.0

Chassagne-Montrachet, Les Ruchottes, 1996
Domaine Bachelet-Ramonet

Quite a fat nose with a touch of grilled nuts and a suspicion of sugar. No undue age. Ripe on the palate. Medium-full body. À point. Lots of fruit. Succulent. Very good indeed. (July 2003)

NOW TO 2013　　　　　　　　　　　　　17.0

Chassagne-Mon trachet, Les Ruchottes, 1996
Domaine Ramonet

Rich, full, concentrated and ample although not as much so as the 1995. But vigorous, classy and balanced. Fine. Only just ready. (N.B.: Bottles vary with this wine. A significant proportion are oxidised.) (May 2005)

NOW TO 2013　　　　　　　　　　　　　17.5

Chassagne-Montrachet, Vide Bourse, 1996
Domaine Bernard Morey

This is really quite evolved on both nose and palate, although better on the latter. But neither tired nor oxidised. The follow-through is fresher, indeed a little dominated by the acidity. It lacks a bit of depth and class. But good, ripe fruit. Very good plus. (October 2005)

DRINK SOON　　　　　　　　　　　　　16.5

Chassagne-Montrachet, Vide Bourse, 1996
Domaine Fernand et Laurent Pillot

No undue colour. Ripe and juicy. Reasonably balanced. Plenty of fruit. No sign of age on the palate. But a lack of zip. Yet very good plus for the vintage. No lack of depth and concentration, and still positive at the end. (April 2006)

NOW TO 2010　　　　　　　　　　　　　16.5

Chevalier-Montrachet, 1996
Domaine Georges Deléger

Full, rich, fat, youthful and gently oaky. Lots of concentration. Very good grip. This is really classy. Lovely creamy-rich Chardonnay. Very fine. (September 2002)

NOW TO 2010+　　　　　　　　　　　　18.5

Corton Blanc, 1996
Domaine Chandon de Briailles

Magnum. Full and vigorous with good depth on the nose. But at the same time a little four-square. Fullish body. Fresh. Ripe. Good grip. Lacks a little flair and real elegance, but very good. (June 2006)

NOW TO 2012　　　　　　　　　　　　　16.0

Corton-Charlemagne, 1996
Domaine Bonneau du Martray

Lovely nose. Real depth and high quality. Vigorous and harmonious. On the palate not quite the concentration at first, it seems. But this is a laid-back, subtle wine. The follow-through is very fine. Long and complex. Fine plus. (June 2006)

NOW TO 2012+　　　　　　　　　　　　18.0

Corton-Charlemagne, 1996
Domaine Bouchard Père et Fils

Ripe, full and gently oaky. *À point.* Good grip. But now plump and ready. Very good depth. Fine plus. (April 2005)

NOW TO 2010+   18.0

Corton-Charlemagne, 1996
Domaine Marius Delarche

"*Réserve.*" Good colour. Fat, ripe and fully ready on the nose. Fullish body. Quite a high level of acidity but quite rich in an appley sort of way. Some oak. Decent class. Very good. (September 2005)

NOW TO 2012   16.0

Corton-Charlemagne, 1996
Domaine Dubreuil-Fontaine

Fullish nose. But a little diffuse. On the palate good acidity but some development. A touch herbal-vegetal. Not too much though. Fullish body. Reasonable fruit. But no real class. (June 2004)

NOW TO 2011   15.5

Corton-Charlemagne, 1996
Domaine Joseph Faiveley

Quite oaky. Rigid. Good fruit but not a lot of dimension. Ripe. A little one-dimensional after the Corton-Charlemagne 1996 from Bouchard Père et Fils. Very good but not brilliant. (April 2005)

NOW TO 2009   16.0

Corton-Charlemagne, 1996
Maison Vincent Girardin

Ripe, gently oaky nose. On the palate the oak is quite marked. But the wine is full bodied, ripe and vigorous. Very good grip. Needs food. Long finish. Fine. (June 2006)

NOW TO 2012+   17.5

Corton-Charlemagne, 1996
Domaine Louis Jadot

Youthful colour. Rich, nicely austere, but ripe and classy, and full and vigorous on the nose. Lots of depth. More than gently oaky. Ample.

Very, very lovely finish. This is very, very fine. *À point* but lots of life left. (June 2005)

NOW TO 2015   19.0

Corton-Charlemagne, 1996
Domaine Michel Juillot

Magnum. The nose is full and rich, but has a little built-in sulphur. Better on the palate. Full body. Good acidity. Just a little heavy though. Somewhat four-square. Relaxed in the glass and was better with food. No lack of fruit. Fine for the vintage. (November 2001)

NOW TO 2016   17.5

Corton-Charlemagne, 1996
Domaine Louis Latour

Magnum. Clean but no great depth or concentration on the nose. Just a touch of built-in sulphur. Medium body. Fully ready. Rather dilute for Corton-Charlemagne. Quite clean on the palate. Balanced and reasonably elegant. But disappointing. And it won't last. (October 2005)

DRINK SOON   16.5

Corton-Charlemagne, 1996
Domaine Rapet Père et Fils

Youthful colour. Discreet, ripe, clean, balanced nose. Hardly oaky at all. Medium to medium-full body. Elegant but rather restrained. Good acidity. Very good but a slight lack of richness. Still very young though. This may develop. (May 2005)

NOW TO 2016   16.0

Meursault, 1996
Domaine Jean-François Coche-Dury

Clean, pure and youthful on the attack. Gently oaky. High acidity, of course. Rich and gently oaky on the palate. Good depth. Lovely fruit. Very long. This is fine for a village wine. (March 2001)

NOW TO 2010   17.0

Meursault, 1996
Domaine des Comtes Lafon

Well matured but no undue age. Ripe and stylish. *À point.* Balanced and positive at the end. Very good for a village example. (June 2006)

NOW TO 2010   15.0

Meursault, Les Caillerets, 1996
Domaine François Mikulski

Medium to medium-full colour. Quite evolved. Only medium weight. Ripe and plump, but no real depth, class or dimension. Quite good at best. (June 2006)

DRINK SOON   14.0

Meursault, Charmes, 1996
Domaine des Comtes Lafon

Splendidly concentrated. Marvellous grip. Extremely profound. None of the usual rasping acidity of the vintage. Very fresh. Full body. Plump. Very fine. But I have had variable bottles. (June 2000)

NOW TO 2015   18.5

Meursault, Charmes, 1996
Domaine François Mikulski

Magnum. Round, ripe and fruity. Good freshness. Medium-full body. Flowery and fragrant. Good plus. (June 2006)

NOW TO 2010   15.5

Meursault, Charmes, 1996
Maison Morey-Blanc

This is very impressive. Medium-full body. Very elegant. Good depth and grip. Long and complex. Very good indeed. (June 2006)

NOW TO 2012   17.0

Meursault, Clos de la Barre, 1996
Domaine des Comtes Lafon

Quite an evolved colour. Also a little oxidised on the nose. This is even more apparent on the palate. Ripe. Good acidity. Plenty of depth. But not what it should be. My own stock is fine: plump, fresh, balanced and succulent (Now to 2012; 16/20). (March 2004)

(SEE NOTE)

Meursault, Désirée, 1996
Domaine des Comtes Lafon

Quite evolved, yet with good acidity. Plump and ripe. Not a lot of body though. Nor much class. This is not that special. Drink soon. (March 2003)

DRINK SOON   13.5

Meursault, Genevrières, 1996
Domaine Bouchard Père et Fils

Very fresh colour. Concentrated. Very youthful. Lovely ripe fruit. Lots of depth and class. This will still improve. It has the weight to match the acidity. Fine. (November 2003)

NOW TO 2016   17.5

Meursault, Genevrières, 1996
Domaine François Jobard

Fresh, fullish, but slightly hard on the nose. More personality, better fruit and less four-square than his 1996 Poruzots. Ripe and long. Very good plus. (June 2006)

NOW TO 2012   16.5

Meursault, Genevrières, 1996
Domaine Rémi Jobard

This is one of the 1996s which has died. Oxidised and over the top. Barely drinkable. (September 2005)

(SEE NOTE)

Meursault, Genevrières, 1996
Domaine Des Comtes Lafon

Some development on the colour. Full, vigorous and ready for drinking on the nose. Yet almost yeasty. Rich and meaty on the palate. Slightly evolved fruit but good grip behind it. This almost suggests a red wine vinified as white: as with Champagne, I get red fruit here, plus quite a lot of volume. Very good grip. Yet very ripe. Atypical. A wine for food. But veal or chicken, not fish. More 1996 than Genevrières. Fine. Ready. (September 2005)

NOW TO 2014   17.5

Meursault, Perrières, 1996
Domaine Joseph Drouhin

Ripe, gently oaky, rich and stylish. Medium-full body. Good acidity. Lovely, peachy fruit. Really quite intense and classy. Fine plus. Will still improve. (March 2000)

NOW TO 2010   18.0

Meursault, Perrières, 1996
Domaine Albert Grivault

Fresh, classy, balanced, youthful on the nose. Slightly lean. But ripe, medium-full bodied.

Fully mature and very good indeed. Lots of depth. Properly minerally. Hardly oaky at all. Long and stylish at the end. (September 2005)

NOW TO 2012   17.0

Meursault, Perrières, 1996
Domaine des Comtes Lafon

Some colour. Quite a lot of evolution. Weird aromatics. Slight vegetal touches. Better on the palate, but a little hard and not very stylish. Medium to medium-full body. This is a bit of a disappointment. The mineral purity of Perrières is there but not in a very elegant way. Better as it evolved in the glass. But only as far as very good. Ready. My own stock is better than this: properly vigorous and minerally. (June 2005)

DRINK SOON   16.0

Meursault, Perrières, 1996
Domaine Guy Roulot

Full. Quite firm. Rich but backward. Minerally and classic. A bit austere. But good depth. Will still improve, and if never very generous, a fine example. (June 2006)

NOW TO 2014   17.5

Meursault, Poruzots, 1996
Domaine François Jobard

Slightly flat on the nose. Fresh on the palate but rather dull. Medium-full body. Foursquare. Quite good. (June 2006)

NOW TO 2010   14.0

Meursault, Tessons, Clos de Mon Plaisir, 1996
Domaine Guy Roulot

Magnum. A touch of built-in sulphur on the nose. Fresh on the palate. Slightly lean but good style. Finishes better than it starts. Very good plus. (June 2006)

NOW TO 2010   16.5

Meursault, Tête de Murger, 1996
Domaine Patrick Javillier

Good nose. Fresh. Plenty of depth. Medium-full body. Ripe, crisp and balanced. Really quite

complex. Lovely fruit at the end. Very good plus. (June 2006)

NOW TO 2012   16.5

Le Montrachet, 1996
Domaine Marquis de Laguiche/
Maison Joseph Drouhin

Magnum. Brilliant nose. Rich, full, complex, vigorous and very classy indeed. This is very lovely. A noble wine with a certain austerity and a huge amount of depth. Splendidly complex. Really exceptional. (June 2006)

NOW TO 2020   20.0

Le Montrachet, 1996
Domaine de la Romanée-Conti

Full, rich, firm and rather more minerally than usual. Lots of depth. Very fine quality. This is very concentrated and very lovely. A great wine potentially. Excellent grip. Very, very youthful. Splendid fruit. This is a yardstick example. A wine for drinking in 2020. (June 2002)

NOW TO 2020   20.0

Nuits-Saint-Georges, Clos de l'Arlot,
Blanc, 1996
Domaine de l'Arlot

Fresh colour. Ripe, gently oaky nose. Good style and depth. Medium-full body. Very good fruit. A finely balanced and finely textured wine. Long and complex. Very good indeed. Still has plenty of life ahead of it. (June 2006)

NOW TO 2010   17.0

Pernand-Vergelesses, 1996
Domaine Jacques Germain

Magnum. Good, fresh nose. A touch of oak. Ripe. Medium-full body. Holding up very well. Very good for what it is. (June 2006)

NOW TO 2010   16.0

Puligny-Montrachet, 1996
Maison Olivier Leflaive Frères

Soft, forward, perhaps a bit slight. Does not seem to have the high acidity of the vintage on the nose. Ripe, clean and stylish though. More to it on the palate. Little oak, but quite rich and with good depth and definition. Just about ready. A very good example of a village wine. (March 2000)

DRINK SOON 15.5

Puligny-Montrachet, Les Caillerets, 1996
Domaine Hubert de Montille

Good colour. Fullish, masculine nose. Plenty of fruit and plenty of backbone. Fresh on the palate. Concentrated. Old viney. Slightly austere at first but very long on the palate. Very good indeed. (June 2006)

NOW TO 2012+ 17.0

Puligny-Montrachet, Les Chalumaux, 1996
Domaine Claude and Hubert Chavy-Chouet

Ripe and fresh, without much depth and concentration, but with good style and balance. Medium weight. À point. Lots of charm. Very good. But a little over-oaked. (September 2002)

DRINK SOON 16.0

Puligny-Montrachet, Les Champs Gain, 1996
Domaine des Comtes Lafon

Full. Slightly clumsy. Lacks grace. The high acidity of the vintage, plus slightly overripe fruit. Ungainly. Quite good only. (June 2000)

NOW TO 2010 14.0

Puligny-Montrachet, Le Clavoillon, 1996
Domaine Leflaive

Fragrant nose. No great grip, concentration or intensity. Medium body. A little one-dimensional and a bit weak. What there is is balanced and elegant, but there isn't enough here. Good at best. (March 2004)

DRINK SOON 15.0

Puligny-Montrachet, Clos de la Garenne, 1996
Domaine Joseph Drouhin

I was not aware that Drouhin could get their hands on this, which as far as I know is a monopoly of the Duc de Magenta and vinified by Jadot. This was a rather over-evolved bottle. Fully ready. Without the concentration and supporting acidity of the Jadot's example, or the vintage. Merely good plus. (March 2001)

DRINK SOON 15.5

Puligny-Montrachet, Clos de la Garenne, 1996
Domaine Duc de Magenta/Maison Louis Jadot

Splendidly mineral. Discreet, ripe, cool and steely. Medium-full body. Pleachy. Lots of depth, class and intensity. Now just about ready. Plenty of reserves. Very fine. Lots of life ahead of it. (November 2002)

NOW TO 2012+ 18.5

Puligny-Montrachet, Les Combettes, 1996
Domaine Étienne Sauzet

Three oxidised/maderised bottles out of six. The better bottles had a much fresher colour. Ripe if not very profound on the nose but no rigid acidity. Medium to medium-full body. Balanced and classy. Soft and fully ready. Complex and better on the palate than on the nose. Fine. (October 2005)

NOW TO 2012 17.5

Puligny-Montrachet, Les Demoiselles, 1996
Domaine Michel Colin-Deléger et Fils

This is à point and not a bit hard or vegetal. Nor is it a bit lacking freshness. Fullish body. Relaxed. Pure but quite oaky. But very elegant. Fine plus. But variable bottles. (November 2005)

NOW TO 2012 18.0

Puligny-Montrachet, Les Folatières, 1996
Domaine Louis Jadot

Lovely nose. Excellent, complex, stylish fruit. Medium-full body. Very fresh, concentrated and complex. À point. Very long and very profound. Fine plus. (June 2006)

NOW TO 2012+ 17.5

Puligny-Montrachet, Les Perrières, 1996
Domaine Louis Carillon et Fils

Understated, complex and very classy. Good acidity, but not a hint of the vegetal aspects one finds so often in this vintage. Fullish body. Will still improve. Fine plus. (February 2003)

NOW TO 2010 18.0

Puligny-Montrachet, Les Perrières, 1996
Domaine Étienne Sauzet

Quite high toned on the nose. Medium to medium-full body. Crisp and minerally. More depth underneath than you might have expected on the nose. Peachy fruit. Balanced and long. Just about *à point*. Very classy. Good finish. (June 2003)

NOW TO 2012   17.5

Puligny-Montrachet, La Truffière, 1996
Domaine Jean-Marc Boillot

Stylish nose. Quite delicate, yet perfectly fresh enough. A touch of oak and a great deal of lovely, very ripe fruit. This is long, most attractive and very impressive. Fine. (June 2006)

NOW TO 2012+   17.5

Saint-Aubin, Clos de la Chatenière, 1996
Domaine Hubert Lamy et Fils

Magnum. Lovely ripe fruit. Medium to medium-full body. Plenty of depth and personality. Long and lovely. This is very good. (June 2006)

NOW TO 2012   16.0

REDS

Beaune, Les Cent Vignes, 1996
Domaine Arnoux Père et Fils

The bottle had been open for some time. Slightly faded. But good stuff underneath. (February 2003)

DRINK SOON   15.0

Beaune, Clos des Mouches, 1996
Domaine Joseph Drouhin

Rich and full, but not the greatest of grip. Yet certainly no lack of acidity. The nose is round, soft, aromatic and spicy. On the palate there is more grip apparent. Very good but not the greatest class and depth. Still youthful. (October 2002)

NOW TO 2012   16.0

Beaune, Aux Cras, 1996
Domaine Germain Père et Fils/
Château de Chorey-lès-Beaune

Good colour. Sophisticated nose. Lovely fruit and delicious, cool, balancing acidity. Fullish body. A little tannin, but ripe and succulent. Very classy. This is splendidly balanced. Will last for ages. (June 2006)

NOW TO 2020+   17.5

Beaune, Grèves, 1996
Maison Roland Remoissenet et Fils

Medium to medium-full colour. Slightly dry on the nose. Decent fruit and grip though. Quite rich on the palate. Good acidity. Slightly rigid. But better than last time out. Good fruit at the end. Good. (October 2001)

NOW TO 2012   15.0

Beaune, Grèves, Vigne de l'Enfant Jésus, 1996
Domaine Bouchard Père et Fils

Medium to medium-full colour. A little development now. Not a heavyweight on the nose, but good fruit and very good class and balance. Very fresh. But not undue acidity. Better on the palate than on the nose. But, nevertheless, a touch of astringency, and it is a bit lean on the follow-through. Is this just a phase? (November 2003)

NOW TO 2012   15.0

Beaune, Lulune, 1996
Domaine Emmanuel Giboulot

Evolved colour. Not very full. Quite developed on nose and palate. Not that concentrated, and it is beginning to lose its fruit. Only fair. (June 2006)

DRINK SOON   13.5

Beaune, Les Marconnets, 1996
Maison Champy

Very good colour. Just about mature. Medium-full body. Good acidity. No lack of succulent fruit. Slightly raw at present. But good depth and grip. This will still improve. Good. (October 2003)

NOW TO 2018   15.0

Beaune, Les Teurons, 1996
Domaine Germain Père et Fils/
Château de Chorey-lès-Beaune

Medium to medium-full colour. Still fresh. Richer than his 1996 Beaune Cras. Good succulence here. Medium-full body. Lovely ripe fruit. Round, rich, ample and seductive. Spicier than the Cras. Lovely finish. Very good. (June 2006)

NOW TO 2015   16.0

Bonnes Mares, 1996
Domaine Georges Roumier et Fils

Full, immature colour. Very, very classy on the nose. Heaps of depth and complexity. The palate is equal to the nose. Fullish, concentrated, complex fruit. Very good grip. Cool, but splendid and very, very long. (June 2006)

2010 TO 2025 +   19.0

Bonnes Mares, 1996
Domaine Comte Georges de Vogüé

Fullish, immature colour. Round, rich, oaky, but backward nose. Fullish and ample. Not as exciting as Georges Roumier's, but classy and concentrated. Very good grip. Very, very long. Lots of depth. Very fine plus. Still needs time. (June 2006)

2010 TO 2025   19.0

Chambertin, 1996
Domaine Leroy

Full colour. Still youthful. Full, rich, austere nose. Stems evident. Very intense and vigorous on the palate. Full body. Very fine, ripe tannins. Excellent grip and very impressive fruit. This is a great wine. Very long and very lovely. (April 2000)

2009 TO 2025   20.0

Chambertin, 1996
Domaine Armand Rousseau

Medium-full colour. Fabulous nose. Rich, ripe and concentrated. Marvellous fruit. Real class. As so often, this is a great wine. Fullish bodied, vigorous, concentrated, intense and with real finesse. Brilliant finish. A great wine. (June 2006)

2010 TO 2030   20.0

Chambertin, 1996
Domaine Trapet Père et Fils

Full colour. Still youthful. Ripe but no great class on the nose. Good concentration. Fullish body. But not the quality of fruit nor the class of Armand Rousseau's. Very good plus. Just about ready. (June 2006)

NOW TO 2018   16.5

Chambertin, Clos de Bèze, 1996
Maison Camille Giroud

Full, vigorous colour. Rich, still closed-in nose. Fullish body. Some tannin. Yet some development. Quite fresh fruit. But slightly clumsy on the palate. Just about ready. Very good plus at best. (June 2006)

NOW TO 2018   16.5

Chambertin, Clos de Bèze, 199
Domaine Armand Rousseau

Full, mature colour. Lovely nose. Rich and intense. Just about ready. Very, very concentrated. Very, very classy. Fullish body. Quite round now. But lots of vigour and with really splendid, classy, rich, concentrated fruit. Very, very long and complex. Very fine indeed. Will still improve. (June 206)

2010 TO 2030   19.5

Chambolle-Musigny, 1996
Domaine Joseph Faiveley

Good colour. Lovely fragrant nose. Medium body. Fresh and ripe. Very good for a village example. (March 2000)

DRINK SOON   16.0

Chambolle-Musigny, 1996
Domaine Michel Gros

Good colour. Slightly austere on the nose still, but softening on the palate. Very lovely fruit. Very good acidity. A proper Chambolle. Medium-full body. Very elegant. Good. (October 2000)

NOW TO 2012   15.0

Chambolle-Musigny, 1996
Domaine Jacques-Frédéric Mugnier

Medium colour. Lovely soft, gently oaky, fragrant nose. Harmonious, succulent and very classy. On the palate just a little tannin. Ripe, subtle and intense. Delicious for a village example. Lovely long, lingering finish. (March 2000)

NOW TO 2012   16.0

Chambolle-Musigny, Les Amoureuses, 1996
Domaine Robert Groffier

Full colour. Lovely fresh, aromatic nose. Very classy. Firmer and fuller than his 1995

Amoureuses. Higher level of acidity. Medium-full body. Very fresh. Gently oaky. Lots of depth and concentration. Even better than his 1995. More depth. Greater dimension. Very fine. (March 2004)

NOW TO 2020 18.5

Chambolle-Musigny, Les Amoureuses, 1996
Domaine Daniel Moine-Hudelot

Good, fullish colour. Plump, ripe, fresh, classy nose. No undue austerity. Medium-full body. Succulent. Just a little tannin but softening nicely. Lovely fruit. Very well balanced. Very Chambolle. Raspberry flavour. Very long. Very subtle and intense. Fine. (October 2005)

NOW TO 2020 17.5

Chambolle-Musigny, Les Amoureuses, 1996
Domaine Jacques-Frédéric Mugnier

Medium-full colour. Just about ready. Very lovely succulent, soft nose. Very lovely fruit. Ripe. Medium-full body. Real elegance and very harmonious. Intense. Classy. Very, very long. Very fine. (June 2006)

2010 TO 2025+ 18.5

Chambolle-Musigny, Les Amoureuses, 1996
Domaine Comte Georges de Vogüé

Good colour. Still youthful. Very lovely nose. Intense, ripe, harmonious and very profound. On the palate still a little tannin. Fullish body. Excellent grip. Real intensity and dimension on the follow-through. Really delicious. Very long. Very elegant. Very fine. (May 2002)

NOW TO 2025 18.5

Chambolle-Musigny, Les Beaux Bruns, 1996
Domaine Ghislaine Barthod

Full, vigorous, youthful colour. Rich, succulent nose. Ripe, fullish bodied and still youthful. Plenty of depth and vigour, if not the class of a real first-division *premier cru*. Slightly austere and a little solid, but very good plus. (June 2006)

2010 TO 2020+ 15.5

Chambolle-Musigny, Les Beaux Bruns, 1996
Domaine Thierry Mortet

Good, youthful colour. Ripe but quite backward nose. Medium-full body. Cool and fresh. Good

vigour and depth. Some class but not great. Slightly austere. (June 2006)

2010 TO 2020 15.5

Chambolle-Musigny, Les Cras, 1996
Domaine Ghislaine Barthod

Good, medium-full colour. Just a bit more than her Charmes. Very Chambolle on the nose. Pure, fragrant raspberry with a touch of chocolate. Quite firm. Some tannin. More austere than the Charmes. Fullish body. Very fine grip. Even more depth at the end. Needs time. Fine plus. (November 2001)

NOW TO 2020 18.0

Chambolle-Musigny, Les Cras, 1996
Domaine Georges Roumier et Fils

Fullish colour. Still youthful. Still a bit austere on the nose. Classy though. Fullish body. Still a little tannin. Needs to round off and get more generous. Ample, long, very stylish and complex. Lovely fragrant finish. Ultimately fine plus. (June 2005)

NOW TO 2024 18.0

Chambolle-Musigny, Les Feusselottes, 1996
Domaine Dr. Georges Mugneret

Medium-full, vigorous colour. Fine, fullish, succulent nose. Very lovely fruit here. Fullish body. Vigorous and still youthful on the palate, too. A little tannin to resolve. High quality. Very classy. Needs time. Fine plus. (June 2006)

2010 TO 2025 18.0

Chambolle-Musigny, Les Fuées, 1996
Domaine Jacques-Frédéric Mugnier

Fullish colour. Lovely but quite austere nose. This is a bit adolescent. Very good fruit. Medium-full body. The tannins are now soft, but the wine has high acidity. A bit 1988-ish. Classy but a touch lean. Long, persistent follow-through though. Very good plus. (October 2002)

NOW TO 2015 16.5

Chapelle-Chambertin, 1996
Domaine Drouhin-Laroze

Fullish colour. Slightly minty on the nose. Medium-full. Good, ripe, plummy fruit. Round and medium-full bodied. Good class and depth. Fresh. No hard acidities. Good structure and vigour. Very good indeed. Just about ready. (October 2005)

NOW TO 2020   17.0

Charmes-Chambertin, 1996
Domaine Denis Bachelet
Medium-full colour. Still immature. Very lovely nose. Rich, ripe, concentrated, classy and succulent. Medium-full body. Very poised, delicious fruit. Lots and lots of depth and class. This is long and very, very classy. Splendid finish. (June 2006)

2010 TO 2025+   19.0

Charmes-Chambertin, 1996
Maison Pierre Bourée et Fils
Good, fresh acidity. Plump, ripe and stylish. Lots of depth. Long. Very good. But quite advanced. (January 2002)

NOW TO 2010   15.5

Charmes-Chambertin, 1996
Domaine Jacky Confuron-Cotétidot
Medium-full colour. A little development. A slightly asutere, stemmy nose. Ripe and sweet underneath. Fullish body. Quite mellow as it developed. Good richness and depth. Not too austere at all as it evolved in the glass. Long and classy. Not a bit rustic or stemmy. Fine plus. (March 2005)

NOW TO 2025   18.0

Charmes-Chambertin, 1996
Domaine Claude Dugat
Fine, full colour. Quite oaky on the nose. Rich, lush and toasted. Fullish body. Very, very concentrated. Tannic, yet soft centred and sweet. Modern but not forced. Very seductive on the palate. Fat as well as cool and fresh. Individual but lovely. Fine finish. Very fine. (February 2001)

NOW TO 2026   18.5

Charmes-Chambertin, 1996
Domaine Dujac
Medium-full colour. Now just about mature. Evolved, smoky, coffee-mocha, round and spicy

nose. Medium to medium-full body. Fresh but no undue hard acidity. Ripe and classy with something just a little lean on the finish. Very good indeed. (October 2005)

NOW TO 2020   17.0

Charmes-Chambertin, 1996
Domaine Frédéric Esmonin
Fullish, immature colour. Slightly banal on the nose. Plump but a bit four-square. Medium-full body. Slightly solid. Some tannin. But no nuance. A little over-extracted and therefore dry at the end. Quite good. (June 2006)

2010 TO 2016   14.0

Charmes-Chambertin, 1996
Domaine Geantet-Pansiot
Good, full, vigorous colour. Slightly dense on the nose. Fullish body. A shade sweet. Decent concentration and balance. Plenty of wine here, but it lacks a little sophistication. Just about ready. (April 2006)

NOW TO 2017   16.0

Charmes-Chambertin, 1996
Domaine Louis Jadot
Fullish colour. Just a little development. Full, closed-in but rich on the nose. More accessible on the palate. Fullish bodied, rich, balanced, fragrant and classy. Good intensity. Lots of vigour. Just about ready. Fine plus. (April 2006)

NOW TO 2026   18.0

Charmes-Chambertin, 1996
Maison Dominique Laurent
Full colour. Still youthful. Sturdy, but rich and youthful on the nose. Fullish body. Very lovely concentrated, old-viney fruit. Just a little rigid still. Will still improve. Good depth. Long finish. Fine. (April 2006)

NOW TO 2020+   17.5

Charmes-Chambertin, 1996
Domaine Armand Rousseau
Medium colour. Now mature. A bit light and diffuse on the nose. Forward and a bit wimpy. Fresh on the palate but only medium body. Nice, attractive fruit and good balance. But a

lack of real concentration. Very good at best. Ready. (April 2006)

NOW TO 2015 16.0

Charmes-Chambertin, 1996
Domaine Christian Sérafin

Fullish colour. Still youthful. Rich, fragrant, succulent, balanced nose. Despite really quite a lot of new oak, this is very impressive. Fullish body. Just about ready. Succulent, vigorous and intense. Very long. Fine plus. (April 2006)

NOW TO 2025 18.0

Charmes-Chambertin, 1996
Domaine Taupenot-Merme

Medium-full colour. Now approaching maturity. Cool, fruity nose, but no real depth and concentration. Nothing special here. The wines are better today. Medium body. No great depth, grip or finesse. Boring. Just about ready. (June 2006)

NOW TO 2012 14.0

Château Corton-Grancey, 1996
Domaine Louis Latour

Fullish colour. Still fresh. Slightly cooked on the nose. Lacks freshness and fragrance. Medium body. Decent fruit, but no great grip, depth or dimension. Rather anonymous for a *grand cru*. Lacks richness. Quite a decent follow-through. But good at best. (October 2005)

NOW TO 2012 15.0

Clos des Lambrays, 1996
Domaine des Lambrays

Magnum. Medium to medium-full, mature colour. Very good, slightly austere fruit on the nose. Cool and crisp. On the palate a little more succulent. Medium to medium-full body. The tannins are now just about resolved. Balanced and stylish. Long. Fully ready. Very good plus but not great. (June 2006)

NOW TO 2016 16.5

Clos de la Roche, 1996
Domaine Dujac

Fresh, medium colour. Fragrant nose. Ripe. Mature. No great weight. But fresh and elegant on the palate. Stylish. Long. Ripe. Classy. Fine. Fully ready.

NOW TO 2018 17.5

Clos de la Roche, 1996
Maison Dominique Laurent

Full colour. A little reduced at first on the nose. Slight austerity behind it. Later it smelled of hot mocha-toffee. On the palate full bodied and concentrated, but the acidity tends to dominate at present. The tannins are softening, and the wine has depth and concentration. Long finish. But slightly vegetal as it developed. Fine. (March 2005)

NOW TO 2028 17.5

Clos de la Roche, 1996
Domaine Leroy

Splendidly full, rich colour. Rich, plump, complex and voluptuous on the nose. Very lovely concentrated fruit here. High class. Excellent harmony. Full, rich, and tannic, but very, very sophisticated and ripe. Lots of depth and dimension. Lovely fruit. (April 2000)

NOW TO 2018 19.0

Clos Saint-Denis, 1996
Domaine Dujac

Mature, medium colour. Rather more evolved than the Clos de la Roche. Slightly more stemmy and less rich and succulent on the palate. Quite fresh but looser knit. Less class. Less dimension. Very good plus. (June 2006)

NOW TO 2014 16.5

Clos de Tart, 1996
Domaine du Clos de Tart

Very full, immature colour. Full, rich, closed-in, backward, tannic nose. A meaty wine. Full body. Some tannin. Quite solid but very concentrated fruit, and very good grip. It doesn't quite have the flair and class it has today, but very good indeed. (June 2006)

2010 TO 2025 17.0

Clos de Vougeot, 1996
Domaine Joseph Faiveley

Fine colour. Closed on nose and palate. Full, tannic, and with very good grip, but not very open at all. Underneath, rich, concentrated and generous. A lot of intensity. This is all in potential. Difficult to taste. But at least fine. (March 2000)

2010 TO 2020   17.5

Clos de Vougeot, 1996
Domaine Anne Gros

Good colour. Some tannin on the nose. Backward. Closed-in. Full, concentrated, cool, very intensely flavoured wine. Lots and lots of dimension. Excellent grip. Very, very long and very, very classy. Very fine. (February 2001)

NOW TO 2026   18.5

Clos de Vougeot, 1996
Domaine Michel Gros

Medium-full colour. Just about ready. Youthful vines (10 years old), but good depth and certainly very good finesse nonetheless. Good, succulent attack if not a follow-through of great intensity. Fine nonetheless. Lovely style. (June 2006)

NOW TO 2020   17.5

Clos de Vougeot, 1996
Domaine Leroy

Big, full, youthful colour. Very ripe, concentrated nose. Almost voluptuous. Super-concentrated. Not a bit austere. Full bodied. Youthful. Still tannic. Very concentrated on the palate. Very good grip. Essence of wine. Not that elegant but fine plus. Still needs 3 to 4 years. (June 2006)

2010 TO 2025   18.0

Clos de Vougeot, 1996
Domaine Méo-Camuzet

Fullish colour. Lovely nose. Rich, full, ample, ripe and with a touch of toffee. Full body. Excellent grip. More floral than the 1995. Higher acidity. Better class. Better fruit. Méo-Camuzet's 1996s are better than his 1995s. This is a very lovely example. (March 2001)

NOW TO 2025   18.5

Clos de Vougeot, Le Grand Maupertuis, 1996
Domaine Jean Tardy et Fils

Good colour. Ripe, rich and succulent on the nose. Cedary on the palate. Medium-full body. À

point. Soft, succulent and attractive. Ripe fruit. Very good, indeed, if not serious. (June 2006)

NOW TO 2019   17.0

Corton, 1996
Maison Champy

Full colour. Chunky nose. No charm. No finesse. Similar palate. Dreary. (June 2006)

NOW TO 2013   13.0

Corton, Hospices de Beaune, Cuvée Charlotte Dumay, 1996
Maison Morey-Blanc

Good colour. Finely poised, classy nose. Just a hint of wood. Medium-full. Pure, and if not that concentrated, at least complex. Some tannin. Good grip. Still youthful and a little raw. Very good indeed. Perhaps fine. But slightly unformed at the end at present, and a slight lack of intensity on the finish. (August 2000)

NOW TO 2018   16.5

Corton, Clos des Cortons Faiveley, 1996
Domaine Joseph Faiveley

Fullish colour. Still youthful. Rich, concentrated, high-quality nose but still very youthful. Fullish bodied and tannic. A bit tight. A little muscular. But fine rather than great. (June 2006)

2009 TO 2025   17.5

Corton, Les Maréchaudes, 1996
Domaine Chandon de Briailles

Magnum. Fullish, youthful colour. High-toned nose. Ripe. Some stems. Medium-full body. Stylish. Supple. Quite complex. Long. Fine. Just about ready. (June 2006)

NOW TO 2020+   17.5

Corton, Les Perrières, 1996
Maison Vincent Girardin

Full colour. Quite austere nose. Still a bit hard. A little more mellow on the palate. Fullish body. The tannins are now beginning to soften, but the acidity is a little high, so a bit raw still. Classy fruit. Complex. Long. Fine. Needs 3 years. (October 2002)

NOW TO 2026   17.5

Corton, Les Renardes, 1996
Domaine Leroy

Medium-full colour, less than the 1995. Less structure than the 1995. Higher acidity. A bit raw on the nose. Slight touch of the vegetal. Fine on the palate. Fresh, fullish and firm. Slightly austere. This will keep well. Very well balanced. (April 2000)

NOW TO 2020   17.5

Echézeaux, 1996
Domaine Robert Arnoux

Fine colour. Splendid nose. Very rich, concentrated and succulent. Lovely balance. Really classy. Fullish body. Very intense. Excellent fruit. A splendid example. Very, very long. Some tannin, but the tannins are very, very ripe. Lovely. (March 2000)

NOW TO 2018   17.5

Echézeaux, 1996
Domaine Jean Grivot

Magnum. Full, backward colour. Backward, too, on the nose. Intense but very closed-in. Big, tannic and a long way from maturity. But very fine quality underneath. Splendidly concentrated fruit. Excellent. (June 2006)

2010 TO 2025+   19.0

Gevrey-Chambertin, 1996
Domaine Armand Rousseau

This is a bit cheap and wimpy. It lacks class, depth and richness. Not very good at all. Ready. (October 2003)

DRINK UP   12.0

Gevrey-Chambertin, Vieilles Vignes, 1996
Domaine Denis Bachelet

Fullish colour. Still youthful. Very lovely, quite concentrated fruit on the nose. Rich, cool and succulent on the palate. Fullish body. Lovely fruit. Very finely balanced. Long. Youthful. Very lovely. (June 2006)

2010 TO 2025   17.5

Gevrey-Chambertin, Vieilles Vignes, 1996
Domaine Alain Burguet

Fullish colour. Still youthful. Decent fruit and depth, if with no real class. Medium-full body. Still a little tannin. Ripe if not very rich or succulent. Slightly austere still. Good, long finish. Very good. Needs time. (June 2006)

2010 TO 2020   16.0

Gevrey-Chambertin, Les Cazetiers, 1996
Domaine Bruno Clair

Good colour. Still youthful. Something on the nose. Just a touch of oxidation. A second bottle was cleaner and fresher, but not really convincing. Medium to medium-full body. Slightly astringent tannins. Ripe but it lacks fat. Quite good plus at best. (June 2006)

2009 TO 2015   14.5

Gevrey-Chambertin, Les Cazetiers, 1996
Domaine Armand Rousseau

Medium-full colour. Good, classy nose. Not that substantial. Fragrant and stylish. Medium to medium-full body. Good acidity. Not exactly on form at present but at least very good. (September 2002)

NOW TO 2015   16.0

Gevrey-Chambertin, Les Cazetiers, 1996
Domaine Sérafin Père et Fils

Fullish, immature colour. Lovely rich, concentrated, oaky nose. Fullish body. Still immature but poised, ripe and very fresh. Classy. Fine plus. (June 2006)

2011 TO 2025   18.0

Gevrey-Chambertin, Les Champeaux, 1996
Domaine Alain Burguet

Good colour. A touch rustic on the nose. More succulence than his Vieilles Vignes and fewer rude tannins, but nevertheless no better. No more finesse. Very good. (June 2006)

2010 TO 2020   16.0

Gevrey-Chambertin, En Champeaux, 1996
Domaine Denis Mortet

Fullish colour. Still youthful. Firm and quite closed on the nose. Fragrant, stylish and not a bit over-extracted. Medium-full body. The tannins are now just about mellow, but the wine is still a little raw. Not yet round and mellow.

Lovely fruit. Excellent balance. Very classy. Fine. (May 2002)

NOW TO 2020   7.5

Gevrey-Chambertin, En Champs, Vieilles Vignes, 1996
Domaine Denis Mortet

Village *appellation contrôlée*. Fullish, youthful colour. A little over-macerated on the nose. Oaky and chunky. Fullish body. Some tannin. Good grip and plenty of fruit. Better on the palate and at the end than on the nose. But a bit too muscular. Good plus. (June 2006)

2010 TO 2018   15.5

Gevrey-Chambertin, Clos Prieur, 1996
Domaine Thierry Mortet

Decent, fullish, youthful colour. A bit four-square on the nose. Chunky. Fullish body. But rather inflexible. It doesn't sing. Quite good. (June 2006)

NOW TO 2014   14.0

Gevrey-Chambertin, Clos Prieur, 1996
Domaine Joseph Roty

Village *appellation contrôlée*; not *premier cru*. Full colour. Firm, closed nose. But a lot of concentrated fruit underneath. Some oak but not excessively so. Full bodied and concentrated. Just a little driven but balanced; when it mellows, it will relax a bit. Very good surely. (March 2000)

NOW TO 2016   6.0

Gevrey-Chambertin, Clos Saint-Jacques, 1996
Domaine Jean-Claude Fourrier

Full colour. Still youthful. Graceful. Slightly closed-in. Ripe, concentrated nose. Not as profound or as concentrated as Jadot's or Rousseau's. Lovely balance nevertheless. Medium-full body. Fragrant. Stylish. Very lovely fruit. Ready. Fine plus. (April 2005)

NOW TO 2022   18.0

Gevrey-Chambertin, Clos Saint-Jacques, 1996
Domaine Louis Jadot

Fullish, immature colour. Very classy nose. Pure, poised, composed, concentrated fruit. Very classy. Very well balanced. Fullish body.

Very concentrated. Very good energy. Marvellous fruit. Very, very long and complex. Excellent. Still needs time. (June 2006)

2010 TO 2025+   19.0

Gevrey-Chambertin, Clos Saint-Jacques, 1996
Domaine Armand Rousseau

Medium-full, mature colour. The nose, though, is still vigorous and even a little closed. Rich and fat, ample and very gently oaky. Medium-full body. Round. Very ripe. Very succulent and seductive. Lovely long, smooth finish. Very fine. *À point* but very vigorous. (April 2005)

NOW TO 2028   18.5

Gevrey-Chambertin, Les Combottes, 1996
Domaine Dujac

Medium-full colour. A touch of maturity. Ripe, sweet nose. Showing the stems. Medium to medium-full body. Ripe, elegant and complex. Not a blockbuster. No undue leanness. Long on the palate. Plenty of depth. Just about ready. Very good indeed. (June 2005)

NOW TO 2017   17.0

Gevrey-Chambertin, Les Corbeaux, 1996
Domaine Denis Bachelet

Medium-full colour. Still youthful. Fragrant, classy, gently oaky, balanced nose. Medium-full body. Nice and succulent on the palate. Splendidly harmonious and intense at the end. Fine. (October 2005)

NOW TO 2025   17.5

Gevrey-Chambertin, Les Corbeaux, Vieilles Vignes, 1996
Domaine Philippe Rossignol

Medium-full colour. Ripe, stylish nose. Good, succulent fruit and very good acidity. Medium-full body. Good tannins. Balanced. Elegant. Long. Good plus. (March 2002)

NOW TO 2014   15.5

Gevrey-Chambertin, Estournelles-Saint-Jacques, 1996
Domaine Frédéric Esmonin

Good colour. Fresh nose. Very pleasant damson fruit. Quite cool. Medium-full body. Good tannins. Ripe in a slightly reserved way on the palate. Good length and class. Finishes long. A laid-back but classy example. Fine. (January 2001)

NOW TO 2018   17.5

Gevrey-Chambertin, Lavaux-Saint-Jacques, 1996
Domaine Claude Dugat

Very fine, full colour. Full, rich, firm, concentrated and oaky on the nose. Splendid depth here. Lots of character. Most impressive for a *premier cru*. Full on the palate. Quite tannic. Not over-extracted though. Just an excellently concentrated and very poised wine. Excellent balance. Lovely fruit. Real complexity and dimension. Very, very long. Very lovely. Very fine or even better. (November 2001)

NOW TO 2027   18.5

Gevrey-Chambertin, Lavaux-Saint-Jacques, 1996
Domaine Bernard Maume

Full colour. Full, meaty and tannic on nose and palate. Quite powerful. A structured wine but one with plenty of depth, grip and concentration. Ample and rich. Vigorous. This is very good indeed. (March 2002)

NOW TO 2020   17.0

Gevrey-Chambertin, Lavaux-Saint-Jacques, 1996
Domaine Denis Mortet

Fine colour. Slightly adolescent at present. More extraction than today but not excessively so. A big wine. Rich, full bodied and concentrated. Lots of depth and dimension. Very good acidity. But quite chunky. Fine. (September 2002)

NOW TO 2020   17.5

Gevrey-Chambertin, Lavaux-Saint-Jacques, 1996
Domaine Armand Rousseau

Medium to medium-full colour. Fragrant, stylish nose. Not that expressive because it lacks a little fat and intensity. Medium to medium-full body. Cool and fragrant. Not a lot of tannin left. A cool vintage, obviously. This has excellent acidity in a slightly lean sort of way, but a slight lack of richness and depth. Some 1972 touches. Yet getting mellow now. Classy finish. Very good. (June 2002)

NOW TO 2010+   16.0

Grands Echézeaux, 1996
Domaine Gros Frère et Soeur

Magnum. Fullish colour. Still fresh. Ripe but quite a lot of oak on the nose. On the palate quite full. Very good grip. Nicely cool and classy, and not a bit too oaky. Profound. Fine plus. Just about ready. (June 2006)

NOW TO 2022   18.0

Grands Echézeaux, 1996
Domaine de la Romanée-Conti

Magnum. Fullish colour. Classy nose. Lovely fruit. Lots of depth and concentration. This is full bodied, rich and abundant. Very well balanced. Long. Just about ready. Fine. (June 2006)

NOW TO 2020   17.5

Griotte-Chambertin, 1996
Domaine Joseph Drouhin

Fullish, youthful colour. Very lovely ripe, quite delicate fruit, but youthful and concentrated. Medium-full body. Balanced, very stylish and vigorous. Not a monster. Just about ready. Very long and very classy. Very fine. (June 2006)

NOW TO 2020+   18.5

Griotte-Chambertin, 1996
Domaine Frédéric Esmonin

Medium-full colour. A little development. Full, rich, slightly robust nose. On the palate there is some very good fruit but a certain astringency about the tannins—or more a rawness. Still youthful. Good austerity. Slightly adolescent. The finish is more ample than the attack. This is classy, complex and quite original. Fine plus. (November 2001)

NOW TO 2027   18.0

Latricières-Chambertin, 1996
Domaine Simon Bize et Fils

Medium-full colour. Quite a lot of the stems on the nose. A bit dry on the palate as a result. Some fruit. But it doesn't sing. Yet it finishes better than it starts. We'll see. (June 2006)

NOW TO 2018   16.0

Latricières-Chambertin, 1996
Domaine Joseph Faiveley

Fine colour. Closed and adolescent on the nose. Rich and full. Slightly robust as Latricières always is, but intense and very well balanced. A big, tannic wine but not a bit burly. Still adolescent. Fine surely. (March 2000)

NOW TO 2020   17.5

Latricières-Chambertin, 1996
Domaine Leroy

Full, youthful colour. Very lovely fruit on the nose. Balanced, poised and fragrant. Multidimensional. Full. Very fine tannins. Very classy. Very harmonious. This is an aristocratic example. Very fine. (April 2000)

NOW TO 2020+   18.5

Latricières-Chambertin, 1996
Domaine Jean Trapet Père et Fils

Good, full colour. No sign of age. Ripe, fullish, stylish, succulent nose. Ample and rich. Medium to medium-full body. It lacks a little concentration and grip. Slightly one-dimensional. And only medium class. Just about ready. Quite good plus. (April 2005)

NOW TO 2015   14.5

Marsannay, Les Longeroies, 1996
Domaine René Bouvier

Lovely, stylish, balanced, vigorous fruit. Long. Complex. Lovely. (January 2002)

NOW TO 2014   15.5

Marsannay, Les Longeroies, 1996
Domaine Bruno Clair

Good, vigorous colour. Quite a soft nose. Medium to medium-full body. Fresh. Plump. Stylish and ripe. Good definition. Good for what it is. (June 2006)

NOW TO 2015   14.5

Mazis-Chambertin, 1996
Maison Camille Giroud

Medium-full colour. Some evolution. The nose is quite developed as well. Slightly barnyardy. Slightly attenuated. Medium-full body. Decent acidity. But not enough concentration and class. Quite good. (April 2005)

NOW TO 2012   14.0

Mazis-Chambertin, 1996
Hospices de Beaune

Made by Alain Corcia for the Troigros restaurant. Full colour. Stewed and chemical on nose and palate. Dirty. No. (April 2005)

(SEE NOTE)

Mazis-Chambertin, 1996
Domaine Philippe Naddef

Full colour. On the nose not too dense or astringent. Rich and full. Quite full on the palate. Fesh. Good grip. Slightly clumsy though. Yet a vigorous finish. Good at best. (April 2005)

NOW TO 2015   15.0

Morey-Saint-Denis, Premier Cru, 1996
Domaine Hubert Lignier

Very full, backward colour. Slightly chunky and solid on the nose. Rich, full and oaky on the palate. Lots of concentration and intensity. But a little overdone. Slightly too much extraction. But very good wine underneath. Very good plus. (June 2006)

2012 TO 2025   16.5

Morey-Saint-Denis, Clos de la Buissière, 1996
Domaine Georges Roumier et Fils

Medium to medium-full colour. Still youthful though. Spicy nose. Quite ripe but quite soft. Medium weight. Indeed even a little slight. But quite rich, balanced and succulent, if no real class. Slightly loose knit at the end. Very good plus. (June 2006)

NOW TO 2015   16.5

Morey-Saint-Denis, En la Rue de Vergy, 1996
Domaine Bruno Clair

Quite a marked acidity. Fresh. Slightly lean. But elegant and very good fruit. Medium body. Still very youthful. (June 2003)

NOW TO 2010   16.5

Musigny, 1996
Domaine Leroy

Splendid full, backward colour. Very lovely nose. Smooth, subtle, fragrant and really lovely. Immaculate harmony. Full body. Very concentrated and intense. Splendid grip. Flowery as well as fragrant. Very, very long and complex. Very fine indeed. (April 2000)

NOW TO 2025   19.5

Le Musigny, 1996
Domaine Comte Georges de Vogüe

Very good colour. Marvellous nose. Very rich, lush and succulent. Totally unmistakable Musigny in its combination of fragrance, delicacy and intensity. Fullish body. Still some tannin. Very pure and fresh. Essence of Chambolle fruit. Very, very long. *Grand vin!* (February 2001)

2012 TO 2030   20.0

Musigny, Vieilles Vignes, 1996
Domaine Comte Georges de Vogüe

Full colour. Still immature. Rich, full, concentrated, backward, oaky nose. Very lovely fruit. Full body. Backward. Splendid concentration. This has depth and intensity. I don't think this is great, but it is very impressive. Still rather closed and austere. This is very fine indeed. (June 2006)

2012 TO 2030   19.0

Nuits-Saint-Georges, Au Bas de Combe, 1996
Domaine Jean Tardy et Fils

Medium-full colour. Mature. Soft nose. Some oak. Medium weight. Decent vigour. Pleasant, plump fruit. Good style. Finishes positively. (June 2006)

NOW TO 2015   15.5

Nuits-Saint-Georges, Aux Boudots, 1996
Domaine Jean-Jacques Confuron

Good colour. Quite oaky all the way through. Rich and fat. Medium-full body. The tannins are now soft. There is plenty of vigour here, and quite a lot of depth and grip. The wine is very attractive, if not having quite the intensity for very fine. Very good indeed. (November 2003)

NOW TO 2018   17.0

Nuits-Saint-Georges, Aux Boudots, 1996
Domaine Jean Grivot

Full colour. Rich, concentrated, quite firm nose. But not too austere. Fullish on the palate. Good tannins. Very good acidity. Lovely fruit. A little reserved at present. Lots of depth and complexity. Very long finish. Very good indeed. Still needs time. (June 2004)

NOW TO 2020+   17.0

Nuits-Saint-Georges, Aux Boudots, 1996
Domaine Gérard Mugneret

Fresh, full colour. Fresh nose. Good acidity. Ripe in a slightly lean sort of way. Medium-full body. Classy. Very fragrant. Kirsch touches. This is medium-full bodied and is now approaching maturity. Very good grip. Long, complex and fresh. Expanded in the glass. Lovely. Fine. (October 2003)

NOW TO 2020   17.5

Nuits-Saint-Georges, Les Chaboeufs, 1996
Domaine Jean-Jacques Confuron

Medium-full, mature colour. Rich, quite concentrated, good style and balance on the nose. Fullish body. Lovely ripe fruit. This is profound and classy. Lovely finish. Lots of character and depth. Just about ready. Fine. (June 2006)

NOW TO 2020   17.5

Nuits-Saint-Georges, Les Chaignots, 1996
Domaine Gérard Mugneret

Medium-full colour. Just a little less profound than his Boudots. richer, fuller but earthier than the Boudots. A slightly bigger wine. Slightly tougher. But no lack of style. Good class. A meaty wine. Fine. (November 2001)

NOW TO 2022   17.5

Nuits-Saint-Georges, Champs Perdrix, 1996
Domaine Alain Michelot

Medium-full colour. Mature. On the nose quite spicy and fully developed. Medium-full body. Stylish. Balanced. Fresh. Good depth. Attractive, ripe fruit. Fully ready. Good long finish. Very good plus. (June 2006)

NOW TO 2020   16.5

Nuits-Saint-Georges, Clos de l'Arlot, 1996
Domaine de l'Arlot

Medium, mature colour. Ripe but slightly stemmy nose. Medium body. Fresh. Good fruit and good intensity. This is quite stylish. The finish is long and positive. Good plus. (June 2006)

NOW TO 2014   15.5

Nuits-Saint-Georges, Clos des Grandes Vignes, 1996
Domaine Charles Thomas

Full colour. Still youthful. Quite firm still on the nose. Still some tannin to resolve on the palate. A fresh, ripe, fullish-bodied wine. Good grip. A little adolescent, but there is depth here. Positive finish. Very good plus for the vintage. (May 2002)

NOW TO 2020   16.5

Nuits-Saint-Georges, Clos Saint-Marc, 1996
Domaine Bouchard Père et Fils

Very good colour. On the nose a little dense, but high quality and very good acidity underneath. Slightly hot in comparison with the Clos des Porrets 1996, but long, fat, succulent and very good indeed. (November 2000)

NOW TO 2020   17.0

Nuits-Saint-Georges, Les Murgers, 1996
Domaine Bertagna

Good, fresh colour. Slightly chunky nose. Medium-full body. Good depth and vigour. Nice, fresh, plump, succulent fruit. Not the greatest finesse but very good. Just about ready. (June 2006)

NOW TO 2017   16.0

Nuits-Saint-Georges, Les Poisets, 1996
Domaine Robert Arnoux

Village wine. Very good colour. Still very youthful looking. Slightly closed on the nose. But lots of substance here. Full body. Really quite tannic, but splendid concentration, grip and intensity. A big wine which needs time. Splendid fruit though. Very good tannins. This is very good, indeed, for a village wine. (March 2000)

NOW TO 2016   16.0

Nuits-Saint-Georges, Les Porrets Saint-Georges, 1996
Maison Bouchard Père et Fils

Good colour. Ripe, sophisticated, balanced nose. On the palate a fine 1996. Classy, fullish bodied, harmonious and attractive. Very good depth. Long and complex. Fine. (November 2000)

NOW TO 2020   17.5

Nuits-Saint-Georges, Les Pruliers, 1996
Domaine Robert Chevillon

Good, fresh colour. Round, ripe, mature, stylish nose. Medium-full body. Nicely fresh and plump. Very good style. Long and complex. Fine. Fully ready. (June 2006)

NOW TO 2019   17.5

Nuits-Saint-Georges, Les Saint-Georges, 1996
Domaine Robert Chevillon

Good, fresh colour. A little bit more depth and concentration than his 1996 Pruliers. Very good fruit on the nose. Ripe on the palate. Not quite the grip or vigour of the Pruliers, but subtle, complex fruit. Very good indeed. (June 2006)

NOW TO 2017   17.0

Nuits-Saint-Georges, Les Saint-Georges, 1996
Domaine Forey Père et Fils

Fullier colour. Firm nose. Closed. A little adolescent. Some tannin. This needs time. At present the structure dominates, and it doesn't seem to have the greatest richness. The finish, however, is fine. Full, sturdy and masculine. Very much middle-Nuits-Saint-Georges. Lovely cassis fruit at the end. Long. Very good depth. Fine plus. (November 2001)

NOW TO 2025   18.0

Nuits-Saint-Georges, Les Saint-Georges, 1996
Domaine Henri Gouges

Good, fullish, fresh colour. Very lovely nose. Riper and richer than many 1996s. Fatter and more creamy as well, which is even more important. Very pure. Very lovely fruit. On the palate medium-full body. A little unresolved tannin. Slightly adolescent. Good grip. When it mellows, this will be very delicious. Underneath there is great class. (September 2003)

NOW TO 2025   18.0

Nuits-Saint-Georges, Les Vaucrains, 1996
Domaine Henri Gouges

Full, youthful colour. Good, rich but backward, tannic nose. Very Vaucrains. A sturdy wine. But very good tannins and very lovely fruit. Backward on the palate, too. Very fine grip. Potentially fine plus. Still needs time. (June 2006)

2009 TO 2022+   18.0

Pernand-Vergelesses, Ile De Vergelesses, 1996
Domaine Chandon de Briailles

Ripe but a little fragile on the nose. Quite evolved. Good style though. Slightly sweet-sour. Lacks a little backbone and grip on the palate. But attractive. Ready now. (October 2000)

DRINK SOON   15.0

Pommard, Clos des Epeneaux, 1996
Domaine du Comte Armand

Full colour. Still youthful. Still a bit closed-in on the nose. But very lovely, classy fruit. Fullish body. Fine plus. (June 2006)

2009 TO 2025   18.0

Pommard, Clos des Epeneaux, 1996
Maison Camille Giroud

Medium-full, mature colour. Very classy on both nose and palate. Fullish body. Very lovely fruit. Excellent harmony. Long. Fully ready. Complex finish. Fine. (June 2006)

NOW TO 2020   17.5

Pommard, Clos des Grands Epenots, 1996
Domaine de Courcel

Magnum. Medium-full, fresh colour. Ripe nose. Slightly spicy. Medium-full body. Good, ample fruit and very good quality if without the flair for better than that. (June 2006)

NOW TO 2020   16.0

Pommard, Les Grands Epenots, 1996
Maison Vincent Girardin

Good colour. Full, firm, stylish nose. Some tannin, but the tannins are well covered. Full bodied, rich, concentrated and gently oaky on the palate. Very good grip. Rich and succulent. Lovely

and fresh, especially on the follow-through. Long. Very good indeed. (March 2000)

NOW TO 2015   17.0

Pommard, Les Jarolières, 1996
Domaine Jean-Marc Boillot

Good colour. Classy nose. Medium-full weight. Volnay touches. Medium-full body. Some tannin. Slightly herbal. Slightly raw. This has good grip and depth, but not a lot of fat, generosity or ripeness. Long. Quite classy. Very good at best. (June 2002)

NOW TO 2018   16.0

Pommard, Les Pézerolles, 1996
Domaine Philippe Billard-Gonnet

Good, full, fresh colour. Ample, ripe nose. Medium-full body. Accessible. Stylish. Good balance. Plenty of vigour. Ripe and positive at the end. Very good. Just about ready. (June 2006)

NOW TO 2018   16.0

Pommard, Les Rugiens, 1996
Domaine Hubert de Montille

Good colour. Rather a dry nose. But more supple on the palate. Medium-full body. Ripe. Good vigour and style. It has depth and finishes well. Very good. (June 2006)

NOW TO 2020   16.0

Pommard, Les Rugiens Bas, 1996
Domaine Aleth le Royer-Girardin

Full colour. Splendid, firm nose. Rich, concentrated, succulent and stylish nose. Classy. Full bodied. Quite tannic. Gently oaky. Lots of depth. This is a fine example. (July 2000)

NOW TO 2018   17.0

Richebourg, 1996
Domaine Jean Grivot

Magnum. Very good colour. Very pure, very concentrated on the nose. Quite lovely. Full, austere and reserved on the palate. Still some tannin. Very intense. Multidimensional. Lots of grip. This is excellent. Very, very long. Still backward. (February 2001)

NOW TO 2030   19.5

Richebourg, 1996
Domaine Gros Frère et Soeur

Magnum. Full, youthful colour. Rich but slightly chunky. Still closed on the nose. This is a little solid. It lacks a bit of grace. I prefer their Grands Echézeaux. Lots of wine here. Needs time. Very good but doesn't sing. (June 2006)

2010 TO 2020+ 16.0

Richebourg, 1996
Domaine Anne Gros

Fine colour. Still very youthful. Rather austere on the nose. Even a slight vegetal, lean touch. Is it always going to be a bit like this, I wondered. On the palate, though, much more round and generous. Full body. Still some tannin to round off. High acidity keeping it fresh. Long and stylish. This is very fine indeed. (February 2004)

NOW TO 2030 19.5

Richebourg, 1996
Domaine Leroy

Fullish colour. Not a lot of maturity. Still very closed-in on the nose. Much less open than the 1995 or 1993. High acidity. Austere. Hidden. Fullish structure. Some tannin. Slightly rigid at present. Nor has it got the fat and richness of the 1992. (April 2000)

NOW TO 2020 17.5

Richebourg, 1996
Domaine Méo-Camuzet

Very fine, full colour. Quite brilliant nose. Marvellous depth, concentration and dimension of fruit. Great aromatic complexity. Still very young and very vigorous. Evolved considerably in the glass. Very ripe. Very complex and very classy. Multidimensional. Full body. No undue tannins. Very long. Brilliant. (March 2001)

NOW TO 2025+ 19.0

La Romanée, 1996
Domaine Bouchard Père et Fils

Very full, rich, immature colour. Splendid quality on the nose. Quite austere. Very lovely rich, ripe fruit. Still backward. Fullish body. Excellent class and very good grip. Now beginning to soften. Very fine. (March 2003)

NOW TO 2028 18.5

Romanée-Saint-Vivant, 1996
Domaine Robert Arnoux

Fullish colour. A touch of development. Full, rich, concentrated and classy on the nose. This has depth and dimension. Fullish body. Quite smooth now. Rich and fresh (rather than marked acidity). Potentially mellow and seductive. Lots of depth and class. Very fine plus. (March 2005)

NOW TO 2030 19.0

Romanée-Saint-Vivant, 1996
Domaine Jean-Jacques Confuron

Good colour. Richly perfumed, quite austere nose. Very classy fruit. Fullish body. Very intense, very lovely coulis of red and black berries here. Not a masculine heavyweight, but excellent grip and length. Very, very classy. Very fine. (February 2001)

NOW TO 2026 18.5

Romanée-Saint-Vivant, 1996
Domaine Alain Hudelot-Noëllat

Good colour. Full, rich, fat, concentrated, opulent nose. Plenty of wine here. Full bodied. Still some tannin to resolve. Very fine grip. This is a bigger wine than Arnoux's or Confuron's. Backward. Very lovely fruit. Lots of dimension here. Very, very long. Very fine indeed. (February 2001)

NOW TO 2020 19.0

Romanée-Saint-Vivant, 1996
Maison Dominique Laurent

Fullish colour. Little sign of maturity yet. Perfumed, oaky, exotic nose. Somewhat artificial and tarty perhaps. Fullish body. A slight residual, reductive flavour. Good tannins. Good grip. But quite a substantial if not slightly lumpy wine. Ample fruit, though, but fine for the vintage at best. (March 2002)

NOW TO 2018 17.5

Romanée-Saint-Vivant, 1996
Domaine Leroy

Full, youthful colour. Firm, rich, concentrated nose. Still a bit austere. Medium-full body. Balanced and classy. A bit lean on the follow-through. Softened up after 15 minutes in the glass. A second bottle was better. Ripe, complex and profound. Lovely finish. Very fine plus. Will still improve. (June 2006)

2009 TO 2025+   19.0

Romanée-Saint-Vivant, 1996
Domaine de la Romanée-Conti

Very good colour. Ripe nose. Quite smooth already. Not too tough. Some of the spices of maturity here. Medium-full body. Still a little tannin. Still needs a little time. Not the greatest fat, richness, and concentration, but very good indeed. (November 2005)

NOW TO 2020   17.0

Ruchottes-Chambertin, 1996
Domaine Frédéric Esmonin

Full colour. Quite a meaty nose. Slightly astringent on the attack. Full and rich. Still needs time. This has good depth. What it lacks is a little class and definition, but very good indeed. (October 2005)

NOW TO 2025   17.0

Ruchottes-Chambertin, 1996
Domaine Dr. Georges Mugneret

Fullish colour. Only a little development. Very lovely, classy nose. Fresh, ripe and complex. Medium-full body. The tannins are now soft, and the wine is just about ready, although still slightly raw. Elegant and balanced. Lovely finish. Fine. (June 2006)

NOW TO 2020   17.5

Ruchottes-Chambertin, 1996
Domaine Georges Roumier/Michel Bonnefond

Fullish colour. Some fat. Rich, fat, concentrated, high-class nose. Full body. Very lovely fruit. Just about ready. Lots of vigour. Still needs a year or two for preference. Excellent follow-through. Very classy. Very profound and very long. Very fine plus. (April 2005)

NOW TO 2030   19.0

Ruchottes-Chambertin, Clos des Ruchottes, 1996
Domaine Armand Rousseau

Medium colour. Fully mature. Ample nose. Ready now. Slightly lean, but good fruit and depth underneath. Medium to medium-full body. Ripe and fragrant. Fresh. Slightly sweet. But lovely, fragrant Pinot Noir. Long and complex. Fine plus. (April 2005)

NOW TO 2020   18.0

Saint-Aubin, Derrière Chez Édouard, 1996
Domaine Hubert Lamy et Fils

Magnum. Very lovely fruit on the nose. Elegant and complex. Medium to medium-full body. But intense, complex and classy. Just about ready. Lovely long finish. Round and seductive. Very good plus. (June 2006)

NOW TO 2018   16.5

Santenay, Clos de Malte, 1996
Domaine Louis Jadot

Fullish colour. Lovely fresh, cherry-flavoured nose. Medium body. No hard edges. Very good acidity. Lovely fruit. This is very well made and stylish for a 1996. Soft but vigorous. (April 2001)

NOW TO 2013   15.0

Santenay, Les Gravières, 1996
Maison Vincent Girardin

Good colour. Rich, quite earthy, quite tannic nose. Good style. Good depth. Medium-full body. Some tannins, but although a bit raw, lovely ripe, juicy fruit as well. Balanced. Long. A bit adolescent but very good for what it is. (March 2000)

NOW TO 2011   16.0

Savigny-lès-Beaune, 1996
Maison Champy

Magnum. Evolved colour. Artisanal nose. Medium to medium-full body. Slightly astringent on the palate. Fresh at the end, but it lacks class. Only fair. (June 2006)

NOW TO 2010   13.5

Savigny-lès-Beaune, Premier Cru, 1996
Maison Champy

Medium-full colour. Good, firm nose. Fresh. Good depth and class. This is a medium-full bodied, stylish, very well-balanced example. Good grip. Not a bit hard. Ripe and complex. Very good. (January 2001)

NOW TO 2015   16.0

Savigny-lès-Beaune, La Dominode, 1996
Domaine Jean-Marc Pavelot

Magnum. Full colour. Still youthful. Rich, full, fat and gently oaky on the nose. Fullish bodied, rich and lovely on the palate. A little tannin still, but the tannins are very well covered. Lots of vigour. Lots of depth. Very good grip. Splendid energy at the end. Very long. Still needs a couple of years. Very good plus. (June 2006)

NOW TO 2015   16.0

Savigny-lès-Beaune, Aux Gravains, 1996
Domaine Jean-Marc Pavelot

Slightly less colour but less advanced than the 1995. Still a touch lean on the nose. Good, classy fruit. Now soft but not yet mellow. Medium body. Very good. But his 1995 is fatter and more seductive. Perhaps this is more elegant though. (June 2003)

NOW TO 2018   16.0

Savigny-lès-Beaune, Les Marconnets, 1996
Domaine Simon Bize et Fils

Medium, well-developed colour. Some stems on the nose. A little weedy. But ripe enough on the palate. Medium to medium-full body. Fresh at the end. Finishes better than it starts. Quite good plus. (June 2006)

NOW TO 2012   14.5

Savigny-lès-Beaune, Les Peuillets, 1996
Domaine Lucien Jacob

Medium-full colour. Still fresh. Ripe, plump, abundant nose. Medium-full body. Good, stylish fruit. Well balanced. Typically Savigny in flavour. Positive finish. Good. (June 2006)

NOW TO 2012   15.0

La Tâche, 1996
Domaine de la Romanée-Conti

Fullish colour. A little development. Very lovely nose. Marvellously complex fruit. Now

beginning to mellow. Real class. Distinguished character. On the palate rather more austere still. Less round. High acidity. Fullish body. Very good tannins, now soft, but the wine needs time to show its generosity. Very fine indeed. (March 2005)

NOW TO 2020+   19.5

Volnay, 1996
Maison Nicolas Potel

Good colour. Very fragrant on the nose. Delicious, succulent, well-balanced Volnay fruit. Quite developed in that there is not a great deal of tannin. Medium weight. Harmonious, long and classy. Very more-ish. Real definition here. (July 2000)

NOW TO 2010   17.0

Volnay, Vendanges Sélectionnées, 1996
Domaine Michel Lafarge

Good colour. Lovely Pinot fruit. Slightly austere. Medium body. A little tannin. This is classy for a village wine. Quite high acidity. Needs to mellow. (August 2000)

DRINK SOON   15.0

Volnay, Premier Cru, 1996
Domaine du Marquis d'Angerville

Medium-full colour. Fresh. Classy nose. Very Volnay. Finely tuned. Fragrant. Medium-full body. Nicely plump. Rich but balanced. Complex, elegant finish. Very good indeed. (June 2006)

NOW TO 2015   17.0

Volnay, Caillerets, Clos des 60 Ouvrées, 1996
Domaine de la Bousse d'Or

Medium to medium-full colour. Accessible nose. Very elegant. Not a blockbuster. Medium to medium-full body. Just about ready. Very fresh. Lovely fruit. Very harmonious. Very complex. Fine. (June 2003)

NOW TO 2020   17.5

Volnay, Carelles, 1996
Maison Camille Giroud

Medium-full colour. Now mature. Quite full on the nose. Rich and plump. Quite muscular for a Volnay. Nicely mature on the palate. Fullish body. Ample. Slightly spicy. Good style. Fine finish. Very good indeed. (June 2006)

NOW TO 2015   17.0

Volnay, Champans, 1996
Domaine Hubert de Montille

Medium-full colour. Still youthful. Fragrant nose. At first a little astringent on the palate, and a lack of charm and succulence. Decent style though. But it doesn't sing. (June 2006)

NOW TO 2010   14.5

Volnay, Clos de la Cave des Ducs, 1996
Domaine Philippe Carré-Courbin

Good colour. Soft, raspberry-flavoured nose. Gently oaky. Medium weight and intensity. Not a lot of tannin. Stylish. Very good, but not the depth or concentration of great. (March 2000)

NOW TO 2009   16.0

Volnay, Clos des Chênes, 1996
Maison Vincent Girardin

Medium-full colour. Just about ready. Fragrant nose. No undue acidity. Soft and classy. Full of fruit. Medium-full body. Round, ripe and most attractive. À point now. Not the depth for fine but very good indeed. Long and fresh. Will keep well. (November 2005)

NOW TO 2019   17.0

Volnay, Clos des Chênes, 1996
Domaine Michel Lafarge

Fullish colour. Some development. Firm nose. Medium-full body. A little tannin. Good acidity, but now quite evolved and round at the end. Just about ready. Lovely long, fresh, elegant finish. Very fine. (June 2006)

NOW TO 2025   18.0

Volnay, Clos des Chênes, 1996
Domaine des Comtes Lafon

Fine colour. Not as stylish or as complete as their Santenots du Milieu 1996. Ripe, succulent, balanced and medium-full bodied. Fine if not great. Slightly more spicy than the Santenots. (October 2000)

NOW TO 2020   17.5

Volnay, Clos des Chênes, 1996
Domaine Jacques Parent

Medium-full colour. Still very fresh. On the nose the wine is medium bodied, fresh and fragrant. Similar on the palate. Very stylish. Still a touch raw but very elegant. Needs to round off. Very good indeed. (March 2005)

NOW TO 2020   17.0

Volnay, Les Pitures, 1996
Domaine Jean-Marc Boillot

Fullish colour. Rich, youthful nose. Very fresh still. Quite chunky on the palate. Some tannin. Slightly austere on the attack but better at the end. But it lacks Volnay fragrance. Good plus. (June 2006)

NOW TO 2015   15.5

Volnay, Santenots, 1996
Domaine Rossignol-Jeanniard

Full, quite developed colour. Ripe, if slightly chunky on the nose. Fullish bodied on the palate. Not the greatest of style, but good fruit and balance if slightly solid. Finishes well. A wine for food. Just about ready. (June 2006)

NOW TO 2018   15.5

Volnay, Santenots du Milieu, 1996
Domaine des Comtes Lafon

Magnum. Full, vigorous colour. Lovely rich, youthful nose. No hard edges. Fullish body. More supple, less chunky than Michel Lafarge's 1996 Clos des Chênes, and so more elegant and finer on the follow-through today. Lovely. Will still improve. (June 2006)

NOW TO 2025   18.0

Volnay, Taillepieds, 1996
Domaine Hubert de Montille

This is very classy. Very intense and concentrated. Quite subtantial. Very well-covered tannins. Velvety underneath. Lots of depth. Above all, real breed. Cool and classy. Very long. Fine plus. (December 2001)

NOW TO 2024   18.0

Vosne-Romanée, 1996
Domaine René Engel

Good colour. Splendid nose. Very lovely fruit and definition for a village wine. A touch adolescent, but ripe and stylish. Long and satisfying. Very good. (October 2000)

NOW TO 2014   16.0

Vosne-Romanée, 1996
Domaine Michel Gros

Medium to medium-full colour. Mature. Lovely ripe, stylish nose. Medium to medium-full body. Lovely fruit. *À point*. Yet very fresh at the end, and long and complex. This is very fine for a village example. (June 2006)

NOW TO 2015   16.0

Vosne-Romanée, Les Beaux Monts, 1996
Domaine Jean Grivot

Full, backward colour. Very fine nose. Backward, firm, pure, rich and concentrated. Very stylish. Lots and lots of depth. Full body. Some tannin still to resolve. Very poised, slightly austere, pure fruit. Very lovely intensity. Splendid grip, of course. This is long and profound, and has a very lovely character. Very fine. (March 2000)

NOW TO 2020   18.5

Vosne-Romanée, Les Brûlées, 1996
Domaine René Engel

Fullish colour. Not very expressive on the nose. But very lovely fruit. Lots of class and very good balance. Fullish body. Concentrated and old viney. Very pure and refined. Excellent grip and a most impressive, profound finish. Very fine. (September 2001)

NOW TO 2026   18.5

Vosne-Romanée, Aux Brûlées, 1996
Domaine Jean Grivot

Very full colour. Just a hint of maturity. Distinctive and very classy on the nose. Very, very lovely fruit. Intense and concentrated. Fullish body. Rich. Now getting mellow but still a touch raw. Very pure and intense. Very lovely fruit. Fine plus. (June 2003)

NOW TO 2020   18.0

Vosne-Romanée, Les Brûlées, 1996
Domaine Gérard Mugneret

Magnum. Medium-full colour. Ripe, succulent nose and palate. Medium-full body. Lovely fruit.

Very classy. Very long and complex. This if fine plus if not very fine. An impressive wine. *À point*, and with a very, very classy and complex finish. (June 2006)

NOW TO 2020   18.0

Vosne-Romanée, Les Chaumes, 1996
Domaine Jean Tardy et Fils

Good colour. Still youthful. Not a lot of nose. Medium to medium-full body. Quite ripe, but not a lot of character or succulence. Somewhat neutral. Fresh finish. (March 2006)

NOW TO 2014   14.0

Vosne-Romanée, Clos des Réas, 1996
Domaine Michel Gros

Monopole. Medium-full colour. Very lovely nose. Succulent, complex and classy. Very harmonious. Lots of dimension here. Medium-full body. Very lovely fruit. Splendidly balanced. Very long and subtle. Very elegant. Fine plus. (June 2006)

NOW TO 2025   18.0

Vosne-Romanée, Les Gaudichots, 1996
Domaine Forey Père et Fils

Medium-full colour. Backward, concentrated nose. Plenty of depth here, but the tannins are dominant at the moment. Full bodied, tannic and quite solid in fact. Very good cassis fruit underneath and very good grip. This is going to need time. But it is certainly very good indeed. (September 2001)

NOW TO 2025+   17.0

Vosne-Romanée, Aux Malconsorts, 1996
Domaine Sylvain Cathiard

Magnum. Full, vigorous colour. Splendid nose. Laid-back. Really classy. Medium-full body. Subtle and harmonious. Long and complex. Great finesse. Very fine. (June 2006)

NOW TO 2025   18.5

Vosne-Romanée, Les Suchots, 1996
Domaine de l'Arlot

Medium to medium-full colour. Slightly sweaty on the nose. A little diffuse. Better on the palate. Medium to medium-full body. Ripe, fresh and oaky. The finish is very stylish, long and subtle. But the wine really needed a bit more concentration and volume. Will develop soon. Very good. (March 2000)

NOW TO 2009   16.0

Vosne-Romanée, Les Suchots, 1996
Domaine Robert Arnoux

Fullish colour. Rich, firm, oaky nose. Already quite generous. Full body. Very good, ripe tannins. A lot of grip and concentration here. This is undoubtedly fine. Lots of depth. Very lovely fruit. Very classy and very long. (September 2001)

NOW TO 2026   18.5

Vosne-Romanée, Les Suchots, 1996
Domaine Jacky Confuron-Cotétidot

Good colour. Ripe, rich, quite classy nose. A touch of the stems. Plenty of depth. Medium-full body. Just about ready. Complex. Good grip. Fine. (June 2006)

NOW TO 2020   17.5

Vosne-Romanée, Les Suchots, 1996
Domaine Jean Grivot

Fullish colour. Just beginning to show a sign of maturity. Very lovely nose. Not a bit too hard or austere. Seductive. The nose is ripe, rich, very complex and very classy. Marvellous finesse. Very composed and laid-back. Medium-full body. The tannins are very ripe and integrated. Plenty of fat. Creamy rich. Very fine grip, of course. Velvety and seductive. Very fine. (December 2001)

NOW TO 2026   18.5

Vosne-Romanée, Les Suchots, 1996
Domaine Gérard Mugneret

Medium-full colour. A little sign of maturity. Looser knit on the nose than Arnoux's, but plump and juicy. Quite accessible already. Good, oaky background. Medium-full body. Succulent and balanced. Lovely ripe fruit. A generous wine with plenty of depth. Fine. (September 2001)

NOW TO 2020+   17.5

1995

The smallest crop of the decade, after 1991, but a very good vintage, indeed, and particularly fine in white wine. These whites were brilliant from the start, but the reds were firmly, even severely, tannic at the outset, and many feared that they would always be a bit hard. They remained so until 2002–2003, when they began to soften up, and very satisfactorily, too, revealing an attractive, plump, ripe succulence underneath and rivalling the 1996s, some of which were being overtaken by their acidities, in elegance. I now prefer the 1995 reds overall.

WEATHER CONDITIONS

There was no real winter in 1994–1995. The early months of the vegetative cycle were dry and mild, indeed fine in March and April. This produced a good *sortie* of buds in both the Chardonnay and Pinot Noir. The bad weather arrived in the middle of May. It snowed on May 13, and the snow remained on the upper slopes. Two days later there was frost on the flatter land below. The weather remained cool and unsettled through June 21 or so—indeed, throughout my visit to sample the 1994 whites in cask, I was wearing a jacket or pullover rather than the normal short-sleeved shirt. The result, naturally, was a long and drawn-out flowering with the inevitable losses resulting from both *coulure* and *millerandage*. The harvest in parts of Chassagne, Chambolle, Gevrey and Marsannay was reduced even further by hail. There were also sporadic outbursts of mildew up and down the Côte. Again, Gevrey-Chambertin was particularly badly affected. The bad flowering affected the red wine crop more than the white. It produced an uneven fruit-setting leading to irregular maturity.

After June 21 the summer arrived, and it then became, paradoxically, too dry and too hot—to the extent of placing stress on the vines and blocking the progress towards maturity. The fine weather continued until September. The two weeks after September 4 were unsettled, and the latter half of this fortnight distinctly rainy, but after the eighteenth the weather cleared. Bouchard Père et Fils began to collect their Pinots on September 21 and their Chardonnays on September 23. Drouhin followed two days later. Most of the Côte de Beaune was picked in dry but cool weather during the following week. By September 30 the harvest was well under way in the Côte de Nuits, and it was at this time that weather broke again. There was a thunderstorm which quickly "turned" the fruit. It became essential to perform a *triage* to eliminate the rotten grapes, both in the vineyard and then later in the winery. Some decided to wait, hoping for a return to finer weather and a gain in sugar content—this eventually came, but a little too late. Most, however, managed to escape at the cost, at the Domaine de la Romanée-Conti for example, of having to reject 30 percent of their crop in their last-picked vineyards: Echézeaux and Grands-Echézeaux.

✣ Rating for the Vintage ✣	
Red	17.5
White	18.5

✣ Size of the Crop ✣ (In hectolitres, excluding generic wine)		
	RED	WHITE
Grands Crus	11,720	3,286
Village and Premiers Crus	173,727	46,575
TOTAL	185,447	49,861

WHERE ARE THE BEST WINES?

- The white wines are impressive and consistent, both geographically and hierarchically.

- Even the lesser red wines of the Côte de Beaune are very good.

- There are lovely red wines in Volnay and in the whole of the southern Côte de Nuits up to Bonnes-Mares.

- The Gevreys are spotty, even at the top levels.

WHEN WILL THE WINES BE AT THEIR BEST?

Despite these wines being 12 years old, there is much to enjoy and admire among the top white wines. The best still have a future. Many of the top red wines, the *grands crus*, have not yet reached their peak. You'll be able to enjoy these well into the 2020s. The *premiers crus* and village wines are ready, although some "only just," and will also keep very well. This is a vintage to enjoy at leisure.

TASTING NOTES

WHITES

Bâtard-Montrachet, 1995
Domaine Jean-Noël Gagnard

Full, rich, firm and gently oaky. The colour shows some evolution. On the palate this has real depth and concentration. Just about *à point*. A very lovely wine. Delicious fruit, and very long and complex. Very vigorous. Very fine plus. Will still improve. (June 2005)

NOW TO 2015   19.0

Bâtard-Montrachet, 1995
Domaine Leflaive

Youthful colour. A concentrated, firm, rather closed-in nose. Full, ample and rich. Plenty of backbone. Still backward. But profound and classy, with very good acidity. This is clean, and has lots of fruit and depth. Only just ready. Fine plus. (March 2006)

NOW TO 2015   18.0

Bâtard-Montrachet, 1995
Domaine Ramonet

Magnum. Youthful colour. Very fresh, vigorous nose. Still a bit closed at first. Full, ripe, concentrated, and rich, but with very fine acidity. Lots of depth and very high quality. Only just ready. Very fine plus. (September 2005)

NOW TO 2015   19.0

Bâtard-Montrachet, 1995
Domaine Étienne Sauzet

Discreet at first on the nose. Rich. Very lovely concentrated fruit and balance. Classy. Intense. Ripe and fat. None of the usual four-square aspect of Bâtard. Still very young. Subtle and complex. Very fine. (March 2001)

NOW TO 2014   18.5

Beaune, Sur les Grèves, 1995
Domaine Germain Père et Fils/
Château de Chorey-lès-Beaune

Quite oaky. Fullish, broad flavoured and slightly spicy. Medium-full body. Good depth and interest. Good plus. (June 2005)

NOW TO 2010+   15.5

Bienvenues-Bâtard-Montrachet, 1995
Domaine Bachelet-Ramonet

A delicate example, yet stylish, fragrant and well balanced. It lacks a little thrust and depth. But it is ripe, fruity and *à point* now. Very good plus. (June 2005)

NOW TO 2011   16.5

Bienvenues-Bâtard-Montrachet, 1995
Domaine Paul Pernot et Fils

Lovely nose. Mature, but vigorous and concentrated. Fullish on the palate. Quite masculine for a Bienvenues-Bâtard-Montrachet, but that is the vintage. Lovely, classy fruit. Very good grip. Mature, but lots of dimension and energy behind it. Very lovely long, complex, classy finish. Very fine plus. (June 2006)

NOW TO 2020   19.0

Bienvenues-Bâtard-Montrachet, 1995
Domaine Ramonet

Some development on the colour. Rich, nutty, mellow and buttery. Full bodied. Splendidly fruity. Slightly smoky. Very good grip. Great class. Very long and complex. Very lovely. Great energy at the end. Very fine indeed. Only just ready. (March 2005)

NOW TO 2020   19.0

Chassagne-Montrachet, Blanchot-Dessus, 1995
Domaine Darviot-Perrin

Fresh colour. The nose is stylish, if without a great deal of depth and concentration. Medium body. Fragrant, balanced and pure. But it lacks weight and complexity. Decent length. Very good. (September 2003)

DRINK SOON   16.0

Chassagne-Montrachet, La Boudriotte, 1995
Domaine Blain-Gagnard

Soft, ripe, classy and now mature on the nose. On the palate medium-full bodied. Fully developed. Gentle, ample, ripe and seductive. But it doesn't have the backbone and depth of Ramonet's 1995 Boudriotte. Very good indeed. (October 2002)

NOW TO 2009   17.0

Chassagne-Montrachet, La Boudriotte, 1995
Domaine Ramonet

Firm, full, rich and classy nose. Still youthful. Lovely on the palate. Very good depth and complexity. Excellent grip. Full body. This is fine and will last very well. Long. Super. (October 2002)

NOW TO 2015   17.5

Chassagne-Montrachet, En Cailleret, 1995
Domaine Louis Jadot

Closed at first. Rich, abundant and very classy on the nose. Similar depth and dimension on the palate. Still very young. It will still get better. Very fresh. Lovely fruit. Fine plus. (June 2003)

NOW TO 2010+   18.5

Chassagne-Montrachet, Les Caillerets, 1995
Domaine Bachelet-Ramonet et Fils

Light golden colour. Quite evolved nose. Some oak. Not much concentration or depth here. A little feeble indeed. But still quite fresh. Honeyed at the end. Quite good plus. (August 2005)

DRINK SOON   14.5

Chassagne-Montrachet, Les Caillerets, 1995
Domaine Marc Colin et Fils

Youthful colour. Fresh, clean, concentrated nose. Lots of vigour and depth. Not a lot of oak. Full, ripe, stylish and complex on the palate. Round and full of energy. Peachy fruit. Still nicely a little austere. Long and multidimensional at the end. This is a fine example. (February 2006)

NOW TO 2012+   17.5

Chassagne-Montrachet, Les Caillerets, 1995
Domaine Jean-Noël Gagnard

Magnum. Ample, ripe, fullish, clean, succulent nose. Fullish body. Gently oaky. Very pure and intensely flavoured. Very good grip. Lots of class. Still youthful and vigorous. This is very fine. Only just ready. (July 2006)

NOW TO 2015   18.5

Chassagne-Montrachet, Les Caillerets, 1995
Domaine Jean Pillot et Fils

Good colour. Mature but still fresh. Rich, full nose. Lots of ripe fruit. Lots of depth. Very gently oaky. *À point.* Not the greatest of vigour now, so drink soon. At first a fine, ample, mature white Burgundy. But got rather sulphury as it evolved. In the end very good at best. (February 2006)

NOW TO 2010   16.0

Chassagne-Montrachet, Les Champs Gain, 1995
Domaine Jean-Noël Gagnard

Marvellously flowery on both nose and palate. Great energy. Very classy. Slight touch of oak. Caroline Lestimé says a touch of muscat on the nose and in the grapes when you eat them. To me, Meursault Charmes characteristics. Fullish body. Very pure. Splendid grip. Lovely. Fine. (June 2002)

NOW TO 2010   17.5

Chassagne-Montrachet, Clos de la Maltroye, 1995
Domaine Jean-Noël Gagnard

Classy, minerally, very vigorous nose. Lovely, balanced, restrained fruit on the palate. Medium-full body. Cool and complex. Very elegant. Very long. Fine. (June 2005)

NOW TO 2010+   17.5

Chassagne-Montrachet, Clos de la Truffière, 1995
Maison Vincent Girardin

Quite evolved on the nose. Rather more so than it should be. Medium to medium-full body. Fragrant. More an up-the-mountain Puligny (La Garenne) in style than a Chassagne. Yet good acidity. Elegant, ripe, peachy fruit. Good positive finish. For reasonably early drinking. But very good plus. (March 2001)

DRINK SOON   16.5

Chassagne-Montrachet, Morgeot, 1995
Domaine Jacques Gagnard-Delagrange

Youthful colour. Rich, youthful nose. Plenty of substance, depth and concentration here. Plus a touch of oak. Fullish body. A lot of complex, ripe, peachy fruit. Lots of class and very fine balance. Still very youthful. Long and lovely. Fine. (October 2005)

NOW TO 2015   17.5

Chassagne-Montrachet, Morgeot, 1995
Domaine René Lamy-Pillot

The colour is now a light gold. Still very fresh, though, on both nose and palate. Very gently oaky. Good depth. Very good grip. No lack of fruit or elegance. Holding up very well. No hurry to drink. Fresh. Yet mellow. Very good indeed. (February 2006)

NOW TO 2010+   17.0

Chassagne-Montrachet, Les Morgeots, 1995
Domaine Bachelet-Ramonet

Fresh, mature colour and nose. Medium to medium-full body. Crisp. Very gently oaky. Not very concentrated. But elegant and quite intense. Ripe and clean. Not a bit heavy. Very good plus. *À point* and no hurry to drink up. (December 2005)

NOW TO 2012   16.5

Chassagne-Montrachet, La Romanée, 1995
Domaine Bachelet-Ramonet

Good freshness, decently balanced and even elegant. But not really enough weight, depth and concentration. Only quite good. (September 2003)

DRINK SOON   14.0

Chassagne-Montrachet, Les Ruchottes, 1995
Domaine Ramonet

Full. Very concentrated. Still very youthful. Very lovely fruit. Real depth. Lots and lots of substance here. High quality. Very fine. (May 2005)

NOW TO 2020   18.5

Chevalier-Montrachet, 1995
Domaine Bouchard Père et Fils

Still a little closed on the nose. Full, rich, very concentrated and very classic. A profound wine.

Fat, youthful, vigorous and very, very fine. Long and lovely. Only just ready. Will still improve. Marvellous after half an hour. (May 2004)

NOW TO 2018   19.0

Chevalier-Montrachet, 1995
Domaine Michel Colin-Deléger et Fils

Evolved colour. Full, concentrated, aromatic nose. A very full wine on the palate. Almost the size of a red wine. Excellent grip. Really rich and fat. Real character. Very profound. Very concentrated. My worry is that it is a bit over-evolved. (February 2003)

DRINK SOON   19.0

Corton-Charlemagne, 1995
Domaine Bonneau du Martray

Full, firm, rich, very concentrated nose. Some oak. Really fine. Marvellous depth and distinction. Excellent. Only just about ready. (November 2005)

NOW TO 2015+   19.5

Corton-Charlemagne, 1995
Domaine Bouchard Père et Fils

Firm, closed, full, backward nose. This is quite a full, rich wine, and it is still developing, indeed a bit adolescent now. Very good grip. Concentrated. Still closed at first. Underneath, there is high quality, just a little oak, and lots of substance. It took time to come out of the glass. Excellent finish. (June 2000)

NOW TO 2020   19.0

Corton-Charlemagne, 1995
Domaine Bruno Clair

Magnum. Very youthful on the nose. Rich, full and minerally. Big and austere, and somewhat adolescent. The wood and fat don't show yet. Classy. But difficult to see quite how good it really is. Very clean, pure and very long. Very good, indeed, upward. (June 2001)

NOW TO 2010+   17.0

Corton-Charlemagne, 1995
Domaine Duchet

Ample, plump nose. Quite developed. Ripe and balanced. Holding up well. This has good depth and class. Very good plus. (June 2005)

NOW TO 2012   16.5

Corton-Charlemagne, 1995
Domaine Michel Juillot

Very classy, clean nose. Full, firm and youthful. Profound. Pure and clean. Rich, mineral and compact. Lots of definition and very fine depth. Multidimensional. Still youthful. Very fine. (November 2001)

NOW TO 2015   18.5

Corton-Charlemagne, 1995
Domaine Louis Latour

A little bit richer and firmer on the nose than the 1996. Medium to medium-full body. A touch of built-in sulphur. Better grip and fruit than the 1996. Not exactly very elegant, but positive finish and very good. (March 2003)

NOW TO 2010   16.0

Corton-Charlemagne, 1995
Maison Roland Remoissenet et Fils

Ripe and fruity. But not a great deal of vigour, real intensity or class. Medium to medium-full body. Balanced. Gently oaky. Decent length. But not the depth of a *grand cru*. Fully ready. Good at best. (March 2001)

DRINK SOON   15.0

Meursault, 1995
Maison Morey-Blanc

Magnum. Juicy, succulent nose. Fullish body. Good depth. Just very gently oaky. Balanced. Long and classy. Good plus. (June 2005)

NOW TO 2010+   15.5

Meursault, Blagny, 1995
Domaine Joseph Matrot

Good grip. Attractive, peachy fruit. Medium-full body. Balanced, rich and long. This is very good. (June 2005)

NOW TO 2010   16.0

Meursault, Les Caillerets, 1995
Domaine François Mikulski

Magnum. Medium to medium-full colour. Slight touch of the stems on the nose. Yet ripe and succulent on the palate. Medium to medium-full body. Good acidity. Attractive. Good plus. (June 2005)

NOW TO 2012   15.5

Meursault, Les Casse-Têtes, 1995
Domaine Patrick Javillier

Ripe and ample, but a bit faded. Medium body. Stylish, balanced and enjoyable nonetheless. Quite good. (June 2005)

DRINK SOON   14.0

Meursault, Charmes, 1995
Domaine Michel Bouzereau et Fils

Youthful colour. Ripe, fresh, mature nose. Not a lot of oak. No great concentration or depth, but clean, fruity and still vigorous. No lack of elegance and balance. Indeed, quite complex at the end. Very good. (August 2005)

NOW TO 2010+   16.0

Meursault, Charmes, 1995
Domaine des Comtes Lafon

Ample and ripe. Well matured. Gently oaky. Fullish body. Rich. Quite exotic. Fully ready. A plump, ample wine. Very good grip. Classy and concentrated. Fine. (June 2005)

NOW TO 2013   17.5

Meursault, Charmes, 1995
Domaine Joseph Matrot

Well-matured colour. Fresh, ripe and concentrated, but still slightly reserved on the nose. Minimal traces of oak. No SO2. Fullish body. Ripe and round. Very good acidity. This expanded in the glass. A lot of depth, concentration and finesse. Individual. Fine. No hurry to drink up. (November 2005)

NOW TO 2010+   17.5

Meursault, Clos de la Barre, 1995
Domaine des Comtes Lafon

Some colour. Quite evolved. Fat nose. A little diffuse. This is not really very exciting. A bit disappointing. Surprisingly neutral. (March 2006)

DRINK SOON   14.0

Meursault, Désirée, 1995
Domaine des Comtes Lafon

Just a little built-in sulphur on the nose. And a bit clumsy anyway, it seems. Better on the palate. A good, oaky base. Good acidity. But it is

all a bit edgy. It lacks harmony. Only fair. Still youthful though. (September 2002)

DRINK SOON   14.0

Meursault, Genevrières, 1995
Domaine Bouchard Père et Fils

This is very impressive. Fresh, concentrated, racy and peachy. This is quite minerally for a Genevrières. Marvellously ripe fruit. Excellent grip. Very, very long. Excellent. Only just about ready. (March 2002)

NOW TO 2010+   18.0

Meursault, Genevrières, 1995
Domaine Charles Jobard

Quite evolved and a touch sulphury. A bit of a disappointment for what it is. Not altogether undrinkable though. Quite full. (July 2001)

DRINK SOON   13.0

Meursault, Genevrières, 1995
Domaine François Jobard

Fresh, youthful, full, firm and pure. Very good grip. This is very classy. Very mineral. Very classic. More Perrières than Genevrières. Long. Fine. Only just ready. (June 2005)

NOW TO 2015   17.5

Meursault, Genevrières, 1995
Domaine des Comtes Lafon

Fullish colour. Slightly more developed than the 1996. Full, rich and vigorous on the nose. Very lovely fruit. Lots of depth and energy. Full bodied and meaty. Gently oaky. Now *à point*. Not quite as much grip at the end as I would have expected, so it is not going to last for decades. But a lovely opulent, fresh, profound, harmonious example. Very typical Genevrières and 1995. Very fine. (September 2005)

NOW TO 2015   18.5

Meursault, Genevrières, 1995
Domaine François Mikulski

Magnum. Quite a deep colour. Fat, buttery nose with a touch of barley sugar. Quite developed. Medium to medium-full body. Yet ripe and still fresh. Good. (June 2005)

NOW TO 2010   15.0

Meursault, Les Gouttes d'Or, 1995
Domaine Pierre Boillot

Fresh colour. Restrained nose. But plenty of depth and concentration here. Quite full on the palate. Very good grip. Rich and concentrated. Just a touch of oak. Still very youthful and vigorous. Lots of class. Fine quality. Will keep very well. (May 2005)

NOW TO 2012　　　　　　　　　　　　　17.5

Meursault, Les Gouttes d'Or, 1995
Maison Joseph de Bucy

Firm nose. Still a bit closed it seems. On the palate firm, good grip, fullish bodied and very stylish. Very long. Will still improve. Fine. (October 2000)

NOW TO 2010　　　　　　　　　　　　　17.5

Meursault, Les Gouttes d'Or, 1995
Domaine des Comtes Lafon

Rich, full, meaty, ripe and very Meursault. Not too four-square. Good grip. Fat, opulent and exotically ripe. Slightly honeyed. Fine plus. (June 2003)

NOW TO 2012　　　　　　　　　　　　　18.0

Meursault, Narvaux, 1995
Domaine Patrick Javillier

Quite evolved but not unduly so. *À point*. Gently oaky. Rich, fat and concentrated. Lots of fruit. Lots of depth together with the Narvaux's minerally-ness. Long. Very good. (June 2000)

DRINK SOON　　　　　　　　　　　　　16.0

Meursault, Les Narvaux, 1995
Domaine Michelot/Mestre-Michelot

Not too heavy a colour, which Michelot's wines can be. Ripe, apricotty nose. Not overripe nor too sulphury, but a little diffuse. Fullish body. Good depth and grip. Rather more to it, and more elegantly presented than the nose would suggest. A little heavy and four-square, but good definition. Positive finish. Good plus. Just about ready. (March 2000)

DRINK SOON　　　　　　　　　　　　　15.5

Meursault, Perrières, 1995
Domaine Robert Ampeau

Very youthful colour. Splendidly ripe, mineral nose. Fullish, round, mellow and profound. Good grip. Very young but now fully ready. Lots of depth. Slightly less grip than I would have expected from Ampeau. But very good indeed. (March 2005)

NOW TO 2012　　　　　　　　　　　　　17.0

Meursault, Perrières, 1995
Domaine Darviot-Perrin

Fresh colour. Very fresh, very youthful, very minerally on the nose. Still a little tight at first. Very pure and clean. Not at all marked by the oak. Very good depth and style. Very good indeed. Only just about ready. (May 2003)

NOW TO 2015　　　　　　　　　　　　　17.0

Meursault, Perrières, 1995
Domaine des Comtes Lafon

Youthful colour. Firm, rich, concentrated, youthful nose. Excellent acidity. Now à point. Full body. Very fresh and clean. Very vigorous. Plenty of depth. Quite firm. Marvellously ripe, minerally and fruity. Great class. Excellent. (June 2004)

NOW TO 2020　　　　　　　　　　　　　19.5

Meursault, Perrières, 1995
Domaine Guy Roulot

Magnum. Very lovely nose. Rich, minerally, ripe and peachy. Classic and *à point*. This is very lovely. Very fresh and vigorous. Very complex. Very elegant. Fine plus. (June 2005)

NOW TO 2012　　　　　　　　　　　　　18.0

Meursault, Poruzots, 1995
Domaine François Jobard

Fullish, rich, fat, meaty and spicy. Vigorous. Lots of depth. This is very good plus. (June 2005)

NOW TO 2012+　　　　　　　　　　　　16.5

Meursault, Tessons, 1995
Domaine Pierre Morey

A monster of concentration. Still splendidly youthful. Very lovely fruit and class. Real *premier cru* quality. Rich. Lots of dimension. Very, very long at the end. Still not ready. (September 2002)

NOW TO 2018   17.5

Meursault, Tessons, Clos de mon Plaisir, 1995
Domaine Guy Roulot

Magnum. Quite a full, firm nose with a little built-in sulphur. A little rigid on the palate. I expected a bit more fruit and vigour here. Only fair. (June 2005)

DRINK SOON   13.5

Le Montrachet, 1995
Domaine Bouchard Père et Fils

Still very closed but very impressive. Full and concentrated on the nose. Excellent grip. Very profound and very lovely. This is still very youthful. Very lovely fruit. Complex and harmonious. Very long. Very aristocratic. Very fine plus. (March 2005)

NOW TO 2018+   19.0

Montrachet, 1995
Domaine du Marquis De Laguiche/
Maison Joseph Drouhin

Very lovely nose. Pure, composed and very profound. Excellent fruit. Harmonious and very classy. This is understated but very, very long and complex. Marvellous. (June 2005)

NOW TO 2015+   20.0

Pernand-Vergelesses, 1995
Domaine Germain Père et Fils/
Château de Chorey-lès-Beaune

Fresh nose. Good fruit. Medium body. Highish acidity. Slightly austere, but clean and not too oaky. Holding up well. Quite good. Drink soon. (June 2005)

DRINK SOON   14.0

Puligny-Montrachet, 1995
Domaine Jean-Marc Boillot

Magnum. Ripe, plump, succulent, vigorous nose. Lots of depth and style for a village wine. Neat and peachy on the palate. Medium to medium-full body. Long. Good plus. (June 2005)

NOW TO 2010   15.5

Puligny-Montrachet, 1995
Domaine Louis Carillon et Fils

Lovely nose. Gently oaky, ripe and concentrated. Excellent acidity. Very pure. Splendid depth and interest for a village wine. Fullish body. Ripe. Lots of vigour. Very fine grip. Excellent fruit. A really lovely example of a village wine. (October 2001)

NOW TO 2010   17.5

Puligny-Montrachet, 1995
Domaine Leflaive

Full. Still very youthful. Firm, concentrated and very vigorous. Confirmation of the return to form of the domaine this year. Not yet ready. Full body. Very good grip. Clean and definitive. Excellent for a village example. (January 2001)

NOW TO 2010   17.0

Puligny-Montrachet, Champ Canet, 1995
Domaine Jean-Marc Boillot

Some hints of noble rot on the nose. Dried apricot and peach. Full body. Very vigorous. Great acidity. Very ample. Very concentrated. Very complex. This is a big wine. Still an infant. Lots of depth. Fine. (June 2006)

NOW TO 2015   17.5

Puligny-Montrachet, Champ Canet, 1995
Domaine Étienne Sauzet

Rich, ripe and exotic. Almost a touch of *pourriture* noble on the nose. Some oak. Medium-full body. Opulent. Fully ready but fresh, complex and very good indeed. (June 2005)

NOW TO 2010   17.0

Puligny-Montrachet, Les Champs Gain, 1995
Domaine Bouchard Père et Fils

Quite evolved on the colour and on the nose. A little oxidised. No. (April 2005)

(SEE NOTE)

Puligny-Montrachet, Les Champs Gain, 1995
Domaine des Comtes Lafon

Plump, ripe, gentle nose. On the palate medium body. Has lost a little of its fruit. But good grip. Good. (June 2005)

DRINK SOON   15.0

Puligny-Montrachet, Les Combettes, 1995
Domaine Robert Ampeau

Very fresh. Stylish, pure and concentrated. Very minimum oak. Fullish body. Intense, pure and youthful. Lovely finish. Fine. (October 2005)

NOW TO 2015   17.5

Puligny-Montrachet, Les Demoiselles, 1995
Domaine Michel Colin-Deléger et Fils/
Mme Françoise Colin

Now mature. A touch of the opulent as well as rich. Fullish body. Ample and balanced. Quite concentrated. Lots of depth and plenty of vigour. This is a fine wine. (December 2003)

NOW TO 2010   17.5

Puligny-Montrachet, Les Folatières, 1995
Domaine d'Auvenay

Lemon gold colour. Intensely flavoured, youthful, very concentrated nose. Just a touch of oak. A wine made for the long term which is only just ready. Full bodied. Rich. Excellent peachy-exotic fruit flavours. Quite powerful. Very fine. (October 2005)

NOW TO 2020   18.5

Puligny-Montrachet, Les Folatières, 1995
Domaine Joseph Drouhin

Quite a developed colour. Full, succulent, gently oaky nose. Rich, ample, very classy wine. Good grip. Lots of depth. Opulent for a 1995 and quite ready to drink. Fine. (March 2001)

NOW TO 2010   17.5

Puligny-Montrachet, Les Folatières, 1995
Domaine Paul Pernot et Fils

Rich, full and classy on the nose. Lots of depth and energy. Full and rich, and subtle and well balanced on the palate. Vigorous. Very fine. (June 2003)

NOW TO 2010+   18.5

Puligny-Montrachet, La Garenne, 1995
Domaine Louis Jadot

Ripe, fullish and firm. Very good acidity. Very vigorous. Lots of depth and complexity for a Garenne. Very good. (June 2005)

NOW TO 2012   16.0

Puligny-Montrachet, Clos de la Garenne, 1995
Domaine Duc de Magenta/Maison Louis Jadot

Full, rich and concentrated. Good grip, of course. Sappy and nutty. Very lovely fruit and vigour. Long and complex. A delicious bottle with a touch of roasted chestnuts at the end. Lots of life here. Very fine. (June 2001)

NOW TO 2015   18.5

Puligny-Montrachet, Les Perrières, 1995
Domaine Louis Carillon et Fils

Fullish, fresh and gently oaky. Very concentrated. Very classy. Very good grip. Lovely fruit. Now just about *à point*. This is balanced, rich, mellow and vigorous. Very lovely indeed. (March 2003)

NOW TO 2010+   18.5

Puligny-Montrachet, Les Pucelles, 1995
Domaine Bouchard Père et Fils

Quite powerful. Lovely rich fruit and great intensity. Very good grip. Fullish body. Ample and flowery. Very pure. This is a lovely example. Very long and complex at the end. Fine. (June 2001)

NOW TO 2013   17.5

Puligny-Montrachet, Les Referts, 1995
Domaine Jean-Marc Boillot

Fullish body. Rich and vigorous. Classy, long and complex. Very good plus. (June 2005)

NOW TO 2010+   16.5

Puligny-Montrachet, La Truffière, 1995
Domaine Jean-Marc Boillot

Some botrytis here on the nose. A touch sweeter on the palate than the rest of the series. Medium to medium-full body. Decent grip. But it lacks a little vigour. Good. (June 2005)

NOW TO 2010   15.0

Saint-Aubin, En Remilly, 1995
Domaine Hubert Lamy et Fils

Magnum. Quite a broad, ample nose. Fullish for a Saint-Aubin. Ripe and peachy. Good grip. Still holding up well. Long. Good. (June 2005)

NOW TO 2010   15.0

Auxey-Duresses, Premier Cru, 1995
Domaine du Comte Armand

Good colour. Just a suggestion of development. Quite firm on the nose. But good, stylish fruit underneath. Fullish body on the palate. Quite a lot of tannin. But underneath, plenty of fruit and very good class. Very good. (July 2000)

NOW TO 2015   16.0

Beaune, Clos Des Couchereaux, 1995
Domaine Louis Jadot

Fullish colour. Quite a full, sturdy nose. Still youthful. But ripe and succulent. Softening nicely. Medium-full body. Elegant, succulent and attractively balanced. Fragrant on the finish. Very stylish. Very fine for a Beaune. Just about ready. (October 2005)

NOW TO 2020   17.0

Beaune, Le Clos des Mouches, 1995
Domaine Joseph Drouhin

Medium-full colour. Round, rich, succulent, even quite concentrated on the nose. Medium-full body. Fresh and balanced. Good depth. Not the class but good plus. Plenty of vigour. (June 2005)

NOW TO 2012   15.5

Beaune, Le Clos des Mouches, 1995
Domaine Christophe Violot-Guillemard

Mediu to medium-full colour. Some brown at the rim now. This is a little dense and tannic, and I fear it always will be. Decent fruit, and good depth and acidity. But the tannins are a little dry. Will they soften? I am not confident. Good at best. (June 2001)

NOW TO 2012   15.0

Beaune, Clos des Vignes Franches, 1995
Maison Vincent Girardin

Good, fullish colour. Still youthful. A little tight on the nose at first. Medium-full body. Some tannin. Good fruit underneath and good acidity, too. Quite concentrated. Quite rich. This is certainly very good. But needs time to soften. (October 2002)

NOW TO 2018   15.0

Beaune, Les Cras, 1995
Domaine Germain Père et Fils/
Château de Chorey-lès-Beaune

Magnum. Good colour. Lovely fragrant nose. Lots of class. A beautifully made, profound wine with lots of energy and depth. Lovely long finish. Very complex. Fine. (June 2005)

NOW TO 2015+   17.5

Beaune, Les Grèves, 1995
Domaine Michel Lafarge

Good colour. Full, rich, meaty nose. Slightly four-square, as usual. On the palate medium-full body. A little rigid and astringent at the end. Could have done with a bit more zip. Quite good plus at best. (June 2005)

NOW TO 2010   14.5

Beaune, Grèves, Vigne de l'Enfant Jésus, 1995
Domaine Bouchard Père et Fils

Medium-full colour. Some development. Ripe, round, fragrant nose. Medium to medium-full body. Now fully à point. Rich. Complex. Succulent. Long. Very classy. Very good indeed. (September 2005)

NOW TO 2015   17.0

Beaune, Les Teurons, 1995
Domaine Duchet

Good colour. Slightly four-square on the nose. Better on the palate. Medium-full body. Ripe and fresh. Decent style. Positive finish. Good. (June 2005)

NOW TO 2012   15.0

Beaune, Les Teurons, 1995
Domaine Germain Père et Fils/
Château de Chorey-lès-Beaune

Good colour. Lovely nose. More minerally and less fragrant than their Beaune Cras. Medium-full body. Ripe, complex and classy. More earthy but very good plus. Long, positive finish. (June 2005)

NOW TO 2015   16.5

Beaune, Les Toussaints, 1995
Domaine Albert Morot

Medium-full colour. Quite high, volatile acidity on the nose. Ripe and quite rich, but rather

over-oaked on the palate. A pity. A nice wine underneath here: balanced and fresh. (June 2005)
NOW TO 2010   14.5

Blagny, La Pièce Sous le Bois, 1995
Domaine Florence Lamy/Lamy-Pillot

Good, just about mature colour. Ripe and vigorous. Sophisticated for a Blagny. Fullish body. Balanced. No aggressive tannins. Not a bit lumpy. Very good for what it is. (November 2005)
NOW TO 2012   15.5

Blagny, La Pièce Sous le Bois, 1995
Domaine Paul Pernot et Fils

Medium to medium-full colour, and just about mature. Classy, fragrant nose. Very good fruit. Soft, supple tannins. Balanced. Ripe and elegant. Plenty of interest. Very good. (June 2001)
NOW TO 2009   16.0

Bonnes Mares, 1995
Domaine Bouchard Père et Fils

This was Bouchard's first vintage: 33 acres bought from Drouhin-Larose. Fine colour. Little sign of maturity. Lovely, succulent nose. Raspberry fruit. Very good tannins. This is fullish and still a way from maturity. But the structure is classy, the fruit concentrated and the acidity very big. This is fine plus. (June 2001)
NOW TO 2030   18.0

Bonnes Mares, 1995
Domaine Fougeray de Beauclair

Medium-full colour. Fully mature. Rich, ripe and slightly artisanal on the nose. Ample. Medium-full body. Fully ready. Fresh. Classier on the palate than on the nose. Long. Fine, positive finish. (June 2005)
NOW TO 2020   17.5

Bonnes Mares, 1995
Domaine Georges Roumier et Fils

Fullish colour. Still immature. Marvellous nose. A proper Bonnes Mares. Splendid concentration and depth. Splendidly rich as well. Almost sweet. Balanced, profound and aristocratic. Multidimensional. A marvellous bottle. (June 2005)
2009 TO 2030   20.0

Bonnes Mares, 1995
Domaine Comte Georges de Vogüé

Full, immature colour. Lots of concentration and breed here. Full but not aggressive on the nose. Lovely high-class fruit. This is an exciting wine. Full body. The tannins are now softening. But it still needs time. Rich, balanced and succulent. Very classy. Very fine plus. (June 2006)
NOW TO 2025   19.0

Chambertin, 1995
Domaine Leroy

Fullish colour. Still youthful. Menthol on the nose. Nicely cool after this oxidised a bit in the glass. But also just a little dense. Not dense on the palate. Fullish body. Excellent balance and structure. Fresh. Very long. Very complex. Very lovely. (April 2000)
NOW TO 2020   19.5

Chambertin, 1995
Domaine Armand Rousseau

Magnum. Medium-full, mature colour. Very lovely, subtle nose. Very concentrated and very lovely. As so often, a great wine. Rather more closed than the Clos de Bèze. Still a bit of unresolved tannin. Marvellous fruit. Splendid balance. The complete example. Still needs time. Very lovely long finish. (June 2005)
2009 TO 2030   20.0

Chambertin, 1995
Domaine Jean Trapet Père et Fils

Very good colour. Ample, rich, fat, opulent nose. Still a little closed but no exaggerated tannins. Fullish body. Rich. Lots of lovely fruit here. Very good grip. Lots of depth and concentration. Lots of class. Lovely finish. Very, very long. This is very fine. (June 2005)
2009 TO 2030   18.5

Chambertin, Clos de Bèze, 1995
Domaine Armand Rousseau

Fullish colour. Ample, rich, ripe, concentrated, succulent nose. Full bodied, profound and very lovely. Splendid depth and energy. Marvellous class and balance. Really splendid. Very, very long and lovely. Just about ready. (June 2005)

NOW TO 2030 19.5

Chambolle-Musigny, 1995
Domaine Georges Roumier et Fils

Magnum. Good colour. Ripe and abundant on the nose. Medium-full body. Still youthful. Lovely fruit for a village wine. Very good grip. Good energy. Clean, vigorous and very long on the palate. Very good plus. (June 2005)

NOW TO 2020 16.5

Chambolle-Musigny, Premier Cru, 1995
Domaine Jean-Jacques Confuron

Medium-full colour. Just about mature. Fragrant nose. Not too oaky. Medium to medium-full body. Slightly rigid on the palate. This lacks suppleness and fragrance. A bit inflexible. Merely good. (June 2005)

NOW TO 2015 15.0

Chambolle-Musigny, Les Amoureuses, 1995
Domaine Amiot-Servelle

Good, fullish, vigorous colour. Lovely fragrant nose. Still quite youthful. Plenty of weight and depth. Ripe, energetic and stylish. Very good grip. Long and very good indeed. Just a slight leanness on the finish as it developed. Only just ready. (February 2006)

NOW TO 2020+ 17.0

Chambolle-Musigny, Les Amoureuses, 1995
Domaine Robert Groffier

Medium-full, vigorous colour. Very lovely nose. Aromatic and succulent. Silky and complex. Medium-full body. Excellent, intensely flavoured fruit and concentration, and really good grip. Very ripe tannins. Splendid follow-through. Intense, sweet and concentrated finish. Very, very long. Very fine. (October 2005)

NOW TO 2020 18.5

Chambolle-Musigny, Les Amoureuses, 1995
Domaine Jacques-Frédéric Mugnier

Medium to medium-full colour. Fully ready. Ripe nose. But slightly diffuse. Medium body.

Lacks concentration, grip and depth. Disappointing. (June 2005)

NOW TO 2012 14.0

Chambolle-Musigny, Les Amoureuses, 1995
Domaine Comte Georges de Vogüé

Fullish colour. Still very youthful. Rich, quite chocolaty, concentrated and intense, but very Chambolle in structure. Very classy. Medium-full body. Some tannin still to resolve. Great class and depth. A really splendid example. Very, very intense. Long and lovely. (June 2001)

NOW TO 2025+ 19.0

Chambolle-Musigny, Aux Beaux Bruns, 1995
Domaine Denis Mortet

Magnum. Huge colour. Rather over-extracted on the nose. Slightly reduced, too. Better on the palate. Rich and full, ripe and succulent, and with very good grip. Slightly overdone but, nevertheless, very good indeed. Will still improve. (June 2005)

NOW TO 2024 17.0

Chambolle-Musigny, Charmes, 1995
Domaine Ghislaine Barthod

Good colour. Very lovely, succulently fruity nose. Lots of lovely ripe fruit here. Medium-full body. Ripe and ample. Plumper, very pure and well balanced. Lovely. Just about ready. (June 2005)

NOW TO 2020+ 17.5

Chambolle-Musigny, Les Cras, 1995
Maison Dominique Laurent

Fullish colour. A little reduced on the nose. But quite full and rich, and not too oaky underneath. Fullish, ripe and intense. Good, ripe tannins. Good grip. Quite a masculine Chambolle but plenty of depth. Fine. (March 2005)

NOW TO 2025 17.5

Chapelle-Chambertin, 1995
Domaine des Tilleuls/Philippe Livera

Medium colour. This is fresh and classy, but it doesn't have quite the depth and individuality of a grand cru. If it were Lavaux Saint-Jacques, it would be fine, but for Chapelle-Chambertin it is only very good indeed. Lovely fruit, though, and classy, oaky and balanced. Long finish. Just about ready but will keep well. (November 2005)

NOW TO 2018   17.0

Chapelle-Chambertin, 1995
Domaine Jean Trapet Père et Fils
Good colour. Aromatic, plump nose. Good, fresh fruit. No undue tannin. Good grip. Medium-full body. Fresh and plump on the palate. Very good vigour and concentration. Ripe, clean fruit. Very good balance. Good definition. Very good indeed. (June 2005)

NOW TO 2019   17.0

Charmes-Chambertin, 1995
Domaine Denis Bachelet
Fullish colour. Only a little sign of maturity. Full, rich, concentrated nose. Quite firm. But by no means tough and tannic. Full body on the palate. Good grip. Just a little unresolved tannin. Very classy and very harmonious. Still a little raw. Lots of depth, dimension and concentration. Lovely fruit. Potentially fine plus. Still needs time. (June 2005)

NOW TO 2028   18.0

Charmes-Chambertin, 1995
Domaine Bernard Dugat-Py
Full colour. Rich, full, ripe and concentrated. Oaky but not excessively so. There is enough wine here to balance it. Fullish body. Very fine, ripe, cool, succulent fruit. Long, energetic and balanced. Very fine. (April 2006)

NOW TO 2020   18.5

Charmes-Chambertin, 1995
Domaine Claude Dugat
Fullish colour. A little development. Brilliant nose. Very composed. Very concentrated. Understated. Fullish body. Complete. Very concentrated. Essence of wine. Still some tannin. This has intensity, vigour and great class. Super. Just about ready. (April 2006)

NOW TO 2035   19.5

Charmes-Chambertin, 1995
Domaine Dujac
Medium-full colour. Fully mature. Soft, ripe, sweet and silky on the nose. Medium to medium-full body. Smooth. Very Dujac. Very fresh and fruity. Very seductive. Long. Fine. Fully ready. (April 2006)

NOW TO 2020   17.5

Charmes-Chambertin, 1995
Domaine Geantet-Pansiot
Medium-full colour. Just a little maturity. Slightly closed on the nose. A biggish, meaty wine with plenty of fruit but a lack of real flair. Fresh, balanced and juicy nevertheless. Good grip. Very good, indeed, if slightly rigid. (April 2006)

NOW TO 2020+   17.0

Charmes-Chambertin, 1995
Domaine Louis Jadot
Fullish, vigorous colour. Ripe, quite structured but rich, concentrated nose. But still closed-in. Full body. No hard edges. Youthful. But the tannins are now absorbed. Lots of class and depth. Vigorous. Fine plus. (April 2006)

NOW TO 2025   18.0

Charmes-Chambertin, 1995
Domaine Henri Perrot-Minot
Medium to medium-full colour. Quite mature. More succulent, less four-square than his 1995 Mazoyères. Medium to medium-full weight. Fresh, ripe and succulent. Not a bit hard. Long, stylish and ready for drinking. Very good finish. Fine. (April 2006)

NOW TO 2018   17.5

Charmes-Chambertin, 1995
Domaine Armand Rousseau
Good, fullish colour. Much less developed than their 1996. Fragrant, concentrated, balanced and classy on the nose. Fullish body. Plump. Very ripe tannins. Smooth and velvety. Lots of intensity and class. Very harmonious. Streets better than their 1996. Lovely, succulent finish. Fine. (April 2006)

NOW TO 2020   17.5

Charmes-Chambertin, 1995
Domaine Jacky Truchot

Fullish colour. Rich nose. Fresh. Lots of depth. On the palate this is now getting quite soft. Not too tannic. Good acidity. Medium-full body. Now just about ready. Decent style, but not the greatest concentration and richness. Very good. (October 2002)

NOW TO 2012   16.0

Charmes-Chambertin, Très Vieilles Vignes, 1995
Domaine Joseph Roty

Very full colour. Still very youthful. Chocolaty nose. Full, rich, concentrated and fat. Quite tannic. Lots of fruit. Very good grip. Slightly dense on the follow-through. Still young. But cool and very long. Not over-extracted—but on the verge. So, fine rather than very fine. Will still improve. (April 2005)

NOW TO 2026   17.5

Chassagne-Montrachet, Clos Saint-Jean, 1995
Domaine Guy Amiot et Fils

Rather more tannic than the 1996. More adolescent. Good grip and concentration. Medium-full body. Rich. Rather more to it than the 1996. I prefer this. Potentially very good. (January 2001)

NOW TO 2012   16.0

Clos des Lambrays, 1995
Domaine des Lambrays

Medium to medium-full colour. Fully mature. Fragrant nose. A touch of the stems. A fresh, medium-full-bodied, stylish wine. Good dimension. Long and complex at the end. Fully ready. Fine. (June 2005)

NOW TO 2020   17.5

Clos de la Roche, 1995
Domaine Dujac

Medium-full colour. Fully ready. Classy, rich, fresh nose. Lots of lovely fruit here. Medium to medium-full body. The fruit is very ripe and very well balanced. Complex and long. Lovely finish. Fine plus. (June 2005)

NOW TO 2020   18.0

Clos de la Roche, 1995
Maison Camille Giroud

Medium-full colour. Full, firm, rich, succulent and old viney on the nose. Rich, full bodied and chocolaty on the palate. Some tannin to resolve. Very good grip. Old viney. Very lovely long, classy finish. Very fine. (June 2005)

NOW TO 2025   18.5

Clos de la Roche, 1995
Domaine Leroy

Medium-full colour. Some evolution. Ripe nose. But nowhere near the depth and grip of the 1996. Medium-full body. Fruity and balanced, but quite open. A little tannin. But not the volume and intensity of the 1996. Very good indeed. (April 2000)

NOW TO 2012   17.0

Clos de la Roche, 1995
Domaine Hubert Lignier

Fullish colour. Rich, fat, concentrated, old viney. Not too oaky. Medium-full body. Cool, ripe and harmonious. Not quite the drive and concentration it could have had. But fine nevertheless. Very classy. Still a little raw. (June 2005)

NOW TO 2025   17.5

Clos de la Roche, 1995
Domaine Armand Rousseau

Medium-full colour. Just about mature. Splendidly rich, concentrated, vigorous nose. Lots of intensity if not the greatest of weight. Very classy. Very profound. Medium-full body. Excellent grip. A lot of class. Very lingering, multi-dimensional finish. Fine plus. Only just about ready. (February 2006)

NOW TO 2025   18.0

Clos Saint-Denis, 1995
Maison Champy

Good colour. Slightly hard, *sous bois* tannins on the nose. A bit astringent on the palate. This is by no means *grand cru* quality. Medium-full body. Lacks succulence. Only fair. (January 2001)

NOW TO 2009   14.0

Clos Saint-Denis, 1995
Domaine Dujac

Medium-full colour. Some development. Ripe, aromatic, slightly jammy nose. Medium-full body. Slightly raw rather than tannic. Still rather closed. Quite spicy. Developed in the glass. Potentially very fine. (March 2005)

NOW TO 2025   18.5

Clos Saint-Denis, 1995
Domaine Henri Jouan

Medium-full colour. Still youthful. Just a touch reduced on the nose. Red fruit flavours. Quite soft. Oaky-toasty. Quite sweet on the palate. Medium-full body. Not a lot of depth, but balanced and even concentrated. Very good intensity at the end. Very good plus. (October 2001)

NOW TO 2015   16.5

Clos Saint-Denis, 1995
Maison Remoissenet Père et Fils

Medium-full, mature colour. Well-developed, spicy nose. Medium-full body. Ample. Just a little tannin. Balanced and just about ready. Good plus, but slightly cooked and lacking real elegance. (March 2005)

NOW TO 2015   15.5

Clos de Vougeot, 1995
Domaine Robert Arnoux

Full colour. A little development. Attractive, fragrant, red-fruity nose. Some development. Medium weight. Slightly hard as it developed. A little tannin. Good grip. Slightly austere still but plenty of depth. Lovely finish. Very good indeed. (October 2001)

NOW TO 2018   17.0

Clos de Vougeot, 1995
Domaine Jean-Jacques Confuron

Medium to medium-full colour. Fully mature. Ripe, rich, vigorous and fragrant on the nose. Medium-full body. Balanced and full of fruit if no great depth or energy at the end. Fully ready. Very good plus. (June 2005)

NOW TO 2015   16.5

Clos de Vougeot, 1995
Domaine Anne Gros

Fine colour. Still tannic on the nose. But underneath, plenty of fruit, depth, grip and concentration. Full bodied. A bit tough at present. But promises well. Potentially fine, I think. (June 2003)

NOW TO 2020   17.5

Clos De Vougeot, 1995
Domaine Louis Jadot

Full colour. Rich, concentrated, aromatic nose. Medium-full body. Not a great deal of unresolved tannin. Very good grip. Lovely fruit. Very classy. Very lovely long finish. Fine plus. (March 2005)

NOW TO 2025   18.0

Clos de Vougeot, 1995
Domaine Leroy

Medium-full colour. Some development now. Full, tannic nose. A little adolescent and lumpy at present. Impressive on the palate though. Still young. The tannins are a little bitter, but ripe and concentrated. Slightly *sauvage* but good cassis underneath. Fine. (April 2000)

NOW TO 2015   17.5

Clos de Vougeot, 1995
Domaine Méo-Camuzet

Quite a full colour but not that deep. Slightly tannic on the nose. But not unduly so. On the palate this is fullish, with very lovely, concentrated fruit. Quite a big, meaty wine. Rich. Very good grip. A touch adolescent. Long and lovely. This is fine plus. (March 2001)

NOW TO 2025   18.0

Clos de Vougeot, 1995
Domaine Dr. Georges Mugneret

Medium-full colour. Full, rich and concentrated on the nose. Fullish body. Good grip. The tannins just about resolved. Fine fruit. Plenty of vigour and depth. Lovely pure Pinot. Fine. (June 2005)

NOW TO 2024   17.5

Clos de Vougeot, "Musigni," 1995
Domaine Gros Frère et Soeur
Magnum. Medium-full colour. Slightly attenuated and overblown on the nose. Medium to medium-full body. Rather thin and weedy on the palate. Nothing special. (June 2005)

NOW TO 2010   13.0

Corton, 1995
Domaine Bonneau du Martray
Medium-full, mature colour. Less classy than their Corton *rouge* 2001 which I tasted alongside. Medium weight on the nose. Fragrant and balanced, but with a slightly stringy, rustic touch and a lack of the texture that is in the wine today. Medium body. Ripe enough and balanced enough. Fragrant and fruity. But not enough class. *À point.* Good plus. (June 2005)

NOW TO 2012   15.5

Corton, 1995
Domaine Bouchard Père et Fils
The colour is still quite young. The nose is still a little tight. And the palate still has quite a lot of unresolved tannin. Fresh red fruit behind it. Slightly vegetal and unripe, but this will round off. This is certainly very good, but I don't think it is fine. It will always be a bit austere. (May 2004)

NOW TO 2020   16.0

Corton, Clos des Cortons Faiveley, 1995
Domaine Joseph Faiveley
Full colour. Rich, backward colour. Full, meaty, oaky, rich on the palate. Still a way to go. Doesn't shout out great quality though. Merely very good indeed. (June 2005)

NOW TO 2025   17.0

Corton, Les Maréchaudes, 1995
Domaine Chandon de Briailles
Medium-full colour. Some of the stems on the nose. Ripe and even sweet underneath. Good energy. Medium to medium-full body. Balanced and stylish. Very good, ripe fruit. Long. Very good indeed. (June 2005)

NOW TO 2015   17.0

Corton, Les Pougets, 1995
Domaine Louis Jadot
Fullish colour. Very fine quality here on the nose. Medium-full body. Gently oaky. Very rich and ripe. Excellent grip. Classy, profound and very, very long. Very fine. Just about ready. (June 2005)

NOW TO 2025   18.5

Corton, Renardes, 1995
Domaine Leroy
Fullish, youthful colour. The nose is a bit closed but concentrated, poised, fresh and balanced. Lots of depth here. More tannin than 1996 but slightly less sophisticated. Big, fat and spicy. Good grip. Long and with plenty of complexity. I prefer (April 2000)

NOW TO 2018   17.0

Corton, Renardes, 1995
Domaine du Prince de Mérode
Good colour. Still youthful. Fresh nose. Spicy. Meaty. Not the greatest class. Fullish body. Ample. Good balance. Attractive if no great style. Good vigour. Only just about ready. Good plus. (October 2005)

NOW TO 2012   15.5

Echézeaux, 1995
Domaine Robert Arnoux
Medium-full colour. Still youthful. Rich, succulent, classy nose. Round and fragrant. Plump and with no hard edges. Medium-full body. Some tannin. Good grip. This is ample and full of fruit. Sweet and elegant. Good intensity. Long. Fine. (October 2001)

NOW TO 2018   17.5

Echézeaux, 1995
Domaine Mongeard-Mugneret
Medium-full colour. Slightly vegetally-chocolate on the nose. Medium to medium-full. Quite evolved. As much astringent as tannic. Underneath plump, ripe and attractively succulent. Good grip. Good style. Very good indeed. (October 2005)

NOW TO 2013   17.0

Echézeaux, 1995
Domaine Mugneret-Gibourg

Very good colour. Still very purple. Cool, composed, classic Pinot nose. Very good grip. No excessive tannin or bulk. Lots of class. Lovely fruit. Medium-full body. Some tannin. Good acidity. Very elegant and poised. Long. Vigorous. Still needs some years. Fine plus. (June 2003)

NOW TO 2020   18.0

Echézeaux, 1995
Domaine de la Romanée-Conti

Medium-full colour. Lovely fragrant nose. Ripe and balanced. Generous and charming. Medium-full body. Lovely fruit. Long, succulent and very seductive. Fine. Fully ready. (June 2005)

NOW TO 2020   17.5

Fixin, Clos Marion, 1995
Domaine Fougeray de Beauclair

Well-matured colour. Slightly artisanal nose. Ripe and succulent. Medium to medium-full bodied. Good grip and vigour. Not too unstylish. Positive finish. Quite good. Just about ready. (June 2005)

NOW TO 2015   14.0

Gevrey-Chambertin, Vieilles Vignes, 1995
Domaine Denis Bachelet

Medium-full colour. Ripe, fragrant and very classy on the nose. Lovely fruit here. Medium to medium-full body. Good acidity. Not the greatest fat, depth or strength. But what there is is complex and harmonious. Balanced. Very good. (June 2005)

NOW TO 2015   16.0

Gevrey-Chambertin, Vieilles Vignes, 1995
Domaine Alain Burguet

Magnum. Fullish colour. A full, quite concentrated, slightly beefy wine. Medium-full body. Still some tannin. Plenty of depth and class. Very good grip. Needs time. Very good indeed. (June 2005)

NOW TO 2020   17.0

Gevrey-Chambertin, Vieilles Vignes, 1995
Domaine Goillot-Bernollin

Full colour. Just a hint of development. Rich, fat, tannic, slightly peppery nose. Slightly spicy. Fullish body. Slightly sturdy but good. (August 2000)

NOW TO 2015   15.0

Gevrey-Chambertin, Premier Cru, 1995
Domaine Bernard Maume

Full, firm, rich, chunky nose. Plenty of depth here. Good class, too. A wine with a lot of backbone. Fullish body. Some tannins. Slightly raw and metallic, and with a pronounced CO_2 as if some of the *malos* took place in bottle. Ripe. Slightly solid, chunky and astringent. It lacks a little style. But good plus. (March 2000)

NOW TO 2009   15.5

Gevrey-Chambertin, Les Cazetiers, 1995
Domaine Bruno Clair

Fullish colour. Classy, fragrant nose. Ripe, nicely austere and very well balanced. Medium-full body. Lacks a little energy, but fragrant, poised and quietly successful. Longer and more complex on the follow-through. Very good indeed. Fully ready. (June 2005)

NOW TO 2015   17.0

Gevrey-Chambertin, Les Cazetiers, 1995
Domaine Sérafin Père et Fils

Good colour. Ripe, full, balanced and fragrant on the nose. Oaky but not excessively so. Fullish body. Rich. Still some unresolved tannin. But good grip and plenty of vigour. Fine. (June 2005)

NOW TO 2020   17.5

Gevrey-Chambertin, Les Champeaux, 1995
Domaine Alain Burguet

Medium-full, mature colour. Slightly overblown on the nose. Slightly weedy on the palate. Young vines at the time. His Vieilles Vignes is immeasurably better. (June 2005)

NOW TO 2010   13.5

Gevrey-Chambertin, En Champeaux, 1995
Domaine Denis Mortet

Bigger and more youthful colour than the 1996. Very full and rich on the nose. Quite a solid, even blockbuster of a wine here. Full bodied and tannic on the palate. But not too solid. Lovely richness, indeed quite a bit fuller than the 1996. No astringency. Very good acidity. This is unexpectedly good. I prefer it to the 1996. Very good indeed. (May 2002)

NOW TO 2020+   17.0

Gevrey-Chambertin, Clos Saint-Jacques, 1995
Domaine Louis Jadot

Full, youthful colour. Firm, concentrated, high-class fruit on the nose. Lots of depth and dimension, but still backward. Full body. Still some tannin. Very good grip. Concentrated, profound and multilayered. Long. Very elegant. Very complex. Very fine but needs time. (June 2005)

NOW TO 2025   18.5

Gevrey-Chambertin, Clos Saint-Jacques, 1995
Domaine Armand Rousseau

At the outset still a little tannic and austere. After 15 minutes, mellow, rich, balanced, fullish and very classy. Long and lovely. Very fine. (June 2004)

NOW TO 2020+   18.5

Gevrey-Chambertin, Aux Combottes, 1995
Domaine Dujac

Medium-full colour. Still youthful. Lovely, fragrant, quite sweet nose. Classy. Medium-full body. No undue tannic structure. Very lovely fruit. The tannins are now soft. Intense. Good grip. Just about ready, but very good intensity and energy. This is very lovely. Very classy. Better than their 1996 Charmes-Chambertin. (October 2005)

NOW TO 2018   18.0

Gevrey-Chambertin, Estournelles-Saint-Jacques, 1995
Domaine Frédéric Esmonin

Fullish colour. Somewhat raw and reserved on the nose. Medium to medium-full body. Not so much tannic as a bit lean. But plenty of depth and quality underneath. Good grip. Potentially ample fruit. What it lacks a little is its elegance. Very good indeed rather than great. (September 2005)

NOW TO 2020   17.0

Gevrey-Chambertin, Lavaux-Saint-Jacques, 1995
Domaine Claude Dugat

Full, firm, youthful colour. Rich, oaky nose. Very good depth and concentration (but not a bit exaggerated). Full body. Very classy tannins. Very pure, rich, ripe fruit. Wholly admirable. Lovely long, vigorous finish. Very fine. Just about ready. (November 2005)

NOW TO 2025   18.5

Gevrey-Chambertin, Lavaux-Saint-Jacques, 1995
Domaine Denis Mortet

Fine colour. Rather less adolescent than the 1996. Not a bit too dense. Very good grip. Lovely fruit. This has both depth and flair. A fine plus 1995. Still needs time, of course, but very promising. Better for the vintage than the 1996 perhaps. (September 2002)

NOW TO 2020   18.0

Griotte-Chambertin, 1995
Domaine Joseph Drouhin

Fullish colour. A touch of brown at the rim. Full, rich, meaty nose. Plenty of depth and not unduly tannic. Full bodied, rich and admirable. Not a bit too much bulk. Good grip. Plenty of depth. Very good concentration on the follow-through. Very fine. Better than the 1996 perhaps. (July 2003)

NOW TO 2026   18.5

Latricières-Chambertin, 1995
Domaine Leroy

Fullish colour. A little development. This is very dense on the nose. Slightly unyielding at present. A little too stewed. Full on the palate. The tannins are less sophisticated than the 1996. Good grip. But not the poise or the flair. Very good indeed. (April 2002)

NOW TO 2016   17.0

Latricières-Chambertin, 1995
Domaine Jean Trapet Père et Fils

Very good colour. Rich but closed-in nose, with a touch of the usual robustness and rusticity of Latricières. Fullish body. Spicy. A little tannin. Good energy. Rich, fat and ample. Long. Good definition. Fine. (March 2004)

NOW TO 2024   17.5

Marsannay, Les Longeroies, 1995
Domaine Bruno Clair

Good, fresh colour. Quite a firm nose. Fullish for a Marsannay. Good grip. Good depth. Still needs to soften. Good fruit. Very good for what it is, but at present a little rigid. (June 2005)

NOW TO 2017   14.5

Mazis-Chambertin, 1995
Domaine Joseph Faiveley

Fine colour. Rich and plummy on the nose. Full, but no longer at all closed and tannic. Vigorous. Good grip. This is ripe and succulent. Elegant. Already quite smooth, very suprisingly. Lots of life. (June 2003)

NOW TO 2025   18.5

Mazis-Chambertin, 1995
Hospices de Beaune

Élevé by Frédéric Esmonin. Full colour. A touch of brown. Rich, ripe, ample and plummy on the nose. Fullish body. Just about ready. Old-viney concentration. Very good grip. Cool and classy. Lovely. Very fine. (April 2005)

NOW TO 2025   18.5

Mazis-Chambertin, 1995
Domaine Philippe Naddef

Medium-full colour. Now some evolution. Firm on the nose, with a touch of mint, but good depth. Not too tough. Medium-full body. Some tannin from the oak. Good grip though. Needs 2 to 3 years to round off. Very good indeed. (April 2005)

NOW TO 2020   17.0

Mazis-Chambertin, 1995
Domaine Armand Rousseau

Medium-full, mature colour. Ripe, round, ample and fragrant on the nose. Medium-full body. Ripe, almost sweet. Very classy. Very harmonious. Long, fragrant and profound. Very fine. (April 2005)

NOW TO 2025   18.0

Mazoyères-Chambertin, 1995
Domaine Henri Perrot-Minot

Medium-full colour. Fresher than his 1995 Charmes-Chambertin. Slight touch of mint.

A little four-square on the nose. Better on the palate. But drier and less complex than his Charmes. Good but no better. (April 2006)

NOW TO 2012   15.0

Monthelie, 1995
Domaine Paul Garaudet

Good colour. Ripe, rich and sturdy. Slightly artisanal. Medium-full body. Slightly four-square. Lacks distinction. (June 2005)

NOW TO 2010   13.5

Monthelie, 1995
Domaine Pierre Morey

Magnum. Medium colour. Fragrant, Volnay-ish nose. Classy. Medium body. Could have been a bit more succulent on the palate. (June 2005)

NOW TO 2010   14.0

Morey-Saint-Denis, Aux Charmes, 1995
Domaine Lignier-Michelot

Medium to medium-full colour. Fully mature. Richer, riper and with more depth than the En la Rue de Vergy. Medium-full body. A little raw still. Balanced and fragrant. Lovely finish. Very good plus. (June 2005)

NOW TO 2020   16.5

Morey-Saint-Denis, En la Rue de Vergy, 1995
Domaine Bruno Clair

Ripe, with a lean, apricotty rather than peachy flavour. An oaky base. Medium to medium-full body. Good grip. But on the palate the oak dominates a bit. A little one-dimensional. But fresh and pleasant. Good. (December 2001)

DRINK SOON   15.0

Morey-Saint-Denis, En la Rue de Vergy, 1995
Domaine Lignier-Michelot

Medium to medium-full colour. Fully mature. Ripe, fragrant, succulent nose. Good depth and style. Medium to medium-full body. Fresh, elegant, if not that complex, but very good for a village wine. Fully ready. (June 2005)

NOW TO 2015   15.0

Musigny, 1995
Domaine Leroy

Fullish, vigorous colour. Firmer than the 1996 on the nose. More structured. Very good grip. Fullish body. Very classy. Splendidly ripe tannins. Aristocratic and harmonious. This is a very lovely example indeed. Very fine plus. (April 2000)
NOW TO 2020   19.0

Musigny, Vieilles Vignes, 1995
Domaine Comte Georges de Vogüé

Fine colour. Still immature. Still a bit closed-in on the nose but potentially very fine. Ripe, very ripe and concentrated. Very lovely fruit. A great deal of class. Fullish body. Still firm. But very good vigour, and lots of personality and class. Still very closed-in. Very fine indeed. (June 2005)
2009 TO 2030   19.0

Nuits-Saint-Georges, Aux Boudots, 1995
Domaine Jean-Jacques Confuron

Good colour. Stylish, succulent nose. Ample and well perfumed. Medium-full body. Good structure and balance. Plenty of depth. Long and stylish. Very good plus. Just about ready. (June 2005)
NOW TO 2018   16.5

Nuits-Saint-Georges, Les Boudots, 1995
Domaine Jean Grivot

Full colour. More than the 1996. Lovely nose. Fat, rich, roast-chestnutty. Plenty of structure but no hard edges. Full on the palate. Some tannin. More than the 1996. Very lovely fruit. Very good grip. Fuller than the 1996, and at least as much depth and character. Very fine. (November 2001)
NOW TO 2026   18.5

Nuits-Saint-Georges, Aux Boudots, 1995
Domaine Méo-Camuzet

Fullish colour. Quite a lot of structure on the nose. But plenty of concentrated fruit to go with it. Fullish body. Very good class. Not quite as concentrated as the Clos de Vougeot, but balanced and stylish. Long. Quite advanced. Could be enjoyed now. Fragrant and complex at the end. Very good indeed. (March 2001)
NOW TO 2018   17.0

Nuits-Saint-Georges, Les Boudots, 1995
Domaine Gérard Mugneret

Medium-full colour. Ripe, fresh, fragrant, balanced nose. Very good fruit here. Medium-full body. A lovely succulent, complex, well-balanced wine. (June 2005)
NOW TO 2020   17.0

Nuits-Saint-Georges, Les Bousselots, 1995
Domaine Robert Chevillon

Full colour. Quite closed and tannic on the nose. Medium-full body. Beginning to soften up on the palate. Slightly earthy. Good grip and concentration. Slightly tough but plenty of depth. Still a little raw, but the tannins are sophisticated. Long and positive at the end. Very good. (March 2003)
NOW TO 2018   16.0

Nuits-Saint-Georges, Les Cailles, 1995
Maison Camille Giroud

Medium to medium-full colour. Fully ready. Rich, mature, concentrated fruit on the nose. Lots of class. Lots of depth. Old viney. Medium-full body. Ripe, ample and profound. Excellent grip. À point. Very long. Fine. (June 2005)
NOW TO 2020   17.5

Nuits-Saint-Georges, Les Cailles, 1995
Domaine Alain Michelot

Medium-full colour now approaching maturity. Soft, ripe and fragrant on the nose. No tough tannins. Elegant and succulent. Medium to medium-full body. Good vigour and depth. Plenty of style and complexity. Attractive, juicy, fresh fruit. Long and nicely pure on the palate. Just about ready. Fine. (November 2005)
NOW TO 2018   17.5

Nuits-Saint-Georges, Les Chaboeufs, 1995
Domaine Jean-Jacques Confuron

Good colour. Vigorous, fresh nose. Ripe and profound. Still a little unresolved tannin. Medium-full body. Ripe, rich and concentrated. Good depth. Still needs a year or so. Good grip. Long and stylish. Better than the Boudots this year. Very good indeed. (June 2005)
NOW TO 2020   17.0

Nuits-Saint-Georges, Les Chaignots, 1995
Domaine Robert Chevillon

Medium to medium-full colour. Fragrant nose. Supple for a Nuits-Saint-Georges—and for a Chaignots. Stylish. Medium to medium-full body. Ripe and elegant. Very good, complex follow-through. Lovely fruit. Fully ready. Very good indeed. (June 2005)

NOW TO 2018   17.0

Nuits-Saint-Georges, Les Chaignots, 1995
Domaine Mugneret-Gibourg

Fine colour. Still very youthful. Very impressive nose. Real depth and concentration. Full body. Very lovely fruit. No hard tannin but quite a lot of backbone. Still needs time. Excellent grip. This is potentially very lovely. (January 2002)

NOW TO 2025   17.5

Nuits-Saint-Georges, Aux Champs Perdrix, 1995
Domaine Alain Michelot

Good colour. Fresh, quite well-matured nose. A touch artisanal. Cleaner as it evolved. Medium body. Lacks a little depth and personality. But balanced and fresh. Good fruit. But a slight absence of richness and complexity. Good plus. Fully ready. (June 2005)

NOW TO 2012   15.5

Nuits-Saint-Georges, Clos de l'Arlot, 1995
Domaine de l'Arlot

Quite fat and quite oaky on the nose. Rich and meaty on the palate. Firm. Still youthful. Aromatic. Vigorous. Good. (June 2005)

NOW TO 2010+   15.0

Nuits-Saint-Georges, Clos des Forêts
Saint-Georges, 1995
Domaine de l'Arlot

Medium colour. Spicy, slightly stemmy nose. A little sweeter than most. Ripe, fragrant, balanced and stylish. Medium to medium-full body. Positive finish. Fully ready. Good plus. (June 2005)

NOW TO 2015   15.5

Nuits-Saint-Georges, Les Damodes, 1995
Domaine Alfred Haegelen-Jayer

Medium to medium-full colour. Some development on the nose. Ripe. Not very tannic. Quite

soft for a 1995. Ample and fruity. Attractive fruit. Very good grip. Medium-full body. Not a bit aggressive, but good depth and vigour. Long. Very good indeed. (September 2002)

NOW TO 2017   17.0

Nuits-Saint-Georges, Les Murgers, 1995
Domaine Armelle and Bernard Rion

Very good colour. Barely mature. Full, voluminous nose. Good depth here. Plenty of weight. A meaty wine. The tannins are not that ripe. Slightly astringent. Yet high acidity. Somewhat unbalanced. Quite good plus but it will never round off. (March 2006)

NOW TO 2011   14.5

Nuits-Saint-Georges, Les Porrets
Saint-Georges, 1995
Domaine Joseph Faiveley

Full colour. Still youthful. Slightly rigid on the nose. Quite oaky. Fullish body. Good grip. Some tannin. Balanced and classy. Plenty of rich fruit. Fine but needs time. (June 2005)

NOW TO 2025   17.5

Nuits-Saint-Georges, Les Porrets
Saint-Georges, 1995
Domaine Alain Michelot

Medium to medium-full colour. Fresh but not very concentrated nose. Stylish and fragrant though. Medium-full body. A little unresolved tannin. Fresh on the palate. It lacks a little richness but positive at the end. Just about ready. Very good. (June 2005)

NOW TO 2016   16.0

Nuits-Saint-Georges, Les Saint-Georges, 1995
Domaine Henri Gouges

Medium-full colour. Now mature. Full, firm, minerally and profound on the nose. High-class fruit. Lots of depth. Full, backward and tannic. Fine plus. But a long way from maturity. (June 2005)

2010 TO 2025+   18.0

Nuits-Saint-Georges, Les Vaucrains, 1995
Domaine Robert Chevillon

Fullish colour. Barely mature. Ripe and succulent, but still a little sturdy on the nose. Softer on the palate. Full of fruit. Medium-full body. Very good grip. Ripe, rich and harmonious. Long and very impressive. Lots of class. Just about ready. Fine. (October 2005)

NOW TO 2020 17.5

Pernand-Vergelesses, 1995
Domaine Rollin Père et Fils
Crisp, fresh, stylish, gently oaky on the nose. For a village wine this is very good indeed. Nicely cool, but concentrated, balanced and elegant. Even some dimension. Good. (October 2001)

DRINK SOON 15.0

Pernand-Vergelesses, Ile de Vergelesses, 1995
Domaine Chandon de Briailles
The first bottle was corked. Another bottle was fresh, medium-bodied and with a stylish nose. Brisk and appley. Good finish. Individual and attractive. Holding up well. Good plus. (June 2005)

NOW TO 2010 15.5

Pommard, Les Chaponnières, 1995
Domaine Philippe Billard-Gonnet
Magnum. Medium-full colour. Fresh nose. Good, classy, fruity nose. Medium-full body. Fragrant. Lacks a little fat on the palate and therefore a little succulence. Better with food. Positive finish. (June 2005)

NOW TO 2015 15.5

Pommard, Les Chaponnières, 1995
Domaine Jacques Parent
Medium colour. Some development. Soft nose. Warm and rich, but not very substantial. Lacks a little character as well. Medium to medium-full body. Quite evolved. The tannins are ripe and now soft. Fresh. The fruit is ripe and sweet. Good length but not much elegance. A little bit innocuous for a 1995 Pommard. Quite good. (March 2000)

DRINK SOON 14.0

Pommard, Clos Orgelot, 1995
Domaine Christophe Violot-Guillemard
Medium to medium-full colour. Some development. Slightly unripe tannins on the nose. Medium to medium-full body. A little earthy,

but good grip and plenty of ripe fruit. A bit unsophisticated. Saved by the quality of the vintage. Quite good. (March 2000)

DRINK SOON 14.0

Pommard, Clos des Epeneaux, 1995
Domaine du Comte Armand
Fresh, medium-full colour. Medium-full nose. Not a great deal of thrust or concentration. Medium-full body. Ripe, balanced but still a little raw. Very good, but lacks the real depth, concentration and personality for fine. (July 2001)

NOW TO 2012 14.0

Pommard, Les Epenots, 1995
Domaine Coron Père et Fils
Round. Medium-full. No great weight. No great sophistication. Clean. Getting ready. But it doesn't have Epenots depth and class. Only fair. (October 2000)

DRINK SOON 13.5

Pommard, Les Rugiens, 1995
Domaine Philippe Billard-Gonnet
Magnum. Good colour. Full, rich, backward nose. This is succulent, meaty and rather better than his Chaponnières. Indeed complex, profound, long and only just ready. Fine. (June 2005)

NOW TO 2020 17.5

Richebourg, 1995
Domaine Jean Grivot
Magnum. Good colour. Very fine, concentrated, rich nose. Lovely fruit here. A great deal of depth. This is full bodied, tannic, splendidly balanced, very vigorous and quite excellent. Splendid drive and energy. Very, very fine fruit. Very, very long. Very fine indeed. (June 2005)

NOW TO 2030 19.5

Richebourg, 1995
Domaine Anne Gros
The first vintage with simply Anne Gros on the label. Very fine colour. Just a hint of maturity. Rich, full, very profound nose. A full-bodied wine. Plenty of structure, but not too solid or tannic. Full and youthful. Still quite a lot of tannin to be

absorbed, more than the 1996. But it is rounder, fatter and richer as well. Yet not quite so elegant perhaps. Like the 1996, emphatically a wine for food. But not yet. (February 2004)

NOW TO 2025   19.0

Richebourg, 1995
Domaine Alain Hudelot-Noëllat

Fullish colour. Just about mature. Ripe, rich, succulent, classy nose. Fullish body. Balanced, intense, very lovely complex fruit. Still quite youthful. Still needs 2 to 3 years. Very lovely long finish. Very complete. Very fine. (June 2006)

2009 TO 2025   18.5

Richebourg, 1995
Domaine Leroy

Fullish colour. Some maturity. A big, ample, meaty, very ripe wine. This is structured, but the structure is hidden behind the richness of the wine. Fresh and clean. Full body. Rich and round. All it needs is time. Lots of dimension. An impressive bottle. Very fine plus. (April 2000)

NOW TO 2020   19.0

La Romanée, 1995
Domaine Bouchard Père et Fils

Fullish colour. Just a hint of maturity. Impressive nose. No undue tannic bulk. Very lovely, rich fruit. Medium-full body. A slight touch of oak. This is suprisingly seductive. Fullish body. Well-covered tannins. Round, rich and most attractive. Not a bit too tough. Fine plus. (March 2003)

NOW TO 2023   18.0

Romanée-Saint-Vivant, 1995
Domaine de l'Arlot

Fullish colour but more mature than the 1993. Ripe and rich, but slightly lumpy, with some of the stems. Fullish body. Sweet and spicy. Less lumpy than the 1993 but a bit rigid nevertheless. Very good, indeed, but not great. (March 2002)

NOW TO 2018   17.0

Romanée-Saint-Vivant, 1995
Domaine Robert Arnoux

Good colour. Sturdier nose than J. J. Confuron's 1995 Romanée-Saint-Vivant. More tannin. Rich,

concentrated and vigorous nevertheless. On the palate fine, but not as fine as Jean-Jacques Confuron's. Very good grip. Rich and full bodied. Still youthful. Lovely fruit. Fine plus. (June 2005)

NOW TO 2020   18.0

Romanée-Saint-Vivant, 1995
Domaine Jean-Jacques Confuron

Good colour. Fine, full, rich, concentrated, complex nose. Lots of depth and lots of class. Full body. Vigorous. Very well balanced. Very pure. Still needs 2 to 3 years. Very fine. (June 2005)

NOW TO 2030   18.5

Romanée-Saint-Vivant, 1995
Domaine Alain Hudelot-Noëllat

Medium-full colour. A little development. Ripe, rich nose (Becky Wasserman says peonies). No aggressive tannins. Lovely fruit. Ample and succulent. This is better than his Richebourg 1995. Better definition. Better grip and distinction. Still a little tannin to resolve. Almost sweet but very fresh. Very, very long and lovely. Very fine plus. (June 2004)

NOW TO 2025   19.0

Romanée-Saint-Vivant, 1995
Maison Louis Jadot

Medium-full colour. Some development. Stylish nose. Not as backward or as concentrated as some. Lovely fruit though. Medium-full body. Good but not too much structure. Ripe tannins. Accessible. Quite concentrated. This is elegant, long and complex. Fine plus. (March 2002)

NOW TO 2026   18.0

Romanée-Saint-Vivant, 1995
Maison Dominique Laurent

Fullish colour. Some development. Full, rich, oaky and exotic on the nose. Not as much grip or definition as the 1996. Similarly, though, it is a bit over-extracted. Some tannin. Lots of oak. Fine fruit but just a little clumsy. I don't think it will ever round off really satisfactorily. Fine at best. (March 2002)

NOW TO 2020   17.5

Romanée-Saint-Vivant, 1995
Domaine Leroy

Full colour. A little development. Splendid nose. Really classy. Marvellously harmonious, intensely concentrated fruit. This is more like a Domaine de la Romanée-Conti Romanée-Saint-Vivant than most of Lalou Bize's wines. Finely tuned. Not a bit overly tannic. Excellent grip. Very, very long and very, very lovely. Excellent for the vintage. (March 2002)

NOW TO 2035   19.5

Ruchottes-Chambertin, 1995
Domaine Frédéric Esmonin

Medium-full, mature colour. Lovely fruit on the nose. Ample. Plump. Cool. Balanced and ripe. Medium-full body. Good structure. Not quite the depth and complexity of his Mazis, but fine and lovely. Profound and long at the end. Just about ready. (April 2005)

NOW TO 2025   18.0

Ruchottes-Chambertin, 1995
Domaine Dr. Georges Mugneret

Medium-full colour. Just about mature. Fine nose. Balanced. Intense. Pure and classy. Medium to medium-full body. Subtle, balanced, very pure and very lovely. Very elegant. Very long. Now ready. (April 2005)

NOW TO 2025   18.5

Ruchottes-Chambertin, 1995
Domaine Georges Roumier et Fils

Fullish, mature colour. Firm nose. Rather closed. A hint of the stems. Cleaner on the palate. Still a little raw and astringent. Very concentrated, very ripe fruit. Medium-full body. Intense, cool and very classy. Very lovely. Indeed very fine plus. (April 2005)

NOW TO 2027   19.0

Ruchottes-Chambertin, Clos des Ruchottes, 1995
Domaine Armand Rousseau

Medium to medium-full, mature colour. Ripe, round nose. More evolved than their Mazis. Charming and fragrant. Medium-full body.

Not as fat as the Mazis or as profound, but very lovely. Intense, ripe and very long. Very impressive fruit. Very fine. (December 2005)

NOW TO 2020   18.5

Santenay, Beaurepaire, 1995
Maison Roland Remoissenet et Fils

Good, if a little heavy, but in Roland Remoissenet's hands, made for drinking a bit later. A little sulphur. Has grip and depth. But it lacks flair. Quite good. (June 2000)

DRINK SOON   14.0

Savigny-lès-Beaune, Bataillière, 1995
Domaine Albert Morot

Medium-full colour. Quite a rich, full, meaty nose. Slightly oaky. Medium to medium-full body. Slightly rigid. Good fruit underneath. And good grip. But a little dominated by the oak. (June 2005)

NOW TO 2012   17.0

Savigny-lès-Beaune, La Dominode, 1995
Domaine Bruno Clair

Medium-full colour. Rich, full, meaty nose. Liquorice and black currant. Plenty of depth. Fullish body. Still very vigorous. Round and opulent. Very good grip. Long and very satisfactory. Very good. (June 2005)

NOW TO 2015   16.0

Savigny-lès-Beaune, La Dominode, 1995
Domaine Jean-Marc Pavelot

Medium-full colour. Ripe, rich, ample, succulent nose. Medium-full body. Very attractive, classy fruit. Round, complex, velvety and very stylish. Lovely long finish. Very good plus. (June 2005)

NOW TO 2015   16.5

Savigny-lès-Beaune, Aux Fourneaux, 1995
Domaine Chandon de Briailles

Medium to medium-full colour. Attractive fruit on the nose. Medium to medium-full body. Ripe and balanced. Decent depth and vigour. Positive finish. Good class. Good. (June 2005)

NOW TO 2012   15.0

Savigny-lès-Beaune, Aux Gravains, 1995
Domaine Jean-Marc Pavelot

Slightly more colour but more advanced than his 1996. Slight touch of almond paste on the nose. Medium to medium-full body. Still a little tannin. Fatter and richer than the 1996. Good grip and depth. Not a bit too sturdy. At present this is the one I prefer. (June 2003)

NOW TO 2018   17.0

Savigny-lès-Beaune, Aux Guettes, 1995
Domaine Simon Bize et Fils

Magnum. Medium colour. Fully developed. Slightly lean and slightly stemmy at first. Round and succulent on the follow-through. Medium body. Quite good. (June 2005)

NOW TO 2010   14.0

Savigny-lès-Beaune, Les Lavières, 1995
Domaine Bouchard Père et Fils

Fullish colour. But much more evolved than the 1990. Now ripe and ready on nose and palate. Balanced and stylish. Fresh. Fullish body. Good grip. Needs another 2 years to get more succulent and sweet, but very good. (June 2003)

NOW TO 2019   16.0

Savigny-lès-Beaune, Les Peuillets, 1995
Domaine Lucien Jacob

Medium to medium-full colour. Slightly rustic on the nose. Medium to medium-full body. A bit farmyardy. Slightly astringent on the palate. Medium body. Decent fruit. Quite good. (June 2005)

NOW TO 2010   14.0

Savigny-lès-Beaune, Les Vergelesses, 1995
Domaine Lucien Jacob

Slightly anonymous on the nose. Better on the palate. Medium body. Fresh, clean, crabapple touches. Holding up well. Quite good plus. (June 2005)

NOW TO 2009   14.5

La Tâche, 1995
Domaine De La Romanée-Conti

Good, fullish colour. Not a bit too tannic on the nose. Ripe, firm and succulent. Very good depth. Lovely fruit. Fullish body on the palate. Some tannin, but the tannins are ripe and well covered. Very good grip. Indeed, quite austere at present. Lots of style and dimension. Real vigour and power. Profound and potentially lovely. Very fine. (March 2003)

NOW TO 2026   18.5

Volnay, Les Caillerets, Ancienne Cuvée Carnot, 1995
Domaine Bouchard Père et Fils

Very good colour. Firm nose. Slightly chunky tannins which dominate at the moment. Medium-full body. Good fruit, but a slight lack of concentration and definition. It needs to soften, but good plus at best for the vintage. (March 2004)

NOW TO 2015   15.5

Volnay, Le Cailleret, 1995
Maison Champy

Magnum. Medium-full colour. This is pedestrian. A bit over-oaked and over-sulphured. A dull wine to begin with. Medium to medium-full body. Decent acidity. Quite nice fruit. But rather astringent. (June 2005)

NOW TO 2010   13.5

Volnay, Champans, 1995
Domaine Des Comtes Lafon

Medium-full colour. Still youthful. Ripe, plump, quite accessible nose. Medium-full body. Still some tannin, but the tannins are ripe and potentially velvety. Good grip. Plenty of depth. Ripe. Getting succulent. Long. Fine. (June 2005)

NOW TO 2020+   17.5

Volnay, Clos Des Angles, 1995
Domaine Rossignol-Jeanniard

Magnum. Medium-full colour. Fragrant nose. Quite developed. Medium to medium-full body. Stylish. Very Volnay. Good fresh acidity. Ripe, succulent fruit. Long. À point. Very good plus. (June 2005)

NOW TO 2015   16.5

Volnay, Clos du Château des Ducs, 1995
Domaine Michel Lafarge

Fullish colour. Still youthful. Fragrant nose. Still a touch raw. Clean, ripe, balanced and very elegant.

Fullish on the palate. Round and a touch spicy. No undue tannic structure. Lovely ripe, succulent fruit on the palate. Long and complex. Very poised. Just about ready. Fine. (March 2005)

NOW TO 2020+   17.5

Volnay, Clos des Chênes, 1995
Maison Camille Giroud

Still fullish. Still with unresolved tannin. Yet some maturity in the flavours. Fullish bodied for a Volnay. Good grip. Will still improve. Like a lot of 1995s, at present a touch burly. But very good wine underneath. (September 2002)

NOW TO 2014   16.0

Volnay, Clos des Chênes, 1995
Domaine Michel Lafarge

Full colour. Less developed than his Clos des Chênes 1996. Firm, full, rich nose. Fuller and richer, more concentrated and more tannic than the 1996. Lots of substance here. Lots of depth. More backward than the 1996. This is very lovely. Splendidly classy at the end. Better than the 1996. (March 2006)

2009 TO 2025+   18.5

Volnay, Clos des Ducs, 1995
Domaine du Marquis d'Angerville

Medium-full colour. Broad, succulent nose. Ripe, balanced and fragrant. Medium-full body. Fully ready. Nicely vigorous. Clean and intense. Quite a lot of depth. Lovely, elegant, fragrant fruit. Very good indeed. (March 2005)

NOW TO 2018   17.0

Volnay, Frémiets, 1995
Domaine Nicolas Rossignol-Jeanniard

Full colour. Ripe. Quite modern. Rather tense. Quite oaky. Slightly forced. Good fruit. Decent tannins. Slightly high, volatile acidity. Not much style. Only quite good. (October 2003)

NOW TO 2014   14.0

Volnay, Santenots, 1995
Domaine Pierre Matrot

Medium to medium-full colour. Soft nose. Fully developed. Round and with good, but not great, style. Medium-full body. Slight touch of astringency. Lacks a bit of velvet and smoothness. Quite fresh on the finish though. But good at best. (June 2005)

NOW TO 2010   15.0

Volnay, Santenots, 1995
Domaine François Mikulski

Magnum. Medium to medium-full colour. Fully developed. A touch of the stems on the nose, but ripe and spicy, and with plenty of interest. Medium-full body. Fresh but a little earthy. Fully developed on the palate. Good plus. (June 2005)

NOW TO 2010   15.5

Volnay, Les Santenots du Milieu, 1995
Domaine des Comtes Lafon

Magnum. Fullish colour. Firm and backward, rich and concentrated on both nose and palate. Good austerity and depth. Long. Full body. Still needs time. Lovely finish. (June 2005)

NOW TO 2020   18.0

Volnay, Taillepieds, 1995
Domaine Hubert de Montille

This is beginning to open up. Medium-full body. Some tannin. Ripe and balanced. Slightly sweeter than the 1996. Getting soft. An attractive bottle with very good fruit and a nicely positive finish. Fine for the vintage. (December 2002)

NOW TO 2020   17.5

Vosne-Romanée, 1995
Maison Dominique Laurent

Good colour. Fullish, ripe, blackberry nose. Plenty of depth. Very good acidity, of course. Rich. Good tannins. Plenty of fat. A lovely example of a village wine, with plenty of life ahead of it. (March 2001)

NOW TO 2015   16.5

Vosne-Romanée, Les Beaux Monts, 1995
Domaine Jean Grivot

Medium-full colour. Still youthful. Slightly burnt, adolescent nose. Full, firm, rich, concentrated and tannic. Rather unforthcoming and not very Pinot expressive. But a lot of depth. Intense, long and balanced. Potentially fine. (April 2005)

2011 TO 2030   17.5

Vosne-Romanée, Les Brûlées, 1995
Domaine Michel Gros

Full, rich, youthful colour. Slight touch of the stems on the nose. Full, rich and tannic. A slight touch of the herbaceous on the palate, but this will disappear. Lots of depth. Lots of dimension. High quality. Very well balanced. Fine plus. (April 2005)

NOW TO 2025   18.0

Vosne-Romanée, Aux Brûlées, 1995
Domaine Gérard Mugneret

Medium-full colour. Fully mature. Rich nose. Quite fat, meaty and slightly spicy in the best sense. Nicely ripe and succulent. Medium-full body. Just about ready. Long, fine and complex. (June 2005)

NOW TO 2020   17.5

Vosne-Romanée, Les Chaumes, 1995
Domaine François Lamarche

Medium to medium-full colour. Some development. Good bead. Clean nose. Some stems evident, but at least some style. Not rustic. On the palate this is a little stringy, but it has the acidity of the vintage and all the fresh fruit, too. So the result is really not bad at all. Good depth. Long. Very good. (March 2000)

NOW TO 2013   16.0

Vosne-Romanée, Les Chaumes, 1995
Domaine Jean Tardy et Fils

Medium-full colour. Just about mature. Some oak. Soft and quite developed. Medium-full body. The tannins now well developed. Now à point. Good grip. Fresh. Decent finish. Very good. (March 2003)

NOW TO 2015   16.0

Vosne-Romanée, Clos des Réas, 1995
Domaine Michel Gros

Ripe, fullish and succulent. Very good, now softening, tannins. Very good fruit. Classy. Slight spice. Fine. (October 2003)

NOW TO 2020   17.5

Vosne-Romanée, Aux Malconsorts, 1995
Domaine Sylvain Cathiard

Magnum. Medium-full colour. Fully mature. Very lovely fragrant nose. Very elegant and beautifully balanced. Medium-full body. Still a little raw. Excellent fruit. Complex and classy. Very lovely character. Long and very fine. (June 2005)

NOW TO 2027   18.5

1994

Nineteen ninety-four was never a Burgundian vintage which generated much excitement. It was a lesser year in both colours, and the best that could be said for it was that it could provide a useful stopgap on the red wine front while we waited for grander vintages such as 1990 and 1993 to mature. In this sense it followed the somewhat looser-knit 1992s. Commercially it has now completely disappeared, and I doubt there are many bottles remaining in any reader's cellars.

But, as our annual 10-year-on tasting in 2004 proved yet again, there are attractive wines—if you stick to the best growers and move up the hierarchy to *premier* and *grand cru*—in all but the most atrocious vintages. In the case of 1994 there are some pleasant surprises among the white wines, too, but more in the sense that a few are still fresh and fruity. The red Côte de Beaunes are tough and have mostly lost what fruit they ever had; however, the Côte de Nuits and the *grands crus* offer many praiseworthy wines, most which can still be kept for the rest of the decade.

WEATHER CONDITIONS

A wet winter built up a high water table in the soil, which was to prove important in a summer which was largely dry. The *sortie* was not particularly abundant, but a swift, early flowering at the end of May, some 15 days in advance of the norm, ensured both a large harvest and the probability of an early one.

Following a savage localised hailstorm in Puligny on June 20, the summer was excellent. August was dry, and in some areas the fruit began to lag behind in development, but a couple of days of rain at the end of the month speeded up the progress toward maturity again. By the first week of September, with everything looking splendidly ripe and healthy, everything was pointing toward an exceptional vintage.

It was not to be. A thunderstorm during the weekend of September 10 ushered in a week or more of heavy rain. Thankfully, the temperature also dropped, and at first these downpours gave no real cause for concern. But as they continued—with most growers starting their harvest on Monday, September 19, in the Côte de Beaune or the weekend before—the fruit began to deteriorate. And the Pinots were not yet ripe. For those with Chardonnay to deal with, there was a pause before these Pinots were attacked. Others, such as Lafarge in Volnay, reversed their usual order, beginning with their generics. Certainly, those who delayed benefited. From September 22 on, the weather improved. Some in the Côte de Nuits were able to wait until the beginning of October. "I had a choice," said Laurent Ponsot, "to pick rotten grapes on the 23rd when most of the Côte de Nuits started picking—or rotten, ripe grapes a week later. The fruit didn't get any worse. But it did get riper."

→ Rating for the Vintage ←	
Red	13.0–14.5
White	13.5

→ Size of the Crop ←		
(In hectolitres, excluding generic wine)		
	RED	WHITE
Grands Crus	12,605	3,504
Village and Premiers Crus	183,337	50,549
TOTAL	195,942	54,053

WHERE ARE THE BEST WINES?

- The reds are both better and more vigorous in the Côte de Nuits than the Côte de Beaune.
- In general the 1994 reds are better than the 1992s.

THE STATE OF MATURITY TODAY

The white wines are now tiring, if not dead. In red there is not a lot of joy still to be had in the Côte de Beaune, except among the superstar domaines. But the top Côte de Nuits reds can still be held. Don't push your luck beyond 2010, however. Best to drink them now.

TASTING NOTES

WHITES

Bâtard-Montrachet, 1994
Domaine Pierre Colin

Brother of Marc Colin of Saint-Aubin, who made this wine. Fresh colour. Broad nose. Fullish and fruity, if with no great zip or elegance. But clean and well made. No great depth, but ripe and balanced. Enjoyable. Reasonably positive finish. Very good plus for the vintage. (April 2005)
DRINK SOON   16.5

Bâtard-Montrachet, 1994
Domaine Richard Fontaine-Gagnard

Quite an advanced colour, but no undue age. Soft nose. Clean but not that expressive. On the palate medium to medium-full body. Fresh. Not heavy. Good, classy fruit. Balanced. Elegant. Good length. Not a brilliant wine in terms of its complexity but fine for the vintage. (April 2005)
DRINK SOON   17.5

Bâtard-Montrachet, 1994
Domaine Jean-Noël Gagnard

Magnum. Rich, fat and just a touch blowsy, yet with very good acidity, on the nose. Just not classy or clear-cut enough for a great vintage. Quite full. Certainly ripe enough and balanced enough. *À point* now. Decent length. Very good indeed, especially for the vintage. (January 2002)
DRINK SOON   17.0

Bâtard-Montrachet, 1994
Domaine Ramonet

This is less vigorous and slightly more sulphury than I would have expected. Rich and ripe, but a slight lack of dimension. Classy nevertheless. But only very good. (March 2005)
DRINK SOON   16.0

Chassagne-Montrachet, Les Caillerets, 1994
Domaine Jean-Noël Gagnard

Fresh, ripe, balanced, classy and succulent. Medium-full. Lots of fruit. Absolutely no sign of age. A lovely bottle. A lot of depth. Very fine for a 1994 and still plenty of life ahead of it. (April 2005)

NOW TO 2009   18.5

Chassagne-Montrachet, Clos de la Maltroie, 1994
Domaine Jean-Noël Gagnard

Ripe and rich on the nose. Just a touch of built-in sulphur. Plenty of weight, grip and fruit on the palate. Positive at the end. Very good plus. (June 2004)

DRINK SOON   16.5

Corton-Charlemagne, 1994
Domaine d'Ardhuy

Lacks a bit of style, and the fruit has begun to dry out. Quite fresh underneath. Quite good. (June 2004)

DRINK UP   14.0

Corton-Charlemagne, 1994
Domaine Bonneau du Martray

Clean, fresh and very stylish on the nose. Very lovely complex fruit. Fullish body. Aristocratic. Lots of life ahead of it. Balanced and vigorous at the end. Very fine. (June 2004)

NOW TO 2010+   18.5

Corton-Charlemagne, 1994
Domaine Louis Latour

Slightly burnt, built-in-sulphury nose. Big, sturdy, over-alcoholic underneath. Fullish body. Ripe. A little built-in sulphur on the attack. Less so on the follow-through. Decent grip. But hot at the end. Unstylish. Ready. (October 2000)

DRINK SOON   14.0

Corton-Charlemagne, 1994
Maison Roland Remoissenet et Fils

Not a lot of nose. Quite ripe, but a bit one-dimensional and a bit blowsy. There really isn't much distinction here, even for this vintage. Fair at best. (March 2001)

DRINK SOON   13.5

Meursault, 1994
Domaine Louis Jadot

A surprisingly good and vigorous example. Full-ish bodied, nutty, balanced and stylish. No sign of age. Very good. (November 2000)

DRINK SOON   16.0

Meursault, Premier Cru, 1994
Domaine Guy Roulot

Magnum. Quite ripe, certainly very stylish. Good depth here and plenty of fruit on the follow-through. Very good. (June 2004)

DRINK SOON   16.0

Meursault, Les Casse-Têtes, 1994
Domaine Patrick Javillier

Magnum. Just a little attenuated on the nose. Ripe on the palate. But drying up a little. Good style and harmony nevertheless. (June 2004)

DRINK UP   15.0

Meursault, Charmes, 1994
Domaine Robert Ampeau

A hint of noble rot here, but rich, ripe and with good depth if not great class. But youthful for a 1994 and good quality. Good but not great. (January 2006)

DRINK SOON   15.0

Meursault, Charmes, 1994
Domaine François and Antoine Jobard

A gentle wine. Soft, quite rich and well balanced. Still very much alive, although more so on the palate than on the nose. Long. Stylish. Very good. (June 2004)

DRINK SOON   16.0

Meursault, Charmes, 1994
Domaine des Comtes Lafon

Surprisingly fresh on the nose. Very good fruit. Just a little oak. Ripe and rich on the palate. Well balanced. Long. Very good indeed. Can still be kept. (June 2004)

DRINK SOON   17.0

Meursault, Charmes, 1994
Domaine René Monnier

Rich, full, concentrated and stylish. Ripe and juicy. Good balance and depth. The palate and the finish are better than the nose. Fine for the vintage. (October 2003)

DRINK SOON   17.5

Meursault, Charmes, 1994
Maison Morey-Blanc

Ripe, gently oaky, mature and classy. Seductive, round and balanced. Lots of depth for the vintage. And plenty of life. *À point.* Fine for the vintage. (September 2001)

DRINK SOON   17.5

Meursault, Clos de la Barre, 1994
Domaine des Comtes Lafon

The colour is still fresh. So is the wine on the nose. This has got good breed, even concentration on the palate, and no lack of vigour. Ripe. Even quite complex. For a village 1994 it is very good indeed. (February 2005)

DRINK SOON   16.0

Meursault, Genevrières, 1994
Domaine François and Antoine Jobard

Fuller and more vigorous than his Charmes. Slightly less fruit on the palate. Balanced and stylish though. Long and complex. Very good. (June 2004)

DRINK SOON   16.0

Meursault, Genevrières, 1994
Domaine des Comtes Lafon

Youthful colour. Soft, flowery, ripe if not sugar-rich nose. A lot more interest and depth here than in the 1998 and 1997. Quite full, clean, fresh, balanced, ripe and even complex. Lots of fruit. Very stylish. Unexpectedly delicious. A very relaxed and harmonious wine. Long and positive at the end. *À point.* Fine for the vintage. (September 2005)

NOW TO 2010+   17.5

Meursault, Genevrières, 1994
Domaine François Mikulski

Magnum. Rich, full and fat. Good concentration. Not quite as stylish as some of these Meursault premiers crus, but good meaty stuff. Still very much alive. (June 2004)

DRINK SOON   15.0

Meursault, Les Perrières, 1994
Domaine des Comtes Lafon

Broad-flavoured, mature, gently oaky nose. Good freshness. Medium body. Good complexity for the vintage. But not the dimension of most of the 1990s vintages. Plump, ripe, balanced and charming. Good, positive finish. Fine for the vintage. (May 2001)

NOW TO 2008   17.5

Meursault, Le Porusot, 1994
Domaine François Jobard

Firm, even hard, and a touch sulphury at the outset. More flesh, fruit and interest as it developed. Good acidity. Not a lot of character, but that is the vintage. Still youthful. Very good. (June 2000)

DRINK SOON   16.0

Meursault, Les Tessons, 1994
Domaine Pierre Morey

Magnum. Slight attenuation on the nose. Has dried up a bit on the palate. This was ripe and stylish but is now just about at the end of its life. (June 2004)

DRINK UP   14.0

Meursault, Les Tessons, 1994
Domaine Guy Roulot

Magnum. Fresh, vigorous, stylish nose. Ripe on the palate. Medium weight. Very well-balanced fruit. Long. Very elegant. Very good plus. (June 2004)

DRINK SOON   16.5

Le Montrachet, 1994
Domaine des Comtes Lafon

Quite a deep colour. Ripe, succulent, slightly exotic nose. Full and very fresh. This is really fine. Not a bit off-vintage-y. Vigorous, profound, fat and classy. No hurry to drink. (March 2005)

NOW TO 2010   19.5

Puligny-Montrachet, Le Cailleret, 1994
Domaine Hubert de Montille

Lovely fruit here. This is still very fresh. Ripe, balanced, fullish. Very stylish. Very lovely. Splendid harmony. (June 2004)

NOW TO 2010+   18.0

Puligny-Montrachet, Les Chalumaux, 1994
Domaine Joseph Matrot

A touch of built-in sulphur on the nose. And the fruit has begun to dry out a bit. Not too bad on the palate. But lacking a little vigour. Decent fruit though. Good. (June 2004)

DRINK SOON   15.0

Puligny-Montrachet, Les Combettes, 1994
Domaine Jean-Marc Boillot

Fresh, ripe, vigorous and really quite oaky on both nose and palate. Full bodied. Quite muscular, even a little sweet. It's very good but also a bit ungainly. (June 2004)

NOW TO 2009   16.0

Puligny-Montrachet, Les Demoiselles, 1994
Domaine Michel Colin-Deléger et Fils

(Mme François Colin). Fragrant, mature but not overly so. Medium to medium-full body. Good fruit if not real dimension or depth. Just a suspicion of oak. Positive finish. Good wine for drinking over the next 2 years. Very good, indeed, for a 1994. (January 2002)

DRINK SOON   15.5

Puligny-Montrachet, Les Folatières, 1994
Domaine Louis Jadot

Rich, full, virile, very stylish nose. Very little age. Ripe and fresh. Quite substantial. Very good grip. Very youthful. Long, complex and elegant. Fine plus. (June 2004)

NOW TO 2010+   18.0

Puligny-Montrachet, Les Folatières, 1994
Domaine Étienne Sauzet

Quite rich but sulphury. Quite full if a little hard at the end. Decent fruit at first. Decent freshness, too, under the sulphur. But after half an hour it began to collapse. Very good for the vintage. (October 2002)

DRINK SOON   16.0

Puligny-Montrachet, Hameau de Blagny, 1994
Domaine Martelet de Cherisey

Crisp and stylish. Still fresh. Not a lot of depth, structure or concentration, but balanced. Long. Very good. Still has life. (June 2004)

DRINK SOON   16.0

Saint-Aubin, Murgers des Dents de Chien, 1994
Domaine Hubert Lamy et Fils

A little bit too advanced now. Fruity, but old. (June 2004)

DRINK UP   13.0

REDS

Beaune, Clos des Ursules, 1994
Domaine Louis Jadot

Very good colour. Still youthful. Ripe and rich, but a bit hard on the nose. On the palate this is beginning to soften up. Still some tannin. Medium-full body. Very good grip. Surprising amount of style and *terroir* definition. Very elegant for a 1994. Lovely finesse and harmony. Really very good indeed, especially for the vintage. (March 2000)

NOW TO 2012   17.0

Beaune, Les Cras, 1994
Domaine Germain Père et Fils/
Château de Chorey-lès-Beaune

Fullish, fresh colour. Slightly unforthcoming and dry on the nose. Decent fruit. Medium-full body. But slightly austere on the attack and dry on the finish. (June 2004)

DRINK SOON   14.0

Beaune, Grèves, 1994
Domaine Michel Lafarge

Fullish, mature colour. Ripe, sumptuous nose. Rich and fullish bodied on the palate. Very good tannins. A vigorous, slightly chunky example. Lovely fruit. Long on the palate. Very good plus. (June 2004)

NOW TO 2010+   16.5

Beaune, Grèves, Vigne de l'Enfant Jésus, 1994
Domaine Bouchard Père et Fils

Medium-full, vigorous colour. Round, ripe, rich nose. The tannins are just a bit clumsy. Decent fruit on the palate but a bit dry. Slightly ungenerous. (June 2004)

DRINK SOON   14.0

Beaune, Vignes Franches, 1994
Domaine Germain Père et Fils/
Château de Chorey-lès-Beaune

Fullish colour. A bit more generous than the Cras, but rather more rustic. Medium-full body. Slightly clumsy. (June 2004)

DRINK SOON · · · · · · · · · · · · 13.0

Bonnes Mares, 1994
Maison Champy

Good, fresh colour. Ripe, round and classy on the nose. A slight lack of fruit and a bit astringent on the palate. But ample fruit. Very good. (June 2004)

NOW TO 2009 · · · · · · · · · · · · 16.0

Bonnes Mares, 1994
Domaine Georges Roumier et Fils

Magnum. Very good colour. Still youthful. Splendid nose. Full, rich, concentrated and very high class. Full, slightly austere on the attack. But very good grip. Good tannins. Ample on the follow-through and very classy all the way through. (June 2004)

NOW TO 2015+ · · · · · · · · · · · · 19.0

Bonnes Mares, 1994
Domaine Comte Georges de Vogüé

Good colour. Impressive nose. Rich, full and still very youthful. Ripe and fullish bodied, but slightly dry, especially after their Musigny. Good depth and fine quality. But this year there is a big difference between the two. (June 2004)

NOW TO 2010+ · · · · · · · · · · · · 17.5

Chambertin, 1994
Domaine Leroy

Medium-full colour. Now mature. Ripe, ample, stylish, fresh nose. Good vigour and definition. A really lovely 1994. Fullish body. Very good fruit. Harmonious and classy, and with very good dimension. Still very young. Lovely. This is very fine for the vintage. (April 2000)

NOW TO 2013 · · · · · · · · · · · · 18.5

Chambertin, 1994
Domaine Armand Rousseau

Magnum. Good colour. Youthful. Very lovely, succulent nose. Excellent fruit and very finely balanced. Slightly softer than the Clos de Bèze, but more succulence, better grip and more dimension. This is still very, very youthful. A very impressive wine indeed. Splendid fruit. Brilliant! (June 2004)

NOW TO 2020+ · · · · · · · · · · · · 20.0

Chambertin, 1994
Domaine Jean and Jean-Louis Trapet

Magnum. Good colour. Classy nose. Plenty of depth here. Rich and succulent. On the palate there is a rich attack and decent grip. But not the depth for fine. Nor the class. (June 2004)

NOW TO 2010+ · · · · · · · · · · · · 17.0

Chambertin, Clos de Bèze, 1994
Domaine Armand Rousseau

Magnum. Good, vigorous colour. Splendid nose. Rich, concentrated, very classy fruit. Fullish bodied on the palate. Very good grip. Splendid energy here. High-quality fruit and balance. Very intense. Excellent. (June 2004)

NOW TO 2020+ · · · · · · · · · · · · 19.5

Chambolle-Musigny, 1994
Domaine Daniel Rion et Fils

Good colour. Soft, fragrant nose. Very Chambolle. Medium-full bodied, but not a bit hard or dense. Mellow, fruity and seductive. Ripe and fruity. Fresh. À point. But it will keep very well. Really very good indeed. (March 2004)

NOW TO 2010 · · · · · · · · · · · · 16.0

Chambolle-Musigny, Les Amoureuses, 1994
Domaine Joseph Drouhin

Medium-full, mature colour. Fragrant nose. Fresh. Very Chambolle. Very lovely ripe, complex fruit. Very elegant. Ripe, fullish, fresh, long and persistent on the palate. This has great style and complexity. Very, very long. Splendidly vigorous and classy at the end. Very fine plus. (June 2004)

NOW TO 2010+ · · · · · · · · · · · · 19.0

Chambolle-Musigny, Les Amoureuses, 1994
Domaine Georges Roumier

Magnum. Good, fresh colour. Sturdier on the nose than the Mugnier Fuées. Very lovely rich, ripe fruit. Very good depth. Fullish body. Some oak. A vigorous, energetic, complex wine. This is very lovely. Really long and classy. Very fine. (June 2004)

NOW TO 2010+   18.5

Chambolle-Musigny, Aux Beaux Bruns, 1994
Domaine Ghislaine Barthod

Magnum. Good, full, fresh colour. Rich, plump and meaty on the nose. Ripe, full and abundant on the palate. Good tannins. Plenty of depth. Just a little four-square but very good. (June 2004)

NOW TO 2009   16.0

Chambolle-Musigny, Aux Beaux Bruns, 1994
Domaine Denis Mortet

Magnum. Medium-full colour. A touch reduced on the nose and a touch astringent on the palate. Good substance. Good fruit. Quite obviously chaptalised. But decent class if no real Chambolle fragrance. Good. (June 2004)

NOW TO 2009   15.0

Chambolle-Musigny, Les Cras, 1994
Domaine Michèle and Patrice Rion

Not *premier cru*. Good colour. Quite an evolved nose. But fragrant and mellow. On the palate this is well matured. Elegant, fruity and positive, but nearing the end. Good plus. (June 2004)

DRINK SOON   15.5

Chambolle-Musigny, Les Cras, 1994
Domaine Georges Roumier et Fils

Magnum. Fresh, medium-full colour. There is an argument for saying that wines of a vintage of only medium depth and concentration should be drunk while still vigorous. And here is a wine to prove the point. All the elegance of good Chambolle. Good fruit and balance. Very good indeed. (December 2000)

DRINK SOON   17.0

Chambolle-Musigny, Les Fuées, 1994
Domaine Jacques-Frédéric Mugnier

Good, fresh colour. Very, very lovely nose. Fragrant and classy. No hard edges. Everything very well integrated. Medium to medium-full body.

Well matured, but fresh, positive, subtle and complex. Very fine. (June 2004)

NOW TO 2009   18.5

Charmes-Chambertin, 1994
Domaine Denis Bachelet

Medium colour. Very lovely nose. Fragrant, stylish, complex and very fresh. Medium-full. Marvellously complex, elegant, fresh fruit on the palate. Excellent grip. Very fine tannins. This is poised and very lovely. Only just ready. Excellent. (June 2004)

NOW TO 2020+   19.5

Clos des Lambrays, 1994
Domaine des Lambrays

Magnum. Lightish colour and lightish, evolved nose. A certain touch of old tea. Fruity and stylish, but a bit evolved on the nose. Yet fresh. Good plus. (June 2004)

NOW TO 2009   15.5

Clos de la Roche, 1994
Domaine Dujac

Medium colour. Stemmy nose. But ripe, fresh, sweet and balanced. On the palate very fresh and intense. Very stylish. Not a hint of any rough tannins. Long and classy. Very fine. (June 2004)

NOW TO 2010+   18.5

Clos de la Roche, 1994
Domaine Leroy

Lighter colour than the 1992. Now evolved. Plump, rich, fresh fruit on the nose. Plenty of interest. A soft, attractive, drinkable wine. Not much dimension, but fresh and not too short. Very good for the vintage. (April 2000)

DRINK SOON   16.0

Clos de la Roche, 1994
Domaine Hubert and Romain Lignier

Good colour. Lovely nose. Very pure, clean fruit here. Balanced, fresh and rich with only just a hint of oak. Slightly less grip and energy on the palate. It is a little astringent at the end but very good plus. (June 2004)

NOW TO 2009   16.5

Clos Saint-Denis, 1994
Domaine Dujac

Light in colour. Fully mature. Light on the palate. No stems. Fully mature. Quite fragrant but a little lighter than expected, and the finish is a little feeble. A bit of a disappointment, even for a 1994. Good at best. (October 2001)

DRINK SOON   15.0

Clos de Tart, 1994
Domaine du Clos de Tart

Magnum. Fullish colour. Meaty nose, but plenty of fruit and grip. Fullish body. A suggestion of astringency at the end, but for the moment good succulence, if slightly lumpy. Good grip. Very good indeed. (June 2004)

NOW TO 2010+   17.0

Clos de Vougeot, 1994
Domaine Robert Arnoux

Fullish colour. Firm on the nose, even to the extent of being a bit burly. Slightly hot. Fullish, meaty and spicy. A little sweet. A touch astringent. This is very good plus, but it doesn't have the class of René Engel's. (October 2001)

DRINK UP   16.5

Clos de Vougeot, 1994
Domaine René Engel

Medium-full colour. Attractive, clean, plump, fresh nose. Medium-full body. Now just about ready. Good tannins. Very good grip. Very good, ample fruit. Balanced, intense and classy. Lovely long finish. Fine. (October 2001)

NOW TO 2010   17.5

Clos de Vougeot, 1994
Domaine Gros Frère et Soeur

Good colour. Fresh nose. Good depth and class. Ripe and succulent on the palate. Rich and fullish bodied. Plenty of fragrance. This is fine. (June 2004)

NOW TO 2010+   17.5

Clos de Vougeot, 1994
Domaine Anne Gros

Good colour. But has evolved fast. On the nose a bit unexciting. Better on the palate. Now only medium bodied. Somewhat diffuse but pleasant. I preferred the 1992. Anne used very little sulphur this year. The wine might have been fresher and more positive had she used a bit more. (June 2003)

DRINK SOON   15.0

Clos de Vougeot, 1994
Domaine Jean Gros

Magnum. Good, fresh colour. Ample nose. This is ripe and really quite profound for vines which were then less than 10 years old. Medium-full bodied, plump, generous, vigorous and with very good grip on the palate. Very long. Very classy. Fine plus. (June 2004)

NOW TO 2010   18.0

Clos de Vougeot, 1994
Domaine Louis Jadot

Good colour. A fullish, meaty wine, but rather astringent all the way through. Difficult to enjoy. The fruit has dried out. (June 2004)

DRINK UP   13.0

Clos de Vougeot, 1994
Domaine Leroy

Medium colour. A little diffuse looking. Fresh and more definitive on the nose than the 1992 though. Medium to medium-full body. A little colour. It lacks a bit of style and flair, but a good, meaty example with a very good finish. (April 2000)

NOW TO 2009   16.0

Clos de Vougeot, 1994
Domaine Méo-Camuzet

Good colour. Still young. Slightly burnt and astringent on the nose. The tannins are not quite integrated. Medium-full body. Better than his Corton. Better grip, riper fruit and more harmony. But not that special. Positive finish though. Very good plus. (March 2001)

NOW TO 2010   16.5

Clos de Vougeot, 1994
Domaine Denis Mortet

Full colour. Quite substantial, but a little lumpy on the nose. Ripe and rich, but rather sturdy on the palate. Not an enormous amount of class. But decent grip. Good plus. (June 2004)

NOW TO 2009   15.5

Clos de Vougeot, 1994
Domaine Georges Mugneret-Gibourg

Good colour. Classy fruit on both nose and palate. Very good grip. Lovely balance and depth. This is ample, generous and succulent. Still very fresh. Fine plus. (June 2004)

NOW TO 2010+   18.0

Le Corton, 1994
Domaine Bouchard Père et Fils

Good fullish, fresh colour. Plump, attractive nose, but on the palate a little astringent at the end. Good energy and substance here. Decent tannins. But only quite good plus. (June 2004)

NOW TO 2009   14.5

Corton, Les Bressandes, 1994
Domaine Chandon de Briailles

Medium to medium-full colour. Round, ripe, quite sweet nose. Some stems. But good style. A bit sweet and bland on the palate. It lacks grip and tails off. Less elegant than on the nose. (June 2004)

DRINK SOON   14.0

Corton, Les Bressandes, 1994
Maison Camille Giroud

Full, fully mature colour. Fat and rich, and ripe and exotic on the nose. Fullish body on the palate. Marvellously complex. Mature, but fresh and complex. Long. Very vigorous still. Fine plus. (September 2002)

NOW TO 2010+   18.0

Corton, Les Renardes, 1994
Domaine Leroy

Good colour. Full, fat, rich, oaky nose. This is high quality. Marvellous depth of fruit, especially for the vintage. Now soft. Now ready. Fullish body. Very classy and balanced. Intense and complex. Fine plus for the vintage. (July 2000)

NOW TO 2010   18.0

Corton, Rognet, 1994
Domaine Méo-Camuzet

Medium-full colour. Still youthful. Slight austerity and astringency on both nose and palate. It lacks a little grip and a little fat. Some unresolved oak tannin. Good but not great. (March 2001)

NOW TO 2010   15.5

Fixin, Clos de la Perrière, 1994
Domaine Joliet Père et Fils

Magnum. Good colour. Slightly robust but not too artisanal on the nose. Decent weight. Good fruit and vigour. No astringent tannins. Balanced. Reasonably stylish. Good. (June 2004)

NOW TO 2009   15.0

Gevrey-Chambertin, Vieilles Vignes, 1994
Domaine Alain Burguet

Good colour. Plump, ripe nose. Stylish and fresh. Vigorous on the palate. Fullish body. No hard edges. Good fat. Ripe. Long. Very good plus. (June 2004)

NOW TO 2010+   16.5

Gevrey-Chambertin, Les Cazetiers, 1994
Domaine Bruno Clair

Good full, fresh colour. Lovely nose. Quite evolved, but complex fruit and lots of class. Similar on the palate. Fully ready in flavour but vigorous in character. Lots of subtle aromas underneath. Long. Very ripe and round. Very fresh. Fine plus. (June 2004)

NOW TO 2010+   18.0

Gevrey-Chambertin, Les Cazetiers, 1994
Domaine Christian Sérafin

Good colour. Ripe, fullish, gently oaky, fragrant nose. More oaky on the palate. Plenty of fruit. Very good vigour. This is more youthful than most. Fresh. Fullish bodied. Succulent. Long. Fine. (June 2004)

NOW TO 2010+   17.5

Gevrey-Chambertin, En Champeaux, 1994
Domaine Denis Mortet

Light-medium, fully mature colour. Mellow nose. Fruity and stylish. But no real depth. Balanced, plump and fruity though. Medium body. Lots of finesse. Long and complex. Fine for the vintage. (May 2002)

NOW TO 2010   17.5

Gevrey-Chambertin, Clos Saint-Jacques, 1994
Domaine Armand Rousseau

Good, fresh colour. Rich, full and vigorous. Especially for the vintage. Medium-full body. Ripe on the palate. Surprisingly classy. Well balanced. This is excellent for the vintage. Long. Stylish. Complex. Lovely. (October 2002)

NOW TO 2018   18.5

Gevrey-Chambertin, Coeur de Roy, 1994
Domaine Bernard Dugat-Py

Good colour. Rich, fullish but not too sturdy nose. Quite a lot of extraction here which masks the fruit. But the fruit and grip are here underneath. A wine for food. Quite good plus. (June 2004)

NOW TO 2009   14.5

Gevrey-Chambertin, Lavaux-Saint-Jacques, 1994
Domaine Bernard Dugat-Py

Very good colour. Rich, full, ample nose. Lots of depth and quality here. Fullish body. Good tannins. Rich and profound. Vigorous and classy. This is fine plus. (June 2004)

NOW TO 2010+   18.0

Grands Echézeaux, 1994
Domaine René Engel

Good colour. Slightly reduced at first on the nose, but good volume and depth. Vigorous, fullish, very stylish. Very good grip on the palate. This is very fine and very lovely. Lots of life here. (June 2004)

NOW TO 2015+   18.5

Latricières-Chambertin, 1994
Domaine Leroy

Medium to medium-full colour. Fully ready. Quite fresh on the nose. Slightly animal and sweaty. Slightly dense. Yet very strawberry. Fine on the palate especially for a 1994. Good

character. Good energy. Good definition and harmony. Long. Fine. (April 2000)

NOW TO 2010   17.5

Marsannay, Les Longeroies, 1994
Domaine Bruno Clair

Fresh, medium colour. Fresh nose. No great weight, but ripe and fruity. This is really surprisingly attractive. Good succulence. Very fresh. A most enjoyable bottle. No sign of age. (June 2004)

NOW TO 2009   15.5

Mazis-Chambertin, 1994
Domaine Frédéric Esmonin

Good colour. Stylish, clean, ample nose. Very impressive for a 1994. Medium-full body. No tannic backbone any more. Succulent and fruity. Fresh and fine quality. No lack of depth. Long. Unexpectedly delicious. Fine plus for the vintage. (April 2005)

NOW TO 2010   18.0

Monthelie, Les Duresses, 1994
Domaine Paul Garaudet

Medium to medium-full colour. No undue age. Round, ripe, generous nose. Even stylish. A bit diffuse and dry at the end though. But quite good. (June 2004)

DRINK SOON   14.0

Château de Monthelie, Sur la Velle, 1994
Domaine Éric de Suremain

Magnum. Soft, intense, classy and fragrant on the nose. Unexpectedly good, succulent and alive for a 1994. Medium body. Very good indeed. A real surprise! (May 2005)

NOW TO 2009   17.0

Morey-Saint-Denis, Clos de la Buissière, 1994
Domaine Georges Roumier

Good colour. A rich, full, quite meaty nose. Ripe but quite sturdy. Fullish body. Good ample attack, but then it falls away a little. Very good plus. (June 2004)

NOW TO 2009   16.5

Musigny, 1994
Domaine Leroy

Medium colour. Fully ready. A touch of SO2 on the nose at first. Pleasant but a little weak after the 1992. Classy on the attack but a little diffuse underneath. Good fruit and grip nevertheless. No long future but very fine for the vintage. (April 2000)

DRINK SOON   18.5

Musigny, 1994
Domaine Jacques-Frédéric Mugnier

Good colour. Marvellous, fragrant nose. Splendid fruit. Medium-full body. Intense. Fresh and classy. Very long. Very complex. Very fine plus. (June 2004)

NOW TO 2010+   19.0

Musigny, 1994
Domaine Comte Georges de Vogüé

Medium-full colour. Fully mature. Elegant but slightly dry on the nose. Medium to medium-full body. Slightly pinched. Decent fruit. Now getting a little dry, but elegant. Fine for the vintage, but their Bonnes Mares is better. (October 2005)

NOW TO 2009   17.5

Nuits-Saint-Georges, Les Bas de Combe, 1994
Domaine Jean Tardy et Fils

Medium to medium-full colour. Soft, gentle, slightly oaky nose. Medium to medium-full body. Soft, ample, ripe and fresh on the palate. A little astringent at the end. But stylish. Good. (June 2004)

NOW TO 2009   15.0

Nuits-Saint-Georges, Les Boudots, 1994
Domaine Jean Grivot

Magnum. Medium to medium-full colour. Now some signs of maturity. Slightly funky, pruney nose. It is lacking a bit of class. But showing good grip. Rather better than the 1992. Now also fully ready. Medium body. Fresher and more stylish. The fruit is purer and seems less chaptalised. Nicely cool at the end. Good, long, positive finish. Fine for the vintage. (November 2001)

NOW TO 2020   17.5

Nuits-Saint-Georges, Les Boudots, 1994
Domaine Jean Tardy et Fils

Good colour. Soft, ripe but slightly neutral on the nose. Medium body. Quite fruity. The tannins are ripe. The wine has balance. The attack is a bit one-dimensional, but the finish shows more character. Decent length and style. Good plus. (June 2004)

NOW TO 2009   15.5

Nuits-Saint-Georges, Clos des Forêts Saint-Georges, 1994
Domaine de l'Arlot

Medium-full colour. Some development. Rich, chocolaty nose. The stemmy character has now diminished. Medium to medium-full body. A certain astringency. But decent fruit if only one-dimensional. Finishes positively. Good. (March 2005)

DRINK SOON   15.0

Nuits-Saint-Georges, Les Porêts-Saint-Georges, 1994
Domaine Joseph Faiveley

Good colour. Rich, fullish, stylish nose. Plenty of depth here. Medium-full body. Ripe. Quite concentrated. Good tannins. Plenty of energy. Quite profound and certainly very stylish. Very good plus. (June 2004)

NOW TO 2010+   16.5

Nuits-Saint-Georges, Les Saint-Georges, 1994
Domaine Forey Père et Fils

Good colour. Full, ripe, sturdy nose. Plenty of substance here and no lack of fruit. Medium-full body. A little four-square. Some obstructive tannin on the attack. But rich enough. Good grip. Good plus. (June 2004)

NOW TO 2009   15.5

Nuits-Saint-Georges, Les Saint-Georges, 1994
Domaine Henri Gouges

Good, fullish, vigorous colour. Lovely ripe, rich nose. Plenty of depth. Lots of class. Medium-full body. Very good, ripe tannins. Very good grip. Lots of wine and lots of enjoyment here. Balanced. Fresh and complex. Very fine finish. (June 2004)

NOW TO 2010+   18.0

**Pommard, Les Chaponnières,
Vieilles Vignes, 1994
Domaine Billard-Gonnet**

Medium-full colour. A little unstylish and sweaty on the nose, but no ungainly tannins. Medium body. On the palate has dried out quite a lot. (June 2004)

DRINK SOON   13.0

**Pommard, Clos des Epeneaux, 1994
Domaine du Comte Armand**

Fullish colour. Still youthful. Very good nose for a 1994. Rich, full and fat. Sophisticated tannins, and a bit more depth and concentration than the 1995 perhaps. But while super for a 1994, not up to the quality of the other 1995s. (July 2001)

NOW TO 2020   18.5

**Pommard, Clos des Epeneaux, 1994
Domaine des Epeneaux**

Full, vigorous colour. In magnum: very dried out. Too much earth and dead leaves. A bad bottle. In bottle: full, tannic, but rich and ripe. Slightly austere but very good indeed. (June 2004)

NOW TO 2010+   17.0

**Pommard, Clos du Verger, 1994
Domaine Billard-Gonnet**

Good colour. Ripe nose. Good fruit here. A medium-full-bodied, meaty example. Quite ripe tannins. No astringency. Fresh fruit. Well made. (June 2004)

NOW TO 2009   15.5

**Pommard, Les Rugiens, 1994
Domaine Billard-Gonnet**

Good, fresh, fullish colour. Ripe, round stylish nose. No hard edges here. Positive. Well balanced. But like most of these 1994s, an absence of real richness. Yet clean, long, positive and very good indeed. (June 2004)

NOW TO 2010+   17.0

**Pommard, Les Rugiens, 1994
Domaine Jean-Marc Boillot**

Good, fresh, medium-weight colour. Ripe, slightly spicy nose and palate. Rather more generous than most. Rich on the palate. Quite mellow. A bit obviously chaptalised, but good plus. (June 2004)

NOW TO 2009   15.5

**Richebourg, 1994
Domaine Anne Gros**

Medium-full, mature colour. Slightly reduced and sweaty on the nose. But ripe and soft. Medium to medium-full body. This is now ready. Fresh, ample, harmonious and very enjoyable. But it lacks the distinction of a top vintage. Reasonably positive at the end. The 1992 is much better. Drink soon. (February 2004)

DRINK SOON   15.5

**Richebourg, 1994
Domaine Jean Gros**

Magnum. Medium-full, mature colour. Ripe, rich, succulent and velvety on the nose. Very lovely, complex fruit. This is ample and fullish bodied on the palate, with very good grip and very fine tannins. Classy fruit and lots of dimension. Excellent. (June 2004)

NOW TO 2015+   19.5

**Richebourg, 1994
Domaine Leroy**

Good colour for a 1994. Just about mature. Ripe, rich and balanced, if just a touch dense. More stylish and more impressive as it evolved. Rich, fullish and oaky. Really excellent for a 1994. Marvellously ample, fresh finish. Very long. (April 2000)

NOW TO 2010   17.5

**Richebourg, 1994
Domaine de la Romanée-Conti**

Full colour. Full, rich, concentrated nose. It got better and better as it evolved in the glass. Fullish body. Sophisticated tannins. Very good grip. Rich and profound with a touch of spice and voluptuousness. Vigorous yet no hard edges. This is a very lovely wine. Excellent for the vintage. (October 2000)

NOW TO 2018   19.0

La Romanée, 1994
Domaine Bouchard Père et Fils
Good, vigorous colour. Fine nose. Rich and meaty, and not a bit off-vintage-y. Fullish body. Ample fruit. Lots of class and very fine balance. This is truly excellent for a 1994. Real depth, vigour and complexity. (October 2005)

NOW TO 2015   20.0

Romanée-Saint-Vivant, 1994
Domaine Robert Arnoux
Good colour. Impressive nose. Rich, full, concentrated and very classy. On the palate this is full bodied and still youthful. Lots of depth and concentration. Very good acidity. A profound and very lovely example. (June 2004)

NOW TO 2020+   19.5

Romanée-Saint-Vivant, 1994
Domaine Alain Hudelot-Noëllat
Good, fullish colour. No undue age. A little dry on the nose but quite classy fruit underneath. Better on the palate. No great richness or concentration. Medium body. Slightly lean. But not too bad. Drink quite soon. It is getting a little thin at the end. (October 2005)

DRINK SOON   15.0

Romanée-Saint-Vivant, 1994
Domaine Leroy
Medium to medium-full colour. Fully mature. Soft, round, ample, ripe nose. Not a great deal of weight and structure. But fresh and attractive. A marvellous 1994. Full and rich, and plenty of definition. Fullish body. Balanced. Very fine. (April 2000)

NOW TO 2010   18.5

Ruchottes-Chambertin, 1994
Domaine Georges Mugneret-Gibourg
Fullish colour. Ripe, fresh, ample nose. Lots of lovely, succulent fruit here. Very youthful. Fullish, plump, fresh and generous. But it doesn't have the grip, concentration, follow-through and sheer flair of, for example, Bachelet's Charmes. Fine plus. (June 2004)

NOW TO 2020+   18.0

Santenay, Longeroies, 1994
Domaine Françoise and Denis Clair
Good colour. This is fresh, stylish, mellow and balanced. Medium body. Good persistence. Long. This is very good, indeed, for what it is. (March 2000)

DRINK SOON   16.0

Savigny-lès-Beaune, La Dominode, 1994
Domaine Bruno Clair
Magnum. Fullish, fresh colour. Ripe nose. Medium to medium-full body. Good fruit. The tannins are ripe, but there is a suggestion of astringency at the end. Lots of style though. Long and complex. (June 2004)

NOW TO 2009   15.5

Savigny-lès-Beaune, La Dominode, 1994
Domaine Jean-Marc Pavelot
Fullish, vigorous colour. Lovely nose. Ripe and rich. On the palate this is medium-full, fat, ripe and energetic. Long and stylish. Very good. (June 2004)

NOW TO 2010+   16.0

Savigny-lès-Beaune, Les Vergelesses, 1994
Domaine Lucien Jacob
Medium colour. Well matured. A bit rustic on the nose. Medium body. Slightly astringent on the palate. This lacks style. (June 2004)

DRINK SOON   13.0

La Tâche, 1994
Domaine de la Romanée-Conti
Good colour. Vigorous nose. Fullish, rich, cool and classy. As always, very individual. The attack is rich and full, vigorous and showing very good grip, but also just a touch of astringency. And the tannins are just a little lumpy. But it is very profound and very fine. It needs food. (June 2004)

NOW TO 2015+   18.5

Volnay, Champans, 1994
Domaine Hubert de Montille
Medium colour. No undue maturity. Rather a thin, austere nose. Medium body. Not much

fruit. Slightly astringent. Not much charm. (June 2004)

DRINK SOON 13.5

Volnay, Clos du Château des Ducs, 1994
Domaine Michel Lafarge

Ripe, rich, succulent nose and palate. Medium to medium-full body. Ample, balanced and fruity-creamy. Fullish body. Balanced and very lovely for a 1994. Lots of class and very long on the palate. (March 2005)

NOW TO 2014 17.5

Volnay, Clos des Chênes, 1994
Domaine Michel Lafarge

Surprisingly good, vigorous colour. Only just about mature looking. Ripe, stylish nose. No lack of depth. Fullish body. Mellow. Good tannins. Plenty of vigour. Remarkably good for the vintage. No lack of charm and succulence. Very fine. (March 2006)

NOW TO 2014 18.5

Volnay, Clos des Ducs, 1994
Domaine du Marquis d'Angerville

This is getting better and better. When I first acquired it, as a bin-end, it was a little tight, the tannins of a not-so-good-year standing out. Now it has mellowed beautifully. Medium to medium-full body. Ripe, succulent, classy and balanced. Even rich. Fine for the vintage. (September 2005)

NOW TO 2010 17.5

Volnay, Frémiets, 1994
Domaine Annick Parent

Medium colour. No undue age. Ripe nose. Medium body. Soft. Quite stylish. Good balance. A suggestion of astringency at the end. Good. (June 2004)

DRINK SOON 15.0

Volnay, Santenots, 1994
Domaine des Comtes Lafon

Medium colour. Fully mature. Not a lot of substance on the nose. But ripe and fruity, and charming on the palate. Only medium body.

But elegant and even quite supple. Fresh. Good, clean finish. Very good plus. (March 2005)

NOW TO 2008 16.5

Volnay, Santenots, 1994
Domaine Joseph Matrot

Good colour. Ripe, rich, mature but vigorous nose. Medium-full and ripe, but at the same time rather astringent on the palate. Yet a positive finish. Would be better with food. (June 2004)

NOW TO 2009 15.0

Volnay, Santenots, 1994
Domaine François Mikulski

Medium colour. Well matured. Round, rich and ripe on the nose. Medium-full bodied, fat and generous on the palate. Very good balance here. No aggressive tannins. Long. No real Volnay elegance but very good plus. (June 2004)

NOW TO 2010+ 16.5

Volnay, Santenots, 1994
Domaine Charles Rossignol-Jeanniard

Medium colour. Well matured. Slightly tight on the nose but fruity. Medium body. No brutal tannins here but not very stylish. (June 2004)

DRINK SOON 14.0

Volnay, Santenots du Milieu, 1994
Domaine des Comtes Lafon

Fullish, vigorous colour. Ripe nose. Quite robust and energetic. Fullish. Some tannin. Decent fruit. Rich at the end. Lacks a little style but very good plus. (June 2004)

NOW TO 2010+ 16.5

Volnay, Taillepieds, 1994
Domaine du Marquis d'Angerville

Medium, but still vigorous colour. Fragrant, clean Pinot nose if without great depth or richness. Medium to medium-full body. Plenty of class and interest. Good fruit and balance. No great concentration, but fresh and enjoyable. Good, positive finish. No hurry to drink up. (February 2005)

NOW TO 2010 16.0

Vosne-Romanée, 1994
Domaine Sylvain Cathiard

Good, fresh colour. Fresh, elegant and rich in a quite oaky, earthy sense. Perhaps a little too much new wood here. The wine is quite fresh. Ripe and succulent. Long. Very good plus. (June 2004)

NOW TO 2010+   16.5

Vosne-Romanée, 1994
Domaine Forey Père et Fils

Good colour. Sturdy nose. A chunky wine with some fruit if no great dimension. Now a bit astringent at the end, although there is good grip here. Quite good plus. (June 2004)

DRINK SOON   14.5

Vosne-Romanée, Clos des Réas, 1994
Domaine Michel Gros

Medium to medium-full, mature colour. Fresh, classy nose. This is much better within its context than the 1995. Medium-full body. The tannins are now soft. This has good fruit and good acidity. A surprising amount of dimension for a 1994. Long. Fine for the vintage. *À point* but no hurry to drink up. (December 2003)

NOW TO 2012   17.5

Vosne-Romanée, Les Suchots, 1994
Domaine Robert Arnoux

Good colour. Ripe and ample on the nose, but just a little sweaty. Better on the palate. Fullish body. Very good, concentrated, ripe fruit. Plenty of depth and grip. Classy and complex. Fine plus.

NOW TO 2010+   18.0

Vosne-Romanée, Les Suchots, 1994
Domaine Jean Grivot

Magnum. Very good colour. Very fine, concentrated, very fresh nose. Excellent tannins here and very high-class fruit. This is surprisingly fresh and youthful on the palate. Medium-full body. Very succulent. Lots of depth, but not a bit hard or astringent. Really very fine. (June 2004)

NOW TO 2015+   18.5

Vougeot, 1994
Domaine Chopin-Groffier

Medium-full, mature colour. Fresh, stylish, individual nose. Good, classy grip and depth. Ripe and quite succulent. No weakness. Good concentration for the vintage and a Vougeot. Classy too. Very good, especially for a village wine. Old viney. (March 2003)

NOW TO 2011   16.0

1993

I said at the outset that, despite some rain during the vintage—and very few vintages are entirely rain-free—1993 was a fine red wine vintage. The colours are excellent, the acidities fine, the structures very good, and the tannins sophisticated. At these top levels, the vintage combines, in the words of Freddy Mugnier, "the velvet texture and richness of 1990, the fruit of 1989 and the acidity of 1988." It was a smallish crop, at least in Pinot Noir, and the wines have concentration. They also have breed.

WEATHER CONDITIONS

Following the 1992 vintage, the autumn was grey and wet, but the winter was largely dry. A hot spell in the last fortnight of March encouraged an early bud-break, and the *sortie* of potential grape bunches turned out to be abundant. The flowering took place successfully, and a few days earlier than normal, during the first ten days of in June.

Spring and summer, right through until August, were warm but wet, frequently interrupted by thunderstorms. As a result, it was the worst season for mildew since 1953. Growers were forced to treat the vines twice as frequently as usual, with Jadot spraying its domaine ten times rather than five. Oïdium was also a problem.

One of the storms took place during the night of June 19–20. A swath of hail caused damage in some of the vineyards of Saint-Aubin and in Blagny, but most seriously in the *premiers crus* of Perrières, Genevrières and Charmes in Meursault and in those *climats* across the border in Puligny: Referts, Combettes and Champ-Canet. The harvest here was more than halved as a result, with Dominique Lafon producing 8.5 *pièces* from his 1.2 hectares of Charmes (16 hl/ha), Thierry Matrot 18 hectolitres per hectare in his Perrières, and Gérard Boudot of Domaine Étienne Sauzet 15 hectolitres per hectare in his Combettes.

The *véraison* took place at the beginning of August, and this was accompanied by a change in the weather. The month that followed was warm and dry—with precipitation of a mere 17 millimetres—and in this heat, the grape skins thickened, a factor that was to be crucial when it came to the harvest. Some of the progress of the fruit toward maturity was retarded, however. The grapes remained blocked, particularly in the best-drained, most meagre soils further up the slope. This seems to have affected the Chardonnays more than the Pinots Noirs.

With the arrival of September, there was a two-day period of rain. This jumpstarted the ripening process again, and the must weight rose rapidly in the 10 days which followed, with the *ban des vendanges* being announced on September 15 in the Côte de Beaune.

The vintage then began. The long-range forecast was not promising, and most growers rushed out to pick their grapes. The reds were now ripe and generally were cleared first, leaving a brief period before the weather changed in which to clear some of the ripest white wine vineyards. Usually, it is the best-exposed sites, the *grands* and *premiers crus*, which arrive at maturity first. But in 1993, it was exactly these which had been *bloqué* in August. The grower was therefore in a dilemma: pick now, just a little unripe—a full degree of alcohol less than in 1992—or wait and perhaps suffer dilution when the announced rain commenced—a no-win situation indeed!

The weather did break, as feared, and on the day of the equinox. But after 3 days of rain, it cleared a little, enabling the rest of the Côte de Beaune harvest to be collected before it deteriorated again at the beginning of October. Conditions were by no means perfect during this period; it was a question of dodging in and out of the showers. But at least the rains were not heavy, nor were they continuous. And it was cool. There was little incidence of rot.

In the Côte de Nuits, the hail damage had occurred earlier, on May 16 and 27, although the June thunderstorm was also deleterious, and the mildew onslaught was, if anything, even worse. All in all, things were not looking good as the *grandes vacances* approached. The August weather though, thankfully, was excellent. A storm on September 10 was beneficial rather than the opposite, for it helped to further ripen and soften the tannins. The *ban des vendanges* was declared, amid some optimism, on September 15, the same day as for the Côte de Beaune.

Sadly, there was rain during the harvest. It rained at the beginning, it rained during the middle, and it rained at the end. But it certainly did not rain everywhere all the time, and most growers were able to stop and start, collecting their fruit when the weather was dry. Few Burgundian domaines are very large, and in this respect, Burgundy benefited in 1993. Most can be picked in a week. With the help of the long-range weather forecast, most growers were able to adapt their picking programs to the best days of the fortnight between September 15 and October 1.

Small berries with a greater concentration of solid to liquid, and not much of them, and fruit—provided the pickers had performed a *triage*—which was healthy, and if not cropped during rain, of good acidity, added up to a promising start. Yet at the beginning, the wines

→ Rating for the Vintage ←	
Red	17.5
White	15.0

→ Size of the Crop ←
(In hectolitres, excluding generic wine)

	RED	WHITE
Grands Crus	11,895	3,577
Village and		
Premiers Crus	181,477	49,681
TOTAL	193,372	53,258

seemed rather neutral, with high acidities. It was only after the *malos* —which were long and drawn out—that the true contours and quality of the 1993 reds began to emerge. In retrospect, these long-lasting *malos* transformed the vintage. The lees were clean, the wines could slowly enrich themselves without danger of mercaptan contamination, and they just went on tasting better and better as summer turned into autumn.

A feature of the 1993s is their excellent, healthy colour. Another is a refreshing acidity: not too high, just what is required to preserve the fruit and maintain the elegance. A third is an intensely perfumed, pure Pinot fruit. If these wines are a little less structured than the 1990s in some cases, at least the tannins are riper and more stylish. There are no hard edges. In sum, the 1993s are more harmonious and *terroir* specific than the 1990s. "As good as the 1990s, but different," said Denis Bachelet. "*Ils pinottent*," said Christian Gouges, meaning that they show a more typical expression of Pinot Noir fruit than this earlier, magnificently rich, but atypical vintage. "They have a flavour of *glacé* (crystalised) fruit," said Jean-Luc Pépin of Domaine Comte Georges de Vogüé. "Harmonious," said Jacques Lardière of Maison Jadot. "An engaging personality," said Robert Drouhin.

Bottle tastings have confirmed the quality of the 1993 reds. The words classic, pure and yardstick occur frequently in my notes. The wines are not as rich or as voluminous as the 1990s, but they are perhaps more elegant. They are certainly more typical. I consider this, with 1990 and 1995, the best of the 1990s red wine vintages after 1999.

WHERE ARE THE BEST WINES?

AND THE STATE OF MATURITY TODAY

The white wines were at their best in Corton-Charlemagne, and one or two of these can still be delicious. Most of the rest are now tired. The reds were always proportionately better as one climbs the hierarchy. They are better, and today more vigorous, in the Côte de Nuits than in the Côte de Beaune. Drink village wines quite soon.

The top reds will still keep very well indeed, well toward the end of the next decade.

TASTING NOTES

WHITES

Bâtard-Montrachet, 1993
Domaine Jean-Noël Gagnard

Magnum. Very good nose. This has individuality. There is good acidity here, plus an interesting spicy aspect. Fullish body on the palate. Slightly lean but not without energy, dimension and even depth. Ripe enough. Slightly austere, but full of complexity. Ready now. It should keep well, though. Very much more to it than the 1994, especially on the follow-through. Very good indeed for the vintage. (January 2002)

NOW TO 2010   17.0

Bâtard-Montrachet, 1993
Domaine Paul Pernot et Fils

Rich, crisp, fresh and with plenty of depth, even elegance. Full body. Quite concentrated. Slightly austere, but not lean. Classy. Very good indeed. (February 2005)

DRINK SOON   17.0

Bâtard-Montrachet, 1993
Maison Verget

This is very classy. Full, rich, concentrated and vigorous. Very good fruit. Lots of ripeness. Not a bit lean. Splendidly fresh. The oak is just right. Very fine. (October 2002)

NOW TO 2010   18.5

Beaune, Sur les Grèves, 1993
Domaine Germain Père et Fils/
Chateau de Chorey-lès-Beaune

Ripe, fresh nose. Good touch of oak. Still lively on the palate. Good fruit. Quite full bodied. It shows well. Very good. (June 2003)

DRINK SOON   16.0

Bienvenues-Bâtard-Montrachet, 1993
Domaine Leflaive

Magnum. Decent, but not with top vigour, class or depth on the nose. Fullish body. Quite

broad-flavoured. It lacks a bit of grip and concentration on the palate. Good at best. (June 2003)
DRINK SOON 15.0

Chassagne-Montrachet, 1993
Domaine Jean-Noël Gagnard

Light to medium colour. Light nose. Quite pretty fruit. Neither weedy, nor rustic. In fact, firm and charming. Quite good. (June 2003)
DRINK SOON 14.0

Chassagne-Montrachet, En Cailleret, 1993
Domaine Guy Amiot et Fils

This is still nicely fresh, honeyed, ripe and generous. Medium-full body. Still very alive. Ripe and harmonious. Good depth. Long. Not a bit tired. Very good indeed. (June 2003)
NOW TO 2010 17.0

Chassagne-Montrachet, Les Caillerets, 1993
Domaine Marc Colin

Quite a developed colour. Nicely plump, fully mature nose. The good base of acidity gives it dimension and vigour. Medium-full body. Ripe and ample with just the merest suggestion of oak. Not a bit lean. Complex and stylish. Plenty of life ahead of it. Very good indeed. (March 2005)
NOW TO 2010 17.0

Chassagne-Montrachet, Les Caillerets, 1993
Domaine Richard Fontaine-Gagnard

Some development on the colour. Not a great deal on the nose, but it is clean and fresh. Medium body. Quite fruity and decently balanced. But altogether, rather neutral. Quite good plus. (May 2005)
DRINK SOON 14.5

Chassagne-Montrachet, Caillerets, 1993
Domaine Jean-Noël Gagnard

Fresh, quite concentrated nose. More to it than their 1996. A 1993 with plenty of personality and fruit. Medium-full body. Clean, fresh and ripe. Still very vigorous. Long. Fine. (June 2006)
NOW TO 2010+ 17.5

Chassagne-Montrachet, Les Chaumées,
Clos de la Truffière, Vieilles Vignes, 1993
Domaine Vincent et François Jouard

Fresh, stylish, fruity and graceful on the nose. Ripe. Medium-full body. Complex and harmonious on the palate. Fine. (June 2003)
DRINK SOON 17.5

Chassagne-Montrachet, Les Chenevottes, 1993
Domaine Jean-Noël Gagnard

Quite evolved. Slightly lean. Not the style of the wines Caroline Lestimé makes today. Medium to medium-full body. Average quality. But improved on aeration. Decent finish. (September 2005)
DRINK SOON 14.5

Chassagne-Montrachet, Morgeot, 1993
Domaine Jean-Noël Gagnard

Light to medium colour. A little more definition and volume on the nose than has the village wine. But not much more vigour on the palate. Decent fresh fruit, though. Quite good plus. (June 2003)
DRINK SOON 14.5

Chassagne-Montrachet, Morgeots, 1993
Domaine Louis Jadot

A slight whiff of tiredness on the nose. Ripe and elegant, but now fading on the palate. Quite good. Drink soon. (June 2003)
DRINK SOON 14.0

Chassagne-Montrachet, Morgeot,
Clos Pitois, 1993
Domaine Roger Belland

Good colour. Plump, ripe nose. Good freshness. Good depth. Medium-full body. Ripe. Really good fruit. Plenty of vigour. Stylish, too. Long. Very good. (June 2003)
NOW TO 2010 16.0

Chassagne-Montrachet, En Pimont, 1993
Chateau de Puligny-Montrachet

Village *appellation contrôlée*. Medium body. Fresh. Not too lean. This is stylish and full of interest for what it is. Vigorous, too. Quite concentrated indeed. Unexpectedly good. (December 2001)

DRINK SOON   16.0

Chassagne-Montrachet, Les Ruchottes, 1993
Domaine Ramonet

Full, firm, fresh and substantial. This has a lot of depth and vitality. Very good grip. Very good fruit. Plenty of life ahead of it. Fine plus. (June 2003)

NOW TO 2008   18.0

Corton-Charlemagne, 1993
Domaine Bonneau du Martray

Real class on the nose. Splendid depth and concentration. Very lovely fruit. Fullish body. Ready but still youthful. Gently oaky. Ripe and balanced. Long and complex. Very fine plus. (June 2006)

NOW TO 2015   19.0

Corton-Charlemagne, 1993
Domaine Jean-François Coche-Dury

Fine nose. Rich and fragrant. Vigorous and minerally. Very classy. This is very concentrated and very lovely. Not a bit tough. Flowery and fruity. Intense and multidimensional. Really excellent. (June 2003)

NOW TO 2010+   19.5

Corton-Charlemagne, 1993
Domaine Joseph Faiveley

Quite a developed colour. Full, fresh but oaky nose. Slightly rigid at first. Really quite oaky on the palate, but crisp and minerally. Yet the oak dominates. Full bodied. Plenty of fruit. But the net effect is a bit heavy. Merely very good. (December 2005)

NOW TO 2010   16.0

Corton-Charlemagne, 1993
Maison Olivier Leflaive Frères

Magnum. Good firm, fullish nose. Still vigorous. A proper Corton Charlemagne. Steely. Fullish body. Ripe and stylish. Fine. (June 2003)

DRINK SOON   17.5

Criots-Bâtard-Montrachet, 1993
Maison Olivier Leflaive Frères

Magnum. Lovely nose. Rich, ripe and classy. Fullish body. Good grip. The fruit is beginning to go, but this is a fine example. (June 2003)

DRINK SOON   17.5

Meursault, 1993
Domaine Jean-François Coche-Dury

Fresh, succulent, ripe and now quite round. Good acidity. Plenty of fruit. Stylish. Slightly hard. But very good. (March 2005)

DRINK SOON   16.0

Meursault, 1993
Domaine Pierre Matrot

Not a lot of fruit. A faint touch of sulphur at the end. Reasonably fresh. But not a lot of interest. Drink soon. (June 2003)

DRINK SOON   13.5

Meursault, En la Barre, 1993
Domaine François Jobard

Slightly austere. Indeed a little lean. But quite classy. Slightly four-square on the palate. Good, though, for a village wine. (October 2002)

DRINK SOON   15.0

Meursault, Les Caillerets, 1993
Domaine François Mikulski

Magnum. Good colour. Fresh, ripe, quite profound nose. Not the greatest of Meursault class: indeed a bit sweet-sour. But quite substantial, quite rich and quite fresh. Quite good plus. (June 2003)

DRINK SOON   14.5

Meursault, Charmes, 1993
Domaine François Jobard

Quite closed on the nose. A bit neutral on the palate. But it is still quite fresh. Good substance but not enough fruit. (June 2003)

DRINK SOON   13.5

Meursault, Clos de la Barre, 1993
Domaine des Comtes Lafon

Youthful colour still. Rich, aromatic, fullish, gently oaky nose and palate. Ripe, concentrated and still very vigorous. Classic nutty Meursault. Lovely. Lots of life ahead of it. (February 2005)

NOW TO 2010   16.0

Meursault, Clos du Cromin, 1993
Domaine Patrick Javillier

A little lean on the nose. It has lost some of its fruit. Fresh, though. Still pleasant. Good structure. Quite good. (June 2003)

DRINK SOON   14.0

Meursault, Les Durots, 1993
Domaine Pierre Morey

Medium colour. Ample, round, attractive nose. Ripe and generous. Medium to medium-full body. Some tannin. Good structure. Balanced and very Volnay-ish. Good class. Very good. (June 2003)

NOW TO 2010+   16.0

Meursault, Genevrières, 1993
Domaine Michel Bouzereau et Fils

Youthful colour. Fragrant, quite minerally nose but not a great deal of vigour or concentration. Yet no lack of depth or elegance. Good fruit. Good balance. *À point* now. To be drunk quite soon. Very good plus. (May 2005)

NOW TO 2008   16.5

Meursault, Genevrières, 1993
Domaine François Jobard

Fresher and fruitier than his Charmes on the nose. A little built-in sulphur. A bit tight. Good substance, but it lacks charm. (June 2003)

DRINK SOON   13.5

Meursault, Genevrières, 1993
Domaine des Comtes Lafon

One bottle a little more evolved than the other. Minuscule harvest because of frost. Acidity to the fore here. Slightly sweet-sour. Medium-full body. A bit rigid. Lacks style. I don't get much pleasure here. But with a careful food accompaniment, it would be more generous. Fair. (September 2005)

DRINK SOON   13.5

Meursault, Genevrières, 1993
Domaine François Mikulski

Magnum. Slight reduction on the nose and a bit astringent on the palate. Some fruit. Good substance. (June 2003)

DRINK SOON   13.5

Meursault, Perrières, 1993
Domaine Michel Bouzereau et Fils

Youthful colour. Ripe, nutty, quite mineral nose and palate. Good fruit. Good depth. Still very fresh. Medium to medium-full body. Plenty of elegance and character. Will still last. Very good plus. (May 2005)

NOW TO 2009   16.5

Meursault, Les Perrières, 1993
Domaine Jean-François Coche-Dury

Magnum. Lovely nose. Rich, concentrated, fresh and classy. This is very lovely, and it will keep well. Very long. Very fine indeed. (June 2003)

NOW TO 2010   19.0

Meursault, Les Perrières, 1993
Domaine des Comtes Lafon

Fuller but slightly leaner on the nose than the 1994. More concentrated. Greater acidity. Medium-full body on the palate. Good oak. Very lovely peachy fruit. Not a bit lean on the follow-through. Not the depth of the 1992, but much more interesting than the 1994. Lots of charm. Very long and complex. Now ready, but no hurry to drink. Very fine for the vintage. (May 2001)

NOW TO 2010   18.5

Meursault, Les Perrières, 1993
Domaine Pierre Matrot

Some SO2—far too much. The fruit has dried out. Past its best. (June 2003)

PAST ITS BEST (SEE NOTE)

Meursault, Perrières, 1993
Domaine Guy Roulot

Youthful colour. Crisp and clean. Slightly lean, but ripe and complex on the nose. Medium to medium-full weight. Very good fruit. Minerally and classy. Quite restrained all the way through. Lovely balance. Peachy, ripe and flowery at the end. Fine. (February 2005)

NOW TO 2010   17.5

Meursault, Porusot, 1993
Domaine Rémi Jobard

Light, mid-gold colour. Fresh nose. Good depth and ripeness. Medium body. Round, soft, fresh and attractive on the palate. Good long finish. Ample for the vintage. No hurry to drink. Very good. (May 2005)

NOW TO 2009   16.0

Meursault, Les Tessons, 1993
Domaine Pierre Morey

The fruit has dried out a bit and the wine has gotten a bit tired. Was quite full. Past its best. (June 2003)

PAST ITS BEST   12.0

Meursault, Tessons, Clos de Mon Plaisir, 1993
Domaine Guy Roulot

Magnum. An attractive, fresh, aromatic example. Fullish body. Good depth, fruit and style. Ample and aromatic. Good plus. (June 2003)

DRINK SOON   15.5

Le Montrachet, 1993
Domaine Bouchard Père et Fils

Well matured, if not slightly tired, on the nose at first. But this improved. Not much depth, though quite fresh on the palate. Decent acidity but not enough concentration. Very good at best. There are better 1993s. (June 2003)

DRINK SOON   16.0

Le Montrachet, 1993
Maison Étienne Sauzet

Quite a deep colour. A fullish, evolved wine on the nose. Rich, ripe and full on the palate. Good acidity, if not the greatest class or dimension. There is a touch of the sweet-sour here. But there is also depth and concentration and plenty of vigour. Not great, perhaps not even fine, but

that is the character of the whites of this vintage. (September 2003)

NOW TO 2009   16.0

Montrachet, 1993
Domaine du Marquis de Laguiche/
Maison Joseph Drouhin

Fullish body. Very lovely fruit. Concentrated, classy, profound and still very fresh. This is quite delicious. Outstanding, indeed, for a 1993. Very elegant and very harmonious. Very long. (June 2003)

NOW TO 2010+   20.0

Musigny, Blanc, 1993
Domaine Comte Georges de Vogüé

Slightly heavy nose with a touch of SO2. Fullish body. Some fruit, but a little four-square. Still vigorous though. But it lacks a little nuance. Very good at best. (June 2003)

DRINK SOON   16.0

Nuits-Saint-Georges, Clos de l'Arlot, Blanc, 1993
Domaine de l'Arlot

Fresh colour. Fresh nose. Ripe and stylish, if without any great depth or concentration. Balanced and attractive, though. But essentially a slight lack of personality. Good plus. (May 2005)

NOW TO 2009   15.5

Puligny-Montrachet, Les Caillerets, 1993
Domaine Hubert de Montille

Fresh and classy, but slightly restrained on the nose. Vigorous, but a little tight. This was the first vintage (though not young vines). Very good. (Now to 2008: 16/20.) A second bottle was more supple and more fragrant. Delicious, in fact. Fine. (June 2003)

NOW TO 2010   17.5

Puligny-Montrachet, Champ Canet, 1993
Domaine Étienne Sauzet

Youthful colour. Delicate, classy nose. Balanced, medium bodied and already very drinkable. Discreet but intense. Long. The oak is very subtle. Very good indeed. (March 2001)

NOW TO 2010   17.0

Puligny-Montrachet, Les Combettes, 1993
Domaine Jean-Marc Boillot

Soft, fruity, plump and vigorous. It needs drinking, but is an attractive, ripe, stylish wine. Very good plus. (June 2003)

DRINK SOON   16.5

Puligny-Montrachet, Les Demoiselles, 1993
Domaine Guy Amiot et Fils

Magnum. Just a touch heavy on the nose. A little SO2, but alive and kicking on the palate. Full bodied, rich and fat. Good grip. Nutty at the end. Not the greatest style, but very good. (June 2003)

DRINK SOON   16.0

Puligny-Montrachet, Les Enseignères, 1993
Maison Verget

Quite a developed colour. Rather over-evolved, if not a bit oxidised on the nose. Decent acidity underneath. But rather thin. No future. Only fair. (May 2005)

DRINK UP   13.0

Puligny-Montrachet, Les Folatières, 1993
Domaine Gérard Chavy et Fils

This is rather evolved. It is also a bit thin and vegetal: indeed, more and more as it evolved. In the glass, it resembled a Coteaux Champenois: yeasty, meagre and with high acidity. Not very exciting at all. (September 2001)

DRINK SOON   12.0

Puligny-Montrachet, Les Folatières, 1993
Domaine Leflaive

Ripe and rich but surprisingly weak-kneed. Where is the grip of the 1993s? Rather tired. A bit sweet and superficial. Only quite good. And it won't really keep. (January 2001)

DRINK SOON   14.0

Puligny-Montrachet, Les Pucelles, 1993
Maison Olivier Leflaive Frères

Magnum. Light nose but soft, ripe and pretty. It is getting a little tired, but it still has fruit. Good. (June 2003)

DRINK SOON   15.0

Puligny-Montrachet, Les Referts, 1993
Domaine Jean-Marc Boillot

A full, rich, juicy wine. Very good acidity. Plenty of depth. *À point.* Vigorous. Concentrated and classy. This is fine. (March 2000)

DRINK SOON   17.5

Puligny-Montrachet, Les Referts, 1993
Domaine Louis Carillon et Fils

Rich, mature nose. Ripe, even a shade opulent. Very good acidity. Medium-full body. Ripe fruit salad with a touch of apple flavour. Lovely finish. Delicious now. Fine plus. (June 2003)

NOW TO 2010   18.0

REDS

Aloxe-Corton, Les Vercots, 1993
Domaine Simon Bize et Fils

Good fullish, quite mature colour. Cedary. Fullish body. Rich. Quite structured. Some tannin. Round. Civilised. Very good. (June 2004)

NOW TO 2015   16.0

Aloxe-Corton, Les Vercots, 1993
Domaine Tollot-Beaut et Fils

Very good colour. Still youthful. Quite oaky. Quite ripe. Fresh. Stylish. On the palate, medium to medium-full. Slightly dominated by the oak, but ripe and with good vigour and class. Long. Good plus. (March 2003)

NOW TO 2010   15.5

Auxey-Duresses, 1993
Domaine Jean-François Coche-Dury

Light, mature colour. Soft, attractively fruity nose. Lots of charm. Fresh. *À point.* Only light-medium bodied, but delicious. (June 2003)

DRINK SOON   15.0

Beaune, Clos des Ursules, 1993
Domaine Louis Jadot

Good colour. Lovely plump, succulent nose. Fullish. Still very youthful. Very lovely fruit. This has lots of class and depth. Fine. (June 2003)

NOW TO 2020   17.5

Beaune, Les Cras, Vieilles Vignes, 1993
Domaine Germain Père et Fils/
Chateau de Chorey-lès-Beaune
Good colour. Rich, full, plump, vigorous, stylish nose. This has class and depth. Medium-full body. Very well balanced. Long and vigorous. Lovely fruit. Fine. (June 2003)
NOW TO 2013+   17.5

Beaune, Aux Cras, 1993
Maison Camille Giroud
Fullish colour. Still very youthful. Rich, fat, classy and profound on the nose. Good grip, but not a bit too austere. Fullish body. Complex. Lots of depth. High quality. Very good. (August 2000)
NOW TO 2015   16.0

Beaune, Grèves, 1993
Domaine Joseph Drouhin
Good colour. Stylish, oaky nose. Medium-full body. Very classy. Balanced, plump, composed and intense. Long and lovely. This is a fine example. (June 2003)
NOW TO 2013+   17.5

Beaune, Les Grèves, 1993
Domaine Michel Lafarge
Fullish colour. Some evolution. Plump and rich. Generous and spicy. Medium-full body. Good acidity. This is developing nicely and will be *à point* in 2003. Good grip. Lovely plump fruit. Concentrated. Long. Fine. (June 2001)
NOW TO 2015   17.5

Beaune, Grèves, 1993
Domaine Tollot-Beaut et Fils
Good colour. Quite a well-matured nose. Sensual but slightly sweet-sour. Yes, getting a little faded on the palate. Decent fruit. Medium to medium-full body. Quite good. (June 2003)
DRINK SOON   14.0

Beaune, Les Marconnets, 1993
Domaine Albert Morot
Quite rigidly oaky on the nose. And on the palate. Far too much. Medium to medium-full body. Quite good fruit and good acidity underneath, but too astringent. (June 2005)
NOW TO 2010   13.5

Beaune, Les Teurons, 1993
Maison Camille Giroud
Full, mature colour. Exotic, funky nose. Slightly reduced. Fullish body on the palate. Fresher than on the nose. Good ripe fruit. Good acidity. Still some tannin to resolve. Perhaps always a little dry at the end and not the greatest of class. But good positive finish. Got cleaner and classier in the glass. Very good plus. (September 2002)
NOW TO 2010   16.5

Beaune, Vignes Franches, 1993
Domaine Michel Bouzereau et Fils
Good medium-full, fresh colour. Decent nose. Quite ripe and balanced, but with an absence of succulence and fragrance. Medium body. A decent bottle, but no excitement here. Slightly one-dimensional and a little hard and austere at the end. Not really ripe enough. (May 2005)
DRINK SOON   14.0

Beaune, Les Vignes Franches, Vieilles Vignes, 1993
Domaine Germain Père et Fils/
Chateau de Chorey-lès-Beaune
Good colour. Plump nose. Good harmonious fruit. Not the quality and balance and intensity of the Cras, but good stuff. Medium to medium-full body. Good grip. Good plus. (June 2003)
NOW TO 2010   15.5

Blagny, La Pièce sous le Bois, 1993
Domaine Joseph Matrot
Good colour. Slightly rustic on the nose. A little overblown on the palate. Medium body. Broad-flavoured. Not a lot of class but reasonable fruit. Not bad plus. (June 2003)
DRINK SOON   13.5

Bonnes Mares, 1993
Domaine Fougeray de Beauclair
Good colour. Slightly evolved on the nose. Fullish body. Quite rich. A little old and tannic. It lacks suppleness. Good at best. (June 2003)
NOW TO 2010   15.0

Bonnes Mares, 1993
Domaine Robert Groffier

Good fullish colour. Still very youthful. Slightly reduced and farmyardy on the nose. This is a pity, for the wine underneath is charming and fragrant, if only medium-full bodied, and a feminine Bonnes Mares. Lovely Pinot fruit. Very finely balanced. If the reduced smell goes, this is fine. Very long and complex. It got better in the glass. (June 2003)

NOW TO 2025   17.5

Bonnes Mares, 1993
Domaine Jacques-Frédéric Mugnier

Good fullish colour. Still quite youthful. A touch reduced on the nose. Ripe and fragrant underneath. Good intensity. Lovely fruit. Medium-full body. Plump, succulent, balanced, fragrant and with very good harmony and concentration. Just about ready. Fine plus. (June 2003)

NOW TO 2020+   18.0

Bonnes Mares, 1993
Domaine Georges Roumier et Fils

Magnum. Very good colour. Full, rich, concentrated, backward and of very high quality. This has very, very lovely fruit. Fullish body. Still needs time. Classy, balanced, complex and very fragrant. Excellent. (June 2003)

NOW TO 2020   19.0

Bonnes Mares, 1993
Domaine Charles Thomas

Very good colour. Rich, fat, almost sweet, meaty nose. A full, little-bit-too-solid wine. This detracts from its class, though it is rich and concentrated. It still needs time. Very good at best. (June 2003)

NOW TO 2020   16.0

Bonnes Mares, 1993
Domaine Comte Georges de Vogüé

Similarly, very good colour to the Amoureuses. Denser on the nose. Still a bit closed and adolescent. Splendid on the palate. Rather more black-fruity. Fullish body. Still some tannin, but the tannins are very ripe and fat. I think I prefer

the sheer flair and the dimension of the Amoureuses, but this is very fine. (May 2002)

NOW TO 2025   18.5

Chambertin, 1993
Domaine Leroy

Fullish colour. Still youthful. Very lovely nose. Ripe, fragrant, complex, classy and very poised. Beginning to open out on the palate. Full. Very fine grip. Clean and long and complex. This is very fine. Very lovely. (April 2000)

NOW TO 2020   18.5

Le Chambertin, 1993
Domaine Denis Mortet

Full colour. Barely mature. At first, very warm, generous, rich and fat on both nose and palate. Full, but no hard edges and not over-oaked. Classy, but fine rather than great. As it developed, it became more and more dominated by the oak. (November 2005)

NOW TO 2020   17.5

Chambertin, 1993
Domaine Jacques Prieur

Quite an evolved colour. Not as full or as fresh as the Musigny 1993. Nothing much on the nose. Dull, tired and neutral on the palate. This is really rather poor for what it is. (June 2000)

DRINK SOON   13.5

Chambertin, 1993
Domaine Armand Rousseau

Full colour. Just a touch of maturity now. Marvellous nose. Rich, full, ripe and profound. Very classy and very complex. Very, very ripe on the palate. Full bodied. Still a little tannin. Vigorous and complex. Lots of depth. Really excellent. Needs another 4 years. (June 2006)

2011 TO 2025+   19.5

Chambertin, 1993
Domaine Jean Trapet Père et Fils

Full colour. Soft nose, but still youthful and unformed. Ripe and plummy. Fullish on the palate. Still a little tannin to resolve. Good grip.

Classy and profound. Vigorous. Fine. Will still improve. (April 2005)

NOW TO 2020   17.5

Chambertin, Clos de Bèze, 1993
Domaine Bruno Clair

Very good colour. Fresh. Fine acidity. Slight evidence of the stems on the nose. Rich, round and very ripe on the palate. Still a little rigid underneath. High quality. Excellent balance. Very fine. (June 2003)

NOW TO 2020   18.5

Chambertin, Clos de Bèze, 1993
Domaine Joseph Faiveley

Full, youthful colour. Rich nose. Some oak. Not a bit too austere or tannic. Full and vigorous on the attack. Slightly austere. But good fruit and depth. Needs a year or two to become more generous. But the potential is there. Fine plus. (September 2005)

NOW TO 2020   18.0

Chambertin, Clos de Bèze, 1993
Domaine Louis Jadot

Fullish colour. A suggestion of maturity. Marvellous nose. Classic. Aristrocratic Pinot fruit. Not a bit too extracted. Fullish body. Very fresh. Just a little tannin. This is very classy indeed. Very, very long and multidimensional. Real class. Real vigour. Brilliant. (June 2003)

NOW TO 2030   19.5

Chambertin, Clos de Bèze, 1993
Domaine Armand Rousseau

Fullish colour. Now just about mature. Lovely fragrant, slightly spicy nose. Just a touch of gingerbread. Fullish bodied, ample and ripe. Just about ready. Gently oaky. Long and succulent. Very fine plus. (June 2005)

NOW TO 2028   19.5

Chambolle-Musigny, 1993
Domaine Bouchard Père et Fils

Good colour. Youthful, plump and vigorous. Good substance for a village Chambolle. Good stylish, balanced fruit. Plenty of substance here. Very good. (June 2000)

NOW TO 2010   16.0

Chambolle-Musigny, 1993
Domaine Jacques Frédéric Mugnier

Good colour. Very classy, ripe, fragrant Chambolle fruit. Not quite so vigorous on the palate. Just a hint of astringency. But very harmonious and classy. Drink quite soon. (June 2003)

DRINK SOON   16.0

Chambolle-Musigny, 1993
Domaine Georges Roumier et Fils

Magnum. Good colour. Rich, and quite full but ample on the nose. Quite an opulent, meaty example. Lovely ripe, balanced fruit. Vigorous and ample and classy. Fine for what it is. (June 2003)

NOW TO 2013   17.0

Chambolle-Musigny, 1993
Domaine Comte Georges de Vogüé

Rich, full, youthful colour. One feels it will still improve. On the palate still very fresh, but just about ready. Fullish body. The tannins are just about resolved. Good acidity. Lovely pure, slightly austere but perfectly ripe fruit. Will improve as it mellows. (June 2005)

NOW TO 2020   18.0

Chambolle-Musigny, Les Amoureuses, 1993
Domaine Robert Groffier Père et Fils

This is quite delicious. Fullish. Very, very lovely cool, harmonious fruit. Great class and depth. A beautiful bottle. Mellow, intense and energetic. (June 2004)

NOW TO 2020+   19.0

Chambolle-Musigny, Les Amoureuses, 1993
Domaine Louis Jadot

Fullish colour. Very, very lovely, fragrant, cool, pure fruit on the nose. Medium-full body. Fully ready. Very lovely fruit. Ripe, rich and almost sweet on the palate. Delicate and reticent. Excellent grip and very well absorbed tannins. Long and lovely. (October 2005)

NOW TO 2025   19.0

Chambolle-Musigny, Les Amoureuses, 1993
Domaine Jacques Frédéric Mugnier

Medium-full colour. Lovely fragrant nose. Very pure. Still quite austere. Quite oaky on the palate. Medium-full body. Good acidity. Good ripe tannins. A wine of high class and luscious fruit. Very intense. Very lovely. Needs time still. (December 2001)

NOW TO 2028   18.5

Chambolle-Musigny, Les Amoureuses, 1993
Domaine Comte Georges de Vogüé

Very good colour. Rich, full and very delicious on the nose. More to it than the 1996. Full bodied, fat and gently oaky. Still some tannin. More structured, as well as more concentrated, than the 1996. Very intense. Really quite powerful. Yet very composed and classy. Excellent fruit. Very fine grip. Enormous length and subtlety at the end. This is brilliant. Very fine indeed. (May 2002)

NOW TO 2025   19.5

Chambolle-Musigny, Les Baudes, 1993
Domaine Ghislaine Barthod

Fullish colour. Still not quite ready. Lovely nose. Both succulent and quite meaty. Very well-balanced. Nothing too hard and austere here. Fullish body. Ripe. Quite firm still. A little bit of tannin to resolve, but long and classy. Very good indeed. (October 2003)

NOW TO 2020   17.0

Chambolle-Musigny, Charmes, 1993
Domaine Ghislaine Barthod

Good colour. Fragrant, classy, vigorous nose. On the palate, a little evolution. Decent, plump attack but then slightly attenuated at the end. Slightly loosening up. It seems to be evolving fast. An unlucky bottle? Only quite good. (June 2003)

DRINK SOON   14.0

Chambolle-Musigny, Les Charmes, 1993
Domaine Daniel Moine-Hudelot

Good colour. Ripe, fresh nose. This is ample, with good acidity and vigour. Medium body.

Some tannin. Slightly one-dimensional on the palate, but clean and fresh and long. Very good. (April 2001)

NOW 2013   16.0

Chambolle-Musigny, La Combe d'Orveau, 1993
Domaine Bruno Clavelier

Fullish colour. Fragrant, classy nose. Soft and plump. Intense and elegant. Medium-full body. Very good ripe tannins. Long and complex at the end. Fine. (March 2002)

NOW TO 2020   17.5

Chambolle-Musigny, La Combe d'Orveau, 1993
Domaine Henri Perrot-Minot

Medium-full colour. Barely mature. Fine, fragrant nose. Nothing exaggerated. Fresh. Ripe. Medium-full body. Very lovely fruit. Smooth and silky. High class. Long, complete and intense. *À point* but with plenty of vigour. (May 2006)

NOW TO 2019   17.5

Chambolle-Musigny, Les Cras, 1993
Domaine Georges Roumier et Fils

Full colour. Still very youthful. Fine, rich, black-fruity nose. Very ripe and succulent. Velvety. Fullish body. Smooth. Lots of depth and concentration. Very fine. (June 2005)

NOW TO 2023   18.5

Chambolle-Musigny, Les Feusselottes, 1993
Domaine Dr. Georges Mugneret

Fullish, fresh colour. Still quite firm on the nose. But plenty of Chambolle fragrance underneath. On the palate, medium to medium-full body. The tannins are now soft. Good acidity. Elegant and full of fruit. Needs another year or so to get really succulent. Still a little austere. And the oak is noticeable on the aftertaste. Long. Very good indeed. (May 2005)

NOW TO 2017   17.0

Chambolle-Musigny, Les Fremières, 1993
Domaine Leroy

Good colour. Rich, fragrant, balanced nose. Just a little unresolved tannin. Red fruit flavours.

Medium-full body. Good acidity. Stylish, concentrated and very good. (March 2004)

NOW TO 2020 16.0

Chambolle-Musigny, Les Fuées, 1993
Domaine Jacques Frédéric Mugnier

Fullish colour. Just beginning to show signs of maturity. At first a little closed-in, both on nose and palate. There are some unresolved tannins here. Underneath, full bodied, ample, rich, not oaky. Excellent class and balance. Long and complex and fine plus. Lots of vigour for the future. Will still improve. (November 2005)

NOW TO 2020 18.0

Charmes-Chambertin, 1993
Domaine Denis Bachelet

Medium-full colour. Just about mature. Fine fragrant nose. Rich, laid-back and very lovely. Medium-full body. Very ripe indeed. Very pure. Very clean. Intense rather than powerful. Very, very long. Excellent. (April 2006)

NOW TO 2025 19.5

Charmes-Chambertin, 1993
Domaine Claude Dugat

Full colour. Still youthful. A bit closed-in, unforthcoming nose. Some new oak. Not as fine as his 1995. Yet on the palate, still pretty damn good. Rich, concentrated fruit and very long and very lovely. Very intense, long finish. (April 2006)

NOW TO 2025 18.5

Charmes-Chambertin, 1993
Domaine Bernard Dugat-Py

Full colour. Still very youthful. Delicious, concentrated fruit on the nose. Rich and profound. Not a bit too oaky or too extracted. Fullish body. Very fine grip. Excellent, multi-layered fruit. Very, very long and lovely. This is very fine. (March 2003)

NOW TO 2026 18.5

Charmes-Chambertin, 1993
Domaine Dujac

Medium to medium-full colour. Fully mature. Soft, fragrant, balanced, elegant, very Dujac nose.

Succulent. Medium to medium-full body. Fresh and balanced. Lovely. Fully *à point*. (April 2006)

NOW TO 2020 18.0

Charmes-Chambertin, 1993
Domaine Hubert Lignier

Rich, full nose. Still youthful. Slightly less concentrated than Bernard Dugat's. But good weight and grip. Juicy and rich. Fullish body. Good tannins. Not the greatest of grip compared with Dugat's, but ripe, succulent and stylish. Fine. (June 2003)

NOW TO 2018 17.5

Charmes-Chambertin, 1993
Domaine Henri Perrot-Minot

Fullish, mature colour. Slightly tough nose. Lacks freshness, nuance and Pinot fruit. Slightly astringent on the attack. Wimpier on the follow-through. Lacks style. (April 2006)

DRINK SOON 13.0

Charmes-Chambertin, Très Vieilles Vignes, 1993
Domaine Joseph Roty

Fine full, rich colour. Still very youthful. Splendid nose. Essence of fruit. Very fine quality. Fullish bodied but very creamy. Brilliantly succulent and rich and concentrated. Excellent grip. Very fine. (April 2006)

NOW TO 2025 18.5

Charmes-Chambertin, 1993
Domaine Jean Armand Rousseau

Fullish, mature colour. Rich, full, meaty, ripe and concentrated on the nose. Very pure. Very clean. Lots of energy. Medium-full body. Composed, succulent, ripe and rich. Very good acidity. Long and fine. (April 2006)

NOW TO 2018 17.5

Chassagne-Montrachet, Clos de la Boudriotte, 1993
Domaine Ramonet

Good colour. Impressive nose. Rich, fullish, plump and classy. Medium-full bodied on the palate. Ripe and concentrated. This is very lovely for what it is. Long and complex. (June 2003)

NOW TO 2013+ 16.5

Chassagne-Montrachet, Clos Saint-Jean, 1993
Maison Camille Giroud

A splendid round, fullish wine. Lots of depth. No hard edges. Unexpectedly smooth. Classy and balanced. Surprisingly delicious. (September 2002)

NOW TO 2010   16.0

Clos des Lambrays, 1993
Domaine des Lambrays

Medium-full colour. Still quite lovely. Soft, fragrant nose. Not a lot of drive or vigour. Medium body. Now fully mature. Ripe, rich and quite intense. Good tannins. This has class. But Dujac's Clos Saint-Denis 1993, tasted alongside it, is better. It has more distinction. But this is undoubtedly fine. (June 2002)

NOW TO 2014   17.5

Clos de la Roche, 1993
Domaine Dujac

Medium-full colour. Just about ready. Fragrant, quite supple nose. Medium-full body. Soft, succulent fruit. Stylish. Long. Fine. (June 2003)

NOW TO 2018   17.5

Clos de la Roche, 1993
Domaine Leroy

Fine fullish colour. The nose is still a bit closed and austere, but there is lots and lots of quality and depth here. Very lovely fruit. Very vigorous. Fullish, rich and balanced. Not quite the delights of the 1996, but very fine nevertheless. (April 2000)

NOW TO 2012   18.5

Clos de la Roche, 1993
Domaine Lignier-Michelot

Good colour. Ripe, fragrant and succulent. Soft, ripe and oaky. Medium-full body. Balanced. Composed and classy. This is very elegant. Lovely long finish. Fine. (June 2003)

NOW TO 2018   18.0

Clos de la Roche, 1993
Domaine Hubert Lignier

Very good colour. Rich, full, youthful and very oaky on the nose. Backward. Full body. Good style and concentration. Very good grip. Lovely fruit. Lots of depth. This is fine plus. (June 2003)

NOW TO 2020   17.5

Clos de la Roche, Vieilles Vignes, 1993
Domaine Ponsot

Good fullish maturity. Vigorous, ripe nose. No austerity. Fullish body. Very ripe tannins. Lovely cool fruit. Balanced. *À point*. Complex. Lots of energy. Very fine. (March 2006)

NOW TO 2020+   18.5

Clos Saint-Denis, 1993
Domaine Joseph Drouhin

Fullish colour. Rich, ripe, concentrated, profound black-fruity nose. Splendidly balanced and complex. Fullish body. Mellow. No aggressive tannins nor rampant acidity. Succulent and classy. Harmonious. *À point* now, but with plenty of life ahead of it. Fine plus. (April 2005)

NOW TO 2019   18.0

Clos Saint-Denis, 1993
Domaine Dujac

Medium-full colour. A suggestion of brown. Aromatic, almost mature nose. Balanced, oaky and intense. Medium to medium-full body. Classy, harmonious, plump and complex. Just about ready, but still a little raw. Very long. Very sophisticated. Very intense at the end. Fine plus. (June 2002)

NOW TO 2018   18.0

Clos de Tart, 1993
Domaine du Clos de Tart

Cuvée Accad. Good colour. Slightly lean on the nose. Some stems. Fresh but slight thin. It lacks charm. This is rather artificial. Not for me. (June 2003)

NOW TO 2010   13.0

Clos de Vougeot, 1993
Domaine d'Ardhuy

Medium to medium-full colour. Smells of toffee. It tastes dry, evolved and slightly reduced. Common. (June 2003)

DRINK SOON   13.0

Clos de Vougeot, 1993
Maison Champy

Good colour. Good fruit on the nose. Fresh, balanced, concentrated and classy. Fullish body. Fresh and harmonious. Old viney. This has a rich, vigorous follow-through. Lots of class and a long, complex finish. Fine plus. (June 2003)

NOW TO 2020   18.0

Clos de Vougeot, 1993
Domaine René Engel

Magnum. Very good colour. Ample, very rich, fat, concentrated nose. Medium-full body. Ripe, rich and intense. Splendid fruit. This doesn't quite have the grip of his Echézeaux, but it is very fine. Usually this has showed better—and the Grands Echézeaux is better still. (June 2003)

NOW TO 2020   18.5

Clos de Vougeot, 1993
Domaine Jean Grivot

Medium-full colour. A little maturity. Very classy and restrained on the nose. Multidimensional in flavour on the palate. Medium-full body. Very good tannins. Very good grip and plenty of succulence to absorb it. Complete. Really delicious finish. Very, very long and complex. Very fine. (October 2005)

NOW TO 2020   18.5

Clos de Vougeot, 1993
Domaine Jean Gros

Magnum. Good colour. Good class on the nose. But nowhere near the intensity and depth of Engel's. Medium body. Good fruit, but slightly one-dimensional. The vines were only 7 years old. Good but not brilliant. (June 2003)

NOW TO 2010   15.0

Clos de Vougeot, 1993
Domaine Alfred Haegelen-Jayer

Fullish colour. Now some signs of maturity. Ripe, plump, attractive nose. Nice and fat and succulent. Medium-full body. Now quite round. Classy, balanced and with plenty of depth. This is a fine example which is now ready but has plenty of vigour and energy. Rich and old viney. Long on the finish. (May 2005)

NOW TO 2020   17.5

Clos de Vougeot, 1993
Domaine Louis Jadot

Full colour. Still a little tannic and austere on the nose. But plenty of fruit and succulence underneath. Lots of finesse, too. Fullish body on the palate. Very fine, plummy fruit. Ripe and rich. Slightly aromatic. Firm. Very good grip. Lots of vigour. Impressive finish. Very fine. Will still improve. (October 2005)

NOW TO 2025   18.5

Clos de Vougeot, 1993
Domaine Leroy

Full, immature colour. Ample, fat, concentrated nose. High class. Lots of depth. Still youthful. Full body. Very lovely succulent fruit. Excellent grip. Very concentrated, very intense and vigorous on the palate. Just about ready. Very fine. Will keep for ages. (March 2006)

NOW TO 2025   18.5

Clos de Vougeot, 1993
Domaine Méo-Camuzet

Medium-full colour, showing a little maturity. A touch of reduction on the nose at first. Rich, ripe, fullish bodied, restrained and classy on the palate. Good structure. No undue oak. Good tannins and good grip. Fat and succulent at the end. Lovely finish. Fine. (October 2005)

NOW TO 2020   17.5

Clos de Vougeot, 1993
Domaine Denis Mortet

Magnum. Medium-full colour. Still vigorous. Spicy, slightly lumpy and over-extracted on the nose. Lacks class. Not very Pinot in character. Medium-full body. Good acidity. Slight touch of sweetness. Better style on the palate than on the nose. Not overdone. Very good indeed, but not fine. It lacks the class for fine. (October 2005)

NOW TO 2017   17.0

Clos de Vougeot, 1993
Domaine Georges Mugneret-Gibourg
Magnum. Very good colour. Rich, full, concentrated and classy on the nose. Still needs time. Full bodied and rich. Very fine grip. This has a lot of depth and style and concentration. Very fine. (June 2003)

NOW TO 2020   18.5

Clos de Vougeot, 1993
Domaine Jacques Prieur
Full colour. Some evolution. Spicy, fat and quite evolved on the nose. Medium-full body. Decent grip and style. Quite fresh. Quite complex. This has a ripe, plump, attractive follow-through and a positive finish. (June 2000)

DRINK SOON   16.5

Clos de Vougeot, 1993
Domaine Jean Raphet et Fils
Medium to medium-full, mature colour. Soft, fragrant, fresh but fully mature nose. Medium to medium-full body. Ripe, fruity, elegant and most attractive. Very harmonious. Not the greatest depth or vigour, or indeed complexity at the end. But very good indeed. (May 2005)

NOW TO 2016   17.0

Clos de Vougeot, 1993
Domaine Daniel Rion et Fils
Medium colour. Mature. A slight haze. Good fresh, succulent, mature wine. No great class, but clean and balanced and with good depth. Very good. (October 2000)

DRINK SOON   16.0

Clos de Vougeot, 1993
Domaine Jean Tardy et Fils
Good colour. Soft and oaky and easy to appreciate on the nose. Quite evolved. Not a lot of grip. Medium body. It lacks zip and dimension. Boring. (June 2003)

NOW TO 2010   14.0

Clos de Vougeot, Grand Maupertuis, 1993
Domaine Anne Gros
Good colour. Very lovely, backward, concentrated nose. Fullish body. Still not together. But splendid concentration and grip. This is potentially very lovely. It just needs time. (June 2003)

NOW TO 2020   18.5

Clos de Vougeot, Musigni, 1993
Domaine Gros Frère et Soeur
Good colour. Ripe, ample and oaky, but a little loose-knit on the nose. The oak dominates on the palate. Medium-full body. But dull. No fragrance. Good at best. The vines were young at the time. (June 2003)

NOW TO 2010   15.0

Corton, 1993
Domaine Méo-Camuzet
Very fine colour. Quite tough on the nose. Tannic. Slightly burly. This is a bit dense. It doesn't quite have the grip. For a 1993, I find it a little disappointing. Good acidity. Slight animal aspects. It lacks a little real fat and richness. Slightly ungainly. Good plus. (March 2001)

NOW TO 2015+   15.5

Corton, Clos du Roi, 1993
Domaine Charles Thomas
Very good colour. Rich, full, meaty and youthful on the nose. Fullish body. Some tannins. But not too solid or lumpy. Still needs time. Rich on the palate. Very good but not brilliant. It lacks fragrance and nuance. (June 2003)

NOW TO 2020   16.0

Corton, Les Languettes, 1993
Maison Camille Giroud
Good colour. Full, rich, sturdy (but not too much) nose. Fullish body. A little tannin. Ripe. Very good acidity. Vigorous. Classy. Very long. Fine. (June 2004)

NOW TO 2019   17.5

Corton, Les Maréchaudes, 1993
Domaine Chandon de Briailles
Good colour. Soft, rich, aromatic nose. Good class and depth. Medium-full body. Ripe, fresh and fragrant. Cool. Composed. Long and elegant. Fine. (June 2003)
NOW TO 2015   17.5

Corton, Les Maréchaudes, 1993
Domaine Michel Mallard et Fils
A bit dry and a bit rustic. Some fruit and depth. But not a lot of style. Drink soon. (February 2003)
DRINK SOON   14.0

Corton, Les Perrières, 1993
Domaine Dubreuil-Fontaine
Medium to medium-full, mature colour. Fragrant, balanced, quite stylish nose. Medium to medium-full body. Good acidity. Lacks a little richness and concentration, but attractive and elegant and positive at the end. Very good. Just about ready. (March 2005)
NOW TO 2017   16.0

Corton, Les Perrières, 1993
Maison Camille Giroud
Full colour. Just a little touch of maturity. Lovely nose. Full. Quite firm. Rich, lush and succulent. Some tannin. Slightly rustic. Quite approachable. Good grip. Slightly astringent at the end. Very good. (June 2001)
NOW TO 2015   16.0

Corton, Les Pougets, 1993
Domaine Louis Jadot
Good, full, immature colour. Ripe, cool, red-fruit flavours. Elegant and with very good acidity. Still slightly lean, but with plenty of depth and just a little oak. Just a little tannin. Fullish body. Still youthful. Fresh. Profound and classy. Fine plus. (November 2001)
NOW TO 2019   18.0

Corton, Renardes, 1993
Domaine Leroy
Medium-full colour. A bit more age than the 1992, surprisingly. Full, elegant nose. Lots of depth and style here. Very good grip. Fullish body. Very well balanced. Slightly sauvage, but that is the character of the *climat*. The stems are evident. Still some tannin. Needs time. Very good indeed. (April 2000)
NOW TO 2015   17.0

Echézeaux, 1993
Domaine Robert Arnoux
Medium-full colour. Just about mature. Lovely fragrant nose. Quite chunky. On the palate, fullish, ripe, balanced, fresh and succulent. Still lots of vigour. Long and fine. (March 2006)
NOW TO 2020   17.5

Echézeaux, 1993
Domaine René Engel
Medium-full colour. Some development. Splendid nose. Very lovely classy, perfumed Pinot Noir fruit. Medium-full body, beginning to round off. Lovely fruit and very fine grip. Relaxed. Balanced. Complex. Fresh and very lovely. (June 2004)
NOW TO 2020+   17.5

Echézeaux, 1993
Domaine Georges Mugneret-Gibourg
Medium-full, still youthful colour. On both the nose and the palate, a little austere, but certainly fragrant and classy. Medium-full body. A little tannin still to evolve. Very good fruit. Plenty of depth. Balanced. Long on the palate. Still needs 2 or 3 years. Very good indeed. (May 2005)
NOW TO 2020   17.0

Gevrey-Chambertin, 1993
Domaine Geantet-Pansiot
Good colour. Ample, rich, oaky nose. Fullish. Some tannin. Very good grip. This is slightly austere and very concentrated. Lots of depth. Still youthful. Very long. This is very good indeed for what it is. (October 2002)
NOW TO 2020   17.0

Gevrey-Chambertin, Vieilles Vignes, 1993
Domaine Denis Bachelet
Good colour. Marvellous nose. Very, very classy, concentrated fruit. Fullish body. Splendidly

concentrated and intense on the palate. Excellent grip and very, very lovely, multidimensional fruit. Excellent for what it is. (June 2003)

NOW TO 2015   17.5

Gevrey-Chambertin, Vieilles Vignes, 1993
Domaine Alain Burguet

Magnum. Good colour. Plump, ripe, vigorous and attractive on the nose. Medium-full body. Slightly chunky. Very good grip—all as usual. And, as usual, a splendid example of a village wine. (June 2003)

NOW TO 2015   16.5

Gevrey-Chambertin, Vieilles Vignes, 1993
Domaine Bernard Dugat-Py

Good colour. Fresh and plummy on the nose. Good class. On the palate, a little forced and chunky. Fullish body. Some tannin. Very good grip. But a bit solid. (June 2003)

NOW TO 2013   14.5

Gevrey-Chambertin, Cuvée de l'Abeille, 1993
Domaine Ponsot

Fullish colour. Still youthful. Soft, fragrant nose. A little astringent. Lacks a little succulence. Medium body. Good fruit, but not supple enough. Quite classy, though. May still soften. Essentially ungenerous and always will be. Quite good at best. (October 2005)

NOW TO 2012   14.0

Gevrey-Chambertin, Les Cazetiers, 1993
Domaine Bruno Clair

Good colour. Very lovely nose. Lots of depth and class, and very harmonious. Medium-full body. À point. Ripe, generous, long and intense. Fully evolved. Fine. (June 2003)

NOW TO 2010   17.5

Gevrey-Chambertin, Les Cazetiers, 1993
Domaine Christian Sérafin

Good colour. Ripe, rich, gently oaky nose. Slightly fatter and more generous than Bruno Clair's, but with not quite the class. Fullish body. Round and oaky, ample and attractive. Good vigour and length. Fine. (June 2003)

NOW TO 2018   17.5

Gevrey-Chambertin, Les Champeaux, 1993
Domaine Alain Burguet

Medium-full colour. Gentle nose. Weaker than his Vieilles Vignes. Fragrant but more evolved. Medium body. Ripe but a little one-dimensional. It lacks a bit of punch and complexity. Good but not exceptional. (June 2003)

NOW TO 2010   15.0

Gevrey-Chambertin, Les Champeaux, 1993
Domaine Denis Mortet

Good full, youthful colour. Fresh, ample, rich, oaky nose. Plenty of substance here, but not over-extracted or over-oaked. Full bodied, ripe and still very youthful. Good grip. No undue tannic structure, though. Very good clean fruit. Plenty of succulence. A classy, virile wine. Will keep well for many years. Only just ready. Very good indeed. (November 2005)

NOW TO 2020   17.0

Gevrey-Chambertin, Les Champonnets, 1993
Domaine Heresztyn

Magnum. Very good colour. Ample, ripe, gently oaky and classy. On the palate, quite chunky. Rich and fullish bodied. Very good grip. Good vigour. A wine for food. Fresh and positive at the end. Very good indeed. (June 2003)

NOW TO 2010   17.0

Gevrey-Chambertin, Clos Saint-Jacques, 1993
Domaine Bruno Clair

Fatter, richer and with more of a chocolate-coffee flavour than his Cazetiers 1993. Full bodied. Now softening. A profound, classy wine. The tannins are very round, and the flavour is very concentrated. Fine plus. (December 2001)

NOW TO 2020   18.0

Gevrey-Chambertin, Clos Saint-Jacques, 1993
Domaine Louis Jadot

Fullish colour. Rich nose, but still a bit tight. Fullish body. Rich, concentrated and full of fruit. Still some tannin. Still rather young, but a wine of splendid depth and class. Excellent grip. Lovely finish. Very fine. (April 2005)

NOW TO 2025   18.5

Gevrey-Chambertin, Clos Saint-Jacques, 1993
Domaine Armand Rousseau

Medium-full, mature colour. Very lovely nose. Succulent, ripe, concentrated fruit. Not a bit tough or heavy. Yet intense and fresh and concentrated and complex. Medium-full body. Lovely fruit. Very fine. (April 2005)

NOW TO 2020+   18.5

Gevrey-Chambertin, Les Combottes, 1993
Domaine Dujac

Medium-full colour. Fragrant, slightly earthy, intense, slightly sweet nose. Quite lovely. Medium to medium-full body. Very smooth and round and soft on the palate. Fully ready. But fresh, concentrated, fragrant, pure and vigorous. Not a bit too stemmy. Slightly. Very good grip. Long and complex. Fine. (May 2005)

NOW TO 2018   17.5

Gevrey-Chambertin, Les Corbeaux, 1993
Maison Denis Bachelet

Good colour. Great composure and class on the nose. Excellent fruit. This is laid-back, even delicate. But intense, balanced and very lovely. Long and complex. Fine. (June 2003)

NOW TO 2018   17.5

Gevrey-Chambertin, Les Corbeaux, 1993
Domaine Heresztyn

Good full, vigorous colour. Ample but slightly sweaty nose. A touch reduced. On the palate, medium to medium-full body. Now soft. Ripe and with no hard acidity, though the acidity is apparent. No lack of vigour here. But a lack of finesse. Improved in the glass as the reduction oxidised. Good. (May 2005)

NOW TO 2010   15.0

Gevrey-Chambertin, Estournelles-Saint-Jacques, 1993
Domaine Louis Jadot

Full colour: more so than their Clos Saint-Jacques 1993. The nose is still a bit pinched. On the palate this is fullish, fragrant, intensely fruity. Beautifully balanced. Very classy.

Drinkable now but better still in 2 years. Lovely. Very long and complex. Fine. (March 2005)

NOW TO 2027   17.5

Gevrey-Chambertin, Lavaux-Saint-Jacques, 1993
Domaine Bernard Maume

Fullish colour. Barely mature. Good class of fruit on the nose. Fullish body, but not a bit dense or rustic. Medium-full body. Juicy and rich. The tannins are now quite absorbed. Lovely balance. Fragrant. Long and complex. Lots of dimension. Fine. (June 2003)

NOW TO 2018   17.5

Gevrey-Chambertin, Lavaux-Saint-Jacques, 1993
Domaine Denis Mortet

Full colour. Ample, slightly austere, oaky but rich nose. Lots of depth and plenty of class. Still youthful. Some tannins. Fullish body. Lovely rich fruit. Very cassis. Lots of depth. Quite extracted but not too much so. Very good indeed. (February 2005)

NOW TO 2020   17.0

Gevrey-Chambertin, Lavaux-Saint-Jacques, 1993
Domaine Vachet-Rousseau

Good fullish colour. Still youthful. Ripe nose with a touch of spice. Mulberry fruit. No great depth or elegance, however. Medium-full body. The tannins are soft and ripe. Fresh and round. Ripe and succulent. The wine is balanced and long on the palate. It is more classy on the palate than on the nose, but not very complex. Still has plenty of vigour, but it might get a bit lean as it develops. There is a slight lack of charm at the end. Very good rather than fine. (March 2005)

NOW TO 2014   16.0

Gevrey-Chambertin, En Motrot, 1993
Domaine Denis Mortet

Magnum. Good colour. Quite a big, fresh, meaty wine on the nose. Plump, ripe, full and vigorous. Good class and balance, too. This is excellent for a village wine. Long and ample at the end. (June 2003)

NOW TO 2015   16.0

Grands Echézeaux, 1993
Domaine Joseph Drouhin

Full, vigorous colour. Profound, closed-in nose. Rich, full, concentrated and with lots of dimension and very fine fruit. Fullish on the palate. Still a little tannin to resolve. Very good grip. Fat and succulent. This is very fine. A wine of harmony and distinction. Very long on the palate. Very lovely. (April 2005)

NOW TO 2025   18.5

Grands Echézeaux, 1993
Domaine de la Romanée-Conti

Fullish colour. Little sign of maturity. Roasted peanuts on the nose. Rich, fat and sweet. Medium-full body. Still some tannin. Still a touch rigid. Good grip. Very good indeed. (April 2004)

NOW TO 2020   17.0

Griotte-Chambertin, 1993
Domaine Joseph Drouhin

Fullish colour. Little sign of maturity. Rich, full, potentially opulent nose. Still a little closed. Lots of depth and concentration. Lots of class. Full bodied, ample, rich, intense and very well balanced on the palate. Very good tannins. Lots of vigour and depth. Excellent long finish. This is very lovely. Multidimensional. Very fine. (July 2003)

NOW TO 2026   18.5

Griotte-Chambertin, 1993
Domaine Frédéric Esmonin

Medium-full colour. Very Griotte (cherry stones) on the nose. Perhaps a touch of the stems. Medium-full body. Just about ready. Sweet and classy and with good intensity. Not a blockbuster. But good style and concentration. Very good length, too. The finish is very long and positive. Fine. (December 2001)

NOW TO 2020   17.5

Latricières-Chambertin, 1993
Domaine Joseph Faiveley

Medium-full colour. Some maturity. Slightly rustic and stemmy on the nose. Sweet and ungainly on the palate. Medium-full body. Slightly astringent. Lacks freshness and distinction. (April 2005)

NOW TO 2011   14.0

Latricières-Chambertin, 1993
Domaine Leroy

Medium-full colour. Slightly more evolved on the nose than a lot of these grands crus. Slight evidence of the stems. Fullish body. Ample and succulent. This is now ready. Ripe and intense. But not a lot of nuance. Fine at best. (June 2003)

NOW TO 2020   17.5

Latricières-Chambertin, 1993
Domaine Ponsot

Fullish, youthful colour. Full, ample, rich, slightly spicy nose. Complex, individual and classy. Now just about ready. Finely balanced. Intense and elegant. Fine plus. (March 2005)

NOW TO 2035   18.0

Marsannay, Le Dessus des Longeroies, 1993
Domaine Fougeray de Beauclair

Good colour. Decent fat, fruit and structure on the nose, if not much style. Fruity and ripe. Medium body. Fresh, but a little common. Quite good. (June 2003)

DRINK SOON   14.0

Marsannay, Les Favières, 1993
Domaine Fougeray de Beauclair

Good colour. Firmer, richer and more stylish than their Dessus des Longeroies. Medium-full body. Ripe. Quite stylish. Fresh and balanced. Long and positive. Good plus. (June 2003)

NOW TO 2013   15.5

Marsannay, Les Longeroies, 1993
Domaine Bruno Clair

Medium colour. Fragrant nose. Quite stylish. Slightly dry on the palate. This is a meaty, medium-bodied, well made wine. Fruity and balanced. But it should now be drunk quite soon. Good. (June 2003)

DRINK SOON   15.0

Marsannay, Les Saint-Jacques, 1993
Domaine Fougeray de Beauclair
Magnum. Good colour. A meaty, gamey wine on the nose. Slightly clumsy on the palate. The fruit is beginning to dry out. Medium to medium-full body. Drink soon. (June 2003)
DRINK SOON   13.0

Mazis-Chambertin, 1993
Domaine Frédéric Esmonin
Medium to medium-full, mature colour. Not as sophisticated as his 1995 Hospices de Beaune on the nose. Medium to medium-full body. Fragrant and ripe on the palate. Fresh. Good fruit. But very good rather than fine. Positive at the end. (April 2005)
NOW TO 2013   16.0

Mazis-Chambertin, 1993
Domaine Pierre Gelin
Medium-full colour. Quite a raw nose. Some stems. A little high-toned and green. Lacks succulence. Medium body. The tannins now rounded off. A lack of real concentration, depth and grip. Quite elegant, but a bit slight for a *grand cru*. Only good plus. (March 2002)
NOW TO 2010   15.5

Mazis-Chambertin, 1993
Domaine Harmand-Geoffroy
Full, vigorous colour. Classy nose. Still a little austere and unformed. Not yet really mellow. Medium-full body. Good tannins. Good acidity. Fragrant Pinot fruit. Ripe underneath. Stylish at the end and nice and long. Very good indeed. Not quite the richness and nuance for fine. But it will still get better. (May 2005)
NOW TO 2018   17.0

Mazis-Chambertin, 1993
Domaine Philippe Naddef
Very full colour. Tough, monolithic nose. Dense and tannic. Fullish body. Some astringency from the wood tannins. Good grip. Very good fruit underneath. Cool and potentially profound. But the oak overwhelms. (April 2005)
NOW TO 2017   16.0

Mazis-Chambertin, 1993
Domaine Armand Rousseau
Medium to medium-full, fully mature colour. Round, sweet and quite evolved. On the palate, not a lot of depth and grip. Fruity and stylish. Ripe, almost sweet. But a slight lack of bite and backbone. Very good at best. His 1995 is better. (April 2005)
NOW TO 2013   16.0

Mazis-Chambertin, 1993
Domaine Vachet-Rousseau
Fullish colour. Just about mature looking. Still a little tight on the nose. But good concentration, fruit and depth. No lack of richness. Fullish body. Just a little oak. Ripe and abundant on the palate. Proper grand cru finesse. Plenty of dimension. Lots of vigour. Just about ready. Fine. (April 2005)
NOW TO 2020   17.5

Mazoyères-Chambertin, 1993
Maison Louis Jadot
Full, rich, youthful colour. Full, rich nose. Slightly four-square, but very good fruit underneath. Plenty of depth. Medium-full body. Ripe. Spicy. Slightly austere. Lacks class, but very good plus. (April 2006)
NOW TO 2020   16.5

Monthelie, 1993
Domaine Paul Garaudet
Magnum. Light mature colour. Good fresh nose. Not too rustic. Plump, fresh, fruity and quite stylish. Good substance and depth. Good. (June 2003)
NOW TO 2010   15.0

Monthelie, Les Duresses, 1993
Domaine des Comtes Lafon
Medium to medium-full, fully mature colour. Ripe, soft and stylish on the nose. Just a touch of oak. Medium body. One can see that the vines are relatively young. Slightly lean but stylish. And with good dimension. Just about ready. Quite good plus. (March 2003)
NOW TO 2010   14.5

Morey-Saint-Denis, 1993
Maison Roland Remoissenet et Fils

Quite youthful, medium to medium-full colour. Now round and fragrant. Good depth for a village wine. Medium to medium-full body. Ample. Even quite stylish. Good plus. (December 2003)

NOW TO 2013   15.5

Morey-Saint-Denis, Vieilles Vignes, 1993
Domaine Hubert Lignier

Good colour. Full, rich, meaty, vigorous, gently oaky nose. Good attack. Plump and fruity. A slight lack of grip makes the flavour a bit one-dimensional. But not too short. Very good. (June 2003)

NOW TO 2010   16.0

Morey-Saint-Denis, Clos de la Buissière, 1993
Domaine Georges Roumier et Fils

Magnum. Good colour. Lovely fresh, fullish nose with more style and fruit and less robustness than usual. A good fullish bodied, meaty wine. Good grip. Ripe. Masculine. Plenty of vigour. Positive finish. Very good plus. (June 2003)

NOW TO 2018   16.5

Morey-Saint-Denis, Les Millandes, 1993
Domaine Heresztyn

Good colour. Fresh, fragrant nose. Lovely ripe Pinot here. Very stylish. Medium-full bodied, balanced and intense. Delicious fruit. Long and classy. Fine plus. (June 2003)

NOW TO 2015   18.0

Musigny, 1993
Domaine Joseph Drouhin

Fullish colour. Very lovely fragrant nose. Not quite the perfection of Jadot's 1993 Musigny, however. Fullish body. Rich and intense, voluptuous and vigorous on the palate. Very finely balanced. Quite opulent fruit. Excellent. Just about ready. (October 2005)

NOW TO 2025   19.5

Musigny, 1993
Domaine Louis Jadot

Fullish colour. Ripe, rich, soft, sweet, fragrant and intense on the nose. Very high quality here. Almost perfect expression of fruit. Just about *à point*. Fullish body. Excellent harmony. Brilliant fruit. Vigorous. Multidimensional. Very great breed. Marvellous long finish. (October 2005)

NOW TO 2030   20.0

Musigny, 1993
Domaine Leroy

Full, immature colour. Still a bit tight on the nose. Closed-in. Full. Quite powerful. On the palate this is still very young but very fine in potential. Excellent fruit. Real depth and class. Good structure and plenty of grip. Very fine. Still needs time. (October 2005)

NOW TO 2038   19.0

Musigny, 1993
Domaine Jacques-Frédéric Mugnier

Magnum. Full colour, especially for a Musigny made by Mugnier. Rich, profound, very classy nose. Full body. Still a little tannin—although the tannins are getting soft—but still a little austere. Lovely intense fruit. Good grip and concentration, of course. This still needs 5 years at least. Very fine indeed. (June 2005)

2010 TO 2030   19.5

Musigny, 1993
Domaine Jacques Prieur

Good colour. Neither fined, nor filtered. Impressive nose. Very good fruit and very good Chambolle definition. Medium-full body. Ripe and stylish. Not as fragrant or as concentrated as the really top Musignys. But a lovely wine. Very good grip. Long, complex and fine plus. Will still improve. (June 2000)

NOW TO 2010   18.0

Musigny, 1993
Domaine Comte Georges de Vogüé

Full, vigorous, rich and concentrated. Still a little austere. Plenty of backbone. Potentially very lovely. But still very young. Very intense, elegant fruit. (March 2005)

2010 TO 2030+   19.0

Nuits-Saint-Georges, Les Bas de Combe, 1993
Domaine Jean Tardy et Fils
Medium-full colour. Soft and quite oaky on the nose. Medium body. Pretty and ripe, but it lacks a bit of concentration and depth. Fresh though, but a little dominated by the oak. Not short. Good. (June 2003)
NOW TO 2010   15.0

Nuits-Saint-Georges, Les Boudots, 1993
Domaine Jean Grivot
Magnum. Fullish colour. Beginning to show maturity. Concentrated, compact, classy nose. Very lovely expression of fruit and roses. On the palate this is now quite accessible. Full body. Just a little tannin. Excellent grip and concentration. Very poised. Splendid balance. Intense and classy. Excellent. The best of the series. (November 2001)
NOW TO 2020   19.0

Nuits-Saint-Georges, Aux Boudots, 1993
Domaine Leroy
Rich, full colour. Barely mature. Firm, very rich, concentrated juicy fruit on the nose. Still some tannin. Full body. Splendidly rich and concentrated fruit. Essence of wine here. Very good grip. This is very well balanced and very profound. Very lovely. Very long. (June 2003)
NOW TO 2020   18.0

Nuits-Saint-Georges, Aux Boudots, 1993
Domaine Méo-Camuzet
Very fine colour. Like his Corton, this is a bit solid and tannic but not as dense as it evolved. Full and austere but rather better mannered, better balanced and more classy. Yet given the vintage, not up to fine quality standard. Intense and with good grip, but only very good indeed. (March 2001)
NOW TO 2020   17.0

Nuits-Saint-Georges, Les Boudots, 1993
Domaine Jean Tardy et Fils
Good colour. Full and vigorous. Soft, round, fragrant and oaky on the nose. Similar on the palate. The oak dominates a bit. But the wine is ripe and full of fruit. Elegant, medium-full bodied, clean and balanced. Just about ready. The finish is long and generous and succulent. Very good indeed. (June 2005)
NOW TO 2020   17.0

Nuits-Saint-Georges, Les Bousselots, 1993
Domaine Robert Chevillon
Good colour. Fresh nose. Plump and fruity without having the greatest class. Medium body. It is drying out a bit now. Decent but not great. The finish is still quite positive. (June 2003)
DRINK SOON   14.5

Nuits-Saint-Georges, Clos des Corvées Pagets, 1993
Domaine Robert Arnoux
Fine colour. Ample, rich, concentrated nose at first. But more austere later on. Medium-full body. Now mature. Mellow. The tannins are now soft. This is very good and long and lovely. But at the end it lacks a bit of sweetness and generosity. Good but not great. (October 2002)
NOW TO 2010   15.0

Nuits-Saint-Georges, Clos des Forêts Saint-Georges, 1993
Domaine de l'Arlot
Medium-full colour. Fresh but slightly stemmy on the nose. Decent structure. Ripe. Medium to medium-full body. Good grip. This is still vigorous. Stylish and fragrant. Good positive finish. Good plus. (June 2003)
NOW TO 2013   15.5

Nuits-Saint-Georges, Clos des Porrets Saint-Georges, 1993
Domaine Henri Gouges
Fullish colour. Some hints of maturity now. Quite firm. Splendidly rich and pure on the nose. A full wine. Still a little tannin to resolve but just about ready. Very good grip. Ample and profound. Very lovely follow-through. Just that little bit more to it than Faiveley's Porêts Saint-Georges. Very fine finish. Fine. (March 2004)
NOW TO 2020   17.5

Nuits-Saint-Georges, Les Lavières, 1993
Domaine Leroy

Village *appellation contrôlée*. Medium to medium-full, mature colour. No great distinction on either the nose or the palate. But ripe, medium to medium-full bodied, round, succulent and balanced. Good. (June 2005)

NOW TO 2014   15.0

Nuits-Saint-Georges, Les Murgers, 1993
Domaine Alain Hudelot-Noëllat

Fullish colour. Just a little brown. Aromatic, classy nose. Medium-full body. This has the grip of the vintage but is now round and complex. The tannins are fully absorbed. Quite rich. Long on the finish. Very good indeed. (May 2005)

NOW TO 2020   17.0

Nuits-Saint-Georges,
Les Porêts-Saint-Georges, 1993
Domaine Joseph Faiveley

Medium-full, mature colour. Ripe, rich and gently oaky. Medium to medium-full body. Still just a little tannin to resolve. Very good grip. Lovely fruit. Generous and seductive. Not a bit sauvage. Long on the palate. Just about ready. Very good indeed. (March 2004)

NOW TO 2018   17.0

Nuits-Saint-Georges, Les Richemones, 1993
Domaine Charles Thomas

Good colour. Big, solid and lumpy. Astringent. Slightly reduced. And the fruit is drying up. Quite full bodied. Quite hot. Too tannic. Unstylish. (June 2003)

NOW TO 2008   13.0

Nuits-Saint-Georges, Les Saint-Georges, 1993
Maison Camille Giroud

Good colour. Rich, full, plump, impressive nose. Full bodied, ripe, quite tannic, structured wine. But good class, good grip and good depth. This still needs time. Very good indeed. (June 2003)

NOW TO 2020   17.0

Nuits-Saint-Georges, Les Saint-Georges, 1993
Domaine Henri Gouges

Good colour. A touch of maturity. Firm, rich nose. A meaty wine. Fullish body. Still some tannin. Good acidity. Still a little rigid. Even a little farmyardy. Adolescent. Yet fine. I have had at least two bad bottles of this wine in the United States. Bad storage, I suspect. (March 2005)

NOW TO 2020   17.5

Nuits-Saint-Georges, Les Vaucrains, 1993
Domaine Robert Chevillon

Fullish, vigorous colour. Mellow but quite sturdy on the nose. Medium-full on the palate. The tannins are nice and round. Succulent and fragrant. Very good clean, pure, Pinot fruit. Very gently oaky. Altogether, a very well made wine. Elegant, long and intense. As is the Robert Chevillon style, a feminine Vaucrains. Long. Lovely. Fine quality. Only just ready, but now *à point*. (May 2005)

NOW TO 2020   17.5

Nuits-Saint-Georges, Les Vaucrains, 1993
Domaine Henri Gouges

Full colour. Still vigorous-looking. Typically rich and profound, yet slightly tough Nuits-Saint-Georges nose. Some tannin still to resolve. Full, rich and meaty on the palate. Good grip and vigour. Now just about ready. Very lovely fruit and a lot of depth. Ripe, complex and long on the palate. Very lovely long finish. This is fine plus. (July 2005)

NOW TO 2020   18.0

Nuits-Saint-Georges, Les Vaucrains, 1993
Maison Dominique Laurent

Rich, full colour. Barely mature. Firm nose, even slightly dense. Lots of oak and tannin. A structured wine. Even a little tough. Full body. Oaky. Good tannins now mellowing. Not the concentration or the purity of Leroy's Aux Boudots. But very good indeed. Slightly dry at the end from the wood. (June 2003)

NOW TO 2015   17.0

Nuits-Saint-Georges, Les Vignes Rondes, 1993
Domaine Daniel Rion et Fils
Good colour. Generous, fresh, quite oaky nose.
Medium to medium-full body. Ripe, mature, fresh,
elegant and quite vigorous. Good plus. (June 2003)
NOW TO 2018   15.5

Pernand-Vergelesses, Ile de Vergelesses, 1993
Domaine Chandon de Briailles
Medium-full, vigorous colour. Fragrant, pure, cool
Pinot nose. Rich and ample underneath. Very
classy. Medium-full body. Just about ready. Vigorous and complex. Good grip. The usual slight
austerity of 1993. But long and with plenty of
dimension at the end. Very good plus. (June 2005)
NOW TO 2018   16.5

Pommard, Chaponnières, Vieilles Vignes, 1993
Domaine Philippe Billard-Gonnet
Good colour. Rich, fresh, ample nose. Plenty of
depth. On the palate, this seems to be losing a
little fruit. It has become a bit sour. Only quite
good. (June 2003)
DRINK SOON   14.0

Pommard, Clos des Epeneaux, 1993
Domaine du Comte Armand
Magnum. This still needs time on the nose,
though it is now soft on the palate. Full and
ample. Very good tannins. This is high class.
Even better than Lafon's Santenots, perhaps.
Very full. Still some unresolved tannins. Very,
very rich and tannic. Very fine. (June 2003)
NOW TO 2018+   18.5

Pommard, Clos du Verger, 1993
Domaine Philippe Billard-Gonnet
Good colour. Fresh, plump, attractive nose.
Medium-full body. Ripe, balanced, fruity and
quite classy and complex. Good follow-through.
It finishes positively. Good plus. (June 2003)
NOW TO 2010   15.5

Pommard, Les Fremiers, 1993
Domaine Coste-Caumartin
You can see the Volnay proximity. Lovely fresh,
juicy fruit on the nose. No hard edges. Good.

But Jean-Marc Pavelot's 1993 Savigny les Narbantons is fatter, more concentrated and more
exciting. (July 2000)
DRINK UP   14.5

Pommard, Les Pézerolles, 1993
Domaine Hubert de Montille
Good colour. Fresh, classy nose. Lots of depth.
Lovely fruit. A fullish, meaty wine wine which
will still improve. Very good grip. Plump and
fine. (June 2003)
NOW TO 2020   17.5

Pommard, Les Rugiens, 1993
Domaine de Courcel
Medium-full colour. Slightly rigid on the nose
and attack. But quite rich; the tannins at the end
are well covered. Good acidity. Fragrant. Plenty
of vigour. Not fine. But full of flavour and very
good indeed. (May 2006)
NOW TO 2020   17.0

Pommard, Les Rugiens, 1993
Domaine Annick Parent
Fullish colour. Still very youthful. Slightly
chunky on the nose. The tannins obtrude a bit.
Slightly dry. Slightly ungenerous. A little too
much structure and not enough fat and succulence. Good fruit, but it also lacks a bit of
dimension. Good plus. (June 2005)
NOW TO 2014   15.5

Pommard, Rugiens Bas, 1993
Domaine Philippe Billard-Gonnet
Good colour. Rich, oaky nose. Full body. Some
tannin. Plenty of depth. Lovely rich, ample follow-
through. This is classy. Very long. Fine. (June 2003)
NOW TO 2013   17.5

Pommard, Les Vignots, 1993
Domaine Leroy
Very full colour. A bit of reduction at first. Under-
neath, surprisingly succulent as well as sub-
stantial. Full bodied and tannic but not dense.
Slightly austere at the end. Needs a bit of gener-
osity, but this will come. Good. (August 2000)
NOW TO 2015   15.0

Richebourg, 1993
Domaine Jean Grivot

Fine colour. Just beginning to evolve. Very lovely nose. Marvellous classy, complex, fresh fruit. Not a bit hard. Fullish body. Excellent ripe tannins. Very fresh. Very round, though not yet ready. Aristocratic presence of very intense, complex, classy fruit. Very, very long. Very, very lovely. This is grand vin. (June 2001)

NOW TO 2030   20.0

Richebourg, 1993
Domaine Anne Gros

Very fine colour. Only a suggestion of maturity. Rich, concentrated, intensely flavoured nose. A great deal of depth here. And dimension, too. On the palate this is beginning to get there. Full body. Very fine grip. Just a little unresolved tannin. Very, very lovely, cool, complex fruit. Long and very lovely indeed. Very pure. This is a great wine. Clearly superior to 1994 and 1995. (February 2004)

NOW TO 2030   20.0

Richebourg, 1993
Domaine Jean Gros

Magnum. Good colour. Very lovely rich nose. Full, concentrated and very aristocratic. This is, as usual, very lovely. Very concentrated, indeed aristocratic, fruit. Everything in place. Great class and depth. Excellent. (June 2003)

NOW TO 2025   20.0

Richebourg, 1993
Domaine Leroy

Fullish, vigorous colour. Very lovely nose. Splendid, harmonious, very elegant fruit. Long and complex. Really profound. Full, rich, generous and harmonious. This is multidimensional. Very lovely. A complete wine. Excellent for the vintage. (April 2000)

NOW TO 2020   19.5

Richebourg, 1993
Domaine Denis Mugneret et Fils

Full colour. Brown at the rim. Not too evolved, but quite spicy on the nose and palate. Fullish body. Rich. Good acidity. Slightly austere, as well as ripe and aromatic. Just about ready. Lovely complex fruit. Fine plus. (April 2005)

NOW TO 2018   18.0

Richebourg, 1993
Domaine de la Romanée-Conti

Medium-full colour. A suggestion of maturity. Splendidly complex, rich, slightly spicy fruit. This has great depth and class. Some evolution now. On the palate this lacks a little fat and fullness. But it is classy and harmonious. The acidity is quite marked. Not as good on the palate as the nose promised. (June 2003)

NOW TO 2020   17.5

La Romanée, 1993
Domaine Bouchard Père et Fils

Fullish, youthful colour. Lovely nose. Classy and not too austere. Fullish body on the palate. Fresh and vigorous. Very good grip. Now ready. Profound and very fine indeed. Splendid finish. (October 2005)

NOW TO 2020   19.0

Romanée-Saint-Vivant, 1993
Domaine de l'Arlot

Medium to medium-full colour. But not a lot of development. Soft, ripe nose. Some oak. Quite concentrated. Some of the stems. Medium-full body. Good richness but some tannins, which are a bit astringent. A little ungainly. But decent grip. Very good indeed. (March 2002)

NOW TO 2019   17.0

Romanée-Saint-Vivant, 1993
Domaine Robert Arnoux

Fine colour. Still immature. Firm on the nose. Closed-in. Rich, but a little light. Lovely fruit underneath, though. Still very youthful. Splendid richness. Very classy fruit. This is a lot better than his 1995. Fullish body. Excellent grip, tannins and intensity. Very lovely finish. Very fine. (March 2002)

NOW TO 2030   18.5

Romanée-Saint-Vivant, 1993
Domaine Jean-Jacques Confuron

Fullish, immature colour. Quite firm-oaky on the nose. Rich, ample fruit behind it. Fullish body. Quite structured. This slightly hides the fruit, but the fruit is delicious and concentrated. Very good grip. Slightly rigid at present, but fine plus. It needs time to soften properly. (June 2003)

NOW TO 2026   18.0

Romanée-Saint-Vivant, 1993
Maison Joseph Drouhin

Medium-full colour. Beautifully elegant nose. Ripe and succulent. Complex and very classy. Medium-full body. Ripe and very classy with just a suspicion of oak. Very Chambolle fruit. This really is Musigny-ish. And it has all the Musigny excitement. Very long. Marvellous fruit. Brilliant finish. Extra special. (December 2001)

NOW TO 2030   19.5

Romanée-Saint-Vivant, 1993
Domaine Louis Jadot

Full colour. Now some maturity. Refined, classy, concentrated and balanced. Most impressive. This is very fine. Fullish body. Very composed. Splendidly classy. Ripe, rich, harmonious and multidimensional. More advanced than Arnoux's. But still needs time. Really lovely. Very, very long and intense at the end. *Grand vin!* (March 2002)

NOW TO 2035   20.0

Romanée-Saint-Vivant, 1993
Domaine Leroy

Fullish colour. Some development. Firm nose. You can find the stems. Still very youthful. Slightly raw and fiery. Medium-full body. Very good grip, but a little lean. It lacks the fat of the 1996. And the ripeness. It reminds me a little of Côte Rôtie. (April 2000)

NOW TO 2018   18.5

Romanée-Saint-Vivant, 1993
Domaine de la Romanée-Conti

Full, rich, immature colour. Marvellous nose. Ample, succulent and seductive. Very classy.

Rich and harmonious. This is just about ready. Rich and classy, but not as complex or as intense as Jadot's. Very discreet and laid-back. Very, very long. A lovely example. Very fine plus. (March 2002)

NOW TO 2025   19.0

Ruchottes-Chambertin, 1993
Domaine Dr. Georges Mugneret

Medium-full colour. Just about mature. Rich, ripe, fragrant, balanced and cool on the nose. Lots of finesse. Medium-full bodied, cool, pure and balanced. I prefer the 1995, which is more concentrated. But this is very lovely. Very composed. Very fine. (May 2005)

NOW TO 2018   18.5

Ruchottes-Chambertin, 1993
Domaine Georges Roumier et Fils

Fullish, fresh colour. A bit reticent on the nose at first, but very fine, pure Pinot. Fullish body. Very classy. Very profound on the palate. Just went on getting better and better. Splendid harmony. Ready, but lots of life ahead of it. Very fine. (November 2005)

NOW TO 2025   18.5

Santenay, Beauregard, 1993
Domaine Roger Belland

Light to medium colour. Fully mature. Good style and depth on the nose. Fresh and ripe. This is à point. Indeed, it needs drinking quite soon. Good fruit. Slightly fading at the end. (June 2003)

DRINK SOON   14.0

Savigny-lès-Beaune, La Dominode, 1993
Domaine Bruno Clair

Quite full colour. Very youthful. Firm nose with a touch of liquorice. Medium-full. A little solid. Quite high acidity. The tannins are now softening, but the wine will get more and more generous as it ages further. Good plus. (August 2000)

NOW TO 2013+   15.5

Savigny-lès-Beaune, Les Dominodes, 1993
Domaine Jean-Marc Pavelot

Good fullish colour. Just about mature. Concentrated but mellow nose. Very lovely old-viney, classy fruit. Balanced, rich, full but with no hard edges. Very lovely. Very long on the palate. A fine example. (June 2004)

NOW TO 2015+ 17.0

Savigny-lès-Beaune, Les Golardes, 1993
Domaine Fougeray de Beauclair

Medium colour. Quite a firm, substantial nose. Earthy in a good sense. Medium-full body. Slightly chunky. But plenty of fruit and good grip. Positive finish. A wine for food. Quite good. (June 2003)

DRINK SOON 14.0

Savigny-lès-Beaune, Aux Guettes, 1993
Domaine Simon Bize et Fils

Medium colour. Slightly dried out fruit on nose and palate. Medium body. Decent acidity but a slight absence of flesh. Quite good. (June 2003)

DRINK SOON 14.0

Savigny-lès-Beaune, Les Lavières, 1993
Domaine Chandon de Briailles

Medium to medium-full colour. Ripe, slightly dry but refined nose. No undue hint of the stems. Medium to medium-full body. Lacks a bit of character, succulence and grip. But good qualilty, nonetheless. No hurry to drink. (May 2005)

NOW TO 2012 15.0

Savigny-lès-Beaune, Les Narbantons, 1993
Domaine Leroy

Fullish, mature colour. Gamey nose. Rich and fullish. Very good grip. Lots of style for a Savigny. Meaty and almost barnyardy. Increasingly so as it developed. Good plus. (June 2003)

NOW TO 2013 15.5

Savigny-lès-Beaune, Les Narbantons, 1993
Domaine Jean-Marc Pavelot

Finely poised. Lovely balance. Concentrated. Definitive. Very stylish. Medium body. Just about ready. Really long and complex. Great class. A super example. (July 2000)

NOW TO 2010 16.0

Savigny-lès-Beaune, Les Vergelesses, 1993
Domaine Simon Bize et Fils

Medium-full, fresh colour. Fragrant and stylish but essentially soft nose. Round, medium-bodied and fully ready. Good fruit. Not a bit stemmy. An elegant wine, but without a great deal of intensity or vigour. Yet complex and very good. (May 2005)

NOW TO 2015 16.0

Savigny-lès-Beaune, Les Vergelesses, 1993
Domaine Lucien Jacob

Medium colour. A little tight, reduced and rustic on the nose. Overall, medium bodied and a bit rustic on the palate. Fresh, though. (June 2003)

NOW TO 2008 12.0

Savigny-lès-Beaune, Les Vergelesses, 1993
Domaine Louis Jadot

Medium to medium-full colour. Still youthful. Fine, aromatic nose. Now just beginning to show the sensual flavours of maturity. Medium-full body on the palate. Very good grip. Ample, succulent fruit. The tannins are now mellow, but the wine is vigorous and complex. Very good. (June 2003)

NOW TO 2018 16.0

La Tâche, 1993
Domaine de la Romanée-Conti

Big colour. Still immature. A bit closed-in on the nose. Very splendid on the palate. Super rich and concentrated. A big wine, but the structure is totally submerged under the richness and concentration of the fruit. Totally excellent. Very, very vigorous. Multidimensional and very, very classy. A great wine, without a doubt. (October 2005)

NOW TO 2038 20.0

Volnay, Les Caillerets, 1993
Maison Champy

Good fresh, fullish colour. Attractive, fresh, youthful, stylish nose. Very good Volnay fruit. Approaching maturity. Medium-full body. Lovely concentrated ripe centre. Long. Very good plus. (January 2001)

NOW TO 2010 16.5

Volnay, Les Caillerets, Clos des 60 Ouvrées, 1993
Domaine de la Pousse d'Or
Very good colour. Delicious, fragrant nose. Intense, pure, elegant and classy. Ripe and complex. Medium-full body. No hard edges. Very lovely fruit. Very long and very subtle. Very lovely. (August 2000)
NOW TO 2023   18.0

Volnay, Champans, 1993
Domaine Jacques Gagnard-Delagrange
Medium colour. Just some maturity. Fragrant but lightish on the nose and palate. Not a great deal of intensity, but ripe and pleasant, elegant and fruity. Medium body. Stylish. À point. Good plus, but not brilliant. (June 2000)
DRINK SOON   15.5

Volnay, Champans, 1993
Domaine des Comtes Lafon
Medium-full colour. Some development. Quite evolved on the nose. Caramelly. Medium to medium-full body. Looser-knit than their 1993 Volnay Santenots. More generous. Not quite the depth it should have. But ripe and classy. Very good plus. (March 2002)
NOW TO 2015   16.5

Volnay, Champans, 1993
Domaine Monthelie-Douhairet
Very good colour. Rather tough on the nose and astringent on the palate. Too stewed. (June 2003)
DRINK SOON   12.0

Volnay, En Chevret, 1993
Domaine Joseph Drouhin
Medium-full colour. Still quite fresh. Soft, elegant, intensely fragrant Pinot nose. Very Volnay. Ripe, very gently oaky, balanced and graceful on the palate. Medium-full body. Good concentration. Very good length. Mellow. Fine finish. A lovely wine with a very long aftertaste. Very stylish. Fine. (May 2005)
NOW TO 2020   17.5

Volnay, Clos de l'Audignac, 1993
Domaine de la Pousse d'Or
Fullish colour. Still not much sign of maturity. Good fragrant nose. Reasonable depth and intensity. Now beginning to soften. Medium to medium-full body. Just a little tannin. Ripe, long, complex and stylish. Very good. (October 2000)
NOW TO 2015   16.0

Volnay, Clos de la Bousse d'Or, 1993
Domaine de la Pousse d'Or
Good colour. Very lovely refined nose. Concentrated, pure and classy. Fullish body. Still a little austere, but the tannins are now softening. Very good acidity. Lots of potential here. Very Volnay. Very classy. (October 2000)
NOW TO 2019   17.5

Volnay, Clos du Chateau des Ducs, 1993
Domaine Michel Lafarge
I have had more than one corked bottle of this wine, exceptionally with Lafarge. Full colour. Still very youthful. Very lovely nose. True intense, fragrant, classy Volnay fruit. Medium-full body. Very good grip. Very well integrated tannins. Can be drunk now. But still very fresh. Will still improve. Complex, subtle and multidimensional. Lovely finish. Very long and very discreet and distinguished. Fine. (September 2004)
NOW TO 2026   17.5

Volnay, Clos des Chênes, 1993
Domaine Michel Lafarge
Fullish, youthful colour. Full, rich and meaty on the palate. Lots of lovely concentrated fruit. Still vigorous, but just about mature. Good grip. Ample. Long. Very fine. (March 2006)
NOW TO 2025+   18.5

Volnay, Clos des Santenots, 1993
Domaine Jacques Prieur
Medium colour. A little evolution. Quite stylish on the nose but a bit dead on the palate. Slightly hot. Lacks flair. Slightly heavy. Quite good at best. (June 2000)
DRINK SOON   14.0

Volnay, Frémiets, 1993
Domaine Annick Parent

Very good colour. Still very youthful. Fragrant, fresh, ripe nose. Classy. Medium-full body. Good tannins. Stylish and complex. Very Volnay. Lovely finish. Very good plus. (June 2006)

NOW TO 2015   16.5

Volnay, Mitans, 1993
Domaine Hubert de Montille

Magnum. Very good colour. Lovely pure fruit on the nose. Rich, backward and concentrated. This is very good plus, but it doesn't quite have the succulence for fine. Slightly tough at the end. But it still needs time. (June 2003)

NOW TO 2020   16.5

Volnay, Ronceret, 1993
Domaine Jean-Marc Boillot

Good colour. Firm nose. Slightly artificial fruit. Chunky on the palate. It lacks a bit of suppleness and flair. It is getting astringent. Only fair. (June 2003)

DRINK SOON   13.5

Volnay, Santenots, 1993
Domaine Robert Ampeau

Medium-full, mature colour. Slightly funky nose. Ripe but slightly exotic. Needs time to open up. Slightly rustic and stemmy on the palate. Slightly sweaty, too. A little ungainly. Will still improve. Very good at best. (October 2005)

NOW TO 2011   15.5

Volnay, Santenots du Milieu, 1993
Domaine des Comtes Lafon

Very full colour. Still very young. Rich, full and concentrated on the nose. Full body. Still some tannin. Very, very rich but quite pronounced acidity (compared with 1995). Long, concentrated, profound and complex. Lots of class. Very fine. (June 2005)

NOW TO 2020+   18.5

Volnay, Les Santenots du Milieu, 1993
Domaine François Mikulski

Magnum. Good colour. Soft, plump, classy nose. Very good fruit. Medium-full body. Smooth. Rich and vigorous. Concentrated and with very good grip. Very long. This is fine. (June 2003)

NOW TO 2018   17.5

Volnay, Taille Pieds, 1993
Domaine du Marquis d'Angerville

Fullish colour. Still vigorous. Lovely fragrant, classy, harmonious nose. Now mellow. Medium-full body. Balanced. Very good tannins. Lots of fruit. Lots of finesse. Vigorous, but *à point*. Fine. (September 2005)

NOW TO 2023   17.5

Volnay, Taille Pieds, 1993
Domaine Hubert de Montille

Half bottle. This is rather more succulent than the Mitans 1993. Fuller. Some tannin. This still needs time. Again, a little austere still, rather than tannic. Good grip. But more concentration. Fine, potentially. (November 2000)

NOW TO 2015   17.5

Vosne-Romanée, 1993
Domaine Sylvain Cathiard

Magnum. Medium colour. Elegant, fragrant, soft nose. This is lightening up a little, perhaps. Good fruit. Medium body. It lacks a little grip and vigour, but good style. *À point*. (June 2003)

NOW TO 2010   15.0

Vosne-Romanée, 1993
Domaine René Engel

Magnum. Good mature colour. Rich, full, plump, ripe nose. This is very good for a village wine. Fullish body. Fresh, concentrated and lovely. Very Pinot. Lovely fruit and very good harmony. Long, concentrated and vigorous. Fine for what it is. Very good indeed. (June 2003)

NOW TO 2016   17.0

Vosne-Romanée, 1993
Domaine Jean Gros

Full, firm, just about mature colour. Rich, fat, full, sweet but vigorous. Earthy. Quite substantial. Lots of depth. Noble quality. Very impressive for a village wine. Nothing too austere. Long and fine. (September 2005)

NOW TO 2013+   17.5

Vosne-Romanée, Les Barreaux, 1993
Domaine Anne Gros

Medium-full colour. Very lovely plump, fresh, ample nose. Like Engel's, this is a splendid village 1993, though quite advanced. Medium-full body. Balanced and elegant. Very good plus. (January 2003)

NOW TO 2010   16.5

Vosne-Romanée, Les Beaumonts, 1993
Domaine Bruno Clavelier

Medium-full colour. Some development. Not a lot on the nose. What there is is plump, harmonious and classy. On the palate, fullish bodied, rich, balanced and just a little spicy. Good depth. Plenty of length. No lack of flair. Very good indeed. (September 2001)

NOW TO 2023   17.0

Vosne-Romanée, Les Beaumonts, 1993
Domaine Jean Grivot

Magnum. Good colour. Splendidly rich, vigorous, concentrated nose. Very fine fruit. Full, rich, generous and marvellously well balanced. This is very lovely. Very impressive. Only just about ready. Very, very long and complex. Great class. Very fine. (June 2003)

NOW TO 2020   18.5

Vosne-Romanée, Les Beaumonts, 1993
Domaine Leroy

Good colour. Ripe, concentrated and exotic on the nose. Very fine mature Pinot here. Fullish body. Balanced, complex and intense. This is fresh and fully mature at the same time. Grivot's has more class, but this is fine plus. Very long and lovely at the end. (June 2003)

NOW TO 2020   18.0

Vosne-Romanée, Les Beaux Monts, 1993
Domaine Clavelier-Brosson

Made by Bruno Clavelier. Medium-full colour. Slightly leaner but more fragrant nose than their 1993 Vosne-Romanée Brûlées. Less fat. Less richness. On the palate, medium to medium-full body. The tannins are now soft. But, again, a little lean. Ready. Attractive, clean Pinot Noir. But it lacks a bit of succulence. Very good at best. (July 2005)

NOW TO 2015   16.0

Vosne-Romanée, Les Brûlées,
Vieilles Vignes, 1993
Domaine Clavelier-Brosson

Made by Bruno Clavelier. Medium-full colour. Soft, refined, fragrant, balanced, pure nose. Medium to medium-full body. Good round, tannic base, supported by a fresh acidity. Now *à point*. Subtle, rich, elegant and very easy to drink. No hard edges. Not the concentration for great, though. But long and complex. Very good indeed. (July 2005)

NOW TO 2018   17.0

Vosne-Romanée, Les Brûlées, 1993
Domaine Bruno Clavelier

(Domaine Clavelier-Buisson). Medium-full colour. Fragrant, stylish, gentle nose. Medium to medium-full body. Clean, ripe, soft Pinot fruit on the palate. Harmonious and classy. Good intensity. Very good indeed. (December 2005)

NOW TO 2015   17.0

Vosne-Romanée, Aux Brûlées, 1993
Domaine René Engel

Magnum. Good colour. Very splendidly concentrated, high-quality nose. Very excellent fruit and depth. Fullish body. Very concentrated. Very vigorous. This is brilliant. Great depth and class. Splendid vigour at the end. All in place. Very fine plus. (June 2003)

NOW TO 2020   19.0

Vosne-Romanée, Les Chaumes, 1993
Domaine Robert Arnoux

Full, rich, firm, backward nose. Very good quality here. Lovely concentrated fruit. Medium-full body on the palate. Very good grip. Still some tannin. Long and satisfying. Very good plus. (October 2002)

NOW TO 2015   16.5

Vosne-Romanée, Les Chaumes, 1993
Domaine Jean Tardy et Fils

Medium-full, mature colour. Soft, very oaky nose. The oak tends to dominate. But there is elegant ripe fruit here, if no great concentration. Medium to medium-full body. Seductive but slightly bland. Very good. (July 2005)

NOW TO 2013   16.0

Vosne-Romanée, Clos des Réas, 1993
Domaine Jean Gros

Medium to medium-full colour. Very refined, quietly successful and concentrated nose. Lovely fruit. Great class. Medium-full body. Balanced, fragrant and elegant. Very good vigour and complexity at the end. Very, very long. Fine plus. (June 2003)

NOW TO 2013   18.0

Vosne-Romanée, Cros Parentoux, 1993
Domaine Méo-Camuzet

Good colour. A touch of maturity. Ripe and oaky but still immature nose. Quite soft on the palate now. Medium-full body. No aggressive tannins. Rich. Good grip. Lots of vigour. Long, complex and classy. Fine plus. (March 2005)

NOW TO 2020+   18.0

Vosne-Romanée, Aux Malconsorts, 1993
Domaine Thomas-Moillard

Full, fairly immature colour. Quite dense as well as tannic on the nose. Underneath, some impressive old-viney fruit. Very good acidity and no lack of concentration or richness. This has a long, intense finish. Fine plus. (September 2001)

NOW TO 2026   18.0

Vosne-Romanée, Les Petits Monts, 1993
Domaine Denis Mugneret et Fils

Good colour. Ripe, fresh, plump nose. This is a delicious, fragrant wine. Very good fruit. Only medium body and not quite the concentration—

or the class—of the very best, but fine nevertheless. Lovely finish. (June 2003)

NOW TO 2013   17.5

Vosne-Romanée, Les Suchots, 1993
Domaine Robert Arnoux

Fullish colour. Rich, full and closed-in on the nose. Sumptuous. On the palate, still youthful. Excellent concentrated fruit. Very classy. Very complex. Very long. Very lovely indeed. An impressive wine. Excellent. (March 2002)

NOW TO 2022   17.5

Vosne-Romanée, Les Suchots, 1993
Domaine Alain Hudelot-Noëllat

Medium-full, mature colour. Rich, fat, fragrant, succulent nose. Medium to medium-full on the palate. Balanced, stylish Pinot Noir fruit. No hard acidity. Ample and round. Lots of depth. Classy and complex. Very good. (May 2005)

NOW TO 2018   16.0

Vosne-Romanée, Les Suchots, 1993
Domaine Gérard Mugneret

Good colour. Fresh nose. Very gently oaky. Good vigour, concentration and depth. Medium to medium-full body. Very good grip. Lovely fruit. This has class. Clean and composed. Just a little lean after the very best. Very good. (June 2003)

NOW TO 2013   16.0

1992

When the wines first came on the market, the 1992 Burgundy vintage was both unfairly denigrated and overpraised. The white wines were hailed in some circles as great, while the reds were dismissed as garbage. As it turned out, both extremes were soon seen as inaccurate. Many of the white wines became blowsy rather quickly. You could separate the really good, the Carillons and the Roulots and the Javilliers—the ones with the grip and the capacity to last—from the rest. Sadly, there were not enough in the former camp, and few wines made it vigorously as far as their tenth anniversaries. Now, of course, they are 15 years old.

For the reds, however, it was a different matter. No one would pretend that 1992 is a great red wine vintage, or even a very good one. It has neither the grip and concentration of 1993 nor the voluptuous richness and weight of 1990, nor indeed the balance and depth of 1991—a year equally but even more unfairly criticised. But what 1992 does have is some very pleasant surprises. At the top levels there are no dogs, but plenty of wines which are still vigorous, with more than enough fruit, acidity and structure to give enjoyment. As always, the essential thing is to stick to the top names and top *climats*. These will not let you down.

WEATHER CONDITIONS

In mild early spring weather the development of the vegetation got off to an early start. May was warm and dry, and some of the more precocious vineyards were in flower by the end of the month, thus ensuring a large harvest which would all ripen at the same time and at an early date. In other vineyards the *floraison* was delayed and suffered in the cold, wet weather of June. These bunches would offer less fruit, and maturity would be uneven and retarded, but paradoxically, they might yield more concentrated wine.

A fine July and August and an early September promised well, but as this last month progressed, the skies clouded over, and the temperature dropped. That final push from maturity to concentration did not come. Most of the Côte de Beaune was harvested in dry weather before two days of rain (33 mm of precipitation on September 22). Thereafter, it was dry until the following weekend, during which period most of the Côte de Nuits was cleared.

WHERE ARE THE BEST WINES?
AND THE STATE OF MATURITY TODAY

- Only a handful of the white wines remain fresh.

- Many minor red wines are now tired. While at the outset, there was no material difference in quality between the Côte de Beaune and the Côte de Nuits, today, fifteen years on, it is naturally the more structured and concentrated Côte de Nuits which have retained their vigour. Nevertheless, drink them soon.

TASTING NOTES

WHITES

Bâtard-Montrachet, 1992
Domaine Delagrange-Bachelet
Soft and mature. A little overblown. A little light. But stylish. Ripe. Good fruit. A little slight on the palate, but quite intense nonetheless. Long. Classy. Very good indeed. (March 2000)
DRINK SOON   17.0

Bâtard-Montrachet, 1992
Domaine Jean-Noël Gagnard
Quite a deep colour. This is different from the generation of wines above. Fullish body. A little more built-in sulphur. Good acidity, especially for 1992. But evolved, more so than the two previous vintages would suggest. More lumpy and four-square. Some botrytis. Full body. Rather more exotic and with less finesse. Rich, long and vigorous. Not too blowsy, but it doesn't have the class of the vintages from 1993 onwards. It was in 1993 that Caroline Lestimé took over responsibility. One can see the difference. Very good plus. (January 2002)
DRINK SOON   16.5

→ Rating for the Vintage ←	
Red	14.0
White	15.5

→ Size of the Crop ←		
(In hectolitres, excluding generic wine)		
	RED	WHITE
Grands Crus	13,278	3,600
Village and		
Premiers Crus	182,261	48,606
TOTAL	195,539	52,206

Bâtard-Montrachet, 1992
Domaine Leflaive

Magnum. Quite a full colour. Rich yet blowsy. Ripe and fullish bodied. Plenty of ripe fruit. But lacks a bit of zip. Slightly heavy. Slight touch of built-in sulphur. Only very good. (July 2003)

DRINK SOON   16.0

Bâtard-Montrachet, 1992
Domaine Michel Niellon

Firm, full and rich. Very good grip. This is firm, profound and very classy on the palate. Still very youthful. Lovely concentrated fruit. Full bodied. Excellent fruit and depth. Fine plus. Lots of life ahead. (March 2002)

NOW TO 2010   18.0

Bâtard-Montrachet, 1992
Domaine Étienne Sauzet

Slightly more floral and less firm than Niellon's Bâtard 1992. Deeper colour, too. More scented on the palate. But good acidity. Refined. Medium-full body. Elegant and complex. This is fine. (March 2002)

DRINK SOON   17.5

Beaune, Sur les Grèves, 1992
Domaine Germain Père et Fils/
Chateau de Chorey-lès-Beaune

Plump and vigorous on the nose. Quite a meaty example. Good depth. Fullish body. Good grip. Holding up well. Very good. (June 2002)

DRINK SOON   16.0

Chassagne-Montrachet, La Boudriotte, 1992
Domaine Ramonet

Firm, youthful nose. Rich, full, cool and really quite minerally for a Chassagne. Flowery. A touch of anise. A touch of oak. Still quite youthful. Very good grip. Fine. Lots of life. (March 2003)

DRINK SOON   17.5

Chassagne-Montrachet, Les Caillerets, 1992
Domaine Jean-Noël Gagnard

Just a little sulphur evident on the nose. A little hidden on the palate. Good rich, classy wine here. But very good indeed, rather than fine. (June 2002)

DRINK SOON   17.0

Chassagne-Montrachet, Les Chenevottes, 1992
Domaine Michel Niellon

This is a splendid 1992. Fullish. Virile. Excellent grip. Very stylish. Lovely, ample fruit. Lots of complexity. Lots of vigour. Fine. (July 2001)

DRINK SOON   17.5

Chassagne-Montrachet, 1992
Domaine du Marquis de Laguiche/
Maison Joseph Drouhin

Just a little faded on the nose. But a classy wine underneath. Still ripe, rich and balanced on the palate. Very good (was very good indeed). (June 2002)

DRINK SOON   16.0

Chassagne-Montrachet, Morgeot, 1992
Domaine Ramonet

Magnum. Splendidly cool and crisp for a 1992. A lot of depth here. Very lovely ripe fruit. Still very vigorous. Ample, ripe, peachy, generous and long. This is fine plus. (July 2000)

DRINK SOON   18.0

Chassagne-Montrachet, La Romanée, 1992
Maison Verget

A typical, somewhat disappointing 1992. Deep colour now. Slight oxidation on the nose. A bit tired on the palate. Not enough grip and concentration and acidity, and now cracking up. Quite decent fruit. Was 16/20; now 14.0 and getting worse. (March 2003)

DRINK UP   14.0

Chassagne-Montrachet, Les Vergets, 1992
Domaine Ramonet

Fresh, ripe, fullish and stylish. Fragrant and peachy. Very good acidity for the vintage. Yet at the same time, the sort of blowsiness of the 1992 vintage. Rich, ripe, round, nutty finish. Very ripe. Classy. Fine. *À point* now. (July 2000)

DRINK SOON   17.5

Chevalier-Montrachet, 1992
Domaine Bouchard Père et Fils

Soft, very ripe—almost overripe—nose. Good depth, grip and class on the palate. Some botrytis here. Good but not great grip. The wine is full bodied, ample and fine plus for the vintage. But essentially it lacks a bit of freshness. (December 2001)

DRINK SOON   18.0

Chevalier-Montrachet, 1992
Domaine Leflaive

Quite rich, but a little flabby on the nose. Fully ready. Medium-full body. Agreeable, but not with the grip or depth or class that it really should have. Very good, but a disappointment for what it is. (October 2000)

DRINK SOON   16.0

Chevalier-Montrachet, 1992
Domaine Jacques Prieur

More evolved than the Meursault Perrières 1992 from Prieur tasted alongside it. Despite decent acidity, it seems a bit flat. Full bodied and rich, but a bit heavy. Now collapsing in the glass. Drink soon. (November 2002)

DRINK SOON   14.0

Corton Blanc, 1992
Domaine Chandon de Briailles

Quite a youthful colour. Fresh nose. Ripe, but no botrytis. Not four-square but not very intense or concentrated. More interest on the palate. Medium-full body. Good crisp fruit. Not very complex, but an enjoyable bottle. No hurry to drink. (May 2005)

DRINK SOON   16.0

Corton-Charlemagne, 1992
Domaine Bonneau du Martray

Full bodied, ripe and lively. Very good grip. Nicely steely. Not a bit of the usual blowsiness of the vintage. Long. Vigorous. Fine. (October 2003)

DRINK SOON   17.5

Corton-Charlemagne, 1992
Maison Champy

Flat and faded on the nose, with some SO2. Loose, watery and common. Past its best. (June 2002)

PAST ITS BEST   12.0

Corton-Charlemagne, 1992
Domaine Joseph Drouhin

Rich, full and mellow but vigorous nose. Gently oaky. Concentrated. Ripe and ample. Fresh and peachy. Fullish body. Lovely fruit. Very fine and still very vigorous. (April 2005)

NOW TO 2010   18.5

Corton-Charlemagne, 1992
Domaine Joseph Faiveley

Slight touch of dry Sauternes. Fullish. Very ample, but very good grip. Very smooth. Rich but dry. Very ripe. Ready. Long. Vigorous at the end. Very fine. (June 2003)

NOW TO 2012   18.5

Corton-Charlemagne, 1992
Domaine Louis Jadot

Full, ripe, rich and concentrated with very good grip, class and depth. Underneath is the real austerity it should have. Still very young. The parcel overhangs the restaurant. Fine plus. (June 2003)

NOW TO 2013   18.0

Corton-Charlemagne, 1992
Domaine Louis Latour

Evolved. Slightly blowsy. Not too sulphury, but rather flat at the end. Good at best. (March 2006)

DRINK SOON   15.0

Corton-Charlemagne, 1992
Maison Roland Remoissenet et Fils

Rich, but it lacks a bit of bite. Quite high in alcohol. Good fruit, but just a little heavy. Very good at best. (March 2004)

NOW TO 2008   16.0

Criots-Bâtard-Montrachet, 1992
Domaine Hubert Lamy et Fils

Youthful colour and a very fresh nose. Just a little lean at first, but it got fatter in the glass. Gently oaky. Discreet. Complex. Classy. This is fine plus. *À point* now. (June 2001)

DRINK SOON   18.0

Meursault, Blagny, Chateau de Blagny, 1992
Domaine Louis Latour

Fresh colour. Broad, fullish nose. Only a hint of wood. Ripe but not overripe. Good acidity. Fulllish on the palate. Fat. Not a great deal of distinction, but an agreeable bottle, if slightly heavy at the end. Good. (May 2005)

DRINK SOON 15.0

Meursault, Blagny, 1992
Domaine Joseph Matrot

Full, ripe and well balanced. Much less sulphur than in Matrot's Puligny-Montrachet les Chalumaux. Cleaner and classier. Good vigour still. Nice and steely, particularly for a 1992. This is fine. (July 2002)

NOW TO 2010 17.5

Meursault, Charmes, 1992
Domaine Pierre Boillot

Fresh colour. Pure, vibrant, clean and very stylish on the nose. Surprisingly fresh. Lots of depth and concentration. Medium-full body. Very good grip. Ripe and concentrated on the palate. Long, subtle and full of vigour. Fine plus. Lots of life ahead of it. A delicious bottle. (May 2005)

NOW TO 2009 18.0

Meursault, Charmes, 1992
Domaine des Comtes Lafon

Fully à point. Fullish bodied, rich and slightly blowsy. But still fresh and succulent. Mellow and opulent. Very good indeed, but not great. (November 2005)

NOW TO 2010 17.0

Meursault, Charmes, 1992
Domaine Joseph Matrot

No undue colour. Fresh, ripe nose. Succulent fruit, if no great depth. Medium-full body. Balanced. Now needs drinking quite soon. Reasonable style, but showing signs of getting a bit thin at the end. Good plus. (May 2005)

DRINK SOON 15.5

Meursault, Charmes, 1992
Domaine François Mikulski

Decent vigour here on the attack, if without a great deal of class. It tails off on the palate. The fruit is beginning to go. Quite good. (June 2002)

DRINK SOON 14.0

Meursault, Charmes, 1992
Maison Morey-Blanc

Some evolution on the nose here. But ripe and classy, nevertheless. Good depth. The finish is impressive. Fine quality. But drink soon. (June 2002)

DRINK SOON 17.5

Meursault, Clos de la Barre, 1992
Domaine des Comtes Lafon

Rich, fat and fading gently on the nose. More vigorous on the palate. A fullish wine with good fruit and individuality and at least decent grip. But like many 1992s, it will not improve further, nor keep. It has classy fruit. But drink it soon. (September 2003)

DRINK SOON 15.0

Meursault, Genevrières, 1992
Domaine des Comtes Lafon

Dominique picked very early, and it shows. Good colour. No undue evolution. Lovely nose. Plump and fruity-salady. Much fresher and more stylish than most. Soft but vigorous. Ample. Very good acidity. Medium to medium-full body. Composed and gentle. Round and complex. Very relaxed. Much less overripe than most. Holding up well. Lovely. (September 2005)

NOW TO 2009 17.5

Meursault, Les Narvaux, 1992
Domaine Patrick Javillier

Magnum. Lovely nose. Classy, cool and minerally. No sign of age. Ripe, ample and very gently oaky on the palate. Complex, long and classy. This is very good indeed. (June 2002)

DRINK SOON 17.0

Meursault, Les Perrières, 1992
Domaine des Comtes Lafon

Quite a deep colour. Quite oaky, too. Ample, but quite developed, if not a bit flabby and oxidised. Is this a good example? More 1992 than Lafon. Rich but blowsy. It lacks zip, but has good concentration. Full bodied. Very good indeed, at best. Drink quite soon. (November 2001)

DRINK SOON   17.0

Meursault, Perrières, 1992
Domaine Joseph Matrot

Fullish, quite well matured colour. A lot of built-in sulphur. Full and rich and with good acidity; concentrated even. But rather four-square and sulphury. Still quite vigorous. Good at best. (July 2001)

DRINK SOON   15.0

Meursault, Les Perrières, 1992
Domaine Jacques Prieur

This is plump, rich and vigorous. Good fruit. Very good acidity for a 1992. Holding up well. Round and ample. Quite full. Not a bit heavy. Very good indeed. (November 2002)

DRINK SOON   17.0

Meursault, Les Perrières, 1992
Domaine Guy Roulot

Magnum. Very fine nose. This is ripe, laid-back, very classy and very concentrated. Lovely minerally fruit. Very classy. Very long. Very fine. (June 2002)

DRINK SOON   18.5

Meursault, Poruzots, 1992
Domaine François Jobard

Fat and rich. Slight SO2 after awhile. Slightly four-square. Minerally in a solid sort of way. Very good grip for a 1992. A wine for food. Clumsy on its own, and the SO2 gets in the way of the enjoyment. Will it throw this off? (August 2000)

DRINK SOON   14.0

Meursault, Tessons, 1992
Domaine Guy Roulot

Magnum. Lovely nose. Ripe, poised, delicate and classy. Impressive fruit and succulence on

the palate. Long and understated. This is very good indeed. (June 2002)

DRINK SOON   17.0

Le Montrachet, 1992
Domaine des Comtes Lafon

Fullish colour. Fullish, mellow, very distinctive on the nose. Thickly textured. Very fine fruit and very good acidity. This is quite lovely. Great class. Great complexity. Great length. Very, very lovely. Excellent. Lots of life ahead of it. (September 2004)

NOW TO 2015+   20.0

Le Montrachet, 1992
Maison Roland Remoissenet et Fils

Fullish colour. Ripe, rich and honeyed. Slightly overripe on the nose. On the palate, this has more concentration and better acidity than was apparent at first. Still vigorous. Good depth and class. Rich. Youthful. Fine plus. (March 2001)

NOW TO 2010+   18.0

Le Montrachet, 1992
Maison Verget

Deep colour. Quite evolved on the nose. Ripe. Slightly sulphury. But decent acidity. Rich. Overblown. A touch of botrytis. Fat. Not the greatest class, but with the depth of Le Montrachet. Very good at best. (April 2005)

DRINK SOON   16.0

Puligny-Montrachet, 1992
Domaine Jean-Marc Boillot

This has rather too much sulphur on the nose. Better on the palate. More residual sugar than some. Fullish body. Fruity but rather unstylish. Quite good. (June 2002)

DRINK SOON   14.0

Puligny-Montrachet, 1992
Domaine Carillon

No fatigue here. Plump, fresh, elegant and fruity. Medium weight. This has aged well. (June 2002)

DRINK SOON   16.0

Puligny-Montrachet, Champ Canet, 1992
Domaine Jean-Marc Boillot

This shows both vigour and class on the nose. Fullish body. Very good depth. Rich and concentrated. Plenty of life ahead of it. This is fine. (June 2002)

DRINK SOON 17.5

Puligny-Montrachet, Champ Canet, 1992
Domaine Étienne Sauzet

Quite a deep colour. Full and slightly reduced on the nose. Cleaner on the palate. Vigorous and rich. Good grip. A lot of concentration here. Slightly youthful. Much more energy than most 1992s. Got better and better as it evolved. Very good indeed. (March 2000)

NOW TO 2012 17.0

Puligny-Montrachet, Les Combettes, 1992
Domaine Joseph Matrot

A bit of built-in sulphur on the nose. Decent acidity, but a slight lack of concentration on the palate. Good fruit but nothing better than good plus. (July 2002)

DRINK SOON 15.5

Puligny-Montrachet, Les Combettes, 1992
Domaine Étienne Sauzet

Fullish, vigorous and with lots of depth and class. This is a 1992 with proper grip. Lovely ripe fruit. The oak is just right. Delicious. (March 2003)

DRINK SOON 18.0

Puligny-Montrachet, Les Pucelles, 1992
Maison Verget

Soft but fresh. Not too "tendre" or blowsy. Quite developed though. Medium to medium-full body. Just a little heavy. Lacks zip. Ripe. Quite scented. Very good rather than great. (March 2002)

DRINK SOON 16.0

Puligny-Montrachet, La Truffière, 1992
Domaine Jean-Marc Boillot

Good colour. Surprisingly firm and vigorous. Quite oaky. Profound and concentrated and classy. Ripe and ample and peachy. This is holding up very well indeed. In fact, it will last well. Very good grip. A lovely bottle. (January 2002)

NOW TO 2010 17.5

Saint-Aubin, En Remilly, 1992
Domaine Hubert Lamy et Fils

A little faded on the nose. It has lost both class and fruit. Past its best. (June 2002)

(SEE NOTE)

REDS

Beaune, Le Clos des Mouches, 1992
Domaine Joseph Drouhin

Medium colour. No undue age. Ripe, plump nose. Similar on the palate. Balanced and stylish. *À point.* Positive finish. Good plus. (June 2002)

DRINK SOON 15.5

Beaune, Les Cras, 1992
Domaine Germain Père et Fils/
Chateau de Chorey-lès-Beaune

Medium colour. No undue age. Lovely nose. Succulent and vigorous. Similar on the palate. Medium-full body. Plenty of vigour. This has both length and depth. Very good. (June 2002)

NOW TO 2009 16.0

Beaune, Grèves, 1992
Domaine Michel Lafarge

Good colour. Quite a sturdy example on the nose. More substance but less class, compared with Jacques Germain's Cras. Medium body. A little astringent. It doesn't have a lot of grip. Good, though. (June 2002)

DRINK SOON 15.0

Blagny, La Pièce sous le Bois, 1992
Domaine Joseph Matrot

This is a little over-chaptalised. Medium-full, round and rich. Nicely balanced but a little sweet. Still vigorous. Quite good. (August 2002)

DRINK SOON 14.5

Bonnes Mares, 1992
Domaine Georges Roumier et Fils

Good colour. Rich, full, fat, classy and succulent on the nose. Slightly austere, as always, compared with de Vogüé's, but full and poised and very fine. (June 2002)

NOW TO 2012+ 18.5

Bonnes Mares, 1992
Domaine Comte Georges de Vogüé
Good colour. Richer, oakier and more sophisticated than Roumier's on the nose. But softer as well. Full bodied and rich on the palate. Very concentrated. This has bags of life ahead of it. Very lovely finish. Very fine plus. (June 2002)

NOW TO 2012+   19.0

Chambertin, 1992
Domaine Bouchard Père et Fils
Fullish, mature colour. Quite fresh on nose and palate. Decent fruit. Plump, if slightly one-dimensional. Balanced. À point. A gentle wine. Now soft and round. Positive, stylish finish. Very good plus, but not great. (November 2002)

NOW TO 2010   16.5

Chambertin, 1992
Domaine Leroy
Medium-full colour. Fully mature. Slightly diffuse on the nose. A little sulphur, too. Not nearly as impressive as the 1994. A bit better on the palate, but a little weak nevertheless. Pretty fruit, but it tails off. (April 2000)

DRINK SOON   16.0

Le Chambertin, 1992
Domaine Armand Rousseau
Mature, fullish colour. But no undue age. Lovely nose. Ripe, slightly spicy and naturally sweet. Very profound and classy. Medium to medium-full body. Soft and round. Long and complex. A brilliant wine for the vintage. (February 2005)

NOW TO 2010   20.0

Chambertin, Clos de Bèze, 1992
Domaine Armand Rousseau
The colour is still very fresh. Less evolved and slightly fuller than Rousseau's Chambertin. A little more muscular on nose and palate. Slightly less sophisticated tannins. Medium-full body. Meaty. Vigorous. Very good fruit and balance but not quite as subtle or as exquisite as their 1992 Chambertin. (February 2005)

NOW TO 2010   19.0

Chambolle-Musigny, 1992
Domaine Comte Georges de Vogüé
Medium to medium-full colour. Fragrant nose. Soft and succulent. No hard edges. Medium body. Slightly bland but ripe and very good for the vintage. Round. À point. (March 2000)

DRINK SOON   15.0

Chambolle-Musigny, Les Feusselottes, 1992
Maison Louis Jadot
Fullish colour. Vigorous nose. Lovely fruit. Plenty of depth. Good substance and very good style on the palate. Rich, cool, balanced and with very good concentration and grip. Fine. (June 2002)

NOW TO 2012   17.5

Chambolle-Musigny, Les Fuées, 1992
Domaine Jacques Frédéric Mugnier
Good colour. Lovely fresh, fragrant nose. Ripe, classy, gently oaky and of medium-full body. Splendidly fresh. This is long and very classy. Fine plus. (June 2002)

NOW TO 2012   18.0

Charmes-Chambertin, 1992
Domaine Denis Bachelet
Good colour. Very, very lovely on the nose. Succulent, balanced and classy. A lot of concentration in a discreet sort of way, especially coming after the Dugat-Py example. Fullish body. Balanced, persistent and very intense and classy. Quite lovely. Very long. Very fine plus. (June 2002)

NOW TO 2012+   19.0

Charmes-Chambertin, 1992
Domaine Bernard Dugat-Py
Good colour. A bit mixed-up on the nose. Some stems evident. Slightly lumpy. Good size, but a little over-extracted. Plump, vigorous and balanced, but this is no better than very good indeed. (June 2002)

NOW TO 2010   17.0

Charmes-Chambertin, 1992
Domaine Dominique Gallois
Good colour. Curious nose. Good succulent fruit, but with a touch of caramel and bitterness.

Better on the palate. Ripe, fullish bodied, mellow, succulent and vigorous. Very good indeed. (June 2002)

NOW TO 2010   17.0

Charmes-Chambertin, Très Vieilles Vignes, 1992
Domaine Joseph Roty

Medium to medium-full colour. Now fully mature. Fat and succulent on the nose. Not too diffuse. Ripe and mellow. Medium body. Decent grip. Fine for the vintage. Still fresh. Positive finish. (April 2006)

NOW TO 2011   17.5

Chassagne-Montrachet, Clos Saint-Jean, 1992
Domaine Ramonet

Medium colour. Quite evolved. Interesting, fragrant nose. Medium body. Fully ready. This is good, but it isn't that vigorous. Good plus at best. (March 2002)

DRINK SOON   15.5

Clos des Lambrays, 1992
Domaine des Lambrays

Good colour. Attractive, fragrant, fresh, plump nose. This has plenty of vigour and depth. Medium-full body. Classy, rich fruit. Fine plus. (June 2002)

NOW TO 2012   18.0

Clos de la Roche, 1992
Domaine Leroy

Full colour for the vintage. Some evolution. Ample, ripe, rich nose. Very good for a 1992. Fresh and delicious. Plump. *À point*. Full body. Charm and attraction. Balanced. Very lovely for what it is. But it lacks a bit of grip. (April 2000)

DRINK SOON   16.0

Clos de la Roche, 1992
Domaine Hubert Lignier

Very good colour. Full, rich and oaky on the nose. Plenty of extraction here. Full, vigorous, youthful and sweet on the palate. Even a bit of tannin. Ripe and opulent. Long. Plenty of life ahead of it. Fine plus. (June 2002)

NOW TO 2012+   18.0

Clos de la Roche, Cuvée Vieilles Vignes, 1992
Domaine Ponsot

Magnum. Vigorous, mature colour. Well matured nose. Medium body. Ripe, fresh and sensual. No weakness. Delicious now. Very fine. (March 2006)

NOW TO 2010   18.5

Clos Saint-Denis, 1992
Domaine Dujac

Good colour. Ripe and plump on the nose. Sweet and quite concentrated on the palate. Good volume. Plenty of fruit and depth here. Lots of vigour. Fine plus. (June 2002)

NOW TO 2012   18.0

Clos de Tart, 1992
Domaine du Clos de Tart

"Vinification Traditionnelle". This is a more complete version of the Accad experimental wine. It is essentially richer and fatter. Good class and vigour. Very fine. (June 2002)

NOW TO 2012   18.5

Clos de Tart, 1992
Domaine du Clos de Tart

"Vinification Accad": an experiment of a few barrels. Most of this was eventually blended back with the wine above. The experiment was not considered a success. Slightly browner colour than the classic. Slightly more stemmy on the nose. Good weight, grip and fruit. Very good. (June 2002)

NOW TO 2009   16.0

Clos de Vougeot, 1992
Domaine René Engel

Magnum. Very good colour. Impressive nose. Fresh, concentrated and classy. Lots of depth. Full, rich and naturally sweet. This is ample and concentrated on the palate. Lots of depth. Lovely long finish. Very vigorous. Very fine. (June 2002)

NOW TO 2012+   18.5

Clos de Vougeot, 1992
Domaine Jean Grivot

This is a very lovely example. Good tannin. Fresh, perfumed nose. Plenty of fruit and depth, and

above all class. Now smooth. Medium body. Balanced and long. Lovely. *À point.* (November 2002)
NOW TO 2008   18.5

Clos de Vougeot, 1992
Domaine Anne Gros

Good colour. Soft, but mellower and fresher and generally more agreeable than the 1994. Medium body. Round. Quite stylish. Quite positive. Very good. (June 2003)
DRINK SOON   16.0

Clos de Vougeot, 1992
Domaine Alain Hudelot-Noëllat

Good colour. Rich, fresh and fullish for a 1992. Plenty of very stylish fruit. Round and plump and very well balanced. This is a lovely example. Long and still very vigorous. (November 2002)
DRINK SOON   17.5

Clos de Vougeot, 1992
Domaine Louis Jadot

Good fullish, youthful colour. Quite firm and very vigorous for a 1992. Lovely fresh, ample fruit. Very good class and grip. Fullish body. Still a little tannin. This is surprisingly lovely. Excellent fruit and balance. Long. Very lovely. Remarkable quality for a 1992. (October 2005)
NOW TO 2015   19.5

Clos de Vougeot, 1992
Domaine Leroy

Medium colour. Fully evolved. A little diffuse, a little one-dimensional on the nose. Medium body. Slightly spicy. Not very stylish. But ripe and not a bit short. I fear it will exhibit more *sous-bois* flavours as it ages. Very good for the vintage. (April 2000)
DRINK SOON   16.0

Clos de Vougeot, 1992
Domaine Dr. Georges Mugneret

Good colour. Lovely fresh, classy nose. Medium-full body. Ample and generous on the palate. This is stylish, even complex. A subtle, classy example. Lovely finish. Fine plus. (June 2002)
NOW TO 2010   18.0

Clos de Vougeot, 1992
Domaine Jean Tardy et Fils

Full colour. No undue age. Mellow, oaky, rich, fat, aromatic and really quite full and concentrated on the nose. Surprisingly succulent for a 1992. Ripe and oaky on the palate. Ample and generous. Splendid for a 1992. Long. Fine. (December 2001)
NOW TO 2009   17.5

Clos de Vougeot, "Musigni", 1992
Domaine Gros Frère et Soeur

Good colour. Nicely plump nose, if without the dimension of Engel's or Grivot's. Similar palate. Ripe and sweet. Decent grip. Very good but not fine. But the vines were young then. (June 2002)
NOW TO 2009   16.0

Corton, Renardes, 1992
Domaine Leroy

Medium-full colour. Still quite youthful. Soft, aromatic nose. Not a lot of strength. But ripe and attractive. Medium body. Gentle. *À point.* Not the greatest of finesse, but fresh and harmonious, if a bit one-dimensional. Very good plus for the vintage. Very pleasant to drink now. (April 2000)
DRINK SOON   16.5

Echézeaux, 1992
Domaine Gérard Mugneret

Medium weight. Fresh and elegant. Good depth; even concentrated. Slightly diffuse on the nose, but good concentration on the palate. Clean and with good fruit and acidity. Fine for the vintage. (October 2003)
DRINK SOON   17.5

Gevrey-Chambertin, Vieilles Vignes, 1992
Domaine Alain Burguet

Good colour. Fresh nose. Vigorous and plump. Medium body. Quite meaty. Good fruit, if not the greatest of depth. But, as usual, of *premier cru* quality. Very good. (June 2002)
NOW TO 2008   16.0

Gevrey-Chambertin, Vieilles Vignes, 1992
Domaine Bernard Dugat-Py

Very good colour. A full, meaty wine for a 1992. Indeed, perhaps a bit too extracted. This detracts from the elegance. Full bodied and rich, if a touch hard. Good grip. Plenty of vigour. A very good example. (June 2002)

NOW TO 2012   16.0

Gevrey-Chambertin, Les Cazetiers, 1992
Domaine Bruno Clair

Good colour. Fragrant nose. Classy, complex and very lovely. It is a bit drier and more evolved than the Clos Saint-Jacques, and it doesn't have the grip. But it is sweet and elegant at the end. Fine. (June 2002)

NOW TO 2009   17.5

Gevrey-Chambertin, Clos Saint-Jacques, 1992
Domaine Bruno Clair

Good fresh colour. Lovely nose. Lots of depth here. Fullish bodied, rich and vigorous on the palate. Lots of class and very good grip. Lovely long finish. This is splendid. (June 2002)

NOW TO 2012+   18.0

Gevrey-Chambertin, Clos Saint-Jacques, 1992
Domaine Armand Rousseau

Medium-full colour. Mature but not unduly so. Aromatic nose. A touch of oak-cedar. Good grip. No great weight, but surprisingly fresh, complex and classy. Soft, ripe, medium-bodied on the palate. Balanced and vigorous but round and mellow. No hard edges. No lack of intensity. This is very classy. Very positive at the end. Plenty of future. Very fine. (May 2001)

NOW TO 2010   18.5

Gevrey-Chambertin, Les Petits Cazetiers, 1992
Domaine Dominique Gallois

Magnum. Good colour. A slight touch of the stems on the nose. This is a vigorous wine on the palate. Good grip and plenty of fruit. But it lacks a little finesse. Positive at the end and with plenty of life, but only very good at best. (June 2002)

NOW TO 2010   16.0

Griotte-Chambertin, 1992
Maison Roland Remoissenet et Fils

Fine colour. No sign of age. Vigorous and fragrant. Fullish body. Lovely fruit. Good concentration.

Ripe and with plenty of depth and intensity. Above all, the class of a *grand cru*. This has plenty of future. (March 2000)

DRINK SOON   18.0

Latricières-Chambertin, 1992
Domaine Joseph Faiveley

Fine colour. Full, rich and vigorous on the nose. This has a lot of depth, substance and concentration for a 1992. On the palate, the attack is good, but then it fades away a little. There is a slight lack of succulence in the middle. Very good plus, at best. (June 2002)

DRINK SOON   16.5

Latricières-Chambertin, 1992
Domaine Leroy

Medium to medium-full colour. Fully ready. Good fresh nose for a 1992. No lack of substance either. Nice and ripe. Medium-full body. Fresh and balanced. This is fine for a 1992. Positive and attractive. Finishes well. (April 2000)

DRINK SOON   17.5

Marsannay, Les Longeroies, 1992
Domaine Bruno Clair

Decent colour. But a little dried up on the nose. Dried herb flavours. It has lost most of its fruit now. Past its best. (June 2002)

PAST ITS BEST   12.0

Mazis-Chambertin, 1992
Domaine Joseph Faiveley

Medium-full, fresh colour. Lovely nose. Full and very clean Pinot. Good acidity. Very classy. Similar on the palate. A wine which is *à point*. The fruit is ripe and velvety. It is a fine bottle. Long and lovely. (June 2000)

NOW TO 2010+   17.5

Mazis-Chambertin, 1992
Domaine Joseph Roty

Good youthful colour. Fragrant, concentrated nose. Fullish body. Very good concentration and intensity. Very good grip. This is quite oaky, and a little rigid on the palate. But very good grip and style. Lovely ripe, concentrated fruit. Fine plus. (March 2000)

NOW TO 2010   18.0

Monthelie, 1992
Domaine Paul Garaudet

Magnum. Good fresh colour. Meaty and plump and quite classy on the nose. Fullish body. Vigorous. Not a lot of depth, but quite good. (June 2002)

DRINK SOON   14.0

Morey-Saint-Denis, Vieilles Vignes, 1992
Domaine Hubert Lignier

Good colour. Fresh, classy, quite concentrated nose. Still quite youthful on the palate. Medium-full body. Complex and balanced. Not the greatest depth or interest on the follow-through, but very good indeed. (June 2002)

NOW TO 2009   17.0

Morey-Saint-Denis, Aux Charmes, 1992
Domaine Lignier-Michelot

Medium colour. Soft and succulent on the nose, if with no great vigour. More to it on the palate. Nicely fresh. Medium size. A plump wine. Positive finish. Very good plus. (June 2002)

DRINK SOON   16.5

Musigny, 1992
Domaine Leroy

Fullish colour for the vintage. Mature-looking. The nose shows fudge and fondant and roasted nuts. Gentle but intense and classy, especially for the vintage. Good grip. More luscious, more consistent and more interesting than the 1994. Medium body. Fine. (April 2000)

DRINK SOON   17.5

Musigny, 1992
Domaine Jacques-Frédéric Mugnier

Medium to medium-full colour. Very lovely fragrant nose. Flowery and silky. No lack of intensity. Medium body. Good freshness. Very complex. Round. Classy. No great depth and richness, but then, it is 1992. But a lovely example of the vintage. (June 2001)

NOW TO 2012   18.5

Musigny, Vieilles Vignes, 1992
Domaine Comte Georges de Vogüé

Good colour. Rather more vigour on the nose than Mugnier's. Rich, fullish bodied, classy and balanced. This is very lovely for 1992. Long, ripe, fragrant and classy. Excellent. (June 2002)

NOW TO 2012   19.5

Nuits-Saint-Georges, 1992
Domaine Jean Tardy et Fils

Medium colour. Soft nose. Oaky but somewhat diffuse. Medium body. Mellow. Decent fruit but nothing special. Good acidity keeping it fresh. But no great depth or excitement. Good plus. (November 2002)

DRINK SOON   15.5

Nuits-Saint-Georges, 1992
Domaine Charles Thomas

Good colour. Good meaty, fresh nose. Medium-full body. Not a lot of grip. Slightly astringent at the end. A little dry. But a good basic. (June 2002)

DRINK SOON   14.0

Nuits-Saint-Georges, Les Boudots, 1992
Domaine Jean Grivot

Medium to medium-full colour. Fully mature. Round, ripe, developed nose. Decent backbone and freshness. Medium body. Soft and round. Quite sweet. Decent freshness, if no great class. Slightly hot and pruney, especially on the finish. Good plus, but it lacks a little elegance. (November 2001)

NOW TO 2010   15.5

Nuits-Saint-Georges, Les Boudots, 1992
Domaine Jean Tardy et Fils

Good colour. Ripe and ample on the nose. Medium-full body. It lacks just a little freshness and zip. But quite succulent, even rich. Just a little one-dimensional at the end. But classy. Very good. (June 2002)

DRINK SOON   16.0

Nuits-Saint-Georges, Les Chaignots, 1992
Domaine Dr. Georges Mugneret

Good colour. Ripe and fragrant on the nose. Ample, rich and generous on the palate. Fullish weight. Well balanced and classy. Lovely finish. This is fine. (June 2002)

NOW TO 2012   17.5

Nuits-Saint-Georges, Les Chaignots, 1992
Domaine Gérard Mugneret

Magnum. An aromatic, well-matured wine on the nose. Quite different from Georges Mugneret's. Medium-full body. A suggestion of astringency. But decent fruit and length, and good finesse. It finishes well. Very good plus. (June 2002)

NOW TO 2009   16.5

Nuits-Saint-Georges, Clos de l'Arlot, 1992
Domaine de l'Arlot

Medium weight. Gently oaky. Now beginning to fade a little. Good acidity, but not a great deal of concentration. Ripe and fruity. Good plus. But drink soon. (August 2002)

DRINK SOON   15.5

Nuits-Saint-Georges, Clos des Porrets Saint-Georges, 1992
Domaine Henri Gouges (?)

Tasteviné. Anonymous, but I think from Gouges: Clos des Porrets. Good fullish, vigorous colour. Soft, clean, fragrant nose. Medium-full body. No sign of diffuseness. Very good acidity in fact. Ripe, fresh, ample and *à point*. Good length. This is very good indeed and shows how good the best 1992s can be. Long and positive. Plenty of life ahead of it. (July 2003)

NOW TO 2010   17.0

Nuits-Saint-Georges, Hauts Pruliers, 1992
Domaine Daniel Rion et Fils

Magnum. Fullish, well matured colour. A little vegetal on the nose. It lacks a little class and succulence. Better on the palate. Decent fruit. Quite ample. Decent freshness. Good plus. (June 2002)

NOW TO 2010   15.5

Nuits-Saint-Georges, Les Murgers, 1992
Domaine Alain Hudelot-Noëllat

Good fullish colour. Little sign of browning at the rim. Fragrant noses, with plenty of structure to support it. Rich, balanced and succulent. Nothing dilute here! On the palate, fullish body and still a little tannin. Good Nuits meatiness, together with good Vosne class. Good grip. Plenty of depth. This will still improve. Long and complex. Ripe and elegant. A very good indeed, if not fine, example. (March 2000)

NOW TO 2012   17.0

Nuits-Saint-Georges, Les Pruliers, 1992
Domaine Henri Gouges

Youthful colour. Still very youthful on nose and palate. Indeed, will be rounder and better in 2 years' time. Medium-full body. Ripe. Plenty of depth and style. Good acidity. Very good fruit. But still needs to mellow. Very good indeed. (December 2001)

NOW TO 2014   17.0

Nuits-Saint-Georges, Les Saint-Georges, 1992
Domaine Henri Gouges

Splendid colour. Full and vigorous. Lovely rich nose. Lots of depth and quality here. Full bodied, rich and meaty. Very good grip. Still bags of life. Lovely ample finish. This is fine plus. (June 2002)

NOW TO 2012+   18.0

Pommard, Les Chaponnières, 1992
Domaine Philippe Billard-Gonnet

Tasteviné, and it fully deserves it. Medium-full body. Very good acidity. Round, fruity, stylish and with plenty of depth and character. Smooth. Complex. Fresh. Very good indeed for the vintage. A lovely bottle. No sign of age. (June 2000)

DRINK SOON   17.0

Pommard, Les Chaponnières, Vieilles Vignes, 1992
Domaine Philippe Billard-Gonnet

Good colour. Fresh, ripe, round, succulent and very enjoyable. Plenty of depth and style. Really very good indeed for a 1992. Not a bit dilute, astringent or without personality. Good for another 10 years still. *À point*. Very good plus. (November 2002)

NOW TO 2012   16.5

Pommard, Clos de Verger, 1992
Domaine Philippe Billard-Gonnet

Tasteviné. Good fresh colour. A touch hard on the nose. Better on the palate. Ripe and balanced. Medium-full body. Attractive fruit. Positive finish. Very good. (June 2002)

NOW TO 2009   16.0

Pommard, Clos des Epeneaux, 1992
Domaine du Comte Armand

Magnum. Fine full, youthful colour. Slightly hard on the nose. Full bodied but rich and tannic on the palate. Good acidity. A meaty wine. Plenty of vigour. Plenty of grip. Very good indeed. (June 2002)

NOW TO 2012+   17.0

Pommard, Clos des Epeneaux, 1992
Maison Camille Giroud

Magnum. Good full, vigorous colour. Youthful, concentrated, sturdy nose. Good fruit on the palate. Decently fresh, but with not a lot of grip. Not astringent or short, though: just not as positive as the best of the Pommards. Very good, nonetheless. (June 2002)

NOW TO 2009   16.0

Pommard, Jarollières, 1992
Domaine Jean-Marc Boillot

Good fullish, fresh colour. Ample and plump on the nose. Fullish body. Meaty and earthy in flavour. But balanced, ripe and vigorous. Very good plus. (June 2002)

NOW TO 2012   16.5

Pommard, Les Pézerolles, 1992
Domaine Hubert de Montille

Good colour. Ripe, plump, rich and vigorous on the nose. Good depth on the palate. Medium-full body. Balanced and intense and very classy. This is very good indeed. (June 2002)

NOW TO 2012   17.0

Pommard, Les Rugiens, 1992
Domaine Philippe Billard-Gonnet

Good fullish, fresh colour. Ripe and rich and ample on the nose. Fullish body. Lots of depth.

Plenty of rich, classy fruit. Good grip. Long and impressive. This is fine. (June 2002)

NOW TO 2012   17.5

Pommard, Les Rugiens, 1992
Domaine Annick Parent

Fresher, fuller colour than expected. Ditto nose. Lovely stylish fruit. This is ready but still fresh and youthful. Pure and stylish. Volnay elegance. Soft but intense and classy. Very good. (August 2000)

DRINK SOON   16.0

Richebourg, 1992
Domaine Jean Grivot

Full colour. Still youthful. Very concentrated. Very high acidity. This is still youthful. Vigorous. Good grip. Very fresh. Very classy. A splendid example. (January 2001)

NOW TO 2010   17.5

Richebourg, 1992
Domaine Anne Gros

Medium-full colour. Quite a lot more developed than the 1994. More stylish on the nose, though. More depth and interest, and more youthful. Medium-full body. Balanced, even rich and even stylish. Very positive at the end. Delicious now. A lovely example of this vintage. Drink soon. (February 2004)

NOW TO 2010   19.0

Richebourg, 1992
Domaine Jean Gros

Fullish colour. Fresh, very concentrated and very classy on the nose. Ample, rich and ripe on the palate. Fragrant, sophisticated and generous. But it doesn't quite have the grip of the finest this year. Fine plus, at best. (June 2002)

NOW TO 2012   18.0

Richebourg, 1992
Domaine Alain Hudelot-Noëllat

Medium-full colour. Fresh, oaky nose. Very good weight and style for a 1992. Lovely balanced, crisp fruit. This has depth and high quality. The wine is not a bit weak or diffuse. Ripe, complex and classy. Very fine for the vintage. No hurry to drink. (November 2003)

NOW TO 2010   18.5

Richebourg, 1992
Domaine Leroy

Medium-full, mature colour. Sweet, fragrant nose. Medium weight. Intense and fruity, if with no great structure or grip or depth on the palate. Soft and generous and attractive. Fully ready. Good length. Very fine for the vintage. (April 2001)

DRINK SOON   18.5

Richebourg, 1992
Domaine Méo-Camuzet

Magnum. Fine colour. Now just about mature. Fine nose. Plenty of depth and vigour. Still fresh. Medium-full body. Classy fruit. Very good acidity. Not the weight and concentration of a great vintage, but the signature of a great *terroir* is here. Very fine indeed for a 1992. (March 2001)

NOW TO 2012   19.0

La Romanée, 1992
Domaine Bouchard Père et Fils

Medium-full, mature colour. This is a lovely 1992. Fresh and plump. Slightly open and slightly more personality than the 1994. Slightly less weight but better acidity. Less to it than the 1994, but it is more accessible at present. Medium body. Surprisingly good fresh finish. Very good indeed for the vintage. (March 2003)

NOW TO 2009   16.0

Romanée-Conti, 1992
Domaine de la Romanée-Conti

Medium colour. A little development. No evidence of the stems. Fragrant and elegant. Soft, plump, ripe and fruity. This is medium bodied. Quite high acidity. Not a lot of richness. Just a suspicion of astringency. But there is vigour here. Classy, but with a slight lack of succulence. Best on the nose. But warmer on the palate with food. (July 2002)

DRINK SOON   18.0

Romanée-Saint-Vivant, 1992
Domaine Robert Arnoux

Good colour. Aromatic, cedar wood nose. Soft and rich with an intriguing sweet-sour touch. Definitely very classy. Ripe fruit. Plenty of depth and length. Plenty of vigour. Fine plus. Perhaps very fine in a 1992 context. (September 2005)

NOW TO 2010   18.0

Romanée-Saint-Vivant, 1992
Domaine Alain Hudelot-Noëllat

Good fresh, medium to medium-full colour. A little muddy and a little diffuse on the nose, but with no sign of age and with good acidity. But not a great amount of richness. More succulence on the palate. Medium-full body. Good fruit. Good vigour and grip. Fruity; really good depth and a positive finish for a 1992. Not great, but very good indeed. (July 2003)

NOW TO 2010   17.0

Romanée-Saint-Vivant, 1992
Domaine Leroy

Medium-full, mature colour. Ample, fat nose. No lack of substance. A slight touch of reduction. Ripe, even sweet on the palate. Fullish body. Good tannins. The attack is fresh. This is very fine for the vintage. (April 2000)

DRINK SOON   18.5

Romanée-Saint-Vivant, 1992
Domaine de la Romanée-Conti

Full colour. Some development. Soft, round and slightly spicy on the nose. Good depth. Quite evolved. On the palate, excellent acidity. Ripe and elegant fruit. No lack of definition or follow-through. Very fine plus. (March 2002)

NOW TO 2013   19.0

Santenay, Clos de Tavannes, 1992
Domaine Jean-Noël Gagnard

Medium colour but not too brown. Soft and fruity on both nose and palate. Good class. Quite fresh. *À point.* Succulent. Good. (June 2002)

DRINK SOON   15.0

Savigny-lès-Beaune, La Dominode, 1992
Domaine Jean-Marc Pavelot

Good vigorous colour. Lovely nose. Plump and quite concentrated. Good energy. Good class. Medium weight. A little sign of age now. But juicy and stylish. Good. (June 2002)

DRINK SOON   15.0

Savigny-lès-Beaune, Aux Guettes, 1992
Domaine Simon Bize et Fils

Lightish, well-matured colour. Gamey nose. A bit light and a little astringent on the palate, but pleasant and quite elegant. The finish is positive. Good. But drink soon. (June 2002)

DRINK SOON   15.0

Savigny-lès-Beaune, Les Lavières, 1992
Domaine Chandon de Briailles

Lightish, well-matured colour. Light nose. Not a lot to it. A little short. Reasonable style, though. But drink soon. Quite good. (June 2002)

DRINK SOON   14.0

La Tâche, 1992
Domaine de la Romanée-Conti

Fullish colour. The nose is ample, fragrant, classy and shows a touch of the stems. On the palate the wine is *à point*, fullish bodied, fresh, plump and succulent. Very fine class. Very long and positive at the end. Very fine indeed. (June 2002)

NOW TO 2012+   19.5

Volnay, Premier Cru, 1992
Domaine Jean-François Coche-Dury

Medium to medium-full colour. No undue maturity. Very lovely ripe, fresh nose. Aromatic. Good acidity. Slightly lean. Slightly boiled-sweety. Certainly has a sweet finish. Yet very lovely fruit. Long, balanced and complex. Very good plus. (March 2003)

NOW TO 2010   16.5

Volnay, Champans, 1992
Domaine Monthelie-Douhairet

Magnum. Good colour. Surprisingly good acidity, even to the point of making the wine a bit austere, particularly as it is big, chunky and tannic for a 1992. Vigorous. Fullish body. Good plus. (June 2003)

NOW TO 2009   15.5

Volnay, Clos du Chateau des Ducs, 1992
Domaine Michel Lafarge

Very good vigorous colour. Ditto on nose and palate. Lots of wine here with a splendid depth and grip for 1992. Ample, classy and succulent. Long, vigorous and positive. Fine plus. (December 2003)

NOW TO 2012   18.0

Volnay, Clos des Chênes, 1992
Domaine Michel Lafarge

Fullish, vigorous colour. Lovely nose. Classy fruit. Vigorous and complex. Impressive on the palate. Concentrated and profound. Lots of life left here. Long and lovely at the end. Fine plus. (June 2002)

NOW TO 2012+   18.0

Volnay, Mitans, 1992
Domaine Hubert de Montille

Good colour. Fresh nose. Real Volnay delicacy, but intensity. Slightly astringent on the palate. But decent fruit, if not a great deal of grip. Very elegant, though, and with a lovely finish. Very good plus. (June 2002)

DRINK SOON   16.5

Volnay, Santenots, 1992
Maison Camille Giroud

Magnum. Medium to medium-full colour. Still youthful. Good nose. Fresh, classy and quite sturdy. Medium-full body. Good depth. Fresh and meaty. This is very good plus. (June 2002)

NOW TO 2009   16.5

Volnay, Santenots, 1992
Domaine François Mikulski

Magnum. Decent colour. No undue age. But a little pinched on the nose. Better on the palate. Quite sweet, ripe fruit. Medium-full body. A little soft-centred at the end, but not weak and still elegant. Very good. (June 2002)

DRINK SOON   16.0

Volnay, Les Santenots du Milieu, 1992
Domaine des Comtes Lafon
Magnum. Fullish, vigorous colour. Fullish, ample nose. Meaty and almost gamey. Rich and full bodied on the palate. Very good grip. Lots of energy at the end. This is fine plus and will keep a long time. (June 2002)
NOW TO 2012+ 18.0

Volnay, Taillepieds, 1992
Domaine Hubert de Montille
Good colour. Lovely nose. This is richer, fuller, firmer and more vigorous than his Mitans. Lovely on the palate. Fullish body. Real depth and grip, even concentration. Long finish. This is fine plus. (June 2002)
NOW TO 2010 18.0

Vosne-Romanée, 1992
Domaine Jacques Cacheux et Fils
Medium body. Fully mature. Evolved nose. A touch of the stems. Not that much class. Quite fresh on the palate. Medium body. Decent depth and vigour. But only medium in style. Positive finish. Quite good plus. (March 2003)
DRINK SOON 14.5

Vosne-Romanée, 1992
Domaine A.F. Gros
Good colour. Fresh and plump and stylish on the nose. Very good for a village example. Open, generous and fragrant on the palate. Medium-full body. Fresh and balanced. This is very good. (June 2002)
NOW TO 2009 16.0

Vosne-Romanée, Les Beaux Monts, 1992
Domaine Leroy
Fullish colour. Firm, concentrated, backward and tannic for a 1992. Fat, rich and oaky. Fullish body. Good grip. Rather more depth and grip and intensity than you would expect for the vintage—though not for Leroy. A fine example for the vintage. (March 2000)
NOW TO 2009 17.5

Vosne-Romanée, Aux Brûlées, 1992
Domaine René Engel
Good colour. Ripe, round and classy on the nose. A little loose-knit on the palate compared with Sylvain Cathiard's Malconsorts, but plump and fresh and stylish. Medium-full weight. Positive finish. Very good indeed. (June 2002)
NOW TO 2009 17.0

Vosne-Romanée, Clos des Réas, 1992
Domaine Jean Gros
Magnum. Very good colour. Lovely round, ripe, laid-back, classy nose. Ample, fruity and succulent on the palate. Rich and fragrant. Very fresh. This is a lovely example. Fine plus. (June 2002)
NOW TO 2012 18.0

Vosne-Romanée, Cros Parentoux, 1992
Domaine Méo-Camuzet
Medium-full colour. Some maturity. Plump, ripe, succulent nose. Good oak base. Medium to medium-full body. Ample and delicious and easy to drink. Not serious, but a fine example of a 1992. (March 2001)
NOW TO 2009 17.5

Vosne-Romanée,
Aux Malconsorts, 1992
Domaine Sylvain Cathiard
Good colour. Nicely rich and ample on the nose. A fullish, meaty but classy wine. Good grip. Plenty of depth. Plenty of vigour. Long at the end. This is fine. (June 2002)
NOW TO 2012 17.5

Vosne-Romanée, Les Suchots, 1992
Domaine Robert Arnoux
Full, barely mature colour. The nose is ripe and classic but still a little closed-in. Very lovely profound fruit, though. Medium-full body. Ripe and rich with well softened tannins. Excellent fresh acidity. Lots and lots of depth and very fine quality. A wine of real distinction which will still get better. Very long. Very lovely. (May 2005)
NOW TO 2015 18.5

Vosne-Romanée, Les Suchots, 1992
Domaine Jean Grivot

Good fullish colour. No undue age. Good nose. No lack of depth. Slightly spicy. Still fresh and vigorous. Slightly sweet on the nose. Medium-full body. Rich and ripe. Good concentration. Not a great deal of style or definition, but that is the vintage. Also a slight lack of zip. But very good within the context of the vintage. (December 2001)
DRINK SOON   16.0

1991

Though not a very exciting vintage for white wine—despite some very pleasant surprises—1991 was a very good red Burgundy vintage. For various reasons, this was not universally acknowledged at the time. Firstly, and most importantly, it was born in the shadow of the great 1990 vintage, and this had followed the charming and successful 1989. Three vintages in a row are difficult to sell. Many merchants had bought such a lot of 1990—and why not?—that they were short of funds for the 1991s. But instead of simply saying (as I tend to in a restaurant when it comes to dessert) "I'm full," many proceeded to denigrate the 1991s. It is true that some of the wines exhibited rather tough tannins at first, but the fruit was present, and there was no lack of acidity. The wise gave them the benefit of the doubt. When the 1991s had settled down in bottle, three years later, it was very apparent that we had—if without the majesty of the 1990s, the sex appeal of the 1989s or the, if austere, elegance of the 1988s—a very good red wine vintage, superior to 1986 and 1987, and, as it would turn out, to 1992 and 1994. Fifteen years on, many of the top wines are still drinking beautifully, and there is ample evidence that those who originally rated it very good were absolutely right.

WEATHER CONDITIONS

It was the year of the three 22s. It froze on April 22; it hailed on June 22; and it hailed again on August 22. Thankfully, however, none of these three depredations affected the standard of the wine—merely the quantity of it. The frost, as it normally does, injured the vines in the plain more than those on the slopes: the generics and the village vines rather than the *premiers* and *grands crus*. Gevrey, Morey and Nuits-Saint-Georges suffered more damage than did Chambolle and Vosne-Romanée, and Chorey-Lès-Beaune, Pommard and Meursault were the most affected areas in the southern sector of the Côte d'Or.

Then followed a cold May, delaying and prolonging the flowering into the second half of June. The hail storm that occurred then was centred in Gevrey-Chambertin, in a swathe that ran the length of the *grands crus* from Charmes to Mazis. But overall, the flowering was irregular, and as a result, *coulure* and *millérandage* were widespread throughout the Côte. The crop would be reduced: a good thing. But maturity would be uneven, and the harvest would be late. The prospects were not auspicious.

But the weather then changed. On the first of July, the summer arrived. For the next ten or more weeks, right up to the harvest, apart from the odd downpour, it was dry and hot. The fruit began to catch up. There was even a fear of prolonged drought blocking the evolution of the ripening process. The Burgundians had shivered in May. In August they had to worry about sunstroke!

→ Rating for the Vintage ←	
Red	16.0
White	13.5

→ Size of the Crop ← (In hectolitres, excluding generic wine)		
	RED	WHITE
Grands Crus	10,855	3,476
Village and Premiers Crus	166,380	45,104
TOTAL	177,235	48,580

The annual Burgundian nightmare is hail after the *véraison*. Inevitably, there are storms in August. Few years go by without a (thankfully) isolated blitz somewhere in the Côte d'Or. The grapes are then bruised, and it is rare that the resulting wine does not show a *goût de grêle*, a sort of hard dirtiness, somewhat like a metallic corky taste.

Chambolle-Musigny was the village chosen to bear the brunt in 1991. (Parts of Savigny and Ladoix, as well as the southern Côte de Nuits Villages, were also affected.) All the way from Le Musigny—but not in neighbouring Grands-Echézeaux or Clos-de-Vougeot, which shows how localised hail damage can be—right up to Clos-de-la-Roche, the vineyards were battered, with the line following that of the *grands* and *premiers crus*.

Remembering 1983, the most punctilious growers such as Jacques Seysses and Christophe Roumier got out their tweezers and carefully removed every single bruised berry which remained on their estate; in the case of Domaine Dujac, seventeen people were employed for three weeks simply to do this. Others resolved merely to *trier* carefully at the time of the harvest and to adjust the maceration times accordingly.

As it happened, the weather following the hail storm was excellent: dry, bright and hot. The most badly affected berries shrivelled up and dropped off. The rest seem to have recovered. There is no hail taint in any 1991s. There were, however, fears that progress towards maturity would be *bloqué*. Certainly, the 1991 Chambolles exhibit unusually high and masculine levels of tannin. But the concentration of fruit is equal to it. Indeed, this is the most successful sector of Burgundy in this vintage: it has produced some excellent wines.

The *ban des vendanges* was declared on Wednesday, September 24. Somewhat unusually—but this was explained by generally lower yields and, therefore, greater concentration—the Côte de Nuits started at the same time as the Côte de Beaune. Some rain fell in the Côte de Nuits on Friday and Saturday, and

rather more throughout the region on Sunday, but it was then fine for at least a week, after which there was a general deterioration in the weather as the late summer disintegrated into autumn. Most growers in the Côte d'Or managed to bring their crop in without the fruit being seriously affected by the rain—indeed Jean Mongeard of Vosne-Romanée says that the first spell unblocked the fruit and increased the eventual sugar levels—but those vines which had not been cleared by October 5 were at risk. Moreover, the rain on the first Sunday affected the white grapes, especially where yields were on the high side, more than the reds. The resultant humidity—fortunately, the weather was cool during the week of September 28 to October 5—caused the Chardonnay grapes to turn quickly into a state of overripeness, diminishing the acidities without adding to the concentration. This fruit needed to be collected fast.

WHERE ARE THE BEST WINES?
AND THE STATE OF MATURITY TODAY

- The vintage is, even more so than usual in Burgundy, better at the top of the hierarchy than at the village and generic levels.

- The reds of the Côte de Nuits are better and now more vigorous than those of the Côte de Beaune.

- The reds are better than the whites, and these white wines are now tired.

- The mainstream villages are better than the villages up in the valleys and in the Hautes-Côtes.

- In the Côte de Nuits, the best wines will be found in Chambolle-Musigny. There are some fine Gevreys, Vosnes and Nuits, (Morey-Saint-Denis and the Clos-de-Vougeot are the most variable), but you must chose your village wines with caution.

- The same can be said for Savigny-lès-Beaune, Beaune, Pommard and Volnay, whose wines of this vintage are better than those of the communes further south.

WHITES

Bâtard-Montrachet, 1991
Domaine Jacques Gagnard-Delagrange

Medium colour. This is ripe and fresh and classy, though being a 1991, it doesn't have a great deal of concentration. Medium weight. No lack of personality. Fine plus for the vintage. Held up well during the meal, but was a little old when I tasted the ullaged bottle the next morning. (May 2001)

DRINK SOON   18.0

Bâtard-Montrachet, 1991
Domaine Pierre Morey

A fat, ripe wine. No lack of fruit. Stylish. Plenty of depth. Approaching its end, but fine. (June 2001)

DRINK SOON   17.5

Beaune, Sur les Grèves, 1991
Domaine Jacques Germain

Quite soft and spicy, even a touch oxidised, on the nose. Better on the palate. Surprisingly honeyed. Still very enjoyable. Good plus. (June 2001)

DRINK UP   15.5

Bienvenues-Bâtard-Montrachet, 1991
Domaine Ramonet

Ripe, gently oaky and classy. Lots of depth for a 1991. Plenty of life and depth for a wine this age. Fine for what it is. (October 2002)

DRINK SOON   17.5

Chassagne-Montrachet, Les Caillerets, 1991
Domaine Jean-Noël Gagnard

Ripe and stylish, but now a little old. Good richness and good depth, nevertheless. Was 17/20; now 14.0. (June 2001)

DRINK SOON   14.0

Chassagne-Montrachet, Les Grandes Ruchottes, 1991
Domaine Paul Pillot

Quite a golden colour. Clean nose. Not too aged. A little dull but not tired. Medium body.

Perfectly pleasant. Surprisingly fresh and enjoyable. (June 2005)

DRINK UP   16.0

Chassagne-Montrachet, Les Ruchottes, 1991
Domaine Ramonet

Some colour now. Firm, rich, fresh, classy nose. Unexpected depth for a 1991. Fullish body. Good grip. Lovely fruit. Not a bit lean. Good positive follow-through. Very fine for the vintage. Even quite rich at the end. One of the best white 1991s I've had. (March 2003)

DRINK SOON   18.5

Corton-Charlemagne, 1991
Domaine Bonneau du Martray

This is superior. Gentle but ripe, rich, balanced and intense. Very classy. Cool and quietly successful. Holding up very well. (June 2001)

DRINK SOON   19.0

Corton-Charlemagne, 1991
Domaine Bouchard Père et Fils

Well matured colour. Quite fresh on the nose, if without much depth or concentration. Classy, if a bit diffuse on the palate. Ripe enough. It lacks a bit of zip, but good. (June 2003)

DRINK SOON   15.0

Corton-Charlemagne, 1991
Maison Champy

Unexpectedly good. Classy, ripe, balanced, even succulent. Fine. Still plenty of life. (January 2001)

DRINK SOON   17.5

Corton-Charlemagne, 1991
Domaine des Héritiers Louis Jadot

Rather faded now. Stylish and ripe underneath, but it has seen better days. Yet after a little hole in the middle palate, it comes back. Very good plus. (June 2001)

DRINK SOON   16.5

Corton-Charlemagne, 1991
Maison Bernard Morey

Quite a developed colour. And similar on the nose and palate as well. Rich. Fullish body.

Reasonably fresh. But not a wine of any great distinction. Quite good at best. (May 2005)

DRINK UP 14.0

Corton-Charlemagne, 1991
Domaine Poulleau Père et Fils

A domaine unknown to me, based in Volnay. Indeed, I do not know how this bottle came to be in my stock at Château Coates. The wine, in fact, is surprisingly good. Fresh and pure. Gently oaky in the background, with no lack of fruit and elegance. Still very fresh and vigorous after 15 years. Fine. (September 2006)

DRINK SOON 17.5

Corton-Charlemagne, 1991
Domaine Rapet Père et Fils

A bit neutral on the nose, though still fresh. Full and rich on the palate. No lack of depth or, indeed fruit. This has both class and dimension. Good grip. As it developed, round and very satisfactory. Good long, positive finish. Very good plus. (July 2002)

DRINK SOON 16.5

Corton-Charlemagne, 1991
Domaine Thomas Frères

This has lots of depth and personality and class for a 1991. Fullish, ripe, balanced and still very fresh. An unexpected amount of fruit. This is, for a 1991, fine at the very least. (July 2002)

DRINK SOON 17.5

Meursault, Les Casse-Têtes, 1991
Domaine Patrick Javillier

Not quite as alive as his Meursault Narvaux 1991. More gentle. Less vigour. No lack of finesse, though. Very good. (June 2001)

DRINK SOON 16.0

Meursault, Charmes, 1991
Domaine des Comtes Lafon

Quite evolved, but rich, balanced and very good indeed and vigorous for the vintage. Quite fat. Good gently oaky base. Holding up well. Very good. (July 2006)

DRINK SOON 16.0

Meursault, Genevrières, 1991
Domaine des Comtes Lafon

Quite a developed colour. The nose is a little neutral but clean and not faded and only just a little vegetal. On the palate the wine is medium-bodied. Still pleasant and fruity and agreeable to drink, if rather one-dimensional. A good effort for the vintage. (September 2005)

DRINK UP 15.0

Meursault, Les Gouttes d'Or, 1991
Maison Joseph de Bucy

Quite evolved in colour and on nose. Ripe and sweet. Not a lot of concentration and acidity, but fresh for the vintage. At least some grip. Drink soon. Very good for the vintage. Much better with food; held up well. (October 2000)

DRINK SOON 16.0

Meursault, Les Narvaux, 1991
Domaine Patrick Javillier

Magnum. Fresh, ripe, plenty of depth and lots of class. Very good balance. Really lovely, stylish, balanced, peachy finish. (June 2001)

DRINK SOON 16.5

Meursault, Perrières, 1991
Domaine des Comtes Lafon

A lovely wine for a 1991. Surprisingly fresh. Good weight and richness. Fruity and balanced. Good depth and class. Fine. (January 2004)

DRINK SOON 17.5

Meursault, Les Perrières, 1991
Domaine Guy Roulot

Magnum. Very laid-back, refined and subtle. This is very classy. Lovely ripe fruit. It now needs drinking quite soon. (June 2001)

DRINK SOON 18.0

Meursault, Les Tessons,
Clos de Mon Plaisir, 1991
Domaine Guy Roulot

Magnum. Fully à point. No undue age. Ripe and succulent. Lots of enjoyment here. Good plus. (June 2001)

DRINK SOON 15.5

Le Montrachet, 1991
Domaine Marc Colin

Clean and fresh. No sign of age. But merely pleasantly fruity. No great depth or interest. The oak is hardly discernable. Pleasant, but not a bit what one would expect for a Montrachet. (April 2005)

DRINK SOON   15.5

Morey-Saint-Denis, Monts Luisants, 1991
Domaine Ponsot

White. Hail in June, so 14 hectolitres per hectare. This is very fresh, very clean and very interesting. Above all, very individual. Though no new oak at all, it seems to have a fat, succulent, almost oaky base. Lovely. Will still keep very well. (September 2002)

NOW TO 2009   17.5

Musigny Blanc, 1991
Domaine Comte Georges de Vogüé

Hot. Alcoholic. Fat and rich. Spicy. Yet good, with plenty of depth. Good quality, if not really classic. Vigorous still. Very good. (June 2000)

DRINK SOON   16.0

Puligny-Montrachet, Les Combettes, 1991
Domaine Jean-Marc Boillot

Showing some age. But very lovely fruit. Laid-back and classy. Good energy, nevertheless. This will still hold up a bit. Fine. (June 2001)

DRINK SOON   17.5

Saint-Aubin, En Remilly, 1991
Domaine Hubert Lamy et Fils

Magnum. A touch faded, but with no lack of fruit, if not as stylish as Lamy's wines are today. Quite good. (July 2001)

DRINK SOON   14.0

REDS

Beaune, Les Bressandes, 1991
Maison Camille Giroud

Full colour. Little sign of maturity. Fullish, slightly tannic nose and attack. A sturdy wine.

Balanced. Quite some tannin, which will always remain. But sweet, ripe and succulent underneath. Very good. (June 2001)

NOW TO 2011+   16.0

Beaune, Clos des Couchereaux, 1991
Domaine Louis Jadot

Half. Good colour. Somewhat hard on the nose and palate, but rich and stylish nevertheless. Medium-full body. This will still improve as it rounds off. Good grip. Really quite concentrated. Very good plus. (December 2000)

DRINK SOON   16.5

Beaune, Clos des Ursules, 1991
Domaine des Héritiers Louis Jadot

Good colour. Just a touch dry and mean on the nose. On the palate, thinning out a touch. Decent style though. Good vigour at the end. Good. (June 2001)

DRINK SOON   15.0

Beaune, Grèves, 1991
Domaine Michel Lafarge

Good colour. Plenty of depth and energy here. Rich and luscious. Ripe and fat. Good structure. Lovely fruit. Long and with good depth. Plenty of future. Very good plus. (June 2001)

NOW TO 2010   16.5

Beaune, Grèves, Vigne de l'Enfant Jésus, 1991
Domaine Bouchard Père et Fils

Very good colour. Just a little maturity. Classy nose. Lots of depth. Full body. Very good tannins. Very good grip. This has both depth and length. Nicely austere. Cool and complex. Lots of finesse. Very good indeed. Will keep very well. (December 2002)

NOW TO 2011+   17.0

Beaune, Les Vignes Franches, 1991
Domaine Jacques Germain

Good colour. Attractive juicy nose. Quite fragrant. Lightening and shortening up, though. A touch astringent at the end. Still juicy, though. Quite good plus. (June 2001)

DRINK SOON   14.5

Blagny, La Pièce sous le Bois, 1991
Domaine Robert Ampeau

Ripe, round, mature and surprisingly rich. Good grip. Elegant. Medium to medium-full body. Lovely fruit. Very good indeed. No hurry to drink. (July 2006)

NOW TO 2010   17.0

Bonnes Mares, 1991
Domaine Georges Roumier et Fils

Full, vigorous colour. Not as fat or as rich on the nose as their 1990. But still impressive. What it lacks is a little grip, a little intensity and a little depth at the end, so fine but not great. (October 2000)

NOW TO 2015   17.5

Bonnes Mares, 1991
Domaine Charles Thomas

Full colour. Rich, full, backward nose. Quite a powerful wine here. Still some tannin. A meaty example. But very sophisticated. Very good grip. Not quite the flair of Vogüé's, but fine plus. Still needs time, though. (June 2001)

NOW TO 2020   18.0

Bonnes Mares, 1991
Domaine Comte Georges de Vogüé

Fullish colour. Splendid nose. Rich, full, concentrated and very classy. Still youthful. Excellent vigour and depth. Lovely grip. Fine fruit. This has a lot going for it. Very fine indeed. Will still improve. (June 2001)

NOW TO 2020   18.5

Chambertin, 1991
Domaine Bouchard Père et Fils

Fine, full colour. Still immature. Fresh, very cassis flavoured. Full body. Still some tannin. This still need time. An austere example at first. But the follow-through is rich, concentrated and of high quality. Very fine at the end. Will still improve. (December 2001)

NOW TO 2020   18.5

Chambertin, 1991
Domaine Louis Jadot

Full colour. Barely mature. Rich, ripe, pure, vigorous and quite full and sturdy on the nose.

Fullish body. Very good grip. Very fine fruit here. This is a very lovely wine indeed. Profound, complex and multidimensional. Excellent. Even better than their 1991 Musigny. Lots of energy. Brilliant. (October 2005)

NOW TO 2015+   20.0

Chambertin, 1991
Domaine Leroy

Fullish colour. Now mature. Very lovely nose for a 1991. Ripe, fragrant nose. Balanced and composed. Good freshness. No hard edges. Medium-full body. Fresh. Neatly balanced. Lots of depth. Lots of class. Excellent for a 1991. (April 2000)

NOW TO 2009   19.0

Chambertin, 1991
Domaine Armand Rousseau

Full colour. Still youthful. Very profound nose. Lots of depth and concentration and richness. Really lovely. Fullish body. Now mellow. The tannins are quite resolved. Excellent freshness. Really high class, multidimensional fruit. Very, very long. Excellent. (March 2004)

NOW TO 2021+   20.0

Le Chamber tin, 1991
Domaine Jean Trapet Père et Fils

The first vintage after the split, made by Jean-Louis. Good vigorous, fullish colour. Stylish nose. No lack of depth. Fullish, fresh and classy. Medium-full body on the palate. Fully ready. Not perhaps the greatest concentration and depth, but a delicious wine. Fully *à point*. Plump and fruity. Nicely fresh finish. Fine. (November 2001)

NOW TO 2010   17.5

Chambertin, Clos de Bèze, 1991
Domaine Armand Rousseau

Medium-full colour. Just about mature. Rich, aromatic, ripe and succulent on the nose. Medium-full body. Very well balanced. Good substance and grip. Concentrated, intense, rich and classy on the follow-through. Very lovely. Ready, but will last well. (March 2005)

NOW TO 2018   19.0

Chambolle-Musigny, Les Amoureuses, 1991
Domaine Georges Roumier et Fils

Fine colour. Very lovely nose. Fullish body. Quite firm. Certainly very concentrated. Very lovely fruit. Great finesse and harmony. Long and very lovely. Will still improve. (June 2001)

NOW TO 2025   18.5

Chambolle-Musigny, La Combe d'Orveau, 1991
Domaine Jean Grivot

Half. Good vigorous colour. Fullish, firm and classy on nose and attack. Good vigour and substance but no hard tannins. Very good acidity. Ripe. Very good fruit. Very stylish. Very good. (June 2000)

NOW TO 2009   16.0

Chambolle-Musigny, Les Cras, 1991
Domaine Ghislaine Barthod

Good colour. Lovely nose. Full but fragrant. Very clean and definitive. Excellent depth. This is very lovely. Still youthful. Will get better and better. (June 2001)

NOW TO 2015   17.5

Chambolle-Musigny, Les Fuées, 1991
Domaine Jacques-Frédéric Mugnier

Medium-full colour. The nose is full mature, if not a touch attenuated. Better on the palate. But it lacks the grip and depth of Ghislaine Barthod's Cras. Merely good. (June 2001)

DRINK SOON   15.0

Chambolle-Musigny, Les Gruenchers, 1991
Domaine Dujac

Good fullish colour. Just about mature. Cool, classy, fragrant, mellow nose. Plenty of depth. Good harmony. No hard edges. Pure. Quite rich. Very good intensity and high quality. Medium-full body. Ripe, even rich on the palate. Classy and vigorous. Long and complex. Very good indeed. Nicely fresh. Will keep well. (December 2001)

NOW TO 2011   17.0

Chapelle-Chambertin, 1991
Domaine Jean Trapet Père et Fils

The first vintage since the split of the Trapet domaine. Fine, vigorous colour. Very classy black-fruity nose. A little unresolved tannin still, but rich, balanced, ripe and profound. On the palate, full body, and very good grip and depth. Just about *à point*. Cool, intense, long finish. Very impressive. This is fine plus. (June 2001)

NOW TO 2011+   18.0

Charmes-Chambertin, 1991
Domaine Claude Dugat

Full, rich, youthful colour. Rull, rich and concentrated on both nose and palate. Very lovely old-vine fruit. Very good grip. Quite structured, but the tannins are very ripe. Excellent quality. Reminds me of a 1993. (April 2001)

NOW TO 2025   18.5

Charmes-Chambertin, 1991
Domaine Bernard Dugat-Py

Fine colour. Lovely old-vine concentrated nose. Lots of depth. Very classy. This is really splendid. The fruit is really rich and distinguished. Very good grip. Fullish weight. Will still improve. (June 2001)

NOW TO 2025   18.5

Charmes-Chambertin, Très Vieilles Vignes, 1991
Domaine Joseph Roty

Medium-full colour. Still vigorous. Lovely nose. Lots of depth, class and interest. Fullish body. Lots of dimension. Vigorous, complex and now sensual. A lot of drive and energy. Yet soft tannins to go with very good grip. Excellent. (April 2006)

NOW TO 2017   19.0

Charmes-Chambertin, 1991
Domaine Christian Sérafin

Good colour. Fresh, plump and not too oaky on the nose. Fullish, vigorous and just about *à point* on the palate. Good ripe fruit. No aggressive tannins. Balanced and stylish. Very good plus. (July 2001)

NOW TO 2001   16.5

Clos des Lambrays, 1991
Domaine des Lambrays

Medium-full colour. Fruity and pretty, but soft-centred. No great vigour, but elegant if quite evolved. This has medium body. It lacks a little vigour. But stylish. Good plus. (June 1991)

DRINK SOON 15.5

Clos de la Roche, 1991
Domaine Dujac

Good colour. Fragrant, very Dujac nose. Intense and concentrated. Medium-full weight. Balanced and lovely, if without the richness of Hubert Lignier's or the sheer brilliance of Ponsot's. Fine, long and very elegant, nonetheless. (June 2001)

NOW TO 2018 17.5

Clos de la Roche, 1991
Domaine Leroy

Good fullish colour. Plenty of interest. Fresh, classy and balanced. An ample example. Medium-full body. *À point.* Balanced and attractive. Not great but very good. (April 2000)

NOW TO 2018 16.0

Clos de la Roche, 1991
Domaine Hubert Lignier

Good colour. Rich, fresh, oaky nose. Plenty of depth and vigour. Fullish body. Some tannin still. Good grip. A wine with class and some power. Long. Very fine. (June 2001)

NOW TO 2018 17.5

Clos de la Roche, 1991
Domaine Louis Rémy

Two bottles. Medium-full, quite fresh colour. Slightly rustic on the nose—the second bottle more so than the first. On the palate plump, quite soft and velvety. Fresh. But neither much dimension nor much class. Quite good at best. (November 2003)

NOW TO 2009 14.0

Clos de la Roche, Cuvée Vieilles Vignes, 1991
Domaine Ponsot

Fine mature colour. Delicious spicy, sensual nose. Quite full. Ripe, rich and silky. Lots of energy. Very long. Delicious. An excellent result. Will still keep. (March 2006)

NOW TO 2016 18.5

Clos de Vougeot, 1991
Maison Champy

Medium-full colour. Fully mature. Somewhat tired on the nose. A lack of class as well as a lack of zip. Medium body. High-ish acidity. But a lack of fruit. Slightly lean. Some astringency. Unexciting. (June 2001)

DRINK SOON 13.0

Clos de Vougeot, 1991
Chateau de la Tour

Good colour. Ripe nose with a touch of butterscotch. Only medium body. Rather thin on the palate. A little astringent, too. The fruit is reasonably stylish, though. Quite good. (June 2001)

DRINK SOON 14.0

Clos de Vougeot, 1991
Domaine Jacky Confuron-Cotétidot

Medium-full colour. Evolved nose. Sweet and spicy but stemmy and unsophisticated. Thin on the palate. Some astringency at the end. No. (June 2001)

DRINK UP 12.0

Clos de Vougeot, 1991
Domaine René Engel

Fullish colour, just about mature. Mellow nose. Rich and concentrated. The tannins are now absorbed. Fullish body. Sophisticated and plump and harmonious. A lot of depth. Lovely finish. Fine plus. (October 2000)

NOW TO 2011+ 18.0

Clos de Vougeot, 1991
Domaine Anne Gros

Very good colour. Admirable nose. Fully mature. Complex, spicy nose. Good structure and grip. Medium-full body. This has both class and depth, as well as plenty of vigour all the way through. Finishes well. Fine. (June 2003)

NOW TO 2013 17.5

Clos de Vougeot, 1991
Domaine Alfred Haegelen-Jayer

Magnum. Good colour. Rich, fragrant, classy nose. Good concentration. Fullish body. Now *à point*. Round and nicely spicy. Full of interest. Very good plus, at the very least. (September 2001)

NOW TO 2010   16.5

Clos de Vougeot, 1991
Domaine Alain Hudelot-Noëllat

Medium-full, mature colour. Ripe and succulent on the nose. Medium-full bodied, rich and juicy on the palate. Deliciously *à point*. Lots of fruit here. Fresh and balanced. Generous and attractive. It does not quite have the class for fine, but neither are there any of the aggressive tannins of the 1991 vintage. Very good indeed. (September 2001)

NOW TO 2010   17.0

Clos de Vougeot, 1991
Domaine Leroy

Good fullish, vigorous colour. Proper old Burgundy nose. The tertiary flavours are now apparent. Still vigorous though. Fullish body. Chocolaty flavours. Quite textured. Very good grip. This is very lovely. Plenty of dimension and a very long finish. Very fine. (March 2005)

NOW TO 2015   18.5

Clos de Vougeot, 1991
Domaine Dr. Georges Mugneret

Good colour. Lovely nose. Full, rich, ripe and vigorous. Fullish on the palate. Plenty of depth. So ripe it is almost sweet. Good grip. This is long, complex and stylish. But the Échezeaux is better this year. (June 2001)

NOW TO 2012   17.0

Clos de Vougeot, Le Grand Maupertuis, 1991
Domaine Anne Gros

Good colour. Very lovely concentrated nose. Poised and classy. Lots of complexity. Fullish body. Ripe tannins. Still vigorous and concentrated. Lots of dimension. A very lovely example. Really long and really elegant. Very fine. (June 2001)

NOW TO 2015   18.5

Clos de Vougeot, Le Grand Maupertuis, 1991
Domaine Jean Gros

Good colour. Full, quite firm and vigorous still on the nose. Considering the vines were only 5 years old at the time, this is surprisingly good. No enormous structure and depth, but balanced and classy. Very good. (June 2001)

DRINK SOON   16.0

Le Corton, 1991
Domaine Bouchard Père et Fils

The crop was 19 hectolitres per hectare. Very full colour. Still very young. Splendidly rich on the nose. Very, very concentrated. Quite splendid. Full body. The tannins are very ripe but very present and vigorous. Austere but balanced, classy and profound. Excellent. And bags of life. This will last me out! Very fine plus. Will still improve. (December 2001)

NOW TO 2020   19.0

Corton, Clos des Cortons Faiveley, 1991
Domaine Joseph Faiveley

Full, rich colour. Still barely mature. Cedary-rich, fat and fruity nose. Very classy and very harmonious. On the palate, really quite soft. Rich and round. Good acidity. Plenty of vigour. Lovely rich fruit. Fully ready. Lots of energy at the end. Very fine plus. (June 2004)

NOW TO 2015   19.0

Corton, Clos du Roi, 1991
Domaine Chandon de Briailles

Good colour. Very lovely, classy nose. This is undoubtedly of *grand cru* quality. Fullish body. Balanced, intense, complex and subtle. Long and intense. Fine plus. (June 2001)

NOW TO 2010   18.0

Corton, Renardes, 1991
Domaine Leroy

Medium-full colour. Just about matured. Refined nose. Lovely fruit and very good grip. Slightly less classy on the palate. Medium-full body. A little tannin still, and these tannins could have been more sophisticated. But ripe and positive. Still fresh. Very good for the vintage. (April 2000)

NOW TO 2010   16.0

Corton, Rognet, 1991
Domaine Méo-Camuzet

Medium-full colour. Still youthful. Fine nose. Fresh and positive. Very pure fruit. The oak is exactly right here. Medium-full body. Nicely cool. Balanced. Stylish. Long. Fine for the vintage. Just about ready. (March 2001)

NOW TO 2012+   17.5

Echézeaux, 1991
Domaine Camille Giroud

Medium-full, mature colour. Pure, ripe, round, succulent nose. Now soft and delicious. On the palate, medium-full body. Just a little unresolved tannin. Fresh. Long. Slightly austere in character. Fine. (June 2004)

NOW TO 2013+   17.5

Echézeaux, 1991
Domaine Jean Grivot

Magnum. Good colour. The nose is slightly lean and herbaceous. Equally on the palate, it is a little odd and confected. They make better wine now. This has certainly got balance and freshness. But the flavours are very curious. (June 2001)

NOW TO 2009   14.0

Echézeaux, 1991
Domaine A.F. Gros

Medium-full colour. Very attractive, plump, ripe fruit on the nose. No huge structure. In fact, rather less on the palate than I would have liked. It continues a bit feebly. Pretty, though, and quite harmonious. But it lacks a bit of grip and punch. Good plus. (June 2001)

DRINK SOON   15.5

Echézeaux, 1991
Domaine Mugneret-Gibourg

Good colour. Splendidly rich, gently oaky nose. Lots of depth. Fullish body. Good vigour. Good class. Impressive fruit. Some tannin. This is ripe, intense, classy and fine. Lovely finish. (June 2001)

NOW TO 2015   17.5

Echézeaux, 1991
Domaine de la Romanée-Conti

Good full, just-about-mature colour. Very good nose. Rich and ample. Vigorous and substantial and fresh. No lack of class and depth. Very classy. Quite gamey. Full bodied and fresh and complex. This is delicious. (October 2005)

NOW TO 2015   18.0

Gevrey-Chambertin, Vieilles Vignes, 1991
Domaine Alain Burguet

Magnum. Fullish colour. Now immature. Quite firm, ripe and rich on the nose. Medium-full body. Vigorous. Good fruit. Very clean and very good acidity. This is classy and has plenty of depth. Long. Very good indeed. (July 2003)

NOW TO 2011   17.0

Gevrey-Chambertin, Vieilles Vignes, 1991
Domaine Bernard Dugat-Py

Good colour. A little tight on the nose. Fresh fruit, if a touch rigid. Full body. Some slightly hard tannins. Good grip. It may relax as it rounds off. Good. (June 2001)

NOW TO 2015   15.0

Gevrey-Chambertin, Les Cazetiers, 1991
Domaine Bruno Clair

Good colour. Quite lean on the nose, but very stylish and complex. Riper on the palate. Good energy and class. Long. Very good indeed. (June 2001)

NOW TO 2015   17.0

Gevrey-Chambertin, Les Champeaux, 1991
Domaine Denis Mortet

Magnum. Good colour. Succulent and fat and ample. Decent class. Ripe and generous. Medium-full weight. Good grip. The finish is vigorous, even intense. This is very good indeed. (June 2001)

NOW TO 2020   17.0

Gevrey-Chambertin, Clos Saint-Jacques, 1991
Domaine Bruno Clair

Medium colour. Now more or less mature. Fresh and juicy. Medium weight. Fragrant nose. Medium to medium-full body. Round, ripe, balanced and attractive, if without the greatest depth and concentration. Very good indeed for the vintage. (October 2003)

NOW TO 2001   17.0

Gevrey-Chambertin, Clos Saint-Jacques, 1991
Domaine Armand Rousseau

Fullish, mature colour. Lovely soft, classy, aromatic, fullish nose. A round, ripe, fresh, balanced wine. Medium-full body. Very elegant. *À point* now. Very lovely fruit. Clean and pure at the end. No hard edges. Very elegant. Very complex. Very long. Very fine. (March 2004)

NOW TO 2018   18.5

Grands Echézeaux, 1991
Domaine Joseph Drouhin

Good colour. Lovely nose. Very poised. Very classy. Ripe, very classy structure. Very good grip. Long, complex and multidimensional. This is excellent. Really elegant. Very fine. (June 2001)

NOW TO 2015   18.5

Grands Echézeaux, 1991
Domaine René Engel

Magnum. Good colour. Lovely nose. Very finely poised. Pure and very stylish. This is a little more *à point* than his Brûlées. The tannins are rounder. Good grip. Lovely plump fruit. A very seductive example. Very fine. (June 2001)

NOW TO 2020   18.5

Grands Echézeaux, 1991
Domaine Robert Sirugue et ses Enfants

Good colour. Evolved nose but fresher on the palate. Very good ripe fruit. Not a lot of acidity. Round. Mellow. Stylish. Long. Very good plus. (February 2006)

NOW TO 2011   16.5

Griotte-Chambertin, 1991
Domaine Joseph Drouhin

Medium-full, mature colour. Lovely, just about mature Pinot on the nose. Ripe, abundant and with plenty of depth. Medium-full body. Balanced, classy, fresh and lovely. This is now *à point* but has plenty of vigour. Good concentration and dimension. Lovely long finish. Very fine for the vintage. (July 2003)

NOW TO 2016   18.5

Latricières-Chambertin, 1991
Domaine Joseph Faiveley

Full colour. Rich, full nose. Some oak. This is ripe and luscious, though still quite sturdy. It will still improve. Rich. Lots of intensity at the end. Full body. Very good grip. Very long. Very fine. (June 2001)

NOW TO 2020   18.5

Latricières-Chambertin, 1991
Domaine Leroy

Good, vigorous-looking, medium-full colour. Sweet, mocha-type nose. Nice and fresh. Seems ready. Another fine example. Fullish body. Lovely fresh fruit. Good ripe tannins. Good grip. Classy and long. Very fine for the vintage. (April 2000)

NOW TO 2015   18.5

Marsannay, Les Longeroies, 1991
Domaine Bruno Clair

Lightish colour. Showing some age now and getting lean. Stylish underneath, though. Light to medium weight. (June 2001)

DRINK SOON   13.0

Mazis-Chambertin, 1991
Domaine Joseph Faiveley (?)

Sélectionné par La Confrérie de Tastevin. Believed to be from Faiveley. Medium-full, mature colour. Round, rich, fragrant, mellow nose. Plenty of fruit. Plenty of class. Medium-full body. Fully ready. Fresh and harmonious. Complex and soft on the palate, but with good underlying energy. A lovely bottle to drink now. Long on the palate. Fine plus. (May 2005)

NOW TO 2015   18.0

Mazis-Chambertin, 1991
Domaine Joseph Faiveley

Medium-full colour. Just about mature. Lovely ample, soft but quite substantial, succulent nose. Fully ready. Ripe, fresh and complex. Mellow, fat and very attractive. This is delicious. Will still last well. Very fine. (September 2004)

NOW TO 2015+   18.5

Morey-Saint-Denis, Les Chenevery, 1991
Domaine Lignier-Michelot
Good colour. Stylish, aromatic nose. Ripe and succulent. A touch of oak. Now ready. Good depth and finesse. Fragrant. Positive. Very good. (June 2001)
NOW TO 2015   16.0

Morey-Saint-Denis, Clos de la Buissière, 1991
Domaine Georges Roumier et Fils
Good colour. Plump, rich, ample and not too firm. Still youthful. A touch rustic on the palate. Medium-full body. Balanced. Good plus. (June 2001)
NOW TO 2010   15.5

Morey-Saint-Denis, En la Rue de Vergy, 1991
Domaine Lignier-Michelot
Good colour. Ripe, succulent, oaky nose. Gentle and balanced. Clean. Very good depth. Ripe tannins. Not the greatest concentration or depth, but attractive style. Fresh. Very good. (December 2001)
DRINK SOON   16.0

Musigny, 1991
Domaine Joseph Drouhin
Fullish, mature colour. Rich, mature, vigorous, classy nose. Quite full. Ripe and very classy. Intense and fragrant. Excellent balance. This is very lovely indeed. Still very youthful. (October 2001)
NOW TO 2025   19.5

Musigny, 1991
Domaine Louis Jadot
Full colour. Barely mature. Fullish, fragrant nose. Plenty of depth. Very fragrant. Fullish body. Balanced. Generous and old viney. Very long. Very fine plus. (October 2005)
NOW TO 2015+   19.0

Musigny, 1991
Domaine Leroy
Medium-full, mature colour. Ripe, subtle, classy and balanced on the nose. Now just about mature. Fullish and intense for the vintage. Fresh and complex. This is a splendid example

of the vintage. Really classy. Very long and very lovely. (April 2000)
NOW TO 2011   19.0

Musigny, 1991
Domaine Jacques-Frédéric Mugnier
Good colour. Plenty of substance here. The nose is rich but still quite firm and austere at first. Lovely on the palate. Splendidly pure, fresh, positive fruit. Great class. Vigorous and very lovely indeed. A great 1991. But delicate. Only medium body. Very, very long. In anybody's terms truly magnificent. Won't keep forever, though. (September 2005)
NOW TO 2010   20.0

Le Musigny, 1991
Domaine Georges Roumier et Fils
Fine colour. Still very youthful. On the nose, a little hidden still. Yet splendid concentrated fruit underneath. On the palate, full bodied, quite sizeable and with very good grip. Tannic, but the tannins are sophisticated. Very lovely fragrant fruit. This is beginning to get there but still needs 2 years. Intense. Very classy. Marvellously long and multidimensional. Real Musigny quality. (October 2000)
NOW TO 2018   19.5

Musigny, 1991
Domaine Comte Georges de Vogüé
Magnum. Medium-full, mature colour. Fragrant and classy on the nose. Still vigorous, even only just ready. Still a little dense. Fullish body. Lots of vigour and very lovely fruit. On the palate, more mature than on the nose. Very harmonious and ample. Real drive and intensity. Very fine indeed. (March 2005)
NOW TO 2020   19.5

Nuits-Saint-Georges, Les Boudots, 1991
Domaine Jean Tardy et Fils
Good colour. Ripe, oaky and succulent. A touch astringent. Fruity and medium-full body. But lacks a little vigour. It will get astringent. Good, merely. (June 2001)
NOW TO 2008   15.0

Nuits-Saint-Georges, Les Bousselots, 1991
Domaine Robert Chevillon
Fullish colour. Some development. Just a little diffuse on the nose. Medium body. Ripe. Slightly spicy-earthy. Good grip. The tannins are now just about softened. This is just about ready. Classy. Very good. (October 2000)
NOW TO 2009   16.0

Nuits-Saint-Georges, Les Chaignots, 1991
Domaine Joseph Faiveley
Medium-full colour. Just a little brown. Slightly austere still. A bit of unresolved tannins and a lack of generosity still. Medium to medium-full body. Ripe underneath, but not very rich. Just about ready. Good but not great. Will always lack a bit of succulence. (June 2005)
NOW TO 2014   15.0

Nuits-Saint-Georges, Les Chaignots, 1991
Domaine Gérard Mugneret
Good colour. Rich, vigorous, succulent nose. Lots of depth and vigour. Full body. Good tannins. Plenty of structure. Very good grip. Fine. Lots of life. (June 2001)
NOW TO 2015   17.5

Nuits-Saint-Georges,
Clos des Argillières, 1991
Domaine Robert Dubois et Fils
Fullish colour. Just about mature. Juicy, fragrant nose; no great class but mellow, the tannins now soft, and with good supporting acidity. Balanced and fruity. Still vigorous, but à point now. Good plus. (August 2001)
DRINK SOON   15.5

Nuits-Saint-Georges, Clos des Forêts
Saint-Georges, 1991
Domaine de l'Arlot
Good colour. Now just about mature. Meaty nose. Some stems. Ripe and juicy on the palate. Good vigour and depth. Sweet and succulent at the end. Very good. (June 2001)
NOW TO 2012   16.0

Nuits-Saint-Georges, Clos Saint-Marc, 1991
Domaine Bouchard Père et Fils
Good mature colour. Ripe, round, velvety on both nose and palate. Fullish body. Rich. Not a bit sauvage. Lots of finesse. Rather more than I expected. Good grip. Long. Very good indeed. (December 2001)
NOW TO 2011+   17.0

Nuits-Saint-Georges, Aux Murgers, 1991
Domaine Méo-Camuzet
Medium to medium-full colour. Still youthful. Quite substantial on the nose. Some tannin. Good ample fruit. Good grip. Medium-full body. Richer and more ample than the Corton, but not quite as individual or as classy. Very good indeed, though. (March 2001)
NOW TO 2012   17.0

Nuits-Saint-Georges, Les Porrets
Saint-Georges, 1991
Domaine Joseph Faiveley
Good colour. Aromatic nose. Succulent and generous. Fullish body. Lots of depth and dimension. Lovely fruit. Very classy. Plenty of depth, fat and vigour. Fine plus. À point. (March 2006)
NOW TO 2015   18.5

Nuits-Saint-Georges, Les Pruliers, 1991
Domaine Lucien Boillot Père et Fils
Good colour. Soft, ripe, vigorous nose. Very fragrant. Sophisticated all the way through. Medium-full body. Ready, but with plenty of grip, depth and future. Now round and succulent. This is very good. (July 2002)
NOW TO 2011   16.0

Nuits-Saint-Georges, Les Pruliers, 1991
Domaine Henri Gouges
Full colour. Barely mature. Lovely rich, plummy nose. Good structure, but very well covered tannins. Full body. Still some unresolved tannin, but just about ready. Ripe. Very good grip. Splendid class for a Nuits-Saint-Georges. Excellent depth and lovely fruit. Nicely austere and profound. Very well made

and harmonious. Real depth and length and complexity. Very vigorous. Will still improve. Fine plus. (November 2001)

NOW TO 2020   18.0

Nuits-Saint-Georges, Les Saint-Georges, 1991
Domaine Michel Chevillon

Good colour. Ripe, fragrant nose. Medium-full on the palate. Fully ready. Underneath, the tannins are just a little rough. But the fruit is ripe, and there is good acidity. It lacks a little concentration and richness. But it is good plus, even very good for the vintage. Good positive finish. (December 2001)

DRINK SOON   16.0

Nuits-Saint-Georges, Les Saint-Georges, 1991
Domaine Robert Chevillon

Good vigorous colour. Lovely nose. High class fragrant fruit supported by very good grip and very fine ripe tannins. Very intense. Very classy. Just about ready. This is most impressive. Lovely. (March 2001)

NOW TO 2010+   18.0

Nuits-Saint-Georges, Les Saint-Georges, 1991
Domaine Henri Gouges

Medium-full, mature colour. Fragrant nose. Balanced, laid-back and classy. Mellow but fresh. Medium-full body. Quite vigorous but now fully mature. Very good fruit and harmony and style. À point. Complex at the end. Fine for the vintage. (September 2003)

NOW TO 2011   17.5

Nuits-Saint-Georges, Les Vignes Rondes, 1991
Domaine Daniel Rion

Good colour. Ripe, plump nose. Plenty of fruit here. Fullish body. Succulent, balanced and virile. Good class, too. Long. Very good. (June 2001)

NOW TO 2012   16.0

Pommard, Les Chaponnières,
Vieilles Vignes, 1991
Domaine Billard-Gonnet

Good colour. Ripe nose. Rather more fleshy and stylish than his Clos du Verger. Medium weight.

A little astringent at the back, but ripe enough and positive at the end. Complex. Quite stylish. Good plus. (June 2001)

NOW TO 2010   15.5

Pommard, Clos des Epeneaux, 1991
Domaine du Comte Armand

Very full colour. Full, solid, meaty nose. Not too muscular though. Very rich. Some tannin. A touch of oak. This is very impressive for a 1991. Very lovely follow-through. Classy and very concentrated. Very fine. (June 2001)

NOW TO 2015   18.5

Pommard, Clos du Verger, 1991
Domaine Billard-Gonnet

Good colour. A little dense on the nose. No lack of fruit on the palate, but some not-very-ripe tannins. Medium-full body. It lacks a little succulence in the middle, but it finishes fresh and positive. Quite good plus. (June 2001)

DRINK SOON   14.5

Pommard, Les Jarolières, 1991
Domaine Jean-Marc Boillot

Very good full, fresh colour. Mellow, ripe, very sophisticated nose. Rich and succulent. Very good tannins on the palate. Very good grip. Complex. Vigorous. Long. Still very youthful. Very good plus. (June 2006)

NOW TO 2015+   16.5

Pommard, Les Jarolières, 1991
Domaine de la Pousse d'Or

Magnum. Ripe, stylish, understated nose. This is balanced and elegant and very well poised. Medium-full body. Very good fruit. Most attractive. Fine. (June 2001)

NOW TO 2010   17.5

Pommard, Les Rugiens, 1991
Domaine Philippe Billard-Gonnet

This is highly competent without having the definition or flair for fine. Medium-full body. Now mellow. Ripe, rich and balanced. No hard tannins. Plenty of character and very good balance. But in the end, though very good, it lacks a little personality. (May 2000)

NOW TO 2009   16.0

Pommard, Les Rugiens, 1991
Domaine Hubert de Montille

Good colour. Refined, subtle nose. Medium body only, and it tails off a little. Stylish. Not as good as his Volnay Mitans. Gentle. Good fruit. But it lacks drive. Quite good. (June 2001)

DRINK SOON   14.0

Pommard, Les Rugiens, 1991
Domaine Pierre Morey

Good colour. Rich, slightly closed-in on the nsoe. Ripe but not the greatest concentration on the palate. Stylish, balanced and long on the palate, nevertheless. Good personality. Very complex and classy. Very good indeed. (June 2001)

NOW TO 2010   17.0

Pommard, Les Rugiens, 1991
Domaine Annick Parent

Very good colour. Lovely nose. Rich and warm and expansive. Ripe. Medium-full body. Just a touch astringent. But very good depth and personality. Drink with food. Fine, long , fresh finish. Very good indeed. (June 2001)

NOW TO 2010   17.0

Richebourg, 1991
Domaine Anne Gros

Medium-full, mature colour. Lots of interest on the nose. A fine vintage and now ready for drinking. Ripe, harmonious, complex and subtle. Medium-full body. Balanced. Plenty of dimension. And the class of the *climat* comes singing through. Very fresh. Very long. Very fine. (February 2004)

NOW TO 2015   18.5

Richebourg, 1991
Domaine Jean Gros

Good colour. Very lovely plump, vigorous nose. Excellent depth and concentration. Medium-full body. Only just about ready. Not a blockbuster, but very lovely fruit. Classy and intense.

Very long. Very lovely. Splendid finish. Very fine plus. (June 2001)

NOW TO 2015   19.0

Richebourg, 1991
Domaine Alain Hudelot-Noëllat

Fullish, mature colour. Lovely nose. Ample and rich. Abundant and fresh. Very, very classy fruit. Full body. Still just a touch of unresolved tannins. Lovely fruit. Very good grip. The aftertaste is rich, mellow, long and multidimensional. This is very fine indeed. (March 2004)

NOW TO 2015   19.5

Richebourg, 1991
Domaine Leroy

Full colour. Still vigorous. Vigorous nose, too. Alive, oaky and intense. Very good concentrated fruit. Full body. Firm. Still a bit of tannin. Still a touch austere. Very good acidity. Very classy. Very fine indeed. (March 2004)

NOW TO 2020+   19.5

Romanée-Conti, 1991
Domaine de la Romanée-Conti

Medium-full colour. Marvellously fragrant, complex nose. Great breeding. Splendidly subtle. Medium-full body. Not as big as La Tâche 1991 but more classy and more intense. Marvellous fruit. Very, very long on the palate. Excellent finish. Even more intense and sweet and profound as it evolved. Really brilliant! (March 2005)

NOW TO 2015   20.0

Romanée-Saint-Vivant, 1991
Domaine Alain Hudelot-Noëllat

Full, mature colour. Soft, classy, Musigny-ish nose. Medium-full body. Mellow. Fresh acidity. Elegant, intense fruit. Plenty of depth and richness and very long at the end. A classy wine and quite delicious now. *À point*. Very fine. (December 2005)

NOW TO 2015   18.5

Romanée-Saint-Vivant, 1991
Domaine Leroy

Full, rich, mature colour. Exotic nose. Rich, lush and succulent. Lovely concentrated fruit. Lots of depth. Full bodied and intense. Quite structured. Fine fruit. Very good grip. This is very lovely. Splendid finish. Bags of life. Very fine indeed for a 1991. (March 2002)

NOW TO 2015   19.5

Romanée-Saint-Vivant, 1991
Domaine de la Romanée-Conti

Medium-full, youthful colour. Marvellous nose. Elegant and laid-back and composed. Fullish body, but velvety. Marvellously complex and delicate and subtle. Splendidly balanced. Very, very long and classy and complex. Very, very intense. Only just ready. Excellent. (March 2005)

NOW TO 2030   19.5

Ruchottes-Chambertin, 1991
Domaine Frédéric Esmonin

Good fullish, mature colour. Aromatic nose. Fragrant. Succulent. Now the secondary/tertiary fragrances. Soft and long. Delicious. Fine plus. (April 2005)

NOW TO 2015   18.0

Ruchottes-Chambertin, 1991
Domaine Georges Roumier

Good colour. Very fine nose. Lovely fruit. Very individual. Splendid balance. Real depth. Full body. Now getting round. It will still improve. Plenty of energy. Not the greatest class, but certainly fine. (June 2001)

NOW TO 2020   17.5

Savigny-lès-Beaune, 1991
Domaine Lucien Jacob

Medium colour. Fresh nose. Plump, ripe and attractive. No great depth, but balanced and succulent. Medium body. Fresh. Good. (December 2001)

DRINK SOON   15.0

Savigny-lès-Beaune, La Dominode, 1991
Domaine Bruno Clair

A lovely wine, now à point. Good colour. Rich oaky nose. Good concentration and very ripe tannins. This could be a 1990, except that this 1990 is still big and brooding, with a long way to go. Nice and substantial on the palate. Well balanced. Ripe and luscious. No hard edges. Lots of class. Fine by any standards. Will last very well. (March 2000)

NOW TO 2011   17.5

Savigny-lès-Beaune, La Dominode, 1991
Domaine Jean-Marc Pavelot

Medium-full colour. Quite rich, if losing just a little of its concentration. Medium-full body. Ripe. Good vigour still. Ripe finish. Good plus. (June 2001)

DRINK SOON   15.5

Savigny-lès-Beaune, Les Fourneaux, 1991
Domaine Simon Bize et Fils

Good colour. Rich, succulent nose. Plenty of depth and fruit. Quite concentrated even. Medium-full body. Round, fat and ripe. Lovely finish. Very long and even voluptuous. Very good. (June 2001)

NOW TO 2010   16.0

Savigny-lès-Beaune, Les Vergelesses, 1991
Domaine Simon Bize et Fils

Medium to medium-full, vigorous colour. Lovely mellow, ripe nose. Medium to medium-full body. Fresh but ripe. Plenty of energy underneath. Complex. Succulent. Still lots of life ahead of it. Very good plus. (June 2006)

NOW TO 2015   16.5

La Tâche, 1991
Domaine de la Romanée-Conti

Fullish colour. Full, rich, concentrated and very lovely on the nose. Real class. Lots of vigour. Full bodied, rich, spicy, gamey and succulent. A touch of gingerbread. Ripe and ample and very lovely. Only just ready. Will keep for ages. Multidimensional. Very, very long. Excellent. (March 2005)

NOW TO 2020   19.5

Volnay, Vendanges Sélectionnées, 1991
Domaine Michel Lafarge

Medium-full, mature colour. Fresh, ripe, succulent nose. Medium to medium-full body. Fragrant. Soft but vigorous. Complex. Very good

indeed for what it is. *À point* but will keep well.
(March 2005)
NOW TO 2011   17.5

Volnay, Les Caillerets, 1991
Domaine Bouchard Père et Fils

Fullish, mature colour. Rich, sweet, caramel and mocha, fully mature nose. Most attractive. Medium-full body. Good grip. Fully ready. Ample and very good indeed for the vintage. (March 2004)
NOW TO 2014   17.0

Volnay, Carelles, 1991
Domaine Jean-Marc Boillot

Very good colour. Very lovely fragrant, clean, classy fruit on the nose. Medium-full body. Equally classy, tannic structure. Long, ample, fresh and almost sweet on the palate. Very silky-smooth. Long. Very good indeed. (November 2002)
NOW TO 2010   17.0

Volnay, Clos de la Bousse d'Or, 1991
Domaine de la Pousse d'Or

Good colour. Lovely nose. Rich and expansive. Fullish body. Lots of depth. Really ripe fruit here. Complex, elegant, very long and lovely. This is fine plus. (June 2001)
NOW TO 2015   18.0

Volnay, Clos des Chênes, 1991
Domaine Michel Lafarge

Medium-full colour. Now mature. Mature, quite concentrated, now sensual nose. Medium to medium-full body. A fully mature Burgundy. Super smooth palate. Fresh. Very good indeed. (March 2006)
NOW TO 2015   17.0

Volnay, Clos des Ducs, 1991
Domaine du Marquis d'Angerville

Fullish colour. Lovely fragrant nose. Medium-full. Very good fruit. This is fullish bodied. Vigorous but now *à point*. Very lovely poised, complex Pinot on the palate. Very lovely, especially for the vintage. Very, very long and complex and fragrant. (October 2002)
NOW TO 2011+   18.0

Volnay, Mitans, 1991
Domaine Hubert de Montille

Good colour. Fresh, elegant and understated. Just a shade lean on the palate but balanced and stylish, long and complex. Very Montille in character. Very good. (June 2001)
NOW TO 2009   16.0

Volnay, Santenots du Milieu, 1991
Domaine des Comtes Lafon

Very good colour. Quite firm and hard on the nose and on the attack. Very good vigour underneath. Fullish body. Ripe and rich. It needs food. Fine. (June 2001)
NOW TO 2010   17.5

Volnay, Taillepieds, 1991
Domaine Hubert de Montille

Good colour. Lovely fragrant nose. Medium weight. Balanced and graceful. Ripe. Now soft and round and full of fruit. Lots of interest. I prefered it to the 1989 today. Fine for the vintage. (October 2003)
NOW TO 2013   17.5

Vosne-Romanée, 1991
Domaine Jacky Confuron-Cotétidot

Medium colour. Quite developed. Rather a pongy nose. Stems and old wood. Fresh on the palate but only medium body and a bit stringy. Unsophisticated. Only quite good. (June 2001)
NOW TO 2009   14.0

Vosne-Romanée, Les Beaumonts, 1991
Domaine Daniel Rion et Fils

Very good colour. Full, vigorous nose. Plump, ripe and fresh if no great finesse. Fullish, ample and fresh on the palate. Nice and ripe and with very good grip and freshness underneath. Not the greatest of elegance but very good plus. Decent finish. (November 2002)
DRINK SOON   16.5

Vosne-Romanée, Beaux Monts, 1991
Domaine Charles Thomas

Fullish, mature colour. Aromatic nose. Plump, stylish and succulent. Fully mature. Fullish weight. Plump, complex and harmonious. Long, complex and classy. Plenty of substance here. Long and positive at the end. Only just ready. Not great but very good indeed for the vintage. Will last and last. (May 2002)

NOW TO 2015   17.0

Vosne-Romanée, Les Brûlées, 1991
Domaine René Engel

Very good colour. Lovely nose. Concentrated and stylish and beautifully balanced. Fullish body. A lovely example. Complex and classy. Long. Only just about ready. Very fine. (June 2001)

NOW TO 2020   18.0

Vosne-Romanée, Clos des Réas, 1991
Domaine Jean Gros

Medium-full, fully mature colour. Plump, ripe, soft, classy nose. Fragrant and elegant. Medium to medium-full body. Harmonious, elegant, intense, silky and very well balanced. Long and lovely. Very composed. Still very vigorous. (March 2005)

NOW TO 2015   17.5

Vosne-Romanée, Les Genevrières, 1991
Domaine Leroy

This is very lovely for a village wine. Ripe, fresh, full of classy fruit. The follow-through doesn't have the greatest depth or complexity, but harmonious and lovely. Still very vigorous. Very good. (October 2002)

DRINK SOON   16.0

Vosne-Romanée, Aux Malconsorts, 1991
Domaine Sylvain Cathiard

Good vigorous colour. Refined and classy on the nose. Some oak. Good balance and succulent fruit. Medium to medium-full body. Complex, stylish, gently oaky and very long on the palate. Almost Vosnay-ish. Fresh but fully ready. Lovely ripe, juicy fruit. Long. Fine. (July 2002)

NOW TO 2011   17.5

Vosne-Romanée, Les Malconsorts, 1991
Domaine Charles Thomas

Fullish, immature colour. Quite a solid nose. Good rich, ripe, meaty wine on the palate.

Fullish body. Structured but no unripe tannins. Good grip. This will still improve. Still very youthful. Good depth. Very good indeed. (June 2001)

NOW TO 2015   17.0

Vosne-Romanée, Les Suchots, 1991
Maison Camille Giroud

Fullish colour. Still very vigorous. Good grip. A classy wine with plenty of depth. Still a little tannin to resolve. Delicious plummy fruit. Fine for the vintage. (September 2002)

NOW TO 2010+   17.5

1990

With a total of nearly 260,000 hectolitres, 1990 was one of the largest crops of recent years, only being surpassed by 1986 and 1982, and a full 10 percent more plentiful than the previous vintage, 1989, itself regarded as generous.

And yet, as if to prove the exception to the general rule, the red wines are truly magnificent—full, rich, and with an exotic cooked-fruit flavour—and the white wines are very good. For quality and consistency, you have to go back to 1959 or 1964 (for reds) to find any year that was so satisfactory both geographically and hierarchically. I said at the outset that I suspected some of the great wines of the 1988 vintage might be superior in the long run, if different, to the great wines of 1990, and I still hold with this view. But further down the scale, the 1990s get the palm. No one who has them in his or her cellar is likely to be disappointed.

WEATHER CONDITIONS

An early and mild start to the growing season produced a prolific *sortie* of productive buds, marred only on the lower slopes at the junction of Savigny, Pernand and Aloxé-Corton by a little frost. The weather then deteriorated in June, and the flowering was prolonged, producing both *coulure* (failure of the flower to set into fruit) and *millerandage* (shot berry).

Volnay was one of the communes most severely affected.

Thenceforth, it was hot and very dry. The younger vines suffered, especially those on the slopes where the soils are thinner and less rich than in the plain. The more mature plants with more complex root-systems were better able to cope, but the progress towards maturation was nevertheless slowed to a standstill. At the end of August and the beginning of September, just when rain was most needed, there were several refreshing thunderstorms (in all, some 80 mm of rain fell in one week), the vines woke up, and they rapidly finished their cycle during three weeks of warm but not excessively hot weather. The red wine harvest began in the Côte de Beaune on September 20, and in the Côte de Nuits, a week or so later. The advent of full maturity, as a result of the prolonged flowering, was irregular, however, and some did not finish their harvest until October 10.

One effect of the drought was that a high proportion of leaves had already fallen from the vines by mid-August. This exposed the fruit; concentrated and dried out the berries; and, incidentally, helped to fix the colour better. Canopy management is not a science understood by many Burgundian *vignerons*, but this gain in colour had occurred accidentally, for the same reason, in one of Charles Rousseau's *cuvées* a couple of years previously. Puzzling over the explanation, he had bounced a theory off the late Gérard Jaboulet in Tain, only to have it confirmed. He subsequently started to deliberately expose his grape bunches to the sun in the final month before the harvest, as do many others these days.

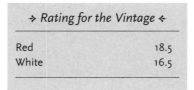

⇥ Rating for the Vintage ⇤	
Red	18.5
White	16.5

⇥ Size of the Crop ⇤ (In hectolitres, excluding generic wine)		
	RED	WHITE
Grands Crus	14,117	3,668
Village and Premiers Crus	188,573	51,926
TOTAL	202,690	55,594

The result, for those who had prudently pruned hard and green-harvested the excessive grape bunches toward the end of July (sensibly knocking off the least favoured bunches in order to mitigate the effects of the prolonged flowering) was a quality of fruit that was second to none. This fruit was abundantly healthy, the skins of the grapes were thick, and the ratio of juice to solid matter was low. It normally requires, says Charles Rousseau (to quote him once again) one kilo of grapes to make one bottle of wine. Or, to put it another way, it takes ten plastic containers of 30 kilos to fill one *pièce*. In 1990 it took twelve. I remember Rousseau pointing out the same fact when I first tasted his 1983s. The result, obviously, is high concentration. For those who did not crop excessively, as Christophe Roumier pointed out, it was necessary neither to chaptalise nor to acidify. Alcohol levels were naturally 12.5° or above, even as high as 14.5° in some exceptional cases.

Nevertheless, for those who harvested at 40 hectolitres per hectare or more, it was necessary to perform a *saignée* to bleed off excess juice before fermentation. *Saignée*, however, is not a cure-all. It is a *faute de mieux*. It is an essential procedure if rain intervenes at the last minute, as it did in 1991. But reducing the harvest of especially the more prolific younger vines to moderate proportions in the first place is far more important. Many of the finest aromatic elements are lost in the *saignée*-d juice. It may concentrate the solids, but it does not of itself increase the acidity.

Many people *saignée*-d their 1990 vats. Jacques Lardière at Jadot *saignée*-d all his *cuvées* 20 percent. Those at Drouhin did only one, but in retrospect felt they could have done more.

WHERE ARE THE BEST WINES? AND THE STATE OF MATURITY TODAY

- In both colours the 1990 vintage is consistent both geographically and hierarchically.

- It is now time to drink the white wines. Many village wines are already a bit tired, but the *premiers* and *grands crus* are still vigorous. In many cases, the 1990 whites are fresher and more enjoyable than the richer but less balanced 1989s.

- It was a proper *vin-de-garde* red wine vintage; the wines were more marked by the year than by their origins and took a long time to mature. Ten years on, the majority of the Côte de Nuits *premiers* and *grands crus* were still dumb. Seven years later, there are still some which will continue to improve. So there is no hurry. Keep some for drinking in 2020.

TASTING NOTES

WHITES

Bâtard-Montrachet, 1990
Domaine Blain-Gagnard

Medium colour. Quite a rich nose. But a little restrained. Good grip on the palate. Medium-full body. Nicely flowery. Quite rich. Good balance. But not a wine with a huge (or *grand cru*) personality. Not heavy, though. But I would have expected a bit more depth and concentration. Very good indeed, at best. (May 2001)

DRINK SOON   17.0

Bâtard-Montrachet, 1990
Maison Champy

First year of "new" Champy. Fresh, youthful colour. Full, rich, concentrated, high quality nose. Still very vigorous. Very fine fruit. Complex and classy. Not a bit heavy. Fine grip. This is fine. (June 2001)

NOW TO 2009   18.5

Bâtard-Montrachet, 1990
Domaine Jean-Noël Gagnard

Rich, fat nose. Very good depth, if no great finesse. Still a little closed. Full bodied and quite solid. Very good fruit here. Nicely concentrated. Rather more sophisticated than the 1992. A wine for food. Just slightly four-square. Very ripe at the end. Long and lovely. Plenty of grip and life ahead of it. Fine. (Some bottle variation here. Another bottle was more vibrant and less four-square [very fine; 18.0]). (January 2002)

DRINK SOON   17.5

Bâtard-Montrachet, 1990
Domaine Pierre Morey

Slightly heavy on the nose. Full, rich and opulent. Ripe but a slight lack of grip and real class. Concentrated nevertheless. Fine but not great. (June 2000)

DRINK UP   17.5

Bienvenues-Bâtard-Montrachet, 1990
Domaine Leflaive

Well developed, to the point of being really quite old. I don't think it even had a great deal of grip and backbone. (May 2004)

PAST ITS BEST (SEE NOTE)

Chassagne-Montrachet, En Cailleret, 1990
Domaine Richard Fontaine-Gagnard

Ripe, rich, full and stylish. And still vigorous. Very Chassagne in character, but not four-square at all. Lovely fruit. Plenty of life. Very good indeed. (June 2001)

DRINK SOON   17.0

Chassagne-Montrachet, Les Caillerets, 1990
Domaine Jean-Noël Gagnard

Youthful colour. Rich, ripe, mature and fresh. Good grip. Good class. No sign of age. Lovely fruit. Long. Very good indeed. (June 2002)

DRINK SOON   17.0

Chassagne-Montrachet, Morgeot, 1990
Domaine Jean-Noël Gagnard

Mature colour. Rich, full nose with just a little residual SO2. Fullish on the palate. Good grip.

Plenty of depth, if without quite the distinction of the wines made by his daughter Caroline Lestimé a few years later. Good plus, nevertheless. (May 2005)
DRINK SOON   15.5

Chassagne-Montrachet, Les Vergers, 1990
Domaine Michel Niellon
Fresh colour. Youthful, only just mature nose. Nicely nutty. Full body. Ripe and profound. Clean and vigorous. Lovely fruit. Lovely long finish. Very fine. (March 2005)
NOW TO 2010   18.5

Chevalier-Montrachet, 1990
Domaine Bouchard Père et Fils
Ripe. Fresh. Rich and balanced. Not the depth of a real Chevalier. But good class. Very good indeed. But not great. (March 2001)
DRINK SOON   16.0

Chevalier-Montrachet, 1990
Domaine Leflaive
A lot better than their 1990 Bienvenues-Bâtard-Montrachet: fuller, fresher, more concentrated. Rich, fat and really quite profound. This is a fine example. But it is not fine. Drink soon. (May 2004)
DRINK SOON   17.5

Chevalier-Montrachet, Les Demoiselles, 1990
Domaine Louis Latour
Deep colour. Honeyed and apricotty. Some oakiness. Round. Quite evolved. Good acidity. Rich. It lacks real *grand cru* class but vigorous and with no lack of depth. Fine. (March 2001)
DRINK SOON   17.5

Corton-Charlemagne, 1990
Domaine Bonneau du Martray
Rich, full, concentrated and very classy indeed. Lots of life yet. Very lovely fruit. A classic example. Very fine. (September 2005)
NOW TO 2012+   18.5

Corton-Charlemagne, 1990
Domaine Bouchard Père et Fils
This was vinified in tank. Never really allowed to breathe properly. Some evolution on the colour.

And on the nose, it shows more age than you would expect. Quite fat and rich. A little oaky. Slightly astringent, too, and a lack of real zip. Ripe but in a slightly dry sort of way. Decent follow-through. But only very good rather than fine. (June 2000)
DRINK SOON   16.0

Corton-Charlemagne, 1990
Domaine Louis Latour
Fresh colour. Fresh nose. But not the greatest depth. A bit too lightweight for Corton-Charlemagne. Ripe, clean, elegant and balanced. Good peachy fruit. Better on the palate than it seemed on the nose. Still vigorous. Fine. (April 2005)
NOW TO 2010   17.5

Corton-Charlemagne, 1990
Domaine Rapet Père et Fils
Very fresh colour. A typical Pernand-side Corton-Charlemagne: steely, high in acidity, slightly lean. Medium to medium-full body. Very clean and pure. I would have expected a bit more richness and fat in 1990. It lacks a bit of generosity. No traces of oak. No shortage of elegance but very good, not fine. No hurry to drink. (May 2005)
NOW TO 2009   16.0

Meursault, Les Casse-Têtes, 1990
Domaine Patrick Javillier
This is elegant, relaxed, gently oaky and very classy. Needs drinking quite soon, but very good plus. (June 2000)
DRINK UP   16.5

Meursault, Charmes, 1990
Domaine Hubert Bouzereau-Gruère
Mature colour, but nothing a bit faded here. Very good acidity. Clean, stylish, fullish, ripe fruit. Plenty of vigour. Very good depth. Nice and rich and nutty, with peachy overtones. Long positive finish. Very good indeed. (July 2000)
DRINK SOON   17.0

Meursault, Charmes, 1990
Maison Champy

Quite classy. Decent depth and fruit. Good weight and grip. Needs drinking soon, but very good. (January 2002)

DRINK SOON   16.0

Meursault, Charmes, 1990
Domaine des Comtes Lafon

Youthful colour. Fresh, flowery, youthful nose. Ripe. Good acidity. Classy and complex. Full-ish, peachy and gently oaky. Ripe and rich and splendidly balanced. Very, very lovely and complex at the end. Very lovely. *À point* but will last well. Very fine. (May 2001)

NOW TO 2010+   18.5

Meursault, Les Genevrières, 1990
Domaine François Jobard

Rather closed and austere. Unforthcoming on the nose. Heavy and sulphury. Yet a good wine underneath. Now drying up. (June 2000)

DRINK SOON   12.0

Meursault, Genevrières, 1990
Domaine des Comtes Lafon

The colour is still fresh, as is the nose. Round, slightly spicy, aromatic and gently oaky; 100 percent new oak then, and bottled after 24 months. Full bodied and ample. Rich and vigorous. A different sort of wine than what is produced today. Bigger and more four-square and more powerful. Excellent grip. Lots and lots of depth. Lovely fruit and no lack of elegance. Very long. Excellent. (September 2005)

NOW TO 2010+   18.5

Meursault, Narvaux, 1990
Domaine Patrick Javillier

Magnum. Ripe, round, fresh, mature and stylish. No undue age at all. A delicious example. Will still last well. (June 2006)

NOW TO 2010+   18.0

Meursault, Les Perrières, 1990
Domaine Jean-Michel Gaunoux

There is a lot of concentration and youthfulness here. Ripe. Vigorous. Good acidity. Underneath,

very good fruit and depth. Now only just about ready. Very classy. Fine. (June 2000)

DRINK SOON   17.5

Meursault, Les Perrières, 1990
Domaine des Comtes Lafon

Some evolution on the colour. Very full on the nose—much fuller than the Charmes. Concentrated. Lots and lots of depth and dimension. Very impressive. Full body. Excellent grip. *À point* and very delicious. Rich, harmonious, profound and multidimensional. Very, very long. Excellent. Burgundy doesn't come much better than this! (May 2001)

DRINK SOON   19.5

Meursault, Perrières, 1990
Domaine Leroy

Ripe, fullish, smoky nose with a touch of built-in sulphur. Concentrated, full bodied, fresh, rich and very youthful on the palate. Surprisingly so. But it lacks flair. Good plus. (March 2005)

DRINK SOON   15.5

Meursault, Perrières, 1990
Domaine Joseph Matrot

Quite evolved, indeed almost too much, on the nose. Better on the palate. Fullish bodied, fat but slightly flabby. Fully evolved. I don't think this was ever that special. (June 2006)

DRINK UP   13.5

Meursault, Les Perrières, 1990
Domaine Guy Roulot

Magnum. Ripe and elegant on the nose. Still fresh. Nicely minerally. Not for very long term keeping, now but long and complex and fine. (June 2000)

DRINK UP   17.5

Meursault, Tessons, 1990
Domaine Pierre Morey

At first the nose is a little pinched. Some SO2. It should have been decanted. This cleared up after a bit to reveal a lovely wine. Medium-full body. Splendidly balanced. Surprisingly classy and intense. Discreet. Complete. Vigorous. Fine. (August 2000)

DRINK SOON   17.5

Meursault, Les Tessons, Clos de Mon Plaisir, 1990
Domaine Guy Roulot

A little sulphur. A little sweet. But underneath, quite stylish. Quite full bodied. Quite good plus. (June 2000)

DRINK SOON   14.5

Le Montrachet, 1990
Domaine Jacques Gagnard-Delagrange

Full, firm, rich and succulent. Lovely nose. Real depth. Not so much a fine acidity as a lot of vigour and intensity. Very classy. Very concentrated. Very lovely ripe fruit and very good grip. *À point* now. Very, very fine. (July 2000)

DRINK SOON   19.5

Le Montrachet, 1990
Maison Louis Latour

Ungainly nose. Full, sulphury and quite evolved. Rich on the palate, but coarse. No. (March 2005)

DRINK SOON   13.0

Morey-Saint-Denis, Clos des
Monts Luisants, 1990
Domaine Ponsot

Aligoté dating from 1911. Fresh colour. Mature, nutty nose. Fresh and crisp. Fullish body. Individual. Fat and rich. Vigorous and complex. Classy. Very fine. Bags of life ahead of it. (March 2006)

NOW TO 2015   18.5

Nuits-Saint-Georges, Clos de l'Arlot,
Blanc, 1990
Domaine de l'Arlot

This is still very fresh, remarkably so for a wine nearly 11 years old. Quite oaky but full of ripe, concentrated fruit very well balanced with the acidity. Quite full, complex, vigorous and classy. Very good indeed. (July 2001)

DRINK SOON   17.0

Nuits-Saint-Georges, La Perrière, Blanc, 1990
Domaine Henri Gouges

Very crisp and youthful on the nose. Individual. Fullish bodied, rich and classy on the palate. Very good acidity. This is fine. (May 2001)

DRINK SOON   17.5

Puligny-Montrachet, 1990
Domaine Jean-Marc Boillot

Just as is should be: ripe, fresh and gently oaky. Very stylish and very well balanced. A lovely example. (June 2000)

DRINK UP   16.0

Puligny-Montrachet, Clos de la Garenne, 1990
Domaine Duc de Magenta/
Maison Louis Jadot

Rich, full and abundant. Ripe and harmonious on the nose. Nutty. Well balanced. This has lots of depth. Very good grip. Aromatic and mineral. High class. Lovely at the end. Still very fresh. Very fine. (November 2002)

NOW TO 2010   18.5

Saint-Aubin, Les Frionnes, 1990
Domaine Hubert Lamy

Magnum. A little too much SO2 here but full, ripe and rich and vigorous. Quite good. (June 2000)

DRINK UP   14.0

REDS

Auxey-Duresses, 1990
Domaine Coche-Bizouard

Very good colour. Barely mature. Full, but slightly sweaty, oxidised nose. Chunky but ripe. Not much elegance here. Rather four-square. On the palate this is a meaty but not exactly very charmingly fruity wine. What merit this has is due more to the vintage than to the wine itself. (July 2000)

DRINK SOON   13.0

Beaune, Les Boucherottes, 1990
Domaine Louis Jadot

Good full, rich, vigorous nose. Quite a lot of class for Boucherottes. Plums and mocha. Fullish body. Still a little tannin, which I think it will always have, in a chewy sort of way. Otherwise, *à point*. Good grip. Rich. Good plus, but not fine. Will keep well. (October 2002)

NOW TO 2015   15.5

Beaune, Le Clos des Mouches, 1990
Domaine Joseph Drouhin

Medium-full, mature colour. Ripe but slightly four-square nose. Nowhere up to the standard of the Clos des Chênes, but ripe and succulent. Medium to medium-full body. Ripe. A slight boiled sweet character, and while quite fresh, not quite with the grip it should have. Now ready. Slightly one-dimensional. Good plus. (March 2003)

NOW TO 2010   15.5

Beaune, Clos des Ursules, 1990
Domaine Louis Jadot

Rich, full colour. Fat, succulent, classy nose. Full-ish body. Vigorous, but now just about *à point*. Lovely ample, ripe, fresh fruit. Long. Lovely. A splendid example of what it is. (October 2003)

NOW TO 2020   17.0

Beaune, Les Cras, Vieilles Vignes, 1990
Domaine Germain Père et Fils/
Chateau de Chorey-lès-Beaune

Very good colour. Still youthful. Full, rich, oaky nose. Quite fat. Very good grip. Still some tannin. Lovely concentrated fruit. Lovely long finish. Only just ready. This is very good indeed. (June 2000)

NOW TO 2010   17.0

Beaune, Grèves, 1990
Domaine Michel Lafarge

Very good colour. Very lovely nose. Rich, quite powerful and vigorous still. Fat, spicy and succulent. Plenty of substance here. Only just ready. Rich at the end. Very good plus. (June 2000)

DRINK SOON   16.5

Beaune, Grèves, Vigne de l'Enfant Jésus, 1990
Domaine Bouchard Père et Fils

Good, full, mature colour. Rich, full, slightly earthy nose. Certainly a success, if without the fragrance of the wines today. Fullish body. Meaty. Plenty of fruit and vigour. Good plus. (September 2005)

NOW TO 2012   15.5

Beaune, Les Marconnets, 1990
Domaine Camille Giroud

Magnum. Good youthful colour. Rich and fat on the nose. Meaty but not dense. Still youthful. Quite a tough wine. Some residual tannin. Good grip. Lacks a bit of grace, but very good. Better with food. Will always be a bit ungainly. (June 2000)

DRINK SOON   16.0

Blagny, La Pièce sous le Bois, 1990
Domaine Pierre Matrot

Fully mature colour. Slightly farmyardy nose. But ample and ripe on the palate. Good acidity. Medium body. Lacks a bit of finesse but quite good. (June 2000)

DRINK UP   14.0

Bonnes Mares, 1990
Domaine Pierre Bertheau et Fils

Medium-full colour. Open, succulent, rich nose. Lovely fruit. Plenty of class. Medium-full body. Ample on the palate. Good grip. A graceful wine, despite a touch of reduction. Medium-full body. Juicy and intense. Soft and juicy at the end. Very attractive, if not as serious as Roumier's or de Vogüé's. (October 2005)

NOW TO 2015   17.5

Bonnes Mares, 1990
Maison Pierre Bourée et Fils

Medium-full colour. Rich, quite evolved nose with a touch of brettanomyces. A little too farmyardy for my liking. Medium-full body. Good depth and grip. This has concentration and an old-viney aspect. Not quite the finesse for a *grand cru*, but it still has vigour and is good plus. (October 2005)

NOW TO 2013   15.5

Bonnes Mares, 1990
Domaine Drouhin-Laroze

Medium-full colour. High-toned, spicy nose. Quite sweet. Just a little suave. Medium to medium-full body. Reasonable depth and very good fruit and balance. This is very good indeed, but it doesn't have the character or class of the best. (October 2005)

NOW TO 2012   17.0

Bonnes Mares, 1990
Domaine Joseph Drouhin

Medium-full colour. Rich, fat, ample nose. Lots of depth and high quality. Very fragrant fruit. Medium-full body. Classy, harmonious, intense and very fine. Very long, lovely finish. Very pure Pinot. (October 2005)

NOW TO 2020   18.5

Bonnes Mares, 1990
Domaine Dujac

Fullish colour. Rich, roasted, toasted nose. Nutty and sweet. Just a touch of the stems. Medium to medium-full body. Ripe, stylish and balanced. Good intensity. But not quite the concentration and fat. The vines were still quite young at the time. Very good indeed. (October 2005)

NOW TO 2015   17.0

Bonnes Mares, 1990
Domaine Joseph Faiveley

Medium-full colour. Big, brutal and slightly chunky on the nose. Yet plenty of rich fruit. Quite oaky. Better on the palate. Yet a bit astringent and four-square at the end. Very lovely succulent fruit. Will it ever round off? I think so. Because there is very good grip here. (October 2005)

NOW TO 2025   18.0

Bonnes Mares, 1990
Domaine Fougeray de Beauclair

Fullish colour. Lovely classy, fullish and very concentrated nose. Fullish body. Ripe. Plump. Not the velvety texture of the best, but impressive fruit. Just a little four-square. But very good vigour at the end. Fine. (October 2005)

NOW TO 2018   17.5

Bonnes Mares, 1990
Domaine Louis Jadot

Fullish colour. Rich, full, backward and still slightly ungainly on the nose. Lots of quality as it developed. Ample and rich and profound. Full body. Very lovely fruit. Really rich and stylish. Splendid depth. This is very fine indeed. Only just ready. (October 2005)

NOW TO 2025   19.5

Bonnes Mares, 1990
Maison Labouré-Roi

Medium-full colour. Quite a sturdy nose without much nuance or succulence. Medium-full body. Slightly solid. Good acidity, but a lack of velvet and composure. It also lacks richness. Quite good. (October 2005)

NOW TO 2010   14.0

Bonnes Mares, 1990
Domaine Georges Lignier et Fils

Medium to medium-full colour. Some stems on the nose. Ripe but a little attenuated. On the palate only medium body. But it has fruit and style and balance. Not rustic at all. Good acidity. A little Dujac-ish in style. Slightly lean, but good plus. (October 2005)

NOW TO 2010   15.5

Bonnes Mares, 1990
Domaine Daniel Moine-Hudelot

Medium-full colour. Ripe nose. Classy. Good weight and depth. Medium-full body. Ample, rich and very satisfactory. Both finesse and complexity. Very good balance. Long and with plenty of dimension. Lovely finish. Fine. (October 2005)

NOW TO 2015   17.5

Bonnes Mares, 1990
Domaine Jacques-Frédéric Mugnier

Fullish colour. Very classy, slightly laid-back and reticent nose but very, very lovely fruit. Fullish body on the palate. Very lovely fruit. Very ripe tannins. Intense and energetic. Rich and with great profoundity and finesse. Very lovely. (October 2005)

NOW TO 2020   19.0

Bonnes Mares, 1990
Domaine Georges Roumier et Fils

Full colour. At first a bit reduced on the nose. When this blew off, a marvellous fruit and depth shone forth. Real breed here. Full, rich and concentrated. Gently oaky. Very, very splendid fruit. Excellent grip. Even better than the de Vogüé example today, but slightly more forward. Multidimensional. Splendidly rich finish. Just about ready. (October 2005)

NOW TO 2025   19.5

Bonnes Mares, 1990
Domaine Charles Thomas

Dense, full colour. Rich, full, masculine wine. Rather four-square. Somewhat muscular. Full bodied on the palate. Rich and tannic. Good concentration. Good grip. Backward, but with plenty of depth. Long positive finish and very good fruit. This is fine plus. Barely ready. (October 2005)

NOW TO 2020   18.0

Bonnes Mares, 1990
Domaine des Varoilles

Medium-full colour. High-toned nose. The acidity shows, but there is not much richness or finesse. Slightly vegetal. On the palate, a little thin. Even a suggestion of astringency at the end. No old-viney fat or concentration here. Disappointing. (October 2005)

DRINK SOON   13.5

Bonnes Mares, 1990
Domaine Comte Georges de Vogüé

Full colour. A great deal of depth and concentration on the nose. Rich, oaky and very promising indeed. Full body. Splendidly rich and concentrated. Marvellous expression of fruit. Still very youthful. Ready, but better still in 5 years. This is quite splendid. Very impressive finish. (October 2005)

NOW TO 2025+   19.5

Chambertin, 1990
Domaine Leroy

Splendid colour. Very full indeed. Full, vigorous, very ample and ripe nose. Fresh, splendid cooked fruit. Real depth and class here. Full body. Very, very rich yet with a fine acidity. Really very lovely. Classy and complex. Excellent. (April 2000)

NOW TO 2028   20.0

Chambertin, 1990
Maison Roland Remoissenet et Fils

Fullish, vigorous colour. Ripe, aromatic and stylish on the nose. Medium-full bodied, ample, rich, balanced and profound. Real *grand cru* quality here. Lots of depth and concentration. Very good grip. Vigorous and very lovely. Very fine. (March 2005)

NOW TO 2016   18.5

Chambertin, 1990
Domaine Armand Rousseau

Medium-full, mature colour. Fully mature, aromatic, complex nose. This is excellent. And fully ready on the palate. Fullish body. Ample, rich, ripe and succulent. Excellent depth and grip. Complex and multidimensional at the end. *Grand vin!* (March 2004)

NOW TO 2025+   20.0

Le Chambertin, 1990
Domaine Jean and Jean-Louis Trapet

Magnum. Good colour. Full, rich, fat and concentrated. Good touch of oak. Very good depth and class and vigour. This is rather better than I remember. Proper Chambertin definition. Lots of substance. Intense, balanced and aristocratic. Very good grip. Only just ready. Bags of life. Very fine. (June 2000)

NOW TO 2015   18.5

Chambertin, Clos de Bèze, 1990
Domaine Armand Rousseau

Full colour. Barely mature. Full, rich nose. Concentrated and vigorous. Chocolaty almost. Fullish on the palate. Lots of wine here. Splendidly balanced. Profound and fruity. Very fine indeed. Now ready, but bags of life left. (April 2003)

NOW TO 2019   19.5

Chambolle-Musigny, 1990
Domaine Dujac

Good fullish colour. Very ripe, fragrant, cool and intense. Really quie rich and succulent. Medium-full body. Good grip. Good structure and texture. Creamy. Vigorous. Complex. Very long. Very good indeed for a village wine. (March 2005)

NOW TO 2016   16.0

Chambolle-Musigny, 1990
Domaine Joseph Faiveley

Fullish, mature colour. Soft, ripe, round and full of fruit. Fully mature. Medium body. Quite delicate. Good balance and intensity. Very classic Chambolle. Very good for what it is. (April 2003)
NOW TO 2008 15.0

Chambolle-Musigny, 1990
Domaine Jacques-Frédéric Mugnier

Medium-full colour. Firm, classy nose. Medium-full body. Very lovely fruit and excellent grip. Poised and definitive. Very complex. Very fresh. Very fine for a village wine. Subtle. Delicious. (March 2000)
NOW TO 2009 16.5

Chambolle-Musigny, 1990
Maison Remoissenet Père et Fils

Fullish, mature colour. Not a lot of depth or elegance on the nose. Medium body. Not a lot of grip or dimension. Decent balance. But essentially dull. (March 2005)
NOW TO 2008 13.5

Chambolle-Musigny, 1990
Domaine Georges Roumier et Fils

Good colour. Now just about ready. Rich, fullish, classy and mellow. Lovely fruit. Succulent and ripe and delicious. Fine for what it is. (January 2001)
NOW TO 2000 16.5

Chambolle-Musigny, Les Amoureuses, 1990
Domaine Joseph Drouhin

Fullish colour. Now mature. Quite oaky on the nose and palate. Rich, full and succulent on the palate. A lovely, ripe, abundant wine with very good balance and a naturally sweet, seductive finish. Very good grip. Lots of depth and class. Fresh, elegant, rich and very long. This is very fine plus. A very lovely wine. Still very vigorous. (December 2003)
NOW TO 2013 19.0

Chambolle-Musigny, Les Amoureuses, 1990
Domaine Georges Roumier et Fils

Medium-full colour. Still a little tough on the nose. Even a hint of reduction and the stems.

Medium-full body. Ripe. Good fruit. But the class of Amoureuses and the sheer distinction of the climat are not here. Very good, but a little disappointing for what it is. Fully ready. (March 2004)
NOW TO 2015 16.0

Chambolle-Musigny, Les Athets, 1990
Domaine Jean Tardy et Fils

Good colour. Very oaky on the nose, and charred oak at that. Some fruit on the palate but rather rigid. Medium-full body. There doesn't seem to be a great deal on the follow-through. A little more fruit than his Nuits-Saint-Georges Aux Bas de Combe though. Quite good plus. (June 2000)
DRINK UP 15.5

Chambolle-Musigny, Les Charmes, 1990
Domaine Ghislaine Barthod

Good mature colour. This is rich and ample. Fullish body. Balanced. Plenty of fruit. Good class. But very good plus, rather than fine. (June 2000)
DRINK SOON 16.5

Chambolle-Musigny, La Combe d'Orveau, 1990
Domaine Anne Gros

Medium-full colour. Fresh, fragrant nose. Very Chambolle in style. This is from the village part of this *climat*. Medium to medium-full. Very well balanced. Beautifully fragrant, intense fruit. Laid-back. Very lovely. Very long. Fine. (June 2000)
DRINK SOON 17.5

Chambolle-Musigny, La Combe d'Orveau, 1990
Domaine A.F. Gros

Village *appellation contrôlée*. Fine colour. Fullish, rich, fat and succulent. Very lovely fruit. Finely balanced. Not as special as the wines Anne produces today. Long and fresh and succulent. Very good. (March 2000)
DRINK SOON 16.0

Chambolle-Musigny, Les Fuées, 1990
Domaine Jacques-Frédéric Mugnier

Most impressive. Good colour. Splendid, rich, concentrated fruit. Medium-full body. Lots of class and depth. Fat and succulent. Very long. Very Chambolle. Fine plus. (June 2003)

NOW TO 2018   18.0

Charmes-Chambertin, 1990
Domaine Denis Bachelet

Medium-full, mature colour. Not as exquisite as the wines today. Just a little lumpy on the nose. On the palate, much more together. Ripe and balanced. Very fresh. Slightly rigid but fine. (April 2006)

NOW TO 2020   17.5

Charmes-Chambertin, 1990
Maison Pierre Bourée et Fils

Medium to medium-full colour. Fully mature. Dried out, rustic nose. Similar palate. Not astringent, but with little grace. Quite fresh and fruity. (April 2006)

DRINK SOON   14.0

Charmes-Chambertin, 1990
Domaine Joseph Drouhin

Full colour. Some development. Slightly cooked fruit on the nose. Full, rich, concentrated, ample and slightly spicy. Plenty of substance. Fullish body. Splendidly rich and exotic on the palate. Very good grip. Fully ready. Plenty of energy. Sweet and long at the end. Fine. (October 2005)

NOW TO 2020   17.5

Charmes-Chambertin, 1990
Domaine Claude Dugat

Medium-full colour. Some development. Lovely ripe nose. Just beginning to come round. Fullish body. Very concentrated and vigorous. Very lovely succulent fruit. Excellent grip. Long. Very fine. (October 2006)

NOW TO 2025   18.5

Charmes-Chambertin, 1990
Domaine Bernard Dugat-Py

Full, vigorous colour. Very lovely fragrant nose. This is quite splendid. Marvellous fruit, and very long and complex. Exquisite. This on the palate is equally lovely. Fullish body. Slightly

spicy. Very good grip. Long, complex, classy and very fine indeed. (April 2006)

NOW TO 2025   19.5

Charmes-Chambertin, 1990
Domaine Dujac

Good fullish, fully mature colour. Soft, velvety, gently oaky, fully ready, open nose. Only of medium weight. On the palate, ripe and fruity, elegant and intense, but not with the greatest weight or depth. Very creamy, very easy to drink. Good grip and class. But it lacks a little something at the end for fine. Very good indeed. (October 2001)

NOW TO 2012   17.0

Charmes-Chambertin, 1990
Domaine Geantet-Pansiot

Good youthful colour. Slightly lumpy and ungainly on the palate. Decent fruit here. But a bit four-square. Lacks flair. Medium-full body. Fat and meaty. Decent fruit and grip. Decent finish. Quite good plus. (April 2006)

NOW TO 2012   14.5

Charmes-Chambertin, 1990
Domaine Georges Lignier et Fils

Fullish, youthful colour. Nicely rich nose. Good fruit. Ample. Long. Fresh. Fullish body on the palate. Medium body. Well matured but fresh and not astringent or short. Ripe and persistent. Medium to medium-full body. Very good. (April 2006)

NOW TO 2015   16.0

Charmes-Chambertin, 1990
Domaine Hubert Lignier

Full colour. Meaty, new oaky nose. This tends to dominate. Rich, full, quite oaky nose. Not too much for most, but a bit rigid for me. Later vintages are better. (April 2006)

NOW TO 2015   16.0

Charmes-Chambertin, 1990
Maison Mommessin

Good youthful colour. Slightly volatile on the nose. Medium-full body. No great tannic structure, but fresh, ripe and juicy. Slightly hot. Good acidity. But altogether, not an enormous amount of finesse. Fully ready. (March 2001)

NOW TO 2008 15.0

Charmes-Chambertin, 1990
Domaine Henri Perrot-Minot
Magnum. Good colour. Still vigorous. On the nose, a little four-square. Fullish body. Good acidity. Slightly solid. Not over-extracted. Not hot, but with a lack of nuance and class. Plenty of fruit. Plenty of vigour. Very good but not great. (April 2005)

NOW TO 2010+ 16.0

Charmes-Chambertin, 1990
Maison Roland Remoissenet et Fils
Medium-full, mature colour. Soupy nose. Lacks freshness and style. Soft, sweet and quite fresh. Yet a bit bland. Medium weight. Quite long. Good but no better. (April 2006)

NOW TO 2011 15.0

Charmes-Chambertin, Très Vieilles Vignes, 1990
Domaine Joseph Roty
Fullish, mature colour. Splendidly ample, very fresh nose. Ripe and succulent. Fullish body. Very intense. Very fine grip. Very, very concentrated. Lots of energy. This is very, very fine. Splendid finish. Very, very long on the palate. (March 2004)

NOW TO 2025 19.5

Charmes-Chambertin, 1990
Domaine Christophe Roumier
Full, fresh colour. Full fresh nose. Lovely slightly restrained fruit. Medium-full weight. High toned. Very classy. Fresh and balanced. Excellent follow-through. Very fine plus. (April 2006)

NOW TO 2025 19.0

Charmes-Chambertin, 1990
Domaine Armand Rousseau
Medium-full colour. Now just about ready. Fragrant, soft-centred nose. Ripe and balanced and fresh and attractive. As always, not the greatest of depth and concentration compared with the best Charmes, but rich and succulent. Now ready. Easy to drink and most enjoyable. (July 2003)

NOW TO 2010 17.0

Charmes-Chambertin, 1990
Domaine Christian Sérafin
Good colour. Quite new oaky on the nose, and I think it always will be. This gives a certain rigidity, also apparent on the attack, to the wine, because, oak apart, it is not that full bodied or concentrated. Medium-full on the palate. Quite rich. The tannins are now absorbed. Lots of woody spices. Good fruit and grip. Positive finish. I think the wines are better today, judging by the 1996s. This is very good indeed. (December 2000)

NOW TO 2010 17.0

Charmes-Chambertin, Vieilles Vignes, 1990
Domaine des Varoilles
Good full, mature colour. Quite rich, fragrant, stylish and mellow on the nose. Mature but still vigorous. Medium-full body. Ripe and abundant. Classy and quite concentrated. Still fresh. Sweet at the end. Very good indeed. (May 2004)

NOW TO 2010 17.0

Clos des Lambrays, 1990
Domaine des Lambrays
Fullish, mature colour. Rich, funky nose. Slight whiff of the stems. Slightly astringent. But plenty of depth. Medium to medium-full body. Ample and sensuous. Also best with food, for it's is a little dry on the follow-through. Yet quite fresh on the finish and very complex. Very good indeed. (September 2004)

NOW TO 2010+ 17.0

Clos de la Roche, 1990
Domaine Joseph Drouhin
Medium-full, mature colour—less than the Clos Saint-Denis. Full, rich, ample, succulent and vigorous on the nose. Less aromatic than the Clos Saint-Denis. More reserved. Masculine.

Splendid fruit on the palate. Very classy. Very long. Very lovely. This is very fine, too. Will still improve. (March 2003)

NOW TO 2020+   18.5

Clos de la Roche, 1990
Domaine Dujac

Medium to medium-full colour. Fully ready. Ripe, soft and fragrant on the nose. Cool, even a little lean. Yet at the same time, almost sweet. Medium to medium-full on the palate. Complex. Fine plus. (March 2005)

NOW TO 2015+   18.0

Clos de la Roche, 1990
Domaine Leroy

Fullish, mature colour. Rich, voluptuous, succulent nose. Plenty of vigour. Full body. Very good energy. Lovely rich fruit. Very plummy. Now ready, but plenty of life still. Rather more structured than pretty well all other 1989s. Long. Fine plus. (April 2006)

NOW TO 2020   18.0

Clos de la Roche, 1990
Domaine Hubert Lignier

Good fullish, mature colour. Meaty nose. Quite oaky. A little dense. But good grip and fruit. Fullish body. Slightly rigid. Still a little unresolved tannin. Underneath, there is some very good, ripe, even rich fruit. And good acidity as well. The net result is very good plus. It lacks flair and nuance for better. (April 2006)

NOW TO 2019   16.5

Clos de la Roche, Cuvée Vieilles Vignes, 1990
Domaine Ponsot

Splendidly full, vigorous colour. Very delicious nose. This is a much more interesting wine than the 1989. Full body. Very fresh. Excellent fruit. Very classy. Very complex. Very special. Only just ready. (March 2006)

NOW TO 2025   19.0

Clos de la Roche, 1990
Domaine Armand Rousseau

Fresh, fullish, mature colour. Ripe, aromatic nose. Medium-full on the palate. Not the greatest

of concentration or depth, but very good plus. Still youthful but fully ready. (April 2004)

NOW TO 2010   16.0

Clos de la Roche, 1990
Domaine Jacky Truchot-Martin

Full colour. No undue maturity. This has all the ample, full richness of the vintage. But underneath, it is a little rustic and stemmy. *À point.* Good plus. (October 2004)

NOW TO 2010   15.5

Clos Saint-Denis, 1990
Domaine Joseph Drouhin

Fullish, mature colour. Lovely rich nose with a very 1990 whiff of mocha/coffee/chocolate. Rich, full bodied and ample on the palate. Very good grip and vigour. Lots of depth. Opulent, long and elegant. Very fine. Only just ready. (March 2003)

NOW TO 2025   18.5

Clos Saint-Denis, 1990
Domaine Dujac

Medium-full, mature colour. Lovely ripe, succulent fruit. Fresh, balanced, mellow and stylish. Medium-full body. Fragrant. Almost sweet. Silky-smooth. Very good well absorbed tannins. Not the depth of his 1990 Clos de la Roche, but long and fine. (October 2004)

NOW TO 2020   17.5

Clos Saint-Denis, 1990
Domaine Heresztyn

Magnum. Medium to medium-full colour. Not a very full, fat or intense nose. But quite decent fruit. A little insignificant for a *grand cru*. Ripe and pleasant, though. But no more than very good plus. (June 2000)

DRINK UP   16.5

Clos Saint-Denis, Vieilles Vignes, 1990
Domaine Ponsot

Splendid full, barely mature colour. Rich, sensuous and finely balanced. Exotic and very distinguished. Very clean uncooked Pinot Noir. Full but very, very fresh and very, very fragrant. This is quite splendid. Complex. Cool. Very, very long and very, very lovely fruit. Undoubtedly a 20/20 wine. Absolutely everything in place. À *point*, but bags of life. More muscular than their Clos de la Roche. (June 2005)

NOW TO 2020   20.0

Clos de Tart, 1990
Domaine du Clos de Tart

Fullish, youthful, barely mature colour. Slight touch of reduction. Full, rich, meaty and now mature. Aromatic, concentrated and succulent. Balanced. Slightly animal/gamey. Very good indeed. (April 2005)

NOW TO 2015   17.0

Clos de Vougeot, 1990
Maison Champy

Medium-full colour. Barely mature. Youthful, fresh nose. Good grip. Not as cooked as some 1990s. Still immature on the palate. Some tannin. Slightly four-square. Ripe and stylish. Will get more succulent as it rounds off. Still far too young. But potentially fine. (January 2001)

NOW TO 2015   17.5

Clos de Vougeot, 1990
Domaine Chopin-Groffier

Fine colour. Pure, balanced, poised and fresh on the nose. Quite high-toned, especially when compared with the Champy. Fullish body. Just a little tannin. Ripe, plump and old viney. Slightly more evolved than most. Spicy. Long. Fine plus. (June 2000)

NOW TO 2010   18.0

Clos de Vougeot, 1990
Domaine Joseph Drouhin

Fullish colour. Some sign of maturity. A rich, fat, slightly caramelly-flavoured wine. Good grip. No lack of substance. Ripe and full bodied and succulent on the palate. Very good grip. This is fat and voluptuous. Plenty of class. Fine. (March 2003)

NOW TO 2015   17.5

Clos de Vougeot, 1990
Domaine René Engel

Full colour. Lovely fresh, ripe, rich nose. Splendidly ample, rich and succulent fruit. This is very lovely. Intense, classy and very clean. Still very youthful, but now à *point* (just about). Very elegant. Rich and opulent. Very fine. (January 2006)

NOW TO 2025   18.5

Clos de Vougeot, 1990
Domaine Jean Grivot

Magnum. Good full immature colour. The nose is still a little closed at first. Fullish body. Still just a little tannin. Lovely, ripe, succulent, classy fruit. Very good acidity. Less 1990 in character, less exotic than a lot of wines. Nicely austere. Complex, fragrant, classy and vigorous. Will still improve. (November 2001)

NOW TO 2024   18.0

Clos de Vougeot, 1990
Domaine Alain Hudelot-Noëllat

Full, mature colour. Round, ripe, sweet, spicy nose. Lots of depth and class. Full, fat and velvety. Good grip. Plenty of texture but vigorous, fresh and very lovely. À *point*. (March 2005)

NOW TO 2015   18.0

Clos de Vougeot, 1990
Domaine Leroy

Medium-full colour. Just about mature. Full, quite firm, cooked fruit nose. Good depth here. Cooler on the palate. Medium-full body. Balanced, rich and poised. A little tannin, but not a bit larger than life. Finishes long and elegant. Fine. (April 2000)

NOW TO 2015   17.5

Clos de Vougeot, 1990
Domaine Mongeard-Mugneret

Magnum. Fine colour. Very excellent fruit. Some oak. Very lovely acidity. Rather more classy than I had expected. Fullish body. Fresh, juicy and succulent. The tannins are now soft, but the wine is vibrant and will still round off. Fine. (October 2000)

NOW TO 2018   17.5

Clos de Vougeot, 1990
Domaine Jacques Prieur

The colour is quite evolved. Not that full. Medium to medium-full body. This has evolved fast and now seems to be losing its grip. Ripe. Pleasant. But won't improve. Quite good plus. (June 2000)

DRINK SOON   14.5

Clos de Vougeot, 1990
Domaine Daniel Rion

Full, still very youthful colour. Still a little austere but pure and unexpectedly (for Rion) classy. Really fine fresh Pinot. Fullish body. Still a little tannin. Good concentration. Very good grip and lots of finesse and energy. Very fine. (March 2004)

NOW TO 2018   18.5

Clos de Vougeot, Grand Maupertuis, 1990
Domaine Anne and François Gros

Fine colour. Still very youthful. Marvellously rich, old-viney nose. Full but now just about mellow on the nose. Very classy. Very concentrated. Excellent grip. This is really delicious. Splendid depth and vigour. But not the definition and class of her wines today. Long finish. Fine plus. (September 2002)

NOW TO 2020   18.0

Clos de Vougeot, Grand Maupertuis, 1990
Domaine Jean Gros

Medium to medium-full colour. Now mature. Soft nose. Balanced and elegant. Lovely and fragrant. Impressive class and distinction, considering the vines were only 4 years old. Very good intensity and length, if only medium body. Really elegant. Fine. (June 2000)

NOW TO 2010   17.5

Clos de Vougeot, Musigni, 1990
Domaine Gros Frère et Soeur

Given the age of the vines, hardly 8 years at the time, this is really very respectable. Good structure. Ripe and succulent. Not to oaky. Good balance, if not great class or depth. (November 2000)

NOW TO 2010   16.0

Corton, 1990
Maison Champy

Good colour. Fullish nose, though not much style. This is evolved and rather thin and insipid now, given *cru* and vintage. Lacks class. Only fair—at best. Drink up. (January 2001)

DRINK UP   13.5

Corton, Bressandes, 1990
Domaine Chandon de Briailles

Medium colour. Fully evolved. Some evidence of the stems on the nose. Not a great deal of weight or concentration: or indeed style. Rather weak on the palate. A little insignificant. Reasonable quality, but no vigour. Only quite good. (June 2000)

DRINK UP   14.0

Corton, Clos des Cortons Faiveley, 1990
Domaine Joseph Faiveley

Fullish colour. Ample on the nose. Good backbone. Ripe and lovely on the palate. Very good grip. Classy. Not a bit tough. But better still in 2 years' time. Fine plus. (January 2006)

NOW TO 2020   18.0

Corton, Clos du Roi, 1990
Domaine Charles Thomas

Fine colour. Reasonable nose. Slightly mean and lean. Ungainly. Medium-full body. Slightly unripe and lumpy. This is only average. Medium body. This is very disappointing. (October 2002)

DRINK SOON   13.0

Corton, Renardes, 1990
Domaine Leroy

Good full colour. Still youthful. Rich, opulent, slightly chocolaty, slightly sauvage underneath. Full body. Slightly cooked fruit. Not as clean or as elegant as 1995, 1996 or 1998. Slightly animal. Slightly lumpy. Very good for the vintage but no better. (April 2000)

NOW TO 2012+   16.0

Echézeaux, 1990
Domaine Dujac

Full, rich nose. Barely mature. Nicely ripe, even a shade overripe, on the nose. Voluptuous.

Medium-full body. Tannins well absorbed. Rich finish. Almost sweet. Long. Most seductive. Very good indeed. (October 2001)

NOW TO 2010+   17.0

Echézeaux, 1990
Domaine Joseph Faiveley

Full colour. Now a touch of maturity. Still a little adolescent on the nose. The tannins are in evidence. Better on the palate. Fullish body. Ample, rich, even exotic. Quite tannic but now softening. The finish is rich and warm. Fine. (September 2002)

NOW TO 2020   17.5

Echézeaux, 1990
Maison Camille Giroud

Full, profound, concentrated and old viney. Splendid richness. Ready but with plenty of vigour. Multidimensional black fruit flavour. Fine plus. (September 2002)

NOW TO 2010+   18.0

Echézeaux, 1990
Domaine Jayer-Gilles

Very full, youthful colour. Quite an extracted nose. But full and with plenty of fruit. Not too tannic, as some of Domaine Jayer-Gilles's wines regularly are. Full body. Quite tannic on the palate. Very good grip. Austere. The fruit is cool. Lacks a little real elegance. Very good plus. (March 2000)

NOW TO 2015   16.5

Echézeaux, 1990
Domaine Manière-Noirot

Good colour. Fresh, stylish nose. But a little lean at first. Medium body. Pleasant, but lacks a little generosity and concentration. Fresh though. But not a lot of style. Rich and vigorous, nevertheless, and it put on weight and style as it developed. Very good. (October 2002)

NOW TO 2010   16.0

Echézeaux, 1990
Domaine Mugneret-Gibourg

Good colour. Splendid nose. Pure and concentrated. Fresh and vigorous. Fullish body. Gently

oaky. Ripe and plummy. Very good grip. Still just a bit of tannin to resolve. Vigorous. Excellent follow-through. Really classy and complex. Fine plus. (June 2000)

NOW TO 2010   18.0

Echézeaux, 1990
Domaine Emmanuel Rouget

Fullish, vigorous colour. Rich, full, youthful, oaky nose. Fullish bodied, concentrated, old viney, harmonious and intense. This is very lovely. Lots of depth. Very, very long. Very, very classy. Very fine. Only just ready. (October 2004)

NOW TO 2025   18.5

Gevrey-Chambertin, 1990
Domaine Jacky Confuron-Cotétidot

Medium to medium-full colour. Now mature. Ample nose. Plump and ripe, but not with a lot of weight. Pleasant, but not with the greatest depth. Slight mocha/liquorice flavours. Decent intensity with backbone. Curiously flavoured. Lots of nice fruit, though. Good plus. (June 2000)

DRINK UP   15.5

Gevrey-Chambertin, 1990
Domaine Denis Mortet

Magnum. Good colour. Fullish, rich, ripe and succulent on the nose. Slightly hot on the palate. Slightly forced. It lacks grace. Good for a village wine, though. Plenty of vigour. Good. (June 2000)

DRINK SOON   15.0

Gevrey-Chambertin, Vieilles Vignes, 1990
Domaine Alain Burguet

Fullish, mature colour. Rich, full, succulent nose. Good class, too. Fullish body. Good grip. Still some tannin to resolve. But there is concentration and depth here. Will still improve. Very good. But perhaps a little pruney: not the sheer elegance for fine. A little sturdy. I have had better bottles. (October 2004)

NOW TO 2020   16.0

Gevrey-Chambertin, Vieilles Vignes, 1990
Domaine Bernard Dugat-Py

Medium-full, mature colour. Slightly muddy on the nose. Soft on the palate. Not the greatest of class. Quite good only. (March 2006)

NOW TO 2010   14.0

Gevrey-Chambertin, Les Cazetiers, 1990
Domaine Bruno Clair

Magnum. Medium to medium-full colour. This is cool and classy but on the light side. Nice chestnut and oak flavours. Slightly lean, but intense, balanced and elegant. Perhaps in 1990 it should have had a bit more weight. Long, though. Very good indeed. (June 2000)

DRINK UP   17.0

Gevrey-Chambertin, Les Cazetiers, 1990
Domaine Joseph Faiveley

Fullish colour. Barely mature. Fullish nose. Still a little tight. Lots of lovely fruit underneath. Medium-full body. The tannins are resolved, and there is good fresh acidity. But it needs time. Currently lacks a little charm. (March 2006)

NOW TO 2020   18.0

Gevrey-Chambertin, Les Champeaux, 1990
Domaine Joseph Drouhin

Full colour. Not yet ready. Full, rich, ample, slightly spicy, slightly chunky nose. A fresh, medium-full bodied wine on the palate. Good ripe tannins. Good acidity. This has plenty of depth and style for what it is (a second-division Gevrey-Chambertin *premier cru*). Long, positive and very good plus. (March 2003)

NOW TO 2012+   16.5

Gevrey-Chambertin, En Champeaux, 1990
Domaine Denis Mortet

Medium-fullish, mature colour. Not with the depth the 1995 or 1993 would indicate. Good, but not the greatest of depth, concentration or finesse on the nose. Medium-full body. Rich, aromatic, slightly cooked fruit. Good grip. This shows the quality of 1990, but for the vintage, it

is not much better than the 1991. Will still last. (May 2002)

NOW TO 2012   15.5

Gevrey-Chambertin, Les Champonnets, 1990
Domaine Heresztyn

Medium-full colour. Good depth and grip, better than the Corbeaux. Slightly more structure. Slightly more freshness and refinement. Good finish. Very good. (June 2000)

DRINK SOON   16.0

Gevrey-Chambertin, Champonnet, Vieilles Vignes, 1990
Domaine des Varoilles

Medium colour. Fragrant on the nose. Medium weight. No lack of fruit, and good acidity. But a touch lean for the vintage. The tannins are now more or less absorbed. But the wine lacks a little richness and succulence. Good plus. (July 2002)

DRINK SOON   15.5

Gevrey-Chambertin, Clos du Meix des Ouches, 1990
Domaine des Varoilles

Village *appellation contrôlée*. From up in the valley beyond Lavaux Saint-Jacques. A monopole, I believe, of the Domaine des Varoilles. Their wines here are always a little lean, but this is to some extent moderated by the vintage. Medium to medium-full colour. Now mature. Fresh, fragrant, pure nose, if of no great weight or concentration. Medium body. Decent complexity and depth. Good balance. Still very fresh. Finishes long and positively, if rather austere. The wine lacks succulence. But very good for a village wine. No lack of originality. (August 2001)

NOW TO 2010   15.5

Gevrey-Chambertin, Clos Saint-Jacques, Vieilles Vignes, 1990
Domaine Fourrier

Medium-full colour. No undue maturity. An element of volatile acidity on the nose. This makes it a bit inky on the palate. Medium to medium-full body. Ripe and balanced and otherwise quite stylish. Now mellow. Slight astringent touches at the end. Good, but not by any means exceptional. Jean-Claude's son, Jean-Marie, produces much better wine today. (November 2002)

DRINK SOON   15.0

Gevrey-Chambertin, Clos Saint-Jacques, 1990
Domaine Louis Jadot

Fullish, mature colour. Still youthful on the nose. Full and rich. Still needs time. Full body. Still some tannin. Very concentrated. Still quite firm. A little more time is still required. But this is very lovely and very profound. Very good grip. Excellent finish. Very fine plus. (April 2005)

NOW TO 2030   19.0

Gevrey-Chambertin, Clos Saint-Jacques, 1990
Domaine Armand Rousseau

Medium-full, mature colour. More mature than the Mazis, less so than the Ruchottes. The nose combines the fruit of the former and the grip of the latter, and then adds some. Very profound. Full, ample, balanced and *à point*. Multidimensional. High class. Very lovely finish. (April 2005)

NOW TO 2020+   18.5

Gevrey-Chambertin, Clos des Varoilles, Vieilles Vignes, 1990
Domaine des Varoilles

Medium to medium-full colour. Still quite youthful. Ripe, mature Pinot Noir, but with no great strength or concentration. Good acidity. Medium body. Quite lean for the vintage. Ripe and stylish, soft and round. The acidity shows at the end. It lacks a bit of generosity. Very good rather than great. (December 2001)

DRINK SOON   16.0

Gevrey-Chambertin, Combe au Moine, 1990
Domaine Fourrier

Fullish colour. Soft, spicy nose. Quite roasted nutty and caramelly, too. Very mellow. Nice and fresh. Medium-full body. Ripe, rich, stylish fruit. Plenty of depth and length. Good concentration. Long and complex. This is very good indeed, even fine. Fully ready. (May 2003)

NOW TO 2013+   17.0

Gevrey-Chambertin, Les Combottes, 1990
Domaine Dujac

Medium-full, mature colour. Slight touch of both stems and mushrooms on the nose. Ripe and mellow and evolved. Medium-full body. Rich, cool and balanced. Fresher than the nose would suggest. Very good grip. Long, complex and vigorous. Lovely finish. Fine. (April 2003)

NOW TO 2013   17.5

Gevrey-Chambertin, Les Corbeaux, 1990
Domaine Denis Bachelet

Medium-full colour. Good nose. As always, class and intensity here. Fullish, rich, ample and concentrated. Beautiful poise and balance. Very lovely fruit. This is living up to all expectations for the vintage. Very long. Very classy. Very lovely. (June 2000)

NOW TO 2010   17.5

Gevrey-Chambertin, Les Corbeaux, 1990
Domaine Heresztyn

Medium to medium-full colour. Ripe, slightly oaky and obvious. Slightly over-evolved. Ripe. But good plus, rather than great. It lacks class and depth for better. (June 2000)

DRINK UP   15.5

Gevrey-Chambertin, Les Fontenys, 1990
Domaine Joseph Roty

Slightly lean on the nose, especially for a 1990. Medium body on the palate. Soft. Not very concentrated. Curiously anonymous. Weak. Lacks grip. OK but not brilliant. (October 2002)

DRINK SOON   14.0

Gevrey-Chambertin, Fonteny, 1990
Domaine Christian Sérafin

Good colour. Now just about mature. Fragrant on the nose. Not aggressive. Not over-macerated. Now fully ready. Sweet and fruity. Good grip. Not cooked. In fact, very elegant and very well balanced. Rich. Medium-full body. More Fonteny than 1990 in character. Fine. (January 2001)

NOW TO 2010+   17.5

Gevrey-Chambertin, En Reniard, 1990
Domaine Alain Burguet

Good colour. Firm-ish, fresh nose. Good style. Ripe. Only medium body and intensity and dimension. But fragrant and stylish. Very good for what it is. (June 2000)

DRINK UP 16.0

Gevrey-Chambertin, La Romanée, 1990
Domaine des Varoilles

Premier cru. Fresh, medium-full, mature colour. The nose now shows secondary if not tertiary flavours: mushroomy, soft, mellow spices and woods. Quite ripe fruit, but not a lot of substance, vigour or intensity, let alone class. Fresh, but with not much dimension. Good. But drink quite soon. (October 2004)

DRINK SOON 15.0

Grands Echézeaux, 1990
Domaine Joseph Drouhin

Fullish colour. Still quite youthful-looking. Splendid nose: rich, full, very classy and profound. Good attack, but slightly reserved. Not quite the volume and richness that I expected on the palate. Yet very fine, certainly. Ample. Very good grip. Better on the follow-through. Still needs 2 years. (March 2003)

NOW TO 2020 18.5

Grands Echézeaux, 1990
Domaine René Engel

Good colour. Fine nose. Lots of volume and depth on the nose. Lovely on the palate. A significant step up on his Clos de Vougeot. Rich and concentrated. Excellent grip. Very lovely, succulent fruit. Very long and lovely. This is very fine. (June 2000)

NOW TO 2010 18.5

Grands Echézeaux, 1990
Domaine Mongeard-Mugneret

Medium-full, well mature colour. Gamey, earthy nose. Not very clean. On the palate, medium to medium-full body. Ripe and with good acidity. Better on the palate than on the nose.

Decent quality. Fully ready. Quite good at best. (October 2005)

NOW TO 2010 14.0

Grands Echézeaux, 1990
Maison Roland Remoissenet et Fils

Good virile colour. Ripe and round and fragrant on the nose. Slightly clumsy and hot on the palate. Medium-full body. Good but not great. Got coarser and coarser in the glass. (March 2001)

DRINK SOON 15.0

Grands Echézeaux, 1990
Domaine de la Romanée-Conti

Fullish, mature colour. Ample, almost sweet, fully mature nose. Rich and ripe and seductive. Medium-full body. Mellow. Intense. Fat and classy. Great class. Very long. Very fragrant. This is very fine. Fully ready. (March 2004)

NOW TO 2020 18.5

Griotte-Chambertin, 1990
Domaine Joseph Drouhin

Good colour. Rich, gently oaky nose. Very finely poised. Beautifully fragrant and splendidly balanced. Rich. Fullish body. Yet intense and delicate. Long and complex. This is very lovely. Classy. Very fine. (June 2000)

NOW TO 2009 18.5

Griotte-Chambertin, 1990
Domaine Fourrier

Medium to medium-full colour. Still youthful. This is more of a 1988 than a 1990. There is a cool, if balanced and elegant, slightly lean touch, and an absence of the usual 1990 richness and exotic spices. Ripe but not rich on the nose. Quite pronounced acidity. Medium body. Fresh and stylish. Good length and complexity. Very good indeed. (December 2000)

NOW TO 2010 17.0

Griotte-Chambertin, 1990
Domaine Ponsot

Medium-full, mature colour. Fragrant nose. Ripe, subtle and fully mature. Medium-full body. Spicy. Good grip. Quite concentrated. But with a slight residual bitterness. And it is not exactly smooth. Lacks a bit of succulence at the end. Very good plus. (October 2004)

NOW TO 2017   16.5

Latricières-Chambertin, 1990
Domaine Camus Père et Fils

Lightish, well matured colour. Stemmy nose. Not too coarse or weedy though. Medium body. Ripe. Quite fresh. Quite stylish. Positive finish. Better than I expected. Good. (April 2005)

DRINK SOON   15.0

Latricières-Chambertin, 1990
Domaine Joseph Drouhin

Fully mature colour. Slightly robust nose. A slight lack of class and a bit of astringency. Medium-full body. Ripe and quite succulent on the palate but a little hot at the end and a little dry. It lacks class. Very good at best. (March 2003)

NOW TO 2010   16.0

Latricières-Chambertin, 1990
Domaine Joseph Faiveley

Fullish colour. Rich, full, oaky nose. Full, concentrated, classy and profound on the palate. Very good acidity. Cool and composed. Complex and multidimensional. Lots of depth and class. Very fine. (April 2005)

NOW TO 2020   18.5

Latricières-Chambertin, 1990
Domaine Leroy

Fullish colour. Splendidly rich, concentrated, oaky nose. A lot of depth and vigour here. Full bodied, rich, aromatic, concentrated and still very vigorous. A meaty example. Exotic and Californian. Classy too. Very fine. (April 2005)

NOW TO 2020+   18.5

Latricières-Chambertin, 1990
Domaine Jean Trapet Père et Fils

Fullish, mature colour. Ripe, ample, concentrated, stylish nose. Plenty of depth. Fullish body. Slightly spicy. Fully mature. Good grip. Just a bit ungainly. Slightly cooked and a bit oxidised. Quite rich. Very good plus. (April 2005)

NOW TO 2010   16.5

Marsannay la Côte, Les Longeroies, 1990
Domaine Bruno Clair

Magnum. This is lovely for what it is. Medium body. Fully evolved. Lovely ripe fruit. Quite complex. Balanced and fragrant. Gentle, fresh and stylish. Quite good. (June 2000)

DRINK SOON   14.0

Marsannay la Côte, Les Saint-Jacques, 1990
Domaine Fougeray de Beauclair

Good colour. Plump, fat, fruity and clean on the nose. This shows well. Medium body. Still quite vigorous. Ample. Good positive finish. Quite good. (June 2000)

DRINK UP   14.0

Mazis-Chambertin, 1990
Domaine Joseph Drouhin

Fullish, mature colour. Lovely fragrant fruit on the nose. Profound and very fresh for a 1990. Fullish body. Mature but vigorous. Ripe, rich and very harmonious. This is very lovely. Lots of depth. Very high quality. Very, very long on the palate. Very fine. (November 2005)

NOW TO 2025   18.5

Mazis-Chambertin, 1990
Domaine Harmand-Geoffroy

Fullish, mature colour. Slightly cooked but ripe nose. The tannins are mellow. Medium-full body. Fresh. Rich. Very good fruit. More classy and harmonious than the nose would suggest. Now à point. Long, lingering, complex finish. Plump and sweet. This is fine. (July 2003)

NOW TO 2015   17.5

Mazis-Chambertin, 1990
Hospices de Beaune

Made by Antonin Rodet. Medium-full, fully mature colour. Rich, concentrated, slightly cooked, slightly reduced nose. This soon blew off. Full, rich, ample, old-viney, creamy chocolate flavours. Still a little tannin. Not a bit too oaky. Excellent grip. Lots of dimension. This is very fine plus. (April 2005)

NOW TO 2020   19.0

Mazis-Chambertin, 1990
Domaine Bernard Maume

Full colour. Rich, fat and rustic, but corked. I don't think it was ever that classy. (April 2005) (SEE NOTE)

Mazis-Chambertin, 1990
Domaine Armand Rousseau

Full colour. Profound, rich, very classy nose. Full and ample. Excellent grip. Very classic. The tannins are now absorbed. This is ready but will keep for ages. Splendid fruit. An exciting example. Very fine. (January 2003)

NOW TO 2018+   18.5

Monthelie, 1990
Domaine Paul Garaudet

Magnum. Medium to medium-full colour. Fresh, plump nose. No lack of style for what it is. Ripe and attractive. Medium-full body. A little astringent. Decent fruit, if not great concentration. Good for what it is. Drink with food. (June 2000)

DRINK UP   14.0

Monthelie, Clos de Meix-Garnier, 1990
Domaine Monthelie-Douhairet

Magnum. Medium colour. Fully mature. Nice fragrant nose. Fresh, juicy nose, but a little astringent on the palate. Slightly better on the finish. Not bad plus. (June 2000)

DRINK UP   13.5

Morey-Saint-Denis, Premier Cru, 1990
Domaine des Lambrays

Medium colour. Mature, aromatic, gamey nose. Medium weight. Good freshness. Good style. Complex and long. Very good. Best with food. (September 2006)

NOW TO 2010   16.0

Morey-Saint-Denis, Clos de la Buissière, 1990
Domaine Georges Roumier

Good colour. Ample, plump nose. Rich and lush, without the rustic edge often apparent here. Chocolate and black cherry on the palate. Still a little unresolved tannin. Fullish body.

Fine potential. Long. Impressive class and balance. Still very fresh. Fine. (June 2000)

NOW TO 2015   17.5

Morey-Saint-Denis, Les Milandes, 1990
Domaine Heresztyn

Medium-full mature colour. Plump, ripe, mature, quite classy nose. Medium-full body. A little tannin to resolve. Rich and fat and ample nevertheless. Balanced and classy. Very good indeed. (June 2000)

NOW TO 2010   17.0

Musigny, 1990
Domaine Leroy

Medium-full colour. Now mature. Gentle for a 1990. Not as big as some, let alone dense. Harmonious and intense, though. Medium-full body only for a 1990. Gently aristocratic and harmonious. Intense and subtle and very Musigny. Long and very fine indeed. (April 2000)

NOW TO 2015+   19.5

Musigny, 1990
Domaine Daniel Moine-Hudelot

Full, youthful colour. Fine but not great nose. Slightly chunky. Lacks a little Musigny fragrance. It doesn't really sing on the nose, especially compared with his Bonnes Mares. I tried another bottle which was much better: properly fragrant, properly classy. This was medium-full bodied, fresh, not a bit cooked, indeed very lovely: long, complex, intense, pure and delicious. (October 2005)

NOW TO 2020   19.0

Musigny, 1990
Domaine Jacques-Frédéric Mugnier

Very full, vigorous colour. Very lovely pure, clean, fragrant nose. Excellent fruit. Medium-full body. Impeccable balance. This is intense and very, very lovely. Essence of Pinot Noir. Now *à point*. Complex and multidimensional. Very, very long. Super! (October 2004)

NOW TO 2025   19.5

Musigny, 1990
Domaine Jacques Prieur

Full colour. Still very youthful. On the nose, still quite a way from maturity. Ripe and rich but a little dense. On the palate this is full bodied. There is still some unresolved tannin. Very good grip. But not a lot of class. It seems a little four-square. Decent length. But a little astringent at the end. (November 2002)

NOW TO 2010   14.0

Musigny, 1990
Domaine Comte Georges de Vogüé

Full colour. Only barely ready. Still quite closed-in on the nose. Coffee and mocha flavours. Full-ish body. Now finally beginning to soften up. Intense. Concentrated. Very lovely raspberry fruit. Very good grip. Just a little tannin still to round off. Excellent long, vigorous finish. Potentially excellent. (March 2005)

NOW TO 2030   20.0

Nuits-Saint-Georges, 1990
Domaine Jean Chauvenet

Magnum. Good colour. Not much sign of age. Slightly austere nose. High acidity. A lack of fat. A curious wine. It lacks the ripeness of most 1990s. Young vines, a bit too much of a harvest and then a bit stewed? Slightly rigid. It won't improve with age. (June 2000)

DRINK UP   13.5

Nuits-Saint-Georges, Au Bas de Combe, 1990
Domaine Jean Tardy et Fils

Good colour. Ample, succulent, quite oaky nose. Ripe, full, slightly rigid, slightly astringent tannins. It lacks flexibility. Only quite good. (June 2000)

DRINK UP   14.0

Nuits-Saint-Georges, Les Boudots, 1990
Domaine Leroy

Fullish colour. Rich, ripe, oaky, exotic nose. Lots of depth. High-toned on the palate. Now just about ready. Oaky. Very good concentration.

Fine grip. This is very long, very classy and very fine. (March 2004)

NOW TO 2027   18.5

Nuits-Saint-Georges, Les Boudots, 1990
Domaine Gérard Mugneret

Medium-full colour. Still quite fresh. Very lovely fragrant nose. Stylish fruit. Very Vosne-ish in style. Medium-full body. *À point.* Smooth, ripe and gently oaky. It lacks just a bit of concentration but is elegant and quite long and very good indeed. (June 2000)

DRINK UP   17.0

Nuits-Saint-Georges, Les Cailles, 1990
Domaine Robert Chevillon

Fine colour. Still very youthful. Lovely fragrant nose. Rich and concentrated. Very stylish. Quite full. Still a little residual tannin. Very good grip. Very good fruit. This is very elegant and lovely. Very good indeed. (January 2004)

NOW TO 2020   17.0

Nuits-Saint-Georges, Aux Chaignots, 1990
Maison Joseph Faiveley

Very good colour. Still youthful. Lovely fragrant nose. Very stylish fruit. Medium to medium-full body. Not by any means a blockbuster. But rich and ample and very well balanced. Elegant. Vosne-ish. Long. Fine. (June 2000)

NOW TO 2010   17.5

Nuits-Saint-Georges, Les Chaignots, 1990
Domaine Dr. Georges Mugneret

Fullish colour. Still vigorous. Succulent, plummy, violets nose. It smells like a classy Vosne-Romanée. Intense. No hard edges yet plenty of substance. Fullish body. Just about mellow. Still a little residual tannin. Very good grip. Lots of class. Lovely fruit and plenty of depth. Very long. Fine plus. (September 2003)

NOW TO 2020   18.0

Nuits-Saint-Georges, Aux Chaignots, 1990
Domaine Gérard Mugneret

Full colour. Tight and tannic—I fear a bit too much so—on nose and palate. Full body. Rich. But is it too stewed? Still very aggressive and solid, if not a bit astringent. Difficult to enjoy. (November 2002)

NOW TO 2014   14.0

Nuits-Saint-Georges, Clos des Forêts Saint-Georges, 1990
Domaine de l'Arlot

Quite full colour. And quite full and rich on the nose and palate. A touch of the stems on the nose. But good depth and succulence. Still youthful. Very good. (June 2001)

NOW TO 2010   16.0

Nuits-Saint-Georges, Clos de la Maréchale, 1990
Domaine Joseph Faiveley

Full colour. Some maturity. Rich, fat, round and quite spicy nose. Fullish body on the palate. A little robust. Still a bit of unresolved tannin. Slightly *sauvage*. Good richness underneath. Needs food. Good plus. (June 2004)

NOW TO 2015   15.5

Nuits-Saint-Georges, Clos Saint-Marc, 1990
Domaine Bouchard Père et Fils

Full colour. Just about mature. Ripe, rich and opulent. A little hot and a vague touch rustic. The wine is fat and plump, but it doesn't have the style of Bouchard's Les Porrets Saint-Georges. Very good. (November 2000)

NOW TO 2010   16.0

Nuits-Saint-Georges, Les Perrières, 1990
Domaine Robert Chevillon

Medium-full, mature colour. Aromatic, cedary nose. More seductive at present than Gouges's 1990 Les Saint-Georges. Medium body. Quite sweet and accessible. Nicely civilised on the follow-through. Balanced. Long. Very good indeed. *À point.* (October 2004)

NOW TO 2020   17.0

Nuits-Saint-Georges, Les Porrets Saint-Georges, 1990
Maison Bouchard Père et Fils

Fullish colour. Just about mature. Lovely stylish, fragrant nose. Just about ready on the palate.

Fullish body. The tannins are now soft. But lots of grip and vigour. Rich, spicy and opulent. Very good indeed. (November 2000)

NOW TO 2010+   17.0

Nuits-Saint-Georges, Les Porrets Saint-Georges, 1990
Domaine Henri Gouges

Fullish colour. Fully mature. Round, ripe, opulent nose. But not very stylish. Drying out a little. Richer on the palate. Fullish body. Smooth. Good, but not a wine with a great deal of finesse. Good. (November 2000)

DRINK SOON   15.0

Nuits-Saint-Georges, Les Pruliers, 1990
Domaine Henri Gouges

Good colour. Lovely nose. Rich, cool and very stylish. Now fully ready. Very good grip. Splendidly elegant fresh fruit. Not a bit aggressive. Long and complex. Quite delicious. Very pure. Very vigorous. Fine plus. (January 2006)

NOW TO 2020   18.0

Nuits-Saint-Georges, Les Saint-Georges, 1990
Domaine Robert Chevillon

Fine colour. Still very youthful. Full, rich nose. Good concentration. A little more stuffing than his 1990 Nuits-Saint-Georges Cailles. More complete. Rich. Quite sturdy still. A little tannin. Very concentrated fruit underneath. Lots of depth. Full body. Vigorous. Lovely finish. Fine. (January 2004)

NOW TO 2025   17.5

Nuits-Saint-Georges, Les Saint-Georges, 1990
Domaine Henri Gouges

Medium-full, mature colour. Quite firm, rich, sturdy nose. Still a little austere. Rather more generous and accessible as it developed. On the palate, fullish body and very good acidity. Still a little tannin. Lovely pure fruit. Very long and very profound. Fine. (October 2004)

NOW TO 2025   17.5

Nuits-Saint-Georges, Les Vaucrains, 1990
Domaine Jean Chauvenet

Magnum. Good full youthful colour. On the ripe side in a slightly austere way. Full body.

Slightly astringent. Cool. The tannins are not yet resolved. Rich underneath, but with a lack of smoothness. Good fruit. Good vigour. Very good but not great. (June 2000)

DRINK SOON — 16.0

Nuits-Saint-Georges, Les Vaucrains, 1990
Domaine Robert Chevillon

Fine colour. Still very youthful. Quite closed-in on the nose. A little tannin still on the palate. A sturdy wine. Full body. Muscular. Plenty of depth but perhaps not the class of his 1990 Saint-Georges. Nor the harmony. Plenty of grip and vigour, though. Certainly very good indeed. (January 2004)

NOW TO 2025 — 17.0

Nuits-Saint-Georges, Les Vaucrains, 1990
Domaine Henri Gouges

Full colour. Barely mature. Full, rich, intense and very profound nose. This is excellent. Full body. Still just a little unresolved tannin. Very fine fruit. Lovely balance. Meaty but classy. Absolutely classic. Very fine. (June 2000)

NOW TO 2010 — 18.0

Pernand-Vergelesses, Ile de Vergelesses, 1990
Domaine Chandon de Briailles

Medium colour. Fully mature. Lightish, fragrant nose. Lacks a little vigour and depth. Good acidity, if a touch lean. Stylish. Could have been a bit richer. Good plus. Drink fairly soon. (June 2000)

DRINK UP — 15.5

Pommard, Les Argillières, 1990
Domaine Lejeune

Medium-full mature colour. Ripe, juicy and succulent. No great density or structure. Slightly strangely jammy on the palate. Medium body. A touch of astringency at the end. Curious flavours. Quite good plus. (June 2000)

DRINK UP — 14.5

Pommard, Les Chaponnières, 1990
Domaine Philippe Billard-Gonnet

Good deep colour. Only just mature. Rich and full and profound on the nose. Good ripe aromatic, slightly cooked Pinot fruit. Very

typically 1990. Fullish on the palate. Splendidly integrated tannins. Good grip. This is stylish, complex and highly satisfactory. Good vigour. Lovely finish. (August 2002)

NOW TO 2010+ — 17.5

Pommard, Les Charmots, 1990
Domaine Ballot-Dancer

Good colour. Quite an evolved nose. Ample and plump, if with no great style. Medium-full body. Meaty. No aggressive tannins. This is now ready. Good grip and good vigour. Plenty of wine here. Reasonable style and depth. Good plus. (July 2000)

DRINK SOON — 15.5

Pommard, Clos des Epeneaux, 1990
Domaine du Comte Armand

Full colour. Impressively lovely, full-but-not-too-sturdy nose. Lots of depth. This has evolved very well. Still some tannin on the palate. Full body. Rich. Concentrated. Intense. Lovely fruit. Fine. (March 2004)

NOW TO 2027 — 17.5

Pommard, Clos des Epeneaux, 1990
Maison Camille Giroud

Rich, full, ample and meaty. Spicy and concentrated. Some tannin. Full, expansive and profound. Still needs time. Fine. (March 2005)

NOW TO 2020 — 17.5

Pommard, Clos des Epenots, 1990
Domaine du Chateau de Meursault/Patriarche

Good colour. Fullish, vigorous but now round and *à point*. Good fruit and depth. Stylish, too. Not a fine wine, but rich and fleshy and very good. (October 2000)

DRINK SOON — 16.0

Pommard, Clos du Verger, 1990
Domaine Philippe Billard-Gonnet

Good, fully mature colour. Ripe nose. Lightish and quite evolved, but no undue age. Elegant and balanced. Good fruit but a little less vigour and succulence than the Argillières. Good. (June 2000)

DRINK UP — 15.0

Pommard, Les Epenots, 1990
Domaine Joseph Drouhin

Fullish, fresh colour. Fullish nose. Good depth. A little oak. Rich and meaty but not a bit dense or solid. Indeed, lots of character and class. Similar on the palate. Full body. Ample, succulent and with plenty of dimension. This is fine. Just about ready. (March 2003)

NOW TO 2015   17.5

Pommard, Grand Clos des Epenots, 1990
Domaine de Courcel

Magnum. Fullish, vigorous colour. Good nose: pure and with good acidity. Somewhat lacking in fat and real concentration though, especially for 1990. Nor does it have the substance of a typical Pommard. Nevertheless, on the palate, if still a little raw, it has good weight and plenty of style and depth. A little unresolved tannin still. Good dimension. Good grip. Medium-full body. Positive finish. Improved on aeration. Very good plus. (November 2001)

NOW TO 2018   16.5

Pommard, Les Grands Epenots, 1990
Domaine Héritiers Armand Girardin

Full colour. Rich, full nose. Quite tannic. But very concentrated. Still backward. On the palate, still a touch rigid, but with lovely old-vine fruit. Lots of depth. High quality. Long and fine. (March 2000)

NOW TO 2015   17.5

Pommard, Les Perrières, 1990
Domaine Jean-Michel Gaunoux

Good colour. Vigorous but not dense on the nose. Quite meaty. Plummy and black fruity. Good grip. Rich. Very good, especially for a village Pommard. Really quite elegant. Plenty of future. Good plus. (June 2000)

DRINK SOON   15.5

Pommard, Les Pézerolles, 1990
Domaine Hubert de Montille

Medium-full, mature colour. Fragrant nose. Slight aspects of old tea though. But more succulent as it developed. On the palate, ripe but

slightly lean on the attack. Richer on the follow-through. Medium to medium-full body. Good grip and energy. Resolved tannins. Pure and elegant. À point. Very good indeed. (October 2004)

NOW TO 2018   17.0

Pommard, Rugiens, 1990
Domaine Philippe Billard-Gonnet

Magnum. Good colour. Barely mature. Full and firm on the nose. At first a bit closed. Rich, fat and meaty. Lovely slightly cooked fruit. But cooked in the best sense. Now round and soft. Good grip. Very good indeed. (October 2005)

NOW TO 2015   17.0

Pommard, Les Rugiens, 1990
Domaine Jean-Marc Boillot

Fullish colour. Still vigorous. Full, quite firm, rich, concentrated nose. Spicy on the palate. Full bodied. Good energy. Lots of depth. Plenty of richness. Long, even complex, at the end. Very good. (June 2006)

NOW TO 2015   16.0

Pommard, Les Rugiens, 1990
Domaine de Courcel

Magnum. Good colour. Rich, quite mocha nose. Fullish. Still a little tannin and some of the tannins are a bit artisanal. Good fruit though, and all the richness and volume of the vintage. Very good. May still improve. It is still a little raw. (January 2003)

NOW TO 2015   16.0

Pommard, Les Rugiens, 1990
Domaine Hubert de Montille

Fine full, youthful colour. Lovely fragrant nose. Quite full but not dense on the palate, letting all the elegance come out. Round and fullish. Sweeter than his Taillepieds. As vigorous but, surprisingly, with a little less tannin. More advanced. This is rich, ample and of fine quality. (June 2000)

NOW TO 2009   17.5

Richebourg, 1990
Domaine A.F. Gros

Full colour. Still youthful. Quite firm on the nose. Rich underneath. Fullish body. Ample and succulent. Now softening. No hard edges. Lovely balance. Fresh and round and complex. Lovely sweet, natural finish. Very fine. (April 2006)

NOW TO 2025   19.0

Richebourg, 1990
Domaine Anne Gros

Very full colour. Still very youthful-looking. Splendidly rich nose. Fresh chocolate, cooked plum tart and black cherry. Full but getting round. Exotic. Fullish body. Just about ready, but keeping it a year or too more would be no bad idea. It will get really velvety. Balanced, rich, cool and stylish. Not as great as the 1993, but nevertheless, very fine indeed. (June 2005)

NOW TO 2025   19.5

Richebourg, 1990
Domaine Jean Gros

Full colour. Still youthful. Rich, fragrant, laid-back nose. Fullish, marvellous poise and intensity. Very delicious pure fruit. Not a bit too cooked. Great class. Intense, powerful and profound. Just about perfect. Will still improve. (April 2006)

NOW TO 2030   20.0

Richebourg, 1990
Domaine Leroy

Full colour. Barely mature. Very lovely nose. Fragrant and intense. Old-viney aromas. Ripe, rich but purer and fresher than most 1990s. Lots of intensity and energy. Very good grip. Still very young. Richer, more tannic, oakier than Jean Gros's 1990 Richebourg. But not as good. Very fine. (April 2006)

NOW TO 2030   18.5

Richebourg, 1990
Domaine de la Romanée-Conti

Full colour. Full, rich, backward nose. Very pure. Very fine acidity. Fresh and very, very classy. Fullish body. Very splendidly rich and jammy (in the best sense). Now about ready. Fat, lush and very seductive. Splendid follow-through and very long, classy finish. Very fine. (March 2002)

NOW TO 2020   18.5

La Romanée, 1990
Domaine Bouchard Père et Fils

Medium-full colour. Only just fully mature. Very curious. Nothing much here. Fruity, balanced and ready. This tastes as if it was vinified with the stems. Fullish body. Rather more to it than it seems at first. Rich, intense, intense, very ample, multidimensional fruit. Very well balanced. Long. Now ready but will keep well. Not great for a 1990. Only fine for the vintage. (March 2003)

NOW TO 2012   17.5

Romanée-Saint-Vivant, 1990
Maison Champy

Full, immature colour. Rich but still closed. Firm and quite substantial. Quite a long way from maturity. Very good grip. Cool fruit. Not too cooked. Full body. Ripe tannins. Very lovely fruit. This is certainly very classy indeed. Very fine at the very least. (January 2001)

NOW TO 2020   18.5

Romanée-Saint-Vivant, 1990
Domaine Jean-Jacques Confuron

Fresh, full colour. Fat, rich, typical 1990 cooked plum tart nose. Full body. Intense. Marvellous grip. Very classy as well as rich and voluptuous. Really profound. Still youthful. Very fine indeed. It will keep for ages. (March 2002)

NOW TO 2030   19.5

Romanée-Saint-Vivant, 1990
Domaine Joseph Drouhin

Fullish, mature colour. This is very lovely. Very fragrant nose. Subtle and ethereal. Fullish body. Mellow. Very concentrated in a feminine sort of way. Very lovely fruit. Excellent balance. Ready and very fine indeed. (March 2003)

NOW TO 2020   19.5

Romanée-Saint-Vivant, 1990
Domaine Alain Hudelot-Noëllat

Very full colour. But fully evolved, if not a touch old. This has has the tertiary aromas of a fully mature wine. Round, full bodied, succulent, sexy and aromatic. Underneath, good acidity. Very lovely fruit. Silky and sensuous. Very lovely indeed. More developed than his 1990 Clos de Vougeot, but more complex and with more finesse. But shorter. I don't think this has been as well stored as it could have been. Usually 19/20. Today 18/20. (March 2005)

NOW TO 2010+   18.0

Romanée-Saint-Vivant, 1990
Maison Louis Jadot

Very full, immature colour. Marvellous fruit on the nose. Splendidly rich and excellently ripe and profound. Really very beautiful. On the palate this is full bodied and still a little tannic. Excellent grip and intensity. Very lovely fruit. Marvellous from start to finish. A great wine. (March 2002)

NOW TO 2034   20.0

Romanée-Saint-Vivant, 1990
Domaine Leroy

Very full, immature colour. Intense nose. After the Jadot, obviously vinified with the stems. High acidity. High toned. Fullish body. Good tannins. Excellent grip. Very classy. Still youthful. Very fine intensity. Slightly less fat, but more vibrant than Jadot's. But excellent, nevertheless. (March 2002)

NOW TO 2034   20.0

Romanée-Saint-Vivant, 1990
Domaine de la Romanée-Conti

Fullish colour. Full, rich, fat, creamy, concentrated nose. Lots and lots of depth. Very fine. A big, meaty wine after their 1991. Very good grip. Very full body. Very rich and concentrated on the palate. Splendid finish. Still very, very vigorous. Very fine indeed. Just about ready. (March 2005)

NOW TO 2030   19.5

Ruchottes-Chambertin, 1990
Maison Louis Jadot

Probably from Frédéric Esmonin. Full, vigorous colour. Quite firm, quite backward, full flavoured nose. Full bodied, firm, rich and meaty. High quality. Lots of depth and concentration.

Very lovely pure, complex fruit at the end. Very fine. Will still improve. (October 2004)

NOW TO 2026   18.5

Ruchottes-Chambertin, 1990
Domaine Dr. Georges Mugneret

Medium-full, mature colour. Youthful, vigorous, cool, high quality nose. Very lovely. Medium-full body. Very composed. Subtle and understated. Rich and ripe and cool and harmonious. Very long and complex. Lovely finish. Very fine. (April 2005)

NOW TO 2020+   18.5

Ruchottes-Chambertin, Clos des Ruchottes, 1990
Domaine Armand Rousseau

Fullish colour. Much fuller than their Mazis. Fresh nose. Quite firm. Very good depth. Fullish body. Good grip. Now à point. Nice plummy-chocolate fruit. Cool. Much more interesting than the Mazis. Long. Very fine. (April 2005)

NOW TO 2020+   18.5

Savigny-lès-Beaune, La Dominode, 1990
Domaine Bruno Clair

Good full colour. Just about mature. Sturdy nose. Some tannin. Rich and full bodied. Very lovely fruit. This will still improve. Ripe. Very good indeed. (June 2000)

NOW TO 2012   17.0

Savigny-lès-Beaune, Les Dominodes, 1990
Domaine Jean-Marc Pavelot

Good fullish, mature colour. Lovely rich nose. Meaty and fat. Still a little tannin. Fulllish body. Very good balance. Rich. Plenty of life. Very good. (June 2000)

DRINK SOON   16.0

Savigny-lès-Beaune, Les Lavières, 1990
Domaine Bouchard Père et Fils

Full, vigorous colour. Barely mature. Rich, fat nose. Ripe, vigorous and succulent. A slight sauvage touch. But this gives it its personality. Good grip. Ready, but bags of life. Lovely spicy/mocha rich finish. Very good. (June 2003)

NOW TO 2019   16.0

Savigny-lès-Beaune, Aux Vergelesses, 1990
Domaine Simon Bize et Fils

Medium colour. Slightly lean, stemmy nose. Good acidity. Medium body. A slight lack of generosity. Lacks substance. Only quite good. (June 2000)

DRINK UP 14.0

La Tâche, 1990
Domaine de la Romanée-Conti

Full colour. Rich and immature. The nose is full and firm. Still closed. But rich and profound. A bit dumb at the start. Full body. Vigorous, even powerful on the follow-through. Splendidly rich fruit. More opulent than the 1993. More volume but less classic. This is a big wine. There is still unresolved tannin here. Strangely, it is more oaky than the rest of these younger wines. I prefer the 1993, as it has more class and balance, but this is rich, opulent, exotic, and still a way from its peak. Very fine plus. (March 2003)

NOW TO 2030 19.0

Volnay, Vendanges Sélectionnées, 1990
Domaine Michel Lafarge

Good substance. Stylish, backward for a village wine. Ripe. Very good grip. Very good for what it is. (October 2000)

NOW TO 2012 15.0

Volnay, Premier Cru, 1990
Domaine Michel Lafarge

Fine colour. Ample, rich and focussed and fragrant on both nose and palate. Medium-full body. Fully *à point*. Mellow, complex and classy. Very good indeed. (June 2000)

NOW TO 2010 17.0

Volnay, Les Angles, 1990
Maison Prosper Maufoux

Good colour. Good nose. Medium-full, fragrant and balanced. On the palate there is good fruit and vigour, but it lacks a bit of richness. Clean and pure, though. Still with a bit of tannin. The finish is good. It will get more generous as it develops. Positive and quite classy at the end. Good. (December 2001)

NOW TO 2015 15.0

Volnay, Les Caillerets, Ancienne Cuvée Carnot, 1990
Domaine Bouchard Père et Fils

Full, rich colour. Fat, full, succulent and aromatic. Still vigorous. Slightly cooked fruit. Full body. Still some tannin. Not the nuance of the wines of today. A little chunky. Good energy, though. Very good for the vintage, but not great. The 1991 and 1985 are better. (March 2004)

NOW TO 2012 16.0

Volnay, Les Caillerets, Clos des 60 Ouvrées, 1990
Domaine de la Pousse d'Or

Magnum. Fully mature colour. Splendid nose. Not quite as intense as Lafarge's Clos des Chênes, nor as concentrated. But very lovely, fragrant, very Volnay fruit. Complex and subtle. Rich and opulent. Not quite as big as the Bousse d'Or. Lovely, though. Fine plus. (June 2000)

DRINK SOON 18.0

Volnay, Champans, 1990
Domaine du Marquis d'Angerville

Good colour. Ample, rich nose. Full and meaty. Fullish and ripe and succulent on the palate. Now velvety. Classy and pure and long and fragrant. Lots of class. Fine plus. (June 2005)

NOW TO 2015 18.0

Volnay, Clos de la Bousse d'Or, 1990
Domaine de la Pousse d'Or

Magnum. Very good colour. Lush, exotic and chocolaty on the nose. Really quite a big wine. Fullish body. Good grip. Virile. Rather more 1990 than Volnay. Splendid fruit. Long and multidimensional. Rich and concentrated. Very good indeed. (July 2001)

NOW TO 2010 17.0

Volnay, Clos des Chênes, 1990
Maison Champy

Good colour. Ample on the nose, but with not much Volnay definition. Fullish body. Rich. A little stewed. Decent acidity but not much class. Quite good. (June 2000)

DRINK UP 14.0

Volnay, Clos des Chênes, 1990
Domaine Joseph Drouhin

Fullish colour. Not yet quite mature. Very lovely fragrant nose. Complex, fragrant and classic. Medium-full body. Harmonious, poised and definitive on the palate. Splendid fruit. This is very long and very lovely. Just about ready. (March 2003)

NOW TO 2015   18.0

Volnay, Clos des Chênes, 1990
Domaine Michel Lafarge

Fullish vigorous colour. Still a little adolescent on the nose. Less together than his 1993 Clos des Chênes. Medium-full body. Good grip. Still a little unresolved tannin. Lovely fruit. The finish is the best part. Great class. Very fine. Will still improve. (March 2006)

NOW TO 2030   18.5

Volnay, Clos des Santenots, 1990
Domaine Jacques Prieur

Good, medium-full colour. Round and ripe and spicy, but well matured. Now a bit astringent. It lacks grip. Not evolving very elegantly. Will get tired very soon. Drink soon. (June 2000)

DRINK SOON   13.5

Volnay, Les Frémiets, 1990
Domaine Annick Parent

Good vigorous colour. Ripe, fresh, quite substantial on the nose. Fullish. Still some tannin. Only just ready. Rich. Almost Pommardish. Very good grip and intensity. Long. Fine. (June 2000)

NOW TO 2010   17.5

Volnay, Les Pitures, 1990
Domaine Jean-Marc Boillot

Good colour. Ripe and oaky. Slightly sweet but vigorous nose. On the palate, perhaps a bit too oaky. Fullish body. Some oaky tannins. Will they resolve? Strong, vigorous finish. Juicy. Very good. (June 2000)

DRINK SOON   16.0

Volnay, Santenots, 1990
Domaine Robert Ampeau

Vigorous, delicious and fully ready. More 1990 than Ampeau in style. Not a bit austere or cool.

Rich, ample, fat and chocolaty. Very good plus. (March 2006)

NOW TO 2018   16.5

Volnay, Santenots, 1990
Domaine Louis Jadot

Medium-full colour. Lovely ripe Pinot nose. Pure, clean, concentrated and fragrant. Lovely Volnay character. Fullish body. A little tannin. Good grip. Ample, vigorous, balanced and very classy. Fine. (March 2000)

NOW TO 2015   17.5

Volnay, Santenots du Milieu, 1990
Domaine des Comtes Lafon

Rich, fat, aromatic and even voluptuous on the nose. Fullish bodied, succulent and sweet on the palate. Just about *à point*. But will keep very well. Fine. (February 2005)

NOW TO 2025   17.5

Volnay, Taille Pieds, 1990
Domaine Hubert de Montille

Fullish colour. Ample but still a bit tight and unformed on the nose. Still very youthful. Full body. Rich, fat and concentrated. Still some tannin. Lots of fruit. Intense. Very fine grip. Lots of wine here. Still needs time. Rather more substantial than the wines today. Very fresh. Fine. (October 2003)

NOW TO 2030   17.5

Vosne-Romanée, Les Beaux Monts, 1990
Domaine Leroy

Full, vigorous colour. Rich, full, vigorous nose. Lots of concentration and depth. Full bodied on the palate. Some tannin still to resolve. Plenty of richness. Very good grip. Long and with plenty of dimension at the end. But is it a bit too concentrated? This is a fine example. (October 2004)

NOW TO 2026   17.5

Vosne-Romanée, Les Beaux Monts, 1990
Domaine Daniel Rion et Fils

Medium to medium-full colour. Fully mature. Ripe, rich, fullish nose. Plenty of fruit, if perhaps without the greatest class. Medium to medium-full body. Soft. Slight aspect of cooked fruit. Fresh though. Good but lacks class and nuance. (March 2005)

NOW TO 2015　　　　　　　　　　　　　　15.0

Vosne-Romanée, Aux Brûlées, 1990
Domaine René Engel

Magnum. Good colour. Rich nose, now beginning to get mellow. Good grip. Not too cooked in flavour. Indeed, very classy. Fullish body. Complex and harmonious and very lovely—especially at the end. (January 2003)

NOW TO 2015+　　　　　　　　　　　　　18.0

Vosne-Romanée, Aux Brûlées, 1990
Domaine Méo-Camuzet

Full, vigorous colour. Barely mature. Full, rich, plump nose. Lots of lovely fruit here. Lots of class. Full on the palate. Plenty of vigour and substance. Nothing too tough or tannic. Yet lots of depth and dimension. Very, very long and complex at the end. A very fine example of a very fine vintage. (March 2001)

NOW TO 2020+　　　　　　　　　　　　　18.0

Vosne-Romanée, Les Chaumes, 1990
Domaine Méo-Camuzet

Medium-full colour. Now fully mature. Fragrant nose. Gently oaky. Very stylish. Only medium-full weight. Medium to medium-full on the palate. Fresh and fragrant. Good class and intensity. Fine for a Chaumes. But Chaumes is only second-division Vosne-Romanée *premier cru*. Fully ready. (March 2004)

NOW TO 2015　　　　　　　　　　　　　　17.5

Vosne-Romanée, Clos des Réas, 1990
Domaine Michel Gros

Quite an evolved colour for the vintage. It seems less full and less fresh than the 1989. Rich and mellow but seemingly not very structured nose. Full bodied on the palate. Very good grip. Rich, vigorous and profound. Lots of life. Good backbone and depth. Long, lush and lovely. Fine for the vintage. (December 2003)

NOW TO 2020　　　　　　　　　　　　　　17.0

Vosne-Romanée, Cros Parantoux, 1990
Domaine Henri Jayer

Full colour. Rich, concentrated nose. This is fat, splendidly profound, and with lovely depth. Very fine fruit. Very good grip. Quite oaky but not excessively so. Only just ready. Vigorous and ripe, almost sweet. Not too cooked fruity. Very fresh. A certain rigidity stops it being great, but very fine. (September 2002)

NOW TO 2020　　　　　　　　　　　　　　18.5

Vosne-Romanée, Cros Parantoux, 1990
Domaine Méo-Camuzet

Fine full, vigorous colour. Very lovely nose. Great class and concentration. Splendid fruit. Full body. Rich. More new oaky than the Brûlées. But not a bit too much. Really excellent concentration and grip. Marvellous depth here. Real dimension at the end and still powerful. This is very fine indeed. (March 2001)

NOW TO 2020+　　　　　　　　　　　　　19.0

Vosne-Romanée, Les Gaudichots, 1990
Domaine Thierry Vigot

Good colour. Still a little tough and four-square on the nose. A little over-macerated. But full bodied and rich. Still with some tannin. Good acidity. And very nice fragrant fruit. Improved in the glass. Plenty of vigour, even class as it developed. Very good indeed. (July 2003)

NOW TO 2018　　　　　　　　　　　　　　17.0

Vosne-Romanée, Les Genevrières, 1990
Domaine Leroy

Fine colour. Lovely rôti nose with chocolate and mocha touches. Rich, fat and full bodied. Very good acidity. The attack is fine. Quite tannic still. Good rich fruit. But on the follow-through, not the dimension of a *premier cru*. Very well balanced. Very good plus. Will still improve. (March 2001)

NOW TO 2015　　　　　　　　　　　　　　16.5

Vosne-Romanée, Aux Malconsorts, 1990
Domaine Sylvain Cathiard

Full, vigorous colour. Firm but rich and classy on the nose. Lovely fruit. Excellent grip. Plenty of energy. Fullish body. Very concentrated. Very long. Very good structure. Lovely. Fine plus. (June 2005)

2009 TO 2025   18.0

Vosne-Romanée, Les Suchots, 1990
Domaine Joseph Drouhin

Full, fresh colour. Rich nose but quite firm still. A little closed. Good ripe tannins, but still needs a year or two to soften fully. Full body. Vigorous. Excellent grip and class. Lovely finish. This is a very fine example. Better than their Clos de Vougeot. (March 2003)

NOW TO 2020   18.5

1989

The 1989s, like the 1985s and for the same reason, are uneven. Some of the wines lack acidity. So how you rate the vintage is a question of attitude. Is a glass half-full or half-empty? Looking at the best (and why not? Why waste one's time with the worst), I would say that the 1989s have fulfilled, indeed exceeded, their early promise. At 10 years old and just about mature, the vintage showed itself to be not only succulent and fruity, but balanced and complex and classy as well. Eight years further on, and now fully *à point,* there is still life in the top red wines, though age is beginning to creep into the whites.

→ Rating for the Vintage	
Red	16.5
White	16.5

→ Size of the Crop ←		
(In hectolitres, excluding generic wine)		
	RED	WHITE
Grands Crus	12,673	3,238
Village and Premiers Crus	178,971	41,573
TOTAL	191,644	44,811

WEATHER CONDITIONS

It was a mild winter; indeed there was no real "winter" to speak of. A modicum of rain in the spring produced a good *sortie,* despite a certain amount of frost damage mainly in Gevrey at the end of April. Again, despite one week of poor weather during the flowering and some hail, which at various times during the summer affected Volnay, Savigny-lès-Beaune, Pernand-Vergelesses, Aloxe and Gevrey-Chambertin again, the fruity-set was successful, and the potential crop of a plentiful size. Thereafter, the summer was hot, though not scorching, and dry, though not parched. The first half of September was particularly fine, and the *ban des vendanges* was declared on September 15 for the white wine grapes and September 17 for the Pinot Noir. In the middle of the harvest, there was a day and a half of rain, though not enough to create any serious problems. Most domaines had completed their collection by October 1.

The first and most important factor was the healthy state of the fruit. It was necessary to *trier* not so much to eliminate any rotten grapes as to prevent any *verjus* (second generation bunches which, though black, would not be fully ripe) from entering the fermentation vat.

It was warm in Burgundy in September 1989, and the grapes were arriving at the wineries at high temperatures. If not cooled immediately, there was a danger that fermentations would develop too quickly. One can see the results of this: short *cuvaisons* and a consequent lack of extraction—pretty wines which lack guts. Those who had the temperature control and could therefore macerate for, say, 20 days rather than 10, gained an advantage.

In 1989 there was a further complication. The skins of the grapes were thin. The ratio of juice to solid was high, and it was consequently difficult to extract the maximum of colour, glycerol and the right sort of tannins. Again, those who could precisely control the temperatures of their fermentations and macerations benefited. Additionally, many performed a *saignée,* particularly for their village wine.

It was also necessary not to pick too late. As the harvest was large, the fruit merely became overripe; it did not concentrate. Moreover, with the acidity levels already on the low side, there was a risk that they would fall even more. This, I feel, is one of the explanations (the size of the crop is the other) why the *grands* and *premiers crus* are disproportionately better than the wines at village level. The village wines, generally from less well-exposed sites, are picked later.

WHERE ARE THE BEST WINES?
AND THE STATE OF MATURITY TODAY

- The white wines were rich and balanced, and tasted well at the ten-year-on tasting. Now they are 18 years old. Only a handful still show any vigour.

- In both colours there was a higher than usual proportional difference as one moved up the hierarchy.

- There are some lovely Volnays; Nuits-Saint-Georges in many cases fail to sing. But in general, the Côte de Nuits are better, as well as obviously being more vigorous than the Côte de Beaunes.

- Drink the village wines now, and most of the better *premiers crus* by 2012 or so. The top *grands crus* can safely be kept until 2020.

TASTING NOTES

WHITES

Bâtard-Montrachet, 1989
Domaine Jean-Noël Gagnard

Softer, riper, richer and more concentrated than the 1990. More open and expressive. More finesse and better acidity. This is honeyed, honeysuckle and flowery. Less solid than the 1990 and rather more sophisticated. Long and complex and classy. Very fine. A really lovely bottle. Better than the 1990. (NB: Marked bottle variation. I definitely had a very good bottle. Others were somewhat tired and vanishing: average at best, 13/20). (January 2002)

NOW TO 2010+   18.5

Bâtard-Montrachet, 1989
Domaine Ramonet

Magnum. Still very young. Full, rich, ample and balanced. Exotic but with very good grip. Still vigorous. Classy. Nutty. Meaty. Full of interest and depth. Fine plus. (April 2002)

DRINK SOON   18.0

Beaune, Clos des Mouches, 1989
Domaine Joseph Drouhin

Magnum. Not much nose, but ripe and honeyed. Meursault-ish. But it lacks a little grip. Still fresh. Spicy, aromatic, gently oaky. Not a bit short, but it lacks a little zip, especially on the attack. Very good. (March 2004)

DRINK SOON   16.0

Chassagne-Montrachet, Morgeot, 1989
Domaine Ramonet

Magnum. Very youthful colour. Very fresh nose. Pure, rich and crisp. Very classy. Fullish bodied, rich and still very youthful on the palate. Excellent acidity. A lot of depth and class. Fine quality. (October 2003)

NOW TO 2009   17.5

Chassagne-Montrachet, Les Vergers, 1989
Domaine Georges Deléger

Quite an evolved colour. But the nose is fresh, rich and concentrated. Fully evolved. Quite exotic. Succulent. Full bodied. Plenty of backbone. Getting a little short and flabby as it evolved. Good plus. Was very good. (March 2005)

DRINK UP   15.5

Chevalier-Montrachet, 1989
Domaine Bouchard Père et Fils

Quite old on the nose at first. Fresher later. Better on the palate. Ripe and rich. Residual minerally aspects still here. Good grip. Not a great wine. Nor does it have the depth it should have. Merely very good indeed. (June 2002)

DRINK SOON   17.0

Chevalier-Montrachet, 1989
Domaine Leflaive

Magnum. Ripe, rich and elegant. Medium-full body. Good attack but not quite the depth and concentration it should have. Balanced, fragrant and elegant but very good rather than great. (April 2001)

DRINK SOON 16.0

Corton-Charlemagne, 1989
Domaine Bonneau du Martray

Fresh colour. Youthful, classy, concentrated nose. Full body. Very good acidity. Still immature. Lots of depth. Very concentrated. Very vigorous. Very fine. (March 2006)

NOW TO 2020 19.0

Corton-Charlemagne, 1989
Domaine Louis Latour

No undue development of colour. Just a touch of sulphur on the nose. Full bodied, firm, rich but just a little hard. Fresh for a 16-year-old wine and very good indeed. But not quite the elegance and texture for fine. Holding up well, though. (October 2005)

NOW TO 2010 17.0

Corton-Charlemagne, 1989
Domaine Leroy

Some development. Close on the nose. Very rich and full and concentrated. Voluptuous. Now *à point*. A fleshy example. Yet with steeliness at the end. This is very fine plus. (April 2001)

NOW TO 2010 18.5

Corton-Charlemagne, 1989
Maison Roland Remoissenet et Fils

Good colour. Ripe nose. This is a little rigid now. Good acidity and quite steely. But there is a lack of succulence and continuity. Yet ripe at the end. Lacks distinction though. Quite good at best now. Was 16/20 in its prime? (April 2001)

DRINK SOON 14.0

Meursault, 1989
Chateau de Meursault

Ripe, fullish, vigorous and not too oaky at all. Rich and honeyed. Very good grip. This is very good indeed. (October 2001)

DRINK SOON 17.0

Meursault, Clos des Perrières, 1989
Domaine Albert Grivault

Youthful colour. This is ripe, crisp, minerally and flowery. Very good intensity. Clean and with good depth and concentration. Rather better than I expected, I must confess. Discreet. Very good indeed. (April 2001)

DRINK SOON 17.0

Meursault, Genevrières, 1989
Domaine Bouchard Père et Fils

A touch of reduction at first. Fat, rich and slightly blowsy. Very mature, almost scented fruit. Not too overly mature. Decent freshness. Very good but nowhere near the class of the 1989. Very good. (November 2003)

DRINK SOON 16.0

Meursault, Genevrières, 1989
Domaine Hubert Bouzereau-Gruère

Well matured colour. Ripe nose. Quite stylish, if with no great concentration, depth or vigour. Medium to medium-full body. Fresh. Attractive. Fully mature and needs drinking soon. Good plus. (May 2005)

DRINK SOON 15.5

Meursault, Genevrières, 1989
Domaine des Comtes Lafon

Good fullish, fresh colour. A big, concentrated wine on the nose. Very, very rich and ripe wine balanced by excellent acidity. Lovely depth and complexity. This is very vigorous and really excellent. On the palate, though, there is just a little heaviness. I prefer the 1990. It has better fruit. This is less flowery and less elegant. Fine plus, but not great. But very, very rich and spicy and exotic. (May 2005)

NOW TO 2009 18.0

Meursault, Le Porusot, 1989
Domaine François Mikulski

A rich, full, concentrated wine; still youthful. Very good grip. This is rich and profound and backward. Needs time. Very good plus. (June 2002)

NOW TO 2012 16.5

Le Montrachet, 1989
Domaine de la Romanée-Conti

Fresh. Very youthful. Very elegant. I expected something richer, more sensual and heavier than this. Very flowery. Long, balanced and delicious. Bags of life. (October 2003)

NOW TO 2009+   19.0

Morey-Saint-Denis, Clos des Monts Luisants Blanc, 1989
Domaine Ponsot

Magnum. 70 percent Aligoté, 15 percent Pinot Blanc, 15 percent Chardonnay. Very fresh, considerably so for a wine 16 years old. Full body. Rich, yet austere. Very lovely with food. Lots of interest. Fine. (June 2005)

DRINK SOON   17.5

Puligny-Montrachet, Les Perrières, 1989
Domaine Étienne Sauzet

Quite an evolved colour. Good delicate flavours, though. Still quite fresh (the second bottle was more evolved). Quite concentrated. Good acidity. Stylish. Good length and depth. Very good plus. (January 2003)

DRINK SOON   16.5

REDS

Beaune, Le Clos des Mouches, 1989
Domaine Joseph Drouhin

Ripe, fullish, *à point* now. No sign of age. Ample and rich. Good acidity. Complex, classy and mellow. Very good indeed. (March 2002)

NOW TO 2010   17.0

Bonnes Mares, 1989
Domaine Joseph Drouhin

Medium to medium-full colour. Mature, but not excessively so. Ripe, very Chambolle nose. Round, soft and succulent. Medium-full body. Very lovely ripe fruit. Good grip. Elegant and complex. Long and lovely. Fine. (October 2000)

DRINK SOON   17.5

Chambertin, 1989
Domaine Bouchard Père et Fils

Very full, rich, mature colour. Ample, nicely evolved nose. Lots of depth here. But quite animal in character. Fullish body. Really quite evolved for 1989. It tastes like it was 10 years older. Ample and rich, though. Lots of substance here. Decent grip. But a slight lack of class. Very good but not great. (November 2002)

DRINK SOON   16.0

Chambertin, 1989
Domaine Leroy

Medium colour. Fully mature. After the 1990, this is a bit loose-knit, but ripe and full of fruit. Medium body. Plump and fruity, but it tails off a bit and it is a bit short. Very good, but no better than that for what it is. (April 2000)

DRINK SOON   16.0

Chambertin, 1989
Domaine Armand Rousseau

Good fullish colour. Very lovely nose. Succulent, ripe, rich and fragrant. Very fresh. Very good acidity for the vintage. *À point* and very delicious. Round, soft and fragrant. Neither the concentration, nor the grip nor the intensity of a really great vintage, but a wine of length and complexity with a very fine lingering finish. (July 2000)

NOW TO 2009   20.0

Le Chambertin, 1989
Domaine Jean Trapet Père et Fils

Good fullish colour. Ripe and fullish on the nose. A little diffuse. It lacks the definition and sheer breed that it should have. On the palate, quite a big, ripe, gently oaky wine. Decent balance. It is still fresh and interesting. And the finish is long and positive. But it is no more than fine. (November 2003)

NOW TO 2011   17.5

Chambertin, Clos de Bèze, 1989
Domaine Armand Rousseau

This is very fine. Fragrant, rich and gently oaky. Sweet, rich, elegant and pure. Medium-full body.

Now *à point* but very vigorous. Most impressive. Very rich and voluptuous and powerful. Very fine indeed; 20/20 for a 1989. (July 2003)

NOW TO 2020   20.0

Chambolle-Musigny, Premier Cru, 1989
Domaine Pierre Bertheau

Quite evolved now. Soft and fragrant but not that concentrated. Medium body. Fruity. Still fresh. But not a lot of grip. So drink quite soon. Good plus. (March 2002)

DRINK SOON   15.5

Chambolle-Musigny, Les Amoureuses, 1989
Domaine Georges Roumier et Fils

Good colour. Just about mature. Very lovely aromatic, fragrant nose. Marvellous classy fruit. Intense and rich. Now mellow. Fullish body. Harmonious. Lots of depth. Fine long finish. Fine plus. Only just ready. (June 2000)

NOW TO 2012+   18.0

Charmes-Chambertin, 1989
Domaine Daniel Taupenot-Merme

Good fresh colour. Mellow, classy nose. Some oak but not too excessive. Indeed a stylish, plump, fresh wine with plenty of character and interest. Long and complex. Very good indeed. (May 2004)

NOW TO 2010   17.0

Charmes-Chambertin, Très Vieilles Vignes, 1989
Domaine Joseph Roty

Full colour. Just about mature. Full, rich and voluptuous on the nose. Sweet and seductive, but I prefer the 1991, let alone the 1990. Rich, fat and succulent. Very fine plus nevertheless, for the vintage. Excellent long finish. (April 2006)

NOW TO 2015   19.0

Clos de la Roche, 1989
Domaine Dujac

The first year, says Jacques Seysses, that we really controlled the harvest. Made less than in 1988. Mature colour. Lovely ripe, succulent nose. Touches of cinnamon. Medium-full body. Lush and rich. Yet balanced. Very seductive. But I prefer the dignity of the 1991 I sampled alongside it. Fine. (October 2001)

NOW TO 2009   17.5

Clos de la Roche, 1989
Domaine Leroy

Good fullish colour. One of the best of these Leroy 1989s. Fat, open and fresh, if not with the greatest class. Evolved fast in the glass, though. Not as good when I returned to it. Slightly astringent. Slightly over-evolved. (April 2000)

DRINK SOON   15.5

Clos de la Roche, 1989
Domaine Hubert Lignier

Magnum. Fullish, mature colour. Rich, ripe, full nose. Very succulent. Almost sweet. Very smooth and mellow. Perfumed and *à point*. Medium body. Fresh. Very lovely ripeness. But exceptional freshness and elegance. One of the best 1989s I have had for ages. Marvellous fruit. Excellent. (June 2003)

NOW TO 2010+   19.0

Clos de la Roche, 1989
Domaine Armand Rousseau

Medium colour. Fully mature. Mellow and supple and medium body only. But with good energy and complexity. It lacks a little real class, though. But certainly very good. Developed in the glass. (December 2000)

DRINK SOON   16.0

Clos de la Roche, Vieilles Vignes, 1989
Domaine Ponsot

Ponsot are the largest growers in Clos De La Roche, with 3.40 hectares, in the heart of the *grand cru*. Medium to medium-full, mature colour. Just beginning to show secondary, fully mature, sensual flavours. Soft. Suggestions of new oak (yet there is none). Supple, fragrant but very rich, concentrated and intense. A wine very much at ease with itself. Fresh, long, gentle, plump, splendidly fruity, complex and very

long on the palate. Very lovely finish. Splendid.
(September 2002)
NOW TO 2015   19.0

Clos de Tart, 1989
Maison Mommessin
Good fullish, mature colour. Lovely fragrant nose.
Plump, rich, medium-full and with plenty of depth
and character. Now mature. Succulent but vigor-
ous and spicy. Good grip. Long. Fine. (October 2001)
NOW TO 2015   17.5

Clos de Vougeot, 1989
Domaine René Engel
Magnum. Full rich colour, only just mature.
Rich, full, fat, spicy but classy nose. Plenty of
substance and depth. Good grip. A fullish, ripe,
multidimensional wine. Lovely fruit. Very rich,
chocolaty-mocha-black fruit flavours. Now getting the tertiary sensual aspects of a mature
wine. Vigorous. Plenty of character and depth
of flavour. Fine plus. Lots of life ahead of it.
(November 2001)
NOW TO 2018   18.0

Clos de Vougeot, 1989
Domaine Leroy
Medium-full colour. Fully mature. Ripe, bal-
anced, aromatic nose. Plenty of succulence. A
fresh, lush example. Fullish body. Very lovely
ripe fruit. Most attractive and very classy, too.
Fine. (April 2000)
NOW TO 2012   17.5

Corton, Vergennes, Cuvée Paul Chanson, 1989
Hospices de Beaune
Elevage Philippe Bouzereau. One bottle perfect.
The other both corked and oxidised. The better
bottle: rich, deep colour. Fine nose. Not over-
oaked. Rich and vigorous. Very good grip. Lots
of class. A delicious wine. (June 2002)
NOW TO 2009   18.5

Echézeaux, 1989
Domaine Jayer-Gilles
Full, vigorous colour. Rich and oaky on the nose.
On the palate, the oak doesn't quite dominate.

The acidity is very good, the fruit is fat and rich.
Good depth. At first, very good indeed, but it got
drier and drier as it evolved. (January 2002)
DRINK SOON   17.0

Echézeaux, 1989
Domaine Henri Jayer
Fine colour. Full, very fresh nose. Lovely, quite
oaky, quite firm fruit. Fullish body on the palate. Slightly rigid but fine and vigorous for the
vintage. Excellent grip. Very pure. Will still
improve. Lovely finish. Fine plus. On aeration
this got better and better. (March 2003)
NOW TO 2015   18.9

Echézeaux, Vieilles Vignes, 1989
Domaine Mongeard-Mugneret
Medium-full colour. Undistinguished nose. Coarse
on the palate. Medium-full body. Some fruit.
Plump, ripe and with good acidity. But it lacks
class. Quite good at best for what it is. (October 2005)
NOW TO 2010   14.0

Echézeaux, 1989
Domaine de la Romanée-Conti
Medium to medium-full, fully mature colour.
Soft, round, elegant and fragrant on the nose.
Sweet and generous. Fresh. Medium-full body.
Very lovely. (March 2005)
NOW TO 2015+   18.0

Gevrey-Chambertin, Vieilles Vignes, 1989
Domaine Bernard Dugat
Medium to medium-full colour. Ripe, rich,
aromatic nose. Good depth. Medium-full body.
Soft. Harmonious. Classy. Long. Impressive for
what it is. (October 2005)
NOW TO 2018   16.5

Gevrey-Chambertin, Les Cazetiers, 1989
Maison Camille Giroud
Full, rich, mature, but still vigorous colour.
Splendidly rich and fat nose. Lots of depth and
quality here. Very good acidity. Lovely cool, bal-
anced fruit. Long, complex and classy. Very fine.
(June 2001)
NOW TO 2010+   18.5

Gevrey-Chambertin, En Champeaux, 1989
Domaine Denis Mortet

Good medium-fullish, mature colour. Now beginning to get soft and aromatic on the nose. Not the depth, concentration or sheer flair of the vintages of today, though. Medium body. Fresh because of the acidity. Lovely fruit, if not great concentration. But elegant. More so than 1991 or 1990. Very good indeed. (May 2002)

NOW TO 2012   17.0

Gevrey-Chambertin, Clos Saint-Jacques, 1989
Domaine Louis Jadot

Medium-full colour. Mature but still vigorous. Took a bit of time to come out of the glass. There is freshness and balance here, but not a great deal of depth and definition. In this sense, it is a typical (good) 1989. Medium-full weight. Ripe and balanced. But there is a slight lack of the excitement one associates with this *cru*. Very good indeed, but not fine. (December 2003)

NOW TO 2009   17.0

Gevrey-Chambertin, Clos Saint-Jacques, 1989
Domaine Armand Rousseau

Good colour. Now a touch of maturity. Soft and fragrant on the nose. No great punch, but profoundly complex in an understated sort of way. Great class. Very lovely fruit. A soft wine, but intense and long on the palate. Fine. *À point*. (March 2000)

NOW TO 2009   17.5

Gevrey-Chambertin, Lavaux-Saint-Jacques, 1989
Maison Joseph Drouhin

Medium-full colour. Rich, ripe, aromatic nose. Slight touch of mocha. Still vigorous. Medium-full body. *À point*. Fresh. Not the greatest fat or concentration, but subtle and with very good grip. Long, cool and classy. Fine. (March 2004)

NOW TO 2020   17.5

Grands Echézeaux, 1989
Domaine Joseph Drouhin

Magnum. Good colour. Rich, ample, spicy and voluptuous on the nose. Fullish, fragrant and ripe

on the palate. Very good grip. Elegant and vigorous. This is very lovely. Impressive finish. (March 2005)

NOW TO 2011   18.5

Grands Echézeaux, 1989
Domaine René Engel

Fullish, fresh colour. Classy, succulent, concentrated nose. Very fresh. Fullish body. Lovely fruit. Elegant and balanced. A beautifully poised wine. Long, complex and still very vigorous. Very fine. (September 2002)

NOW TO 2010   18.5

Grands Echézeaux, 1989
Maison Roland Remoissenet et Fils

Under the label of Royale Club. Good colour. Rich, fragrant, mature nose. Sliglty bulky, but concentrated and stylish. Fullish body. Round, ripe and sweet. Very good acidity. Stylish and concentrated. Lots of drive at the end. This is fine plus. (October 2000)

DRINK SOON   18.0

Grands Echézeaux, 1989
Domaine de la Romanée-Conti

Medium-full, fully mature colour. Firmer, richer and more earthy on the nose than their 1989 Echézeaux. Fullish body. Some tannin. Rich. Meaty. Not as ethereally fragrant as the Echézeaux, but fine plus. Bigger and fatter. (March 2005)

NOW TO 2018+   18.0

Griotte-Chambertin, 1989
Domaine Joseph Drouhin

Medium-full, mature colour. Ripe, opulent, sweet and seductive on the nose. Lovely rich fruit here. Medium-full body. Rich. *À point*. Very lovely fruit. Classier than the 1991 and longer and with more dimension on the follow-through. Surprisingly good acidity. Lots of concentration. Very lovely and seductive. Will keep well. (July 2003)

NOW TO 2018   18.5

Latricières-Chambertin, 1989
Maison Camille Giroud

Ample, ripe and luscious. Very good support and grip. Fullish body. Still fresh. A lovely seductive wine. Splendid fruit. Fine. (September 2002)

DRINK SOON   17.5

Latricières-Chambertin, 1989
Domaine Leroy

Medium to medium-full colour. Fully mature. Soft, ripe, almost sweet nose. Quite gentle. Medium-full body. Fully evolved. Lacks a bit of style but has more harmony than the 1990. Very good. (April 2000)

DRINK SOON   16.0

Mazis-Chambertin, 1989
Domaine Bernard Maume

Medium-full colour. Just about ready. Ripe, fragrant, youthful, quie chunky nose. Similarly, a bit chunky on the palate. Fullish bodied, ripe and vigorous, but it lacks fat, velvet and real class. Yet still plenty of life and no lack of pleasure here. Very good plus. (October 2001)

DRINK SOON   16.5

Morey-Saint-Denis, Clos des Ormes, 1989
Maison Joseph Faiveley

Medium to medium-full colour. Soft, fragrant nose. Not a great deal of depth or real class. Less good on the palate. Medium body. No great succulence or intensity. Stylish but a little weak. Fresh, though. (September 2001)

DRINK SOON   16.0

Le Musigny, 1989
Domaine Joseph Drouhin

Fullish, vigorous colour. Magical nose. Marvellous fruit. Ripe and vigorous and of superb finesse. Fullish on the palate. Mellow, velvety, intense, concentrated and complex. Splendid fruit. Very Musigny. Absolutely *à point* now but still very vigorous. Great class. Great wine without a shadow of a doubt. Very, very long, aromatic and subtle at the end. (October 2005)

NOW TO 2020   20.0

Musigny, 1989
Domaine Leroy

Medium to medium-full colour. Ripe, sweet nose, hinting at getting a bit diffuse. There is

a little astringency here. And it lacks real definition. Not up to the quality of wines in later vintages. (April 2000)

DRINK SOON   16.5

Musigny, 1989
Domaine Jacques-Frédéric Mugnier

The second bottle was better than the first. The first lacked a bit of energy, was medium-full bodied, and was very well balanced and very classy. Certainly very fine. The second seemed more concentrated and richer. Quite lovely. Now ready. (June 2003)

NOW TO 2010   18.5

Nuits-Saint-Georges, Les Chaignots, 1989
Domaine Robert Chevillon

Good fullish colour. Fully mature. Rich and sumptuous on the nose. Ripe and full bodied. Good acidity and good tannins and good depth. Still nicely austere. Very raspberry in flavour. Long and vigorous on the finish. Very good indeed. Only just ready. (January 2002)

NOW TO 2014   17.0

Nuits-Saint-Georges, Les Chaignots, 1989
Domaine Alain Michelot

Magnum. Medium to medium-full colour. Ripe, fragrant and elegant. You can see more Vosne than Nuits here. Good class and good grip. *À point.* Fresh and balanced. Positive. Very good indeed. No hurry to drink. (January 2004)

NOW TO 2010   17.0

Nuits-Saint-Georges, Les Chaignots, 1989
Domaine Dr. Georges Mugneret

Medium-full colour. Ripe, quite rich, plump nose. Plenty of fruit here and a good grip, if not really very full and concentrated. Medium to medium-full body. Good style. Well balanced. Very good indeed, but not fine. There is not enough to it. (January 2003)

NOW 2010   17.0

Nuits-Saint-Georges, Aux Chaignots, 1989
Domaine Gérard Mugneret

Magnum. Good full, vigorous colour. Ripe, attractive nose. Lots of fruit. Good freshness.

Plump and attractive. On the palate full bodied, fresh, generous, rich and classy. A lovely bottle. Fully *à point*. Juicy and delicious. Fine. (December 2001)

NOW TO 2009　　　　　　　　　17.5

Nuits-Saint-Georges, Aux Murgers, 1989
Domaine Méo-Camuzet

Good colour. Medium-full and just about mature. Ripe on the nose but a little unresolved wood tannin. Slightly astringent. If anything a slight lack of fruit. On the palate, fullish body. A little astringent. But ripe and ample and sweet. It lacks a little class. Good plus. (March 2001)

DRINK SOON　　　　　　　　　15.5

Nuits-Saint-Georges, Les Porrets Saint-Georges, 1989
Domaine Joseph Faiveley

Good colour. Full, fresh and vigorous. Similar on the nose and palate. Very good grip for a 1989. Ripe, succulent tannins. Rich, juicy and classy. Plenty of life left here. Fine. (May 2004)

NOW TO 2015　　　　　　　　　17.5

Nuits-Saint-Georges, Les Saint-Georges, 1989
Domaine Henri Gouges

Medium, mature colour. Riper, richer, spicier but less fresh nose than the 1991. Medium to medium-full body. Decent fruit but not a lot of grip and concentration. Very good plus, but not brilliant. It lacks real class and complexity. It should be drunk quite soon. (September 2003)

DRINK SOON　　　　　　　　　16.5

Richebourg, 1989
Domaine Anne Gros

Fine, full, mature colour. Grilled nuts and coffee on the nose. Fresh, stylish and very composed. This is absolutely *à point*. Medium-full body. Velvety-smooth. Today, more enjoyable to drink than the 1990, though the latter is more concentrated and better in the long run. Ripe and complex. Very elegant and very harmonious. Very long and lovely. Very fine indeed. (February 2004)

NOW TO 2020　　　　　　　　　19.5

Richebourg, 1989
Domaine Leroy

Medium to medium-full colour. Fully mature. High-toned nose. Lovely poised, balanced, elegant fruit. Medium-full body. A slight lack of grip compared with many of the preceeding wines. Sweet and ripe and voluptuous nevertheless. (April 2000)

DRINK SOON　　　　　　　　　17.5

Richebourg, 1989
Domaine Méo-Camuzet

Fullish colour. Rich, oaky, sweet, fullish and quite structured. Full, but not too tannic or dense. Very ripe. Lush and sexy and very fine. A little obvious. (June 2004)

NOW 2015　　　　　　　　　18.5

Richebourg, 1989
Domaine de la Romanée-Conti

Medium-full, fully mature colour. Rich and fat but less expressive on the nose than the 1989 Romanée-Saint-Vivant. Fullish body. Still some tannin. Very ripe and exotic. Voluptuous and almost sweet. This will still improve. Very vigorous. Lovely long finish. (March 2005)

NOW TO 2020+　　　　　　　　19.0

La Romanée, 1989
Domaine Bouchard Père et Fils

Fullish colour. Fully mature. More to it than the 1990. A lot more depth on the nose in a slightly burnt-caramel, exotic sort of way. Medium-full body. Quite sweet without being cooked. Very seductive. Good freshness. No hard edges. Good depth. Good intensity. More to it and with a better finish than the 1990. Fine plus. (March 2003)

NOW TO 2012　　　　　　　　　18.0

Romanée-Saint-Vivant, 1989
Domaine Louis Jadot

Good full, vigorous colour. This is very fine on the nose. Ripe, exotic but very well balanced on the palate. Lush and succulent. Very seductive. Almost as good as the 1990. But more exotic. Super-duper and only just ready. (March 2002)

NOW TO 2025　　　　　　　　　19.5

Romanée-Saint-Vivant, 1989
Maison Jaffelin

Full colour. Now just about mature. Slightly dense on the nose. Chunky. Even slightly coarse. A little tannic. A little stewed. Did this come from Michel Voarick? Lots of lovely ripe fruit on the palate. But a little inelegantly put together. Fine but not brilliant. It deteriorated in the glass. (March 2002)

NOW TO 2014   17.5

Romanée-Saint-Vivant, 1989
Domaine Leroy

Medium to medium-full colour. Much looser-knit looking than the 1990. Round, ripe, sweet but without the structure and vigour of the 1990. Medium-full body. Fresh, ripe and succulent. But it lacks the wight and thrust of the 1990. Very fine. (April 2000)

NOW TO 2011+   18.5

Romanée-Saint-Vivant, 1989
Domaine de la Romanée-Conti

Medium-full, fully mature colour. Very lovely complex, slightly chocolaty nose. Medium-full body. Very finely balanced. Excellent fruit. Harmonious. Fragrant. Still some tannin. Great energy. Very long. Very fine. (March 2005)

NOW TO 2018   18.5

Romanée-Saint-Vivant, 1989
Domaine Charles Thomas

This is really very disappointing. Medium bodied, unbalanced and unstylish. A disgrace for what it is. Indeed not really very pleasant to drink, even for a wine of less pretention. (November 2002)

DRINK SOON   12.0

Ruchottes-Chambertin, 1989
Domaine Bonnefond

(Christophe Roumier.) Medium-full, mature colour. Still quite firm on the nose. Rich, concentrated and fullish. Youthful. Very good grip for a 1989. Ample, classy, concentrated fruit. Lovely wine. Just about ready. Very fine. (October 2002)

NOW TO 2011+   18.5

Ruchottes-Chambertin, Clos des Ruchottes, 1989
Domaine Armand Rousseau

Medium to medium-full colour. Well matured. Unexpectedly, a little stemmy on the nose. Sweet but slightly rustic on the palate. No great elegance. Good but not great. Medium body. Decent acidity, but not very fresh. (April 2005)

DRINK SOON   15.0

Santenay, 1989
Maison Camille Giroud

Good colour. Full and rich and just about ready. Plenty of depth and quality for a village Santenay. Rich and meaty. Slightly sauvage. Good grip. Elegant sweet finish. Very good for a village example. (June 2001)

NOW TO 2010   16.0

La Tâche, 1989
Domaine de la Romanée-Conti

Medium-full, fully mature colour. Splendid nose. Super-concentrated. Multidimensional. Fullish. Riper tannins than the 1989 Richebourg. Real depth here. Full bodied, balanced, profound and complex. Very exciting. A marvellous bottle. Only just ready. (March 2005)

NOW TO 2020+   20.0

Volnay, Les Caillerets, Ancienne Cuvée Carnot, 1989
Domaine Bouchard Père et Fils

Good full, vigorous colour. Quite lean, pure nose. Very good acidity. Good class, too. Quite full for a Volnay. Succulent and complex. Long and vigorous. Fine. (March 2001)

NOW TO 2010   17.5

Volnay, Clos des Chênes, 1989
Domaine Joseph Drouhin

Fullish, youthful colour for a 1989. Elegant, fragrant, aromatic nose. Round and rich. Good fullish structure. Vigorous but mellow. Plenty of life left. Fine. (March 2004)

NOW TO 2010+   17.5

Volnay, Taillepieds, 1989
Domaine Hubert de Montille

Good fresh, fullish colour. Ripe, fragrant, fleshy and sweet on the nose. Medium-full body.

Succulent, especially for de Montille. Ripe. Balanced. Fresh. Classy. (June 2005)

NOW TO 2015   17.0

Vosne-Romanée, 1989
Domaine Emmanuel Rouget

Fullish, still vigorous colour. Rich, vigorous nose. Lovely Pinot. A bit tight and perhaps, I think, it will always be a bit too tight for its own good. Good but too rigid for a 1989. No seductive appeal. Yet much better as it developed. Very good indeed. (November 2005)

NOW TO 2020   17.0

Vosne-Romanée, Aux Brûlées, 1989
Domaine Méo-Camuzet

Very good colour. Fullish. Still fresh. Ample, rich nose. A touch of spice. Plenty of vigour. Fullish body, but now perhaps beginning to lighten up at the end. Nice fruit. Still fresh and attractive. Got better in the glass and seemed to put on weight. Very good indeed, but not brilliant. (March 2001)

DRINK SOON   17.0

Vosne-Romanée, Clos des Réas, 1989
Domaine Michel Gros

Full, rich, vigorous colour. Ripe, fresh and quite concentrated nose. Very good fruit here. Very succulent. Medium-full body. Absolutely à point. Fresh and juicy. Soft and mellow. Excellent finish. Delicious. Excellent balance for the vintage. Most seductive. Fine plus for the vintage. (December 2003)

NOW TO 2013   18.0

Vosne-Romanée, Cros Parantoux, 1989
Domaine Henri Jayer

Very full colour. Still very young. A big, oaky, concentrated, slightly over-extracted wine. Splendid fruit on the palate. Rich. Still vigorous. Not too much oak or tannin. Good grip. Fresh and youthful. Slightly rigid. But fine, nevertheless. (January 2000)

NOW TO 2010   17.5

Vosne-Romanée, Les Suchots, 1989
Maison Camille Giroud

Good colour. Ripe, slightly rustic, sweet and full bodied on the nose. A little overblown perhaps.

Fullish bodied and fresh on the palate. Good tannins. Good concentration. Soft and mellow and velvety. Not the greatest grip, definition and class, but very good plus. (March 2000)

DRINK SOON   16.5

1988

If 1988 did not make much of an impact as a white wine vintage, it was, right from the start, hailed for its red wines as very good indeed. The acidity of the 1978, combined with the lush, concentrated fruit of the 1985, was how I described it myself, having had a second look at the wines, by that time in bottle, in the early months of 1990. I went on to declare it the best vintage for a generation. It was not cheap, but it was worth it. The wines were classically structured, with a potential for development and long aging, which was exciting. There was a depth, a dimension and a finesse in the best 1988s which was truly fine.

Many years have now passed, during which we have had a number of very good, indeed better, vintages: 1990, 1993, 1995, 1999, 2002, 2005. In the meantime, I have occasionally heard or seen criticism expressed over the 1988s: *The 1988 reds were not as good as all that. The wines were lean and hard. The acidity level was too high. There was a lack of charm.* For those who sought instant gratification, facile easiness-to-drink, the 1988 reds were not their glass of wine. But this was the fault of the critic, not of the 1988s. By definition, a serious wine cannot be facile. A wine made for the long term will not give instant gratification in its youth.

Today, almost 20 years on, we can see that the 1988 reds have fulfilled all their early promise. Many are still vigorous. There is a great deal of harmony in these wines and a high note of elegance. They are somewhat aloof, and some are still—and always will be—a little austere. But they have real class, are very consistent, geographically and hierarchically, and can continue to be kept for some time.

WEATHER CONDITIONS

The 1988 weather conditions can be summarised as follows: spring was warm; the flowering took place without mishap; July, August and the first part of September were dry and hot; and after a lull in the middle of the month, the weather improved and was, in general, excellent throughout the red wine harvest. What this produced was a large red wine crop: 11 percent more than in 1987, though 12 percent less than that of 1986—and moreover, and crucially, one in a ripe and extremely healthy condition at the time of harvest. There was no rot and no hail damage, and the ambient temperature was warm but not too hot when the grapes were brought in to the winery. The result? Very easy fermentations. No problems either with runaway temperatures which needed to be watched over day and night, nor with cold musts which would need heating up to get them going. As Charles Rousseau said to me:

"You'd have to have been a real idiot not to produce good wine in 1988. If you did make a mess of things, you'd better go and choose another *metier*."

→ Rating for the Vintage ←	
Red	17.5
White	14.5

→ Size of the Crop ← (In hectolitres, excluding generic wine)		
	RED	WHITE
Grands Crus	12,797	3,533
Village and *Premiers Crus*	170,056	46,434
TOTAL	182,853	49,967

WHERE ARE THE BEST WINES? AND THE STATE OF MATURITY TODAY

- The white wines were uneven, better proportionately as one climbed the hierarchy, but now for the most part well past their best.

- The best reds are to be found in Volnay and in Chambolle-Musigny.

- Drink lesser wines now. The better *premiers* and *grands crus* still show plenty of vigour. There is no hurry to consume these.

TASTING NOTES

WHITES

Chassagne-Montrachet, Morgeot, 1988
Domaine Ramonet

Youthful, rich, concentrated and elegant. Fullish. Lots of depth. Peachy, apricotty and honeyed. None of the usual four-square aspects of Morgeot, nor the leanness of the vintage. A lovely wine. *À point*, but with lots of vigour. (January 2001)
DRINK SOON   18.0

Corton-Charlemagne, 1988
Domaine Bonneau du Martray

Crisp, cool, elegant and complex. Very fresh. Medium-full body but not great concentration and depth. Yet very classy. Delicious. Lots of life ahead of it. Fine. (July 2003)
NOW TO 2010   17.5

Corton-Charlemagne, 1988
Maison Roland Remoissenet et Fils

Fresh, firm nose. Rich and nutty for a 1988. Good depth. Quite full. Improved in the glass. This is much better even than the 1995, let alone 1986, 1992 and 1994. Fine. (March 2001)
DRINK SOON   17.5

Criots-Bâtard-Montrachet, 1988
Domaine Hubert Lamy et Fils

Fresh for a wine of 15 years of age. A touch of built-in sulphur. Not as refined as today. Medium-full body. Some fruit. Slightly pedestrian and one-dimensional. Good but not great. Drink fairly soon. (June 2003)
DRINK SOON   15.0

Meursault, Genevrières, 1988
Domaine François Jobard

Still a touch of SO_2. Full, rich and austere. Got better and better in the glass. Not magic. Slightly clumsy on the palate. But still fresh. Good plus. (January 2006)

NOW TO 2010   15.5

Meursault, Genevrières, 1988
Domaine des Comtes Lafon

Quite an evolved colour. Flowery, fresh nose. No great richness but balanced and quite elegant. Medium to medium-full body. The acidity is very good but not dominant and has preserved the style. Slight touch of candied fruits. Good length. Holding up well. Very good indeed. (September 2005)

DRINK QUITE SOON   17.0

Meursault, Genevrières, 1988
Domaine Pierre Morey

Quite an evolved colour. Fresh nose. Rich and full. Mellow. Surprisingly ample. Lots of dimension. Still youthful. Long and complex. Very good indeed, even for the vintage. Lovely finish. (March 2005)

DRINK SOON   17.5

Meursault, Perrières, 1988
Domaine Robert Ampeau

Mature colour. A little neutral on the nose at first. But plenty of depth, ripeness and vigour. Ample. Fresh. Lovely fruit. Excellent for the vintage. Still bags of life. (October 2005)

NOW TO 2012   19.0

Meursault, Perrières, 1988
Domaine des Comtes Lafon

Rich, full, austere and not a bit too oaky. Fullish on the palate. Ample. Splendidly balanced. Real quality here. Very fine. (January 2006)

NOW TO 2010+   18.5

Le Montrachet, 1988
Domaine du Marquis de Laguiche/
Maison Joseph Drouhin

This is still quite youthful. Ripe, rich, profound and very classy on the nose. On the palate, full bodied, energetic, intense and very aristocratic. This must be the best 1988 white. Splendid depth and concentration. Very vigorous, long,

complex and very, very classy. Excellent. Only just about ready. (March 2005)

NOW TO 2020   20.0

REDS

Beaune, Hospices de Beaune,
Cuvée Nicolas Rolin, 1988
Domaine Louis Jadot

Fullish, youthful colour. Austere but elegant on the nose. Firm acidity. Slightly ungenerous. Medium-full body. Good but not great. Still vigorous. (October 2004)

NOW TO 2010   15.0

Beaune, Les Cent Vignes, 1988
Maison Camille Giroud

Very good colour. Ripe, succulent nose. Lovely juicy fruit here. Round, balanced, very ripe palate. Medium to medium-full body. Some tannin. Good grip. This is stylish, ample and very good plus. Not a bit austere. (October 2000)

DRINK SOON   16.5

Bonnes Mares, 1988
Domaine Drouhin-Laroze

Fullish colour. Still quite youthful. Good fruit, but not the greatest degree of class. Ample, sweet, ripe and fullish. Good balance. Slightly one-dimensional, though. Slightly artificial in its fruit. Not a bit too lean, though. Good plus. (October 2003)

NOW TO 2020   15.5

Bonnes Mares, 1988
Domaine Charles Thomas

Decent colour. Quite fresh. But rather weak for a 1988. Decent fruit but not at all enough depth and concentration and dimension for a Bonnes Mares. Average at best. (November 2002)

DRINK SOON   14.0

Bonnes Mares, 1988
Domaine Comte Georges de Vogüé

Medium to medium-full colour. Still quite youthful. Ripe, plummy, fresh nose. Fullish, but not hard or austere or tannic. Plenty of fat and succulence. Very Bonnes Mares (rather than Musigny)

in character. Fullish body. Ample. Ripe. Rich and mellow. Very fine. Impressive and very classy. Very fine indeed. Lots of life ahead of it. (June 2005)
NOW TO 2020   19.0

Chambertin, 1988
Domaine Joseph Drouhin
Fine barely mature colour. At first a little austere but after 10 minutes it began to get sweeter and sweeter. Lots of class. Very lovely fruit and of course very good grip. Fullish body. Mellow, concentrated, subtle and fragrant. Very lovely long, lingering finish. Very fine plus. (October 2001)
NOW TO 2015   18.5

Chambertin, 1988
Domaine Armand Rousseau
Fine, full, vigorous colour. Ample, rich, minerally nose. Very classy. Very classic. Fullish body. Ripe, smooth, balanced and complex. Very lovely indeed. (September 2005)
NOW TO 2015+   20.0

Le Chambertin, 1988
Domaine Louis Trapet
Full, fully mature colour. Rich, ripe and spicy on the nose. Medium-full body on the palate. A slightly lack of concentration and distinction but balanced and ripe, if not exactly very rich. A little ungenerous. Very good indeed at best. (March 2001)
DRINK SOON   17.0

Chambertin, Clos de Bèze, 1988
Domaine Armand Rousseau
Full colour. Firm and full on the nose. Some tannin still a little evident. Rich and vigorous and profound. This is fuller, richer and more vigorous than his 1988 Clos Saint-Jacques and a better wine. Excellent grip. Splendidly energetic and virile. Excellent finish. This is very fine indeed. (October 2002)
NOW TO 2015+   19.5

Chambolle-Musigny, 1988
Domaine Chopin-Groffier
Good colour. This is quite a substantial wine. Ripe. Good acidity. Fragrant. Fullish bodied.

Vigorous. Still youthful. Quite firm. But very good. Plenty of life ahead of it. (March 2000)
NOW TO 2015   16.0

Chambolle-Musigny, Les Fuées, 1988
Domaine Jacques-Frédéric Mugnier
Medium-full, mature colour. Fragrant, supple, intense nose. Just about ready. Complex and stylish. Very well balanced. Long. Fine. (March 2000)
NOW TO 2010+   17.5

Chambolle-Musigny, Les Amoureuses, 1988
Domaine Joseph Drouhin
Full colour. Less developed than the 1990. More austere nose. Better acidity. More classic. But less sex appeal. Much less oaky. The tannins are more obvious. Fullish body. Very well balanced. Very long and complex. Very fragrant and Chambolle-ish. A lovely example. And an interesting foil to the 1990. Both are very fine. Which you prefer is a question of taste. But this is not as rich or as complex as the 1990, or as sweet at the end. The 1990 is better, in my view. Still very vigorous. (December 2003)
NOW TO 2013   18.5

Chambolle-Musigny, Les Amoureuses, 1988
Domaine Georges Roumier et Fils
Medium-full colour. Still fresh. Light, fragrant and reticent on the nose. Yet very elegant. Medium-full body. Silky-smooth. Very lovely fruit. Very finely balanced. Complex, classy and very fine. Lovely finish. (June 2005)
NOW TO 2020   18.5

Chambolle-Musigny, Les Amoureuses, 1988
Domaine Comte Georges de Vogüé
Medium-full, mature colour. Lovely aromatic nose. Fullish bodied, ample, ripe and classy. An intense, very fragrant, very lovely, multidimensional example. Very complex. Fine plus. (March 2001)
NOW TO 2010+   18.0

Chambolle-Musigny, Charmes, 1988
Domaine Ghislaine Barthod
Medium-full, mature colour. Quite soft now, almost deceptively so for a 1988. Lovely fruit.

Good substance. Ripe and stylish. Good acidity. Not a bit severe. Quite concentrated. Fresh and succulent. Very good. (November 2003)

NOW TO 2010   16.0

Charmes-Chambertin, 1988
Domaine Denis Bachelet

Medium-full colour. Still very fresh-looking. Very fresh, but ripe and succulent on the nose. No hard edges here. Medium to medium-full body. Splendidly balanced, mellow tannins. Great vigour. Lovely sweet fruit. Yet very fresh at the end. Clean and intense. Very fine. Ready now, but will keep very well. (June 2004)

NOW TO 2020   18.5

Charmes-Chambertin, 1988
Maison Pierre Bourée et Fils

Medium to medium-full colour. Fully mature. Fat, mature, rather rustic nose. Fullish body. Quite mature in its flavours. Decent acidity. But it lacks class and balance. Clean at the end, though. (April 2006)

DRINK SOON   15.5

Charmes-Chambertin, 1988
Domaine Joseph Drouhin

Fullish, mature colour. Lovely fragrant nose. Ripe and rich. Laid-back. Very harmonious. Very classy. Lovely fruit. Medium-full body. Soft, mature, ripe and balanced. Long, complex and very elegant. Very lovely. Very fine. (April 2006)

NOW TO 2015   18.5

Charmes-Chambertin, 1988
Domaine Dujac

Medium colour. Fully mature. Soft and sweet. This is a corked bottle. Essentially, it is more Dujac than Charmes. Probably 16.0 or 17.0. Fully ready. (April 2006)

NOW TO 2012 (SEE NOTE)

Charmes-Chambertin, 1988
Domaine Joseph Faiveley

Full, vigorous colour. Just a little maturity. Firm but rich on the nose. Ripe and succulent. Not a bit hard. This is fullish bodied. Now *à point*.

Very long, complex and stylish. Better and better as it developed. Very fine. (April 2006)

NOW TO 2018   18.5

Charmes-Chambertin, 1988
Domaine Bernard Maume

Medium-full, mature colour. Slightly dense on the nose. Earthy, too. Slightly rustic. A bit rigid on the palate. The tannins stick out. Decent fruit. Good grip. Better with food. Long positive finish. (April 2006)

NOW TO 2011   15.5

Charmes-Chambertin, Très Vieilles Vignes, 1988
Domaine Joseph Roty

Full, rich, immature-looking colour. Splendidly concentrated. Full, rich and very vigorous. Excellent fruit. Very ripe, even exotic. Real intensity here. Very good grip. Very, very long on the palate. Still youthful. Very fine indeed. (April 2006)

NOW TO 2025   19.5

Charmes-Chambertin, 1988
Domaine Armand Rousseau

Medium to medium-full colour. Fully mature. Ripe and soft, but no great vigour. Yet splendidly harmonious. Medium body. Cool. Composed. Ripe at the end. Very long. Very silky smooth. Fine plus. (April 2006)

NOW TO 2015   18.0

Clos de la Roche, 1988
Domaine Armand Rousseau

Medium to medium-full colour. More opulent than this 1988 Charmes-Chambertin, but still fresh. Medium to medium body. Generous. Earthy. Good grip. This is rounder than the Charmes. Less fragrant. Less class, but fatter. Very good plus. (October 2002)

DRINK SOON   16.5

Clos de la Roche, Cuvée Vieilles Vignes, 1988
Domaine Ponsot

Magnum. Medium colour. Fully mature. Touches of caramel on the nose. Ripe butterscotchy palate. Almost sweet. Vigorous but medium bodied. Slightly too sweet yet fresh enough. Fine but not great. (March 2006)

NOW TO 2015   17.5

Clos de Vougeot, 1988
Domaine René Engel

Fine, fresh colour. Lovely nose. Cool and classy. Ripe and fullish and not a bit lacking succulence. Complex, classy and now *à point* but with plenty of vigour. Quite high acidity but no lack of generosity. This is fine. (September 2002)

NOW TO 2015   17.5

Corton, Le Clos du Roi, 1988
Domaine Chandon de Briailles

Good fresh colour. Fresh and fragrant on the nose. Soft and round and medium to medium-full body on the palate. Plenty of charm. Very good fruit. And no lack of class. Fine. (May 2003)

NOW TO 2013   17.5

Echézeaux, 1988
Domaine Mongeard-Mugneret

Medium colour. Mature, but no undue age. Slightly dirty rather than corked, because it didn't seem to get any worse. Medium to medium-full body. Slightly lean. But some decent fruit. A clean bottle would be quite good but no better. (March 2006)

DRINK SOON   14.0

Echézeaux, 1988
Domaine de la Romanée-Conti

Fullish colour. Opulent nose. Not a touch lean. Round with a slight touch of caramel and mocha. Opulent and seductive as it developed. Medium-full body. Rich and ripe. Lots of depth. Slightly oaky. Very good grip. Lovely balance. Soft, long, intense and even sweet at the end. Fine. (October 2002)

NOW TO 2010+   17.5

Gevrey-Chambertin, Vieilles Vignes, 1988
Domaine Denis Bachelet

Fullish, fresh colour. Obviously bottled with more than the usual amount of CO_2 in the wine. But this has just kept it fresh. Not much nose. A

little austere at first, but round and ripe underneath. Very good. (April 2000)

DRINK SOON   16.0

Gevrey-Chambertin, Clos Saint-Jacques, 1988
Domaine Michel Esmonin et Fille

Fullish colour. Now fully mature. Soft, round, plump nose. Slight touch of the stems. Decent class, but not the greatest amount. Medium body. Lacks real concentration. But fresh and pleasantly fruity, if without great depth and class. OK but not brilliant. Declined in the glass. Drink soon. (April 2005)

DRINK SOON   14.0

Gevrey-Chambertin, Clos Saint-Jacques, 1988
Domaine Louis Jadot

Fullish colour. Still youthful. Very full, rich, concentrated, chocolaty nose. Splendid depth of flavour. Real dimension. A little closed-in still. The attack is OK, the finish brilliant. Full body. Very, very rich and concentrated. Excellent grip. Very fine plus. (April 2005)

NOW TO 2025   19.5

Gevrey-Chambertin, Clos Saint-Jacques, 1988
Domaine Armand Rousseau

Fullish, mature colour. Richer and more concentrated than the Ruchottes. More ample. More depth. More complete. Full bodied, rich and very concentrated. Marvellous fruit. Great intensity and class. Marvellous finish. Excellent. Only just ready. (April 2005)

NOW TO 2025   19.0

Gevrey-Chambertin, Le Poissenot, 1988
Domaine Geantet-Pansiot

Fullish, vigorous colour. Succulent, rich nose. Very good style and depth. Fresh and plump. Fullish body. Lovely fruit. Ripe, fat and generous. Good intensity. Fragrant and really quite classy. Fine. (March 2001)

NOW TO 2010   17.5

Grands Echézeaux, 1988
Domaine de la Romanée-Conti

Full colour. Splendidly sweet, lush and succulent. Rather fuller, richer and more concentrated than the 1988 Echézeaux. A full and very lovely wine on the palate. Excellent acidity. Most impressive. This has a great deal of depth. Very, very lovely fruit and balance. Significantly better than the 1988 Echézeaux. Much more intensity and energy. Very fine. (October 2002)

NOW TO 2012+ 18.5

Griotte-Chambertin, 1988
Domaine Joseph Drouhin

Full colour. Now mature. Fragrant, indeed delicate. Fullish. Quite oaky. Very lovely cool, classy fruit. Medium-full body. Ripe. Now getting mellow. Fine acidity. Complex. Long. Very subtle, long and harmonious. Very, very long finish. A lovely wine. (March 2002)

NOW TO 2020 18.5

Latricières-Chambertin, 1988
Maison Joseph Drouhin

Medium-full, well matured colour. Very lovely, cool, stylish nose. Not a bit too austere. Complex, classy and ample. Medium-full body. Very good grip. Generous and very lovely and very long at the end. Very fine. (April 2005)

NOW TO 2015 18.5

Latricières-Chambertin, 1988
Domaine Joseph Faiveley

Fullish, round, ripe and succulent. Not a bit austere. Lovely fragrant Pinot fruit. A delicious wine. (February 2005)

NOW TO 2020 17.5

Mazis-Chambertin, 1988
Domaine Joseph Faiveley

Medium-full colour. Slightly chunky, coffee-flavoured nose. A bit dense. Fullish body. Good depth and grip. Slightly ungainly on the attack but better on the follow-through. Good fruit. Vigorous. Still youthful. Fine. (April 2005)

NOW TO 2015 17.5

Mazis-Chambertin, 1988
Domaine Armand Rousseau

Medium, well matured colour. Soft, ripe, aromatic nose. Ample, ripe, plummy and full of fruit. This is very seductive. Round and rich and with very good grip. Medium-full body. Complex. Fine plus. (April 2005)

NOW TO 2015 18.0

Musigny, 1988
Domaine Comte Georges de Vogüé

Good colour. Fullish. Very classy. Just about softened up. Splendid fruit and lovely harmony. Ripe. Getting luscious. Above all, real breed. Very fine plus. (June 2001)

NOW TO 2025 19.0

Nuits-Saint-Georges, Les Chaignots, 1988
Domaine Robert Chevillon

Very good colour. Still vigorous. Really quite opulent for a 1988. Rich, full and fat on the nose. Concentrated and classy. Excellent fruit. Very good grip. Yet not a bit austere. Good tannins. Vigorous and fine. Better than their 1989 Chaignots. Fuller, richer and more concentrated. (January 2002)

NOW TO 2020 17.5

Nuits-Saint-Georges, Aux Chaignots, 1988
Domaine Mugneret-Gibourg

Medium to medium-full, mature colour. Fine classy, concentrated, balanced nose. Very lovely fruit. Medium to medium-full body. Fragrant and intense. Complex. Plenty of life ahead of it. Fine. (March 2001)

NOW TO 2010 17.5

Nuits-Saint-Georges, Les Perrières, 1988
Maison Camille Giroud

Medium-full, mature colour. Soft, ripe, gentle nose. Very classy. Medium to medium-full body. Well matured. Ripe, round, sweet and succulent. Atypical. Not a bit lean or austere. Most attractive. Very good plus. (June 2004)

NOW TO 2010+ 16.5

Nuits-Saint-Georges, Les Pruliers, 1988
Domaine Henri Gouges

Full, mature colour. Firm, rich, slightly robust nose. Fullish, meaty and concentrated. Very good grip. Not as elegent as Mugneret-Gibourg's

1988 Nuits-Saint-Georges Chaignots. But harmonious and multidimensional. Plenty of life ahead of it. (March 2001)

NOW TO 2012   17.0

Nuits-Saint-Georges, Les Saint-Georges, 1988
Domaine Henri Gouges

Medium to medium-full colour. Interesting slight roast-chestnut-caramel spice on the nose. Medium-full body. Fresh, ripe and vigorous. Good weight. Not austere. The finish is positive and this is altogether better than the 1989, but it is a little clumsier than the 1991. Very good indeed. (September 2003)

NOW TO 2011   17.0

Pommard, Clos des Boucherottes, 1988
Maison Joseph Drouhin

Medium-full, mature colour. Still a little closed and austere on the nose. More generous as it developed. Medium-full body. Good backbone. Good grip. Now mellow. Plenty of style, depth and vigour. Very good. (March 2001)

NOW TO 2010   16.0

Pommard, Clos des Epeneaux, 1988
Domaine du Comte Armand

Full colour. Barely mature. Substantial nose. A little four-square. On the palate, big, full bodied and tannic. Too much so for its own good. Rich and fruity. But too big and astringent. Slightly one-dimensional. Yet good acidity. Only quite good. Will it ever resolve itself? (March 2002)

NOW TO 2015   14.0

Richebourg, 1988
Domaine Gros Frère et Soeur

Good colour. Ripe, rich and gently oaky. Still youthful. Not a bit too austere. Plump and classy. Medium body. Sweet and ripe but not that complex. Good grip but a slight lack of depth. Still very fresh. Fine but not great. (March 2002)

NOW TO 2012   17.5

Richebourg, 1988
Domaine de la Romanée-Conti

Full colour. Rich, full and meaty on the nose. A suggestion of the tannic structure on the palate.

Bigger, of course, than their 1988 Romanée-Saint-Vivant. More bulky. But a great deal more richness and concentration. Very long. Very classy. Very concentrated and multidimensional. This is aromatic, voluptuous and very fine indeed. Splendid. (October 2002)

NOW TO 2015+   19.5

La Romanée, 1988
Domaine Bouchard Père et Fils

Fine colour. Much better than the 1990 and 1989. Slightly austere on the nose. But lots of depth and vigour. This is full bodied, youthful, rich and very well balanced. Lots of dimension. Really quite structured. Lovely finish. Very fine for the vintage. Will still improve. (March 2003)

NOW TO 2025   18.5

Romanée-Saint-Vivant, 1988
Maison Jaffelin

Fullish, mature colour. Much more elegant and balanced than the 1989. Fragrant. Sandal-woody. Round, ripe and attractive. No undue tannins. Fresh, generous and fullish bodied. Very lovely. A major improvement on the 1989. Long, complex and classy. This is very fine. (March 2002)

NOW TO 2020   18.5

Romanée-Saint-Vivant, 1988
Domaine de la Romanée-Conti

Fullish, mature colour. Lovely fragrant, flowery, elegant nose. Very Romanée-Saint-Vivant in style. On the palate it is medium-full bodied, laid-back, rich and full of fruit. But leaner and not as rich or as voluptuous as the 1989. Very fine plus, though. (March 2002)

NOW TO 2020   19.0

Ruchottes-Chambertin, 1988
Domaine Frédéric Esmonin

Medium-full, mature colour. Slightly tough on the nose. But good depth here, if a little ungainly. On the palate full body, very good concentration of fruit and good grip. Quite oaky. Slightly light but not a bit lean. Fine finish. Lots of depth and class. Fine. (April 2005)

NOW TO 2015   17.5

Ruchottes-Chambertin, 1988
Maison Louis Jadot

Very full, still immature colour. The nose is still closed. On the palate, slightly tannic and astringent. Ripe, fullish and concentrated. Even rich. But a little sturdy. The structure is apparent. Just a touch over-macerated. Yet plenty of fruit and succulence, even sweetness. Very good indeed. (October 2001)

NOW TO 2012   17.0

Ruchottes-Chambertin, Clos des Ruchottes, 1988
Domaine Armand Rousseau

Fullish, vigorous, mature colour. A little more developed than the 1990. Fresh, stylish, balanced, vigorous nose. Crisp but elegant at the end. Medium-full body. Ripe. Raspberry-flavoured. Very fresh. Leaner than the 1990, but complex. Lots of dimension. Very long. Very classy. (December 2003)

NOW TO 2010+   18.0

Savigny-lès-Beaune, Les Dominodes, 1988
Domaine Bruno Clair

Good, fullish, vigorous colour. Very pure and fragrant on the nose, with a slight underlying tannic austerity. On the palate medium to medium-full body. Ripe, pure, classy, balanced and even intense. By no means a blockbuster, but elegant, complex, fresh and harmonious. Lovely long finish. Very good indeed. A lovely example of what it is. Unexpected style for a Savigny. (May 2003)

NOW TO 2010+   17.0

La Tâche, 1988
Domaine de la Romanée-Conti

Full colour. Still very vigorous. Very lovely nose. As big as their 1988 Richebourg, but with less obvious tannic structure. Marvellously concentrated fruit. Full and succulent. Yet more opulent than the Richebourg. Still very vigorous. Excellent grip. Really brilliant fruit. Very, very lovely. Excellent. (October 2002)

NOW TO 2015+   20.0

Volnay, Les Caillerets, 1988
Domaine de la Pousse d'Or

Medium-full colour. Just about mature. Ripe. Very stylish. Lovely fresh, plummy nose. Medium to medium-full body. Intense. Long. Not a bit lean. Complex at the end. Fine. (November 2000)

NOW TO 2010+   17.5

Volnay, Caillerets, Clos des 60 Ouvrées, 1988
Domaine de la Pousse d'Or

Magnum. Fullish, mature colour. Fragrant, succulent and even sweet on the nose. No austerity. Fullish body. Ample. Good grip. A suggestion of cedar wood. Ripe and quite rich. Very good vigour. Plenty of class. Lovely long finish. Fine plus. (November 2002)

NOW TO 2010   18.0

Vosne-Romanée, Les Beaux Monts, 1988
Domaine Leroy

Good colour. Fragrant, but now mature on the nose. Quite sensuous. Not a bit too austere. Medium-full body. Rich and ripe. Good grip. A generous example. Long. Soft. Fully ready. Very good indeed. (October 2002)

NOW TO 2010   17.0

Vosne-Romanée, Les Chaumes, 1988
Domaine Méo-Camuzet

Medium to medium-full colour. Ripe, youthful nose. Round and fresh but without any undue austerity. Medium body. Some oak. Not a great deal of concentration. But balanced and elegant. Very good but it lacks a little succulence and charm. (October 2005)

NOW TO 2018   16.0

Vosne-Romanée, Les Chaumes, 1988
Domaine Daniel Rion et Fils

This is fullish bodied but fragrant, balanced and ripe, without anything austere and lean about it. Lovely fruit. Really very elegant. Complex, long and soft at the end. Very good indeed. (October 2003)

NOW TO 2013+   17.0

Vosne-Romanée, Clos des Réas, 1988
Domaine Jean Gros

Good fullish, mature colour. A slight touch of reduction on the nose. This is still youthful. This medium to medium-full bodied, balanced and classy, but the acidity is quite marked. Still needs a couple of years to round off. Very good indeed. (January 2004)

NOW TO 2020   17.0

Vosne-Romanée, Cros Parantoux, 1988
Domaine Henri Jayer

Full, barely mature colour. Fullish, rich, concentrated and quite solid. But not too oaky. Plummy. Very well balanced. Lots of quality and depth. No austerity. Just very good grip. Very good fruit. Seductive. Very fine plus. (June 2005)

NOW TO 2020   19.0

Vosne-Romanée,
Les Gaudichots, 1988
Domaine Forey Père et Fils

Good fullish colour. Just about mature. Ripe nose. Nothing a bit too austere about it. Medium-full body. Quite concentrated. Clean, ripe and rich. Good energy at the end. Vigorous and à point. Good length. Very good indeed, if not fine. (March 2003)

NOW TO 2016   17.0

Vosne-Romanée, Les Gaudichots, 1988
Domaine Thierry Vigot

Good colour. Slightly earthy (but not rustic—just a little dry) on the nose. It "warmed up" in the glass, though. Medium-full body. Decent acidity, but could have been riper and had more personality. Very good. (May 2003)

NOW TO 2010   16.0

Vosne-Romanée, Les Suchots, 1988
Maison Camille Giroud

Good colour. Generous on the nose for a 1988. No austerity here. Medium-full body. Ripe and accessible and really quite seductive. Classy. Very good acidity. Long and complex. Fine plus. (June 2003)

NOW TO 2015   18.0

Vosne-Romanée, Les Suchots, 1988
Domaine Gérard Mugneret

Magnum. Full, mature colour. Fullish, ripe, rich and ample on the nose. Still very fresh. Full, rich and vigorous on the palate with a hint of new oak. Lots of depth and character. Very good grip. Round and very lovely. Long. Very fine. (November 2002)

NOW TO 2010+   18.5

1987

Twenty years old, and the product of a mediocre growing season, the 1987s never promised a great deal and are now well past their best. The white wines were rather thin and dilute; the reds were variable, at their best at the outset in the Côte de Beaune, but only of interest at *premier cru* level and above. Many of the Côte de Beaunes had already begun to dry out by 1997. At the 10-year-on tasting we found some agreeable Côte de Nuits. But I doubt that there is anything which will give much pleasure today.

WEATHER CONDITIONS

It was not a very auspicious summer. As one grower said to me, "We only had 6 weeks of fine weather in 1987: 3 in March and 3 in September." After a cold January, the early spring was dry. April was miserable, and May not much better, though there was an improvement towards the end of the month. The *sortie*, though large, was a fortnight late, and indifferent weather in June retarded the flowering until the end of the month.

The climate continued to be disappointing. Though there was not much *coulure*, there was widespread *millerandage*—albeit less in the Chardonnays than in the Pinots, which had flowered earlier when the weather was poorer still. Moreover, hail in parts of Meursault further reduced the size of the eventual crop, fortuitously as it turned out, for in those cooler corners further up in the hills where the flowering took place even later and in slightly better conditions, the crop was larger, but consequently more dilute.

It was not until the beginning of September, with growers already anticipating the worst, that the weather improved. Three weeks of sun saved the crop. After September 20 the weather broke, diluting the concentration which had been building up. There were several days of rain, but at the same time there was a cool north wind. This dried the fruit and prevented the formation of rot. Indeed because of the *millerandage*, the mature berries in each bunch were separated from each other, and so there was less incidence of *pourriture grise* than in 1986 and 1985. The harvest was generally under way by September 27 and at first took place under clear skies. From October 3 or 4 onwards it was intermittently wet, not just during the rest of the harvesting period but right through the winter.

⇘ Rating for the Vintage ⇙	
Red	14.5
White	13.5

⇘ Size of the Crop ⇙ (In hectolitres, excluding generic wine)		
	RED	WHITE
Grands Crus	11,018	2,785
Village and Premiers Crus	159,322	36,593
TOTAL	170,340	39,378

TASTING NOTES

WHITES

Bâtard-Montrachet, 1987
Domaine Ramonet

Magnum. Some depth and age to the colour now. Ripe, mature, fullish, oaky nose. Plenty of depth, energy and concentration on the palate. I was amazed when I heard it was 1987. This is really delicious. Long, lovely and very fresh indeed. Very fine indeed, especially for the vintage. (January 2001)

DRINK SOON   19.0

Meursault, Charmes, 1987
Domaine Robert Ampeau

As usual, quite ample and very fresh for the vintage. Good acidity. Medium to medium-full body. But at the end, a little four-square and not exactly elegant. Very good plus for the vintage. (April 2001)

DRINK SOON   16.5

Le Montrachet, 1987
Domaine de la Romanée-Conti

Full colour. Rich, fat and youthful. Slightly heavy. Some botrytis. Good energy. Plenty of depth. Unexpectedly full, vigorous and concentrated for the vintage. A slight lack of real class but certainly fine. (May 2005)

NOW TO 2009   17.5

Puligny-Montrachet, Les Combettes, 1987
Domaine Robert Ampeau

Fresh colour. Fresh for what it is on the nose. Could have been 1997. Medium weight. Not a lot of vigour. But quite fresh and ample and juicy fruity. Better on the palate than on the nose. Really very attractive. No hurry to drink. Very good indeed. (October 2005)

NOW TO 2010   17.0

Puligny-Montrachet, Les Pucelles, 1987
Domaine Leflaive

This is now a well matured wine, but one with plenty of interest, nevertheless. There is fruit and balance, and a honeyed finish. But no great depth or dimension. Nor is there a great deal of class. For a 1987, it has quality and has held up well. Very good plus within the context of the vintage. (August 2001)

DRINK SOON   16.5

REDS

Beaune, Les Grèves, 1987
Domaine Michel Lafarge

Ripe, soft, plump and fragrant. Medium to medium-full body. Balanced and fresh. This has both depth and good intensity. Lovely fruit. Positive and classy. Still vigorous. (March 2002)

NOW TO 2011   16.0

Chambertin, 1987
Domaine Louis Jadot

Good colour. This is very classy and very fresh for a 1987. Medium body. Fragrant and very stylish. Still quite oaky. Now refined, round, soft, gentle and harmonious. Very long. Very classy. No sign of earthy, dead leaf tannins. Very fine. (April 2001)
NOW TO 2009   18.5

Chambertin, 1987
Domaine Ponsot

Medium colour. Quite mature nose. Ripe, rich, individual, fragrant and very, very clean. Medium structure. No dead leaves tannins. Mellow. Complex. Not the greatest of depth and length, but very fine for the vintage. (April 2001)
DRINK SOON   18.5

Gevrey-Chambertin, Clos Saint-Jacques, 1987
Domaine Louis Jadot

Fresh, mature colour. Round, ripe, fresh, oaky nose. On the palate, medium to medium-full body. Good fruit. Balanced. Still has vigour and life. Classy and remarkably good for the vintage. Fine plus for the vintage. (April 2005)
DRINK SOON   18.0

Latricières-Chambertin, 1987
Domaine Joseph Faiveley

Good mature colour. No undue age. A slight lack of vigour on both nose and palate, but no lack of fruit and balance. Some style. Medium body. At least very good indeed for the vintage. (October 2001)
DRINK SOON   17.0

Romanée-Saint-Vivant, 1987
Domaine de la Romanée-Conti

(Marey-Monge.) Medium mature colour. Fragrant nose. But a bit light. Well developed. Not the depth and the succulence of the 1986. Medium body. Decent freshness and fruit. But a little one-dimensional. There is no doubt that this is fine for the vintage but, after the 1986, not special. (March 2002)
DRINK SOON   17.5

1986

A very large crop: the biggest in recent years after the 1982. But larger in retrospect in *rouge* than in *blanc*. It was a vintage which was variable from the outset. Vintage rain separated the quality of the Côte d'Or reds into good Côte de Nuits (though not exceptional) and disappointing Côte de Beaunes. The white wines, though, seemed very much better, and there were many at the outset who opined for 1986 over 1985. As these wines have evolved, these rosy expectations have proven hollow. Too many white wines were made with overripe grapes and rapidly coarsened up, even dried up in bottle, though there were honourable exceptions. Today, even the best reds now show undue age.

WEATHER CONDITIONS

The winter of 1985–86 was cold, but the excesses of 1985 were avoided. There was no frost damage. Spring was cool, wet and miserable, retarding the development of the viticultural cycle, but June was warm and sunny. More importantly, it was exceptionally dry, enabling the flowering to take place successfully thus ensuring a crop which, barring disaster, would be large. July was a little hotter and a little drier than the norm, and August was, at first, also dry and fine. From the middle of the month onward, however, the weather was patchy, and as the climate deteriorated further, fears of the quality of the harvest began to mount. September was somewhat cooler and considerably wetter than the average: 115 millimetres of rain fell, compared with under 10 millimetres in 1985. It was also humid, particularly between the two most important downpours of September 12 to 15 and September 24 to 25. This humidity, having arrived when the grapes were already almost at maturity, encouraged the spread of rot, and for the most part, as far as the Pinot Noir was concerned, it was *pourriture grise*. What the onset of this did, in its turn, was to encourage some growers to start their harvest as early as September 20. Those who did, or who started as soon as the rain stopped on September 25, have made weak, watery wine in huge quantities: wine of no merit.

Thankfully, after the clouds had blown away on September 25 the barometer rose, the humidity was rapidly chased off by a cool, drying wind from the north, and there was no further rain until the third week of October, by which time all the white grapes had been gathered in safety.

The best growers delayed starting their harvest until the beginning of October, by which time the Chardonnay grapes had benefited from the drying wind and were concentrated and fully ripe: indeed, some even had the beginnings of *pourriture noble*, which gave the wines some extra fatness, but at the expense of reducing the acidity. The grapes gained as much as half a degree of potential alcohol per day in maturity during the vital week after the rain had ceased. The size of the white wine harvest was as large as anticipated, but in those *climats* not affected by frost in the previous vintage, it was no larger than in 1985. That of the red wine harvest, though, despite a great deal of *triage*, was much greater.

✢ Rating for the Vintage ✢	
Red	12.0–14.5
White	13.5–16.5

✢ Size of the Crop ✢ (In hectolitres, excluding generic wine)		
	RED	WHITE
Grands Crus	14,877	2,957
Village and Premiers Crus	197,856	48,302
TOTAL	212,733	51,259

TASTING NOTES

WHITES

Bâtard-Montrachet, 1986
Domaine Leflaive
Magnum. Quite a deep colour. Quite a lot of botrytis on the nose. Decent acidity but a lack of purity. Fullish body. Some clumsiness. Some astringency. Quite good at best. Oxidised in the glass. (October 2001)
DRINK SOON   14.0

Bienvenues-Bâtard-Montrachet, 1986
Domaine Louis Carillon et Fils
A little reduced at first. Fully ready. Rich, full and concentrated. Slightly dead, but a good bottle. Should be fine and vigorous. (March 2003)
DRINK SOON   15.0

Chevalier-Montrachet, Les Demoiselles, 1986
Domaine Louis Jadot
Rich. Full. Very good acidity. Now quite decadent. Very good concentration. Still with excellent vigour. Very fine plus. (October 2002)
DRINK SOON   19.0

Corton-Charlemagne, 1986
Domaine Michel Juillot
Fresh colour. Surprisingly youthful. Rich, ripe, clean and succulent. Classy. *À point*. Very good indeed. It lacks a little class to be really fine. (May 2001)
DRINK UP   17.0

Corton-Charlemagne, 1986
Maison Roland Remoissenet et Fils
Very evolved colour. Almost too old. This is confirmed on the palate. Old and madeirised. Well past its best. (March 2001)
PAST ITS BEST (SEE NOTE)

Meursault, Blagny, 1986
Maison Louis Jadot
Fine at first. Fresh, ripe and full of interest. No lack of grip. But declined after 30 minutes. (August 2000)
DRINK SOON   14.5

Meursault, Charmes, 1986
Domaine des Comtes Lafon
Full, rich and sensuous. Ripe and delicious. Fat. Good grip. Well matured. Still fresh. On the verge of overripeness. Perhaps not the greatest

of class, but seductive and attractive. Good positive finish. Fine. (October 2002)

DRINK SOON   17.5

Meursault, Genevrières, 1986
Domaine des Comtes Lafon

Quite an evolved colour. The nose is also developed. A little oxidised. A certain nuttiness and overripeness. Broad and a little sweet-sour. Fat and, if not very elegant, certainly no lacking interest. Medium-full body. A wine for food. Slightly astringent at the end now. Yet a certain sweetness all the way through. Others admired it, but not my taste. No real *terroir* definition. (September 2005)

DRINK SOON   15.0

Le Montrachet, 1986
Domaine des Comtes Lafon

Deep colour. But no undue age. Honeyed. A little botrytis. A suggestion of sweetness. Cool and fresh. Soft. Very ripe. Balanced, fresh and classy. Holding up very, very well. *À point*. No hurry to drink. Very fine indeed. But didn't hold up in the glass for very long. (June 2005)

NOW TO 2009   19.0

Puligny-Montrachet, Champ Canet, 1986
Domaine Louis Carillon et Fils

Distinct botrytis on the nose. Almost sweet on the palate. Quite evolved. Fullish bodied, rich and aromatic. Decent acidity at the end. Nicely ripe and stylish. Very good, but not as good as his 1986 Perrières. (September 2001)

DRINK SOON   16.0

Puligny-Montrachet, Les Combettes, 1986
Domaine Leflaive

Lightish colour. Pretty. Not botrytised, but not very concentrated or with very much grip. A little bland, in fact. On the palate, a suggestion of built-in sulphur. This is thin and unexciting, despite having a decent length. Better than the Pucelles. Quite good. (June 2000)

DRINK SOON   14.0

Puligny-Montrachet, Les Combettes, 1986
Domaine Étienne Sauzet

Magnum. Lovely nose. Very good grip. Quite full and firm. Quite a big wine. Good fresh fruit. Still vigorous. Fine quality. Still holding up well. (July 2004)

NOW TO 2010   17.5

Puligny-Montrachet, Les Perrières, 1986
Domaine Louis Carillon et Fils

Still holding up very well. A lovely mature white Burgundy. Melons and peaches with a suggestion of oak underneath. No fade. Great class. Still plenty of depth and interest. A lovely bottle. Fine. (November 2001)

DRINK SOON   17.5

Puligny-Montrachet, Les Pucelles, 1986
Domaine Leflaive

It is some time since I last saw this. Five or more years ago I found it overweight, unbalanced, flabby and rather disappointing. This bottle is full, alcoholic, meaty and rather heavy, but the acidity is there. The wine is overripe and rather coarsely honeyed at the end, but by no means a disaster. Better with food. There are touches of the southern Rhône here. (August 2001)

DRINK SOON   1.0

REDS

Bonnes Mares, 1986
Domaine Georges Roumier et Fils

Magnum. This was the first year Christophe green-harvested. Good full, vigorous, mature colour. Surprisingly attractive, fresh and clean. Yet gamey-sensual fruit. They late-harvested here and benefited from a better *arrière-saison*. Very complex. Soft and really delicious. Good energy and depth and even backbone. Long. A splendid example. Fine plus/very fine for what it is. (June 2003)

DRINK SOON   18.5

Bonnes Mares, 1986
Domaine Charles Thomas

Full, mature colour. No astringency on the nose, which is full and firm but fresh and stylish. Very rich and ample. Very good acidity. Fullish body. The whole thing has vigour, intensity and class. Very long. Very velvety-smooth. Splendid for a 1986. Really fine. (May 2002)

NOW TO 2009   17.5

Clos de la Roche, 1986
Domaine Hubert Lignier

Medium, well-matured colour. The nose is diffuse, but there is some fruit, as well as a little astringency. The finish is clean, though. Not dry. Most enjoyable. Good fresh, slightly over-ripe, fruit. For a 1986 this is fine, if a little one-dimensional. (April 2003)

DRINK SOON   17.5

Mazis-Chambertin, 1986
Domaine Philippe Naddef

Surprisingly full, vigorous colour. Rich nose. Slightly four-square. But not too oaky. On the palate this has excellent acidity, is full, rich and sweet. Quite structured, but not too much so. Nice and fat. Good grip. Much more concentration and grip than most 1986s. Much more vigour and substance. Very fine for what it is. (October 2001)

DRINK SOON   18.0

Musigny, 1986
Domaine Jacques-Frédéric Mugnier

Good fullish, mature colour. Ripe nose. Fresh. Spicy. Not the greatest grip or purity. Yet excellent for the vintage. Better on the palate. Medium-full body. Lots of concentrated fruit. Good freshness. Even complexity. And long and classy and silky at the end. The palate is very lovely here. 20/20 for the vintage and unexpectedly still will last well. (September 2005)

NOW TO 2010+   20.0

Richebourg, 1986
Domaine Jean Gros

Medium colour. Yet still very fresh after 20 years. Gentle nose. Soft, ripe and sweet. Fragrant old rose (though not in any way fading) aspects. On the palate this is fully à point, and it was wise not to leave this too long, as I think from here it may begin to lose its bite. Medium

body. Oaky. Ripe and balanced. Indeed no lack of class, length and complexity. Got better and better and more vigorous in the glass. A lovely mellow wine. Very long on the palate. Very fine for the vintage. (November 2001)

DRINK SOON   18.5

Romanée-Saint-Vivant, 1986
Domaine de la Romanée-Conti

(Marey-Monge.) Good fullish colour. Now mature. Rather richer and more succulent and with more depth than the 1987. Similar on the palate. Soft but plump, fat and ample. Good grip. Medium-full body. Really rather good for the vintage. Still has life. Very fine. (March 2002)

NOW TO 2010+   18.5

Volnay, Clos de l'Audignac, 1986
Domaine de la Pousse d'Or

Fullish colour. Ripe. Plump. Good substance. Rich and stylish. Medium-full body. Fresh. Good tannins. Very good plus. (October 2003)

NOW TO 2016   16.5

1985

The year 1985 was a splendid white wine vintage and a year for reds which were ripe, generous, succulent and medium-full bodied. Where there was a question mark over these reds was in their vigour. Some were a little too loose-knit. I remember a friend warning me when I was about to set up a 10-year-on tasting in London that we would find half the reds fully ready, even at the "drink soon" stage, while the other half would still need 3 or 4 years to mature. He was absolutely right.

WEATHER CONDITIONS

The key to the answer, as so often, lies in the weather. The 1985 season commenced with a bout of really savage frost, with the temperature descending to −18°C in Chablis, a level at which even the vine is vulnerable. Although the thermometer did not fall quite so low in the Côte d'Or, in plots where there were young vines, where there was a hollow in which the frost could collect, or where, for one reason or another, plants were simply particularly susceptible, much damage was done. Some vines were killed outright. Others did not produce in 1985. A few suddenly gave up the ghost in the years to come. Not since 1956 was there such arctic weather in Burgundy.

In the Côte d'Or, the overall effect of the frost, though overplayed at the time, was important but not serious, in terms of both the 1985 crop and the long-term. Much of the damage was in AC Bourgogne *rouge* vineyards, not in the village wines, though a little pocket of *premiers crus* in Gevrey, where the land dips between the *grand cru* of Charmes and the main road, suffered badly, as did part of the low-lying ground behind the walls of Clos Vougeot, and also parts of Aloxe and Chorey. In these areas, large-scale replanting was necessary. Estimates of the total losses added up to 250 hectares in the Côte d'Or, plus 70 in the Saône et Loire and 50 in the Yonne (Chablis). This represents just under 3 percent of the area under vines in the Côte d'Or.

Following the cold winter, the spring and early summer progressed without mishap. The flowering was a little late, but on those vines not affected by the frost, a perfectly satisfactory number of flowers set into fruit. Up to the beginning of August, the climate was neit-her exceptionally good nor worryingly bad, but then a perfect *fin de saison* set in. August and September were extremely dry, with barely 10 millimetres of rain falling during those two months (an unprecedented drought), and, though August was not particularly warm, September was really quite hot. This transformed the crop from something uneven, behind-hand and unpromising at the beginning of the month to something ripe, uniform, healthy and concentrated by the last week when the harvest began to get under way.

The harvest progressed swiftly and safely. There was no rot; there had been no hail. It was hardly necessary to pick over the bunches either in the vineyard or in the *chai* to eliminate anything rotten. All the fruit was ripe; all of it was healthy. At the Domaine Rousseau in Gevrey-Chambertin, the crop required twenty-five pickers for 6 days. In 1986 it would require fifty for 12. It was an easy harvest: no rain and no vinification problems, despite the fine weather, and no lack, it seemed, of either bunches of fruit or juice.

→ Rating for the Vintage ←	
Red	16.5
White	18.5

→ Size of the Crop ← (In hectolitres, excluding generic wine)		
	RED	WHITE
Grands Crus	9,699	2,506
Village and Premiers Crus	129,445	44,066
TOTAL	139,144	46,572

WHERE ARE THE BEST WINES? AND THE STATE OF MATURITY TODAY

- The white wines were consistent and slow to evolve. At the very top levels, there are still some magnificent bottles, even today.

- Twenty-two years on, there are many *premier* and *grand cru* reds which show no signs of age, even in the Côte de Beaune, where Volnays in particular stand out. These are quite delicious now and can still be kept.

TASTING NOTES

WHITES

Bâtard-Montrachet, 1985
Domaine Jean-Noël Gagnard

This is very classy. Full bodied. Clean, concentrated and vigorous. Indeed, very youthful still. Lovely ripe acidity. Peachy. Long. Very fine. (October 2002)

DRINK SOON   18.5

Chassagne-Montrachet, La Boudriotte, 1985
Domaine Blain-Gagnard

This is very lovely, and very fresh still. Indeed, splendidly so. Soft, but fresh, concentrated, vigorous and harmonious on the palate. Lovely fruit. Fine. (October 2002)

DRINK SOON 17.5

Chassagne-Montrachet, Les Caillerets, 1985
Domaine Jean-Noël Gagnard

Marvellous nose. A splendid wine of real class and quality. Still very fresh. Very profound. Ripe and succulent. Full and concentrated. Real depth. *Grand cru* quality. Very fine indeed. A splendid example. (December 2001)

DRINK SOON 19.5

Corton-Charlemagne, 1985
Domaine Bonneau du Martray

Splendidly youthful colour. This is a wine of amazing vigour and very splendid quality. Fullish body. Complex, relaxed, very vigorous fruit. Very fine grip of acidity. Long and profound. Excellent. Indeed, really great. Absolutely no sign of age. (June 2005)

NOW TO 2010+ 20.0

Corton-Charlemagne, 1985
Domaine Louis Latour

Deep colour. Honeyed nose. Quite evolved. Even a touch of oxidation. Some fruit still and still fresh. But now beginning to lose its grip. Lacks a bit of elegance. (March 2003)

DRINK SOON 15.0

Meursault, Genevrières, 1985
Domaine des Comtes Lafon

Fullish, but not too old a colour by any means. Compared with the 1986, this is classic. Full, rich, nutty and gently oaky. Lovely harmony. Lots of depth. Still vigorous, though not for very much longer perhaps. A powerful wine, like the 1989. Very fine grip. Lovely finish. Very fine. (September 2005)

NOW TO 2010 18.5

Meursault, Perrières, 1985
Domaine Robert Ampeau

The colour is still very fresh indeed. Vigorous, full, pure and full of fruit on the nose. Nutty and minerally. Remarkable energy for a 20 year old wine. Very little oak. Long and very lovely. (October 2005)

NOW TO 2010+ 18.0

Montrachet, 1985
Domaine Ramonet

Rich, fat, nutty, concentrated and very fresh. Splendid depth and vigour. Very lovely fruit. Profound and multidimensional. Gentle finish. Long, complex and absolutely delicious. Full body. Very, very long indeed. This is super. Great wine. (April 2006)

NOW TO 2015 20.0

Morey-Saint-Denis, Monts Luisants, Blanc, 1985
Domaine Ponsot

A very vigorous vine. Ripe and complex. Excellent grip. Quite full. Lots of depth. Will last and last. Lovely. (January 2001)

NOW TO 2010 18.0

Puligny-Montrachet, Les Combettes, 1985
Domaine Robert Ampeau

Surprisingly fresh nose. Ripe, ample and nicely steely-peachy. Good vigour. Plenty of depth and very good grip. Fine. (October 2005)

NOW TO 2012 17.5

Puligny-Montrachet, Les Pucelles, 1985
Domaine Leflaive

Full and mature, but profound and splendidly vigorous. This is very lovely. Marvellous fruit. *Grand cru* quality. Not a whisper of age. Very long, rich finish. (December 2000)

DRINK SOON 19.0

REDS

Beaune, Les Grèves, 1985
Domaine Michel Lafarge

Fullish, ample, round, ripe and fully mature. This is rich and aromatic and very good plus.

Plenty of vigour. Long and satisfying at the end. (October 2000)

DRINK SOON   16.5

Beaune, Les Grèves, 1985
Domaine Albert Morot

An interesting wine. At first a little lean and austere for the vintage—despite previous decanting—but as it developed, it seemed to get sweeter and more succulent. A reserved wine, nevertheless. But certainly very good plus. (April 2001)

DRINK SOON   16.5

Beaune, Perrières, 1985
Domaine Leroy

Full colour. Brown at the rim. Rich, mellow and sophisticated on the nose. Medium-full bodied, round, balanced and delicious on the palate. Plenty of energy still. Long on the palate. Very good. (June 2005)

NOW TO 2012   16.0

Beaune, Les Teurons, 1985
Domaine Albert Morot

A lightish colour for a 1985. Fully mature. Ample nose. Quite pronounced acidity, plus an aspect of the stems. Medium body. A bit on the lean side for 1985. One hesitates to suggest that there might be some 1984 in here. But the wine doesn't taste much like a 1985. Elegant but rather lacking in sweetness and succulence and fat, which, after all, are the signatures of 1985. Some new oak on the aftertaste. Curious. But good. (May 2001)

DRINK SOON   15.0

Bonnes Mares, 1985
Domaine Joseph Drouhin

Medium-full, mature colour. Fragrant, mature nose. Not the geatest richness and fat and intensity, but very good indeed. Good follow-through. Round, ripe, balanced and lovely. Long and lingering at the end. (October 2000)

DRINK SOON   17.0

Bonnes Mares, 1985
Maison Roland Remoissenet et Fils

Very good colour. Ripe, cool, aromatic nose. Good acidity. Some oak. A full, rich, succulent, balanced wine. Very splendidly cool and classy. Excellent subtle depth and harmony. Vigorous, long and very complex. Very fine. (March 2001)

NOW TO 2010   18.5

Chambertin, 1985
Domaine Joseph Drouhin

Good vigorous colour. Immediately a wine of substance, class and dimension. Splendidly pure, vigorous Pinot on the nose. Profound and rich and with very good grip. Fullish on the palate. Ample, complex and distinguished. This is very fine indeed and will keep for ages. (December 2003)

NOW TO 2013+   19.5

Le Chambertin, 1985
Domaine Leroy

Excellent colour. Barely mature. Marvellous nose. Very concentrated. Very rich. Very fresh and multidimensional. On the palate, a full bodied wine with plenty of backbone. Now rich, velvety and mellow, but with amazing vigour for a 1985. Real breed here. Excellent. A great wine. (January 2003)

NOW TO 2020+   20.0

Chambertin, 1985
Domaine Armand Rousseau

Fullish, mature colour. Fully mature nose. Delicate. Ethereal and fragrant. On the palate, soft and silky yet intense and classy. Well matured. Lovely balance. Great class. A bit more evolved than last time out, but very lovely indeed. Splendidly complex. Splendid finish. (October 2005)

DRINK SOON   20.0

Le Chambertin, 1985
Domaine Jean Trapet Père et Fils

Medium-full, mature colour. Rich nose, now mature, with spicy vegetal touches. Quite full. Ample, plump and balanced. It lacks a little class and richness and concentration and definition, but it has good acidity. Long on the palate. Still very fresh. Very good indeed. (August 2001)

DRINK SOON   17.0

Chambolle-Musigny, Premier Cru, 1985
Domaine Jacques-Frédéric Mugnier

Medium to medium-full colour. Well matured. This is quite developed. Medium to medium-full body. Aromatic. Definitely an old Burgundy. Sensuous flavour now. Better on the palate than on the nose. His 1988 Fuées is rather better. Yet plump, fresh and complex. Very good. (March 2000)

DRINK SOON   16.0

Charmes-Chambertin, 1985
Domaine Denis Bachelet

Fine full, mature colour. Vigorous but gentle nose. Intense but understated. Very poised. Very together. Fullish body. Essence of fruit. Perfect harmony. Very, very long and very, very classy. An excellent wine. (April 2006)

NOW TO 2020   19.0

Charmes-Chambertin, 1985
Domaine Joseph Faiveley

Fullish colour. Still very young. On the nose, rich, full, tannic and even sturdy but splendid fruit underneath. Splendidly balanced. Full on the palate. Excellent grip. Very lovely balanced, rich fruit. Plums and black currants. A lovely example. Lots of depth. Fine plus. (March 2002)

NOW TO 2012+   18.0

Charmes-Chambertin, 1985
Maison Moillard

Medium-full colour. Fully mature. Somewhat corked. Medium-full body. Rather rigid. No better than quite good. (April 2006)

NOW TO 2011   14.0

Charmes-Chambertin, Très Vieilles Vignes, 1985
Domaine Joseph Roty

Full, vigorous colour. Very lovely nose. Intense, concentrated and still very youthful. Splendid fruit. Fullish body. Very rich on the palate. Quite oaky. Marvellously concentrated. Very vigorous. Real quality and depth here. An exotic example. Excellent. Will last for ages. (January 2001)

NOW TO 2020   19.0

Clos de la Roche, 1985
Domaine Dujac

Medium-full, mature colour. Quite well-matured but still very fresh on the nose. Good acidity, but not as much as in the 1990. Medium-full body. Mellow but succulent and fresh. Fine plus. (June 2004)

NOW TO 2010   18.0

Clos de la Roche, 1985
Maison Joseph Faiveley

Medium-full colour. Fully mature. Big, fat, earthy and slightly reduced. A bit ungainly. Better as it evolved. Full body. Still a firm tannic element. Ripe, stylish, vigorous and balanced. Lots of energy. Fine but not great. (March 2006)

NOW TO 2020+   17.5

Clos de la Roche, Cuvée Vieilles Vignes, 1985
Domaine Ponsot

Magnum. Fullish, mature yet vigorous colour. Lovely slight grapefruit touch to the fruit on the nose. Medium body. Individual but evolved. Lacks a little energy. Fresh, though. Very good rather than great. (March 2006)

NOW TO 2012   16.0

Clos Saint-Denis, 1985
Domaine Dujac

Medium-full, mature colour. Soft, mature but intense and vigorous nose. Good grip. Mellow and complex. Very lovely fruit. Very classy. Long and multidimensional and with lots of freshness and potential for aging. (September 2002)

NOW TO 2010+   17.5

Clos de Tart, 1985
Domaine du Clos de Tart

Medium-full colour. Rich nose. Even a little sweetness. Slight toughness. But underneath, good depth and concentration. Slightly four-square, though. Slightly inflexible. Decent acidity. Still vigorous, if slightly ungainly. Ripe finish. Good length. Very good plus. (October 2002)

DRINK SOON   16.5

Corton, 1985
Domaine Joseph Drouhin

Good colour. Still virile. Lovely nose. Fragrant, ripe and stylish. Lots of fruit and very good depth and grip. Medium-full body. Still fresh. Nice masculine Kirsh flavours. Long. Very fine.

(January 2001)

DRINK SOON 18.0

Corton, 1985
Domaine Charles Thomas

Full, rich, mature colour. Sensual, fully mature Pinot fruit on the nose. More evolved than the Bonnes Mares 1986. It is fuller, fatter, richer and more aromatic. But is it classier? Here there is a suspicion of astringency and lumpiness. It is best drunk with food. Plenty of vigour and life still. It is very good indeed. (May 2002)

NOW TO 2009 17.0

Corton, Les Bressandes, 1985
Domaine Chandon de Briailles

Good, vigorous colour. Rich and mellow on the nose with a definitive flavour of the stems. Ample, ripe, vigorous and classy on the palate. *À point*, but with plenty of life left. Medium-full body. Good grip. Complex and intense and long and rich and delicious. Fine plus.

(July 2003)

NOW TO 2013 18.0

Corton, Clos des Cortons, 1985
Domaine Joseph Faiveley

Full, vigorous colour. Still barely mature. Firm nose. Still a little unforthcoming. More so on the palate. Quite firm but full bodied, ripe and succulent. Very good grip. Juicy. Balanced. Fresh but *à point*. Long and vigorous. Bags of life. Very fine. (July 2006)

NOW TO 2020 18.5

Corton, Le Clos du Roi, 1985
Domaine Dubreuil-Fontaine

Medium to medium-full colour. Well matured, slightly rustic on the nose. The fruit is a little dried out. It is better on the palate, even if a bit aged. Fresh. Medium body. Good acid-ity. Decent style. Slightly lean at the end. Very good. (March 2006)

DRINK SOON 16.0

Corton, Les Pougets, 1985
Domaine Louis Jadot

Magnum. Good fullish, mature colour. Black cherry nose. Still quite austere. Firm. Very good acidity for a 1985. Balanced. Fullish body. Now soft. Ripe. Fruity. Long and complex. Fine, but not quite the richness for great. (November 2002)

NOW TO 2020 17.5

Chateau Corton-Grancey, 1985
Domaine Louis Latour

Medium to medium-full colour. Still fresh. Pleasant, if a bit one-dimensional on the nose. But good acidity and plump fruit. Not cooked. This is *à point*. It didn't gain anything in the glass. But it is medium bodied and is perfectly pleasant. (June 2000)

DRINK SOON 14.5

Echézeaux, 1985
Domaine Henri Jayer

Quite an evolved colour. Much more so than their 1989. Rather aggressive nose. Strangely herbaceous. Better on the palate. Soft but fresh. Round. Lovely ripe, concentrated fruit. Quite oaky. A bit rigid at the end. But lots of vigour. Will it ever really soften up? Very good indeed. As it evolved, it got more and more raw and rigid. Was the wood properly seasoned? (March 2003)

NOW TO 2010 17.0

Echézeaux, 1985
Domaine Jean-Pierre Mugneret

I've never encountered this Mugneret before, but there are many in this area. Good colour. Full and still quite vigorous. Somewhat funky on the nose. A little reduced and not entirely clean. Medium body. Now soft. Not exactly elegant, but fresh. Needs drinking. (December 2001)

DRINK SOON 13.5

Echézeaux, 1985
Domaine de la Romanée-Conti

Magnum. Fullish, mature colour. Rich, ripe and classy and balanced on the nose. Lovely profound fruit on the palate. This is really fine. Plump, vigorous, cool and complex. A lovely bottle. Fine plus. (July 2003)

NOW TO 2015   17.5

Echézeaux, Vieilles Vignes, 1985
Domaine Mongeard-Mugneret

Medium-full, mature colour. Fragrant nose. Rather more class than their 1989. Medium to medium-full colour. Round and succulent. Not fine but very good indeed. *À point* and not for the long term. (October 2005)

NOW TO 2010   17.0

Fixin, La Croix Blanche, 1985
Domaine Bruno Clair

Magnum. Medium, mature colour. Pure, slightly lean, but ripe and classy. Medium body. Not the greatest of depth or concentration on the palate. But soft and pleasant. Good. (October 2003)

DRINK SOON   15.0

Gevrey-Chambertin, Vieilles Vignes, 1985
Domaine Alain Burguet

Rich, fat, ripe, stylish and balanced. Full body. Virile. Elegant. This is very lovely for what it is. Still bags of life. Very good indeed. (October 2003)

NOW TO 2013+   17.0

Gevrey-Chambertin, Vieilles Vignes, 1985
Domaine Christian Sérafin

Fullish, youthful colour. Still quite firm and closed on the nose. Fullish on the palate. Quite chunky. Some tannin. No undue oak or tannin, though. The follow-through shows excellent acidity and succulent fruit. Cool, classy and fragrant. Very good indeed. (March 2002)

NOW TO 2010+   17.0

Gevrey-Chambertin, Clos Saint-Jacques, 1985
Domaine Louis Jadot

Medium-full, rich, well-matured colour. Aromatic, fragrant, old-vine Burgundy on the nose.

Medium-full body. *À point*. Properly sensual. Sweet, ripe, fresh finish at the same time. This is very lovely. Lots of life ahead of it. Just a little tarty at the end. (November 2002)

NOW TO 2015   18.0

Gevrey-Chambertin, Cl os Saint-Jacques, 1985
Domaine Armand Rousseau

Medium-full colour. Rich, full, concentrated and very profound on the nose. This is very composed and lovely. Fullish body. Very fine fruit. Very vigorous, too. Very lovely. Very fine. (April 2005)

NOW TO 2012   18.5

Gevrey-Chambertin, Lavaux-Saint-Jacques, 1985
Maison Leroy

Good full, vigorous colour. Still quite youthful. Some tannin here. Even a little chunky. But mellowed in the glass. Full bodied, ripe, succulent and concentrated on the palate. Very good grip. Still years ahead of it. Not great but very good indeed. (October 2001)

NOW TO 2015   16.5

Grands Echézeaux, 1985
Domaine René Engel

Magnum. Medium-full, mature colour. It took some time to come out of the glass. Rich and ripe. Slightly earthy tannins. Good grip. Medium-full body. Not as classy as today, but balanced. Reasonable fruit, but a bit short. Very good. (October 2003)

NOW TO 2009   16.0

Grands Echézeaux, 1985
Domaine de la Romanée-Conti

Very good colour. Still barely ready. Marvellously rich nose. Fullish body. Rich. Very ripe. Now mellow but very vigorous. Excellent fruit. This is very lovely. Multidimensional. Still very youthful. Very long. Very complex. Very, very classy and *terroir* expressive. Very fine. (March 2001)

NOW TO 2020   18.5

Griotte-Chambertin, 1985
Domaine Joseph Drouhin

Fullish colour. Properly mature. Rich, vigorous, opulent and classy on the nose. Very lovely fruit here. Splendidly balanced. Fullish bodied, plump and *à point*. Fresh for a 1985. Very smooth and silky. This is a lot better than the 1989, indeed. Very, very lovely indeed. Everything in place. Very, very long. Lovely lingering, complex finish. Excellent. Will last well. (July 2003)

NOW TO 2020   19.0

Latricières-Chambertin, 1985
Domaine Joseph Faiveley

Full colour. Fuller than that of their 1988. More structure, more depth and vigour. Very classy. Lovely at the end. This is very fine, and holding up very well. (Feburary 2005)

NOW TO 2025   18.0

Latricières-Chambertin, 1985
Domaine Ponsot

Fine full, mature colour. Lovely fragrant nose. This is very, very lovely. Ripe, rich and smooth. Really very fine grip. Concentrated and complex. Lots and lots of depth. Perhaps the most classy Latricières I have ever had. Really very fine. (January 2004)

NOW TO 2020   18.5

Latricières-Chambertin, 1985
Domaine Jean Trapet Père et Fils

Medium colour. Fully mature. Sweet, slightly stemmy nose. Evolved. Soft. Not very classy. Slightly over-chaptalised. Decent grip and a positive finish. But good plus, at best. (April 2005)

DRINK SOON   15.5

Mazis-Chambertin, 1985
Domaine Joseph Faiveley

Fullish colour. Now mature. Splendidly ripe, profound nose. Just a hint of mint. Very classy. Some mocha. Medium-full body. Now mellow. The tannins are now soft. Very lovely succulent fruit. Balanced. Very long. Absolutely *à point*. Very delicious. Very lovely long finish. (October 2001)

NOW TO 2010+   18.5

Mazis-Chambertin, 1985
Domaine Armand Rousseau

Medium-full rich colour. Slightly reduced on the nose. The second bottle was fresher. Better after an aeration. Fresh, soft and fragrant. Medium-full weight. Classy. Cool. Balanced and fine. Not great, but a lovely bottle. Long and complex at the end. (January 2006)

NOW TO 2015   18.0

Musigny, 1985
Domaine Jacques-Frédéric Mugnier

Well matured on the nose. Rich, aromatic, soft and complex. Underneath, a very classy wine. More elegant on the palate than the nose because it is fresher and more vigorous. Lovely finish. Quite delicious. Very fine. (Feburary 2005)

NOW TO 2020+   18.5

Le Musigny, 1985
Domaine Jacques Prieur

Medium-full, fully mature colour. Fragrant nose. Just a little clumsy. Good fruit. Medium body. Clean and classy. But simple. Good freshness. Decent depth. This is not concocted, but it lacks the intensity and character of real Musigny. Rather vegetal as it evolved. Good at best. (March 2001)

DRINK SOON   15.0

Nuits-Saint-Georges, Les Boudots, 1985
Domaine Louis Jadot

Fullish, fresh colour. Lovely vigorous, fragrant, classy nose. Fullish body. Ripe, balanced and very elegant on the palate. Very good grip. Still has vigour. Ripe and harmonious. Very Vosne-ish. Long and lovely. (October 2000)

NOW TO 2010+   18.0

Nuits-Saint-Georges, Les Damodes, 1985
Domaine Jayer-Gilles

Full, vigorous colour. Oaky on the nose and while ripe and juicy, slightly bitter. On the palate, there is a wine of depth and richness and good grip. But the oak tannins dominate, and always will. This is a bit aggressive and bitter on the follow-through, after a succulent sweet entry; 100 percent new oak doesn't work here! (August 2001)

DRINK SOON   15.5

Nuits-Saint-Georges, Les Saint-Georges, 1985
Hospices de Nuits

Elevé by François Germain. Full colour. Well matured if slightly muddy nose. Fullish body. Quite a meaty wine. Ripe and with good acidity but not that much richness or finesse. Quite a muscular follow-through. *À point*. A typical, slightly four-square Nuits-Saint-Georges. Good plus. (March 2003)

NOW TO 2008   15.5

Pommard, Les Chanlins-Bas, 1985
Domaine Monthelie-Douhairet

Still a full, vigorous colour. Ripe, round and slightly rustic, but smooth enough on the nose and palate. Good grip. Average elegance. Not tough. A bit one-dimensional. Still plenty of life, though. Good but not special. (October 2003)

NOW TO 2011   15.0

Pommard, Clos de la Commaraine, 1985
Domaine Jaboulet-Vercherre

Fullish, mature colour. Chunky nose. Slightly tough. Not much class. Slightly soupy. Medium to medium-full body. Slightly astringent. Slightly spicy. Lumpy and coarse. Got more and more astringent at the end as it developed. (March 2002)

DRINK SOON   13.5

Pommard, Clos de Verger, 1985
Domaine Pothier-Rieusset

Medium-full colour. Now fully mature. But no undue age. Ripe, quite sweet, mellow nose. A touch rustic in the background. Medium body. Good balance. But not a lot of class. Good though. Still lovely. (October 2000)

DRINK SOON   15.0

Pommard, Les Epenots, 1985
Maison Camille Giroud

Good full, mature colour. Ripe nose. Plump, fresh but soft. Medium-full body. Decent depth and fruit. But not quite with the richness and flair and dimension for better than very good. (June 2003)

NOW TO 2010   16.0

Pommard, Les Rugiens, 1985
Domaine Hubert de Montille

Magnum. This is still very fresh, if not still a little austere. Fine ripe tannins. Medium-full body. Slightly lean on the palate, but very lovely fruit. Still very, very fresh. Even concentrated. Little in the way of mature-wine sensuousness in the flavour. Yet long, classy and very good indeed. This will still improve. It will, I hope, be more generous. (June 2001)

NOW TO 2010+   17.0

Richebourg, 1985
Domaine Jean Gros

Full colour. Still vigorous. Not quite as expressive on the nose as other bottles I have had. On the palate it is fine but not great. The fruit is losing its vigour. The acidity is a little to the fore. I have had better bottles. A second bottle was similar. This should be a 20/20 wine. (March 2004)

(SEE NOTE)

Richebourg, 1985
Domaine de la Romanée-Conti

Good colour. Slightly lean on the nose. I thought it was 1988. Medium-full body. Very classy. Ripe and quite substantial, and richer and richer as it evolved. A touch of oak. Lovely fruit. Very complex. Lovely. Fine plus. (October 2000)

NOW TO 2009+   18.0

La Romanée, 1985
Domaine Bouchard Père et Fils

Magnum. Fine, full colour. Still youthful. Lovely rich, full nose. A structured wine with a great deal of depth and succulence. Mellow, sweet and fresh. Very lovely pure fruit. No lack of vigour and structure. This is ample and succulent and very lovely indeed. Mellow, opulent and very fresh. A great wine. (March 2003)

NOW TO 2010+   19.5

Romanée-Saint-Vivant, 1985
Domaine Alain Hudelot-Noëllat

Medium-full colour. Now mature. Fresh nose. Ample fruit. Concentrated and classy. Fragrant and vigorous. Not as classy as the Domainee de

La Romanée-Conti, but still very impressive. Ripe, mature, balanced and classy. Now fully ready, but with no hurry to drink. Fresh and complex. Very fine. (March 2002)

NOW TO 2010+   18.5

Romanée-Saint-Vivant, Les Quatre Journeaux, 1985
Domaine Louis Latour

Good fullish colour. Well matured. Open, dry, flabby nose. No grip. No concentration. On the palate, a bit corked, but nevertheless, no joy here. All the fruit has been squeezed out of it. Astringent all the way through. Artificially sweet. Rather coarse. Drink soon (14/20). A second bottle was fresher and much better. Medium-full body. Plump, classy and balanced. Much more sophisticated. Gently oaky. Rich and lots of depth. Fine at the end. (March 2002)

NOW TO 2010   18.0

Romanée-Saint-Vivant, 1985
Domaine de la Romanée-Conti

(Marey-Monge.) Good fresh, full colour. Lovely fragrant nose. Balanced and classy. Pure and velvety-smooth. Yet very fresh. Marvellous intensity and depth. Softer than the 1990 of course, but still very fresh, complex and vigorous. Very fine for the vintage. Will still keep well. (March 2002)

NOW TO 2010+   18.5

Ruchottes-Chambertin, 1985
Maison Leroy

Full, vigorous colour. Splendidly concentrated, full, youthful nose. Very, very concentrated on the palate. Evidence of the stems. Excellent grip. Not the greatest of class, but fine plus. (March 2006)

NOW TO 2025+   18.5

Savigny-lès-Beaune, Les Vergelesses, 1985
Domaine Robert Ampeau

Medium colour. Nice youthful fragrant nose. Medium body. Nicely intense. Ripe and mature but vigorous. Good acidity. There is a slightly lean background here but no lack of quality. Good. (November 2005)

DRINK SOON   15.0

La Tâche, 1985
Domaine de la Romanée-Conti

Fullish, mature colour. Intense, very high quality Pinot on the nose. Full but soft and mellow on the palate. Really profound and with splendid vigour. Ready, but I am sure will last like this for ages. Excellent balance. Very lovely fruit. Very, very lovely. Very, very long. Excellent. (April 2006)

NOW TO 2020   19.5

Volnay, Les Caillerets, 1985
Domaine Bouchard Père et Fils

Medium-full colour. Fully ready. Fragrant, ripe, attractive nose. Still fresh. Medium-full body. Fresh. Quite rich. Lots of fruit. Very good acidity. Fresh and fragrant. Long and complex. Fine for the vintage. It will last well. I prefer this to the 1990. (March 2004)

NOW TO 2015   17.5

Volnay, Les Caillerets, 1985
Domaine Yvon Clerget

Fully mature colour. But with plenty of energy and intensity all the way through. Medium weight. Lovely fragrant fruit. Very Volnay. Very silky now. Lovely lingering finish. Fine. (September 2000)

DRINK SOON   17.5

Volnay, Champans, 1985
Domaine Hubert de Montille

This is full, well-structured, rich and fat. I thought it was a Pommard. Intense, succulent and still very young. Very good grip. Lots of depth. Very complex. Very classy. Very long. Bags of life ahead of it. Both full bodied and very elegant. Sumptuous. This is fine. (January 2003)

NOW TO 2020   17.5

Volnay, Clos de la Bousse d'Or, 1985
Domaine de la Pousse d'Or

Medium-full colour. No undue age. Rich, full and classy on the nose. On the palate, fullish bodied, pure and youthful. Very good grip. This is cool and very classy. Lovely fruit. Very long.

Very impressive. Real depth. Lots of life ahead of it. Fine plus. (March 2002)

NOW TO 2010+   18.0

Volnay, Clos des Chênes, 1985
Domaine Michel Lafarge

Fullish colour. This is a splendid wine and will still get better, though it is delicious now (especially if decanted in advance). Marvellously rich, succulent, concentrated nose. Excellent Pinot fruit. Classic Volnay. Fullish on the palate. Ample, rich, naturally sweet. The flavours are now getting complex, sensuous and mature. Multidimensional. This is very fine. Very lovely complex, fragrant finish. (January 2003)

NOW TO 2020+   18.5

Volnay, Les Mitans, 1985
Domaine Hubert de Montille

Fullish colour. Very fresh, youthful and stylish. Very lovely complex fruit. Medium-full body. Succulent and very elegant. Lots of dimension. Not a bit too austere. Very, very long on the palate. Fine plus. (September 2001)

NOW TO 2010+   18.0

Volnay, Taillepieds, 1985
Domaine du Marquis d'Angerville

Medium to medium-full colour. Very fragrant, elegant nose. Fine acidity for the vintage. Silky-smooth and intense. Medium body. Very fresh. Very complex. Very well balanced. A lovely example with a long, vigorous finish. Fine. (June 2000)

NOW TO 2009   17.5

Volnay, Taillepieds, 1985
Domaine Hubert de Montille

Good fullish, fresh colour. Fragrant nose. Slightly lean and with a suggestion of the stems (50 percent in those days). Medium-full body. Ripe, plump, balanced, vigorous and classy. Fragrant. Long. Still very fresh. Lovely. (June 2005)

NOW TO 2015   18.0

Vosne-Romanée, Clos des Réas, 1985
Domaine Michel Gros

Full and mature, but with fresh-looking colour. A rich, fully mature wine with all the complex spices of maturity. Multidimensional and complex. Medium-full body. Sweet and fresh. Old-viney concentration. This is very profound and very lovely. A delicious bottle. Long and lingering at the end. Fine plus for the vintage. It will still last well. (December 2003)

NOW TO 2010+   18.0

Vosne-Romanée, Les Suchots, 1985
Maison Joseph Drouhin

Full, vigorous colour. On the nose and the palate, the wine is stylish, balanced and very good indeed. The attack lacks a little personality, but the finish is more interesting. Yet I don't think there is a lot of concentration and depth here. Elegant and long, but very good plus, not fine. (April 2003)

NOW TO 2009   16.5

1983

Since the outset, opinions have been divided about the 1983 vintage. "Garbage," said an American magazine about the Domaine de la Romanée-Conti 1983s. These and other wines certainly were atypical. The tannins were solid and rather dry, and the wines, once the puppy-fat had disappeared, were unwieldy in their youth. Burgundy, we used to tell ourselves, is not the full bodied, warm-hearted wine the old books told us about. It is a wine of fragrance and delicacy, intensity but not muscle. And just as we were getting the message across, along came the 1983s to refute us. Many who wrote about the 1983s were confused. Some lambasted the whole vintage because they found a few big-name wines in Gevrey-Chambertin with rot, and others of equal standing in Vosne-Romanée demonstrating a taint of hail. Then the 1985s came along, and everybody jumped overboard in pursuit of their bubbly, charming fruit: a no-problem vintage we could all enjoy relatively young. And so we could forget about the 1983s.

And I began to feel like an Old-Testament prophet. But I have stuck to my guns. The best 1983s, I have always felt, would exceed—in concentration, in intensity and in complexity, not to mention, in the long-term, in finesse—the best of the 1985s. It is now clear that there *are* some great wines in this vintage. The rotten and the hail-tainted should not prevent us from acknowledging this fact.

The white wines, on the other hand, were very much less exciting. Rain during the early part of September, when the berries were more or less physiologically ripe, caused widespread rot. Some of this was noble rot, and one or two "Meursault-ernes" were made as a result. Elsewhere, even when clean—the rotten berries having been eliminated—the wines were heavy and alcoholic. All these whites are now old.

WEATHER CONDITIONS

The start was not auspicious. The early spring was late, very cold and particularly wet. Budding was normal, but humidity was high, and there were fears that rot might develop prematurely in the vineyards. However, the end of May saw a marked improvement. June brought the sun and dry weather, and the flowering took place in the middle of the month in excellent conditions. It looked as if it were going to be a good-sized crop and, numbering the usual 100 days between the onset of the flowering and the date of picking, a harvest which would not be too late.

The weather continued to be fine, except for a particularly bad hail-storm in Vosne, Vougeot and Chambolle in July (of which more later), right up until the end of August. It was particularly hot and dry, and, as will be seen, this was the salvation, or at least one of them, of the 1983 harvest.

September, however, brought rain. Not just a little much-needed moisture, but almost continual downpours, for 2 whole weeks. The growers began to fear for the worst. Luckily, just in time, the rain stopped. Because of the heat during July

and August, the grapes had built up very thick skins and did not seem to be too affected by the early September inundation. Moreover, with the fine weather came great heat. The fortnight prior to the start of the harvest (September 25) saw temperatures in the upper 20s Celsius. The fruit was therefore able to become super-ripe and super-concentrated with extract, sugar and acidity levels all increasing as the water evaporated in the grapes.

This is the secret of the success of the best of the 1983 vintage. The hot weather arrived when the grapes were already more or less fully ripe; most of the tannins, therefore, though dominant, are round and well covered. In 1976, a vintage with which the 1983 has been much compared, the heat occurred earlier when the grapes were still in their infancy. The sap, to some extent, could not flow through the plant as easily as it should because of a lack of rain, and the skins were thickened and scorched. In 1976, the tannin, therefore, was less round and less ripe, and the wines were often too hard and tough for their own good.

So the 1983 fruit was super-ripe and super-concentrated. As one grower pointed out: in 1983 the grapes ripened in 90 days and not 100. Most people picked after 100 days, so the fruit had an element of *sur-maturité* not seen in Burgundy for more than 20 years. Who would need to chaptalise the 1983s?

Yet there were problems. Not all the 1983s are quite as marvellous as the above might indicate. Despite the hail having occurred before the *véraison* (when the grapes begin to soften and change colour), some wines were affected. More display rather dry tannins and a touch of rot as a result of the wet start to September.

→ Rating for the Vintage ←

Red	12.0–18.5
White	13.5

→ Size of the Crop ←
(In hectolitres, excluding generic wine)

	RED	WHITE
Grands Crus	11,955	3,038
Village and		
Premiers Crus	143,435	36,527
TOTAL	155,390	39,565

Sadly, sorting tables were not as prevalent then as they are today.

WHERE ARE THE BEST WINES? AND THE STATE OF MATURITY TODAY

- The white whines are now old.
- The red wines are variable. A lot have dried up. Only the very best *premier* and *grand cru* examples are still vigorous. But these will still keep.

TASTING NOTES

WHITES

Bâtard-Montrachet, 1983
Domaine Louis Jadot

Quite a developed colour. But not excessively so. Full, rich and aromatic, but not heavy or oily. Very good acidity, thanks to Jacques Lardière's policy of stopping the malo. Nevertheless, aspects of the southern Rhône. But no undue botrytis. A meaty wine. Still vigorous. A splendid, multifaceted, mature wine. Delicious. Fine. (March 2003)

DRINK SOON   17.5

Corton-Charlemagne, 1983
Domaine Bouchard Père et Fils

Quite a deep golden colour. Ripe, rich nose. Almost like a vendange tardive. Yet balanced and elegant and with plenty of depth. Suggestions of sweetness on the palate. Plenty of interest. If not a great deal of class. Still has vigour. Very good. (June 2000)

DRINK SOON   16.0

Meursault, Perrières, 1983
Domaine Pierre Morey

Magnum. Pierre's first year when he could refridgerate the must. Alternately, very hot and very stormy. Huge rush to maturity. Lots of damage from *ver de la grape*-caused rot. Most picked too late: they just weren't ready early enough. This is a very clean wine, but definitely a vendange tardive. There is even now a residual sweetness. But very concentrated. But with a dry finish. Surprisingly fresh, vigorous

and well-balanced. A curiosity, but fine. Bags of life. (August 2000)

NOW TO 2010   17.5

REDS

Chambertin, 1983
Domaine Ponsot

Medium to medium-full colour. Fresh, especially for 1983, a vintage whose colours browned very early. Rich and concentrated, if slightly tight on the nose. Touches of minty toothpaste on nose and palate. Fullish body. A slightly hard/earthy character but fresh, lively and very concentrated. Very good grip. Evolved in the glass. Individual and complex. Amazingly youthful for a 1983. Still even a bit austere and will still improve. Will still last well. Fine. (March 2006)

NOW TO 2015+   17.5

Chambertin, 1983
Domaine Armand Rousseau

Fine full, vigorous colour. Marvellously rich nose. Full body. Some tannin. Vigorous. Excellent depth and grip. Completely clean and truly exciting. Lots of substance here. Powerful, vigorous and very classy. This is not quite great: perhaps it lacks just a little class. But it is profound, multidimensional, fat and vigorous. Very, very lovely. Proof that at its top level, 1983 is quite superior to 1985. (December 2001)

DRINK SOON   19.5

Chambertin, Vieilles Vignes, 1983
Domaine Jean Trapet Père et Fils

Full colour. No undue brown at all. Rich, robust, toffee flavours on the nose. Vigorous and powerful. Full and concentrated. Spicy and sweet. Quite alcoholic. Good grip. There is a lot of depth and power here. And a really very fine wine. Complex at the end. Mocha flavours. (January 2001)

DRINK SOON   19.0

Chambertin, Clos de Bèze, 1983
Domaine Clair-Daü

Mature colour. Medium weight. Fragrant, clean, classy and pure. No undue undergrowthy smells, nor rot nor hail taint. Mature but clean and balanced. Now lightening up a bit. But classy, long and still fresh. Fine quality. (October 2000)

DRINK SOON 17.5

Charmes-Chambertin, 1983
Domaine Joseph Drouhin

Fullish colour. Fully mature. Fragrant nose. Fresh for the vintage. Rich and concentrated as well. Excellent for a 1983. No astringency. Just a full, very fat, rich and succulent wine. Excellent concentration. Lots of vigour. Very sweet and yet very fresh. Very long. Lots of time left. This is very fine. (April 2006)

NOW TO 2012 18.5

Charmes-Chambertin, 1983
Maison Leroy

Medium-full, fully mature colour. No undue age. On the nose, some of the astringency of the vintage. Slightly rigid. Yet very fine fruit. Not as fine as Drouhin's. But more vigour and more depth. Still youthful. Fine plus. (April 2006)

NOW TO 2015 18.0

Clos de la Roche, Vieilles Vignes, 1983
Domaine Ponsot

Full, evolved colour. Rich, full, succulent, aromatic, soft nose. Fully mature, if not loosening up now. But ripe and sweet and still vigorous. Not a trace of any rot or hail. Long, concentrated, classy and lovely. (October 2002)

DRINK SOON 18.5

Clos de Vougeot, 1983
Domaine Alain Hudelot-Noëllat

Full but quite old colour: properly brown at the rim. Splendid aromatic nose. Toffee, mocha, exotic and velvety. Not a bit astringent. Nor any off-flavours or hail taint. Fullish but now beginning to lighten up. Ample, ripe, rich and spicy. Residual sweetness. Obviously the product of a hot year. But not hot and alcoholic at the end. Good acidity. Not a hint of dryness on the finish. At first opulent and seductive, if not of great finesse. But it didn't hold up very well in the glass. Got a bit dirty on the finish. Merely very good. (Febuary 2004)

DRINK SOON 16.0

Clos de Vougeot, 1983
Domaine Dr. Georges Mugneret

Magnum. Fine colour. No signs of age. Rich and concentrated but fresh, not cooked on the nose. Lots of depth and dimension. Full bodied. Still a little tannic. But very concentrated on the palate. Real essence of wine. Very fine grip. This is vigorous and fresh and very fine. A lovely bottle. Proving again how good the best 1983s can be. Bags of life. This is very fine. Bravo! (January 2000)

DRINK SOON 18.5

Gevrey-Chambertin, Clos Saint-Jacques, 1983
Domaine Armand Rousseau

Very fresh, fullish colour. Ripe, spicy, even sweet, on the nose. Not a bit astringent, nor coarse or rotten. Very fresh on the palate. Full bodied, rich and sweet. *À point*. Very concentrated. Much more so than their 1985. Very fine grip. Lots of life. Very fine plus. (May 2001)

NOW TO 2012 19.0

Gevrey-Chambertin, Lavaux-Saint-Jacques, 1983
Domaine Henri Magnien

Fullish, mature colour. No undue age. Still vigorous. Nothing rotten or hailed-on here. Rich and opulent, but with a slight chocolate and astringent touch. Clean. No dead leaves. Still plenty of life. Very good. But a wine for food. (August 2000)

DRINK SOON 16.0

Le Musigny, 1983
Domaine Joseph Drouhin

Magnum. Full, rich colour. Fragrant, yet spicy nose. At a high level, the elegance of Musigny is fighting with the exoticism of the vintage. The vintage wins. Spicy, full, mature and rather less elegant than the 1985. Smooth and sweet at the end. Fine, but not very fine. (September 2005)

NOW TO 2012 17.5

Pommard, Les Rugiens, 1983
Domaine Hubert de Montille

Magnum. Quite a full, vigorous colour. On the nose, a touch chunky and astringent. Slight dryness but less than with most, because there is an underlying richness in the wine. Good grip. Quite a powerful wine for a 1983. Good depth. Harmonious. Good finish. But I fear the astringency will take over from now on. It is also losing its generosity and sweetness. Now a little austere. Very much better with food. Not nearly as ungenerous. Very good plus. (June 2002)

DRINK SOON   16.5

Romane-Saint-Vivant, 1983
Domaine de la Romanée-Conti

(Marey-Monge.) Fullish, well matured colour. Quite an earthy nose. Rather more mature than the 1985. And less classy and less concentrated. Less grip, too. On the palate, this is soft and ripe. No hail taste or anything. Indeed, very fine grip. More fruity than the 1989. But indeed as much, if not more, interest on the palate. Very fine. (March 2002)

NOW TO 2010+   18.5

La Tâche, 1983
Domaine de la Romanée-Conti

Fullish, mature colour. Fullish nose. Aromatic, rich, exotic, concentrated and complex. Splendidly intense. Very lovely. Very seductive. Full bodied. Clean and pure. Quite a big wine, almost as big as the 1990. Much bigger than the 1985. Exotic and lovely. Not a bit astringent or overbalanced. Long and multidimensional. A really splendid example, if not really very elegant. Very fine. (March 2003)

NOW TO 2022   18.5

Volnay, Champans, 1983
Domaine Monthelie-Douhairet

Good vigorous colour. But well-matured. Slightly dry and astringent on the nose. Better on the palate. Good attack. Fresh and plump and with good acidity. Slightly astringent at the end. Good but not brilliant. Not the greatest of class. (September 2002)

DRINK SOON   15.0

Volnay, Champans, 1983
Domaine Hubert de Montille

The first year that Étienne vinified with Hubert. A huge *triage* after an attack of grape worm. Fullish colour. Concentrated and spicy. Rich and succulent. Very good grip and intensity. Quite meaty and structured. Bags of life. Fine. (December 2001)

NOW TO 2009+   17.5

Volnay, Les Mitans, 1983
Domaine Hubert de Montille

Magnum. Full, mature colour. No undue age. Very lovely fragrant nose. All the rich, almost exotic aspects of the vintage but none of the astringency or overripeness. Long, mellow, profound and delicious. Very well balanced. (September 2001)

DRINK SOON   17.5

1978

One of the smaller crops of the decade. Only 1981, 1975 and 1971 were significantly lower. The year 1974, however, was almost identical in size.

The white wines were blessed with good acidity. They were quite full, had good structure and were ripe, racy, balanced and stylish. As they evolved—and were compared with the 1979s—which one preferred became a question of individual taste: the charm and instant appeal of the one, or the sometimes rather austere rigidity (but certainly the depth) of the other. In the long run, the 1979s won, in my view, but there were plenty of equally good if not better 1978s. Today, not unexpectedly, after nearly 30 years, they are well past their best.

The reds, too, had good acidity. At first they were clean and richly fruity and had a lot of style. They were clearly better than, if not as big as, the 1976s, but they did not quite have the refinement of the 1971s. On the other hand, they were more even and lasted better.

Today, the mark of the 1978 vintage is a finesse and consistency throughout the Côte;

this is not one of those vintages (both 1979 and 1980 spring to mind) in which one can single out a section of the *vignoble* as being superior to the rest. The wines had a vigour and a harmony which gave them structure to last. Pleasant as they were in their youth, the best had—and some still have—the extra dimension and character of maturity. While in the final analysis, few wines have the richness, the succulence and the generosity to make them really fine, 1978 is a very good vintage, and at the top levels, it is still holding up.

WEATHER CONDITIONS

The 1978 weather pattern followed that of 1977 and was echoed by both 1979 and 1980—though not by 1981. The resulting wines were different, but one important factor links these four successive harvests: in each, the progress of the vine was severely delayed by poor weather in the spring. Where 1978 differed from the other years was in the quality of the weather in late summer and early autumn. From the very lip of disaster, the vintage, miraculously, was not just rescued into the realms of the acceptable, but promoted into the ranks of the successful. From the first week of August, when the vine was almost a month behind schedule, the sun shone, and the grapes were enabled to swell and ripen without interference. The fine weather continued until mid-October, when, more than a fortnight late, the vintage was finally ready to begin.

At the beginning, it hardly seemed possible that the miracle had happened. As late as the first of October, sugar readings in the vineyard indicated below 10 (alcoholic) degree wines, suggesting that a lot of chaptalisation would be required: the legal limit is the amount of sugar which will increase the alcoholic degree by 2°. My supplier of Bourgogne Aligoté and Montagny—for I was a wine merchant in those days—Roger Rageot, the Director of the Buxy Cooperative in the Côte Chalonnaise, told me that the grapes gained 2° in the last fortnight.

TASTING NOTES

WHITES

Bâtard-Montrachet, 1978
Maison Roland Remoissenet et Fils
Ripe, rich but still vigorous colour. Very lovely, rich, fat and concentrated nose. Very lovely on the palate. Complex, full, vigorous and very profound. Rich and very lovely. This is a very fine wine indeed. (July 2003)

NOW TO 2013   19.0

Corton-Charlemagne, 1978
Domaine Bonneau du Martray
Cool. Nutty. Fullish body. Plenty of depth. Ripe and aromatic. Still vigorous. Complex and long. This is fine. (April 2005)

NOW TO 2010   17.5

Corton-Charlemagne, 1978
Domaine Louis Latour
Magnum. Quite a deep colour. Fat, ripe, rich but not a bit heavy. Ample and quite stylish. Long. Very good indeed. (April 2005)

DRINK SOON   17.0

Meursault, Genevrières, 1978
Maison Roland Remoissenet et Fils
A bit reduced at first. But this blew away. Good colour. Quite fresh but well matured. Has lost a little of its concentration and grip. Reasonable class. But holding up very well for a 24-year-old white. (January 2003)

DRINK SOON   17.0

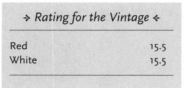

→ Rating for the Vintage ←	
Red	15.5
White	15.5

→ Size of the Crop ← (In hectolitres, excluding generic wine)	RED	WHITE
Grands Crus	8,546	2,103
Village and Premiers Crus	115,606	29,670
TOTAL	124,152	31,773

Le Montrachet, 1978
Domaine du Marquis de Laguiche/
Maison Joseph Drouhin

This is excellent. Truly classy. Very vigorous. Fullish bodied, rich and excellently balanced. Rich and aristocratic. Marvellous depth and concentration. Really very lovely. A great wine. Bags of life. (June 2000)

DRINK SOON 20.0

REDS

Chambertin, 1978
Domaine Jean Trapet Père et Fils

Medium colour. Well matured. Fullish, rich nose. A slight hardness here. Fullish, balanced, round and ripe on the palate. Still fresh. Not as seductive as Dujac's Combottes, but quite firm and with plenty of depth and energy. Fine. (March 2006)

NOW TO 2012+ 17.5

Chambolle-Musigny, 1978
Maison Roland Remoissenet et Fils

Good mature colour. Full, vigorous, fragrant and complex on the nose. Full and concentrated and with a lovely intensity of fruit on the palate. Very ripe but excellent grip. Lovely. Youthful for a 1978. Was probably ex-Vogue. Will still last very well. (March 2001)

NOW TO 2009 17.5

Chambolle-Musigny, Les Amoureuses, 1978
Domaine Robert Groffier

Healthy colour. Delicate, aromatic but fresh nose. Very lovely fragrant, intense, classy fruit. Medium-full body. Still youthful. Long, complex and with great finesse. Very fine. (March 2005)

NOW TO 2010 18.5

Chambolle-Musigny, Les Cras, 1978
Domaine Ghislaine Barthod-Noëllat

Good vigorous colour. At first I thought this was corked. But as it didn't get any worse, save to leave a certain aftertaste of slightly unclean wood, I concluded it wasn't. For despite this, there was much to enjoy. The wine is still vigorous.

Medium-full weight. Good supporting acidity, as you would expect with this vintage. Indeed, quite firm for a Chambolle. The fruit is a bit curate's-eggy. Good plump, ripe Pinot but with a certain dead-leaf, unclean-wood aspect on the finish. Yet not a bit undrinkable. Good, certainly. Other bottles may be even better. (May 2001)

DRINK SOON 15.0

Charmes-Chambertin, 1978
Domaine Hubert Camus

Good colour. Still fresh. The nose is a touch lean. On the palate, a little more fruit and succulence and no lack of style (more than today in my experience), but it has seen better days. The acidity is still keeping it fresh, of course. (October 2000)

DRINK SOON 16.0

Charmes-Chambertin, 1978
Domaine Dujac

Deeper colour than some Dujacs. Fully mature. No undue age. Soft, open, sweet, fresh and sensual. Medium body. Getting sensual. Not the greatest of depth. Not for very long term keeping. (April 2006)

NOW TO 2012 16.0

Charmes-Chambertin, 1978
Maison Camille Giroud

Medium to medium-full, mature colour. Fresh, ripe, complex, very classy nose. Medium-full body. Lovely balance. Lots of depth. Very good grip. Complex, naturally sweet at the end. Ripe. Gently spicy. Fresh and lovely. (June 2004)

NOW TO 2010+ 18.0

Clos de la Roche, Vieilles Vignes, 1978
Domaine Ponsot

Good, still fresh colour. Ripe nose. Good vigour. Nicely crisp fruit, but rich underneath. Fullish body. Elegant. Long. Very fine. (March 2006)

NOW TO 2012 18.5

Clos Saint-Denis, 1978
Domaine Dujac

Magnum. Medium to medium-full colour. Stylish nose. Lots of depth. At first a bit earthy (low fill), but this shook off, or most of it. Good fruit. Very good grip. Classy. Long. If clean, certainly fine. (July 2004)

NOW TO 2010+   17.5

Clos de Vougeot, 1978
Domaine Leroy

Still full and firm, even slightly austere on the nose. Quite tough. Plenty of depth. Good grip and plenty of fruit. Very good indeed. But not exactly soft and relaxed. Yet got mellower in the glass. Fine plus. (October 2002)

NOW TO 2010   18.0

Clos de Vougeot, 1978
Maison Roland Remoissenet et Fils

Full, not-too-mature colour. Full, fresh and rich, but slightly four-square on the nose. Better on the palate. Full and quite meaty. Good acidity. Plenty of depth and fruit, but not the nuance and class of fine. Good vigour. Very good indeed. (October 2003)

NOW TO 2010   17.0

Corton, 1978
Domaine Bonneau du Martray

Good colour. Soft, mellow and fullish. Classy. This is rather better than the reputation of the red wine at the time would suggest. Slightly earthy. Good vigour. Very good. (October 2002)

DRINK SOON   16.0

Echézeaux, 1978
Domaine de la Romanée-Conti

Good colour. Very impressive nose. Very fresh, sensual and subtle. Full and fat. Fullish body. Lovely fruit. Soft and mellow. Complex and classy. Still very vigorous. Very fine. (March 2001)

NOW TO 2010   18.5

Gevrey-Chambertin, Aux Combottes, 1978
Domaine Dujac

Medium-full colour. Still fresh. Very fragrant, ripe nose. Medium-full body. Fresh and mellow. Very, very composed and elegant. Very lovely. À *point* and showing no sign of age. Delicious. Fine plus. (March 2006)

NOW TO 2012+   18.0

Latricières-Chambertin, 1978
Domaine Ponsot

Fullish, fresh colour. Ripe, classy nose. Sensuous and aromatic now. Fullish body. Vigorous. Good grip. Lots of depth. Long. Fine plus. (April 2005)

NOW TO 2010+   18.0

Musigny, 1978
Maison Roland Remoissenet et Fils

Full, mature colour. Very rich nose. Even a slight touch of reduction at first. Full but very fragrant and intense. Very good grip. This has depth and class. Not the greatest of subtlety and finesse, but fine plus. (October 2003)

NOW TO 2013   18.0

Pernand-Vergelesses, Les Vergelesses, 1978
Domaine Rapet Père et Fils

Medium colour. No undue age. Slightly lean but fruity and stylish on both nose and palate. Medium body. Ripe and stylish. Long. Fresh. Really quite plump. Very good for what it is and holding up well. (June 2005)

NOW TO 2010+   15.0

Pommard, Les Pézerolles, 1978
Domaine Hubert de Montille

Fullish, mature tannin. This has a lot of finesse. Ripe, concentrated, classy and pure. Very complex. Very harmonious. Long. Fine. (November 2000)

DRINK SOON   17.5

Pommard, Les Rugiens, 1978
Domaine Jean Boillot et Fils

Quite firm on the nose. The acidity is reasonably marked. Now a touch lean and vegetal. Medium-full body. Quite a lot riper on the palate than the nose would suggest. Good fruit. Good energy. Good class. Long. Very good. (October 2002)

DRINK SOON   16.0

Pommard, Les Rugiens, 1978
Maison Camille Giroud

Brilliantly fresh, fullish colour for a wine which is now 25 years old. Fullish, slightly earthy, fresh, quite substantial nose. Full body. Very good tannins. Fine acidity. Rich fruit. Concentrated and very stylish. Long and impressive. Lots of vigour. Not a bit lean. Fine plus. (June 2003)

NOW TO 2010 18.0

La Romanée, 1978
Domaine Bouchard Père et Fils

Full, rich colour. Lots of vigour. Fresh but very 1978 on the nose. A slight austerity here. Riper on the palate. Medium-full body. This is classy but a little aloof. Very good acidity. Good structure. The follow-through is multidimensional and very, very classy. Very good length and a lovely long finish. Very fine plus. (March 2003)

NOW TO 2015 19.0

Romanée-Saint-Vivant, 1978
Domaine Cathiard-Molinière

Full, rich colour. Still vigorous. A bit evolved and rustic on the nose. Somewhat dried out. Decent fruit. But always a little coarse, I think. Medium-full body. It was better 5 years ago. Decent but not special. Drink up. (March 2002)

DRINK UP 15.0

Romanée-Saint-Vivant, Les Quatre Journeaux, 1978
Domaine Louis Latour

Fullish colour. Good depth and class on the nose. Still plenty of vigour. Well-balanced. Fullish body. Good tannins. A little sweet perhaps, but harmonious, complex, long and positive. Fine. (March 2002)

DRINK SOON 17.5

Romanée-Saint-Vivant, 1978
Domaine Charles Noëllat

Medium-full, mature colour. Quite evolved now. Medium to medium-full body. Good concentration and balance. Plenty of fruit and depth and with good grip. Was fine once, now very good indeed. Still very enjoyable. (March 2002)

DRINK SOON 17.0

Romanée-Saint-Vivant, 1978
Maison Roland Remoissenet et Fils

Under the label of Royale Club. Good colour. On the nose, ripe but a little lean at the end.

Riper on the palate. Fullish body. Good soft tannins. Rich and stylish. Very finely balanced. Long and complex. Absolutely no sign of age. Very vigorous. Lovely. Fine plus. (October 2000)

DRINK SOON 18.0

La Tâche, 1978
Domaine de la Romanée-Conti

Fullish colour. Well matured. More colour than the 1976. Full, rich, vigorous, aromatic, complex and fat and very ripe indeed on the nose. Full bodied. Creamy-rich. This is very, very vigorous. Excellent grip. Multidimensional. Really profound and very, very lovely. Very fine plus. (March 2003)

NOW TO 2020+ 19.0

Volnay, Clos de la Bousse d'Or, 1978
Domaine de la Pousse d'Or

Good colour. Lovely ripe, classy nose. Lots of depth and class. Very generous. Medium-full body. Very complete. Mellow and profound and complex. This is long and lovely. This is fine and will last very well. (October 2002)

NOW TO 2010+ 17.5

Volnay, Clos des Ducs, 1978
Domaine du Marquis d'Angerville

Good full, mature colour. Slightly austere but classy, fragrant nose. Ripe, even sweet, on the palate. Medium-full body. Harmonious. Lovely fruit. Very long and complex. Very fine. Still holding up very well. (April 2005)

NOW TO 2010+ 18.0

Volnay, Frémiets, 1978
Maison Camille Giroud

Youthful, mature, medium-full colour. One bottle a little thin and acidic—even with some volatile acidity. The second bottle is fuller, fatter, fresher and purer. Medium-full body. Fragrant, balanced and very stylish. Very Volnay. Long and fragrant and classy. Very good indeed. (June 2001)

DRINK SOON 17.0

Vosne-Romanée, Les Chaumes, 1978
Domaine Robert Arnoux

Fullish, rich, mature colour. Aromatic, ripe, stylish, complex, but slightly austere nose. Round and sweet on the palate. Good grip and freshness. Ripe and succulent. Long on the palate. Good finesse. (October 2001)

NOW TO 2010   17.0

Vosne-Romanée, Les Suchots, 1978
Maison Roland Remoissenet et Fils

Medium-full colour. Mature, but not unduly so. A touch of drains or something on the nose. Sweet and concocted on the palate. This is rather dreadful. No. A rogue bottle? (March 2006)

(SEE NOTE)

1976

The year 1976 was a sizeable crop, as large as 1970, though down on both 1972 and 1973, and, as it would turn out, 1977.

After a string of poor years, 1976 was almost bound to be overwritten, especially as it was the product of an absolutely gorgeous hot summer and an early harvest. And so it was. But we had to beware of now reacting in an opposite direction. There are a lot of parallels between 1976 and 1983.

The white wines were big, spicy, alcoholic and unbalanced. They lacked that *sine qua non*, good acidity. Controls were not what they are today, and more than one wine, in cask, was oxidised. Most were far too blowsy. They did not last.

As in other very concentrated years, more fruit was required to yield a barrel's worth of must than usual: not 300 kilograms, but more like 400. The wines had good colour and plenty of ripe, if rather "cooked," fruit; they were high in alcohol, lowish in acidity and, of course, unduly high in tannin.

At the outset, they were hard, but had plenty of flavour and extract. The Côte de Beaune seemed less unbalanced than the Côte de Nuits. But the wines looked like *vins de garde* with richness and substance.

In general, the vintage is uneven. Some wines were past it at 10 years. Others were too tannic, and the tannins were too unsophisticated: they never got there. But search hard, and even today you will find some good, if rather tough, wines. Few, sadly, are really elegant, and it is this which marks the vintage down.

→ Rating for the Vintage ←	
Red	14.5
White	13.0

→ Size of the Crop ← (In hectolitres, excluding generic wine)		
	RED	WHITE
Grands Crus	11,146	2,012
Village and Premiers Crus	142,613	28,077
TOTAL	153,759	30,089

WEATHER CONDITIONS

The summer, as I have indicated, was hot and dry. The harvest was abundant, but in these conditions, the very last grape was able to get to full ripeness and concentration, even as early as the second week of September. Moreover, the fruit was very healthy and was collected in good conditions (much better than in Bordeaux), well before the weather began to deteriorate towards the end of the month.

TASTING NOTES

WHITES

Chevalier-Montrachet, 1976
Maison Roland Remoissenet et Fils

Full, but not a bit heavy. Very clean. Surprisingly good vigour and grip. Really properly steely. Holding up remarkably well. Fine. (July 2004)

DRINK SOON   17.5

Corton-Charlemagne, 1976
Domaine Bonneau du Martray
Rich and grapey. Full and lush. There is a suggestion of the sweet and sour. Good acidity, but also overripe. Lots of character. But definitely a wine for food. (July 2001)

DRINK SOON   17.5

Meursault, Charmes, 1976
Domaine Leroy
Remarkably fresh. No undue botrytis. Still plenty of fruit. Good acidity. Lightened up a bit in the glass. The fat disappeared. Good, but not great now. (October 2001)

DRINK UP   15.0

REDS

Chambolle-Musigny, Les Amoureuses, 1976
Domaine Daniel Moine-Hudelot
Medium-full colour. Fresh. Plenty of weight on the nose. Vigorous. Good fruit. Still very much alive. Medium-full body. Nice and juicy. Even some of the elegance of Amoureuses coming through. Not tough. The finish is most agreable. Still long. Still vigorous. Long, fragrant and classy. Very good plus. (December 2001)

DRINK SOON   16.5

Chambolle-Musigny, Les Cras, 1976
Domaine Ghislaine Barthod-Noëllat
Good fullish, vigorous colour. Rich, fragrant nose with some of the 1976 structure underneath. Plenty of vigour here, and not a bit dense. Fullish, aromatic, balanced and rich on the palate. Most enjoyable. This is long and very good indeed. Complex and classy at the end. (March 2003)

NOW TO 2010   17.0

Clos de la Roche, 1976
Domaine Dujac
Very good mature colour. Really quite full for a Dujac wine. Full nose. Slightly animal. Good grip. Quite meaty, but not a bit of astringency. Full bodied. Vigorous. Mellow. Profound. This is a splendid wine for food. Rich, but with very

good acidity. Ripe, aromatic, surprisingly clean and vigorous. Very fine. (September 2002)

NOW TO 2010   18.0

Clos de la Roche, Cuvée Vieilles Vignes, 1976
Domaine Ponsot
Full vigorous, mature colour. Very fresh, concentrated, complex nose. Absolutely not a trace of astringency anywhere. Splendidly rich and vigorous. Very lovely harmony. Very long. Excellent. (March 2006)

NOW TO 2020   20.0

Clos de Vougeot, 1976
Maison Camille Giroud
Fullish colour. Mature but not dense or hard. Full and concentrated and spicy. A big, beefy wine. Nothing aggressive. Yet full and tannic at the outset. Still some tannins. Ripe and spicy and full of secondary flavours. Still has muscle. Funky and sweet and classy at the end. Long and lovely. (June 2004)

NOW TO 2010   17.5

Corton, Bressandes, 1976
Maison Camille Giroud
This is very lovely. Full colour. Still very youthful. Plump and very fresh. Not a touch of astringency. Fullish body. Vigorous. Yet fully mature. Complex, aromatic and classy. Very long. Very fine. (November 2005)

DRINK SOON   18.5

Corton, Clos du Roi, 1976
Maison Camille Giroud
Fine, full, youthful colour. On the nose, a little dry but remarkably unastringent. On the palate, full bodied, rich and quite fat. Good acidity. Plenty of dimension. No dryness. No tightening up. Fine. (March 2005)

DRINK SOON   17.5

Gevrey-Chambertin, Clos Prieur, 1976
Domaine Jean Trapet Père et Fils
Good fullish, mature colour. Not a bit dry or astringent. Ripe, ample, classy and vigorous.

Fullish bodied, balanced and with good depth. This is very good plus. (October 2003)
NOW TO 2010   16.5

Gevrey-Chambertin, Clos Saint-Jacques, 1976
Maison Roland Remoissenet et Fils

Full, vigorous colour. Muddy nose. Fruity, but it lacks class. Fullish body. Fruity on the palate. Slightly lumpy. Slightly rigid. OK but not special. (April 2005)
DRINK SOON   15.0

Griotte-Chambertin, 1976
Domaine Joseph Drouhin

Fullish colour. Surprisingly purple, especially for the vintage. Fresh, vigorous nose. Complex spies. Very good fruit. Very lovely. On the palate, a meaty wine. But with plenty of class and very good grip. Medium-full body. The tannins are now soft. Not a bit astringent. Very good acidity. This is surprisingly good. Slightly four-square, but that is 1976. (July 2003)
NOW TO 2010   17.5

Latricières-Chambertin, 1976
Maison Camille Giroud

Good fullish colour. No undue brown. Gingerbread and liquorice on the nose. Ripe and spicy. Fresh and complex. Fullish body. Ripe tannins. No astringency. Ample and plump. Balanced and classy. Long finish. Very fine. Indeed, one of the best 1976s I have had for ages. No hurry to drink. (May 2005)
NOW TO 2010+   18.5

Nuits-Saint-Georges, Les Pruliers, 1976
Maison Camille Giroud

Very good colour. Mature, but no undue age. Slightly dense on both nose and palate. Good but not brilliant acidity. Ripe, but just a little one-dimensional. Medium-full body. Good but not great. (June 2001)
DRINK SOON   15.0

Romanée-Saint-Vivant, 1976
Domaine Charles Noëllat

Surprisingly full, rich, mature colour. Rich, full, fat, ample and vigorous on the nose.

Fresh, fullish bodied, fragrant and full of fruit on the palate. No undue astringency at all. No great class, but a little diluted. Very good plus. (April 2004)
DRINK SOON   16.5

Romanée-Saint-Vivant, 1976
Domaine de la Romanée-Conti

(Morey-Monge.) Medium to medium-full colour. Fully mature. Ripe nose. Very fresh. No undue astringency. Medium-full body. Smooth. Classy. Not that concentrated. But an unexpectedly lovely bottle to drink now. Balanced, long and still alive. Very fine. (March 2002)
DRINK SOON   18.5

La Tâche, 1976
Domaine de la Romanée-Conti

Medium-full, well matured colour. A surprisingly un-tough, not dense wine. Now fragrant, almost ethereal. Very classy. This is now only medium bodied on the palate. It has begun to soften up, even to dry out. Slightly astringent on the follow-through. Slightly lean at the end. But not a bit aggressive nor astringent on the finish. Very good indeed. (March 2003)
DRINK SOON   17.0

Volnay, Premier Cru, 1976
Domaine Hubert de Montille

Slightly fading colour now. A little astringent on the nose. More fruit on the palate but lightening up now. Quite rich, originally. A little past its best perhaps, but nevertheless quite stylish. Good. (September 2002)
DRINK SOON   15.0

Volnay, Les Caillerets, Ancienne
Cuvée Carnot, 1976
Domaine Bouchard Père et Fils

Good full, fresh colour. A little tight on the nose. But reasonably fruity. A little rigid on the palate. Slightly astringent. Decent acidity, but with a lack of fat and succulence. Quite good. It won't improve. (March 2004)
DRINK SOON   14.0

Volnay, Champans, 1976
Maison Camille Giroud

Full, mature colour. Fragrant. Good acidity. Fullish but not a bit chunky. Balanced. Complex. Classy. Still very fresh. Very good finish. Very good plus. (June 2001)

DRINK SOON   16.5

Volnay, Clos des Chênes, 1976
Domaine Michel Lafarge

Medium-full colour. No undue age. Fine nose. Pure, rich, and spicy in the best sense. Full-ish body. Absolutely no astringency. Very ripe tannins. Unexpectedly pure and with very good grip. A splendid success in a uneven vintage. Will still last. (May 2004)

NOW TO 2010   17.5

Vosne-Romanée, 1976
Domaine Gérard Mugneret

Magnum. Medium colour. Fully mature. Ripe. Very fruity. No astringent tannins. Fresh and stylish. Medium body. *À point*. A very well-made, very pleasant wine. Long. Very good. (October 2003)

DRINK SOON   16.0

Vosne-Romanée, Les Suchots, 1976
Maison Camille Giroud

Good colour. Still very fresh and vigorous. Full, rich nose. Slightly dense but not off-puttingly so. Nor is it astringent. Medium-full body. Ripe and balanced. Fresh and stylish. No dryness. Fat and long. Fine. But lacks a little charm. (June 2003)

DRINK SOON   17.5

1971

This was the smallest vintage of the 1970s: 60 percent lower than the 10 year average. The year 1973 would produce almost twice as much, and 1982 almost three times the meagre 1971 crop.

The 1971 vintage was one of the first that I was responsible for buying as a merchant. The choice was fraught with danger. For while the vintage was generally fine, there was a lot of hail damage and *goût de grêle* in the wines in the Côte de Beaune, particularly in Volnay and Pommard: and there were similar problems in Nuits-Saint-Georges and Vosne-Romanée. There were also, it seemed to me—though none of the reports commented on it, and it was a small, essentially concentrated vintage—one or two wines which, while they were well-coloured and seemed ripe and fruity enough, did not have the length or grip I would have expected.

The whites were exceptional, and, of course, there was no problem with a hail taste. They were full, balanced and concentrated. They had real *terroir* definition and were very classy indeed. They lasted very well, but now, over 35 years later, can hardly be expected still to be vigorous.

At the start, the red wines had a good colour and plenty of concentrated ripe fruit, and they seemed also to have good acidity. There were flaws in many of the Côte de Beaune reds, and you had to pick and choose in Nuits-Saint-Georges and in Vosne-Romanée. Two domaines which were affected—and two of the few which offered wine in bottle then—were Henri Gouges and the Domaine de la Romanée-Conti. Yet the latter are brilliant. And, if carefully chosen, in many of the rest there was much to excite.

While everyone seemed determined to rate the 1971s as *vins de longue garde*, I was a little hesitant. They had more breed, certainly, than the 1969s. They were less lush and spicy. But they were less tannic and less alcoholic. Did they really have the grip and the volume? At the top levels, yes. But lower down the scale—perhaps a little surplus 1970 had been added to compensate for the short crop?—I thought not, or not always. Few 1971s are still alive, but some of those that are, are very fine.

As the 1971s have evolved, we have been able to separate the pleasantly ripe but best-at-8-to-10-years sheep from the firmer, more concentrated and long-lasting goats. Now, at getting on 35 years old, no wine should be criticised for needing drinking soon. And there are still some magnificently vigorous examples (the top Rousseaus, for instance). There are some very fine 1971s, and these have real breed.

WEATHER CONDITIONS

The spring was generally mild, and the buds burst early, but it was a small *sortie*, and the subsequent crop was further reduced by a cold and wet June, causing widespread *coulure* and *millerandage*. July was hot and dry; August, as so often, was unsettled, with a period of storms and cool weather in the middle of the month when much of the Côte was affected by hail: three successive waves in the afternoon of August 19. But then there was a return to fine weather in September. The *vendanges* began early, around September 15, and a small harvest of grapes was gathered in excellent conditions.

→ Rating for the Vintage ←	
Red	16.0
White	18.0

→ Size of the Crop ←		
(In hectolitres, excluding generic wine)		
	RED	WHITE
Grands Crus	7,533	1,527
Village and Premiers Crus	83,926	17,674
TOTAL	91,459	19,201

TASTING NOTES

WHITES

Criots-Bâtard-Montrachet, 1971
Domaine Delagrange-Bachelet

Magnum. Full mature colour. Fresh, well-matured nose. Holding up very well. Still succulent. Very good grip. Lovely cool crab-appley/peachy fruit. Complex. Long. Fine plus. (July 2006)

DRINK SOON   18.0

REDS

Beaune, Bressandes, 1971
Domaine Albert Morot

Light to medium colour. Well matured nose. The acidity is a bit dominant on the attack. Softer on the follow-through. Ripe. Fragrant. Stylish, long, classy and complex. Very lovely. Fine. (April 2005)

DRINK SOON   17.5

Beaune, Grèves, Vigne de l'Enfant Jésus, 1971
Domaine Bouchard Père et Fils

Magnum. Mellow, cedary nose. Soft. Still fresh. Good ripe fruit. Aromatic and sweet coffee flavours. Good style. Balanced and still vigorous. Long. Quite sweet at the end. Very good indeed. (October 2002)

DRINK SOON   17.0

Bonnes Mares, 1971
Maison Camille Giroud

Very fine colour. Very lovely nose. A fresh, juicy, plump, mellow wine. No hard edges. Excellent grip. Very classy. Full body. Somewhat austere still. Very classy. Not a bit rough and really very fine. Plenty of vigour. (October 2001)

DRINK SOON   18.5

Chambertin, 1971
Maison Camille Giroud

Fullish, vigorous, mature colour. This is fine, concentrated and profound. Full body. Very fine grip. Splendid fruit. A big, meaty, youthful example, as you would expect from Camille Giroud. Long and fresh. Lots of life ahead of it. Very fine. (June 2001)

NOW TO 2010   18.5

Chambertin, Clos de Bèze, 1971
Domaine Charles Thomas

Fullish, fully mature colour. Lovely sensual nose. But splendidly fresh still. Fullish weight. Very ripe but with excellent balancing acidity. Very harmonious. Very classy, intense finish without a trace of undue age or astringency. Plenty of vigour. Right up at the top of the tree, this wine. Very fine indeed. (May 2002)

NOW TO 2009   19.5

Charmes-Chambertin, 1971
Domaine Louis Latour

Good fresh colour. Ripe nose. Crisp and stylish. Medium-full body. Quite meaty. Rich, balanced and clean. Vigorous. Lots of energy. No sign of age. This is fine. (April 2006)

NOW TO 2012   17.5

Clos de Vougeot, 1971
Maison Camille Giroud

Fullish, mature colour. No undue age. Rich, ample, creamy, old-viney nose. Fresh. Complex. Delicious. Full bodied on the palate. It was quite a chunky wine in its youth. Today, definitely a wine for food. Quite substantial, if not with residual tannins. Good grip. Lovely complex fruit, but lacking in generosity and succulence. Slightly austere. But very classy. Fine. (Septmber 2004)

NOW TO 2010   17.5

Clos de Vougeot, 1971
Domaine Louis Jadot

Half. Because of hail damage and macerated for 12 to 14 hours only with pigeage and heating having added extra tannin. This is holding up very well. Still youthful. Full of interest. Very good. (June 2000)

DRINK SOON   16.0

Corton, Les Pougets, 1971
Domaine Louis Jadot

Fullish, fully mature colour. The nose is a little understated and a little dry. On the palate though, this is smooth, complex, classy and generous. Fullish bodied, vigorous and with a lot of depth. Lovely long finish. *À point*. Delicate. But will keep very well. (November 2002)

DRINK SOON   18.5

Echézeaux, 1971
Domaine de la Romanée-Conti

Medium, fully mature colour. Well matured, fragrant, almost sweet nose. Very expressive. Profound and ethereal. Fully mature yet vigorous and complex on the palate. Intense. Spicy. Long and fine plus. But it collapsed a bit in the glass. (March 2005)

NOW TO 2009   18.0

Gevrey-Chambertin, Clos Saint-Jacques, 1971
Domaine Gérard Seguin

Lichine label. Medium, fully mature colour. Lovely succulent nose. Round. Medium-full body. Balanced and profound. Still vigorous. Lovely fruit. Long and aromatic and very lovely. Very fine. (April 2005)

NOW TO 2010   18.5

Grands Echézeaux, 1971
Domaine de la Romanée-Conti

Medium-full, mature colour. Refined nose. Balanced and classy. Fresh. Not a blockbuster. Complex and classy. Very delicious. Fullish body. Ripe and rich. Vigorous but mellow. Very lovely ample fruit. Excellent balance and great finesse. Mature but vigorous. Really delicious. Unexpectedly rich for what it is. Very fine. A second bottle had mocha touches on the nose and was sweeter on the palate. A little older but still vigorous. Fine plus. (September 2005)

NOW TO 2010+   18.5

Nuits-Saint-Georges, Les Perrières, 1971
Maison Camille Giroud

Very good full, youthful colour. Aromatic nose. Still a little tight at first. It needed time to come out. Fullish body. Ample and very well balanced. Lovely cool fruit. Splendid structure and vigour for a 1971. Very stylish. Long. Fine. (June 2001)

DRINK SOON   17.5

Nuits-Saint-Georges, Les Vaucrains, 1971
Maison Camille Giroud

Full, rich colour. No undue maturity. Fresh, complex, mature nose. Vigorous. Fullish body. Balanced and nicely funky in flavour. Good long finish. Plenty of depth and energy. Quite a big wine. (June 2004)

NOW TO 2011+   17.5

Richebourg, 1971
Maison Camille Giroud

Fine mature colour. Shows a little age on the nose. Refined but getting a little thin. The fruit is classy but it is losing its sweetness. Medium to medium-full body. Fine but declining. (June 2001)

DRINK UP   17.5

Romanée-Saint-Vivant, Les Quatre Journeaux, 1971
Domaine Louis Latour

Lightish, well mature colour. Quite old, but no under senility. Fragrant. No undue sweetness. Soft, elegant and medium-bodied on the palate. This is very classy. No astringency. Sweet, pure and quietly energetic. Lovely. Very fine. (March 2002)
DRINK SOON   18.5

Romanée-Saint-Vivant, 1971
Domaine Marey-Monge/
Domaine de la Romanée-Conti

Magnum. Fine colour. Full, aromatic, profound and aristocratic nose. Fullish on the palate. Round and ripe. Subtle and silky. Marvellous fruit. Excellent finish. Still very, very fresh in this size. Very, very intense and very, very lovely. (March 2005)
NOW TO 2011+   19.0

Romanée-Saint-Vivant, 1971
Domaine de la Romanée-Conti

Magnum. Remarkable fine, fresh, full colour. Very, very lovely nose. Very fresh. Round and vigorous and fullish and succulent. The most lovely, classy, complex, rich, ripe fruit. Sweet and soft and seductive. This is a very lovely wine indeed. Impeccable balance. Very fine plus. It seems as if it will last for ages, despite being over 35 now. (March 2003)
NOW TO 2012+   19.0

La Tâche, 1971
Domaine de la Romanée-Conti

Magnum. Excellent, full, fine colour. Marvellously profound, poised, aristocratic nose. Very fresh. Very, very complex. Ethereal. Medium-full body. Fabulous fruit. Intense and profound. Quite fabulous. One feels that it has been like this for the last 15 years and will stay like this for the next 15. Extraordinary length and multidimensional. Perfection! (March 2005)
NOW TO 2020   20.0

Volnay, En Chevrets, 1971
Domaine Henri Boillot

Magnum. Aged colour now. Medium weight. Well matured. Soft, sweet and balanced. Stylish

and complex. Very Volnay. Nice and ripe. Good length. It needs to be drunk quite soon but is very good. (September 2002)
DRINK SOON   16.0

Vosne-Romanée, Les Suchots, 1971
Maison Camille Giroud

Fine, full, vigorous colour. Ravishingly elegant. Cool, concentrated, laid-back and complex. Smooth and succulent. Splendidly balanced. Silky and multidimensional and vigorous. Very, very long. Very fine plus. One of the freshest 1971s I have sampled for some time. (June 2004)
NOW TO 2011+   18.5

1969

In total contrast to Bordeaux, 1969 was a very successful harvest in Burgundy, though a small one, and it is much to be preferred to 1970 (and more consistent than 1971). Indeed, one could well argue that, with 1966, this was the best vintage of the decade after 1964. The white wines were very good indeed: firm, rich, concentrated, intense and really classic examples that lasted very well indeed, the best since 1959. Naturally, they are now old.

The red wines are a different matter. Full and rich and ripe, yes. But balanced and elegant? Not quite so high on the scale. There is a robust quality about many 1969 Burgundies, and in some cases, the tannins obtrude. The 1964s are more complete. The 1966s, though a little less structured, can show finer Pinot Noir fruit. Yet there is much enjoyment still to be found in this vintage, and the best wines are still vigorous.

WEATHER CONDITIONS

The climate, however, was not all that auspicious. Spring was late, the flowering delayed and protracted, leading to widespread *millerandage*, which reduced the crop, and it wasn't until July that the summer really began. Thereafter, though September was uneven, the weather in general was fine and hot, thus enabling the maturation to catch up a little. The vintage was nevertheless a little late, but the harvest was collected in good weather.

TASTING NOTES

WHITES

Meursault, Charmes, 1969
Domaine Leroy

Fresh colour. Youthful nose, especially for a wine of this age. Expanded in the glass. Round, fleshy, rich and balanced. Fully mature on the palate. Lots of depth and plenty of vigour. Full bodied, fat and quite mineral. Very fine indeed. (March 2005)

DRINK SOON   19.5

REDS

Beaune, Clos des Ursules, 1969
Domaine des Héritiers Louis Jadot

Tasted at Jadot in Beaune. Medium-full, vigorous, mature colour. Very lovely fragrant nose. Old roses. Soft, round, classy and complex. Ripe and full and mature. Mellow black-cherry flavours. Very good acidity. Totally lovely for what it is. Fine. (June 2001)

DRINK SOON   17.5

Chambertin, 1969
Domaine Leroy

Fullish, mature colour. Rich, vigorous, sweet, and high acidity nose. Fullish on the palate. Vigorous but complex, classy, fragrant and very harmonious. Very lovely classy fruit. Excellent grip. This is really very fine indeed. Magnificent! (March 2002)

NOW TO 2010+   19.0

Chambolle-Musigny, Les Amoureuses, 1969
Domaine Comte Georges de Vogüé

Medium, fully mature colour. Mellow nose. Aromatic. Stylish. Complex. Very interesting fruit

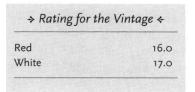

⇢ Rating for the Vintage ⇠	
Red	16.0
White	17.0

⇢ Size of the Crop ⇠ (In hectolitres, excluding generic wine)		
	RED	WHITE
Grands Crus	8,084	1,499
Village and Premiers Crus	92,673	19,759
TOTAL	100,757	21,258

and spice flavours. Fully ready. Medium-full body. Very good grip. Touches of caramel and mocha. Very long. Spicy. Very seductive. Ready but very vigorous. Fragrant, lush and rich. Very, very long finish. Very fine. (April 2005)

DRINK SOON   18.5

Charmes-Chambertin, 1969
Domaine Moignon

Medium-full, well matured colour. Quite fragrant, in a slightly soupy way, on the palate. At the end, a little lean. Medium body. Good but not great. (April 2006)

DRINK SOON   15.0

Clos de la Roche, 1969
Domaine Dujac

Has Jacques Seysses ever produced better? Still amazingly youthful. Very good colour. Fragrant, classy nose. Fullish bodied, vigorous, rich and profound on the palate. Very, very complex and intense. Very long. Very vigorous. Not a hint of age. Very fine. (December 2003)

NOW TO 2010   18.5

Clos de Vougeot, 1969
Domaine Joseph Drouhin

Medium-full colour. Fully mature. This is a little earthy and with dead leaves and stems on the nose. But quite rich and with good acidity on the palate. Medium-full body. Classy. Ripe in a slightly austere way. Long and intense. Plenty of vigour. Fine. (July 2000)

DRINK SOON   17.5

Clos de Vougeot, 1969
Domaine Jean Grivot

Magnum. Medium-full, well mature colour. Sweet, ripe, exotic nose. Well matured. This has lightened up a bit. It is more like a 1971 than a 1969. On the palate, medium body, sweet, round, balanced and fresh. But exotic rather than fullish and spicy. Very sensuous. Long on the finish. Lovely. (November 2001)

NOW TO 2010   17.5

Echézeaux, 1969
Domaine Leroy

Medium-full, mature colour. Ripe, rich nose. Gingerbread touches. Sweet and spicy. Fullish body. Chunky. Very fresh. This has a lot of class and concentration. Old viney. Lovely cool character. Still really surprisingly youthful. Long. Excellent. (March 2002)

NOW TO 2010+   18.5

Gevrey-Chambertin, Lavaux-Saint-Jacques, 1969
Maison Roland Remoissenet et Fils

Good fresh, medium-full colour. Rich and aromatic nose. Surprisingly fresh and vigorous. Ripe and fruity. Fullish body. Mellow. Balanced. Long at the end. Was fine. Now very good plus. (March 2004)

DRINK SOON   16.5

Grands Echézeaux, 1969
Maison Roland Remoissenet et Fils

Vigorous, fullish colour. Ripe, voluptuous nose. Plenty of freshness still. Full, fat, fresh and sweet. Fully mature, but cool and distinguished. Still very long and complex at the end. Very fine. (March 2005)

NOW TO 2010   18.5

Grands Echézeaux, 1969
Domaine de la Romanée-Conti

Slightly low level. Fully mature colour. Lovely mellow nose. Intense. Exotic. Gamey. Very good grip. Medium-full body. Long. Vigorous. Fine plus. (April 2004)

NOW TO 2010+   18.0

Griotte-Chambertin, 1969
Domaine Joseph Drouhin

Good, well matured colour. The nose is sweet, mellow, slightly spicy and well matured. So is the palate. But there is no lack of grip here. Not

a vestige of astringency. Smooth, vigorous, ripe and classy. Lots of richness and depth. More than the nose would suggest. Very classy and very intense at the end. Very fine. (March 2002)

DRINK SOON   18.5

Musigny, 1969
Domaine Jean Hudelot

Full, very vigorous colour. Rich, round, fragrant nose. Good substance. Velvety. Still very fresh. Ripe. Good acidity. Very fine fruit. Still lots of energy and life ahead of it. Lots of class and lots of depth. This is very fine plus. (March 2005)

NOW TO 2010   19.0

La Romanée, 1969
Domaine Bouchard Père et Fils

Low ullage and the cork crumbled. Somewhat maderised. Good mature colour. Medium to medium-full body. Slightly astringent. And yet sweet on the finish. This was very fine in the first place. And it is still enjoyable. But past its best. (March 2003)

PAST ITS BEST   15.0

La Romanée, 1969
Maison Camille Giroud

Good fullish, mature colour. Ripe, sensuous and quite delicious on the nose. Very complex and very classy. Rich, full bodied, fresh and very fine. Excellent grip. This is very lovely. (June 2001)

DRINK SOON   19.0

Romanée-Saint-Vivant, 1969
Domaine de la Romanée-Conti

(Marey-Monge.) Fullish, mature colour. Fragrant and well developed on the nose. Complex and classy. Medium-full body. Plump, harmonious and subtle. But the Latour 1969 is greater. Fine, though. (March 2002)

DRINK SOON   17.5

Romanée-Saint-Vivant, Les Quatre Journeaux, 1969
Domaine Louis Latour

Fine full, mature colour. Firm nose. Quite full, indeed a little sturdy at first. Rich, full bodied and fat on the palate. Old viney. Profound. Long and lovely. Even better than the 1971. Really splendid. Very fine. (March 2002)

NOW TO 2010   18.5

Santenay, Les Gravières, 1969
Domaine Philippe Mestre

Full, vigorous colour. Barely mature. Ripe, fleshy, succulent nose. Not too alcoholic, nor too robust. Indeed, fat and classy. Fresh. Slightly animal, but attractively so. On the palate this is full and quite robust. Good grip. A chunky wine. Yet fresh and with good depth. Positive finish. Very good. (December 2001)

DRINK SOON   16.0

La Tâche, 1969
Domaine de la Romanée-Conti

Medium colour. Browner than the 1970. But fuller, fatter, more spicy and more vigorous on the nose. This is a meaty wine. Gamey, too. Rich and fat. Good structure and depth. Very good grip. Complex and classy at the end. This is fine. And still holding up well, despite the appearance. (March 2003)

DRINK SOON   17.5

Volnay, Champans, 1969
Maison Camille Giroud

This is very delicious. Ripe, fullish, rich and very profound. Very Volnay. Laid-back and classy. Medium-full body. Still very, very fresh. Long and complex. Fine plus. (June 2001)

DRINK SOON   18.0

Volnay, Clos des Ducs, 1969
Domaine du Marquis d'Angerville

Magnum. Fragrant nose. Ripe, succulent, vigorous and delicious on the palate. Fullish body. Still very fresh, if not concentrated and vigorous. Very classy. Lovely harmony. Very long. Still holding up very well. Very fine. (July 2004)

NOW TO 2010+   18.5

1966

The year 1966 ranks in my view jointly with 1969, in being, after 1964, the best of the decade's red wine vintages in Burgundy, though judging by a tasting I did in 1996, the wines seemed to be holding up less well (see *Côte d'Or*). (The 1966 Domaine de la Romanée-Conti wines, on the other hand, showed better than they did when we made a similar tasting of the 1964 vintage).

There is much that was highly satisfactory about the 1966s. They had balance and elegance; they were clean, pure and intense; most had plenty of character; and the best had no lack of vigour. Best of all, they had a poise lacking in the 1969s and sometimes overwhelmed by the richness and substance in the 1964s.

WEATHER CONDITIONS

The weather pattern was mixed, with clement conditions in June, leading to a larger than normal harvest, and then rather poorer weather throughout July and most of August. September, however, was splendid, with enough short showers of rain to keep the progress towards maturity on an even keel. The harvest commenced in the last week of the month and took place under sunny blue skies.

TASTING NOTES

WHITES

Puligny-Montrachet, Les Combettes, 1966
Maison Roland Remoissenet et Fils

Says Henri Clerc on the label. Splendidly youthful colour. Ripe, rich, fat and vigorous on the nose. Still plenty of fruit. Remarkable for a 40-year-old wine. Good grip on the finish. Drink soon. (June 2000)

DRINK SOON   17.0

REDS

Charmes-Chambertin, 1966
Domaine Louis Latour

Good fullish, mature colour. Sturdy, well matured nose. Slightly dense. Medium-full body. A little sweet. Fresh but lacks real class. Very good at best. (April 2006)

DRINK SOON   16.0

Clos de Vougeot, 1966
Domaine Charles Noëllat

Well matured colour. Fresh, vigorous nose. This has style and depth. Lovely fruit. Fullish body. No undue age despite the colour. Rich and vigorous. Balanced. Lots of depth. This is very good indeed. I bought this for Malmaison from the Vannier collection. Still holding up well. Fine. (October 2003)

DRINK SOON   17.5

Le Corton, 1966
Domaine Bouchard Père et Fils

Fullish, well matured colour. Quite a full, mocha-flavoured, rich nose. Medium-full body on the palate. Fragrant. But a bit funky. This is now getting towards its end. Shows well but slightly astringent at the end. Fine but drink soon. (April 2005)

DRINK SOON   17.5

Corton, Les Renardes, 1966
Domaine François Gaunoux

Domaine in Meursault. Medium to medium-full colour. Mature but not unduly so. Getting a little tired and astringent now on the nose. But there is quality underneath. Medium body. Some very good fruit here. Rich and opulent, but it is now loosening up and getting a little short. Slightly dry at the end. Very good plus, nevertheless. (December 2001)

DRINK SOON   16.5

Grands Echézeaux, 1966
Maison Leroy

Good fullish, mature colour. Definitely stemmy on the nose. Sweet. Medium to medium-full. Ripe. Medium-full body. Spicy and aromatic. Lots of depth. Soft. Still very fresh. Very fine for the vintage. Still very, very long. (April 2005)

NOW TO 2010+   18.5

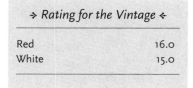

> → *Rating for the Vintage* ←

Red	16.0
White	15.0

> → *Size of the Crop* ←
> (In hectolitres, excluding generic wine)

	RED	WHITE
Grands Crus	10,682	2,146
Village and *Premiers Crus*	115,134	27,070
TOTAL	125,816	29,216

Mazis-Chambertin, 1966
Domaine Pierre Gelin

Medium, fully mature colour. But very classy nose. Fragrant and positive and silky. Medium body. Sweet and succulent. Very good grip. Long, clean, elegant and lovely. Very, very fresh. Very fine. Drink soon. (April 2005)

DRINK SOON   18.5

Le Musigny, 1966
Domaine Comte Georges de Vogüé

Very lovely nose. Rich, mellow, complex, succulent, lovely slightly roasted flavours. Medium-full body. Ripe, concentrated and intense. This is very lovely. Very long and very refined. Naturally sweet at the end. (October 2002)

DRINK QUITE SOON   19.0

Pernand-Vergelesses, Ile de Vergelesses, 1966
Domaine Chandon de Briailles

Light colour. Now really very tawny. Fragrant but ethereal. A little past it on the nose. Yet undoubtedly classy, even quite persistent. This is not dead yet. Rather too soft. Yet there is still more than a vestige of very elegant, complex fruit. Very pure. Very classy. Very long. Still enjoyable. Once very good indeed. Now very good. (December 2001)

DRINK UP   16.0

Romanée-Saint-Vivant, Les Quatre Journeaux, 1966
Domaine Louis Latour

Medium-full, slightly cloudy colour. I think I had a glass with a little of sediment in it, compared with others round the table. Rich, full and succulent on the nose. Lovely fruit. Ripe and classy. Fullish body. Fragrant, balanced and classy. This is very lovely. Not too sweet. Lots of depth, concentration and class. Long and vigorous. Very fine. (March 2002)

NOW TO 2010   18.5

Romanée-Saint-Vivant, 1966
Domaine de la Romanée-Conti

(Marey-Monge.) Clear, medium-full, mature colour. Impressive nose. Very lovely fruit. Balanced and stylish. Lots of depth. Really rich on the palate. Not quite as vigorous as Latour's 1966, but more composed and more intense. Very long, very complex and very classy. Very fine indeed. (March 2002)

DRINK SOON   19.5

La Tâche, 1966
Domaine de la Romanée-Conti

Fullish colour. Good freshness. Good acidity. This is rich and quite masculine. Ripe and stylish. Lots of distinction. But just a touch austere next to the de Vogüé's 1966 Musigny. Slightly hard. (October 2002)

DRINK SOON   18.0

Volnay, Clos des Chênes, 1966
Maison Roland Remoissenet et Fils

Vigorous colour. On the nose very youthful for a 1966. On the palate, too. I would have said a very vigorous 1985. Full bodied, round, ripe, elegant, almost sweet. Good structure. Now mellow. Lots of depth. Yet not a lot of real Volnay class. Very good indeed. (March 2001)

NOW TO 2010   17.0

Vosne-Romanée, Beaux Monts, 1966
Domaine Charles Thomas

Full, fully mature colour. Ripe, mature but just a little rigid on the nose. Better on the palate. More supple, and yet with good substance and energy on the follow-through. Mineral in character. Nicely ripe; almost sweet. It expanded in the glass. Balanced, long and classy. A soft, delicious, mature Burgundy, with plenty of vigour. Fine. (May 2002)

NOW TO 2009   17.5

Vosne-Romanée, Les Malconsorts, 1966
Domaine Thomas-Moillard

Magnum. Firm, full, vigorous colour. Surprisingly so. Almost dense. A big, quite sweet, slightly old-fashioned wine. Suave. Not exactly very elegant, but vigorous, balanced and meaty. Good, but not great because it is not very elegant. (January 2004)

NOW TO 2010   15.0

1964

I did not buy the 1964 vintage—I was a student travelling the vineyards of France at the time—but I am sure I would have enjoyed doing so. My first encounter with them was when they were first offered *en primeur* in late 1966 or early 1967, after they had been bottled and shipped. From the start, I loved the vintage. To this day, I rate it with 1949 and 1952 as the best of what I call "old-fashioned" Burgundy.

I mean old-fashioned in the best sense: low yields, concentrated wines, genuine Pinot and Pinot *fin*. I do not mean Rhône or Algeria-bolstered soupy stuff, *ersatz* Châteauneuf-du-Pape with a little Beaune or Nuits-Saint-Georges added—what used to be enjoyed in Britain and other northern European countries, but which had no more relation to good de Vogüé or Rousseau than a MacDonald's has to a fillet of beef.

For Burgundy was old-fashioned then. Tractors had hardly begun to appear in the vineyards. Horses and oxen were still more commonplace. There was electric light in the cellar, but otherwise little had changed for 100, even 200 years. Fermentation took place in wood, not in stainless steel, ice and cold water were the only methods of controlling the temperature, and the *pigeage* was performed by the proprietor and his male children, naked in the vats. Women were not admitted. Empiricism was the order of the day. The new wine would begin to ferment again in the spring. We thought this was in sympathy with the evolution of the vines for next year's crop. No one had heard about malo-lactic fermentation.

"Rich, ample and concentrated" said a review at the time. Aromatic, nicely (but not excessively) alcoholic, with a good touch of spice, I would add. And the wines had good acidity. The quality of the red wines was even throughout the Côte, from Santenay to Gevrey-Chambertin. Some of the whites were a little heavy. They are and were at their best on the hill of Corton.

The red wines showed every promise of a long and successful life, and this is how they have turned out. Today the 1964s remain a splendid and consistent vintage, and many still have a future, even at more than 40 years of age. For those who like sensual wine (and who does not, of those who love ripe Burgundy?) this is a marvellous vintage. I still buy it where I can, and I am rarely disappointed.

WEATHER CONDITIONS

The year 1964 was the best vintage of the decade, and an almost perfect summer. The spring was cool, but the flowering was swift and untroubled. June was warm, July was very hot, and there was just enough rain in August to keep the evolution of the vines on an even keel. There were some showers in September, which enabled the tannins to ripen properly, and a large-sized vintage of small berries with thick skins, display-ing a splendid ratio of solid to liquid, was gathered from Septem-ber 18 onwards in fine weather. When it did begin to rain, as it did in Bordeaux from October 8 onward, the Burgundy harvest was safely evolving into wine in the growers' cellars.

→ Rating for the Vintage ←

Red	17.5
White	16.0

→ Size of the Crop ←
(In hectolitres, excluding generic wine)

	RED	WHITE
Grands Crus	12,168	2,047
Village and Premiers Crus	117,095	24,900
TOTAL	129,263	26,947

TASTING NOTES

WHITES

Morey-Saint-Denis, Monts Luisants, 1964
Domaine Ponsot

At first it seemed a bit tired. But as it evolved, it became fresher and fresher and more and more profound. 100 percent Aligoté at the time. Remarkable depth, interest and vigour. Very individual. Delicious. (January 2001)

DRINK SOON   19.0

REDS

Beaune, Grèves, Vigne de l'Enfant Jésus, 1964
Domaine Bouchard Père et Fils

Magnum. This is very lovely. Full colour. Still very youthful. Rich, aromatic, fresh and com-plex nose. Lots of class. Full and velvety. Very good concentration and grip. Still very youthful on the palate. Impressive. Fine mature Bur-gundy. Very long and lovely. (June 2002)

NOW TO 2010+   17.5

Beaune, Les Teurons, 1964
Domaine Bouchard Père et Fils

Fine, fullish, mature colour. Lovely aromatic nose. Mocha touches. Mellow. Fullish body. Aromatic. Soft but vigorous. Complex and classy. Very ripe. Lovely sweet finish. Fine. (November 2003)

NOW TO 2010   17.5

Bonnes Mares, 1964
Domaine Bouchard Père et Fils

Domaine. Full and mature, but not with an old colour. Refined mocha nose, which is very typical of 1964. Soft, fragrant and volup-tuous. Well matured but very fresh. Medium-full body. Very smooth and silky. Rich and very, very long, fragrant and classy. Very fine. Still has life. (June 2004)

NOW TO 2010+   18.5

Bonnes Mares, 1964
Domaine Comte Georges de Vogüé

Medium-full, mature colour. No undue age. Very lovely fragrant, classy nose. Fullish, very intense and freshly balanced. Sweet at the end. Aristocratic. Very, very lovely. Very long. Very fine. (March 2001)

DRINK SOON   19.0

Chambolle-Musigny, Les Amoureuses, 1964
Maison Roland Remoissenet et Fils

Fine, vigorous colour. Very lovely fragrant, plump nose. Very good grip. Fullish body. Ample and vigorous. No sign of age. Rich, ripe, sweet and classy. Lovely intense fruit. This is very fine. (March 2001)

DRINK SOON   18.5

Chambolle-Musigny, Les Charmes, 1964
Maison Roland Remoissenet et Fils

Good fullish, fresh colour. As with all old Remoissenet wines, almost uncannily fresh on the palate. Medium-full body. Fragrant. Very Chambolle. Ripe, mellow, succulent and elegant. Very good balance. Good class. Long. This is very good indeed. (March 2003)

NOW TO 2010   17.0

Chapelle-Chambertin, 1964
Domaine Pierre Ponnelle

Funky on the nose at first, but ripe, sweet and vigorous underneath. Plenty of concentration and vigour on the palate. Cleaned up after a while. Fullish body. Very fine. (October 2001)

NOW TO 2010   18.5

Charmes-Chambertin, 1964
Maison Leroy

Medium to medium-full colour. Well matured. Very fine, fresh nose. A lot of concentrated wine here. Fullish body. Old-viney. A touch sweet. But naturally so. Long and vigorous. Very fine. (April 2006)

NOW TO 2015   18.5

Charmes-Chambertin, 1964
Maison Roland Remoissenet et Fils

Fullish colour. Lovely nose. Balanced and quite delicate. Fullish bodied, ripe, well matured and fragrant on the palate. It has now lost a bit of its sweetness. Yet pure and elegant and complex and succulent, nonetheless. Fine. (January 2002)

DRINK SOON   17.5

Clos de Vougeot, 1964
Maison Chanson Père et Fils

Medium colour. Fully mature. Light, fragrant nose. Quite fresh. Good elegance. A little dilute on the palate and now lightening up further. Quite fresh but a bit too soft. Good at best. (April 2004)

DRINK UP   15.0

Clos de Vougeot, 1964
Chateau de la Tour

Good full, vigorous colour. Rich, meaty nose. Plenty of depth and quality here. Very youthful. Full, concentrated and meaty on the palate. Very good grip. Fragrant and elegant. Long. Fine. (December 2001)

DRINK SOON   17.5

Clos de Vougeot, 1964
Domaine Jean Grivot

Magnum. Fine, vigorous colour. Very, very lovely nose. Marvellous fruit. Great poise, class and complexity. Medium-full body. Rich, ample and mellow. Succulent and multidimensional. Very lovely. Very fine indeed. (July 2003)

NOW TO 2010+   18.5

Clos de Vougeot, 1964
Seigneurie de Posanges/Maison Remoissenet

(From Jean Gros.) Medium-full, now fully mature colour. Open, accessible, classy, succulent nose. Very ripe cassis. Very good acidity. Lots of class in a quite gentle sort of way. Medium-full body. Very lovely balance. À *point*. Great class. Very lovely lingering finish. Will last very well. The balance is marvellous. This is very fine. (October 2001)

NOW TO 2010+   18.5

Corton, 1964
Maison Charles Kinloch

Medium-full, mature colour. Ripe, funky, sweet and seductive on the nose. Touches of gingerbread. Medium to medium-full body. Not a lot of tannin. Fragrant and intense. A sexy example. Good ample fruit and with plenty of grip. Long. Fine. *À point*, but plenty of life ahead of it. (September 2005)

NOW TO 2015   17.5

Corton, Les Bressandes, 1964
Maison Camille Giroud

Very full colour. Rich, vigorous and very promising. A touch of oak on the nose which is lovely and rich and concentrated. On the palate, very fresh for a wine over 40 years old. Rich and concentrated. Round, fresh, balanced and fragrant. Silky and very long and subtle at the end. Very classy. Very lovely. Will still keep for ages. Very fine. (September 2005)

NOW TO 2015   18.5

Grands Echézeaux, 1964
Maison Leroy

Good fullish, mature colour. Less stemmy than their 1966. Richer but less sweet. Lots of depth. Full bodied, rich, profound, classy and still very vigorous. Very lovely fruit. Mellow but very long. Fine plus and full of life. (April 2005)

NOW TO 2010+   18.0

Le Musigny, 1964
Domaine Joseph Faiveley

Full, firm and vigorous on the nose and also in the colour. Marvellous quality. Profound, multidimensional and very, very classy. Full bodied, ample and very, very fresh and vigorous. No hard edges. Marvellous follow-through. Seductive. Essence of wine. Bags of life. Quite perfect. (March 2001)

NOW TO 2010   20.0

Nuits-Saint-Georges, Premier Cru, 1964
Maison Leroy

Tastevinage label. Full, vigorous colour. Cool and fragrant. Fruity and complex. Very ripe. Very vigorous. A quite substantial wine. Rich, velvety and profound. Very lovely fruit. Real depth and class. Especially so for a Nuits-Saint-Georges. Fine plus. Still bags of life. (March 2005)

NOW TO 2010   18.0

Pommard, Les Epenots, 1964
Maison Leroy

Medium colour. Fully mature. Full, rich, aromatic. Ripe nose with a touch of green olives. Medium-full body. Good fruit. But not the usual 1964 fat. Plenty of depth and very youthful. I don't find this very seductive. But very good indeed. (March 2003)

DRINK SOON   17.0

Richebourg, 1964
Domaine de la Romanée-Conti

Fullish, rich, mature colour. Marvellous nose. Aromatic, classy and very intense. Splendid fruit. Medium-full body. Rich and spicy. Lovely mocha flavours. Still very vigorous. Very lovely. (April 2001)

DRINK SOON   18.5

Romanée-Saint-Vivant, 1964
Maison Roland Remoissenet et Fils

Vibrant, medium-full colour. Suspiciously vigorous colour. Rich. Quite high volatile acidity. A little concocted. It has been recorked. Medium-full body. Slight underlying oak. Slight astringency. Yet a fine wine. Not only rebottled but refreshed. Not as long or as classy as Louis Latour's. Yet fine intensity and still bags of life. (March 2002)

NOW TO 2010   17.5

Romanée-Saint-Vivant, 1964
Maison Henri de Villamont

Medium, well matured colour. Thinning on the nose. Rather coarse and lumpy underneath. Dirty on the palate. Clumsy and astringent. No. Never was anything better than "fair." Past its best. (March 2002)

PAST ITS BEST (SEE NOTE)

Romanée-Saint-Vivant, Les Quatre Journeaux, 1964
Domaine Louis Latour

Magnum. Splendidly full, rich colour. Lovely nose. Fat, rich and voluptuous. Really quite concentrated. An ample, fullish, sumptuous wine. Full body. Very good grip. Really splendid depth and concentration of fruit. Excellent. (March 2002)

NOW TO 2010   19.5

Santenay, Les Gravières, 1964
Domaine de la Pousse d'Or

Mature colour, lightening up now. Soft, fragrant, rich but slightly earthy nose. Mellow, concentrated, complex and very rich on the palate. A lot of depth and very fine quality for what it is. Still vigorous. Medium-full body. Sweet and almost caramelly, but with very fine grip. Long. Lovely. (May 2003)

NOW TO 2010   17.0

La Tâche, 1964
Domaine de la Romanée-Conti

Some ullage. Full, vigorous colour. There is a little maderised flavour on the nose. But underneath, the wine is full, rich and profound. Still enjoyable. Full bodied. Quite tannic but not astringent. Very, very rich and concentrated and vigorous. Lots of depth and grip. A wine for food. This bottle is very fine. Better bottles, great, I suspect. A huge wine. (March 2003)

NOW TO 2010   18.5

Volnay, Les Caillerets, Ancienne
Cuvée Carnot, 1964
Domaine Bouchard Père et Fils

Fullish, mature colour. No undue age. Lovely, fully mature nose. Cedary, ripe, profound, complex and spicy. Fullish body. Fresh and succulent. Gently sweet at the end, and very long. Aromatic and subtle. Very lovely. Fine. Will still keep well. (March 2004)

NOW TO 2010+   17.5

Volnay, Les Caillerets, Clos des 60 Ouvrées, 1964
Domaine de la Pousse d'Or

Imperiale. This is truly excellent. I have tried this in magnum and double magnum, I think. In this size, it is as if it were a 1978, even a 1975. Round and mellow. But full bodied and intense. Rich, fat and expansive. Splendid vigour. Very fine. (July 2000)

DRINK SOON   18.5

Volnay, Champans, 1964
Domaine Hubert de Montille

Fine, mature colour. Fragrant, complex, classy but slightly delicate nose. Not the volume of the Taillepieds, as I remember it. But fullish bodied, round, even fat. Very complex. Very lovely ripe fruit. *À point.* Fine. Delicious. (January 2003)

DRINK SOON   17.5

Vosne-Romanée, 1964
Maison Morin Père et Fils

Good mature colour. Fully ready. Ample, succulent and voluptuous. Good grip. Fullish body. Ample. Plenty of depth. Especially so for a village wine. Long. Very good indeed. (November 2005)

DRINK QUITE SOON   16.0

Vosne-Romanée, Les Suchots, 1964
Maison Camille Giroud

Fully mature colour. Fullish but decidely developed. Rich, cool, fragrant nose. Very complex. Very fresh. Slightly chocolaty. Balanced. Well matured. Long. Sweet and positive at the end. Very fine. Will still keep. (June 2006)

NOW TO 2010   18.5

Vougeot, 1964
Maison Morin Père et Fils

Good fullish, fully mature colour. Aromatic nose. Medium-full body. Ripe, sweet and vigorous. Not the greatest finesse, but ample, rich and meaty. And with good grip. Probably surplus Clos de Vougeot. Still vigorous. Very good. (November 2005)

DRINK SOON   16.0

1962

Right from the very beginning, the 1962 Burgundy vintage—rather like the 1972s in the end—resisted being put into a Bordeaux straightjacket. Here was a vintage which, in many respects, especially in white, was every bit as good as 1961, and of course, it was much more abundant. But it was overshadowed by 1959 and would also be by 1964. For the 1962s the word generous is extremely apt. Ample, plump and fruity, with a coming-out-to-embrace-you immediate charm: these were other attributes showered on it at the time. Unsaid was the implication that, for all its appeal, the 1962s would not be real stayers. A parallel would be the 1985s today. Balance, ripeness and finesse: they were all there. But what about the backbone?

As it turned out, there are more than a few 1962s at the top level which, even after 45 years, have plenty of vigour. On the basis of the wines below, I would still be prepared to have a punt at any 1962 of reasonable *provenance* and appearance. The vintage is holding up very well indeed. Dare I suggest it's outlasting the 1962 Bordeaux? And these have lasted rather better than expected.

WEATHER CONDITIONS

The year 1962, in contrast with 1964, was a late developer right from the beginning. The bud-break was late; April and May were cold and sunless, though dry; and as a result, the flowering—though it was successful—was late, not occurring until the second half of June. From then on, the weather improved, progressively warming up through July until August, which was hot and sunny, with some welcome rain at the end of the month. September was good, if not brilliant, but the harvest did not begin until October 8. Again, it was a large crop. And the quality was very good.

TASTING NOTES

WHITES

Bâtard-Montrachet, 1962
Domaine François Gaunoux

Clean, but seemingly slightly faded in its fruit at first. On oxidation, it got richer and

	Rating for the Vintage
Red	15.5
White	17.0

→ Size of the Crop ← (In hectolitres, excluding generic wine)		
	RED	WHITE
Grands Crus	9,870	1,592
Village and Premiers Crus	100,089	20,197
TOTAL	109,959	21,789

plumper. Old but not faded. Decadent. Delicious with white truffles! Held up very well in the glass. (October 2002)

DRINK SOON   17.0

Chevalier-Montrachet, 1962
Domaine Bouchard Père et Fils

Quite a deep, but not aged colour. Very lovely fresh, ripe, honeyed nose. Not a bit of age Full body. Very classy. Splendid depth of flavour here. Fine acidity. Very complex. It got better and better in the glass. Lots of vigour. Very fine indeed. (December 2001)

DRINK SOON   19.0

REDS

Chambertin, Clos de Bèze, 1962
Domaine Clair-Daü

Good, vigorous, medium-full colour. On the nose it has lost a little of its fruit. A little too lean really now, I fear. Sweeter on the palate. Fullish body. Good fruit. Good grip. It has lost a little of its class. Despite the vegetal nose, the wine is very pleasant to drink. Soft, mellow and long. No sign of astringency. Very good indeed. (January 2001)

DRINK SOON   17.0

Charmes-Chambertin, 1962
Maison Joseph Drouhin

Medium to medium-full colour. Well matured. Showing a little age on the nose. But lots of finesse here. Fragrant. Mellow. Long. Classy. More vigorous on the nose than on the palate. Very fine. (April 2006)

DRINK SOON   18.5

Grands Echézeaux, 1962
Domaine de la Romanée-Conti

Recorked in 1996. Full, vigorous, mature colour. Quite full and masculine on the nose. Fragrant and refined. Slightly sweet, caramel spice in the background. Full bodied, rich, opulent, ripe and high class. Lots of vigour. Very good grip. This is still very youthful. Long. Very well covered tannins. Very lovely indeed. Got better and better in the glass. Will last another 20 years. Fine plus. (1962 at the domaine perhaps even better than 1964, which was abundant. It was a lot better than 1961.) (November 2002)

DRINK SOON   18.0

Richebourg, 1962
Domaine de la Romanée-Conti

Magnum. Splendid colour. Fragrant, elegant, rich, mineral, fat and very, very lovely. Full bodied, smooth, rich and profound. Soft and silky. Very ripe and succulent. This is very lovely indeed. Fresh as a daisy. Very long. Absolutely no sign of age. Very fine indeed. (October 2004)

NOW TO 2014+   19.0

La Romanée, 1962
Domaine Bouchard Père et Fils

Medium-full, mature colour. No undue age. Ample, fragrant nose. Delicate and lovely. Really quite soft on the palate. Mellow and laid-back. Very fresh and elegant, but with a slight lack of energy. Long and complex. Fine. Drink quite soon. (March 2003)

DRINK SOON   17.5

Romanée-Conti, 1962
Domaine de la Romanée-Conti

Good full colour. Mature, but no undue age. Splendid nose—really exquisite musk and caramel touches, but it doesn't quite live up to it on the palate. A touch of secondary fermentation, but nevertheless, rich and ripe and even caramelly. On the palate there is a slight prickle (noticeable in other DRC 1962s). Marked acidity. Fullish body. Mellow. Delicious, nevertheless. The La Tâche 1962 is fuller, fatter and today better on the palate. Fine plus. (September 2001)

DRINK SOON   18.5

Romanée-Saint-Vivant, 1962
Maison Moillard

Medium to medium-full colour. Ripe, vigorous nose. Plenty of depth and vigour on the palate. Fullish body. Classy, concentrated and old viney. Lots of character. No undue age. Pure, rich and complex. Very fine. (March 2002)

NOW TO 2009   18.5

La Tâche, 1962
Domaine de la Romanée-Conti

Fullish, surprisingly vigorous colour. Slight undergrowth and green-twigginess on the nose. A little carbon dioxide. Fullish bodied, fresh and vigorous on the palate. Still very youthful. Less to it than both 1964 and 1959, but otherwise, the most impressive of the 1960s. Cool. Very elegant fruit. Surprisingly young. Long and vigorous. Very lovely. (March 2003)

NOW TO 2010   19.0

1961

This is a vintage about which it is difficult to generalise. There are some extremely good wines. But in general, I prefer the 1962s. They are not as uneven. Some 1961s lack succulence and generosity. The reputation of the vintage in Burgundy was much helped by the excellence of the wines in Bordeaux. In reality, the wines are good, but they are by no means great. Both 1959 and 1964 were clearly superior vintages.

WEATHER CONDITIONS

It was an irregular growing season. The spring was unnaturally warm, leading to an early development of the buds. The flowering conditions, however, were cool, reducing the crop through *coulure*, and it was then not really hot until August, and even then, only patchily. September was fine though, right through until the end of the harvest, but the ripeness and concentration of the fruit were uneven.

REDS

Aloxe-Corton, 1961
Maison Leroy

Good fullish, mature colour. Nutty, rich and caramelly on the nose. Fullish, smooth, vigorous and balanced. Good grip. Nice long, intense finish. This has unexpected depth and class for a village wine. Good length. Good vigour. Very good. (October 2003)

NOW TO 2009   16.0

Beaune, Clos du Roi, 1961
Domaine Doudet-Naudin

Full colour. Meaty but slightly sweaty. Slightly reduced and not very Pinot-ish. Spurious crap on the palate. (October 2003)

DRINK SOON   11.0

Beaune, Grèves, Vigne de l'Enfant Jésus, 1961
Domaine Bouchard Père et Fils

Fullish, mature colour. Very lovely fragrant nose. Plenty of class. Plenty of fruit. Plenty of vigour. Ripe. Slight mocha spice. Very flowery. Very intense. Very composed. Very harmonious. Still very young. Not a trace of astringency. Very fresh. Very lovely. (June 2000)

DRINK SOON   18.0

Beaune, Les Toussaints, 1961
Maison Roland Remoissenet et Fils

Good vigorous, mature colour. Full, robust, rich nose. Still vigorous. Slightly rigid perhaps. Fullish on the palate. Good style and depth. It lacks a bit of finesse and nuance. In fact, it tastes quite Pommard-ish. But there is good fruit and vigour and acidity here. Good plus. (May 2003)

DRINK SOON   15.5

Chambolle-Musigny, Les Amoureuses, 1961
Maison Joseph Drouhin

Fine, mature colour. Very lovely aromatic nose. Not a trace of age. Beautifully harmonious. Very lovely Chambolle fruit. Quite delicious. Very elegant. Very fragrant. Very long. Very lovely. (June 2000)

DRINK SOON   18.5

Clos Saint-Denis, 1961
Domaine Pierre Ponnelle

Medium-full colour. Quite a developed nose. Sensuous. Slightly vegetal. It has lost a little of its concentration, grip and class. On the palate, sweet, ripe, fruity and still very enjoyable. Medium-full body. Very good indeed. (October 2001)

DRINK SOON   17.0

Le Corton, 1961
Domaine Bouchard Père et Fils

(This was at lunch chez Bouchard.) Very fine, barely mature colour. Though 40 years old, this will last for at least another 20. Fullish body. Sweet, fresh, aromatic, complex and profound. Very, very long and very, very lovely. Excellent! (November 2003)

NOW TO 2025   20.0

Latricières-Chambertin, 1961
Domaine Drouhin-Laroze

Medium colour. Fully mature, if not lightening up. Rich and slightly sweet, with just a hint of fade on the nose. Medium body. Soft and succulent, but now loosening up. Pleasant fruit. Decent length at the end. Some style, but good rather than great. (December 2001)

DRINK UP   15.0

→ Rating for the Vintage ←	
Red	15.5
White	16.0

→ Size of the Crop ← (In hectolitres, excluding generic wine)		
	RED	WHITE
Grands Crus	7,496	1,365
Village and Premiers Crus	76,182	16,943
TOTAL	83,678	18,308

Latricières-Chambertin, 1961
Domaine Joseph Faiveley

Tasteviné. Medium to medium-full colour. Now soft and fragrant. Sweet and mellow. Cherry-raspberry flavours on the nose. Medium-full body. Rich and harmonious. Understated. Discreet. Fine plus. (April 2001)

DRINK SOON   18.0

Mazis-Chambertin, 1961
Domaine Pierre Ponnelle

Medium-full colour. Vigorous. But less so than the 1959, which I tasted alongside. On the nose the fruit is lovely but fading a little, losing the aromatic elements. Still really delicious on the palate. Still sweet and very lovely. A splendid wine. But the 1959 is better still. (October 2001)

DRINK SOON   18.5

Nuits-Saint-Georges, Clos des Forêts Saint-Georges, 1961
Domaine Jules Belin

"Cuvée Hors Ligne." Fine, full colour. Rich, fragrant, voluptuous, very concentrated nose. Animal and sensual. Full bodied, exotic, oaky underneath. Very essence of wine. Almost like a 1961 claret. Sweet but pure and balanced. Still very young. Yet no hard edges. Full but not tannic. Very lovely. Very fine. (December 2001)

DRINK SOON   18.5

Nuits-Saint-Georges, Clos des Grandes Vignes, 1961
Domaine Charles Thomas

Fine colour. Full and mature, but no sign of decay. Lovely nose. Really concentrated and sweet. Vigorous and unexpectedly classy. Essence of wine. Quite new oaky. Good structure. Still a little tannin and backbone, though now quite silky. Very lovely fruit. Naturally sweet. Long and refined. Delicious! (May 2002)

NOW TO 2009   17.5

Richebourg, 1961
Domaine Gros-Renaudot

Bottled by Jean de Besse, *négociant* in Beaune. Fine, full, mature colour. Still very youthful.

Lovely silky-smooth, rich, chocolate nose. The acidity is a touch on the volatile side, which meant that it didn't hold up too well in the glass—it had been decanted an hour previously. But exotic, velvety and delicious. Sweet at the end. (October 2001)

DRINK SOON   18.5

Richebourg, 1961
Domaine de la Romanée-Conti

Full, mature colour. Surprisingly rich, full and vigorous. Very concentrated. Multidimensional. This is very closed and ungainly at the outset. But rich, rich, fruity, mellow and very fine indeed as it developed. (March 2006)

NOW TO 2015+   19.0

La Romanée, 1961
Domaine Bouchard Père et Fils

Magnum. Fullish colour. Showing a bit of age now on the nose. Much better on the palate. This is soft, fragrant, sweet and juicy. Fresh and surprisingly pure. Medium to medium-full body. Splendidly balanced. Velvety and complex and classy at the end. Very lovely. Very fine. (March 2003)

DRINK SOON   18.5

Ruchottes-Chambertin, 1961
Domaine Thomas-Bassot

Fullish, mature colour. Pretty, but now a bit over the top. Some sweetness, but too old. A bit astringent and fruitless at the end. (July 2003)

(SEE NOTE)

Savigny-lès-Beaune, Les Lavières, 1961
Domaine Bouchard Père et Fils

Good full colour. "Old fashioned" nose. Full, rich but rustic. Vigorous, though. On the palate it is beginning to lose its sweetness. A sturdy wine. Good. (June 2003)

DRINK SOON   15.0

1959

A large, glorious and early vintage. You have to go back to 1949 and forward as far as 1990 for something as successful as this, though 1964 was not far behind. The whites lasted very well, though at more than 45 years on, it is no surprise that they are now old. The best of the reds, even at this age, are still vigorous—virile indeed.

The whites were full, concentrated and rich: right at the verge of sur-maturity without being over the top. Acidities were nevertheless enough, and the flavours were opulent without being heavy or too exotic.

The red wines are full, ample, rich and generous. There is structure and backbone, acidity and grip, and much that is both complex and classy. You can taste the heat of the summer, for there is plenty of warmth in the wines. But there is no lack of fresh fruit or elegance either. A classic vintage of depth and concentration.

→ Rating for the Vintage ←

Red	18.5
White	17.5

→ Size of the Crop ←
(In hectolitres, excluding generic wine)

	RED	WHITE
Grands Crus	7,255	1,836
Village and		
Premiers Crus	108,722	23,321
TOTAL	115,977	25,157

WEATHER CONDITIONS

Fine weather in early June, following a mild spring, enabled the vines to flower swiftly and successfully, ensuring not only a large and early harvest, but one of even maturity. July and August were very hot and dry. Early September brought just enough rain to keep the maturation progress on an even keel. And the harvest took place in ideal conditions, beginning two weeks earlier than usual on September 14.

TASTING NOTES

WHITES

REDS

Beaune, Les Toussaints, 1959
Maison Roland Remoissenet et Fils
Marvellous colour. Remarkably vigorous and full bodied. Rich and concentrated. Fat, ample and voluptuous. Still sweet. Very classy. Fullish and plump and indeed classy and very lovely. Still lots of vigour. Very good indeed. (July 2003)
NOW TO 2010   17.0

Bonnes Mares, 1959
Maison Camille Giroud
Full, mature colour but with no sign of age. Sensual nose. Ample. Fully mature. On the palate this is rich and plump. Very good acidity. Fresh. Soft. Silky. Very good intensity. Not perhaps the greatest class, but full bodied, meaty and fine. (June 2001)
NOW TO 2009   17.5

Charmes-Chambertin, 1959
Domaine Paul Bouchard
Good vigorous colour. Tough nose. Solid palate. Medium-full body. Quite vigorous. But no flair. Clean finish, though. Good. (April 2006)
NOW TO 2012   15.0

Charmes-Chambertin, 1959
Domaine Doudet-Naudin
Good vigorous colour. Old fashioned. Short and sweet and rather rustic. Decent freshness. Not bad. (April 2006)
DRINK SOON   13.0

Charmes-Chambertin, 1959
Domaine Pierre Ponnelle
Fullish body. Very smooth. Rich, rich and silky. Concentrated and sweet. Classy and vigorous. Soft at the end. Very fine. (March 2006)
NOW TO 2012+   18.5

Clos de Vougeot, 1959
Domaine Clair-Daü
Magnum. Medium colour. Fully mature. Fragrant but quite aged nose. Yet complex and profound, ripe and classy. As it evolved it seemed

to put on weight. Rich and fat. Well matured but classy, refined, long and elegant. Lingering finish. Fine. (January 2001)

DRINK SOON   17.5

Clos de Vougeot, 1959
Domaine Charles Thomas

Fine full, vigorous-yet-mature colour. Lots of bottles rather vinegary. Even a good bottle showed a little of this on development. Fullish body. Very opulent. Mocha and other flavours which are not found in the 1966 and the 1961. *Rôti*. Evidence of a very hot year. Quite evolved. Now very sensual. But still full and lively. But the Nuits-Saint-Georges Clos des Grandes Vignes 1961 is rather more vigorous and more concentrated. I prefer it. But this is fine. (May 2002)

DRINK QUITE SOON   17.5

Grands Echézeaux, 1959
Maison Leroy

Fullish, vigorous colour. Fragrant and slightly pruney but very fresh on the nose. On the palate soft, intense and very velvety. Lovely ripe, rich fruit. Fresh and vigorous at the end. Very, very fine. Still bags of life. Absolutely no sign of age. (March 2005)

NOW TO 2010+   19.0

Grands Echézeaux, 1959
Maison Roland Remoissenet et Fils

Magnum. Quite a vigorous, mature colour. Ripe, mellow nose. Rich and profound. Very 1959. Slightly spicy, but lots of ripeness and depth. Abundant. Fine plus. Still vigorous. (March 2005)

NOW TO 2020+   18.0

Mazis-Chambertin, 1959
Domaine Pierre Ponnelle

Medium-full, vigorous colour. Very lovely nose. Rich, sweet and vigorous. Marvellously complex

and aromatic. Lovely nutty-caramel flavours. Fullish bodied, rich and still fresh on the palate. Perhaps the finish is not quite as good as the nose. Indeed the finish of the 1961, which I tasted alongside, is more vigorous, if this is more complex. (October 2001)

DRINK SOON   18.5

Le Musigny, 1959
Domaine Louis Jadot

Fine colour. Very rich, full, creamy nose. Quite high volatile acidity but not enough in any way to spoil the wine. Profound and very classy indeed. Full bodied, intense and rich. Very fresh, very plump and succulent on the palate. Lots of depth and dimension. Excellent. Really very lovely. Really very long. Very vigorous. Very fine indeed. (October 2001)

DRINK SOON   19.5

Nuits-Saint-Georges, Les Vaucrains, 1959
Maison Camille Giroud

Surprisingly fresh, mature, full colour. Rich, full, slightly caramelly nose. Full. Still very fresh. Amazingly so for a 48- year-old wine. Lots of energy. Lovely complexity. Great class and harmony. Brilliant. Will still keep very well. (June 2006)

NOW TO 2010   19.0

La Tâche, 1959
Domaine de la Romanée-Conti

Full, rich, youthful colour. Lovely nose. Really profound and concentrated. Full bodied, rich, vigorous and powerful on the palate. Great depth here. Still firm and very youthful. This is really excellent. Multidimensional, rich fruit. Not a bit too hot or robust. Just a lot of very concentrated, very lovely wine. Very, very long. Complex. Excellent. (March 2003)

NOW TO 2020   20.0

2007 Vintage Assessment

A PRELIMINARY REPORT

One of the most climatically curious vintages has ended happily. Up to the end of August, growers were anticipating a disaster. The sun then started shining, and 10 weeks of the most spectacular autumn followed. The leaves on the trees and vines did not begin to fall until Hospices time, with the first really proper frost occurring on the night of November 12. The resulting colour in the interim was truly magnificent. Sadly, it was a very early harvest; so not all could fully benefit. Nevertheless, there was much early satisfaction with 2007 to be discerned, as buyers and journalists toured Burgundy to sample the 2006s.

After a mild and dry winter—only one severe frost occurred, at the end of January—Burgundy enjoyed its summer in April, with temperatures as high as the 30s (85 plus Farenheit) and 4 weeks of abundant sun. Thereafter, apart from a week in mid-May, when the vines flowered some 3 weeks early, the weather remained wet, cold and miserable for two and a half months. Even after July 14, it continued to be patchy, with more days of cloud and rain than days of sun. Unsettled weather persisted until the last week of August, when, right at the last minute the clouds cleared, and temperatures improved.

Overall, it was a very wet summer indeed. Mildew and rot remained a constant threat. With hindsight, it became clear that, even more than usual, it was crucial to not over-crop, dangerous to not pay daily attention to the state of health of the vines and advantageous to (if possible) delay the date of the harvest.

Every year there is hail somewhere; in 2007 it fell to the *climat* of Charmes-Chambertin to bear the brunt. There were three hailstorms in Chablis, variously ravaging the village of Chichée and the *premiers crus* of Montée de Tonnerre and Mont de Milieu, and later, Vaillons.

Early on, the authorities announced that the Ban des Vendanges would be August 18; they did not expect everyone to immediately rush out to harvest, but they wanted to give total liberty to each domaine to choose its own picking date. The vintage started first in the Côte de Beaune, around Monday, September 3. This was followed a week or so later by the Côte de Nuits, Chablis and the Maconnais and Beaujolais. Normally, the last two regions commence a good 10 days—and in the case of the Beaujolais, 2 weeks—before the Côte d'Or. The late pickers, the Côte Chalonaise and the Hautes-Côtes had the best of it, as they were able to profit more from the return to fine weather.

It hardly needs to be said that it was essential to *tri,* to eliminate substandard fruit before fermentation. As a result, most estates produced a reduced crop, some announcing 25 percent less than in 2006 (which was by no means large).

The Chablis results are variable. Alcohol levels are reasonable, but acidities are low. Many wines will be rather soft and ephemeral. Growers producing whites in the Côte de Beaune, especially those who picked later than most, are rather more enthusiastic, and many consider 2007 to be better than 2006. As far as the reds are concerned, the vintage is considered superior in the Côte de Nuits, in comparison with the Côte de Beaune, with *vignerons* in Gevrey-Chambertin even prepared to compare their 2007s with their 2005s. In the Maconnais and the Beaujolais, the 2007 vintage is said to be good (better than 2006), but not great.

Appendix One

Where alternative marks are given, this indicates a variation, either between the wines themselves or between one end of the Côte and the other. See the individual vintage assessments for further information.

Marks given out of 20:

13.0 = Not bad

14.0 = Quite good

15.0 = Good

16.0 = Very good

17.0 = Very good indeed

18.0 = Fine plus

19.0 = Very fine indeed

— = Never of much consequence: now dead and buried

( ) = Now old

Please note: In every vintage, however bad, the very best growers make surprisingly good wine. The reverse, sadly, is also true.

	RED	WHITE		RED	WHITE
2005	19.0	18.5	1992	14.0	(15.5)
2004	14.0–16.0	16.5	1991	16.0	(13.5)
2003	12.0–15.0	10.0–12.5	1990	18.5	16.5
2002	18.0	19.0	1989	16.5	(16.5)
2001	14.0–16.0	14.5	1988	17.5	(14.5)
2000	13.0–15.5	15.5	1987	(14.5)	(13.5)
1999	18.5	17.5	1986	(12.0–14.5)	(13.5–16.5)
1998	16.0	(14.5)	1985	16.5	(18.5)
1997	14.0	(14.0)	1984	—	—
1996	16.5	15.5	1983	(12.0–18.5)	(13.5)
1995	17.5	18.5	1982	(14.5)	(16.0)
1994	13.0–14.5	(13.5)	1981	—	—
1993	17.5	(15.0)	1980	(13.0–16.0)	(12.0)

	RED	WHITE		RED	WHITE
1979	(14.5)	(16.0)	1966	(16.0)	(15.0)
1978	15.5	(15.5)	1965	—	—
1977	—	—	1964	17.5	(16.0)
1976	(14.5)	(13.0)	1963	—	—
1975	—	—	1962	(16.0)	(17.0)
1974	—	—	1961	(15.5)	(16.0)
1973	—	—	1960	—	—
1972	—	—	1959	18.5	(17.5)
1971	(16.0)	(18.0)	1952	(18.5)	(16.5)
1970	(14.5)	(14.5)	1949	(19.0)	(18.0)
1969	16.0	(17.0)	1947	(16.5)	(15.0)
1968	—	—	1945	(18.5)	(16.0)
1967	(14.5)	(15.0)			

Appendix Two

RATING THE VINEYARDS OF THE CÔTE D'OR

RED

★★★ *Three Stars*

Romanée-Conti

La Tâche

Richebourg

Romanée-Saint-Vivant

Grands-Echézeaux

Clos-de-Vougeot (top)

Le Musigny

Clos de la Roche

La Romanée

Chambertin

Chambertin, Clos de Bèze

Mazis-Chambertin (*haut*)

Ruchottes-Chambertin (*bas*)

Corton, Clos du Roi

★★ *Two Stars*

La Grande-Rue

Echézeaux

Clos de Vougeot (lower parts)

Bonnes-Mares

Clos de Tart

Clos des Lambrays

Clos Saint-Denis

Chapelle-Chambertin

Charmes-Chambertin

Corton (except Clos du Roi)

Griotte-Chambertin

Latricières-Chambertin

Mazis-Chambertin (*bas*)

Mazoyères-Chambertin

Ruchottes-Chambertin (*haut*)

Gevrey-Chambertin, Clos Saint-Jacques

Chambolle-Musigny, Les Amoureuses

★ *One Star*

Gevrey-Chambertin: Les Cazetiers;
    Estournelles-Saint-Jacques;
    Lavaux-Saint-Jacques; Les Combottes

Chambolle-Musigny: Les Fuées;
    Les Cras; La Combe d'Orveau

Vosne-Romanée: Les Beaumonts (*bas*);
    Les Brûlées (north side); Les Suchots
    (upper section); Cros Parentoux;
    Les Malconsorts

Nuits-Saint-Georges: Aux Boudots;
    Les Saint-Georges; Les Vaucrains;
    Les Cailles; Les Porrets/Clos des Porrets

Pernand-Vergelesses: Ile de Vergelesses

Pommard: Les Petits Epenots;
    Les Rugiens (*bas*)

Volnay: Les Caillerets (*dessous*);
    Clos des Chênes (*dessous*); Taille-Pieds;
    Les Santenots-du-Milieu

WHITE

★★★ *Three Stars*

Le Montrachet

Chevalier-Montrachet

Corton-Charlemagne (the *lieu-dit* Le
    Charlemagne and the southerly
    part of En Charlemagne)

★★ *Two Stars*

Corton-Charlemagne (the rest)

Bâtard-Montrachet

Bienvenues-Bâtard-Montrachet

Criots-Bâtard-Montrachet

Meursault, Les Perrières (*dessous*)

Puligny-Montrachet, Les Caillerets

★ *One Star*

Meursault: Les Genevrières (*dessous*);
    Les Charmes (*dessous*); Les Perrières (*dessus*)

Puligny-Montrachet: Les Combettes;
    Les Perrières; Les Pucelles; Les Folatières
    (lower section); Clos de la Garenne

Chassagne-Montrachet: Blanchot *Dessous*;
    En Remilly; Les Caillerets; La Grande
    Montagne; Les Grandes Ruchottes;
    La Romanée

Appendix Three

RATING THE DOMAINES AND THE *NÉGOCIANTS*

Cote d'Or

★★★ *Three Stars*

D'Auvenay, Saint-Romain

Denis Bachelet, Gevrey-Chambertin

Bonneau du Martray, Pernand-Vergelesses

Louis Carillon et Fils, Puligny-Montrachet

Sylvain Cathiard, Vosne-Romanée

Jean Grivot, Vosne-Romanée

Anne Gros, Vosne-Romanée

Michel Gros, Vosne-Romanée

Michel Lafarge, Volnay

Comtes Lafon, Meursault

Leflaive, Puligny-Montrachet

Leroy, Vosne-Romanée

Ramonet, Chassagne-Montrachet

Romanée-Conti, Vosne-Romanée

Guy Roulot, Meursault

Armand Rousseau, Gevrey-Chambertin

De Vogüé, Chambolle-Musigny

★★ *Two Stars*

Marquis d'Angerville, Volnay

Comte Armand, Pommard

Ghislaine Barthod, Chambolle-Musigny

Bouchard Père et Fils, Beaune

Chandon de Briailles, Savigny-lès-Beaune

Bruno Clair, Marsannay

Jean-François Coche-Dury, Meursault

J.J. Confuron, Nuits-Saint-Georges Prémeaux

Joseph Drouhin, Beaune

Claude Dugat, Gevrey-Chambertin

Bernard Dugat-Py, Gevrey-Chambertin

Dujac, Morey-Saint-Denis

René Engel, Vosne-Romanée

Joseph Faiveley, Nuits-Saint-Georges

Fourrier, Gevrey-Chambertin

Henri Gouges, Nuits-Saint-Georges

Gros Frère et Soeur, Vosne-Romanée

Louis Jadot, Beaune

Henri Jayer, Vosne-Romanée (for the wines
made up to his retirement)

Lambrays, Morey-Saint-Denis

Leroy, Auxey-Duresses

Liger-Belair, Vosne-Romanée

Méo-Camuzet, Vosne-Romanée

Denis Mortet, Gevrey-Chambertin

Jacques-Frédéric Mugnier,
Chambolle-Musigny

Perdrix, Nuits-Saint-Georges Prémeaux

Ponsot, Morey-Saint-Denis

Georges Roumier et Fils, Chambolle-Musigny

Clos de Tart, Morey-Saint-Denis

★ *One Star: Côte de Nuits*

Amiot-Servelle, Chambolle-Musigny

D'Ardhuy, Corgoloin

Arlaud Père et Fils, Morey-Saint-Denis

Robert Arnoux, Vosne-Romanée

Bertagna, Vougeot

François Bertheau, Chambolle-Musigny

Louis Boillot et Fils, Chambolle-Musigny

Alain Burguet, Gevrey-Chambertin

Jean Chauvenet, Nuits-Saint-Georges

Robert Chevillon, Nuits-Saint-Georges

Jacky Confuron-Cotetidot, Vosne-Romanée

Damoy, Gevrey-Chambertin

Drouhin Laroze, Gevrey-Chambertin

David Duband, Chevannes

Dupont-Tisserandot, Gevrey-Chambertin

Sylvie Esmonin, Gevrey-Chambertin

Régis Forey, Vosne-Romanée

Geantet Pansiot, Gevrey-Chambertin

Robert Groffier et Fils, Gevrey-Chambertin

Olivier Guyot, Marsannay

Heresztyn, Gevrey-Chambertin

Alain Hudelot-Noëllat, Vougeot

Humbert Frères, Gevrey-Chambertin

Olivier Jouan, Arcenant

Gilles Jourdan, Corgoloin

Lamarche, Vosne-Romanée

Thibault Liger-Belair, Nuits-Saint-Georges

Hubert Lignier, Morey-Saint-Denis

Lignier-Michelot, Morey-Saint-Denis

Alain Michelot, Nuits-Saint-Georges

Georges Mugneret/Mugneret-Gibourg,
Vosne-Romanée

Gérard Mugneret, Vosne-Romanée

Sylvain Pataille, Marsannay

Perrot-Minot, Morey-Saint-Denis

Nicolas Potel, Nuits-Saint-Georges

Louis Rémy, Morey-Saint-Denis

Rossignol-Trapet, Gevrey-Chambertin

Joseph and Philippe Roty,
Gevrey-Chambertin

Christian Sérafin, Gevrey-Chambertin

Robert Sirugue et ses Enfants,
Vosne-Romanée

Taupenot-Merme, Morey-Saint-Denis

Jean and Jean-Louis Trapet,
Gevrey-Chambertin

Vougeraie, Nuits-Saint-Georges Prémeaux

★ *One Star: Côte de Beaune*

Robert Ampeau et Fils, Meursault

Roger Belland, Santenay

Albert Bichot, Beaune

Simon Bize et Fils, Savigny-lès-Beaune

Jean-Marc Blain-Gagnard,
  Chassagne-Montrachet

Jean Boillot, Volnay/Maison Henri Boillot,
  Meursault

Jean-Marc Boillot, Pommard

Michel Bouzereau et Fils, Meursault

Yves Boyer-Martenot, Meursault

Chanson Père et Fils, Beaune

Château de Chorey-lès-Beaune,
  Chorey-lès-Beaune

Marc Colin et Fils, Saint-Aubin

Colin-Deléger, Chassagne-Montrachet

De Courcel, Pommard

Domaine des Croix, Beaune

Vincent Dancer, Chassagne-Montrachet

Didier Darviot-Perrin, Monthelie

Arnaud Ente, Meursault

Richard Fontaine-Gagnard,
  Chassagne-Montrachet

Jean-Noël Gagnard, Chassagne-Montrachet

Vincent Girardin, Meursault

Camille Giroud, Beaune

Alain Gras, Saint-Romain

Patrick Javillier, Meursault

François and Antoine Jobard, Meursault

François and Vincent Jouard,
  Chassagne-Montrachet

Hubert Lamy et Fils, Saint-Aubin

Latour-Giraud, Meursault

Latour-Labille et Fils, Meursault

Olivier Leflaive Frères, Puligny-Montrachet

René Lequin Colin, Santenay

Château de la Maltroye, Chassagne-Montrachet

Matrot, Meursault

Prince Florent de Mérode,
  Ladoix-Serrigny

François Mikulski, Meursault

Monthelie-Douhairet, Monthelie

Hubert de Montille, Volnay

Les Deux Montilles, Volnay

Bernard Morey, Chassagne-Montrachet

Pierre Morey/Morey-Blanc, Meursault

Lucien Muzard et Fils, Santenay

Michel Niellon, Chassagne-Montrachet

Alain Patriarche, Meursault

Jean-Marc Pavelot, Savigny-lès-Beaune

Paul Pernot et Fils, Puligny-Montrachet

Jean Pillot et Fils, Chassagne-Montrachet

Château de Puligny-Montrachet,
  Puligny-Montrachet

Rapet Père et Fils, Pernand-Vergelesses

Jean-Claude Rateau, Beaune

Roblot-Monnet, Volnay

Nicolas Rossignol/Rossignol-Jeanniard, Volnay

Aleth Le Royer-Girardin, Pommard

Étienne Sauzet, Puligny-Montrachet

Jean-Marc and Anne-Marie Vincent,
  Santenay

★★ *Two Stars*

Billaud Simon	Domaine des Malandes
Vincent Dauvissat	Louis Michel
Benoît Droin	Christian Moreau et Fils
Joseph Drouhin	Raveneau
William Fèvre	Gérard Tremblay, Domaine des Iles
Maison Jadot	

★ *One Star*

Christian Adine, Domaine de la Conciergerie	Daniel Étienne Defaix
Barat	Corinne and Jean-Pierre Grossot
Jean-Claude Bessin	Moreau-Naudet
Alain Besson	Pinson
Domaine de Chantemerle, François Boudin	Denis Race
Christophe et Fils	Francine and Olivier Savary
Domaine du Colombier, Thierry Mothe	Servin
Jean Collet et Fils	Laurent Tribut
Daniel Dampt	Domaine de Vauroux, Anne and Olivier Tricon
Bernard Defaix et Fils	Vocoret

★ *One Star*

Stéphane Aladame, Montagny

Guillemette and Olivier Besson, Givry

Jean-Claude Brelière, Rully

Michel Briday, Rully

Luc Brintet, Mercurey

Joseph Faiveley, Domaine des Croix Jacquelet, Mercurey

Dujardin-Perrotto, Givry

Vincent Dureuil-Janthial, Rully

Christophe Grandmougin, Rully

Henri and Paul Jacqueson, Rully

Joblot, Givry

Michel Juillot, Mercurey

Bruno Lorenzon, Mercurey

François Lumpp, Givry

François Raquillet, Mercurey

André Delorme, Domaine de la Renarde, Rully

Antonin Rodet, Mercurey

Cave des Vignerons de Buxy

A and P de Villaine, Bouzeron

Appendix Four

CÔTE D'OR: THE SIZE OF THE CROP
(in hectolitres, excluding generic wine)

Sadly, the statistics I have been able to obtain for the older vintages do not allow me to parallel these production figures with surface areas. The areas producing generic and non-generic wine are not separated. However, in 1949, a total of 8,980 hectares was under production in the Côte d'Or. This is not much different from the area in 2005: 9,650 hectares, of which 5,857 hectares produced village, *premier* and *grand cru*, and 3,793 hectares produced generic wine.

	RED	WHITE	TOTAL
2006			
Grands Crus	12,738	4,004	16,742
Village and *Premiers Crus*	165,281	65,327	228,808
Total	178,019	67,531	245,550
2005			
Grands Crus	13,214	3,692	16,906
Village and *Premiers Crus*	175,674	58,817	234,491
Total	188,888	62,509	251,397
2004			
Grands Crus	12,547	4,078	16,625
Village and *Premiers Crus*	164,592	67,053	231,645
Total	177,139	71,131	248,270
2003			
Grands Crus	9,093	2,884	11,977
Village and *Premiers Crus*	117,896	43,142	161,038
Total	126,989	46,026	173,015
2002			
Grands Crus	13,114	3,726	16,840
Village and *Premiers Crus*	170,522	62,385	232,907
Total	183,636	66,111	249,747

	RED	WHITE	TOTAL
2001			
Grands Crus	13,955	3,935	17,890
Village and *Premiers Crus*	174,216	60,185	234,401
Total	188,171	64,120	252,291
2000			
Grands Crus	14,199	3,989	18,188
Village and *Premiers Crus*	180,748	59,353	240,101
Total	194,947	63,342	258,289
1999			
Grands Crus	15,297	4,187	19,484
Village and *Premiers Crus*	208,830	67,051	275,881
Total	224,127	71,238	295,365
1998			
Grands Crus	11,907	3,605	15,512
Village and *Premiers Crus*	168,473	51,340	219,813
Total	180,380	54,945	235,325
1997			
Grands Crus	12,076	3,727	15,803
Village and *Premiers Crus*	159,608	54,752	214,360
Total	171,684	58,479	230,163
1996			
Grands Crus	14,548	3,874	18,422
Village and *Premiers Crus*	190,154	56,905	247,062
Total	204,702	60,779	265,484
1995			
Grands Crus	11,720	3,286	15,006
Village and *Premiers Crus*	173,727	46,575	220,302
Total	185,447	49,861	235,308
1994			
Grands Crus	12,605	3,504	16,109
Village and *Premiers Crus*	183,337	50,549	233,886
Total	195,942	54,053	249,995
1993			
Grands Crus	11,895	3,577	15,472
Village and *Premiers Crus*	181,477	49,681	231,158
Total	193,372	53,258	246,630
1992			
Grands Crus	13,278	3,600	16,878
Village and *Premiers Crus*	182,261	48,606	230,867
Total	195,539	52,206	247,745
1991			
Grands Crus	10,855	3,476	14,331
Village and *Premiers Crus*	166,380	45,104	211,484
Total	177,235	48,580	225,815
1990			
Grands Crus	14,117	3,668	17,785
Village and *Premiers Crus*	188,573	51,926	240,499
Total	202,690	55,594	258,284

	RED	WHITE	TOTAL
1989			
Grands Crus	12,673	3,238	15,911
Village and *Premiers Crus*	178,971	41,573	220,544
Total	191,644	44,811	236,455
1988			
Grands Crus	12,797	3,533	16,330
Village and *Premiers Crus*	170,056	46,434	216,490
Total	182,853	49,967	232,820
1987			
Grands Crus	11,018	2,785	13,803
Village and *Premiers Crus*	159,322	36,593	195,915
Total	170,340	39,378	209,718
1986			
Grands Crus	14,877	2,957	17,834
Village and *Premiers Crus*	197,856	48,302	246,158
Total	212,733	51,259	263,992
1985			
Grands Crus	9,699	2,506	12,205
Village and *Premiers Crus*	129,445	44,066	173,511
Total	139,144	46,572	185,716
1984			
Grands Crus	8,939	1,902	10,841
Village and *Premiers Crus*	123,492	31,815	155,307
Total	132,431	33,717	166,148
1983			
Grands Crus	11,955	3,038	14,993
Village and *Premiers Crus*	143,435	36,527	179,962
Total	155,390	39,565	194,955
1982			
Grands Crus	17,933	4,002	21,935
Village and *Premiers Crus*	233,894	53,397	287,291
Total	251,827	57,399	309,226
1981			
Grands Crus	7,115	1,859	8,974
Village and *Premiers Crus*	83,685	25,036	108,721
Total	90,800	26,895	117,695
1980			
Grands Crus	9,959	2,518	12,477
Village and *Premiers Crus*	141,410	35,023	176,433
Total	151,369	37,541	188,910
1979			
Grands Crus	10,630	2,796	13,426
Village and *Premiers Crus*	148,905	45,007	193,912
Total	159,535	47,803	207,338
1978			
Grands Crus	8,546	2,103	10,559
Village and *Premiers Crus*	115,606	29,670	145,276
Total	124,152	31,773	155,835

	RED	WHITE	TOTAL
1977			
Grands Crus	11,413	2,191	13,604
Village and *Premiers Crus*	138,156	35,375	175,351
Total	149,569	37,566	187,135
1976			
Grands Crus	11,146	2,012	13,158
Village and *Premiers Crus*	142,613	28,077	170,690
Total	153,759	30,089	183,848
1975			
Grands Crus	7,451	1,680	9,131
Village and *Premiers Crus*	87,971	18,354	106,325
Total	95,422	20,034	115,456
1974			
Grands Crus	10,090	2,064	12,154
Village and *Premiers Crus*	115,498	22,590	138,088
Total	125,588	24,654	150,242
1973			
Grands Crus	12,758	2,801	15,559
Village and *Premiers Crus*	156,857	33,404	190,261
Total	169,615	36,205	205,820
1972			
Grands Crus	12,273	2,216	14,989
Village and *Premiers Crus*	147,956	28,292	176,248
Total	160,229	30,508	191,237
1971			
Grands Crus	7,533	1,527	9,060
Village and *Premiers Crus*	83,926	17,674	101,600
Total	91,459	19,201	110,660
1970			
Grands Crus	12,756	2,356	15,112
Village and *Premiers Crus*	141,018	27,985	169,003
Total	153,774	30,341	184,115
1969			
Grands Crus	8,084	1,499	9,583
Village and *Premiers Crus*	92,673	19,579	112,432
TOTAL	100,757	21,258	122,015
1967			
Grands Crus	9,931	1,617	11,548
Village and *Premiers Crus*	102,061	15,717	117,778
Total	111,992	17,334	129,326
1966			
Grands Crus	10,682	2,146	12,828
Village and *Premiers Crus*	115,134	27,070	142,204
Total	125,816	29,216	155,032
1964			
Grands Crus	12,168	2,047	14,215
Village and *Premiers Crus*	117,095	24,900	141,995
Total	129,263	26,947	156,210

	RED	WHITE	TOTAL
1962			
Grands Crus	9,870	1,592	11,462
Village and *Premiers Crus*	100,089	20,197	120,286
Total	109,959	21,789	131,748
1961			
Grands Crus	7,496	1,365	8,861
Village and *Premiers Crus*	76,182	16,943	93,125
Total	83,678	18,308	101,986
1959			
Grands Crus	7,255	1,836	9,091
Village and *Premiers Crus*	108,722	23,321	132,043
Total	115,977	25,157	141,134
1957			
Grands Crus	6,379	914	7,293
Village and *Premiers Crus*	54,225	9,118	63,343
Total	60,604	10,032	70,636
1952			
Grands Crus	6,845	1,184	8,029
Village and *Premiers Crus*	61,509	12,991	74,500
Total	68,354	14,175	82,529
1949			
Grands Crus	5,620	759	6,379
Village and *Premiers Crus*	47,567	8,196	55,763
Total	53,187	8,955	62,142

Appendix Five

CÔTE D'OR SURFACE AREAS: A SUMMARY
(in hectares, excluding generic wines)

Compared to 10 years ago, the white wine surface area has grown by 17 percent, and the area under Pinot by 3 percent. There are 377 red wine *premiers crus* and 162 white wine *premiers crus*, a total of 539, of which, 393 are found in the Côte de Beaune and 146 in the Côte de Nuits. Please note that in some villages, such as Chassagne-Montrachet, the same *climat* can produce both red and white wine.

2005 DECLARATION

Côte de Beaune	Total	Village AC	Total
Village AC *rouge*	1,474	Village AC *rouge et rosé*	2,555
Village AC *blanc*	720	Village AC *blanc*	765
Premier cru rouge	1,162	Total	3,320
Premier cru blanc	484		
Grand cru rouge	95	*Premier Cru*	
Grand cru blanc	88	*Premier cru rouge*	1,561
Total	4,023	*Premier cru blanc*	529
		Total	2,090
Côte de Nuits			
Village AC *rouge et rosé*	1,113	*Grand Cru*	
Village AC *blanc*	45	Grand cru rouge	361
Premier cru rouge	399	Grand cru blanc	89
Premier cru blanc	10	Total	450
Grand cru rouge	266		
Grand cru blanc	1	TOTAL *ROUGE ET ROSÉ*	4,509
Total	1,834	TOTAL *BLANC*	1,348
		TOTAL *SURFACE AREA*	5,857

Appendix Six

PRICE MOVEMENTS

These four tables show the movement of *ex cellar* prices of four top domaines over the last 35 years. Where there are gaps, it means the wine was not bought.

Domaine Chandon de Briailles
(Prices in FF per bottle until 1999)

WINE/YEAR	69	70	71	72	73	74	75	76	77	78
Red Wines										
Savigny-lès-Beaune	9			16	16	16		25		
SLB *1er cru* Fourneaux										
SLB *1er cru* Lavières	9			16				27		30
Pernand *1er cru* Les Vergelesses										
Pernand *1er cru* Ile des Vergelesses	10	12		17	17	17		28		33
Aloxe Corton *1er cru* Valozières										
Volnay Caillerets										
Corton Maréchaudes			20	22						
Corton Bressandes	12.5	16		22	24	24		45		48
Corton Clos du Roi	12.5	16			24	24		50		52
White Wines										
Pernand Vergelesses *1er cru* Ile Blanc										
Corton Blanc										
Corton Charlemagne										

WINE/YEAR	79	80	81	82	83	84	85	86	87
Red Wines									
Savigny-lès-Beaune	28	33	35	35	37.5	30	38	38.5	38
SLB *1er cru* Fourneaux									
SLB *1er cru* Lavières	30	38	40	40	43	40	45	44	45
Pernand *1er cru* Les Vergelesses							36.5		39.5
Pernand *1er cru* Ile des Vergelesses	33	42	44	44	47	44	55	54	55
Aloxe Corton *1er cru* Valozières	45	52			63		80	78.5	70
Volnay Caillerets									
Corton Maréchaudes					66	71.5	90	89	100
Corton Bressandes	52	65	67	67	75	80	100	97	120
Corton Clos du Roi	56	70		83	91.5	90	120	108	140
White Wines									
Pernand Vergelesses *1er cru* Ile Blanc									
Corton Blanc				83	100	100	130		150
Corton Charlemagne									

WINE/YEAR	88	89	90	91	92	93	94	95	96
Red Wines									
Savigny-lès-Beaune	40	40	42	42	42	45		45	47
SLB *1er cru* Fourneaux	45	45	48	48	48	50		52	54
SLB *1er cru* Lavières	50	50	55	55	55	125[a]		59	62
Pernand *1er cru* Les Vergelesses			50	50	50	50		55	57
Pernand *1er cru* Ile des Vergelesses	58	58	60	60	60	65		65	67
Aloxe Corton *1er cru* Valozières						58		60	70
Volnay Caillerets									
Corton Maréchaudes	110	110	110	100	100	100		110	115
Corton Bressandes	135	120	140	120	120	120		130	135
Corton Clos du Roi	150	150	150	130	130	130		140	150
White Wines									
Pernand Vergelesses *1er cru* Ile Blanc	60	60	60	60	65	65		80	80
Corton Blanc	160	160	160	160	160	160		180	180
Corton Charlemagne							New	200	200

WINE/YEAR	97	98	99		00	01	02	03	04
Red Wines									
Savigny-lès-Beaune	47	47	47	*EUROS*	7.62	8.38	8.38	9.50	9.50
SLB *1er cru* Fourneaux	54	54	54		8.69	9.15	9.15	10.50	10.50
SLB *1er cru* Lavières	62	62	65		10.37	10.82	12.75	12.50	12.50
Pernand *1er cru* Les Vergelesses	57	57	57		9.15	9.60	9.60	11.00	11.00
Pernand *1er cru* Ile des Vergelesses	67	70	70		11.13	11.60	11.60	14.00	14.00
Aloxe Corton *1er cru* Valozières	70	70	72		10.98	12.20	12.20	16.00	16.00
Volnay Caillerets			New		15.55	16.01	15.00	17.50	17.50
Corton Maréchaudes	115	115	115		18.29	19.06	19.06	21.00	21.00
Corton Bressandes	135	135	140		22.41	23.17	23.2	25.5	25.5
Corton Clos du Roi	150	150	160		25.61	26.37	26.37	30.00	30.00
White Wines									
Pernand Vergelesses *1er cru* Ile Blanc	80	80	80		13.42	14.18	14.63	15.50	15.50
Corton Blanc	180	180	180		28.84	29.73	30.00	33.00	33.00
Corton Charlemagne	200	200	200		32.01	32.78	33.00	36.00	36.00

[a]Magnums only

Domaine R. Engel
(Prices per bottle in FF until 1999)

WINE/YEAR	78	79	80	81	82	83	84
Vosne Romanee	42			50			60
VR *1er cru* Brûlées	45	47			60	60	67
Echézeaux		50		55	55	70	75
Clos Vougeot	60	62		70	70	90	100
Grands Echézeaux				60			

WINE/YEAR	85	86	87	88	89	90	91
Vosne Romanee	70	55	57	60	63	63	61
VR *1er cru* Brûlées	75	73	77	80	83	83	81
Echézeaux	90	85	90	95	100	100	100
Clos Vougeot	135	130	140	150	160	160	180
Grands Echézeaux	135	130	150	180	180	180	180

WINE/YEAR	92	93	94	95	96	97	98
Vosne Romanee		63	63	65	75	85	90
VR *1er cru* Brûlées		83	83	85	95	105	110
Echézeaux		105	105	110	110	125	135
Clos Vougeot		165	165	175	180	180	185
Grands Echézeaux		185	185	190	195	205	210

WINE/YEAR	99		00	01	02	03	04
Vosne Romanee	95	*EUROS*	14.94	15	17	19	20
VR *1er cru* Brûlées	130		20.27	20.50	22.50	25	26
Echézeaux	160		25.15	25.70	30	33	35
Clos Vougeot	195		30.18	30.50	34	37	40
Grands Echézeaux	230		35.10	36	38	41	45

Domaine Henri Gouges
(Prices per bottle in FF until 1999)

WINE/YEAR	59	62	66	69	70	71	72	76	77
Red Wines									
Nuits St. Georges				12.50	12.50	14	15	26	
NSG *1er cru* Clos Porrets	9	12	13	16	16	18	19	30	30
NSG *1er cru* Pruliers		11	13	16	16	18	19	30	30
NSG *1er cru* Vaucrains	9		14		18	20	21	32	34
NSG *1er cru* Les St Georges			14		18	20	21	32	34
White Wines									
NSG *1er cru* Clos Porrets Blanc									
NSG *1er cru* Perrière Blanc									

WINE/YEAR	78	79	80	81	82	83	84	85	86
Red Wines									
Nuits St. Georges	36	46	50		42	52	45	55	55
NSG *1er cru* Clos Porrets	40	50	59		62	72	65	75	75
NSG *1er cru* Pruliers	40	50	59		62	72	65	75	75
NSG *1er cru* Vaucrains	52	61		65	75	68	80	80	80
NSG *1er cru* Les St Georges		52	61		65	75	68	80	80
White Wines									
NSG *1er cru* Clos Porrets Blanc									
NSG *1er cru* Perrière Blanc									

WINE/YEAR	87	88	89	90	91	92	93	94	95	96
Red Wines										
Nuits St. Georges		60	62	62	61	60	65	61	68	71.50
NSG *1er cru* Clos Porrets	75	82	85	85	83	84	90	83	96	107
NSG *1er cru* Pruliers	75	82	85	85	83	84	90	83	96	107
NSG *1er cru* Vaucrains		95	95	95	95	102	110	100	119	130
NSG *1er cru* Les St Georges	80	95	95	95	95	102	110	100	119	130
White Wines										
NSG *1er cru* Clos Porrets Blanc			100	100					93	
NSG *1er cru* Perrière Blanc			110	110	105	110	108		119	130

WINE/YEAR	97	98	99	00	01	02	03	04
Red Wines			*EUROS*					
Nuits St. Georges	75	77	78	12.49	13.74	14	14.70	14.25
NSG *1er cru* Clos Porrets	110	113	115	18.60	20.46	21.34	22.84	22.41
NSG *1er cru* Pruliers	110	113	115	18.60	20.46	21.34	22.84	22.41
NSG *1er cru* Vaucrains	136	140	143	22.89	25.18	30.49	32.63	32.02
NSG *1er cru* Les St Georges	36	140	143	22.89	25.18	30.49	32.63	32.02
White Wines								
NSG *1er cru* Clos Porrets Blanc			115					
NSG *1er cru* Perrière Blanc	136	145	145	22.56	25.18	30.49	30.50	30

Domaine Armand Rousseau
(Prices in FF per bottle until 1998)

WINE/YEAR	66	69	70	71	72	73	74	75	76	77
Gevrey Chambertin		11	12	18	18	20	24		28	30
GC 1er cru Lavaux St. Jacques	9	13	14	18	22		28		32	35
GC 1er cru Cazetiers		13	14	22	20				32	35
Mazy Chambertin	11	16	17	26	28	27	32		40	40
Charmes Chambertin	12	17	18	28	30	28	32		44	45
Clos de la Roche	12	20	20	30	32		36		46	50
Ruchottes Chambertin										55
GC 1er cru Clos St. Jacques	15	22	22	35	36	30			50	55
Chambertin	20	30	30	45	47	44	50		65	70
Chambertin Clos de Bèze	21	30	30	45	47	44	50		65	70

WINE/YEAR	78	79	80	81	82	83	84	85	86	
Gevrey Chambertin	42	42	50		47.50	55	50	60	55	
GC 1er cru Lavaux St. Jacques	48	48			60		60	75	70	
GC 1er cru Cazetiers		50				65	65	80	75	
Mazy Chambertin	58	55	75		75	85	80	100	90	
Charmes Chambertin	58	60	75		75	85	80	100	90	
Clos de la Roche	65	65			85	95	90	110	100	
Ruchottes Chambertin	70	70			90	100	95	120	110	
GC 1er cru Clos St. Jacques	75	75			100	120	110	140	130	
Chambertin	100	100			130	160	150	190	175	
Chambertin Clos de Bèze	100	100			130	160	150	190	175	

WINE/YEAR	87	88	89	90	91	92	93	94	95	96
Gevrey Chambertin	55	70	70	72	70	70	75	70	80	92
GC 1er cru Lavaux St. Jacques	70					90				
GC 1er cru Cazetiers	75	90	90	92	90		98	90	105	120
Mazy Chambertin	90	120	120	125	120	120	130	120	140	160
Charmes Chambertin	90	120	120	125	120	120	130	120	140	160
Clos de la Roche	100	130	130	135	130	130	140	130	150	175
Ruchottes Chambertin	110	140	140	145	140	140	150	140	160	185
GC 1er cru Clos St. Jacques	130	170	170	175	170	170	185	170	200	230
Chambertin	175	210	210	220	210	210	230	210	250	290
Chambertin Clos de Bèze	175	210	210	220	210	210	230	210	250	290

WINE/YEAR	97	98		99	00	01	02	03	04
Gevrey Chambertin	98	105		16.50	17	17	19	22	
GC 1er cru Lavaux St. Jacques				22	22	23	25	29	
GC 1er cru Cazetiers	130	140	*EUROS*	22	22	23	25	29	
Mazy Chambertin	175	185		29	29	29	31	36	
Charmes Chambertin	175	185		29	29	29	31	36	
Clos de la Roche	190	200		31	31	31	34	40	
Ruchottes Chambertin	200	220		34	34	36	40	48	
GC 1er cru Clos St. Jacques	250	270		42	43	45	49	56	
Chambertin	310	350		54	55	57	61	71	
Chambertin Clos de Bèze	310	350		54	55	57	61	71	

Appendix Seven

MEASUREMENTS AND CONVERSION TABLES

SURFACE AREA

1 hectare = 100 ares = 10,000 square metres = 2.471 acres.

An *ouvrée* corresponds to the amount of land one worker can cultivate by hand in one day. It measures 4.285 ares.

A *journal* (plural *journaux*) is the equivalent of the area one worker can cultivate per day with the help of a horse and plough. A *journal* equals 8 *ouvrées*. There are 2.92 *journaux* per hectare.

CAPACITY

1 hectolitre = 100 litres = 22 gallons = 133.3 bottles = 11.1 cases.

1 Burgundian *pièce* = 228 litres = 304 bottles = 25.33 cases.

A *feuillette* is a half-size cask; a *quarteau* is a quarter-size cask. A *queue* is two *pièces*, a *tonneau* four. A *demi-muid* is an undefined term for a larger cask. Today, *demi-muids* of 500- or 600-litre capacity are becoming increasingly common for white wines.

YIELD

In general, one vine will yield three quarters of a bottle of wine.

In most vintages, ten plastic containers of 30 kilos each (300 kg) will produce 1 *pièce* (228 l) of wine. Sometimes the fruit contains less juice, in which instance, twelve or thirteen containers (360–390 kg) are required.

Most of the best growers aim to produce a maximum of three quarters of a *pièce* per *ouvrée* (18 *pièces* per ha) for village wine (39.91 hl/ha) and proportionately less for their better wines. One *pièce* per *ouvrée* (53.22 hl/ha) is considered excessive.

The law normally allows (*rendement de base* plus 20 percent *PLC*) 42 hectolitres per hectare for *grand cru rouge*, 48 for *grand cru blanc*, 48 for *rouge* and 54 for *blanc*, respectively, for village and *premier cru* red and white. See page 18 for recent changes to the law.

Given a yield of 1 *pièce* per 300 kilos of fruit, 1 ton per acre is equivalent to 19.08 hectolitres per hectare.

Bibliography

Abric, Loïc. *Le Vin de Bourgogne au XIXème Siècle*;
   Editions de l'Armançon, Dijon, 1993.
Andrieu, Pierre. *Petite Histoire de la Bourgogne et de son
   Vignoble*; La Journée Vinicole, Montpellier, 1955.
Anon. *Histoire et Chronique du Village de Pommard*;
   1995.
Arlot, John and Fielden, Christopher. *Burgundy,
   Vines and Wines*; Davis-Poynter, London, 1976.
Arnoux, Claude. *Dissertation sur la Situation de
   Bourgogne*; London, 1728 (Facsimile edition
   published by Daniel Marcrette, Luzarches, 1978).
Bazin, Jean-François. *Le Clos de Vougeot*, in the series
   Le Grand Bernard des Vins de France; Jacques
   Legrand, Paris, 1987.
Bazin, Jean-François. *Le Montrachet*, in the series
   Le Grand Bernard des Vins de France; Jacques
   Legrand, Paris, 1988.
Bazin, Jean-François. *Chambertin, La Côte de Nuits
   de Dijon à Chambolle-Musigny*, in the series
   Le Grand Bernard des Vins de France; Jacques
   Legrand, Paris, 1991.
Bazin, Jean-François. *La Romanée-Conti, La Côte de
   Nuits de Vosne-Romanée à Corgolin*, in the series
   Le Grand Bernard des Vins de France; Jacques
   Legrand, Paris, 1994.
Beeston, Fiona. *The Wine Men*; Sinclair, Stevenson,
   London, 1991 (Bruno Clair and Jacky
   Confuron-Cotéditot).
Bertall. *La Vigne*; Plon, Paris, 1878.

Biss, Austin and Smith, Owen. *The Wines of Chablis*;
   Writers International Ltd., Bournmouth, 2000.
Blanchet, Suzanne. *Les Vins de Bourgogne*; Editions
   Jéma, Marmonde, 1985.
Bourguignon, Claude. *Le Sol, la Terre et les Champs*;
   Editions Sang de la Terre, Paris, 1989.
Broadbent, Michael. *The Great Vintage Wine Book II*;
   Mitchell Beazley, London, 1991.
Cannard, Henri. *Balades en Bourgogne*; Dijon, 1988.
Cannard, Henri. *Montagny*; Dijon, 2001.
Chapuis, Claude. *Corton*, in the series *Le Grand
   Bernard des Vins de France*; Jacques Legrand,
   Paris, 1989.
Coates, Clive. *Côte d'Or, A Celebration of the Great
   Wines of Burgundy*; Weidenfeld and Nicolson,
   London, and University of California Press,
   Berkeley, 1997.
Coates, Clive. *An Encyclopaedia of the Wines and
   Domaines of France*; Weidenfeld and Nicolson,
   London, and University of California Press,
   Berkeley, 2000.
Coates, Clive. *The Great Wines of France*; Mitchell
   Beazley, London, 2005 (articles on DRC,
   Drouhin, Anne Gros, Jadot, Lafon, Leflaive,
   Leroy, Rousseau, Ramonet, Raveneau, Vogüé).
Courtépée, M. and Béguillet, M. *Description
   Générales et Particulières du Duché de
   Bourgogne*, 7 vols 1775–85, 2nd edition in 4 vols;
   Dijon, 1848.

Danguy, M.R. and Aubertin, M. Ch. *Les Grands Vins de Bourgogne: La Côte d'Or*; H. Armand, Dijon, 1892.

Dion, Prof. Roger. *Histoire de la Vigne et du Vin en France des Origines au XIXème Siècle*; Paris, 1959.

Drouot, Henri. *La Côte d'Or*.

Ducourneau, Alix and Monteil, Armand-Alexis. *Bourgogne, Histoires des Abbayes, Communes et Châteaux*; Paris, 1844. Reprint Belna Editions, Beaune, 1992.

Duijker, Hubrecht. *Wijnwijzer Bourgogne*; Het Spectrum, Ulrecht, 1986.

Durand, E. and Guichard, J. *La Culture de la Vigne en Côte d'Or*; Arthur Batault, Beaune, 1896.

Eyres, Harry. *Wine Dynasties of Europe*; Lennard, 1990 (Jean Grivot).

Fielden, Christopher. *White Burgundy*; Christopher Helm, London, 1988.

Fourgeot, Pierre. *Origines du Vignoble Bourguignon*; Presses Universitaire de France, Paris, 1972.

Fried, Eunice. *Burgundy, the Country, the Wines, the People*; Harper and Row, New York, 1986.

Gadille, Rolande. *Le Vignoble de la Côte Bourguignonne*; University of Dijon, 1967.

Garnot, Benoît. *Vins, Vignes et Vignerons en Bourgogne du Moyen Age à l'Époque Contemporaine*; Annales de Bourgogne, 2001.

Gwynn, Stephen. *Burgundy*; Constable, London, 1934.

Halliday, James and Johnson, Hugh. *The Art and Science of Wine*; Mitchell Beazley, London, 1992.

Hanson, Anthony. *Burgundy*, 2nd Edition; Faber and Faber, London and Boston, 1995.

Hyams, Edward. *Dionysus: A Social History of the Wine Vine*; Thames and Hudson, London, 1965.

Jefferson, Thomas. *Jefferson and Wine*; E.R. de Treville Lawrence Sr., Vinifera Wine Growers Association, The Plains, VA, 1976.

Jeunet-Henry, François (M. and Mme). *L'Historique de la Vigne et du Vin de Bourgogne par la Chronologie et l'Anecdotique*; La Pensée Universelle, Paris, 1994.

Johnson, Hugh. *The World Atlas of Wine*, 4th Edition; Mitchell Beazley, London, 1994.

Johnson, Hugh. *Wine Companion*, 3rd Edition; Mitchell Beazley, London, 1991.

Johnson, Hugh. *The Story of Wine*; Mitchell Beazley, London, 1989.

Jullien, A. *Topographie de Tous les Vignobles Connus*; Paris, various editions from 1816 onward.

Kramer, Jane. *Letter from Europe* (article on Mme Monthelie-Douhairet); The New Yorker, 1 Jan., 1990.

Kramer, Matt. *Making Sense of Burgundy*; William Morrow, New York, 1990.

Lachiver, Marcel. *Vins, Vignes et Vignerons: Histoire du Vignoble Français*; Fayard, France, 1988.

Landrieu-Lussigny, Marie-Hélène. *Le Vignoble Bourguignon, Ses Lieux-Dits*; Jeanne Laffitte, Marseille, 1983.

Laurent, Robert. *Les Vignerons de la Côte d'Or au XIX Siècle* (2 vols); University of Dijon, 1958.

Lautel, Dr. Robert. *Terroirs des Bourgognes*; Revue des Oenologues.

Lavalle, Dr. Jean. *Histoire et Statistique de la Vigne et des Grands Vins de la Côte d'Or*; Dusacq, Paris, 1855.

Leneuf, Noël, Lautet, Robert and Rat, Pierre. *Terroirs et Vins de France*; ed. Charles Pomerol, Total-Editions-Presse, Paris, 1984.

Léon-Gauthier, Pierre. *Les Clos de Bourgogne*; Librairie de la Renaissance, Beaune, 1931.

Loftus, Simon. *Puligny-Montrachet: Journal of a Village in Burgundy*; Ebury Press, London, 1992.

Luchet, Auguste. *La Côte d'Or*; Levy, Paris, 1858.

Lynch, Kermit. *Adventures on the Wine Route*; Farrer, Strauss and Giroux, New York, 1988.

Marsh, Sarah. *The Contribution of Pinot Noir Clones to the Vineyards of the Côte d'Or* (Dissertation for the MW exam, 2005. Privately printed.).

Morelot, Dr. *Statistique de la Vigne dans le Département de la Côte d'Or*; Dijon, Paris, 1831.

Motsch, Elizabeth. *Ciels Changeants, Menaces d'Orages; Vignerons en Bourgogne*; Actes Sud, 2005.

Moucheron, E. de. *Grands Crus de Bourgogne, Histoires et Traditions Vineuses*; Dupin, Beaune, 1955.

Norman, Dr. Remington. The Great Domaines of Burgundy, 2nd Edition; Kyle Cathie, London, 1996.

Olney, Richard. *Romanée-Conti*; Flammarion, Paris, 1991.

Parker, Robert. Jr. *Burgundy*; Simon and Schuster, New York, 1990.

Peynaud, Emile. *The Taste of Wine*; MacDonald Orbis, London, 1987. (Trans. Schuster, Michael).

Peynaud, Emile. *Connaissance et Travail du Vin*; Dunod, Paris, 1981.

Pitiot, Sylvain and Poupon, Pierre. *Nouvel Atlas des Grands Vignobles de Bourgogne* (2 vols); Jacques Legrand, Paris, 1999.

Redding, Cyrus. *A History and Description of Modern Wines*; London, 1833, and many editions thereafter.

Rigaux, Jacky. *Ode aux Grands Vins de Bourgogne*; Éditions l'Armançon, 1997.

Rigaux, Jacky. *Gevrey-Chambertin*; Éditions l'Armançon, 1999.

Rigaux, Jacky. *Le Terroir et le Vigneron*; Éditions Terres en Vues, 2006.

Robinson, Jancis. *The Oxford Companion to Wine*; OUP, Oxford, 1994 (esp. contributions by Jasper Morris and Mark Savage on Burgundy, Mel Knox on barrels).

Robinson, Jancis. *Vines, Grapes and Wines*; Mitchell Beazley, London, 1986.

Robinson, Jancis. *The Great Wine Book*; Sidgwick and Jackson, London, 1982 (articles on Laguiche, Domaine de la Romanée-Conti, De Vogüé).

Rodier, Camille. *Le Vin de Bourgogne*; Dijon, various editions from 1921 onward.

Rodier, Camille. *Le Clos-de-Vougeot*; Venot, Dijon, 1948.

Roupnel, Gaston. *La Bourgogne*; Paris, 1923.

Rozet, Georges. *La Confrérie des Chevaliers du Tastevin*; Editions EPIC, Paris, 1950.

Rozet, Georges. *La Bourgogne, Tastevin en Main*; Horizons de France, Paris, 1949.

Sadrin, Paul and Anny. *Meursault*, in the series *Le Grand Bernard des Vins de France*; Jacques Legrand, Paris, 1994.

Seward, Desmond. *Monks and Wine*; Mitchell Beazley, London, 1979.

Simon, Joanna (Ed.). *Harrods Book of Fine Wine*; Mitchell Beazley, London, 1990 (article on Drouhin by Serena Sutcliffe).

Sutcliffe, Serena and Schuster, Michael. *Guide to the Wines of Burgundy*; Mitchell Beazley, 1992.

Sutcliffe, Serena (Ed.). *Great Vineyards and Wine Makers*; MacDonald, London, 1982 (articles on Ampeau, Comte Armand, Bouchard Père et Fils, Clair-Daü, Dujac, Gouges, Louis Latour, Leflaive, Rousseau, Varoilles and de Vogüé).

Vergnelle-Lamotte. *Mémoires sur la Viticulture et l'Oenologie de la Côte d'Or*; Dijon, 1846.

Vienne, H. *Essai Historique sur la Ville de Nuits*; Dijon, 1845. Reprint Laffitte Reprints, Marseille, 1976.

Wallerand, Jean-Claude and Coulais, Christian. *Bourgogne, Guide des Vins*; Gilbert and Gaillard, Solar, France, 1992.

Younger, William. *Gods, Men and Wine*; The International Wine and Food Society, Michael Joseph, London, 1966.

Yoxall, H.W. *The Wines of Burgundy*; The International Wine and Food Society, Michael Joseph, London, 1968.

INDEX

Page numbers in bold font denote the entry's principal reference or references.

Moreau-Naudin, 45

Morein, 47

Moret-Nominé, **199**

Morey, 84, 104, 118, **119–120**

Morey, Albert, 272

Morey appellation, 104, 106

Morey, Bernard, 261, **280**

Morey Blanc, S.A., **254**

Morey-Coffinet, Michel, 261

Morey Cooperative, 107

Morey, Jean-Marc, 261, **280**

Morey, Marc, 261, **280**

Morey, Pierre, **254**, 261

Moreys, 169

Morey-Saint-Denis, 70, 77, 83, **104–116**, 118, 123
  recommended sources in, 92, 120, 121, 122, 262,
    263

Morey-Saint-Denis (village of), 137, 138

Morey (village of), 132

Morgeot, 272, 273, 275

Morgeot *blanc*, 275

Morgeot *rouge*, 275

Morot, Albert, 203, **214**

Mortet, Denis, 85, **100**, 127

Mortet fam., 74

Mortet, Thierry, **100**

Mosnier, Sylvain, Dom., **62**

Mothe, Thierry, Dom, 53, **62**

moths, 19

Mouton, Gérard, Dom., **307**

La Moutonne (*grands crus*), 43

Les Moutottes, 187

Mugneret, Denis, 134

Mugneret, Dominique, 136, **146**

Mugneret, Georges, 127, **146**

Mugneret, Gérard, **146**

Mugneret-Gibourg, 136, **146**, 149

Mugneret, Jean-Pierre, 135, **170**

Mugnier, Jacques Frédérick, 118, 119, **124**, 156

Les Murées, 273

Aux Murgers, 72, 150, 151, **152**, 153

Les Murgers des Dents de Chien, 269

Murray, David, **285**

Muscadet, 67

Le Musigny, 71, 117, **118–119**, 119

Le Musigny *blanc*, 118

must, 21

Muteau, Général, 212

Muzard, Lucien et Fils, 285, **286**

Naddef, Philippe, **82**, 88

En Naget, 184

Naigeon-Chauveau, 87, 104, 119

Nantoux, 168

Les Narbantons, 195, 196

Les Narvaux, 243

Naudant, Jean-René, 135, 170

Naudin-Ferrand, Henri, 136, **170**

Les Naugues, 299

négoce, 62, 224, 267

négociants
  overview, 3, 6–7, 178
  abuse by, 151
  of Aloxe-Corton, 189
  of Beaune, 50, 202, 210, 214, 222, 224, 241, 264
  of Chassagne-Montrachet, 280
  of Côte Chalonnaise, 297, 298
  of Echevronne, 163
  importance of, 203
  of Meursault, 248, 254, 256, 298
  of Nuits-Saint-Georges, 149, 158, 162
  oldest, 209
  of Pommard, 223
  of Puligny-Montrachet, 260, 263
  of Saint-Aubin and Gamay, 269
  of Santenay, 286
  of white wine, 230

Nerthus, Dom., 231

New Haven, 314

Newman, Christopher, 88, **111**, 119

Nié, Louis, **286**

Niellon, Michel, 261, **280–281**

Ninot, Dom., **298**

No. 1, 162

Noël-Bouton fam., 295

Noël-Bouton, Jérôme, **297–298**

Noëllat, 163

Noëllat, Michel et Fils, 127, 136 **147**

Les Noirots, 71, 118, 121

Noisot, Claude, 79

nomenclature, 4–5. *See also* classification systems

Norman, Remington, 8, 116

Nouveau, Claude, **288–289**

Nudant, Dom., 182, **186–187**

Nugues, Sulvie and Jean-Claude Pigneret, Dom., **310**

Nuits, 151

Nuits *blanc*, 152

Nuits *premier crus*, 157

Nuits-Saint-Georges, 50, 72–73, 84, 91, 137, **149–162**,
    165, 166
  recommended sources in, 122, 139, 205

Nuits-Saint-Georges Clos des Corvées, 162

Nuits-Saint-Georges *premiers crus*, 149, 162, 165

Nuits-Saint-Georges village wines, 150, 152

Nuits-Saint-Georges whites *(blancs)*, 152, 159, 162

Nuits-Saint-Georges (wine), 151

oak, 25, 27, 48–49, 146

Odoul-Coquard, **114**

Odoul-Coquard, Thierry, 87